SWEDEN

openhagen

D0706727

Königsberg

Danzig

EAST PRUSSIA

Vistula

Stettin

Oder

Poznań

Warsaw

BERLIN

Frankfurt
a.d.O.

P O L A N D

A N Y

Dresden

Breslau

Oder

Vistula

Elbe

Prague

Cracow

Pilsen

(to Poland 1938)

C Z E C H O S L O V A K I A

1938

Danube

(to Hungary

Vienna

Bratislava
(to Hungary
1938)

Tisza

Budapest

T R I A

Graz

H U N G A R Y

0   50   100   150 km

YUGOSLAVIA

GERMANY AND THE SECOND WORLD WAR

I

The Build-up of German Aggression

Germany
and the
Second World War

Edited by the
Militärgeschichtliches
Forschungsamt (Research
Institute for Military History),
Freiburg im Breisgau, Germany

VOLUME I
The Build-up of
German Aggression

WILHELM DEIST
MANFRED MESSERSCHMIDT
HANS-ERICH VOLKMANN
WOLFRAM WETTE

Translated by
P. S. FALLA
DEAN S. McMURRY
EWALD OSERS

CLARENDON PRESS · OXFORD
1990

Oxford University Press, Walton Street, Oxford OX2 6DP
Oxford New York Toronto
Delhi Bombay Calcutta Madras Karachi
Petaling Jaya Singapore Hong Kong Tokyo
Nairobi Dar es Salaam Cape Town
Melbourne Auckland
and associated companies in
Berlin Ibadan

Oxford is a trade mark of Oxford University Press

Published in the United States
by Oxford University Press, New York

© *1990 Deutsche Verlags-Anstalt GmbH, Stuttgart*

British Library Cataloguing in Publication Data
Germany and the Second World War.
Vol. 1, The build-up of German aggression.
1. World War 2
I. Deist, Wilhelm, 1931– II. Militargeschichtliches
940.53
ISBN 0–19–822866–X

Library of Congress Cataloging-in-Publication Data
Ursachen und Voraussetzungen der deutschen Kriegspolitik. English.
The build-up of German aggression / Wilhelm Deist ... [et al.];
translated by P. S. Falla, Dean S. McMurry, Ewald Osers; edited by
the Militärgeschichtliches Forschungsamt (Research Institute for
Military History).
p. cm. — (Germany and the Second World War; v. 1)
Translation of: Ursachen und Voraussetzungen der deutschen
Kriegspolitik.
Includes bibliographical references.
1. World War, 1939–1945—Causes. 2. Germany—Politics and
government—1933–1945. 3. Germany—Military policy—History—20th
century. I. Deist, Wilhelm. II. Germany (West)
Militärgeschichtliches Forschungsamt. III. Title. IV. Series:
Deutsche Reich und der Zweite Weltkrieg. English; v. 1.
DD256.5.D43413 vol. 1
[D741]
943.086 s—dc20
[940.53'437]   *90–7134*
ISBN 0–19–822866–X

Typeset by Burns & Smith Ltd., Derby
Printed in Great Britain by
Courier International Ltd.
Tiptree, Essex

Editor's Preface to the English Edition

THE publication in English of the first volume of *Germany and the Second World War* provides a welcome opportunity to explain to a wider international public the plan of this ten-volume work and the scope of the volumes that have so far appeared in German. It also affords an opportunity for the editors to assess the reception of the first four volumes by historians, especially military historians, as well as by readers of a younger generation, and by those who themselves lived through the Second World War.

The translation offers the English-speaking public a history of the war from a German point of view, and that in two senses. The narrative embodies the results of German research and concentrates attention on the National Socialist rulers of the Reich, whose decisions are treated against the background of Germany's human and material resources and are related to the effects of the war. The strategy and potential of Germany's adversaries are also included in the general picture.

The sixteen contributors to the first four volumes were all born between 1923 and 1948: accordingly, some of them were of an age to experience the war at first hand. The later volumes will be chiefly the work of younger scholars. In all cases the authors were at liberty to work without any instructions that could in any way hamper their academic freedom of research. It has aroused some surprise, as well as discussion and criticism, that members of a single institute, in their contributions to a collective work such as the present, should openly express divergent points of view and accept the fact that a synthesis, however desirable in itself, could not invariably be attained. This has been the case, for instance, with Volume IV, where it seemed to the authors that an 'agreement to differ' was preferable to an enforced uniformity.

In its conception and method the work differs fundamentally from the old style of military history. The modern view of military history as a branch of historiography has led to an interdisciplinary and comparative approach, so that the work embraces political, economic, and social factors in a comprehensive account; this method has met with general approval, though there has been occasional criticism of the degree of emphasis laid on different aspects. The original idea of a 'history of society in wartime' reflected the need, felt especially in Germany, to make up lost ground in the domain of social history. This approach has been generally welcomed, though if pursued too exclusively it could lead to neglect of the military factors that often decide the fate of nations. However, in the first four volumes the two points of view complement each other harmoniously. Some of the authors have concentrated on traditional military-historical research, which it has been possible to undertake since the German archives were released from Allied custody, and which will also be an objective of future volumes.

The purpose of the ten-volume work is to describe the course of the Second World War and to 'place' it in the history of Europe and the world. Even more than the first world-wide conflict born of a struggle for hegemony in Europe, the war of

1939–45 marked a historical turning-point. When it ended, the German Reich stood before the 'grave of its past' (Gerhard Ritter). By launching the war, Germany had drawn the whole world deeply into its own history; it now lay in ruins and had lost its national unity and identity. At the same time the European age had irrevocably come to an end—the age 'in which the world was governed from Europe and world history was concentrated in the old continent' (Count Peter Kielmansegg). Europe was no longer the hub of world events.

Our authors believe that the study of the origins of the Second World War, and of the National Socialist war policy in particular, cannot be confined to the years of Hitler's chancellorship from 1933 onwards. The increasing economic, military, and political strength of the Kaiser's Germany led it to put forward new claims in its ambition to become a European great power and eventually a world power alongside Great Britain. The abandonment of Bismarck's policy of restraint was epitomized in 1895 by the German sociologist Max Weber, who observed that the foundation of the Reich in 1871 was a 'youthful prank that Germany had played in its old age, and one which would not have been worth the cost unless it was intended to mark the beginning of a world-power policy and not just the end of one.'

The change from a Bismarckian to a world-power policy did not merely reflect the attitude of the economic and social élite. As Hans Plehn wrote in 1913: 'It is an almost universal feeling throughout the country that we shall only win our freedom to play a part in world politics through a major European war.' This does not constitute a proof of sole German war guilt in 1914, but it provides an indication of the nature of Germany's part in bringing about the First World War.

The background of Prusso-German history confronts scholars with the question of a 'special German way' and that of 'constant features in German history' (Andreas Hillgruber). The idea of the continuity of Germany's great-power policy and hegemonism, and the part played in it by dominant economic and social circles, has fascinated German historians in particular and is still a subject of lively debate, as can be seen in the present work. The problem is brought into sharper focus by an examination of possible alternatives and the meaning of what actually happened. But the prelude to the Second World War cannot in fact be fully explained by the continuity of the politico-strategic ideas of ruling circles. Hitler's aims went far beyond those of the Weimar revisionists, and for that reason he refused the opportunity offered by the British policy of appeasement, which would have satisfied virtually all the territorial demands of German revisionists of the 1920s.

Mindful of the interconnection of foreign, domestic, and economic policy with military and ideological factors, the authors of Volume I have started out from different viewpoints and have concentrated on various fields of enquiry which appeared relevant to the causes and preconditions of the German policy of aggression. This fruitful diversity of approach within the framework of military history will be a characteristic of future volumes also.

It is accepted by historians that after the National Socialist 'seizure of power' in 1933 the regime was able to establish an 'understanding' (Klaus-Jürgen Müller), based on fundamental identity of purpose, with the military leaders, big business, and large sections of the bourgeoisie, and that this provided Hitler with support during the early years of his rule. However, differences soon developed between Hitler and the military leaders, especially as regards Germany's readiness for war and above all the extent of the risk involved in a major conflict. There was no agreement on policy or strategy. On many levels the 'Führer state' was afflicted by a grave lack of co-ordination. Thus, the rearmament programme was subject to constant variation, and, more seriously, there was no vestige of co-ordination between the measures of the respective fighting services. The military leaders, for their part, were conscious of the nightmare of the four-year struggle of the First World War and saw the very existence of the Reich as being once more threatened.

Against this background the authors of Volume I point out in their Conclusion that it would be a superficial interpretation of the continuity thesis to argue that 'the policies of the Nazi regime were essentially a continuation of traditional tendencies and lines of development'. The hodgepodge of Hitler's ideas, blending a Darwinian racial ideology with calculations of power politics, was so remote from traditional Western values, to which the older ruling circles were still largely attached, that the latter's 'understanding' with the dictator cannot be regarded as an expression of continuity in the usual sense.

The German invasion of Poland on 1 September 1939, which began the Second World War, has been attributed not only to Hitler's war policy but also to 'German militarism' in general. However, research has convincingly shown that there was no broad public support for Hitler's action: unlike the situation in 1914, the great majority of Germans in 1939 considered it a fatal error to resort to war as an instrument of policy. Although nearly all political groups before 1933 had professed a warlike ideology, and despite the strenuous propaganda efforts of the regime, the prevailing mood among the population was one of deep apathy, for reasons which the authors of Volume I are unable fully to explain. It is equally hard to account for the fact that despite increasing depression and war-weariness, the bulk of the population stood firm until the very last day of the war without any signs of widespread resistance.

The Second World War is far too recent for a balanced, self-contained account to be possible, and moreover the Soviet archives are still closed to Western scholars. A beginning has none the less been made with the exploration and analysis of the immensely complicated interrelations of events. Among questions that remain to be studied more deeply is the part played by Germany in the rivalries of European powers in the imperialist era. In this context we may notice a move away from the narrow type of analysis which treated the events of the two world wars as a process 'growing, like a tree, out of purely German roots' (Ludwig Dehio).

Among questions that need further elucidation, readers and reviewers of the present work have singled out that of the causes of the German–Soviet war, the respective responsibilities and basic aims of Hitler and Stalin. The authors of Volume IV (published in Germany in 1983) were unable to record any generally accepted view. Given the intricate mixture of ideological vision and political ambition on the part of the two dictators, the authors themselves differed in their assessments, and their work reflects the prevailing divergence of interpretations. It seems beyond doubt, however, that Hitler and Stalin were both inspired by ideological dogma as well as considerations of foreign policy.

Historians still argue over Stalin's intentions in 1941, when, after a huge process of rearmament and after the drastic purge of Red Army leaders, he deployed his forces close to the frontier in what—in the opinion of one of the contributors to Volume IV—was clearly an 'offensive configuration', reflecting a politico-military doctrine of the offensive. It is undisputed that Stalin's intentions and his security interests were determined by a power-political and ideological calculation that did not exclude an offensive policy. On the contrary, a war between the capitalist-imperialist powers no doubt seemed to Stalin to afford an opportunity of transforming the balance of power on the European continent. It is less probable that he intended to attack Germany in 1941 than that he planned to intervene militarily as late as possible, after the contending powers had exhausted themselves. The view disseminated by the German leaders at the time, that Hitler had invaded the Soviet Union to forestall imminent hostile action by Russia, is rejected in Volume IV of the present work and was not substantiated by the discussion which took place in German periodicals in 1986 on the subject of the 'war between the dictators'.

Hitler and Stalin both regarded the use of military force as a means of asserting and enlarging their respective spheres of power and influence. There is no doubt that Hitler initiated the German–Soviet war; but historians will long continue to discuss the view put forward in Volume IV, that 'This was Hitler's real war.'

As the foregoing remarks will have shown, the present work must for many reasons be regarded for the time being as no more than part of a structure, just as every period of history is a transitional stage opening up new vistas in the light of the past. The work is not intended to provide a self-contained, cut and dried view of history; as befits a free society, the way is clear for controversy and criticism, for each generation is entitled to form its own interpretation of events. The international comparison of results and standards of judgement, which the English translation of this work is intended to promote, will be of especial importance for this purpose.

The Institute and the authors would like to convey their special thanks to the publishers and translators, especially Mr P. S. Falla, for their unstinting efforts to ensure the very high standards attained in this work. Thanks are also due to Dr Wilhelm Deist for supervising every stage of the translation project, and to Mr Wilfried Rädisch for his editorial assistance, especially with the bibliographies.

In revising their contributions for this edition the authors have, where possible, taken account of the various works which have appeared since the publication of the German edition in 1979.

Dr GÜNTER ROTH,
Brigadier-General,
Director,
Research Institute for
Military History

Preface to the German Edition

THE Second World War brought about fundamental and irrevocable changes in Europe and the world. The past decades have seen a complete transformation of the international system as it existed before 1939; the shift of power to new global centres; profound changes in political and social conditions in the world outside Europe; a completely new aspect of warfare; and revolutionary progress in technology. All these developments are to a large extent the result of the course and outcome of the war, which can thus be seen as a major turning-point in history. Its causes and effects are rightly an object of continued study to all those who seek to understand the world as it is today.

The central part that Germany played in bringing about and waging the Second World War, with its far-reaching consequences for so many nations, and the heavy burdens endured by the German people itself during the war and subsequently, will long be the subject of research and historical enquiry. It is a special responsibility of German historians to investigate these fateful events. There already exists a profusion of analyses and accounts of the war years, in which attention is paid to political, military, economic, and social aspects. The Research Institute for Military History is primarily concerned with the military aspects of events and their consequences.

The first two inspectors-general of the Federal German defence forces, Generals Heusinger and Foertsch, created favourable conditions for the performance of this task by enlarging the scope of the Institute, and took an interest in the first discussions concerning research into the history of the Second World War. In view of the deficiency of sources and staff limitations, the Institute first devoted itself to studies of individual problems. But it soon became clear that such studies, useful as they might be, were insufficient in the long run. As the post-war generation in Germany grew to occupy positions of responsibility, questions concerning the reasons for the war were raised more and more pressingly in a general form, making clear the need for a synthesis of the accounts so far produced and, above all, a comprehensive source of information for readers interested in history. Meanwhile, the release of military archives from British and American custody provided further material for a general history of the war from the German point of view.

However, the terms of reference for the present study and for the Institute's work in general diverged from the tradition of nineteenth-century military historiography and the method followed in the multi-volume German official history of the First World War, which was only partially adequate from the historian's point of view. Since 1945 the conditions of work on military history have undergone a basic change. In the Federal German Republic, as elsewhere, historiography has transcended the national limitations that characterized earlier works. Military history has become a recognized subdivision of history in general, and, unlike the 'general staff' histories of former times, includes political, economic, and social problems within its purview. Again, whereas the older style of military history aimed at producing a 'definitive' account from the editors' point of view—a purpose that was also reflected in the anonymity of the contributors—it was considered that military historians nowadays should enjoy to the full the freedom of academic enquiry guaranteed by the Federal constitution. There is no longer room for considerations of any kind that stand in the way of forming and publishing conclusions based on intensive research. Certainly, Moltke's principle that the prestige of military leaders must be safeguarded in the interest of soldierly comradeship—a view that held sway for many years, and had its adherents in foreign armies also—would be quite rejected today.

The planning and execution of the present work have been basically determined by this modern interpretation of military history. What it entails from the point of view of scholarship is explained in the Introduction to this volume by the chief historian of the Institute. As regards the individual contributors, in contrast to 'official histories' of the nineteenth and early twentieth centuries the authors of its separate Parts are named and take full academic responsibility for their work.

In a collective work by historians of different schools it cannot be assumed that agreement will prevail on all points of research. The judgements expressed by individual authors are partly shaped by basic personal views that are not subject to regulation. Naturally, there has been an endeavour to arrive at agreed conclusions: this is most clearly seen in the principles of arrangement and criteria of selection, but finds a limit at the point where scholarly judgement is involved. Thus, the work contains interpretations of history behind which different viewpoints and basic attitudes can be discerned. 'Pluralism' of this kind should be an advantage, not a disadvantage, to critical readers such as the Institute would wish to reach. Those who experienced the war themselves, and the generation whose outlook has been decisively affected by its events and consequences, will form conclusions on the basis of their own knowledge and interests, using the findings of the present study. As to scientific interpretation, the multiplicity of views is a matter of daily experience.

Accordingly, the Institute hopes that the present work will not only impart fresh impulses to the historical investigation of the Second World War, but also provide a wider public, including members of the Federal armed forces, with an account that will assist their understanding of the war with all its consequences for Germany, Europe, and the world.

On the publication of Volume I, I express my thanks to all members of the Research Institute for Military History who took part in planning and preparing the work, and especially in formulating its general conception. Gratitude is due, not least, to my predecessors in the directorship. I also thank the authors for their work on Volume I and the volumes soon to follow.

During the preparation and production of this work the Institute has received assistance from numerous archives, authorities, and academic institutions, both in Germany and abroad. It is my duty and pleasure to express thanks for this help, which I hope will continue in the future.

Dr OTHMAR HACKL,
Colonel, GS
Director,
Research Institute for
 Military History,
1976–85

Contents

PART II

The National Socialist Economy in Preparation for War

List of Figures and Maps

FIGURES

MAPS (endpapers to volume)

The figures and maps are taken from originals by Hans Gaenshirt, Vera Kluge, and Rolf Schindler of the Cartographic Section, Research Institute for Military History.

Notes on the Authors

Dr WILHELM DEIST (b. 1931). Publications: *Militär und Innenpolitik im Weltkrieg 1914–1918* (Quellen zur Geschichte des Parlamentarismus und der politischen Parteien, 2nd ser., Militär und Politik; Düsseldorf, 1970); with H. Schottelius (eds.), *Marine und Marinepolitik im kaiserlichen Deutschland 1871–1914²* (Düsseldorf, 1981); *Flottenpolitik und Flottenpropaganda: Das Nachrichtenbureau des Reichsmarineamtes 1897–1914* (Beiträge zur Militär- und Kriegsgeschichte, 17; Stuttgart, 1976); *The Wehrmacht and German Rearmament* (London, 1981; pbk. 1986); (ed.), *The German Military in the Age of Total War* (Leamington Spa, 1985); contributions to collective works and periodicals on the military history of the Wilhelmine Empire and the Weimar Republic.

Professor Dr MANFRED MESSERSCHMIDT (b. 1926). Publications: *Deutschland in englischer Sicht: Die Wandlungen des Deutschlandbildes in der englischen Geschichtsschreibung* (Düsseldorf, 1955); *Die Wehrmacht im NS-Staat: Zeit der Indoktrination* (Hamburg, 1969); *Militär und Politik in der Bismarckzeit und im Wilhelminischen Deutschland* (Darmstadt, 1975); *Die politische Geschichte der Preußisch-Deutschen Armee 1814–1890* (Handbuch zur deutschen Militärgeschichte 1648–1939, vol. ii, sect. IV. 1; Munich, 1975); *Die preußische Armee: Strukturen und Organisation 1814–1890* (Handbuch zur deutschen Militärgeschichte 1648–1939, vol. ii, sect. IV. 2; Munich, 1976); numerous contributions to collective works and periodicals on German military history in the nineteenth and twentieth centuries, including legal-historical aspects.

Professor Dr HANS-ERICH VOLKMANN (b. 1938). Publications: *Die deutsche Baltikumspolitik zwischen Brest-Litovsk und Compiègne* (Cologne and Vienna, 1970); with F. Forstmeier (eds.), *Wirtschaft und Rüstung am Vorabend des Zweiten Weltkrieges* (Düsseldorf, 1975); *Kriegswirtschaft und Rüstung 1939–1945* (Düsseldorf, 1977); 'Politik, Wirtschaft und Aufrüstung unter dem Nationalsozialismus', in M. Funke (ed.), *Hitler, Deutschland und die Mächte* (Düsseldorf, 1976), 269–91; 'Zum Verhältnis von Großwirtschaft und NS-Regime im Zweiten Weltkrieg', in K. D. Bracher, M. Funke, and H.-A. Jacobsen (eds.), *Nationalsozialistische Diktatur 1933–1945* (Düsseldorf, 1983), 480–508; *Wirtschaft im Dritten Reich: Eine Bibliographie*, 2 vols. (Koblenz, 1980–4). Further publications on twentieth-century German history, especially relations with the East European states.

Dr WOLFRAM WETTE (b. 1940). Publications: *Kriegstheorien deutscher Sozialisten: Marx, Engels, Lassalle, Bernstein, Kautsky, Luxemburg* (Stuttgart etc., 1971); 'Friedensforschung, Militärgeschichtsforschung, Geschichtswissenschaft: Aspekte einer Kooperation', in *Aus Politik und Zeitgeschichte*, 7 (1974); with K. Holl (eds.) *Pazifismus in der Weimarer Republik: Beiträge zur historischen Friedensforschung* (Paderborn, 1981); with G. R. Ueberschär, *Bomben und Legenden: Die schrittweise Aufklärung des Luftangriffs auf Freiburg am 10. Mai 1940. Ein Dokumentarischer Bericht* (Freiburg, 1981); with G. R. Ueberschär (eds.), *'Unternehmen Barbarossa': Der deutsche Überfall auf die Sowjetunion 1941. Berichte, Analysen, Dokumente* (Paderborn, 1984); with R.-D. Müller and G. R. Ueberschär, *Wer zurückweicht wird erschossen! Kriegsalltag und Kriegsende in Südwestdeutschland 1944/45* (Freiburg, 1985); *Geschichte und Frieden: Aufgaben historischer Friedensforschung* (AFB-Texte; Bonn, 1987); *Gustav Noske: Eine politische Biographie* (Düsseldorf, 1987).

Note on the Translation

THE Prefaces, Introduction, and Parts I and IV of the text were translated by P. S. Falla; Part II by Ewald Osers; Part III and the Conclusions by Dean S. McMurry. The translation as a whole was edited and revised by P. S. Falla.

In the Bibliography information has been added concerning English translations of German and other foreign-language works. These translations are cited in the footnotes and have been used whenever possible for quotations occurring in the text.

Abbreviations

AA	Auswärtiges Amt: ministry of foreign affairs
A. Ausl/Abw	Amt Ausland/Abwehr: counter-intelligence (foreign countries)
Abt.	Abteilung: department
a.D.	außer Dienst: retired
ADAP	*Akten zur deutschen auswärtigen Politik*: Documents on German Foreign Policy
ADB	Allgemeiner Deutscher Beamtenbund: General Association of German Civil Servants
ADGB	Allgemeiner Deutscher Gewerkschaftsbund: General Association of German Trade Unions
AHA	Allgemeines Heeresamt: general army office
AStA	Allgemeiner Studentenausschuß: General Students' Committee
AWA	Allgemeines Wehrmachtsamt: armed forces general office
BA	Bundesarchiv (Federal German archives), Koblenz
BA-MA	Bundesarchiv-Militärarchiv, Freiburg im Breisgau
Bb.	Briefbuch: register of mail
BDM	Bund Deutscher Mädel: League of German Maidens
BMW	Bayerische Motorenwerke: Bavarian Motor Works
BVP	Bayerische Volkspartei: Bavarian People's Party
BZ	Behördenzentrale: administration centre
CC	Central Committee
Chef H.Rüst u. BdE	Chef der Heeresrüstung und Befehlshaber des Ersatzheeres: chief of army armaments programmes and commander of replacement army
CID	Committee of Imperial Defence
Comintern	Communist International
CP	Communist Party
CPSU	Communist Party of the Soviet Union
DAF	Deutsche Arbeitsfront: German Labour Front
DBFP	*Documents on British Foreign Policy*
DDF	*Documents diplomatiques français*
DDI	*Documenti diplomatici italiani*
DDP	Deutsche Demokratische Partei: German Democratic Party
DFG	Deutsche Friedensgesellschaft: German Association for Peace
d. Gen.St.	des Generalstabes: of the general staff
DGFK	Deutsche Gesellschaft für Friedens- und Konfliktforschung: German Association for the Study of Peace and Conflict
DGFP	*Documents on German Foreign Policy*
Dipl.Ing.	Diplomingenieur: academically trained engineer
DNB	Deutsches Nachrichtenbüro: German news agency
DNVP	Deutschnationale Volkspartei: German National People's Party
DRC	Defence Requirements Committee
DStP	Deutsche Staatspartei: German State Party

DVFP	Deutsch-Völkische Freiheitspartei: German Party of the People's Freedom
DVP	Deutsche Volkspartei: German People's Party
E-	Ersatz: replacement
FdU	Führer der Unterseeboote: leader of U-boats
Frhr.	Freiherr: baron
FRUS	*Foreign Relations of the United States*
GBW	Generalbevollmächtigter für die Kriegswirtschaft: plenipotentiary for the war economy
GDR	German Democratic Republic
Gen.Feldm.	Generalfeldmarschall: field marshal
Genst.	Generalstab: general staff
Gestapo	Geheime Staatspolizei: secret state police
g.Kdos.	geheime Kommandosache: top secret (military)
g.Rs.	geheime Reichssache: top secret (political)
Gruppf.	Gruppenführer: lieutenant-general (SS)
ha.	hectare
Ha.-Pol.	Handelspolitische Abteilung: trade-policy department
HC Deb.[5]	*House of Commons Debates*, 5th series
HJ	Hitlerjugend: Hitler Youth
HJ	*Historical Journal*
HL	Heeresleitung: army command
H.Wa.A.	Heereswaffenamt: army ordnance office
HZ	*Historische Zeitschrift*
i.Br.	im Breisgau
IFTU	International Federation of Trade Unions
IfZ	Institut für Zeitgeschichte (Institute for Contemporary History), Munich
i.G.	im Generalstab: in the general staff
IMT	*International Military Tribunal* (*see* Bibliography, s.v. *Trial*)
JCH	*Journal of Contemporary History*
JMH	*Journal of Modern History*
KdF	Kraft durch Freude: 'Strength through Joy'
KK	Korpskommando: corps headquarters
K.Kpt.	Korvettenkapitän: lieutenant-commander
KPD	Kommunistische Partei Deutschlands: German Communist Party
KPD-O	KDP-Opposition: Communist Opposition
KTB	Kriegstagebuch: war diary
KZ	Konzentrationslager: concentration camp
L.Dv.	Luftwaffendruckvorschrift: air-force regulation
L-Offizier	Landesschutzoffizier: local defence officer
LSI	Labour and Socialist International
Lw	Luftwaffe: German air force
Lw Fü.Stab	Luftwaffenführungsstab: air-force command staff
Mefo	Metallurgische Forschungsgesellschaft: Metallurgical Research Company (*see also* Glossary)
MG	Maschinengewehr: machine-gun

MGFA	Militärgeschichtliches Forschungsamt: Research Institute for Military History
MGM	*Militärgeschichtliche Mitteilungen*
Mob-	Mobilmachungs-: mobilization
mot	motorisiert: motorized
MPA	Marinepersonalamt: navy personnel office
MR	*Marine-Rundschau*
MT	motorized transport
MWa	Marinewaffenamt: navy ordnance office
MWehr	Marinewehramt: naval defence office
NDB	*Neue Deutsche Biographie*
NF	Neue Folge: new series
NS	Nationalsozialistisch: National Socialist
NS	New series
NSBO	Nationalsozialistische Betriebszellenorganisation: National Socialist Factory Cells Organisation
NSDAP	Nationalsozialistische Deutsche Arbeiterpartei: National Socialist German Workers' Party
NSDStB	Nationalsozialistischer Deutscher Studentenbund: National Socialist German Students' Association
NSFK	Nationalsozialistisches Fliegerkorps: National Socialist flying corps
NSKK	Nationalsozialistisches Kraftfahr-Korps: National Socialist motorized corps
Ob.d.L.	Oberfehlshaber der Luftwaffe: commander-in-chief of the Luftwaffe
OKH	Oberkommando des Heeres: army high command
OKL	Oberkommando der Luftwaffe: air-force high command
OKM	Oberkommando der Marine: navy high command
OKW	Oberkommando der Wehrmacht: high command of the armed forces
O.Qu.	Oberquartiermeister: senior quartermaster (= assistant chief of staff)
PA	Politisches Archiv des Auswärtigen Amtes (political archives of the foreign ministry), Bonn
PK	Propaganda-Kompanie: military propaganda unit
PRO	Public Record Office, London
PVS	*Politische Vierteljahresschrift*
RAD	Reichsarbeitsdienst: Reich Labour Service
RAF	Royal Air Force
RDI	Reichsverband der Deutschen Industrie: Reich Association of German Industry
R.d.L.	Reichsminister der Luftfahrt: Reich minister of aviation
RGBl.	*Reichsgesetzblatt* (Reich Law Gazette)
RM	Reichsmark (currency)
RMVP	Reichsministerium für Volksaufklärung und Propaganda: Reich ministry for popular enlightenment and propaganda
RSHA	Reichssicherheitshauptamt: Reich central security office

RVDP	Reichsverband der Deutschen Presse: Reich Association of the German Press
S	Schilling (Austrian currency)
SA	Sturmabteilung: storm troops
SD	Sicherheitsdienst: security service
SOPADE	Sozialdemokratische Partei Deutschlands: German Social Democratic Party (in exile in Prague)
SPD	Sozialdemokratische Partei Deutschlands: German Social Democratic Party
SS	Schutzstaffel: guard detachment
StA	Staatsarchiv (state archives), Nuremberg
t.	tonnes
T1, 2	army departments of Truppenamt (*see* Glossary)
TA	Truppenamt: troops office (*see* Glossary)
USPD	Unabhängige Sozialdemokratische Partei Deutschlands: Independent German Social Democratic Party
USSBS	*United States Strategic Bombing Survey*
VDA	Verein für das Deutschtum im Ausland: Association (People's League) for Germans Abroad
VfZG	*Vierteljahrshefte für Zeitgeschichte*
VGAD	Verstärkter Grenzaufsichtdienst: reinforced frontier surveillance service
WA	Wehrmachtamt (*see* Glossary)
Wa.A.	Waffenamt: army ordnance office
WFA	Wehrmachtsführungsamt: operations staff of the armed forces
WFK	Weltbund für internationale Freundschaftsarbeit der Kirchen: World Council of Churches for International Friendship
Wifo	Wirtschaftliche Forschungsgesellschaft: Economic Research Company
WiJ	Wirtschaftstab (economy department) of the army ordnance office
WPA	Wehrpolitisches Amt: combat-policy office (of the National Socialists)
Wi Rü Amt	Wehrwirtschafts- und Rüstungsamt: war-economy and armaments office
WStb	Wehrwirtschaftsstab: war-economy office
W Wi	Wehrwirtschaftliche Abteilung: war-economy department
WWR	*Wehrwissenschaftliche Rundschau*
ZA	Zentralabteilung: central department
z.b.V.	zur besonderen Verwendung: for special duties
ZfG	*Zeitschrift für Geschichtswissenschaft*
ZMG	*Zeitschrift für Militärgeschichte*
ZStA	Zentrales Staatsarchiv (central state archives), Potsdam

Glossary of German Terms

THE following list comprises titles, names of institutions, etc. which are not translated in the text (or not at each occurrence), and also some typically Nazi terms whose connotations are not fully rendered in a literal translation. Some further terms are glossed in the Abbreviations.

Altreich	The 'Old Reich', i.e. Germany prior to the absorption of Austria (or, in context, prior to some other accession of territory).
Anschluss	The union of Austria with the Reich.
Buna	Sodium butadione rubber, a synthetic substitute for rubber developed in Germany with a view to achieving German self-sufficiency in rubber products.
Freikorps	Rightist paramilitary units or 'private armies' in post-1918 Germany.
Führer	Leader; Hitler's title as supreme head of the Party, state, and armed forces, and embodiment of the people's will.
Gau	Region: main territorial unit in the Nazi party structure.
Gauleiter	'Regional leader': head of a *Gau*.
Geschäftsgruppe	'Working committee' of the Four-year Plan administration.
Gleichschaltung	'Co-ordination', i.e. Nazification of all branches of German life from 1933 onwards.
Heeresleitung	Army command in the ministry of defence prior to 1935.
Heimwehr	Austrian rightist paramilitary organization (to 1936).
Junker	Member of the Prussian landed aristocracy.
Kampfbund für den gewerblichen Mittelstand	'Combat Union for the Trading Middle Class': militant association of retailers (in opposition to 'Jewish-controlled' chain-stores).
Land (pl. *Länder*)	The constituent states of Germany; controlled by Reich governors from 1933 onwards.
Landtag	State legislature.
Lebensraum	'Living-space' for Germany, with connotation of conquest in the east.
Luftwaffe	The German air force.
Machtergreifung	'Seizure of power': Hitler's appointment as Chancellor on 30 Jan. 1933. This took place in legal form, but the Nazis deliberately stressed its revolutionary aspect.
Marineleitung	Navy command (cf. *Heeresleitung*).
Mefowechsel	Bills of exchange secured on a fictitious 'metallurgical research' company, as a camouflaged means of financing rearmament.
Ministeramt	'Ministerial office' in the ministry of defence, for political and military matters; subsequently known as the *Wehrmachtamt*.

Ministerialdirektor	(approx.) Under-secretary in a ministry.
Ministerialrat	(approx.) Counsellor in a ministry.
Mitteleuropa	Central Europe (often in context of German hegemony or economic influence).
Ostmark	'Eastern March': name used to denote Austria after the Anschluss.
Panzerschiff	Armoured vessel, 'pocket battleship'.
Reichskanzlei	Reich chancellery.
Reichskommissar, -iat	Reich commissioner, commission.
Reichskristallnacht	'Night of broken glass': the German pogrom of 9–10 Nov. 1938.
Reichslandbund	Reich Agricultural Association.
Reichsleiter	Reich director: title of high Party official responsible for a particular area, e.g. foreign policy, propaganda, etc.
Reichsnährstand	Reich Foodstuffs Corporation.
Reichswehr	Name of the armed forces from 1920 to 1935. See also *Wehr*, *Wehrmacht*.
Stahlhelm	'Steel Helmet': nationalist ex-servicemen's organization.
Totenkopfverbände	'Death's Head' units of the SS.
Truppenamt	'Troops office' in the ministry of defence until 1935: code-name for the general staff, prohibited by the treaty of Versailles.
Verfügungstruppen	'General service troops': militarized formations of the SS (*see* Abbreviations).
Volk	People, race, nation, ethnic stock.
völkisch	Pertaining to the *Volk* (with racialist, mystical, and sentimental-traditionalist overtones); patriotic, nationalist.
Wehr	Defence (as in *Reichswehr*, *Wehrmacht*); also a prefix in numerous compounds with militaristic associations, e.g. *Wehrwille* (military spirit), *Wiederwehrhaftmachung* (remilitarization, sc. of the German people), etc.
Wehrmacht	The German armed forces (from 1935 onwards).
Wehrmachtamt	Title given to the *Ministeramt* (q.v.) from 1935 onwards.
Westwall	The 'West Wall': fortifications in the west of Germany, a line of defence extending from Luxemburg to Switzerland. Known colloquially in Britain as the 'Siegfried Line'.
Wilhelmstrasse, the	Term denoting the German ministry of foreign affairs (from its address in Berlin).

Introduction

THE Second World War and the events leading up to it are the subject of a vast number of academic studies. The archives of the countries involved provide ever-new source-material for research. Some important records, it is true, remain unavailable, either because they were destroyed as a result of the war or because certain states, e.g. the Soviet Union, follow a less liberal policy. However, as far back as the 1960s it was noted that the profusion of studies of specific problems or aspects, such as foreign policy, strategy, the war effort of particular states, or the history of particular services, was in striking contrast to the reluctance of scholars to co-ordinate the mass of material into a comprehensive account. Any deficiency of source-material can no longer be regarded as a serious obstacle to doing so: a much graver deterrent, in all probability, is the enormous bulk of the existing literature and documentation. For example, a recent bibliography on the subject of 'Italy in the Second World War' runs to over 900 pages and comprises over 9,000 items.

The Research Institute for Military History has embarked on the compilation of a ten-volume general account under the title *Germany and the Second World War*. The small group of contributors are aware that such a work cannot aspire to completeness in any particular field or to fill many gaps in the state of research. It is rather a question of attempting to bring order into a multiplicity of data.

The Institute's specific obligation to the academic world is to use for its benefit the extensive holdings of the Military Archives in Freiburg. Historians and researchers have repeatedly expressed the wish that this object might be combined with that of producing a general account of the Second World War.

The suggestion that this might be an 'official' account is open to misunderstanding. It is not the Institute's task to produce work expressing 'the viewpoint of the Federal Republic of Germany'. Such a viewpoint does not exist and therefore cannot be given. By a valuable tradition, the Institute enjoys academic freedom in its work and publications. The authors on its staff are responsible to the learned world for their research and conclusions. In the case of a collective work the question arises as to how the independence of individual authors is to be reconciled with the need to produce, as far as possible, a unified and self-consistent account. It will be the task of the present team of authors to cope with this difficulty. *Germany and the Second World War* will be produced in accordance with the working tradition of the Institute. Owing to staff limitations the volumes can only be tackled successively, but further volumes will be published as rapidly as possible.

In their preliminary consideration the authors had in view the general accounts of the war that have been undertaken or completed in various countries. These illustrate the difficulties involved even when their subject-matter is deliberately restricted, as e.g. in the American publication *The United States Army in World War II*, planned to comprise eighty-five volumes, of which many have already been published. The British *History of the Second World War* has made clear in its various series the number of angles from which the subject can be approached, and has shown what military, political, and social aspects require to be treated in a history of the Second World War. From the Eastern bloc we have the six-volume Soviet *History of the Great Patriotic War*; the Soviet *History of the Second World War 1939–1945* in twelve volumes (1973–82) and *Deutschland im zweiten Weltkrieg*, published in six volumes in East Berlin (1974–86). These works differ radically from those of the West in having a political as well as an academic function. They are intended to provide historical justification for the post-war position of the Soviet Union by connecting the victories of the Red Army with world-wide decolonization and liberation movements. The East German work can also be read as a political and ideological forecast of German history.

We cannot here enumerate, or describe even in a general way, the various studies of the Second World War that have been produced by learned institutions throughout the world. The exchange of ideas has been furthered by many international symposia and reports on projected research in a number of countries. French colleagues are to be thanked for taking the initiative of bringing together historians of the subject in the Comité International d'Histoire de la Deuxième Guerre Mondiale. The Research Institute for Military History has long benefited from international co-operation and kept itself abreast of current and projected research.

The Institute's members have based their work on the realization that they too must adopt specific angles of approach in order to cope with the huge mass of material. We shall attempt to give a brief account of the principles of selection, organization, and treatment. Perhaps the best way of doing so is to cast a glance at the plans for a history of the Second World War that were formulated in Germany in the 1960s. These were based on an interpretation of the conflict as involving, on the one hand, the authoritarian and totalitarian regimes of Germany, Italy, and Japan, with aims limited to particular regions, and, on the other, the Western democracies and the Soviet Union, representing ideas of world order. In this schema the aggressors were portrayed as exponents of neo-imperialistic power politics. Or again the theme was that of a struggle between ambitions of regional hegemony and universal principles of order in the totalitarian age, and the conflict between nationalist expansionism and the 'status quo' powers.

However, it was already apparent in the 1960s that such an approach would not do. Alongside works that failed to discern any conscious purpose in German policy leading to the Second World War, there were already studies of the National Socialist regime from the specific point of view of warlike preparations. Subsequent research showed ever more clearly that the structure of the regime was bound up with the question of the causes and purpose of the war. Alongside the totalitarian thesis which placed Hitler at the centre of all decision-making in the Third Reich, others painted a picture of administrative chaos in which the advance towards war was a more or less accidental effect of internal political developments. However, analyses based on economic arguments referred more and more often to long-term planning and the regime's endeavours to achieve autarky as a preliminary to war.

Then, from the mid-1960s onwards, scholars reverted to earlier themes, such as Hitler's ideas concerning international affairs and whether his 'programme' of the 1920s could be recognized in his foreign policy moves after 1933. Given this evolution of the direction of research, it seemed clear that a general survey was needed which would embrace questions of the structure of the regime, its policies and programmes, economic developments, and rearmament. The working title 'The Third Reich in the World War' was adopted as a basis for continued consideration of the project, the results of which were made known from time to time.

It was clear from the beginning of the Institute's deliberations that a linear account like the Reichsarchiv history of the First World War was no longer a feasible mode of treatment. At the time such an account represented the maximum attainable level of agreement. Even then, it is true, the initial intention was to provide more than simply a history of military events, the war economy, and the state of war armaments; but the plan suffered from irreconcilable differences among those responsible for it. Psychological and political obstacles such as those that stood in the way of a comprehensive account of the First World War in Germany no longer exist today. Hence, it was possible at the planning stage to consider freely what conclusions were to be drawn from the then state of research and from the fact that certain aspects and areas of the subject had been investigated more thoroughly than others. While, for instance, the war at sea or particular operations in Europe and elsewhere have been studied in great detail, there are gaps as regards some aspects of the pre-war period and economic and social developments during the war itself. However, it was clear from the outset that the Institute could not embark on an economic and social history of Germany from 1933 to 1945. The task was essentially to produce a military history—not, however, a 'war history' of the traditional kind, confined to military events, but a history of the German people in wartime.

The Institute has been concerned for some years with the task of formulating an up-to-date conception of military history. It has expressed its views on this problem in several publications. It may nowadays be taken as agreed that military history is part of history in general, and is not concerned only with problems that bear some practical relation to the soldier's profession. It is also recognized that the military historian must apply the methods of historical science if he wishes to achieve adequate results. Given the interdependence of military, political, economic, and ideological factors, and the other social forces that determine the shape and structure of an era, his field of interest is both enlarged and complicated. If he seeks to ascertain and lay down basic guidelines for the investigation of historical processes, he will also have to engage in a dialogue with sister disciplines without losing sight of his own particular interest. His enquiry must include the subjects of these disciplines in so far as their problems make this necessary. The present authors have approached their task without committing themselves beforehand to any particular theory as to the structure and policy of the National Socialist state—either that of totalitarianism or any of the interpretations of Fascism. They do, however, adhere to the view that National Socialism is to be regarded as a particular form of Fascism. This view, which is not meant dogmatically, is based on recognizable parallels in the manifestation of Fascist movements. This approach does not involve the danger that has been described as 'generalizing the concept of Fascism' at the expense of 'the distinction between totalitarian and democratic politics'. Within that concept, as here applied, it remains entirely possible to decribe Hitler's position from a basis of specific research rather than on a priori assumptions. We have seen it as an object of our enquiry to explain Hitler's part in the National Socialist system and to do so from the point of view of the preparation and conduct of war. In this way foreign, military, and economic policy assume greater importance than other spheres which Hitler may have had less interest in controlling.

However, while possibilities of interpretation are thus left open, it should be said at once that the 'agent theory', long regarded as authoritative by Marxist historians, can be ignored as contrary to the facts. This theory, formulated by Georgi Dimitrov at the Seventh Congress of the Comintern and endorsed in 1933 at the Thirteenth Plenum of the Executive Committee of that body, was expressed as follows: 'Fascism is the overt terrorist dictatorship of the most reactionary, chauvinist, and imperialist elements of finance capital.' Hitler cannot be regarded as a puppet of finance capital. No one but he enjoyed mass support in Germany before and during the war, especially from 1936 onwards; it was he who set the course for the war which broke out on 1 September 1939, and it is thus correct to speak of his 'unleashing' that war.

However, the respective parts played by Hitler, the military, big business, and the rest of the state apparatus during 1933–45 cannot, in many cases, be identified in such a way that it is meaningful to enquire who gave the orders or who carried them out. Long-term processes, such as those necessary to speed up rearmament despite the shortage of raw materials and foreign currency, acquired a momentum of their own, from which their authors could not disengage without abandoning their objectives. The same may be said of the 'necessities' occasioned by the war. Scholars have disagreed as to the methods by which the ever-new problems were dealt with; but it remains true that no one supplanted Hitler at the helm. There was a complete or partial identification of interests, and from 1 September 1939 onwards all were agreed that the war must be won. The potential centres of resistance achieved no co-ordination; their base was too narrow for any successful action.

During the preparation for war and during the war itself, it is possible to identify forms of co-operation or collaboration with Hitler on the part of various leading groups in Germany, but in these cases terms like 'alliance' or 'coalition' are hardly appropriate except in the initial stage of Nazi rule. The more Hitler consolidated his position by success in foreign affairs, the less accurate are descriptions implying a kind of contractual agreement between independent partners. The notion of a polycracy among official bodies may suitably designate the variety and, from time to time, the conflict of interests at the highest levels under Hitler; and certainly it is possible to discern a trend towards a degree of independence at the middle and lower levels, which has been called a manifestation of 'polyarchy'. But, however useful such conceptual approaches may be in detail—e.g. the often cited notion of 'pluralism'—it remains a fact that all the parallel initiatives and the conflicting intentions, plans, and strategies were circumscribed by the policy of rearming at high speed and gaining a favourable position for the start of a war, the purpose and objectives of which were ultimately determined by Hitler alone. It was quite consistent with this that various relatively powerful leaders and props of his regime emphasized different aspects of the rearmament process: this applied to Goebbels, Ley, Himmler, Rosenberg, the Wehrmacht, and several other bodies. Similarly, the respective services did not always see eye to eye on matters of armament and organization; different views were taken of strategic and operational questions; and there were similar divergences over economic policy. It even occurred that individual highly placed functionaries concerned with foreign affairs, the economy, or defence regarded this or that move by Hitler as premature or misguided; but this did not signify a serious challenge to his overriding power. What stands out is the consistency of the German effort to attain hegemony in Europe. In Hitler's unswerving plan, with its racial ideology, that hegemony was furthermore intended to solve the problem of 'space' for generations to come. Domestic, foreign, and economic policy were all harnessed to that end. The scale of rearmament pointed in this direction even before 1939. Day-to-day foreign policy and propaganda were designed to protect the rearmament process and make it possible to gain vantage-points so that the great overall aim could be progressively realized. In a sense, foreign policy itself was geared to the economic policy of arming for future expansion, and was made subservient to the developing requirements and 'necessities' of what had become an irreversible process.

Historians have spoken of Hitler's even more ambitious dreams of world supremacy. These remained in the sphere of intentions only, leading to few decisions of importance to the actual preparation and conduct of the war. Indeed, the conditions in which it was launched precluded such far-reaching ideas, for which Germany simply did not possess an adequate economic or military basis.

The Second World War, involving in the end over sixty belligerents, took on dimensions with which Hitler, the Wehrmacht, and the German economy did not reckon in 1939. The design of the present work is determined by the course taken by the war, its extension to other countries and areas, and the progressive exploitation of the human and material resources, first of Germany and ultimately of the greater part of Europe.

The volume describing the origins of the war is followed by three volumes dealing with the establishment of hegemony in Europe, the extension of German rule over Poland, Denmark, Norway, Holland, Belgium, Luxemburg, France, Yugoslavia, and Greece, and finally the North African campaigns and the invasion of the Soviet Union. The German–Soviet war is treated in particular detail. This was a war for the realization of Hitler's essential programme, and the failure of 'Operation Barbarossa' marked the beginning of a change of fortune, the end of the blitzkrieg. In that war the German leadership was confronted most acutely with the problems of coalition warfare. In these four volumes emphasis is laid on the strategic design of the belligerents, the course of military operations, and the dependence of plans on economic potential and the armaments situation.

Volume V deals with the organization of the German power-sphere in Europe up to the summer of 1941. It is intended to display a cross-section in a way that cannot be attempted in the narrative volumes. The German occupation still dominates the memory of the countries concerned more powerfully than the short campaigns in which they were defeated. If only for this reason, a military history compiled from the German point of view must describe the German rule in Europe with all its features and accompanying phenomena, as well as the organization of the human and material resources of the German power-sphere for the purpose of carrying on the war.

Volume VI describes the extension of the European war into a world war. It poses the question whether the events in Europe and the Pacific are to be regarded as two separate wars, or whether, given the American war aims and Hitler's ultimate intentions, it is correct to speak of *the* Second World War. Subsequent volumes will deal with Germany's loss of the initiative after Stalingrad and the allied landings in North Africa. A further 'cross-section' volume will describe the situation of 'fortress Europe' in the context of Germany's desperate endeavours to mobilize her forces against the Allies' strategic bombing and against resistance and liberation movements, and to consolidate her defences against the expected invasion of the Continent. The war economy, deportations, the exploitation of the occupied countries, and the fate of Jews in Hitler's empire will be described, as will the situation in Germany and the developments that led to the attempt on Hitler's life on 20 July 1944, with the resulting further shift of power in favour of the Party and the SS.

The remaining volumes will be devoted to military operations involving the Allied advance to Germany's frontiers, the retreat from France, the Soviet Union, Poland, and the Baltic States, and the collapse of the Third Reich. Finally, an attempt will be made to sum up the results of the war and the consequences of total defeat for the German people.

Despite excursions to the Pacific area, the work as a whole is conceived from a European and even a specifically German viewpoint. But, given the scale of the conflict in Europe, the extension of German rule over a large part of the Continent, and Germany's partnership, unequal though it was, with a number of allies, it will be necessary to depict a portion of European history which is largely a tale of violence, injustice, and exploitation.

Germany's efforts before the war to manœuvre herself once more into the position of a great power belong to the context of European history. Her domestic and foreign, economic and armaments policies that led to war were a matter not only of interest but of direct concern to her European neighbours. The treaty of Versailles affected all Europe, and the way in which National Socialist Germany overcame that unhappy heritage of the First World War became the dominant theme of European politics after 1933. It can indeed be said that the events leading up to the Second World War were determined by the attitude of the nations of Europe to the experiences and consequences of the war of 1914–18. These were not only matters for soldiers and statesmen, but for nations and societies as well. Accordingly, the authors of the present work are fully aware that its Germano-centric plan must not be allowed to obscure the European and world-wide horizon of events.

The work is not primarily addressed to professional historians. It is intended to be of use to students of all ages who are interested in history, and in particular to contribute to the spread of historical knowledge in the Federal German armed forces. For this reason numerous references to primary and secondary sources are given in the notes. However, the authors have avoided detailed treatment of historical controversies, which are already known to scholars and will not be missed by the general reader.

Volume I is entitled *The Build-up of German Aggression*. The working group headed by Wilhelm Deist has chosen this title as a concise statement of its viewpoint. The German leaders, with their plans for achieving all-out rearmament and a comprehensive state of national discipline and ideological conformity, set out to remedy as fast as possible the effects of the world economic depression. Their objective, apart from stabilizing the country economically and socially, was certainly not to reinforce the international security system, but to make Germany once again a great power so that she could profit from the undermining of that system—which, admittedly, was called in question by other powers as well. Our first volume is divided into four parts describing the preparation for war in the field of propaganda and home policy, economic planning, armaments, and foreign policy. These contributions do not constitute comprehensive history of the pre-war years. In many respects a more detailed study would have been desirable. Thus, social policy could only be dealt with selectively, chiefly from the point of view of whether it set bounds to the ruthless exploitation of labour and, to some extent, protected living standards against the financial demands or rearmament. Hitler's decisions in this respect were no doubt influenced by his study of events during the closing phase of the First World War. However, a balanced treatment of this theme is impossible pending the investigation of important areas of economic and social history. The authors also had to refrain from offering an independent treatment of financial policy and from going into details of military technology or the history of state, Wehrmacht, and party organization; these, however, are not hard to find in the specialized literature. There is no systematic treatment of anti-Semitism, since, although inextricably involved with Nazi ideology, propaganda, home and foreign policy, and with the regime's often proclaimed war aims, it did not have a decisive effect on direct preparations for war.

As the conclusions are intended once again to make clear, the co-ordination of the four contributions has been attempted only in terms of the theme 'preparation for war'. The reader will judge how far it has been successful. The difficulties of such an undertaking are known to all who have sought to investigate this period of

German history. Little direct record exists of policy-planning by Hitler and his closest associates. There was in Berlin no 'cabinet' to which, in the normal course of business, all important proposals would be submitted for discussion and decision. Hitler's style was entirely different. His role was completely unlike that of a Western prime minister. His statements to various representatives of the state, the army, the party, and the business world, even when they coincided in point of time, were often irreconcilable with one another.

Hitler's curious reluctance to discuss his 'programme' with army leaders and heads of the foreign ministry, so as to draw strategic and foreign-policy conclusions in good time, was due partly to the fact that he could afford to leave such problems in suspense, since in any case there was sufficient will to co-operate in material and ideological respects. Another reason was that in Hitler's mind 'ideal' combinations conflicted with the constraints brought about by actual developments, which in foreign affairs were themselves often a reaction of German moves.

Thus, as regarded the decision-making process in Berlin, the study of the origins of the Second World War is confronted with difficulties bound up with the organization of the National Socialist state, with Hitler's style of leadership, his 'programme', and the manner of its progressive realization, which was affected by the reactions and initiatives of other powers as well as the economic 'necessities' of rearmament. Without attempting any general statement as to the role of the individual in history, it remains the case that Hitler ultimately gave direction to the policy of preparing for aggressive war—despite all procedural hesitations, despite much uncertainty and dependence on the structures of a modern industrial state, poor in raw materials, with its élite classes likewise imbued with revisionism. The European war that broke out on 1 September 1939 would not have done so but for Hitler. Very probably, sooner or later, a different war would have broken out with the lines differently drawn, but that is not our subject here.

The authors of this volume have received help and advice from many colleagues and institutions. Meetings of historians have assisted in the preparation of the work.

Special thanks for critical advice and comments are due to Professors Volker R. Berghahn (Warwick), Charles Bloch (Paris, Tel Aviv), Francis L. Carsten (London), Fritz Fischer (Hamburg), Michael Geyer (Ann Arbor), and Timothy W. Mason (Oxford).

Documents from the following archives have been used: National Archives, Washington; Public Record Office, London; Bundesarchiv, Koblenz; Bundesarchiv-Militärarchiv, Freiburg; Politisches Archiv des Auswärtigen Amtes, Bonn; Archiv des Instituts für Zeitgeschichte, Munich. The authors express their thanks for kind co-operation in this connection.

MANFRED MESSERSCHMIDT,
Chief Historian,
Research Institute for
  Military History,
1970–88

PART I

Ideology, Propaganda, and Internal Politics as Preconditions of the War Policy of the Third Reich

WOLFRAM WETTE

I. Militarist and Pacifist Ideologies in the Last Phase of the Weimar Republic

1. The Problem: Militarism in the Weimar Republic and the Second World War

Whereas in August 1914 the Germans went to war in a spirit of nationalist fervour, there was little sign of enthusiasm or jingoism in September 1939. The prevailing mood on the day of the invasion of Poland was characterized by a foreign observer[1] as one of apathy. Karl Wahl, the Gauleiter of Swabia, who visited many parts of the Reich at that time, described his impressions as follows: 'Nothing on the journey reminded me of 1914: no enthusiasm, no joy, no cheering. Wherever you went there was an uncanny quiet, not to say depression. The whole German people seemed to be gripped by a paralytic fear which made it incapable either of applauding or of expressing discontent.'[2] Another observer at a later date similarly described the contrast with the enthusiasm that swept Germany in 1914: this time people seemed full of anxiety, and he spoke of the 'dull obedience of the masses disciplined by terror into blind mechanical loyalty and also bewildered and stupefied by a militant propaganda.[3] A majority of the German population at the outbreak of war was 'loyal, but reluctantly so'.[4]

The picture painted by these observers was confirmed by the official agencies concerned with assessing public opinion. These described the population as calm and self-possessed, but depressed and apathetic.[5] It is known how coolly Hitler was greeted by the Berliners who turned out, not in large numbers, on that Friday, 1 September, when he drove from the new Reich Chancellery to the Kroll Opera House to give an account of his actions to the Reichstag.[6]

The shock caused by the announcement that hostilities had begun was intensified by the British and French declarations of war on 3 September. Hitler himself is said to have been taken aback, as he had counted on Western neutrality. After Poland had been crushed in a few weeks, on 6 October Hitler made a speech in the Reichstag offering peace, but on terms that involved the Western powers acquiescing in the conquest of Poland.[7] The 'peace' speech and the lack of any Anglo-French action on land were regarded by the German people as parts of a single phenomenon, the man in the street taking them as a confirmation of his hopes that hostilities would soon cease. Peace rumours persisted, although they were constantly denied and the mass media continued to stir up warlike sentiments.

---

[1] Thus the American correspondent W. L. Shirer, quoted in Steinert, *Hitlers Krieg*, 91.
[2] Wahl, *Deutsches Herz*, 246.   [3] Ritter, *Resistance*, 139.
[4] Krausnick and Graml, 'Widerstand', 482.
[5] Steinert, *Hitlers Krieg*, 91–2.
[6] Dröge, *Widerstand*, 78 (also for the following passage).
[7] Hitler's speech to the Reichstag, 6 Oct. 1939, in Domarus, ii. 1377–93; here 1388 ff.

Thus, when the Second World War was unleashed by the German invasion of Poland, the mood in Germany was one of passivity, anxiety, shock, and disquiet. A profound gap seemed to divide the National Socialist leadership from large sections of the population, who did not want war and certainly not a world war. However, the German people as a whole behaved as the government wished it to: it obeyed, in reluctant loyalty.

How is this behaviour to be explained? Why did the Germans 'follow Hitler dumbly into war and do nothing to prevent themselves being dragged into the abyss'?[8] How could it be that millions of people conformed to a policy which meant no less than a risk of physical extinction for every one of them, whether his part in the war was active or passive? They did so, moreover, despite the fact that many of them must have had vivid memories of the horrors of 1914–18. Was it because the German people tacitly supported the National Socialist regime—or did they dissent from it but see no means of opposing it by word or deed, all-powerful as it appeared to be? Had the principle of leadership and obedience already installed itself in such a way that the Germans had degenerated into a 'will-less mass'? Or was war simply accepted as something decreed by fate, a quasi-natural phenomenon in a world ruled by national egotism? And did the German people, over and above this, harbour specific political hopes and wishes—such as frontier revision, colonies, or the general strengthening of Germany's position in Europe and the world—for the sake of which they were prepared to go to war once again?

No one will dispute that these questions must be answered if we are to form a valid judgement as to the causes and preconditions of the Second World War. But it is easier to state the questions than to answer them; and the present state of research[9] does not allow us to dismiss any of them as irrelevant.

What are the facts and events that must be taken into account in order to provide an adequate explanation of the origins of the Second World War? Historians give very different answers to this question. There is, however, a fair measure of agreement that an analysis confined to the period immediately before the outbreak of war, e.g. the year 1939, is bound to leave important factors out of account. It would be inadmissible thus to disregard the manifold strands of continuity in the realm of ideology and foreign policy, in military and economic matters, and in many other respects.

Among the ideologies of importance in this connection, special interest of course attaches to the National Socialist philosophy of war and the use of force, which from 1933 onwards formed the basis for the remilitarization (*Wiederwehrhaftmachung*) of the German people both materially and psychologically. None the less, an analysis of the war ideology of National Socialism does not provide a sufficient answer to what is here our main question, namely what was the attitude of the German people towards war or, more generally, the use of force as an instrument of policy. We need to know this in relation to the population as a whole and to that part of it which was politically articulate—and, in the absence of contemporary opinion polls, our

[8] Steinert, *Hitlers Krieg*, 93.
[9] Cf. Deutsch, *Kriegsursachenforschung*, and Gantzel, *System*.

enquiry must begin with the articulate élite. Certainly an intensive ideological indoctrination took place in 1933–9; but to be fully effective this must have been grafted on to existing mental habits and traditions.

It follows that the ideological background to the Second World War must be seen in a longer historical perspective. In what follows we shall look back to the closing years of the Weimar Republic. Whereas after 1933 the public expression of opinion in Germany underwent massive restriction and by degrees was narrowed down to one opinion only, that of the regime, in the pre-Hitler period all political and social groups enjoyed freedom to publish and propagate their views. As is well known, they used this freedom most extensively during the Republic's period of crisis (1923–33). To many observers Germany at this time gave the impression of a regular battleground for the most different and in some cases the most eccentric ideas and ideologies. Today it is no easy matter to analyse and define these ideas and to classify them into basic tendencies. It is scarcely possible to give a complete picture of the many-faceted spectrum of opinions; instead we are obliged to make a selection from the standpoint of their political importance.

In this survey we shall consider particularly the leaders and spokesmen of political parties, of the churches and other important interest-groups, including students, for example. Our object is to discover what ideological positions were adopted by the leaders of political opinion in the last years of the Weimar Republic with regard to the range of questions that may be loosely defined as related to 'war and peace.' More precisely, which of the politically articulate social groups at that time were prepared in principle to accept or contemplate the use of military force as an instrument of foreign policy, and which other groups were opposed to this or advocated a policy of peaceful understanding with other countries?

If it should appear that a definite military or warlike ideology was already widespread before 1933—perhaps even more so than the anti-democratic mood of the time—then this would throw some light on the period immediately before the outbreak of war. It would explain in part how it was possible in September 1939 for the National Socialist propaganda machine to switch more or less suddenly from peaceful protestations to a warlike note. If a majority of the German nation or its political spokesmen during the inter-war years already thought in terms of war rather than peace, if they were militaristic rather than pacifist,[10] it would follow that the National Socialists—whose object was to condition the whole population psychologically for war—needed only to apply their technique of persuasion to the minority who believed in the settlement of conflict by peaceful means.

Particular attention is due here to the 'warlike' or 'military' spirit (*Wehrgedanke*) which was extolled by the various right-wing groups in the Weimar period, and to which parties of the centre, and even in some cases of the left, felt obliged to show respect during the last years of the republic. What did this slogan mean in its

---

[10] In the present study the terms 'militarism' and 'pacifism' are used as a basis of analysis. Both are fundamental historical concepts that have an acknowledged place in German politico-social studies, making it possible to 'analyse structures and major connections of events'. Cf. *Geschichtliche Grundbegriffe*, preface, vol. i, pp. xiii–xiv. On the historical concept of militarism cf. ibid. iv, 1–47; on pacifism, ibid. 767–87.

various interpretations? Was it aimed at breaking asunder the 'chains of Versailles'? Was it identical with an aggressive, warlike ideology, or was it merely a doctrine of national defence resting, at least in part, on a rational foundation?

Here it should at once be pointed out that the treaty of Versailles had confronted Germany with two alternatives that may be summarily expressed as follows. She could either pursue a policy of peaceful understanding with the victors of the First World War—which did not rule out a revision of the treaty, but did mean renouncing an active policy of military strength; or, in line with traditional German nationalism, she could attempt to regain a position of military and political power by evading the restrictions of Versailles.[11] Given the military impotence of the Weimar Republic, those who advocated the 'reawakening of the fighting spirit' (*Wehrwillen*), and who attacked the policy of compliance with the treaty, thereby signified their hope that in the long run, and at the proper time, the cultivation of the fighting spirit would be followed by actual rearmament, making possible a foreign policy that would not entail compromise for the sake of friendly relations. At all events, many champions of the ambiguous notion of 'defence' did not believe in peaceful understanding but in power politics in one form or another, and the effect of their propaganda was to gain adherents for this attitude. Their ideology concerning the state and defence matters was, it can be shown, largely bound up with traditional ideas of the primacy of foreign policy and the recovery of Germany's position as a world power.[12]

Immediately after the end of the Second World War the historian Friedrich Meinecke[13] formulated the alternative in similar terms. The Weimar majority, he wrote, had been firmly determined

to throw off, or at least to loosen, one by one, the fetters of the Versailles treaty, by working patiently and slowly through steady if meagre compromises with the victorious powers. It was at that time the only politically realistic method possible for gradually doing away with the restrictions. Any other method threatened sooner or later to lead to war, and any war to lead again, as happened later, to a catastrophe for Germany.

To prevent any misunderstanding of the scope and basis of the following survey, it should once more be expressly pointed out that the question of the attitude of particular leaders of opinion to war and the use of force is not to be identified with the much more general question of the degree of sympathy or antipathy felt for the National Socialist regime by the parties, associations, churches, and other groups under consideration. We shall be primarily concerned with that aspect of their ideology that relates to the use of force in politics and especially in foreign policy. Our subject is thus a different one from that which concentrated on the opposition between democracy and dictatorship, and which was not concerned, or only marginally so, with the part played by warlike ideologies as a precondition of

---

[11] Salewski's interpretation in 'Sicherheitspolitik' is open to question. On the question as to the extent to which, and the period during which, conciliation (*Verständigung*) became a specific foreign policy of the Weimar governments, see now the basic analysis in Krüger, *Außenpolitik*.

[12] Cf. Hillgruber, *Großmachtpolitik*.

[13] Meinecke, *Catastrophe*, 44.

German war policy. In the light of this purpose, the question as to the relation of particular non-National Socialist groups to National Socialism before 1933 becomes a question as to their closeness to, or distance from, the National Socialist ideology of war and the use of force, while after 1933 it is a question of their readiness to co-operate with the regime in preparing for war on the home front by propaganda and other means.

Under the general heading of 'militarism' we shall group the ideologies of those who advocated a policy in which military force was to play a decisive role and military methods of organization were to be applied to society in general. 'Militarism' is indeed more than an ideological phenomenon—it also relates to economy, social order, armaments, home policy, and other fields; but it is characteristic of the form it took after the First World War, and the debate concerning it in inter-war Germany, that the subject was narrowed to ideological matters and to the civilian attitude of mind, while other equally important aspects of militarism were neglected.[14] The militarist ideologies of the Weimar period gave expression to certain values and attitudes according to which 'soldierly' qualities were held up for admiration and emulation. To quote an expert on the ideologies represented by the militant political associations of the Weimar period:

'Soldier' was a term of praise in itself, denoting the 'better' or more 'active' member of the nation, and also a model for those concerned with politics. To be a soldier meant subordination, service, self-sacrifice—all virtues which, properly understood, no community can do without. But it also meant a specific attitude in political matters, ideological 'backbone', the habit of thinking in terms of command and obedience, the leadership principle, hierarchical order, military subordination, and discipline in political affairs as well.[15]

The type of militarist outlook that was widespread in the Weimar period included, in addition to these ideas, that of the natural necessity of war. A future war as an instrument of national policy was an inseparable part of the militarist outlook.

In contradistinction to 'militarism', the general term 'pacifist' includes all ideologies which—again in the context of the actual historical situation of Weimar Germany—were opposed to military aggression and any measures preparatory to it. Those who thought in this way advocated the renunciation of force; they were for reaching a peaceful understanding with other countries, a compromise with the victors of 1918, and peaceful revision of the treaty of Versailles. Those aims were common to all moderate and radical pacifists, whatever their other differences. During the Weimar period there were numerous forms of pacifism; all expressed a

---

[14] Berghahn, *Militarismus*, 16. According to Berghahn there is as yet no theory of militarism that is recognized by all political schools of thought, so that the concept is still 'vague and controversial' (ibid. 31). The definition used here is convenient for the purposes of our investigation. Cf. now also Berghahn, *Militarism*. On militarism in the Weimar Republic in general, and the differences between it and the militarism of the Empire, cf. *Militär und Militarismus*, and Geyer, *Aufrüstung*. These works examine the interrelation of military, industrial, administrative, and social factors against the background of the dynamic process of the industrialization of war. They deal only incidentally with the militarist ideologies that are in the forefront of the present study.

[15] Rohe, *Reichsbanner*, 111–12.

desire for peace, but many held to a radical formulation of extreme idealistic positions which debarred them from achieving a realistic peace policy;[16] this was the essential weakness of a section of the pacifist movement in Weimar days. In the account which follows we shall include under the broad heading of pacifism the policy of the parties which formed the 'Weimar coalition', in so far and for as long as they did not abandon the basic principles of the policy of peaceful understanding.[17] This variant of pacifism could be associated with a firm belief in the need to possess armed forces.

We shall devote much attention to the militarist ideologies of the last years of the Weimar Republic, as they are at least indirectly connected with the question of responsibility for the Second World War. Certainly the National Socialist government of Germany brought about this particular war and is beyond question responsible for the time of its outbreak and the first military moves, as a government which unleashes a war has the immediate initiative on its side. But it was not only the National Socialists who considered it legitimate to wage war in support of German power: many other groups and parties in Germany thought the same. The racialist (*völkisch*), anti-Semitic, authoritarian, and militaristic traditions of the Kaiser's Germany were no less alive among large parts of the population in the 1920s than was nationalism itself. The Nazis rode this wave of feeling and made it serve their purpose.

The various pacifist tendencies by which many Germans were influenced in Weimar times were seen by the National Socialist regime as an obstacle to their essential aim of remilitarizing Germany materially and psychologically and preparing it for war. To remove the obstacle was in large measure the task of propaganda, which, as we shall see in Chapter I.II below, had to take account of pacifist sentiment among the workers and the left-of-centre bourgeoisie, so that the strategy of psychological mobilization for the intended war was pursued in a variety of ways. The fact that the mood of the German people in September 1939 was so different from that of August 1914 is perhaps to be explained by the continuing effect of pacifist ideologies. The National Socialist regime's measures of domestic and social policy, as described in Chapter I.III, also appear in retrospect as closely bound up with the policy of preparation for war.

To conclude these preliminary remarks, it should be said that in this context neither ideologies, nor National Socialist propaganda, nor the regime's internal policy will be dealt with as separate themes. The object is rather to analyse all three with a view to discovering whether and to what extent they must be regarded as causes and preconditions of German war policy.

[16] In Nov. 1924 Carl von Ossietzky wrote with reference to radical-pacifist positions: 'German pacifism was always illusionary, starry-eyed, or doctrinaire—mistrustful of political methods and of the leaders who used them. It was a philosophy, a religion, a set of dogmas that had never been transformed into energy. It might occasionally succeed in making a few slogans catch on, or holding a successful meeting, but it never created a mass organization: the people always stood aside from it' (Ossietzky, *Pazifisten*, 38 f.). On organized pacifism cf. I.1.8 below.

[17] This non-dogmatic concept of pacifism is fully discussed in the present author's 'Probleme des Pazifismus', 9–25, esp. 13 ff.

2. The National Socialist Ideology of Violence and Hitler's War Plans

The use of force played such a prominent role in the ideology and political practice of German Fascism that, after the defeat of 1945, the ideas of 'Fascism' and 'violence' were virtually equated in everyday speech. Considering the melancholy results of the National Socialist policy of war and racialism,[18] no one will deny the justice of this fact. In the Second World War, which Germany unleashed, 27 million soldiers of all nations died in battle, while altogether 25 million civilians lost their lives, over 5 million of them as victims of Nazi racial policy.

But the connection between Fascism and violence is only imperfectly understood if attention is confined to the Second World War and its consequences. 'Force' must be regarded as a general term[19] comprising the whole range of manifestations of the non-peaceful policy of National Socialism. The historical development of that policy may be divided into four phases: first, the vehement advocacy of a specific ideology of force; second, the mobilization of the masses by terrorist methods as a means towards conquest by force; third, the terrorist use of force in home affairs for the purpose of establishing a dictatorship and militarizing the whole of society in preparation for war; and fourth, the extension of violence to foreign territories by means of expansionist warfare.

If 'violence' is further understood[20] to mean not only the direct power to kill or injure in body or mind, but also the suppression of political liberties and the practice of lawlessness, injustice, and exploitation, then Fascism in its German form once again exemplifies the definition to the uttermost.

The glorification of war and conflict, the terrorist use of force, and resort to war are the most obvious common features of Fascism in European countries, especially Germany and Italy. To them may be added the totalitarian claim to power, the dictatorial principle, and the propagandist cult of the Leader, the use of terrorist paramilitary bands, and so on. Although there were certainly many differences between Italian Fascism, German National Socialism, and other Fascist movements, it is possible to identify similar basic patterns which suffice to relate the movements to a single type which can be generally called 'Fascism'.[21] The argument over the misleading term 'left-wing Fascism' (or 'Fascism of the left'), which came into the use in the 1960s,[22] has shown that clarity of definition tends to be lost when one element of Fascism, in this case violence, is singled out and substituted for the whole.

The academic and political discussion concerning Fascism is far from being closed.[23] Some objection to the use of the term has arisen from liberal theories of

---

[18] Jacobsen, *Der Zweite Weltkrieg*, 30.   [19] Sauer, 'Mobilmachung', II ff.; cf. also I.III.4 below.
[20] On the concept of violence see Galtung, 'Gewalt', 55–104; Gronow and Hilppö, 'Violence', 311–20; Rammstedt, *Gewaltverhältnisse*. For a critique of Galtung cf. Matz, *Politik und Gewalt*, 70 ff.
[21] Erdmann, *Zeit der Weltkriege*, 362; also Thamer, *Verführung*, 22 ff. (the author of this latest comprehensive account of the Third Reich also holds to the concept of Facism).
[22] The term was coined by J. Habermas: cf. Kernig, 'Kriegslehre', 86.
[23] Cf. e.g. *Theorien über den Faschismus*; *Texte zur Faschismusdiskussion*; Clemenz, *Gesellschaftliche*

totalitarianism: the term, it is contended, is so general as often to obscure more than it explains, and is thus unhelpful to scientific discussion. Politically, again, it is argued that Fascism is a 'Soviet formula',[24] a polemical expression tending in some degree to 'trivialize' the notion of totalitarian dictatorship.[25]

However, the concept of Fascism was used before 1933 by Liberals,[26] Social Democrats,[27] Catholics,[28] and other non-Communists, not in the sense given to it by Soviet Marxist theory, but the precise opposite.[29] Consequently it is not the case that anyone who used the concept is merely parroting a 'Soviet formula'.[30] Moreover, the objections advanced against the term lend some colour to the mistaken view, which may have serious political consequences, that National Socialist Fascism, as National Socialism, was simply one form of socialism among others. This misunderstanding might lead one to overlook the fact that the Nazis ferociously combated and persecuted the Social Democrats, Communists, and trade unionists under the opprobrious general heading of 'Marxism.'

The actual course of the National Socialists' conquest of power, their policy of oppression and preparation for war, is traced elsewhere in this volume. As regards militarist tendencies in the Weimar Republic, with which we are concerned here, the following problems are of interest. Firstly, we have to analyse the National Socialist ideology of force,[31] more especially as it was expressed in the philosophy of the Party's chief personality, Adolf Hitler; secondly, we have to show how the Führer's conception of foreign policy took shape on the basis of that ideology; thirdly, we shall enquire whether Hitler's warlike intentions were common knowledge before 1933 or whether they were disregarded by the public.[32] This will lead to the further question whether Hitler's ideology of force was specifically National Socialist or whether there were other political groups in the Weimar period which found it natural to think in similar terms.

Hitler's attitude towards the use of force in politics was not primarily based on functional considerations or purely rational calculation, but rather on a particular 'philosophy', namely the bizarre mixture of metaphysics and biology according to which conflict in general and war in particular were to be regarded as natural laws which neither an individual nor a nation could flout without incurring destruction. 'He who would live must fight. He who does not wish to fight in this world, where

---

Ursprünge; Mansilla, *Faschismus*; Wippermann, *Faschismustheorien*; Schulz, *Faschismus*; *Faschismus als soziale Bewegung*; Saage, *Faschismustheorien*; Winkler, *Revolution, Staat, Faschismus*.

[24] Bracher, *Schlüsselwörter*, 104; cf. also 26–7.

[25] Bracher, 'Faschismus', 551.

[26] e.g. Stresemann: see I.1.6 below, also I.1.3 n. 89.

[27] Cf. e.g. the terminology used by the Fourth Congress of the Socialist Workers' International in a resolution in summer 1931 on 'The situation in Germany and Central Europe and the Working Classes' Fight for Democracy', repr. in Braunthal, *Geschichte der Internationale*, ii. 570 ff., here p. 571. Cf. also Wette, 'Stimmzettel', 358–403, esp. 375 ff.

[28] Cf. e.g. Riesenberger, *Friedensbewegung*, 261 ff.

[29] For a critique of the Communist theory of Fascism cf. I.1.9 below.

[30] Bracher, *Schlüsselwörter*, 104.

[31] On this point see Jacobsen's article 'Krieg'.

[32] Cf. Lange, *Hitlers unbeachtete Maximen*.

permanent struggle is the law of life, has not the right to exist.'[33] Elsewhere in *Mein Kampf* Hitler speaks of 'the eternal laws of life on this earth, which are and will remain those of a ceaseless struggle for existence'.[34]

The central idea of a 'struggle for life' (*Lebenskampf*),[35] which Hitler repeatedly invoked in the first volume of *Mein Kampf* and which was no doubt influenced by Darwin,[36] did not necessarily mean war in all circumstances, but it included the notion of war from the beginning. Hitler always regarded war as 'one of the obvious ways of attaining political ends. The ends might change, but the means were axiomatic.'[37] In a chapter of his 'Second Book' (written in 1928 but not published till after his death) entitled 'War and Peace in the Struggle for Life' he traced the idea of the 'permanent struggle' in world history as follows:

History itself is the presentation of the course of a people's struggle for existence. I deliberately use the phrase 'struggle for existence' here because in truth that struggle for daily bread, equally in peace and war, is an eternal battle against thousands upon thousands of resistances, just as life itself is an eternal struggle against death. For men know as little why they live as does any other creature in this world. Only life is filled with the longing to preserve itself.

The 'two most powerful life-instincts' are hunger and love. The 'law' that 'self-preservation and continuance are the great urges underlying all action' applies equally to individuals and peoples. But 'the possibility of satisfaction is limited, so the logical consequence is a struggle in all its forms'. In particular, living-space is limited, and hence there arises 'the compulsion to engage in the struggle for existence'.[38]

This leads to a particular view of politics, which is 'in truth the execution of a nation's struggle for existence'.[39] It is not essentially warlike or essentially peaceful, but must 'always choose the weapon of its struggle so that life in the highest sense of the word is served'.[40] According to this view the difference between the concepts of peace and war 'sank into nothingness', since 'the stake over which politics wrestles is always life itself'.[41] Hence Hitler's conviction that the task of truly great legislators and statesmen was never 'limited preparation for war' but rather 'the unlimited, inner, and thorough training of a people'.[42] In this way war was presented as a normal condition, a regular occurrence, to be distinguished from peace only by the amount of force involved. Hitler also expounded his idea of unlimited forcible conquest in a pamphlet written for industrialists in 1927 entitled

---

[33] Hitler, *Mein Kampf* (trans.), 242.

[34] Ibid. 554.

[35] On the origin of Hitler's *Lebenskampf* concept see Lange, 'Terminus "Lebensraum"'.

[36] Zmarzlik, 'Sozialdarwinismus', 246 ff.; Jäckel, *Hitlers Weltanschauung*, 118.

[37] Jäckel, *Hitlers Weltanschauung*, 32. Cf. now also the sequel: Jäckel, *Hitlers Herrschaft*, maintaining that Hitler consistently pursued his two chief aims—the conquest of *Lebensraum* in the east and the annihilation of the Jews in Europe—in accordance with the programme he had set himself in the 1920s.

[38] *Hitler's Secret Book* (trans. of *Hitlers zweites Buch*; cited below as *Secret Book*), 5–6.

[39] Ibid. 7.

[40] Ibid. 12.

[41] Ibid. 7.

[42] Ibid. 32.

Der Weg zum Wiederaufstieg (The Road to Recovery), which declared that the supreme task of politics was to 'secure the natural satisfaction of no less natural imperialism'.[43]

As for the various forms of pacifism that played a prominent part in the ideological quarrels of the Weimar period, these could only appear to Hitler as unnatural 'humanitarian nonsense', which did not deserve the name of policy since they violated the natural law of the permanent struggle for life.[44] Pacifism was 'vicious' and its adherents were 'enemies and opponents of all heroic racial (*völkisch*) virtues', seeking to persuade people that they need not 'be ready to fight for markets for their goods with the shedding of their blood'.[45] By presenting pacifists as the enemies not only of heroic ideals but also of capitalist competition, Hitler created a bogy with which he hoped to frighten the industrialists who might be so important in his rise to power.[46] In his address to businessmen in January 1932 he spoke once again of competition as the application of the fighting principle to economics;[47] once again he equated pacifism and anti-capitalism, at the same time proclaiming his 'inexorable decision to destroy Marxism in Germany down to its very last root'.[48]

In the same way as Hitler spoke of pacifism, so from the outset he spoke and wrote of humanitarianism in tones of hatred and contempt. According to *Mein Kampf*, the 'consuming fire' of the instinct of self-preservation will cause 'so-called humanitarianism, which connotes only a mixture of fatuous timidity and self-conceit, [to] melt away as under the March sunshine. Man has become great through perpetual struggle. In perpetual peace his greatness must decline.'[49] To the National Socialist leader, man's humanity was 'only the handmaiden of his weakness, and at the same time actually the cruellest destroyer of his existence'[50]—a negative quality, not a virtue of any kind. Hence, the Spartans' practice of exposing sick, weak, and deformed children was 'more decent and in truth a thousand times more humane than the wretched insanity in our day which preserves the most pathological specimens'.[51]

Implicit in the 'right of the stronger' as thus proclaimed was a further principle of social Darwinism that held a central place in Hitler's world of ideas. The 'aristocratic principle of Nature',[52] that the strong must conquer and the weak go to the wall, was also an 'iron law of necessity' applying to the life of nations,[53] and therefore a higher or master race must one day dominate the world.

---

[43] Hitler, 'Weg zum Wiederaufstieg', 51.
[44] *Secret Book*, 15–16. On Fascist anti-pacifism see also Goebbels, 'Faschismus', 316–17.
[45] *Secret Book*, 23–4, 99.
[46] Cf. Nitschke, *Der Feind*.
[47] Hitler's address to West German industrialists on 27 Jan. 1932, repr. in Domarus, i. 68–90; Baynes, i. 777–829.
[48] Baynes, i. 823.
[49] *Mein Kampf* (trans.), 124.
[50] *Secret Book*, 17.
[51] Ibid. 18.
[52] *Mein Kampf* (trans.), 65.
[53] Ibid. 242.

According to Hitler, the common purpose of home and foreign policy was to prepare and carry out the increase of power by warlike means. 'The forging of the sword is a work that has to be done through the domestic policy which must be adopted by a national government. To see that the work of forging these arms is assured, and to recruit allies (*Waffengenossen*), is the task of foreign policy.'[54] At all times it is a question of 'the employment of force',[55] i.e. a policy of violence.

As early as 13 November 1918, in one of his very first recorded speeches, Hitler expressed the conviction that Germany's misfortune 'must be broken by German iron'.[56]

Hitler's belief in the creativeness of force was a constant feature of his thinking from the time when he took up politics at the end of the First World War. In this respect he differed little from such contemporaries as Oswald Spengler, Carl Schmitt, Georges Sorel, Mussolini, and others, who also worshipped violence as heroism and saw the world as divided into friends and enemies.[57] The idea that war was a legitimate use of force was certainly widespread at that time, abroad as well as in Germany. Despite the experience of the First World War, most contemporaries took it for granted that disputes among states must in the last resort be settled by force of arms.

Hitler's views on the role of force in history were crystallized long before the formulation of his foreign-policy programme, which dates from 1928. Chronologically as well as logically, the conception and adoption of specific aims and moves in foreign affairs were preceded by the abstract ideology of force. The latter knew no bounds of space and time and, by definition, laid no claim to be a functional political theory, in the sense of contending, for instance, that war was justified for the sake of achieving a just peace. The ideology was more in the nature of a permanent declaration of war, regarded as having a mystic value of its own.[58] It seems necessary to recall this fact, since when studying 'Hitler's ultimate aims'—the Greater German Reich, colonialism, world domination[59]—and particular stratagems underlying National Socialist war policy, and in seeking after the event to infer specific decisions by the Führer, it is only too easy to overlook the fact that rational calculation and arguments based on consistency of purpose constitute only one aspect of the problem.

In order to judge the circumstances which led to Hitler's appointment as chancellor, and also the contemporary assessment of his policy of rearmament and war, it is of importance to enquire whether his ideology of force and his concrete ideas concerning war were fully known and understood before 1933. It has been said that *Mein Kampf* was regarded as unreadable by friend and foe alike, and become 'the least read best-seller in world literature'.[60] None the less, by January 1933 there

---

[54] Ibid. 498. For the close interrelation between home and foreign policy cf. also *Secret Book*, 80, 85 ff.

[55] *Secret Book*, 24.   [56] Quoted from Jäckel, *Hitlers Weltanschauung*, 31.

[57] Cf. Lenk, '*Volk und Staat*', 106 ff.   [58] Cf. e.g. Broszat, *The Hitler State*, 307–8.

[59] Cf. Moltmann, 'Weltherrschaftsideen'; Hildebrand, *Reich*; *Weltherrschaft im Visier*; Thies, *Architekt*.

[60] Jäckel, *Hitlers Weltanschauung*, 13. On reactions to *Mein Kampf* before 1933 cf. now Schreiber's analysis *Hitler-Interpretationen*, and Koebner (ed.), *Weimars Ende*.

existed 287,000 copies of Hitler's polemic work,[61] and we may assume they were acquired more or less voluntarily, in contrast to later times, when the book was forced on its recipients. Certainly it does not follow that every purchaser read *Mein Kampf*, but it is even less likely that its contents were not generally known. Admittedly, it would seem that before 1933 it was not read in its entirety even by the Nazi faithful.[62]

Böhme, the former Social Democratic mayor of Brunswick,[63] does not believe that many members of his party were familiar with the book's contents. However, we know from Paul Löbe (SPD), a former president of the Reichstag, that the SPD members of that body received many reports on the main themes of *Mein Kampf*,[64] so that it cannot be said they were completely uninformed. Indeed, as early as 1930 the SPD group in the Reichstag produced a very accurate prognosis of what might be expected from the National Socialists.[65] It is all the more surprising that neither the Communists and Social Democrats, nor the Centre and liberal Democrats, thought of exposing Hitler's ideas on war in a massive propaganda campaign to discredit the National Socialist party.

A study of contemporary journalism leads to similar conclusions. By and large, political writers took little notice of *Mein Kampf*. Only Theodor Heuss, in a book on Hitler published in 1932,[66] referred to his basic ideas on foreign policy, in particular territorial expansion in the east. In a number of other writings which dealt extensively with National Socialism,[67] Hitler's ideas on war were either ignored or mentioned only in passing.

Politicians and journalists in Austria, Switzerland, France, Italy, Great Britain, the USA, and even Poland[68] similarly took little notice of Hitler's book before 1933, and in any case did not take it seriously. The only exception was the Soviet Union. Both Stalin and Litvinov, the commissar for foreign affairs, had read a Russian translation of *Mein Kampf* from cover to cover before 1933,[69] and consequently knew that Hitler's Germany was a threat to the USSR.[70]

Contemporaries repeatedly explained the failure to take account of Hitler's views as set out in *Mein Kampf* by pointing to the book's size, its confused and repetitive nature, the turgid and tedious style, and unendurable long-windedness. But the intellectual arrogance that found expression in such criticism had the fateful consequence that National Socialist ideology was not only dismissed as pseudo-philosophy but was neither taken seriously nor deemed worthy of refutation.[71]

---

[61] Hammer, 'Hitlers "Mein Kampf"', 163.
[62] Lange, *Hitlers unbeachtete Maximen*, 145 ff.
[63] Ibid. 162.
[64] Ibid. 61.
[65] *Jahrbuch der SPD 1930*, 31; and cf. I.1.7 below.
[66] Heuss, *Hitlers Weg*.
[67] Knickerbocker, *German Crisis*; Oehme and Caro, *Drittes Reich*; Andernach, *Hitler*.
[68] Lange, *Hitlers unbeachtete Maximen*, 75–130. Cf. also Bacon, *Press Opinion*; Kimmel, *Aufstieg*; Illert, *Deutsche Rechte*; Granzow, *Mirror*; Sheldon, 'Hitler-Bild'.
[69] Lange, *Hitlers unbeachtete Maximen*, 131 ff.
[70] Snell, *Illusion*, 22.
[71] Lange, *Hitlers unbeachtete Maximen*, 66, 154; also Bracher, *Dictatorship*, 168.

Moreover, Hitler was effective chiefly as a speaker rather than a political writer, and his propagandist rhetoric was often more cautious than his polemical manifesto of 1925. This was especially true of his foreign policy, which in any case dropped out of view for a time after the Nazi electoral success in September 1930.

Moreover, conservative circles took the view that political propaganda was one thing and the exercise of governmental power another. People reassured themselves and one another with the cliché that Hitler's bark would no doubt be worse than his bite.

Between 1933 and 1939 National Socialist propaganda dropped suggestions in the foreign press that Hitler intended to withdraw *Mein Kampf* and eventually publish a revised edition. Far from this, Hitler authorized mass printing on a scale that was to reach 9,840,000 copies by 1943.[72] It is thus clear than anyone who wanted to know what Hitler said and planned could easily find out. At the very least, his ambitious plans of warlike expansion were not unknown,[73] and, as they contained 'elements of purposeful planning and designs for the future',[74] it was not possible simply to dismiss them as absurd.

3. The Militarism of the 'Nationalist Opposition'

The 'nationalist opposition' of the Weimar period was not a parliamentary opposition in the constitutional sense, but rather a parliamentary and extra-parliamentary group of political parties, paramilitary and veterans' associations, political sects, clubs, and literary coteries which, whatever their differences, shared the common aim of overthrowing the hated Weimar 'system' and establishing an authoritarian nationalist state. The nationalists were, in short, not only opposed to the republican parties but to the Weimar form of government and democracy as such.

The 'nationalist opposition' in this sense existed throughout the Weimar period, although the concept was first brought into wide public notice by Hugenberg in 1929. This was on the occasion of one of the first common actions of the anti-republican right, the referendum against the Young plan for German reparation payments. The participants were the German National People's Party (DNVP), the Stahlhelm (ex-soldiers' league), the Reichslandbund (National Agricultural Association), and the NSDAP (the Nazi party). In 1931 a loose organization of the nationalist opposition was created in the form of the 'Harzburg front', a right-wing political alliance representing the DNVP, NSDAP, Stahlhelm, Reichslandbund, the Pan-German Association, and leading spokesmen of the large estate-owners, heavy industry, and the Reichswehr. Supporters of the Harzburg front were also to be found in the many patriotic (*völkisch*), agrarian, and small traders' associations, as well as among a majority of academics in and outside the universities, organized student bodies, and numerous intellectuals. From this time on, the NSDAP gradually took over the leadership of the whole anti-republican right.

[72] Lange, *Hitlers unbeachtete Maximen*, 148.   [73] Sauer, 'Mobilmachung', 58.
[74] Jacobsen, *Der Zweite Weltkrieg*, 20.

(a) The Stahlhelm

The Stahlhelm association of ex-servicemen[75] was the largest and most influential paramilitary organization of the political right. Founded on 25 December 1918,[76] in the midst of the revolutionary transition from the empire to the republic, it developed in a pronouncedly political direction, unlike other ex-soldiers' associations, which concentrated on upholding military tradition. From the mid-1920s onwards the Stahlhelm had about 400,000–500,000 members, all former front-line soldiers. Some were members of the nobility, others of the middle or lower-middle class; their political views were conservative and nationalistic.[77] Foreign countries regarded the association, which paraded in uniform, as one of the paramilitary bodies that were preparing for a war of revenge and could play the part of an army reserve in case of conflict. The Reichswehr, too, saw the Stahlhelm as a potential reserve and, given its fanatically militarist views, welcomed it as a counterweight to pacifist tendencies on the political left.[78]

Franz Seldte, the founder of the Stahlhelm, was a factory-owner and an ex-officer; until 1927 he belonged to the Deutsche Volkspartei (DVP), though in opposition to Stresemann. His deputy, Theodor Duesterberg, a former professional soldier and general staff officer,[79] first inclined towards the Deutsch-Völkische Freiheitspartei (DVFP), a splinter-group of the radical right, and afterwards became an influential member of the DNVP. In 1928 the Stahlhelm had fifty-one members of the Reichstag representing the DNVP and nine representing the DVP—a respectable-sized parliamentary group.[80] After 1928 it moved closer and closer to the DNVP, and from the autumn of 1930 was increasingly under National Socialist influence. Despite this link between its leaders and the parties of the anti-republican or moderate right, the Stahlhelm professed a non-party ideology—which, however, only meant that its members did not have to belong to any particular right-wing party. That ideology was rooted in the authoritarian tradition of the Kaiser's Germany and the shared experience of the trenches in the First World War, which was felt as a symbol of national unity transcending party ties.

The anti-republican character of the Stahlhelm was manifest from the early 1920s onwards. Some of its members supported the Hitler *putsch* of November 1923. After its failure they continued to regard themselves as active opponents of the 'system' of Weimar democracy and as exponents of an authoritarian state, a 'national dictatorship'[81] inspired by military ideas of organization and action. There was

---

[75] Cf. Seldte, *Stahlhelm*; Duesterberg, *Stahlhelm*; Klotzbücher, *Stahlhelm*; Berghahn, *Stahlhelm*.

[76] Duesterberg, *Stahlhelm*, 7: 'The Stahlhelm was a product of its time, of the Marxist revolution of 1918.'

[77] For the front-line soldiers, nationalism was a product of the First World War: 'When we went to war, we were German soldiers. When we came back, we were both Germans and human beings' (Schauwecker, 'Erlebnis', 179).   [78] Rohe, *Reichsbanner*, 172–3.

[79] In 1933 Duesterberg was refused admission to the NSDAP because of his Jewish origin. Cf. Messerschmidt, *Wehrmacht*, 42.

[80] Berghahn, *Stahlhelm*, III n. 6; Klotzbücher, *Stahlhelm*, 312–13.

[81] On 4 Nov. 1923 the Stahlhelm executive called on the Reich chancellor 'to set up a national dictatorship immediately'. The document is reproduced in Seldte, *Stahlhelm*, 46; cf. also Klotzbücher, *Stahlhelm*, 80 ff.

already talk of a 'Third Reich'—not in quite the same sense as Hitler's, but the latter was certainly closer to Stahlhelm ideas than to the parliamentary republic.

Relations between the Stahlhelm and the NSDAP were not institutionalized until fairly late, as Hitler forbade members of his party to belong to both organizations. They joined forces in order to destroy the republic in 1931, with the creation of the Harzburg front.[82] From then onwards the Stahlhelm became one of the chief forerunners of Hitler's dictatorship—to some extent consciously, to some extent against its will.[83] Seldte became minister of labour in Hitler's cabinet in 1933, and held the post until 1945.[84]

There is no doubt that the NSDAP and the Stahlhelm were united in hostility to democracy,[85] liberalism, and socialism, as well as in the emphasis they laid on militarism. Does this mean they were united in planning a future war? Did the Stahlhelm members contemplate the use of force to restore Germany and increase her power? Did the front-line soldiers wish to return to the front? What was meant by their oft-repeated slogans concerning the 'front-line spirit' (*Frontgeist*) and 'ideal of the front-line soldier' (*Frontsoldatenidee*)?

These ideas did not necessarily signify a cut-and-dried programme in foreign affairs, to be achieved by means of a new war. What they chiefly reflected was the Stahlhelm's irrationalism.[86] As Eduard Stadtler, head of its training department from 1928, once put it, the front-line ideology was 'something mysterious and inexpressible, as indefinable as the experience of war from which it is derived'.[87] Duesterberg spoke with equal mystery of 'the renewal of the German people in the spirit of the old-time front'.[88] The war, which was the central theme of discussion in Stahlhelm circles, was stylized into an occurrence beyond imagination, the breeding-ground of glorious forms of human life. This glorification of the war owed much to the literary group associated with 'soldierly nationalism', which we shall consider in due course.

The front-line ideology, or that of war, was politically relevant in so far as it offered a model for society in peace-time. The Stahlhelm's objective was, so to speak, a fellowship of the trenches transferred to peaceful conditions, a 'front-line state'[89] organized on military lines, i.e. on the principle of leadership, with the élite

---

[82] For the Stahlhelm's role in the Harzburg front see Klotzbücher, *Stahlhelm*, 232–73.

[83] According to Duesterberg (*Stahlhelm*, 151), most of the Stahlhelm leaders were opposed to Hitler. But the documents he himself cites include words addressed to Hitler by the Bavarian Stahlhelm leader, von Lenz: 'All we care for is the victory of our shared ideal, and that is the same whether you call it Stahlhelm or NSDAP' (ibid. 22).

[84] For the Stahlhelm rallying to the Third Reich see Klotzbücher, *Stahlhelm*, 273–310; for its dissolution in 1935 cf. Berghahn, 'Ende des "Stahlhelm"'.

[85] On the Stahlhelm's idea of democracy cf. Duesterberg's illuminating remark: 'Nothing can be more democratic than to have faced death together' (*Stahlhelm*, 8).

[86] Cf. Seldte's remark to Hitler on 12 Aug. 1935: 'My men are not political creatures, but old soldiers' (Berghahn, 'Ende des "Stahlhelm"', 449) For their lack of interest in politics cf. also Klotzbücher, 114 ff.

[87] Stadtler, *Seldte* (1930), 21.   [88] Duesterberg, *Stahlhelm*, 9.

[89] The journal *Der Stahlhelm* (1 Feb. 1925) declared that the aim of the association was a 'state of front-line soldiers' (Seldte, *Stahlhelm*, 55). See also Berghahn, *Stahlhelm*, 97, 99; Klotzbücher, *Stahlhelm*, 112–29.

of front-line soldiers in charge.[90] Such ideas caused Stresemann to comment in September 1928 that the Stahlhelm must be expected to develop into 'a kind of Fascist party'.[91] It was several times in danger of being banned, but was saved by Hindenburg's intervention: paradoxically, the president of the republic was an honorary member of this anti-republican association.

The front-line ideology was, however, more than just metaphysics. Among other things, it stood for vehement rejection of the military provisions of the treaty of Versailles. A message[92] proclaimed to 132,000 members at the association's Eighth Congress in Berlin in May 1927 announced:

The Stahlhelm is resolved to combat all softness and cowardice that seeks to weaken and destroy the German people's sense of honour by the abandonment of its military sovereignty and warlike spirit (*Wehrrecht und Wehrwillen*). The Stahlhelm declares that it refuses to recognize the state of affairs brought about by the dictat of Versailles and later arrangements. It therefore demands the recognition of the national state for the benefit of all Germans, the restoration of Germany's military sovereignty, and effective revocation of the admission of war guilt, which was extorted by blackmail.

It is typical of the Stahlhelm's irrational philosophy of war that Seldte rejected the notion of war guilt altogether, holding that war could only be regarded as 'a natural catastrophe'.[93] It was senseless to speak of German war-guilt, since 'the essence and nature of Germanness make it certain in advance that Germany can never be an aggressor.'[94] Similarly, the claim to 'our rightful sovereignty in defence matters' was not founded on a rational analysis of the situation affecting Germany's security in the years of the Weimar Republic, but on such generalities as 'our eternally threatened position in the centre of Europe' and the 'centuries-long inroads of Asiatic hordes'.[95]

The Stahlhelm held numerous militant demonstrations, often only a few miles from the Polish frontier, at which aggressive demands for 'living-space' in the east could be heard. In October 1928 Seldte declared that it was the 'destined task' of a 'policy of liberation in the east' 'not only to hold on to what is German but also to recover what has been seized from us and to conquer new lands, to create more living-space'.[96] At a meeting of leaders of the Central Rhine branch of the Stahlhelm in October 1927 Duesterberg deplored the German government's renunciation of an aggressive war in the east.[97] At the Silesian rally of front-line soldiers in 1930 he declared that freedom must be gained by force of arms. It was an illusion to think that Germany could recover all it had lost by a policy of understanding and compliance with treaties.[98] In 1932 Seldte demanded the return

---

[90] Seldte, *Stahlhelm*, 17: 'We give notice of our claim to take over the leadership of Germany.'
[91] Berghahn, *Stahlhelm*, 116; Klotzbücher, *Stahlhelm*, 81, 316.
[92] Text of message in *Der Stahlhelm* (5 May 1927), 1; repr. in e.g. *Deutsche Parteiprogramme*, 553–5, and Berghan, *Stahlhelm*, 105–6.   [93] Seldte, *Stahlhelm*, 14.
[94] Ibid. 15.   [95] Duesterberg, *Stahlhelm*, 152.
[96] *Der Stahlhelm* (28 Oct. 1928), quoted from Klotzbücher, *Stahlhelm*, 130.
[97] *Der Stahlhelm* (16 Oct. 1927), quoted from Klotzbücher, *Stahlhelm*, 131.
[98] *Der Stahlhelm-Student* [organ of the Langemarck (Stahlhelm) Students' Association], 9–10 (1929–30), 10, quoted from Klotzbücher, *Stahlhelm*, 131.

of 'our colonies and the territories seized from us, which are so necessary for providing the living-space that our cramped and suffering people (*unser Volk in Not und unser Volk ohne Raum*) so badly needs'.[99]

The Brandenburg branch of the Stahlhelm, in an appeal of 2 September 1928, expressed its hostility to the status quo as follows: 'We hate with all our soul the present constitution of the state . . . because it deprives us of the prospect of liberating our enslaved fatherland and cleansing the German people from the lying aspersion of war guilt; of gaining necessary living-space in the east and enabling the German people to bear arms once again.'[100] This document anticipates all three phases of Hitler's policy: first, the abolition of the parliamentary system; secondly, the rearmament and remilitarization of the German people; and thirdly, the objective of 'gaining'—in other words conquering—living-space in the east.

At Breslau in 1931, at the tenth nation-wide rally of former front-line soldiers, the Stahlhelm leaders uttered a scarcely veiled demand for a war with Poland. Addressing a parade of over 100,000 Stahlhelm members in uniform, Seldte recalled that the German army which fought the war of liberation against Napoleon had assembled in Silesia, and indicated his belief that a new war of this kind was at hand. On the last day of the rally he delivered a so-called 'target speech': 'Seldte gives the order "About turn!" and points out the goal to his entire field-grey army—the Eastern Front. And to his question whether they recognize the goal, the whole army answers "Yes!"'[101] Duesterberg underlined the demonstration with the threatening words; 'The Polish gentlemen should realize from their own chequered history that both Germany and the Russian giant will one day recover their strength. The Polish state is not a national state.'[102] Summing up, the Stahlhelm leader declared: 'at Breslau we once more clearly demanded the return of West Prussia, Upper Silesia and the Corridor, and the satisfaction of our claim in the east.'[103]

The Breslau rally brought a shower of protests from the Poles and French. The German ambassador in Paris reported that Briand had described it as 'probably the most warlike manifestation in Germany since the peace treaty'. The Stahlhelm's hatred of Poland was deep-seated. Rampant prejudice prevailed: Poland was regarded as Germany's most dangerous enemy, a state that had no right to exist and that could only be dealt with by extermination.[104]

A year later, when many Stahlhelm members had joined the Nazi party, Siegfried Wagner, a retired major who was one of the Stahlhelm's political leaders and 'eastern experts', described his vision of a Great German Reich at a rally in Magdeburg attended by several thousand members, including Seldte and Duesterberg:

[99] Seldte, *Stahlhelm*, 16. The slogan 'Volk ohne Raum' (People without space) was coined by Hans Grimm, a German writer on colonial themes, as the title of a book published in 1926, which reached a circulation of 265,000 by 1933. Cf. Lange, 'Terminus "Lebensraum"'.

[100] The appeal is reprinted in Kleinau, *Soldaten der Nation* (1933), Appendix, 55 ff.

[101] Seldte, *Stahlhelm*, 120.   [102] Quoted from Berghahn, *Stahlhelm*, 169.

[103] Seldte, *Stahlhelm*, 17.

[104] Thus Berghahn, *Stahlhelm*, 170 ff., with further references.

The first task will be to secure our torn and threatened eastern frontiers against the aggressive Polish power with its thirst for conquest. This will lead to a new spatial consolidation of the German east, crowned by a new political organization of the whole area between Germany and Russia's real frontier. This will take place under German leadership in a new supranational embodiment of the imperial idea (*Reichsgedanke*), to the benefit of all the small nations that cannot in the long run subsist by themselves, and also to the advantage of our own race (*Volkstum*), which will find new tasks and additional work to perform in those regions.[105]

In the light of these unequivocal contemporary documents it was of little avail for Duesterberg, after the Second World War, to attempt to establish the legend that the Stahlhelm had been a peaceable league of veterans firmly opposed to Hitler.[106] The leading spirits of the Stahlhelm certainly did not regard it as the first task of politics to prevent a new war. On the contrary, as Wilhelm Kleinau put it, they regarded war as 'an indispensable instrument of policy'.[107] As the Stahlhelm became politicized and radicalized from 1925 to 1930 it developed into an organization overtly hostile to the republic,[108] as well as to the foreign policy of peaceful understanding represented by the parties of the 'Weimar coalition'.

(b) The Deutschnationale Volkspartei (DNVP)

As already mentioned, personal ties between the Stahlhelm and the DNVP were very close. As the Stahlhelm was the most important of the right-wing militarist organizations, so the DNVP in the 1920s—i.e. until its members began to join the NSDAP *en masse* in the autumn of 1930—formed the parliamentary core of the 'national opposition' to Versailles and to the parliamentary system itself. The party proclaimed itself 'Christian, *völkisch*, and national';[109] it took part in the governmental process during the phase of stabilization of the Weimar Republic, which lasted several years, but it remained throughout a 'party of monarchist convictions'.[110]

In internal affairs the DNVP was hostile to the 'detested November state' and the republican parties. The slogan 'Down with Weimar!' meant a return to the monarchy and the establishment of a strong authoritarian state in which soldierly ideals would also be rules of social conduct. With the watchwords 'Struggle and power' and 'Down with the shameful peace of Versailles and the politicians of "fulfilment"',[111] the DNVP opposed all attempts to come to an understanding with the victors of the First World War. The party also objected on principle to the League of Nations and in 1926 voted against Germany's accession to the League, for which Stresemann was responsible. Although the DNVP leaders did no more than hint at the fact in public, their contemplated policy was a war of revenge.

The party's idea of tactics can be seen from a letter of 9 January 1920 addressed by

[105] *Kreuz-Zeitung* (7 May 1932), 7; quoted from Berghahn, *Stahlhelm*, 224.
[106] Duesterberg, *Stahlhelm*, 9–10, 122, 152.
[107] Kleinau, *Stahlhelm und Staat*, 35.
[108] Klotzbücher, *Stahlhelm*, 132–3.
[109] Dörr, *Deutschnationale Volkspartei*, 311.
[110] Ibid. 5; also Hiller von Gaertringen, 'Monarchismus'.
[111] Dörr, *Deutschnationale Volkspartei*, 209 and *passim*.

Oskar von der Osten-Warnitz to a fellow member, Siegfried von Kardorff.[112] Osten-Warnitz thought it inadvisable to 'give prominence to the *revanche* idea'; on the other hand, a formula must be found

which would make it clear that, as a matter of fixed policy, we shall never accept the crying injustice and the intrinsic impossibilities of the treaty of Versailles, but shall constantly work for its revision 'by peaceful means'. The Entente cannot object to such a formulation, and we can make the mental reservation that if peaceful means do not achieve our end we may have to resort to others.

While the 'Principles of the DNVP' as published in 1920 used fairly innocuous formulations such as a 'newly strengthened Reich' and a 'strong and consistent foreign policy based on German interests alone',[113] it was clear from later statements that this meant nothing but dictatorship, rearmament, and a war of revenge. On 19 May 1924 the deputy chairman of the party, Hans Schlange-Schöningen—a retired cavalry officer and a Junker landowner—addressed to the chairman, Alfred Hugenberg, a strictly confidential memorandum[114] advocating a dictatorship 'of which we should speak as little as possible, but which is bound to be our object'. Once the dictatorship was established, it must be a principle of party policy to 'secure a respite in foreign affairs so as to build up our state power and military preparedness (*Wehrhaftigkeit*)'. The writer continued: 'The only way I can see of having peace in foreign relations is cold-bloodedly to let the French have the Rhine and the Ruhr for a time, so that we can get Germany on its feet again and one day reconquer the lost territories . . . We must play for high stakes, or all is lost: history teaches that you cannot save a nation with half-measures.'

In a speech[115] in the summer of 1925 Karl Gottfried Gok—a DNVP member of the Reichstag and vice-chairman of the firm of Blohm & Voss AG—described the party's aims as follows:

Our programme must be: Down with Stresemann. Down with the lie about war-guilt. Revision of the treaty of Versailles . . . No talk of reconciliation until the crime of Versailles is expunged. Radical nationalism and the duty to hate must be our message until the wrong done to us is wiped out. But too few of us are resolute! Down with Weimar and Versailles! More courage to stand up for principles—this is what the time requires. We must openly proclaim our extremism, even if we are decried as fanatics. If we are cowardly and irresolute we can no more win the battle for our future than we were able to win the last war. . . . Once we have reconquered our place in the sun, hate can disappear. Then, and only then, will be the time for international reconciliation.

Naturally, the DNVP in its official utterances, such as its manifesto for the Reichstag election of 1928,[116] guarded itself against the charge that its foreign policy was aimed at new wars. It countered such ideas with the ambiguous formula: 'We

---

[112] Quoted from *Weltherrschaft im Visier*, 17 n. 34 (source: ZStA Potsdam, papers of Count Kuno von Westarp, file 114, fos. 15–16).

[113] The document 'Grundsätze der DNVP' is reproduced in *Deutsche Parteiprogramme*, 533–42, here 536; also in Dörr, *Deutschnationale Volkspartei*, 503–12, here 505.

[114] Reproduced in Dörr, *Deutschnationale Volkspartei*, 490–3, here 492–3.

[115] Reproduced ibid. 517–22, here 512–13.

[116] Reproduced ibid. 549–52, here 549; also in *Reichstags-Handbuch* 1928, 157–60, here 158.

are not so foolish as deliberately to expose our unarmed people to the foeman's knife.'

The election of Alfred Hugenberg, a Pan-German and captain of industry, as the DNVP's new chairman on 20 October 1928 inaugurated a new phase of the party's uncompromising attack on the Weimar Republic, during which it sought to disguise its expansionist ideas in foreign affairs by peaceful slogans. In a public speech on 19 September 1931 at the tenth nation-wide party congress at Stettin,[117] Hugenberg spoke of a 'people without space' and a 'people in chains', of 'our children's longing' for 'freedom and space', which the German people could only achieve by its own efforts. 'The solution is not a world economy or imperialism under a mask of hypocritical pacifism, not Pan-Europe and a customs union, not international capitalism, foreign credits, and world banks, but the untrammelled freedom of any great nation to act in its own interest and to do away with the errors, the internal paralysis and external slavery, that stand in the way of its vigorous self-help.' When Hugenberg spoke of 'great works of peace' to be undertaken, he meant in concrete terms that Germany must have her African colonies back, that her 'energetic race' needed new space for settlement in the 'German East'—for 'the reconstruction of the east, far beyond the old German borders [!], can only be achieved by Germany'. In addition Hugenberg inveighed against the 'Marxist-cityfied paralysis of the brain' which gave rise to 'fatalistic and un-German theories', and appealed to 'faith in the West'. As for his own imperialist programme, it represented 'the spirit of peace in its highest sense'.

Next day, at the same congress, Hugenberg spoke on internal policy.[118] He referred to the 'extermination of Marxist influences' as the foundation of the programme of national salvation, and branded the social democrats, the Centre party, the Deutsche Volkspartei, and their adherents as responsible for Germany's misfortunes. The DNVP must stand together with the patriotic associations, the Stahlhelm and the National Socialists, forming a solid national opposition, so as to put down Bolshevism and create an orderly system. Hugenberg also attempted to gain support from women, 'whose pride and suffering it has been through the centuries to be mothers of German soldiers', and he sought an alliance with the Protestant church.

As a majority of Protestant clergymen were attracted to the nationalist cause in any case,[119] Hugenberg could be sure that the call for increased activity on the part of the national opposition would not be without effect on them. The ideological links between the DNVP and the Protestant church had been reaffirmed in a pamphlet of 1931, written by a pastor named Wilm and distributed by the party, entitled *The Attitude of Evangelical Christians towards Pacifism*.[120] This work described humanitarian and Christian pacifism as a 'dangerous madness' that could

---

[117] *Hugenbergs weltwirtschaftliches Programm* (1931), 3–4, 14–15.

[118] *Hugenbergs innenpolitisches Programm* (1931), 4, 17 ff.

[119] Cf. I.I.4 below.

[120] *Stellung des evangelischen Christen* (1931), 2–7. Cf. also *Warum bekämpfen wir Deutschnationalen den Pazifismus?* (1924).

only be of profit to Bolshevism. Christians must be in favour of 'the authoritative, self-defending (*wehrhaft*) national state', which must be the 'highest authority'. Pacifism, which refused to acknowledge the immediate God-given authority of the armed and disciplined state, was guilty of 'absolute disobedience to the divine order and commandment'. Thus, 'reformed Christianity based on the Bible stood in the same relationship to pacifism as true faith to idolatry'. Pastor Wilm did not shrink from declaring it to be that teaching of Scripture that 'war remains the ultimate and profoundest imperative of the state'. Even if 'the connection between Christianity and preparedness for war filled millions of Germans with hatred of Christianity', it must be upheld 'even though we are called murderers and warmongers'. The slogan 'No more war' meant ruin and was 'contrary to the clear message of Holy Writ', so that the evangelical Christian must reject pacifism as 'impious'. Since a war waged by a desperate people for its life and future was 'a thousand times more moral' than a shameful peace, in Germany's special position there was only the alternative of an authoritarian state 'on a soldierly foundation', a state of 'noble warriors'.

What was still comparatively abstract in the Christian-nationalist ideology of militarism, namely the direction in which the aggressiveness it justified was to be unleashed, was indicated with precision in speeches by the DNVP leaders. Freiherr von Freytagh-Loringhoven, a specialist in public law and a member of the Reichstag, enumerated the following aims at a meeting of party leaders on 25 June 1932: eradication of the 'war-guilt lie', cancelling of reparations, recovery of independence in defence matters, frontier revision, especially in the east, the return of colonies, the 'establishment of a Great German Reich'. Afterwards thought could be given to 'acquiring new territory to provide space for the German people, liberating it from the smoke of cities, settling in once more as a land-dwelling nation (*Bauernvolk*) sound in body and mind'.[121] Apart from Hitler's specifically racist ideology, a speech like this contained everything that he and the NSDAP were to embody in their political programme after 1933.

In electoral terms, after its great success in 1924 (6.2 million votes, or 20.5 per cent of the electorate) the DNVP suffered one defeat after another.[122] In 1928 it obtained 14 per cent of the vote, in 1930 7 per cent, and in July 1932 5.9 per cent. Hugenberg's co-operation with Hitler over the referendum against the Young Plan in 1929 brought as little advantage to the DNVP as did the formation of the Harzburg front composed of the NSDAP, the DNVP, the Stahlhelm, the Pan-German Association, other 'patriotic' organizations, and representatives of heavy industry and the big banks. The rightward shift of bourgeois voters accrued entirely to the NSDAP.

In 1933 Hugenberg joined Hitler's cabinet as minister for the economy and also for food and agriculture. His role as 'economic dictator' lasted only a few months, however. During the world economic conference in London in 1933 there came to light the draft of a speech by Hugenberg in which he sought to overtrump the Nazis by demanding the return of Germany's African colonies and the opening up of

---

[121] *Nationale Außenpolitik* (1932), 3, 16.
[122] Cf. Milatz, *Wähler*, 122 ff.; Hiller von Gaertringen, 'Ende der DNVP', 248.

space for settlement in Eastern Europe.[123] Aggressive tones of this kind were inconvenient to Hitler during the phase of secret rearmament and soothing 'peace speeches', and he used the opportunity to get rid of Hugenberg. The latter resigned on 27 June 1933, 'because he had received a vote of no confidence for his stand in London'.[124] On the same day the DNVP declared itself dissolved. The party had served its purpose in Hitler's eyes, and he had no further use for it.

(c) Soldierly Nationalism: A Literary Movement

The liveliest intellectual force among the conservative-nationalist groups consisted of young writers and publicists who are usually referred to by the paradoxical term 'conservative revolutionaries'.[125] Their ideas had a strong influence on the nationalist parties, circles, and associations of all kinds, especially the Stahlhelm. They included the numerically small group of intellectuals who from about the mid-1920s took it upon themselves to treat the theme of war repeatedly in literary terms. As war and the nation were the central preoccupation of this literary group, their ideology has been aptly defined as one of 'militant' or 'soldierly' nationalism.[126]

Among the members of this group were the brothers Ernst and Friedrich Georg Jünger, Werner Beumelburg, Edwin Erich Dwinger, Franz Schauwecker, Helmut Franke, Friedrich Hielscher, Wilhelm Kleinau, Albrecht Erich Günther, Ernst von Salomon, Gerhard Günther, and Wilhelm von Schramm, to mention only some of the best-known. They were all born in the 1890s and had served at the front in the world war. They regarded the war as an experience that had left a decisive mark upon them.[127] As they rejected all forms of organization and every kind of binding political programme, they belonged to none of the conservative parties. What united them was a particular attitude of mind that had been formed by the war and which they thought it important somehow to preserve in the years that followed.

This did not in itself make them unique. Many other parties and associations cultivated the memory of the unbreakable fellowship of front-line fighters. On the political right this attitude often went with hostility to the republic, which was considered as unheroic, unwarlike, unsoldierly, pacifist, and defeatist. The nationalist and anti-democratic interpretation of the war experience became one of the most effective bonds of conservative union,[128] especially as the democratic left almost entirely abandoned the emotive field of military tradition to the political right.[129]

---

[123] The draft of Hugenberg's speech, dated 14 June 1933, is printed in *DGFP*, c. i, No. 312.

[124] See minutes of cabinet meeting, ibid. 607–8; and cf. Bracher, *Dictatorship*, 282 ff.

[125] Cf. Mohler's apologia, *Konservative Revolution*; also Klemperer, *New Conservatism*; Sontheimer, *Antidemokratisches Denken*, 143 ff.; Gerstenberger, *Konservatismus*; Greiffenhagen, *Dilemma*; Grebing *et al.*, *Konservatismus*.

[126] Prümm, *Soldatischer Nationalismus*.

[127] Thus Ernst Jünger: 'War is our father: we were formed as a new generation in the glowing womb of the trenches, and we proudly acknowledge our origin' (preface to Friedrich Georg Jünger, *Aufmarsch* (1928), p. xi).

[128] Prümm, *Soldatischer Nationalismus*, vol. i, p. v.

[129] Rosenberg, *German Republic*, 132–3.

The way in which conservatives of all kinds sought to assimilate and stylize the war experience can only be fully understood against the background of earlier trends. In the previous century conservative theoreticians had developed a philosophy of war which represented it as a law of nature, a process ordained by destiny. The idea of perpetual peace, stemming from the Enlightenment era, appeared to them an unnatural Utopia. Indeed, conservative theory regarded war as positively beneficial,[130] as a means whereby nations were rejuvenated and unified.

These elements of the conservative philosophy of war thus had only to be absorbed and actualized in the literary portrayal of 1914–18. Some new angles were introduced, as in Ernst Jünger's aesthetic approach; but in general the glorification of war by the ex-soldier literati of the 'conservative revolution' under the Weimar Republic was in line with the earlier tradition.

Many of the former front-line soldiers—some were fighters for fighting's sake, but others were nationalists by conviction or patriots with little interest in politics—became active Freikorps members in the first years of the republic; after the Freikorps were disbanded they gravitated to right-wing veterans' organizations (*Wehrbünde*). Among the soldiers who were prevented by the Versailles restrictions from exercising their profession at this time, those who took to writing did not express any political creed in the narrower sense, but rather a subjective, individual glorification of the experience of the war years.[131] The politicization of that experience came after 1924, when the economic situation began to settle and the violent international conflicts of the immediate post-war years subsided. During this phase of so-called stability the experience of war and the question of war-guilt were no longer as topical as before, so that the front-line writers found themselves isolated for some years. But although less in the public eye they remained active, and indeed developed a sense of mission.[132] By degrees their ideology permeated the right-wing opposition parties and the numerous ex-servicemen's associations inspired by military traditions: the Werwolf, the Jungdeutscher Orden, the Bund Oberland, the Bund Wiking, and others. Such bodies as these, and above all the Stahlhelm, afforded an effective propaganda platform to writers like Friedrich Georg Jünger, Schauwecker, Franke, and Kleinau, and especially Ernst Jünger, beyond dispute the foremost exponent of 'soldierly nationalism'.[133] In 1924–6 the group had as its mouthpiece the Stahlhelm journal *Die Standarte*. When the front-line writers subsequently broke with the Stahlhelm, regarding it as bogged down in reactionary nationalism, they tried unsuccessfully for a few years to bring about a fusion of the other veterans' associations. Then, in the final period of the republic, the group enjoyed a literary success: their war books sold in mass editions and exercised direct influence over a wide public.

The ideology of 'soldierly nationalism' presented itself as a bundle of irrationalities, amid which, with some difficulty, four main strands can be

---

[130] Cf. Greiffenhagen, *Dilemma*, 258 ff.; Sontheimer, *Antidemokratisches Denken*, 134–5.

[131] Prümm, *Soldatischer Nationalismus*, i. 38.

[132] Ibid.; also Schwarz, *Konservativer Anarchist*, 65. The latter emphasizes that Ernst Jünger and his circle did not cease to preach the gospel of militarism in the years of prosperity from 1925 to 1929.

[133] Prümm, *Soldatischer Nationalismus*, i. 57.

identified: firstly, the experience of the world war was glorified and idealized; secondly, the particular experience was broadened into a glorification of war and the warlike spirit in general; thirdly, this went with a strong sense of nationalism; and fourthly, the writers of this school called for the establishment of an ex-servicemen's state with a mission of imperialism and conquest.

In sharp contrast to the pacifist interpretation of the war experience, the nationalist front-line writers set out to make people forget the sorrows and destruction of war and to emphasize its positive aspects. 'We shall try to expunge from our memory the negative, conditional part of the war, that which is dedicated to corruption [*sic*]—since it is normal for memory to behave in this way, and only to preserve what is great, lively, and life-giving.'[134] As these words show, the writers in question were not basically concerned with a political, social, or economic analysis of the world war, or with any form of verifiable knowledge or rational argument. Theirs was a world of intuition and feeling, a glory divorced from reality. Enquiry into the causes of the war was beyond their horizon. They were content to regard war in general as the 'father of all things', or , as the widely read Oswald Spengler put it more forcefully still: 'In the beginning was War.'[135] According to Ernst Jünger, in seeking to understand the nature of war it was of secondary importance 'in what century the war was waged, for what ideas, and with what weapons'.[136]

These writers did not have in mind a particular war in its specific historical context, but war as such. As Friedrich Hielscher put it, a man must be 'a warrior for war's sake', and this would assure him of 'supreme peace of soul'.[137] In this social-Darwinist philosophy, with its emphasis on fighting, the distinction between war and peace disappeared: they became 'two aspects of the same continuous transformation that we call life'. 'War is always with us, and peace is always with us. For every life achieves fulfilment by destroying other lives.'[138] Heroism was everything and humanity nothing. 'The born warrior takes no account of humanitarian aspects: he cannot, for he is totally imbued with the fatefulness of war.'[139] A moral, ethical, or legal judgement of war seemed no less absured than distinguishing between wars of aggression and defence. All this belonged to the despised sphere of rational analysis, which, according to Albrecht Erich Günther, only served to paralyse instinct. 'Naturally every war is a war of self-defence, for both sides even: either the new creation (*das Werdende*) is defending its vital rights against the stifling pressure of the existing order, or that order is defending its own vital rights against the destructive force of the New. Hence [the humanitarian] argument can only interest us for its propaganda value, its instinct-paralysing

---

[134] Schramm, 'Kritik' (1930), 35.
[135] Spengler, *Untergang*, ii. 448 (1922) = trans. ii. 363.
[136] E. Jünger, 'Mobilmachung', 11 (1930).
[137] Hielscher, 'Verwandlung', 131 (1930).
[138] Ibid. 129.
[139] F. G. Jünger, 'Krieg und Krieger', 63 (1930). Cf. the same author's pamphlet *Aufmarsch des Nationalismus*, 56 (1928): 'There is no value in the chatter of weak-spirited humanitarianism, which springs from a cowardly desire for peace and quiet and which, by its babbling, denies everything that life and blood affirm in battle.'

effect.' It was thus self-evident that the 'defence of vital rights' included the right to attack.[140] Pursuing this idea, Ernst Jünger told his fellow countrymen that they should be proud if the world 'felt them to be a supreme danger to itself.'[141]

The 'unabashed application of the principle "Art for art's sake" to warfare',[142] which was typical of the ideology of 'soldierly nationalism', reached an extreme form in the notion that war, irrespective of any practical or political aim, was in itself one of the noblest arts. For true soldiers, Wilhelm von Schramm wrote, the world war had been a grave disappointment: not because of Germany's defeat, but because 'it was not fought for the profounder ideals of war'. It did not express the notion of war 'as an art, as the highest and noblest form of human conflict, the artistic version, obeying its own laws, of the struggle among nations'; it had been fought for 'practical aims and material profit' instead of being the 'high, serious game of bloodshed' (*blutiges Spiel*) which 'at all times had made men what they were'.[143]

The socialist writer Walter Benjamin once subjected to a close analysis the collective work *Krieg und Krieger*, from which several of our quotations are taken, and passed a devastating verdict on it:

This should be said in all bitterness: confronted with a scene of total mobilization, the German love of nature underwent an unprecedented upsurge. The spirits of peace that had imbued the landscape with contemplation were driven out, and, as far as one could see over the edge of the trenches, everthing in sight had become a tract of German idealism; every shell-hole was a problem, every barbed-wire entanglement an autonomy, every explosion a maxim; the firmament by day was the cosmic interior of the steel helmet, and by night the moral law over it.

However, Benjamin continued, the representatives of the new nationalism, who exalted war as a metaphysical abstraction, were not mere idealists. 'What was developing here beneath the mask of a wartime volunteer and a post-war mercenary was in fact the unmistakable form of a Fascist class-warrior, and when these writers speak of the nation they mean a state ruled by that class.' They were the 'war engineers of the ruling class', and as such they were the 'counterpart of the senior official in formal dress. God knows', Benjamin warned, 'that their bid for leadership is to be taken seriously, their threat is not an idle one.'[144]

'Soldierly nationalism' did in fact play a double role in this fashion. On the one hand it propagated a metaphysical cult of war for its own sake, and on the other it put forward an unmistakable claim to leadership on behalf of the élite of the front-line generation. It was this claim that constituted what critics have called, rather imprecisely, the 'politicization of the war experience'.[145] The writers of this school exalted wartime comradeship as the ideal model of a national community and the

[140] Günther, 'Intelligenz', 90–1.
[141] E. Jünger, 'Mobilmachung', 26.
[142] Benjamin, 'Faschismus', 39 (1930).
[143] Schramm, 'Kritik', 38–41.
[144] Benjamin, 'Faschismus', 39–40.
[145] Sontheimer, *Antidemokratisches Denken*, 115 ff., Prümm, *Soldatischer Nationalismus*, i. 38 ff., esp. 186 ff.

basis for the political regeneration of Germany, and on this they founded a specific political demand for a state ruled by front-line soldiers. The first task of such a state would be to put an end to the 'feeble' and 'unheroic' foreign policy of the democratic parties, aimed at conciliation and the peaceful revision of the treaty of Versailles.

On this basis, 'soldierly nationalism' developed a positively classic ideology of militarism.[146] Military ideas of order were applied to peacetime conditions by way of an emotional projection of the war experience, without any vestige of an attempt on the writers' part to analyse the principles of an advanced industrial society.

The conception of an 'ex-servicemen's state', which we have already spoken of in the context of the Stahlhelm, functioned primarily as an authoritarian, nationalist challenge to the democratic system of Weimar. As such it differed, at best, only in degree from the National Socialist regime that came into being after 1933. But the liquidation of the detested Weimar system was only one of its objectives. The Frontsoldatenstaat was also to pave the way for warlike conquest. Warfare was the all-time heroic ideal, and war must again be waged—not necessarily a particular war such as one of revenge against France or a preventive war against Poland, but a war for war's sake.

The literary advocates of 'warlike nationalism' surpassed themselves in dreams of imperialism which went far beyond those of the Pan-Germans of 1914 and in no way fell short of Hitler's. In 1926 Friedrich Georg Jünger declared that the nationalist movement must ceaselessly hammer into the German mind the idea of imperialism 'projected to an infinite degree'. 'Nothing is more important, more urgent than to keep alive imperialist determination everywhere, to steel it and make it ready for the fray. For any struggle that we may be engaged in tomorrow or the day after will be a struggle for existence. . . . It will decide who is to rule the earth.'[147] As the *Frontsoldatenstaat* was intended to develop 'Germanness (*das Deutsche*) in a new aggressive form', 'every additional screw in a machine-gun, every improvement in gas warfare [was] more important to it than the League of Nations'. The task of Germanness was not to co-operate in the League of Nations but to create the 'Imperium germanicum'.[148] As F. G. Jünger declared, 'the nationalist mentality is necessarily at the same time an imperialist one'.[149].

His brother Ernst Jünger expressed the conviction that 'it can only be good for the world if we are its leaders (*die ersten*)'.[150] His war diary *Feuer und Blut* was an argument, with racialist overtones, for imperialist expansion by force, unlimited by any specific territorial goal. It can be seen how little difference there was between the ideas of warlike nationalism and Hitler's programme, which also from the beginning embodied notions of world conquest. According to *Mein Kampf*, 'A state which, in an epoch of racial adulteration, devotes itself to the duty of preserving the

---

[146] Berghahn (*Militarismus*, 18) describes E. Jünger's writings as 'modern militarism of the first water'.

[147] F. G. Jünger, *Aufmarsch*, 60–1 (1928; first published in 1926 as vol. ii of the series *Der Aufmarsch*).

[148] Ibid. 68–9.

[149] Ibid. 63.

[150] E. Jünger, *Wäldchen 125* (1925), quoted from 4th edn. (1929), 178–9.

best elements of its racial stock must one day become ruler of the earth.'[151] Ernst Jünger wrote: 'The urge to press on without restraint is something we have in our blood as our Germanic heritage, and we hope it will one day develop into an imperialism which will not be aimed, like yesterday's puny imperialism, at gaining a few privileges, border provinces, or Pacific islands, but will really go for the highest stake (*das Ganze*).'[152] What Jünger was advocating here, without any attempt at political justification, was the idea of violence for its own sake.[153] The vision of a Germanic world empire as its reward was expressed very vaguely and rather gives the impression of an optional extra, a sop reluctantly offered to those who were not yet completely converted to political irrationalism.

(d) The Student Body

The undergraduates of the Weimar Republic were the academics of the Third Reich. For this reason if for no other, they deserve special attention. As is well known, the great majority of students not only failed to support the republic but were actively hostile to it. Especially from 1927 onwards, extreme right-wing views found acceptance and were actively propagated by many German students and university teachers. The students were the only section of the population of which a large proportion, even before January, 1933, formed themselves into a representative association dominated by National Socialists.[154] This majority of the students were among the most active pioneers of the Third Reich.

One reason for this state of affairs was that the students were largely drawn from the middle or lower-middle class.[155] Members of this class, especially small tradesmen and the like,[156] had been largely impoverished by the war and inflation. When the great depression set in in 1929 they were again threatened socially, economically, and politically, to a greater extent than other sections of the community, with the result that as a whole they inclined markedly to support National Socialism. Ninety-five per cent of university students in the Weimar period belonged to the bourgeoisie, and only a tiny proportion to the working class: for instance, in Prussia in 1925 the proportion of the latter was 425 out of 31,000 students, or 1.3 per cent. The class character of the academic world was obvious: sons and daughters of the labouring masses were no more numerous at the universities than those of the small officer caste.

The social composition of the student body was matched by its political orientation and organizational structure. About 60 per cent (78,000 out of 132,000

---

[151] Hitler, *Mein Kampf* (trans.), 560.

[152] E. Jünger, *Feuer und Blut* (1925); quoted from 4th edn. (1929), 66.

[153] Prümm (*Soldatischer Nationalismus*, i. 208–9) speaks in this connection of Jünger's 'overheated military fantasy'. Schwarz (*Konservativer Anarchist*, 59) calls Jünger a 'congenital militarist' (*Gesinnungsmilitarist*). As the American historian Weinberg emphasizes ('Friedenspropaganda', 128), it would be difficult to find a glorification of war in the style of Ernst Jünger in any other country.

[154] Cf. Faust, *Studentenbund*, i. 13–14; ii. 17–22.

[155] For the social composition of the student body cf. Bleuel and Klinnert, *Studenten*, 190–1; Faust, *Studentenbund*, i. 112 ff.; more recently Kater, *Studentenschaft*.

[156] Cf. Winkler, *Mittelstand*, and id., 'Protest'.

students at Reich universities) belonged to student associations (*Korporationen*),[157] which had given a special character to academic life since the nineteenth century. Their members constituted the strongest and politically most influential group at the universities. At most 5 per cent of students belonged to groups representing parties of the 'Weimar coalition'. In particular, the largest democratic party, the SPD, had no influence at the universities. Those students who were not organized in party-political groups—about a third of the total—tended to share the outlook of the Korporationen. The great majority of middle-class academic youth rejected political parties althogether, but especially the democratic parties: they supported the idea of a national movement independent of party, which would do away with the whole 'democratic riff-raff', create an authoritarian nation, and restore Germany to its former greatness. Anti-Semitism was rife at the universities, especially in the medical schools and such associations as the Kyffhäuser-Verband der Vereine deutscher Studentenschaften, the Allgemeiner Deutscher Burschenbund, the Deutsche Burschenschaft, and the Kösener Senioren-Convents-Verband.[158] Political irrationalism was equally popular: instead of reason and understanding, life was to be guided by faith, instinct, emotions, and will-power.

The great majority of the student body was right-wing in its opinions even before the victorious rise of the National Socialist German Students' Association (NSDStB). This body, founded spontaneously by students in 1926, described itself in militant language as 'the fighting cell of the Movement on the university front'.[159] After a lean period of a year or two it began to take off in 1928 under the leadership of Baldur von Schirach, a close associate of Hitler's who ensured that it gave up its leftist position and conformed to the latter's purposes. The most important effect of the 'new course' was an amicable arrangement with the Korporationen, traditionally the strongest university associations. This required no great effort of assimilation, given the range of ideas that the two sides had in common: anti-rationalism, anti-Semitism, nationalism, the community spirit (Volksgemeinschaft), hatred of democracy and parliamentarianism, and the 'front-line soldiers' myth,[160] plus the idea of a corporate state with a 'leader' and a strong defence capacity.

The front-line myth and the militarist ideology to some extent receded into the background[161] after the mid-1920s, when the ex-servicemen left the universities; but they enjoyed a comeback from 1928–9 onwards. The younger generation of students, who had not served in the war, for the most part adopted the myth whole-heartedly and idealized the previous generation and its experiences, taking a

---

[157] For the names of the associations and their membership numbers see Bleuel and Klinnert, *Studenten*, appendix, pp. 261–2; on the following passage see ibid. 8, 174–85.

[158] Cf. ibid. 130–55 (on anti-Semitism in the medical schools, esp. 153–4); Kater, *Studentenschaft*, 145–62.

[159] Faust, *Studentenbund*, i. 12.

[160] Details ibid. 128–52. 'The Korporationen were on the right politically . . . There was little difference between their programme and the National Socialists'' (ibid. 139).

[161] On what follows see Bleuel and Klinnert, *Studenten*, 101 ff., 197 ff.; Faust, *Studentenbund*, i. 94 ff., 129; ii. 98 ff.

lively interest in the glorification of war as preached by such authors as Jünger, Schauwecker, Beumelburg, and others.

The revival of enthusiasm for war and army matters found political expression in student demands for 'reawakening the warlike spirit (*Wehrwillen*)', military training, and the promotion of military sports, the creation of professorships in defence matters, and the combating of all forms of pacifism. The NSDStB, from the moment of its foundation, consciously propagated a warlike ideology. This found favour with the student corporations as it was skilfully linked with the idea of defending honour by force of arms, a notion which was then uncritically translated into political terms.[162] Thus, the corporations' ideal of honour continued to form the basis for successful propagation of a militarist ideology.

From the end of the 1920s the military-mindedness of the student body rapidly increased. At every student rally stress was laid on Germany's military weakness, her need of proper defences, and the students' own readiness to fight for their country. The students assented with enthusiasm to the Nazi maxim that 'our nation must be rescued from the fog of international Jewish pacifism'.[163] The wave of militarism also found expression in new organizations: the Stahlhelm-Studentenring and the Langemarck-Stiftung der deutschen Studentenschaft. In the protest against the Young plan, in which the DNVP, the National Socialists, and the Stahlhelm joined forces, the Stahlhelm-Studentenring and the Deutsche Burschenschaft took part on a corporative basis.[164] At a rally in 1929 the latter body voted to set up a 'freedom fund' to promote defence activities (*Wehrarbeit*), which for some years past had comprised not only theoretical discussion but also practical military training. Holiday camps run by officers on military lines—often called *Wehrsportlager*—were more and more frequently organized by the most varied student associations. In 1931 the council of the Deutsche Studentenschaft reported that its main activity in the past year had consisted in *Wehrsport* and propaganda work.[165] The arrangement between the NSDStB and the corporations led to a dynamic expansion of the former, its principal accretion of strength coming from the Deutsche Burschenschaft.[166] The triumphal advance reached a peak for the time being in the 'conquest' of the Deutsche Studentenschaft (DSt), the largest and most influential voluntary association of German students, which in 1931 elected a National Socialist as its chairman. A year later its governing body abolished all democratic rules of procedure and introduced the 'leadership' principle. In the last five years of the Weimar Republic, without any particular help from the NSDAP, the National Socialist student organization established itself securely in nearly all German universities. At the elections to the Allgemeiner Studentenausschuss (AStA: General Students' Committee) in the winter term of 1930/1, at which the number of those voting was over 50 per cent at all universities and over 90 per cent in some, the NSDStB obtained an absolute majority in eleven universities and a

---

[162] Bleuel and Klinnert, *Studenten*, 117; Faust, *Studentenbund*, i. 94.
[163] Faust, *Studentenbund*, i. 95.   [164] Bleuel and Klinnert, *Studenten*, 108, 195.
[165] Faust, *Studentenbund*, i. 96.
[166] Bleuel and Klinnert, *Studenten*, 206; cf. also Bracher, *Weimarer Republik*, 132 ff.

relative one in ten more.[167] This showed that even before Hitler came to power the great majority of German students had espoused a militant and radical nationalism combined with hatred of all forms of internationalism and pacifism.

In this way the generation of students who had been too young to fight in the First World War ranged themselves beside those members of the war generation who idealized warfare and regarded peace as a mere period of preparation for the next trial of strength. The young men who were students at German universities in 1929–33 were in their late twenties to mid-thirties in 1939, when Germany invaded Poland and unleashed the Second World War. Since their student days they had at least inwardly accepted the idea of a fresh conflict, even if they did not actually wish for one.

4. THE ATTITUDE OF THE PROTESTANT CHURCH

The Protestant clergymen who, between the wars and especially in the last years of the Weimar Republic, expressed opinions on matters of war and peace, and thus took part in the process of forming public opinion, were guided by theological traditions which in part went back to Luther,[168] in particular his version of the doctrine of just and unjust wars. This rested on the premiss that wars were bound to recur, being an inevitable destiny imposed by God on sinful man. By connecting the notion of warfare with that of original sin, and indeed establishing a direct causal link between them, orthodox Lutheran theology helped to bring about the situation 'that citizens accept the political decision to make war as something imposed on them by fate'.[169] The view of war based on the theology of original sin helped to implant in Protestantism, internationally considered, the system of thought and behaviour that has been described by critics as 'Christian militarism'.[170]

The earlier tradition of Protestantism with its acceptance of war had reached its apogee during the First World War, in Germany as in other countries. Pastors and theologians in 1914 adopted an attitude of unqualified nationalism, in the light of which it went without saying that the German cause was a righteous one. This view was described as follows in the first half of the 1920s by Martin Schian in a work entitled *Die deutsche evangelische Kirche im Weltkrieg*, published on behalf of the German Evangelical Church Committee:

The Evangelical churches in the German Reich have always adopted a national standpoint, being convinced that they did nothing to detract from their Christian character by rendering to Caesar what was Caesar's. This attitude was not due to their close connection with the state or the episcopal supremacy of the secular ruler;[171] in their view it was self-evident, and to maintain it seemed to them a moral duty.[172]

---

[167] Bleuel and Klinnert, *Studenten*, 213–14; further election results in Faust, *Studentenbund*, ii. 140–7 (appendix).

[168] Cf. Deschner, *Kirche und Krieg*; *Christentum und Militarismus*.

[169] Huber, 'Evangelische Theologie', 213–14.

[170] Cf. Russell, 'Christentum und Militarismus', 21–109.

[171] Since the Reformation each temporal sovereign was the overlord of the German Evangelical church in his dominions, with the title of 'supreme bishop' (*summus episcopus*).

[172] Schian, *Arbeit der evangelischen Kirche*, 17.

This nationalism was combined with the idea that God was the lord of peoples and the disposer of battles. At the outbreak of the First World War the idea of the 'German God', which goes back to Ernst Moritz Arndt, was frequently invoked by many representatives of the Evangelical church.[173] Hence, the great majority of its pastors believed, and asserted in numerous wartime sermons, that Germany was fighting for a just cause[174]—a position adopted, *mutatis mutandis*, by the patriotic churches of other countries also. Many Protestant pastors in Germany went so far in their sermons as to denigrate and disparage the nation's enemies.[175] Only a few dissentients such as Martin Rade, professor of theology at Marburg, dared to call in question the moral justification of the war,[176] and attempts made by liberal or social theologians to challenge the prevalent 'war theology'[177] were of very little avail. As long as the war continued, the national-conservative majority of German Protestantism—what was called 'national Protestantism'[178]—favoured a victors' peace with annexations; only a liberal minority advocated a compromise peace such as the Centre party, the social democrats, and the left-wing liberals sought to achieve after 1917.

The revolution of 1918–19 came as a terrific shock to German Protestantism.[179] Many theologians saw it as 'a betrayal of the national cause that was supposed to be victorious up to the end of the war, an act of treason against the monarchical form of state as ordained by God'.[180] These theologians had seen their ideal embodied in the German empire of 1871—as it were the Protestant form of state *par excellence*—and had in addition identified it closely with the social system and standards of imperial Germany. The overthrow of the monarchies meant for the Evangelical churches the end of episcopal supremacy, so that it became necessary to establish the church on a new constitutional foundation. As ecclesiastical Protestantism remained wedded to the idea of the monarchical, authoritarian state, it considered itself, *vis-à-vis* the republic, as a kind of trustee for the old state which had disappeared. A parliamentary state based on parties did not seem to it the kind of authority it could acknowledge.[181] Anti-republicanism remained one of the chief marks of political Protestantism during the whole Weimar period.

Certainly German Protestantism in the 1920s was far from being monolithic. It included liberal and Christian socialist groups and a variety of other tendencies.[182] But without question national Protestantism, i.e. the conservative, nationalist

---

[173] Huber, 'Evangelische Theologie', 140.

[174] Ibid. 155.

[175] Pressel, *Kriegspredigt*, 75, 127 ff., 141, 151 ff.

[176] Huber, 'Evangelische Theologie', 181 ff.

[177] Ibid. 215.

[178] Defined in Huber and Schwerdtfeger, 'Friedenshandeln', 558: an important trend in 19th- and 20th-cent. Protestantism, strongly influenced by nationalism and offering religious arguments for national supremacy.

[179] Greschat, *Protestantismus*, 11.

[180] Pressel, *Kriegspredigt*, 28.

[181] Erdmann, *Zeit der Weltkriege*, 214–15; Christ, *Politischer Protestantismus*, 78 ff., 385, 388; Pressel, *Kriegspredigt*, 28, 295–6; Huber, 'Evangelische Theologie', 186; Gaede, 'Protestantismus', 417 ff.

[182] Cf. Kupisch, 'Strömungen der Evangelischen Kirche'; Christ, *Politischer Protestantismus*, 385 ff.; Scholder, 'Kirchen im Dritten Reich', 11 ff.

outlook, was dominant. According to a special study, between 1919 and 1933 about 70–80 per cent of Evangelical pastors were of this persuasion.[183] They mostly voted for the DNVP and felt attached to the nobility, the military, big business, landowners, and the wealthy bourgeoisie, as can be seen from the membership of representative church institutions.[184] At the elections to the Constituent Assembly in 1919 several Protestant newspapers had exhorted their readers to vote for the DNVP,[185] and in the following years the great majority of representatives of the Evangelical churches in Germany opted for the 'national opposition'. Officially the church regarded itself as above party,[186] but, like the Stahlhelm, it interpreted this non-partisanship as a vote for the right. As Otto Dibelius put it: 'The church is politically neutral, but she votes German-national.'[187] The majority of pastors not only agreed with the political right in opposing democracy, liberalism, and socialism, but also in being anti-pacifist. To form an idea of the extent to which national Protestantism affected political attitudes in general, it must be recalled that in 1924 the Evangelical churches officially comprised 40 million members, or over 60 per cent of the German population, and that among these about 11 million, or 19 per cent of the population, were actually church-goers. These latter belonged mainly to the middle and upper ranks of society; Protestants among the working class were for the most part non-practising.[188]

In the 1920s scarcely any question was discussed more vehemently among Protestants than that of the Christian attitude to war and peace[189] and the connected political problems of the day: rearmament, ex-soldiers' and militarist associations, and the policy of compromise in foreign affairs. The national Protestant school of thought agreed on these points with the political right.[190] Accordingly it refused to accept the fact of Germany's military defeat; it did much to spread the 'stab in the back' legend,[191] and it was firmly opposed to pacifist ideas.[192]

A prominent member of the school, the theologian Gottfried Traub, editor of the periodical *Eiserne Blätter* and a DNVP member of the National Assembly, carried anti-pacifism so far that in 1919 he wanted the phrase 'reconciliation of nations' deleted from Article 148 of the constitution (referring to the aims of education), thus arousing sharp protests from Evangelical Protestants.[193] In the last days of the republic, at a time of surging nationalism, the same Traub held forth on the 'moral right to wage war'.[194] Another pastor, Hans Asmussen, felt called on to rebut the notion that war was un-Christian.[195] Paul Althaus, a theologian and professor of

---

[183] Dahm, *Pfarrer*, 9 and *passim*.
[184] Gaede, 'Protestantismus', 417–18.
[185] Cf. Greschat, *Protestantismus*, pt. 1, docs. 33, 36, 37, 39, 43, 44, 45, 50.
[186] Cf. Wright, *'Above Parties'*; Dahm, *Pfarrer*, 104–9,
[187] Dahm, *Pfarrer*, 104. Cf. in general Thalmann, *Protestantisme et nationalisme*.
[188] Wright, *'Above Parties'*, p. vi.
[189] Christ, *Politischer Protestantismus*, 141.   [190] Ibid. 55 ff.
[191] Gaede, 'Protestantismus', 375; id., *Kirche*, 24–31.
[192] Christ, *Politischer Protestantismus*, 151.
[193] For details see Gaede, *Kirche*, 51–2.
[194] Traub, 'Geisteskampf der Gegenwart'.
[195] Asmussen, *Politik und Christentum*, 99.

conservative and nationalist views, was one of those at the end of the 1920s who called in scarcely veiled language for a war in order to overthrow the treaty of Versailles. In an essay entitled 'War and Christianity' he wrote: 'As if, given a hypocritical peace intended to perpetuate a status quo convenient to the majority, it may not be right to long for open war as being, in such a case, probably the more moral expression of relations between two nations.'[196]

Amid such voices from right-wing Protestantism, the Evangelical authorities ordained that special services of mourning be held to mark the tenth anniversary of Versailles on 6 June 1929. At that time Martin Rade of Marburg warned against the danger to peace represented by constant recriminations against the treaty and by revisionist demands. 'Our church', he declared, 'is committing a sin against our people by making out that the situation is desperate and hopeless. Those who pay attention to it can only say to themselves: "Our only hope is another war".'[197] Indeed, his fellow pastor Althaus did not shrink from saying this. 'The only man who can truly enter into an era of peace among nations is he who in his heart can say "Yes" to war.'[198] To Althaus's mind there was no doubt that real conflicts could only be resolved by war.

Twelve years after 1918, when the wave of nationalist war literature reached its height for the first time, Otto Dibelius, an authoritative representative of the Evangelical church,[199] general superintendent for the Kurmark (electoral march of Brandenburg), raised the question 'Whether war can be in accordance with God's will'. His book on the subject, entitled *Arguments and Answers*, set out to give guidance to the faithful in a situation in which, as he saw it, the pacifist and militarist camps were drawn up 'in fixed and opposing ranks'.[200] He began by saying that one who honoured 'the noble aspects of war' was not thereby necessarily denying the message of the Christian gospel.[201] He then proceeded with historical reflections which amounted to undiluted social Darwinism. 'In human history one act of violence follows another, one war succeeds another. Destiny depends on an unceasing combat of all against all . . . There has always been war. All that we call culture has been shaped by the great decisions achieved on battlefields. The rise and fall of nations has been sealed by bloody wars . . . That and that alone is the content of history. War, war, ever again war!'[202] In short, 'war among nations is part of the natural order; religion has nothing to say against this, nor has Christianity'.[203] As to the adverse effects of war, Dibelius dismissed these as unimportant.[204] He also argued that war was recognized by international law as a method of settling disputes

---

[196] P. Althaus, 'Krieg und Christentum', in *Die Religion in Geschichte und Gegenwart*[2] (1929), iii. 1311; quoted from Christ, *Politischer Protestantismus*, 146.

[197] Quoted from Gaede, 'Protestantismus', 391, 386.

[198] Althaus, *Staatsgedanke*, 64–5.

[199] According to Kupisch ('Strömungen der Evangelischen Kirche', 384) Dibelius was one of the most influential men in the Evangelical church in Prussia in the Weimar period, esp. on account of his much-read book *Das Jahrhundert der Kirche* (1926).

[200] Dahm, on the other hand, takes the view (*Pfarrer*, 119–20) that it was not a question of 'two hard-and-fast blocs confronting each other', but that there were numerous intermediate shades of opinion.

[201] Dibelius, *Friede*, 22.   [202] Ibid. 27–8.   [203] Ibid. 57.
[204] Ibid. 52.

among states.[205] This was a remarkable standpoint in view of the signature in 1928, two years before, of the Kellogg Pact outlawing war.[206]

In a chapter entitled 'The Joy of War' Dibelius wrote that the soldier longed for times in which he could develop the occupation which was the main purpose of his life. This would 'never be otherwise . . . And it is not only the soldier who rejoices, but all who long for something out of the ordinary.'[207] Statements like this hardly conceal the glorification of war and the military profession. The latter, Dibelius exclaimed, was 'a glorious station in life'—more to be respected than that of the craftsman, the merchant, or the bourgeois. Warlike displays moved him to enthusiasm: 'Parades, manœuvres! Even the most doctrinaire pacifist must feel an electric shock run through his blood when he hears military music.'[208] Dibelius had correspondingly sharp words for pacifists. Their propaganda, he informed his readers, 'need not be taken seriously'; more, it 'sprang from an ideology to which the Christian felt himself definitely opposed'.[209] He denounced the history of the peace movement since 1850 as 'a history of people who tried to interfere in the life of nations with rational arguments and bloodless ideals of humanity.'[210] Christian pacifism, he maintained, consisted of 'being ready to sacrifice oneself joyfully for the nation'.[211] Hence, the church—unlike what might be expected of socialists, Communists, democrats, and 'vast numbers of the unprincipled [!] of all kinds'—would never call on its members to refuse military service or sabotage a war, but would command them to obey the authorities, 'which is a basic doctrine of Christianity'.[212] In conclusion: 'This is the spirit in which the Christian goes to war . . . He will face the foe and refuse no service that he is ordered to perform. He is serving his God when he fights for the Fatherland.' . . . This is what the church ordains.'[213]

These words, written in 1930, were in accord with the tradition of the Evangelical church in Germany.[214] An occurrence in the same year was symbolic of the pattern of forces within the church: the German Evangelical Church Congress at Nuremberg elected as its president a retired lieutenant-general, Count Vitzthum von Eckstädt, who presented himself wearing the insignia of the Iron Cross, first

---

[205] Ibid. 55. This was a very widespread view, as shown by Dahm, *Pfarrer*, 118–19.

[206] Cf. Krüger, 'Friedenssicherung', and Wehberg, *Ächtung des Krieges*. On the attitude of German public opinion to the idea of outlawing war cf. the present author's 'From Kellogg to Hitler', 71–99.

[207] Dibelius, *Friede*, 58. Dahm (*Pfarrer*, 120–1) takes a more favourable view: he considers that Dibelius, as a conservative, answered 'no' to the question whether war could be in accordance with God's will. In my opinion this cannot be sustained, although it can clearly be seen that Dibelius was at pains to distinguish between abstract theological considerations and practical ones. Despite the view of K. Scholder (cf. 'Dibelius', 90–104, esp. 93), who maintains that Dibelius's *Friede* opposed any glorification of war, I am of the opinion that, with its emphasis on obedience to authority and the Christian's duty to serve in war, the book cannot have exercised any influence against war and in the direction of peace.

[208] Dibelius, *Friede*, 59.

[209] Ibid. 15–16.

[210] Ibid. 73.

[211] Ibid. 196, 204.

[212] Ibid. 199–200.

[213] Ibid. 210.

[214] Dignath-Düren, *Kirche*, 13.

class, and based his eligibility on the fact that he had served forty years as an officer.[215]

Dibelius's book was clearly not just a metaphysical treatise on war, but a set of concrete political instructions to the faithful. As the great majority of Protestant church leaders in Germany were of his way of thinking, it may be taken that, to say the least, the Evangelical church took no action to prevent war. It is also to be noted that German conservatism was largely rooted in theology: it constantly appealed to Christian authority, and used religious arguments to buttress conservative values.[216] General Ludwig Beck spoke for many when he quoted the saying of the elder Moltke that war was 'a link in God's world order'. Beck considered it senseless to bother one's head about the abolition of war: 'War cannot be abolished. Any reflection on man's imperfection as ordained by God must come back to this conclusion again and again.'[217]

Compared with the nationalist majority, those groups within the Evangelical church which felt it their duty to adopt pacifist positions had scarcely any influence in politics. Among organizations there was the German section of the World Alliance for Promoting International Friendship through the Churches, whose object was 'to cultivate a spirit of friendship among nations so as to combat movements leading to hatred and war', and which included Dietrich Bonhoeffer among its members;[218] the Evangelischer Friedensbund, founded in Berlin in 1931, which sought to unite Evangelical pacifists of left-wing inclinations;[219] and various Christian-socialist and liberal-democratic groups. A comparison of the circulation figures of publications of the Evangelical pacifists with those of the nationalist Protestants will give an idea of their relative influence. *Die Christliche Welt*, edited by Martin Rade, ran to 3,000 copies, and F. Siegmund-Schulze's *Eiche* to 2,000, while the *Sonntagsblatt des arbeitenden Volkes*, edited by the Christian socialist E. Eckert, had a circulation of 14,300. By contrast, the national-conservative church newspapers and the conservative Sunday press sold about 2 million copies, or a hundred times as many.[220] An analyst of the Evangelical press and other publications concludes that 'their [the pacifists'] output was not small, but the opposition camp was very strong—not only sceptics, but those who rejected pacifism on principle and upheld the values and dignity of war'.[221] The situation within political Protestantism, with nationalists and pacifists opposing each other on the question of war and peace, was more or less paralleled in party terms: the nationalist Protestants gravitated towards

[215] Gaede, 'Protestantismus', 417. On the social origins of delegates to the congress cf. Balzer, *Klassengegensätze*, 37–8.
[216] Greiffenhagen, *Dilemma*, 15, 23.
[217] Beck, *Studien*, 247, 251, 257. Moltke wrote on 11 Dec. 1880 to Bluntschli, the professor of international law at Heidelberg: 'Perpetual peace is a dream, and not even a beautiful one; war is a link in God's providence. In war the noblest human virtues are developed: courage and self-denial, the sense of duty and readiness to sacrifice one's life. If it were not for war, the world would sink into a morass of materialism' (*Gesammelte Schriften und Denkwürdigkeiten*, iii. 254).
[218] Boyens, 'Stellung der Ökumene', 426.
[219] Christ, *Politischer Protestantismus*, 271–2.
[220] Gaede, 'Protestantismus', 416–17.
[221] Christ, *Politischer Protestantismus*, 169.

the conservative and *völkisch* parties, and the pacifists towards the democrats and socialists.[222]

The relationship of political Protestantism to the NSDAP before 1933 is only of marginal concern here. The collective work *Die Kirche und das Dritte Reich*,[223] published in 1932, presents a wide range of arguments which led Evangelical theologians to sympathize with National Socialism. Some hostile comments are included,[224] but more or less pro-Fascist utterances are very numerous: it is often emphasized that 'wide Evangelical circles followed National Socialism with a high degree of political confidence'.[225] One contributor warned against 'distorting the biblical hope of peace into political pacifism';[226] another celebrated National Socialism as a movement in which 'heroism is born again', so that 'the cross of Christ and the *Hakenkreuz* (swastika) . . . must grow more and more into a unity'. S. Nobiling, a pastor in Berlin and a declared National Socialist, interpreted this as involving the express approval of war as an instrument of policy.[227]

Thus, the alliance of nationalism, militarism, and religion that had characterized the war theology of 1914-18 lived on in the Weimar Republic and—though we cannot pursue this in detail here—in the Third Reich, where it was fortified with the idea of a crusade against Bolshevism and world Jewry.[228] As in the past, pacifist attitudes were held by only minority groups of German Protestants.

On 2 September 1939, the second day of the war against Poland, the German Evangelical church issued an official call to its members in the following terms:

Since yesterday our German people has been engaged in a fight for the land of its fathers, so that German blood may return to German blood. The German Evangelical church has always been loyally associated with the destiny of the Germany people. It has provided weapons of steel with the invincible force of God's word: the confidence of faith that our nation and every one of us is in God's hands, and the strength of prayer making us strong in good and ill fortune. So in this hour too we unite ourselves with our people in prayer for the Führer and the Reich, the whole of our armed forces, and all those who do their duty for the Fatherland on the home front.[229]

While this appeal was free from exaggerated nationalist rhetoric, it made clear to all that the Evangelical church was not opposed to Hitler and his war policy, and the Protestants were once more enjoined to obey the secular power. The National Socialist regime had reason to be satisfied.

---

[222] Gaede, 'Protestantismus', 393-8, 417; Christ, *Politischer Protestantismus*, 155-6.

[223] Ed. by Leopold Klotz. For the interpretation cf. Dahm, *Pfarrer*, 203 ff.

[224] For example, an anti-Fascist and pacifist line was taken by Professor E. Fuchs of Kiel: *Kirche und Drittes Reich*, i. 34 ff.

[225] Ibid. i. 20, 36-7, 38.

[226] Thus the pro-Nazi Professor H. Dörries of Göttingen: ibid. ii. 41.

[227] Ibid. ii. 80, 84-5.   [228] Huber, 'Kirche', 167.

[229] Text of appeal in *Gesetzblatt der Deutschen Evangelischen Kirche*, (1939), No. 19; here quoted from Messerschmidt, 'Militärseelsorgepolitik im Zweiten Weltkrieg', 49. The documentation with commentary by Brakelmann (ed.), *Kirche im Krieg*, while observing all necessary qualifications, concludes (p. 19) that from 1939 onwards 'mainstream Protestantism' had 'chosen its course and broadly shared responsibility with the National Socialist party and state for the war, which it supported to the end'.

5. THE CATHOLIC CHURCH AND THE CENTRE PARTY: WAR THEOLOGY, INTERNATIONAL UNDERSTANDING, AND OBEDIENCE TO AUTHORITY

The traditional moral theology of the Catholic church also distinguished between just and unjust wars:[230] the faithful were allowed to serve in the former, while participation in the latter was a sin. A 'just' war must be fought for a just cause at the behest of a legitimate authority. It must only be undertaken as a last resort, and measures against the enemy must be compatible with the natural law. These four criteria had been recognized by Catholic theologians and jurists for centuries. During the period of Christian nation-states the Popes, as rulers of the universal church, found themselves in a dilemma which they sought to escape by refraining from designating any particular war as just or unjust. Instead, the Vatican addressed peace appeals to the belligerents and itself observed neutrality; at the same time it allowed the church authorities of each country to support the national government, so that in practice the bishops always took the line that their own country's war was a just one.

A trend towards nationalism had been perceptible among German Catholics before 1914, parallel to the weakening of internationalism in the church as a whole. Like most of their compatriots, German Catholics were swept by a wave of enthusiasm at the outbreak of the First World War. Since the days of the *Kulturkampf* they had been under suspicion in many quarters for alleged lack of loyalty to the empire, and, like the social democrats, were not fully integrated into imperial society. Accordingly, most of them welcomed the war as a test of patriotism, giving them a chance to show that they were loyal Germans and not hostile to the regime.[231]

This was true of clergy as well as laity. An analysis of Catholic war sermons between 1914 and 1918 brings to light the same mixture of nationalism, conservatism, warlike spirit, and religion which was characteristic of Protestants, Jews, and other religious groups. The theologian Karl Barth spoke of a 'single World War theology' reflected in the similar language and content of the war sermons of all denominations.[232] Catholics, like the nationalist Protestants, adopted the ideology of a special 'German mission'.[233] Some theologians went so far as to identify the German cause with the divine purpose, so that Germany was fighting a 'holy war'.[234] The influential Catholic philosopher Max Scheler believed that he heard 'the sacred voice of God' in the 'loud speech of weapons'.[235] He and many Catholic priests regarded the war partly as a punishment and call to repentance, but also as a revelation and divine judgement.[236] War and peace, according to Catholic

---

[230] Cf. Russell, 'Christentum und Militarismus', 26 ff., and the literature cited there. For the following passage cf. Lewy, *Catholic Church*, 261.

[231] Hammer, *Kriegstheologie*, 73; also Missalla, *Gott mit uns*, 32, 123–4.

[232] Pressel, *Kriegspredigt*, 21; Huber, 'Evangelische Theologie', 136–7.

[233] Erdmann, *Zeit der Weltkriege*, 87 ff., esp. 89–90.

[234] Missalla, *Gott mit uns*, 67; cf. also 88, 110 ff.

[235] Cf. Scheler, *Genius des Krieges*, (1915), preface and pp. 117–52. On Scheler cf. also Erdmann, *Zeit der Weltkriege*, 90–1.

[236] Thus e.g. Scheler, *Genius des Krieges*, who also believed in war as 'leading men to God'.

sermons, were not the result of human action but of moral and religious changes. Here a specifically fatalist attitude came into play, as it did in war sermons that concentrated on consoling the faithful and thus made it easier to withdraw into the sphere of private devotion.[237]

The church frequently urged its members to subscribe to war loans as an 'obligation of conscience'. If the war could not be waged for lack of money, a preacher wrote, 'enemy hordes from all quarters of the earth' would destroy the Germans' land and livelihood; the country would be overrun by 'a deluge of wild Cossacks and negro soldiers, the French enemies of the church and the Russian enemies of the Pope'.[238] Similar appeals were made in the Second World War, when the clergy urged Catholics to contribute to the various collections for the purpose of overcoming shortages in the war economy.[239] In 1914–18 Catholic priests, like Protestant pastors, glorified the soldier's death in action: 'A warrior's death is no death. He is transfigured by the radiance of immortality and eternal life.'[240] Michael von Faulhaber, bishop of Speyer and afterwards cardinal, saw it as the task of the Catholic clergy to preach sermons that would 'strengthen souls for military duties', and by their pastoral care to serve the 'sacred cause of the Fatherland'.[241]

Like the Catholic clergy, the representatives of political Catholicism supported the war; the Centre party in the Reichstag, in particular, was determined not to be outdone in patriotism.[242] In the first years after 1914, Catholic church leaders and the Centre party both supported a hegemonistic war-aims policy.[243] Only in the middle of 1917 was it possible for Matthias Erzberger, who had till then been an extreme annexationist, to bring his party round to the idea of a conciliatory peace and co-operation with the liberals and socialists. This was an anticipation of the 'Weimar coalition' of the SPD, Centre, and DDP, which was to be the effective support of the first German republic.

During the republican period the foreign policy of the parties of political Catholicism, viz. the Centre and the Bavarian Volkspartei (BVP),[244] was firmly oriented in a peaceable direction. In several speeches the leaders pleaded for the reconciliation of nations and peaceful co-operation. A plea for the League of Nations was already contained in the 'Policy Guidelines for the German Centre Party' in December 1918, and continued to be the basis of the party's foreign policy.[245] In 1919 the Centre, led by Matthias Erzberger, accepted the treaty of

---

[237] Missalla (*Gott mit uns*, 127–8, 129–30) saw the actual political element as consisting in this fatalism. 'Anyone who, everywhere and in all occurrences, seeks for traces of divine intervention and divine providence, who ignores all worldly factors and refers everything simply and solely to God, is in the last resort making human beings and the whole world a puppet-show manipulated by a higher power' (ibid. 130).

[238] Missalla, ibid. 110 ff., here 111.

[239] Zahn, *Catholics*, 25.

[240] Missalla, *Gott mit uns*, 115; other striking examples in Faulhaber, *Waffen des Lichtes*.

[241] Faulhaber, *Schwert*, pp. vi–vii.

[242] Lutz, *Demokratie im Zwielicht*, 21; also Missalla, *Gott mit uns*, 33.

[243] Erdmann, *Zeit der Weltkriege*, 90.

[244] Cf. Morsey, 'Zentrumspartei', and Schwend, 'Bayerische Volkspartei'.

[245] Cf. *Bürgerliche Parteien*, ii. 908–9.

Versailles, and from then on it supported the 'policy of fulfilment'[246] which was intended to convince the world of Germany's honest determination to meet her obligations and pay reparations. In the long term the Centre politicians thought a revision of the treaty might be possible by means of improved relations with the Western powers. Stresemann's foreign policy[247] was unreservedly backed by the Centre party, including the Locarno treaty and Germany's entry into the League of Nations. At the same time the Centre attached great importance to its national and patriotic image.

On 21 January 1927 the Centre party in the Reichstag drew up a *National Political Manifesto*[248] confirming its support for international co-operation, peaceful development, and membership of the League. The manifesto also described the Reichswehr as a 'political necessity'. 'There can be no state authority without power. This is what gives the German people's army its essential foundation and its task.' As the Centre regarded state and military power as linked in this way, it supported the military budget throughout the 1920s. In the public controversy about the building of an armoured vessel in 1928–9 it again voted for the necessary funds.[249] The party leaders were not over-concerned with the problem of finding a specific security justification for their position. They considered their moderate attitude towards the military provisions of Versailles as something quite natural. The use of military force 'in defence against unprovoked attack' was a principle undisputed in political Catholicism,[250] based on the theory of just and unjust war.

Towards the end of the 1920s the right wing of the Centre party, which favoured co-operation with the very right-wing DNVP, became increasingly influential. At the election of new officers at the party congress in Cologne in 1928 Monsignor Ludwig Kaas, a right-winger and a professor of ecclesiastical law at Trier, was elected chairman in opposition to the Christian trade-unionist Adam Stegerwald and the representative of the Catholic workers' movement, Josef Joos.[251] The main reason for Kass's election was that, as a priest, he was expected to be able to compose the differences within the party,[252] and the Centre wanted to consider itself 'a party with its ideology rooted in religion'.[253] But the election was more than an expression of the desire to 'revert to the party's religious heritage'[254] and strengthen its ties with the church: it also denoted a shift to the right. The conservative, authoritarian, corporatist bourgeois element had prevailed over the working-class left wing, and the party continued to evince anti-parliamentarian tendencies.[255]

Monsignor Kaas, who was also the party's foreign affairs spokesman, continued

---

[246] The 'policy of fulfilment' was inaugurated by J. Wirth of the Centre party, Reich chancellor in 1921–2. Cf. Rosenberg, *German Republic*, 152–3.   [247] Cf. I.I.6 below.

[248] Text in *Deutsche Parteiprogramme*, 494 ff.; cf. also Joos, *Ideenwelt des Zentrums*, 60.

[249] Cf. Wacker, *Panzerschiff 'A'*, 65, 143–4.

[250] Schulte, 'Zentrum', 48–9.   [251] Morsey, *Politischer Katholizismus*, 18–19.

[252] Morsey, 'Zentrumspartei', 285 ff.; *Bürgerliche Parteien*, ii. 925.

[253] Becker, 'Zentrumspartei', 357. Hence also the prominence of the Catholic clergy in the party's leadership: see Böckenförde, 'Katholizismus', 319.

[254] Morsey, 'Zentrumspartei', 289.   [255] Plum, *Gesellschaftsstruktur*, 205.

to support Stresemann's policy of conciliating the Western powers, and was opposed to a 'head-on fight' against the arbitrary provisions of Versailles.[256] It was his hope, however, that by peaceful means 'the nation might be able to ascend to freedom and world status'.[257] In the Reichstag debate on 19 November 1928 he argued even more clearly for a 'change in the thrust of our foreign policy', meaning above all a more aggressively revisionist policy towards Poland.[258]

In 1930–2 Heinrich Brüning of the Centre party was chancellor of the Reich, governing by emergency decrees independently of parliament. The very fact that he presented his government as a 'cabinet of former front-line soldiers' made it clear that he was not the man to check the growing militarization of the state and of public opinion. As is well known, the army high command of 1918–19 provided the republic with its president (Hindenburg) in 1925 and its defence minister (Groener) in 1928, and from 1929 onwards the Reichswehr steadily increased its influence in domestic affairs.[259] Brüning evidently did not find it especially difficult to fit into the Hindenburg–Groener constellation. His statement that he was able to 'report' to the president that he had formed a cabinet was an illustration of his political outlook.[260] It was also typical that when Brüning first met Hitler on 6 October 1930 he appealed to the latter 'as an old front-line soldier' to tolerate his (Brüning's) plans for a restoration of the monarchy[261] and also his version of a revisionist policy.[262] When Hitler replied that his own object was to destroy both the left-wing socialists and the reactionaries in home affairs, and in foreign affairs to crush the hereditary enemy, France, and Russia as the stronghold of Bolshevism, Brüning demurred and, according to his own account, tried to convince Hitler that 'a frontal attack before one was sufficiently armed on the home front would lead to complete failure and chaos in Germany'. Brüning also favoured coalitions of the Centre and the NSDAP in the provincial (Land) parliaments.[263] This policy was subsequently continued by Kaas, who in November 1932 sought Hindenburg's support for the idea of a government of 'national concentration' including the NSDAP.[264] In his speech to the Reichstag on 16 October 1930 Brüning for the first time openly demanded military equality of rights for Germany, in accordance with his principle of working for an early revision of the treaty of Versailles. Equality of rights also implied equality of armaments, which German diplomacy veiled under the term 'disarmament'.[265] It was a sign of the altered political climate in the Brüning period that in the Reichstag debate of 24–5 February 1932, in which party leaders vied with one another in showing how patriotic they had been in 1914–18, the chancellor

[256] Cf. Kass's speech at Dortmund on 17 Oct. 1929, in *Schulthess* (1929), 191–2.
[257] Kaas, 'Außenpolitik' (1928), 16; id., 'Völkerbund' (1929), 122–3.
[258] *Bürgerliche Parteien*, ii. 926.
[259] Cf. Rosenberg, *German Republic*, 268–702; Geyer, *Landesverteidigung*, 1–2; on Groener see Deist, III.1.2 below.
[260] Brüning, *Memoiren*, 168; on Brüning's anti-pacifism see also I.1.10 below.
[261] The BVP was also in favour of restoration: see Schwend, 'Bayerische Volkspartei', 481 ff.
[262] Brüning, *Memoiren*, 192–5.   [263] Ibid. 196.
[264] Morsey, *Politischer Katholizismus*, 70 ff.; on the Centre party's coalition policy see also Junker, *Zentrumspartei*, 72 ff.
[265] Bloch, *Hitler*, 15; Rautenberg, *Rüstungspolitik*, 12 ff., 22.

himself claimed that on 9 November 1918 he had been in command of a unit whose task was to defeat the revolution.[266]

It is true that political Catholicism had come to terms, much sooner than Protestantism, with the republic born of the revolution: it had at an early date established a positive relationship towards the new state and had developed into a Centre party which was one of its pillars. Throughout the Weimar period, the Catholic Centre occupied a key position in parliamentary affairs.[267] However, its relations with the republic were of a pragmatic character: that is to say, it supported the republican system but did not, as a party, commit itself to republicanism as such.[268] Joos, a member of the Reichstag and of the party's left wing, in an essay on the party's political ideas in 1928 cited a statement by Gröber, formerly the chairman of its parliamentary section, to the effect that Catholics believed that 'all authority was from God, the republic no less than the monarchy', and that the citizen owed an equal duty of obedience to either regime.[269] Joos's statement was in itself a clear defence of the republic against adherents of the monarchy, some of whom were still to be found in the Centre party. But the argument was to prove equally valid in altered circumstances, with the result that the Centre—which was able to maintain its nation-wide share of 11-12 per cent of votes in 1928-33[270]—by no means proved a reliable defender of democracy in the republic's last years. In Brüning's time, particularly, the party systematically discouraged the respect felt by the Catholic population for the parliamentary regime and flirted with experiments in dictatorship,[271] at the same time distancing itself more and more clearly from the social democrats. Catholic political circles regarded parliamentary democracy as no more than a historical phenomenon, the presence or absence of which was to be accepted for the sake of the continuity of the state.[272]

According to the ideas held in the Catholic church and parties based on Catholic doctrine concerning authority sanctioned by the divine will, the attitude of the Centre and the Bayerische Volkspartei towards the government legally formed by Hitler in 1933 was largely predetermined: a majority of those concerned were prepared to accept it as legitimate. The bishops in conference at Fulda on 18 March 1933 gave their official blessing, in contrast to their previously adverse attitude to the NSDAP, by urging the faithful to 'show obedience to legal authority and conscientiously perform their civic duties, rejecting as a matter of principle any illegal or subversive behaviour'.[273] The concordat between the Vatican and the Hitler government, and—probably connected with it—the Centre party's support for the Enabling Law,[274] nipped in the bud any latent disposition to resist the

[266] *Verhandlungen des Reichstages* (446), 2230-1.
[267] Morsey, *Politischer Katholizismus*, 16.
[268] Erdmann, *Zeit der Weltkriege*, 214.
[269] Joos, *Ideenwelt des Zentrums*, 27.
[270] For the history of votes cast for the Centre party and seats obtained by it cf. Morsey, *Politischer Katholizismus*, 15.
[271] Instances in Morsey, 'Zentrumspartei', 291 ff.
[272] Plum, *Gesellschaftsstruktur*, 205.
[273] Text in Lewy, *Catholic Church*, 39; see also Morsey, *Politischer Katholizismus*, 153 ff.
[274] Thus recently Scholder, *Kirchen*.

National Socialist regime.[275] while the concordat enhanced the latter's prestige both in Germany and abroad.

Altogether it is clear that the Catholic church in Germany endeavoured at all costs to reach a *modus vivendi* with the National Socialist regime in 1933, and that afterwards it supported and collaborated with the regime as long as its own essential interests were respected.[276] Catholics who were not National Socialists were first politically paralysed by their own leaders and then integrated by them into the National Socialist state. The government for its part, and especially Hitler himself, treated relations with the church as a question of power to be decided pragmatically. There was no question, for instance, of caring whether religion and the Nazi ideology were compatible; all that interested Hitler was how far the church would lend itself to the furtherance of his racial and expansionist policies.[277]

As the church's traditional ideas of authority determined the attitude of political Catholicism towards Hitler's government after January 1933, so the clergy's attitude to Hitler's war policy was governed by Catholic ideas of a just and unjust war. It must be pointed out here that the Catholic church had long been sceptical or hostile towards markedly pacifist ideas. The Catholic peace movement during the Weimar period—with such organizations as the Friedensbund Deutscher Katholiken, the Christlich-Soziale Reichspartei (a political splinter-group), and publications such as the *Rhein-Mainische Volkszeitung* and the *Katholische Friedenswarte*—had little influence and no practical effect on the official church, as the movement could not count on the bishops' support. It was typical that throughout the twenty years of Weimar the Catholic bishops ignored the nation-wide congresses of the Friedensbund, although it was by no means a radically pacifist body and supported the doctrine of the 'just war'.[278] Far from the Friedensbund being protected by the concordat, it was not even mentioned.[279] The Vatican and the bishops' conference at Fulda thought it more important to obtain a secret protocol[280] providing that if and when Germany introduced universal conscription—which of course involved a breach of the treaty of Versailles—men studying for the priesthood would be exempt from military service; the clergy were also to enjoy special privileges in the event of war, such as being employed as chaplains or on ambulance duties.

In general the concordat contributed much to ensuring 'general support for Germany's cause in the Second World War'.[281] If it was the case that 'with very few exceptions German Catholics fought Hitler's war to the bitter end as a matter of course',[282] this was not only out of conviction or because they feared the con-

---

[275] Lewy, *Catholic Church*, 90.

[276] Böckenförde, 'Katholizismus', 321–2, 355; Junker, *Zentrumspartei*, 156 ff.; Plum, *Gesellschaftsstruktur*, 203–4, 208–9; Morsey, 'Zentrumspartei', 353 ff., 369–70, 388, 412, also doc. 23, p. 448. A still harsher judgement in A. Grosser's afterword to Friedländer, *Pius XII* (German edn, 167). For an appreciation of resistance by the churches cf. I.III.3 below. For the general relationship between Catholicism and National Socialism see *Katholische Kirche im Dritten Reich*.

[277] Erdmann, *Zeit der Weltkriege*, 435.

[278] Riesenberger, *Katholische Friedensbewegung*, 10, 53 ff., 58. For the principal figures in the Catholic peace movement see I.11 below. For their lack of success cf. Walter Dirks's foreword to Riesenberger.

[279] Lewy, *Catholic Church*, 84.   [280] Ibid. 85–6; cf. also Deist, III.11.2 (*a*) n. 26 below.

[281] Zahn, *Catholics*, 104 ff.   [282] Ibid. 79.

sequences of disobedience, but also because the clergy and especially the bishops expressly called on them to do so. In addition, as in the first war, the Catholic press and organizations set the example of open support for what they considered the national cause, urging the faithful to stand fast on the field of honour 'in defence of their fatherland and fellow countrymen'.[283]

An outstanding example was the army bishop Rarkowski, who exercised direct spiritual authority over Catholics serving in the armed forces.[284] On the day of the invasion of Poland he addressed a ringing call to German troops:

In this grave hour, when German people face a test of their resolve under fire and have come forward to fight for their natural and God-given rights, I address myself to you soldiers, you who are in the forefront of this battle and who have the honourable task of protecting and defending the security and life of the German nation with the sword . . . Each of you knows what is at stake for our people in these stormy days and each man sees before him, as he goes into action, the shining example of a true fighter, our Führer and Supreme Commander, the first and bravest soldier of the Greater German Reich, who is now with you at the fighting front.[285]

Hitler's war was given a religious stamp of approval, not only by the fire-eating Rarkowski but also the bulk of the German clergy at all levels.[286] Large sections of opposition groups within the church likewise called for 'obedience to the Führer' and 'loyalty to the Führer and Reich'.[287] In mid-September 1939 the bishops issued a pastoral letter[288] calling on Catholic soldiers to do their duty:

In this decisive hour we encourage and enjoin our Catholic soldiers to obey the Führer and devote themselves wholly to doing their duty in a spirit of joyful sacrifice. We urge the faithful to pray fervently that God's providence may bring the war to a conclusion and a peace that shall be full of blessing for our people and country.

In 1941, when war with the Soviet Union began, church leaders of both denominations vied with each other in calling for war on Bolshevism: after 1933 they had very soon adopted uncritically Hitler's picture of the need to choose between it and National Socialism.[289]

The history of the attitudes of the Catholic church to the question of war and peace is one of adaptation, as can be illustrated from the change in Faulhaber's position. In the First World War, as bishop of Speyer, he used the pulpit to propagate military and patriotic ideas,[290] while during the Weimar period he made some speeches that were decidedly pacific in tone.[291] In a sermon in February 1932, at the time of the opening of the Geneva conference on disarmament, he

---

[283] Ibid. 88 ff.
[284] Cf. ibid. 213–58; also Lewy, *Catholic Church*, 236 ff.
[285] The document is reproduced in Friedländer, *Pius XII*, 34.
[286] Ibid. 33; also Lewy, *Catholic Church*, 148–9.
[287] Scholder, 'Kirchen im Dritten Reich', 15.
[288] Reproduced in Lewy, *Catholic Church*, 226.
[289] Examples ibid. 205 ff., 229 ff. and *passim*; see also Scholder, 'Kirchen im Dritten Reich', 15; also Lemhöfer, 'Bolschewismus', 131–9.
[290] See n. 241 above. [291] Faulhaber, *Rufende Stimmen* (1931), 444–54.

emphasized the need to disarm and to work actively for peace, and declared that the conditions justifying war were much less often fulfilled at the present day than in the past.[292] At the beginning of the Nazi period Faulhaber was the only Catholic church leader in Germany who spoke publicly of a basic contradiction between the Christian faith and the National Socialist philosophy,[293] by which he meant anti-Semitism and racism; none the less, in 1939 he joined the rest of the Bavarian hierarchy in issuing an official call to arms. The Catholic newspapers published in his area of influence were especially prominent in their unconditional support for Hitler's war.[294]

6. POLITICAL LIBERALISM IN THE SERVICE OF NATIONALISM: THE DEUTSCHE VOLKSPARTEI AND THE DEUTSCHE DEMOKRATISCHE PARTEI

The liberals in Weimar days were represented politically by two parties: the right-wing Deutsche Volkspartei (DVP), as successor to the National Liberals, and the left-wing Deutsche Demokratische Partei (DDP). The DVP claimed to be a party of the political centre and to represent the interests of the *Mittelstand* of small craftsmen and traders; however, for a long time it chiefly stood for anti-republican rightist tendencies. For instance, it was not until 1927, the eighth year of the republic, that the DVP consented to take active part in a commemoration by the Reichstag of the anniversary of the adoption of the Weimar constitution.[295] In 1925–9 Gustav Stresemann, who had founded the DVP in 1919, more than once played with the idea of replacing it by a new, genuinely republican party of the bourgeois centre, perhaps in alliance with the left-wing liberals.[296] One reason for this plan, which did not come to fruition, was the prevalence in the DVP of anti-socialist right-wing views: these did not suit Stresemann, as he needed SPD support for his foreign policy. The DVP's claim to represent the interests of craftsmen and small businesses was only partly true. In practice the home and economic policy of the DVP—which was represented in all Reich governments between 1922 and 1932—was often dominated by heavy industry with its two great associations, the Reichsverband der deutschen Industrie and the Vereinigung der deutschen Arbeitgeberverbände. Stresemann himself, who was for many years chairman of the party, observed in 1929 that it was 'more and more a party of industry only'.[297] Under universal suffrage the DVP would never have gained a single seat in the Reichstag if it had openly declared itself a party of big business: it had to conceal the fact if it was to keep a hold on its supporters, who mostly came from the urban middle class, the propertied bourgeoisie, and the higher civil service.[298]

---

[292] Zahn, *Catholics*, 152–3; Riesenberger, *Katholische Friedensbewegung*, 58.

[293] Scholder, *Kirchen*, i. 660–1.

[294] Zahn, *Catholics*, 154 ff., 169.

[295] Turner, *Stresemann*, 234.

[296] Rosenberg, *German Republic*, 272.

[297] Stresemann's letter of 13 Mar. 1929, quoted in Turner, *Stresemann*, 252.

[298] On the composition and electoral potential of the DVP cf. Booms, 'Deutsche Volkspartei', 525; Döhn, *Politik und Interesse*; also the article 'Deutsche Volkspartei (DVP) 1918–1933' in *Bürgerliche Parteien*, i. 645–66.

Stresemann, who was chancellor in August–November 1923 and foreign minister in several cabinets thereafter, determined the foreign policy of the republic from 1923 until his death on 3 October 1929. His contemporary Carl von Ossietzky, a far from uncritical observer, declared that he had 'a degree of political talent unique in Germany', which made him one of the chief statesmen of the Weimar era. 'His object was to convert the right wing to a reasonable policy, and in that he suffered his great defeat. He wanted to convince the nationalists, but they rejected him.'[299] What was the policy that Ossietzky, himself a pacifist, called a 'reasonable' one?

In 1914–18 Stresemann had been a vociferous annexationist and advocate of a 'victor's peace', a position not far removed from that of the Pan-Germans.[300] Unlike many incorrigible nationalists, however, he began in the early 1920s to realize that, whether one liked it or not, it was out of the question for Germany with her drastically reduced military potential to pursue a policy of power in the old style. He therefore rejected the idea of a war of revenge as unrealistic, and became an advocate of peaceful revision of the Versailles terms that were regarded as unjust. As he argued in 1925, any attempt to improve Germany's position must have as its basis 'firstly the changes in the power situation due to the unfortunate outcome of the world war, but also the ideals of the League of Nations, whose purpose is to prevent wars of aggression by outlawing the aggressor and by compulsory arbitration'.[301] As, in home affairs, Stresemann became a *Vernunftrepublikaner* (one who accepted the republic on practical grounds), so in foreign affairs he accepted the need to base Germany's policy on the situation brought about by the loss of the war.

The first important stage in this policy was the Franco-German settlement under the Locarno treaty of 1925 and Germany's admission to the League of Nations in the following year: Germany was given a permanent seat on the Council in recognition of her status as a great power. Then came the partial settlement of the reparations issue, and in 1928 the signature of the Kellogg pact, which represented a peak in post-war efforts to provide for the peaceful settlement of international conflicts.[302]

It was a symbolic recognition of the European dimension of Stresemann's policy that in 1926 he was the first German to be awarded the Nobel prize for peace,[303] along with Aristide Briand, the French foreign minister, and Sir Austen Chamberlain, the British foreign secretary. This was primarily a reward for his efforts, sealed by the treaty of Locarno, to wipe out the wartime antagonism between Germany and France. It was indeed Stresemann's great merit to have achieved peaceful relations with France, at least for a time, and to have gone some way to overcome the 'hereditary enmity' of the two countries. It was indicative of his position *vis-à-vis* his own party, and also of the general situation in Germany,

---

[299] Ossietzky, 'Abschied von Stresemann', *Weltbühne* (8 Oct. 1929), 537–9; repr. in Stresemann, *Schriften* (ed. Harttung), 409, 411.

[300] For an appraisal of Stresemann see also Messerschmidt, IV.1.4 below, and Thimme, *Stresemann*.

[301] From an article published anonymously in the *Magdeburgische Zeitung* (26 Nov. 1925); repr. in Stresemann, *Schriften*, 341–2.

[302] Wehberg, *Ächtung des Krieges*.

[303] Cf. Harttung (ed.), *Friedens-Nobelpreis*.

that he was several times compelled to excuse himself for this policy of reconciliation in the West. He did so with the statement, whose political significance remains a matter of controversy, that the question of Germany's eastern frontiers was still open[304] and that her revisionist demands might be met in that quarter.

In view of such statements it may be asked whether Stresemann did unambiguously seek to guide his fellow countrymen into the path of conciliation and friendly relations with the rest of Europe, or whether he was not, directly or at least indirectly, a supporter of power politics. Certainly he and his party aimed for a comprehensive revision of the Versailles 'system' and hoped to see Germany recover its former power.[305] The DVP's inaugural manifesto of 18 December 1918,[306] with its demands for the territorial integrity of the Reich, union with Austria, and the right to colonies, made it clear that the party thought in terms of restoring Germany's position as it had been before 1914. After Versailles, treaty revision and Germany's readmission to the circle of great powers were, in the DVP's view, the proper aims of any German national policy. Stresemann took account of this in an article he wrote for the press in 1925 on the aims and methods of his revisionist policy:

The object of German foreign policy . . . must be to work for the revision of our Eastern frontier, the impossibility of which is today recognized on all sides. A further object must be to assert Germany's claim to colonial activity and to posses colonies once more. Finally, we must stand up for the right of national self-determination, a principle which the Allies have treated with unheard-of cynicism and turned into an illusion as regards the union of German Austria with Germany . . . To advance towards these aims does not require any warlike means, which are lacking to Germany, but it presupposes co-operation with those powers on whose decision these matters at present depend.[307]

In addition to the revision of Germany's eastern frontiers at Poland's expense, the union with Austria, the return of the Saar and Memel territories, Eupen-Malmédy, and if possible also the Sudetenland, Stresemann hoped to recover Germany's old colonies and to acquire new ones.[308] These aims were the corner-stones of his policy of treaty revision and great-power status.

It has been maintained that these revisionist and colonial aims were the true long-term basis of Stresemann's foreign policy, and that even his attitude towards France was 'above all a pragmatic and functional one',[309] since there was no hope of Germany recovering her great-power status without French acquiescence.

Stresemann's adoption of a policy of peaceful understanding most probably did not mean that he was opposed to a policy that might in case of need have been pursued by military means. Stresemann had always admired the army, and regarded the *Reichswehr* as a sacrosanct institution that must be protected from the social

---

[304] Cf. Bracher, *Krise Europas*, 863.

[305] Erdmann, *Zeit der Weltkriege*, 259.

[306] Bürgerliche Parteien, i. 652.

[307] *Hamburger Fremdenblatt* (14 Sept. 1925); repr. in Stresemann, *Vermächtnis*, ii. 172.

[308] Maxelon, *Stresemann*, 297–8.

[309] Ibid. 290. Stresemann's policy towards Britain followed the same objectives. Cf. Weidenfeld, *Englandpolitik*, 290 ff.

democratic demand for parliamentary control. It is also certain that he and the governments to which he belonged[310] knew the main facts about Germany's secret rearmament; he did not put a stop to these activities, and felt no obligation to obey to the letter the Versailles restrictions on German armament.[311] On the contrary, he facilitated secret rearmament and sharply attacked well-known pacifists—such as Ludwig Quidde, Hermann Kantorowicz, and Friedrich Wilhelm Foerster—for divulging the facts concerning it.[312] However, when Stresemann died in October 1929 Germany was only a third-rank military power; and when, in 1929–30, louder voices were heard calling for military equality and early and complete revision of the treaty of Versailles, this did not represent a continuation of Stresemann's policy but a form of nationalism which despised peaceful methods as a sign of weakness.

Throughout his life Stresemann was a nationally minded statesman intent on securing a revision of what the German people as a whole regarded as an unjust treaty. To that extent he undoubtedly contributed to the fact that 'national revisionist aims kept alive dangerous illusions among large sections of the German people'.[313] In his own estimation, too, he was a 'power politician', whose chief aim was to restore Germany to her position as a world power. However, his historical greatness lay in the fact that he endeavoured to persuade his contemporaries, especially those on the political right, that the policy of revisionism should be conceived as a policy of understanding and pursued only by peaceful means. In an obituary notice Ossietzky predicted that before long the 'internationalists', so much detested by the 'nationalists', would be the only ones to take up and continue Stresemann's policy of peaceful compromise, and that they 'might perhaps one day defend his good name against his own political friends'.[314]

After Stresemann's death the DVP, which had never been truly loyal to him as its chairman, fell wholly under the unfluence of its own right wing, representing heavy industry. From the end of 1929 the party moved steadily rightwards under the chairmanship of Ernst Scholz. By its abrupt rejection of a plan to increase social insurance contributions it played a large part in the downfall of Hermann Müller's SPD cabinet—the last in the history of the Weimar Republic to have a parliamentary majority behind it. Eduard Dingeldey, who became chairman of the DVP at the end of 1930, was one of those who, for whatever tactical reasons, wished to bring the National Socialists into the government.[315] But by then the DVP had long ceased to be an important factor in domestic politics. In the Reichstag election of 1930 it lost a third of its seats, reducing its strength to thirty. In July 1932 they dwindled to seven: the DVP's supporters had deserted it for the DNVP and the NSDAP.

The left-wing liberals of the Weimar period were united in the Deutsche Demokratische Partei (DDP), the result of fusion between the Progressive People's

[310] Including that of Hermann Müller, the social democratic Reich chancellor; cf. Deist, III.1.1 below.
[311] Turner, *Stresemann*, 277–8.
[312] Bloch, *Hitler*, 13.
[313] Maxelon, *Stresemann*, 298.
[314] Ossietzky, 'Abschied von Stresemann', in Stresemann, *Schriften*, 408–12, here 412.
[315] Booms, 'Deutsche Volkspartei', 528.

Party and the left wing of the National Liberals. Unlike the DVP, the DDP from its inception took a decidedly pro-republican line, and together with the Centre and the SPD it formed the 'Weimar coalition'. Its supporters were mostly intellectuals, white-collar workers, and members of the *Mittelstand* of small businesses:[316] from this point of view, like the DVP, it was a typically middle-class party.

In foreign affairs, as early as 1918–19 the DDP was distinguished by a somewhat naïve pacifism[317] which was to colour its foreign policy, albeit in a watered-down form, for the next two decades. Specifically, this meant support for a policy of conciliation, for the League of Nations, and for international law. The DDP rejected war as a means of policy, but a majority made an exception for defensive war. Among the latter was Ludwig Quidde, chairman of the Deutsche Friedens-gesellschaft and subsequently a Nobel prize-winner, and Walter Schücking, a noted expert on international law.[318] In an official publication of 1928 on the party's attitude to pacifism[319] the executive distanced itself from the radical pacifists who rejected even wars of defence; it advocated 'organizational pacifism', meaning the development of the League of Nations and international arbitration, co-operation among nations, and the limitation of armaments with a view to their abolition.

However, this 'organizational' or moderate pacifism was not interpreted as anti-military. On the contrary, its advocates also proclaimed their support for the 'military spirit' (*Wehrgedanke*), which played so large a part in Weimar politics. True, the DDP was to a large extent uninterested in questions of military policy,[320] although for nearly eight years (March 1920–January 1928) it provided a minister of defence in the person of Otto Gessler. However, Gessler—a monarchist of authoritarian views, a representative of the DDP's right wing, and a decided opponent of the radical pacifists in his own party—thought of himself not so much as a party politician but rather as a servant of the state, standing above party and concerned chiefly to defend Reichswehr interests.

The lack of unity of the DDP as regards military policy was especially clear during the Reichstag election campaign of 1928, in which the question of building a pocket battleship played a large part. The DDP at first opposed the project, but changed its mind after the cabinet was formed: this led to a violent controversy with the radical pacifist wing and the Deutsche Friedensgesellschaft, in which DDP members occupied important posts.[321] Next year, in 1929, the DDP executive approved a set of guidelines for the party on military questions,[322] in which they again advocated peaceful coexistence with other nations 'subject to our own national dignity'; they also called for compromise, mutual understanding, and a just peace. 'Organizational pacifism' was reaffirmed by rejecting wars of aggression and

[316] Cf. *Bürgerliche Parteien*, i. 302, 311.

[317] Albertin, *Liberalismus*, 198, 414.

[318] Cf. Acker, *Schücking*.

[319] For the debate on pacifism in the DDP cf. also Stephan, *Linksliberalismus*, 332 ff.

[320] Schustereit, 'Wehrfragen'.

[321] Cf. *Bürgerliche Parteien*, i. 320; Wacker, *Panzerschiff 'A'*, 27 ff., 92 ff.; Schustereit, 'Wehrfragen', doc. 8, pp. 160 ff.

[322] Reprinted in Schustereit, 'Wehrfragen', doc. 11, p. 170.

acknowledging the role of the German armed forces as the instrument for the defence of the republic. In general these guidelines were very similar to those of the SPD in the same year.

The DDP with its moderate pacifism also believed it possible to combine support for the 'military spirit' with a determined policy of treaty revision. In 1919 it had been one of the parties that refused to assent to the treaty of Versailles, and its programme of that year declared that a revision of the treaty was the most important aim of German foreign policy. The DDP also declared that Germany had a 'right to possess colonies' and to enjoy equal status in Europe.[323] In later years it was especially Erich Koch-Weser, the party's chairman from 1924 to 1930, who made himself the spokesman of revisionist claims. Refusing to recognize Versailles as a basis of peaceful international relations, he called for the union of Germany and Austria, a 'settlement of Germany's eastern frontiers', the liberation of the Rhineland and the Saar, the return of Eupen and Malmédy, self-determination for Alsace, Lorraine, and the Sudeten Germans, and frontier adjustments with Denmark.[324] Koch-Weser emphasized that war was ruled out as a means of solving these questions and that the revision of Versailles must be achieved through the League of Nations.[325] The objective of restoring Germany's international position and equality of rights was evidently the lowest common denominator of foreign policy capable of uniting the two opposite wings of the DDP.

The Deutsche Staatspartei (DStP) succeeded the DDP when the latter was dissolved in 1930, and from the start adopted a nationalist tone. At its inaugural congress on 9 November the foreign-policy spokesman, Professor Erich Obst of Hanover, spoke of colonies, a 'nation without space' in the east, and the demand for German freedom to rearm.[326] Disturbed by this militant programme, Ludwig Quidde concluded that the new party, unlike its predecessor, would have no room for national pacifism, and that he himself could therefore not belong to it.[327] The DStP took a further step to the right by merging with two nationalist and anti-republican organizations, the Jungdeutscher Orden and the Volksnationale Reichsvereinigung. However, while this prompt adaptation to the nationalist trend caused many members of the former DDP's left wing to quit the DStP, the latter did not succeed in rallying middle-class voters. In the years after 1930 it never gained more than 1 per cent of votes, and dwindled into a splinter-group of no importance. Left-wing liberalism ceased to exist in the final phase of the Weimar Republic. Its former potential adherents moved to the right; only a minority joined the SPD, such as Anton Erkelenz, a member of the employees' wing of the DDP, and the historian Ludwig Bergsträsser.

In the Reichstag election of September 1930 the NSDAP gained more votes from

---

[323] *Bürgerliche Parteien*, i. 306. On the DDP's policy of peaceful revision cf. Stephan, *Links-liberalismus*, 116–17, 173, 333–4; Schustereit, *Linksliberalismus*, 68 ff.

[324] Koch-Weser, *Außenpolitik* (1929), 138–42.

[325] Block (*Hitler*, 14) describes Koch-Weser's demands as an 'outspokenly imperialistic . . . programme'.

[326] Stephan, *Linksliberalismus*, 484; *Bürgerliche Parteien*, i. 324–5.

[327] Stephan, *Linksliberalismus*, 481.

the German Nationals than from the two liberal parties, but in the next year or two these latter were the chief losers. In the election of 31 July 1932 the Nazis deprived them of over 2 million votes altogether. Both the socialist parties—the SPD and the KPD—and also the two Catholic parties, the Centre, and the Bayerische Volkspartei, maintained their numerical strength in the years of crisis, so that the NSDAP grew chiefly at the expense of the parties representing business and the middle class.[328] The traditional middle-class parties—the DVP, the DDP, the Wirtschaftspartei, and a number of lesser groups—still obtained about 25 per cent of all votes in 1928; by November 1932 this had fallen to 5 per cent.

From the beginning of the world depression it had been clear that the German middle class was prepared to jettison the republic if the latter seemed to be harmful to its interests. However, while the middle and lesser bourgeoisie did much to assist Hitler's rise to power, this does not mean that they necessarily approved all aspects of his aggressive foreign policy. What motivated their support from 1929–30 onwards was not so much foreign policy as economic distress and the threat, or reality, of a decline in their social status. Hitler seemed to be the man who would remedy this, while his aggressive nationalism struck a responsive chord also.

The close interrelation between home- and foreign-policy aims can be paralleled from the history of the First World War.[329] At that time German public opinion was divided into two camps under the slogans of a 'victors' peace' and a 'compromise peace' (*Verständigungsfrieden*). These were associated with rival aspirations in home affairs: in the first case the preservation of the old monarchical and militaristic order, in the second case democracy, political equality, and social justice. During the crisis of the Weimar Republic, home and foreign objectives were similarly linked. The National Socialist watchword 'Germany, awake!' was not, in the first instance, a call to war with France and Poland to wipe out the 'shameful treaty' of Versailles; it meant a war with the SPD and the Centre party to maintain or reconquer the privileges of the middle class.

That all the middle-class voters who now supported the NSDAP wholeheartedly endorsed the foreign policy of Hitler's *Mein Kampf* is neither provable nor probable.[330] There was indeed an ostensible identity of class interests, as National Socialist propaganda promised the middle class everything it needed for its own protection. In addition, many members of that class identified emotionally with the militarist trappings of the NSDAP—the uniforms, parades, and military symbolism, harmonizing with the middle class's respect for authority and discipline. A part was played in this by shared memories of the 'heroic days' of the world war, transmuted into dreams of the future. Earlier demands for the revision of Versailles and the return of Germany's colonies fitted into the same pattern, creating an ideological climate in which voters could be mobilized with the war-cry 'Germany, awake!'

---

[328] For a detailed analysis of the election results of 1930–2 see Winkler, *Mittelstand*, 175–6; also Saage, 'Antisozialismus'.

[329] This comparison is taken from Rosenberg, *German Republic*, 282.

[330] Winkler, *Mittelstand*, 181.

7. The Policy of Peaceful Understanding: Social Democracy, the Reichsbanner Schwarz-Rot-Gold, and the Trade Unions

All shades of social democracy in the Weimar period were united in opposition to war and in favouring an active policy of peace and disarmament. This was a traditional attitude, rooted in the expectations of members of the party and those who supported it.

'There is in Germany only one great peace party and one great peace-loving association: that is, the social democratic movement.'[331] This statement by a leading social democrat, Wilhelm Sollmann, at the party congress at Leipzig in 1931 expressed the SPD's idea of itself as a peace party and correctly defined its place in the party spectrum of the late Weimar period.

The official party ideology was based, in the past, on a conception derived from Marx's theory of history, often summarized in the formula 'capitalism equals war, socialism equals peace'. Wilhelm Dittmann, who had represented the Independent Socialists (USPD) on the Council of People's Commissioners in 1918, thus described his party's peace policy at the Magdeburg congress in 1929, which was especially concerned with defence matters:

To strengthen the power of the working class—that alone is the way finally to overcome the war spirit, to do away with armaments, to abolish war itself along with the capitalism that exploits and oppresses human beings. Just as exploitation and oppression lead to class antagonism and the class war, so also do they create national antagonism and warfare. Only when socialism has done away with exploitation and oppression in home affairs, so that class antagonism and class warfare are abolished, will there likewise be an end of antagonism among nations. This, comrades, is the noble objective we must always keep in view. But we can only reach it in stages, step by step . . . Socialism is the force that will bring lasting peace to the world.[332]

However, opinions differed sharply within the SPD as regards the concrete steps whereby the 'noble ultimate objective' was to be approached. Since 1917 at the latest—the time of the joint peace resolution of the SPD, the Centre, and the Progressive People's Party—a majority of the SPD had dropped the idea of achieving socialism by international revolutionary action. Instead, the party had increasingly included in its programme[333] elements that belonged largely to a bourgeois-liberal tradition, such as the rejection of war as an instrument of policy; the settlement of international disputes by compulsory arbitration: the development of international law; agreements on disarmament and the reduction of armaments; the strengthening and democratization of the League of Nations; and support for any foreign policy designed to improve relations among nations.

There was also disagreement within the party over defence policy.[334] The

---

[331] *Sozialdemokratischer Parteitag 1931, Protokoll*, 181.

[332] *Sozialdemokratischer Parteitag 1929, Protokoll*, 119.

[333] Cf. the SPD's Görlitz Programme of 1921 and its Heidelberg Programme of 1925, both reprinted in *Programme der deutschen Sozialdemokratie*, 83–4, 91–2; also 'Richtlinien zur Wehrpolitik' (guidelines on defence policy) adopted at the 1929 congress, *Sozialdemokratischer Parteitag 1929, Protokoll*, 288–9.

[334] Described in Wacker, *Panzerschiff 'A'*; and Drechsler, *Sozialistische Arbeiterpartei*.

conflicting views were for some years not debated openly, but at Magdeburg in 1929 the issue was raised whether it was compatible with the policy of peace and disarmament, on which all were agreed, to acknowledge that the Weimar Republic could not do without an army and navy. Contrary to the views of a strong minority, composed of a radical pacifist and a 'class warfare' group, the congress finally adopted 'guidelines on defence policy'[335] which stated that as long as there was a risk of imperialist and Fascist states launching new wars for the sake of power, the German republic must have armed forces 'to protect its neutrality and the political, economic, and social achievements of the working class'. Given the party's anti-militarist past, it required much travail before such a statement could be officially adopted. However, it failed to achieve the hoped-for effect: relations between the party and the military remained cool, if not hostile. In the years of crisis after 1930 the Reichswehr did nothing to protect the republic, let alone the achievements of the working class; instead, it intervened in domestic politics by supporting the anti-democratic right.

If the social democrats rejected the use of force in foreign affairs, they applied the same principle at home. The rules of parliamentary democracy, it was thought, provided a sufficient guarantee that conflicts would be resolved peaceably and without violence.[336] Occasionally, however, social democrats threatened to use force against opponents of the Weimar system of government. Thus, for instance, Wilhelm Dittmann declared at Magdeburg: 'In case of emergency we social democrats will also use force to defend ourselves, either at home or abroad.'[337]

The organization that he had in mind for this purpose was the Reichsbanner Schwarz-Rot-Gold (named after the black–red–gold republican tricolour).[338] Founded in 1924 in response to acts of violence by the radical right and as a counter to conservative and reactionary 'defence associations', its purpose was to unite those ex-soldiers who believed that the democractic republic must be defended against its enemies of both right and left. The immediate cause of its foundation (under the title 'Bund republikanischer Kriegsteilnehmer') was Hitler's unsuccessful coup in Munich in November 1923. Thus, initially at all events, its pro-republican objective was combined with an anti-Nazi one. In the last phase of the republic, from the election of September 1930 to Hitler's assumption of power in January 1933, this opposition to Nazism revived in a much-intensified form and dominated the German political scene. In those years the Reichsbanner increasingly developed into a militant anti-Fascist association, as the task of protecting the republic became identical with that of combating the growing power of the NSDAP and its nationalist allies.

In party-political terms the Reichsbanner stood close to the Weimar coalition of the SPD, the Centre, and the DDP. Any supporter of the republican regime could join it, and all three coalition parties were represented at its inaugural assembly.[339]

[335] *Sozialdemokratischer Parteitag 1929, Protokoll*, 288.
[336] Cf. Wette, 'Stimmzettel', 363 ff.
[337] *Sozialdemokratischer Parteitag 1929, Protokoll*, 116.
[338] Cf. Rohne, *Reichsbanner*.
[339] Ibid. 274.

Its national executive, elected in 1926, comprised thirteen social democrats, four members of the DDP, and three of the Centre. As these figures indicate, social democratic influence was dominant from the beginning. Social democrats continued to hold the leading positions until 1933: this was logical, as the SPD and the trade unions furnished over 80, probably over 90, per cent of the membership.[340] Sociologically speaking, the Reichsbanner was primarily an organization of urban workers.

In point of numbers, the Reichsbanner was the strongest militant organization of the Weimar period. In 1924, the first year of its existence, it recruited over 2 million members. In 1925, according to its leaders, it had about 3 million members, and in the following years the figure is said to have risen to $3\frac{1}{2}$ million.[341] This far exceeded the membership of the Stahlhelm, the Reichsbanner's natural opponent in the extra-parliamentary arena. Thus, the latter was a factor of importance in the domestic power-struggle. However, though its members gave themselves a militant air by parading in uniform, it was in the last resort not a civic militia but a propaganda organization; its methods of persuasion were traditional social democratic ones such as orderly large-scale marches—not, for instance, the use of arms. This was also true of the amalgamation of the SPD, trade unions, Reichsbanner, and workers' athletic associations which was formed late in 1931 under the martial title of the 'Iron Front'.

Since members of the Reichsbanner, like those of the Stahlhelm, were ex-servicemen, the question arises of what psychological effect the war had had on them. Had they too remained 'eternal soldiers', exalting the heroic virtues and politicizing the military experience? Or was the Reichsbanner, as Goebbels contemptuously called it, a 'flock of pacifist sheep, incapable of defending themselves'?[342] In contrast to the right-wing veterans' organizations, which regarded the war, all in all, in a highly favourable light, the Reichsbanner did indeed represent a moderately pacifist outlook. Its members with one accord rejected a war of revenge or aggression and fully supported the conciliatory policy of the republican parties. On the other hand, the Reichsbanner leaders had no hesitation in approving the idea of armed resistance to aggression from outside: they were whole-heartedly in favour of national self-defence, as indeed were practically all members of the republican parties.

During the crisis of the Weimar Republic the Reichsbanner 'gradually turned away from pacifist positions and laid increasing emphasis on national defence'.[343] In 1932 Karl Höltermann, who had succeeded Hörsing as national Reichsbanner leader, stressed the latter's willingness to take part in frontier policing and territorial defence, and thus to be considered as a reserve army or national militia in

[340] Ibid. 328. At the end of 1932 the party chairman Otto Wels estimated that the SPD provided no less than 95% of Reichsbanner members; see Schulze, *Anpassung*, 77.

[341] Rohe, *Reichsbanner*, 73-4; also Deutsch, *Antifaschismus*, 101. For the most part this was due to collective accession by various republican organizations and associations for self-defence: cf. Rohe, *Reichsbanner*, 71-2.

[342] Goebbels, *Revolution*, 32.

[343] Rohe, *Reichsbanner*, 191-2.

the event of an external threat. However, despite this concession to the nationalist and militarist trend that increased in strength in the late 1920s, the Reichsbanner never indulged in any glorification of war. On the contrary, peace and conciliation were its watchword, as is shown by a typical pamphlet of 1928: 'We hate war. Not because we are cowards, or cannot or will not fight. We hate war because it is a disgrace to civilization . . . German youth must learn to despise the romanticizing of war, and to fight for a world of peace.'[344]

If nevertheless the Reichsbanner sometimes emphasized the 'ex-service' note, it was in order to appeal to the spirit of comradeship among those who had served in the trenches together. Thus, for instance, Höltermann began a radio address with these words:

The man who is now addressing you was born in 1894; he served at the front and thus shared in the fellowship of war. And therefore I turn first to my comrades from the trenches and beg them to listen to me, as one comrade would listen to another in the same dugout. Think, as I speak to you, of the comradeship of those days, however much our political paths may have diverged since then.[345]

By appeals of this kind, combined with the argument that the war had made it possible to create a democratic Germany, 'the true legacy of our dead', it was hoped to persuade at least some members of the war generation to support the new state and the parties on which it rested. The Reichsbanner would have no truck with a front-line ideology of the right-wing type, i.e. the politicization of warlike virtues and their application to the domestic power-struggle. Its members did not, like those of the Stahlhelm, read such authors as Beumelburg, Dwinger, Schauwecker, Ernst and Friedrich Georg Jünger; they read the pacifist writings of Bröger, Remarque, Renn, Unruh, Witkop, and Barbusse.[346] There was indeed some overlapping: names like Flex, Alverdes, Binding, and Witkop appear in both lists; but the emotional emphasis in Reichsbanner circles concentrated on the element of fear, horror, and bloodshed—the misery and despair, the destructive side of war.

Thus, the Reichsbanner was undoubtedly one of the Weimar groups which regarded war as an illegitimate and ineffective means of policy, which would have nothing to do with its apologists, and believed in the peaceful settlement of international disputes. Reichsbanner members saw the experience of war as imposing on them a special obligation to work for a lasting peace settlement. From 1927 onwards they made contact with similar ex-servicemen's associations in the former enemy countries. Special importance was attached to reconciliation with France and to relations with corresponding French associations, in particular the Union Fédérale des Anciens Combattants and the Fédération Nationale des Combattants Républicains, both left-wing organizations.[347] While the Reichsbanner endeavoured to make its war experience serve as the cause of a peaceable

---

[344] The pamphlet was reprinted in the journal *Reichsbanner* (15 Nov. 1930), as *Jungbannerbeilage* (supplement for young people); quoted here from Rohe, *Reichsbanner*, 146 n. 3.

[345] The address was reprinted in *Reichsbanner* (21 Nov. 1931); quoted here from Rohe, *Reichsbanner*, 136–7.

[346] Rohe, *Reichsbanner*, 142.   [347] For these contacts cf. ibid. 147–57.

European order, the Stahlhelm regarded such foreign contacts as harmful to the national interest. True, the nationalist right in Germany from time to time flirted with the idea of an 'ex-servicemen's international'; but in practice its chief aim was to politicize the war experience as a means of strengthening national integration.

If we have frequently spoken here of 'pacifist' attitudes without defining them closely, it is because, in the case of the Reichsbanner and also of the SPD, pacifism was a state of mind rather than a specific political concept.[348] In any case, from 1923 onwards German foreign policy was Stresemann's private domain, and for some years the SPD confined itself to supporting his attempts to come to terms with the victor nations and achieve a peaceful revision of the treaty of Versailles.

What has been said about the character of the SPD's pacifism was also true of the third pillar of social democracy, the free trade-union organizations. These were the Allgemeiner Deutscher Gewerkschaftsbund (ADGB), the central association of unions representing the various branches of industry; the Allgemeiner Freier Angestelltenbund (AfA-Bund) of white-collar workers; and the Allgemeiner Deutscher Beamtenbund (ADB), civil servants; the last two were amalgamated with the ADGB in 1923. The trade-union organizations, with between 4 and 5 million members,[349] were among the most influential social bodies in Weimar Germany. A congress of trade-unionists at Nuremberg in 1919 had decided on a policy of neutrality as between the three left-wing parties, the SPD, USPD (Independent Socialists), and KPD (Communists); this no longer had any practical application after the dissolution of the USPD and the expulsion of Communists from the ADGB. It remained only to regulate relations with the SPD, which was done on the basis of a principle, laid down as far back as 1905, of 'coexistence with equal rights'.[350] In practice there was some division of labour: the party looked after 'major policy', while the unions concentrated on matters of economic, social, and wage policy.[351] Naturally the division could not be hard and fast. In the latest phase of the Weimar Republic the ADGB, while in principle at one with the SPD, showed a disposition to use the whole of its power in general political matters. This showed itself in the discussion over economic democracy[352] and also when, in 1930, the chancellor Hermann Müller 'came a cropper'[353] on account of the threatened reduction of unemployment relief. Other instances were the handling of the reparations question, with all its importance to the economy and to foreign relations;[354] the job-creation programme; and finally the argument as to what methods

---

[348] Rosenberg, *German Republic*, 155; details now in Wette, 'Sozialdemokratie', 281–300.

[349] Membership details at different dates in the ADGB *Jahrbücher* (Yearbooks); summary in *Sachwörterbuch der Geschichte Deutschlands*, i. 42–3.

[350] On relations between the SPD and the trade unions see Seidel, *Gewerkschaftsbewegung*, 54 ff.

[351] This can be seen clearly from the ADGB Yearbooks.

[352] Cf. *Wirtschaftsdemokratien*, also Tarnow, *Stellungnahme*.

[353] The result of ADGB action was described in these terms by the union leader F. Tarnow in a speech of Aug. 1932, repr. in Heer, *Burgfrieden*, 118–49, here 120. On the fall of the Müller government cf. also Fülberth and Harrer, *Sozialdemokratie*, 226.

[354] On the union's demand for 'an end to reparations' cf. the pamphlet *Gewerkschaften* (1932) and the ADGB *Jahrbuch 1931*, 251–2. On the conflict between the ADGB and the SPD over reparations see Heer, *Burgfrieden*, 38–45.

the organized workers should adopt to prevent the continued undermining of parliamentary democracy and the rise of National Socialism.[355] In several cases there were serious conflicts between the SPD and ADGB leaders. For example, the latter tried to make contact, over the heads of the SPD, with the governments ruling by presidential decree from 1930 onwards. Again, over the question whether the Reichsbanner should support Chancellor Schleicher's plan for a Reichskuratorium für Jugendertüchtigung (Reich Institute for the Training of Young Men),[356] the unions, in opposition to the social democratic executive, were in favour of co-operation with the Stülpnagel committee, which sought to make the defence associations serve the interests of the Reichswehr.

However, the division of labour between the SPD and the ADGB had the effect that in foreign affairs the unions in Weimar years, while generally supporting an anti-militarist and conciliatory policy, did not concern themselves in detail either with foreign affairs or with defence. Such matters were as a rule left to the international trade-union congresses, which passed many resolutions on the international struggle against militarism and threats of war.[357]

As regards disarmament, the secretaries of the International Federation of Trade Unions (IFTU) and the Labour and Socialist International (LSI) kept in close touch with one another from the mid-1920s onwards, though they did not come forward with proposals for public guidance.[358] When, after several years' preparation, the Council of the League of Nations at last convened a disarmament conference to be held in February 1932, the two international trade-union bodies set up a joint disarmament commission.[359] Its functions were first, to work out a programme of co-operation in anti-war propaganda, and second, to formulate the demands of the international workers' movement in regard to disarmament.

The joint disarmament programme of the IFTU and the LSI was published in July 1931.[360] To mobilize public opinion it was proposed to organize large-scale demonstrations, world-wide mass petitions, and frontier meetings of workers' associations in neighbouring countries. Socialist parliamentary groups were enjoined to support disarmament in their national parliaments. In a joint resolution the two international bodies declared that only the creation of a socialist order could finally bring peace, but that the task meanwhile was 'to foster the germs of peace that [were] already present in the existing order'. Disarmament must be based on equality and not be used as an opportunity for rearmament. In other words, the trade-union bodies did not share the intention of German governments from 1930 onwards, as well as the Reichswehr and the political right wing, to use the Geneva

---

[355] See in general Matthias, 'Sozialdemokratische Partei', 101–278, and id., 'Untergang', 281–316. In the opinion of Otto Wels, the SPD chairman, the trade-union leaders bore the main responsibility for the abstention of the 'Iron Front' from active measures of resistance. Cf. Schulze, *Anpassung*, pp. xvii–xviii, and Wette, 'Stimmzettel', 383 ff.

[356] Details of the controversies in Schulze, *Anpassung*, 72 ff. and *passim*.

[357] Cf. e.g. the resolution of the 1922 IFTU congress in Rome, reprinted in Schwarz, *Handbuch der deutschen Gewerkschaftskongresse*, 267–8; and resolution of the 1922 ADGB congress at Leipzig, ibid. 266.

[358] Cf. Hilferding's self-critical remarks in 'Krieg', 385, 390.

[359] For what follows see ADGB *Jahrbuch 1930*, 321 ff..

[360] For the disarmament campaign see ibid. 322; text of resolution, 323–4.

conference as a pretext for the legalization of the German rearmament programme; they wished to bring about 'complete, general, and controlled disarmament' on the part of all powers, including the victors of the First World War.

The propaganda campaign ran its course accordingly during the months preceeding the opening of the conference in February 1932. A petition[361] prepared by the two internationals was endorsed in Germany alone at 2,437 meetings organized by the SPD, which were attended by more than 600,000 people. The ADGB also collected petitions of its own. A similar campaign took place in other countries, so that finally the chairmen of the joint disarmament committee of the IFTU and the LSI presented a petition to the Geneva conference on behalf of 25 million voters and 14 million trade-union members.

The international campaign was unable to prevent the conference from becoming 'a lamentable spectacle', as it was dubbed in retrospect by W. Schevenel, the secretary-general of IFTU.[362] But the campaign was significant in that it once more emphasized the desire of organized labour for peace, as demonstrated in many thousand grass-roots meetings as well as in national parliaments and at the international level.

One cannot answer simply 'yes' or 'no' to the question whether the social democratic workers' movement perceived clearly enough before 1933 that once the National Socialist party had come to power in Germany it would set its course towards war. From 1930 onwards the social democrats adopted the term 'Fascist', which was already part of Communist vocabulary, to describe the Nazis as a counter-revolutionary movement. In so doing they were not thinking primarily of naked physical force, as used, for instance, by the Nazi 'storm troops', but of the prospect of a Fascist dictatorship, seen as the antithesis to peaceful democracy.[363] Thus, their main attention was centred on the Nazis' aspiration to power in home affairs; isolated warnings of a warlike foreign policy being pursued by a Fascist government were on the whole disregarded. Nevertheless, a statement by the social democratic members of the Reichstag, dating from the late autumn of 1930, shows clearly that a broadly accurate view was taken of the Nazi threat:

A Hitler government would aim to follow the Italian example by destroying all workers' organizations and creating a long-term state of siege. It would abolish freedom of the press and of assembly and other political rights, bringing about a permanent danger of civil war at home and a foreign war of revenge. This would mean the economic collapse of Germany and the end of an independent German nation, with all the frightful consequences that would ensue for the working people.[364]

Despite this remarkable accurate prediction, the SPD in the following years made scarcely any attempt to discover, from the writings and speeches of leading Nazis, what exactly would be the direction and methods of their foreign policy. True, the

---

[361] For text see ADGB *Jahrbuch 1931*, 247. On the disarmament campaign in general, ibid. 'Der Kampf um die Abrüstung', 247–52.

[362] Ibid. 249.

[363] Wette, 'Stimmzettel', 375–6; Lademacher, 'Gewalt', 415 ff.

[364] Statement in the social democratic press, repr. in *Jahrbuch der SPD 1930*, 21 ff.

SPD parliamentary spokesman, Rudolf Breitscheid,[365] speaking at the party congress at Leipzig in 1931, referred in general terms to the threat of violence from German Fascism, but he was evidently not convinced that if the 'Hitlerites' came to power they would put into practice what they had so loudly proclaimed. Wilhelm Sollmann[366] warned against elements in Germany which wanted to use force to crush the Bolshevik experiment in Soviet Russia; any such attempt, he declared, would meet with decided resistance from German social democrats, whose foreign policy was one of peace with all nations, Bolshevik Russia included. 'The leaders of bloodstained world capitalism and, for the most part, the priests of the Christian churches, which defend world war and world capitalism' were, he maintained, the last people to have the right to force an allegedly higher civilization on the Soviet Union. In 1931 Alexander Schifrin, one of the most active social democratic publicists in the final phase of the Weimar Republic, mentioned the ideas put forward by Hitler and Rosenberg concerning German expansion into Poland and western Russia,[367] but took the view that these ideas of armed conquest were basically not new: they were a variant of the general attitude of aggressive nationalism, which was devoid of any singleness of purpose:

There was complete confusion as to the basic questions: in what direction were we to march, with whom and against whom? For instance: France as the main enemy, firm integration in the Fascist bloc of south-east European states, plus reliance on Britain and an anti-Russian policy for Britain's sake (the NSDAP's strategic plan favoured by Hitler and Rosenberg)? Or perhaps an anti-French attitude combined with eastward expansion (von Seeckt, probably also von Schleicher)? Or, on the contrary, a capitalist-nationalist party of co-operation with France, membership of the Western bloc, and, when it grew stronger, an all-out attack on the Soviet Union (Papen, Rechberg, Klönne, the *Ring* [a conservative journal] and Jungdo [Jungdeutscher Orden] school of thought)? Or, finally, no Western alliance, final break with the West, expansion to the south-east, and close relations with the Soviet Union (the Brockdorff–Rantzau tradition, adopted by the 'Action Circle')? This covered a 180-degree range of possibilities, from a war of revenge to a military alliance with the Soviet Union. Thus, there was total confusion as to what the basic direction of policy would be: for or against France? for or against Russia? An alliance with the Anglo-Saxon world, or a challenge to it? An alliance with Fascist Italy, or an attitude of reserve? It was not even clear who was the 'hereditary enemy', or to which foreign countries we owed 'Nibelung loyalty' and were owed it by them in return.[368]

Thus, although the SPD saw the Nazis as constituting a threat of war, they had no clear idea what the latter's foreign policy might be. In 1932–3 the top echelons of the party did not even discuss this question,[369] nor did it play a prominent part in the SPD's anti-Fascist propaganda. The first social democrats to utter the cry 'Hitler means war!' were those who escaped to Prague in the spring of 1933.[370] If the

[365] *Sozialdemokratischer Parteitag 1931, Protokoll*, 93–4; cf. also 100–1.
[366] Ibid. 110–11.
[367] Schifrin, 'Hakenkreuz', 112.
[368] Id., 'Gegenrevolution', 391–2 .
[369] Cf. minutes in Schulze, *Anpassung*.
[370] On the executive of the SPD in exile ('SOPADE') cf. *Mit dem Gesicht nach Deutschland*.

warning was not clearly heard at an earlier date it may have been in part because the glorification of war was no monopoly of National Socialism and other *völkisch* organizations, but pervaded the whole of the anti-republican right.[371] It may be added that the various parties and associations which stood for a strong national and military policy had no clear idea of Hitler's intentions either.

To sum up, German social democracy in the Weimar period, true to its pacifist tradition, desired peace and understanding with all nations: party members and voters were of one mind with their leaders in this. However, from the time of Noske's resignation in 1920 the SPD had scarcely any influence on the foreign or defence policy of the Weimar Republic. Instead it concentrated, as in the past, on issues of domestic and social policy. Like the other democratic parties, it proved unable to implant in the national mind a sufficiently widespread conviction of the link between national and democratic ideas. As a result, it was increasingly easy for right-wing slogans to prevail among the undecided. None the less, the peace policy and the social democratic advocacy of non-violence had a lasting effect on the political consciousness of the German working class. This tradition was still alive in 1939, though by then it could not express itself openly.

8. ORGANIZED PACIFISM: AN ISOLATED MOVEMENT

The label 'pacifist' was applied in Weimar times to a large number of very different positions.[372] Their lowest common denominator consisted in opposition to an aggressive national policy, to the outward signs of militarism, and to anti-democratic forces. Pacifists either completely rejected the use of military force for the solution of internal or international disputes, or at least wished to restrict it to very narrow limits. On the specific questions of how peace was to be achieved or preserved and how the desired state of peace was to be envisaged, opinions differed widely. Organized pacifism in Weimar Germany did not succeed in formulating an agreed peace policy.

Within the broad range of pacifist convictions two main currents could be discerned in the 1920s, a moderate and a radical one.[373] The long-standing opposition between these from the start impeded efforts to form a single pacifist front. Moderate pacifism, based on organizational principles of international law, was in line with the pre-war pacifist movement. Its object was, by means of a thoroughgoing reform of the League of Nations, to create a system of collective security on which an international peace settlement could be based. This 'League of Nations pacifism' did not, in principle, rule out a war of self-defence legitimized by the League. Radical, anti-militarist pacifism, on the other hand, was opposed to military service, to any use of force, and to any preparation for war. It wished to prevent war by non-violent means, such as a general strike and refusal to perform

---

[371] See I.1.3–6 above.

[372] Cf. Scheler's analysis, *Idee des Friedens* (1931), distinguishing eight varieties of pacifism: heroic, Christian, liberal-economic, juristic, Marxist-socialist-Communist, big business, imperialistic, and cultural. For the spectrum of pacifist organizations cf. also *Pazifismus*.

[373] Scheer, *Friedensgesellschaft*, 354–81, 557 ff.

military duties. In addition, radical pacifists proclaimed the need of social change to overcome causes of strife in the world. In this respect they came close to the socialist way of thinking.

After 1918 the membership of pacifist organizations increased.[374] A strong influx of social democratic support altered the character of the movement, which before the war had been largely bourgeois and liberal. The largest (30,000 members) and most influential pacifist association, the Deutsche Friedensgesellschaft (DFG), drew its support in Weimar days equally from bourgeois and socialist elements. According to a survey in 1927, nearly half its members belonged to the SPD, a quarter to the DDP, and about 5 per cent to the Centre, while another 25 per cent had no party allegiance. Thus, the SPD and DDP were regarded as the parties to which pacifists could most readily look for the fulfilment of their aims.

The DDP was strongly in favour of international understanding, the League of Nations, and the political and economic unification of Europe. These ideals were close to those of organizational pacifism, and a number of leading pacifists were DDP members, including Quidde, Gerlach, Count Kessler, Freiherr von Schoenaich, and Schücking. However, in the world of party politics the ideals in question were more and more overlaid by considerations of national interest, so that in the course of twenty years the pacifist element in the party became increasingly marginal. Radical pacifism was from the outset quite unacceptable to a majority of the DDP; and after 1930 the party (now renamed Deutsche Staatspartei) scarcely offered an adequate field of activity even to moderate pacifists.

On the other hand, the views of the SPD and DFG on peaceful foreign relations were almost identical. This similarity encouraged many to be members of both institutions. There was, however, room for dispute over defence matters, as a majority of the SPD supported the military defence of the democratic state. In the debate over pocket-battleship construction in 1928 this attitude was firmly opposed by radical pacifists. The latter subsequently took over the leadership of the DFG, and in September 1931 finally broke with the SPD.

In 1921 several pacifist groups for the first time united to form an umbrella organization, the Deutsches Friedenskartell. By the mid-1920s this was supported by twenty-two organizations with over 50,000 members. Though a considerable increase of strength over pre-war organized pacifism, this did not constitute a factor of the same order as the mass associations, the Stahlhelm and the Reichsbanner. In 1929 the Friedenskartell broke up owing to insuperable conflict between the moderates and radicals. After the latter had gained control of the DFG, the moderates withdrew from that body. Thus, the crisis of organized pacifism in Germany occurred exactly at the time when the nationalist opposition formed a united front in the shape of the 'Reich committee for the German referendum against the Young plan and the war-guilt lie'.[375] It was not by chance that the crisis of the German peace movement coincided with the period of dissolution of the Weimar state. After 1929 it was no longer possible to create a united pacifist front.

Altogether the organized peace movement had little influence on Reich policy,

---

[374] The following data are from Scheer, *Friedensgesellschaft*, 397–415, 497–521.   [375] Ibid. 495–6.

the republican parties, or the general public. 'German pacifism remained an outsiders' movement in a society that had preserved its basic conservative structure in military and administrative matters, in the economic and judicial systems. It was . . . beyond the movement's power to alter these, and consequently it remained in the same marginal position as in the Wilhelmine empire'.[376] The organized peace movement did not succeed in enlisting for its own rational purposes the war-weariness and longing for peace that large sections of the population had felt immediately after the war.

After the breach in 1929 between the moderate and radical pacifists, the DFG with the latter in charge became more and more isolated. It had no further prospect of influencing the republican parties. Moreover, the radical pacifists did nothing in 1930–3 to strengthen the hand of the largest republican party, the SPD. The DFG became more and more of a non-parliamentary left-wing opposition, consuming its energies in the fight against what it regarded as the fatal policy of the SPD. The pacifist splinter-groups, the Radikaldemokratische Partei and the Sozialistische Arbeiterpartei Deutschlands, founded in 1930 and 1931 respectively, remained ineffectual minorities. Membership of the DFG shrank to a few thousand in 1932–3. In the last phase of the republic the pacifist organizations had lost all power of attraction. Pacifists were pariahs of society. Since they saw the war coming earlier than most—their slogan 'The Third Reich means war!'[377] dates from the autumn of 1929—they were a permanent target of obloquy from the 'nationalist opposition'. Significantly, the DFG and its subsidiary organizations were destroyed by the Nazi regime as early as the first half of March 1933. Their leaders were either arrested or deprived of a livelihood by being dismissed from teaching posts; many ended in concentration camps.

9. ABSTRACT WARNINGS AGAINST IMPERIALISM: THE KPD AND THE COMINTERN

The election manifesto of the German Communist Party (KPD) in August 1930 proclaimed the 'national and social liberation of the German people' and promised that if the party came to power it would tear up the treaty of Versailles, cancel Germany's international debts and reparation payments, and recover the territory lost in 1919, which would be incorporated in a Soviet Germany.[378] The party thus struck a nationalist chord by adding these demands to the international and revolutionary elements of its programme. It did so in awareness that the NSDAP was threatening to gain considerable influence, not least by combining the appeal of nationalism with that of socialism. 'In practice this mounted to forming an ideological front with the National Socialists and against the republican parties, which were committed to the policy of "fulfilment" in foreign affairs.'[379]

---

[376] Ibid. 559–60.　　　　　　　　　　　　　　　　　　　　　　　[377] Ibid. 542.
[378] Text of programme in *Der deutsche Kommunismus*, 58 ff.; cf. also Trotsky's criticism of national Communism, ibid., doc. 95, pp. 302–3.
[379] Duhnke, *Die KPD*, 21.

The KPD's nationalist slogans did not mean that it intended to pursue an aggressively revisionist policy after the manner of the nationalist right; they were primarily a tactical manœuvre to prevent the massive flow of votes to the NSDAP. At the same time, a policy of strength that was liable to involve Germany in conflict with the Western powers was much more congenial to the KPD than was the 'fulfilment' policy of the republican parties. This was because, from the mid-1920s onwards, the KPD had been completely dependent on the foreign-policy interests and needs of the Soviet Union; and its behaviour between the wars can only be understood in the light of this fact.

The fear of an anti-Soviet coalition of the capitalist powers was a nightmare to Soviet politicians and diplomats. In accordance with Lenin's doctrine that new wars were inevitable in the imperialist era, the Soviet leaders believed that the exacerbation of capitalist crises would bring about armed conflicts among capitalist countries and must also lead to their attacking the Soviet Union. They were convinced that the existence of the Soviet Union had had the effect of transferring the class struggle from the national to the international plane.

The practical consequence of the theory of the inevitability of war was that the Communist International (Comintern), which functioned as the mouthpiece of Soviet interests, required all the national Communist parties, in their programme and actual policy, to give absolute priority to the defence of the Soviet Union. This was one of the key points in the debate at the sixth world congress of the Comintern, which was held in Moscow in the autumn of 1928 and which—on the strength of predictions that the crisis of capitalism was about to be intensified—decided upon an ultra-left course, i.e. an intensification of the battle for world revolution.[380] Nikolai Bukharin, reporting on the international situation on behalf of the Executive Committee of the Comintern, warned his hearers that the complexity of relations among capitalist states should not obscure the fact that the main under-lying tendency was towards the formation of an anti-Soviet bloc.[381] The danger of war—meaning an attack by capitalist states on the Soviet Union—was the key to the whole international situation.[382]

Bukharin's propaganda line brought out with especial clarity the purely ideological basis of the theory of an impending imperialist war. 'We do not need a confused accumulation of facts: what we have to do is discern amid all facts and tendencies the central factor, the central problem of the danger of war.'[383] The British delegate, Bell, spoke of the causes and conditions of 'the' war in even more sweeping and dogmatic terms. 'All Communists understand that wars are inevitable under the capitalist system and that their causes lie in imperialist rivalry for raw materials and markets, in the fight to safeguard investment opportunities.'[384] The congress was in agreement that despite their antagonist relations the imperialist

---

[380] Cf. Flechtheim, *Die KPD*, 249 ff.

[381] *Protokoll 6. Komintern-Kongreß 1928*, i. 39–40; cf. also 1928 programme of the Communist International in *Der deutsche Kommunismus*, doc. 4, pp. 46 ff., esp. 52 ff.

[382] *Protokoll 6. Komintern-Kongreß 1928*, i. 526; cf. also 531–2.

[383] Ibid. 536.

[384] Ibid. 506.

powers—Britain, the United States, France, Italy, and Germany—had a single common enemy in the proletarian state of the Soviet Union, and that this enmity conjured up the prospect of a new war.

While thus proclaiming the inevitability of war, the Communists in their day-to-day propaganda condemned all wars on moralistic grounds and presented themselves as champions of peace. *Vorwärts*, the principal organ of the German Social Democrats, pointed out this contradiction in a criticism of the theses of the sixth Comintern congress and what it called 'the warming-up of the old, vulgar-Marxist theory' of the inevitability of war. 'If war does break out, the further course of events is inevitable too: imperialist war leads to civil war, world revolution, and the world-wide triumph of the Soviet system. Long live world revolution—or rather, since that would only be the second stage, long live war!'[385] Although the Communists vehemently denied this interpretation, it followed logically from their theory. It was also clear that the Communist slogan of 'fighting imperialist war' had nothing pacific about it. Indeed, it was expressly dissociated from pacifism and connected with the exhortation to fight for the proletarian revolution:[386] for the Russian experience in 1917–18 had proved the effectiveness of peace propaganda in bringing about such a revolution. Now and later, the slogan of 'fighting against war' was used in the same sense of fighting for the revolutionary aims of international Communism, expressed unambiguously in the formula 'transformation of the imperialist war into a civil war'.[387]

At the same time Communist anti-war propaganda pursued the strategic aim of delaying as long as possible what was believed to be the inevitable imperialist war against the Soviet Union.[388] Thus, for instance, Stalin at the fifteenth congress of the Communist Party of the Soviet Union in October 1927 stated that in view of continued Western preparations for an attack it was very important 'to delay the war with the capitalist world, inevitable though it was', so that the Soviet Union might face it in better conditions.[389] This implied realization of the Soviet Union's unpreparedness for war was the decisive factor in Soviet foreign policy throughout the Stalin era.[390] It was also the basis of the policy of working for collective security in Europe, pursued by the Soviet Union from 1934 to 1938 (entry into the League of Nations in 1934; treaties of mutual assistance with France and Czechoslovakia in 1935), and of Soviet opposition to appeasement, seen as an attempt by Britain and France to divert German expansionism against the Soviet Union.

The Comintern thesis of the inevitability of a new imperialist war and the fear of an attack on the Soviet Union are also to be seen as the background to the massive attacks launched by the German Communists against the SPD's foreign policy of conciliation and a more pro-Western orientation. Ernst Thälmann, the German

---

[385] *Vorwärts* (27 July 1928), quoted in *Protokoll 6. Komintern-Kongreß 1928*, i. 528.
[386] *Faschismus*, 7–8 and 77 ff.; cf. also *Protokoll 6. Komintern-Kongreß 1928*, i. 79, 234, 568 ff., and Flechtheim, *Die KPD*, 329.
[387] 1928 programme (n. 381 above), in *Der deutsche Kommunismus*, doc. 4, p. 56.
[388] Cf. Lenin, *Works*, xxxi. 448; Stalin, *Works*, x. 52–3.
[389] Stalin, *Works*, x. 296.
[390] Cf. Duhnke, *Die KPD*, 300; Allard, *Stalin*, 7 ff.

Communist leader, said at the Moscow congress in 1928 that counter-revolutionary social democracy had adopted a pro-capitalist policy in all matters and fully supported the warlike intentions of the capitalist bourgeoisie against the Soviet Union; he even declared that social democracy was 'the motive force as regards war preparations against the Soviet Union'. Consequently, he argued, the Communists' fight against imperialist war was a fight against the German bourgeoisie and social democrats.[391] At the twelfth congress of the KPD in June 1929 Thälmann again denounced the social democrats as the most active champions of German imperialism and its policy of war with the Soviet Union.[392]

The Communist assessment of the world situation took virtually no account of the question of the nature of the war policy of the National Socialist leaders. Since the theory laid down that fresh wars were inevitable, the intentions of particular parties or politicians in capitalist countries were of secondary importance. Moreover, the Communists' theory of Fascism prevented their analysing the expansionist aims of the NSDAP thoroughly and in good time. The theory more or less equated 'Fascist' with 'non-Communist', which led, among other things, to the bizarre conclusion that social democracy was the left wing of 'Fascism' and the NSDAP its right wing. The branding of the social democrats as 'social Fascists', which went back to 1924,[393] not only exposed the whole absurdity of the Communist notion of Fascism; it also prevented even a partial degree of co-operation between the KPD and the SPD against the true Fascists, and condemned in advance the subsequent overtures for a united front.

From 1928 onwards the Communists made a wholesale identification between democrats and Fascists. Similarly, they identified the rule of the imperialist bourgeoisie with 'unremitting war against the broad masses in capitalist countries' and the 'steadily increasing danger of war among nations.'[394] On 15 June 1930 the Politburo of the KPD declared that Fascism in Germany was 'by no means confined to Fascist associations of militants and murderers, the National Socialists, the Stahlhelm, and so on', but included 'all the important bourgeois parties' and the 'social Fascist agents' of the bourgeois state apparatus.[395] The Brüning government was described as 'openly Fascist', and the government of Prussia under the social democrats Braun and Severing was also accused of following a 'Fascist course'.[396] Thus, when the KPD spoke of fighting Fascism it had in mind all the parties it considered counter-revolutionary[397]—in other words all non-Communist parties,

---

[391] *Protokoll 6. Komintern-Kongreß 1928*, i. 16–17, 302; programme, loc. cit. (n. 387 above).
[392] *Protokoll XII. Parteitag der KPD* (1929), 72. Cf. also Duhnke, *Die KPD*, 28–9, 298 ff.; and Flechtheim, *Die KPD*, 258 ff.
[393] *Protokoll 5. Komintern-Kongreß 1924*. For Stalin's 'social Fascism' thesis see Stalin, *Works*, vi. 252–3; further documents in *Der deutsche Kommunismus*, 182–90. Cf. also Bahne, 'Sozialfaschismus', 211 ff.   [394] *Faschismus*, 87.
[395] Politburo resolution in *Der deutsche Kommunismus*, doc. 44, pp. 150–1.
[396] Thälmann, *Revolutionärer Ausweg*, 23; *Der deutsche Kommunismus*, doc. 47, pp. 157–8.
[397] On the interpretation of Fascism as counter-revolution cf. *Komintern und Faschismus*, 15–32, documented by articles from *Inprekorr* (*Internationale Pressekorrespondenz*, the Comintern organ from 1921 to 1933) and *Rundschau*, its successor from 1933 to 1940. The KPD referred to the NSDAP as 'Fascism (National Fascism)': cf. *Der deutsche Kommunismus*, doc. 5, pp. 58 ff.

including, first and foremost, the social democrats. They were the chief adversary: National Socialism was only 'the second arch-enemy of the German working class'.[398] Even after the dramatic advance of the NSDAP in 1930–2 the KPD did not alter its tactics, and gave no serious consideration to forming a united front with the social democrats against the Nazis. Neither the 'united front from below', which figured in Communist propaganda from May 1932, nor the 'anti-Fascist action' also organized by them was aimed at jointly combating the National Socialists; they were directed against the social democratic leaders.[399]

Altogether the Communists' abstract and undifferentiated theory of Fascism led them fatally to misjudge the true German Fascism represented chiefly by National Socialism. As late as 1932 the KPD leaders did not consider the Nazis a serious danger,[400] but merely a secondary instance of the general evolution of the bourgeoisie towards Fascism in the final phase of capitalist development.[401] As all German governments between 1928 and 1933 had already been stigmatized as 'Fascist' or at least 'semi-Fascist', the true character of Nazism was not understood. In this way the KPD, at least indirectly, helped the Nazis to gain power; at all events it did practically nothing before 1933 to hinder the Fascist advance.

In terms of voting strength, the KPD in the last phase of the republic grew to be the third largest German party. In September 1930 it obtained 4.6 million votes, in November 1932 actually 5.9 million, compared with 7.2 million for the SPD and 11.9 million for the NSDAP. However, as the KPD's warnings against imperialist war did not specifically refer to the NSDAP but to capitalist and bourgeois parties in general, including the SPD, it can safely be said that they did no harm to the NSDAP, since no one was obliged to make the connection. Only isolated warnings against the Nazis' war policy came from the KPD before 1933.[402]

Stalin, the Soviet government, and the Comintern knew from 1933 at the latest of Hitler's expansionist ideas as set out in *Mein Kampf*.[403] A writer in the journal *Communist International*, in an analysis of Hitler's foreign policy published in that year, predicted a Nazi attack on the Soviet Union with especial reference to *Mein Kampf*.[404] The KPD likewise realized after 1933 that the actual Fascist regime in Germany—and not the abstract imperialist world of the West—was pursuing a war policy, and urged its supporters to take counter-action. For years, however, it refused to admit to itself that, persecuted and driven undergound, it had scarcely any power to prevent the catastrophe.

[398] Article in *Inprekorr*, 70 (19 Aug. 1930); document in *Komintern und Faschismus*, 153–4, also Allard, *Stalin*, 16 ff.; cf. documents in Steinberg, *Widerstand*, 219 ff. See also the statement by the Central Committee of the KPD on the works council elections of 1930: 'To be a Communist is to be a mortal enemy of social fascism' (*Der deutsche Kommunismus*, doc. 57, pp. 186–7).

[399] Duhnke, *Die KPD*, 51. Cf. *Der deutsche Kommunismus*, doc. 61, pp. 194–5. The KPD policy is documented in Weber, *Hauptfeind Sozialdemokratie*.

[400] Cf. Thälmann's speech to the Central Committee of the KPD in Feb. 1932: *Der deutsche Kommunismus*, doc. 47, pp. 157–8.

[401] Duhnke, *Die KPD*, 51.

[402] In 1932 Thälmann warned that a vote for Hitler was a vote for war: cf. I.II.6 below. A radically different view in *Geschichte der deutschen Arbeiterbewegung*, v. 10.

[403] Lange, *Hitlers unbeachtete Maximen*, 131 ff.; Allard, *Stalin*, 30.

[404] Quoted from Duhnke, *Die KPD*, 304.

The Communists were strongly opposed to an imperialist war, i.e. one fought by the capitalist countries against the Soviet Union, since it would threaten the destruction of the 'first socialist state'. As we have seen, this opposition to war had nothing to do with pacifism, or with a general rejection of force as an instrument of policy. It was a dogma of German Communists, as of others, that future revolutions would take the same course as the Russian one of 1917, which meant that force would play a part.[405] In the final phase of the Weimar Republic the KPD presented itself as a revolutionary party which had no concern for the rules of the bourgeois republic and whose ideology sanctioned the use of force in order to create a classless society in which force would no longer be necessary.[406] Thus, for instance, the International Anti-Fascist Congress organized by the Communists in Berlin in 1929 declared that the fight against Fascism must be carried on in all sections of polit-ical and economic life, 'without refraining from any means, including armed revolutionary mass action'.[407] It also declared that the overthrow and destruction of Fascism could only come about 'by the violent overthrow and complete destruction of the social order of which Fascism is the result and the expression, namely decaying capitalist society'.[408] It remained true, however, that this revolutionary attitude was more of a myth than a reality,[409] at any rate as far as preparing for an armed uprising was concerned. The KPD made no such preparations in the months before 30 January 1933 or at any time afterwards. It was no more able than the SPD to offer effective resistance to the National Socialists after they had assumed power. After the Reichstag fire, the Nazis themselves were unable to produce evidence of a KPD plot for an armed uprising.[410]

The paramilitary Roter Frontkämpferbund (RFB), which was founded in 1924 and continued to exist illegally after being banned in 1929, possessed arms and was evidently capable of offering resistance, as were sections of the social democratic 'Iron Front'.[411] Its purpose, however, was not to engage in armed combat but primarily to spread the idea of proletarian readiness for defence and to protect Communist assemblies and demonstrations.[412]

Members of the KPD and RFB took part in nearly all the indoor and street fighting that became a permanent feature of election campaigns in the last days of the republic. However, at the end of 1930 the Comintern condemned physical violence against the Nazis as 'sectarian', and on 10 November 1931 the KPD adopted a resolution condemning isolated acts of terror and 'senseless' armed

---

[405] The Comintern programme of 1928 stated that 'Communists scorn to conceal their views and intentions. They openly declare that their aims can only be achieved by the violent overthrow of every existing social order' (*Der deutsche Kommunismus*, doc. 4, p. 57).
[406] Flechtheim, *Die KPD*, 326 ff.; recently Bahne, 'Gewaltproblem', 683.
[407] *Faschismus*, 79.
[408] Ibid. 80.
[409] Duhnke, *Die KPD*, 13 ff.
[410] Mommsen, 'Reichstagbrand', 391 ff.
[411] Duhnke, *Die KPD*, 43–4.
[412] Herbell, *Staatsbürger*, 282–3; Schuster, *Frontkämpferbund*, esp. 236 ff., referring to the 'legend' and 'bogy' of an armed Communist uprising. Cf. also the inaugural appeal of 1924 in *Der deutsche Kommunismus*, doc. 20, pp. 93–4.

attacks against individual Fascists. According to Comintern instructions, the ideological struggle was the chief method to be used against National Socialism, and accordingly KPD representatives turned up at NSDAP meetings to argue the Communist position.[413]

With its thesis of the inevitability of imperialist war the KPD helped to spread a fatalistic ideology which, if it did not increase the likelihood of war, did not diminish it either. It maintained that according to the iron law of history the world-wide rule of the imperialist bourgeoisie would be overthrown in a series of bloody civil wars, revolutions, revolts, and international wars, and would then give place to Comintern rule.[414] The ideological justification of force as a means towards creating a non-violent society was also hardly calculated to encourage the idea of a peaceful settlement of political conflict.

10. THE WAVE OF WAR BOOKS AND FILMS FROM 1929 ONWARDS

A profound change in the political attitudes of large sections of society is generally reflected in literature and the cinema, as well as in the tastes of the reading and film-going public. Conversely, it can be said that if books and films of a particular tendency start to attract the interest of a wide public from a fairly precise point of time onwards, this can be regarded as the sign of a change in political trends.

It was clear to observers during the last years of Weimar that Germany was experiencing a flood of nationalist war books and war films, and that there was a decline in cultural products with a pacifist trend. Is it possible in retrospect to evaluate the change more precisely?

After Hitler's assumption of power, works were published in foreign countries concerning the Nazis' secret rearmament and ideological preparation for war.[415] Notice was also taken of the development of literature since 1933.

The British journalist Dorothy Woodman[416] wrote in 1934: 'There is no end to the writing of war books. It is impossible to give even an approximate list of their titles.'[417] She spoke of the outlawing of anti-war literature and the 'militarization of literary production'. In a book published in 1936 concerning Hitler's war against the peace-fighters in Germany[418] the same writer calculated that the number of new titles under the heading of 'military science' had more than doubled from 1932 to 1935: figures for the succecssive years were 198, 256, 385, and 433. She concluded: 'The military spirit, the war spirit, the will to war is to be inculcated into the German people while its official leaders seek to bamboozle the world with their talk of peace.'

---

[413] Duhnke, *Die KPD*, 21–2, 34. On the anti-terror resolution see also Flechtheim, *Die KPD*, 279.

[414] Flechtheim, *Die KPD*, 329.

[415] *Hitler Rearms* (1934); *Hitlers Luftflotte startbereit* (1935); *Das deutsche Volk klagt an* (1936).

[416] I owe to Prof. F. L. Carsten of London the information that Dorothy Woodman was a journalist working for the *New Statesman* weekly, and that the name was not (as stated by Rautenberg, *Rüstungspolitik*, 464) a pseudonym for the émigré publicist and KPD member Herbert H. Schreiber.

[417] *Hitler treibt*, 432 ff., cf. the English version, *Hitler Rearms* (1934), esp. 244–6.

[418] *Das deutsche Volk*, 54–5.

Given the political situation, writers like Woodman were naturally concerned to warn the international public of the evidence for longer-term Nazi intentions. The development of literary trends before 1933 was of little account compared with this specific indoctrination.

The trend in question is confirmed, albeit from the opposite political point of view, in a dissertation of 1936 by Günther Lutz on the subject of 'Shared experience in war literature', with references to some 400 titles.[419] The writer deals with works that reflect 'the inner link between the front-line community and our present national community', and distinguishes them sharply from the 'efforts of coffee-house literati, deserters, and aliens',[420] i.e. war books with a pacifist tendency. From his extensive survey the writer concluded that the output of war books reached a high-water mark in 1915 but began to diminish in the following year. It had not revived until 1928, when a new spate of works was apparently produced in response to the attempts of 'alien-minded literati' such as Remarque 'to sully the memory of those who fell in the world war'.[421]

An analysis of Lutz's bibliography gives the following statistics concerning the output of nationalist war books. In 1916–28 the number of new titles remained steady at about ten per year. After 1929 the curve rose steeply to a peak in 1930 and another in 1933. The average in 1929–33 was considerably higher than in 1915; the 1933 figure was double that for 1915, though one was a year of peace and the other of war.

An analysis[422] based on the index of German books in print in 1925–35 confirms strikingly that the militarist and anti-pacifist trend began some years before Hitler's accession to power. The number of war books rose from about 200 in 1926 to about 300 in 1929 and over 400 in 1930; in 1931 and 1932 it fell back to about 300, and then reached a peak of over 500 in each year from 1933 to 1935. If we now consider titles concerned with 'defence questions', the curve ascends continuously from under 10 in 1929 to over 50 in 1935.[423] The number of books dealing with future wars was especially high in 1930–2. Books on problems of peace, which might be classified as pacifist in the widest sense, show an opposite trend, the graph falling steadily from 1929 to 1933. From 1933 onwards no pacifist literature was printed in Germany. It must also be noted that throughout the two decades the number of pacifist publications was only about one-tenth that of nationalist war books, so that altogether in 1929–30 a clear change set in in favour of the latter.

This was also the period of mass editions of works of 'soldierly nationalism'.[424] Werner Beumelburg's *Gruppe Bosemüller* had an immediate print-run of 30,000 copies in 1930, then reached 65,000 in 1933 (90,000 in 1935, 170,000 in 1940). His best-seller *Sperrfeuer um Deutschland* was printed in 100,000 copies in 1930 alone,

---

[419] Lutz, *Gemeinschaftserlebnis*, 20, 85, 92.

[420] Ibid. 10–11.

[421] Ibid. 11, 95.

[422] Present author's calculation, based on inspection of several thousand titles.

[423] The public debate on defence policy came to an end in 1935, as the militaristic conception of society had by then been put into practice (Hillgruber, 'Militarismus', 41).

[424] The following data are taken from the *Deutsches Bücherverzeichnis*, vols. xv–xxii.

rising to 140,000 in 1931, 150,000 in 1932, and 166,000 in 1933 (216,000 in 1935, 328,000 in 1938). Edwin E. Dwinger's books also sold in tens of thousands, as did those of Ernst Jünger, Franz Schauwecker, Franz Seldte, and other representatives of 'soldierly nationalism' or the 'conservative revolution'.[425]

It is true that Erich Maria Remarque's *Im Westen nichts Neues* (All Quiet on the Western Front) was printed in one million copies in Germany in 1930, and two million in foreign countries.[426] This was an anti-war novel in so far as it told an unvarnished tale and avoided heroics. For this reason it aroused a violent reaction from the nationalist right, where it was described as an insult to the honour of front-line fighters. Schauwecker spoke of the 'war experience of a sub-man', and F. G. Jünger contemptuously described the book as one which 'did not represent the heroic fight of the German armies, but uttered feeble complaints against war'.[427] But Remarque's runaway success remained an isolated case. Moreover, later in 1930 it became clear that the nationalist right, encouraged by the NSDAP triumph at the September election, was not prepared to let it go unchallenged. On 5 December the first showing in Berlin of the film from Remarque's novel was disrupted by violent demonstrations, chiefly on the part of National Socialists,[428] and a second showing had to be cancelled. A few days later the NSDAP organized large public meetings to protest against the film; the veterans' associations also protested violently. The Länder of Saxony, Bavaria, and Württemberg appealed to the chief film censor in Berlin to withdraw the film's certificate. It was a sign of the times that the censor's office acceded to the request and banned further showings on the pretext that the film was harmful to Germany's reputation abroad.

The Centre party—Brüning was at this time Reich chancellor—supported the ban. Brüning, who had described his government as one of front-line soldiers,[429] approved the ban on grounds of international peace: he thought such productions contributed to a nervous atmosphere and that a firm line should also be taken with other pacifist films and plays. When the social democratic government of Prussia opposed the ban, Brüning described its attitude as 'very dangerous from the point of view of foreign relations'. He also advised the Centre party to take more account of new types of activity ('parades, small-bore shooting, etc.').[430] The Reich minister of the interior, Joseph Wirth, who was also a member of the Centre party, likewise supported the ban:[431] he agreed with Brüning that 'certain feelings must be respected' and 'regard paid to certain attitudes of mind'.

The film world, like that of literature, was an arena in which political quarrels were fought out.[432] Tendencies in German film-making from 1930 onwards were

---

[425] Cf. Prümm, *Soldatischer Nationalismus*, 75, with a list of the chief war books of 1930. Further details in *Deutsches Bücherverzeichnis*.

[426] Prümm, *Soldatischer Nationalismus*, 75.

[427] Sontheimer, *Antidemokratisches Denken*, 119–20; cf. also Rohe, *Reichsbanner*, 143.

[428] *Schulthess* (1930), 243; cf. also Kracauer, *Caligari*, 131; Sontheimer, *Antidemokratisches Denken*, 119–20; Reimann, *Goebbels*, 143–4.

[429] Bracher, *Weimarer Republik*, 468.

[430] *Protokolle Zentrumspartei*, 500 ff. (meeting of parliamentary executive committee, 12 Dec. 1930).

[431] Ibid. 517 (meeting of parliamentary party, 20 Feb. 1931).

[432] Kracauer, *Caligari*, 138.

closely in line with the boom in war-glorifying literature. Films of social criticism and pacifist tendency were increasingly displaced by 'national epics' in which the chief characters were warriors, leaders of men, and heroic rebels.[433] Typical of these were the films of Luis Trenker, which exalted military virtue and represented war as something which transcended the individual and which he had to accept without question. As the film historian Kracauer observes: 'Trenker's mountaineer was the type of man on whom a regime bent on war could safely count.'[434]

The patriotic war films made for the home market were a symptom of the decline of the Weimar Republic in so far as they supported authoritarianism and, like the corresponding novels, portrayed the heroism of war. 'There is no doubt that the desire for authoritarian models which found satisfaction in the patriotic epics of 1930-3 was a decisive factor in Hitler's favour. Broad sections of the population, including some intellectuals, were mentally prepared for the kind of system that Hitler gave them.' What German films offered to the imagination, Germany provided in real life. 'Trumpets rang out without ceasing, and the "little man" on his living-room sofa felt himself transported into stirring times. The thunder of battle resounded, with one victory celebration after another. Everything was just as he had seen it on film.'[435]

As we have seen, the rise of militarist tendencies and the decline of pacifist ones in literature, the cinema, and other politicized areas of entertainment began in the late 1920s and early 1930s, and it has frequently been interpreted as a reaction to the sensational success of Remarque's book.[436] There may be some truth in this, but it overlooks the fact that the ideological development affecting literature, the cinema, and popular taste was related to the change in socio-economic conditions since the beginning of the world depression. It is in fact noteworthy that the spate of right-wing war books coincided with the onset of the slump and that they found a ready audience at that time. It is plausible to infer that the consumers of this literature had lost faith in the pacifism of the 'system', i.e. the conciliatory policy of the Weimar politicians, and were turning towards solutions based on force and authoritarianism.

After a short phase of toleration of the republic, the bourgeoisie in particular adopted attitudes in the last years of Weimar 'which denigrated its liberal traditions as signs of weakness and exalted methods of force and brutality. Like the "conservative revolutionaries", so the bourgeoisie now came to regard the democratic mechanism as antiquated and unsuitable. It accepted the retrospective glorification of war as the ideal state of society.'[437] Hence the boom in right-wing books and films in which war, violence, and qualities of leadership were exalted. There was a demand for the stimulus offered by 'soldierly nationalism' and other literature exalting irrational, nationalist, authoritarian, and heroic ideologies: for they suggested that simple solutions might be found to the economic and political crisis, instead of the much harder work of discovering its true causes and its consequences for everyone. The nostalgia for war had a compensatory function:

---

[433] Kracauer, *Caligari*, 152-8, 164, 171 ff.   [434] Ibid. 171.   [435] Ibid. 180-1.
[436] Lutz, *Gemeinschaftserlebnis*, 11; Sontheimer, *Antidemokratisches Denken*, 118.
[437] Prümm, *Soldatischer Nationalismus*, 70-1.

In contrast to the negative present, war appeared as an ideal condition that united the whole nation, levelled social differences, and assigned a place to everyone in a clear authoritarian structure. At a time of acute crisis there was enormous emotional power in the recollection of heroic deeds performed together in the past. The memory of national greatness at a time of personal and social distress enabled men to forget their subjective and collective misery and to take a pride in their own personality and standing.[438]

As the above analysis shows, the year 1933 did not bring any marked change in the popularity of either militarist or pacifist books and films, but rather confirmed the trend of the past few years. The Fascist movement did not cause this trend; it may have intensified it, and certainly made use of it. The spate of militarist and nationalist books and films helped to create a climate in which the most aggressive political force and the one most vehemently opposed to democracy, socialism, and pacifism, namely the NSDAP, could develop in a few years from a splinter-group into the largest political party.

The new fashion in literature and the cinema which set in in 1929 completes the picture that emerges from an analysis of ideological trends in the parties, the principal associations, and the churches at the end of the Weimar period, in relation to the use of force in politics. As the economic crisis grew more acute and the parliamentary system fell into decline—two phenomena that were closely connected—pacifist attitudes gave way to a militaristic glorification of war or a fatalistic acceptance of it. Militarism expressed itself in the exaltation of war and soldierly virtues, in laments for the failure of the first, 'pacifist' German republic, in the increasingly loud demand for spiritual and material 'rearmament', and in all kinds of aggressive and nationalist watchwords. Intentionally or not, this development was assisted by a fatalistic attitude towards future wars, rooted in theology or historical theory and inherent in ideologies of a Christian or Communist stamp.

A consistent policy of international understanding, renouncing force as an instrument of foreign policy, had ceased to command articulate majority support in Germany before 1933. The legitimacy of war was taken for granted, and the ideologies we have described as militaristic and fatalistic were probably even more widespread in the German population than was opposition to democracy.

There are no reliable surveys to bear this out for certain; and none of the Reichstag election campaigns in 1930–3 were fought primarily on foreign policy. The voter was not invited to choose between war and peace. Hence, the trends described here cannot be expressed in exact percentages, but only as 'predominant ideological tendencies'.

The upshot was that the advocates of a policy of strength in the last phase of the Weimar Republic met with increasing sympathy, especially among the bourgeoisie. This does not mean that a majority of the German population supported Hitler's war plans in 1933. These were indeed largely unknown, as the book setting out his programme belonged to the category of an unread best-seller. But it is our view that a majority of the population—influenced by Fascist, reactionary-monarchist, and

[438] Ibid. 74.

conservative-nationalist parties and associations—was ripe for a degree of militarization of the social fabric, whatever the exact form it might take. And this responsiveness did not, to say the least, exclude eventual acceptance of the use of methods of force in foreign affairs.

Given this state of mind on the political right wing and among its supporters, Hitler and his associates could be confident that their policy of material and psychological rearmament would probably meet with joyful assent rather than resistance. If they could succeed in throttling bourgeois pacifism and destroying workers' organizations that stood for international peace and understanding, there would be no obstacle to further ideological preparation for war.[439] Hitler and his propagandists even felt safe in preaching international peace for some years[440] as a diversionary manœuvre, without the fear that this would cause any weakening of the German people's readiness for violent methods.

[439] Cf. I.III below.
[440] Cf. I.III,3, 5; also the survey in Wette, 'Difficult Persuasion'.

II. Propaganda Mobilization for War

1. National Socialist Propaganda before 1933

AFTER the fiasco of the Munich *Putsch* in November 1923 Hitler prescribed the adoption by the NSDAP of a policy of 'legality'. To achieve power, the party had first to divest itself of the image of a radical nationalist splinter-group and acquire a mass following that could be translated into a growing number of seats in the Reichstag. The political task was thus 'to bring back into the rightist camp the masses which were drifting leftwards under the parliamentary system, or at any rate a sizeable proportion of them'.[1] In so far as the NSDAP succeeded in this, it was the natural rival of the socialist and democratic parties, and the latter's political and trade-union organizations served it as a model: the political enemy was to be beaten with his own weapons.

The objective, as before, was to destroy the republican regime. In a Reichstag speech on 9 March 1929 Goebbels declared in all frankness that it was the NSDAP's intention 'to do away with the system itself, not simply to mitigate the effect of diseased phenomena'.[2] Thus, the methods of carrying on the fight, imposed by the Weimar constitution, were purely a matter of tactics. The purpose was not to obtain a large number of parliamentary seats in order to introduce constructive policies, but to use the Reichstag as one among several possible ways of attaining absolute power. Like the democratic parties, the parliamentary system was to be beaten with its own weapons.

Since the policy of 'legality' made it necessary to mobilize mass support, the main emphasis of political work had to be centred on propaganda. Hitler had recognized at an early stage the importance of propaganda in the domestic political struggle, and had displayed his own skill in that direction during the first phase of the party's history, from 1919 to 1923. During his imprisonment at Landsberg, when he was writing *Mein Kampf*, he made a thorough study of the objectives and methods of political propaganda, returning again and again to the object-lesson of Allied propaganda in the First World War. The principles he deduced from it [3] were that propaganda 'must appeal to the feelings of the public rather than to what is called their understanding'; it must 'be presented in a popular form and must . . . not be above the heads of the least intellectual level of those to whom it is directed'. Thus, 'its purely intellectual level will be all the lower in proportion to the size of the mass of people whom it is desired to affect'. Propaganda had nothing to do with scientific instruction: rather, as the masses' power of apprehension was very limited, their understanding small, and their forgetfulness great, the propagandist must confine himself to a very few points and hammer them home in the form of slogans until

[1] Alff, *Faschismus*, 22.
[2] Goebbels, *Revolution*, 17.
[3] Hitler, *Mein Kampf* (trans.), ch. on 'War Propaganda', esp. 156 ff., 159 (= original, 193 ff., 197–8).

even the simplest member of the audience absorbed the right idea. The effectiveness of stereotypes and the constant repetition of slogans was impressed on Hitler by the technique of Allied wartime propaganda and also by American methods of commercial advertising.[4] It was the National Socialist propagandists who introduced these ideas into German politics. To sum up, the method consisted of using a small number of slogans, keeping to a low intellectual level, taking account of the masses' proneness to sentiment and slowness of understanding, avoiding fine distinctions, and tirelessly repeating the simplest points a thousand times over. This, in Hitler's view, was the secret of success in political propaganda; by observing these principles, it could be turned into a first-class weapon.

This was a contrary conception to the methods of the democratic and socialist parties, which had always relied chiefly on rational persuasion. Their basic conviction, derived from traditions of the Enlightenment, was that, in election campaigns as at other times, the first consideration was to develop the voter's political consciousness so that he would be capable of taking decisions in accordance with his own interests. Against this, National Socialist propaganda chose to dispense with explanation and appeal instead to the irrational, demagogically stirring up economic and political fears and harping on emotional clichés for the identification of friends and enemies. The Nazi propagandists put so much trust in these methods that they did not even pretend to be able to justify their policy rationally. Hitler expressed his position on this at a public meeting in 1927: 'Make no mistake, with us too the important thing is faith, not knowledge.' People must believe in a cause. Only faith creates the state. What makes people fight and die for religious ideals? Not knowledge, but blind faith.'[5] Thus, intellectual conviction was consciously and explicitly rejected. Until 1933 public demonstrations were the Nazis' chief method of political agitation. Their purpose was not to put forward specific plans to justify their political views, but to use methods of suggestion to put across the political faith of National Socialism, which was itself not defined in any detail. The rational element in a Nazi propaganda speech amounted simply to a calculation of its propaganda effect.

The content of such a speech was confined for the most part to vehement denunciation of the status quo: an outburst of hatred for the Weimar 'system', the Jews and the Jewish world conspiracy, the Marxists and pacifists who wanted to make Germany defenceless, the 'November criminals', the 'shameful' treaty of Versailles and the burden of reparations, inept democratic politicians, economic distress, social discord, and national humiliation. As far as the future was concerned, the recipe was to promise everything to everyone, avoiding precise commitments as far as possible, and suggesting to every social group that if the NSDAP came to power the interests of that group would be specially favoured. Hitler presented himself as the radical embodiment of opposition to the odious present and as the strong man, the leader whose faith and strength of will would

---

4 Hitler, *Mein Kampf* (trans.), 163; also Lukács, *Zerstörung der Vernunft*, 573, and Winckler, *Funktion faschistischer Sprache*, 92–3.
5 *Adolf Hitler in Franken*, 56.

bring about a happier, freer, greater, and more powerful Germany. In this way all malcontents were attracted to the NSDAP with vague promises and filled with 'blind faith'.

Thus, unlike the traditional liberal and socialist ideologies, Fascist ideology and propaganda did not purport to express particular class interests. On a later occasion Goebbels openly, and with a certain pride, admitted this when he said that National Socialism had 'never had a doctrine in the sense of discussing problems or particular issues. Its ambition was to achieve power. Only after that would there be any question of drawing up or implementing a programme. If anyone asked us how we intended to solve this or that problem, we would reply that we did not yet know. We had our plans right enough, but we did not choose to expose them to public criticism.'[6] In this way ideology degenerated into propaganda and mere tactical calculation, in which words had no meaning and whose only purpose was the attainment of power.

A further characteristic of National Socialist propaganda was the use of a vocabulary of violence—a range of terms which constantly reflected the will to use force, and made it very clear what would be left of the party's protestations of legality if and when those who used such language actually came to power. Hitler's own speeches, in particular, were studded with obscene attacks on his political opponents. He regularly depicted them as the vilest criminals—thieves, swindlers, saboteurs, bandits, and murderers—against whom none but the most ruthless methods should be employed.[7] The scapegoats were further dehumanized by animal comparisons: such terms[8] as 'bug', 'vermin', 'parasite', 'maw-worm', 'viper' were intended to prevent the hearer feeling any sympathy for the opponent; instead, the comparison with a small but treacherous creature made it natural to think of extermination. Hitler's all-out defamation and denunciation of his political rivals was a linguistic expression of the violent character of his policy, which he himself described in such terms as 'brutal', 'ruthless', 'inexorable', 'pitiless', 'merciless', 'uncompromising', and 'fanatical'. In Hitler's language the adversary has to be crushed, destroyed, annihilated, done away with, exterminated, or extirpated, and this must be done with ruthlessness, brutality, and fanaticism. In addition, purely objective descriptions such as national, international, democratic, Jewish, Marxist, and pacifist were, by Nazi propaganda, distorted into terms of abuse.

A further instrument of propaganda technique was the 'ideological cult' which the National Socialists already handled with virtuosity during the phase leading up to the seizure of power.[9] The use of symbols and rituals was planned and executed with precision. True, the success of these methods was mainly due to the fact that the 'movement' did not create entirely new forms but made use of existing tendencies, applying to its own purposes much that was already current in

---

[6] Secret statement by Goebbels on 5 Apr. 1940 to invited representatives of the German press; extracts in Jacobsen, *Der Zweite Weltkrieg*, 180–1; cf. also Hillgruber, *Germany and the Two World Wars*, 56–7.

[7] Grieswelle, *Propaganda*, 79.

[8] For the following passage see Winckler, *Funktion faschistischer Sprache*, 63 ff., cf. also Bein, 'Parasit'; Burke, 'Rhetoric'; Bork, *Mißbrauch*.

[9] Cf. Gamm, *Kult*, and Vondung, *Magie*; the latter uses the term 'ideological cult'.

nationalist circles. Thus, the party imitated the cult of heroic, warlike, national, and racial ideals and symbols which had already prevailed in the Kaiser's Germany. It also borrowed much from particular aspects of the youth movement, such as the romantic fire ritual, the equinoctial celebrations, and amateur theatricals, and also such terms as 'Führer' (leader), 'Gau' (district or region, with archaic overtones), or '"Heil"-Gruss' (salute with outstretched arm).[10] Other models were found in military life, the Christian churches, and Italian Fascism.

Hitler and Goebbels knew how strongly unpolitical human beings, in particular, could be affected by ideological symbols. Such symbols helped to dethrone the intellect and liberate emotions; and this manipulative effect was vital to a party which had come forward with a political faith but no actual political programme. Already in the 1920s the NSDAP evolved a specific type of demonstration[11] in which ritual had an acknowledged place. At the beginning of a mass meeting the SA would perform a martial entry with banners, military music, and the roll of drums, and form up with their swastika flags and standards into a 'speaker's guard of honour'. Then battle-songs were sung to get the audience into the right mood before the speaker appeared. When he did so, often after several hours of waiting, the tension was released in tumultuous cries of 'Sieg Heil'.

Hitler probably found the most fruitful suggestions for his propaganda methods in Gustave Le Bon's *La Psychologie des foules*.[12] He applied the teachings of mass psychology to the organization of mass meetings, which he regarded as superior to all forms of written propaganda. As he observed in *Mein Kampf*, the individual who has felt isolated and in fear of solitude acquired in this way

the picture of a great community, which has a strengthening and encouraging effect on most people . . . If, on leaving the shop or mammoth factory, in which he feels very small indeed, he enters a vast assembly for the first time and sees around him thousands and thousands of men who hold the same opinions; if, while still seeking his way, he is gripped by the force of mass suggestion which comes from the excitement and enthusiasm of three or four thousand other men in whose midst he finds himself; if the manifest success and the consensus of thousands confirm the truth and justice of the new teaching and for the first time raise doubts in his mind as to the truth of the opinions held by himself up to now—then he submits himself to the mystic fascination of what we call mass suggestion.[13]

Hitler and some of his closer associates were indeed masters of mass psychology, and displayed a certain originality in this field.[14] Here, and not in the so-called National Socialist *Weltanschauung*—which was little more than a mishmash of clichés and slogans[15]—was the key to the success of Fascist propaganda.

In the electoral battle which continued from 1930 to 1933 it became clear that the NSDAP was better organized than the other parties, and in consequence was able to

[10] For details see Vondung, *Magie*, 13–32.
[11] Cf. ibid. 34 ff., and Grieswelle, *Propaganda*, 35–42.
[12] Le Bon, *Psychologie*.
[13] Hitler, *Mein Kampf* (trans.), 397–8.
[14] Thus Bracher, *Dictatorship*, 140.
[15] Cf. Lenk, *'Volk und Staat'*.

conduct propaganda campaigns such as Germany had never known before. The NSDAP reaped its reward for having spent the relatively peaceful years before the world depression in systematically expanding its organization, its propaganda apparatus, and the SA.[16] The latter had long ceased to be merely a security corps for assemblies and bodyguard for party leaders, and had become a regular private army, capable of intimidating opponents by demonstrative acts of force and even by its mere presence. When the NSDAP and the SA initiated acts of terror on the streets or paraded in large numbers, in uniform, at mass demonstrations, it was not meant as a rehearsal for civil war; rather it reflected the discovery that a show of force can be attractive as well as repellent. Thus, violence as embodied by the SA belonged to the armoury of psychological mobilization.[17]

When the party was refounded in February 1925, a central propaganda commission was set up under Goebbels to co-ordinate meetings and public-speaking arrangements. This body, the predecessor of the later Reichspropagandaleitung der NSDAP (Reich Propaganda Leadership Unit) controlled the activities of Nazi spokesmen, principally members of the Reichstag and the Land parliaments, who enjoyed the benefit of attendance allowances, free travel, and parliamentary immunity. As Goebbels said in 1927: 'Any elected representative is *ipso facto* a Party official, whom the state is kind enough to pay for his services.'[18] In 1928, under the auspices of the Reichspropagandaleitung, an 'NSDAP speakers' school' was founded in order to cultivate uniformity of style. With its help the party put up about 1,000 speakers in the Reichstag election of autumn 1930, who appeared at about 34,000 meetings and bore the brunt of the campaign. Speeches at public demonstrations continued to be the chief propaganda method. The party newspapers and the Hugenberg press often carried Hitler's speeches and those of other leaders such as Goebbels, Strasser, Frick, and Feder, thus providing extra publicity; but this was only an echo of the mass demonstrations with which the NSDAP filled the streets and assembly-halls. Wherever Hitler went he used the most up-to-date technical aids. For instance, during the Presidential election of 1932 and the Landtag elections of the same year he travelled by air and was thus able to speak in four or five major cities each day. Only the radio network was out of bounds to the Nazis until 1933.

It was largely thanks to their effective mass propaganda campaigns that the Nazi party, which in 1928 was still a negligible quantity with twelve Reichstag seats, achieved spectacular electoral success in the last phase of the Weimar Republic. But this does not suffice to explain how it was that at that time such resounding successes could be attained in Germany by a party which, however well equipped organizationally and from the psychological and tactical points of view, had so little of a concrete message to deliver. The explanation is partly a matter of social psychology.

---

[16] Bracher, *Dictatorship*, 143 ff. Cf. also Horn's study from the organizational point of view, *Marsch zur Machtergreifung*.

[17] Sauer, 'Mobilmachung', 12 ff.

[18] Quoted from Grieswelle, *Propaganda*, 28.

The rise of the NSDAP coincided in time with the decline of the economy, and the two were closely connected. It was only the situation caused by the economic depression that provided Nazi propaganda with a fruitful soil. Its mass adherents came from the middle classes, who—including the intellectuals among them—felt the crisis as a threat to their social and economic security and privileges. In many quarters it was actually seen as a threat to their livelihood, producing an atmosphere of panic and despair.[19] It was this that created the real basis for the success of National Socialist propaganda among the masses.

As many sections of the population, not only the middle classes, were decidedly immature politically, fear for their livelihood did not lead them to take action on their own account, but to call for a leader who would get rid of the despised republican politicians and effect a miraculous once-and-for-all cure. This was an expression of helplessness, leading them to shift responsibility on to the most radical leader-figure in the nationalist and counter-revolutionary camp.

A further factor was that the middle classes, which formed the most important political support of the NSDAP, had never had great esteem for the parliamentary system. The traditions of the authoritarian state were, by contrast, alive among them, and the Weimar Republic, racked by crisis, had not succeeded in replacing these traditions by democratic ones. For this reason the slogan 'Down with the Weimar system!' met with a wide response, although the economic crisis was more the fault of capitalism than of parliamentary democracy or the parties connected with it.

Finally, certain philosophical traditions helped to prepare the ground for Fascist propaganda. For more than a century the down-grading of reason and the intellect, the uncritical glorification of intuition, hostility to progress, and belief in myths had been established features of philosophical irrationalism.[20] This, although an international phenomenon, had become a prevailing tendency in Germany alone. With its reactionary political implications, it was not only an academic discipline but—in a popularized form and in the language of black-and-white propaganda—it played a dominant part in the various educational institutions, in day-to-day journalism, and in literature. As National Socialism gathered strength, the militant hostility to reason on the part of reactionary philosophers and authors became a serious factor in politics. The economic and social crisis after 1929 baffled the understanding of many of its victims, and this created a vacuum that political irrationalism was ready to fill, not necessarily in the guise of Fascist propaganda. Its slogans and clichés functioned as a substitute for the much more difficult process of explaining the highly complex workings of a capitalist society that had run into a crisis.

In this situation, the possibility of identifying with a leader-figure who appeared as a miraculous deliverer provided compensation for the actual or apprehended threat to one's livelihood. Anti-Semitic, racialist, anti-democratic, and anti-socialist

---

[19] Cf. Lukács, *Zerstörung der Vernunft*, 68–73.
[20] Ibid. 10–11, 565–6, and *passim*; also Fest, *Hitler*, 371 ff., 'German Catastrophe or German Consistency?'

slogans identified scapegoats for personal misfortunes, canalized pent-up feelings of aggression, and so contributed to radicalizing the potentially anti-democratic middle-class section of the electorate. Finally, anti-capitalist agitation by the left wing and the SA suggested the possibility of overcoming the class conflict in a future 'community of the people' (Volksgemeinschaft: cf. Chapter I.III below).

The desperate mood of the middle classes, the authoritarian tradition, and philosophical irrationalism, together with an underdeveloped sense of democracy, may explain the successes of National Socialist propaganda, but not Hitler's actual appointment to the chancellorship. Although the NSDAP had risen in a few years from a splinter-group to the strongest party in the Reichstag—at the election of July 1932 it received 37.8 per cent of the votes cast—it still had no parliamentary majority. Thus, Hitler's appointment was not the unavoidable consequence of the electoral successes won by the party's unrivalled propaganda campaign. It was due to collaboration with Hitler on the part of the traditional political right wing and sections of heavy industry, the large estate-owners, and the military, which began with the formation of the 'Harzburg front' in the autumn of 1931.[21]

2. Ideological *Gleichschaltung*: Propaganda, the Mass Media, and Control Systems, 1933–1939

Hitler's appointment to the chancellorship on 30 January 1933 marked the victory of the dictatorial and militarist tendencies which had gained ground in the final phase of the Weimar Republic and had increasingly influenced policy under the chancellors Brüning, Papen, and Schleicher. Like his three predecessors, Hitler was not supported by a parliamentary majority but was the head of a presidential cabinet governing by emergency decrees in accordance with Article 48 of the Weimar constitution. In its personal composition, the National Socialist government was a new edition of the 'Harzburg front'.[22] Papen was vice-chancellor; the Nationalists were represented by Hugenberg, the Stahlhelm by Seldte, and these groups were backed by influential industrial and agrarian circles. The three National Socialists in the government were counterbalanced by eight conservative ministers. Hence, one could hardly speak of Nazi predominance, except perhaps in the sense that the National Socialist members of the government had clearer political ambitions than their colleagues.

In the first weeks and months of its existence the new government took decisions which drastically altered the domestic balance of power in the Nazi's favour. Firstly, the decree of 4 February 1933 'For the Protection of the German People' rigorously curbed the rights of the press, of assembly, and of free speech; it thus created an important basis for the monopolization of political news, the suppression

---

[21] Since the foundation of the German national state these traditional élites had been the champions of Germany's claim to great-power status. Lines of continuity are traced, with attention to some conclusions in the present volume, in Fischer, *Bündnis der Eliten*, and some essays in *Auf dem Weg ins Dritte Reich*. Cf. also *Nationalsozialistische Machtergreifung*, sect. 2, 'Das Bündnis der Eliten als Voraussetzung der nationalsozialistischen Herrschaft'.

[22] Cf. now *Die Regierung Hitler*, pt. 1. *1933/34*.

of hostile opinions, and the policy of ideological *Gleichschaltung* (enforced uniformity) in the following years. Shortly afterwards, the pretext of the Reichstag fire was used to extract from the president a further decree 'On the Protection of the People and State'. This was issued on 28 February and largely abrogated basic rights, creating a permanent state of emergency. Finally, with the Enabling Law of 23 March 1933, for which all bourgeois parties voted, including the Centre, the government took to itself full legislative powers despite the opposition of the persecuted left-wing parties. Thereafter, step by step the regime destroyed what was left of the parliamentary system of government, deprived its political opponents of influence, and created a dictatorial system without parallel in German history.[23]

It has already been pointed out that this gradual conquest of power was supported by the non-Nazi members of the government and the military, industrial, and agrarian circles whom they represented. This fact should not be obscured by the conflicts which certainly existed within the ruling group. The same is true as regards the *Gleichschaltung* of ideology. This could not have come about without the open co-operation or, at the very least, reluctant compliance of a large number of recognized opinion-formers. 'The effective spread of propaganda and the rapid regimentation of cultural life would not have been possible without the invaluable help eagerly tendered by writers and artists, professors and churchmen.'[24] Intellectual co-ordination often took the form of self-censorship, while manipulation and compulsion also did their part in ensuring the success of Nazi policy.

Hitler himself never left it in doubt that he intended to secure an ideological monopoly and would use the power of government to achieve this by every possible means. As he declared in *Mein Kampf*, 'a *Weltanschauung* is intolerant and cannot permit another to exist side by side with it. It imperiously demands its own recognition as unique and exclusive, and a complete transformation in accordance with its views throughout all the branches of public life.' This 'transformation', or regimentation, had no use for 'the intelligence and independent spirit of the rank and file' of party members, but only the 'disciplined obedience' with which they followed their intellectual leaders.[25] Thus, Hitler required blind intellectual subjection for the purpose of an effective system of domination at home, which in turn was the precondition of foreign domination to be achieved by war. Accordingly, after 30 January 1933 his government purposefully set about gaining control of the mass media and subjecting them to his aims.

By a decree of 13 March 1933[26] the government created a new *Reichsministerium für Volksaufklärung und Propaganda* (RMVP: Ministry for Popular Enlightenment

---

[23] Several collective works appeared on the occasion of the 50th anniversary of Hitler's appointment as chancellor, summing up the state of research concerning the Nazi dictatorship. Among these may be mentioned: *1933: Wie die Republik der Diktatur erlag*; *Nationalsozialistische Diktatur 1933–1945*; *Ploetz: Das Dritte Reich*; and *Das Dritte Reich: Herrschaftsstruktur und Geschichte*.

[24] Bracher, *Dictatorship*, 311–12, with numerous examples. On the willing co-operation of large sections of the population with the regime cf. I.III.1 below, esp. the works cited in n. 11 thereto.

[25] Hitler, *Mein Kampf* (trans.), 378, 381.

[26] See *RGBl.* i (1933), 104. Concerning the division of authority see *Kriegspropaganda*, 123 ff.; on the following passage see also Sywottek, *Mobilmachung*, 23 ff.

and Propaganda). With this institution, also a complete novelty in German history, Hitler incorporated into the state apparatus a section of the National Socialist party organization, including its personnel. However, the Reich propaganda department of the party continued to exist, so as to maintain in this sector as in others the dualistic system of rule by both party and state. The propaganda ministry was organized on the lines of the party office and was divided into sections to direct and oversee particular media. It possessed an infrastructure at provincial and local level, corresponding to the National Socialist regional (Gau) and district (Kreis) propaganda offices. To ensure uniformity the party and state institutions were often placed under a single authority at the top.

Joseph Goebbels, who now became propaganda minister, had been appointed by Hitler NSDAP Gauleiter of Berlin in 1926. In 1928 he had become Reich propaganda director of the NSDAP, in which capacity he did much to bring about the party's electoral successes in 1930–3.[27] Goebbels was the intellectual among the top Nazi leaders. His rise from the rank of a provincial agitator to that of a minister was due to his exceptional rhetorical gifts and also to his political flexibility and ingenuity in the use of all instruments suited to propaganda purposes. Before 1933 he had already managed to make himself indispensable by presenting a superhuman image of Hitler, the Führer, as a political genius, and thus creating the myth that was to exert a spell over many Germans until the last years of the war.[28]

Goebbels was the moving spirit of Nazi propaganda policy. He created the apparatus, issued the directives, and saw that they were put into effect. When Hitler was not himself speaking, Goebbels acted as his mouthpiece. All threads were in his hand, since in addition to being propaganda minister and head of the party's Reich propaganda office he was president of the Reichskulturkammer (Reich Cultural Institute). This body, set up by a law of 22 September 1933, was the third propaganda institution of the Nazi state, with the function of rigorously censoring, supervising, and regimenting 'intellectual workers' of all kinds.

Shortly after the propaganda ministry was set up, Goebbels described its functions as follows. 'It is the ministry's task to bring about an intellectual mobilization in Germany. It thus plays the same part in things of the mind as the defence ministry does in guarding the nation (*auf dem Gebiet der Wache*).'[29] This mobilization of the mind, Goebbels went on, was perhaps even more necessary than the material rearmament of the nation. It was to be achieved by instilling a uniform mental attitude into every member of the population.

Hitler, Goebbels, and the radio expert Hadamowsky had long realized that in this process of ideological standardization or *Volksführung* (leading or directing the people) a key part would be played by the radio as the most modern of the mass

---

[27] Cf. Heiber, *Goebbels*; Schaumburg-Lippe, *Dr. G*; Reimann, *Goebbels*.

[28] Cf. Bramsted, *Goebbels*, 189 ff., 'Goebbels and the Creation of the Führer Myth'; also Schaumburg-Lippe, *Dr. G*, 125 ff.; Reimann, *Goebbels*, 65 ff. For a recent analysis of the susceptibility of a large part of the population to this myth see Kershaw, *Popular Opinion*.

[29] Goebbels, 'Die zukünftige Arbeit und Gestaltung des deutschen Rundfunks', speech of 25 Mar. 1933, repr. in *Goebbels-Reden*, i. 82–107, here p. 90.

media.[30] It was therefore only consistent when the government immediately took control of the broadcasting system. Within a few days of his appointment as minister Goebbels summoned the directors and senior officials of the radio companies and informed them, in a speech bristling with threats, what their function was to be in future. 'We make no bones about it: the radio belongs to us and nobody else. We intend to use it in the service of our ideas, and no one else's will be allowed a hearing . . . Broadcasting is to be co-ordinated and subordinated to the aims that the government of national revolution has set itself. Directions for this purpose will be given by the government.'[31] In the following year (1934) the propaganda ministry assured itself of even closer control by making the broadcasting stations economically dependent on the Reich instead of the Länder, as they had hitherto largely been, and transferring all shares in them to the Reich Broadcasting Company.[32] In this way the radio department of the ministry had complete economic control of the stations, while the content of broadcasts was controlled by its subsidiary departments.

However, National Socialist radio policy was not confined to the supervision and control of programmes. The party attached importance to increasing the popularity and effectiveness of broadcasts by encouraging the public to take advantage of the new medium, which was still young and not as yet widespread. In close co-operation with a body of industrialists, known from September 1933 as the Werberat der deutschen Wirtschaft (Advertising Council of the German Economy), the RMVP set afoot the mass production of cheap radio sets and encouraged their sale.[33] Thus, the profit-making interest of the big electronic concerns, and the interest of the industry in selling receiver sets, went hand in hand with party policy. Already in 1933, 1,500,000 small radios (*Volksempfänger*, 'people's sets') were sold, and at the outbreak of war 70 per cent of German households owned a radio, three times as many as in 1932.[34] These sets were made so as to receive the national broadcasting station and the nearest local one, but not any foreign stations.

The increase in the number of listeners was a considerable help to Nazi propaganda. But the ministry, not content with this, arranged through local party offices for the collective reception of important broadcasts; it also built up a network of *Funkwarten* (radio monitors),[35] who provided an additional means of control and a kind of 'audience research', helping to prevent the repetition of propaganda that had missed its aim.

Goebbels rightly believed that 'radio would be as important in the twentieth century as the press was in the nineteenth',[36] and accordingly the RMVP devoted

---

[30] Cf. Hadamowsky, *Propaganda* (1933); id., *Rundfunk im Dienste der Volksführung* (1934); id., *Dein Rundfunk* (1934). Cf. also Stark, *Propaganda* (1930).

[31] *Goebbels-Reden*, i. 87, 89.

[32] Sywottek, *Mobilmachung*, 30 ff.; details in Pohle, *Rundfunk*.

[33] Scheel, *Ätherwellen*, 61–9.

[34] Bramsted, *Goebbels*, 74. Exact figures for 1932–5 in Goebbels, *Rundfunk* (1935), 7–8.

[35] Bramsted, *Goebbels*, 74–5.

[36] Cf. his speech of 18 Aug. 1933 at the opening of the first radio exhibition after the seizure of power, 'Der Rundfunk als achte Großmacht', in Goebbels, *Signale*, 197.

its utmost attention to this medium.[37] From the outset the radio department of the ministry functioned as, in Nazi parlance, the 'command centre' or 'general staff' of German broadcasting.[38]

The co-ordination of the press proved more difficult than that of the radio, as a huge variety of publications had survived from the Weimar period. In no other highly industrialized country were there so many daily and weekly papers as in Germany before 1933.[39] Until then, the Nazi press did not constitute a high percentage of them, and its finances were in a bad way. This was soon remedied after January 1933, as the regime took violent action against KPD and SPD papers, confiscated their printing-presses and editorial offices, and sold them at knock-down prices to the National Socialist regional press.[40] In an exhibition of 'self-discipline' the Verlegerverein (Publishers' Association)[41] remained silent when 150 Communist and social democratic newspapers were suppressed; thereafter the Association openly collaborated with the regime, encouraged by the fact that bourgeois papers were not molested for the time being.[42] The professional organization of journalists and editors[43] was brought into line by the appointment of Hitler's press chief Otto Dietrich to be its new president. A draconian measure followed with the Reich Schriftleitergesetz (Press Law) of 4 October 1933, threatening with the loss of employment any journalist who did not write 'in accordance with the national Socialist *Weltanschauung*'.[44]

Rolf Rienhardt, one of the principal executants of Nazi press policy, expressed forcefully the regime's totalitarian claims:

The National Socialist philosophy regards the press as a means of educating the people into National Socialism. The press is thus an instrument of the National Socialist state. The National Socialist philosophy claims absolute validity and does not tolerate the advocacy of other political doctrines. Accordingly, a state depending on the National Socialist movement recognizes none but a National Socialist press.[45]

To complement this control of the press, a gigantic financial concern was created. Max Amann—the publisher of the party newspaper *Völkischer Beobachter*, and now also president of the Reich press chamber—together with his deputy Rolf Rienhardt and other associates, bought up a large number of publishing houses, film

---

[37] On the respective functions of the Reich propaganda office of the NSDAP, the Reichsrundfunk-kammer, the Reichsrundfunkgesellschaft, the Reichssendeleiter and so on, cf. Pohle, *Rundfunk*; Wulf, *Presse und Funk*; Bramsted, *Goebbels*, 54.

[38] Müller, *Reichsministerium*, 22; Hadamowsky, *Rundfunk im Dienste der Volksführung*. Similarly, Otto Dietrich, the Reich press chief, called the press department of the propaganda ministry the 'general staff of the German press'. See Sänger, *Politik der Täuschungen*, 275.

[39] Details in Hale, *Press*, 3, 143 ff; also Koszyk, *Sozialdemokratische Presse*, and id., *Deutsche Presse*.

[40] These acts of violence were legitimized *ex post facto* by the 'law on the confiscation of Communist property' of 26 May 1933 and the 'law on the confiscation of the property of enemies to the people and state' of 14 July 1933.

[41] Full title: Verein Deutscher Zeitungsverleger (VDZV).

[42] Details in Hale, *Press*, 80, 92–3, 111–12, 115 ff.

[43] Renamed Reichsverband der Deutschen Presse (RVDP).

[44] Cf. Abel, *Presselenkung*, 20 ff.; Bramsted, *Goebbels*, 44–5.

[45] The Rienhardt memorandum of 1935 is reprinted in Hale, *Press*, 154–5,

companies,[46] news agencies, and advertising firms, so that the Eher-Verlag (his original firm) in a few years became the largest economic enterprise in Germany.[47] By 1939 the NSDAP had achieved economic control of about two-thirds of all German newspapers.[48] About 2,000 papers remained in private hands, but these, like other organs of opinion, were closely supervised as regards content.

As the regimentation of newspapers became more thorough, their quality declined. Total circulation fell by about 10 per cent between 1933 and 1939, chiefly because many Germans found their uniform contents boring and repellent.[49] Later the regime created a weekly with more intellectual appeal entitled *Das Reich*,[50] which was intended to remedy the situation.

The third pillar of National Socialist propaganda and control was, as already mentioned, the Reich chamber of culture. This comprised subordinate chambers for each of the various branches of cultural life—the press, radio, theatre, films, music, literature, and the fine arts.[51] The division of functions was similar to that in the propaganda ministry.[52] The organization reflected the regime's intention to regiment all aspects of political and intellectual life, and to be seen to be doing so by means of an all-embracing, ever-present apparatus of control and propaganda. With the threefold system composed of the propaganda ministry, the propaganda department of the party, and the Reich chamber of culture, each with its subordinate bodies, public opinion was 'formed' by the Nazi dictatorship,[53] in other words artificially created in accordance with official directives.

Naturally, so widely ramified a system led to conflicts of authority.[54] Goebbels's ministry, for instance, competed for influence with the foreign ministry and with the ministry for science, education, and culture under Bernhard Rust. For years also Goebbels was at odds with Alfred Rosenberg, who at the beginning of 1934 was appointed to supervise all forms of ideological training within the party. Even within Goebbels's empire, e.g. in the press department, there prevailed a kind of 'planned chaos', a confusion of authority which was never quite resolved. This was exactly what Hitler wanted, as in other areas of command, since the 'divide and

---

[46] On economic concentration in the film industry cf. Becker, *Film*, 116 ff., 210 ff.

[47] The stages are described in Hale, *Press*, 136 ff.; tables showing the number and circulation of National Socialist papers, and the rise of the Eher-Verlag, in Koszyk, *Deutsche Presse*, 385 ff.

[48] According to Hale, *Press*, 257 ff.; Abel (*Presselenkung*, 67) even speaks of 70–80% of German newspapers being under the economic and personal control of the NSDAP.

[49] Cf. Hale, *Press*, 230–1; Abel, *Presselenkung*, 61 ff.

[50] This journal, planned by Rienhardt from 1937 onwards, first appeared in May 1940. Cf. Martens, *Das Reich*, and Abel, *Presselenkung*, 74 ff.

[51] For the functions of the chambers cf. Bramsted, *Goebbels*, 76–9. On the Reich film chamber and National Socialist film propaganda cf. Becker, *Film*.

[52] Cf. Bramsted, *Goebbels*, 61–71. The diagram showing the organization of the propaganda ministry is reproduced in Abel, *Presselenkung*, 110–21. Cf. also *Kriegspropaganda*, 120–90.

[53] Addressing foreign press correspondents on 6 Apr. 1934, Goebells said: 'Public opinion is not only a matter of atmosphere and feeling; it is largely the effect of deliberate influence . . . Public opinion can be created' (Goebbels, *Signale*, 128).

[54] Cf. Bollmus, *Amt Rosenberg*; Bramsted, *Goebbels*, 50 ff.; Abel, *Presselenkung*, 13 ff., 68 ff., 104; Hale, *Press*, 88 ff.

rule' system enhanced his own absolute authority.[55] It was part of his technique not to define duties with precision, and the conflicts that resulted should not be given undue significance, still less interpreted as symptoms of resistance to the regime.[56]

The success of the policy of ideological *Gleichschaltung* was due in part to the readiness with which many bourgeois intellectuals toed the line, and the determination with which the regime pursued its aim while taking care to preserve a semblance of legality. It was also due to the fact that Goebbels's ministry began its work not only with the enthusiasm of novelty but also with a well-qualified staff. The Nazi propagandists who entered government service in this way were on the average about ten years younger than the party élite as a whole.

They came from the upper middle class of imperial (and Weimar) Germany. The percentage of their fathers in occupations enjoying a top prestige in imperial Germany, such as landowners and holders of military and ecclesiastical posts, was higher than that of other Nazi groups analyzed. The educational level attained by the future propagandists was high too. More than half of them had attended a university. . . . Many of them had served as officers in the First World War and subsequently found it difficult to obtain employment in post-war Germany.[27]

In other words, the Nazi propagandists belonged to the class of former front-line soldiers and out-of-work intellectuals who had suffered especially from their loss of social status in the 1920s and attached themselves to the NSDAP as the most radical and militant of the right-wing groups.

Emergency decrees, the enabling law of March 1933, the law establishing the Reich chamber of culture, and the press law of October 1933 provided the legal façade for the supervision and control of public opinion. The organizational back-up consisted of several competing agencies. Gradually all non-Nazi publishing firms and professional organizations were forced into line, a huge press trust was created, and the broadcasting system was taken completely under control. At a daily press conference in the propaganda ministry[58] detailed instructions were given concerning the treatment of issues by all media, the themes to be emphasized, and the language to be employed. Thus, organizational, material, personal, and technical conditions were created for the comprehensive manipulation of opinion, so that the public 'responded more or less automatically to the changing appeals and directives'.[59] Compared to other areas of government activity, in which *ad hoc* decisions were the rule, the centralized propaganda apparatus under Goebbels functioned very successfully in the ensuing years. True, there were conflicts of authority here as in other institutions, especially at lower levels, but the government was able at all times to assert its propaganda line effectively.

[55] Cf. Broszat, *The Hitler State*; Diehl-Thiele, *Partei und Staat*; Hüttenberger, *Gauleiter*; id., 'Polykratie'; Bollmus, *Amt Rosenberg*.

[56] Bracher, *Dictatorship*, 341–2.

[57] Bramsted, *Goebbels*, 57–8.

[58] On the press conferences cf. Sänger, *Politik der Täuschungen*; Abel, *Presselenkung*, 37 ff.; Bramsted, *Goebbels*, 88–9; *Kriegspropaganda*, 26–48.

[59] Bramsted, *Goebbels*, 455.

3. THE POLICY OF DECEPTION: HITLER'S AND GOEBBELS'S 'PEACE SPEECHES',
1933–1936

In the years before 1933 National Socialist propaganda had proved itself one of the most effective ways of conquering power by mobilizing mass opinion. After Hitler became chancellor it acquired a double function. In the first place it had to assist in building up the system of totalitarian rule. For this purpose the increasing power of the state, the party, the Führer, the armed forces, and the Gestapo had to be loudly proclaimed and hammered into the consciousness of every citizen. Secondly, the material and organizational preparations for war had at first to be completely concealed from foreign countries and also from most of the German public, or, when this was no longer possible, played down as simply defensive in character. In performing these tasks Nazi propaganda functioned above all as a means of concealment and intimidation. The transmission of ideology was of secondary importance. 'Public enlightenment' was never a matter of straightforward information. What Hitler, Goebbels, and the German propaganda agencies carried on systematically in 1933–9 is seen in retrospect to have been one single campaign of deception on a massive scale, with the chief propagandists of the regime writing and speaking as if they were the leading spirits of organized pacifism in Germany.

Only a few days after forming his government, Hitler held a secret meeting with the Reichswehr commanders[60] at which he announced his war policy in unmistakable terms and set in motion the necessary rearmament measures.[61] Then and afterwards, nothing was more often emphasized in public speeches than the firmly peaceful intentions of the new rulers. Assurances of peace for all time were the stock-in-trade of National Socialist propaganda until 1939. However, from about 1936 onwards, as the party consolidated its power on the home front, these protestations were more and more often coupled with verbal sabre-rattling. In the first years of Nazi rule, when secret rearmament was in progress, the regime generally abstained from threatening gestures and confined itself to glorifying old-style conservative and nationalist virtues that were now part of the state ideology: generosity, heroism, manliness, self-sacrifice, discipline, team spirit, ardent devotion to the state and to the national cause.

Goebbels was later to preen himself on the success of the deceptive propaganda thanks to which the Nazi regime had built up its power without interference from abroad. In the spring of 1940 he declared in retrospect:

We have managed up till now to keep our opponents guessing as to Germany's real aims, just as our opponents on the home front up till 1932 had no idea what we were aiming at. They didn't realize that when we vowed to stick to legal methods it was just a trick—we wanted to acquire power legally, but not to use it legally . . . After all, they might have throttled us . . . As it was, they let us get through the danger zone. It was just the same in foreign affairs . . . In 1933 a French prime minister ought to have said—and I would have done, if I had been the French prime minister—'The man who has become German chancellor is the man who

---

[60] Transcript of Hitler's speech in Jacobsen, *1939–1945*, 95–6; repr. in Vogelsang, *Reichswehr*; trans. in *Documents on Nazism*, 508–9.   [61] For details see Deist, III.II below.

wrote *Mein Kampf*, in which he says such and such things. This man cannot be tolerated in our neighbourhood. Either he goes, or we shall march in.' That would have been quite logical, but they didn't do it. They let us alone, we got through the danger zone without let or hindrance, we skated round all the dangers, and then—when we were ready, well armed, better than they—they chose that time to start the war!'[62]

Apart from the statement that it was the other side who started the war, this summing-up by Goebbels is quite correct. If the regime was able to get through the 'danger zone', in other words the first phase of remilitarization—first clandestine, then open rearmament—it was in large measure due to the skilful propaganda which at that stage dealt mainly in slogans that had been popular with the whole of the political right wing in Weimar days,[63] such as 'equal rights' (*Gleichberechtigung*) and the revision of Versailles. The object was to give the impression to foreigners and Germans alike that the regime had no other intention in foreign affairs than to continue the moderate policy of peaceful revision as pursued by the Weimar governments.

One of the standard themes of propaganda that recurred with only slight variations in 1933–6 was the assertion that Nazi Germany sincerely desired peace. Hitler himself inaugurated the peace offensive in his first broadcast on 1 February 1933, when he read out his 'Proclamation of the Government to the German People'. This stated that the national government were 'impressed with the importance of their duty to take part in securing and maintaining that peace which the world needs today more than ever before'.[64] A day or two later, in an interview with British and American journalists, Hitler declared that he had often been misrepresented as making 'bloodthirsty and firebrand speeches against foreign countries', but that anyone who, like him, had experience of war knew what a waste of resources it involved. Accordingly, 'nobody wanted peace and tranquillity more than himself and Germany'.[65] The reference to the First World War, and the theme that no one who had fought in it wanted to repeat the experience, were seldom absent from Hitler's later 'peace speeches'.[66]

In his speech to the Reichstag on the enabling law on 23 March 1933 Hitler again emphasized that the German people wished to live at peace with the world and 'to extend a hand in sincere understanding to every nation'.[67] In a Reichstag speech on

---

[62] n. 6 above.

[63] The continuity of slogans and objectives is stressed in Bloch, *Hitler*, ch. 1. Wollstein, *Revisionismus*, is less informative. A division of functions between the foreign ministry and the propaganda ministry with regard to propaganda in foreign countries was agreed as early as 24 May 1933: see *DGFP*, c. i. No. 261, pp. 483 ff.

[64] Domarus, i. 191–4, here 193 = Baynes, ii. 1001–2. On peaceful protestations see also Hagemann, *Publizistik*, 211 ff.

[65] Domarus, i. 199–200 = Baynes, ii. 1003.

[66] Cf. e.g. Hitler's speech at the opening of the Reichstag session at Potsdam on 21 Mar. 1933 (Domarus, i. 228 = Baynes, ii. 1014); his interview with the *Daily Telegraph* correspondent on 2 May 1933 (Domarus, i. 265; cf. Baynes, ii. 1085); his speech at Munich on 9 Nov. 1933 commemorating the *putsch* of Nov. 1923 (Domarus, i. 328 = Baynes, ii. 1137); and his interview with the British correspondent Ward Price on 5 Aug. 1934 (Domarus, i. 432 = Baynes, ii. 1181).

[67] Domarus, i. 235; cf. Baynes, ii. 1017.

foreign policy on 17 May 1933, which was extolled by propaganda as a great *Friedensrede* (peace stand) and published in several languages,[68] he declared that a new war would be 'utter madness' and would only increase the imbalance in Europe, and that the German government 'earnestly desired to prevent such a development by means of honest and active co-operation'.[69] Goebbels backed this up with a broadcast stating that Hitler had many times solemnly proclaimed that the German government and people had no more earnest wish than to go about their work and earn their daily bread in peace with themselves and their neighbours.[70]

In September 1933 Goebbels appeared in Geneva during the League of Nations conference on disarmament. Addressing representatives of the international press in very moderate terms on 'National Socialist Germany and its responsibility for peace', he again expressed regret that Nazi policy in the past months had met with 'lack of understanding, mistrust, and even opposition' in foreign countries.[71] It was absurd, he declared to assert that the new Germany was getting ready to pursue a policy of expansion by force. German foreign policy had nothing to do with ideas of war and *revanche*. It would be a good thing, he believed, if these two words could be expunged from the international vocabulary. Germany needed a solution to the economic crisis more than any other country, and it was simply unfair to accuse the German government of wanting war when its whole constructive work was 'imbued with the spirit of peace'.[72]

A few weeks later, on 14 October 1933, Hitler announced his decision to withdraw from the disarmament conference and from the League of Nations. At the same time Goebbels held a press conference at which he read out Hitler's Proclamation to the German People, reiterating his 'policy of sincere love for peace and readiness to reach an understanding'.[73] Also on 14 October, Hitler, evidently anxious to allay foreign suspicions, made a broadcast in which he again scouted the idea of war.[74] However, at an internal meeting on the 18th he recognized the danger that France might react to Germany's withdrawal from the League by at least re-occupying the Rhineland; it was therefore important that German propaganda should avoid 'the slightest suggestion of chauvinism or the spirit of *revanche*'.[75]

During 1933 Hitler gave several interviews to sympathetic foreign journalists[76] on the theme that he felt insulted by continued allegations that he wanted war. In his New Year proclamation of 1 January 1934 and his Reichstag speech on 30 January

---

[68] e.g. the pamphlets *Das junge Deutschland will Arbeit und Frieden* (1933; published in German, Dutch, English, French, Norwegian, Portuguese, and Spanish); Hitler, *Reden für Gleichberechtigung und Frieden* (1934); id., *Deutschland will Frieden und Gleichberechtigung* (1934); *Die Reden Hitlers als Kanzler* (1934); Hitler, *Frieden und Sicherheit* (1933); *Des Führers Kampf um den Weltfrieden* (1936). Cf. also Hadamowsky, *Hitler kämpft um den Frieden Europas* (1936).

[69] Domarus, i. 273 = Baynes, ii. 1046.

[70] 'Volk an die Arbeit', broadcast by Goebbels, 17 July 1933, in id., *Signale*, 185.

[71] Goebbels, *Signale*, 234.   [72] Ibid. 245 ff.

[73] Domarus, i. 306–7 = Baynes, ii. 1089.

[74] Hitler's broadcast of 14 Oct. 1933, in Domarus, i. 314 = Baynes, ii. 1103.

[75] Domarus, i. 317.

[76] Cf. ibid. 319, 332–3 = Baynes, ii. 1105, 1147.

1934 he again professed Germany's desire for peace, this time emphasizing her relations with Russia and Poland.[77] The German–Polish non-aggression treaty of 26 January 1934 did in fact improve relations between the two countries, which had been far from cordial, and until 1938 it was regarded in foreign countries as a hopeful sign.[78] Peaceful protestations again accompanied Hitler's dramatic moves in 1935: the announcement on 9 March of the creation of the Luftwaffe, and on 16 March the introduction of universal conscription. The line was that these were purely defensive measures and that peace was still 'the profoundest and most sincere wish of the German people'.[79] In the new law the title of 'defence minister' had been altered to 'war minister', and Hitler accordingly thought it necessary to make another 'peace speech' in the Reichstag on 21 May 1935. In this he sought to palliate the adverse effect of the law by declaring that National Socialist Germany wanted peace 'because of its most fundamental convictions', and that 'the restoration of the German defence force [would] contribute to this peace'.[80]

Another standard theme of Nazi propaganda was anti-Bolshevism, with which Hitler had already made play in his address to the Industrialists' Club at Düsseldorf on 27 January 1932. On that occasion he stated that 'But for us, already today there would be no more bourgeoisie alive in Germany; the question "Bolshevism or not Bolshevism" would long ago have been decided.'[81] From then onwards Hitler and his propagandists continued to exploit this cliché to the effect that the only alternative to Bolshevism was nationalism (or National Socialism), and that the former stood for chaos, 'red terror', collapse of the German economy and of the Western world, and so on.

This 'bulwark' thesis[82]—the claim to have saved Germany and Europe from Bolshevism and defended 'Western civilization'—was repeated incessantly by Nazi propaganda in the pre-war years. To begin with it accompanied the persecution of Communists, socialists, trade-unionists, and other opponents of the regime within Germany's frontiers. Between 1933 and 1935–6 the Nazi leaders liked to emphasize that anti-Bolshevism at home in no way prevented friendly relations with the one country governed by a Bolshevik regime, namely the Soviet Union.[83] During that period the business of anti-Soviet propaganda was left to an ostensibly private organization, the Gesamtverband deutscher antikommunistischer Vereinigungen, later known as the 'anti-Comintern'.[84] This two-pronged policy *vis-à-vis* the Soviet Union was given up around the time of the outbreak of the Spanish civil war. At the party rally in September 1935 Goebbels spoke of Germany's 'world mission' to

[77] Domarus, i. 357 = Baynes, ii. 1161 ff.
[78] Broszat, *Polenpolitik*, 188–91. On the German–Polish non-aggression pact of 1934 see also Messerschmidt, IV.II.I and esp. IV.III.I (a) below.
[79] Domarus, i. 476 = Baynes, ii. 1198
[80] Domarus, i. 506, 514 = Baynes, ii. 1220, 1246.
[81] Domarus, i. 86–7 = Baynes, i. 822; on anti-Bolshevik propaganda in general cf. Sywottek, *Mobilmachung*, 104 ff.
[82] Bracher, *Dictatorship*, 395–6.
[83] Cf. e.g. Hitler's Reichstag speeches of 23 Mar. 1933 (Domarus, i. 236 = Baynes, ii. 1019) and 7 Mar. 1936 (Domarus, i. 587 = Baynes, ii. 1281).
[84] Cf. Sywottek, *Mobilmachung*, 105–6; also Messerschmidt, II.v.6 below.

combat Bolshevism,[85] while at the 1936 rally Bolshevism was denounced as a constant menace out to destroy Europe and the world.[86] On such occasions the Soviet Union was represented as the breeding-ground and stronghold of every imaginable cruelty, inhumanity, brutality, injustice, deceit, and barbarism.[87] During the Spanish civil war (1936–9) the whole of this anti-Bolshevik vocabulary was applied to all supporters of the Spanish republic, who were indiscriminately denounced as 'Marxists', 'Bolsheviks', 'Marxist bandits and incendiaries', or 'Bolshevik murder gangs'. The Spanish republican government were called the 'Soviet rulers', the territory controlled by them was 'Soviet Spain', and the civil war itself figured in Nazi propaganda as 'Soviet Russia's war'.[88]

To anticipate a little, it may be noted here that after the conclusion of the Hitler–Stalin pact of 23 August 1939, whereby the ideological arch-enemies agreed on a division of booty in Eastern Europe, the Nazi anti-Bolshevik campaign was suspended until the invasion of the Soviet Union. The fact that it was possible thus to switch it off for a limited period shows to what extent anti-Bolshevism was a propaganda ploy that could be used for quite different ends according to circumstances.

Another standard theme was the assertion that the German government stood firmly for disarmament and arms control and was at all times ready to conclude non-aggression pacts. The call for disarmament was, however, in fact addressed exclusively to the rest of Europe: Germany, it was claimed, had long since disarmed in accordance with the treaty of Versailles, and had been waiting for years for other states to disarm as they had promised.[89] The complaint that one-sided disarmament was unjust and that others must disarm to Germany's level was cultivated in advance as a pretext for Hitler's withdrawal from the disarmament conference and the League of Nations.

The demand for equal rights for Germany—a propaganda theme second in frequency only to Hitler's protestations of peace—appealed to an irrational sense of injury that was certainly felt by the German people at large. Its main practical thrust, however, was in relation to armaments, as was openly admitted. Thus, Hitler in his 'peace speech' of 17 May 1933 emphasized that Germany demanded 'genuine equality of rights in the sense of the disarmament of other nations'; adding immediately, however, that if other states were not prepared to disarm, Germany must still maintain her claim to equality[90]—in other words, to rearm to their level. Goebbels combined the two main propaganda themes in the concise formula that Germany was 'fighting for peace and equal rights'.[91]

---

[85] *Parteitag der Freiheit 1935*, p. 126.

[86] Goebbels, 'Der Bolschewismus in Theorie und Praxis', in *Parteitag der Ehre 1936*, 97–124, here 103.

[87] Sywottek, *Mobilmachung*, 107.

[88] Ibid. 115. On the Spanish civil war see Messerschmidt, IV.v.2 below.

[89] Cf. Hitler's Reichstag speech of 23 Mar. 1933 (Domarus, i. 234 = Baynes, ii. 1018) and Goebbels's Sportpalast speech on 20 Oct. 1933, in *Signale*, 270–1.

[90] Domarus, i. 274, 276 = Baynes, ii. 1049, 1052.

[91] Goebbels, *Signale*, 250 ff.; cf. also the titles in n. 68 above, where the terms 'peace' and 'equal rights' are reiterated.

Naturally, this scarcely veiled announcement of an intent to rearm was linked with the statement that Germany had nothing in mind but her national security and was far from harbouring any aggressive ambitions. Her sole desire was 'to be able to preserve her independence and defend her frontiers'.[92] In October 1933, when the British correspondent Ward Price pointed out to Hitler that a large proportion of Germany's young men were receiving military training in labour camps or as members of the SA and other institutions, and that people in Britain and France were alarmed lest these youths should one day be tempted to put their military skills to practical use, Hitler would not hear of such arguments.[93] In August 1934—only six months before the announcement that Germany once more possessed an air force, which was a clear breach of the treaty of Versailles—Hitler indirectly admitted to the same journalist that Germany was building up a large air force, but at once added the standard reference to 'Germany's measures of self-defence'.[94] The same argument was used to justify the reintroduction of universal conscription. According to a government statement of 16 March 1935,[95] this was intended 'to bring to an end the unworthy and in the last resort menacing state of powerless defensiveness' of the Reich and to increase its security. German rearmament was purely defensive and thus served to maintain peace.

Another standard propaganda theme was the peaceful revision of the treaty of Versailles. The principle of nationality was usually invoked in this context. The Versailles system, it was declared, had not succeeded in drawing frontiers in accordance with ethnic boundaries, and it was in everyone's interest to solve these problems reasonably once and for all.[96] Germany wanted treaty revision, but only by peaceful means. When Hitler declared that 'National Socialism knows no policy of correcting frontiers at the expense of foreign peoples',[97] he was careful to leave open the possibility that they might be corrected at the expense of foreign states. However, his propaganda continued to insist that it was Germany's wish 'to consider and solve all outstanding questions dispassionately by way of negotiation'.[98]

One of the most ambiguous slogans, and hence the most useful for deception purposes, was that concerning the restoration of Germany's 'honour'. This was used to comprise everything that was considered slanderous in the Versailles treaty and its consequences: the 'war-guilt lie', reparations, arms limitations, and so on.[99] Thus, Nazi propaganda claimed that Germany's 'defenceless' state was unworthy and dishonouring. Hitler and Goebbels, with their keen sense of atmosphere, knew

[92] Thus Hitler in his Reichstag speech of 17 May 1933 (Domarus, i. 276 ff. = Baynes, ii. 1052 ff.); and Goebbels in Geneva on 28 Sept. 1933, in *Signale*, 246.

[93] Domarus, i. 321; cf. Baynes, ii. 1105.

[94] Domarus, i. 433 = Baynes, ii. 1182. Göring, the Reich air minister, spoke similarly to Ward Price on 11 Mar. 1935: see *Dokumente der deutschen Politik*, iv. 214-15.

[95] Domarus, i. 494-5 = Baynes, ii. 1208 ff.

[96] Cf. Hitler's 'peach speech' of 17 May 1933: Domarus, i. 271 ff. = Baynes, ii. 1041 ff.

[97] Hitler's broadcast of 27 May 1933 prior to the Danzig election: Domarus, i. 279 = Baynes, ii. 1061.

[98] Proclamation to the German people, 15 Oct. 1933: Domarus. i. 307 = Baynes, ii. 1091.

[99] Cf. Goebbels's speech of 28 Sept. 1933, in *Signale*, 264; and Hitler's speech of 14 Oct. 1933 (Domarus, i. 306 = Baynes, ii. 1089).

how to strike an injured note when these supposedly sensitive questions of German honour came on the *tapis*. The linked ideas of peace, honour, and equal rights were a cloak for peace propaganda directed at foreign countries, while at home they were used to justify rearmament and the expansion of Nazi power.

Nazi propaganda admitted with remarkable frankness that the establishment of an authoritarian system—officially called the 'restoration of stability in home affairs'—was not an end in itself but merely the basis for a dynamic foreign policy.[100] Goebbels, for instance, in his Sportpalast speech on 7 November 1933[101] declared that the government was well aware that the great issues between Germany and the rest of the world could only be tackled when Germany had once more achieved inner security and unity; consequently, the fight to achieve these aims was a matter of foreign policy as well as home policy. 'True, we did not speak of foreign policy, but we always meant it. We intended to broach foreign problems as soon as we could be sure of having a united and determined people behind us.' In the previous six months this had not been lost sight of for a moment.

When we did away with parties, when we passed the law setting up Reich governors so that Germany was no longer a clutter of small states, when we overthrew Communism and restored unanimity of national sentiment (*Einheit des Volksdenkens*), it was not simply because we desired all this from the domestic point of view. No, it was because we knew that the moment would soon come when we would have to call upon the whole nation, and when we need the confidence of the whole nation over some foreign issue there must be no parties or organizations or local interests to which the world might appeal against us. So it was all done according to a plan,[102] bit by bit, one stroke after another. In the first month we overthrew Communism, in the second we eradicated it completely; the parties were eliminated in the third and fourth months, and the parliamentary system in the fifth.

This was how the German people had regained its 'internal security'.

Thus, the standard themes of National Socialist propaganda in 1933–6 were peace, anti-Bolshevism, disarmament, equal rights, internal and external security, peaceful treaty revision, and the nationality principle, Germany's national honour, and stability in home affairs. All these were popular themes and, as far as the verbal assurances of the new rulers went, they could quite well be interpreted as a continuation of Weimar policies.

The Nazis' anti-Bolshevik propaganda, which did good service in consolidating their rule at home,[103] was directly related to the version of anti-Bolshevism that had prevailed among the right-wing parties in Weimar days. It was characteristic of this version that it did not make clear at first sight what exactly was meant by 'Bolshevism'. When the nationalist right inveighed against the 'Bolshevik danger' this did not imply, first and foremost, any concrete military or revolutionary threat

---

[100] Cf. Hitler's address to the Industrialists' Club on 27 Jan. 1932 (Domarus, i. 86 ff. = Baynes, i. 822 ff.), and his speech on the enabling law (Domarus, i. 235 = Baynes, ii. 1016–18).

[101] Defending Germany's withdrawal from the League of Nations and the disarmament conference; cf. *Signale*, 282, 301.

[102] The reference to a 'plan' was mere propaganda.

[103] See I.III.I below.

from the Soviet Union or the German Communists. It referred rather to a largely irrational picture, based vaguely on historical experience, in which domestic and foreign attributes of the enemy were inextricably mingled. The smear-word *Kulturbolschewismus* (cultural Bolshevism), current in Weimar days, did not relate to Soviet Russian culture or that of German Communists; in nationalist eyes it was the entire cultural scene of the republic that deserved to be stigmatized as 'Bolshevik'. It was typical of the vague lineaments of the Bolshevik bogy that the Stahlhelm national executive, on the occasion of the tenth ex-servicemen's rally in Munich at the beginning of June 1929, proclaimed that the veterans' movement had 'for years been carrying on the fight against Bolshevism at home and abroad'.[104] Similarly, Hugenberg, chairman of the National People's Party (DNVP), addressing the Harzburg rally on 11 October 1931, declared on behalf of the whole 'national opposition' that 'our country must be preserved from the chaos of Bolshevism' by the establishment of 'governments under national leadership' in Prussia and in the Reich.[105] Again, in October 1930 the Stahlhelm demanded that the social democratic Prussian government under Braun and Severing be swept away as a 'barren Marxist dictatorship'.[106] These expressions show clearly that the terms 'Bolshevism', 'Communism', and 'Marxism' were used indiscriminately in nationalist propaganda during the Weimar years, to denigrate not only the Communist Party but the social democrats and the trade unions, and indeed from time to time the Centre party and the Democrats also.

Against this background it can be understood that the anti-Bolshevik propaganda of the National Socialist regime made an impression on the German bourgeoisie and that of foreign countries. Above all, the petty bourgeoisie, who had been accustomed since the Kaiser's time to fear the 'red' international as the real threat to their material and social well-being, believed the claim that the Nazi party was the only alternative to Bolshevism and was, if only for that reason, legitimized by history. The integrative effect on German society of such propaganda, with an appeal dating back decades, is not to be underrated.

As regards continuity in foreign policy,[107] or rather in its propaganda aspect, it should be noted here that the social democratic party in the Reichstag made no objection to Hitler's intentions as he outlined them in 1933. In a speech on the enabling bill, which the SPD opposed on grounds of home policy, their spokesman Otto Wels declared: 'As to the Chancellor's demand for equal rights in foreign affairs, we social democrats support it all the more firmly since we have at all times fought for it as a matter of principle.'[108] The principal liberal newspaper of the Weimar period—the *Frankfurter Zeitung*, which was still largely untouched by Nazi regimentation[109]—also supported the new regime's foreign-policy line, as for the

---

[104] *Schulthess 1929*, 86.

[105] The resolution moved by Hugenberg for the 'national opposition' is reproduced in *Schulthess 1931*, 225. [106] See *Schulthess 1930*, 200.

[107] On continuity in foreign policy and the execution of Hitler's 'peace policy' see Messerschmidt, IV.I.5 below. [108] Domarus, i. 239.

[109] Cf. Bramsted, *Goebbels*, ch. 5, 'The Strange Case of the *Frankfurter Zeitung*', esp. 126–7 and 135 ff. As regards the paper's chief editor, Rudolf Kircher, cf. also Sänger, *Politik der Täuschungen*, 175–6.

first four or five years of his rule Hitler gave the impression of being an advocate of peace in Europe. When bourgeois-liberal journalists declared that the nation was convinced of the government's sincere desire for peace and understanding they rendered a signal service to the regime, especially as the *Frankfurter Zeitung* was known to be taken seriously in foreign countries, whereas the Nazi-controlled press was not.

4. THE ROLE OF THE ARMED FORCES IN PSYCHOLOGICAL PREPARATION FOR WAR

On 3 February 1933, a few days after he became chancellor, Hitler held his first meeting with senior Reichswehr commanders.[110] He sought an alliance with the military leaders, knowing that he could not assert his own rule without their support. But in addition to an alliance for domestic purposes with those who held a monopoly of armed force, the purpose of the meeting was to initiate the policy of preparation for war.

In his address Hitler disclosed far-reaching war plans with very little concealment—'the conquest of new *Lebensraum* in the east, and its ruthless Germanization'—and described the internal measures that were required by way of preparation. Young people were to be hardened and their military spirit encouraged by all possible means. The whole nation, young and old, was to be imbued with the idea that Germany could only be saved in battle. No pacifist ideas would be tolerated; the armed forces were to be built up, and universal conscription reintroduced.

The prospect of psychological, material, and personal remilitarization was so much in the interest of the Reichswehr leaders that Hitler could be sure of their active support. Blomberg, the new defence minister, no doubt spoke for all of them on 3 February 1933 when he stated that Hitler's government was 'the realization of what many of the best of us have desired for years', offering a basis for the 'militarization of the nation as a whole'.[111] The programme of rearmament and remilitarization embodied an identity of interests between the National Socialist government and the army,[112] which was to prove in subsequent years an important element of stability for the regime.

In proclaiming the strengthening of the military spirit as the main educative purpose of his government Hitler gave satisfaction to a demand that the army leaders had been pressing on the Weimar governments unsuccessfully for ten years and more. The military regarded the need for more effective 'psychological mobilization' as proved by the experience of the First World War[113] and especially its conclusion, which they chose not to regard as a military defeat but as due primarily to non-military causes.

---

[110] See n. 60 above.   [111] Vogelsang, 'Dokumente', 432–3.
[112] Cf. Müller, *Heer*, 34, 37 ff., 43, 66; Hüttenberger, 'Polykratie', 423 ff., also Deist, Part III below. Messerschmidt, in *Wehrmacht*, I and *passim*, speaks of a 'partial identity of aims' between the *Reichswehr* and the NSDAP.   [113] See esp. Sywottek, *Mobilmachung*, 13 ff.

General Ludendorff and Grand Admiral von Tirpitz had stated in their war memoirs, as early as 1919, that the civil government had not succeeded in arousing the German people's will to victory, and that this had been a main cause of Germany's defeat.[114] Then in the first half of the 1920s a number of influential nationalist military writers—including the retired General Friedrich von Bernhardi and the army officers Kurt Hesse and George Soldan[115]—studied the propaganda policy of the First World War in order to draw lessons for the next. Their main conclusion was that propaganda must be used to prepare the German people thoroughly for a future war, and that in the war itself greater importance must be attached to propaganda than in the past. After the experience of 1914–18 the next war could hardly be envisaged as anything but a total conflict,[116] in which 'psychological warfare' might even be the deciding factor. Consequently, psychological mobilization was of no less importance than personal and material preparation for war.

The defence ministry itself was at that time similarly concerned with the problem of propaganda in and before a future war. Given the severe restrictions imposed by the treaty of Versailles on personal and material armament, psychological preparation for war seemed a fruitful and reliable sphere of activity, especially when cloaked in innocent-sounding terms such as 'strengthening the defensive spirit' or 'fostering defensive attitudes'. There is no doubt that the defence ministry took it for granted that a new war was inevitable and required that the population be prepared for it 'mentally and psychologically' (*geistig und seelisch*) by means of planned propaganda.[117] In March 1924 a ministry 'memorandum on psychological preparation for war'[118] complained that the republican governments were evidently incapable of 'preparing the nation mentally for war' (*das Volk geistig auf den Krieg einzustellen*). The task must therefore be undertaken single-handed for the time being by the Wehrmacht as the body 'responsible for the military idea (*Wehrgedanke*) and for future mobilization', with assistance from 'rightist circles, the patriotic associations and organizations of the old army, which conduct propaganda by word and deed for the military idea'. At the same time a sharp struggle must be waged against the opponents of war, who saw a warmonger underneath every uniform and in everyone who stood up for the military idea. This was necessary if only for the sake of 'self-preservation'. In addition it was necessary to gain the confidence of sections of the population that were as yet lukewarm in military matters, since, according to the theory of total war, it could not be waged

---

[114] Ludendorff, *War Memories*, 361, 367–9, 382–3; Tirpitz, *Memoirs*, 321 ff. For a critique of these assertions cf. Fraser, *Germany*, 3–28.

[115] Bernhardi, *Vom Kriege der Zukunft* (1920; trans. = *The War of the Future*); Hesse, *Feldherr Psychologos* (1922); id., *Persönlichkeit und Masse* (1933); Soldan, Der *Mensch und die Schlacht der Zukunft* (1925); in detail Sywottek, *Mobilmachung*, 14 ff.

[116] On the theory of total war cf. Kernig, 'Krieg', in *Sowjetsystem*, iii. 1066 ff., esp. 1079–80; also Wehler, '"Absoluter" und "totaler" Krieg', and Senghaas, *Abschreckung*, 40 ff.

[117] Cf. Reichswehrministerium, Zentralabteilung, No. 342/23 I (1923), in BA-MA RW 6/v. 37 (previously OKW/2377).

[118] Reichswehrministerium, No. 266/24. II z. of March 1924; 'Denkschrift über die geistige Kriegsvorbereitung des Volkes', ibid.

without their willing co-operation. Finally, the memorandum enumerated arguments by means of which the ground could be made ready for the 'psychological preparation of the whole nation' for war.

As can be seen from the criticism of republican governments which the Reichswehr disapproved of as unsound in defence matters, or even pacifist, the army's idea of psychological mobilization was implicitly hostile to the parliamentary system and the political parties on which it rested. In the first half of the 1920s the Reichswehr was only prepared to co-operate with the government of the day on condition that the latter did something for national defence. Not until about 1925 did the army begin to see that there was no foreseeable prospect of treaty revision by force of arms, and to give up Seeckt's idea of an early return to great-power ambitions.[119] Then, however, the years of economic and political crisis after 1929 opened up new possibilities of psychological mobilization. Senior Reichswehr officers turned increasingly to ideas of the militarization of society as a whole,[120] demanding that the whole population be organized in peacetime in full and permanent readiness for war.

Some attempts to realize this idea were made in the last days of the republic. A presidential decree of 13 September 1932 set up the Reichskuratorium für Jugendertüchtigung (Reich Institute for the Training of Young Men)[121] with the object of bringing together the different defence associations under state supervision. Thus, the military leaders were able to influence pre-military training as they desired. General von Schleicher, the defence minister in von Papen's government, emphasized to the chancellor in a letter of October 1932[122] that the task was to toughen up the whole of the rising generation for war. He called for the expansion of voluntary labour service, the 'integration of Prussian youth-training into the general plan for the training of young people', 'compulsory physical exercise in schools', the 'reorganization of the academic working year' and a number of other measures. The Hitler government was able to build on these theoretical and practical steps towards psychological mobilization, in the same way as on the rearmament and job-creation programmes initiated in the Weimar period.

The policy of psychological, material, and personal remilitarization which Hitler expounded to the Reichswehr commanders on 3 February 1933 precisely fitted the latter's ideas, as may be guessed from what we have said about their attitude in Weimar days. Clearly there was nothing original about Hitler's military programme or that of the NSDAP. It took up the theory of total war, already developed in military circles, and emphasized the importance of psychological and propaganda factors in preparing for and waging a future war. Like Ludendorff, Tirpitz, and other leading military officers and writers, Hitler saw it as the cardinal error of German statesmen in the First World War that their propaganda had not been

---

[119] Cf. Geyer, *Aufrüstung*, 25–64, and Deist, III.1.1 below.

[120] Hillgruber, 'Militarismus', 38 ff., based on Geyer, *Landesverteidigung*.

[121] On the Reichskuratorium für Jugendertüchtigung see Geyer, *Landesverteidigung*, 188 ff.; and, on its directives concerning defence-related sports, cf. Mägerlein, *Wehrsport* (1933).

[122] Der Reichswehrminister, No. 486/32 (secret), of 17 Oct. 1932; repr. in Schützle, *Reichswehr*, appendix, 1–3.

skilful or inspiring enough.[123] Constantin Hierl,[124] the NSDAP expert in military matters, was fully in accord with Reichswehr ideas when he declared at the party rally in 1929 that the 'coming war' would follow the trend towards total war and that accordingly economic and propaganda warfare would play a larger part than in the past.

Thus, the remilitarization programme was a joint responsibility of the nationalist right, the Reichswehr, and the NSDAP. The only change brought about by the formation of Hitler's government was to increase the chance of its being implemented. Whereas the Reichswehr in Weimar days had regarded itself as the sole legitimate 'upholder of the military idea and future mobilization', the government itself now took on the task of strengthening the warlike spirit, thus fulfilling the Reichswehr's demands of the past decade. In future the two authorities could share their activities on a basis of common interest. The practical effect was that Goebbels's apparatus looked after major propaganda campaigns, while the defence ministry (later the war ministry) concentrated on popularizing the armed forces and making organizational plans for future psychological warfare. In this sphere as in others there arose conflicts of authority, which Goebbels's ministry generally resolved in its own favour.[125]

On this basis the Wehrmacht was able to keep its own propaganda apparatus to a relatively modest scale.[126] The body initially responsible for such work was the press section of the defence minister's office. In 1938, when the high command was reorganized, this section was absorbed into the propaganda department of the Wehrmacht high command (OKW).[127] That department represented the army and navy, while the air ministry had a press section of its own.[128] The steady flow of propaganda directed at the public on behalf of the armed forces was co-ordinated, first and foremost, by a daily press conference at the propaganda ministry. There the Wehrmacht press officers, who attended along with those of other ministries, gave regular guidance on the treatment of military matters and those involving military policy. The general principle in such questions was that 'no information should be divulged with regard to internal political preparations for war, especially those involving the NSDAP'.[129] The war ministry, to improve its own image and promote the education of the whole nation in a military sense, began in November 1936 to publish an illustrated fortnightly journal, *Die Wehrmacht*,[130] 'to exert

[123] Sywottek, *Mobilmachung*, pp. xxv ff.

[124] Hierl, *Wehrpolitik*, 8 ff.; Hierl subsequently became Reichsarbeitsführer (head of the state labour service).

[125] Cf. *Kriegspropaganda*, 127 ff.; Messerschmidt, *Wehrmacht*, 239 ff.

[126] Sywottek, *Mobilmachung*, ch. on '"Propagandainstitutionen" der Wehrmacht', 36 ff., here 41; further details in Messerschmidt, 'Öffentlichkeitsarbeit'.

[127] Cf. Kaiser, 'Amtsgruppe Wehrmachtpropaganda', also *Kriegspropaganda*, 133 ff.; Wedel, *Propagandatruppen*, 153.

[128] On the latter's functions and methods cf. 'Anleitung für den Pressedienst. Geheim. Erlassen vom Reichsminister der Luftfahrt und Oberbefehlshaber der Luftwaffe' (Berlin, 1938).

[129] Press directive of 19 Jan. 1938; text in Sänger, *Politik der Täuschungen*, 163. Cf. also further press directives on military matters, ibid. 167, 270 ff.

[130] Cf. Sywottek, *Mobilmachung*, 38–9; Messerschmidt, *Wehrmacht*, 159. On the dispute whether *Die Wehrmacht* should be published by the NSDAP or the OKW cf. Hale, *Press*, 259 ff.: Amann,

authoritative influence on the formation of public opinion in all defence matters'. By the outbreak of war this journal had a circulation of 750,000, which suggests that it was not unsuccessful in its chief aim of increasing the popularity of the armed forces.[131]

The broadcasting system was of course also available for Wehrmacht propaganda. Here the content of bulletins was agreed between the OKW press department and the central broadcasting authority. The press department remained responsible for the 'supervision of literature relating to military policy or the military spirit',[132] with the result that everything published on defence policy showed features of warlike propaganda.[133] To increase the effect of such literature other institutions such as the Deutsche Arbeitsfront (DAF: German Labour Front) were associated with the distribution. Finally, military propaganda was carried on by Wehrmacht officers delivering a wide range of lectures in factories and labour-service camps. In the provinces this task fell to the press liaison officers of middle and lower commands, who in 1939 were rechristened Wehrmacht propaganda officers.

In addition to this propaganda, aimed at nation-wide psychological mobilization, from 1936 onwards the Wehrmacht set about preparing itself organizationally for psychological warfare.[134] Since the National Socialist leadership and the Wehrmacht were both convinced that in a future conflict the 'propaganda war' would be of equal importance to the 'armed struggle' and to 'economic warfare',[135] there was no dispute as to the need for special units; the only question was whether they should be set up under the propaganda or the war ministry. The solution adopted was that the Wehrmacht, aided by the Reich propaganda offices, set up Propaganda-Kompanien (PK: military units) with sections for war-reporting in word and picture, film and radio, and for loudspeaker propaganda; by the outbreak of war there were fifteen of these sections, while the propaganda ministry exerted influence in matters of staffing and propaganda content.[136] In the winter of 1938–9 Keitel and Goebbels reached an 'agreement on wartime propaganda'[137] providing that the propaganda ministry would be responsible for a future propaganda war. Thus, the Wehrmacht's psychological activity was incorporated in Goebbels's propaganda organization.[138]

In the first years of National Socialist rule the Wehrpolitisches Amt der NSDAP

---

representing the Eher-Verlag, finally won the day against Keitel (for the high command). Cf. also Murawski, *Press* (1937).

[131] 680,000 in July 1939; 1 million in Nov. 1939 (Hale, *Press*, 264; Sywottek, *Mobilmachung*, 38–9).

[132] Details in Sywottek, *Mobilmachung*, 39–40, and Messerschmidt, *Wehrmacht*, 148 ff.

[133] Cf. Scherke and Vitzthum, *Bibliographie der geistigen Kriegführung* (1938).

[134] Cf. Wedel, *Propagandatruppen* (Wedel rose to be major-general and head of the Amtsgruppe Wehrmachtpropaganda in the OKW); also Scheel, 'PK-Einheiten', 447 ff.

[135] Cf. Blau, *Propaganda* (1935), and id., *Geistige Kriegführung* (1937), by a specialist in the Psychologisches Laboratorium of the war ministry. Cf. also the study by the chief of staff of the OKW dated 19 Apr. 1938, on 'Die Kriegführung als Problem der Organisation', in *IMT* xxxviii. 35–50 (doc. 211–L).

[136] Scheel, 'PK-Einheiten', 499–55; *Kriegspropaganda*, 127 ff.; Wedel, *Propagandatruppen*, 18 ff.

[137] Wedel, *Propagandatruppen* 22–3; Messerschmidt, *Wehrmacht*, 241.

[138] Messerschmidt, *Wehrmacht*, 241–5; *Kriegspropaganda*, 128 ff.

(WPA: the Party's Combat Policy Office), directed by Epp and Haselmayr,[139] tried to assert its overriding authority in all matters of defence education and training. The defence ministry, however, objected to this intrusion into its monopoly of arms-bearing, and in March 1935 the WPA was dissolved. This was probably not a very hard decision for Hitler to take, as, apart from the propaganda and war ministries, there were numerous other institutions and organizations concerned with the 'remilitarization' of the German people.

One of these was the Deutsche Gesellschaft für Wehrpolitik und Wehr-wissenschaften (German Association for Military Policy and Military Sciences), under the retired General von Cochenhausen, a successor body to the Wehrwissenschaftliche Arbeitsgemeinschaft (Military Science Association) set up in 1929. The new association gradually developed into a contact-centre for all persons and institutions concerned with military science, policy and propaganda.[140] The universities and schools made their contribution to psychological rearmament, as did the Hitler Youth, the SA, the Reich labour service, and the Bund Deutscher Mädel (BDM: League of German Maidens).[141] The NSDAP itself was also active in the field of defence propaganda. The general picture is one of constant indoctrination of the German people with soldierly and heroic ideals, buttressed by a wide array of institutions.

The process of extolling military virtues was a basic feature of psychological mobilization in the pre-war years. Especially in the first years after 1933, the propaganda machine had a complex and contradictory task to perform. On the one hand, material rearmament had to be shielded from the attention of foreign countries by constant protestations of peace; but, on the other, the fighting spirit (*Wehrwille*) of the German population had to be awakened and strengthened.[142] This could not be done by openly aggressive propaganda, which would have deprived the 'peace offensive' of credibility. Hence, propaganda under Goebbels's direction took the form of preaching old-fashioned heroic and authoritarian ideals in somewhat general, emotional terms, avoiding the mention of specific targets of aggression. Typical of this policy were the films on military themes which were made from 1934 onwards with the object of increasing the army's popularity. By skilfully blending peaceful protestations with praise for military virtues, a favourable basis was created for the intended switch, in due course, to a more aggressive interpretation of the 'fighting spirit'.

In the year before the outbreak of war Goebbels again stepped up the theme of popularizing the Wehrmacht,[143] while in the forces themselves intensive measures

---

[139] Cf. Baum, 'Wehrpolitisches Amt'; Messerschmidt, *Wehrmacht*, 241.

[140] On the concept of 'military science' and the profusion of terms with the prefix 'Wehr' cf. Linnebach, *Wehrwissenschaften* (1939); also Binz, *Wehrgrundlagen* (1935); *Erziehung zum Wehrwillen* (1937); Messerschmidt, *Wehrmacht*, 166 ff.; Wohlfeil, 'Wehr-, Kriegs-, oder Militärgeschichte?'; Sywottek, *Mobilmachung*, 43 ff.

[141] Details in Sywottek, *Mobilmachung*, 32 ff., 45 ff., 73–91. On particular aspects: Dahle, *Einsatz einer Wissenschaft*; Geißler, *Dekadenz*; Stellrecht, *Soldatentum* (1935); Frank, *Kämpfende Wissenschaft* (1934); id., *Deutsche Wissenschaft und Judenfragen* (1937). Cf. also I.III.3 below.

[142] Cf. Sywottek, *Mobilmachung*, 49–63 ('Wehrpropaganda in der "Risikozone"').

[143] Cf. ibid. 166 ff.

were taken to prepare psychologically for the coming war of aggression. These measures showed once again that the propaganda of the political and military authorities was fully co-ordinated in every detail.[144] As an example we may cite a directive by Brauchitsch, the army commander-in-chief, concerning the language to be used by officers in orders of the day commemorating the twenty-fifth anniversary of the First World War at the beginning of August 1939.[145] According to this, the Third Reich was to be presented as the 'front-line soldiers' victory', a fulfilment of the legacy of the two million comrades who had given their lives in 1914–18. The 'misery of the "system"' was a thing of the past, and Germany had recovered her 'honour and freedom'. Political and military leaders were now 'inspired by a common ideology'. In direct reference to the impending war Brauchitsch, following a Goebbels directive, ordered that the present situation should be compared with that of 1914 as follows: 'Once again envy, discontent, and hatred are arrayed against Germany, once again the encirclers are at work.'[146] With this falsification of history the armed forces and the civil population were alike prepared for what was to come.

Even more than other aspects of National Socialist propaganda in the 1930s, military propaganda is to be regarded as an important link between the militarist and nationalist tendencies of the closing phase of the Weimar Republic, as described in Chapter I.1, and the aims of the Nazi regime. The propaganda carried on by the Wehrmacht made a substantial contribution to the psychological mobilization of the German population for the war unleashed in 1939.

5. From Peaceful Protestations to Sabre-rattling and the Advance Disclaiming of War-guilt, 1936–1939

National Socialist propaganda did not switch abruptly from the peace theme to massive threats of force or to anything that could be recognized as a direct preparation for war. The evolution took place, but it was skilfully spread over two or three years. From the spring of 1936 onwards hypocritical assurances of Germany's love of peace were combined with clear allusions to her recovered strength. In 1933–5 Goebbels's watchword had been 'We are not a sabre-rattling Germany';[147] but from 1936 onwards heed was paid to the maxim of the party's fighting days, that, to be effective, propaganda must be accompanied by a show of strength and by the actual use of force.[148] As German power increased, sabre-

---

[144] Cf. also I.II.5 below.

[145] The 'keywords' are reproduced as a document in Messerschmidt, *Wehrmacht*, 237.

[146] Ibid.; on encirclement propaganda cf. I.II.5 below.

[147] Goebbels, *Signale*, 270–1.

[148] Hadamowsky declared (*Propaganda*, 22) that propaganda and the use of force were 'never absolute opposites', but were complementary. Propaganda comprised 'all degrees of the effective influencing of individuals and masses—from the sudden arousal of attention and the amicable persuasion of an individual to the other extreme of loud mass propaganda; from the loose organization of what has been achieved to the creation of official or semi-official institutions, from individual acts of terror to mass terror, from the legitimate use of force by the stronger party . . . to the military enforcement of obedience and discipline under martial law.' Cf. also the summing-up of Nazi propaganda methods in Bramsted, *Goebbels*, 450.

rattling now became a regular feature of the regime's utterances. Even when propaganda was concerned with foreign affairs, it was always aimed at the German population as well, showing clearly the closeness with which home and foreign policy were mixed.

The Nazi regime's treaty violations and aggressive acts in 1936–9 followed a similar tactical pattern. First, the intended political aim was prepared for by propaganda; then a *fait accompli* was created by a swift military stroke. Then came assurances to alarmed foreign opinion that Germany had no further territorial claims and that the maintenance of peace continued to be its supreme object; but at the same time care was taken to point out that Germany had regained its military strength.

When, on 7 March 1936, German troops reoccupied the Rhineland,[149] which had been demilitarized by the treaty of Versailles, the effect of surprise was fully realized, especially as world opinion was then preoccupied by the Italo-Abyssinian war, while German military preparations had been of the utmost secrecy. After the *fait accompli* Hitler was at pains to assuage the anxiety expressed in protests received or expected from foreign countries.[150] He spoke of the German people's 'inborn love of peace' and described its alleged militarist intentions and 'latent desire for aggression' as a mere bogy, the product of 'fervid imagination'. To complete the lulling of foreign opinion and concealment of his designs he proceeded to put forward a seven-point programme of 'security for Europe', with every assurance of pacific intentions including the offer of a non-aggression pact. This move, of course, had no other purpose than to divert attention from the Rhineland coup.

The German press was instructed on 7 March to represent the occupation—which was a clear breach not only of Versailles but of the Locarno treaty of 16 October 1925—as a reply to the alleged violation of Locarno by the Franco-Soviet pact of May 1935 (in Nazi language the 'Russian pact'). Hitler now assured the rest of Europe that he had no territorial claims to put forward.[151] The German media were instructed not to use the term 'military action', as 'no fear of war must be allowed to arise'. The press must spread confidence, as the government would need the public's support for 'future actions'.[152] To secure popular endorsement of the Rhineland coup after it had taken place, Hitler ordered a general election, to be fought on the slogan of 'international peace, reconciliation, and understanding'. At the same time the press was instructed to avoid 'spineless liberalist pacifism' and to make it clear that Germany was an 'honour-loving people' that would not be done out of its rights, especially military ones.[153] On 28 March, on the eve of the election

---

[149] On the occupation of the Rhineland cf. Deist, III.II.2, and Messerschmidt, IV.v.1 below.

[150] Cf. Hitler's Reichstag speech of 7 Mar. 1936, in Domarus, i. 583, 585, 594–5 = Baynes, ii. 1274, 1277, 1297–9.

[151] Domarus, i. 596 = Baynes, ii. 1300. On the Franco-Soviet pact see Messerschmidt, IV.iv below.

[152] Press directives of 7 and 9 Mar. 1936 by Aschmann, the foreign ministry spokesman, and Brauweiler, head of the foreign press department of the propaganda ministry, in Sänger, *Politik der Täuschungen*, 78–9.

[153] Press directive of 11 Mar. 1936, ibid. 83.

(which produced for the first time the afterwards familiar manipulated vote of 99 per cent in the government's favour), Hitler delivered a speech including the statement 'I do not believe there is a man in the world who has done more than I have to speak and fight for peace.'[154]

The reoccupation of the Rhineland, which was achieved without bloodshed and aroused only verbal protests, was naturally celebrated by German propaganda as a great victory and as the completion of the fight for Germany's equality of rights.[155] Hitler had already achieved the return of the Saar (13 January 1935), the reintroduction of conscription (16 March 1935), and the naval treaty with Britain (18 June 1935) allowing Germany to build ships in excess of the Versailles limitations. With these successes and the reoccupation of the Rhineland he had gained a great deal of what the Weimar governments had vainly striven for, and Germany was once more recognized as a great power. Altogether, then, it was no great problem for Nazi propaganda to present Hitler as the executor of Weimar revisionism.

A further event of international importance in 1936 was the holding of the Olympic games in Germany.[156] This provided Nazi propaganda with a welcome opportunity to introduce foreign sportsmen and journalists to a peace-loving Germany, which moreover could point to a successful record on the home front. The government had solved the problem of six million unemployed; to the benefit of all Europe it had overcome Communism, its only enemy; and the German people could point with pride to its social achievements.[157] In Berlin foreign observers were shown an anti-Bolshevik exhibition entitled 'World Enemy No. 1', which no doubt struck a responsive note in view of the anti-Communism felt in other Western countries.[158] Anti-Semitic propaganda was suspended for the duration of the games, by a direct order to the press.[159] In general the media were instructed to 'use extreme tact' in their reports and comments, so as to avoid any misunderstandings.[160] Finally, Germany gained credit for the excellent organization of the games.

Internally, the games certainly did much to enhance Hitler's prestige. Abroad, however, contrary to widespread opinion, they were not a success, as was admitted in a secret report by the propaganda ministry. An international press campaign had been going on for three years and, in December 1935, nearly achieved its object of preventing the games being held in Germany; a large part of world opinion was hostile to the Nazi leaders, and the foreign press did not change its attitude as the games proceeded.[161]

Hitler's order of 26 July 1936 for the formation of the Condor Legion of bomber aircraft which took part on Franco's side in the Spanish civil war was not made

---

[154] Hitler's speech of 28 Mar. 1936 (Domarus, i. 614 ff.; cf. Baynes, ii. 1320–1).

[155] On the successive stages cf. Deist, III.II.2 (c), and Messerschmidt, IV.II and IV.III below.

[156] Cf. Krüger, *Olympische Spiele*; Bramsted, *Goebbels*, 150 ff.

[157] Hagemann, *Publizistik*, 208.

[158] Sänger, *Politik der Täuschungen*, 109–10.

[159] Press directive of 3 Aug. 1936; see Sänger, *Politik der Täuschungen*, 108.

[160] Press directive of 15 Aug. 1936 by government spokesman Berndt; Sänger, *Politik der Täuschungen*, 111.

[161] Krüger, *Olympische Spiele*, 11, 228 ff.; Ueberhorst, *Olympische Spiele*, 82.

known to the German public. Only after the troops returned on 20 May 1939,[162] when the web of deception could no longer be preserved, was the Legion first mentioned in the German press.

A few weeks after the Olympic games the National Socialist 'party rally of honour' was held at Nuremberg, from 8 to 14 September 1936. Hitler used it as the occasion to announce the extension of the period of conscription to two years and to inaugurate a Four-year Plan, of which Göring was put in charge.[163] The word 'war' was now back in the official vocabulary—the defence ministry had been renamed 'war ministry' a year earlier—and it aroused no special attention when Hitler, at the conclusion of the rally, cried out to his soldiers: 'The battle standards (*Kriegsfahnen*) of the new Reich wave before you for the first time.' By way of demonstrating German power Hitler continued to emphasize that 'the people, the party, and the armed forces' were 'linked in indissoluble fellowship'.[164] The Soviet Union, at least, was bound to regard it as an undisguised threat when the Führer combined his constant theme of the world danger of Communism with the boast that 'the new German army now stands before the gates of Germany.'[165] Such references to the increasing military and economic power of the Reich introduced a new phase of German propaganda: the transition from soothing words to intimidation.[166]

A year later, at the 1937 rally, Hitler uttered still plainer threats of military action; he referred again to the alleged world-wide danger of Bolshevism, which he used in relations with the West as the justification for Germany's own feverish rearmament.[167] The National Socialist state, he declared, had forged weapons for itself in order to 'crush with lightning speed' any attempt to introduce Bolshevism into Germany. He added the direct threat: 'That we have been in the past good soldiers—that assuredly the world will not have forgotten. That today we are still better soldiers—for that the world can take our word.' In any case, he boasted, the time was past when a defenceless Germany could be forced to submit to anything whatever.[168] Shortly afterwards he once again made it clear to the service chiefs that he was not concerned with retaliation against foreign interference but with carrying out his own aggressive plans.[169]

In February 1938 Hitler dismissed the war minister, von Blomberg, and made himself commander-in-chief of the three services, on the ground of the close links between them and the state. He took this opportunity to demonstrate once again the completeness of his power to foreigners and to the German people. On 20 February, in a 'report' to the Reichstag on the first five years of Nazi rule,[170] he declared: 'The German army of peace is drawn up. A powerful air force protects our homeland. A

---

[162] Sänger, *Politik der Täuschungen*, 145. On the operations of the Condor Legion see Maier, *Guernica*.
[163] Cf. Volkmann, II.v below.
[164] Hitler's speech on 14 Sept. 1936 (Domarus, i. 644; cf. Baynes, ii. 1327–31).
[165] Domarus, i. 646.
[166] Hagemann, *Publizistik*, 219; Sywottek, *Mobilmachung*, 104 ff.
[167] On anti-Bolshevik propaganda cf. esp. Sywottek, *Mobilmachung*, 110–20.
[168] Hitler's speech on 13 Sept. 1937 (Domarus, i. 726 ff., here 731 = Baynes, i. 688 ff., here 711).
[169] Cf. Hitler's secret speech on 5 Nov. 1937. The 'Hoßbach memorandum' is reprinted in Domarus, i. 747–56; trans. in *Documents on Nazism*, 521 ff. Cf. also Bussmann, 'Hoßbach-Niederschrift'.
[170] Hitler's Reichstag speech on 20 Feb. 1938 (Domarus, i. 796 ff.; cf. Baynes, ii. 1387–8).

new naval power guards our coasts. As part of the huge increase in general production we have been able to carry through an unprecedented rearmament programme.' He spoke further of 'defence to the last breath', of 'blind loyalty and blind obedience', of 'lightning-swift action' if foreign countries should think of interfering, and of the 'steel and iron' that would protect the German homeland.

In 1938 came the forced Anschluss with Austria in March, the Munich agreement in September, and the entry of German troops into the Sudeten area in October. All these events were marked by increased aggressiveness in Nazi propaganda. Peaceful protestations were still heard as well, but they were clearly overshadowed by the threat that Germany was henceforth prepared to 'go the limit' and would no longer put up with compromises.

According to the official version, the entry of German troops into Austria on 12 March 1938[171] was no more than a 'friendly visit'. The aggression was played up as another of Hitler's 'works of peace', which had saved Austria from being engulfed in civil war like Spain.[172] Having achieved the Anschluss without firing a shot, Hitler was able to boast that 'Germany has once more become a world power . . . Behind this decision stand now 75 million people, and before it stands henceforth the German army.'[173] 'No power in the world can any longer subdue us to its will.'[174]

In the months after the Anschluss Goebbels's ministry carried on an intensified campaign against Czechoslovakia.[175] Alleged Czech atrocities against the Sudeten Germans were denounced with increasing vehemence. The press and radio were given exact instructions from time to time as to the scale of the attack, while Hitler continued to make preparations for a military 'solution' of the so-called crisis. At the end of September 1938 the British premier Chamberlain, the French premier Daladier, Mussolini, and Hitler met for the last-minute conference which ended in the Munich agreement. Czechoslovakia, which was not represented at the conference, was obliged to vacate the Sudeten districts by 10 October, whereupon they were occupied by German troops.

Although there was relief both in Germany and abroad that war had again been averted, to his close associates Hitler seemed rather disappointed than pleased by his bloodless victory. However, the propaganda machine soon adjusted to the new situation, praising the Führer to the skies for having once more saved the peace of the world. This secured him 'almost legendary prestige' with the German people, large sections of whom seem to have completely identified with the Führer's cause after Munich.[176] For his part Hitler concentrated all the harder on his next objectives, 'destroying' rump Czechosolvakia and annexing the Memel territory

---

[171] Cf. Rosar, *Gemeinschaft*; Botz, *Eingliederung Österreichs*; also Messerschmidt, IV.v.7 (*a*) below.

[172] Cf. Domarus, i. 819 = Baynes, ii. 1424; also Sänger, *Politik der Täuschungen*, 200 ff.

[173] Domarus, i. 828, 830 = Baynes, ii. 1431, 1435. A similar directive to the press on 1 Oct. 1938: 'Today [Germany] is a great power of the first rank—militarily, socially, and in every way it stands at the head of all nations.' See Sänger, *Politik der Täuschungen*, 246.

[174] Hitler's speech to a mass meeting at Graz on 3 Apr. 1938: Domarus, i. 843 = Baynes, ii. 1451.

[175] Cf. Bramsted, *Goebbels*, 167 ff.; also Sywottek, *Mobilmachung*, 121 ff.

[176] Steinert, *Hitlers Krieg*, 77 ff.

from Lithuania. Both these were achieved in March 1939 after due preparation in the propaganda and military fields.

The National Socialist institutions for the study of public opinion had reported a general fear of war during the Sudeten crisis, followed by universal relief after Munich.[177] Thus, Hitler knew that despite months of propaganda against Czechoslovakia the psychological mobilization for war left much to be desired. He therefore thought it necessary to accelerate the switch from soothing phrases to the show of strength and threat of force, with the primary object of conditioning the German population for war; intimidating foreign countries was only a secondary aim.

On 10 November 1938 Hitler expounded the new propaganda line to a meeting of about 400 German journalists and publishers. The deputy Führer Rudolf Hess was present, together with the heads of the propaganda apparatus: Goebbels, Rosenberg, Max Amann (president of the Reich Press Chamber), Karl Hanke (state secretary of the propaganda ministry), and Otto Dietrich (press chief of the Reich).[178] At this secret meeting Hitler not only announced that propaganda was to be switched to preparation for war, but declared in all frankness that his peaceful protestations of past years were purely deceptive manœuvres, intended to mislead opinion at home and abroad and to provide a cover for German rearmament. The speech is worth quoting at some length.

For decades circumstances have compelled me to talk about almost nothing but peace. Only by continually stressing Germany's desire for peace and her peaceful intentions could I achieve freedom for the German people bit by bit and provide the armaments which were always necessary before the next step could be taken. It is obvious that such peace propaganda also had its doubtful aspects, for it can only too easily give people the idea that the present regime really identifies itself with the determination to preserve peace at all costs. This would not only lead to a wrong assessment of the aims of this system, but above all it might lead to the German nation, instead of being prepared for every eventuality, being filled with a spirit of defeatism which in the long run would inevitably undermine the success of the present regime. It was only out of necessity that for years I talked of peace. But it was now necessary gradually to re-educate the German people psychologically and to make it clear that there are some things which *must* be achieved by force if peaceful means fail. To do this it was necessary not to advocate force as such, but to depict to the German people certain diplomatic events in such a light that the inner voice of the nation itself gradually began to call for the use of force. That meant, to portray certain events in such a way that the conviction automatically grew in the minds of the broad mass of the people: If things cannot be settled amicably, force will have to be used, but in any case things cannot go on like this.

Hitler went on to tell his hearers that the new propaganda line had been planned months before and brought gradually and increasingly into effect. The 'pacifist gramophone record' was 'played out' as far as Germany was concerned; no one would believe it any more.[179]

[177] Ibid. Cf. also Messerschmidt, IV.v.7 below.
[178] *Völkischer Beobachter*, 11 Nov. 1938.
[179] Cf. Treue, 'Rede Hitlers', 182–3; text also in Domarus, i. 973–7, here 974; trans. in *Documents on Nazism*, 549.

Erich Kordt, who was present at the meeting, summed up its purpose by saying that Hitler had given the press two years to 'awaken the German people's will to war'.[180] In addition Hitler had made it clear how little the peaceful disposition of the German people suited his plans.

During the year that elapsed between Munich and the outbreak of war in September 1939 the German population were subjected to systematic psychological mobilization for war, not least on account of the lukewarmness they had shown during the Sudeten crisis. On 19 October 1938 the propaganda ministry issued a directive on 'popularizing the armed forces', which laid down that intensive propaganda was to be conducted from then onwards to increase the German people's confidence in itself and in its military resources.[181] In the ensuing months the propaganda institutions of the state, party, and Wehrmacht used every available means to publicize the armed forces and keep them in the centre of attention, thus creating and strengthening an emotional bond between the services and the people. The campaign, which was planned and carried out in detail, was also designed to impart a sense of military superiority over all Germany's potential opponents.

In addition to 'popularizing the armed forces' the programme gave indications, vague at first, of a war aim, viz. to safeguard Germany's food supply by increasing its 'living space'.[182] This cardinal feature of National Socialist policy had in the previous years only been discussed at secret high-level meetings. Towards the end of 1938 party functionaries were once more reminded of it, and Hitler's Reichstag speech of 30 January 1939[183] inaugurated an official campaign on the theme of *Lebensraum*. The propaganda line[184] was to point to the existence of 'have' and 'have-not' nations, indicating that Germany would not submit to being kept in the latter class for all time and that her demands must be listened to. She wanted peace, as always, but a price must be paid for it, namely the satisfaction of her 'legitimate, vital, and inalienable claims'.

Thus, in 1939 Germany's demand for territorial expansion in Europe was still coupled with general protestations of peace. German propaganda called for the equalization of power and possessions between the 'haves' and 'have-nots', and on this basis contended that 'true peace' would be served not by maintaining the status quo but by bringing about a just equilibrium. Addressing the national-conservative elements of the German public, Goebbels played on old anti-Versailles feelings, the demand for a 'place in the sun', and proper recognition of Germany's status in the world; while Germans who had formerly belonged to the workers' parties were appealed to by the notion of a 'class struggle among nations'.[185]

The extinction of rump Czechoslovakia in March 1939 could not, even with the

---

[180] Cf. Kordt, *Wahn und Wirklichkeit*, 133; quoted from Treue, 'Rede Hitlers', 180.

[181] Sywottek, *Mobilmachung*, 166–7.

[182] On the switch to *Lebensraum* propaganda cf. ibid. 180 ff.

[183] See Domarus, ii. 1047–67 (here 1052–3) = Baynes, ii. 1567 ff.

[184] Cf. Bramsted, *Goebbels*, 183 ff.; Sywottek, *Mobilmachung*, 197.

[185] Cf. Goebbels, *Zeit ohne Beispiel*, 157 ff.; Bramsted, *Goebbels*, 408; Sywottek, *Mobilmachung*, 184, 197.

greatest ingenuity, be justified on racial grounds; instead, for the first time emphasis was given to *Lebensraum* propaganda. Then, in the spring and summer, two new themes were introduced in direct preparation for war: first, the cry of 'encirclement', and second, the imputation of war guilt to the other side should Germany's claim to *Lebensraum* not be satisfied.

The slogan of 'encirclement' made its appearance in March 1939. It had of course an earlier history, and in the years before 1914 the theme of 'Germany beset by enemies' had contributed not a little to the population's readiness for war.[186] Now it was once more suggested that peace-loving Germany was under military threat from a ring of hostile powers, instigated by the British warmongers.[187] Britain, which sought thus to throttle Germany, was a prototype of the 'satisfied' states and in addition stood for world Jewry, 'world democracy', and thus 'world Bolshevism'. Besides Britain, which was the chief bogy, France and the distant United States were branded as 'encircling' powers. The intended effect was clear: the German population was to be persuaded that it was in the same situation as in 1914, surrounded by envious neighbours and warmongering competitors, biding their time for an attack on the peace-loving Reich, whose just and vital demands they refused to meet.

A further important element was the charge of responsibility for the coming war.[188] Ever since 1919 the war-guilt clause of the treaty of Versailles had been interpreted as a moral judgement, and indignation at the 'war-guilt lie' had been fuelled for the past two decades; it was natural therefore that the Nazis attached importance to blaming Germany's adversaries in advance. As a kind of rehearsal during the Sudeten crisis in 1938 Goebbels had given instructions that not Hitler, but the Czechoslovak premier Beneš, was to be portrayed as choosing between war and peace, and therefore saddled with war-guilt in anticipation.[189] During 1939 German propaganda was similarly at pains to plant responsibility for the coming war on Britain and, to a lesser extent, France and the United States. The Nazi leaders knew that despite all their efforts the idea of war was unpopular, and they therefore wished to present it in advance as a defensive struggle. Nothing was left undone to drive home the parallel with 1914. The prospect of a 'war forced on Germany' would, the leaders hoped, help to mask their aggressive designs and remedy the nation's lack of enthusiasm for war.

---

[186] The term was used in 1906 by the German chancellor, Prince Bernhard von Bülow, to describe the policy of the Anglo-French Entente. For its refutation cf. Bernstein, *Einkreisung* (1919), and Kantorowicz, *Englische Politik* (1929). For parallels in the pre-history of the First and Second World Wars cf. Fraser, *Germany*, 134 ff. On the socio-political roots of the ideology of encirclement cf. Dahrendorf, *Society*, 131; also Dehio, *World Politics*, and Berghahn, *Tirpitz-Plan*.

[187] Cf. Goebbels's articles in the *Völkischer Beobachter*: 'Die Einkreiser' (20 May 1939); 'Nochmals: Die Einkreiser' (27 May 1939); 'Das schreckliche Wort von der Einkreisung' (1 June 1939); repr. in id., *Zeit ohne Beispiel*, 144 ff., 188 ff. Also Bramsted, *Goebbels*, 183 ff.; Sywottek, *Mobilmachung*, 199 ff.; Messerschmidt, *Wehrmacht*, 237.

[188] Details in Sywottek, *Mobilmachung*, 186 ff. and Fraser, *Germany*, 99 ff.

[189] Details in Bramsted, *Goebbels*, 173 ff.; also relevant press directives in Sänger, *Politik der Täuschungen*, 243.

War against Poland was decided upon by May 1939 at the latest.[190] By then the Poles had refused the German suggestion that they should join in the anti-Comintern pact and support Germany's territorial ambitions at Soviet expense, either actively or at least by refraining from opposition. Instead, the Poles had accepted the British and French offer of a guarantee against a vital threat to their independence—whereupon Hitler had retaliated on 28 April by denouncing the German–Polish non-aggression pact of 1934.[191]

Thus, from May 1939 onwards Hitler was merely concerned to await a 'suitable opportunity' to attack Poland.[192] That opportunity had first to be manufactured, and in the intervening few months Goebbels's propaganda was notably restrained. There was as yet no massive attack on or denigration of Poland, as had been the case with Czechoslovakia in the previous year. Stress was laid on the encirclement theme, with Britain as the chief enemy and instigator of war, using Poland as a cat's paw. This, with slight variations, remained the basic pattern during the whole summer of 1939. Only in August, especially the second half of the month, did an orchestrated anti-Polish campaign set in, after the well-tried model of 1938. As was realized both in Germany and abroad, this was an immediate prelude to war. Propaganda during the previous months had touched on the theme that the status of Danzig required revision so that its citizens could come 'home to the Reich'; the principle of nationality, it was declared, had been flouted when the Polish state was restored in 1919. Then, in August, the full-scale propaganda onslaught began. Day by day the mass media produced sensational accounts, mostly pure inventions, of bestial and terrorist acts against Germans in Poland, while the Polish government was accused of preparing for an expansionist war on Germany. The domestic purpose of this multiform propaganda was to make the German population feel threatened, to create a sense of solidarity with the allegedly persecuted Germans in Poland, and to make it appear that military action was unavoidable. The allegations of Polish warlike intentions towards Germany fitted into the well-tried technique of pinning war-guilt on the adversary in advance. The Polish mobilization on 30 August afforded a welcome opportunity to present Germany's own measures as defensive. Then, as is well know, fabricated Polish 'attacks' in the frontier area served as a pretext for German 'counter-measures'.

It thus went without saying that when Britain and France declared war in September 1939, and also later, Nazi propaganda took the line that Germany was engaged in a righteous war that was not of her seeking.[193] The German press obediently declared that war was the result of deliberate British policy and that Germany's actions were defensive, the response of a prudent leadership. The propaganda of deceit had for the time being reached its climax.

---

[190] Cf. Hitler's address to military chiefs on 23 May 1939 concerning his intention to attack Poland at a suitable opportunity: *DGFP* D. vi, No. 433, pp. 574–80, here 576.

[191] Cf. Messerschmidt, IV.VI.4 below.

[192] On the following passage see Sywottek, *Mobilmachung*, 209–33.

[193] Cf. German White Books published by the foreign ministry in 1939: *Urkunden zur letzten Phase der deutsch-polnischen Krise* and *Dokumente zur Vorgeschichte des Krieges*. Further examples in Steinert, *Hitlers Krieg*, 93–4; cf. also Fraser, *Germany*, 133 ff.

6. Fear of War and Hopes for Peace among the German Population

The behaviour of the German population in September 1939 can only be partly explained by the effects of government propaganda. At least equally important in determining its attitude were the authoritarian, nationalist, and militarist tendencies described in the first chapter of this study, which became prevalent in the last phase of the Weimar Republic.

The left-wing parties failed to make the Führer's warlike ideas a central issue in the election campaigns of 1930–2. Ernst Thälmann, the KPD leader, who stood for the Reich presidency in the spring of 1932, did indeed utter the warning 'A vote for Hitler is a vote for war.'[194] But this was only a repetition of earlier Communist predictions of war as a consequence of imperialist policies: it owed nothing to any detailed study of the NSDAP's programme or the statements of its leaders. The Social Democrats in the Reichstag expressed anxiety in the autumn of 1930 that, if Hitler came to power, there would be danger of civil war at home and a war of *revanche* in Europe;[195] but it was a long time before the Social Democratic Party as a whole came to realize that Hitler did indeed stand for war. Only from mid-1933 did the party's executive (SOPADE), now in exile in Prague, make the danger of war its central theme.[196]

Thus, before 1933 few people in Germany fully realized that if the National Socialists came to power they would deliberately plan for a new war, and moreover one with more far-reaching aims than the revision of Versailles. But, apart from this widespread ignorance of actual Nazi intentions, large sections of the population, influenced by militarist ideologies, were in what might be called a state of latent readiness for war—a psychological disposition to approve or at least tolerate a war policy.[197] In other words, large parts of the population were in a frame of mind such that they could not be expected to support a pacific policy or actively to oppose a warlike one.

Although the climate of opinion was thus favourable to the Nazi leaders even before 1933, they did not at first seek to inflame it further or advocate war as the solution to all outstanding difficulties, but instead presented a peaceful façade for the next two or three years. We have seen many of the domestic and foreign reasons for this. On the home front, an important factor was that the regime could not estimate how those parts of the population that were influenced by bourgeois-pacifist or socialist ideas would react if they knew their rulers' true intentions.

The Nazi leaders knew that peace-loving traditions were alive especially among the German working class, and in home propaganda they were at pains to avoid any suggestion that might have aroused the fear of war at an inconvenient time, in other words before German rearmament was complete. This anxiety was carried so far that an official reprimand was administered to the Vaterländischer Frauenverein

---

[194] *Deutsche Widerstandskämpfer*, i. 24; cf. also I.1.9 above.
[195] *Jahrbuch der SPD 1930*, 21.
[196] Matthias, *Sozialdemokratie und Nation*, 18 ff.   [197] Cf. I.1.10 above.

(Patriotic Women's League), an unimportant organization which, in 1934, stated in a circular to its members that 'We must get ready larger supplies of clothing so as to be prepared if war should break out'.[198] In March 1935, on the reintroduction of universal conscription, several German newspapers published articles to the effect that there was serious talk of war in Italy and France; these elicited a 'most emphatic' warning from the authorities that 'there must be no working-up of a war psychosis'.[199] On the occasion of the reoccupation of the Rhineland in March 1936 several local authorities reported that there was serious fear of foreign complications;[200] the press was thereupon instructed to build up confidence, as 'no fear of war must be allowed to arise'.[201] When German troops entered Austria on 12 March 1938 the press liaison officer strictly prohibited the use of the word 'war'.[202] In September 1939, when the war against Poland had actually begun, the regime still had not the courage to say so. At the government press conference on 1 September the assembled journalists were told that there must be 'no headlines containing the word "war". As the Führer said in his speech, we are only striking back.'[203] Thus, throughout the period of preparation for war the Nazi rulers were most careful to keep any suggestion of war out of official announcements. There is no doubt that measures of this kind, supplementing peace propaganda, reflected the rulers' fears that their authority might be seriously threatened if a war panic were to spread. Hitler's announcement that the NSDAP would hold its 'nation-wide peace rally' at Nuremberg in September 1939[204] must likewise be regarded as part of a camouflage policy inspired by the fear of resistance to his plans, and designed to stabilize conditions on the home front. It may also have been intended to provide a fall-back position in the unexpected event of international developments forcing Hitler to desist from his warlike intentions.[205]

The propagandists of the Third Reich were pretty closely informed, by their research organizations, as to what the population felt concerning the prospect of war. Regular reports on 'attitudes and atmosphere', as the jargon had it, were furnished by the Gestapo, the security service (SD), the various Party headquarters, local judicial authorities and public prosecutors, Reich propaganda centres, and the army high command. These institutions did not conduct polls but relied on 'participating observers', i.e. an army of informers. In 1937 the SD alone employed between 30,000 and 50,000 anonymous informers in addition to a central staff of

---

[198] Sänger, *Politik der Täuschungen*, 266.

[199] Ibid. 64–5. On 9 June 1935 Kurt Jahnke, head of the press department of the propaganda ministry, repeated as a paramount directive: 'No war psychosis! Any news that might run contrary to this is to be treated as propaganda put out by enemies of Germany.' Evidence of grave anxiety and war psychosis among the German people is contained in a political-situation report of 13 June 1935 by the district president (Regierungspräsident) of Aachen, repr. in Vollmer, *Volksopposition*, 229.

[200] Situation report by the Gestapo, Aachen, for Mar. 1936: ibid. 370–1.

[201] Sänger, *Politik der Täuschungen*, 79.

[202] Ibid. 201.

[203] Ibid. 392. On the foreign-political aspect of this formulation cf. concluding paragraphs of Messerschmidt, IV.VI.4 below.

[204] Cf. Burden, *Nuremberg Rallies*, 161 ff.

[205] Cf. Messerschmidt, IV.VI.4 below.

about 3,000; that is to say, there was about one SD man for every 2,500 of the population.[206] These figures show how close was the network of spying and supervision. Certainly, the quality of reports left much to be desired before the war, and was only satisfactory from 1939 onwards; but even during the years of peace these sources could be relied on to report typical widespread opinions and emotional reactions to current events. In general the public-opinion reports, especially those of the SD, were tolerably accurate despite a tendency to optimism in some cases.[207] As such they were valuable to the authorities, and enabled the propaganda apparatus to react appropriately to popular trends.

The various public-opinion reports compiled in 1933–9 suggest that 'the Germans were not in an aggressive warlike mood, but full of resignation, fear of war, and longing for peace'.[208] This is the general impression from reports connected with the reintroduction of conscription, the reoccupation of the Rhineland, and the march into Austria. When the Sudeten crisis came to a head in the autumn of 1938 the German population seems to have been more affected than previously by a 'general war psychosis' or fear of warlike developments. A report dated 1 October, the day on which German troops marched into the Sudeten area, declared that:

There is no enthusiasm for warlike complications arising out of the Sudeten German question. People are oppressed by the uncertainty of the political situation. No one wants to think of a war against Britain and France. The education of the whole people to shoulder the tasks and trials of a total war is still far from complete.

Many are depressed, chiefly on account of serious fear that war would sooner or later put an end to economic prosperity and would have disastrous results for Germany.

Due to the foreign situation and the prospect of war, which is for the most part openly spoken of, the general feeling is one of gravity and anxiety; a general war psychosis.[209]

Two months later a report on the 'general atmosphere' once again indicated that 'the population'—not further defined, unfortunately—had, during the Sudeten crisis, desired nothing but peace. The language of the report is clear:

Everywhere there was much tension and anxiety; people did not want war at any price. This was especially the case with former front-line fighters . . . Listening to foreign broadcasts caused confusion and vacillation among the great majority of politically unsophisticated people. Political training and education, especially in defence preparedness, are still quite

---

[206] Höhne, *Order*, 218; Dröge, *Widerstand*, 53–4.

[207] This conclusion, based on close examination of the sources, is independently arrived at by Steinert (*Hitlers Krieg*, 40–8, here 45) and Dröge (*Widerstand*, 45–68, here 60). The SD (Security Service) reports from 1938 onwards, but not those of 1933–8, are now fully documented in *Meldungen aus dem Reich*. The earlier period is partly covered by the regional documentation in *Lageberichte der Geheimen Staatspolizei über die Provinz Hessen-Nassau 1933–1936*.

[208] Steinert, *Hitlers Krieg*, 26. This is also confirmed by Kershaw's recent investigation in *Popular Opinion*, based on reports on the state of feeling in Bavaria. Kershaw (p. 126) attributes the absence of any rebellion against the regime in Sept. 1939 to the Hitler myth, which aroused 'elemental feelings of loyalty'.

[209] Summary of economic reports of the military economic inspectorate, compiled by the military economic staff of the OKW, 1 Oct. 1939, in BA-MA RW 19/87.

insufficient. This is true of all but a very few of those in lower positions of authority. In this area failure is almost complete.[210]

This report by the military economy staff of the high command of the Wehrmacht was confirmed by those of the Reichssicherheitshauptamt (RSHA: Reich Central Security Office). During the Sudeten crisis, all reports agreed, there was general depression and war psychosis,[211] which gave way to a burst of enthusiasm and relief when the Munich agreement was signed. The avoidance of war was greeted with joy everywhere, lifting from the population 'the heavy anxiety of its concern for the maintenance of peace'. All was now optimism and admiration for the Führer's statesmanship. Matters took a similar course next spring, with the absorption of Bohemia-Moravia and the Memel district.[212] At first there was a certain nervousness, here and there some fear of war, and a movement to convert capital into material assets. Then, when Hitler's latest moves were accomplished without bloodshed and without incurring sanctions from the Western powers, enthusiasm and admiration for the Führer knew no bounds. These successes seem to have won him the support of practically all sections of society.

From the various public-opinion reports it appears clear that the years of 'peace' propaganda directed at the German public by its Nazi rulers had not been without effect. The official slogans had been widely believed and not seen as the deception they were. From the regime's point of view these side-effects threatened to develop into a serious danger, as they interfered with the objective of creating a war mentality: this was the case at least from the autumn of 1938 onwards. Hitler had shown his awareness of the problem years earlier, on 17 January 1935, when the British journalist Ward Price questioned him on the remark by a French statesman that Germany would pursue a conciliatory policy only until the Reichswehr believed itself capable of winning a war. Hitler replied: 'This statesman of yours can never have been at the head of a nation. Otherwise, how could he think it possible to preach peace to a people for ten years on end, and then suddenly launch them into war?'[213] This reply was of course part of Hitler's usual technique of evasion, but there was a grain of truth in it, as was uncomfortably clear during the Sudeten crisis. Thus, in the speech on 10 November 1938, already mentioned, Hitler found himself obliged to scrap the 'pacifist record', as he called it, and step up the process of psychological mobilization for the war he intended to wage.

According to the opinion reports, from May until well into August 1939 there were no signs of a war mentality among the German population. No one seems to have expected France or Britain to take action. According to the reports, while there was confidence in the Wehrmacht there was no desire at all for another war: people trusted in the Führer's statesmanship to achieve his aims by peaceful means. Only a minority seem to have thought that war was on the cards—at most a localized

---

[210] Summary economic report of the military economic staff of the OKW, 30 Nov. 1938, in BA-MA RW 19/87.
[211] Steinert, *Hitlers Krieg*, 77 ff.
[212] Ibid. 80.
[213] Interview with Ward Price, 17 Jan. 1935, in Domarus, i. 476 = Baynes, ii. 1198.

campaign against Poland, but certainly not a world war.[214] In the second half of August, when anti-Polish propaganda was in full spate, some decrease in optimism was observed, but up to the last people remained confident that war would be avoided as before. The Hitler–Stalin pact of 23 August seemed fully to justify this view.

The outbreak of war consequently came as a severe shock, and the opinion reports fully confirm the first-hand impression of many contemporaries[215] that the mood of the population at the beginning of September 1939 was one of depression. The reports also indicate that numerous peace rumours[216] began to circulate from the very beginning of hostilities. After each new victory people clearly hoped that the war was really over, and cast about for evidence that would justify their belief. Each new development was interpreted in terms of this wishful thinking.

The Nazi regime had failed in its all-out effort to produce a mood of warlike exhilaration comparable to that of August 1914. If the results of the government's propaganda are judged against the aim that it set itself, it must be counted as ineffective. Gratified as the Germans were by Hitler's many bloodless successes in foreign affairs up to the end of 1938, they were none the less afraid of another war. The regime's campaign of psychological and material preparation for war had managed to silence, but not extinguish, the peaceable traditions of the socialist workers' movement and bourgeois pacifism. These traditions continued, and had derived temporary though illusory nourishment from the government's protestations of its desire for peace. Even in the intensive final phase of psychological mobilization between November 1938 and September 1939 it was not possible entirely to neutralize the effects of the reiterated peaceful protestations of earlier years.

At the same time, government propaganda did have some success in deceiving the population as to the Nazi rulers' true intentions and those of foreign countries. Minds were confused by the multiplicity of slogans—plutocrats, world Jewry, world Bolshevism, encirclement, *Lebensraum*—and, on top of all, the Hitler–Stalin pact. Was the old picture, with Bolsheviks and Jews as the main enemy, now out of date? Were the real villains the Anglo-American plutocrats, or the Poles in league with them? Or was it true, as the government claimed, that all these forces together were encircling peace-loving Germany and threatening it with war? Those in charge of propaganda saw clearly enough that they would not succeed in inducing large sections of the population to approve and support the regime's war policy. Consequently, they deliberately introduced a medley of slogans in which there was not one enemy but several; threats were to be expected from every quarter, and the government itself was not the architect of events but was forced into action by them. By thus diversifying its propaganda the regime brought about a general sense of impending danger, while taking care not to specify the exact nature of the threat. This atmosphere combined with the traditional fatalistic attitude towards war, of which we spoke in Chapter I.1 above. Given the population's acceptance of war as something decreed by fate, the propagandists managed, by gestures of strength and

[214] Steinert, *Hitlers Krieg*, 84.　　[215] Cf. I.1.1. above.　　[216] Dröge, *Widerstand*, 87.

the conjuring up of threats, to produce that minimum of readiness to fight which manifested itself in the reluctant loyalty of the German people when war actually broke out.

Another factor in producing this attitude was the disciplining and intimidation, over the past years, of all groups which might be regarded as possible opponents on the home front. This will be described in the following chapter.

III. Organizing Society in Preparation for War

THE domestic programme of the NSDAP called for the destruction of the parliamentary system and the multi-party state and the regimentation of all special-interest associations. However, this uniformity was not an end in itself, designed to bring about a lasting peaceable order; it was only a method of creating preconditions for the conquest of *Lebensraum*. The main purpose of Nazi home policy was to convert the whole of German society into a weapon of aggression.

Hitler had repeatedly made this clear even before 1933. According to *Mein Kampf*, the object of domestic policy was to forge a sword, while it was for foreign policy to ensure that the forging proceeded in safety and to seek allies.[1] Later he used the formulation that 'domestic policy must furnish the native (*völkisch*) instrument of strength to foreign policy'; it must 'put an end to the cancer of democracy', 'strengthen the will to fight' (*Wehrwille*), and encourage the spirit of nationality against the 'evil cesspit of pacifism', by rearmament and eventually by creating a new body politic that would 'overcome . . . the cleavage between the classes'. The close connection between Nazi internal and external policy is seen especially in Hitler's definition of the former: its function was to bring about 'the regaining of our people's strength for the prosecution of its struggle for existence and thereby the strength to represent its vital interests abroad'.[2] In 1930 Goebbels coined that formula that the purpose of home policy was to 'shape the nation' as a 'preliminary to foreign policy, the object of which was in turn to ensure its *Lebensraum*'.[3]

In the view of Hitler and his associates this 'formative' process had to take account of the experience of the world war and the revolution of November 1918. According to the nationalist version, Germany had not suffered a military defeat but a 'collapse', brought about on the one hand by the mistakes of imperial policy and propaganda and on the other by the treachery of 'Marxist Jewish wire-pullers', who had staged the revolution and thus plunged a dagger into the back of the undefeated army. To prevent anything similar happening again, the 'wire-pullers' and their organizations had to be eliminated.[4]

According to the concept of total war, as we have seen in the propaganda context, Germany could only win a future war if the whole people took part in preparing for it and fighting as a united racial community. Therefore the first blow must be

[1] Hitler, *Mein Kampf* (trans.), 498 (amended; original, p. 689).
[2] *Hitler's Secret Book* (cited below as *Secret Book*), 79–80, 85; Hitler's address to Reichswehr commanders on 3 Feb. 1933, in Jacobsen, *1939–1945*, 95–6, and Vogelsang, 'Dokumente', 434–5.
[3] Goebbels, 'Um die deutsche Scholle' (speech at demonstration in Munich, 11 May 1930), in id., *Revolution*, 27–8.
[4] Cf. e.g. Goebbels, *Revolution*, 98–9. This was also the view of the conservative nationalists who later resisted Hitler: cf. Graml, 'Resistance Thinking', 8.

struck against the socialist and Communist organizations which were standard-bearers of the class struggle. An attempt could then be made to court the working class, which was indispensable to the war programme, by gradually prising it away from the revolutionary ideology of Western socialism, which was traditionally inclined to pacifism. The NSDAP believed that it could fill the resulting vacuum with its own ideology and organizing power. The systematic oppression and ideological 're-education' of the 1930s were thus the outcome of the party's 'historical analysis' of the First World War and the revolution.

1. *GLEICHSCHALTUNG* and VOLUNTARY CO-OPERATION

The regime devoted most of its energy in 1933–4 to disarming, persecuting, and partially liquidating opposition elements within and outside the party. During this phase internal policy, in the sense of consolidating the seizure of power, was indeed the government's primary concern. However, each step on the way to achieving a totalitarian order was at the same time a step towards preparing the intended war of conquest. In this sense the whole National Socialist home policy of 1933–9 was geared to preparation for war.

As is well known, Hitler was able to achieve the principal stages in his planned assumption of power during the first year of his chancellorship. This success was only to a small extent the result of shrewd tactics on his part; for Hitler's conservative and nationalist colleagues in the coalition government fully shared his aim of doing away with the parliamentary system and establishing a permanent authoritarian regime. To ensure their willing co-operation Hitler was at pains to couch his initial statements in a moderate, statesmanlike tone, extolling national, conservative, and Christian values.[5] His colleagues were also in agreement that the Communists and social democrats should be excluded from public life as quickly as possible, if necessary by force. The coalition government practised and sanctioned the use of force, while concealing it as far as possible behind a smokescreen of protestations of legality.

Within four days of forming his government, the new chancellor set about gaining the co-operation of the chief army leaders. He attached key importance to the role of the military in consolidating his power, as is clear from the fact that in addressing the army commanders on 3 February 1933 he unfolded to them the essential features of his whole long-term policy. Thus, the military leaders were aware of his plans for conquest and expansion from the outset. At the same secret meeting he described in all frankness his intentions on the home front: the ruthless eradication of 'Marxism' and pacifism, and the nation-wide inculcation of a fighting spirit by means of a 'strictly authoritarian regime'; all this as a preparation to overthrowing the treaty of Versailles and 'conquering fresh *Lebensraum* in the east, which was to be ruthlessly Germanized'.[6] His emphasis on the 'joy of war'

[5] e.g. the 'Proclamation to the German Nation' of 1 Feb. 1933, in Domarus i. 191 ff. (cf. Baynes, i. 112 ff., ii. 1001–2).

[6] Jacobsen, *1939–1945*, 95–6.

(*Wehrfreudigkeit*) confirmed the army chiefs in the conviction that, in contrast to the republican era, the government and the Reichswehr were once again pursuing a common interest.

In February 1933 President von Hindenburg approved several emergency decrees by which the conquest of power was pushed forward at a rapid rate. At the same time the civil service was deeply penetrated by National Socialists. Göring, as Prussian minister of the interior, carried out numerous dismissals and new appointments. The principal police forces were staffed by National Socialists, mostly senior SA officers. The police were ordered to co-operate closely with the nationalist associations (the SA, the SS, and the Stahlhelm) and 'to shoot without question'[7] where the left wing was concerned. Göring also set up an auxiliary police force, 50,000 strong—mostly members of the SA and SS—and began to organize the Gestapo (secret state police). At the beginning of February all Communist demonstrations were banned in Prussia. The KPD headquarters in Berlin was occupied on 24 February. At the first cabinet meeting on 30 January Hugenberg, for the nationalist party, had proposed an official ban on the KPD , but Hitler waited for some weeks before taking this (largely formal) step. Then, on 27 February, the Reichstag fire—which the Communists had nothing to do with—was used as a pretext to accuse them of an attempt at revolutionary subversion. About 4,000 KPD functionaries were arrested, and many local offices of the SPD and its newspapers were occupied by the authorities. Rapidly exploiting the state of panic generated by his own propaganda, on 28 February Hitler secured approval for the Decree for the Protection of the People and the State (the 'Reichstag fire decree'), which suspended all basic rights and in practice legalized any arbitrary action by the government. It was this decree, rather than the enabling act of 23 March, which created in constitutional terms a state of emergency in Germany which was to last until 1945. In the first weeks of March the police in Prussia alone arrested over 10,000 persons on the basis of the decree of 28 February.

Despite the anti-Communist measures and a massive campaign of intimidation, in the Reichstag election of 5 March 1933 the National Socialists received only 43.9 per cent of votes;[8] thus, Hitler was still technically dependent on the German Nationalists, with whose aid he could claim a bare majority of 51.9 per cent. These figures incidentally show that a large number of right-wing supporters had gravitated to the NSDAP.

In the first half of March, under the slogan of 'national unity', the Nazis enacted summary measures transferring the authority of the German Länder to the central power, thus destroying the federal system and the restrictions it had hitherto imposed. By dint of massive pressure from above and below and terrorist activity by the SA, the Land governments were compelled to resign and give way to 'national' cabinets; in addition Reichsstatthalter ('governors') were appointed as Hitler's direct representatives. Nazi propaganda whitewashed the government-inspired terror with phrases like 'nationalist uprising' and 'national awakening', calculated to

[7] Bracher, Sauer, and Schulz, *Machtergreifung*, 73.
[8] Details in Bracher, *Dictatorship*, 256–7.

appeal to the nationalist bourgeoisie. The Potsdam ceremony on 21 March—a theatrical prelude to the first Reichstag session of the Third Reich—was likewise marked by Hitler's renewed professions of loyalty to national-conservative ideals. These had the desired effect on Hindenburg and the generals, bishops, diplomats, and parliamentarians as far as the Centre party.

On 23 March the Reichstag voted the enabling law. In so doing it virtually abdicated its own authority, conferred full legislative powers on the Reich government, and thus abolished the 'separation of powers'. By this time all the Communist deputies had been arrested or were in hiding, while some SPD deputies were in 'protective custody'. The SPD members still in the Reichstag were the only ones who voted against the bill. Party government was now at an end; the bourgeois parties had consented to their own extinction. Thus, in barely two months the first phase of the political struggle had ended with a complete victory for Hitler.

The paradoxical slogan of the 'legal revolution' helped Hitler and his propagandists to present each successive stage of the seizure of power as a legal constitutional act. This was of the utmost importance, appealing as it did to the loyalty and sense of discipline of both the bourgeoisie and the bureaucracy.[9] In the civil service and the legal profession, the regime's cloak of legality did more than anything else to induce readiness to co-operate. Despite many actual breaches of the law and the constitution,[10] the new regime was able to take over the state system more or less intact, thus completely making up for its own shortage of trained administrative personnel. Besides the willing co-operation of the old élite, the influx of members into the NSDAP was a visible sign of opportunist adaptation to the new order.[11] Some 1,600,000 new members[12] joined the party in February–March 1933; sarcastically known to their new comrades as 'March converts', they were almost exclusively former members of the bourgeois parties. Particularly striking was the number of civil servants, academics, and lawyers.

After the Communists came the trade unions. The whole policy of the trade-union leadership since 1932, and especially their address of loyalty to Hitler on 20 March 1933, showed that their spirit of resistance had long been broken and that they were painfully anxious to adapt to the new system. In the hope of at least preserving their organization, the union leaders of their own accord called on their members to celebrate May Day 1933 together with the National Socialists and under the latter's banner. This was of no avail, however. On the following day the SA and SS commandeered the union offices, their businesses and banks, and arrested the principal officials.

---

[9] Cf. ibid. 210, 216, 249, 258; Broszat, *The Hitler State*, 11–12, 241 ff., also Mommsen, *Beamtentum*; Runge, *Beamtentum*; Fest, *Hitler* (trans.), 412.

[10] For the violations of law see Bracher, *Dictatorship*, 266.

[11] No social history of Germany in the Nazi period has yet been written. Recent years, however, have seen the publication of numerous local and regional studies which can be regarded as preliminary to a general account of political behaviour in the Third Reich. Despite variations in detail, the general effect is to show that the National Socialist regime enjoyed considerable support from the outset. Among these studies may be cited: Burckhardt, *Eine Stadt wird braun; Bayern in der NS-Zeit* (and five further volumes in the projected series with this title); *Lebensgeschichte*, vol. i.

[12] Broszat, *The Hitler State*, 199–200.

The SPD was disposed of with equally little trouble. Condemned to passivity by its legalistic attitude, it was considered no more than a minor threat by the NSDAP. On 10 May 1933 the party's offices, newspapers, and property were confiscated, as were those of the Reichsbanner, with no resistance in either case. On 22 June an edict of Göring's dissolved the SPD as an 'organization hostile to the state and people'; by the same token its parliamentary mandates were invalidated.

Other political groups either dissolved themselves in the summer of 1933 or were merged with National Socialist organizations. The German State party, the German People's party, the National People's party, the Stahlhelm, the Bavarian People's party—all disappeared almost unnoticed, as did the Centre party itself on 5 July 1933. The majority of organizations combined their self-dissolution with assurances to Hitler that they, or their members, wished to co-operate with the new state. The same voluntary submission was forthcoming from associations representing industry, craftsmen, trade, and agriculture. As early as 14 July 1933 the NSDAP was able to assert its own political monopoly by a 'law against the formation of new parties'. Thus, the single-party state was firmly established within less than six months of Nazi rule.[13] Future political decisions could only be taken legally within the Nazi party. It had taken Mussolini, Hitler's model, six years to achieve the same result in Italy. With some reason, Nazi propaganda spoke of a 'pitiful collapse' of the old political forces from right to left. It did indeed seem that the demise of Weimar democracy was not especially painful even to its former supporters.

The speed with which the Hitler regime asserted itself cannot be explained only by SA terror or by the superior astuteness of the NSDAP leaders. Of no less importance was the unforced co-operation of the army, the bureaucracy, the judicial system, the business world, and politicians of the conservative or nationalist persuasion. The total seizure of power was only made possible by an alliance between the right-wing opponents of democracy and the National Socialist mass movement.

After the establishment of the one-party dictatorship, based formally on the law of 14 July 1933, the party leaders let it be understood that the revolution was at an end. This announcement was addressed not least to the NSDAP itself, and the SA in particular. The members of the SA and the party rank and file had as yet received no economic or social reward, nor were they satisfied with the measure of state power they enjoyed;[14] they wished to extend to the full their control over the state. It was in Hitler's interest, on the other hand, to check their dynamism at this stage and make them content with what they had. This was the purpose of the slogan of the 'unity of party and state', proclaimed in the law of 1 December 1933. The Führer, as party leader and head of the government, sought to bring about a kind of division of labour. The NSDAP was to serve as an instrument for educating the German people and as a breeding-ground of party officials, while the state administration would remain in the hands of the trained bureaucracy. So the law of 1 December did not abolish the dualism of party and state, but laid down that the

[13] This phase of the 'seizure of power' is documented in *Hitlers Machtergreifung 1933*.
[14] On the composition of the SA cf. Jamin, *Zwischen den Klassen*.

Führer's authority would function in order to resolve any personal or institutional conflicts.[15] Neither at this time nor later was there any systematic fusion of the party with the state bureaucracy. In accordance with the principle of 'divide and rule', Hitler allowed full scope to the rivalry between state and party authorities and made no attempt to remedy the confusion that resulted. Instead of the orderliness of which it boasted, the National Socialist regime was a chaos of conflicting authority, the very reverse of an efficient, frictionless administrative machine.

The summer of 1934 witnessed two further decisions of importance to the consolidation of the regime. Firstly, the formal duality of power between president and chancellor ended with Hindenburg's death on 2 August, when the two offices were combined in Hitler's person. Secondly, Hitler bound the Reichswehr to himself once and for all, and satisfied its claim to be the sole armed force in the state, by means of the blood-bath on 30 June in which Röhm and other SA leaders were killed, thus clipping the wings of the party's private army.[16] The culmination of his personal power was reached on 2 August when, in accordance with suggestions by Reichswehr officers, it was enacted that the army would henceforth take a personal oath of allegiance to Hitler. Thus, within a year and a half the National Socialists, in alliance with heavy industry, the Reichswehr, and the bureaucracy, had subjected the German state and society to their rule. The only 'right' that the population still enjoyed was to endorse the regime's political acts by acclamation after the event. The regime used such plebiscites to affirm, again and again, the unity of the government and people, and hence the legitimacy of their own rule.

In terms of Hitler's dictum that the task of home policy was to 'furnish the native instrument of strength to foreign policy',[17] the state of affairs at the end of 1934 could be regarded as a considerable initial success, at least as regards the monopoly of political power. Single-party rule, the elimination of the Länder, and the centralization of government had been achieved, together with Hitler's absolute personal authority; the non-Nazi parties had been destroyed or dissolved, the opposition within the party had been beheaded, the associations of private interests had been brought into line, the influence of conservative and nationalist elements in the government had been cut down to size. The following years (1935–8) saw the consolidation of this monopoly of internal power.

2. BRIBERY BY MEANS OF SOCIAL BENEFITS

Like the rest of the regime's domestic policy, its social policy was designed to unite the population behind the government and so prepare it indirectly for the requirements of the war of conquest. The main problem, though not the only one, was to ensure the loyalty, or at least the acquiescence, of the working class. The Nazi leaders clearly recognized the decisive importance of the workers' attitude,

---

[15] Cf. *Der 'Führerstaat'*, and the works cited above in I.II.2 n. 23.
[16] Cf. Höhne, *Mordsache Röhm*.
[17] *Secret Book*, 79.

once more against the background of the First World War. In 1916–18 the workers had increasingly rebelled against the economic hardships they were subjected to, and had formed the nucleus of a much broader-based revolt against the continuation of the war.[18] This goes to explain Hitler's expressed fears that economic distress might lead to 'attempts at subversion', and his statement that 'one cannot for long keep a people below an otherwise generally valid living standard by an appeal to known facts or even to ideals'.[19] In other words, to prevent matters developing as they had in the past, the economic hardships of the working class must not exceed a certain level. It was necessary, moreover, to keep the workers in line by means of social concessions that would compensate for their deprivation of political rights. For Hitler and his associates were well aware that the war they intended could not be waged without the workers' co-operation, whether in the armed forces or the factories.

As wage-earners and their dependants made up about half the German population, the NSDAP had sought to curry favour with them even before 1933. These attempts, however, had been chiefly a matter of election tactics and were not very successful. Before Hitler's assumption of power National Socialism had hardly weakened the attachment of the working class to its own political and trade-union organizations. The left wing of the NSDAP, led by the brothers Gregor and Otto Strasser,[20] stressed the anti-capitalist elements of the party programme, but it was no more influential than the National Socialist Factory Cells Organization (NSBO), which was supposed to act as a 'shock troop' agency on the shop-floor. Although this organization claimed 300,000 members by the end of 1932,[21] it remained of secondary importance within the party; the independent trade unions at that time had about 6 million members. At the works council elections in 1932, NSBO candidates obtained only 4 per cent of the votes cast.[22] The mass of NSDAP voters belonged to the old and new middle class of small businessmen, not to the working class.[23]

With the destruction of its political and trade-union associations in the first months of Hitler's chancellorship, the working class lost the right to organize itself politically or to defend its own economic interests. The National Socialist government sought to fill this vacuum in several ways: (1) by ideological appeals; (2) by measures of social welfare; (3) by creating sham trade unions; (4) by brutal terrorism.

In the first place, an attempt was made to win over the workers by flattering propaganda and a specific ideology of labour. Appeals to idealism, patriotism, and the work ethos, slogans such as 'labour is a title of nobility', watchwords implying

[18] Kocka, *Klassengesellschaft*; Feldmann, Kolb, and Rürup, 'Massenbewegungen'.
[19] *Secret Book*, 95–6 (trans. amended; original, p. 121).
[20] Cf. Kühnl, *Nationalsozialistische Linke*.
[21] Mason, *Arbeiterklasse*, 3; Grebing (*Arbeiterbewegung*, 213) gives the membership of the NSBO in Dec. 1932 as 170,000.
[22] Broszat, *The Hitler State*, 139.
[23] On the NSDAP's electoral potential cf. Winkler, *Mittelstand*; Schweitzer, 'Nazification', in id., *Big Business and the Third Reich*.

equality of status ('workers with hand and brain', 'creative workers of all classes')—all these devices were used to create confidence and make it easier to get rid of the ADGB (the general trade union organization), whose officials were stigmatized as 'Marxist shop-floor bosses'. From the beginning, and especially from the mid-1930s onwards, Nazi propaganda directed at the workers made increasing use of militarist terminology.[24] The provision of jobs was officially called the 'labour battle'; one spoke of 'committing' or 'engaging' the labour force, and the worker in an arms factory was a 'soldier of the machine'. Finally, as part of the militarization of society, all workers were dubbed 'soldiers of labour'. Thus, the concept of a society organized and disciplined on military lines was clearly reflected also in the National Socialist organization of the working class. The compulsory labour service introduced by a law of 26 June 1935 similarly combined the state direction of labour with pre-military training for the (mostly juvenile) unemployed.

It was, none the less, hardly to be expected that the German workers, reared in anti-militarist traditions, could be bamboozled by militant-heroic watchwords into putting up with the loss of freedom and, in due course, supporting a war policy. Accordingly, the question was whether the regime could carry through an economic policy friendly to workers' interests which would improve the lot of the suffering masses in concrete, measurable terms. It must be recalled that the world depression of 1929–33 had put at least a third of the German labouring population out of work. Industrial workers were especially hard hit. In 1933 an average of 40 per cent of all classes of such workers were unemployed. Hunger, fear, and despair were rife. When the system of state insurance broke down under the weight of the unemployment figures, only about a tenth of the 6 million registered as unemployed in December 1932 were in receipt of a dole that itself barely permitted survival.[25]

This situation provided the regime with an opportunity to gain the workers' allegiance if, now that the world depression was gradually coming to an end, they were able to take prompt action to cure unemployment. The regime's job-creating measures, consisting essentially of a continuation of Schleicher's programme, were in fact a striking success. The propaganda claim that Hitler had put an end to unemployment was at first only partly true, as in the summer of 1935 almost 3,000,000 were still registered, and in December 1935 the figure was still 2,500,000; but in 1936 the level of employment throughout industry was approximately the same as in 1929. Between the beginning of 1933 and the autumn of 1936 the number of unemployed fell by almost 5 million. The figure for those still out of work was comparable to that for the years 1926–9 and was basically due to structural causes arising from rationalization. Even this residual unemployment was to some extent mopped up by the armament boom of 1936–9.[26]

The job-creation programme had varying effects on the workers' standard of living. As there was no state wages policy in the true sense but only a free-for-all labour market, wages went up appreciably in the armament industries but not in

---

[24] See Ley, *Soldaten der Arbeit*; Bracher, *Dictatorship*, 419–20; Bork, *Mißbrauch*, esp. 19–23.
[25] Mason, *Arbeiterklasse*, 25.
[26] Ibid. 55 ff.; Broszat, *The Hitler State*, 137. Cf. also Volkmann, II.v.5 below.

others. In 1936 the everyday life of most German workers was probably still one of poverty and privation.[27] However, accelerated rearmament began with the announcement of the Four-year Plan in September 1936; by May 1938 the labour surplus had been absorbed, and wages rose sharply. In industry the rise was of the order of 11 per cent. Despite the increased cost of living, the purchasing power of the working population increased appreciably. The real weekly wage of many in the consumer-goods industry at the beginning of the war was probably still some way lower than in 1929, but on the whole most Germans, including industrial workers, were as well off in 1939 as at the end of the 1920s.[28] The general standard in 1939 was certainly higher than in 1933, and was more or less comparable with that of 1928.[29] Many at the time thought the degree of prosperity unrivalled in German history, and, while National Socialist propaganda depicted the achievement in the usual superlatives, they were basically not contrary to the ascertainable truth. 'To the many thousands who before 1933 either had become unemployed or had never been employed at all, the loss of trade union organizations and social freedom was, in the final analysis, less important than the fact that with Hitler came full employment, mobility and opportunities for advancement— regardless of the methods or consequences.'[30] Only a few, no doubt, realized that the considerable increase in the gross national product was almost exclusively reflected in arms production and did little to raise the purchasing power of the working population. After the bitter years of unemployment, the decisive factor for millions of workers was that they had a job again.

The third method by which the National Socialist leaders tried to win over the workers' loyalty was by creating a sham trade union, the Deutsche Arbeitsfront (DAF: German Labour Front). This body, headed by Robert Ley, was improvised on 6 May 1933, a few days after the destruction of the free unions. Its function was 'to educate all working Germans for the National Socialist state and the National Socialist way of thought'[31]—implying in this context the superseding of class antagonism, at least as a matter of mental attitudes. Propaganda also sought to give the impression that the DAF was the fulfilment of the dream of a great unified trade-union system, which it had not been possible to realize in Weimar days. According to the ideology of a single national community (*Volksgemeinschaft*) employers also came within the category of 'all working Germans', and their organization (the Reich Corporation of German Industry) was duly absorbed into the DAF in November 1933. At the same time state institutions were appointed to carry out arbitral functions in the economic and social sphere, particularly the Treuhänder der Arbeit (Trustees of Labour) under Seldte, the labour minister. In practice their role amounted to defending the employers' interests and abolishing the right to conclude collective agreements. The law of 20 January 1934 'for the

---

[27] Mason *Arbeiterklasse*, 72.
[28] Ibid. 113 ff.
[29] Schoenbaum, *Revolution*, 113 ff.
[30] Bracher, *Dictatorship*, 421–2; Broszat, *The Hitler State*, 155.
[31] Quoted in Broszat, *The Hitler State*, 146. On the DAF cf. also Bracher, *Dictatorship*, 412–13, 273, and Mason, *Arbeiterklasse*, 40; see Volkmann, II.ii.4 below.

ordering of national labour', drafted by Seldte and Hugenberg's successor, the economic minister Kurt Schmitt, indicated how the regime envisaged the new economic order: the National Socialist 'national community' was to develop from the fiction of a 'works community' composed of 'works leaders' (the employers) and the work-force or 'retinue' (*Gefolgschaft*, a word with overtones of feudal loyalty). This basic social law of the Third Reich also led in the end to the curtailment of workers' rights, increased state regulation, and the favouring of employers' interests.

The DAF, though conceived as an instrument of social integration without class bias, was in general viewed with scepticism by the workers, despite the advantages it provided in the way of leisure activities, the Kraft durch Freude (KdF: strength through joy) movement,[32] and so on. Certainly it was not regarded as an adequate substitute for the banned trade unions. Up to the mid-1930s the DAF had no success in changing the attitude of industrial workers, who were largely indifferent to politics and reacted with fear, resignation, or embitterment rather than showing any disposition to adapt themselves to the new regime.[33] However, from 1936 onwards the situation in the labour market improved with accelerated rearmament, and in due course, as full employment was reached, labour became a scarce commodity. In these circumstances the DAF acquired a certain weight of its own and was able to some extent to represent the workers' economic interests *vis-à-vis* management and state institutions.

In 1938, as part of the preparation for war, the regime extended the working week to sixty hours and imposed further restrictions on movement and the choice of occupation, as well as additional regulations on the 'deployment of labour'.[34] These measures aroused discontent which could not be diverted by constant appeals to national solidarity, right thinking, and the spirit of sacrifice.[35] Some visible improvement in the standard of living was necessary, but was of course hard to reconcile with the intensified rearmament which swallowed up a large part of the national income. For fear of the incalculable consequences of social distress the regime, now and later, maintained a policy of social concessions: even in 1939–40 it refrained from cutting back the production of consumer goods. Nevertheless, as appears from the reports of the official bodies monitoring public opinion, this policy of 'bribery'[36] by social concessions did not succeed in transforming the working population into a willing tool of Nazi expansionism.[37] Dissatisfaction continued to be regularly voiced by the workers, as well as by the peasantry, craftsmen, minor clerks and employees, and junior officials; the same was true of

[32] Cf. Buchholz, *Die nationalsozialistische Gemeinschaft 'Kraft durch Freude'*; Moyer, *The Kraft durch Freude Movement*.

[33] Cf. documents in Vollmer, *Volksopposition*, and Thévoz, Branig, and Lowenthal-Hensel, *Pommern*.

[34] Cf. Schoenbaum, *Revolution*, 106–8; Mason, *Arbeiterklasse*, 139, 146–7.

[35] e.g. in connection with the 'Winter Relief' collections. Cf. Goebbels's account of 10 Oct. 1939, in *Goebbels-Reden*, i. 1 ff., and Bramsted, *Goebbels*, 102 ff.

[36] Term used by Mason, *Arbeiterklasse*, 13 and *passim*, and previously by Fraser, *Germany*, 97. Cf. now also Kranig, *Lockung und Zwang*.

[37] Mason, *Arbeiterklasse*, 158.

denominational organizations.[38] The attitude of the working class as a whole seemed to have changed little.

Oscillating between terrorist violence and concern for the workers' material needs, the regime in some cases shrank from applying rigorous measures. It observed caution, for instance, in the application of the compulsory service decree of 22 June 1938[39] for the construction of the Western fortifications. This is another indication that the regime had not succeeded by 1939 in completely stabilizing the home front. 'Hatred of National Socialism in working-class circles was certainly less pronounced in 1938 than in 1933; but awareness of specific collective interests in conflict with those of the ruling groups remained largely unaffected, and expressed itself in innumerable acts of solidarity at the place of work.'[40]

None the less, in September 1939 the German workers behaved as obediently as all other Germans. They did not succeed in putting up any effective resistance to the unleashing of the war. During the First World War hundreds of workers had gone on strike, and their actions had finally contributed to the ending of the war and the overthrow of the monarchy. By contrast, there were no strikes during the Second World War, and no developments comparable with the revolutionary upheaval of 1918–19.[41]

Karl Marx, in his analysis of Bonapartism, examined the interrelation of home and foreign policy and argued that in certain historical conditions the launching of a foreign war is a direct consequence of antagonisms within a society.[42] Thus, Napoleon III in the 1850s and 1860s periodically waged wars in order to prevent an open outbreak of the class struggle in France; internal difficulties were glossed over and diverted to foreign issues, and in this way the emperor kept himself in power. In line with this analysis, attempts have often been made to explain the outbreak of particular wars in terms of social imperialism. Such factors seem to have played an important part in the origin of the First World War.[43] Was this also the case in 1939? Studies of Germany's economic situation in that year have shown that Hitler not only intended a war of expansion and planned it systematically, but that he needed it to avoid the economic disaster that threatened to occur as a result of many years' overstraining of the economy by accelerated rearmament, with scarcely any restriction on consumer-goods production.[44] Hitler, it is argued, could not hope to achieve with Germany's natural resources the arms superiority he needed to carry out his war plans; he therefore 'was content to gain time which enabled him to achieve initial successes at least. Once the war was started it would have to feed itself.'[45] On this view, the wasteful use of resources under the Four-year Plan

---

[38] Steinert, *Hitlers Krieg*, 76. On the situation of the middle class cf. Saldern, *Mittelstand*.

[39] *RGBl.* (1938), i. 652, and ibid. (1939), 206; also Mason, *Arbeiterklasse*, 669 ff.

[40] Mason, *Arbeiterklasse*, 149.

[41] The chief reason for this was the Nazi terror: I.III.4 below.

[42] Cf. Wette, *Kriegstheorien*, 44 ff.

[43] Cf. Berghahn, *Rüstung*; Hallgarten and Radkau, *Industrie*; Bracher, afterword to Sauer, 'Mobilmachung', 372, stating that Hitler's basic conception was 'social-imperialist and expansionist'.

[44] Cf. *Wirtschaft und Rüstung*, esp. contributions by Milward and Mason; also Part II of the present volume.

[45] Sauer, 'Mobilmachung', 101.

carried with it the compulsion to launch a war if economic policy was not to end in a complete catastrophe.

The limitations of Germany's economic resources certainly led to a preference for blitzkrieg strategy and may have played a part in the timing of the attack on Poland.[46] But the effects of the socio-political situation were, at most, indirect. The regime was not compelled to launch a war in the autumn of 1939 so as to divert attention from major social conflicts or class struggles that threatened its position. However, it was one function of the 1939 war to forestall social dangers that were otherwise bound to develop owing to the contradictions of economic policy.[47]

3. EMIGRATION AND RESISTANCE

The unbridled terror during the first months after Hitler's accession to power showed clearly how the new rulers intended to deal with their political opponents. To escape the concentration stadien, thousands now took the sad decision to emigrate, rightly supposing that their lives were in danger if they remained in Germany.[48]

Those who emigrated included all kinds of opponents of the regime: democrats, social democrats, Communists, trade-unionists, pacifists, human-rights activists, members and supporters of the Confessing Church, and members of socialist splinter-parties such as the German Socialist Workers' Party (SAPD), the Communist Party-Opposition (KPO), and the Internationaler Sozialistischer Kampfbund (ISK: Militant Socialist International). The bulk of the *émigrés*, however, were Communists and Social Democrats.

Among those without party affiliations were over 2,500 writers and academics,[49] including Bertolt Brecht, Thomas and Heinrich Mann, Robert Musil, Joseph Roth, Stefan Zweig, Sigmund Freud, Ernst Cassirer, Max Horkheimer, Theodor W. Adorno, Alexander Rüstow, Veit Valentin, Herbert Marcuse, Albert Einstein, and Max Born—altogether a savage bleeding of German cultural and intellectual life.

While the *émigré* writers and scholars did their best to make a livelihood in the neighbouring European countries, which were often less than welcoming, their works were being burnt in Germany. Left-wing, pacifist, and Jewish literature that had been noted on the black lists of the propaganda ministry figured prominently in the notorious *auto-da-fé* of 10 May 1933.[50]

The exiles formed themselves from the outset into groups of various orientations, which remained separate. There was no political 'emigration' in the sense of an

[46] Cf. Thöne, *Entwicklungsstadien*; Dülffer, 'Beginn des Krieges', 459 ff., 468 ff.

[47] Following Mason, *Arbeiterklasse*, 164, rather than Schoenbaum, who ascribes less importance to the socio-political sources of conflict.

[48] For the following passages see Grossmann, *Emigration*, 31–9. The classification of refugees into 'political' and 'Jewish' is open to dispute, since National Socialist racism was political and many Jews were political opponents of the regime. However, this terminology was used by the League of Nations commissioner for refugees (Grossmann, p. 43).

[49] On the cultural exodus see Maas, *Exilpresse*; Pross, *Emigration*; Möller, *Exodus der Kultur*.

[50] Bracher, *Dictatorship*, 324–5; Bramsted, *Goebbels*, 68. Details in *10 Mai 1933*. On the historical background: Krockow, *Scheiterhaufen*.

intellectually homogeneous community, still less a concerted organization. The sole bond uniting all the *émigrés* was their rejection of Nazi rule and desire to help bring about its downfall.

According to the League of Nations high commissioner for German refugees,[51] by the end of 1935 65,000 persons had left Germany, including 40,000 Jews, 5,000–6,000 Social Democrats, 6,000–8,000 Communists, 2,000 pacifists and others with no party affiliation, 1,000 members of the Catholic party, and a further group of 2,000 not identified by party or race; to these figures were added 4,000 refugees from the Saarland. In 1934–5 there were more political than Jewish refugees, but this changed in the following years. By the outbreak of war about 300,000 had fled from Germany, of whom about 250,000 were Jews. The number of those persecuted and excluded from society is completed by the 300,000 Germans who, according to a Gestapo figure, were in prison or concentration camps for political reasons at the outbreak of war. Most of these belonged to the workers' movement.[52]

By imprisoning its more conspicuous political opponents or driving them into exile, the National Socialist regime neutralized most of those who might have constituted focal points of active resistance. The exiles for their part endeavoured for years to thwart Nazi war policy from outside the country. Their flight from the Reich was, in this sense, anything but a flight from political commitment.

At an early stage the exiles denounced Hitler's rearmament measures and the psychological mobilization of the German population for war.[53] They warned foreign countries unceasingly of Germany's aggressive intentions. From the outset they unmasked the regime's peaceful protestations as the enormous deception that they were. They composed numerous pamphlets and factual studies[54] intended to influence public opinion and strengthen resistance groups in Germany. As regards the success of this 'truth offensive', it must be recognized that in foreign countries little attention was paid to the *émigrés* down to the beginning of the war. The European host countries[55] tolerated the political refugees but mistrusted them, and hardly encouraged their anti-Nazi activity; some countries, such as Switzerland, in fact hindered it considerably.

Although the *émigrés* thus counted for little in terms of power, the National Socialist regime feared them as a dangerous influence on public opinion.[56] Their very existence was a refutation of the alleged identity between National Socialism and Germany. Moreover, the regime overrated the *émigrés*' ability to influence foreign countries and develop contacts with the opposition inside Germany. The *émigrés* were outside the immediate reach of the German persecuting agencies; so, to

---

[51] See Grossmann, *Emigration*, 43.
[52] *Der lautlose Aufstand*, 149.
[53] Cf. the contemporary publications *Hitler Rearms* and *Das deutsche Volk klagt an*. Also T. Mann, 'Briefwechsel mit Bonn' (1936), in id., *Schriften zur Politik*, 99–100; Matthias, *Sozialdemokratie und Nation*; *Mit dem Gesicht nach Deutschland*; *Geschichte der deutschen Arbeiterbewegung*, v. 129 ff., 159 ff.
[54] Cf. e.g. Gittig, *Tarnschriften*.
[55] On the attitude of the host countries see Grossmann, *Emigration*, 40.
[56] On the following passage see Tutas, *Nationalsozialismus und Exil*, 281 ff.

reduce them to silence, the regime extended its 'brown arm'[57] beyond Germany's frontiers, applying the internal methods of terrorist repression to political refugees abroad. Official German institutions in foreign countries were ordered systematically to record and keep watch on all *émigrés*. It was the task of Goebbels's propaganda apparatus to denigrate them as politically, intellectually, and morally inferior and as criminals, so as to convince German and foreign opinion that they were in no way to be trusted. In addition National Socialist diplomacy did its best to induce the governments of the host countries to suppress the exiles' publications and political activity; these efforts were not without effect, especially in those countries that felt directly threatened by the growing military power of Germany. Also, from about 1935 onwards the regime took measures against particular exiles, including deprivation of citizenship and the use of relatives as hostages, and not excluding kidnapping and murder.[58] According to James G. McDonald, the League of Nations high commissioner, over 4,000 Germans were deprived of citizenship by September 1935;[59] by mid-1939 the figure had risen to 11,000, of whom 88 per cent were of Jewish origin. An important motive of the regime's brutal policy was no doubt the fear that its intentions might be unmasked. No one must be allowed to assert with impunity that Hitler represented an acute danger of war.

Just as there was no unity of thought and action among the political *émigrés*, so there was no unified resistance movement within Germany, either before or during the war. Opposition groups of different orientations came to the fore at different times with different aims and methods. Hence, no generalizations can be made about resistance on the home front. Moreoever, the range of activities that could be so described included anything from inner non-participation or inactive opposition to disobedience and anti-regime activity, and it is an insoluble problem to decide what exactly constituted resistance and what did not.[60]

From the very beginning, in Weimar times, the two great workers' parties,[61] the SPD and the KPD, had fought the rising Fascist movement. However, except for some socialist splinter-groups—and in particular the left oppositional wing of the KPD[62]—the organizations of the workers' movement had long misjudged German fascism. In 1933-4 many Social Democrats and Communists still believed that the National Socialist regime could not last long and would collapse by reason of its own contradictions. Apart from this false estimation, there was little agreement between the workers' parties in the fight against Fascism. The Communist theory

---

[57] Term used by Grossmann: *Emigration*, 67.

[58] Tutas, *Nationalsozialismus und Exil*, 13, 20 ff., 281 ff., with reference to particular cases.

[59] Grossmann, *Emigration*, 67 ff.; Tutas, *Nationalsozialismus und Exil*, 151 ff., cf. also Misch, *Ausbürgerungslisten* (1939), and *Ausbürgerung deutscher Staatsangehöriger 1933-45.*

[60] On the concept of 'resistance' cf. e.g. Büchel, *Deutscher Widerstand;* Bracher, *Dictatorship*, 402; *Stand und Problematik der Erforschung des Widerstandes.* The latest research is reflected in *Widerstand gegen den Nationalsozialismus*, parts 2, 3, and 4 of which deal with resistance before the outbreak of war in 1939.

[61] On resistance by the workers' movement see Abendroth, *Sozialgeschichte*, 116 ff., 145 ff.; id., 'Widerstand', 76-96; Grebing, *Arbeiterbewegung*, 216 ff.; also the regional studies in Klotzbach, *Nationalsozialismus*; Steinberg, *Widerstand; Widerstand und Verfolgung in Wien.*

[62] Cf. *Faschismus in Deutschland: Analysen der KPD-Opposition aus den Jahren 1928-1933.*

of 'social Fascism',[63] which denigrated Social Democracy as the 'chief support of Facism on the left', ruled out any co-operation between them. The small intermediate groups that split off from the two main parties saw the need for all socialists to work together, but they commanded no support worth mentioning and no practical influence.

The KPD was forced underground directly after the Reichstag fire, when its chief officials were arrested. The ADGB (trade-union federation) and parts of the SPD for a time pursued an illusory policy of adaptation to the regime, till they too were banned. In May 1933 some members of the SPD executive escaped to Prague, where they formed an executive in exile (SOPADE).[64] This body attempted to establish itself as the foreign headquarters of the SPD, but soon came into conflict with the party officials remaining in Germany, who for the most part submitted to the Nazi regime, with only a few engaging in active resistance. Neither the Social Democrats[65] nor the trade-unionists[66] nor the Reichsbanner were prepared to carry on an organized underground struggle, and the rank and file waited in vain for any initiative from their top leaders. Hence there arose, to begin with, only loosely knit social democratic groups, which largely confined themselves to maintaining old personal contacts and, in the long term, preserving the ideal of social democracy. Their contacts with one another were also limited. Their clandestine publishing activity was mostly local in character and meant little in terms of power. From 1935 onwards at the latest, the opposition groups were themselves aware of this. They believed less and less in the possibility of active resistance, an idea which was replaced by that of 'passive mental loyalty' (*passive Gesinnungstreue*).[67] The chances that anti-Fascist propaganda and conspiracy might succeed were far outweighed by the dangers and sacrifice involved, and resignation inevitably set in. From 1936–7 social democratic opposition in Germany consisted of no more than political discussions in very small groups. Intellectual disaffection of this kind was clearly no threat to the regime. Similarly, political 'whisper-jokes'[68] and rumours[69] had very little to do with true resistance.

Communist anti-Fascism was indeed more consistent than that of the social democrats, inasmuch as the KPD leaders and many loyal party officials, including junior ones, at no stage came to terms with the Hitler regime, but sought to create an anti-Fascist people's movement that would overthrow it from within. Although thousands of leading officials, including the party chairman Ernst Thälmann, were arrested as early as February–March 1933,[70] their supporters in the following years

---

[63] See Bahne, 'Sozialfaschismus', 211–45; also I.1.9 above.

[64] Cf. Matthias, *Sozialdemokratie und Nation*; Edinger, *Exile Politics*; and the documentation in *Deutschland-Berichte der Sozialdemokratischen Partei Deutschlands (SOPADE) 1934–1940*.

[65] Cf. recently Schulze, *Anpassung*. On the interpretation of 'illegality' (*Illegalität*) cf. *Widerstand und Verfolgung in Wien*, i. 9.

[66] Cf. *Gewerkschaftliche Monatshefte*, 26 (1975), No. 7, with articles by H. Mommsen, H. Skrzypczak, B. Engelmann, G. Beier, H.O. Hemmer, and others; Esters and Pelger, *Gewerkschafter*.

[67] Klotzbach, *Nationalsozialismus*, 141; for the following passage, also ibid. 141–5.

[68] Cf. Gamm, *Flüsterwitz*, 11.

[69] Dröge, *Widerstand*.

[70] Cf. *Deutsche Widerstandskämpfer*; Berthold, 'Faschistischer Terror', 14–15.

carried on an underground struggle in which great sacrifices were made with little regard to the disproportion between effort and result. The Communists too had no real chance of undermining the regime. From the middle of 1934 onwards it was clear to the KPD and to its Comintern masters that the attempts to form a broad popular anti-Fascist movement had failed completely. A reorientation took place, leading in summer–autumn 1935 to the Comintern decision to give up the tactics of forming a united front from below (by detaching social democratic workers from their own parties), and instead to work for a popular front of all anti-Fascists 'to bring down the Hitler dictatorship and prevent war'.[71] Such a front indeed came into existence in France and Spain, but not in Germany. One of the main reasons was that the Communists continued to mistrust the Social Democrats, whom they had for more than a decade stigmatized as 'social Fascists'. After 1935 the possibility of resistance grew increasingly remote. The regime's successes in foreign policy and in reducing unemployment helped to stabilize the home front and to isolate the illegal remnants of the workers' movement. Contact between resistance-groups and the population became more and more tenuous. The passive attitude of the Western powers to the annexations of 1938–9, and especially the Hitler–Stalin pact of August 1939, afforded no prospect of any encouragement to resistance inside Germany. Finally, such will to resistance as remained was broken by the Gestapo and SS. Arrests on even a vague suspicion of subversive activity, followed by long terms of imprisonment, continued to be the order of the day even after the destruction of organized resistance in 1934;[72] indeed, they were increasingly common right up to the outbreak of war.

Thus, the activity of opposition groups from within the workers' movement was almost completely paralysed by 1939. Beside the repressive measures we have mentioned, conscription into the Labour Service and the Wehrmacht played its part in weakening the coherence of potential resistance elements and communication between them.

In order to prepare and wage war, German Fascism had to destroy the workers' movement. It had achieved this so thoroughly by 1933–4 that at the outbreak of war the regime had scarcely reason to fear a symbolic anti-war demonstration, much less actual rebellion. The question whether a popular front could have prevented war must remain hypothetical. At any rate it was too late by 1935. At the beginning of the 1930s a combination of all left-wing opponents of National Socialism might have halted its progress. Given the internal political conditions in the mid-1930s, with the regime firmly in the saddle, an illegal battle would have had to be fought with practically no chance of success.[73]

---

[71] Cf. *Geschichte der deutschen Arbeiterbewegung*, v. 101–28; Duhnke, *Die KPD*, 150 ff.

[72] According to Abendroth, *Sozialgeschichte*, 145, by the beginning of the war 225,000 Germans had been sentenced to a total of nearly 600,000 years' imprisonment for political offences. Berthold ('Faschistischer Terror', 14) states that of the KPD's 300,000-odd members in 1933 about half were persecuted, imprisoned, or put in concentration camps; tens of thousands of party members and officials were murdered.

[73] Reichhardt, 'Widerstand der Arbeiterbewegung', 209 ff., states that according to the general estimate no more than 10% of former members of the workers' parties were prepared to continue the struggle after 1933.

While there was, none the less, a measure of resistance to National Socialism among the workers throughout the years 1929–39, opposition from the upper ranks of society did not begin until 1938. A military opposition took shape for a short time in connection with the Sudeten crisis.[74] The public heard nothing of it, as the plans to overthrow Hitler were hatched in the utmost secrecy. The thinking that gave rise to the attempt was largely that of General Ludwig Beck, the army chief of staff. In May 1938, after Hitler had more than once unfolded his war plans to the top military leaders,[75] Beck submitted a memorandum in which he gave both military and political reasons for thinking that the prospects for a policy of expansion in 1938, which must naturally first be directed against Czechoslovakia, were anything but favourable.[76] Beck feared that Germany was insufficiently prepared from the point of view of military organization and armaments, and might be involved in a long war against a coalition of superior strength in political, military, economic, and psychological respects. This did not mean that he was opposed to war on principle;[77] but—like Admiral Günther Guse, the naval chief of staff—he was opposed to Hitler's policy towards Czechoslovakia 'on account of the political and strategic situation at this moment', believing that it would lead to a world war which Germany could not win at that juncture.[78] Thus, the officers concerned, thinking in traditional terms of power politics, based their opposition on essentially military grounds. Beck himself did not disapprove of the Hitler regime as such and in any case was neither prepared nor able to act independently of traditional military norms. Having failed in his attempt to persuade Hitler through the proper channels, he had no alternative but to resign and retire to private life. His successor, General Franz Halder, took the decisive step of joining the conspiracy in September 1938, the object of which was to overthrow Hitler by a *coup d'état*.[79] The chief motive, as before, was to prevent a war which, in the plotters' opinion, could only lead to defeat. Preparations for the coup were organized by a group of senior officers, and it was to be put into operation the moment Hitler seemed about to launch the country into war. However, the course of events was basically affected by the appeasement policy of Britain and France, leading to the Munich agreement and the cession of the Sudeten area without hostilities. This removed the ground for action by the conspirators, who gave up their attempt. Thus, there was no actual attempt at resistance by the conservative opposition before the war.

We may refer briefly to opposition from the churches.[80] This, like the conservative opposition, was not directed against the National Socialist regime as such, but was essentially concerned with safeguarding the autonomy of the ecclesiastical sphere against *Gleichschaltung*. This applies equally to the activity of

[74] On the following see Müller, *Heer*, 300–77; Bracher, *Dictatorship*, 483–94; also Deist, III.iii.4, and Messerschmidt, IV.v.7 (*b*) below.

[75] e.g. on 5 Nov. 1937 and at the end of Jan. 1938; cf. Müller, *Heer*, 234, 301.

[76] Text of memorandum in Foerster, *Beck*, 100–5; for the interpretation, Müller, *Heer*, 300 ff.

[77] Cf. his lecture 'Die Lehre vom totalen Krieg' in Beck, *Studien*, 231–58.

[78] Müller, *Heer*, 309 ff.; a different view in Graml, 'Resistance Thinking', 7 ff.; on Guse cf. also Deist, III.ii.3 (*c*) below.

[79] On the conspiracy of Sept. 1938 see Müller, *Heer*, 345 ff.

[80] Summary in Bracher, *Dictatorship*, 469 ff.

the Confessing Church. Altogether church opposition was directed to confessional interests in the narrower sense and led to direct political resistance only in the case of one or two exceptional individuals, such as Alfred Delp or Dietrich Bonhoeffer. The churches as such did not take any action against the war.

To sum up: the Hitler regime was overthrown only by Germany's complete military defeat in the Second World War. Neither the political *émigrés* who attacked the Nazi rulers from outside, nor the various opposition groups within Germany, were able to threaten the regime seriously or prevent war. From the mere point of view of political strength, there is no doubt that the political emigration and the internal resistance were completely overshadowed by their opponent. The history of the *émigrés* and of the active resisters in Germany is one of suffering, persecution, and failure, not of political success.

The conservative opposition did not wish to prevent a war of conquest as such, only the launching of one at what they thought was an unfavourable moment. The left-wing opposition tried to overthrow the regime and so prevent war altogether. The failure of these convinced enemies of National Socialism is due to many causes. They include the impossibility of the free formation of public opinion, the regime's methods of terrorism and repression of all dissidents, and the deafness of foreign governments to the well-grounded warnings of the political *émigrés* and the internal German opposition. More important than all this is the fact that the National Socialist regime commanded widespread acceptance in Germany in the 1930s. Especially in the years of Hitler's foreign-policy successes, the regime was supported by the great majority of the German people.

4. TERROR AS A MEANS OF DISCIPLINE

The essence of Fascism is violence. 'Physical and intellectual violation—this is what it believes in, practises, loves, honours, and glorifies.' The meaning and purpose of the National Socialist state system can only be 'to condition the German people for the "coming war", while remorselessly excluding, suppressing, and exterminating any opposing factor; to turn the nation into an infinitely obedient instrument of war, afflicted by no critical thought, spellbound in blind, fanatical ignorance'.[81] This apt description of the role of force in international and German Fascism was formulated in 1937–8 by a German writer of bourgeois origin who had emigrated and been deprived of citizenship: Thomas Mann.

National Socialism indeed practised violence at every stage of its development. Torture and political murder, waves of arrests, concentration camps, street terror, and war—all these were variations on its philosophy of power, an ideology in which military and terrorist violence both had a fixed place.

As part of the domestic preparation for war, the function of state-directed terror was to intimidate and eliminate political opponents and to nip potential resistance in the bud. Whenever compliance could not be secured by propaganda and the

---

[81] T. Mann, *Schriften zur Politik*, 104, 110. On Fascism and violence see also I.1.2 above.

control of information, socio-political concessions, and the *Gleichschaltung* of political and social organizations, the machinery of force was brought into action. Like all the methods in the regime's armoury, terror against actual or supposed political opponents was not an end in itself but a part of the strategy by which the German people was to be forged into an obedient, efficient instrument of war. Thus, the terror by which the population was kept in line from 1933 to 1939 was an integral part of the regime's preparation for war.

Even before Hitler became chancellor it was plain to all that street terror and political murder were no less important than propaganda in the Nazi techique of mobilization, despite all claims that the party wished to achieve power by legal means. At that stage the violent aspect of the 'movement' was chiefly embodied in its paramilitary organization, the Sturmabteilung (SA: 'storm troops'). This organization was founded in 1920 and, a few years later, showed itself to be one of the most active and strongest of the radical right-wing fighting groups in Bavaria. From then on the SA supported the National Socialist battle for power by the use or threat of physical force; it also transmitted to the NSDAP the 'front-line spirit' in its political form. Its cadres, significantly, were largely former officers and members of the Freikorps, and Röhm, its chief, was the prototype of a leader of mercenaries.[82] However, the SA was not merely an instrument of terror. With its disciplined marches and parades it presented the picture of a future orderly deployment of power, while its military bands and the solemn dedication of colours appealed to those sections of the population which were enthusiastic for military spectacles of all kinds.[83]

During the first five weeks after the middle of June 1932, when the temporary ban on the SA was lifted, street fights, for which the Nazis were chiefly responsible, accounted for 99 dead and 1,125 injured.[84] Among the many political acts of terror, a case that received especial publicity was the bestial murder at Potempa in Upper Silesia of a Communist worker by five SA men. When they were sentenced to death under an emergency decree of 9 August 1932 against political terror Hitler, in a published telegram, assured them of his 'unbounded devotion', thus ostentatiously allying himself with political crime.[85]

This was a foretaste of the brutal violence with which the promised 'destruction of Marxism' was to be carried out in the first months of 1933. Up to July 1933 an estimated 50,000 persons—Communist functionaries, social democrats, left-wing intellectuals, and pacifists—were arrested and sent to improvised concentration camps. During the same period SA terror claimed 500 or 600 dead.[86] Göring, who organized the mass arrests and terror in Prussia, declared at a mass meeting on 3 March: 'I am not here to dispense justice, only to destroy and exterminate—that is

[82] Bracher, *Dictatorship*, 170–1, 176–7.
[83] Broszat, *The Hitler State*, 19.
[84] According to the former Prussian premier Otto Braun, *Weimar*, 252.
[85] Broszat, *The Hitler State*, 25.
[86] Fest, *Hitler* (trans.), 401. Cf. also the 1933 figures for political offences in Broszat, *The Hitler State*, 332.

all.[87] Hitler himself was not behindhand. Never, he declared in speeches before the Reichstag election of 5 March 1933, would he desist from the task of 'extirpating Marxism and its attendant phenomena in Germany'.[88] At the same time, Goebbels on Hitler's orders depicted the Führer as a statesman urging moderation, while the SA took upon itself the odium of violence and radical behaviour. This hypocrisy was compounded by juridical measures[89] such as the 'Reichstag fire decree', intended to cast a cloak of legality over the random terror of the SA as well as more systematic violence—a tactic which clearly had a considerable amount of success in deluding the public.

By 1933 the SA was about 500,000 strong, or five times as large as the Reichswehr in purely numerical terms. In 1934 it had 4 million members.[90] This increase of strength and the resulting competition with the Wehrmacht contained the seeds of a serious conflict. Moreover, in the first months of Hitler's chancellorship the SA developed a terrorist dynamism of its own that could become dangerous to the regime as the latter began to consolidate itself after the mass arrests. Once the NSDAP had achieved political power in the Reich, the SA really had no further part to play. Accordingly, Hitler tried to divert it into the task of training young people. Röhm, however, saw the SA as the nucleus of a new army, and he wished in addition to preserve it as a political force capable of controlling 'the state'.

In order to make good his claim to totalitarian leadership, Hitler decided to resolve this conflict by violence also. In the blood-bath of 30 June 1934, inaccurately styled the 'Röhm *putsch*',[91] the SA leaders were cold-bloodedly liquidated. To preserve the façade of legality once again, this act of mass murder was passed off as 'emergency defence of the state'. Hitler was able to count on the 'tacit complicity of the Wehrmacht leaders',[92] who had all along regarded the SA as a dangerous rival. After the violent elimination of its leaders the SA played no further part worth mentioning, but sank to the level of a military sports association. Despite all propaganda to the contrary, the murder of the SA leaders was nothing but a politically sanctioned crime. As such it belongs to the series ranging from the Potempa affair and other terrorist acts of the 'time of struggle' to the regime's later policies of war and genocide.

With the destruction of the SA began the rise of the SS (Schutzstaffel, 'guard detachment'). This organization, originally set up to guard the person of party leaders and ensure order at meetings, grew considerably in importance after Heinrich Himmler was appointed Reichsführer SS on 6 January 1929. While the SA, which rather belonged to the tradition of radical right-wing paramilitary associations, developed into a mass army of brownshirts from 1929 onwards, the SS—which at that date was only about 1,000 strong—grew, under the influence of Himmler's ideas of order and élitism, into a kind of police force within the party. By

[87] Göring, *Reden und Aufsätze*, 27.
[88] Domarus, i. 205, also 206–11; cf. Baynes, i. 254, 665–6.
[89] Bracher, *Dictatorship*, 435.
[90] Höhne, *Order*, 91–2.
[91] Bloch, *Die SA*.
[92] Bracher, *Dictatorship*, 300 ff.; cf. also Deist, III.II.2 (*b*) and III.III.3 below.

the outbreak of war, ten years later, it could claim to constitute the 'hard core' of the party's forces.[93] In August 1931 Reinhard Heydrich began, under Himmler's instructions, to build up a separate intelligence service within the SS, the so-called Sicherheitsdienst (SD: Security Service), which began as a secret police unit within the NSDAP and, from 1933 onwards, spread a network of spies throughout Germany. On 27 September 1939 the SD and Gestapo were merged into the Reichssicherheitshauptamt (RSHA: Reich Central Security Office) under Heydrich.[94]

The SS did not become a feared and mysterious instrument of government until its fusion with the political police forces of the Länder, including the Gestapo (secret state police), which latter Göring as premier of Prussia had built up from April 1933 onwards.[95] By dint of conflicts with his rivals, lasting over several years, Himmler acquired ever-increasing police powers, culminating with the Führer's decree of 17 June 1936, which placed the whole German police system under the SS. Himmler, as Reichsführer SS and chief of the German police, was now in charge of a huge, centralized apparatus that was already largely independent of control by the Reich minister of home affairs.

The term 'SS state',[96] which has become part of the vocabulary of the subject, is designed to emphasize that the SS took shape as a special organization directly responsible to Hitler and independent of the state administration; it asserted its priority over the latter on the strength of its special political task, and so established itself, alongside the older institutions over which it took precedence, as a state within the state. It claimed not only to safeguard the new political order but actually to mould it to its own design, without being subject to any laws or to judicial examination of its acts. The Prussian law of 10 February 1936 had already laid down that acts of the Gestapo were not subject to judicial review by the state authorities.[97]

From the middle of 1936 Himmler with his new title seriously advanced the claim to subject every human being in the Reich or within its power to thoroughgoing control and supervision, and to persecute and imprison in concentration camps all opponents of the regime, whether of the right or the left, Jews or adherents of the Christian churches. Up to the outbreak of war this was the principal activity of the SS. It was Himmler who transformed the improvised SA terror of the first months of the regime's existence into the bureaucratically planned and executed system of curbing opposition by means of concentration camps. At the same time, fulfilling what had been the SA's ambition, he created, alongside the Wehrmacht and in competition with it, a second military force, later called Waffen-SS (the Armed SS).[98] At the outbreak of war this body numbered 28,000 men. Although paid from the budget of the finance ministry, it was subject to no civil authority, but only to

---

[93] *Anatomy,* 346.
[94] Höhne, *Order,* 226 ff.; *Anatomy,* 437 ff.; Broszat, *The Hitler State,* 275–6.
[95] On the organizational history see Zipfel, 'Gestapo'; also Delarue, *Histoire de la Gestapo.*
[96] Based on Kogon, *Theory and Practice*; also *Anatomy*; summary account in Bracher, *Dictatorship,* 438 ff.
[97] Text in *Anatomy,* 151.
[98] Cf. ibid. 233–49, 343–4; and Deist, III.III.3 below.

Himmler as Hitler's representative. Units of the Armed SS—Totenkopfverbände (Death' Head units) and Verfügungstruppen (militarized formations), recruited on a voluntary basis—took part in the Polish operations in September 1939 within the framework of regular army units.

In describing the different organs of terror and discipline the present account has considered these chiefly from the organizational point of view. This may give the impression that the 'Hitler state'—that strange dual phenomenon, composed of 'old' institutions on the one hand and, on the other, the SS operating an extra-legal state of its own—conformed to the picture of a perfectly organized and highly efficient system such as that depicted by older theories of totalitarianism.[99] However, recent studies of the internal policy of the Third Reich have shown that there was a gulf between the totalitarian claim and the reality. The NSDAP itself was a highly contradictory formation, a conglomerate of ideologies, subordinate bodies, rival cliques, and groups of leaders, held together solely by Hitler as Führer and by his instrument, the SS. In the same way the 'Hitler state' was not totalitarian in the sense of maximum efficiency; it was a jungle of competing authorities, confused in structure and in part badly administered. Its power rested partly on its intimidating ambiguity, partly on a well-organized system of repression, and partly on Hitler's technique of contriving that the ministries, organizations, and other authorities were in constant rivalry with one another.

It was also not the case that the regime's policy of terror was uniformly intensive and affected all sections of the population equally. Certainly, any critic of the National Socialist state risked incarceration, and even in outwardly stable years the Gestapo arrested thousands of dissidents. Between October 1935 and May 1936, for example, 7,266 persons were arrested on account of 'activity for the KPD and SPD'.[100] None the less, as the regime consolidated itself during the winter of 1936–7 the number of concentration-camp inmates fell to under 10,000, and four of the seven camps were closed down.[101] This reduction in the incidence of terror was due to the fact that after the suppression of the SA in the summer of 1934 conservative ideas of order came more to the fore, as did conservative elements in the state itself, and these gave at least as strong an imprint to the system as did the NSDAP.[102] In the showdown of 1934 Hitler had himself decided against the SA and in favour of the conservative elements, especially the Wehrmacht.

A new wave of terror did not set in until 1937–8, with the acceleration of rearmament and preparations for war. Its object was to ensure that the relative stability of the previous years did not turn into political stagnation, which could not suit the regime's war policy. Persecution was now extended to elements 'harmful to the nation', such as 'anti-social elements'—beggars, tramps, gypsies, psychopaths, alcoholics, and the mentally ill. 'Shirkers'—e.g. any who left their jobs 'without sufficient reason'—homosexuals, and Jehovah's Witnesses were imprisoned in

---

[99] Cf. Arendt, *Totalitarianism*; for the controversy cf. Jänicke, *Totalitäre Herrschaft*; Schlangen, 'Totalitäre Herrschaft'; Greiffenhagen, Kühnle, and Müller, *Totalitarismus*.

[100] *Anatomy*, 424 ff.   [101] Bracher, *Dictatorship*, 448

[102] Broszat, *The Hitler State*, 213–14.

camps 'as a preventive measure'; the device of 'protective arrest', introduced after the Reichstag fire, gave a semblance of legality to the preventive treatment of all potential opponents of the regime.[103] 'The mixture of political, criminal, punitive and preventive considerations, characteristic of the new phase of concentration-camp policy that began in 1937, brought a renewed increase in the camp population'.[104] Thousands of political arrests were made in connection with the annexations of 1938—Austria and the Sudetenland—while the pogrom of 9 November 1938 (Reichskristallnacht, 'night of broken glass') brought, for the time being, another 35,000 Jews into the camps.[105] Apart from other motives, the need for manpower on SS production-sites played an important part.

The fresh wave of terror against the 'enemy within' was intended to arouse the warlike spirit once again as a direct prelude to mobilization for a war of conquest. Once internal enemies had been pilloried it was easy to identify them with external ones. A further reason for the arrests lay in the sphere of labour policy. Such measures as the order of 22 June 1938,[106] intended to provide additional manpower for the arms sector, met with considerable resistance from the working class in particular, so much so that the authorities refrained from applying it strictly.[107] The later arbitrary measures of repression must be seen against this background. They were not only an expression of the totalitarian claims of the 'SS state', but also of the rulers' mistrust of some of their own subjects.

Himmler admitted this indirectly in a speech to senior SS officers on 8 November 1938, with reference to the barely averted war over the Sudeten crisis. It was, he said, the task of the SS to nip any revolutionary development in the bud. 'One thing I can guarantee—that as long as I am in charge of the SS, in a war at home there won't be any shirkers or anyone who even dreams of making a revolution.'[108]

Thus, the many terrorist measures of the SS, the Gestapo, and the SD in the last year before the launching of the war against Poland were a sign of the regime's weakness, inasmuch as terror was always resorted to when the political leaders had to admit the limitations of their power to push forward mobilization for war at the speed and on the scale they desired.

5. THE MILITARIZED 'NATIONAL COMMUNITY'

The idea of the 'national community' (*Volksgemeinschaft*), like almost all the rest of the Nazi ideology, did not originate with Hitler's movement. It was introduced into the political vocabulary by the youth movement and the neo-conservatism of the early 1920s, and adopted by National Socialist propaganda in the same way as many other conservative and nationalist slogans. The term was used primarily in opposition to the idea and reality of the class society and of those political parties

[103] *Anatomy*, 402 ff., 437 ff.
[104] Bracher, *Dictatorship*, 449.
[105] *Anatomy*, 445 ff.
[106] Repr. in Mason, *Arbeiterklasse*, 669 ff.
[107] Ibid. 250 ff.
[108] Himmler, *Geheimreden*, 48.

and associations which regarded class divisions as the essence of the capitalist system. It was also a slogan of opposition to the party system and to the organization of society into more or less autonomous 'estates' and interest-groups. The notion of a 'community' expressed the idealistic feeling that social antagonisms and tension between classes could be transcended by a sense of belonging to the same national and ethnic stock (Volkstum), without the need to do away with the class system as such. The Marxist principle that human consciousness is determined by the individual's social situation was to be overthrown in the euphoria of ideological equality. National Socialist propaganda used the idea of *Volksgemeinschaft* above all in the field of social policy, to justify the destruction of the unions and gain the loyalty of the working class; at the same time, racialist ideas increasingly became the criterion of national solidarity.

Just as the regime was able to draw on conservative and nationalist traditions in its home policy and social ideology—not least the tradition of fellowship among those who had fought in the trenches of the First World War[109]—in the same way the racial aspect of the idea and policy of *Volksgemeinschaft* echoed a widespread, latent anti-Semitism. Hitler's policy towards the Jews[110] showed with brutal clarity to what extent the National Socialist idea of *Volksgemeinschaft* was rooted in a distinction between friends and enemies. Anyone who, according to arbitrary definitions, did not belong to the community was denounced as harmful and parasitic: in the name of an imaginary 'sound popular instinct' (*gesundes Volksempfinden*) he was subjected to political, economic, legal, and moral discrimination, deprived of basic rights, exposed without protection to officially sanctioned terrorism, and finally destroyed by the regime's machinery of mass murder. This treatment of 'noxious elements' was meted out not only to Germans of Jewish race but also to other minorities, such as Jehovah's Witnesses, as well as the 'anti-social' and the 'work-shy'. Once political opposition had been eliminated, these categories functioned as the actual 'enemy within', on whom aggressions were discharged on the scapegoat principle. During the phase of preparation for war the regime staged the persecution of these alleged enemy groups not primarily as a matter of racial ideology, but rather as one method of shaping the nation in accordance with the specious formula of *Volksgemeinschaft*.

On 1 May 1933, the first 'Labour Day' held under National Socialist auspices, Goebbels gave an address to young people on the *Volksgemeinschaft* theme, which was to be a staple of propaganda gatherings in the coming years. The social vision proclaimed by Hitler's chief propagandist was a characteristic expression of the heady brand of idealism with which the doctrine was dispensed to the public.

On this day the whole nation at all levels, in all its professions, occupations, and estates, acknowledges the dignity and blessedness of labour. On a day when in former times we heard the rattle of machine-guns and the hate-inspired songs of the class struggle and the Internationale, in this first year of Hitler's government the German people is assembled in

---

[109] Cf. I.1.3 and I.1.10 above.
[110] Summary in Bracher, *Dictatorship*, 450 ff., 520 ff.; also Krausnick in *Anatomy*, 23 ff. See also I.III.4 and I.III.5 above.

unanimous, unswerving loyalty to the state, the race (*Volk*), and the German nation to which we all belong. Every difference is wiped away. The barriers of class hatred and the arrogance of social status that for over fifty years divided the nation from itself have been torn down. Germans of all classes, tribes (*Stämme*), professions, and denominations have joined hands across the barriers that separated them and have vowed henceforth to live as a community, to work and fight for the fatherland that unites us all. . . . The class struggle is at an end. The idea of the national community rises above the ruins of the bankrupt liberal-capitalist state. . . . Thus the German people marches into the future.[III]

The National Socialist regime sought to resolve antagonisms and overcome class conflict, not by any radical change in social owership but by the propagation of a common political creed. The ulterior purpose was clearly indicated by Goebbels's references to marching together into the future. The object was to ensure that the 'united national community' (*geschlossene Volksgemeinschaft*)[112] would be capable of 'seeing through' the next war, unlike the situation in 1914–18, when first the home front and then the internal political truce collapsed.

Given this war-oriented objective, National Socialist propaganda used the terms *Volksgemeinschaft* and *Wehrgemeinschaft* more or less interchangeably,[113] thus accurately reflecting the policy of remilitarizing the whole German people. From the regime's point of view—of course not openly expressed—the ideal form of *Wehrgemeinschaft* or 'brotherhood in arms' was a thoroughly organized and militarized society that allowed itself to be used by the Führer as an instrument of war. As a high officer of the SA put it in 1939: 'All German people, wherever they stand and whether they are at present in uniform or not, are soldiers. . . . Each one must serve the community and subordinate himself to it, since he depends on it and cannot exist without it. In the event of war the whole nation, from children . . . to the most aged, and including women as well, are part of the defensive struggle.'[114]

The creation of *Wehrgemeinschaft* by the National Socialist regime was the fulfilment of what the Wehrmacht and the nationalist opposition had vainly pressed for throughout the Weimar period.[115] The government could therefore be sure of the enthusiastic assent of rightist circles. This was one of the major causes of the loyal co-operative of the old conservative élite with the National Socialist leaders, without which the relative internal stability of the Third Reich would have been unattainable. Among other things it meant that the old administrative apparatus could be left virtually intact: out of a million and a half civil servants, only 1 or 2 per cent were affected by the purges.[116]

One of the chief practical tasks of the *Volksgemeinschaft* policy was to enrol and organize every form of labour potential for the coming war. The jargon for this was

---

[III] Goebbels, 'Zur Feier der deutschen Jugend am 1. Mai 1933', in *Goebbels spricht*, 99 ff.; Hitler used almost identical terminology in a 'Call to Workers' in the *Völkischer Beobachter* (2 May 1933), 1 ff.

[112] This slogan was also the key motif of the 1937 party rally: cf. *Parteitag der Arbeit*, 92, 278 and *passim*.

[113] Cf. *Volksgemeinschaft — Wehrgemeinschaft* (1936).

[114] SA-Hauptsturmführer Simon in *Der SA-Führer*, 4 (1939), 19–20; quoted from Sywottek, *Mobilmachung*, 85.

[115] Cf. I.I.3 and I.II.4 above.

[116] Mommsen, *Beamtentum*, 13–14, 21; figures, 54 ff.

Menschenverteilung or 'distribution of human material'. Göring, the commissioner for the Four-year Plan, described the policy as follows at a session of the Reich Defence Council on 18 November 1938:

Every German, male or female, aged between 14 and 65 must in effect have a mobilization order in his or her pocket, indicating where they are wanted. In a future war we cannot do without either the 14- or the 60-year-olds—everyone can be given something to do. We must get hold of them all and give them their different tasks, so that one man goes into the army and another into the factory, or one worker stays in the factory while another goes off to the front and lets his wife take over ... We must see that young people are properly directed from the beginning; unnecessary skills must be replaced by necessary ones, all human resources must be used to the full, the greatest care must be taken to determine where people are needed and where they are not, and to decide where they belong at the critical moment, overriding as far as possible all stupid bureaucratic restrictions.[117]

In 1936–9, during the phase of accelerated rearmament and prepartion for war, the regime's labour policy and the accompanying *Volksgemeinschaft* propaganda laid stress on this aspect of mobilizing all the German people's reserves of civil and military strength.

According to the boasts of Nazi ideologists and propagandists at the outbreak of war, the 'constructive work' of 1933–9 achieved its object of unifying the German people and finally overcoming class differences. For instance, a few days after the attack on Poland Göring declared,[118] with a significant allusion to the 'civic truce' of August 1914, that the whole German nation was now in the struggle as one man, a 'devoted (*verschworen*) community' of 'soldiers in arms and soldiers of the factory floor'. Looking back on the wonderful achievements since the seizure of power, one of the 'greatest and most tremendous', he claimed, 'and the most immortal of all our Führer's great services to the nation', was the creation of the *Volksgemeinschaft*.

Was this true or mere propaganda? What had the regime achieved in the social sphere apart from the 'distribution of human material'? Was the 'national community' a reality or not?

After the elimination of parties, the free trade unions, and the Land governments, the liquidation of opposition within the party and the regimentation of all associations representing particular interests,[119] the regime proceeded to 'take in hand' and train the German people by means of a many-faceted system of compulsory organizations. The conquest of state power was to be followed by the complete subjection of society, so that every single individual was available to serve the government's purposes.

The horizontal and vertical organization of the NSDAP[120] was in many ways well adapted to the achievement of this purpose.[121] At Reich level it included central

---

[117] Text in Mason, *Arbeiterklasse*, 909–33, here 928–9.
[118] Göring's speech at the Rhein-Metall-Borsig-Werke, 9 Sept. 1939; repr. in Mason, *Arbeiterklasse*, 1044–7, here 1046–7.
[119] Described in I.II.2 and I.III.1 above.
[120] Diagram in Zentner, *Illustrierte Geschichte*, 242; details in Horn, *Führerideologie*, but only for the period before 1933.
[121] For the process of transmission see Bracher, *Dictatorship*, 237 f.

offices for matters of organization, finance, propaganda, the press, foreign and colonial policy, and so on, with corresponding offices at Gau (region) and Kreis (district) level. The hierarchy of command descended from Führer to Gauleiter,[122] Kreisleiter, Ortsgruppenleiter (local branch leader), Zellenleiter (cell leader), and finally Blockwart (block warden).[123] Around these party offices were grouped the 'party formations'. (*Gliederungen*): the SA and SS, the NS-Kraftfahr-Korps (NSKK: automobile corps), the Hitlerjugend (HJ: Hitler Youth), the students' union (NSDStB), the Dozentenbund (academic teachers' union), the NS-Frauenschaft (women's association), and the NS-Fliegerkorps (flying corps). An outer circle comprised 'associated' bodies such as the German Labour Front (DAF), the people's welfare organization, the war victims' welfare organization, the doctors', teachers', and lawyers' unions, the league of German technicians,[124] and the Reich association of civil servants. Then there were numerous special organizations directly controlled by the NSDAP,[125] such as the Todt Organization, responsible for roads and buildings, the Reichsarbeitsdienst (RAD: Reich Labour Service), the Reich colonial league, the air-raid precautions organization, the Verein für das Deutschtum im Ausland (VDA: League for German Interests Abroad), and so on. Both the 'associated' organizations and the party formations for specific professions enjoyed a monopoly status, which did not prevent their competing fiercely with one another. Like the NSDAP itself, they were organized on the 'Führer' principle. Membership was generally compulsory. The teachers' union, for instance, had about 320,000 members in 1937 and controlled 97 per cent of teachers in all schools.[126] In the German Labour Front (DAF) compulsory membership for all employers and workers was introduced in mid-1936. By the beginning of the war the DAF had about 22,000,000 members,[127] thus controlling nearly half the German population. From the summer of 1935 onwards all German youths were obliged to perform labour service,[128] and membership of the Hitler Youth became compulsory at the end of 1936.

Thus, in the political practice of the National Socialist regime *Volksgemeinschaft* meant the organization of the whole of society so as to confirm the loyalty of party members and supporters and provide them with a field of activity, while those who were hostile or indifferent were to be supervised, spied on, and controlled even in their leisure time. Every member of a family was organized in some way, and the regime thus had a listening-post in almost every household. How far membership of the mass organizations signified positive loyalty to the state on the part of each individual is another matter; at all events the extremely high degree of organization is not to be taken as proof of loyalty in every case.

[122] Cf. Hüttenberger, *Gauleiter*; Diehl-Thiele, *Partei und Staat*, 37 ff.
[123] The manner in which the leaders of local party groups and cells 'looked after' the population is described in Diehl-Thiele, *Partei und Staat*, 161 ff.
[124] Cf. Ludwig, *Technik*.   [125] Cf. Broszat, *The Hitler State*, ch. 8, pp. 262–93.
[126] Zentner, *Illustrierte Geschichte*, 377.
[127] See Schumann, *Nationalsozialismus*.
[128] On the Reich Labour Service cf. the autobiographical account *Dienst*, by K. Hierl, former Reichsarbeitsführer.

Another method used by the regime to give the impression of a *Volks-gemeinschaft* was the preaching and symbolization of equality. It did not matter that social differences had scarcely changed at all. The object was not economic equality but an equality of attitudes based on the conviction that it was important to belong to the same community. Sociological reality was irrelevant: what mattered was to take pride in being a German national of German race.

No effort was spared in propaganda to demonstrate this ideal form of equality. The annual processions on 'National Labour Day', for example, presented a picture of employers and workers, hardly distinguishable in outward appearance, marching side by side. Everyone ate the same pea-soup in public on the occasion of the 'winter relief' collection. A similar piece of symbolism could be seen in the fact that a prince of Schaumburg-Lippe was Goebbels's adjutant and a prince of Hesse was Göring's secretary.

Again, the awarding of offices, orders, distinctions, uniforms, and badges was made the opportunity for a ritual reversal of social status. Anyone who not only conformed but made a public show of right thinking could become an official in one of the party organizations or associated bodies and thus belong to the government élite. In this way there came into being literally millions of office-holders whose dignity did not necessarily carry any real influence. This ingenious system of rewards exploited the human desire for recognition and also the ingrained respect for authority that, as in the past, characterized large sections of the German population. The symbolism of *Volksgemeinschaft* was intended to foster self-esteem and gain the loyalty of those on whom the regime had conferred an apparent improvement of status.

Young people especially encountered the *Volksgemeinschaft* in the form of an elaborate system of compulsory education and indoctrination, to the pressure of which they were helplessly exposed. Hitler himself had described the stages of this system at the 1935 party rally:

The boy will join the Jungvolk, the young lad will join the Hitler Youth, and then he will move on into the SA or the SS or the other organizations, and the SA men and SS men will one day join the Labour Service and then the army; and the soldier of the people will in due course return to the party organization, the SA, or the SS, and our nation will never again go to ruin as, to our sorrow, it once did.[129]

This scheme became a reality by 1 December 1936,[130] when a law was passed turning the Hitler Youth into a state organization.[131] Henceforth all young people of both sexes, who had already been indoctrinated with Nazi ideals at school,[132] were obliged to enrol in the successive youth-groups from the age of ten to eighteen. Boys

---

[129] Domarus, i. 534.

[130] See *Gesetze des NS-Staates*, 81 ff.

[131] Cf. the autobiographical *Hitler-Jugend* by B. von Schirach, former Reichsjugendführer; Klose, *Gleichschritt*; Brandenburg, *Geschichte der HJ*; Koch, *Hitlerjugend*; Klönne, *Jugend im Dritten Reich*; Boberach, *Jugend unter Hitler*; *Betrogene Generation*; Wortmann, *Baldur von Schirach*.

[132] Cf. Eilers, *Schulpolitik*; *Erziehung und Schulung im Dritten Reich*; Scholtz, *Erziehung und Unterricht*.

from ten to fourteen belonged to the Deutsches Jungvolk (German Young Folk) and from fourteen to eighteen to the Hitler Youth; girls from ten to fourteen belonged to the Jungmädelbund (Young Maidens) and from fourteen to eighteen to the Bund Deutscher Mädel (BDM: League of German Maidens). Girls from eighteen to twenty-one were then enrolled in a branch of the BDM called Glaube und Schönheit (Faith and Beauty). In addition, as a first introduction to the National Socialist community, there were 'children's groups' belonging to the NS-Frauenschaft and the Deutsches Frauenwerk (women's groups) in which children were taken care of between the ages of six and ten.

Each of these organizations was supposed to offer young people some occupation or diversion suitable to their age and outwardly unpolitical. With banners, songs, and uniforms, camp-fire romanticism and high-flown speeches, the regime did succeed in gaining the allegiance of a great many young people. These more or less unpolitical activities were accompanied by purposeful indoctrination and practical training for warlike pursuits. In the Hitler Youth boys of eleven learnt to shoot with small-bore rifles; all were encouraged to strive for the sharp-shooter's badge; games evolved into war games; in education the dominant ideal was that of physical fitness and fighting spirit.[133] Reason and understanding were down-graded so as to paralyse the critical faculty; hate was stirred up against a series of enemies within and without; blind obedience was inculcated, together with adoration of the Führer. The official directive for secondary-school teachers of German laid down that they must strengthen the minds of young people and make them 'conscious of their Germanness, self-confident, militant (*wehrhaft*), and ready for action'.[134] When Hitler proclaimed that German youth of the future should be 'slim and slender, swift as greyhounds, tough as leather, and hard as Krupp steel', this simply meant they were to be efficient for war purposes.

Thus, the young people who grew up in the 1930s and had gone through school, the Jungvolk, the Hitler Youth, the SA, the labour service, and the Wehrmacht had not only been subjected to continuous ideological indoctrination but also to uninterrupted military training.

On the one hand the regime took over the old educational institutions; on the other it set up its own training establishments so as to breed an especially loyal generation of leaders for the state and party.[135] This would make it possible to complete the transformation of the élite, which, for lack of trained Nazi personnel, had so far only just begun. For this purpose the first Ordensburgen ('Order Castles' for political and physical training of the élite) and National Political Institutes of Education ('Napolas') were set up in 1933, and in 1937 the Adolf Hitler Schools.

In addition to compulsory organization and education, a factor in promoting *Volksgemeinschaft* was the uncertainty of the law, not so much in civil matters but in anything that could be called political. Any hint of opposition carried the

---

[133] Cf. Stellrecht, *Soldatentum* (1935); id., 'Wehrerziehung' (1937); Krieck, *Nationalpolitische Erziehung* (1933); Schirach, *Revolution* (1938); Bracher, *Dictatorship*, 326–42.
[134] Quoted from Zentner, *Illustrierte Geschichte*, 348.
[135] Cf. Ueberhorst, *Elite*; Bracher, *Dictatorship*, 330–4.

suspicion of high treason.[136] The SS and Gestapo,[137] subject to no judicial authority and bound by no rules of procedure, struck terror into dissidents. The regime's practice of working more and more by *ad hoc* decrees and improvised 'measures' rather than through the laws[138] created a state of fear and uncertainty in which no one really knew what was still allowed or already forbidden. The jungle of authorities—party, official, semi-official—was a source of impenetrable confusion to the 'little man'. Functionaries were able to extend their powers unchecked, or to dodge responsibility almost at will.[139] All this meant that the ordinary citizen, especially if he still had some reservations about the regime, finally felt deprived of rights, threatened from every side, and unable to influence events in any way.

A population thus atomized and regimented was incapable of forming any political intentions of its own, still less of planning opposition to the regime. This was a decisive step towards the creation of a 'will-less mass' which could be used by the regime in almost any direction when the time came, provided certain tactical rules of legitimacy were observed and so long as a basic standard of living was maintained.

On the material side of the *Volksgemeinschaft* policy the regime's tactics were not unskilful, in that favours and burdens were distributed more or less evenly among all classes:

If no social group did well in the Third Reich, no social group did badly—or so badly that its discontent was not compensated by the contentment of another group. Labour's defeat was business's triumph, agriculture's frustrations labour's relief, small business's misfortunes the consumer's reward, the consumer's aggravation agriculture's compensation. *Kraft durch Freude* was reinforced by *Kraft durch Schadenfreude.*[140]

There were also more opportunities of advancement, greater social mobility, and at least some loosening of the old class divisions.[141] As all sections of the population were regimented, though with different degrees of intensity , there may indeed have been a certain psychological equalization which the lower social classes perceived as a narrowing of the gap between them and the old upper classes.[142] It is nevertheless the case that the National Socialist regime left intact the private-capitalist character of the economy and neither wanted any profound social change nor was forced to allow any against its will.

Just as the National Socialist 'factory community' with the entrepreneur as 'leader' and the work-force as his 'followers' did nothing to alter social reality, so the *Volksgemeinschaft* was far from conforming to the picture of harmony suggested by Nazi propagandists. There was no question of its putting an end to social

---

[136] On 'law and justice' see Broszat, *The Hitler State*, 328 ff.; Bracher, *Dictatorship*, 302 ff,; and Johe, *Justiz*.

[137] Cf. I.III.4 above.

[138] Fraenkel, in *The Dual State*, speaks of a 'dualism of measures and norms of state behaviour' (*Maßnahmen- und Normen-Staat*); see also Diehl-Thiele, *Partei und Staat*, 8 ff.

[139] Cf. Broszat, *The Hitler Staat*, 347 ff.

[140] Schoenbaum, *Revolution*, 295-6.

[141] Cf. ibid. 61 ff.

[142] Broszat, *The Hitler State*, 155-6.

antagonisms. The *Volksgemeinschaft* idea was from start to finish an instrument of integration in the service of preparations for war. The gulf between pretence and reality explains the ceaseless efforts of Nazi propaganda to drive home with threats and blandishments the conviction that former class antagonisms had been swept away by the new national fellowship.

The aim of the Hitler regime was, by organizing society in all its aspects, to extend into everyday life the authoritarian rule of the Führer state.[143] The *Volksgemeinschaft* propaganda and the educational strategy that went with it were designed to make this political and social exercise of authority palatable to the population—which did not constitute a homogeneous group, sociologically or politically—and compensate it for the effective denial of its rights. It will probably never be exactly known how far the dictatorship was able in this way to break down the inner solidarity of particular classes and groups and to substitute an emotional identification with the whole community, or how far the claim to have done so was mere demagogy. Undoubtedly the uncertainty of law, and the fear of denunciation and reprisals that was closely bound up with the system of compulsory organization, contributed in large measure to the resigned attitude of the German people at the outbreak of war. The average, simple citizen who had welcomed the regime's bloodless victories in foreign affairs between 1933 and 1938, but who had not completely shed his reservations concerning it and above all did not want a war, found himself entangled in a web of compulsion, intimidated and incapable of deviating from the system.

[143] For the concepts 'authoritarian' and 'totalitarian' cf. Greiffenhagen, Kühnl, and Müller, *Totalitarismus*, esp. 50 ff.; also Bracher, *Kontroversen*.

PART II

The National Socialist Economy in Preparation for War

HANS-ERICH VOLKMANN

I. From International Economy to Large-area Economy

1. THE WORLD DEPRESSION IN GERMANY AS A CRISIS OF THE LIBERAL ECONOMIC SYSTEM

APART from the treaty of Versailles, which left an unmistakable imprint on the political behaviour of broad sections of German society during the Weimar era, the world depression was certainly the event of that period which most profoundly and lastingly affected the public consciousness. It had its origin in the United States, where, after a prolonged phase of prosperity combined with an irrationally optimistic belief in the continuation of the boom, the first depression phenomena began to appear in 1929 as a result of a widening gap between production and demand, leading to ever greater uncertainty in the economic sphere. A hitherto well-nigh unbridled readiness for speculation succumbed, in October of that year, to an alarmed sobering-up at the New York Stock Exchange and led to its crash. The consequences were a decline in production, a slump in prices, and mass unemployment; because of the interlinked nature of international trade and capital, these consequences did not remain confined to the United States. Even though they hit Germany with full force, their overall effect was certainly no worse than in other industrialized countries, albeit differentiated in detail and degree. Austria, for example, experienced a deeper slump of its economy; in Britain the depression was of longer duration; the United States had, proportionately, a larger number of unemployed, and especially of unprovided-for unemployed. What made the great depression different in Germany was not so much its purely economic as its political effect and dimension. In Germany it acted as the acid test of democracy, just when the middle strata, which were particularly affected by the depression, were beginning to lose faith in purely economic solutions to economic problems and were falling victim to National Socialist propaganda. 'For Germany the crisis of the capitalist economy effectively coincided with a crisis of confidence in the idea of the democratic state and of parliamentary government; this is what lent it its weight.'[1] It is significant that the rise of the NSDAP from a right-wing radical splinter-group to a party capable of government was in direct ratio to the decline of the economy of the Weimar Republic. Even though this indisputable fact should not lead us to conclude that National Socialism arose from exclusively economic causes, the economic circumstances between the end of 1929 and 1932–early 1933 certainly contained essential conditions for the feasibility of a National Socialist regime.

Alongside the middle classes the big agrarian and industrial entrepreneurs similarly became alienated after 1930 from the democratic state—hesitantly at first,

[1] Dederke, *Reich*, 199. On the slump cf. Kindleberger, *World in Depression*; Kuczynski, *Ende der Weltwirtschaftskrise*; *Staats- und Wirtschaftskrise*.

but permanently. In any case, they had never been enamoured of that state, even though, at least during the period of economic stability after 1925, they had used it to pursue their political as well as economic ends. Having been largely identified in the past with the principle of liberal world-market-oriented trade, this democratic state was now losing its stature and credibility in tandem with the breaking-up of the world market. And the world-wide depression resulted in a shrinkage of the world market in practically every field. The longer the depression continued, the more the conviction gained ground in economic circles that this was not a transient but a more permanent phenomenon. From this conviction there arose a readiness to call the long-term validity of the existing international economic system into question; the wish to replace it by some other system, e.g. a national one, was increasingly voiced. An economic approach was emerging which was focused no longer on the international but instead on the national market, and which saw as its ideal not an international division of labour but the development and extension of a national economy. While the idea of a narrow domestic economy was rejected, foreign economic relations were being given a different character. The characteristic of a future economy was increasingly being defined as the creation of a large, multinational, but closely integrated economic sphere.

In Germany the great depression resulted in a dismantling of the liberal economic system, in parallel with the disintegration of democracy, and in the progressive establishment of a state-led economic upturn which found its most marked expression in the Third Reich.

The world-wide depression hit Germany not so much by the familiar destabilization in the monetary sphere, resulting from the withdrawal of short-term loans and credits placed in Germany, as by the consequences of the decline in international trade. German commerce and industry, and hence the jobs related to them, were essentially export-dependent. Also, Germany's vital need for imported foodstuffs and raw materials had to be largely paid for by exports. The disintegration of the world market was the more disastrous for the Reich as its measure of self-sufficiency had been gravely diminished by the surrender of its territories, imposed by the treaty of Versailles, and by a simultaneous population increase within its now reduced territory. This loss of territory meant the loss of 75 per cent of German iron-ore production, 26 per cent of lead production, and 7 per cent of German industrial enterprises. The agricultural surplus areas of West Prussia and Posen (Poznań), ceded by Germany, had accounted for 18 per cent of its potato yield, 17 per cent of rye and barley, and 13 and 11 per cent respectively of its wheat and oats harvest. While international trade was functioning, Germany's growing production for export had managed to achieve a certain balance by means of imports. With the world-wide depression this no longer applied. The declining volume of world trade resulted in shrinking exports for Germany, and these led to increasing unemployment. This in turn caused a decline in purchasing power, together with a drop in domestic demand, and in turn this led to even greater unemployment.

The last three Weimar governments could no longer find a way out of this vicious circle. Wedded as they were to traditional economic thought, they tried, by means of half-hearted though steadily growing state intervention, to restore validity to the fundamental principle which had become highly questionable during the world-wide slump and had in part been invalidated—that of a free-market economy. In other words, they endeavoured, by simulating the prerequisites of the market-economy system, to set its mechanism going once more. Although, or rather because, these endeavours failed, the presidential cabinets—less in concrete terms than by dint of the method used—were in fact preparing the ground, in both economic theory and economic policy, for the policy of the National Socialist regime, based on a state-engineered boom.

The Brüning government committed itself to a policy of redressing the adverse state budget, and hence to a cut in public expenditure, even when, by the spring of 1931, the number of unemployed exceeded the 4-million mark. Instead of adopting an anticyclical approach, i.e. attempting to compensate for declining export production by stimulating domestic demand, Brüning pursued a restrictive financial policy (e.g. by his emergency decree of 8 December 1931) which was openly aimed at triggering economic stimuli by the traditional liberal method of lowered prices and wages. However, the more restrained public finance became, the more demand declined and all the more rapidly did the economic crisis become aggravated. Indeed, it may be assumed that the enormous economic difficulties were 'not all that unwelcome' to the chancellor[2] since, serving another essential purpose of his policy, they could be readily adduced as proof of Germany's inability to continue to make reparation payments.

Brüning's continued support for industrial exports, inherited from his predecessors in office, was bound to fail in view of the disrupted state of world trade, and also because of his pronouncedly protectionist agrarian policy. This appeared to be called for by the especially difficult position of agriculture. Ever since the phase of economic stabilization (1925–8) German farmers had been at a disadvantage compared with other occupational groups. The world-wide drop in farm prices during the depression, caused by general agricultural over-production, hit German agriculture with especial severity because, owing to its less favourable climate and structural conditions by comparison with the classic agricultural countries, it had to bear a high level of overheads. Producer prices were slumping continually, and with them sales profits, while indebtedness was rising in parallel with this trend. In 1931 alone some 177,000 hectares of agricultural land was sold by forced public auction.[3] With his agrarian protectionism, especially favouring the large estates of East Germany—a policy reflected among other things by an endeavour to erect customs and trade barriers in the hope of creating an agricultural zone that would be largely independent of the world market and hence price-neutral—Brüning found himself in conflict with the interests of big industry and exporting industry, whose aim it was, at least temporarily, to reintegrate themselves

---

[2] Brüning, *Memoiren*, 286; cf. ibid. 475.
[3] Cf. Petzina, *Wirtschaft*, 99.

at all costs into the international economy. This conflict of objectives between agrarian protectionism and support for industry—a conflict conducted not only between agricultural and industrial associations but also within the cabinet—was to continue through Papen to Schleicher; in consequence, measures of agricultural and industrial policy not infrequently led to mutual paralysis. The fact was that no presidential cabinet, dependent as it was on the favour of the Reich president, could afford to offend against his own large-scale agrarian interests. Thus, the governments from Brüning to Schleicher progressively lost the confidence not only of extensive industrial circles but also of the lower-middle and middle classes, and indeed of the peasant strata.

The job-creation programmes of the presidential cabinets probably represented the clearest measures of state intervention during the Weimar era, even though Brüning here too exhibited extreme restraint. When in May 1932 he had to resign the chancellorship things had not progressed beyond certain plans, and these envisaged a level of expenditure of RM135m.—a mere drop in the ocean in view of the millions unemployed.

Papen and Schleicher deviated from Brüning's line in economic policy by endeavouring to lead the economy rapidly out of depression into an upturn phase.[4] If Brüning's principal economic goal may be defined as the rehabilitation of public finance, then his successor Papen aimed at a 'stimulation of private initiative'.[5] By an emergency degree of 14 June 1932 he enacted the job-creation programme drafted by his predecessor, without substantial modification: there was no marked increase in the resources earmarked for its execution—no decisive boost of the domestic economy through an expansion of public spending. Although the Papen government, in mid-August 1932, decided that 'economic measures should be given priority' over any other state-political measures and that 'swift action' was 'of the utmost importance',[6] all steps continued to be along the lines of traditional liberal economic thought. As the recession seemed to have bottomed out about the middle of 1932, the chancellor believed that he could confine himself to limited intervention in an economy whose trend was seen as being cyclical: 'At the present stage of the depression, a very advanced stage and presumably not too far from its end, it may be assumed that any attempt to stimulate the economy will, in all likelihood, help achieve its natural continuation in an actual upswing of the economy.'[7] The job-creation programme was now buttressed by indirect subsidies for enterprises: tax bonuses were granted by the state in return for the recruitment of new employees and for prompt payment of taxes.[8] Even so, success was not achieved, or at best was extremely questionable. What happened was that unexpected side-effects appeared. Employment of new labour, which did take place, albeit on a limited scale (the rise in employment between August and October 1932

---

[4] Cf. Marcon, *Arbeitsbeschaffungspolitik.*
[5] Kuczynski, 'Wirtschaftspolitische Konzeptionen', 217.
[6] Cabinet meeting, 13 Aug. 1932, quoted from Dorpalen, *Hindenburg*, 338.
[7] Speech by Papen, 28 Aug. 1932, quoted from *Schulthess 1932*, 146.
[8] *RGBl.* (1932), i. 425.

was 160,000 persons), turned out to be predominantly a mere redistribution of manpower, and actually had detrimental results in those areas 'where enterprises, on the strength of employment premiums, were able to undercut their competitors'. The uncompetitive enterprises suffered a drop in orders and offset their shortage of work by dismissals.[9]

The second effect, already hinted at, was the onset of a price collapse. In conjunction with the legally permissible cut in standard wages by up to 50 per cent for newly enrolled manpower, a revival of domestic trade was not to be expected. As for the tax bonuses (for which RM1,500m. was set aside) to which anybody was entitled who was liable for a certain amount of turnover tax, land tax, business tax, or any similar tax (with the exception of manual and office workers), this was carved up into minute amounts and at the very best (e.g. in large-scale enterprises) amounted to a mere 1 per cent of the total turnover; it was thus scarcely a motivation for investment, especially at a time when industry and small trade had unutilized production capacities on their hands. The effect of this policy of investment stimuli has been ironically described by the quip 'What Papen with his programme achieved in a quarter, anyone else without an economic programme would have needed three months to achieve.'[10] Yet his economic policy should not be judged quite so negatively. A limited upturn undeniably took place. There was a slight increase in the indices for the output both of capital goods and of consumer goods, even though they remained below those for the comparable period in 1931 (Table II.1.1).

Stock Exchange quotations also improved slightly (though only temporarily). This would certainly not have been the case without the economy-stimulating measures, whose psychological effect should not be underestimated (Table II.1.2).

There was, however, nothing like a breakthrough, because the root problem, the

TABLE II.1.1. *Indices for capital and consumer goods 1931–1932, seasonally adjusted* (1928 = 100)

	Capital goods		Consumer goods	
	1931	1932	1931	1932
July	71.3	49.4	88.6	76.0
August	64.2	47.5	85.8	74.9
September	62.4	49.3	84.1	76.7
October	54.3	49.4	85.2	78.5
November	54.5	51.4	84.3	78.9
December	52.6	51.4	80.7	78.2

Source: Kroll, *Weltwirtschaftskrise*, 414.

[9] *Jahresbericht der Gewerbeaufsichtsbeamten und Werkbehörden 1931/32*, section on Prussia (Berlin, 1933), 30, quoted from Kuczynski, 'Wirtschaftspolitische Konzeptionen', 218.
[10] Kuczynski, 'Wirtschaftspolitische Konzeptionen', 221.

TABLE II.1.2. *Indices of Stock Exchange quotations: monthly averages 1932 (1924–6 = 100)*

	Mining and heavy industry	Metal-processing, engineering, and vehicles	Electrical engineering	Chemicals	Building and related trades	Textiles and clothing
July	51.5	26.4	51.8	51.6	26.0	33.7
August	54.1	28.7	55.7	53.5	29.4	34.9
September	61.6	34.9	63.3	60.5	36.8	41.7
October	58.3	34.0	59.4	58.8	35.2	40.4
November	59.6	34.1	59.6	59.5	35.1	41.0
December	65.7	35.4	62.9	62.1	37.3	42.5

Source: Kroll, *Weltwirtschaftskrise*, 416.

integration of the millions of unemployed into the production process, remained unsolved. Papen was therefore denied the approval of his programme by a parliamentary majority. The programme was also rejected by Hitler with the blanket observation that he considered it 'partly inadequate, partly ill-thought-out, partly quite useless, and indeed dangerous'.[11] When nevertheless Hitler subsequently came back to it, it was given a completely different function.

The same was true of the agricultural policy sector. Here Papen continued Brüning's protectionist policy, largely by means of a quota system for imports of agricultural produce; naturally, as under his predecessor, this proved an obstacle to a revival of foreign trade. Only the National Socialists succeeded, admittedly by a totally different economic policy, in resolving this conflict in their own way.

The Schleicher government, which succeeded Papen's cabinet, decisively intensified the shift towards state intervention. Together with the dismantling of the democratic parliamentary system, the validity of economic liberalism was being increasingly questioned. The new chancellor, while in principle continuing along Papen's road of stimulating the economy by means of job-creation and tax bonuses, did so far more purposefully. While the Papen government had hoped to restore the German economy through incentives for private enterprise, Schleicher and his colleagues doubted whether state incentives would suffice to restart the patently defective mechanism of the liberal-market system in such a way that it would continue to function smoothly in line with the economic laws valid in the past. Instead the chancellor favoured a policy of overcoming the effects of the world depression in Germany by measures ensuring a state-led boom. This idea found expression in the establishment of a commission for employment under the directorship of the Prussian Landrat (district administrator) Gereke. In the opinion of that body the goal of 'directing as many unemployed as possible back into the production process [could] only be achieved by a more vigorous application than hitherto of the principle that, especially in times of crisis, "the working class . . . [should] by the performance of public works, in particular of such as are needed anyway" (Max Wirth)' be helped towards wages and bread.[12]

The alternative to stimulation of private initiative was therefore restoration of the economy by the public provision of employment. Implementation of such a concept, in whatever form and on whatever scale, required indirect and direct state supervision. The so-called Gereke plan thus represented 'the first organic step towards a new economic order, towards a planned economy',[13] a step later to be followed by others under National Socialism. As a matter of principle the means of production remained under the control of their former, usually private, owners. The state figured merely as contractor and customer. The Schleicher government, in contrast to Papen's cabinet, was thus practising direct job-creation. Whereas

[11] Letter from Hitler to Papen, 16 Nov. 1932, quoted from *Schulthess 1932*, 206.
[12] Draft from the Reich commissioner's office, 17 Feb. 1932, quoted from Kuczynski, 'Wirtschaftspolitische Konzeptionen', 221–2. On the job-creation programmes of the Reich government prior to Hitler cf. Boelcke, *Deutsche Wirtschaft*, 13–29.
[13] Kuczynski, 'Wirtschaftspolitische Konzeptionen', 222 n. 28.

indirect job-creation may be understood as 'investment activity encouraged by measures on the revenue side of the state budget' (tax bonuses, tax relief, etc.), direct job-creation implied 'investment performed or induced by the provision of state resources'.[14] The Reich commissioner had resources allocated to him for the execution of a programme which primarily envisaged the improvement of the infrastructure of the domestic economy. In order to avoid inflationary side-effects it was again to be financed through tax bonuses, but these were now to be for as large amounts as possible and issued only for public works.

However, even the Schleicher–Gereke plan failed to achieve the hoped-for results. This was due to several causes. For one thing, state finance was to be used as effectively as possible; the Reich commissioner therefore tried to ensure that, in the placing of orders, 'the entrepreneur's profit' was limited 'to the smallest possible scale'.[15] In consequence, entrepreneurs were less than eager to accept such public orders. Moreover, where they were put into effect the regulations called for the use of the largest possible work-force, with the result that the placing of such state contracts did little to achieve a revival of the domestic economy in the industrial sphere, more especially in mechanical engineering, which had been badly hit by the world-wide depression and which was of particular importance to any economic upturn. Added to this was the fact that the government neglected to strengthen or expand buyer demand, and hence the domestic market, by wage increases. In fact, wages were steadily declining. In these circumstances it was clear to Gereke himself that 'such major successes' as would have brought about a true turning-point in economic life and simultaneously a stabilization of political conditions could 'not possibly be achieved' in the short run, e.g. 'by the autumn of 1933'.[16]

This realization gave rise on 28 January 1933 to a Short-term Programme (*Sofortprogramm*) for job-creation, with an allocation of RM500m. for the issue of tax bonuses, even though the amount earmarked by Papen for that purpose had not yet been exhausted. Since the available total still did not seem to the government to be sufficient for the implementation of the envisaged programme, it was contemplated that the firms which received public orders could make drafts on the contracting body and that these drafts would be accepted by state financial institutions and discounted by the Reichsbank. This plan of Schleicher's, however, was not implemented.

When his government resigned the situation in Germany was as follows. Although the economic crisis had reached its absolute peak in the winter of 1931–2, the ensuing improvement remained slight; indeed, in a number of areas economic difficulties were still increasing. Unemployment reached its zenith in February 1932, though in January 1933 it once more exceeded the 6-million mark. Regardless of this fluctuation, income per capita (here given as RM per month) had been steadily declining:[17]

---

[14] Schiller, *Arbeitsbeschaffung*, 2–3.
[15] Implementing regulation on job-creation, 6 Jan. 1933: *RGBl.* (1933), i. 12.
[16] Gereke, 16 Jan. 1933, at a ministerial conference, quoted from Vogelsang, *Reichswehr*, 488.
[17] These figures according to Dederke, *Reich*, 278.

1928 = 1,453   1931 = 1,201
1929 = 1,436   1932 = 1,094
1930 = 1,372

Industrial wages exhibited the same downward trend as prices. This was true of capital goods (the drop in annual average prices between 1929 and 1932 was 14.6 per cent) and more particularly of consumer goods (where the drop over the same period was 31.5 per cent). Agricultural wholesale prices between 1929 and 1932, measured by annual averages, dropped by a total of 29.9 per cent.[18] While the volume of agricultural production actually showed a slight rise, the value of the produce dropped from RM13.9m. in 1928/9 to RM8.8m. in 1932, i.e. by 36.7 per cent.[19]

The process of industrial shrinkage best reflects the course of the recession. In terms of volume German industrial production showed a decline of 43.1 per cent between 1927/8 and 1932/3, though this was greatly exceeded by the fall in prices of approximately 50 per cent (gross value).[20] Table II.1.3 illustrates the full extent of the fall in production in a number of important industries.

In spite of the slight recovery during the Papen era Stock Exchange quotations of securities exhibited a permanent decline; this was one of the reasons for reluctance to invest. The annual averages for the overall index of quotations are shown in the following list (1924–6 = 100):[21]

1927 = 158.0   1930 = 109.2
1928 = 148.4   1931 = 80.5
1929 = 133.9   1932 = 54.5

In certain areas, such as mechanical engineering—one of particular importance to Germany—share prices dropped by 70 per cent. In the paper industry and in shipbuilding they even dropped by 80 per cent.[22]

The fact that Schleicher lost the vote of confidence and hence his chance of implementing his programme for the revitalization of the economy was certainly due also to a steadily growing conviction among industrialists, landowners, and, above all, economists and economic journalists that a recovery could no longer be accomplished solely by occasional impulses from the state. A long-harboured latent mistrust of the parliamentary democratic state, and hence also of the future viability of the accepted liberal free-trade principle of world ecnomics, was now surfacing in ever widening circles. Surely that principle had been conspicuously upset by the effects and after-effects of the First World War, when intensified industrial development outside Europe had resulted in a shift of the international economic centre of gravity. Former raw-material sources and marketing areas suddenly emerged as tough competitors of the classic industrialized nations, which in turn

[18] Kroll, *Weltwirtschaftskrise*, 91.
[19] Fischer, *Wirtschaftspolitik*, 56.
[20] Kroll, *Weltwirtschaftskrise*, 95.
[21] Ibid. 106.
[22] Ibid. 107.

TABLE II.1.3. *Production indices of important commodities during the great depression in Germany* (1928=100)

	Iron	Non-ferrous metals	Engineering	Motor-vehicles	Ship-Building[a]	Construction overall	Coal[b]	Gas	Electricity	Oil	Textiles	Footwear	Glass	Paper
1929	109.9	98.2	100.9	94.0	123	100.3	108.6	105.8	117.9	111.8	92.4	103.8	94.1	101.9
1930	80.1	89.5	83.1	62.4	105	88.3	93.6	102.2	113.2	190.1	90.0	100.7	81.4	96.8
1931	56.9	69.7	59.5	43.9	30	55.9	78.1	98.8	99.6	248.5	87.7	93.6	61.7	86.7
1932	38.9	60.8	38.4	26.0	3	37.7	68.9	93.2	90.4	250.7	80.0	85.3	49.0	79.9

[a] New ships laid down.
[b] Hard coal, coke, lignite, and briquettes from hard coal and lignite.

Source: Kroll, *Weltwirtschaftskrise*, 97.

were compelled to seek new slots for themselves in the structure of world trade, thereby further aggravating the depression. Thus, there arose, especially in Germany, an inclination to withdraw from international economic ties, the more so as most European and overseas states seemed to regard protectionism and protective tariffs as more suitable attributes of an economy-stimulating trade policy than free trade through most-favoured-nation arrangements. The world-wide depression and the disintegration of the Weimar Republic had combined to strengthen a widespread belief that the country was on the verge of a historic turning-point, one which must bring with it a total transformation of political and economic conditions.[23]

The voices of those who, as so-called economic-policy and economic-theory 'reformers', had been prophesying the failure of economic automatism and had been calling for an active, comprehensive, state-led upturn policy, were becoming even louder and ever more numerous. Such a policy would be most consistently realized within a closed, and if possible self-sufficient, area.

Thus, the concept of autarky became a subject of discussion, though it gave rise also to a great many misunderstandings. It became topical when, after the experience of the depression, the understandable wish arose to free Germany from its international currency ties in order to shield it in the future from the kind of monetary upheavals triggered by the crash of the New York Stock Exchange on the eve of the great depression. The lower the economic barometer fell, the more did the slogan of autarky experience a boom. Autarky—as a contemporary author observed—had 'all of a sudden become one of the most frequently encountered words in the daily press and periodicals'.[24] Two aspects firmly established the wishful thinking about autarky in public political consciousness: an excessive national awareness and considerations of economic policy. 'The hypertrophied nationalism of today', a Swiss author wrote, 'is the best spring from which the dubious plant of the autarky movement draws its strength.'[25] Autarky, in the formulation of a Frankfurt professor of economics in 1932, was 'the economic ideal of nationalism' generally.[26]

Although this statement characterizes the fundamental attitude of many supporters of autarky, there were nevertheless quite a few who realized that self-sufficiency within the given borders was impossible for Germany. They demanded the maintenance of foreign-trade connections, though these must no longer be left to the free interplay of market forces; instead, given a world-wide policy of high protective tariffs, they must be shaped in line with Germany's national and economic needs. One of the most prominent journalistic champions of this trend demanded that foreign trade should 'no longer be allowed to drift schematically or wildly; instead one must at least draw up a basic plan as the basis from which one may operate with a measure of safety'.[27] And a famous and highly regarded

---

[23] Cf. Predöhl, 'Epochenbedeutung'.
[24] Nell-Breuning, 'Autarkie', 28; cf. Hoffmann, 'Autarkie'.
[25] Keller, 'Autarkie', 770.   [26] Gerloff, 'Autarkie', 13.
[27] Ferdinand-Friedrich Zimmermann, alias Ferdinand Fried, quoted from Grotkopp, *Krise*, 218. This work presents the ideas of the 'reformers' at length and demonstrates their effect.

academic economist—speaking in effect for a whole string of others—agreed with him by referring to the need for a 'purposeful planned shaping . . . of international economic processes from a national centre'.[28]

Contemporaries realized that such a policy, aiming at economic freedom of action, must come up against constraints. International economic relations were too close and too many-sided for any one state to be able to pursue a totally independent trade policy—unless, of course, the (already punctured) principle of free trade and most-favoured-nation treatment were replaced by the bilateral principle, though this would essentially limit any foreign-trade activity to exchanges between raw-material and agricultural countries on the one side and industrialized states on the other, always assuming that these were mutually complementary. One important and original publicist and economist, who had a decisive influence on the economic discussion during the final phase of the Weimar Republic and more particularly on the 'reformers', felt certain, as many autarky champions did, that any imports needed could be met by exports on a bilateral basis. After all, he argued, 'the need to market their products is at least as pressing in the raw-material countries as the need to export is in Germany'.[29]

This idea of a mutually complementary exchange of goods represents a point of departure for area-oriented or area-linked foreign trade. Out of the reformers' discussion concerning a policy of state-led boom came the idea of *Groß-raumwirtschaft*, large-area economy. The supporters of such a purposeful policy of state-directed boom did not discuss these increasingly interesting problems of economic reorganization within Europe merely as individuals; there came into being a number of economic-policy societies and associations which made that set of problems the central issue of their activity. Within the Studiengesellschaft für Geld- und Kreditwirtschaft (Society for the Study of Monetary and Loan Economics), for instance, this body's most active publicist considered autarky realizable only within a continental framework. If the necessity arose for Germany to pursue a policy of import restrictions and self-sufficiency with regard to raw materials and foodstuffs, then this could be no more than an interim solution. The aim must be a multinational closed trading sphere. For the reformers the 'hands of the economic world clock . . . pointed towards increasing autarky, towards the endeavour to achieve the greatest possible self-suffiency within enclosed economic areas'.[30] The postulated ultimate aim was a European economic sphere recruited from 300 million people, one that would, 'ranking equal, if not superior', take its place alongside America's sphere of hegemony, alongside the British Empire, and alongside the emerging Sino-Japanese and finally the Russian large-scale areas.[31] A particular role was played by the Studiengesellschaft für Mittel- und Südosteuropa (Society for the Study of Central and South-East Europe) and by the Mitteleuropäischer Wirtschaftstag (Central European Economic Forum), which,

---

[28] Werner Sombart, in a lecture given in 1932 on the future of capitalism, quoted from Grotkopp, *Krise*.

[29] Friedländer-Prechtl, 'Dynamik', 22.

[30] Id., *Wirtschaftswende*, 132.

[31] Ibid, 134.

influenced by the Langnam Association, the Reich Association of German Industry, and the German Industry and Trade Forum, represented heavy-industry interests in central Europe and endeavoured to keep open the economic doors to south-east and eastern Europe, and indeed open them wider. The goal, ultimately, was the creation of 'a German-dominated large-area economy in central and south-east Europe'.[32] Models of an integrated European economy were being developed everywhere—models known by the names of the Pan-European idea,[33] the Central Europe Plan, and Zwischeneuropa (Inter-Europe, or the 'lands between').

The concepts of Central Europe and Inter-Europe were at the focus of reflections in the Tatkreis (Action Circle), where the problem of Europe's economic-political structure under German leadership was being discussed extensively and thoroughly. It will suffice here to introduce, as representatives of the attitude of a large number of members of this influential, politically conservative circle, three of its best-known figures. The first is the political writer Gieselher Wirsing, who advocated a union of Germany with 'Inter-Europe' (i.e. Austria, the Baltic States, Poland, Czechoslovakia, Hungary, Yugoslavia, Bulgaria, and Romania). In 1930 he proposed an agricultural division of labour 'in the German–Inter-European sphere' with a view to weaning the predominantly agricultural countries from their monoculture and over-production, and guiding them towards purchasing power through the marketing of deliberately cultivated agricultural produce in short supply. If that were achieved there would no longer be any fundamental difficulties about the sale of German industrial products. Wirsing's aim was not 'to fit the entire industrial production of, say, Germany, Austria, and Czechoslovakia into that zone, but only a sufficiently large portion of it to ensure that the fate of these countries will no longer be totally dependent on the receptive capacity of world markets'.[34] In 1931 he regarded Germany, because of the emerging closed markets of America and Japan, as being already forcibly condemned to an autarky which, however, might still be avoided by its own initiative. 'But unless the alternative—a colony of the West or extrication from capitalist entanglement, even by supreme sacrifices in our standard of living—is presented with full force we shall find ourselves succumbing to the paralysing policy of the stronger competitor.[35]

Hans Zehrer, one of the most influential representatives of the Action Circle, looked beyond Central Europe. He was already reflecting on an 'outline of a European economic programme on the basis of geo-political regional thought opposed to the "economic nationalism of others"'. As a prerequisite of such an economic programme he listed 'first of all the internal structure of Germany on a planned-economy, state capitalist, authoritarian basis as well as an uncompromising (because demanded, above all, by the economy) foreign-policy reorientation towards the east and south-east'.[36]

---

[32] Frommelt, *Paneuropa*, 99.

[33] For the literature cf. Volkmann, 'Außenwirtschaftliches Programm', 262 nn. 76–7.

[34] Wirsing, *Zwischeneuropa*, 290. The manuscript was completed by the autumn of 1930.

[35] Id., 'Zwangsautarkie', 438.

[36] Hecker, 'Die Tat', 136.

A third member of the Action Circle, Ferdinand Friedrich Zimmermann, also known as Ferdinand Fried, set his targets for spatial ideas even higher. He proceeded from the argument that 'even though the idea of economic spheres is still rejected as a principle, as being the antithesis to free trade, there is nevertheless an increasing meeting of minds on the idea of a synthesis of the south-east European area'.[37] Considering that economic blocs were taking shape everywhere in the world, while 'the whole of the "south-east" [was] still an expanse of ruins',[38] the temptation for Germany to build up that area according to its own concept was great. He saw the intended German–Austrian customs union as a milestone on the road to a new order in eastern central Europe: this union might 'perhaps' bring about 'the decisive turn towards the new direction which points us to the future'. Provided the customs union between Germany and Austria took place, he could see 'the new contours of the world gradually emerging as though on an exposed photographic plate in the developer'.[39] Germany-Austria could then provide the nucleus around which the central and south-east European area might group itself, if possible with the inclusion of Greece, providing a link to Turkey and Persia. This sphere would have to seek a northern connection with the Baltic States, constituting an area which 'eventually in the east' might find 'its powerful economic backing in Russia'. The economic symbiosis between central Europe and Russia, as envisaged by Zimmermann, could be further extended westwards to Belgium and Holland, and northwards to Scandinavia. For how much longer these areas would be able to support themselves on what was left of their colonial empires in Africa and south-east Asia was 'a question of time'.[40] Friedrich Zimmermann's ideas were absorbed in many respects into National Socialist thinking, especially as he was an early active supporter of the NSDAP and maintained close contacts with its leaders.

The popularity of the central European idea is proved, among other things, by the activity of the eponymous institute which published a widely noticed series of studies. In a collection of articles, for which Reich Minister Treviranus himself had even written an introductory message, large-area economics was described as the 'road to European unity'.[41]

Underlying these concepts was a common endeavour, modified as it may have been in detail, to restore the relative economic unity of the German Reich and Austria-Hungary, which had been destroyed by the creation of the European post-war states and hence by the erection of a multiplicity of tariff barriers. This would serve to strengthen both the domestic European market and the competitiveness of that area *vis-à-vis* the colonial powers, the United States, and Japan in the world market. After all, a clear tendency towards the establishment of self-sufficient large-scale areas under the control of those states could be seen on all sides, and this trend was intensified by the world depression:[42] Britain had, with the Ottawa agreements

---

[37] Fried, *Autarkie*, 127.
[38] Ibid. 142.
[39] Fried, *Ende des Kapitalismus*, 264.
[40] Ibid. 265.
[41] *Großraumwirtschaft.*
[42] Raupach, 'Auswirkungen', 51.

(1932), created its own virtually closed economic area, within which the colonies enjoyed preferences, and France was by then regarded as self-sufficient in the agricultural sphere.[43] Bolshevik Russia, too, had largely restricted and oriented its foreign trade to the importation of modern investment goods.

It may have been significant that the Institute for Social and Political Sciences of the University of Heidelberg started publication of a series of studies (under the general editorship of Arnold Bergsträsser, Jakob Marschak, and Alfred Weber) which demonstrated Europe's integration in the field of manufacturing industry and set out to describe the interlocking foreign-trade patterns among European countries. The first of these studies arrived at the remarkable conclusion that European foreign trade 'predominantly [served] the international economic complementation of Europe' and that, in consequence, 'the domestic European market . . . [was] more important to the countries belonging to it than was the rest of the world'.[44] This study also listed the evidence for the decline of European trade with the extra-European world, from 37 per cent of the world-trade volume in 1914 to an average of 31 per cent for the period 1925–30. By way of contrast, increasing sales were recorded in the overseas market by the United States and by Japan. The conclusion drawn from this state of affairs—one that was bound to confirm the champions of autarky in their views just as it was bound to shake liberal economists and entrepreneurs in the attitude to free-trade and -market economics—was thus formulated: 'Even though one may believe that industrialization of new countries will not damage the old European industrialized countries in the long run, the decline of Europe's share in world trade should nevertheless be a warning signal to us to reflect on the common European interest and the need for economic co-operation among all countries of Europe.'[45]

It was no accident that the International Trade Conference of March 1930 had placed the problems of closer economic co-operation within Europe in the forefront of its discussions, or that the German Industry and Trade Forum in 1931 felt a need to examine 'to what extent German economy . . . might be strengthened through a closer relationship of the European countries with each other'.[46]

2. THE NATIONAL SOCIALIST 'ALTERNATIVE'

The theory of autarky was thus developed as an alternative to the free-trade principle in world economics. Its protagonists among academic economists were at first exposed to violent attacks from the liberal economic establishment, and its followers among the ranks of entrepreneurs were initially regarded as rank outsiders. They therefore sought political backing, and this they found in the NSDAP. Since the elections of September 1930 this party represented not only a weighty factor of political life in Germany but its *Lebensraum* (living-space) theory

[43] Bousquet, *Autarkie*.
[44] Gaedicke and Eynern, *Integration*, 21.
[45] Ibid. 126.
[46] BA R II/1291.

seemed to provide just the right intellectual umbrella for the growth of the idea of autarky—the more so as the party still lacked a clearly defined economic programme. Before the world depression the National Socialists had 'made no serious contribution to economic theory, but merely argued about economic problems in a pseudo-scientific manner',[47] so that their economic concepts at the time could certainly be described as 'a conglomeration of confused ideas'.[48] However, the central ideological postulate for an extension of German living-space provides the key to their economic-policy thinking and subsequent action. After all, the National Socialist movement explicitly formulated the claim that 'it will always let its foreign policy be determined by the necessity to secure the space necessary to the life of our people'.[49] This claim, which formed part of the ideological foundations of the National Socialist programme, was without doubt primarily motivated by power-political and racial-policy considerations. However, when 'the large-scale provision of nutritional and settlement space for the growing German people' was proclaimed as 'the task of German foreign policy',[50] this revealed its markedly economic component, which initially meant a predominantly agricultural-economic component. If Germany once more wished to play a part in the concert of European powers—and the National Socialists were firmly resolved that this should be so—then in their view their prime need was the consolidation of economic conditions. This was understood to mean above all the safeguarding of the nutrition of a population growing by an estimated 900,000 each year, an aim which Hitler regarded as the prerequisite of an active foreign policy.

Three roads were, in Hitler's view, available towards the solution of this problem:

1. internal colonization, which—regardless of possible mechanization and automation in agriculture and the envisaged intensification of soil-yields through increased fertilization—was bound to be subject to distinct limits.

2. '[acquisition of] new land . . . in order to . . . settle the surplus millions and thus continue to maintain the nation on the basis of self-sufficiency in foodstuffs': this possibility was given preference by National Socialism over the next alternative,

3. '[production] by industry and commerce . . . for foreign demand, in order to meet our living requirements from the proceeds': in other words, through international trade.

Underlying the demand for an extension of the peasantry and of agricultural production was the desire to establish a healthy balance between agriculture and industry—not least with a view to the stabilization of internal political conditions. 'A solid stock of small and medium farmers' seemed 'the best protection which a nation could have against social ills'.[51] Simultaneously a state of relative nutritional autarky was being striven for in order to safeguard, at least partially, 'the freedom and independence of the nation, especially at critical junctures in its history'.[52]

[47] Krause, *Wirtschaftstheorie*, 17.   [48] Cf. Fischer, *Wirtschaftspolitik*, 51.
[49] *Hitler's Secret Book* (trans. of *Hitlers zweites Buch*; cited below as *Secret Book*), 45.
[50] Feder, *Programm*, 10.   [51] Hitler, *Mein Kampf* (trans.), 126.
[52] Ibid.

Realization of the (for the moment) unalterable colonial-policy pattern led Hitler to strive for an arrangement with Britain; hence, for him and his party 'the only possibility . . . of carrying a sound territorial policy into effect was that of acquiring new territory in Europe itself'.[53] In consequence the National Socialists saw their economic task in putting a stop to 'the colonial and trade policy of pre-war times', and this they did by 'turning [their] eyes towards the lands of the east'.[54] 'If new territory were to be acquired in Europe . . . it must be mainly at Russia's cost, and the new German Empire should set out on its march along the same road as was formerly trodden by the Teutonic Knights, this time to acquire soil for the German plough by means of the German sword and thus to provide the nation with its daily bread.'[55] Thus, even before the world-wide depression, Hitler preferred territorial expansion of the German economic sphere to the development of the country's position in international trade. 'The chatter about the peaceful conquest of the world by commercial means' the leader of the NSDAP regarded as 'the most completely nonsensical stuff ever raised to the dignity of a guiding principle in the policy of a state.'[56]

From the living-space theory, based as it was on radical ideology and power policy, there followed, quite logically, the demand for a self-contained trading state in the form of a large-scale economic sphere dominated by Germany. An eastward extension of the area of settlement and an expansion of agricultural land was bound to halt the farming population's exodus from rural areas and hence progressive industrialization; above all, it was bound to help reduce Germany's dependence on exports, a dependence criticized by Hitler on foreign-political grounds. 'A people which no longer needs to shunt off its rising rural generations into the big cities as factory-workers, but which instead can settle them as free peasants on their own soil, will open up a domestic sales market to German industry which can gradually remove and exempt it from the frenzied struggle and scramble for the "place in the sun" in the rest of the world.'[57] Moreover, 'in view of the limitations of our own raw materials and the ensuing threatening dependence on other countries' the creation of a large-scale economic sphere incorporating eastern Europe seemed to National Socialists to be an urgent need.[58]

Even the early National Socialist concept of agricultural policy was planned with a long-term view and deliberately included in its calculations the element of military aggression. Its implementation implied that the German people must 'organize [its] national forces and set them on the path which will lead them away from that territorial restriction' and win new territory 'not only as the source of our maintenance but also as a basis of political power'.[59] As such an expansion was not ultimately attainable by peaceful means Germany would have to 'proceed to the

---

[53] Ibid. 127.
[54] Ibid. 533.
[55] Ibid. 128.
[56] Ibid. 131.
[57] *Secret Book*, 210.
[58] Ibid. 99.
[59] Hitler, *Mein Kampf* (trans.), 526.

greatest possible concentration of its forces internally', i.e. it would have to rearm on a considerable scale. With a view to settlement in the east and the establishment of a large-scale economic sphere the National Socialists set themselves as their 'greatest' political task 'the formation of a superior strong land army',[60] because 'the sword must come before the plough and an army before economics'.[61]

In the first instance the party did not draw any programmatic economic conclusion from the ideas just presented. The party programme, drafted by Gottfried Feder and Adolf Hitler, contained a string of ambiguous slogans such as 'creation of a corporate state', abolition of 'interest-slavery' (*Zinsknechtschaft*), and 'common weal comes before private profit'.[62] The last of these, together with the adjective 'socialist' in the party's name, and finally the writings of 'left-wing' National Socialists (e.g. the Strasser brothers), gave rise to the suspicion that the party was paying tribute to some new variant of Marxist ideology. 'The danger that friend and foe may fail to realize the meaning of certain slogans, that they may overestimate some of them and, consciously or unconsciously absorbing Marxist ideas and terminology, construe a totally false picture from fragments' seemed 'exceedingly great'.[63]

Evidently, all that was needed for the first major electoral success in September 1930 was general criticism of economic conditions in the Weimar Republic. Subsequently, however, at a time when, as a result of world-wide depression, the political climate in Germany was largely determined by economic factors, the need began to be realized for a detailed economic programme that went beyond platitudes. It was necessary to refute 'in a convincing manner the old claim of our opponents that National Socialism does not understand economics and would, if it came to power, wreck the economy'.[64] Believing that the party's accession to power or failure would depend on future arguments about domestic policies, Hitler 'devoted especially careful consideration to economic matters' after 1930.[65]

From 1930 onward the NSDAP did not concern itself in its propaganda with criticizing the economic policy of the presidential cabinets in detail, but rejected it fundamentally by placing the current economic problems into the framework of its 'own programme for a revolutionary transformation of conditions in Germany'.[66] In other words, the National Socialists were trying to offer a serious alternative to market economics, an alternative which eventually called itself 'autarky within a large economic area'.

The party's endeavours to formulate a credible economic programme were favoured by the circumstance that, as a result of the general political and economic conditions of the 1930s, a number of representatives of economic theory and practice were drawing closer to the NSDAP by their wish to replace the market- and

---

[60] *Secret Book*, 210.
[61] Ibid. 99.
[62] Cf. Barkai, *Wirtschaftssystem*, 25–30.
[63] Reupke, *Nationalsozialismus*, preface.
[64] Oestreich, *Walther Funk*, 80.
[65] Ibid.
[66] Ibid. 81.

world-trade-oriented system with one that would receive its economic impulses from the state and would be geographically determined. The NSDAP unhesitatingly accepted these opponents, not infrequently 'reformers' and autarky champions, into its ranks and/or claimed their programme for itself, adapting it along its own lines in conjunction with its living-space theory. Of considerable importance in the formulation of a clearly defined and practicable economic concept of the NSDAP, and also typical of the influence of the so-called reformers on economic thought within the party, was the work of the founder of the Studiengesellschaft für Geld- und Kreditwirtschaft, Dräger, published under the title Arbeitsbeschaffung und produktive Kreditschöpfung (Job Creation and Productive Creation of Credits) in the series Nationalsozialistische Bibliothek (Library of National Socialism) in 1932. It provided the intellectual guideline for the speech made in the Reichstag on 10 May 1932 by Gregor Strasser, the Reichsorganisationsleiter (Reich director of organisation) of the NSDAP, and for the *Wirtschaftliches Sofortprogramm der NSDAP* (Short-term Economic Programme of the NSDAP), subsequently published as a mandatory directive for the party's propaganda and electioneering helpers. In line with this publication fundamental directives were proclaimed for future National Socialist economic policy, such as the draft of a generous state-sponsored job-creation programme, to be financed by deficit spending. The Short-term Economic Programme moreover contained a trade-policy component which, after 1934, determined Schacht's foreign-trade line—the principle of bilateralism practised under the 'New Plan'. Strasser called not only for a stimulation of the domestic economy through measures taken by the state but also for a revival of the domestic market, especially through the promotion of agriculture. In his view an increase in agricultural yields was to take place alongside the development of a closed economic sphere designed initially to safeguard the nation's food supply more effectively. The Short-term Programme assumed that it was possible to step up the yield of German agriculture within a few years to such an extent that the Reich would become largely independent of imports of foreign foodstuffs. Measures to stimulate the revival of agricultural production would in turn stimulate domestic demand in related industries (mechanical engineering, chemicals). Better utilization of German soil—as indeed the efforts towards nutritional self-sufficiency generally—would, according to the basic ideas formulated in the Short-term Programme, create over a million jobs in agriculture and generally result in higher employment in other branches of the economy. The autarky efforts thus aimed, as a first step, at a forced 'development of the domestic market with an involvement of industry'.[67] National Socialism, in consequence, was determined to 'apply any import restrictions which might result in German workers or German peasants being given bread and work'.[68]

Whereas Germany's potential for agricultural self-sufficiency was assessed over-optimistically, the industrial sphere was viewed more soberly. Nevertheless, National Socialism was aiming at a loosening of world-wide economic ties, if only

[67] Speech by Strasser, 10 May 1932, quoted from 'Nationale Handelspolitik,' 6.
[68] *Wirtschaftliches Sofortprogramm*, 17.

with an eye to safeguarding the job-creation programme through stimulation of domestic production. Consideration proceeded from the fact that in 1931 some 1.5 to 1.7 million workers were employed in German exports. If exports were throttled back the result—because of the drop in foreign-currency earnings—would be a corresponding decline in imports. If such reductions through foreign-trade controls were largely confined to finished goods, then new jobs might be created in Germany for their manufacture. Moreover, since it was to be expected that, as a result of the world depression as well as the protectionist policy of other countries, German export industry would 'despite its intentions be unable to maintain its level of employment, let alone restore it to its former figures' (in other words, unemployment was determined also by foreign trade), it was widely held that such unemployment could be mitigated solely 'by the creation of new work for an expanded domestic market'.[69] In this sense 'the shaping of an autarkic economy' implied 'planned orientation, determined by the domestic market, towards a necessary and achievable minimum volume of foreign trade and its extension in terms of quality and nature'.[70] Gottfried Feder in this connection called for an 'examination of the need for the importation of raw materials, promotion of exports of finished goods, restriction of exports of vital domestic products'. The burden of the job-creation measures was the demand for a 'switch from a liberal capitalist economy to a domestic economy aiming at a sensible autarky'.[71]

At the same time the champions of autarky who were allied with the National Socialists or who were active within the party never postulated as an ultimate economic objective the ideal of domestic supplies through self-sufficiency, such as the formula 'back to linen, rye bread, and Uckermark tobacco'.[72] There was no question in the minds of the autarky supporters in the NSDAP that self-sufficiency for Germany, in the strictest sense, was 'a downright impossibility'.[73] Implementation of autarky to them did not mean, as their critics suggested time and again, the 'remodelling of the German economy into an organism totally cut off from the outside world'; for them it was not tantamount to a 'hermetical sealing of . . . frontiers and total isolation from foreign markets'.[74] Even though National Socialism endeavoured to replace the liberal-individualistic principle of economics by another, trade policy occupied a major place in programme discussions after 1930. Whereas the liberal economic model of foreign trade was seen—at least in theory—as free and world-wide trade, the NSDAP now proclaimed a national trade policy instead of an international one. Sensible autarky called for a fundamental turn in foreign-trade policy; in the final analysis it implied that no more should be exported than was required for the importation of indispensable raw materials and foodstuffs and of such commodities as were 'unavailable or available in insufficient measure' or could not be manufactured in Germany in sufficient quantity.[75] To

---

[69] Lüttgens, *Autarkie*, 19.   [70] Ibid. 29.

[71] Expert opinion by Feder on job-creation, *c.* summer 1932, BA, Kleine Erwerbungen NSDAP NS 20/122.

[72] Epstein, *Akkumulation*, 20.

[73] Gerloff, 'Autarkie', 14.   [74] Maurer, *Grundlagen*, 48.

[75] Speech by Gregor Strasser, 10 May 1932, quoted from 'Nationale Handelspolitik', 7.

ensure this required the introduction of foreign-trade controls and quotas, and these Strasser demanded in his Short-term Economic Programme. 'Autarky therefore implies the devising of an import and export plan which would proceed from necessary import requirements and seek to meet these by way of a planned exchange of goods'.[76] Such an economic system the National Socialists described as *Nationalwirtschaft*, a national economy which would have to be a guarantee for the German nation that its economy would in future be largely protected against crises in the economies of other countries. Germany's economic autarky was regarded as 'accomplished only when economic unassailability has been attained, i.e. an economic position which cannot, or certainly not decisively, be affected by foreign manœuvres or events'.[77] Such a state of affairs, in the opinion of Schacht, the future Reichsbank president and Hitler's Reich minister of economic affairs, could not be achieved so long as foreign countries were able to impede Germany's economic development. In consequence there was a need for optimal rearmament. In Schacht's opinion there were only two ways of escaping foreign economic pressures: 'One way is that of a strong military capability and a strong military determination which, at the decisive moment,' would defend 'the nation's existence and vital rights'. The other way must lead to economic co-operation with Germany's neighbours. It was necessary 'to make it clear, time and again, that real economic advantage' lay and should be pursued 'hand in hand with that of our neighbours'.[78]

In the event of a National Socialist government one would therefore expect certain consequences in foreign-trade policy in the shape of a transformation of the existing system of trade agreements, accompanied by notice of termination of current trade agreements at the earliest possible date. Foreign trade, moreover, would be conducted on the basis of bilateral agreements, as far as possible eliminating foreign currencies, i.e. on what is known as the clearing system. This meant that, whenever new agreements were concluded, the liberal principle of free trade would have to yield to that of reciprocity (the exchange of goods of equal value and/or equal quantity). Under the clearing system any foreign-trade assets accruing would be mutually credited and compensated. An 'attempt would therefore always be made to establish an equilibrium with a country in respect of its exports to and its imports from Germany'.[79] This principle of reciprocity would moreover be complemented by that of preference instead of most-favoured-nation treatment. In such a system of agreements the decisive criteria for a differentiated treatment of economic partners would have to be political, geographical, or economic facts, such as existing or potential alliances or geographical contiguity. These demands were in fact contained in the Short-term Economic Programme. Preferential agreements might well affect the development of closer economic relations or alliances between individual countries as 'the partners to the treaty conceded to each other or to a specific third party privileges which were not extended to any other countries'.[80] A

---

[76] Fried, *Autarkie*, 48.
[77] Albert, *Nationalwirtschaft*, 8.
[78] Schacht, *Grundsätze*, 61.
[79] 'Nationale Handelspolitik', 7.
[80] Massakas, *Präferenzzölle*, 11.

foreign trade policy thus conceived would, according to National Socialist wishful thinking, lead 'quite naturally to amalgamation'.[81]

At this point, therefore, National Socialism performed the mental connection between the theory of autarky and large-area economics on the one hand and that of living-space on the other, with its racially ethnic (*völkisch*) and power-political motivations—theories which had already been developed outside the NSDAP. Autarky in the National Socialist sense therefore meant nothing other than economic imperialism aimed at 'the creation of an economic sphere self-sufficient within itself in production and consumption', which 'would, however, have to be based upon such large areas and such rich resources that it would satisfy all the vital economic . . . requirements of its members'. Moreover, autarky meant 'an opening up of markets, and a conquest of markets that would not rely on [the nation's] own strength, on the efficiency of domestic production, or on free competition, but that sees its weapons in the attainment of convenient preferential positions and in a monopolistic exclusion of competition'.[82] Yet the NSDAP resolutely rejected any labelling of such an economically motivated expansion drive as an 'imperialist power display', let alone as 'a striving for world dominion'. It regarded it solely as the result of what it believed to be the 'correct realization . . . that creation has implanted in man's soul the drive for self-preservation'. Autarky did not, as a member of the Reich Economic Council of the Party formulated it, necessarily entail 'war at all costs'. It could be brought about 'also in an entirely peaceful, diplomatic way'.[83]

This opening up and conquest of markets was to be striven for in the first instance by foreign trade, i.e. by peaceful means. Yet it was bound to have some rigid premisses and to entail consequences which were in striking conflict with a market economy and free trade, such as planned-economy interventions by the state. Central economic-planning authorities were to balance the performance of the German national economy against the requirements of the population and to regulate imports and exports in accordance with national-economic requirements as defined by the party and the state.

Foreign trade had to be switched towards eastern and south-eastern Europe, principally because, in the National Socialist view, for Germany to have its raw-material bases predominantly in territories from which it might be cut off in the event of complications was a totally unsatisfactory state of affairs. It was therefore part of the National Socialist trade-policy directives, as contained in the Short-term Economic Programme of 1932, that for raw-material requirements beyond the capacity of German domestic production preference was to be given to friendly European countries, especially if these were prepared to import finished goods from Germany to complement the purchase of their raw materials.[84]

Beyond south-eastern Europe a National Socialist Germany intended to permeate

---

[81] Fried, *Autarkie*, 126.
[82] Gerloff, 'Autarkie', 13.
[83] Pfaff, *Wirtschafts-Aufbau*, 10.
[84] *Wirtschaftliches Sofortprogramm*, 17.

the entire central and east central European area and to place the economies affected, 'by way of a necessary complementation of German and their own autarky, into firm economic-policy relations with the German state and economic sphere'.[85] In the view of the autarky champions Germany was thus facing the tremendous and forward-looking task of 'really organizing an economic sphere for the first time'.[86]

The period following 1933 demonstrated the masterly skill and also the ruthlessness with which the National Socialist regime perceived and implemented this task. Wherever the trade-policy card failed to win the trick, there, as the economic literature from NSDAP circles made quite clear even before the 'seizure of power', 'recourse to the sword' appeared 'not only as a necessity but also as a right'.[87] Thus, the element of war was deliberately taken into consideration in the shaping of economic policy. During the world-wide depression the NSDAP not only adopted the idea of autarky within a large-scale economic sphere but amplified this concept, originally based on trade policy and contractual principles, by introducing an aggressive power-political component. The image of life as a struggle meant that war was regarded not only as an integral part of politics but was also transferred into economics. In National Socialist circles there was a conviction that 'only under the compulsion of warlike conflicts would the nations be ready to embark on the road towards a greater and more secure existence'; this was true also of economic needs, regardless of how these were formulated. 'To show absolute consideration for the wishes of every individual state' would be 'to favour an atomization of political living-spaces and to thwart any healthy development towards greater forms of existence'.[88] Autarky, to remain within the National Socialist vocabulary, was defined as 'the vital right of every people and every nation so to shape its economy that it becomes a fortress within which, in the event of trade-policy, currency-policy, or indeed warlike complications, it cannot be brought to its knees by hunger or by thirst'. Autarky had to be equated with 'separation of the nation's needs according to economic-policy and military-policy points of view'.[89]

National Socialist autarky policy, as consistently practised after 1933, was based on a multiple-step plan formulated even before Hitler's accession to power. Accordingly, the most immediate economic task of a National Socialist Germany was 'utilization of the available area, exhaustion of all the potential' available to achieve maximum self-sufficiency, to ensure the country's ability to rearm regardless of possible foreign pressures. In this way the prerequisites would be created for pursuing 'the expansion of . . . Reich territory through the recovery of stolen land (eastern Germany, the *Nordmark* [North Schleswig], Eupen-Malmédy, Alsace, etc.)' by alternate application of diplomacy and military action. The next step would be aimed at the 'creation of Greater Germany through the annexation of

---

[85] Daitz, *Ostraumpolitik*, 10.
[86] Fried, *Autarkie*, 127.
[87] Pfaff, *Wirtschafts-Aufbau*, 10.
[88] Obst, *Großraumidee*, 20/21.
[89] According to the NSDAP's expert on large-area economics, Werner Daitz, quoted from Ringer, *Handel*, 20.

areas inhabited by Germans and German in sentiment which, even before the world war, did not belong to the Reich' but to which, in the National Socialist view, a 'claim cannot be disputed':[90] the areas meant were Austria, the Sudeten region, and certain parts of Poland. Only when the economic and rearmament potential of a German Reich thus strengthened by territorial accretion made this possible would a final military effort be made to mark out the living-space in the east in its definitive dimension. To confine oneself to existing boundaries seemed to the National Socialists to be 'just as impossible on economic as on political grounds'.[91]

To this eastern orientation of the living-space idea the National Socialist programme-makers very soon added a western component. As early as 1931 an agricultural expert of the NSDAP suggested that in the pursuit of living-space projects one should not 'one-sidedly turn one's gaze to the east'. There was 'certainly less . . . counter-pressure in the west'. There was 'fine farmland also over there in the west, less than half utilized according to our ideas of cultivation and work'.[92] Shortly before the beginning of the Second World War a certain body of opinion in Germany altogether refused to tie itself down to any fixed living-space. Living-space was no longer seen as a static shape but as a variable magnitude responding to a nation's urge towards expansion: 'The nation's manifestation of life emerges most conspicuously from the flexibility of the living-space boundary, which . . . by its nature is a genuine boundary of movement'.[93]

Hitler and other NSDAP leaders were anxious to work out their economic programme for a state-stimulated upturn and, ultimately, for a withdrawal from international ties in favour of an economic sphere of hegemony in Europe, not only in co-operation with economic theoreticians but also in close contact with the world of industrial entrepreneurs. Even though the NSDAP intended to get their take-over of political responsibility legitimated by a heavy vote, the party nevertheless realized that it also needed the approval and confidence of the élite of industrial leadership. That was why Hitler had been trying between 1927 and 1928 to win the Ruhr industrialists over to his objectives by means of lectures, even though he had then been unable to offer them any clear economic programme. Approaches were also being made to numerous other entrepreneurs. The frequently heard assumption that these endeavours had led heavy industry, with the exception of a few leading figures, to be favourably disposed towards the party at an early date has been questioned even by historians who are regarded as anything but friends of big business.[94]

Although certain responsibilities had been institutionalized within the party at an early date, the NSDAP was for a long time without a body capable of tackling economic problems with proper authority. Not until 1929 did Hitler bring Otto Wagener, an ex-officer and former *Freikorps* commander, chairman of the board of a

---

[90] Albert, *Wiederaufrüstung*, 18.
[91] Ibid. 19.
[92] Willikens, *Agrarpolitik*, 46.
[93] Durach, 'Begriff Lebensraum', 288.
[94] Hallgarten, *Hitler*, 96.

sewing-machine company and active also as an assistant professor of economic policy and manufacturing, into the party's headquarters (*Reichsleitung*) in Munich, where he planned to establish an economic-policy department; this was eventually set up on 1 January 1931. Its task was to make practical preparations 'which would at any time enable National Socialism, on its accession to power, to take in hand also the rebuilding of the German economy'.[95] Wagener's appointment meant that Gottfried Feder was being pushed towards the margin of the leading group within the NSDAP. Feder, who until then had regarded himself as an authorized economic-policy spokesman for his party, was a graduate engineer with only amateurish insights into economic affairs, so Hitler did not consider him qualified to produce practicable or expert economic plans, let along subsequently to translate them into politics. Besides, vague slogans of Feder's invention such as the 'abolition of interest-slavery' and 'common weal comes before private profit' repeatedly aroused the mistrust of certain groups of entrepreneurs, who feared possible socialization and expropriation plans in the event of the National Socialists seizing power in the foreseeable future. Although Feder retained the chairmanship of the 'Economic Council of the Reichsleitung of the Party', he no longer exerted any decisive influence on the moulding of economic-policy opinion within the NSDAP. Instead he took over the ideas developed by Wagener and his staff and presented them to the public. Within the economic-policy department a division of labour was soon established, with men from economic life increasingly taking over various posts. Thus, the section for industry went to a former member of the Flick concern (Dr von Lucke), and that for trade to a member of Siemens-Schuckert AG (Cordemann, husband of Werner Siemens's granddaughter). The economic-policy department furthermore had working parties to advise it; these were headed by prominent scientists (e.g. Professor Jens Jessen, University of Kiel) or representatives of industry and banking. Thus, a director of the Deutsche Bank (von Stauss) and a member of IG-Farben (Dr Fischer) held important posts in the 'Working Party for International Economics'.

With a view to intensifying the dialogue with industry, Hitler commissioned Wilhelm Keppler, an industrialist who had joined the NSDAP at an early date, to 'reshape the party's economic programme in co-operation with the large-scale entrepreneurs'.[96] This 'personal economic adviser' to Hitler, who was believed in party circles to be heading for a great career, had established vital and solid contacts between the NSDAP and top leaders of big business by founding what became known as the Keppler circle. He succeeded in establishing contacts with several major industrialists and banks, and also with wholesale trade and big landowners. Eventually he enrolled twelve interested figures in a quasi-institutionalized discussion and working party, whose task it was to develop an alternative economic programme to government policy and to win over the German entrepreneurial world into opposition to the republic and in favour of a take-over of governmental power by National Socialism.

[95] Schmidt-Pauli, *Männer um Hitler*, 148.
[96] Testimony by Keppler in the Flick trial at Nuremberg, quoted from Hallgarten, *Hitler*, 97.

What response the ideology of autarky would find among representatives of practical economic management also depended to a large extent on the economic press. Here the NSDAP undoubtedly benefited from the fact that the conservative and nationalist right wing controlled some influential economic publications and that two of their most gifted editors had been instrumental in introducing the autarky programme into the party, while at the same time championing it in business circles. The first of these was the business editor Otto Dietrich, later to become Hitler's press chief but at the time working for the nationalist *München-Augsburger Zeitung*. As the son-in-law of the former president of the Alldeutscher Verband (All-German Union) and publisher of the *Rheinisch-Westfälische Zeitung*, the political mouthpiece of the Ruhr mining industry, Dietrich was in a position to influence the *rapprochement* between National Socialists and the political right wing.

The other prominent journalist was Walther Funk, the future Reich minister of economic affairs and Reichsbank president. He joined Hitler's service in 1930 as an additional economic adviser. Besides his close relations with industry he also had contacts with influential conservative circles. Last but not least, he was a personal friend of President von Hindenburg.

Before joining the NSDAP Funk, as editor of a leading Berlin Stock Exchange journal, already had the reputation of being an accomplished and skilful writer and an expert on economic matters, 'who was time and again consulted on economic problems by important business circles and in particular by the right-wing political parties'.[97] He was a member of the NSDAP's economic council, which was attached to the party's economic policy department and headed by Feder, though Funk was eventually to neutralize Feder's work. In the opinion of an attentive observer of the political scene in the Brown House in Munich, the headquarters of the NSDAP, Hitler had drawn on the advice of 'such an experienced adviser and acknowledged efficient economic policy expert' because he seemed 'to offer a certain guarantee that he would not lose his way among theories but . . . embark on practical roads . . . which would diverge from the rutted and bumpy tracks of the present system'—meaning the liberal principle of market economy.[98] During 1931 and 1932 Funk was one of Hitler's most important contacts with German business, and he actually succeeded, by making use of his personal contacts, 'not only in standing up effectively to the arguments' of many an industrialist, 'but in convincing him and enlisting him as a supporter'. Any such 'success represented a moral, political, and economic enhancement of the party's fighting strength, and helped demolish the prejudice that National Socialism was merely a party of class hatred and class struggle'.[99]

Funk had for some time been a member of the board of the Gesellschaft für deutsche Wirtschafts- und Sozialpolitik (Society for German Economic and Social Policy), which, while not enjoying the scholarly reputation of the Verein für

---

[97] Schmidt-Pauli, *Männer um Hitler*, 92.
[98] Ibid. 95.
[99] Oestreich, *Walther Funk*, 84.

Sozialpolitik (Association for Social Policy,[100] with which it should not be confused), was a group supporting broad economic interests—one might call it a lobby—with outstanding German firms and business associations, as well as science, administration, and politics represented on it.[101]

The Society controlled the journal *Neue Wirtschaft* (New Economics), nominally a non-party publication but in practice, since 1930, increasingly propagating National Socialist economic policy. Walther Funk as editor-in-chief was responsible for its contents. The journal devoted ample space to the autarky idea and voiced its conviction that 'the system of a national economy characterized by strong autarkic tendencies would'—even abroad—'dominate the next few decades'.[102]

An agency of considerable propagandist efficacy in favour of the idea of autarky was the Wirtschaftspolitischer Presse-Dienst der NSDAP (Economic Policy Press Service of the NSDAP), published by Wagener 'after arrangement with various industrialists' (*sic*), which supplied information to publications, economic-interest associations, and chambers of commerce and, according to its publisher's calculations, reached a regular readership of over half a million. Here the NSDAP's foreign-trade programme was formulated as 'expansion of key industries' into 'an autarkic "closed economic sphere"' . . . embracing the whole of eastern and south-eastern Europe'.[103]

To conclude from all this that German industrial big business succumbed at an early date to the fascination of the National Socialist formula of 'autarky within a large economic sphere' and therefore helped National Socialism into the saddle would be rash and, thus put, incorrect. Indeed, until the end of 1932 there was certainly among business circles a widespread scepticism of National Socialism. Their traditional export orientation was too deeply rooted to be dropped on a whim without much heart-searching. Just as deeply rooted was an uneasy suspicion of intended socialization and nationalization. Nevertheless, or rather for this reason, German business, following the great electoral success of September 1930, decided to take a closer look at the NSDAP's economic policy, even though 'its aims were not readily detectable'.[104] From 1930 the 'Revier' (Ruhr mining area) in particular had regarded the NSDAP as a force that should not be underestimated, which was why closer ties were established with it after the autumn elections. Following the enormous increase in votes for the party, many Ruhr industrialists found themselves faced with the choice of 'either rejecting National Socialism from the outset . . . with all the damaging effects this might [possibly have for them] in the event of its confidently expected participation in the government, or else to show

---

[100] Cf. the publications of the *Verein für Sozialpolitik*.

[101] Cf. Volkmann, 'Außenwirtschaftliches Programm', 268 ff.

[102] Schürmann, 'Weg zur Autarkie', 3.

[103] Schulz, *Aufstieg*, 625. Of particular interest is the presentation by Zumpe, *Wirtschaft und Staat*. Although the author writes from a GDR-Marxist point of view, the National Socialists are no longer portrayed as the henchmen of big capital and of the big landowners. The assumption now is one of complicity, which comes close to the thesis of the identity of interests assumed in the present book. The study is distinguished by expert knowledge, a wealth of material, and an effort to make differentiated judgements. Even non-Marxist historiography will in future have to take account of it.

[104] Reupke, *Nationalsozialismus*, 7.

interest in it. . . . Heavy industry opted for the latter alternative', as one of its representatives admitted after 1945.[105]

The persistent lack of success shown by the presidential governments in overcoming the depression, and the increasing polarization of agrarian and industrial groups, resulted in a growing influx of industrial entrepreneurs into the NSDAP, accompanied by their efforts to exert a deliberate influence on the shaping of its economic programme in line with their own views. The front of the so-called nationalist opposition brought together at the Harzburg rally (11 October 1931), representing the reactionary right wing of politics and economic life, was admittedly oriented not in favour of the National Socialists but against the Weimar Republic, more particularly against the Brüning government. Even so, the agreed demand for a strong state and for 'restitution of German military sovereignty and armament parity' meant the acknowledgement that all participating political groupings, and hence also the NSDAP, were potential coalition partners and therefore capable of sharing governmental responsibility.[106]

From 1932 onward the balance of political decisions among industrial big business and banking seemed very gradually to be swinging in favour of the NSDAP, whose concept of a state-triggered upturn and an autarkic large-scale economic sphere appeared to offer an alternative programme to that of the presidential governments. A still clearly perceptible reserve *vis-à-vis* the party was due primarily to fear that the economic policy which it proclaimed would involve a planned economy, in whatever form or intensity, as well as to fear of the party's suspected hostility to private ownership. In order to dispel such misgivings Hitler addressed the Düsseldorf Industrial Club on 27 January 1932 with an unambiguous declaration in favour of private enterprise and entrepreneurial initiative and responsibility; these he believed could be safeguarded only in an authoritarian state based on the leadership principle. He considered it illogical 'to base industrial life on the idea of achievement, on the value of the individual, and hence in practice on the authority of the individual and yet to deny this authority of the individual in politics and to replace it by the law of the larger number, by democracy'.[107] Hitler promised to curtail the influence of organized labour upon the economy and to alleviate the world-wide depression by the territorial expansion of the Reich's economic base.

It is difficult to assess the success of this address, especially as it avoided all precise detail. But in the spring of 1932, when political conditions in Gemany were increasingly shifting towards the right and in the direction of an authoritarian regime, when National Socialist participation in government or even exclusive National Socialist government had moved into the realm of the possible, big business still, out of uncertainty about the Nazis' economic programme, largely lacked the necessary resolution to break with the existing government, expecially as

[105] Heinrichsbauer, *Schwerindustrie*, 38.
[106] *Dokumente zur deutschen Geschichte 1929–1933*, 43.
[107] *Vortrag Adolf Hitlers*, 10.

no other that would better serve its interests was yet in sight. Hjalmar Schacht, the former Reichsbank president who had been in sympathy with the NSDAP since Harzburg, therefore thought the time had come to define the Party's economic ideas and to bring them into harmony with those of industry. In agreement with Hitler and business friends he set up a study-centre designed 'in joint work to achieve complete agreement between the fundamental views of National Socialism and what would be expected of private enterprise'.[108]

This institution, supported also financially by banks and well-known business firms, co-operated closely with the Keppler circle. In order to gain business support for Hitler as chancellor it was necessary to eliminate all those items in the programme which suggested the existence of socialization or nationalization tendencies within the Party. In consequence the Short-term Economic Programme was pulped in the autumn, because it included the socialization of monopolies and state supervision of joint-stock companies.[109] During the period which followed the National Socialists and their sympathizers in big business left no stone unturned to present the NSDAP as favouring the employers. Gradually even industrial circles which still maintained some reserve of scepticism towards the Party came to believe that National Socialism intended to 'preserve the true foundations of private ownership in business'.[110]

Although the elections of November 1932 resulted in a considerable loss of votes for the NSDAP, while von Papen failed to achieve a reliable majority for himself in the Reichstag, evidence was accumulating that industry, big landowners, and banks would withdraw support from von Papen. Typical of this trend was the petition addressed by representatives of these economic groups to von Hindenburg, calling, as is well known, for Hitler's appointment as chancellor—even though its historical implication has been the subject of considerable controversy. It has been pointed out that 'the political convictions of the signatories of this petition . . . [were] not typical of these big businessmen in November 1932',[111] especially as the list of petitioners might have been extended by other well-known names from among prominent entrepreneurs. However, the correspondence files of the banker von Schröder, who acted as secretary in this matter, contain a number of letters from captains of industry testifying beyond any doubt to their support for the petition. They merely considered it inopportune to vote so demonstratively for the NSDAP and its leader.[112] A few days after the petition there was a meeting in Düsseldorf of the Langnam Association, an organization representing various branches of Rhineland-Westphalian industry and commerce, as well as large portions of the heavy and mining industries, which had by then reoriented themselves to the domestic market. The meeting adopted a positive and open-

---

[108] Letter from Schacht to Hitler, 12 Apr. 1932, quoted from Stegmann, 'Großindustrie', 450.

[109] *Wirtschaftliches Sofortprogramm*, 28 ff.

[110] *Berliner Börsen-Zeitung* (6 Apr. 1932), quoted and interpreted in *Mitteilungen der Deutschen Arbeitgeberverbände* (15 Apr. 1932), 110. Similar views were expressed by a representative of the Rheinische AG für Braunkohlenbergbau und Brikettfabrikation. Cf. Schneider, *Unternehmer*, 113.

[111] Turner, *Faschismus*, 25; text of petition in Kühnl, *Faschismus*, 160 ff.

[112] Cf. Volkmann, 'Außenwirtschaftliches Programm', 272.

minded attitude towards autarky endeavours within the framework of a German-dominated Europe. Whereas this body had 'only a few weeks ago cheered von Papen', there emerged 'the surprising fact that almost the whole of industry' now wanted 'the appointment of Hitler, regardless of circumstances'.[113]

At the beginning of 1933 an arrangement was made between the NSDAP and the Deutschnationale Volkspartei (DNVP: German National People's Party), envisaging the formation 'by the cold method'—i.e. without new elections—of a coalition government headed by Hitler. This had been preceded by negotiations between the Keppler circle and industrial leaders, resulting in broad agreement on the National Socialist economic programme. There was now an expectation among wide circles of entrepreneurs of 'an economic upturn through the placing of state orders'.[114] What was expected in particular was a stimulation of the domestic market through rearmament, as promised by Hitler, through an extension of the transport network and, in this context, the promotion of motor-vehicle manufacture, shipbuilding, and aircraft construction financed by public funds. The IG-Farben AG now also aligned itself with the party's economic programme: here the crucial factor was no doubt the National Socialist promise that a process for the production of synthetic motor fuel and rubber, developed at great cost, would be utilized on a big scale in connection with rearmament. This assurance was underpinned in the Wirtschaftliches Aufbauprogramm der NSDAP (Economic Development Programme of the NSDAP), which replaced the Short-term Economic Programme as the party's new electoral platform, by the declaration of intent that, in the event of a National Socialist assumption of government, there would be a vigorous expansion of the domestic raw-material basis.

The fact that at about the end of 1932 and the beginning of 1933 large sections of German industrial business were reconciling themselves—from an economic point of view—to a government controlled by the National Socialists and to the policy propagated by them was due not solely to the party's (by then credible) assurances that, regardless of those controls which were inevitably linked with a policy of autarky, it would 'not abolish the entire capitalist economic structure and the right to private property'.[115] Two factors were decisive in inclining the entrepreneurs to approve the policy of autarky: first, retention of their ownership of the means of production, together with the chance of profit-maximization, and second, the NSDAP's promise to resolve the economic problems inherited from the Weimar Republic, and to achieve this by way of territorial extension and market expansion. 'A single large market, an enlarged area of production, organization, and transportation, with its prospects of more efficient and thus less expensive production of goods—that was what they were longing for.'[116] After the turn of 1932–3 a major part of representative German finance and business was therefore

---

[113] Information given by Scholz, head of a press bureau financed by the industrialists Wolff and Flick, to Franz Bracht, Schleicher's future minister of the interior, 16 Nov. 1932, quoted in Kühnl, *Faschismus*, 163.
[114] Testimony of the banker von Schröder to the Nuremberg Tribunal, quoted ibid. 175.
[115] *Der Große Brockhaus*, xiii (Leipzig, 1932), 209.
[116] Thiele, *Großraumwirtschaft*, 158.

prepared, more or less unhesitatingly, to make common cause with the National Socialists.[117]

As Germany's export-oriented industry was no longer succeeding in making its mark or holding its place in the world market, it became increasingly attracted to a solution which promised 'dramatically to improve conditions of surplus-value production and realization in the domestic market and, in the longer term, to prepare for the territorial expansion of that domestic market'; in this way an alternative to a world-market-oriented export policy would be implemented through an enlargement of the market, to be forcibly achieved by political and, if necessary, military means.[118] These plans and ideas had long been familiar to industrialists from their own reflections. It is possible that the National Socialist endeavours 'to make Germany autarkic were welcomed by certain industrial enterprises not out of idealism but as an opportunity to enlarge their own spheres of power. Hitler's economic programme'—at least according to the testimony of the banker Schröder, an early sympathizer of National Socialism—'was known to business as a whole and was welcomed by it'.[119] The hopes and desires of numerous figures in economic life were focused on having a strong authoritarian government after the economic upheavals of the past, one which would stay in power for a prolonged period and would thus be able to provide a guarantee of long-term solutions to economic problems. The call for more state action eventually grew too loud to be disregarded once an arrangement had become possible with the NSDAP to the effect that 'business should guide itself towards the solution of the problems placed before it by the political leadership'. Consolidation of the economy meant stabilization of political conditions—and this was understood by industry to mean not only the struggle against Communism but also a far-reaching elimination of the influence of organized labour. A National Socialist government was further expected to introduce compulsory organization of trade associations, though these would govern and represent themselves and 'would themselves have to ensure a balance of production'; it was even expected that the new organizations would exert a greater influence on economic policy than they had in the past.[120]

When Schleicher, Papen's successor, set about implementing an unorthodox economic policy, and when an alliance between 'the military and the working class' appeared to be within the realm of the possible, industrial business felt faced with a political alternative, a choice between National Socialism and Marxism.[121] By late 1932 or early 1933 the moment had arrived: 'The continuous threat of civil war by the German Communist Party'—that, at least, was how it appeared to industrial leaders—'its cultural propaganda denying all European thought, its hostility to religion . . . its brutally proclaimed totalitarian principle' gave rise 'to the belief, in ever widening circles, even among very deliberate and sensibly thinking

[117] In detail in Sohn-Rethel, *Ökonomie*, 90–9; Volkmann, 'Politik, Wirtschaft und Aufrüstung'.
[118] Kadritzke, *Faschismus*, 163–4.
[119] Testimony of the banker von Schröder to the Nuremberg Tribunal, quoted from Kühnl, *Faschismus*, 175.
[120] Ibid. 174–5.
[121] Turner, *Faschismus*, 27; cf. Winkler, 'Unternehmerverbände', 368 ff.

individuals, that, compared with Communism, National Socialism was the lesser evil.'[122]

Whereas the *rapprochement* between NSDAP and industry was progressing hesitantly, if enduringly, and whereas extensive identity of interests, especially between Hitler and heavy industry on the basis of their common expansionist aims, was not achieved until the turn of 1932–3, the specific conditions in the agrarian sector between the National Socialist party and agriculture had led to an earlier and closer affinity. This was largely due to the significance in terms of racial ideology which the German Fascist movement assigned to the peasantry as the biological stock of the German people and potential reservoir of settlers for the Germanization of a larger living-space to be acquired for Germany in the future.

Thus, an agrarian-political concept soon crystallized within the National Socialist programme. Although National Socialist policy with regard to the peasantry and agriculture had been based on an impetus towards rearmament and a war economy ever since the 1920s, this was further intensified when the agronomist R. Walther Darré made himself available to the NSDAP leadership in 1930 as adviser on agricultural matters. He possessed the requisite expertise and a capacity for theoretical and abstract thinking, as well as a talent for writing and a high measure of organizational skill; these he put to the Party's service to utilize the voting potential of the peasantry. Possessed by the same fanatic racial mania as Hitler, he saw, like his leader, 'the peasantry as the life-source of the Nordic race'.[123] His 'blood-and-soil' theory matched Hitler's ideas concerning the need for an enlargement of German living-space, and thus, still under the Weimar Republic, he built the foundation on which the National Socialist regime was to base its rearmament-conditioned autarky policy in the agrarian sector after 1933. Darré wished to see agriculture as the centre of the national economic production process. 'In an economy based on and guided by the idea of the Volk, agriculture, as the custodian and guarantor of the nutritional base . . . [should be] not a part of that economy . . . but its precondition.' It must be the foremost task of the people's (*völkisch*) state to safeguard its population's food supplies from its own territory, 'so as not to be, in this vital area, at the mercy of foreign countries'.[124] If agriculture was assigned the task of ensuring a people's and a state's foodstuffs from its own resources, industry would be able to concentrate on a more receptive domestic market and reduce its dependence on foreign countries, because 'certain laws, so to speak, automatically come into being for the building up of the domestic market'. However, a state organism consolidated in this manner was, as he put it, subsequently subject to a kind of natural expansionist urge, since 'its relationship to its territory . . . likewise follows certain laws, from which conclusions [may] in turn be derived for its foreign policy'.[125] To Darré there was no doubt that Germany had

[122] Heinrichsbauer, *Schwerindustrie*, 36.

[123] Title of his book, *Das Bauerntum als Lebensquell der nordischen Rasse*, published in Munich in 1929.

[124] 'Zur Wiedergeburt des Bauerntums' (1 July 1931), in Darré, *Blut und Boden*, 65.

[125] Ibid. 66.

too little space for a strong growing race.[126] Again in agreement with Hitler, he believed that it was necessary 'to gain the needed space where . . . it offered itself naturally', i.e. in the east.[127] The blood-and-soil theory established 'the moral right to recover as much land in the east as is necessary . . . to establish harmony between the ethnic body (*Volkskörper*) and its geopolitical space', which implied a 'life-and-death' struggle. National Socialism demanded that the German people be prepared for this conflict 'and also for the realization that in this struggle . . . there can be but one slogan: simply to be victorious'.[128]

For the purpose of capturing the rural vote, in March 1930 Hitler formulated an 'official party proclamation on the NSDAP's attitude to the rural population and agriculture', which contained these principal ideas:

1. increased agricultural production with the objective of 'essentially feeding ourselves from our own land and soil';
2. creation of a highly efficient agricultural economy with sufficient purchasing power to reduce German industry's dependence on exports;
3. the German peasantry's role as the foodstuff-producing estate, representing the 'mainstay of the people's health', 'the nation's fount of youth and the backbone of its military strength' for the conquest of the living- and settlement-space regarded as necessary.[129]

By persistent work the National Socialist movement had already won the sympathies of wide agricultural circles during the final years of the Weimar Republic. Admittedly, during the first few years of the Party's existence its demand in the official programme for a 'land reform adapted to national requirements, the introduction of a law on the expropriation without compensation of land for public-interest purposes'[130] initially met with rejection on the part of big landowners and caused small and medium-sized farmers to fear for their property. Hitler therefore found himself compelled in April 1928 to supplement the twenty-five theses of the party programme, declared to be unalterable, by the assurance that 'the passage on "expropriation without compensation" refers only to the creation of legislative facilities for the expropriation, if necessary, of land acquired in an illegal manner or not managed in line with the nation's interest'. As the NSDAP stood 'on the platform of private ownership' the formula referred to could be directed solely 'against Jewish land-speculation companies' but not against the German peasantry.[131]

It was only when the Party, by a great propaganda effort, disseminated its thesis on agrarian policy in 1930 and simultaneously launched an expert-advice service in

---

[126] 'Stellung und Aufgaben des Landstandes in einem nach lebensgesetzlichen Gesichtspunkten aufgebauten deutschen Staate' (1 Sept. 1930), in Darré, *Erkenntnisse*, 163.
[127] Ibid. 164.
[128] Ibid. 165.
[129] Quoted from Feder, *Programm*, 7; cf. Merkel, *Agrarpolitik*, 87–91.
[130] Feder, *Programm*, 20–1.
[131] Ibid. 21.

rural areas that it gained real influence in the countryside. One of its measures was the introduction of a so-called 'Land Policy Apparatus' (Agrarpolitischer Apparat), consisting of agricultural experts whose task it was 'rather like a delicately ramified root-system to penetrate into all rural affairs, cling fast to them, and endeavour to envelop them so that eventually nothing could take place in the agricultural sphere throughout Reich territory' that the NSDAP was not able to 'keep in sight and basically to dominate'.[132] The supra-regional weekly *Nationalsozialistische Landpost* (National Socialist Rural News), published from the late summer of 1931 onwards, intensified Party influence on the peasantry, and this wooing for the favour of the rural voters inevitably produced results.

Table II.1.4 allows a comparison of Reichstag election votes for the NSDAP from 1928 to 1933 in six predominantly rural constituencies (East Prussia, Pomerania, Schleswig-Holstein, East Hanover, Hesse-Darmstadt, and the Palatinate) with six predominantly urban constituencies (Berlin, Westphalia South, Düsseldorf East, Chemnitz-Zwickau, Merseburg, Hamburg). In 1928 the difference between town and country was scarcely significant. Two years later, however, out of every 100 voters the NSDAP was gaining 4.7 more in rural than in urban areas. This disproportion increased to 12.6 by July 1932 and to 12.8 by 1933.[133]

TABLE II.1.4. *Average share of NSDAP vote in six rural and six urban constituencies 1928–1933* (%)

	1928	1930	1932 (I)	1932 (II)	1933
Predominantly rural	2.8	22.6	47.1	42.4	52.4
Predominantly urban	2.4	17.9	34.5	29.9	39.6

Source: Gies, 'NSDAP', 343.

With these electoral successes agrarian policy gained increasing importance within the NSDAP's propaganda plan; this is confirmed by the establishment in 1932 of the office for agrarian policy in the Party's Reichsleitung. Beyond the capture of votes in the countryside, however, the intentions of the National Socialists were directed towards a penetration of vocational organizations in agriculture. Conditions for this seemed particularly favourable at the beginning of the 1930s when, added to the general material hardships in agriculture and the effects of the world economic depression, there was dissatisfaction among farmers with the organizations representing their interests; these seemed mainly engaged in fierce rivalry and political argument with each other. As a result, unbridled

[132] Circular from Darré, 27 Nov. 1930, to the Agrarpolitischer Apparat, quoted from Gies, 'NSDAP', 347.
[133] Cf. ibid. 343 n. 10a.

National Socialist propaganda and infiltration succeeded, within the span of a single year (autumn 1931 to November 1932), in crushing the Christlich-nationale Bauern- und Landvolkpartei (Christian National Peasant and Rural Party)—which in 1930 still had 19 deputies in the Reichstag—so that its voters henceforward predominantly voted for the NSDAP. At the same time began the ideological and individual infiltration of the most important organization of the peasantry, the Reichslandbund (National Agricultural Association), which was predominantly oriented towards the big landowners. One of its two directors, H. von Sybel, made his first contacts with the National Socialists in 1931 and eventually represented them in the Reichstag from July 1932 onwards. Towards the end of 1931 the Reichslandbund elected Darré's deputy in the NSDAP's Reichsleitung to be its fourth president, and in the spring of 1932, in the second electoral round, it openly supported Hitler's candidacy for the post of head of state. These spectacular successes would certainly not have been possible if 'strivings towards autarky and glorification of the peasantry, as performed by Darré's blood-and-soil ideology' had not 'long been the objective of the political endeavours of this peasantry association and its followers'.[134]

Bibliographical Note (1989)

The relationship between National Socialism and the leaders of the economy continues to be the subject of new studies. It was also the theme of a series of lectures at the University of Augsburg. Regrettably, the lecturer narrowed down the problem to the support given to Hitler by big business, without making clear the motives of economic policy which ultimately led German big business to turn away from the Weimar Republic and towards National Socialism. The National Socialist alternative to the free market and world-wide economy, i.e. autarky within a large economic area, as formulated with the co-operation of renowned representatives of big business, was not fully understood by the author. Cf. Bernecker, 'Kapitalismus und Nationalsozialismus'. Neebe, *Großindustrie*, 176 ff., 274 n. 17, questions the thesis that big business ultimately supported the National Socialist economic policy for its autarky and large-area economic programme. Such a rash judgement can only be arrived at if one works exclusively from documents without tracing the co-operation of big business and National Socialism in economic policy beyond the period 1930–3. Neebe lacks the history-of-ideas approach to the subject. The same flaw is unfortunately exhibited also in the extensive and worthwhile study by Turner, *German Big Business and the Rise of Hitler*. Both studies are based exclusively on documentary sources and the primary and secondary political-history literature, without the least regard to the literature on economic policy and economic theory of the period analysed by them (cf. also Volkmann, *Wirtschaft im Dritten Reich*, i, esp. 23–47). They are thus unable to mark out the intellectual background against which political and economic decisions were made. Both authors tend towards a personalized view of history, but this cannot ultimately explain why German private industry came to such a speedy arrangement with National Socialism as soon as the latter came to power, or why during the Third Reich almost complete identity of economic objectives was achieved,

[134] Ibid. 376; cf. Denecke, *Agrarpolitische Konzeptionen*; Gessner, *Agrarverbände*, 258–63.

with the result that conflicts remained almost entirely confined to the organizational and administrative sphere. Turner is still deeply rooted in the totalitarianism theory. A very differently structured study is that by Teichert, *Autarkie*. It reveals the ideological background against which economic policy, and especially foreign-trade policy, was possible and was being realized in practice. The author refers in particular to the spate of articles on geopolitical and strategic thinking; this had an influence which should not be underrated on the formulation of economic, and more especially foreign-trade, theory and programmes. The study establishes the existence of a link between radically motivated expansionism, in the sense of living-space theory, on the one hand, and a power-political and eventually economically motivated expansionism on the other.

II. The National Socialist War Economy

1. THE WAR-ECONOMY SYSTEM

WITH what was termed 'Wehrwirtschaft' (military or war economy) the NSDAP propagated an economic principle that was new in modern German economic history. It differed from other, earlier forms of economic management not so much in the relatively high share allotted to rearmament or economic preparations for war generally as in the ideological principle underlying it, the fact that it was 'inspired by a totally different attitude of mind' and was 'subject to different internal laws',[1] the ones formulated in the theory of the large economic area and living-space. Wehrwirtschaft was understood by the National Socialist regime to mean 'the remoulding, in peacetime, of the economy for war on the basis of military considerations'. This not only entailed the primacy of rearmament throughout economic life but also reflected the view that under National Socialism 'economic policy must be the tool of rearmament policy', as openly admitted by the regime and its leaders.[2] After all, the military—and among them more especially the war-economy experts—had drawn what they believed to be the only correct and decisive conclusion from the unexpectedly heavy battles of *matériel* in the First World War, as manifestations of modern war in the technological age, and from the supply difficulties caused by the Allied blockade: the conclusion that any future economic preparations for war should not be confined to the operational needs of the fighting forces. Instead, they were to ensure equally the satisfaction of the needs of the armed forces and of the civilian population in order to achieve readiness for and endurance in war, in both the material and the psychological sense. Future military conflicts, of the kind that the armed forces under National Socialism did not rule out and that Hitler deliberately intended to provoke, were presented by military-political writers in Germany as a so-called total war, one which was bound to make 'quite different demands upon the people than did the world war, for it will require the nation to place its mental, physical, and material forces in the service of the war'.[3] That kind of war required special economic measures, in the sense that 'in the economic sphere, too, the fighting forces and the nation' must 'constitute a powerful unity'.[4] The prerequisite was a general orientation of all economic life in Germany towards war, in particular through the transformation of the liberal market-economy system into a state-guided economy, the so-called war economy. This was charged with 'the task of preparing the overall economy, in peacetime, for total war'.[5] It was up to the war economy to ensure that 'the nation's entire

---

[1] Statement by Reich Press Chief Dietrich, quoted from Weil, 'Literatur', 201.
[2] Brockdorff, 'Weltwirtschaft und Weltrüstung', 492.
[3] Ludendorff, *The Nation at War* (1936), 22.
[4] Ibid. 55.
[5] Zinnemann, 'Wechselwirkungen', 491.

economic and professional life [would be] up to the demands of a total war'.[6] If the armed forces therefore understood the term 'war economy' to cover not only rearmament measures but a multitude of other measures within the nation's economy, this view was in line with that of leading politicians of the National Socialist era. Thus, the state secretary in the Reich ministry of economic affairs, Brinkmann, simply saw the war economy as 'the new shape of the peacetime economy', with, in particular, two specific tasks to be implemented—ensuring that 'the economic requirements of the armed forces are met' and providing for 'the preparation and execution of economic mobilization'.[7]

The large number of so-called war-economists—and this term covers military men, journalists, and academic economists—were all agreed that war-economy preparations in peacetime had to take place in these areas:

1. determination of the amount of raw materials needed for the economy as a whole, and more particularly for supplying the armament industry with the principal basic raw materials such as coal, iron, copper, lead, zinc, etc.;
2. provision of fuels;
3. storage of goods and raw materials not available in the future domestic war-zone;
4. compilation of a record of all industries concerning their productive capacities and, if necessary, expansion;
5. regulation of the employment of manpower with a view to the necessary call-up of workers to the forces in the event of war;
6. reorganization of transport in the light of military and economic conditions;
7. organization of food supply;
8. systematic rearrangement of external economic relations with a view to blockade-proof supplies;
9. financial cover for peacetime and subsequently wartime rearmament.

Generally speaking, the demands of the war economists were for 'a planned state-managed economic organization, the prerequisite of which [must be] a study of the economy based upon precise statistical data'.[8]

A mere four days after Hitler's assumption of the chancellor's post the direction of his economic policy emerged clearly when as the head of government, addressing the commanders-in-chief of the army and navy, he expressed the view that the present economic problems could no longer be resolved by classic economic means—such as an intensified German presence in world markets—but solely by the extension of the territorial basis of the Reich. To 'intensify exports [was] useless' in view of the limited absorption capacity of the world market and of excess production everywhere. There was therefore a need for settlement, especially in order to safeguard food supplies; for this, however, the German people's living-space was insufficient and must therefore be enlarged. In consequence, building up the armed forces was 'the most important prerequisite of attaining that goal: . . .

[6] Fischer, *Wehrwirtschaft*, 21.
[7] Brinkmann, *Wirtschaftspolitik*, 68.
[8] Statement by Major (retd.) Hesse, a university teacher, 'Entwicklung', 292.

viz., conquest of new living-space in the east'.[9] That was the power-political and economic-policy guideline to which all economic life in the Third Reich now had to adapt. As early as 8 February 1933 Hitler made it unmistakably clear to his cabinet that the *Wiederwehrhaftmachung* (remilitarization) of the German people was his foremost concern. Setting the economic course for the next four or five years, he demanded during a budget discussion 'everything for the armed forces'; it was therefore universally agreed that the resources needed by the armed forces would be safeguarded first of all, and that only then would the question be examined of how much could be spent in the civilian sphere.[10] The priorities for the entire economic process were thereby laid down; specifically this meant that 'the economy of the Reich . . . [must] be primarily aligned along the needs of German rearmament' and that 'all special interests [must] take a back seat compared with this goal'.[11]

The National Socialist programme for living-space and autarky was therefore, as has just been shown, not merely a propaganda line prior to 1933 but continued to be an essential directive when the party was in power. The preconditions for its implementation had to be brought about by means of the war economy, but it was not of course possible to do this in the ideal way conceived by the theoreticians. The National Socialist rulers had to make allowance for the traditional ruling élites in economic life, especially in big business.[12] When Hitler assumed the reins of government, relations between National Socialism and big business rested upon a great measure of identity of interests; even so, however, both sides had undertaken certain obligations and were compelled to make concessions. 'Relations between the exponents of government' can therefore be 'described as a "pact" of big business, Reichswehr, and National Socialism',[13] a pact which did not permit the introduction of a system that would embrace the whole of the economy in the way repeatedly and emphatically demanded by the military. Thus, the means of production remained largely in private ownership. Big business, moreover, retained control of enterprises and also, in a limited way, of the markets. It further continued to have the decisive say concerning top-management personnel, who were anyway used to acting in concert. Finally, big business possessed an intact organization which enabled it effectively to formulate its interests *vis-à-vis* the state and the military. For their own part, the National Socialists had realized at an early date that entrepreneurs must be allowed sufficient latitude for private enterprise even under the war economy—partly as a corrective to planning errors by the state, and partly because they clung to the belief that 'only free and independent individuals, capable of disposing freely over their work and their yield, are imbued with a serious sense of responsibility towards their work, so that only on this soil can forceful personalities emerge and only on the soil of freedom and responsibility can a sense of common weal flourish'. They therefore opposed the elimination of

[9] Quoted from Vogelsang, 'Dokumente', 435.
[10] Minutes of meeting, 8 Feb. 1933, *DGFP*, c. i. 37.   [11] Weil, 'Literatur', 201.
[12] The term 'big business' (*Großwirtschaft*) is intended to refer 'not only to industrial-interest associations but to the complex of managements of large enterprises, interwoven with the top echelons of firms in trade and industry' (Hüttenberger, 'Polykratie', 423 n. 17).
[13] Ibid. 423.

entrepreneurial initiative, of the profit motive, and of competition.[14] For political and psychological reasons the task of the economy had to continue to be the satisfaction of identifiable economic demand, and this meant that private profit and money-making remained linked with it.

In the view of the military, however, freedom in the choice of employment, in price and wage settlement, in profit creation, and ultimately in supply and demand could only be allowed so long as there was no need for 'prices and sales to be regulated from a superior level, by the state or an economic community, in the spirit of economic guidance'.[15] On this point the armed forces and Hitler held identical views. His policy was, after all, designed 'to compel business to serve the common weal to its own advantage', as he characterized the relationship between the state and the business world.[16] If it was intended, in this division of labour, to translate the primacy of rearmament into reality by the ambitious plan of achieving a vastly advanced state of rearmament within a few years, then a different economic system was needed from that of the Weimar Republic, viz. an institutionalized legal framework for the economy, one which allowed for interventionist measures. A range of tools was needed for laying down rearmament priorities, for pulling 'the whole of economic policy together into integrated effectiveness in line with the requirements of the war economy'.[17] War economy in the National Socialist state was not equivalent to a planned economy in the strict sense. Instead, the regime demanded for itself 'merely the right to steer the economy in the direction required by state policy', while being willing to leave 'economic initiative and the execution of individual economic decisions to the free judgement of the individual and to free private business'.[18] Because the National Socialist regime was reluctant to pursue its rearmament intentions 'by the roundabout route of an economic bureaucracy to be set up by the state',[19] it sought other ways of making the economy subservient to the objectives of rearmament policy. There was, in consequence, no restructuring of the inherited market system in the sense of a centralist solution in 1933. The intention was instead to influence the market-economy steering mechanism by *dirigiste* measures on the part of the state. The economic system introduced step by step after 1933 may be assigned to the 'guided-market economy' or 'organized capitalism' type:[20] the state set the economic goals, it laid down the economic priorities, it even acted on a considerable scale as the customer, i.e. generally as a directing agency, while entrepreneurs managed their business on their own responsibility in line with the state's directives. The National Socialists felt under an obligation to 'observe the intrinsic laws of all economic matters' because they feared that any violation of these might have to be paid for dearly in economic consequences.[21]

---

[14] Feder, *Deutscher Staat*, 23–4.
[15] 'Die Begriffe der Wehr-, Friedens- und Kriegswirtschaft', 256–7.
[16] Quoted from Köhler, *Des Führers Wirtschaftspolitik*, 7.
[17] Korfes, *Wehrwirtschaftslehre*, 53.
[18] Fischer, *Wehrwirtschaft*, 26.
[19] Speech by Hitler to the Reichstag, 23 Mar. 1933, quoted from *Schulthess 1933*, 70.
[20] Cf. Rubbert, 'Marktwirtschaft'; Schweitzer, 'Organisierter Kapitalismus'.
[21] Goebel, 'Durchführung', 157.

This fear was reflected also in the regime's readiness to confine itself to the form of a so-called 'leader economy' (*Führerwirtschaft*), which permitted a certain measure of decentralization, delegation, and ultimately also self-management within the framework of an entrepreneurial association. However, this latitude granted to business by the state had to have its limit 'whenever the great advantages of shared responsibility and private initiative' were in danger of being 'outweighed by the disadvantage that uniform planning and smooth fulfilment of the plans might be jeopardized'. Even though the regime thus eschewed the introduction of a perfect planned-economy system, believing instead in a compromise between state *dirigisme* and private entrepreneurial responsibility as an ideal model for its war economy, the political leadership, to enforce its will in rearmament matters, nevertheless had to have at its disposal the 'complete range of all conceivable degrees of intensity, starting with the command in the form of orders and prohibitions, through general instructions, directives, and recommendations, advice and financial benefits, all the way down to complete *laissez-faire*'.[22]

In order to be in a position to translate the state tasks into economic production the National Socialist government first of all proclaimed the principle of 'professional self-management': branches of the economy amalgamated into cor- porations would receive the state's directives for passing on to individual enterprises. Conversely, they were responsible for entrepreneurial action to the originator of the political order.[23]

If the National Socialist government wished 'so to shape the conditions of the economic process that economic agents will, in pursuit of their own interests, adapt themselves to the overall economic goals',[24] then it had to be one of its most pressing tasks to restructure the organization of the economic unions and associations inherited from the Weimar era and/or assign new tasks to them, or else impose new personnel. This was necessary on two grounds:

1. It was essential to strip them of their political influence. For 'in a strong state'—the National Socialist regime argued—'the business world does not need any political organizations' any longer. What would be conceded to it was 'a coalition for the representation of the professional interests of the different industries' on the basis of the corporate idea.[25] The leading figures at the head of such professional representative bodies would now have quite different tasks from 'possibly conducting economic policy in the manner of a political leader'. It was to be made impossible in the future for the so-called leaders of industry to oppose National Socialist policy. Instead they would be obliged to support it.[26]

2. These bodies were to be used as a conveyor belt for the transmission of the state's rearmament intentions to the overall economic process. 'State guidance of the economy, representing not a planned economy but a purposeful guidance of the

[22] All quotations in this paragraph are from Weigmann, 'Problemlage', 33.
[23] Cf. Krüger, *Berufsständischer Gedanke.*
[24] Hegelheimer, *Wirtschaftslenkung*, 45.
[25] Köhler, *Des Führers Wirtschaftspolitik*, 13.
[26] Ibid. 14.

economy in the direction of the state's political goals, instead of a free economy, requires the abolition of a multifarious and often even chaotic pattern of associations and its replacement by a sensibly articulated structure.'[27] War economy, after all, represented an economic system whose 'contents [were] . . . determined not by those in the economy but by extra-economic events, principally by the political and military leadership'.[28]

At the centre of National Socialist policy concerning associations was, above all, a desire for concentration—the amalgamation of parallel or competing organizations—since it was 'more convenient . . . for the authorities to deal with a few large ones rather than with a lot of little ones'.[29] This claim to guidance, voiced by the party and state leadership, encountered no more than feeble opposition among interest-groups and associations,[30] mainly because by the summer of 1933 there was scarcely any doubt left that state control of the economy in the National Socialist sense did not imply a planned economy proper, in its full-blown guise, but merely a purposeful guidance of the economy in line with the state's political objectives in place of the earlier economic system governed by the market.

2. ORGANIZATION AND CONTROL OF AGRICULTURE

As Reichsbauernführer (Reich agricultural leader) Darré observed in a memorandum to Hitler, 'the entire efforts of agricultural policy since the seizure of power' had been 'characterized by preparation for the possibility of war'.[31] When in his government statement of 2 February 1933 the Führer declared the 'rescue of the German peasantry for the sake of maintaining the nation's basis of nutrition and hence of life' to be the demand of the hour,[32] undertaking to rescue agriculture from its destitution within four years, his purpose was to ensure agricultural self-sufficiency as one aspect of blockade-proof rearmament. After all—to use National Socialist terminology—'the German people's freedom to rearm (*Wehrfreiheit*)' could be 'secured in the long run only . . . if it also enjoyed nutritional freedom'. From this conviction there followed 'first of all a systematic ordering of production' and the creation of the prerequisites of 'overseeing and controlling production down to the last farmstead'.[33] To achieve this goal the farming community was the first occupational group to be subjected, after 1933, to what was called *Gleichschaltung* (forcible co-ordination).

Agriculture's alignment with the National Socialist regime's rearmament requirements was implemented, in its first phase, by a unification of associations, described by the National Socialists as a 'corporate restructuring'. Thanks to the

---

[27] Völtzer, 'Sozialismus', 15.
[28] Goebel, 'Durchführung', 156.
[29] Lenel, *Ursachen*, 348.
[30] Cf. Esenwein-Rothe, *Wirtschaftsverbände*, 5.
[31] Herferth, 'Faschistischer Reichsnährstand', 1054.
[32] *Schulthess 1933*, 36.
[33] Brummenbaum, a department head in the Reichsnährstand, in 1935 at a meeting of 'Peasant Leaders in Goslar, quoted from Hoeft, 'Agrarpolitik des deutschen Faschismus', 1226.

propagandist and subversive activity pursued by the party among rural political associations prior to 1933 this led to rapid success. The reorganization started in the spring of 1933.[34] After the March elections the Reichslandbund—by then infiltrated by the NSDAP— promoted on its own initiative the *Gleichschaltung* of agrarian interest-organizations with Hitler's state and appealed for 'unification of agriculture'. The representatives of large estates did not regard the reshaping of agricultural conditions as assured on the lines they themselves favoured unless 'first of all, and throughout the whole Reich territory, a *Gleichschaltung* of the rural political apparatus and the NSDAP peasantry bodies with the Reichslandbund' was effected.[35] In consequence a body known as the Reichsführergemeinschaft took over the external representation of the entire German peasantry on 4 April. This was headed by R. Walther Darré. The following day the Deutscher Landwirtschaftsrat (German Agricultural Council), as the umbrella organization of the chambers of agriculture, assured 'the government of national regeneration of its unreserved and unanimous obedience and support'[36] and, quite consistently, elected Darré its president in May 1933; the Raiffeisen Association, followed by the board of the Landhandelsbund (Rural Trade Association) had placed themselves under the Council the previous month.[37] On 13 September 1933 the government enacted a law through Darré, who was by then minister for food and agriculture, whereby the various branches of the agricultural economy (including forestry, horticulture, fishery, and hunting, as well as agricultural co-operatives, rural trade, and the processing and improvement of agricultural produce) were to be reorganized through mandatory membership of the central organization, the Reichsnährstand (Reich Foodstuffs Corporation).[38]

At the beginning of 1934 the agricultural co-operatives were incorporated in the Reichsnährstand. This new body, however, did not operate merely as a vocational representative body; in the Reichsnährstand the regime had created for itself an instrument which placed 'individuals along with their farmsteads, i.e. the entire production base, firmly in the hands of a leader, just like a well-organized and disciplined army'.[39] Subordinated to the administrative and expert supervision of the minister for food and agriculture, and subject to auditing by the audit office, the Reichsnährstand functioned as a state-institutionalized compulsory organization for the restructuring of the entire food-supply economy in line with whatever regulatory or planning interventions were deemed necessary. Its primary task was the implementation of the 'market order' set up between 1934 and 1935 as a preliminary stage for the future 'war food-supplies order', since 'between the peacetime economy based on the market order and the war economy [there was] no

---

[34] For the regulations and laws enacted by the National Socialist regime cf. *Chronik der Agrarpolitik*.

[35] 'Hannoverscher Landbund', 24 Apr. 1933, quoted from Hoeft, *Agrarpolitik des deutschen Imperialismus*, 33.

[36] Quoted from Fischer, *Wirtschaftspolitik*, 78.   [37] Cf. Herferth, *Reichsnährstand*, 80 ff.

[38] Cf. Farquharson, *Plough*, 43 ff.; on the overall subject of National Socialist agricultural policy cf. the relevant chapter in Henning, *Landwirtschaft*, 211–28. The author underrates the function of agricultural policy in preparing for war.

[39] Reischle, *Kann man Deutschland aushungern?*, 85.

difference in kind but only in degree'.[40] Market associations henceforward not only fixed the prices of agricultural produce but also regulated their transportation and sales, and ultimately determined the delivery quotas which had been introduced by the state. Thus, the market order, 'thanks to the preliminary work done on it while still at peace, and for peacetime, provided the basis on which the entire foodstuffs distribution under the war foodstuffs economy was built up'.[41] A consistently observed and practised market order seemed indispensable to the National Socialist government for the solution of all agricultural tasks in preparation for war, in particular the safeguarding of the country's food basis. It was seen as a guarantee that shortages and possible difficulties could be overcome or eliminated by systematic stockpiling, that unreliable production units could be controlled, and that trends towards rising prices could, if necessary, be counteracted.[42] Linked to the system of guaranteed sales and fixed prices was the intention of keeping consumer prices low in the long run and indirectly 'stabilizing industrial wages as the most important cost factors in rearmament'.[43]

However, these governmental endeavours were opposed by the programmatic intention of the party to improve farmers' incomes, largely in order to check the drift from the land. And in fact a rise in prices of agricultural produce was recorded until the end of 1934, designed to make up for the loss of income caused by the world-wide depression. Producer prices in agriculture rose between February 1933 and November 1934 by roughly 30 per cent compared with those of 1932. However, to keep armament expenditure within calculable limits the peasants were eventually subjected, for the sake of stable industrial wages, to a policy of declining prices, and thus to reduced income. A successful outcome of the proclaimed agricultural 'production battle', which of course was largely identical with rearmament efforts, absolutely ruled out any substantial raising of consumer prices of agricultural produce. Thus, the agricultural market order was ultimately determined by 'allowance for the purchasing power of urban consumers, in particular industrial labour'.[44] In the end the prices of agricultural produce were lagging behind those of the years 1928–9 (Table II.II.I).[45]

Agricultural politicians were pleased to note that the fixed prices of agricultural produce during the rearmament phase, 'in order to stabilize the relation between wages and the prices of the most essential foodstuffs', remained 'at a level favourable to the large capital for armament'.[46]

Finally the Reich farm inheritance law (Reichserbhofgesetz) of 29 September 1933[47] should also, though not exclusively, be viewed in the light of the war economy. It restricted the right of free disposal by owners of farms ranging from 7.5

[40] Merkel and Wöhrmann, *Bauernrecht*, 37. Cf. Herferth, *Reichsnährstand.*
[41] Reischle, *Agrarpolitik*, 74.
[42] Merkel, *Agrarpolitik*, 83.
[43] Kruedener, 'Zielkonflikt', 348.
[44] Meinhold, *Grundlagen*, 60.
[45] *Gefüge und Ordnung*, 124.
[46] Hoernle, posthumous papers, quoted from Melzer, *Studien*, 28.
[47] *RGBl.* (1933), i. 685.

TABLE II.II.I. *Price-trends in agricultural produce 1928/9–1938/9*[a]

	1928/9 (RM/100 kg)	1938/9 (RM/100 kg)	Change (%)
Pigs	142.00	100.00	−30
Cattle	75.00	68.00	−9
Rye	21.10	18.40	−13
Wheat	21.60	20.00	−7
Potatoes	5.80	5.00	−14
Vegetables	16.60	11.60	−30
Butter	352.00	254.00	−28
Eggs (per 100)	10.20	8.20	−20

[a] On price-trends in agriculture up to 1936 cf. Barkai, *Wirtschaftssystem*, 147–8.

Source: Reischle, *Agrarpolitik*, 57.

to 125 hectares (though in practice there was no upper limit); these were henceforward entailed. In this way farmers and their heirs were tied to their land, and so an almost constant supply of manpower was created; children, women, and relatives of pensionable age were deliberately included as the pull of the armaments industry rapidly triggered off a rural exodus. The law further resulted in a process of concentration at the expense of small peasants. By 1939 the size of agricultural and forestry enterprises rose from 13.6 to 18.5 hectares, over 35 per cent, in line with the government's intentions of mechanization and consolidation of farmland. Without the farm inheritance law (and this conviction was voiced in the Reichsnährstand) it would have been 'quite impossible to perform the economic tasks with which the German rural population . . . was faced.'[48]

It is worth noting that this enforced organization of agriculture initially took place solely through representatives of the party—virtually independently of the ministry in question (and indeed by way of undermining its competence and responsibility), at least while Hugenberg was in charge of both the ministry of economic affairs and the ministry of agriculture. When on 27 June 1933 Darré took over ministerial responsibility for agriculture and food supplies, agricultural policy came under the control of a man in whose hands all the important threads of agricultural production and distribution came together. Until 1945 the agricultural and foodstuffs sector remained firmly under the responsibility and control of the party, also in terms of personnel. Only in this field was a genuine symbiosis of party and state achieved, the more so as all important party and organizational posts were bracketed with state-administration ones. Attempts to transfer this model to trade and industry failed.

[48] Reischle, *Agrarpolitik*, 24.

3. THE ALIGNMENT OF TRADE AND INDUSTRY WITH THE DEMANDS OF REARMAMENT

Even before the establishment of the coalition government under Hitler at the end of January 1933 the NSDAP had succeeded in winning over considerable sections of the middle class from trade and industry.[49] The world-wide depression since 1929 had hit trade, crafts, and small entrepreneurs especially hard and thus made them susceptible to the slogans of the NSDAP, from which they expected an improvement in the economic situation. 'Ideological penetration, political direction, economic "actions" and organized infiltration' by the party had 'exerted a profound effect on the middle class'.[50] The commercial middle class attributed its economic hardships not only to the world-wide depression but also to its own political isolation. Standing as it did between the influential industrial and agrarian associations on the one hand and well-organized labour on the other, it found itself between the fronts politically as well as economically. It was because of this situation that even before the depression trade and crafts in the Weimar Republic had not only called for financial improvements but, as the Reichsverband des Deutschen Handwerks (Reich Association of German Craftsmen) declared to the Reich government towards the end of 1931, 'demanded a fundamental change in German economic policy because the one-sided favouring of capitalist and trade-union forces, in conjunction with the public direction of the economy,' had 'increasingly narrowed down the living-space of the trading middle class'.[51] Trade and the crafts found themselves at the mercy of the interests of collectivist forces and longing for a secure place in the structure of society, a place of equality alongside other economic groups. This almost nostalgic desire for a system of guilds on the medieval pattern was in line with the NSDAP's programmatic declaration in favour of some corporate state, of whatever form, that would open up for the crafts and trade the prospect of equal treatment within the hierarchy of the economic and political élites. As the party programme postulated 'the creation of a healthy middle class and its preservation'[52] the NSDAP succeeded in penetrating the organizations of the trading middle class in much the same way as it did the agricultural organizations, and this provided a good starting position for their subsequent alignment with the goals of National Socialism. Alongside the amalgamation within the Reichsnährstand of agricultural forces active in production, processing, and trade, the organization of trades and crafts likewise seemed in 1933 to be progressing successfully according to corporate principles. Initially the National Socialists gained control of artisans' and trade associations through the infiltration of members of the NS-Kampfbund für den gewerblichen Mittelstand (National Socialist Combat Union for the Trading Middle Class) into appropriate controlling bodies and posts. However, the activities of the protagonists of the corporate idea

---

[49] Cf. Winkler, *Mittelstand*.   [50] Schweitzer, *Big Business in the Third Reich*, 88.
[51] Memorandum of the Reich Association of German Crafts, 25 Nov. 1933, quoted from Chesi, *Struktur der Handwerksorganisation*, 25.
[52] Feder, *Programm*, 20.

caused some anxiety in the course of 1933, above all in Hitler's mind, lest a vocational and corporate organization 'in National Socialist guise' should grow to uncontrollable political and economic potency. Even so, the establishment of 'corporations' and vocational chambers was proclaimed on 3 May 1933 and a Reich 'corporation' was successfully set up for the crafts (1 October 1933), the head of the Kampfbund für den gewerblichen Mittelstand being appointed its president.

The Prussian minister president (Göring) and the Reich minister of economic affairs (Hugenberg), however, felt obliged in the early summer of 1933 to oppose the endeavours for a corporate structure within the trading middle class. Trade and crafts were brought together in a corporate manner in so-called Reich groups after the Kampfbund für den gewerblichen Mittelstand had been dissolved or absorbed into other organizations. This restructuring took place in parallel with the reorganization of industrial associations.[53]

The trading middle class was strictly organized by the state, as can be shown by the example of craftsmen, the most important middle-class form of trade within the war economy. In order to place rearmament orders in a planned way and to ensure that their execution could be monitored, a Reich central office for craft deliveries was set up between the Reichshandwerksmeister (Reichs Crafts Master) as the representative of the Reich Corporation of German Crafts on the one hand and the industrial enterprise on the other; this Reich Central Office was to be in charge of placing orders through specialized regional delivery co-operatives. This structure greatly facilitated economic mobilization for the purpose of rearmament. The fact that the crafts had 'set up special centres which accepted major orders and saw to their share-out and execution' was to be 'welcomed from the point of view of national defence'.[54] In order to render this *dirigiste* system more effective, and simultaneously to release skilled workers for industry, the policy on crafts was aimed at a radical reduction in the number of small enterprises, e.g. through the third Order on crafts (18 January 1935), in compliance with which the number of craft enterprises diminished by 153,390 between 1936 and 1938.[55] An implementation regulation for the Four-year Plan (first quarter of 1939) provided an instrument for combing out 'unviable' or overmanned craft enterprises with a view to transferring their proprietors or the craftsmen employed in them as skilled workers, to be retrained if necessary, 'to economically more necessary and useful tasks' in the field of rearmament.[56] The Reich Corporation of German Crafts established a dense network of supply co-operatives throughout the Reich, so that the crafts, in their own estimation of their importance, represented 'a decentralized, scarcely vulnerable part of the war economy'.[57] Wehrmacht orders were in fact a favourite area of activity of the craft organizations: for instance, they made themselves responsible for the execution of half the fortifications on the western frontier.

---

[53] Cf. II.ii.2 above.
[54] Vorwerck, 'Berufsständische Ordnung', 326.
[55] 'Festigung der Handwerkswirtschaft', 129.
[56] Goetze, 'Festigung', 123.
[57] *Handwerk, Helfer der Wehrmacht*, 1.

Clothing, equipment, and general-service carts of the armed forces came very largely from craft enterprises. In addition, major construction jobs were performed by craftsmen in connection with the building of barracks and housing for civilian employees of the armed forces.

Yet there is no denying the fact that, contrary to the NSDAP's proclaimed policy concerning the middle class, the crafts were being largely sacrificed to the interests of rearmament—i.e. the interests of big industry favoured by the state for its modern serial and mass production—and that they were able to justify their existence only where they directly served war preparations or warfare itself, or provided indispensable services to the population.

The reorganization and concentration of industrial associations progressed in separate phases, the first reorientation taking place under the motto of 'corporate reorganization', promoted both by the NSDAP's corporate state ideologists and by industrial interests, though from different motivations. The end result was the corporate restructuring of the whole of trade and industry. While the party ideologists were trying to ensure NSDAP influence on economic developments, largely through membership of the industrial associations, industry chose the road of *Selbstgleichschaltung* (voluntarily toeing the party line), with the ulterior motive of preserving its institutional independence. Very shortly after the Reichstag elections of March 1933, won (albeit manipulated) by the National Socialists with a clear majority, Krupp, as president of the Reich Association of German Industry, felt constrained to assure Hitler that 'German industry' regarded itself 'as an important and indispensable factor in the building up of the nation' and was therefore ready 'to co-operate in this task'.[58] Proposals were presently put forward for a simplification of the pattern of associations, with a simultaneous application of the leadership principle, but these were unable to prevent the appointment of the NSDAP economic expert Wagener and another party functionary to the posts of Reich commissioners for the Reich Association of German Industry and for the remaining trade and industry associations. However, before they could begin any activity the Federation of German Employers' Associations voluntarily amalgamated with the Reich Association of German Industry to become the Reich Corporation of German Industry. The aim of this merger, performed in line with the corporate idea proclaimed by the NSDAP ever since its establishment, was to escape, up to a point, from the control and influence of state and party, while simultaneously demonstrating readiness to seek a 'synthesis between political leadership and economic necessities'.[59] With this step industry was following in the tracks of trades and crafts. Under the slogan 'rationalization of the system of associations' Krupp von Bohlen und Halbach, as president of the new overall industrial federation, now introduced the 'leader principle'—i.e. the number of decision-makers in the member associations was reduced to one. The Reich

---

[58] Letter from Krupp to Hitler, 24 Mar. 1933, quoted from Czichon, *Wer verhalf Hitler zur Macht?*, 83–4.

[59] Letters from Krupp to Hitler, 4 and 25 Apr. 1933, quoted from Bracher, Sauer, and Schulz, *Machtergreifung*, 632.

Corporation moreover refused recognition of lesser interest-groups as such and thereby ensured a streamlining of the pattern of industrial associations.

As an insurance against party intervention a National Socialist ideologist from the ranks of industry was demonstratively elected secretary; he supported a corporate structure, though 'not at the expense of big business or entrepreneurial independence'. As he saw it, it would be sufficient 'to transform the top-level associations, based on contracts under private law, into state or semi-state organizations in order to implement the party's intentions concerning reorganization on corporate lines'.[60] The big industrialist Fritz Thyssen, an early follower of the NSDAP, set up an institute for corporate affairs in Düsseldorf in the spring of 1933—actually with Hitler's consent—which opposed the National Socialist Combat League for the Middle Class and endeavoured, within the framework of a corporate structure, to protect and consolidate industrial interests against state and party demands and requests. However, the institution had a short life—only until 1935.

Leading NSDAP functionaries and Hitler himself regarded these corporate self-administering organizations as unsuited to the enforcement of economic controls aiming at rearmament,[61] and for that reason they were no longer promoted in the industrial sphere after the summer of 1933. The non-party minister of economic affairs, Schmitt, who succeeded the German Nationalist Hugenberg, worked towards a so-called 'organic structure' of trade and industry (as opposed to a corporate one), in order to safeguard 'in a hitherto unique manner the possibility of the implementation of the wishes of the Reich government in the economy'—as against those of the NSDAP.[62] His so-called organic structural model was based on a specialized and regional pattern of organization, designed to guarantee an optimal opportunity for state intervention throughout trade and industry, including the crafts, to ensure that war-economic intentions were carried out. The new corporation, which united six branches of industry in compulsory membership, took its cue from the demand that in future 'the departmental minister responsible should inform the six leaders of the individual Reich groups of trade and industry of his intentions, to ensure that these intentions penetrate by the fastest and simplest administrative route down to the last link of the economy'.[63]

For his plans Schmitt could count on support from Hitler and the armed forces. The latter expected a regulation, shortly to be introduced in agreement with them, concerning 'the safeguarding and organization of the financial, human, and material resources necessary for the defence of the Reich within the scope of the entire national economy', and as a first step demanded immediate measures for the maintenance and expansion of the existing armament industry.[64] There was a

---

[60] Memorandum by Reupke, member of the NSDAP and of the Reich Association of German Industry, first quarter of 1933, quoted from Esenwein-Rothe, *Wirtschaftsverbände*, 192.

[61] Cf. Darré's speech to the economic and social policy committee of the Reich Association of German Industry, 11 Jan. 1934, referring to future price and market regulations. Text in Darré, *Blut und Boden*, 365–73.

[62] Guth, 'Wirtschaft', 879 (my italics). [63] Ibid.

[64] General directive of the minister of economic affairs, 1 July 1933, BA–MA Wi I F 5/406.

danger that the increasingly close coalition between the party's corporatist ideologists and trade and industry might, for one thing, get the better of the head of government and that, for another, the implementation of a corporate model, with its inevitable experimenting, might result in sight being lost of the ultimate goal—the gearing of the economic process to rearmament—or in excessively slow progress towards it. On 6 July 1933 Hitler therefore made it clear beyond any doubt that in the organization of the economy practical experience must not be neglected in favour of 'a certain idea', by which was meant the corporate ideology.[65] A day later, addressing the Reichstatthalter (Reich governors), he declared that the National Socialist revolution would have to be steered on to an evolutionary track. Unemployment could not be cured by economic commissioners, new organizations, or theories. What was needed instead was strict economic-political control, and that must lie solely in the hands of the minister of economic affairs. Henceforth the party was identical with the state and should not, in matters concerning the economy, arrogate to itself any competences of the Reich government.[66] In the early summer of 1933 Hitler and Schmitt came to an agreement under which the corporate system was rejected in favour of the 'organic structure' of trade and industry.[67] The minister of economic affairs, as director-general of the Allianz insurance company, and himself a representative of big business, was hoping for the approval of big business for this agreement, which entailed the restructuring and change in function of industrial associations. After all, he was in a position to offer a *quid pro quo* which he had negotiated in exchange for the surrender of the right to corporate self-management. Agreement had been reached on a separation of different branches of the economy into two political spheres of interest: the NSDAP would be assigned agriculture as its domain, while the areas of competence of the ministries of finance and of economic affairs were to be open to influence by big business. The risk of a possible loss of control by the state as a result of that division of labour was considered slight by Hitler compared with the threat to his freedom of economic-political manœuvre represented by the corporate system. After all, there was basic consensus between him and the industrial leaders on the priority to be enjoyed in the economy by rearmament and war preparations, looking towards the creation of a German-dominated closed European trade and economic sphere, and hence the reorientation and restoration of an industry which had very largely lost its foreign markets in the world-wide recession. The law of 27 February 1934 concerning preparations for the organic development of the German economy eventually cleared the road for the ministry of economic affairs directly to transmit state and party intentions to the industrial associations. The ministry was empowered

1. to recognize industrial associations as the sole representatives of their branch of the economy;
2. to set up, dissolve, or amalgamate economic associations;

[65] Quoted from Bracher, Sauer, and Schulz, *Machtergreifung*, 681.
[66] *Frankfurter Zeitung* (1 Sept. 1933). Cf. Barkai, *Wirtschaftssystem*, 90 f.
[67] Cf. Schweitzer, 'Organisierter Kapitalismus', 36.

3. to amend or supplement the statutes and articles of incorporation of economic associations, and especially to introduce the leadership principle;
4. to appoint or recall the leaders of economic associations;
5. to attach entrepreneurs and enterprises to economic associations.[68]

These measures, which dragged on for over a year, did not seem to the Wehrmacht to be effective enough. On 20 May 1934 it vigorously remonstrated with Hitler because compulsory organization of the economy had still not been adopted. Referring to the views of the commanders-in-chief of the three services, Blomberg proposed to the chancellor that, for all economic measures to be planned and executed with regard to rearmament, he should appoint an officer who, holding the rank of state secretary, would answer directly to the minister of economic affairs. Such an arrangement, the Wehrmacht believed, would ensure the co-ordination of the rearmamant programmes for army, navy, and air force, as well as their preferential implementation within the overall economic system. That officer, moreover, should centrally direct the tasks of all ministries in so far as they were related to rearmament and war preparations.[69] This demand eventually crystallized in a proposal of 20 June 1934 addressed by the Heereswaffenamt (Army ordnance office) to the chancellor that he himself should assume control of the economy and appoint an economic delegate with dictatorial powers who, supported by a working party composed of representatives of industry, trade, the banks, agriculture, the Wehrmacht, and the party, would have the task of pursuing a policy of systematic economic war preparations. The ordnance office further proposed that all departments concerned with economic matters, including the German Labour Front,[70] should be subordinated to the new economic dictator. As a first official action the defence minister, who fully identified himself with the ordnance office memorandum, expected an instruction to all party and other authorities to refrain from taking any economic measures without prior consultation with and approval from the economic delegate.[71] Even though these ideas, tending as they did to curtail the rights of the traditional administration, were rejected, the corporate-system ideologists in the NSDAP clearly suffered a first setback. Blomberg's intervention actually resulted in the abolition of the above-mentioned Reich commissioner posts and in the political isolation of their incumbents. Wagener was even forced out of his post of head of the NSDAP's economic department, which was subsequently given to Wilhelm Keppler, a man from the ranks of medium-sized business, who was simultaneously promoted to be Hitler's economic delegate in the Reich chancellery, though without being equipped with the full powers the Wehrmacht leaders would have liked to see.

Moreover, Schmitt, minister of economic affairs, had to vacate his post as a result of Blomberg's attack. Ready in the wings to succeed him was Hjalmar Schacht, one-

---

[68] *RGBl.* (1934), i. 185.
[69] Schweitzer, 'Organisierter Kapitalismus', 42.　　　　　　　　　　　　　　　[70] Cf. II.ii.4 below.
[71] Letter from Blomberg to Hitler, 20 June 1934, BA-MA Wi I F 5/406; memorandum of the army ordnance office to Blomberg, 20 Apr. 1934 (text in Barthel, 'Rüstungswirtschaftliche Forderungen', 90–2).

time president of the Reichsbank under the Weimar Republic and reappointed to that office by Hitler's government. He attached supreme importance to 'the concentration of all, but absolutely all, economic and financial forces' for the much-invoked 'militarization of our nation',[72] thereby agreeing with the demands made by Hitler and the Wehrmacht. For a while the corporate-system ideologists in the party, above all Gottfried Feder, acting as state secretary in the ministry of economic affairs, and Keppler, the NSDAP's economic expert and initially a champion of corporate interests in industry, succeeded in blocking Schacht's appointment. It required Hitler's instruction to the party for restraint in matters of economic policy, as well as vigorous interventions with Keppler on the part of the Wehrmacht office, for Schacht to be installed as minister of economic affairs *pro tempore* (he served from 3 August 1934 until 26 November 1937). Schacht liquidated all initial signs of an emerging corporate system and relieved its protagonists of their posts. Feder lost his position in the ministry of economic affairs and vanished from public politics, while Keppler was debarred from entering Schacht's ministry. Kessler, a representative of the electrical engineering industry, appointed by Schmitt under the leadership principle as 'director of the economy', was relieved of his post and the institution abolished. The president of the Chemical Association, Pietzsch, a convinced National Socialist and personal economic adviser to the Führer's deputy Hess, had to resign his post. The NSDAP's direct influence on trade and industry was thus largely eliminated and the corporate idea was politically dead. By the end of November 1934 Schacht was in a position to apply the full powers legislatively enacted by his predecessor to enforce the compulsory organization of trade and industry in Reich groups and specialized groups with their subdivisions (Fig. II.II.I). Each Reich group and the main groups in industry were henceforth headed by a director, to be appointed or dismissed by the Reich minister of economic affairs, and to be responsible for representing the interests of his group within the economy and beyond it, in accordance with the national interest. Simultaneously the Reichswirtschaftskammer (Reich chamber of the economy) was set up as a link between the state and business enterprise; its president was appointed by the minister of economic affairs.[73]

The new structure of trade and industry, therefore, was not an end in itself but served the direction and operative employment of the economy for the purpose of rearmament; it was to be 'a sharp sword in the hand of the National Socialist state apparatus' for fighting the 'battle' of war preparations.[74] Once introduced, the principle of organization remained virtually unchanged until 1945, even though over the years the National Socialist regime set up additional agencies for putting its ideas concerning the armament economy into effect.

By 1938 the military were able to observe with satisfaction that 'the present organization of trade and industry' had 'been extensively involved in the

---

[72] Schacht in a speech at Königsberg, 1935, quoted from Müller, *Zentralbank*, 24.
[73] First regulation implementing the law on the preparation for the organic structure of the German economy, 27 Nov. 1934, *RGBl.* (1934), i. 1194–9.
[74] Starcke, *NSBO*, 159.

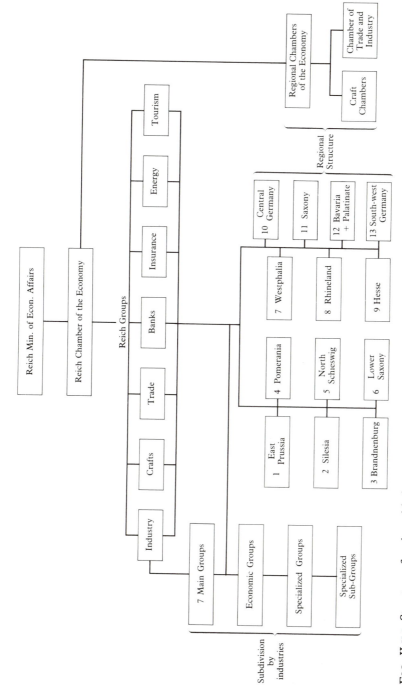

FIG. II.III.I. Structure of trade and industry

Source: Erbe, *Wirtschaftspolitik*, 53.

preparatory work of economic mobilization', that it was functioning 'smoothly on the whole',[75] and that it was being 'utilized for rearmament on a large scale'.[76] It could therefore be stated that 'soon after assuming power the National Socialist state . . . carried out a complete reorganization in all areas of the German economy and . . . this organization was from the outset oriented towards the defence capability which had been demanded by the Wehrmacht for many years'.[77] Hitler's understanding of the relationship between state and economy had prevailed: that it was not the task of political authority to resolve economic problems but to pose them. In his view the economy was merely one of the instruments used by the state in pursuance of its racial and power-political objectives.[78]

However, any expectations that Schacht would mould the newly created economic organizations into a tightly organized apparatus for the enforcement of his policy of economic war preparations were soon disappointed. Though a supporter of a certain measure of state direction of the economy, he was at the same time so much in the grip of his inherited liberal economic ideas that he applied his almost dictatorial powers in the economic sphere only in certain sectors. By reason of his professional and social background and education he felt a considerable degree of sympathy for what is called a free economy, whose representative he ultimately was. He even dared to attempt to rescind compulsory membership of trade and industry corporations, but failed in the face of opposition from the military. Ever since the autumn of 1931 Blomberg had demanded the introduction of compulsory organizations as a guarantee of the concerted implementation of armament-industry mobilization.[79] In return for eventually conceding this, Schacht obtained a relatively wide freedom of action for the trade corporations. Although the minister of economic affairs determined the direction and goals of production, although he increasingly intervened in the distribution process (raw materials, foreign currency, orders), and although a special department set up in his ministry laid down the principles of the policy to be pursued by the compulsory organizations, the latter were granted, and made good use of, the concession that they could elect their leaders from within their own ranks, though in agreement with the minister. In practice, therefore, they represented their concerns, both amongst each other and *vis-à-vis* the state, in much the same way as they had done before. Thus, it was Schacht who first introduced what was, after his term of office, laid down as a right: industry's so-called self-responsibility. This could work only because three prerequisites were assured. First, it was based on an identity of interests between industry, state, and Wehrmacht with regard to a common political and economic goal, the creation of a large-scale economic sphere and living-space. Second, the

<hr>

75 Comment by OKW W Stb (High Command of the Armed Forces War Economy Staff), 1 Mar. 1938, on Reichsleiter Ley's bill, BA-MA Wi I F 5/320.
76 Head of war economy staff to Reich ministries and chamber of the economy, 14 Jan. 1938, BA-MA Wi I F 5/203.
77 Lecture by Thomas to a class of assistant professors, 28 Feb. 1939, *IMT* xxxvi. 111-12.
78 Hitler, *Mein Kampf* (trans.), 136.
79 Letter from Blomberg to the minister of economic affairs, 20 Oct. 1933; cf. Schweitzer, 'Organisierter Kapitalismus', 45.

political leadership possessed no strategic objective that was formulated even in outline according to direction or time-scale, towards which remilitarization could have oriented itself. Wehrmacht and economy therefore initially pursued rearmament based on the premises of total war and engaged in a general economic preparation for war. At its focus, in the first instance, stood the expansion of the capacity of industrial production for equipping a mass army, for opening up German raw-material sources, and for developing and manufacturing ersatz or so-called 'German' materials to ensure blockade-proof supplies for the army and the population.

However, this so-called 'rearmament in breadth' had to be followed, according to Wehrmacht intentions derived from the concept of total war, by a second phase, that of rearmament in depth. In other words, calculations were based on a relatively prolonged period of rearmament, during which the economic process was to be directed, as comprehensively as possible, towards a kind of warfare involving all the forces of the nation, with the aim of eventually attaining an optimum of economic readiness for war, not confined to the sphere of armaments.

Finally, Schacht's leadership principle was tolerated because the National Socialist regime, in order to ensure the domestic stabilization of its rule and regardless of the primacy of rearmament, had to make allowance for the increase in economic expectations which followed the change of government in 1933, as well as for the rise in public purchasing power due to the rearmament boom. Such allowance could not be made within a tightly centralized rearmamant economy.

It is obvious that this principle of self-management conflicted with any nationalization of the armament industry. In any case, such a drastic measure was ruled out on financial grounds. Where would the state have found the money to finance the heavy investment needed for the entension of the requisite production capacities? A nationalized armament industry would have expanded much more slowly than a privately owned one. The state therefore confined itself to laying down the armament industry's targets as well as the share-out of commodities and raw materials within an economy that continued to be governed by competition; it was moreover assumed that the industry would, in the interests of its own profit, help correct any planning errors which might be made by the state. For these reasons the National Socialists wanted 'not nationalization of armament enterprises but the most considerable industry possible, one that could be rapidly switched to supplying modern armed forces with their military requirements'.[80] Schacht regarded the inherited economic pattern and system as the downright prerequisite of comprehensive rearmament and economic war preparations. 'Guns, aircraft, submarines or whatever else is necessary for national defence', he observed in a speech in December 1935, could 'not be visualized without resorting to the highest stage of development of the capitalist economy'.[81] Provided that the state's general economic-political guidance remained unchallenged and inviolate, i.e. provided the primacy of rearmament was accepted and implemented, the private capitalist

---

[80] Ruprecht, 'Rüstungsindustrie', 243.

[81] Schacht's observations quoted from Schweitzer, 'Organisierter Kapitalismus', 49.

system could remain functionally intact. As this prerequisite appeared to be granted, Schacht successfully resisted the agitation of fanatical National Socialists from the 'left-wing' camp and from the earlier Feder tendency, who wished to lead the economy out of the anonymity of capital and who were calling for the dissolution of joint-stock companies. The minister of economic affairs, however, regarded just that type of entrepreneur as particularly suited to the militarized economy because, mostly on a big-business scale, they were generally able to make investments for the expansion and rationalization of armament production through an increase of capital stock without drawing excessively on the state's financial capacity.

Big business altogether enjoyed particular favour and intensive support during the Third Reich because, in terms of the rearmament economy, it was highly efficient. For that reason the concentration of enterprises was pushed forward, regardless of the middle-class policy proclaimed before 1933. In particular, the National Socialist state devoted greater and more favourable attention to cartels, compared with the Weimar period. The cartel law enacted on 15 July 1933, during Schmitt's short tenure of the ministry of economic affairs, ensured on the one hand better control of the concentration of economic power and, on the other, the guidance of entire industrial branches, or sections of them, in the direction of production desired by the state. The law authorized the minister not only compulsorily to amalgamate enterprises into cartels but also to use investment prohibitions and directives for programming those cartels towards rearmament. Assignments of raw materials and orders were likewise more easily handled, without recourse to state sub-organizations, and thus largely avoiding an over-inflated economic bureaucracy, because the cartels themselves made these individual regulations.

Furthermore, the price structure remained easier for the state to oversee.[82] Generally speaking, until 1938 the National Socialist regime practised considerable restraint with regard to price-setting, even though it had inherited the necessary legislative and, to some extent, organizational instruments as assets from the bankrupt estate of the Weimar Republic. Prior to 1936 there was no state-controlled price-fixing. The commissioner for price surveillance, appointed as early as 1931, confined himself, as his title suggests, to price supervision, which seemed dispensable by the time he was relieved of his office in mid-1933. Brüning's deflationary policy was no longer compatible with the marked economic revival. So long as industry possessed spare capacity, the more so as a wage-freeze had been decreed during the phase of job-creation, there was no danger of inflationist tendencies emerging. When towards the end of 1934 a price commissioner was once more in office, this was for the purpose of monitoring a price rise (intended and accepted by the party and more especially by the Reichsnährstand) in the area of medium-sized and small enterprises, particularly for agricultural produce. The fact was that the temporary price rises in the agricultural sphere mentioned above, achieved through the NSDAP's efforts in favour of the farmers, were being

---

[82] On cartel policy cf. Swatek, *Unternehmenskonzentration.*

criticized by the public and causing political dissatisfaction; this mood was to be checked by the demonstrative appointment of a price commissioner. The workers, in particular, 'wished to share in the successes of agriculture and of those trades which had been favoured by job-creation'.[83] The National Socialist regime, however, had no wish for a prices–wages spiral because it was anxious to check the inflationary tendencies already inherent in the rearmament boom. For that reason 'the struggles against unemployment and for militarization (*Wehrhaftmachung*) of the German people' were 'priority tasks, demanding the maintenance of the present level of wages'.[84] Regardless of this view by the government the work of the price commissioner was doomed to failure anyway because the Reichsnährstand, in the person of Darré and with party support, was trying to prevent any influence being exerted on agricultural policy by a government-appointed commissioner, and because the price commissioner was in fact demanding a return to market-economy conditions as the best method of price regulation—which was in direct opposition to the economic philosophy of National Socialism. He therefore resigned his post in mid-1935, and it remained vacant until the Four-year Plan took effect.[85]

4. KEEPING THE WORK-FORCE IN ORDER: TRUSTEES OF LABOUR AND THE GERMAN LABOUR FRONT

Hitler's much-heralded intention of abolishing the trade unions and thereby implementing the leader principle within each enterprise in favour of the employers no doubt increased the latter's readiness to agree to stronger economic steering measures applied from without by the state. A mere three weeks after his assumption of the chancellorship the new head of government assured an audience of prominent industrialists that he desired nothing more ardently than an upturn in the economy, parallel to the stabilization of power-political conditions. This he regarded as closely linked with the 'question of the creation of the armed forces', but in his opinion everything was indissolubly tied to one precondition, the extinction of Marxism, of which he believed the labour organizations to be an emanation.[86]

The measures initiated immediately after the election of March 1933 were not merely designed to eliminate the rights and freedoms of labour as potentially disturbing factors in the economic rearmament process and its division of labour. For the employers they also represented a considerable enhancement of their powers of control; especially in view of the profits to be expected from re-armament and territorial expansion, they were willing to pay for this with a curtailment of entrepreneurial decision-making in other areas and with the loss of certain aspects of political influence. As a first step the law on works representatives and economic associations (4 April 1933) postponed all due intra-enterprise elections

---

[83] Remark by State Secretary Krohn of the ministry of labour, Aug. 1935, quoted from Barkai, *Wirtschaftssystem*, 146.

[84] Cf. Dickert, *Preisüberwachung*; Barkai, *Wirtschaftssystem*, 147–50.

[85] Cf. II.v below.

[86] Cf. Hitler's remarks at a meeting with industrialists, 20 Feb. 1933, *IMT* xxxv. 47.

by six months; it simultaneously authorized the provincial authorities to relieve of their office any workers' representatives opposed to the National Socialist system 'in a sense hostile to the state or to the economy' and to 'appoint in the place of the excluded . . members . . . new representatives from among eligible members of the work-force'.[87] This meant that the intra-enterprise influence of the trade unions was practically eliminated. The total liquidation of the labour organizations followed in May 1933. A skilful psychological move in preparation of their destruction was the proclamation of May Day as the Day of National Labour. Before the excitement of the mass celebrations on that occasion had worn off, the trade-union headquarters was occupied on 2 May 1933, trade-union assets were confiscated, and leading officials arrested; these were initially replaced by representatives of the Nationalsozialistische Betriebszellenorganisation (NSBO: National Socialist Factory Cells Organization), founded in 1929 as a rival to the unions. For two reasons, however, no National Socialist unified trade union was set up: for one thing, the NSBO had failed to make any appreciable inroad into the labour force and, for another, the government feared the influence of 'left-wing' National Socialists on any such unified trade union, resulting in inner-party conflicts which would be bound to lead to friction and damage to the rearmament economy.[88]

Some of the tasks previously performed by the trade unions were basically transferred to two institutions—the Deutsche Arbeitsfront (DAF: German Labour Front) and the Trustees of Labour—while others were dropped altogether. Until reorganization through a promised 'social constitution' one of the duties of the Trustees of Labour was to be the preservation of industrial peace[89] as the most important prerequisite for the smoothest possible execution of armament production. On behalf of the state these trustees acted as mediators between work-force and employers, especially in wage matters, by creating the prerequisites of collective agreements. The law on the regulation of national labour (20 January 1934) subsequently shifted the balance (already only nominal) between workers and employers in favour of the employers, who were designated 'leaders of their enterprises' while the workers were demoted to 'followers'.

The German Labour Front united both groups as the organization of 'German toilers with hand and brain'. Fudging the provisions of the law on the regulation of national labour, its activities were aimed at 'safeguarding industrial peace' by stimulating 'among enterprise leaders an understanding of the justified demands of their staff, and among staff an understanding of the situation and potential of their enterprise'.[90] In fact the German Labour Front served to control the working capacity and enhance the will to work of the German population, and ultimately served the purpose of, 'alongside material rearmament, also educating the people themselves towards an optimal readiness for battle and performance, as was considered indispensable by the supreme leadership in the realization of its political

[87] *Ursachen und Folgen*, ix. 626.
[88] On the position of the left wing in the NSDAP cf. Kühnl, *Nationalsozialistische Linke*. On National Socialist trade-union policy see Schumann, *Nationalsozialismus*.
[89] Law of 19 May 1933, in *Ursachen und Folgen*, ix. 642.
[90] Hitler's order on the character and objective of the German Labour Front, 24 Oct. 1934, ibid. 655.

intentions and with a view to the preparations for war'.[91] In particular it played a part in the training of skilled workers and apprentices and the up-grading of suitable unskilled workers to supplement their number, especially in case the former should be called up and thus withdrawn from industry. Finally, the Labour Front had to help ensure that, if necessary, any shortfall of male labour in the rearmament or war economy was made up by female labour. Altogether the German Labour Front aimed at 'intensifying pro-military (*wehrfreudig*) attitudes in the enterprises'.[92] This was achieved largely by way of its subordinate leisure organization, Kraft durch Freude (KdF: Strength through Joy), designed to keep the people, who were working even harder and longer hours in the rearmament economy, able and willing to work, by means of recuperation and diversion. As 'working hours are making high and strenuous demands on toiling individuals, they must be offered, during their leisure hours, the best of the best in food for the soul, mind, and body'.[93] It was also important to remind workers through propaganda of their duty to make sacrifices in the service of rearmament and subsequently the war economy—to motivate them 'for material, physical, and psychological commitment to the national community (*Volksganze*)' and to convince them of the need to 'renounce personal advantages, higher wages, political gains, and similar special wishes'.[94]

With a view to the aggressive actions laid down in its programme and included in its political calculations, the National Socialist regime regarded it as desirable to rehearse the public in good time, i.e. during the limited period of peace, in a certain attitude of material renunciation so that, should restrictions become necessary at the outbreak of or during a war, the regime would be protected against the possibility of unrest. 'The inner unity of the national order in peacetime was to ensure that it was instantly equal to the demands of war.'[95]

5. ADMINISTRATION OF THE WAR ECONOMY

An indispensable prerequisite of a properly functioning war economy, in the view of the military, was an organization which would be responsible for the co-ordinated determination of the requirements of the different services—such co-ordination to be based on strategic objectives—and which, moreover, would harmonize the armed forces' increasing demands with available production potentials. The Wehrmacht believed itself to be entitled and able to assume that task. There still existed, from Weimar days, an economic staff within the army, and there was a similar body within the navy; neither body, however, was able to organize or execute the necessary 'systematic economic mobilization',[96] especially as the air force had appeared on the scene as a third customer. Initially the three services each followed

---

[91] Reichhardt, *Arbeitsfront*, 188.
[92] Report by Thomas, Nov. 1936, BA-MA Wi I F 5/113.
[93] Speech by Ley, 27 Nov. 1933, in *Ursachen und Folgen*, ix. 645.
[94] List of main points for a report by Thomas, chief of the war economy staff, 20 Nov. 1936, BA-MA Wi I F 5/113.
[95] *Stellung der Sozialpolitik*, 40.
[96] Thomas, *Wehr- und Rüstungswirtschaft*, 62.

their own road towards equipping themselves with what material they needed; in the autumn of 1934, however, an 'office for defence economy and weapons affairs'—subsequently (October 1935) the 'war economy staff department'—was set up in the Reich war ministry, or (from February 1938) within the high command of the armed forces, as a centralized control-post of the war economy. However, the commanders-in-chief, fettered by their separate-service thinking, skilfully prevented the new institution from being given any power of command, so that it remained unable to 'concert Wehrmacht armament in a way to match requirements'.[97] These requirements, in the absence of a strategic concept, were in any case a matter for argument, and such argument was frequently and with varying success indulged in by the different services. As the economic and armaments staff only rarely succeeded in co-ordinating the armament plans or measures of the Wehrmacht branches, its influence on the rearmament economy was altogether limited. However, taking the three services together, and considering that no precise military objective was initially aimed at by the political leadership, they did in fact widely influence production and investments through the demands their extensive armament programmes were making on the economy.

In continuation of an inter-ministerial committee set up in 1929–30 the Hitler cabinet decided on 4 April 1933 to establish a Reich defence council; in view of the fact that rearmament was affecting a large area of political and social life, this council included as permanent members not only the representatives of the three services but also five government ministers.[98] Whereas this body existed only on paper, the Reich defence committee, as a subordinate organization, was to direct 'the mobilization of the state and people, corresponding to military mobilization';[99] this was to be done by establishing working schedules as a basis for the war preparations carried out by the Reich departments, for which the defence (war) minister was ultimately responsible.

It was the task of the ministry of economic affairs to create the overall economic preconditions for the realization of these armament-related plans. In general terms it had 'the task of making all economic preparations for the conduct of war', by legislative initiatives as well as by control measures and specific intervention in the economic process. It therefore had to take all measures which had to be 'put into effect, while still at peace, to strengthen our economic rearmament'.[100] The Reich Defence Law of 21 May 1935 strengthened the position of the ministry of economic affairs. The Reichsbank president, who was in charge of the ministry, was now given the title of Generalbevollmächtigter für die Kriegswirtschaft (GBW: Plenipotentiary for the War Economy). In this capacity he assumed control of 'economic preparations for the event of war', and all ministries concerned were now subject, 'while still at peace', to the instructions of the plenipotentiary in matters

---

[97] Ibid. 64.
[98] Meinck, 'Reichsverteidigungsrat'.
[99] Jodl to the Nuremberg Military Tribunal, *IMT* xv. 346.
[100] Schacht's progress report on economic mobilization, 30 Sept. 1934, quoted from Mendelssohn, *Nürnberger Dokumente*, 16.

related to 'the preparation of the war economy and the provision of finance for the conduct of war'. Any questions relating directly to mobilization were to be settled 'in closest mutual agreement' between the war minister, von Blomberg, and Schacht.[101] In the summer of the same year, however, the minister of economic affairs was stripped of important responsibilities, as 'armament enterprises' (*R-Betriebe*) producing to the requirements of the armed forces were transferred to the supervision of the Wehrmacht; the plenipotentiary for the war economy remained responsible for 'war-essential' and 'life-essential' enterprises (*k- und l-Betriebe*), i.e. those concerned respectively with the rest of the rearmament and war-production programme and with supplying the population. Because the two domains were closely interlinked (e.g. in respect of primary products and deliveries, and power requirements), this arrangement proved unsatisfactory, resulting in considerable conflicts of competence, and hence in damage to rearmament. The difficulties which emerged, however, were not all 'due to the division of the economy'[102] but also to differences of opinion on fundamental economic issues, especially as the Wehrmacht was not prepared to show anything like the same consideration of overall economic problems that the plenipotentiary for the war economy had to show in his capacity of Reichsbank president and minister of economic affairs. Within the economic sectors assigned to it the Wehrmacht was more efficient in assigning orders and practising meticulous production control than the plenipotentiary. This was because it set up war-economy inspectorates in all military districts, complete with subdivisions, whereas the plenipotentiary initially installed relatively ineffective branch offices (subsequently Land economic offices) of the ministry of economic affairs. Their powers of enforcement, however, were inadequate to achieve a degree of mobilization of 'k' and 'l' enterprises comparable with that of the armaments industry. The main complaints of the Wehrmacht about the plenipotentiary were that he did not give sufficient priority to ensuring the manpower, raw-material, and machinery requirements for armament enterprises, that he was too slow in preparing for the close-down of inessential enterprises in the event of mobilization, and that he was neglecting the transport system; the war-economy staff therefore felt permanently obliged to intervene in these matters. Quite apart from considerations of domestic policy, the lack of clear dividing-lines between the duties of the different authorities, both generally and particularly within the war-economy administration, was an obstacle to a thoroughgoing rearmament ecomony.

Among other reasons, total mobilization of economic forces for rearmament and war preparations generally was unrealizable because of the expectations of the public, e.g. in the consumer area. In view of these expectations it could only have been implemented at the risk of internal political conflict. Until 1936 this attitude represented an indisputable obstacle to the rearmament economy. Nevertheless, the skilful manner in which job-creation and -direction were linked to rearmament, and

[101] Resolution of the Reich government concerning the Reich defence council, 21 May 1935, *IMT* xxx. 63.
[102] Thomas, *Wehr- und Rüstungswirtschaft*, 75.

its success in providing a boost to the economy, earned the new rulers considerable credit among workers as well as employers, so that they possessed the necessary freedom of manœuvre to adopt a tougher economic line when this became necessary after 1936.

III. Job-creation and Armament Boom

1. JOB-CREATION AND INDIRECT REARMAMENT

ALTHOUGH agreement had been reached between the NSDAP and large sections of industry on the need for a change-over from world trade to large-area economics stimulated by state initiatives, at the beginning of Hitler's chancellorship there was still no consensus on the methods for a rapid cure of the economic crisis. Schacht had explicitly warned the leader of the National Socialist party against announcing a detailed economic rescue programme during the election campaign; he was anxious to avoid undesirable discussion and differences with individual branches of the economy. To please all economic groupings was obviously impossible. They were instead to be confirmed in the belief that a cabinet led by the National Socialists would watch their interests and implement their ideas. As soon as the new government took office, agriculture, industry, and trade submitted to the chancellor their plans for the recovery of the economy. The agrarians advised the new head of government to aim at foodstuff autarky within a self-enclosed economy; this was in line with National Socialist ideas concerning a successful way out of the depression and a foreign-trade reorientation in the future.[1] There was also agreement between the National Socialist leadership and the Deutscher Industrie- und Handelstag (German Industry and Trade Forum), which called for job-creation through an export promotion drive that would assure employment for 3 million people.[2] This demand was motivated not so much by the hope, still perceptible in 1932, of recapturing the world market and receiving state subsidies to ensure German competitiveness, as by the expectation that the government, in line with its proclaimed plans for safeguarding food supplies, would see to it that bilateral exchanges of goods with the European agricultural countries were intensified.

Hitler for his part was firmly resolved to place the stimulation of the economy consistently in the service of his power-political and territorial expansion plans. An examination of state-stimulated measures, planned or initiated after February 1933, from this point of view makes it clear that job-creation during the first two years of National Socialist rule represented the first step towards extensive rearmament as part of at least a long-term plan for a war of conquest aimed at the establishment of a German power-political and economic area of hegemony in Europe.[3]

Realizing that 'periods of rearmament . . . are invariably periods of general economic upturn',[4] the National Socialists skilfully combined job-creation with a

---

[1] Memorandum of the Deutscher Landwirtschaftsrat, 23 Feb. 1933, BA R 43 II/308a.

[2] Memorandum of the Deutscher Industrie- und Handelstag, 1 Feb. 1933, PA, Wirtschaft I, Allgemeine wirtschaftliche Lage, xv.

[3] Cf., in agreement with this thesis, Fischer, *Wirtschaftspolitik*, 61. Other studies, proceeding from economic theory, sometimes underrate this in their interpretations. Cf. Wolffsohn, 'Großunternehmer'; id., *Industrie*, 107 ff.

[4] Lampe, *Wehrwirtschaftslehre*, 3.

consolidation of the economy designed to stabilize their political system. On 1 February 1933 Hitler revealed to the public his main economic objectives, though confining himself to such generalities as promising the 'rescue of the German peasant to preserve the base of the nation's food supplies and hence its life' and the 'rescue of the German worker by a gigantic and comprehensive assault on unemployment'.[5] A few days later, speaking to his ministers, he added some details to his statement, to the effect that job-creation had to be seen as an indispensable part of rearmament and that—bearing in mind the existing political and economic circumstances and possibilities—all state orders placed within the framework of job-creation must, at least indirectly, serve the growth of military strength. 'Any publicly supported job-creation measure must be judged according to whether it is necessary' for the 'remilitarization of the German people. This consideration must always and everywhere come first.' If war was included in political calculations, then, in the view of the minister of transport, 'the entire German transport network must be in working order . . . in an emergency'. 'Development of German waterways', in particular, was 'in the military interest'.[6] Likewise, from the point of view of the military, weapons and equipment for the forces must not be neglected, which was why early consideration should be given 'above all to the material underpinning of armaments'.[7] In fact, 'rearmament played a not inconsiderable part . . . in the creation of employment.'[8]

Hitler elucidated the meaning and tasks of his government's job-creation measures in the most unmistakable manner when he told Gereke, the commissioner for employment in Schleicher's government, who for the time being remained in office: 'Liquidation of unemployment will be our National Socialist achievement! We shall remilitarize the German people. We shall build barracks and airfields. We shall build roads and autobahns on strategic principles. We shall develop the newest and most modern aircraft. All this will help alleviate unemployment.'[9]

On grounds of both foreign-policy and domestic considerations Hitler was anxious to conceal from the public, and also from certain economic groups still sceptical towards him and his government, the extent of his rearmament efforts. He therefore warned his cabinet colleagues 'to avoid furnishing precise data on any economic programme of the Reich government'.[10] Job-creation through deliberate state demand, based on indirect rearmament programmes, as hinted to Gereke,

---

[5] *Schulthess 1933*, 36.

[6] Excerpt from minutes of ministerial conference, 8 Feb. 1933, *DGFP*, c. i. 35–7, here 36. (The excerpt does not contain the passage referred to in n. 10 below.)

[7] Ibid.   [8] Schacht, *My First 76 Years*, 362.

[9] Gereke, *Landrat*, 157–8. Cf. also Boelcke, *Deutsche Wirtschaft*, 8–9, where it is pointed out that, among others, W. Lauterbach, an official in the Reich ministry of economic affairs, had called for state investments for job-creation and hence for a general cranking-up of the economy as early as 1931. 'The orders to industry triggered by such investments, together with the purchasing power of the newly engaged workers (which would be a completely new factor, because wages would be financed through additional credits), would change the supply-demand ratio at a stroke . . . Labour from the vast army of unemployed would, as it were, be sucked up again by enterprises at a more or less rapid pace and spread over the economy as a whole. The movement, once initiated, would propagate independently.'

[10] Minutes of ministerial conference, 8 Feb. 1933, IfZ Fa 203/1, quoted from Petzina, 'Hauptprobleme', 40.

naturally resulted in a growth of the national product and was therefore eminently suitable for domestic propaganda exploitation. For that reason Schleicher's Short-term Programme (*Sofortprogramm*) was promptly brought down from its shelf and put into effect, the more easily as the finance for its implementation had been allocated by the last presidential cabinet.[11] It was suitable for 'camouflage of the work for an enhancement of national defence', the euphemism for rearmament and preparation for war. Hitler realized that the initial phase of rearmament would be the most difficult and most dangerous in terms of foreign policy. The immediate task was to get through the period of impotence that would elapse between staking the claim to remilitarization and securing its acknowledgement or acceptance by the Western powers (as well as by Poland, which was thought capable of a preventive strike)—in short, to emerge from the zone of real risk during the first stage of rearmament. The Short-term Programme set the signals for German rearmament. Out of its financial provisions (altogether RM500m., of which RM400m. was allocated to Länder and municipalities and RM100m. to the Reich budget), in February 1933 the Wehrmacht demanded RM50m. out of the RM70m. assigned to the job-creation fund set up by the Schleicher cabinet, for the purpose of phase one (1 April 1933 to 31 March 1936) of a reconstruction programme, dated 7 November 1932, for a quantitative and qualitative expansion of the peace-time army. The Wehrmacht believed it could spend the entire sum budgeted for it in 1933. The commissioner for aviation, who had agreed with the defence minister a three-year minimum programme of RM127m. for the build-up of the Luftwaffe, claimed an instalment of RM42.3m. for 1933; the amounts remaining in the Short-term Programme were to serve the promotion of small-scale suburban housing developments and canal construction.

The chancellor was extremely dissatisfied by the exiguousness of the sums demanded for the objectives in question. Only reluctantly did he take note of Blomberg's view 'that the rate of rearmament could not be accelerated any further in the coming year'. More especially, he regarded the sum assigned for rearmament in the air by 1936 as totally inadequate, and left no doubt that he himself was thinking in terms of a quite different scale of rearmament even for the immediate future. In his view rearmament 'demanded thousands of millions'. In the end the decision to allocate the sums in the way proposed was adopted, though Hitler added the emphatic statement that 'in future, in any clash between demands for the Wehrmacht and demands for other purposes, the interest of the Wehrmacht must under all circumstances have precedence. Decisions concerning the allocation of finance under the Short-term Programme must be made on the same lines.' The functional change which Schleicher's programme had undergone is illustrated by Hitler's instruction that priority must be given to so-called national defence, and that any militarily non-essential works envisaged by Länder, municipalities, or

---

[11] The more recent literature assigns to Gregor Strasser a central role in connection with the National Socialist job-creation programme. Cf. Boelcke, *Deutsche Wirtschaft*, 29–38. This also contains an indication that Hugenberg, the minister of economic affairs in Hitler's coalition cabinet, was sceptical if not hostile to the so-called Reinhardt programme (ibid. 59).

other public bodies must be cut down as far as possible.[12] To avoid any misunderstanding, it should be borne in mind that the financial means made available from the Short-term Programme under the Schleicher–Gereke plan were not intended to cover the total rearmament costs in 1933, but merely to contribute to the financing of a framework programme of rearmament. The bulk of rearmament proceeded under the army's Second Armament Programme, drafted before the 'seizure of power'; this was designed by its authors to commence on 1 April 1933 and to be completed by 1938, regardless of the form of state or government. Financed by money from the Short-term Programme, it was so vigorously launched that it proved possible to shorten the original scheduling to two years, so that in the view of the army the programme should now be 'more or less completed in 1934 with the financial means of 1933'. Any remaining gaps would have to be made good in the budget year 1934, or at the latest 1935.[13]

If, in order to produce the expected political and economic and psychological effect, rearmament was to stimulate the economy rapidly but yet permanently, it had to be on a scale which transcended traditional financial possibilities and practices. A state-induced armament-led boom could not be launched or seen through by men who adhered to conventional budgetary ideas of the kind customary under the presidential cabinets, or who wanted to finance rearmament from a limited state budget. Hitler needed a person who was able to produce money in different ways, i.e. through the Reichsbank. He therefore believed a change at the top to be an indispensable prerequisite of his rearmament policy. When in mid-March the acting Reichsbank president Luther was replaced by Schacht, the chancellor had found a man who seemed prepared—and, as it turned out, remained willing for a number of years—to finance the extensive rearmament programme in an unconventional way, through an initially unlimited creation of money. Rearmament was to become financially supportable through productive creation of credits.

Nothing now stood in the way of job-creation through rearmament. The National Socialist policy for mastering the depression by a state-led stimulation of the economy differed from that of the presidential cabinets not so much in concept as in its consistent application to a different objective, that of rearmament with the goal of creating an ultimately self-sufficient large-scale economic area. With his very first step Hitler succeeded in meeting agriculture's demands for autarky and mechanization and, thereby, in vitally stimulating and increasing industrial production by replacing the collapsed world market with a secure domestic one that was expanding thanks to armament orders.

It was towards the end of May 1933 that the chancellor finally won over the leading figures of industry and banking; this was at a meeting specially called to discuss the job-creation measures which transformed Schleicher's Short-term Programme in the direction of rearmament and superseded it. As on previous

---

[12] Hitler to the cabinet committee for employment, 9 Feb. 1933, BA R 43 II/536. Cf. Deist, III.II.1 below.

[13] Cf. Geyer, 'Rüstungsprogramm', 134, 158.

occasions, Hitler again stressed the importance of private enterprise, especially of big business, and expounded his plans for the restimulation of production. He did not conceal that the state gave priority to those job-creation measures which strengthened Germany in its struggle for an 'equal' place alongside the other great powers—i.e. to rearmament. In this connection he mentioned autobahn construction, which, he pointed out, combined job-creation and an improvement of the nation's strategic position in an ideal manner.

Hitler succeeded in convincing his audience that job-creation and hence the revival of the economy would be carried out not at their expense, but instead through tax-relief measures at the state's expense, and—it should be noted—against the material interests of the work-force.[14]

Two days later he gave orders in cabinet, in line with an announcement back in February, that entrepreneurs were not to be burdened with higher taxes than in 1932, the peak year of the depression, and that the shortfall to the exchequer was to be offset by cuts in the social-welfare budget.[15] As soon as the leaders of the German economy became aware of this policy, and regarded it as guaranteed by the person of the renowned financial expert Schacht, they declared themselves ready to support it virtually *en bloc*—the more so as Fritz Reinhardt, the newly appointed state secretary in the ministry of finance, had just submitted fully worked-out proposals for practical job-creation for the revitalization of the economy and for its financing, essentially by fiscal means and depreciation, proposals which, according to contemporaries, came as 'a pleasant surprise even to many experts'.[16]

The National Socialist job-creation measures were contained in the two so-called Reinhardt programmes (1 June and 21 September 1933).[17] These, as they were primarily concerned with the building sector, also benefited private housing and agriculture, and likewise served towards the improvement and renovation of municipal and industrial institutions and transport installations. Nevertheless, they frequently had an indirect bearing on rearmament. At any rate, these programmes managed to provide work for over 50 per cent of the roughly 6 million unemployed in January 1933: the number of unemployed fell from 6,013,618 in January 1933 to 2,798,342 at 31 March 1934.[18] Following appropriate regulations concerning fiscal and depreciation relief, the 'law on voluntary donations for the promotion of national labour' came into force in July 1933; this was the only form of donation enjoying tax advantages, and between mid-July and the end of October it yielded RM35m. for the financing of job-creation. The time for donations ran until 31 March 1934.[19] In view of these clearly serious and brisk initiatives by the state, big business confidently left the economy in the hands of a National Socialist government and believed that it could now dispense with the Deutschnationale

---

[14] Record of conference between Hitler and industrialists, 29 May 1933, BA R 43 II/536. Cf. Wolffsohn, *Industrie*, 124–7, who fails to see this connection because he does not place the economic measures in the context of the overall political concept of job-creation.

[15] Record of ministerial conference, 31 May 1933, BA R 43 II/536. Cf. also Petzina, 'Hauptprobleme', 46–7.

[16] Grotkopp, *Krise*, 283.

[17] *RGBl.* (1933), i. 323–9; 651 ff.

[18] Cf. Berndt, *Vierjahresplan*, 86.

[19] Reinhardt, *Arbeitsschlacht*, 80.

Volkspartei (DNVP: German National People's Party) and its minister of economic affairs and of agriculture, Hugenberg, as an alternative political force.

Job-creation was increasingly taking place by way of indirect armament orders in the form of measures for the improvement of the Wehrmacht's infrastructure. The military very soon 'lumped together anything that . . . seemed apt to create employment, regardless of cost or the manner of financing'.[20]

The Wehrmacht first of all gave notice of a financial requirement of approximately RM425.5m. to be spread over a four-year period. This sum was used predominantly for road-building on army-owned land, construction of fortifications, clothing and food stores, and especially for rail- and bridge-building, and to a large extent also for the housing of civilian Wehrmacht employees, barracks, and refinery plant. The navy, in its job-creation drive, concentrated on the extension and construction of shipyards and ports (e.g. Heligoland), docks, lockgates, etc., as well as armament enterprises (e.g. Krupp) and, on a lesser scale, the establishment of 'shadow enterprises' (firms which would produce items of armament only in case of need), preliminary work for the housing of shipyard workers, and the equipment of shipyards and naval bases with tugs and vehicles. Further, it went ahead with the establishment of training centres, hospitals, and depots.[21] The Reich aviation ministry initially confined its demands mainly to the creation of anti-aircraft defence installations; by dint of day- and night-shifts Göring's ministry was set up at a high cost, and certain prerequisites of aerial rearmament were created at the same time. Göring 'immediately extended manufacture and increased air traffic beyond the extent of necessary traffic, so as to be able to train a large number of pilots'.[22]

The rearmament aspect is particularly significant in connection with the job-creation measure that had most impact on public consciousness, autobahn construction. However, contrary to widespread belief, this had no more than a minimal effect on the labour market and hence on economic recovery. In assuming, under the law of 27 June 1933,[23] the responsibility and financing of this project, first planned in the Weimar era, the state was motivated not only by transport and economy-boosting considerations but also by political and strategic aspects. Hitler for one was convinced that 'mobilization . . . [could] not be effected on our existing roads'[24] and he therefore made no secret of the fact that with the construction of the *Reichsautobahnen* he was 'primarily . . . [pursuing] military objectives'.[25] The

---

[20] Conference at the Wehramt, 19 May 1933, quoted from Stelzner, *Arbeitsbeschaffung*, 240. The new biography by Pentzlin, *Hjalmar Schacht*, likewise fails to see the connection between indirect rearmament and job-creation. The economic upturn during the first half of the 1930s is mistakenly attributed solely to private and civilian investments (pp. 199 ff.); their considerable importance for rearmament is not realized.

[21] Lecture by Flottenintendant Thiele, 13 July 1944, *IMT* xxxv. 569–99. Cf. Stelzner, *Arbeitsbeschaffung*, 241.

[22] Göring to the Nuremberg Tribunal, *IMT* ix. 280. Cf Deist, III.II.I below.

[23] *RGBl.* (1933), ii. 509–10.

[24] Hitler at a conference with industrialists, 29 May 1933, BA R 43/II/536.

[25] Report of Dorpmüller, director-general of the Reich railways, to the board of management, 27–8 Nov. 1934, quoted from Watzdorf, 'Autobahnbau', 68.

insignificant economy-boosting effect of autobahn construction clearly emerges from the small number of workmen employed on it during the phase of active job-creation.

Even allowing for the fact that for each autobahn workman there was another in the supply industry, the job-creating and economy-boosting effect remained slight. Although originally accompanied by a great deal of propaganda and presented as a social and economy-stimulating measure—because it was 'undesirable for the *Reichsautobahn* to be publicly described as part of the rearmament programme'—by 1936 it was, at least partially, admitted to the public that 'the *Reichsautobahnen* represent the Führer's road-building programme, which, as he had repeatedly stated, is being implemented simultaneously with our rearmament tasks'.[26]

The military were involved in all stages of planning, even though their demands were not always met. There was also not infrequent Wehrmacht criticism of the extravagant *Reichsautobahn* construction: the military would have preferred to see an acceleration of direct rearmament instead (Table II.III.I).[27]

Autobahn construction, together with other road-building projects, provided the

TABLE II.III.I. *Employment of labour in* Reichsautobahn *construction 1933–1938*

	Month (end of)	Directly employed on construction or on the *Reichsautobahnen* staff
1933	December	4,000
1934	March	46,000
	June	38,600
	September	71,500
	December	84,600
1935	January	39,700
	February	51,800
	March	77,000
	April	96,700
	May	112,200
	June	117,100
	September	118,000
	December	72,300
1936	March	86,000
	April	106,300
	June	130,000
	September	112,000
	December	80,000

Source: Stelzner, *Arbeitsbeschaffung*, 95; cf. also Lärmer, *Autobahnbau*, 54.

[26] Document from Todt's office, 6 Oct. 1936, quoted from Lärmer, *Autobahnbau*, 57.
[27] On this set of issues cf. Ludwig, 'Strukurmerkmale', 50–3.

basis for an increase in motor-vehicle use in Germany; this was further promoted by the abolition of motor-vehicle duty on 10 April 1933. The accelerated manufacture of motor-vehicles of all kinds after 1933 was not merely intended to stimulate the economy generally or to improve transport conditions. Motorization of industry was designed 'some day to facilitate a necessary motorization of the army'.[28] Although the public would undoubtedly have wished to see a greater measure of individual choice in vehicles, this had to take second place to the demand of the military for a numerically high level of motor-vehicles in business and private ownership. 'The larger the number of vehicles employed in civilian motor transport,' the Wehrmacht argued, 'the more rapidly and comprehensively can motorized army formations be made available at the outbreak of war. Purposeful unified organization and an increase in the rate of motorization of the economy and of civilian vehicle use were therefore, long before the war, in line with our rearmament planning.'[29]

Increased motor-vehicle production was considered the more urgent by government, business, and military as Germany was lagging far behind other countries in motor-vehicle use and, despite all appropriate efforts after 1933, continued to do so for a number of years. With one in every seventy-five inhabitants owning a motor-vehicle in 1933, Germany occupied the eleventh place in Europe. As late as January 1938 France and Britain, both with one motor-vehicle per nineteen inhabitants, held joint first place, while Germany, with one vehicle per forty-four inhabitants, lay in seventh place, even though no other country had such a high growth-rate in motor-vehicle production (Table II.III.2).[30]

2. Job-creation and Direct Rearmament

Realizing the strict limitations on the manpower potential which could be absorbed by civilian and indirect rearmament projects under the Short-term and Reinhardt Programmes, the National Socialist government decided deliberately to link job-creation with direct rearmament. The genuinely economy-reviving stimuli, which had been lacking in the job-creation programmes of earlier governments, were now to be provided by direct armament orders. The tie-up between job-creation and rearmament was to ensure the smoothest possible transition from the market economy to a rapid rearmament boom. It is against this background that one should view the impatient urgings of the Wehrmacht for armament orders to be placed with domestic industry and for sufficient finance to be made available from the job-creation programme to pay for those orders. At the end of March 1933 Blomberg intervened with the commissioner for employment for speedier allocation of money, as 'preliminary work on the orders [was] completed'.[31] No sooner had the law on

[28] 'Die Industrie', 27.

[29] Schell, 'Krieg', 506. Henning, 'Kraftfahrzeugindustrie', attempts a differentiated assessment of the topic of motorization but, by making insufficient allowance for central issues of National Socialist policy, misjudges its significance in the rearmament economy.

[30] Wehner, 'Verkehrswesen', 41.

[31] Letter from Blomberg to the commissioner for employment, 31 March 1933, BA R 2/18665.

TABLE II.III.2(*a*). *Motor-vehicle production in the principal industrialized countries 1933–1936 (1932 = 100)*

	1933	1934	1935	1936
Germany	204	338	478	585
USA	140	201	287	323
Britain	126	147	171	198
France	112	118	105	114
Italy	144	149	155	144

Source: Wehner, 'Verkehrswesen', 42.

TABLE II.III.2(*b*). *Motor-vehicle production in Germany*

	Motor-cars	Motor-buses and -trucks	Delivery vans	Tractors
1928	108,029		41,104	
1932	43,430	8,234		1,593
1933	92,160	13,261		3,168
1934	147,330	27,325		4,968
1935	205,092	41,528		8,494
1936	244,289	57,312		12,864
1937	269,055	62,404		18,025
1938	274,849	63,470		27,915

Source: Wehner, 'Verkehrswesen', 41.

donations for the promotion of national work been passed (1 June 1933), with the necessary implementation regulations yet to be enacted (these did not happen until 24 July 1933), than the Wehrmacht leaders demanded a first instalment of RM13.5m. from the fund for armament purchases.[32]

The prerequisites of a tie-up between job-creation and direct rearmament existed even before 1933. This interdependence had the advantage that the unemployed, unlike those employed on autobahn construction, could be found jobs at their places of residence. Conditions for placing major indirect armament orders as early as 1933–4 proved favourable in the sense that industry had unused production capacity at its disposal; this was 'the reason why armaments were very soon given priority'[33] over civilian job-creation orders. Moreover, the running-in period for armament production was greatly reduced by the fact that from the Weimar era, alongside the armament enterprises approved by the victors of Versailles, there also existed illegal

[32] Minister of defence to minister of finance, 8 July 1933, BA R 2/18718.
[33] Schacht, *My First 76 Years*, 362.

ones which had free capacity available and possessed the necessary know-how in armament manufacture.[34] 'Only thanks to this secret activity of German enterprise, and also on the basis of experience gained meanwhile in the manufacture of peacetime products, was it possible after 1933 to switch directly to the new tasks of remilitarization and to master a variety of entirely new problems.'[35]

The Wehrmacht initially registered all enterprises which might be considered for armament orders, and by mid-1934 had reserved 2,800 firms with approximately 750,000 workers. These accounted for at least 15 per cent of German industrial production, with individual production quotas substantially higher:[36]

Engineering, apparatus, and vehicles	59%
Iron and steel	56%
Optical and precision engineering	46%
Rubber and asbestos	45%
Metal-smelting	36%
Leather	27%
Chemicals	25%

Subcontractors and suppliers were not included in the reservation procedure. Naturally, there could be no question yet of immediately taking up these firms' entire production capacity with armament orders; nevertheless, the economy was beginning to prepare itself for the expected armaments boom. Industry's reorientation to the armament requirements of the Third Reich has often been dated from 1935, a year chosen because of the low level of investment in the production-goods industry. However, this neglects the fact that, for one thing, there existed unused production capacity and, for another, the growth-rate between 1932 and the following year was already considerable (over 20 per cent), while in 1934 production more than doubled compared with the previous year (Table II.III.3).[37]

The rise of investment from the summer of 1933 to the summer of 1934 was revealed mainly in these four areas:[38]

	% increase
Domestic orders of machinery (value)	77
Net domestic consumption of iron	71
Building-industry production	67
Licencing of goods vehicles	81

[34] Cf. Hansen, *Reichswehr und Industrie.*

[35] Gustav Krupp in a speech at Berlin University, Jan. 1944, quoted from *Der Nürnberger Prozeß*, ii. 32–3.

[36] Report of the ministry of economic affairs on the tasks set it by the defence council, 30 Sept. 1934, *IMT* xxxvi. 184–5. The figures are percentages.

[37] Cf. Petzina *et al., Sozialgeschichtliches Arbeitsbuch*, iii. 65–6. Although the figures for pure investments differ from Table II.III.3 for certain data, they reflect the same trend. In this connection it is interesting to note that the housing boom so spectacularly proclaimed by National Socialist propaganda was conspicuously lagging behind rearmament efforts. Between 1933 and 1939 housing was considerably below the 1929 level on an annual comparison, and it was only in 1937 that it barely exceeded the figure for the great depression year of 1930 (ibid. 125).

[38] Figures from Stelzner, *Arbeitsbeschaffung*, 121.

TABLE II.III.3. *Investment in German industry 1928–1938* (1928 = 100)

	Production-goods industry		Consumer-goods industry		Industry overall	
	RMm.	%	RMm.	%	RMm.	%
1928	1,717	100.0	898	100.0	2,615	100.0
1932	245	14.3	194	21.6	439	16.8
1933	309	18.0	248	27.6	557	21.3
1934	700	40.8	360	40.0	1,060	40.5
1935	1,221	71.1	415	46.2	1,636	62.6
1936	1,637	95.3	522	58.1	2,159	82.6
1937	2,208	128.6	635	70.7	2,843	108.7
1938	2,952	171.9	739	82.3	3,691	141.1

Source: Albert, *Wiederaufrüstung*, 68.

Although the Wehrmacht did not start until the autumn of 1933 to specify its immediate armament requirements,[39] it had nevertheless done some preliminary planning. The army at any rate had defined its medium-term demands in its so-called first and second rearmament programme before 1933.[40] As part of the extension of the transport network the aviation industry, for example, stepped up its production to more than ten times that of the preceding year. Although these were still predominantly civil aircraft, they were eminently suitable for refurbishing for military purposes. Göring, moreover, gave instructions for 'bomber aircraft [to be] developed from commercial aeroplanes.[41] After the summer of 1933, however, detailed plans existed for the raising of a military air fleet, and the necessary economic and manufacturing measures for its construction were taken in the course of the same year (Table II.III.4).[42]

By the end of the first half of 1933 the Reich aviation ministry had placed several major orders with industry. Thus, in August 1933 Junkers received a large-scale order for approximately 1,000 Ju-52 machines and several hundred training aircraft, and the Dornier works one for 1,000 Do-11 and Do-13 machines;[43] these were clearly covert bombers, for whose appropriate armament German weapon manufacturers began to work in 1934,[44] even though the aircraft were not completed that year. It is certainly worth noting that manpower in the aviation industry increased from 3,500–4,000 in 1933 to 72,000 in 1935. Tank production

[39] Letter from Blomberg to the chiefs of the army and navy command and to the minister of aviation, 25 Oct. 1933, *IMT* xxxiv. 487–91.
[40] Geyer, 'Rüstungsprogramm'.
[41] Göring to the Nuremberg Tribunal, *IMT* ix. 280. Cf. Deist, III.II.4 below. On aerial rearmament cf. Gehrisch, *Entwicklung*.
[42] Cf. Deist, III.II.4 below.
[43] Irving, *Rise and Fall*, 45.
[44] Foreign ministry memorandum, 10 Aug. 1934, PA II FA, 'betr. Umbau der deutschen Wehrmacht', Abr 44, vol. i.

TABLE II.III.4. *German aircraft production 1932–1939*

	Total No.	No. of military aircraft
1932	36	—
1933	368	—
1934	1,968	840
1935	3,183	1,823
1936	5,112	2,530
1937	5,606	2,651
1938	5,235	3,350
1939	8,295	4,733

Source: Wehner, 'Verkehrswesen', 46–7.

likewise started up in July 1933, when Krupp embarked on a comprehensive 'agricultural tractor programme', though in fact this was the first serial manufacture of armoured fighting vehicles.[45] The following year Auto-Union was induced to build Wehrmacht vehicles, the department concerned, 'owing to the prevailing necessity, being camouflaged under the name of BZ (*Behördenzentrale*: administration centre)'.[46] Iron and steel works began to increase their manpower from 1933 onwards, though the extent of this varied from one firm to another. The following instances are worth noting: about 500 new workers were engaged during the first four months of 1933 by Rheinmetall, an enterprise manufacturing heavy guns, machine-guns, and field-howitzers; the work-force of the Mauser rifle factory increased from 800 to 1,300 in the course of January. The Berlin-Karlsruher Industriewerke increased its work-force by 35 per cent during the first half of 1933; the Bochumer Verein during the same period engaged about 400 new workers; and the work-force of the Rheinsdorf gunpowder factory rose from 2,000 to 5,200.[47] By mid-November the navy had ordered combat equipment worth RM41.48m. from eight firms, not including shipbuilding orders worth over RM70m.[48] These instances could be multiplied.

An early start was also made on the setting up of a so-called 'shadow industry', production facilities which would be taken up only in the event of mobilization or war. This, however, did not meet with the unreserved approval of the Wehrmacht, which instead demanded increased manufacture of weapons and equipment.[49] The Wehrmacht also included in its rearmament planning the possibility that military conflicts might be provoked by Germany's violation of the Versailles limitations. Within an economic heartland, already defined under the Weimar Republic, known

[45] Stelzner, *Arbeitsbeschaffung*, 184 n. 2. Cf. Deist, III.II.2 below.
[46] Kirchberg, 'Kraftfahrzeugindustrie', 119.
[47] Cf. Benoist-Méchin, *Historie de l'armée allemande*, iii. 162.
[48] Chief of navy command to chief of army command, 15 Nov. 1933, BA-MA RH 8/v. 941.
[49] Stelzner, *Arbeitsbeschaffung*, 223.

as *Innerdeutschland* and thought to be relatively invulnerable, the Wehrmacht promoted the enlargement of approximately ninety-five firms between the summer of 1934 and the spring of 1935. Further it initiated the establishment of approximately sixty new firms, mostly of medium size, within that region, which of course resulted in a corresponding creation of jobs.[50] By December 1934 eighteen factories within this 'protected area' (e.g. Borsig in Tegel, Krupp-Gruson in Magdeburg, and the Bochumer Verein in Hanover) had embarked on the production of infantry weapons and certain types of heavy guns, though output failed to reach the targets expected by the Wehrmacht.[51]

Without these armament orders (at first indirect but also in some cases direct) the drop in unemployment of roughly 50 per cent during the first year of National Socialist rule cannot be explained. At the end of 1934, in view of the increasing momentum of the armaments boom, the government suspended any specific promotion of job-creation, even before its economic '"detonator" could be fully effective'.[52] After all, the rearmament drive was resulting in 'a multitude of jobs' and offering a sufficient 'guarantee of a steadily growing number of fellow Germans (*Volksgenossen*) being employed in the realization of that great task'.[53] Investment in 1933 was certainly neither exclusively nor predominantly due to direct armament orders; it was due instead to industry's intention of being ready for such orders in good time. The state was therefore able, after a certain running-in phase of the armament economy, basically to leave the absorption of the unemployed in the production process to the internal dynamics of the rearmament boom which had been triggered by indirect and direct armament orders.

The start of the 'second armament programme'[54] in the spring of 1933 certainly produced a marked stimulation of the economy, which was acquiring an increasingly armament-oriented character, but this was not accompanied by a second major inroad into the remaining pool of unemployed. Unemployment in fact declined only slowly, though steadily, as the economy accelerated. This was due to the fact that by then it was no longer a matter of finding a job for just any unemployed person but of the right man being needed in the right job. The following list shows the annual average number of unemployed (in millions):[55]

1933	4.804	1936	1.592
1934	2.718	1937	0.912
1935	2.151	1938	0.429

The government-initiated revival of the economy continued, by and large, in 1934, 'with Wehrmacht orders [playing] a considerable part'.[56]

---

[50] Wehrmacht office to army command, navy command, and ministry of aviation, 10 Apr. 1935, BA-MA RH 8/v. 941.

[51] Report by chief of army ordnance office, May 1934, BA-MA RH 8/v. 957.

[52] Honigberger, *Zielsetzung*, 19.

[53] Report by Professor Nöll von der Nahmer at the 1938 conference of the German Labour Front's banking and insurance section, quoted from Kuczynski, *Studien*, 153.

[54] Cf. Deist, Part III below.   [55] Figures according to Albert, *Wiederaufrüstung*, 54.

[56] Notes for a report by the defence economy and weapons office, 17 Nov. 1934, BA-MA RW 19/82.

Comparison with the decline in unemployment in Britain and the United States (Table II.III.5) shows that the conquest of unemployment in Germany was not due to any world-wide economic recovery but very largely to the state's economy-stimulating measures—i.e. to indirect and direct rearmament. Anyone dividing National Socialist economic policy into a phase of job-creation followed by one of rearmament fails to understand the link between politics and economics in the Third Reich.

The publicly financed cost of job-creation through rearmament can now no longer be reliably established. The difficulty of arriving at even reasonably accurate orders of magnitude is due, for one thing, to the fact that official statistics were manipulated so that an exact separation into military and civilian job-creation is no longer possible.[57] Thus, all kinds of motorized armament items are listed in the statistics simply as vehicles of various types. For another thing, the boundaries between civilian and indirect rearmament measures are necessarily blurred. As job-creation demonstrably benefited rearmament to a high degree it is impossible to draw a sharp line between job-creation costs and rearmament costs. A considerable portion of the budget items set out in Table II.III.6 should therefore be looked upon as rearmament expenditure.[58]

National Socialist job-creation should be understood not only as an economic primer but also with regard to its rearmament and, more especially, system-stabilizing importance. In other words, the growing political credibility of the National Socialist regime since the summer of 1933, and especially its maintenance, depended largely on full employment. This was the only guarantee that the identity of interests between big business and the state would continue and that labour, which had for the most part been well organized before 1933, would continue to be politically reliable. Any armament-linked full employment, however, must inevitably be limited in time, because of its dependence on volume—unless, of course, the military equipment was brought into operation in a war. Only thus could the armament-linked state-led boom be perpetuated, and full employment be made downright indispensable. Job-creation, in consequence, was 'not just "a boost" through public finance' but, 'as revealed by its links with transport, settlement, and defence policy, the principal nodal and channelling-point' required by 'the creation of a new German economic and territorial order'.[59]

3. WAR ECONOMY AS CRISIS ECONOMY

Mobilization of the armament economy did not start only with the introduction of general conscription. Even in 1933 pure rearmament expenditure considerably exceeded the annual totals of the Weimar era in scope and tempo, most of the finance going into a structural reorganization, which was at first scarcely noticed by

---

[57] According to the Federal statistical office the non-encoded data were destroyed during the war.

[58] On the problem of job-creation and rearmament financing cf. also Hübener, *Arbeitsbeschaffung*.

[59] From the introduction by the Heidelberg economist Carl Brinkmann to the thesis by K. Schiller, *Arbeitsbeschaffung*.

TABLE II.III.5. *Total unemployed in Germany, Britain, and USA (1933-1935)*

	GERMANY				BRITAIN				USA			
	Peak[a]		Later fig.[b]		Peak[a]		Later fig.[b]		Peak[c]		Later fig.[d]	
	No.[e]	%[f]	No.[e]	%[f]	No.[e]	%[f]	No.[e]	%[f]	No.[e]	%[f]	No.[e]	%[f]
Overall economy	6.01	9.2	2.97	4.5	—	—	—	—	13.69	10.69	11.33	9.0
Industry, trade, and transport	5.47	8.4	2.80	4.3	2.96	6.4	2.33	5.0	—	—	—	—

[a] Jan. 1933.
[b] Jan. 1935
[c] Mar. 1933
[d] Dec. 1934
[e] Millions.
[f] of population.

Source: Wagemann, *Zwischenbilanz*, 100.

TABLE II.III.6. *Public expenditure on civilian job-creation 1933–1934* (RMm.)

	By end of 1933	Total by end of 1934
1. Public construction (waterways, roads and underground engineering, public buildings, bridges, etc.)	855.6	1,002.4
2. Housing	723.3	1,280.0
3. Transport	950.8[a]	1,683.9[b]
4. Agriculture and fishing (improvements, rural settlements, etc.)	337.4	389.2
5. Promotion of consumer goods	70.0	70.0
6. Other purposes	164.0	568.0
TOTAL	3,101.1	4,993.5
Compare:		
7. Rearmament expenditure	1,900.0	5,900.0

[a] *Reichsautobahnen* account for RM50m. of this figure.
[b] *Reichsautobahnen* account for RM350m. of this figure.

Source: Barkai, *Wirtschaftssystem*, 181.

observers but which proved vital to the future direction of the rearmament economy. The purposeful manner in which the government led by the National Socialists proceeded along its road of rearmament economy was illustrated, a mere two and a half months after the seizure of power, by the law on a population, vocational, and enterprise census,[60] designed to establish the data needed for an 'economic preparation for war'.[61]

Financing of rearmament outside the job-creation programme was likewise speedily embarked upon. Statistical data on armament expenditure by the Third Reich vary considerably. The difficulty of arriving at a precise figure is due to the circumstance that not only Wehrmacht costs but also a large portion of public and private investment must be included in rearmament expenditure. In attempting to do this it is not always possible to determine whether, and if so to what extent, such investment served to meet private-enterprise or rearmament-economy requirements. Hitler, in one of his threatening speeches at the outbreak of war, named a sum allegedly spent on purely military expenditure since 1933: 'For over six years I have worked on building up the German armed forces. During that period over 90,000 million was spent on building up our Wehrmacht. Today it is the best-equipped in the world and stands far beyond comparison with that of 1914.'[62]

[60] 12 Apr. 1933. *RGBl.* (1933), i. 199–200.
[61] Bracher, Sauer, and Schulz, *Machtergreifung*, 798.
[62] Domarus, ii. 1315.

While Hitler's figure, because of its intended propaganda effect, was on the high side, it seems likely that the data given after 1945 by Schacht, the Reichsbank president at the relevant time and temporary minister of economic affairs, and by Schwerin von Krosigk, the minister of finance, who were concerned to justify themselves and minimize their responsibility for war preparations, were too much on the low side (see the various estimates in Tables II.III.7[63] and II.III.8[64]).

The only figures which can be established with any accuracy are amounts totalling RM60,900m. directly spent by the Wehrmacht, though this sum does not, of course, include all rearmament expenditure, least of all that of the civilian departments, such as the ministries of the interior, transport, and labour, as well as the Four-year Plan authority. Private investments are also excluded from the sum.

State expenditure, and more particularly military expenditure, at any rate increased so enormously between 1934 and 1938 that it could not be met from taxation, nor did it remain in step with the rise in national income. In 1938 state expenditure was approximately RM30,000m., of which only RM17,700m. could be

TABLE II.III.7. *Some estimates of rearmament expenditure 1933–1939, by calendar year* (RM000m.)

	1	2	3	4	5	6	7
1933	0.746	0.7	—	1.9	0.746	0.72	1.5[a]
1934	4.197	4.2	4.433	4.1	4.197	3.3	2.8
1935	5.487	5.5	5.934	6.0	5.487	5.15	5.5
1936	10.273	10.3	10.743	10.8	10.273	9.0	11.0
1937	10.961	11.0	14.515	11.7	10.961	10.85	14.1
1938	17.247	17.2	20.325	17.2	17.247	15.5	16.6
1939[b]	11.906[c]	32.3	13.907[c]	30.0	—	—	16.3[c]
TOTAL	60.82[d]	81.12[e]	69.86[f]	80.7	48.9[g]	44.52[g]	67.8[h]

[a] Feb.–Dec. 1933.
[b] Some entries go up to 31 Aug., others are for the whole year.
[c] 1 Apr.–31 Aug. 1939.
[d] 1 Apr. 1934–31 Aug. 1939.
[e] 1933–9. If indirect rearmament expenditure is included the total increases by RM3,000m.–RM4,000m.
[f] 1 Apr. 1934–31 Aug. 1939. By including estimated expenditure of civilian authorities, Schweitzer, 'Wiederaufrüstung', 618, arrives at RM70,000m.–RM74,000m.
[g] Low figure because 1939 is not included.
[h] If expenditure on the maintenance and training of the NSDAP's paramilitary units, as well as Länder and municipal expenditure on rearmament, are added to this total one arrives at RM78,000m. Cf. Eichholtz, *Kriegswirtschaft*, 32.

Sources (by column): (1) Stuebel, 'Finanzierung', 4129; (2) Fischer, *Wirtschaftspolitik*, 102; (3) Schweitzer, *Big Business*, 331; (4) Carroll, *Design*, 184; (5) Minister of Finance Schwerin von Krosigk in the Wilhelmstrasse trial, quoted from Erbe, *Wirtschaftspolitik*, 39; (6) Ibid. 25, 100; (7) Eichholtz, *Kriegswirtschaft*, 31.

[63] On this table cf. also Hennig, 'Industrie', 122.
[64] On the table as a whole cf. Hennig, 'Industrie', 123.

TABLE II.III.8. *Some estimates of rearmament expenditure by budget year*
(*1 Apr.–31 Mar.*) *1933–9* (RM000m.)

	1	1	1	2	2	3	4
1932/3	—	—	1.0	—	—	0.6	—
1933/4	1.9	—	3.0	1.9	1.9	0.7	1.9
1934/5	1.9	2.25	5.5	1.9	2.8	4.1	1.9
1935/6	4.0	5.0	10.0	4.0	6.2	5.5	4.0
1936/7	5.8	7.0	12.5	5.8	10.0	10.3	5.8
1937/8	8.2	9.0	16.0	8.2	14.6	11.0	8.2
1938/9	18.4	11.0	27.0	18.4	16.0	17.2	18.4
TOTAL	40.2	34.25	75.0	40.2	51.5	49.4	40.2

Sources (*by column*): (1) Data from the Länderrat (Council of Länder) of the US Zone of Occupation (Schacht's data from his evidence to the Nuremberg Tribunal); cf. Kuczynski, *Studien*, 128; (2) Klein, *Preparations*, 264; Hillman, 'Comparative Strength', 45; (3) Köllner, *Rüstungsfinanzierung*, 82; (4) Wagenführ, *Industrie*, 17.

met from taxes. In that year state expenditure amounted to 35 per cent of the national income. Rearmament expenditure could therefore be financed only by state indebtedness based on credit expansion, i.e. by deficit spending. Hence, from an early date (31 May 1933) the Reichsbank assumed 'the financing of rearmament to a considerable extent', at first mainly by so-called 'Mefo' bills, in order, 'out of nothing—and initially, moreover, under camouflage—to achieve a state of rearmament which would render possible a foreign policy which demands respect'.[65] Four major German firms had founded the Metallurgische Forschungsanstalt (Metallurgical Research Institute) with a capital of RM1m.; enterprises receiving armament orders from the Wehrmacht were able to draw bills on it, and these were guaranteed by the state and discounted by the Reichsbank. The Wehrmacht was in fact able to make its first payment in 1933 by 'Mefo' bills. With the 'Mefo' bills presented to it the Reichsbank covered the printing of banknotes, so that the money supply increased without an increase in the supply of goods in the markets.

The fact that Germany's accelerated rearmament remained totally camouflaged until March 1935 and, for reasons of military secrecy, partially concealed beyond that date meant that 'the banknote printing-press was resorted to at the very beginning of the entire rearmament programme', whereas, in the view of economic experts, this form of financing should have stood at the conclusion of rearmament.[66] The danger of inflation inherent in 'Mefo' bills was realized at the time. By 31 March 1938 some 12,000 million of these bills had been spent, of which about a half had been deposited with the Reichsbank, while the other half entered into monetary circulation, causing the notes in circulation to increase by RM6,000m. If one con-

[65] President of the Reichsbank board to Hitler, 7 Jan. 1939, *IMT* xxxvi. 366.
[66] Memorandum by Schacht, 3 May 1935, *IMT* xxvii. 50.

siders the Wehrmacht's pure rearmament expenditure, then the 'Mefo' bills can be said to have covered 50 per cent of armament purchasing costs between 1934 and 1939. Between 1934 and 1936 their share amounted to approximately 20 per cent (Table II.III.9).[67]

TABLE II.III.9. *Wehrmacht rearmament expenditure by budget years 1934/5–30 Aug. 1939*

	Sum (RMooom.)	Proportion covered by 'Mefo' bills	
		RMooom.	%
1934/5	4.1	2.1	51.2
1935/6	5.5	2.7	49.0
1936/7	10.3	4.4	42.7
1937/8	11.0	2.7	24.6
1938/9	17.2	—	—
1939 (1 Apr.–30 Aug.)	11.9	—	—
TOTAL	60.0	11.9	20.0

Source: Stuebel, 'Finanzierung', 4131.

Because of their inflationary effect, in 1937 the Reichsbank president refused to issue any further 'Mefo' bills. He did in fact approve one more non-recurrent credit in the sum of RM3,000m., but only on condition that from the spring of 1938 onwards the 'Mefo' system would no longer be practised. In fact no more 'Mefo' bills went into circulation after 31 March 1938. In 1939, when they should have been redeemed by the state after a five-year term, the state was not in a position to do so.

For that reason the most important means of financing rearmament, alongside the 'Mefo' bills, were now non-interest-bearing *Reichsschatzanweisungen* ('U-Schätze': Reich treasury notes) and *Lieferschatzanweisungen* (supply treasury notes), which came into circulation from 1938/9 onwards. Between May and October 1939 so-called *NF-Steuergutscheine* (New Finance Plan tax vouchers) were issued on the basis of the 'New Finance Plan'. They were used to pay for supplies and other services to the Reich to an amount of 40 per cent of the invoiced totals. Interest-bearing long-term *Reichsanleihen* (Reich bonds) and *Schatzanweisungen* (treasury notes) were also floated as early as 1933.[68]

On the whole, however, the political decision-makers of the Third Reich regarded rearmament financing as a problem which only required a short- or medium-term solution, i.e. until such time as a certain state of rearmament was reached and the

[67] On rearmament and war financing cf. more recently Boelcke, *Kosten*. This contains not only the definition of the two concepts but also a presentation, in the context of the overall political development, of financial measures for the preparation and execution of the war.

[68] On rearmament financing cf. Boelcke, 'Probleme'.

problem finally solved through territorial expansion. They did not hesitate, therefore, to burden the state with a heavy debt for the purpose of rearmament (Fig. II.III.1). The goal of the National Socialist rulers was the fastest possible attainment of the highest possible level of rearmament, in order to expand their political and economic sphere of influence by limited military operations.

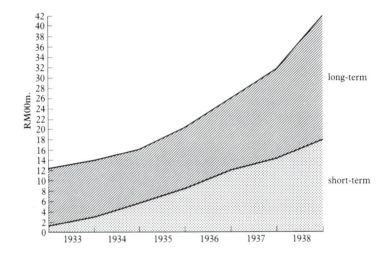

FIG. II.III.1. The gross Reich debt, 1933–8

For that reason, alongside specific measures of subsidized job-creation and, at least initially, a rather haphazard allocation of armament orders, preparations were made for a systematic military mobilization on a broad economic basis. A typical example was the initiative, taken by industry in May–June 1933, to establish and develop a German mineral-oil industry by producing synthetic motor-fuel through the hydrogenation of coal. This project was in line with the National Socialist demand for partial autarky to make rearmament proof against economic blockade and political pressure. Although the production of synthetic fuel on a major scale had until then been dismissed because of the uneconomic nature of the process, this did not stop the National Socialist regime from going ahead. On 14 December 1933 the so-called petrol agreement was concluded between IG-Farben-Industrie and the state: the enterprises undertook to produce between 300,000 and 350,000 tons of motor fuel annually, while the Reich extended a ten-year purchase and price guarantee. IG-Farben thereupon increased its staff from 112,600 at the end of 1933 to 134,700 in the following year.[69] A short while afterwards the ministry of economic affairs used the law to force the lignite and fuel industry, and the cellulose manufacturers, into compulsory cartels to ensure that production was organized and increased in the direction demanded by the state. The National Socialist

[69] Benoist-Méchin, *Historie de l'armée allemande*, iii. 162 n. 2.

government had used such special directive measures within individual industries from the very beginning of its rule in order to define clear focal points of production. In line with its rearmament intentions these were in the sector of production goods, and were applied (from March 1933) through a series of bans on investment and enlargement in the consumer-goods industry. The ensuing larger percentage growth of the production-goods index compared with the consumer-goods index is shown in Table II.III.10.

TABLE II.III.10. *Industrial production trends in Germany 1932–1934 (1928 = 100)*

	1932	Dec. 1933	% Increase	July 1934	% Increase
Overall index	61.2	75.1	23	89.5	19
Production goods	50.2	66.1	32	84.3	28
Consumer goods	77.6	88.6	14	97.4	10

Source: Report by the Reichskreditgesellschaft on Germany's economic situation at the turn of 1934–5, quoted from Gossweiler, 'Übergang', 70.

In order to assign to raw materials vital for rearmament a degree of priority above other commodities the National Socialist government at first took a few rather hesitant steps towards a *dirigiste* foreign-trade policy. Rather than tighten up the not very stringent foreign-currency regulations inherited from the Brüning era, it decided in favour of rationing raw materials. The minister of economic affairs was authorized on 22 March 1934 'to supervise and regulate dealings in industrial raw materials and primary products, especially their acquisition, distribution, storage, sale, and use' and 'to that end to set up special supervision centres for particular types of goods'.[70] This authority, however, was initially applied only to foreign trade.

Regardless of the regimentation described above, after eighteen months of National Socialist government the Wehrmacht continued to express extreme dissatisfaction with the result of the orientation of industrial production towards rearmament requirements. Blomberg, reporting to Hitler on 20 May 1934, accused Schmitt, the minister of economic affairs, of failing 'so far to take the absolutely necessary measures for economic mobilization'.[71] He linked his general criticism of economic preparations for rearmament with the specific demand that a production programme for synthetic fuels should at long last be developed and pushed forward. In the second half of June 1934 Blomberg demanded of the chancellor a thorough investigation into whether, in view of the close interrelations of rearmament and the industrial shift of emphasis, 'the good and welcome decision in the *military* field'

[70] *RGBl.* (1934), i. 212.
[71] Quoted from Schweitzer, 'Organisierter Kapitalismus', 42.

was in harmony with 'the measures of government authorities in the *economic* field' to date.[72] At any rate the top echelons of the Wehrmacht regarded the equipment of a twenty-one-division army as safeguarded on the basis of industry carrying three to four months' supplies. On the other hand, there was still the question of the extent to which the further development of the armed forces, on the scale planned for them, could be vigorously advanced.

Detailed Wehrmacht criticism focused on inadequate supervision of raw-material dealings and the absence of measures for ore extraction and metal production. German ore deposits were being opened up at a slow pace, construction of hydrogenation plant was being delayed, the state was not energetic enough in pushing ahead with the production of synthetic rubber and other plastics and substitute materials, and above all was neglecting the textile sector, where bottlenecks existed in wool and cotton supplies.

The first signs of crisis, not to be underestimated in their extent, in fact appeared in the National Socialist economy in mid-1934 and posed a serious threat to rearmament. For the most part they were due to shortages caused by raw-material problems and resulted in the following symptomatic upheavals.

In mid-July 1934 the second-largest copper electrolysis plant closed down owing to lack of raw materials. Opel announced the shut-down because of insufficient allocation of non-precious metals. The predominantly foreign nickel-suppliers threatened to liquidate their stocks stored in Germany because of missed dates of payment. For the same reason 'a major volume' of rubber had already been shipped out of Hamburg harbour. The Deutsche Edelmetallwerke, faced with a shortage of raw materials, gave notice that it would have to suspend 'deliveries of alloy steel for especially important Wehrmacht purposes' at the end of July, and the Dynamit-Nobel AG similarly saw no way of maintaining production (especially of explosives) beyond July.[73]

The economic crisis of the summer of 1934 presented itself as a foreign-trade crisis, even though its roots lay essentially in the domestic economic actions of the Third Reich. At a superficial glance it merely reflected the world-wide depression in the foreign markets: international trade continued to show a falling trend beyond 1932 (when it was RSM52,100m., reducing to RM47,800m. in 1933) though some of this was due to depreciation in certain countries (in terms of volume it showed a slight rise). In these tight conditions it would have required quite exceptional efforts for Germany to increase its foreign trade. There were several obstacles to such an increase. For one thing, a depreciation of the Mark would have been necessary in order to enhance competitiveness, but this would, at the same time, have resulted in an appreciation of Germany's foreign debts. For another thing, some important trade partners (e.g. the United States, Britain) imposed trade sanctions on the National Socialist state because of its persecution of the Jews. Thirdly, the export-impeding effect of the government's rearmament orders allocated to German

---

[72] Cf. comment by Blomberg, 20 June 1934, BA-MA Wi I F 5/406.

[73] Defence Minister to Keppler, the Führer's delegate for the economy, 19 July 1934, BA-MA Wi I F 5/406.

industry should not be underrated: these offered a long-term production basis with assured sales. Added to this was the fact that the Third Reich's agricultural protectionism resulted in increased demands on the engineering industry, one of Germany's most important export industries. There was thus a convergence of foreign-trade depression with its shrinking exports and of the fact that capacity was largely taken up by domestic manufacture. And, finally, an erroneously conceived ideological striving for autarky (also motivated by the desire to rearmament) had a detrimental effect on the foreign-trade balance sheet.

This export paralysis, with its variety of causes, was confronted, on the other side, by an import demand substantially revived by the rearmament boom—resulting not only from an increased requirement of essential raw materials, animal feed, and feeding-stuffs for stockpiling against an emergency, but also from an increased call for consumer goods due to a higher level of employment and, hence, an increase in wages and general purchasing power.

In practice the rearmament boom resulted in diminished exports from 1933 onwards:[74]

> 1933 (4th quarter):   RM1,260m.
> 1934 (1st quarter):   RM1,090m.
> 1934 (2nd quarter):   RM990m.

In the spring of 1934, for the first time since 1929, Germany again had a balance-of-payment deficit. Simultaneously there was a rise in imports, with the percentage increase in imports of raw materials and primary products exceeding that for foodstuffs and stimulants (coffee, tobacco, etc.), as shown in Table II.III.11).

TABLE II.III.11. *Percentage changes in imports compared with previous six-month period*
1933–1934

Imports	2nd half 1933		1st half 1934	
	Value	Quantity	Value	Quantity
Foodstuffs, beverages	−0.5	+1.3	−6.2	−4.1
Raw materials and primary products	+2.7	−1.3	+16.0	+16.0
TOTAL IMPORTS	+0.4	+1.3	+8.8	+10.0

Source: Gossweiler, 'Übergang', 76.

It is significant, however, that of these imports a real 44.8 per cent was accounted for by consumer goods and only 15.5 per cent by the production-goods industry—which ran totally counter to the government's rearmament intentions.[75] Schacht therefore tried emphatically to convince business that 'the less is

[74] *Konjunkturstatistisches Handbuch 1936*, data according to Gossweiler, 'Übergang', 76.
[75] Cf. Volkmann, 'Außenhandel und Aufrüstung', 86.

consumed, the more work can be applied to rearmament', since he realized full well that 'life-style and scale of rearmament' were 'in reverse proportion to one another'.[76] As the gap between imports and exports widened, so the Reichsbank's already insignificant foreign-currency reserves (RM400m. at the start of 1934) shrank to a minimum of RM76.8m. in July 1934)[77] so that the Wehrmacht office saw the rearmament situation as 'disquieting in the extreme'.[78]

The autumn of 1934 witnessed another exacerbation of the overall economic situation, as shown by the following typical instances. The textile industry was suffering from serious bottlenecks (the cotton-processing enterprises held only two weeks' supply of raw materials), which the government was trying to overcome by a provisionally enacted thirty-six-hour week and part-time work; stocks for rubber production were sufficient for two months; and fuel reserves could meet requirements for about three to three-and-a-half months. The military were now urging that 'all public projects not absolutely essential from a military or political point of view be set aside in the interest of rearmament, thereby reducing the financial burden and the raw-material demand on the Reich'.[79] Imports of foodstuffs, raw materials, and goods for private and civilian needs were drastically cut back, but this failed to improve the overall economic situation. In theory the government was suddenly faced with the alternative of either consistently pursuing the war economy in its originally outlined form, with all the economic risks this entailed, or of finding some economically defendable balance between the requirements of rearmament and the overall economy, which would have retarded the growth of German military strength for a number of years. Naturally, any slowing down of the pace of rearmament was out of the question for the National Socialist rulers. Accordingly, upon Schacht's recommendation, they decided on total foreign-trade control through central foreign-currency and raw-material rationing on the basis of the so-callled New Plan of September 1934, which marked phase two of the National Socialist war economy.

---

[76] Schacht, *'Finanzwunder'*, 11.

[77] Gossweiler, *'Übergang'*, 76.

[78] Notes by Thomas for a report to the defence minister and chief of the army command, 16 Apr. 1934, BA-MA Wi I F 5/3260.

[79] Thomas, *Wehr- und Rüstungswirtschaft*, 87.

IV. The National Socialist Economy under the 'New Plan'

1. NATURE AND STRUCTURE OF THE 'NEW PLAN'

IN the late summer of 1934 Reichsbank President Schacht became, in addition, minister of economic affairs of the Reich and of Prussia. From that moment he was determined, in spite of the world depression, to stabilize the revival of the German economy by means of a *dirigiste* foreign-trade policy; his 'New Plan' of September 1934 was intended to steer the development of foreign trade towards a rearmament economy. Whatever divergent statements he may have made after 1945, he based all his economic considerations and measures on the thesis that 'implementation of the rearmament programme . . . [was] *the* task of German policy' and that 'everything else must be subordinated to that objective'.[1] The primary foreign-trade principle henceforward was 'No purchases unless they can be paid for, and then only those urgently needed'[2]—from the rearmament point of view. In practice the 'New Plan' aimed at extensively cutting back on imports of finished articles and consumer goods and restricting them, as far as possible, to foodstuffs and animal feed which could not be produced in Germany (or not in sufficient quantity), as well as to armament-related raw materials and special commodities. In other words, the function of foreign trade was to 'procure such goods as were not available domestically, or not on a sufficient scale,[3] the decision as to what or how much was needed lying ultimately with the state. This marked the transition from foreign-currency control—first initiated during the Brüning era and intensified after the Nationalist Socialist 'seizure of power'—to actual import control. From now on the state regulated imports by means of a priority list for raw materials, foodstuffs, and animal feed, thus at the same time deciding on their productive utilization. Strict control over raw materials, however, was not introduced until 1936. Instead, the state confined itself to ensuring, by setting up supervisory authorities, that raw materials were being used along the desired lines, i.e. according to rearmament priorities. With the 'New Plan' the National Socialist regime had fashioned a tool for itself not only, according to a contemporary admission, to ensure 'economic recovery' but also 'the militarization (*Wehrhaftmachung*) of the German Reich'.[4] Naturally, this armament-oriented foreign trade was bound to militate against any increase of supplies to the civilian population. To the National Socialist regime, however, in agreement with the Wehrmacht, it was a matter of course that 'a major part of . . . imports [could] not yet be directly devoted to improving the standard of

---

[1] Memorandum by Schacht on the financing of German rearmament, 3 May 1935, *IMT* xxvii. 50.
[2] Schacht, *Deutschland*, 15.
[3] Grävell, 'Störungen', 44.
[4] Flaig, *Untersuchung*, 81.

living' so long as the nation was 'still on the road of strengthening the country's defence'—in plain language, rearmament.[5] In fact, without considerable imports from abroad, Germany was unable to remedy its drastic shortages of raw materials. Thus, there was a shortage of most metals needed for modern armaments. German deposits of bauxite, zinc, nickel, and copper only accounted for a minute portion of what was needed, chromium was not mined at all, and two-thirds of the requirements of lead and iron had to be imported. Stocks of metal had shrunk to such an extent that some firms were already forced to draw on their stockpiles built up for the event of war. Germany's dependence on textile raw materials amounted to approximately nine-tenths, and the shortage of unvulcanized rubber and motor-fuel was even worse. There were shortages also in the areas of agriculture and forestry.

The 'New Plan' ensured that the intended priorities in imports were observed and that, at the same time, overall imports were kept relatively low in spite of the rapidly growing demands of the armament industry (Table II.iv.1).

TABLE II.iv.1. *German imports 1933–1936* (RMm.)

	Total imports	Finished goods
1933	4,203.6	715.8
1934	4,451.0	575.6
1935	4,159.0	408.1
1936	4,218.0	397.4

Source: Statistisches Jahrbuch für das Deutsche Reich (1941–2); Table according to Kroll, *Weltwirtschaftskrise*, 481.

The restructuring of the foreign-trade pattern in terms of goods was linked, first, with a shift towards countries which were suppliers of raw materials and, second, with the development of an accountancy system which largely eliminated cash payments in foreign currency. From the turn of 1933–4 the government had endeavoured to concentrate foreign trade on countries which, by virtue of their surplus production of agricultural, forestry, and raw materials, were in a position to fill the painful gaps in the German rearmament economy.

The second principle underlying the 'New Plan' was 'Buy from your customers'. In other words, Germany was trying to offset its imports by exports on a bilateral basis or, through clearing accountancy with the country concerned, to balance the value of imports and exports, i.e. to achieve an even balance of trade. Thus, the Third Reich was reverting to 'the ancient system of barter, albeit in different forms, allowing for increased and more varied turnover'.[6]

---

[5] Brinkmann (state secretary in Reich ministry of economic affairs), 'Außenhandel', 387.
[6] Dix, 'Handelspolitik', 1131.

Suitable countries for such a foreign-trade pattern were industrially under-developed ones with surplus raw materials and agricultural produce, and countries which had a heavy domestic demand for manufactured and production goods and therefore seemed ready to absorb German products—e.g. the countries of Central and South America. In general, however, it was intended to shift the focus of foreign trade, especially of imports, from overseas to Europe, in order to ensure for Germany secure sources of industrial and agricultural raw materials from her own neighbours. Such a reorientation had to be effected swiftly to avert potential foreign threats triggered off by Germany's remilitarization. Germany's accelerated rearmament involved not only the risk of preventive foreign military intervention, of which her rulers were fully conscious, but also the possibility of an economic blockade, which would have disastrous consequences to planned and current rearmament. Greatly concerned, State Secretary for Foreign Affairs von Bülow wrote to his minister in the late summer of 1934: 'In view of our isolation and our present weakness economically and as regards foreign currency, our opponents do not even need to expose themselves to the hazards, the odium, and the dangers of military measures. Without mobilizing one man or firing one shot they can place us in the most difficult situation by mounting either a covert or an overt financial and economic blockade against us.'[7] Aiming as it did at blockade-proof rearmament, National Socialist Germany was obliged 'to increase those of its imports which came from Europe and cut down, in the same measure, on overseas imports'.[8] Close economic studies had shown that even before 1933 the foreign trade of European countries had been predominantly directed to the European sphere; moreover, an analysis of the commodities exchanged revealed that the economic dependence of European countries upon one another was greater than that on extra-European countries, since 'the different parts of Europe . . . complement each other favourably'.[9] The share of extra-European countries in the imports of European countries (excepting Britain) between 1925 and 1930 amounted to only 26 per cent, and in the case of exports the proportion was only 19.7 per cent of the exports of continental European states.[10] In consequence, National Socialist Germany was anxious to attract to itself the highest possible percentage of the trade which the continental European countries had until then carried on with the rest of the world and, more especially, to divert it from Britain. At the time of the Weimar Republic and during the initial phase of the National Socialist regime European trade partners accounted for four-fifths of German exports, with one-fifth going overseas. German imports, on the other hand, were made up about equally of imports from overseas and from the Continent. After 1934–5 that ratio shifted in favour of Europe (Table II.iv.2).

While 'war-economy considerations' inclined the National Socialist leaders at an early date 'to consider the greatest possible switch of raw-material imports from

[7] Von Bülow to Neurath, [16] Aug. 1934, *DGFP*, C. iii, No. 162, here p. 330.
[8] Oesterheld, *Wirtschaftsraum*, 115.
[9] Gaedicke and Eynern, *Integration*, 1.
[10] Ibid. 9.

TABLE II.iv.2. German imports and exports 1934–1935

	Imports from				Exports to			
	Europe		Overseas		Europe		Overseas	
	RMm.	%	RMm.	%	RMm.	%	RMm.	%
1934								
1st qu.	592.6	51.7	554.7	48.3	840.2	76.8	254.1	23.2
2nd qu.	590.3	51.2	562.5	48.8	768.1	77.4	223.9	22.6
3rd qu.	651.8	61.7	404.9	38.3	774.2	77.8	231.2	23.0
4th qu.	725.8	66.4	368.2	33.6	805.9	74.9	269.3	25.1
1935								
1st qu.	716.8	64.2	399.5	35.8	688.7	71.2	278.2	28.8

Source: Kühn, Verlagerungen, 13.

overseas towards areas reachable by overland transport', trade-policy considerations pointed chiefly to the Balkans.[11] The countries of south-east Europe possessed a considerable wealth of mineral deposits, the extraction of which might be greatly intensified, as well as agricultural surpluses which were difficult to sell in the world market but could readily be marketed in Germany.

German efforts to intensify economic relations initially met with ready understanding on the part of the governments of the south-east European states—so long as the power-political and economic motives behind German economic policy, which after 1938 clearly aimed at the incorporation of the Balkans in a large-scale German economic sphere, had not yet become too obvious. Germany's endeavours to increase her agricultural and raw-material imports and to find a secure market for her manufactured goods were in harmony with the efforts of the south-east European countries to overcome their structural and marketing difficulties by exporting to a country which, with its lack of colonies, was the only country in Europe to purchase major quantities of south-east European export goods—agricultural produce and industrial raw materials—and that at high prices and continually, while supplying south-east Europe with 'the products wanted by its inhabitants and needed for its industrialization'.[12] The south-east European share in German foreign trade steadily increased from 1934 onward, in both percentage and value (Tables II.iv.3–4). Of particular importance were bauxite supplies from Hungary and Yugoslavia (Table II.iv.5). Romanian oil supplies to the Reich were seen as indispensable:[13]

[11] Report by Rosenberg on the activity of the foreign policy office of the NSDAP in 1933–4, IMT xxv. 36.

[12] Weber, Außenhandelsverflechtung, 29.

[13] Figures (in '000 t.) are from the German Legation in Bucharest; quoted from Hillgruber, Deutschrumänische Beziehungen, 249.

1933	187	1937	532
1934	255	1938	450
1935	688	1939	1,272
1936	900		

The importance to Germany of these oil deliveries 'should not be underrated, either on economic or on military-policy grounds', which was why 'the successful utilization of the south-east European sphere' seemed 'indispensable to the German economy'.[14]

TABLE II.v.3. *Germany's share in the foreign trade of south-east Europe and the Danubian countries respectively, 1933–1940 (%)*

	Imports		Exports	
	South-east Europe	Danubian countries only	South-east Europe	Danubian countries only
1933	18.44	19.55	15.35	14.15
1934	19.66	17.88	22.72	19.56
1935	25.92	25.01	25.69	21.94
1936	33.77	34.02	29.62	26.46
1937	32.86	32.80	26.32	23.52
1938[a]	40.07	41.28	40.73	29.99
1939[b]	50.61	56.58	46.08	49.72
1940[c]	54.01	62.32	46.36	50.82

[a] Including Austria.
[b] Including the 'Protectorate'.
[c] Greece until outbreak of war with Italy in October of that year.

Source: Schulmeister, *Werdende Großraumwirtschaft*, 52 (also in Sundhaussen, 'Südosteuropa', 236).

TABLE II.iv.4. *Germany's trade with south-east Europe (RMm.)*

	1934	1935	1936	1937	1938[a]
Bulgaria	53.0	81.3	105.2	140.0	140.7
Yugoslavia	67.8	98.3	152.4	266.6	225.9
Romania	109.9	143.7	195.5	309.9	289.2
Hungary	103.5	140.8	176.5	224.6	219.8
Turkey	118.4	160.7	197.9	208.9	267.4
Greece	84.6	107.6	131.9	189.5	204.7

[a] Figures for the 'old Reich', i.e. Germany in her 1937 frontiers.

Source: Kühn, *Verlagerungen*, 27.

[14] Halsmayr, *Grundlagen*, 4.

TABLE II.iv.5. Bauxite extraction and deliveries from Hungary and Yugoslavia 1934–1939 (1,000 t.)

	Hungary			Yugoslavia		
	Extraction	Total exports	Exports to Germany	Extraction	Total exports	Exports to Germany
1934	185.0	106.2	103.8	84.8	91.8	65.6
1935	211.1	227.6	219.5	216.2	171.2	160.0
1936	329.1	341.6	336.0	292.2	253.1	232.9
1937	532.7	479.7	465.7	354.2	388.4	384.9
1938	540.7	362.4	358.2	406.4	379.7	379.7
1939	495.0	570.2	565.7	314.3	266.5	257.5

Source: Griff nach Südosteuropa, 14.

The 'New Plan', with its foreign-trade policy based on clearing and compensation agreements and on geopolitical considerations, was aimed primarily at ensuring, in both the short and the medium term, the indispensable supplies required by the war economy. The objective, from a military and strategic point of view, was to surround German territory with a ring of friendly or neutral trade partners, to establish a *cordon économique*—to seek trade partners in areas 'where, in the event of complications, [they were] within range of our weapons'.[15] Beyond this objective, the 'New Plan' aimed in the long run to create a large-scale German economic area as far as this was feasible by economic means. Following Germany's domestic refashioning in terms of economic organization and aims, long-term incorporation in an organically growing large-scale economic area . . . [had] to be seen as one of the next major tasks of economic policy'. Such a policy need not necessarily be confined to 'dealings with immediate neighbour economies';[16] extensive ties might well develop also between non-contiguous countries, as was the case with regard to south-east Europe. Admittedly, the territorial rearrangements connected with the annexation of Austria and the break-up of Czechoslovakia were intended to create different conditions. Linked with bilateral trade was the intention to force Germany's trade partners into the greatest possible measure of dependence, in order thus to gain possession of 'more or less extensive "economic areas"'.[17] In fact the National Socialists regarded the economic conditions of south-east Europe as structured in such a way that industrialized Germany would have secure markets in the agricultural countries, while these in turn could to a large extent meet [Germany's] requirements of imported agricultural products',[18] the same being true of industrial raw materials. In the context of large-area economy, however, trade with south-east Europe served not only to ensure indispensable imports in peacetime and in the event of war through an increase in the neighbourly exchange of goods, but also to establish political relations by means of economic ones. In the view of its protagonists, autarky had to lead 'away from world trade towards the phase beyond the country's own economy, i.e. an area economy (*Raumwirtschaft*), the alliance economy (*Bündniswirtschaft*) of a bloc of nations'.[19] To the National Socialists this meant, specifically, that 'even when Germany's straitened conditions have been overcome, there would be no reversal of the major shift in foodstuff and animal-feed imports from overseas and western Europe to south-east Europe so long as close economic ties with the south-eastern states seem politically desirable'.[20] South-east Europe had become one of the obvious and unalterable objectives of German hegemonist strivings.

2. ASSURANCE OF SUPPLIES THROUGH FOREIGN-TRADE EXPANSION

The task of 'anchoring' Germany's requirements of foodstuffs, animal feed, and raw materials 'in foreign-trade agreements to such an extent that a maximum of

---

[15] NSDAP Reichstag member Dr Hunke, 'Die Lage', 482.
[16] Posse (state secretary in the ministry of economic affairs), 'Großraumwirtschaft', 282.
[17] Fried, *Autarkie*, 126.   [18] Link, 'Außenhandelspolitik', 87.
[19] Ibid. 86.   [20] Weidemann, *Gestaltung*, 66.

reciprocal obligations' would stem from them[21] was tackled vigorously during the first half of the 1930s, and with considerable success. From 1934, for instance, the Third Reich had been making every effort 'to make the German market indispensable to Yugoslav exports';[22] this was achieved by the conclusion of a trade treaty which was regarded in Berlin 'as an exemplary illustration of the line pursued by the trade policy of the National Socialist government'. The essence of that agreement was an attempt 'to attune the two economies to one another from production onwards', i.e. to align the Yugoslav economy to German requirements. The treaty was therefore regarded 'as a preliminary stage to the large-area economic development initiated by the Third Reich'.[23] As Germany could offer both a receptive market for Balkan agricultural produce and the means of production and investment needed to encourage south-east European industrialization and the accelerated exploitation of their raw materials, the Balkan countries, being short of capital and relying on their agricultural and mineral exports, found a natural trade partner in Germany, with its highly developed industry on the one hand and its need of agricultural imports on the other.[24]

In the case of Hungary there was already talk of a 'German–Hungarian economic community', described in Budapest itself as an almost 'classic example of trade policy reverting to a healthy basis'.[25]

In accordance with its large-area concept, as well as obvious rearmament considerations, National Socialist Germany was aiming, beyond south-east Europe, 'at penetrating the East European belt of states' in its entirety and tying the territories concerned 'into firm relations with the German political and economic area'.[26] Two of the Baltic States, Estonia and Latvia, provide an illustration of this. These two countries' percentage share in supplying Germany's needs was relatively slight; on the other hand, their exports formed an important complement within a large-scale economic area dominated by Germany. Their importance within the overall pattern of German foreign trade, moreover, lay in the specific composition of their surplus products. The two Baltic seaboard states held first place among suppliers of calf-hides—a commodity in particularly short supply in Germany—and second place among exporters of flax, another commodity of considerable importance in view of the grievous lack of raw materials for German textiles. Finally, Estonian phosphorite deposits proved to be 'the only ones directly accessible to Germany'.[27] Second to Denmark, these two Baltic states together supplied the largest quantity of butter to the Reich, with its notoriously huge shortage of fats. In addition, Germany imported from these states appreciable

[21] Grävell, 'Störungen', 109.
[22] Foreign ministry circular to German embassies, 21 June 1934, quoted from Schönfeld, 'Rohstoffsicherungspolitik', 216.
[23] Posse, Großraumwirtschaft', 283.
[24] Cf. Raupach, 'Auswirkungen', 52.
[25] Statement by the Hungarian minister in Berlin in the periodical *Der Vierjahresplan*, quoted from Kühn, *Verlagerungen*, 23–4.
[26] Stated by the NSDAP's expert on large-area economics, Daitz, *Ostraumpolitik*, 9–10.
[27] *Wirtschaftsnachrichten der Volkswirtschaftlichen Abteilung der IG-Farben-Industrie*, 6 Oct. 1939, 'Die Versorgung mit Faserstoffen, Häuten und Fellen', BA-MA Wi I F 5/3184.

amounts of other foodstuffs and animal feed which, in the event of war, might be augmented, through a German blockade of the Baltic, by the quantities normally shipped to Britain.[28]

'Germany's large-area economic mission in the Danubian and Baltic region'—the camouflage phrase for German hegemonistic plans[29]—was complemented in a northerly direction, where interest centred on raw materials and, in particular, on Sweden's industrial products. In its trade with that country the Reich was interested mainly in 'increasing the proportion of armament-relevant raw materials' in its imports.[30] Following the conclusion of the clearing agreement of August 1934, the graph of German iron-ore imports from Sweden showed a steady rise, both quantitatively and as a percentage of total Swedish exports. German military circles saw 'the importance of the Swedish economy primarily in the possibility of obtaining adequate quantities of high-quality iron ores, vital to the manufacture of weapons-grade steel',[31] even in the event of a British naval blockade (Table II.iv.6).

TABLE II.iv.6. *Extraction and exports of iron ore from Sweden until 1936 (1,000 t.)*

	Extraction	Exports		
		Total	To Germany	
			Quantity	%
1926	8,466	7,656	5,817	76.0
1927	9,661	10,716	8,682	81.0
1928	4,669	5,093	3,646	71.6
1929	11,468	10,899	7,382	67.7
1930	11,236	9,387	6,725	71.6
1931	7,071	4,496	2,803	62.3
1932	3,299	2,219	1,578	71.1
1933	2,699	3,151	2,257	71.6
1934	5,253	6,870	4,695	68.3
1935	7,932	7,710	5,509	71.4
1936	11,250	11,198	8,248	73.6

Source: Wittmann, *Schweden*, 486.

In addition to the Scandinavian countries the Third Reich concluded clearing agreements with its western and southern neighbours. Thus, the arrangements with the Netherlands and Switzerland 'pointed the new direction in which Germany wished to reach an arrangement and agreement with other national economies',[32] its

[28] Cf. Volkmann, 'Ökonomie und Machtpolitik', 492.
[29] Erbsland, *Umgestaltung*, 63.
[30] Wittmann, *Schweden*, 112.
[31] Reich agency for foreign trade, 16 Jan. 1934, quoted ibid. 118.
[32] Posse, 'Großraumwirtschaft', 283.

ultimate hope being to manœuvre them into economic and hence also political dependence.

Altogether the National Socialist regime was satisfied with the results of the 'New Plan'. Not only had the negative balance of payments of 1934 been transformed into a positive one (Table II.iv.7), but important milestones had been planted along the road to a large-area economy.

Up to 1937 imports of ores were increased by 132 per cent in volume, those of crude oil by 116 per cent, and those of unvulcanized rubber by 71 per cent, while imports of manufactured goods were cut back by 63 per cent. In Schacht's view the figures vividly demonstrated 'the contribution of the New Plan to the implementation of rearmament and to assuring our food supplies'.[33] There was also a general increase in imports of raw materials (Table II.iv.8).

Despite the shift in foreign-trade emphasis under the 'New Plan' and despite extensive adaptation by the Third Reich's trade partners to German raw-material requirements, both in industry and agriculture, it did not prove possible to satisfy the rearmament-linked high demand without also importing from countries outside the European economic bloc whose contours were beginning to emerge. In addition to the priority task of creating a close large-scale economic area with all its advantages of import and export stability, trade policy had to exploit every export opportunity as a means of financing the imports which were vital to rearmament. The prospects of such endeavours could hardly have been worse in 1935. Although an increase in vital raw-material imports for the benefit of the rearmament economy was recorded, the brunt of 'getting the balance of payment into the black was borne almost exclusively by the countries with which we have clearing agreements'.[34] In other words, the increased volume of exports was not matched by increased foreign-currency earnings, which alone would have made it possible to pay for raw-material imports to meet the growing demands of the armament industry. What emerged was the picture of an armament industry working virtually to capacity, in three shifts, while its raw materials were rapidly running out (Table II.iv.9).

The anxiety was gaining ground in the Wehrmacht 'that through purely domestic economic activity we are getting poorer every day, that without exports we cannot earn foreign currency, and that without foreign currency there can be no rearmament'. Those in authority began to realize that 'the vigorous revival of the economy or—put more accurately—rearmament and job-creation'[35] had been achieved only by eating into raw materials accumulated in the past and by running up considerable debts with the clearing-account countries, who were able to absorb only a limited volume of German manufactured and production goods. By the end of 1935 the rearmament programme had to be regarded as seriously threatened, with reserves declining from March to September as follows (p. 256, foot):[36]

[33] Schacht, *'Finanzwunder'*, 27–8. Schacht's biographer, Pentzlin, has viewed and assessed the 'New Plan' solely from foreign-currency aspects. The rearmament and large-area economics background has remained hidden from him. Cf. Pentzlin, *Hjalmar Schacht*, 222–3.

[34] Memorandum by the war ministry, 6 May 1938, BA-MA Wi vi/386.

[35] Memorandum by the defence economy and weapons office, 18 Feb. 1935, BA-MA Wi F 5/383.

[36] Report on the 12th meeting of the Reich defence committee, 14 May 1936, BA-MA Wi I F 5/701; cf. Volkmann, 'Außenhandel und Aufrüstung', 91.

TABLE II.iv.7. *Foreign-trade results and Reichsbank gold reserves 1928–1937 (RMm.)*

	Foreign trade total	Exports	Imports	Balance of exports against imports	Av. gold and foreign-currency reserves
1928	26,277	12,276	14,001	− 1,725	2,405.5
1929	26,930	13,483	13,447	+ 36	2,506.3
1930	22,429	12,036	10,393	+ 1,643	2,806.0
1931	16,326	9,599	6,727	+ 2,872	1,914.4
1932	10,406	5,739	4,667	+ 1,072	974.6
1933	9,075	4,871	4,204	+ 667	529.7
1934	8,618	4,167	4,451	− 284	164.7
1935	8,429	4,270	4,159	+ 111	91.0
1936	8,986	4,768	4,218	+ 550	75.0
1937	11,379	5,911	5,468	+ 443	70.0[a]
1938	10,706	5,257	5,449	− 192	
1939	10,860	5,653	5,207	+ 446	

[a] Approximate figure.

Source: Volkmann, 'Außenhandel und Aufrüstung', 85.

TABLE II.IV.8. *German imports of principal raw materials 1933-1936* (RMm.)

	Wool	Cotton	Unvulcanized rubber	Iron ores	Fuels and lubricants
1933	266.2	307.0	25.1	58.8	127.5
1934	322.6	260.2	42.3	88.3	124.4
1935	248.1	329.7	45.5	123.4	144.6
1936	229.4	257.7	66.2	168.3	169.2

Source: Statistisches Jahrbuch für das Deutsche Reich (1941–2); cf. Kroll, *Weltwirt-schaftskrise*, 481.

TABLE II.IV.9. *Reserves of vital rearmament raw materials in short supply 1934–1935* (1,000 t.)

	1 Apr. 1934	1 Sept. 1935
Cotton	95	68
Wool	67	48
Silk	—	—
Flax	11	8
Hemp	8	6
Jute	30	22
Leather	—	76
Magnesite	12	10
Linseed	120[a]	80[a]

[a] Equivalent to 45,000 t. of linseed oil.
[b] Equivalent to 26,000 t. of linseed oil.

Source: Volkmann, 'Außenhandel und Aufrüstung', 91.

	Decline of reserves
Iron ore	more than one-third
Copper, lead	nearly two-thirds
Zinc	more than two-thirds
Wool, worsted yarn	more than half
Cotton	more than half
Jute	nearly two-thirds
Hides, furs	nearly half
Unvulcanized rubber	more than two-thirds

The armament industry's reserves had shrunk to one or two months' supplies. From the point of view of the war economy the economic development was 'in no way satisfactory'. By the spring of 1935 the Wehrmacht realized that the 'strengthening of our economic instruments of power . . . and the consumption of raw-material reserves' had been effected through 'financial anticipation of the future', i.e. the expectation of territorial aggrandisement.[37] The military therefore regarded the reincorporation of the Saarland in 1935 as 'a welcome accretion of strength for the war economy'.[38] When, in the face of this situation, the leaders of the state and the Wehrmacht nevertheless demanded extensive rearmament, the minister of economic affairs, Schacht, without 'wishing to deny or change [his] often-voiced support for the utmost possible rearmament', nevertheless felt 'in duty bound to point out the economic limitations of such a policy'.[39]

As Schacht, with growing urgency, was arguing his case that exports were 'the indispensable basis of any acquisition of foreign currency and raw materials, and hence also of rearmament',[40] the Wehrmacht began to press for state promotion of exports. A personal initiative by Hitler in the spring of 1935 collapsed in the face of the export weariness of enterprises engaged on state-sponsored direct or indirect armament orders, and also over the question of what an armament-oriented industry might be able or permitted to export without impairing the rearmament economy. The answer to this question was as simple as it was absurd: war material, which was in great demand in a widely rearming world and promised to yield ample supplies of foreign currency.[41] Exports of military equipment were therefore stepped up, but they proved as controversial on account of their rearmament-obstructing nature as their economic benefits were questionable. In any case they accounted for only a fraction of total German exports and their currency earnings were unsatisfactory, as the chief customers were industrially underdeveloped countries, the demand from which was in sharp contrast to their lack of internationally acceptable currency.

3. DOMESTIC MEASURES AIMING AT AUTARKY

As exports failed to provide sufficient finance for the purchase of the necessary raw materials, foodstuffs, and animal feed, the 'New Plan' was paralleled by efforts for greater autarky at home; in the agricultural sector these aimed at achieving 'foodstuff freedom' (*Nahrungsfreiheit*) through intensification and restructuring of production. The reason was that in 1935, alongside the raw-material bottlenecks in the industrial sector, there emerged supply difficulties in the agricultural sector. Although it was just about possible to 'safeguard vital foodstuffs' for supplying the population, the poor harvest of 1934—on Hitler's own admission—resulted 'occasionally . . . in a temporary shortage of some foodstuff or other'.[42] However, these shortages were not due solely to below-average harvest yields but also to

---

[37] Report of the defence economy and weapons office on the economic situation, 1 May 1935, BA-MA RW 19/82.
[38] Note for report on the economic situation, 16 Mar. 1935, ibid.
[39] Letter from Schacht to Blomberg, 24 Dec. 1935, *IMT* xxxvi. 292.
[40] Ibid. 295.
[41] Cf. Volkmann, 'Außenhandel und Aufrüstung', 94 ff. and annex.
[42] Hitler at the Reich Party rally 1935, quoted from 'Reichsparteitag und Wirtschaft', 292.

increased demand on the part of the public, who, thanks to the rearmament-led economic revival, were enjoying increased purchasing power. In fact, the shortages all had their origin in the rearmament economy. One reason was that, in the allocation of foreign currency, raw materials vital to rearmament always enjoyed priorty over imports of foodstuffs. The slogan of 'guns instead of butter', proclaimed by Rudolf Hess, the deputy Führer, therefore meant that imports of foodstuffs 'simply had to take second place to imports of industrial raw materials'.[43] Moreover, the National Socialist government, ever since coming to power, had practised stockpiling in preparation for war, as 'a nation . . . could win a war only if its leaders saw to it that it was at least modestly fed'.[44]

Stockpiling, above all, was aimed at supplying the forces in the event of war. To the National Socialists it was 'a fact confirmed by experience a thousand times over that supplying an army with food was no less important than supplying it with ammunition, and that persistent hunger was one of the most effective obstacles to achieving victory'.[45] Dependence on conquered territories was to be kept to a minimum. Stockpiling of food was managed by 'Reich agencies' (*Reichsstellen*). The Reich agency for grain, for instance, alone spent RM26.5m. in 1933 on foreign purchases and storage.

The setting up of foodstuff and grain stores was promoted by the granting of loans to mills and to the trade for the establishment of silos and other storage facilities (RM6.3m. in 1935), these loans as a rule covering 33.5 per cent of the building costs. The money was allocated by a commission in which the war minister and the air minister ensured that 'location (of storage facilities) took account of military considerations'.[46] The necessary reserves were of course siphoned off the civilian market, taken either from domestic production or from imports.

As the factors governing agricultural production rendered a rapid switch-over from peacetime to wartime production impossible, the food economy was subject to 'the law of permanent readiness'. In other words, agricultural production had to be programmed well ahead, to ensure that transition from peacetime to wartime economic conditions could proceed smoothly. The intended 'war-proof (*wehrsicher*) form of nutrition' could be realized only if the productive forces of the German soil were fully exploited, so as to approximate the objective of partial autarky.[47] Moreover, the cultivation of agricultural crops had to be regulated, so that in the event of a blockade Germany would be in a position to feed itself for a considerable period of time.

This was the objective of the agricultural 'production battle' proclaimed by the Reich agricultural leader, Darré, in 1934; it reflected the demands of the 'New Plan' within the sphere of farming. The 'production battle' was to create conditions to enable the German nation, in a warlike conflict, essentially to feed itself with what

[43] Schwichtenberg, *Erzeugungsschlacht*, 23.

[44] Ibid. 20.

[45] Meinhold, *Erzeugungsbedingungen*, 2.

[46] Directives for storage construction, quoted from Hoeft, *Agrarpolitik des deutschen Imperialismus*, 44. This is also the source for the figures.

[47] Schwichow, 'Ernährungswirtschaft', 258.

was produced by its own farmers. For that reason all regulations relating to German agriculture 'from 1934 onwards must be virtually viewed as measures for a total war'.[48] In practice, therefore, the 'production battle' served the stepping-up of agricultural production as a prerequisite of blockade-proof rearmament, as well as 'the saving of foreign currency in favour of military consolidation and industry', so that Germany should be able to 'complete its rearmament'.[49] The need for an increase in production to safeguard food supplies in a war emerged from the admission by leading agriculturists that 'the complications which can arise in a war, such as blockade, were always on the cards since 1934, though not with the same severity, because of our shortage of foreign currency'.[50] The experience of the First World War had taught the National Socialists a lesson in war economy: 'A state which does not possess within itself the economic resources needed for the conduct of a war is bound to find itself in such a degree of dependence that the success of its struggle is in jeopardy from the outset.'[51] In consequence, 'the main emphasis of food policy, viewed from a war-economy angle', was on 'security through our own strength'.[52] In consistent application of the slogan of the 'production battle'—'Cultivate the soil labour-intensively and produce what the German people lacks'[53]—imports of foodstuffs and animal feed were subject to considerable restrictions from 1934 onwards (Table II.iv.10).

TABLE II.iv.10. *German Imports 1931–1936* (t.)

	1931–3[a]	1934	1936
Grain	2,640.07	1,880.53	538.10
Vegetables	340.92	317.81	237.70
Butter and cheese	124.67	95.54	103.29
Eggs	123.44	75.96	79.81
Fats and blubber	439.70	330.93	328.07
Oleaginous crops	2,365.87	2,214.19	1,429.23
Animal feed	734.46	144.22	190.21

[a] Presumably annual averages (though this does not emerge from Melzer's presentation).

Source: Melzer, *Studien*, 16.

In spite of all regulatory interventions by the Reichsnährstand, the farm economy failed to reach the high level of self-sufficiency aimed at; this may be shown by the example of cereal cultivation. Although the Third Reich had a realistic chance of meeting its domestic requirement of bread grain, this was not consistently utilized.

[48] Speech by Herbert Backe, state secretary in the Reich ministry of food, to Reichsleiter and Gauleiter, 6 Feb. 1934, quoted from Herferth, *Reichsnährstand*, 228.
[49] Schwichtenberg, *Erzeugungsschlacht*, 22–3.
[50] Darré's agricultural production plan of 27 Nov. 1939, quoted from Melzer, *Studien*, 17.
[51] Heß, 'Wehrwirtschaft', 2187.   [52] Hauser, 'Wehrwirtschaft', 2090.
[53] Press service of the Reichsnährstand, 14 Dec. 1934, quoted from Melzer, *Studien*, 16.

Owing to a price policy dispensing with incentives, a lack of fertilizers, and a reduction of the cultivable acreage (e.g. as a result of autobahn construction or the establishment of army training-grounds and airfields), a stagnation in grain production came about, to be followed by a retrogressive trend after the outbreak of war. Requisitioning of agricultural land by the Wehrmacht[54] and construction of fortifications resulted in the break-up of 140 villages and the partial evacuation of 225 rural communities between 1933 and 1938. In addition, over 30,000 farmers and farm workers, along with their families, were made to abandon approximately 5,600 enterprises with a total acreage of about 120,000 hectares during the last two years before the outbreak of the war, for the purpose of building the Westwall.[55] Altogether the productive agricultural acreage diminished by approximately 596,000 hectares between 1934 and 1935 alone (Table II.iv.11).

TABLE II.iv.11. *Productive agricultural acreage in Germany 1932–1939*

	Farmland in use (1,000 ha)	% of area used as:		
		Arable land and gardens	Meadows	Pastures
1932	29,370	72.2	18.7	9.1
1933	29,365	72.2	18.7	9.1
1934	29,348	72.2	18.7	9.1
1935	28,752	70.2	19.7	10.1
1936	28,747	70.3	19.6	10.1
1937	28,724	70.4	19.5	10.1
1938	28,537	70.2	19.6	10.2
1939	28,535	70.1	19.8	10.1

Source: Woermann, 'Erzeugungsschlacht', 117.

Under these conditions the absolute yields rarely reached the figures for 1913. Frequently the per-hectare yields likewise lagged behind those for that year (Table II.iv.12). The record harvests of 1938 and 1939 were due to exceptionally favourable weather conditions; as a result, yields of basic agricultural foodstuffs, compared with the referential period of 1928–32, rose by approximately 20 per cent and the arable yields overall by approximately 15 per cent (Table II.iv.13).

Despite every effort to achieve autarky, the food balance sheet for the mid-1930s showed a deficit, as indicated in the following list, where the right-hand column gives the percentage shortfall in domestic production in 1934/5:[56]

---

[54] Law on land acquisition for Wehrmacht purposes, 29 Mar. 1935, *RGBl.* (1935), i. 467–8.
[55] Cf. Melzer, *Studien*, 18.
[56] From Kroll, *Weltwirtschaftskrise*, 530.

Grain, potatoes, sugar, beef, milk	0–2
Ham, freshwater fish, vegetables	3–10
Pork	10–20
Fruit	10–20
Poultry, eggs	20–30
Sea fish	30–40
Fats (incl. butter, lard, and margarine)	40–50
Legumes	50–60
Vegetable oils	95–9

This arose from the dual demands on agriculture—on the one hand, to meet the increased private domestic demand arising from a higher standard of living and, on the other, to satisfy the demands of a stockpiling economy preparing for war.

TABLE II.IV.12. *Average per-hectare grain yields in Germany 1908–1944* (t.)

	1908–13	1928–32	1934–38	1944
Rye	1.86	1.72	1.73	1.68
Wheat	2.27	2.07	2.25	2.14
Oats	1.98	1.91	2.02	1.82
Barley	2.12	2.00	2.16	1.94

Source: Checiński, 'Umstellung', 330.

TABLE II.IV.13. *Crop yields in the* Altreich *1928–1942* (10,000 t.)

	Grain and pulses	Potatoes	Sugar beet	Food crops	Fodder beet	Hay
1928–32	226[a]	104	28	358	37	138
1933	257	104	21	382	40	133
1934	215	111	26	352	42	107
1935	224	103	26	353	44	133
1936	224	116	30	370	47	160
1937	228	138	38	404	51	150
1938	268	127	39	434	46	149
1939	251	129	42	422	47	145
1940	220	133	41	394	48	128
1941	217	109	40	366	46	136
1942	213	126	41	380	52	124

[a] Annual averages.

Source: Woermann, 'Erzeugungsschlacht', 119.

About the end of 1935 and the beginning of 1936 the hard-line rearmament course—marked by a restrictive import policy in the agricultural sector, in order 'to relieve the balance of trade and to release foreign currency for armament imports'[57]—was no longer tenable. Even during 1935 it had to be accepted that, because of the tight animal-feed situation, supplies to the army were suffering,[58] and the foodstuff situation similarly called for at least a temporary adjustment of economic priorities. So as not to jeopardize political stability at home the National Socialist regime, though not without differences of opinion within the government and some infighting, decided to increase currency allocations to ensure food supplies, at the expense of rearmament-related raw-material imports; this resulted in serious shortages in industrial production, especially for the Wehrmacht.

If the regime had insisted on the drive towards foodstuff autarky because of rearmament, the German food situation in 1936 would have needed a bumper harvest 'to avoid a sizeable shortage of the most important foodstuffs'.[59]

A source of particular anxiety to the National Socialist leadership was the country's dependence on the world market in the textile sector. Here too there was a clash between consumer and rearmament interests, especially as the Wehrmacht had given notice of a large requirement of material for uniforms. The severity of the situation emerges from a suggestion by Reich Agricultural Leader Darré in 1935, to the effect that every farmer should 'plant a few square metres of flax' and make the Führer a present of the yield, so that 'every soldier . . . might have fatigues woven from it'.[60] Moreover, the Reich government promoted domestic sheep-breeding, making RM8m. available for this purpose in 1935. The measures initiated were not only to meet immediate demand but 'to lay the first modest foundation of an emergency stock of wool for our uniform-cloth industry'.[61]

The Reich government, inspired 'by a powerful militant determination'—in other words, guided by its decision to wage a war for living-space—realized at an early date that it would possess the necessary elbow-room only if it was able to 'oppose any external economic pressure by its own strength'.[62] In consequence it had to strive to exploit and process all domestic mineral reserves regardless of economic profitability. In 1934 Hitler entrusted Keppler, his then personal adviser on economic matters, with the 'special responsibility for raw materials and industrial materials'; this entailed 'implementing all such economic measures as seemed necessary in view of the foreign-currency situation in order to bring about the replacement of foreign raw materials by those of domestic production'.[63] This realignment was to be based on exact scientific and technical data on German raw-material deposits, the minister of economic affairs having been previously charged

[57] Kruedener, 'Zielkonflikt', 338.

[58] Letter from Darré to Schacht, 14 Jan. 1936, BA-MA Wi I F 5/614.

[59] Memorandum from the department for central observation of the economy, 'Die deutsche Rohstoff- und Ernährungslage in ihrer volkswirtschaftlichen Verflechtung', BA-MA RW 19, Anh. 1/231.

[60] Quoted from Kroll, Wehrwirtschaftskrise, 449.

[61] Report from the war ministry on the state of the economy in areas within the responsibility of the army food and supplies department, 1 June 1935, BA-MA RW 19/81.

[62] Schwichtenberg, Erzeugungsschlacht, 21.

[63] Letter from Keppler to Kehrl, quoted from Kehrl, Krisenmanager, 60.

(by a law of 4 December 1934) with the systematic exploration of workable deposits.[64] In future private owners of land would have to permit, or themselves undertake, state-planned prospecting on their property. Moreover, the law laid down in detail the obligation of anyone prospecting below ground to report and specify his findings.

This kind of data-gathering, however, required a period of several years, and that was why, in all these areas, action was based on the criteria of economic urgency. Top priority belonged to supplies of motor-fuel, on which the operational readiness of a modern motorized army crucially depended. When the National Socialists came to power German dependence on foreign mineral oil amounted to approximately 70 to 75 per cent, a fact which greatly worried the military and political leadership and triggered off a search for ways of stepping up domestic supplies. The project of intensified crude-oil extraction, promoted by the long-time party ideologist and, for a short while, acting state secretary in the ministry of economic affairs, Gottfried Feder, though supported by Hitler, apparently failed to meet with the appropriate response from the mineral-oil industry. Although development and exploratory drilling dramatically increased between 1933 and 1934, the figure remained almost constant from 1935 to 1938: to be exact, development drillings showed a slight increase, while exploratory drilling work showed a decline after 1937 (Figs. II.IV.I, 2).

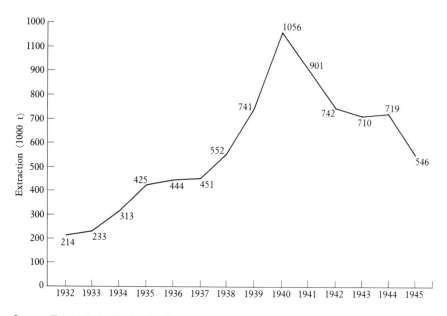

Source: *Taschenkalender für den Bergbau*, 243.

FIG. II.IV.I. Petroleum extraction in Germany, 1932–45

[64] Kolshorn, 'Erfassung', 263.

At the same time there was an extensive development of the processing of imported oil (Table II.iv.14).

Although crude-oil production increased by approximately 90 per cent between 1933 and 1936, the total volume remained far below the planned orders of magnitude; from the military point of view the German oil deposits were too unproductive and therefore too insignificant to meet the growing demand. After all,

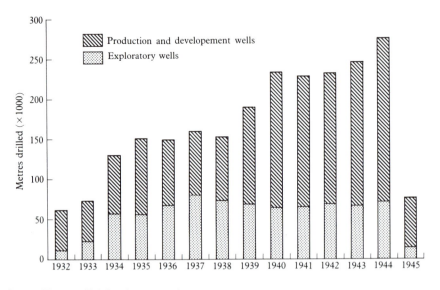

Source: Kasper, *Erdölgewinnung*, 236.

FIG. II.IV.2. Drilling in Germany, 1932–45

TABLE II.IV.14. *Production and consumption in the mineral-oil industry 1933–1936* (1,000 t.)

	Oil production	Synthetic-fuel production	Mineral-oil consumption	
	I	2	3	4
1933	233	108.4	2,238	2,810
1934	313	153.2	2,564	3,295
1935	425	240.8	2,973	3,835
1936	444	475.9	3,497	4,590

Sources (by column): (1) *Taschenkalender für den Bergbau*, 243; (2) *Deutsche Mineralölwirtschaft*, 624, 627; (3) *Statistisches Handbuch*, 501; (4) Birkenfeld, *Treibstoff*, 218 (though his data come from diverse documents and altogether err on the high side).

consumption of mineral oils increased by approximately 56 per cent between 1933 and 1936.

The National Socialist regime therefore turned its attention to the chemical industry: this was not only to be Germany's saviour from dependence on foreign mineral oil but was further intended to meet the economy's overall requirements so far as necessary 'to ensure national raw-material supplies through our own efforts'.[65] At the Reich Party rally of 1935 Hitler charged the chemical industry with the task of replacing raw materials which were unavailable, or available only in insufficient quantities, or whose importation would be endangered in the event of a conflict, by substitute materials (*Ersatzstoffe*)—'through the production of our own materials (*Werkstoffe*) to make Germany independent of imports'. Hitler was referring particularly to the production of petrol from coal, which, 'launched on a maximum scale', must in future, as new hydrogenation plants went on stream, result in the domestic production of 'a high percentage of German motor-fuel requirements'.[66] Whereas the production of synthetic petrol during the early phase of the regime served the general motorization of the country and only indirectly benefited the rearmament economy, its expansion during Schacht's tenure of the ministry of economic affairs was increasingly governed by war-economy considerations. Although the production costs of synthetic petrol were considerably higher than for petrol from crude oil, this did not stop the National Socialists from producing motor-fuel from domestic raw materials by the hydrogenation of coal, 'as the decisive considerations were strategic, not merely economic, aspects'.[67] Nevertheless, the minister of economic affairs opposed the Wehrmacht's demand for the appointment of a 'special commissioner for the mineral-oil economy', to control the industry according to rearmament criteria and thus prepare the way for mobilization. But this controversy between Schacht, the raw-materials commissioner Keppler, and the Wehrmacht—more particularly the commander-in-chief of the air force, as an especially interested customer for motor-fuel—did not spring solely from differences of opinion. Schacht was not greatly worried about any disruption of the economy as a whole. He merely claimed that he was entitled to fill the new post with a person from the ministry of economic affairs, a person enjoying his confidence, and he wanted his claim to prevail.

Despite the rapid rise in the output of hydrogenation plants—by approximately 330 per cent between 1933 and 1936—reorganization in favour of domestic supplies in the event of war was not even within sight. German oil deposits and the production of the hydrogenation plants combined were still not yielding any appreciable domestic output by 1936, except in the areas of petrol and heating-oil (Table II.iv.15).

Current requirements and stockpiling had to be met from domestic production plus imports. Following the failure of negotiations with importers concerning voluntary storage, an organization called Wirtschaftliche Forschungsgesellschaft

---

[65] 'Chemische Industrie', 482.
[66] *Parteitag der Freiheit*, 37.
[67] Hellmer, 'Kohlehydrierung', 1481.

TABLE II.IV.I5. *Domestic oil-production as a proportion of total requirement 1934–1936 (%)*

	1934	1935	1936
Combustion-engine fuels	40.0	45.0	50.0
Diesel fuels	9.5	8.0	9.5
Heating-oil	38.0	42.3	42.0
Engine-oil	18.6	17.1	17.5

Source: Kasper, *Erdölgewinnung*, 49.

mbH (Wifo: Economic Research Company Ltd.) was set up on 24 August 1934 with the assignment from the state to provide for 'the establishment and maintenance of enterprises and plants of industry, trade, and crafts', in particular 'the establishment and maintenance of experimental and research plants for the promotion of the industries concerned'.[68] This vaguely worded definition of its aim, designed for public consumption, was supplemented for internal use by the more specific definition of 'construction of Reich-owned large-scale and intermediate storage-tank sites, as well as . . . the maintenance of national reserves for Wehrmacht purposes'.[69] During the period which followed, Wifo stockpiled considerable quantities, especially of aviation fuel, from imports and German production:

Year-end	Mineral oils (t.)
1935	76,758
1936	273,465
1937	420,976[70]
1938	589,665

The stockpile at the end of 1938 represented the pre-war peak, even though it fell far short of the requirement specified on 22 May 1935 by the war-economy staff in the event of general mobilization—8,000 tonnes of light motor-fuels and 1,060,000 tonnes of light aviation fuels.[71]

To counter the chronic shortage of textile raw materials, the ersatz industry's second focus was 'the development and manufacture of German fibre materials'; this was 'tackled resolutely'.[72] A whole string of new factories was set up for the

---

[68] Articles of association, 24 Aug. 1934, quoted from Birkenfeld, *Treibstoff*, 58.

[69] Report of the ministry of economic affairs at the end of Dec. 1937 on the preparations taken for economic mobilization by the plenipotentiary for the war economy, *IMT* xxxvi. 256.

[70] This figure includes 117,634 t. of Leuna aviation fuel and 163,943 t. of imported and other fuel. ('Leuna fuel' was motor and aviation fuel made at Leuna in Saxony by the hydrogenation of coal.)

[71] Data according to Birkenfeld, *Treibstoff*, 59.

[72] Hitler at the Reich Party rally 1935, *Parteitag der Freiheit*, 37.

manufacture of rayon and rayon staple, dispersed throughout Germany to avoid excessive production losses in the event of air raids. Production of both rose sufficiently not only to satisfy domestic consumption but also to permit stock-piling.[73] However, as wool and cotton, because of their different characteristics, could not be readily replaced by synthetic fibres, the raw-material situation in the textile industry continued to be precarious.

Particular attention was paid by the government to safeguarding supplies of unvulcanized rubber, which initially depended entirely on overseas imports. The tight currency reserves were scarcely adequate to meet the growing demand, resulting from increased motor-vehicle use by the public and the military, let alone to build up reserves for the event of war. With a view to controlling consumption of one of 'the most important raw materials of the entire rearmament and war economy', the ministry of economic affairs set up a supervisory agency for caoutchouc and asbestos on 9 May 1934.[74] Although it introduced a quota system, this had to be supplemented within the Wehrmacht by the following restrictions in order to overcome the shortages:

1. extensive cut-back on motor-vehicle transport;
2. use of small and medium-sized vehicles wherever the terrain permitted;
3. restrictions on the use of rubberized materials wherever possible (ban on the use of such materials for floor or stair-runners);
4. development of rubber-free gas-suits.[75]

It was hoped that by the recycling of old rubber—launched in the Third Reich under the motto of 'Struggle against Waste'—and especially by the manufacture of synthetic rubber (Buna), for which IG Farben took out a patent, Germany would free itself from its dependence on foreign countries as far as rubber was concerned. Before any other potential user, the Wehrmacht had shown interest in Buna manufacture, the technical problems of which had been solved at the beginning of the 1930s. Other potential users, however, were slow to overcome their psychological inhibitions about using ersatz materials (in official usage they were called 'German materials') in their own manufacturing processes; these reservations applied to ersatz materials generally and more especially to synthetic rubber, and militated against its mass production and hence its more or less economic manufacture and marketing. The war-economy staff even had to face some resistance to the introduction of Buna within the Wehrmacht itself. After protracted consultations the three services undertook to promote Buna development in the following precisely delimited areas and to permit use of the new material for the purposes indicated:

1. army: tyres, rubberized materials for anti-gas protection, seals and gaskets, engine suspensions, low-voltage cables;

---

[73] Cf. Table II.v.13 below.

[74] Paper by Hedler, OKW/Wi Rü Amt, *Kautschuk und Versorgungslage im Kriege*, BA-MA Wi I F 5/614.

[75] Directives for economy measures issued by the Reich war minister, 7 Sept. 1936, ibid.

2. navy: battery cases, high-voltage cables;
3. air force: fuel-tank claddings.[76]

Yet in spite of insistent urging by the war-economy staff it did not prove possible, before 1936, to promote Buna manufacture at a pace that would satisfy Wehrmacht demands. The reason was that in addition to the development of extensive production plants it was necessary to set up processing plants before a major transition from unvulcanized rubber to the German ersatz material could be embarked upon.

Solution of the iron-ore problem proved especially difficult, even though iron-ore extraction rose dramatically, by approximately 167 per cent between 1933 and 1936 (Table II.IV.16). Iron and steel production increased proportionally, so that shortages did not at first appear.

TABLE II.IV.16. *German iron-ore production and imports*
1934–1936 (1,000 t.)

	Extraction of utilizable iron ore	Imports
1933	2,550	
1934	3,671	8,265
1935	5,290	14,061
1936	6,812	18,469

Source: Note for a report by Thomas, early Apr. 1937, BA-MA Wi VI/202.

At the same time, the country's high degree of dependence on imported iron ore—the most important raw material for armaments—was an ever-present threat to full mobilization. That threat had to be reduced. As Germany was unwilling to 'allow its freedom to rearm, regained at long last, to be jeopardized by shortage of iron',[77] it was compelled increasingly, and in disregard of cost, to extract and smelt low-grade iron ore, while improving the dressing process. Even so, in 1936 Geman production of iron ore amounted to only some 18 per cent of requirements; there was therefore no question of unlimited freedom to rearm.

In the non-ferrous sector some remarkable successes were scored in ore extraction and metal production. But here too dependence on foreign countries remained considerable, especially with regard to copper, tin, and nickel (Tables II.IV.17–22). Even so, the growth-rate in lead production from German ores between 1933 and 1936 was about 15 per cent, that of zinc 23 per cent, and that of aluminium 416 per cent.[78]

---

[76] Cf. Treue, *Gummi*, 258.
[77] Schacht addressing iron-works experts, 1 Dec. 1935, quoted from Kroll, *Weltwirtschaftskrise*, 512.
[78] Data given by Schacht in a letter to Göring, 5 Aug. 1937, *IMT* xxxvi. 568.

TABLE II.IV.17. *German iron and steel production*
1928–1939 (million t.)

	Pig iron	Crude steel	Rolling-mill products
1928	11.7	14.3	13.2
1929	13.2	16.2	14.2
1932	3.9	5.7	5.6
1933	5.2	7.6	7.3
1934	8.7	11.9	10.6
1935	12.8	16.4	12.2
1936	15.3	19.2	14.3
1937	15.9	19.8	15.1
1938	18.0	22.6	16.4
1939	17.4	22.5	16.2

Source: *Statistisches Handbuch*, 288.

TABLE II.IV.18. *German copper-ore extraction and imports 1935–1936* (1,000 t.)

	Production by Mansfeld'scher Kupferschieferbergbau AG	Copper-ore extraction from lead/zinc-ore mines	Imports of copper ore
1935	1,106.4	7.39	400.54
1936	1,105.6	3.48	482.47

Source: Note for a report by Thomas, early Apr. 1937, BA-MA Wi VI/202.

TABLE II.IV.19. *German zinc-ore extraction and imports*
1935–1936 (1,000 t.)

	Zinc ore mined	Imports of zinc ore
1935	180.63	17.24
1936	197.93	120.64

Source: Note for a report by Thomas, early Apr. 1937, BA-MA Wi VI/202.

TABLE II.IV.20. *German tin imports 1934–1936* (1,000 t.)

	Imports of tin ores	Imports of tin
1934	0.60	13.47
1935	1.23	11.82
1936	1.56	9.18

Note: There is no information about tin ore mined in this period.
Source: Note for a report by Thomas, BA-MA Wi VI/202.

TABLE II.IV.21. *German lead-ore extraction and imports 1935–1936* (1,000 t.)

	Rich lead ores mined	Poor lead ores mined	Lead/zinc ores (mixed ore)	Imports of lead ore
1935	54.89	45.15	118.54	83.98
1936	57.98	41.77	144.83	99.30

Source: Note for a report by Thomas, BA-MA Wi VI/202.

TABLE II.IV.22. *German nickel-ore extraction and imports 1934–1936*[a] (1,000 t.)

	Imports of nickel ore	Imports of nickel
1934	37.61	5.4
1935	29.01	6.1
1936	17.65	3.4

[a] There was virtually no mining of nickel ore until 1934. From 1936 production is estimated at approximately 75 t. per month.

Source: Note for a report by Thomas, BA-MA Wi VI/202.

Hard-coal production was satisfactory and permitted exports of major quantities, while bauxite-mining, though intensified, remained far below the increase in imports (Table II.IV.23).

TABLE II.IV.23. *German bauxite extraction and imports*
1934–1936 (1,000 t.)

	Bauxite mined	Imports of unpurified bauxite
1934	6.6	326.5
1935	8.3	505.5
1936	N.A.	981.2

Source: Note for a report by Thomas, early Apr. 1937, BA-MA Wi VI/202.

When the Wehrmacht drew up a war-economy balance sheet a year after the enactment of the 'New Plan' it was certainly able to point to appreciable economic success. In foreign trade the 'New Plan' had made it possible to secure 'the raw materials needed for the realization of the defence programme, as well as an indispensable additional importation of foodstuffs and animal feed'. Admittedly Germany's debts with its clearing partners had grown considerably. All in all, however, in the opinion of authoritative Wehrmacht circles, 'the rearmament programme . . . has so far been implemented, albeit with difficulties'. 'In rearmament-economy terms', therefore, 'the principal demands which the forces make of the economy have been met. Unfortunately, however, the Reich's economic readiness for war has not been increased.'[79] That readiness continued to depend on reliable imports of foreign raw materials. Economic revival under the 'New Plan' had taken place at the expense of the economic substance of the Reich. In order to satisfy the most pressing nutritional and industrial needs, the country's raw material and food reserves had been depleted during 1934 and 1935. Along with a diminution of the stocks of textile raw materials, stockpiles of ore and metals had been drawn upon in 1935 in an ever increasing measure. That process could not be repeated. By the spring of 1936 stocks in the agricultural and industrial sectors had 'shrunk to the minimum necessary for orderly operation'. For the rest of 1936 there was now the prospect of no longer being able—as during 1934 and 1935—'to live on stockpiled reserves', so that, if a hard economic course of rearmament continued to be followed, 'Germany's raw-material supplies for the first time looked like being seriously threatened'.[80]

If overall economic production was to be kept at the same volume as in the past, if trade and industry, rearmament, and food supplies were to be held at existing levels, German imports would have to be stepped up by nearly one-quarter of the 1935

---

[79] Report by the defence economy and weapons office on the economic situation, 1 Oct. 1935, BA-MA RW 19/82.
[80] Secret report on the department for the central observation of the economy, 'Die deutsche Rohstoff- und Ernährungslage in ihrer volkswirtschaftlichen Verflechtung', 19 May 1936, BA-MA RW 19, Anh. I/231.

volume, 'without even taking into account the urgently needed topping-up of depleted reserves'. In the opinion of authoritative circles it could hardly be expected 'that the necessary surplus earnings of hard currency would be in fact achieved'. As for increasing Germany's foreign indebtedness, the government could see 'no possibility at the moment', since the trade partners with whom Germany had so far failed to settle her clearing accounts had already, in 1935, 'suspended deliveries as soon as outstanding debts reached a certain level'.[81]

[81] Report by Ministerialdirektor Wohlthat of the ministry of economic affairs to the Reich defence committee, 14 May 1936, secret document, BA-MA Wi F 5/701. A Cologne doctoral thesis interestingly establishes the connection between Germany's leaving the League of Nations in the autumn of 1933 and the autarkic trade policy. The author argues that the bilateralization of Germany's foreign-political relations, upon leaving the League, moved along generally parallel lines to foreign trade relations. 'With its departure from the League of Nations . . . and the ensuing attempts . . . to establish a new bilateral security system among the states of central Europe, the Reich effected, at the foreign-policy and diplomatic level, a breach with the post-1918 international order in the same way as, by switching foreign-trade relations towards the south-east by means of trade and clearing agreements and by the implementation of the "New Plan" in 1934, it permanently turned away from the liberal world economic system' (Dengg, *Deutschlands Austritt aus dem Völkerbund*, 427).

V. The War Economy under the Four-year Plan

1. MOTIVATION AND OBJECTIVES

By 1936 the rearmament efforts of the Third Reich had reached a scale which, allowing for the country's overall economic needs, seemed just about feasible—at least from the point of view of the minister of economic affairs. In all his calculations and measures Schacht had always proceeded from the view 'that the productive capacity of the economy represented the natural limit of rearmament',[1] and this he thought had been reached, if indeed not exceeded, by 1936. The war economy had arrived at a point where a decision had to be made between either slowing down the pace of rearmament in favour of intensified export efforts—a decision which would have been justifiable, seeing that the war preparations were general rather than specifically aimed at a fixed date—or maintaining the rearmament drive at an undiminished pace, though at the expense of the population, of the maintenance and development of the Party machine, and of the construction of ostentatious public buildings.

A third option, finally, was the tightening-up of armament production by aiming at a limited strategic objective at the earliest possible moment. A decision along these lines, which would have required intensified economic *dirigisme*, was beginning to take shape in the spring of 1936. To Hitler any relaxation of the rearmament drive was out of the question. 'To ensure further militarization' (*Wehrhaftmachung*) he therefore instructed Göring at the beginning of April to 'examine and order all necessary measures' in governmental and Party institutions.[2]

Göring, with a reputation for energy but totally incompetent in economic matters, had been picked at Schacht's suggestion, who little suspected that the air minister with his unconditional devotion to Hitler would soon turn into a powerful rival. Göring made it clear that rearmament would be maintained within the overall economic process by arguing 'the political need for an unchanged pace of rearmament'.[3]

---

[1] Statement by the former minister of finance in Hitler's government, Schwerin von Krosigk, in 1945, quoted from Schweitzer, 'Wiederaufrüstung', 595.

[2] Directive by Hitler, 4 Apr. 1936, PA, Büro Reichsminister, Akten betreffend Erlaß des Führers zur Verbesserung der Rohstoff- und Devisenlage.

[3] Minutes of meeting of the expert committee on export matters, 15 May 1936, Secret, BA R 26 1/36. In the mean time two biographies of Göring have been published. One of these (Overy, *Göring*) deals extensively with the Luftwaffe chief's economic role, though it overrates his function and his opportunities for strictly aligning the economy towards war production by way of administrative regulations. Göring's personality as the man responsibile for the Four-year Plan is unduly emphasized, with no regard for the fact that behind the so-called strong man there were, both in the Four-year Plan administration and in the Reich ministry of economic affairs, as well as in other economic policy bodies, leading representatives of business itself. Thus, there was nearly always a harmonization of interests

Despite this slogan and all appropriate efforts, serious disturbances occurred in production in the summer of 1936, resulting in an acute threat to the rearmament programme. Insufficient reserves of foreign currency and raw materials caused widespread economic upheavals and delays in Wehrmacht orders. Whereas in most areas industrial stockpiles in 1934 had been sufficient for four to six months, by May 1936 they only covered requirements for one to two months. One result of that situation was the fact that in the summer of 1936 ammunition factories were working to only 70 per cent of their capacity. Typical shortages occurred in unvulcanized rubber, where stocks held by rubber-processing firms shrank to a day's supply. Most serious of all was the situation with non-ferrous metal. Raw-material requirements of the Wehrmacht could no longer be met; indeed, certain enterprises had temporarily to be closed down. The motor-vehicle industry was eventually compelled to switch to short time (two or three working days per week).[4] The Wehrmacht also complained of inadequate allocations of heavy leather. The overall situation with regard to raw materials and more especially the extent of dependence on foreign supplies can be gauged from the data on requirements and domestic production set out in Table II.v.1.

Whereas increased production and food supplies had until recently, despite all efforts to step up domestic production capacity, been ensured 'largely by the consumption of stocks of foreign raw materials and foreign foodstuffs', this was no longer possible in the future 'owing to the growing exhaustion of stockpiles' and the shortage of foreign currency. In the view of responsible economic circles 'a turning-point had been reached'[5] which did not permit 'thoroughgoing measures by the Reich government to be postponed for much longer'.[6] For the first time also a shortage of skilled workers was beginning to be felt, especially in the machine-tool and engineering industries. In order to cope with it, enterprises frequently enticed the coveted workers away from a rival by tempting wages, which led the war ministry to urge that 'appropriate measures be taken to put a stop to this practice, which jeopardizes both rearmament and the wage level'.[7]

In his new post Göring made desperate efforts to overcome that critical supply-phase by stimulating foreign trade. At three sittings a 'raw-materials and foreign-currency staff', composed of Party, state, Wehrmacht, and business representatives, examined all possible ways of stepping up exports. The international situation, however, proved just as unfavourable as that at home. Not only had the lucrative armament orders in Germany produced a marked reluctance to export, but so had

---

between private enterprise and the state, and this continued during the Second World War. The second biography (Martens, *Göring*) has appeared in the form of a doctoral thesis. Its author, a disciple of Klaus Hildebrand, shows, like his academic teacher, little appreciation of the interdependence of politics and economics. In consequence he fails to see the economic implications of National Socialist expansionist policy, and Göring fails to acquire any economic profile.

[4] Minutes of ministerial council, 4 Sept. 1936, *IMT* xxxii. 489 ff.
[5] Ministerialdirektor Wohlthat, ministry of economic affairs, at the 12th meeting of the Reich defence committee, 14 May 1936, BA-MA Wi I F 5/701.
[6] Report by the war-economy staff on the economic situation, 1 Aug. 1936, BA-MA RW 19/8.
[7] Ibid.

TABLE II.v.I. *Survey of raw-material position, 2 May 1936* (1,000 t.)

	Iron ores		Aluminium		Unvulcanized rubber		Cellulose	
	Peacetime (1936)	In case of mobilization in 1938	Peacetime (1936)	In case of mobilization in 1938	Peacetime (1936)	In case of mobilization in 1938	Peacetime (1936)	In case of mobilization in 1938
Total requirements of Wehrmacht and economy (estimate)	9,500	11,000	105	160	75	85		Depending on natural-fibre imports
Production (entire Reich territory)	1,800	1,800	96	96	1	1	12–70	12–70
SHORTFALL	7,700	9,200	9	64	74		Any production increase would be taken up by the market	
SURPLUS	—		—		—			
Existing provisional plans for extended domestic production		1,200[a]		—		24	Increase initially to 70,000 t. by end of 1936	

[a] Keppler's proposal.

Source: Expert opinion by the chief of the war economy staff. Gen. Thomas, on economic war preparations to date, 1 Mar. 1939, *IMT* xxvii. 122–34, here 134.

the paperwork connected with state-controlled foreign trade. Public orders in the end left entrepreneurs too little latitude in the export field to create the necessary conditions (acquisition of foreign currency) for ensuring imports of raw materials vital for rearmament or imports of foodstuffs and animal feed—which were just as vital for wartime supplies. Thus, Göring's attempt to persuade the captains of industry to realize the country's needs and do their duty, i.e. to develop personal initiative, were doomed to failure, even though he had thought this approach more promising than compulsory measures enacted 'by the state on the strength of its authority'.[8]

Along with the realization that it was impossible to find a recipe for a swift and decisive restimulation of foreign trade, the conviction was gaining ground that, under the pressure of circumstances, imported raw materials would have to be supplemented by an intensive exploitation of the country's mineral wealth. As it could not be expected that direct or indirect Wehrmacht requirements of raw materials would diminish in the foreseeable future, the military war-economy organization saw no alternative to an intensified working of domestic raw-material deposits and a substantial increase in the use of synthetic materials in order to improve the situation in the rearmament economy.[9] In this assessment of the situation it agreed with the ministry of economic affairs. Its state secretary Brinkmann demanded no less than an all-out effort by 'the German inventive spirit . . . to open up the vast territory of ersatz and new materials'.[10] This inevitably demanded heavy investments. In view of the enormous claims made by rearmament, however, the public purse was not at first willing, as it had been in the days of the job-creation programme, to participate to any significant extent in the financing of such investments. The ministry of economic affairs was instead determined to let 'the economy itself, and more especially industry and the banks, bear the main burden'.[11] Although Hitler regarded this demand as correct in principle, he doubted that an economic policy shaped by Schacht and his economic concepts would be able to produce the desired result, i.e. in an increasingly difficult economic situation ensure the maintenance of the pace and scale of rearmament. Even if such doubts were to prove unfounded, the fact remained that any in-depth rearmament oriented towards the concept of total war—not, of course, officially proclaimed as such but tacitly pursued in agreement between the war minister and the minister of economic affairs—could not have been satisfactorily completed until the mid-1940s. For Hitler this would have meant an intolerable postponement of his plans. This the Führer was not prepared to contemplate in 1936. Instead he was determined to pursue his overall ambitions single-mindedly in the future and, whenever possible, to exploit any shifts in the European balance of power (such as might, for instance, arise in the course of the Spanish Civil War) to pursue his own

[8] Minutes of meeting of the expert committee on export matters under the raw-materials and foreign-currency staff, 30 June 1936, quoted from Riedel, 'Rohstofflage', 311.
[9] Report by Thomas, 9 June 1936, quoted from Wagner, 'Wehrmachtführung', 185.
[10] Brinkmann, *Wirtschaftspolitik*, 75.
[11] Ibid. 83.

hegemonistic ambitions on the Continent, even though he had not yet decided on the sequence of his thrusts—France or living-space in the east. What mattered then was the pursuit of an economic policy which would make it possible to create within a foreseeable period an operational, numerically large, effective army, with modern equipment, capable of successful operation in campaigns limited both in time and space. Such a policy made it possible to promote rearmament with relatively limited resources and, by an alternation of military aggression and diplomatic pressure, progressively to enlarge the economic base of the Reich by territorial accretions. Henceforward the war economy, in view of the existing situation, was to be guided by the requirements of what was later to be called blitzkrieg. Effectively this meant the concentration of efforts on the material equipment of the armed forces, i.e. the neglect of in-depth rearmament in favour of rearmament in breadth. It also meant the intensification of economic efforts to render possible an early operational employment of the Wehrmacht; this was to be ensured by an enlarged economic administrative machine furnished with extended powers. This emphatic priority for rearmament could not fail to have repercussions on the consumer needs of the public.

Such a measure of performance by the economy and such a measure of renunciation by the entire population needed thorough propaganda and careful timing if they were to be understood and accepted as necessary, and if the process was not to endanger social or political stability. The Reich Party rally scheduled for Nuremberg at the beginning of September 1936, with its cheering masses, provided the ideal sounding-board for the proclamation of an economic plan that was to be judged almost exclusively in terms of rearmament economy. At that 'Party Rally of Honour' Hitler announced his Four-year Plan; he justified it by the 'goal of German economic policy', which was 'the improvement of the living standard of the broad masses',[12] with simultaneous efforts to pursue the rearmament necessary for the country's defence against the Bolshevik danger from outside—a danger invariably invoked by the National Socialist regime. In fact, however, the Four-year Plan, as Wehrmacht circles correctly pointed out, was 'war economy in its pure form',[13] i.e. economic peacetime preparations for planned acts of aggression. The acclamation of the masses—'almost every sentence of the proclamation was received by the congress with tumultuous cheers which at the end grew into a prolonged demonstration for the Führer'[14]—provided Hitler with the authority to impose on the public a renunciation of wages and consumption and to steer economic demand 'in those directions' which 'emerged from the potential of our own domestic production'.[15] The National Socialist movement, Hitler avowed, was not 'greatly concerned whether butter would occasionally be in short supply' or 'whether there would be a slight shortage of eggs'.[16] Production, not wages, mattered if the aim was to make Germany self-sufficient in raw materials within four years. In a secret

---

[12] *Parteitag der Ehre*, 39.
[13] Manuscript of an article by Thomas, chief of the war-economy staff, Dec. 1936, BA-MA Wi I F 5/113.
[14] *Parteitag der Ehre*, 47.   [15] Ibid. 41.   [16] Ibid. 40.

memorandum of August 1936, outlining the Four-year Plan and containing the economic justification of his war policy, Hitler once more developed the familiar economic aims of National Socialism. Just as National Socialist policy generally served no other aim than 'to enable our people and Reich to assert their life', so the economy too had this sole and exclusive task. It had to be unconditionally enlisted in 'our nation's struggle to assert itself', a struggle that was now imminent. The point was that full employment and the growth of the national product had led to greater demand by the public, and that could not be 'satisfied by Germany's domestic economy'. Nor could any substantial increase in agricultural performance or the substitution of lacking raw materials 'by artificial methods' be expected at present.

On the basis of such an assessment of the situation two demands became imperative for Hitler. The first was to initiate at once all measures which, with the aim of autarky, would ensure 'for the future a final solution', through 'an expansion of living-space and of [Germany's] raw-material and foodstuff base'. The second requirement was to seek 'temporary relief' for the intermediate period, until such an expansion of living-space, which was basically conceivable only in military terms, could be accomplished.[17] This amounted to an unconditional exploitation of German mineral resources and productive capacities for the purpose of rearmament, to be pursued regardless of cost. Pointing out that 'four precious years' of National Socialist rule had meanwhile elapsed without the appropriate rearmament measures having been taken, Hitler set out the following tasks: 'I. The German army must be operational within four years. II. The German economy must be fit for war within four years.'[18]

As for the objection that the 'foodstuffs and raw materials' necessary for the realization of this programme were 'lacking', Hitler described it as 'totally irrelevant'[19] provided the attempt—made until then and demonstrably unsuccessful—to combine direct rearmament and war-economy stockpiling was abandoned. In his view no state could succeed in 'stocking up in advance the quantities of raw materials needed for a war'.[20] He therefore emphatically demanded that full economic mobilization should neglect long-term stockpiling and confine itself to sufficient armaments, equipment, and food supplies. This instruction suggests both his later blitzkrieg concept and his intention to exploit occupied or annexed territories.

Thus, implementation of the new economic concept meant nothing other than short-term intensive economic efforts aimed at such military actions as would achieve a partial extension of the economic base,[21] which in turn was to provide sufficient substance for renewed rearmament initiatives aimed at an autarkic living-space as the final objective. The motto was 'Achieve the highest possible degree of

---

[17] Treue, 'Hitlers Denkschrift', 206 (trans. in *Documents on Nazism 1919–1945*, 401–8, here 403–4).

[18] Ibid. 210 (trans., 407–8).

[19] Ibid. 206 (trans., 404).

[20] Ibid. 207 (trans., 405).

[21] Anticipating later accounts, reference may be made here to the annexation of Austria, the incorporation of the Sudetenland, and the establishment of the Protectorate of Bohemia and Moravia.

rearmament for military and economic policy' as the prerequisite of the 'assumption of Germany's foreign-policy leadership in Europe'.[22]

Specifically, Hitler called for a ruthless mobilization of the economy, concentrated on certain priority areas, in particular the raw-material sector, in order that foreign currency might be saved and 'channelled towards those requirements which, whatever the circumstances, can only be met by imports'[23]—such as foodstuffs, where Germany's dependence on foreign countries amounted to 15–20 per cent. While production of all raw materials and ersatz materials was to be stepped up rapidly, the memorandum singled out the following priorities:

1. increase in mineral oil-extraction at a rate that would enable Wehrmacht requirements to be met within eighteen months;
2. mass production of synthetic rubber and manufacture of rayon staple from wood as the primary material;
3. satisfaction of Germany's requirement of industrial lubricants by appropriate processing of coal;
4. increase in iron-ore extraction regardless of the ferric content of the ore; in this area, as in the production of raw materials and ersatz materials generally, the cost and economic viability aspect was to be disregarded.

The Four-year Plan marked the beginning of the second phase of National Socialist economic policy, one that was bound to have drastic consequences because its objectives were set so high that they inevitably exceeded Germany's economic potential and could not but lead to territorial expansion.

2. THE INSTITUTIONAL ANCHORING OF THE PLAN

Hitler's economic objectives, as laid down in the Four-year Plan, were linked with criticism of the existing administration, in particular the ministry of economic affairs and Schacht personally, and therefore foreshadowed not only structural changes in the apparatus of economic management but also personal consequences at the top. Hitler's sermonizing to his minister of economic affairs and plenipotentiary for the war economy, that it was not for governmental economic institutions 'to worry their heads over production methods',[24] was clearly a reaction to Schacht's violent criticism of the new economic programme: it was obvious that Schacht was not—or not yet—willing to be responsible for steering the new autarky course which aimed at aggression.

It was not as though Schacht suddenly rejected rearmament or economic preparations for war, however. He merely wanted to pursue and complete them by other economic ways and means, and over a longer period of time. He had warned Göring before, in the spring of 1936, against judging 'the raw-material situation solely from the angle of German domestic production', i.e. he had voiced

[22] Proposals of the war-economy staff on the implementation of the Four-year Plan, 37/40, 5 Sept. 1936, BA-MA Wi I F 5/1083.
[23] Treue, 'Hitlers Denkschrift', 208 (trans., 406).
[24] Ibid.

misgivings about an exaggerated policy of autarky.[25] Being a supporter of in-depth rearmament, just like the army's war-economy administration, Schacht turned to Blomberg as soon as Hitler had informed him of the contents of the Four-year Plan, in the hope of finding an ally in him. He asked him—in his view 'the only one among all the ministers to whom Hitler might perhaps have listened'[26]—to dissuade the Führer from his intended economic programme. The attempt 'to use all our energies to make us independent of foreign countries through domestic production'[27] was in Schacht's view irresponsible in economic terms: for one thing, because production of substitute materials was still suffering from teething troubles; for another, because setbacks had been suffered in the production of motor-fuel; thirdly, because Buna could not be produced in major quantities until mid-1937; and fourthly, because smelting of low-grade ore was still presenting considerable problems. An intensified policy of autarky within the existing frontiers of the Reich, at a time of increasing rearmament demands, involved the danger, in Schacht's considered opinion, that the country 'might no longer [be able to] hold out throughout the necessary intermediate period' until domestic raw-material production reached a satisfactory level.[28] The minister of economic affairs therefore advocated an intensified promotion of exports as a prerequisite of assured supplies and—albeit slowed-down—rearmament. On the other hand, given the pace of rearmament, extensive development of German production of raw materials and ersatz materials was bound to result in a shortage of manpower and a reduction of productive capacities in export industries, and hence a threat to foodstuff imports.

However, Blomberg did not prove an advocate of Schacht's cause. On the contrary, the Four-year Plan was readily endorsed by the Wehrmacht. At last the political leadership appeared willing to assign to rearmament the necessary priority in the economic process. The Four-year Plan was hailed as 'an enterprise of great boldness and determination in the economic field': there was no doubt 'that in our authoritarian state the implementation of the programme would be successfully accomplished according to schedule and with the desired production targets'.[29] Despite this statement the war-economy staff and, more particularly, its representative Thomas found it difficult to accept the principle of rearmament in breadth that was inherent in the Four-year Plan.

Hitler himself dismissed any objections to his programme, especially with regard to still insufficiently developed production methods or deficient technical installations. Instead he declared it to be industry's task to overcome any possible obstacles to production and in this connection to prove its much-vaunted private-enterprise flexibility. If industry disappointed the expectations vested in it, 'the National Socialist state would itself solve this task',[30] and it would then 'no longer need any private enterprise'.[31] This patent threat suggests that Hitler, by distancing

[25] Minutes of meeting of the ministerial council, 12 May 1936, *IMT* xxvii. 137.
[26] Schacht, *My first 76 Years*, 370.
[27] Note by Thomas on a conversation with Schacht, 2 Sept. 1936, *IMT* xxvii. 153.
[28] Ibid. 154.
[29] Report by the war-economy staff on the economic situation, 1 Oct. 1936, BA-MA RW 19/83.
[30] Treue, 'Hitlers Denkschrift', 209 (trans., 406).   [31] Ibid. 208 (trans., 406).

himself from Schacht's economic policy, was also striving for a qualitative change in the relationship between state and big business, primarily by means of an intensified and differentiated *dirigisme*, designed to ensure priority for rearmament over any private-enterprise or departmental special interests.

The creation of the Four-year Plan organization, superimposed at least conceptually on existing economic control bodies, might seem at first glance to confirm that assumption in general terms. Moreover, the appointment of the commander-in-chief of the Luftwaffe, Hermann Göring, as commissioner for the Four-year Plan would not make it unreasonable to suppose that the overall economy of the Third Reich would henceforth be dictated by the interests of the military.

Actual conditions, however, refute this supposition. They show that, up to the very beginning of the war, while the entrepreneurial scope of big business may have been progressively—though only partially—restricted, its influence on economic policy increased.[32] This is true especially of the big chemical firms, with IG-Farben at their head, which were among the driving forces for increased autarky and full mobilization. IG-Farben owned the patents for synthetic processes of particular importance to rearmament (e.g. Buna manufacture, synthetic motor-fuel production), hence the management's emphatic support for the idea of far-reaching autarky. Only the rearmament-led, and subsequently war-governed, mass production of synthetic fuels and Buna, as well as of other chemical ersatz and primary substances, could recover the high development costs incurred and, of course, beyond a break-even point yield considerable profits. IG-Farben had therefore set out its ideas on the development of the German war economy in a memorandum as early as 1935, and this did not fail to influence the decision of the National Socialist leadership to proclaim its Four-year Plan.[33] In the opinion of the enterprise the prerequisites of waging a modern war existed only if 'the totality of productive forces was subordinated to a single aim on the basis of long-term preparation'. If that was to be achieved there was no avoiding the need 'to create a reorganized war economy which would enlist every last man and woman, the last piece of productive equipment or machinery, as well as every last quantity of raw material for the manufacture of products vital to warfare, and to fit all manpower, productive installations, and raw material into an economic organism directed on strict military lines'. Just as IG-Farben wished to see fundamental priority being assigned within industrial production to the manufacture of weapons and equipment for the fighting forces, so it believed that, in addition 'the entire output of industry, crafts, and small trade, as well as of agriculture, must be included . . . as vital to war . . . in the framework of an all-embracing war economy'.[34]

This view was in agreement with that of the Wehrmacht and of Hitler. Looking for an individual who could, in line with the leadership principle, assume responsibility for the fulfilment of that task, the head of government picked Göring.

[32] Cf. Volkmann, 'Verhältnis'.

[33] Cf. Treue, *Wirtschaftsgeschichte*, 53. The road to co-operation between IG-Farben and the National Socialist rulers has been clearly described by Borkin, *Unheilige Allianz*. For details of multiple personal links between the chemical enterprise and Göring's Four-year Plan authority see ibid. 67 ff.

[34] Memorandum by IG-Farben AG, beginning of 1935, quoted from *Anatomie des Krieges*, 130.

In his post of commissioner for raw materials and foreign currency he had proved himself an obedient and energetic agent of the Führer's will: he was therefore charged with 'preparing the German economy for war'.[35]

In his new capacity Göring was entitled to issue decrees and regulations and to give instructions to all authorities—including the ministers concerned—as well as to party bodies and their branches and associated organizations, whenever such instructions bore upon economic policy.[36] Determined to interpret his rights generously, Göring did not confine himself to the establishment of a personal staff which would have endeavoured to ensure the implementation of the Four-year Plan within the framework of existing rearmament agencies, and would have supervised those bodies. Instead he created an authority eponymous with Hitler's memorandum, within which certain specialized groups, known as Geschäftsgruppen (working committees), were assigned their own areas of responsibility, which not infrequently coincided with those of existing bodies. Altogether the Four-year Plan took over responsibility for the manufacture and distribution of raw materials and primary materials, for agricultural production, and for employment of labour, price surveillance, and currency matters. The heads of the individual Geschäftsgruppen not infrequently held office in the Four-year Plan organization simultaneously with a similar post in other governmental or party authorities. One instance of such a dual function was provided by the Geschäftsgruppe for food supplies, whose direction was entrusted to State Secretary Backe of the Reich ministry of food and agriculture, while a senior official of the ministry of labour and the president of the Reich institution for labour exchanges and unemployment insurance between them shared the duty of heading the Geschäftsgruppe for manpower employment.

As one of the NSDAP's representatives in the Four-year Plan the Gauleiter of Silesia, Wagner, took over the Geschäftsgruppe for price control with the rank of Reich commissioner; that group, being the supreme Reich authority in its sphere, had ministerial character and was the only institution in the Four-year Plan with a subordinated administrative apparatus, in the form of price formation and surveillance authorities, all the way down to district level. Performance of such dual functions was intended to prevent competing or uncoordinated activities, while at the same time ensuring Göring's influence on the overall economic process, just as, the other way round, governmental and party authorities concerned with rearmament matters endeavoured to make their ideas, or demands and interests, carry some weight within the Four-year Plan organization. However, only the armed forces, and more particularly the Luftwaffe, succeeded in achieving this to any extent, by working through Göring himself. Initially the most important Geschäftsgruppe, the bureau for German raw materials and synthetics, was likewise headed by a senior officer (Colonel Löb) of the air ministry. The appointment of the personnel of the Four-year Plan authority underlined the increasingly clear rearmament goal of the new economic policy.

---

[35] Minutes of meeting of the Reich Defence Council, 18 Nov. 1938, BA-MA Wi I F 5/560.
[36] Decree on the implementation of the Four-year Plan, 18 Sept. 1936, *RGBl.* (1936), i. 887.

At the same time, numerous representatives of the world of industry occupied important—albeit not the most important—posts in one or another economic-policy institution of a governmental character, such as the machinery manufacturer and Gau (regional) economic adviser Pleiger, the textile industrialist and likewise Gau economic adviser Kehrl, the IG-Farben director Krauch, and the chemical expert Eckell from the same enterprise. This personal bracketing of course served to tie private enterprise to the state, just as, conversely, industry managed to assert its interests within the economic bureaucracy and hence in economic policy generally—the more so as Göring, a layman in the field of economics, lacked any deeper insights into economic matters either at national or plant level.

The organization of the Four-year Plan as set out in Fig. II.v.1 was not to be of long duration. Already in 1937 the first changes, both personnel and structural, were carried out. They affected primarily the Geschäftsgruppe for raw-material distribution under the minister-president of Baden, Köhler, which was dissolved for inefficiency, its powers being transferred to newly created bodies, such as that for recycling of used materials and for foreign trade. In response to pressure from the Wehrmacht Göring appointed Colonel von Hanneken of the army ordnance office to be plenipotentiary for iron and steel. Henceforward Hanneken, responsible for the regulation of that market, became a model for subsequent 'plenipotentiaries' as, owing to over-bureaucratization, the Four-year Plan authority was progressively becoming too inflexible. Even Göring found himself compelled to admit that the bureaucratic unwieldiness of the machine was putting the 'punctual execution of the Four-year Plan' in jeopardy.[37]

The work of the Four-year Plan further suffered as a result of clashes of competence with the Wehrmacht and more particularly with Schacht, the minister of economic affairs, who was also plenipotentiary for the war economy. From this conflict Göring emerged in the autumn of 1937 as at least the partial victor, after fundamental differences on the pace, financing, and intensity of rearmament had induced Schacht to resign from both his official posts. Göring, charged with the provisional performance of Schacht's duties, carried out an intra-departmental reorganization which gave him an opportunity to place persons enjoying his confidence in key positions and, at the same time, to merge certain functions of the ministry with the Four-year Plan authority before Walther Funk—state secretary in the propaganda ministry and a man loyal to Göring—received from his hand the decree appointing him Reich and Prussian minister of economic affairs and plenipotentiary for the war economy at the beginning of 1938. In theory Funk, now that he had these two positions, was confirmed in all of Schacht's former functions and powers,[38] although the Wehrmacht, appealing to Hitler's decree of 4 February 1938—under which the high command of the armed forces was in charge of 'the unified preparation of the Reich's defence in all areas'[39]—wished to assume responsibility also for economic war preparations.[40] However, as Funk was very

---

[37] Göring, 'Jahreswende', 707.

[38] Letter from Lammers to Funk, 6 Apr. 1938, *IMT* xxxvi. 281.　　　　　[39] *Schulthess 1938,* 17.

[40] Letter from the war-economy staff to department L (Landesverteidigung) of the OKW, 27 Apr. 1938, *IMT* xxxvi. 275–8.

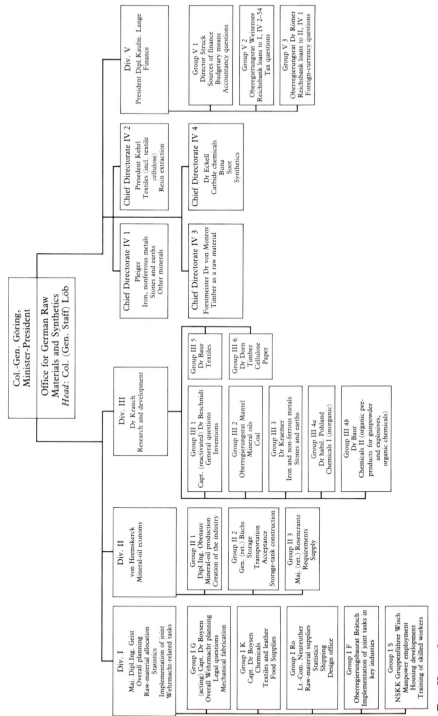

FIG. II.V.I. Organization chart of the Four-year Plan authority (as of 1 Aug. 1937).

much under Göring's influence, 'the activities of the plenipotentiary for the economy practically ceased'.[41] There remained a certain dualism between the army's war-economy staff and the Four-year Plan organization, further exacerbated by the fact that Göring, as commander-in-chief of the Luftwaffe, particularly favoured that service in rearmament matters. With Hitler's support Göring had advanced to be supreme leader of the economy, though the Wehrmacht continued to be responsible for armament production and also retained its say on weapon manufacture.

The Prussian ministry of state, headed by Göring as minister-president, functioned as the seat of the Four-year Plan organization. Following the *Gleichschaltung* of the Länder (provinces), it thus came to perform a new function. Originally all fundamental questions were to be discussed in the 'inner cabinet' (*Kleiner Ministerrat*), consisting of the war minister, the minister of finance, the minister of economic affairs, the minister of food, the Prussian minister of finance, and Special Minister Kerrl. Göring, however, succeeded quite soon in downgrading this body to a purely consultative role, especially as collective discussions ran counter to the leadership principle. The 'inner cabinet' had been set up less for economic reasons than as a concession to departmental ministers.

Greater importance attached to the 'general council', whose members were to harmonize the economic plans of the various ministries with those of the Four-year Plan, and then to ensure the implementation of these harmonized measures. It was therefore up to the general council to act as a kind of co-ordinating body and to ensure 'in day-to-day business the necessary collaboration between the various departments participating in the Four-year Plan'.[42] But this body similarly failed to cope with the problems assigned to it. Instead it developed into a once-weekly working party, where specific questions of the Four-year Plan as well as general economic matters were discussed, and where, in consequence, a lively interministerial exchange of ideas took place.

Private enterprise was able to exert a greater influence on the policy of the Four-year Plan inside the 'war-economy council' which Göring, as acting minister of economic affairs, set up within the Reich chamber of the economy at the end of January 1938. On it were 'outstanding figures' from German private enterprise, whose duty it now was to translate the decisions of the Four-year Plan into practical economic policy, in other words to 'make an all-out effort to strengthen the German economy, in order to ensure that it was equal to any demands which might be made on it for the safety of the German nation'.[43] Hitler, moreover, had urged the creation of a 'war-economy leaders' corps' as early as 1936; it was to consist of the war minister and the commanders-in-chief of the three services, as well as entrepreneurs and managers who had given meritorious service to rearmament. The

[41] Göring at the Nuremberg Military Tribunal, *IMT* ix. 288.

[42] Decree on the reorganization of the ministry of economic affairs and the continuation of the Four-year Plan, quoted from Petzina, *Autarkiepolitik*, 58.

[43] Deutsches Nachrichtenbüro (German News Agency), afternoon and evening edn., vol. v, No. 147, 31 Jan. 1938, BA R 43 II/308.

National Socialist regime expected that by such appointments, presented as a distinction, the key figures in big business would be tied more closely to the system. 'Appointment as war-economic leader places these public figures under a special obligation of loyalty to the state and the Wehrmacht', the *Völkischer Beobachter* proclaimed.[44] To ensure the implementation of the Four-year Plan with regard to trade and industry, the supervisory agencies set up earlier were now extended so as to regulate the systematic control of the flow of commodities, i.e. the acquisition and utilization of raw materials and semi-finished goods by industry and the crafts.

However, this *dirigiste* tool, suitable also for regulating the market through price and wage controls, rationing of manpower, and the distribution and allocation of raw materials and other means of production and consumer goods, did not fuse into an apparatus of economic control covering and embracing all spheres of the economy. Entrepreneurial and administrative initiative continued, outside the Four-year Plan, to enjoy relatively great latitude, revealing both the interests of various government departments and—to a limited extent—industry's striving for profit, even if not motivated by rearmament. This opportunity for harmonization of interests proved to be a corrective to administrative planning errors within the war economy; up to a point it guaranteed satisfaction of demand outside the rearmament area and thus, to a great extent, provided for the National Socialist system the social and political peace it needed. On the basis of this realization Göring, even under the Four-year Plan, and wherever this could be justified, guided the German economy on a loose rein, so that the principle of 'organized capitalism' remained on the whole intact, even if one might prefer to describe it, in terms of economic-planning categories, as 'controlled chaos'.

3. Control of Manpower, Wages, and Consumption

Whereas the initial phase of the National Socialist war economy was characterized by the endeavour to fit the large number of unemployed into the production process, the onset of the rearmament boom, even before the enactment of the Four-year Plan, revealed striking evidence of a shortage of manpower, especially in the field of skilled labour, and this operated 'directly as a seriously retarding factor in the forced rearmament drive under the Four-year Plan'.[45] By the spring of 1934 the change from a job-creation policy to one of manpower employment 'as an element of Germany's defence and war economy' had been completed.[46] Whereas the provision of jobs had previously been directed towards leading the unemployed—largely also with a view to system stabilization—towards a sufficiency of wages and bread, if necessary regardless of their training, the task now was to find for blue-collar and white-collar workers employment appropriate to their skills and experience. Laws passed in May and August 1934 created the legal prerequisites of

---

[44] *Völkischer Beobachter*, 15 Dec. 1937, quoted from *Dokumente zur deutschen Geschichte, 1936–1939*, 66.

[45] Mason, *Arbeiterklasse*, 133.

[46] Cf. the title of Trompke's doctoral thesis *Arbeitseinsatz*.

geographical manpower planning; for instance, they authorized the Reich institution for labour exchanges and unemployment insurance to stop the drift of labour from rural areas to urban and industrial ones, in order to safeguard the agricultural 'production battle'. A regulation issued on 29 December 1934, prompted by the needs of rearmament, aimed at 'safeguarding the manpower requirements of the metal industry'.[47] Likewise, before the drafting of the Four-year Plan the Reich government introduced the *Arbeitsbuch*, a worker's employment book, 'in order to ensure the efficient distribution of manpower in the German economy' and to curtail the free movement of labour, the individual's right to change his place of work.[48] Henceforward blue-collar and white-collar workers could only be given jobs if they were in possession of that *Arbeitsbuch*, which was issued by labour offices. It had to contain details of enrolment and dismissal, as well as the name of the employer. This enabled the state to practise some kind of control over the manpower situation. At an early date the National Socialist government tried to offset the manpower shortage by a better utilization of what were now called the *Gefolgschaft*, the staff or 'retinue', of an enterprise. By mid-1934 a regulation came into force which authorized the labour trustees to extend the daily working hours in vital rearmament enterprises beyond the statutory eight-hour day. Every employer was henceforward entitled to have supplementary work done, in accordance with his own judgement, on thirty days in a year.[49]

In addition to the extension of working hours, after 1935 there was also an increasingly intensive utilization of labour and a saving of manpower through mechanization and rationalization of production processes, e.g. through conveyor belts. In the consumer-goods industry, on the other hand, the aim was a shortening of hours and hence a reduction of wages. In this way it was intended to induce those working in this branch of the economy to switch over, in increasing numbers, to the producer-goods industry. Between 1933 and 1936 there was in fact an increase in the performance of industrial workers, varying according to the individual industry's importance to rearmament (see Table II.v.2).

By 1936 the above measures were no longer sufficient, especially in the metallurgical and construction sectors, where considerable shortages occurred. As the implementation of the Four-year Plan demanded an optimal exploitation of Germany's manpower, the Four-year Plan organization now assumed control of employment in order to meet the manpower needs of important governmental and economic projects. This control began (on 7 November 1936) by making it a duty of the iron, metallurgical, and construction industries to train apprentices, 'whose number must be in an appropriate ratio to that of . . . the skilled workers employed'.[50] As for the problem of skilled labour itself, an attempt was made to solve it by means of enlistment controls, prohibition of enticement, etc., but this did

---

[47] Cf. Petzina, *Autarkiepolitik*, 158.

[48] Law of 26 Feb. 1935, *RGBl.* (1935), i. 311. On labour legislation and the labour constitution cf. Kranig, *Lockung und Zwang*.

[49] Decree on the amended version of the ordinance on working hours, 26 July 1934, *RGBl.* (1934), i. 803.

[50] *Reichsanzeiger* (Reich Gazette), 626 (9 Nov. 1936).

TABLE II.v.2. *The performance of an employed industrial worker 1932–1936*
(1932 = 100)

	Industry overall	Armaments industry		Consumer industry	
		Iron and steel	Vehicles	Textiles	Foodstuffs
1933	101	115	135	109	99
1934	102	130	145	104	96
1935	107	143	163	96	98
1936	110	149	173	103	96

Source: Böhm, *Entwicklung*, 113.

not prevent a painful manpower shortage towards the end of 1937, because of the raised production targets of the Four-year Plan. It was further aggravated by the colossal demand on the part of the firms involved in the construction of the Westwall.

Suddenly there was an increased demand not only for industrial workers but also for building workers, in particular for skilled bricklayers. In the autumn of 1937 against 450,000 employed bricklayers there were a mere 110 temporarily unemployed ones, evidence that the manpower potential in this occupation was fully exhausted. To remedy the shortage of underground construction workers it became the practice to enlist unemployed bakers, butchers, barbers, printers, and textile- and leather-workers, but their performance, outside their own skills, naturally proved unsatisfactory. Unemployment among skilled metal-workers was in some cases below 100: in the autumn of 1937 it was 41 for lathe operators, 42 for machine-tool makers, and 25 for precision engineers.[51] Any relaxation of the labour market, any reduction in over-employment, was out of the question for the Berlin rulers unless they wished to renounce their political programme. The German Labour Front did not conceal from its members among the workforce what, in political terms, this was all about and what was expected of them: as the Labour Front explained, the Third Reich was

endeavouring to replace by intensified work the space and the goods now denied to it. If, for instance, it is necessary instead of high-grade foreign ore to smelt inferior domestic ore, then a greater number of working hours must quite simply be expended in order to produce the same amount of iron. If, furthermore, it is necessary artificially, by means of complicated chemical and industrial processes, to produce petroleum and the products obtained from it, which elsewhere are obtained from nature with only a slight effort, then this too means an increased investment of labour, just as do all efforts to extract higher yields from our limited arable land . . . If, therefore, Germany has to expend an increased amount of labour, then it

[51] Syrup, 'Maßnahmen zur Regelung', 144.

is obvious that the demands made on our workers become the greater the more determined our nation is not to lag behind the other nations of the world in its standard of living and military equipment.[52]

In the summer of 1938 Göring therefore found himself compelled to regulate the supply of manpower for politically important tasks by a decree of 22 June which provided for mandatory employment over limited periods.[53] In practice—and this was not even publicly denied in Germany—this meant 'a far-reaching curtailment of the free movement of labour',[54] designed to ensure the optimal utilization of human labour for the purpose of rearmament. 'Since the enactment of the Four-year Plan and of mandatory employment' the attempt was being made to solve 'the question of manpower employment in the economic and military sphere from the point of view of total militarization and the definitive economic safeguarding of the Reich'.[55]

Just as in the area of employment, there was also a close link between the Four-year Plan and price and wage policy. The overburdening of production capacities by rearmament orders and the resulting shortages of raw materials and manpower naturally entailed a danger of price and wage increases. If the state was to be able to calculate the costs of rearmament in the long term, National Socialist 'price policy could not be denied considerable defence-policy importance'. The government, above all, had to ensure a relative stability of prices and a balance between wages and prices in order to forestall inflationary trends. Generally speaking, a price was to be aimed at which would 'meet the general economic purposes of the Four-year Plan, i.e. the achievement of economic freedom and independence in peace as in war, while at the same time improving all the prerequisites of productivity'.[56] Although there had been state supervision of prices since 1931, this had been confined to corrective intervention. In the phase of direct economic preparations for war the National Socialist regime now switched to a policy of active price formation. In consequence, the Reich commissioner for price control, appointed by the law of 29 October 1936 and under the authority of the Four-year Plan, was charged with the supervision of prices 'of goods and services of every kind, especially everyday needs, throughout the field of agricultural, craft, and industrial production, and [with overseeing] traffic in commodities and goods of every kind, as well as other remunerations'.[57] At the end of November 1936 the most drastic price-policy measure was enacted: a price freeze, which became the starting-point for future policy aimed at what was called an 'economically fair price'.[58] Such a price was arrived at 'when the separate economic groups' part-shares in the final price' were in line with 'the value of their performance for the national economy'.[59] In

---

[52] *Jahrbuch 1939*, i. 82–3.
[53] *RGBl.* (1938), i. 652.
[54] Trompke, *Arbeitseinsatz*, 109.
[55] Ibid. 110.
[56] Meinhold, 'Volkswirtschaftliche Grundsätze', 572.
[57] *RGBl.* (1936), i. 927.
[58] Ibid. 955.
[59] Meinhold, 'Volkswirtschaftliche Grundsätze', 587.

practice this meant that an attempt had to be made to calculate and establish the price on the basis of costs by applying a number of directives and regulations. This was done primarily to fix the prices of orders by the state, where directives regulated the manner of cost-definition and prescribed calculation and profit-margins; these were then reflected also in price-formation in the private area. In this way the intended stabilization of price levels was largely successful: between 1934 and 1939 the cost-of-living index rose by a mere 5 per cent, while the wholesale-price index for industrial manufactured goods and rearmament-related means of production actually showed a slight decline. The overall wholesale-price index rose by only 8 per cent over that period—only a little over 1 per cent annually.

The rearmament-oriented price control outlined above would have remained ineffective without a parallel wages policy. Wages, after all, were a particularly important cost factor in the war economy. As with all other economic measures, those concerning wage policy also had to relate to 'the recovery of the political freedom and the remilitarization of the German people'.[60] In consequence, the wage structure in the National Socialist state reflected a wage policy that was designed to 'serve the rebuilding of the German economy and . . . the rearmament of the Wehrmacht'.[61]

Put differently: stable wages meant stable prices, and these benefited primarily the state as the purchaser of armaments. To the National Socialists this meant that 'wages as such had to be kept stable, so that, by and large, no general changes in wage levels could be tolerated'.[62]

There were also cyclical reasons for avoiding, as far as possible, any excessive rise in wages because this would have inevitably resulted in an increased demand for consumer goods—something to be avoided. After all, as Schacht made clear in 1938, 'the less is consumed, the more work can be expended on rearmament. The higher consumption rises, on the other hand, the more manpower has to be left in consumer-good manufacture. Standard of living and scale of rearmament are therefore in an inverse ratio. The less I consume the more I save, and the more I save the more I can put into rearmament.'[63] Rearmament priorities therefore demanded a shift from the manufacture of consumer goods to that of production and rearmament goods. Because ever since 1933 rearmament had been swallowing up a growing proportion of the national revenue, the public's purchasing power had to be restricted in order to limit demand for consumer goods and prevent any attempts to raise living standards; thus, raw materials, capital, and foreign currency could be channelled predominantly into heavy industry. 'Rearmament . . . demanded a postponement of an extension of consumer-goods production in favour of the production of rearmament items, and thus from the very outset resulted in a limited consumer market, which, moreover, shrank further as consumption tended to increase.'[64]

---

[60] Seldte, *Sozialpolitik*, 23.
[61] Mansfeld, 'Grundsätze', 30.
[62] Seldte, *Sozialpolitik*, 24.
[63] Schacht, *'Finanzwunder'*, 11.
[64] Mansfeld, 'Grundsätze', 30.

This was best achieved by a wage freeze, which actually succeeded at the beginning of National Socialist rule, when a large number of unemployed waited to be absorbed into the production process. However, as the first shortages appeared in the labour market the wage freeze was circumvented not only by employers wishing to keep their workers or to enlist new ones, but also by the German Labour Front, which was anxious to consolidate and extend its position within the National Socialist oligarchy. The increased demands made on production by the Four-year Plan after August 1936 triggered off a wave of across-the-board wage increases. Workers, realizing their new market value, tried to exploit the (to them) favourable situation, while employers realized that the new production targets set for them could be reached only by wage incentives or by additional manpower, which in turn could as a rule only be attracted by tempting wage levels.

This trend proved exceedingly dangerous to the rearmament economy. Enticement of workers was most marked in the sectors which had been suffering from a manpower shortage anyway, such as agriculture and the export industries. Their output suddenly seemed at risk, which was tantamount to a loss or increased expenditure of foreign currency, and hence to diminished imports of goods and raw materials vital to rearmament. The public's purchasing power increased,[65] resulting in a marked growth over a short period in consumer-goods production to the detriment of rearmament, as well as in wage rises in the consumer industry. In 1936 the average annual rise in income in the consumer-goods industry—6.5 per cent, compared with 4.5 per cent for the rest of industry—was higher than anywhere else.[66] This situation changed as the Four-year Plan came into effect. After the beginning of 1937 order-books in the production-goods industry filled at such a rate that wage rises were now being caused 'mainly by the industries directly or indirectly connected with rearmament'. In the spring of 1937 the German average wage was approximately 8 per cent[67] and weekly income approximately 19 per cent above the figures for the autumn of 1933.[68] After that date the wage differentials between the industries working for production goods and rearmament on the one hand and the consumer-goods industry on the other began to widen. Industrial peace and the stability of the ruling system seemed threatened. Added to this was a trial of strength between the wage-freeze supporters—the trustees of labour, the minister of labour, and Göring—on the one side, and the German Labour Front, agitating in favour of the wage-earners, on the other. This conflict Göring succeeded in settling in his favour. In the course of 1937 the shaping of wage policy became the responsibility of the Four-year Plan.

Two possible ways of halting the rise in wages offered themselves: first, a ban on changing one's place of work, which would put a stop to attracting workers by high wage incentives, and second, a restrictive wage policy operating with fixed

[65] Mason, *Arbeiterklasse*, 113.
[66] Report of Reich statistical office on the trend of real work-earnings in 1936, ibid. 239.
[67] In Dec. 1936 7.3%.
[68] Report of Reich statistical office on the trend of real work-earnings in the first quarter of 1937, Mason, *Arbeiterklasse*, 312.

minimum and maximum wages. Both roads were chosen, though not with complete consistency. Although the commissioner for the Four-year Plan issued a number of decrees which made enlistment of new workers as well as changing one's place of work—especially in the iron, metal-working, and chemical industries and in construction—subject to approval by the labour office concerned, these regulations, despite the fines and prison sentences threatened in the event of violation, had no great effect and scarcely contributed to a solution to the problem. 'The offer of dazzling wages and fantastic salaries on the one hand, and the enforced raising of existing piece-rates without extra pay, the refusal . . . of disciplined work, all the way to the deliberate manufacture of rejects in order to get out of an existing employment contract'—these were 'no rarity in the factories'.[69]

The systematic implementation of rearmament would be called in question if 'enterprises, guided by their own interests and often against the interests of the community, entice workers away from one another, denude important plants, and, contrary to the Führer's orders, start a wave of across-the-board wage increases, which only give rise to grave social tensions and most seriously endanger the existing wage structure'.[70] Hourly earnings continued to rise steadily during 1937. By December they were 0.8 per cent above the September figure and 2.6 per cent above that for the previous December.[71] Although the authorities responsible—e.g. the ministry of labour, the Reich institution for labour exchanges, and the Reich trustees of labour—vigorously deplored the unwelcome trend in wages and employment, they were 'patently unable to call a halt to it'. In mid-January they agreed 'to use all suitable means to prevent a further wage rise that was not based on a particular performance but on the economic boom and the shortage of skilled workers'. Whereas past regulations only provided for the fixing of minimum wages, there was now a determination also to put an upper limit on work emoluments and to intervene with mandatory regulations 'wherever a tendency was observed that threatened to be detrimental to the implementation . . . of rearmament'.[72] The prerequisites for direct state intervention in wage formation, however, were created only by the decree of 22 June 1938. Henceforth the Reich trustees and the newly appointed special trustees of labour had to monitor wages and working conditions in general and to take all measures necessary 'to prevent any impairment of militarization or of the implementation of the Four-year Plan by wage trends or other working conditions'. Finally, they were authorized to set 'mandatory upper and lower wage limits'.[73]

However, these measures mostly remained on paper. Lacking a bureaucratic apparatus of their own, the trustees of labour were not in a position to put them into

[69] Report of war-economy inspectorate VI to the war-economy staff, 2 Sept. 1938, Mason, *Arbeiterklasse*, 275.

[70] Letter from the commissioner for price control to the Four-year Plan commissioner, 12 Dec. 1937, ibid. 750.

[71] Report of Reich statistical office on the trend of real work-earnings in the fourth quarter of 1937, ibid. 412.

[72] Letter from the Reich and Prussian minister of labour to the Four-year Plan commissioner, 21 Jan. 1938, ibid. 757.

[73] Decree on wages, 26 June 1938, *RGBl.* (1938), i. 691.

effect. Instead they confined themselves to spot-checks and exemplary fines, which remained relatively ineffective. It is not surprising, then, that during the first twelve months following the enactment of the decree the rate of wage rises was even higher than during the preceding period. Hourly wages in industry rose by an average of 5 per cent, and weekly wages between June 1938 and June 1939 by approximately 9 per cent.[74] Until the outbreak of war the regime no longer had wage development under control, even though it lagged behind the increased performance of the workers. As the National Socialist regime frankly admitted, 'the reconstruction of the Wehrmacht and economy . . . was made possible by the renunciation of many hopes in the field of wage policy';[75] see Table II.v.3.[76]

Curtailment and control of consumption in favour of rearmament production have to be seen as fundamental pillars of the National Socialist war economy. Both were practicable, up to a point, by means of a price and wage policy. But ultimately only direct control of public consumption, as well as of industry, could hold out any hope of satisfactory results. Yet before 1939 the National Socialist rulers were reluctant—in the interests of keeping the system stable—to apply this radical measure. They confined themselves to attempts to redirect demand from scarce goods to those in plentiful supply, to measures ensuring preferential use of domestic products, in order to relieve the foreign-currency balance for importing goods vital to rearmament, and to the attempted replacement of high-quality goods by those of inferior quality.

These endeavours, affecting mainly the area of foodstuffs, were further intensified after the proclamation of the Four-year Plan: 'Nutrition should, as a matter of principle, focus on the products of German soil and adjust to the seasonal pattern of production and harvest'.[77] The government contented itself with an indirect control of consumption through import controls, but largely also relied on vigorous propaganda. This was based on monthly recommendations, compiled after 1937 by a working party for consumption control set up within the Four-year Plan; the Wehrmacht was represented on it with a vote, and stood up for its interests. Only in the area of fat supplies, because of the high degree of dependence on imports, was direct control of consumption practised by the state.

Outside the food sector there were efforts, largely of an educational character, to influence consumption in the home and in small industrial enterprises. Special importance was attached to freeing German synthetics of their reputation as ersatz substances and upgrading them by calling them 'German materials'.

4. AGRICULTURAL AND FOOD POLICY

If, as Hitler declared, the Four-year Plan aimed at 'nothing less than the economic and military strengthening of the Reich',[78] then special efforts were called for in

[74] Cf. Mason, *Arbeiterklasse*, 155. [75] Mansfeld, 'Grundsätze', 31.
[76] On the problem of labour in the Third Reich cf. the case study by Yano, *Hüttenarbeiter*, which, apart from its specific subject, is of fundamental importance. [77] Moritz, 'Ergänzungen', 117.
[78] Speech by Hitler, contents reproduced in report by the war-economy staff on the economic situation, 1 Feb. 1937, BA-MA RW 19/84.

TABLE II.v.3. *Wages policy in the Third Reich*

	Wages[a]						Official cost-of-living index[a]	Undistributed profits of earning associations as % of national revenue	Gross wages[b]		
	Nominal hourly		Effective hourly	Effective weekly		As % of national income			Engineering	Foodstuffs	Clothing
	Contract	Effective		Nominal	Real						
	1	2	3	4	5	6	7	8	9	10	11
1929	122	133		149	118	56.6	128				
1932	100	100	100	100	100	57.0	100				
1933	97	97	99	102	104	56.0	98	0.5	100	100	100
1934	97	99	99	110	109	55.0	100	1.4	113	101	96
1935	97	101	100	112	110	54.6	102	2.6	118	101	91
1936	97	102	101	117	112	53.5	103	3.6	120	101	96
1937	97	105	104	121	115	52.7	104	3.9	122	102	95
1938	97	108	107	126	119	52.4	104	4.9			
1939	98	111		131	123	51.8	105				

[a] 1932 = 100.
[b] 1933 = 100.

Sources (by column): (1)–(6) Petzina, *Autarkiepolitik*, 167; (7) Bry, *Wages*, 255; (8) Andexel, *Imperialismus*, 94; (9) Kuczynski, *Darstellung*, 103; (10)–(11) ibid. 171–2.

agricultural policy, since safeguarding the country's food supplies was a preliminary of any war preparations. Even though the Four-year Plan had 'in fact begun in agriculture in 1934, with the production battle',[79] the target set in 1936, of eliminating the possibility of Germany being starved out in any future war, was not in fact reached.[80] On the contrary, the precarious food-supply situation was one aspect of the general economic crisis of 1936. The high degree of Germany's dependence on imports of certain foodstuffs and animal feed made the risk of war appear even more serious. Neither the shift of imports from overseas to south-east Europe nor Germany's efforts at autarky at home had yet produced the hoped-for results in terms of assured food supplies; not only were no emergency stockpiles set up in 1936, but existing ones had already to be drawn upon (Table II.v.4).

TABLE II.v.4. *German foodstuff reserves 1935–1939* (1,000 t.)

	1935	1936	1937	1938	1939
Bread-grain	5,697	5,021	3,082	4,400	9,136
Fodder-grain	2,871	2,890	3,711	4,216	5,593
Potatoes	14,748	12,083	13,743	16,665	15,461
Sugar	1,009	1,027	1,085	1,455	1,410
Vegetable oils and fats	310	147	132	216	472
Oil-cake	223	204	259	331	487
Grease and lard	6	7	16	13	14

Source: Wartime nutrition plan of the Nutritional Research Centre (German Academy of Agricultural Sciences); table from Herferth, *Reichsnährstand*, 239.

It seemed an obvious step, therefore, to assign to agricultural policy a special priority position within the Four-year Plan; this led to the incorporation of the Reichsnährstand (Reich Foodstuffs Corporation) into Göring's institution.

From the beginning of 1937 the state had been using a guidance system in agriculture which was in fact a package of educational work, loans, and, on a limited scale, price incentives. A regular advisory and educational campaign was launched, which, though sporadically employed in 1934–5, systematically informed and instructed the farming community on the tasks and means of the production battle—on the correct use of the soil and on livestock keeping—emphasizing that activities should be restricted to the cultivation and production of absolutely vital

[79] Herbert Backe, 'Bauerntum und Vierjahresplan', 14, quoted from Schwichtenberg, *Erzeugungsschlacht*, 24.
[80] Ibid.

products, with the ultimate objective of achieving a high degree of self-sufficiency. At the same time, Darré, the Reich agricultural leader, issued an appeal on 23 March 1937 for an 'efficiency contest of the German rural community', which would be an incentive to every farmer to 'do his duty towards the people and the state'.[81] These measures were accompanied by price cuts for fertilizers and higher prices for agricultural produce to be delivered to storage. Reduced-rate loans were made available for the purchase of farm machinery, and finally the National Socialist regime did not even shrink from administrative compulsion: the 'decree for safeguarding agriculture' (23 March 1937)[82] authorized the commissioner for the Four-year Plan to prescribe the crops to be grown wherever an owner of agricultural land had not been guided in his cropping plan by the principle of 'safeguarding the nation's food supply'. The idea was to extend the arable acreage at the expense of grazing and pasture, with an eye to planting crops yielding textile fibres and fats, as well as cattle-feed, in order to relieve the foreign-currency balance. This attempt failed, however. All that was achieved was a shift of emphasis in arable crops (Table II.v.5).

TABLE II.v.5. *Cultivated area per farming year (1928–1939)* (1,000 ha.)

	1928	1933	1934	1935	1936	1937	1938	1939
Rape-seed	16.8	5.2	26.7	47.0	54.6	49.9	61.9	46.7
Flax	14.5	4.9	8.8	22.3	44.1	56.9	44.9	83.2
Hemp	0.8	0.2	0.4	3.6	5.6	7.5	12.7	20.3
Maize-grain	2.1	3.7	16.3	15.8	19.3	38.3	65.8	27.6
Sugar-beet	454.0	304.0	357.0	373.0	389.0	455.0	502.0	537.0
Winter barley	183.0	271.0	307.0	388.0	436.0	439.0	517.0	329.0
Lucerne	285.0	315.0	319.0	369.0	404.0	418.0	412.0	409.0
Lupins	46.0	53.2	57.3	61.6	81.7	98.6	101.6	77.1

Source: Petzina, *Autarkiepolitik*, 93.

Simultaneously an effort was made by the state to tackle the seemingly insoluble problem of a shortage of farm labour. On the one hand it was conceded that, but for the drift of manpower from the countryside into the towns, rearmament could 'not have been carried out as quickly or as completely'[83] as it had been. On the other hand the withdrawal of manpower from agriculture had begun to jeopardize the targets of the 'production battle' as early as 1938.[84]

Ever since 1933 there had been a marked and permanent drop in rural manpower. By 1939 it amounted to approximately 1.4 million, though it should be remembered

[81] Quoted from Schwichtenberg, *Erzeugungsschlacht*, 27.
[82] *RGBl.* (1937), i. 422–3.
[83] *Leipziger Neueste Nachrichten*, 20 Nov. 1940.
[84] State Secretary Backe at the Sixth Farmers' Rally (1938), in *NS-Landpost*, 2 Dec. 1938.

that this downward trend, especially on large estates, was due to a decline in the number of itinerant foreign workers. Along with the drift of regular agricultural workers into industry, another factor in the decline of the manpower potential was an increasing reluctance by the members of a farmer's family to supplement the labour of the head of their household (Table II.v.6).[85]

TABLE II.v.6. *The agricultural work-force 1907–1939*[a] (000s)

	1907	1925	1933	1939
Unit leaders and family members:				
Permanent	6,539	8,919		8,085
Non-permanent	2,485	2,126		707
TOTAL	9,024	11,045	10,208	8,793
External manpower				
Permanent	2,148	2,306	2,055	1,956
Non-permanent	1,720	987	812	849
TOTAL	3,868	3,293	2,867	2,805
GRAND TOTAL	12,892	14,338	13,075	11,597

[a] Within the Reich frontiers of 1919.

Source: Rolfes, 'Landwirtschaft', 753.

In order to cope with the manpower shortage (by the end of March 1937 there were 97,000 vacancies in agriculture and only 8,600 fully employable unemployed),[86] a generous housing programme was launched,[87] but owing to insufficient allocations of building materials this was only partially implemented. In addition, the Landdienst (rural service) of the Hitler Youth became a regular and essential part of agricultural manpower;[88] likewise, the Reich Labour Service, intended to comprise some 300,000 members by April 1939, was predominantly employed in agriculture, especially in what was called the Landeskulturwerk (land-cultivation scheme), whose list of tasks included bringing some 21m. hectares of new land under the plough or making used acreage more productive.[89]

[85] It is worth noting that the performance of agricultural enterprises was maintained to a considerable extent by the fact that the family members of independent farmers increasingly took the place of foreign labour. Whereas in 1933 some 48% of persons gainfully employed in independent agricultural enterprises consisted of family members, the figure by 1939 was 53.5%. Cf. Petzina *et al.*, *Sozialgeschichtliches Arbeitsbuch*, iii. 57.

[86] Mangels, 'Facharbeitermangel', 350.

[87] Cf. Syrup, 'Maßnahmen zur Versorgung', 209.

[88] For 1934 alone a sum of RM44m. was made available.

[89] *Der Vierjahresplan*, i (1937), 222.

Collectively, all these measures had a definitely beneficial effect on agricultural production. In important areas, e.g. bread-grain, pulses, eggs, and fats, there was a marked increase in production. But this bore no relation to the material or financial input. By 1938 experts were doubtful about the possibility of still further stepping up agricultural production. It was feared that 'limits would emerge in the course of the production battle', due to 'the operation of the law of diminishing returns and a deterioration in the ratio of the prices of farm produce and production costs'. It was no secret that farming enterprises found themselves compelled by the shortage of manpower to pay above-tariff wages without being able to recover these increased costs in their prices, as these were fixed by the state. In view of these circumstances the moment was rapidly approaching, or had possibly even arrived, 'when a further production increase . . . would no longer strengthen but rather weaken the economic viability of farm enterprises'.[90] Besides, as production increased, so, thanks to all-round improved wages, did consumption. Whatever success the policy of safeguarding foodstuffs may have achieved—the degree of self-sufficiency in respect of basic foodstuffs showed a continuous rise until 1939—was gained at the expense of renouncing a broad spectrum of foodstuffs, especially from abroad (Table II.v.7).

TABLE II.v.7. *Home-grown supplies of major foodstuffs*
1927/8–1938/9 (av. %)

	1927/8	1933/4	1938/9
Bread-grain	79	99	115
Pulses[a]	62	50	71
Potatoes	96	100	100
Vegetables	84	90	91
Sugar	100	99	101
Meat	91	98	97
Eggs	64	80	82
Fat	44	53	57
TOTAL AVERAGE	68	80	83

[a] Except lentils.

Source: Petzina, *Autarkiepolitik*, 95.

It proved impossible, however, to meet civilian and Wehrmacht requirements without agricultural imports: between the launch of the Four-year Plan and the outbreak of war these imports increased regularly by approximately 50 per cent in volume, and thus accounted for some 40 per cent of all imports. In detail, and with

[90] State Secretary Backe on the situation in agriculture; supplement to report of war-economy staff on the economic situation, 1 Feb. 1938, BA-MA RW 19/93.

regard to certain years, the food-supply situation must have appeared totally unsatisfactory from a war-economy point of view. In the spring of 1937, for instance, the supply situation was so difficult that, 'as a bridging operation until the next harvest the major part of foreign currency acquired in a special way'—this was revenue from exports of war material—had to be expended.[91] In the budget year 1937/8 there were still 'no national reserves for the event of full mobilization', and the Wehrmacht judged 'the prospects for making a start on stockpiling', even with imported produce, to be 'slight' in the area of fats, where the shortage was particularly serious.[92] Here the gap amounted to 40–50 per cent. It undoubtedly represented the most serious strain on German food supplies, which was why the National Socialist regime decided to draft a 'fat plan', which would regulate production, processing, importation, and consumption. Its principal objective was to urge the public to use more domestic fats, such as rape-oil and butter, in order to save foreign currency. See Table II.v.8.

TABLE II.v.8. *Butter production and consumption 1928–1940* (1,000 t.)

	Consumption	Net imports	Domestic production		
			Farm butter	Dairy butter	Total
1928–32	500.0	113.0	187.0	200.0	387.0
1933	507.6	59.1	195.0	253.4	448.5
1934	513.0	61.8	170.0	281.2	451.2
1935	523.0	71.0	140.0	312.0	452.0
1936	571.5	75.4	112.5	383.6	496.1
1937	603.7	86.8	100.0	416.9	516.9
1938	600.0	92.4	97.5	410.1	507.6
1939	638.3	90.6	34.5	463.2	597.7
1940	756.7	129.7	54.0	573.0	627.0

Source: Checiński, 'Umstellung', 331.

There was, in addition, a second problem with agricultural supply which was of considerable concern to the regime, the shortage of animal feed, which directly affected the Wehrmacht. In view of the chronic shortage of oats it found itself compelled to feed more barley to its horses. Even so, some 30 per cent of fodder-

[91] Note on conference of the commanders-in-chief with the war minister, 13 Apr. 1937, BA-MA Wi I F 5/1196. For the principal types of cereals, potatoes, and sugar-beet an increase in yields had been achieved between 1934 and 1938, especially through increased application of fertilizers, at least by comparison with the middle and late 1920s. However, the average yields for the harvest years 1939 to 1944 again showed a decline. Throughout the period of National Socialist rule the average levels of 1909–13 were never achieved. Cf. Petzina *et al.*, *Sozialgeschichtliches Arbeitsbuch*, iii. 60, table b.
[92] War-economy staff survey of the food situation 1937–8, 1 Jan. 1938, BA-MA RW 19/86.

cereals still had to be imported in 1938. The overall cereal yield in 1939 was only marginally above the figure for 1913. Thus, 'neither the war-economy goal of the Four-year Plan—independence in the event of war—nor the trade-policy goal—redressing of the foreign-currency balance—was attained'.[93] Towards the end of 1937 the minister of food and agriculture presented a gloomy prospect of the future—entirely in line with what was actually to happen—by pointing to the dangers threatening agriculture from the raw-material and manpower situations. In his opinion 'not only could no improvement be expected in either direction during 1938, but an exacerbation of the situation must be feared. 'The production battle', in consequence, 'could not only not be maintained on the scale that might be possible and would be desirable, but it could not even be seen through.'[94] The National Socialist regime therefore hoped to approach the safeguarding of the food supplies needed for war by means of military expansion in 1938–9. The prerequisite was 'an all-out effort' in the agricultural sector, 'in order to rearm German industry and the German army for the Führer in the shortest possible time'.[95]

5. THE FOUR-YEAR PLAN AND INDUSTRIAL MOBILIZATION

Given that both the Wehrmacht and the economy were, according to Hitler's directive, to be ready for war within a four-year period, it would have been necessary to base the Four-year Plan upon exactly calculated requirements, to be seen as overall production targets but allowing priority to rearmament. In point of fact the Reich statistical office had carried out a survey in 1936, embracing 300 branches of industry with 180,000 firms and recording 'work-force composition according to sex, age, and training, as well as consumption of raw materials, ancillary materials, fuel and power for production purposes, performance capacity, domestic and foreign sales, and stocks of materials and finished goods at the beginning and the end of the year'.[96] The data thus obtained served as the basis of a plan for 1938; this, however, had to be modified repeatedly and eventually amounted to little more than a guideline. One reason was that the figures demanded by the Wehrmacht services in the event of mobilization, as also the requirement totals established by the plenipotentiary for the war economy, were notably imprecise. Another reason was that the key figures referred to rearmament and civilian consumption in 1936, and therefore failed to take into account not only the increase in consumption due to growing mass earnings but also the increased consumption of raw materials and manpower due to the extension or development

---

[93] Petzina, *Autarkiepolitik*, 95.

[94] Report by Darré on the harvest and food-supply situation, Nov. 1937, BA-MA Wi I F 5/695.

[95] Remark by Darré, quoted from Melzer, *Studien*, 22. Grundmann, *Agrarpolitik*, has pointed out the conflict, to which National Socialist agricultural and food policy were exposed, between ideological demands and military-political and military-economic necessity. The intentions and problems associated with the law on farm inheritance show that an anti-modernist 'peasant' ideology was unable, under the pressure of the armament needs of a modern expansion-oriented industrial country, to meet the foodstuff requirements of a society preparing for war.

[96] Report at the end of 1937 on preparations for economic mobilization by the plenipotentiary for the war economy, *IMT* xxxvi. 253.

of production capacities, which alone could ensure the implementation of the Four-year Plan. Flawed as it was by these imponderables, the Four-year Plan inevitably required improvisation and continuous intervention by the state, to a degree far in excess of what had originally been expected.

Regardless of frequent changes in target figures, the Four-year Plan laid down two industrial priority areas: (1) the intensive extraction and processing of domestic raw materials in the sectors of coal, iron and steel, non-ferrous metals, electricity, and petroleum; (2) the expansion of the chemical industry in connection with the manufacture of Buna, synthetic motor-fuel, and fibre materials. Hitler's personal expectations were particularly high in the last two areas. On 29 April 1937, to thunderous applause, he declared to senior party officials at the castle of Vogelsang in the Eifel: 'We shall complete our first two gigantic Buna factories this very winter, and with them we shall meet our entire rubber requirements. By next year we shall meet our total motor-fuel requirements from our own production.'[97]

The boosting of industrial production largely depended on the extension of basic industries, especially coal-mining, as coal was not only a source of power but also the raw material for synthetic substances. Mineral oils were acquiring growing importance. Next in importance came the safeguarding of food supplies and the development of the network of waterways and of shipbuilding, as a prerequisite of an efficient German transport system linked to the rest of central and south-east Europe. Further investment priorities were the chemical industry and power generation. See Table II.v.9.

The Four-year Plan saw the continuation of the endeavours—which had been going on since 1933—to make Germany self-sufficient in mineral oil, both through an intensification of German crude-oil extraction and through extension of the filtration process. As by 1936 the proportion of synthetic motor-fuel already amounted to approximately 30 per cent, governmental and industrial leaders at first believed that Hitler's directive—to make Germany independent of foreign mineral oils within the next eighteen months—could be implemented. The tight situation in raw materials and manpower, however, gave rise to considerable delays in the development of the necessary industrial plant, so that the production target envisaged for 1938 (Table II.v.10) was nowhere near reached.

It is true that a considerable increase of German mineral-oil production from domestic raw materials was recorded under the Four-year Plan. Petroleum production had gone up by approximately 63 per cent, while the output from hydrogenation plants showed an increase of approximately 69 per cent—though this should be viewed as the result of extensions of capacity effected before the proclamation of the Four-year Plan. It should also be borne in mind that mineral-oil consumption had risen by some 24 per cent between 1936 and 1939. Altogether, Germany's dependence on foreign mineral oil by 1939 amounted to just under 50 per cent, so that Hitler's time-limit of eighteen months for self-sufficency eventually had to be extended until 1940. See Table II.v.11.

[97] BA tape-recording F 2a-EW 67207–672245.

Production of synthetic rubber (Buna) also lagged behind the planned targets—for technological as well as economic reasons. The material was developed by IG-Farben in 1927, but intensive testing had been made impossible by its high production costs. An agreement made in 1935 between the chemical concern and

TABLE II.v.9. *Distribution of investment 1937[a] (%)*

	Plan II[b]	Plan III[c]	Plan IV[d]
Mineral oil	16.7	22.6	28.3
Buna rubber	6.0	7.8	6.9
Other chemicals	27.3	12.5	8.2
Waterways, ports, and shipbuilding	21.2	17.8	16.0
Base metals	4.1	3.6	3.7
Iron and steel	2.7	5.1	3.8
Textiles	4.0	5.1	5.1
Food	3.1	7.3	16.0
Coal	0.5	2.2	2.1
Energy	11.0	13.3	7.6
Timber	1.0	0.3	0.7
Machines and technical products	2.3	2.2	0.8
Leather and guts	0.1	0.2	0.1
Housing	—	—	0.7

[a] Plan I (15 Oct. 1936) has not so far been found in archives.
[b] 10 Jan. 1937.
[c] 27 May 1937.
[d] 31 Dec. 1937.

Source: Petzina, *Autarkiepolitik*, 83.

TABLE II.v.10. *Mineral-oil programme for 1938 under the Four-year Plan[a] (1,000 t.)*

	Total production	Motor-fuel	Aviation fuel	Diesel oil	Heating oil	Lubricating oil	Paraffin
Estimated requirement	4,990.0	2,675.0	80	1,200.0	550.0	485	—
Envisaged production	5,482.8	3,003.5	80	1,115.1	599.2	485	200

[a] Overall plan of 27 May 1937 (adjusted to 1938 requirements).

Source: Birkenfeld, *Treibstoff*, 230.

TABLE II.v.11. *Production and consumption of mineral-oil products 1937–1939 (1,000 t.)*

	Crude-oil extraction	Production of synthetic fuel	Mineral-oil consumption	
	I	2	3	4
1937	451	852.9	3,507	5,080
1938	552	1,056.0	4,287	6,150
1939	741	1,434.1	4,365	

Sources (by column): (1) *Taschenkalender für den Bergbau*, 243; (2) *Deutsche Mineralölwirtschaft*, 624, 627; (3) *Statistisches Handbuch*, 501; (4) Birkenfeld, *Treibstoff*, 218 (though his data come from diverse documents and altogether err on the high side).

Hitler's Raw Materials Commissioner Keppler on the construction of a plant producing 200 tonnes of Buna per month was scuttled both by the ministry of economic affairs—because of the unfavourable price-gap between synthetic and natural rubber—and by the Wehrmacht, which made purchase of major quantities of tyres subject to more prolonged series of tests. Eventually, thanks to the joint efforts of Göring and the IG-Farben managing director Krauch, mass production of Buna was launched through state-guaranteed purchases and credits, and through compulsory financial participation by the tyre industry in the development and extension of the factories concerned. Difficulties in obtaining the necessary materials again caused delays in plant construction, so that reaching the targets (Table II.v.12) by 1938 was out of the question.

In 1938 the target figure of 29,000 t. had to be set against a mere 5,000 t. of actual production, or approximately 5 per cent of German domestic consumption. A year later Buna production amounted to roughly one-quarter of the target under the Four-year Plan. Not until 1942 did the decisive breakthrough in production occur.

TABLE II.v.12. *Planned Buna production 1937–1940 (1,000 t.)*

	1937	1938	1939	1940
Schkopau plant	4	24	24	24
Dorsten-Minden plant		5	24	24
Fürstenberg plant			12	24
Buna plant IV[a]			20	24
TOTAL PLANNED	4	29	80	96

[a] Location not yet decided.

Source: Schweitzer, 'Vierjahresplan', 379.

In the mean time the Wehrmacht was forced to impose 'drastic restrictions on the use of motor vehicles in order to save rubber and fuel', as the worsening shortage of foreign currency precluded any filling of the gap through imports of natural rubber. 'Germany started the war with practically no stockpile of natural or synthetic rubber.'[98]

Indisputable success, on the other hand, was achieved under the Four-year Plan in the production of artificial fibres (Tables II.v.13a, b). The establishment of the necessary production plants had to be financed by existing textile firms, who also had to process the rayon staple and rayon fibres in a certain proportion to natural fibres. Whereas in 1932 Germany only managed to meet 5.2 per cent of its requirements of textile raw materials, and in 1936 some 31 per cent, 1938–9 production amounted to 43 per cent of requirements. Complete autarky, however, was achieved only during the war.

TABLE II.v.13(*a*). *Planned production of synthetic fibres 1936–1940* (1,000 t.)

	1936	1937	1938	1939	1940
Rayon	95.0	196.0	211.5	244.0	424.0
Rayon staple	48.8	94.2	140.3	219.4	298.4

Source: Schweitzer, 'Vierjahresplan', 376.

TABLE II.v.13(*b*). *Actual production of synthetic fibres 1935–1943* (1,000 t.)

	1935	1936	1937	1938	1939	1940	1942	1943
Rayon	44.0	45.4	57.2	66.0	74.0			96.0
Rayon staple	19.6	45.0	105.0	160.0	204.0	250.0	328.0	

Sources: Kehrl, *Krisenmanager*, 90–1; Kroll, *Weltwirtschaftskrise*, 502 (1936 and 1937 rayon-production figures only).

Of vital importance to the war economy, needless to say, was the manufacture of basic chemicals; as a result of measures taken under the Four-year Plan these were produced in approximately the envisaged quantities (Table II.v.14).

One of Germany's most vital industrial materials was coal. Notwithstanding the growing importance of oil, coal remained the basis of power supplies and of the major part of ersatz-material and synthetics production. Moreover, coke output and steel production were indissolubly linked as primary factors in the rearmament economy. The lamentations indulged in by the National Socialists about Germany's

---

[98] USSBS, *Overall Report: European war* (Washington, 1945), 46.

TABLE II.v.14. *Production of basic chemicals 1936–1938* (1,000 t.)

	Actual Production			1938 plan	Plan fulfilment (%)
	1936	1937	1938		
Sulphuric acid	1,440	1,650	1,850	1,977	93
Chlorine	190	230	280	295	95
Caustic soda	270	350	450	488	92
Soda	800	940	1,100	1,210	91

Source: Petzina, *Autarkiepolitik*, 101.

lack of natural wealth certainly did not concern coal deposits, which did make self-sufficiency possible, and which therefore occupied a special place in the Four-year Plan. On the basis of a 1936 production total of approximately 158.3m. t. of hard coal and 161.4m. t. of lignite, Göring's organization laid down the rates of increase for the period up to 1940 given in Table II.v.15.

TABLE II.v.15. *Planned increment in coal production 1937–1940* (1,000 t.)

	1937	1938	1939	1940
Hard coal	3,450	12,900	17,400	20,400
Lignite	6,350	24,150	30,150	34,000

Source: Schweitzer, 'Vierjahresplan', 363.

Because of a shortage of manpower, however, attainment of the target was beset by numerous difficulties. Nevertheless, following extensive mechanization in the mines, along with measures to improve miners' pay and social benefits, and thanks finally to the compulsory recruitment of mineworkers, the 1940 target was actually reached in 1938. From 1936 to 1938 mining of hard coal rose by 18 per cent, that of open-cast lignite by 23 per cent, and coke production by 22 per cent. This high performance, however (see Table II.v.16), was achieved not so much by expansion as by the utilization of existing, previously unused, capacities. Total extraction of hard coal in 1938, for instance, was only 5 per cent up on the 1929 figure (for the Reich territory including the Saarland).

Along with the solution to the mineral-oil problem, the Four-year Plan was concerned, as a second priority, with an intensified extraction of domestic ores, 'in order to raise Germany's iron production to the very utmost'[99] and thereby reduce

[99] Treue, 'Hitlers Denkschrift', 209 (trans., 406).

TABLE II.v.16. *Actual coal production 1937/8–1939/40* (1,000 t.)

	1937/8	1938/9	1939/40
Hard coal	188,007	187,481	204,797
Lignite	187,228	199,464	211,606

Source: Schweitzer, 'Vierjahresplan', 364.

the country's dependence on imports. In the past the war industry stood or fell with Swedish supplies, but in view of the disorganization of German foreign trade and resulting payment difficulties these imports had to be regarded as in jeopardy. There was the further danger that, in order to preserve its neutrality, Sweden might altogether stop its iron-ore exports in the event of war. Thus, if 'the defence programme . . . was to be fully implemented, even with Germany cut off from imports of foreign ore', [100] German ores of inferior quality would have to be resorted to, and in good time. If, in addition, Germany had an opportunity of continuing 'to import cheap ore, so much the better. The existence of the country's economy, and above all the conduct of the war must not, however'—in Hitler's opinion—'be dependent on this.'[101]

At the suggestion of Hitler's economic adviser, Keppler, a number of metallurgical plants, even before the proclamation of the Four-year Plan, had experimented with the processing of so-called acid or Dogger ores, but had rejected an extension of the practice on grounds of cost. Initially, therefore, the iron and steel industry was reluctant to accept the view that 'stepping up domestic ore extraction is the most urgent command of the hour'.[102] The industry argued that it was unable for technical reasons to produce a cheap kind of pig iron from German ore with a 26 per cent iron content similar to that obtained from Swedish 45 per cent ore, but Hitler, with his belief in the need for economic independence, dismissed this objection as 'irrelevant', just as he did the reminder that, 'if the idea were to be proceeded with, all German blast-furnaces would have to be reconstructed'. To him the question was not 'what we would rather do, but only what we are able to do'.[103]

But on this point, too, opinions differed greatly between the smelting industry and the Four-year Plan authority. More than that: for the first time in the Third Reich an industrial group went into open opposition—not against rearmament as

[100] Göring at a meeting of the working party for the iron-producing industry, 17 Mar. 1937, quoted from Petzina, *Autarkiepolitik*, 102. Coal-production in the Ruhr (per man and per shift) was also considerably increased between 1933 and 1936. But in 1937 production dropped back to the 1932 level and continued to decline further until the end of the war. Cf. Petzina *et al.*, *Sozialgeschichtliches Arbeitsbuch*, iii. 62.
[101] Treue, 'Hitlers Denkschrift', 209 (trans., 406).
[102] Kellermann, director of Gutehoffnungshütte smelting-plant, to Keppler, 16 Sept. 1936, quoted from Riedel, *Eisen*, 96.
[103] Treue, 'Hitlers Denkschrift', 209 (trans., 406).

such, but because of the possible entrepreneurial risks associated with it. In the autumn of 1936 the bureau for German raw materials and synthetics informed the smelting industry 'that the order had been issued from the highest quarter that German metallurgical plants must under all circumstances be sufficiently equipped with German ores, and that this order must be obeyed'.[104] Simultaneously it was suggested to the industry that the centralized mining of Dogger ores should be carried out by an ore supply company, to be financed by contributions, because Germany was already 'in a state of mobilization and war,' even though there was 'no shooting yet'. To avoid the danger of the blast-furnaces going out as a result of the non-importation of foreign ore, it was necessary 'to descend into German soil while there is time'.[105]

Yet the metallurgical industry refused to invest in a venture whose economic soundness seemed to it highly questionable—especially as it had a prominent champion of its cause in the person of Schacht, the minister of economic affairs. The conflict around the extension of the German ore-base thus acquired a second dimension: from being a trial of strength between an industrial interest-group and state power it turned into an intragovernmental struggle for power, for control of German economic policy. While Göring time and again demanded that 'the economic interest of an individual enterprise' must yield to 'the economic interest of German life altogether',[106] Schacht pointed to the interaction of the two economic factors. If one product became more expensive, he argued, a general rise in prices must inevitably follow. If the smelting of 30 per cent ore, compared with 60 per cent ore, required double the blast-furnace capacity, double the manpower, and an increased volume of transport, then this could only have repercussions on the entire rearmament economy. Such an action would, on a major scale, tie up productive forces already in short supply, and any cost–benefit effect would be lost. 'I cannot and must not operate uneconomically whenever I feel like it because I would thus be using up the German nation's economic substance; and that economic substance has not yet grown so large that we can use it up as we like,' Schacht declared to the Reich chamber of the economy.[107]

His alternative to the Four–year plan—to slow down the pace of rearmament—though supported by the metallurgical industry, was no longer under discussion. There could be no mistaking Hitler's statement at the International Automobile and Motor-Cycle Show in February 1937 that private enterprise must either prove itself capable of solving the iron-ore problem or else forfeit the right 'to continue as a free industry'.[108] As existing iron and steel stocks were falling far short of requirements and had to be rationed, the National Socialist regime ordered the total exhaustion of all mines in operation, regarding their ruthless exploitation as

[104] Note by Rohne, 'Ilseder Hütte, 'On the foundation of the Hermann Göring works at Salzgitter-Watenstedt in 1937 and the resulting effects on ore management by the Ilseder Hütte plant', quoted from Riedel, *Eisen*, 109.

[105] Göring in a speech on the implementation of the Four-year Plan, 17 Dec. 1936, ibid.

[106] Ibid. 111.

[107] Speech by Schacht, 22 Jan. 1937, in *Deutsche Wirtschaftszeitung*, 34 (1937), 153.

[108] *Schulthess 1937*, 40.

'absolutely justified' in view of future territorial conquests.[109] The smelting industry, seeing its future threatened, agreed—at least verbally—to process inferior ores, especially as the state, reluctant to call for unreasonable financial sacrifices, promised that 'no one' would 'suffer economic collapse.'[110]

Meanwhile, apart from a few test drillings etc., nothing was being done by industry that might have helped expand Germany's iron-ore base. In the summer of 1937 the shortages in the iron and steel sector resulted in dangerous bottlenecks in rearmament. The Wehrmacht had to content itself with less than half its stipulated steel quota. In consequence, army barracks were not being completed, which led to major difficulties in the accommodation and training of troops. Deliveries of motor-vehicles and ammunition remained below the level considered necessary. The fortification programme, scheduled for completion by 1942, was extended to 1948. Strategic railway construction work was only partially embarked upon. The navy found itself unable, on the basis of its steel allocations, to carry out naval development within the framework of the London naval agreement. 'The battle for steel' was being 'conducted with all, including impermissible, means: every authority believed its own order to be the most important' and pressed 'for its execution in every possible way'.[111]

In this situation Göring decided on action. On 23 July 1937 he set up a company entitled the Hermann Göring Ore-Mining and Ironworks as the nucleus of the subsequent Hermann Göring-Werke. Its first task was the exploitation of the Salzgitter ores. The necessary privately owned deposits were sequestrated. In the autumn of 1937 the state assumed control over the manufacture of all steel capacities in private ownership and reserved to itself the right to issue licences for the establishment of all smelting and steelmaking plants.

These measures, of course, were effective in increasing iron and steel production only in the medium and long term. The targets of the Four-year Plan were not reached in 1937; in 1938 they were reached only through the additional production from Austria following the Anschluss (Table II.v.17).

TABLE II.v.17. *Domestic production of iron ore in 1936–1940* (ore content × 1,000 t.)

	1936	1937	1938	1939	1940
First plan	2, 141	3, 158	3, 568	4, 230	5, 157
Supplementary plan	2, 141	3, 158	3, 981	5, 223	7, 045
Production	2, 258	2, 758	4, 265	5, 600	5, 698

Source: Schweitzer, 'Vierjahresplan', 367.

[109] Göring at a meeting of the working party for the iron-producing industry, 17 Mar. 1937, quoted from Riedel, *Eisen*, 125.   [110] Ibid. 127.

[111] Thomas's report to Hitler on the economic situation concerning rearmament, July 1937, BA-MA Wi I F 5/114.

The armaments industry also had a considerable demand for non-ferrous metals; because of rising consumption it was becoming increasingly difficult to get any closer to the desired objective of independence from foreign imports. Although production was steadily increasing, the coefficient of self-sufficiency, especially with regard to heavy metals, remained almost constant (Table II.v.18).

TABLE II.v.18. *Domestic supply of non-ferrous metals 1934–1938*
(% of consumption)

	1934	1935	1936	1937	1938
Copper	45	43	43	39	41
Zinc	67	68	70	74	78
Lead	64	61	59	60	68

Source: Petzina, *Autarkiepolitik*, 109.

Wherever possible, the attempt was made to replace heavy by light metals, often aluminium. With a 70 per cent rate of increase over two years Germany overtook the USA in 1938 as the world's biggest producer of aluminium (29 per cent of world production). Here too, however, manufacture did not keep pace with demand, and aluminium was in turn often replaced by magnesium, which was available in sufficient quantities. From an overall point of view, however, the Four-year Plan failed to ensure Germany's supplies of non-ferrous metals from domestic production, if only because nearly 100 per cent of the primary material for aluminium production, just like the metals indispensable for the manufacture of high-grade steel, had to be imported. This circumstance illustrates the degree to which rearmament was vulnerable to economic influences from abroad.

6. FROM FOREIGN TRADE TO A LARGE-AREA ECONOMY

Although the Four-year Plan assigned to foreign trade no more than a supplementary role, economically motivated by rearmament, the implementation of Hitler's rearmament demands nevertheless vitally depended on foreign trade. After all, the economic measures set in motion after the autumn of 1936 could not possibly yield any results for a number of months, especially as major investments were needed as a prerequisite of any appreciable increases in production. Thus, to avoid any relaxation of the rearmament effort during the intervening period, existing reserves of raw materials had to be drawn upon until such time as the Four-year Plan began to produce economic results—the more so as, in the government's view, these reserves were too slight anyway to provide 'any reliable support . . . in the event of war'.[112] If stocks of raw materials were almost too short for maintaining

---

[112] Minutes of council of ministers, 4 Sept. 1936, *IMT* xxvi. 490.

rearmament on the same scale and at the same pace as hitherto, even for a while, they were quite definitely insufficient for an enlargement of industrial capacities to the level required for the implementation of the Four-year Plan, let alone 'for the simultaneous successful execution of rearmament'.[113] Clear-sighted individuals realized that, even when the running-in period of the Four-year Plan was over, expectations of its effect on rearmament had been pegged too high and that self-sufficiency in the sectors listed by Hitler, especially given the time-limits set by him, was feasible only on a modest scale and indeed demonstrably impossible with regard to many rearmament-relevant products and basic materials.

Conditions in the world market initially favoured a stepping-up of German exports. The militarization of the Third Reich triggered off a certain rearmament dynamic, not only among its smaller neighbours, who were feeling threatened, but also among the great powers; fanned by the Spanish Civil War this resulted in a world-wide, albeit temporary, economic upturn. In order to make the most of the favourable moment, all German authorities responsible for the rearmament economy agreed 'for the time being to place exports . . . above everything else, even above rearmament'.[114] A committee composed of representatives of the Four-year Plan, the ministry of economic affairs, and the war ministry endeavoured to achieve a balance between the obviously inevitable 'conflicting interests of exports, Wehrmacht claims, and the demands of the Four-year Plan'. Whether an export order was, for compelling reasons, to be subordinated to the claims of the Wehrmacht and the Four-year Plan would be decided case by case.[115]

At first sight these efforts appeared to be successful: there was an appreciable increase in foreign trade in 1937, in both exports and imports. Nevertheless, the foreign-trade surplus fell short of that of the previous year by more than RM100m. Foreign-currency and gold reserves reached a new low, and there was no hope of achieving anything approaching the imports which would have been necessary to attain the greatly increased production targets of the Four-year Plan. The growth of foreign-trade turnover occurred predominantly in the first half of 1937 and was due to a short-lived boom on the world market. Thus, in 1937 German foreign trade rose by 24 to 30 per cent in value, but only by 18 to 19 per cent in volume. This was due to the price rises caused by the boom of both imports and exports. But these higher import prices proved a considerable burden to the German balance of payments because imported foodstuffs and animal feed had to be paid for almost invariably in foreign cash, and on a considerable higher scale than originally calculated. These agricultural imports therefore foiled the original objective of 'employing foreign-currency reserves in order, as far as possible, to bridge the running-in period for the maximum enhancement of German self-sufficiency'.[116] The renewed setback in world trade during the latter half of 1937 was an additional major factor in the poor

---

[113] Expert opinion by Max Ilgner, deputy member of the board of IG-Farben, on export promotion within the Four-year Plan, 5 Mar. 1937, PA Büro Unterstaatssekretär, Rohstoffausschuß, Jan. 1937–Feb. 1938.

[114] War-economy staff report on the economic situation, 1 May 1937, BA-MA Wi vi/202.

[115] Decree of the Reich and Prussian minister of economic affairs, 25 May 1937, BA R 13 I/501.

[116] Report by Ministerialdirektor Neumann, ministry of economic affairs, 10 Feb. 1938, BA R 26 iv/4.

start of the Four-year Plan in its first year. In 1938 imports and exports showed a marked decline, with a negative balance of trade. This failure could in no way be attributed to the new short-lived world-wide depression; it was primarily due to domestic economic causes. As Schacht had pointed out in the spring of 1937, promotion of exports was of little use so long as 'German manufacturers very often neglected export deals in favour of lucrative and risk-free domestic business.'[117] In actual fact, rearmament orders now accounted for such a high proportion of overall industrial production that there was scarcely any unused capacity left for exports—especially in the iron and steel and electrical engineering industries, where export opportunities existed.[118]

TABLE II.v.19. *Share of major industries in Wehrmacht orders (1936)*[a]

	Total sales by the industry (RMm.)	Total sales by 'R enterprises'	
		RMm.	%
Aircraft engines	275.0	275.0	100
Airframe construction	610.0	598.0	98
Firearms	77.0	66.0	86
Shipbuilding	500.0	435.0	87
Nitrocellulose and raw cellulose	99.0	81.0	82
Welded-steel plants	2.4	1.8	76
Storage batteries	52.0	39.0	76
Manufacture of cables and insulated conductors	348.0	254.0	74
Tyres	196.0	137.0	70
Motor-vehicles	1,426.0	970.0	68
Railway-wagons	107.0	67.0	63
Vehicle-parts	376.0	231.0	62
Paper-machinery	138.0	79.0	57
General engineering	1,924.0	1,092.0	57
Pyrotechnical industry	14.0	8.0	56
Ingot steel	1,534.0	827.0	54
Explosives	214.0	117.0	54
Steel-rolling mills	2,266.0	1,193.0	53
Optical and precision engineering	407.0	210.0	52
Rubber-reclaiming plant	9.5	5.0	52
Clothing machinery	132.0	69.0	52
Motor-vehicle trailers	266.0	139.0	52
Nickel, tungsten, and other smelters	79.0	40.0	51
Blast-furnace plants	841.0	420.0	50
Bicycles	125.0	61.0	49
Metal hardware	930.0	456.0	49

[117] Letter from Schacht to Göring, 2 Apr. 1937, *IMT* xxxvi. 284.
[118] Cf. Table II.v.19.

TABLE II.v.19 (*cont.*)

	Total sales by the industry (RMm.)	Total sales by 'R enterprises'	
		RMm.	%
Clocks	57.0	28.0	49
Textile machinery	176.0	84.0	48
Rubber goods	221.0	99.0	45
Electric machinery and apparatus	1,712.0	743.0	44
Small batteries and cells	20.0	9.0	43
Metal-rolling and -pressing	757.0	315.0	42
Iron and steel foundries	880.0	363.0	41
Metal foundries	222.0	92.0	41
Fittings and mountings	174.0	71.0	41
Stoves and ovens	177.0	70.0	39
Rubber footwear	25.0	10.0	39
Office machines	143.0	55.0	38
Photochemical industry	112.0	43.0	38
Foodstuff machinery	165.0	62.0	37
Wire and related items	501.0	181.0	36
Speaking equipment and gramophone records	10.0	3.5	36
Hot-pressed items (metal industry)	50.0	18.0	36
Other iron and steel items	1,192.0	425.0	36
Incandescent light-bulbs	87.0	30.0	34
Agricultural machinery	267.0	87.0	33
Machine tools	642.0	205.0	32
Carbon, carbon disulphide, and thiocyanate compounds	9.0	3.0	31
Thomas slag-mills	67.0	21.0	31
Tanneries	570.0	170.0	30
Detonating substances and electric detonators	28.0	8.0	29
Processed foodstuffs	167.0	48.0	29
Dressings and bandages	26.0	7.0	28
Pianos and organs	20.0	6.0	28
Slag industry	28.0	7.0	25
Asbestos goods	39.0	9.0	24
Surgical cotton wool	7.7	1.8	24
Netting	7.3	1.6	21
Leather and saddlery goods	236.0	50.0	21
Heavy woven fabrics	86.0	17.0	20
Steel construction	398.0	81.0	20
Worsted yarn-spinning	274.0	53.0	19
Organic acid and other organic chemicals	36.0	7.0	19
Baskets and wicker furniture	22.0	4.0	18

TABLE II.V.19 (*cont.*)

	Total sales by the industry (RMm.)	Total sales by 'R enterprises'	
		RMm.	%
Cutlery	103.0	19.0	18
Cellulose acetate, viscose films, and other cellulose products	59.0	11.0	18
Tinware	422.0	73.0	17
Rayon and synthetics	303.0	50.0	17
Plywood	96.0	16.0	17
Tools	175.0	28.0	16
Locks and metal fittings	118.0	18.0	15
Boilers and appliances	212.0	31.0	15
Metal foundries	43.0	7.0	15
Suit- and dress-material weaving-mills	821.0	122.0	15
Watches	43.0	6.0	15
Wooden articles	175.0	24.0	14
Leather transmission-belts	42.0	6.0	13
Flax mills	59.0	7.0	12
Toys	77.0	9.0	12
Ferrous alloys	84.0	9.0	11
Meat products	565.0	60.0	11
Barrels	34.0	4.0	11

[a] Industries with a less than 10% share of 'R enterprises' in their total sales are not included in this table.

Source: BA R 13 1/641: list of 'R enterprises' for July 1937.

Besides, as was openly admitted, the distribution system for raw materials was not working properly. For one thing, there was a shortage of the necessary raw materials. For another, it was impossible, in the preliminary industries which manufactured individual parts, to establish 'whether the raw material contained in the individual parts was intended for export or for the domestic market'.[119] Thirdly, rearmament and the Four-year Plan had absorbed such large numbers of skilled workers that there was a manpower shortage, which hindered the execution of export orders. And finally, the scope and urgency of orders for the Wehrmacht and the Four-year Plan authority prevented industry from accepting and executing export orders at short notice.

The high level of German indebtedness (RM500m. in the summer of 1937) to a number of clearing countries, especially south-east Europe and Turkey, represented a further obstacle to the maintenance, let alone extension, of German foreign trade.

[119] Letter from Schacht to Göring, 2 Apr. 1937, *IMT* xxxvi. 284.

This was due to the fact that Germany—because of its weakness in exports and also because these trade partners, which were to a great extent industrially underdeveloped, had only a limited receptiveness for German manufactures—had purchased more than it had sold. But until that balance was settled, the creditor countries held back their exports to the Reich. In these dire straits the Four-year Plan authority decided to use Germany's remaining foreign securities and channel them, along with the last remnants of foreign currency, towards rearmament-related purposes. In vain did Schacht vigorously protest against this project. If the intention was to 'bring rearmament to a certain level as fast as possible', then, in his unchanged opinion, it was necessary in all economic considerations 'to give priority to the idea of the largest possible accumulation of foreign currency, and hence the greatest possible acquisition of raw materials, through exports'.[120] If, on the other hand, 'the last reserves [were] to be eaten up, without provision being made in any other way for emergencies during the next few years', i.e. 'before the successes of the Four-year Plan really made themselves felt in practice', the minister of economic affairs had no wish to share the responsibility.[121] Making it clear to the Four-year Plan commissioner and Hitler himself that he regarded their foreign-currency, manufacturing, and financial policy 'as incorrect', Schacht in the early autumn of 1937 resigned his posts of minister of economic affairs and plenipotentiary for the war economy, but retained his post of Reichsbank president.

Among the National Socialist leaders the realization had meanwhile gained ground that, while exports were necessary, 'our envisaged tasks cannot be solved by exports alone',[122] at least not within the narrow framework of the domestic economy. No decisive improvement was achieved during the first phase of the Four-year Plan either in raw and primary materials or in agricultural produce, the less so as meat and fat supplies were largely dependent on animal-feed imports. There was a continuing large measure of dependence on foreign imports with regard to the very products which would be difficult to replace in the event of war.

At the beginning of November 1937, four and a half years after coming to power, Hitler, in the presence of the minister of foreign affairs and a very restricted circle of top Wehrmacht leaders, sketched out the state of affairs, both in general and, more particularly, in economic terms. The touchstone of what had been achieved, he declared, must be the safeguarding and preservation of the ethnic mass (*Volksmasse*). As on previous occasions, he presented autarky as the ultimate goal of National Socialist economic measures. Such autarky was only conditionally feasible in the area of raw materials; 'in the area of foodstuffs the question of autarky had to be answered with a flat No'. Enhancement of agricultural production had been paralysed by increased consumer demand. No further appreciable increase in production could be expected in agriculture, as the soil, even with the intensified application of artificial fertilizer, had ceased to become

[120] Letter from Schacht to Göring, 5 Aug. 1937, ibid. 573.
[121] Ibid. 575.
[122] Letter from Göring to Schacht, 22 Aug. 1937, ibid. 554.

more fertile but, on the contrary, was 'already showing signs of exhaustion'.[123] The way out of this all-round incipient stagnation, 'the only . . . salvation, which might appear to be a mere dream' was, according to Hitler, 'the acquisition of greater living-space'. The point was not to secure an increase in population 'but in agriculturally useful space', as well as 'raw material regions' which, in line with his ideas set out in *Mein Kampf*, were 'to be sought in Europe and not overseas'.[124]

Towards the end of 1937 Hitler, basing himself on the military power attained by then, was ready to risk the long-considered step towards the creation of a European integrated economy by way of territorial expansion. On the part of the Wehrmacht this intention met with support even in quarters where, regardless of Hitler's blitzkrieg concept, the principle of in-depth rearmament and the doctrine of total war had not yet been abandoned. This doctrine not only postulated military operations aimed at the physical and material annihilation of an enemy army; it also included economic warfare, with the aim of either weakening or destroying the economic base of a potential or actual opponent, or of expanding and stabilizing one's own economic position. To the chief of the war-economy staff it was of the essence of any future war that it would 'grow beyond the framework of military operations' into a 'means of economic warfare'.[125] If Thomas now accepted a blitzkrieg, it was only for 'securing and expanding our limited economic strength' as the prerequisite of and preparation for a major war that would bring about German hegemony in Europe. Brief aggressive operations, limited in time and space, had to precede the military conflict with the decisive adversaries, in order to offset the economic shortages arising from the narrow limits of German space and resources, wherever this goal seemed impossible of achievement by peaceful means.

In the view of leading political, military, industrial, and even academic economic circles the strained conditions within the German economic area towards the end of 1937 urgently called for its 'enlargement, because the burden on the economy was so heavy that military efficiency and security could no longer be enhanced'.[126]

---

[123] Record by Col. Hoßbach, dated 10 Nov. 1937, of conference at the Reich chancellery on 5 Nov. 1937, *IMT* xxv. 404–5.

[124] Ibid. 406. The thesis that National Socialist Germany had been consistently working towards the creation of an autarkic large-area economic zone, ultimately also by military means, ever since Schacht's 'New Plan', which inaugurated a Europe-centred foreign-trade policy under Berlin's aegis, is finding increasing support in the relevant literature. Thus, the Dutch historian Capelle writes (*Economie en buitenlandse handel,* 67): 'From the point of view of trade policy Germany applied herself to creating a "large area economy" by means of territorial expansion by force. This increasingly isolated Germany from the world market.'

[125] Report by Thomas to the war academy, 2 Apr. 1934, BA-MA Wi I F 5/3308.

[126] According to the Kiel economist Predöhl, quoted from Meier, *Außenhandelsregulierung,* 55.

VI. Rearmament Economy and Aggression

1. THE ECONOMIC EXPLOITATION OF SPAIN DURING THE CIVIL WAR

IN agreeing to Franco's request for military support against the Republican forces, Hitler combined his hope of containing Communist influence in Europe with his intention of drawing Spain into the Third Reich's economic orbit, chiefly in order to develop and channel Spain's wide range of agricultural products and industrial raw materials into Germany's rearmament economy. Such a policy of economic partnership, to be enforced by pressure from intervention troops, met with the support of the Four-year Plan authority and also the Wehrmacht. After all, 'the best rearmament position' was enjoyed by a state 'which either possessed gold for purchases abroad' or had an ally 'who would supply it with raw materials from his own reserves'. As the National Socialist state had virtually no gold reserves left, 'such an ally might save Germany a lot of trouble'.[1]

Economic issues therefore played an important part in German policy towards Spain during the Civil War of 1936–9. Spain's principal agricultural exports, such as oil and citrus fruit, as well as tinned fish, were all commodities in great demand but in short supply in Germany, as were the minerals available in Spain. During the Civil War Spain headed the list of European producers of lead and was one of Europe's most important producers of copper. Morever, it held top place among world producers of zinc ore and mercury, while tin, tungsten, silver, gold, bismuth, antimony, and sulphur were produced in lesser quantities. Of particular importance, because of their low sulphur and very high iron content (up to 60 per cent and over), were Spain's famous iron-ore deposits, some of which were worked by the open-cast method. After Sweden and France, Spain held the third place among Germany's suppliers of iron ore, accounting for approximately 50 per cent of the Third Reich's imports of pyrites. This was a raw material of increasing importance for the manufacture of synthetic materials by the chemical industry. After the outbreak of the Spanish Civil War the IG-Farben concern was faced with 'the very dangerous situation of no longer being able to import sufficient quantities of pyrites for the production of sulphuric acid'.[2]

As an agricultural country rich in raw materials but industrially still underdeveloped, Spain might, in the long run, prove an ideal partner in a European clearing system tailored to German needs and to those of the projected large-scale economic sphere. Throughout the Civil War the National Socialist regime therefore pursued an economic policy aimed at 'the safeguarding of German interests in . . . the rearmament area'[3] but also designed, beyond this immediate objective, 'not to

---

[1] Speech by Thomas to the war-economy advisory council, 15 Mar. 1937, BA-MA Wi I F 5/1196.

[2] Travel account by Gattineau, IG-Farben, quoted from Schieder, 'Spanischer Bürgerkrieg', 177.

[3] Instruction to Warlimont, the German liaison officer with Franco, quoted from Abendroth, *Hitler*, 124.

industrialize Spain, but, as a country clearly complementary to Germany, to utilize its raw-material base on the one hand, while on the other keeping it and strengthening it as a buyer of German industrial exports'.[4]

At the beginning of the Civil War Germany's economic involvement in Spain was directed towards securing the largest possible quantities of raw materials in compensation for German deliveries of war material. Immediately after his appointment as commissioner for the Four-year Plan Göring took the first firm steps towards restarting Spanish exports to the Reich, which had virtually petered out since the beginning of the upheavals in Spain. As a result of German intervention in the Civil War considerable amounts of raw materials were safeguarded by the late summer of 1936, and the first consignment of copper ore (2,000 t.) was unloaded in the port of Hamburg by the end of September.[5] Shortly afterwards the Hisma company in Seville, which handled German deliveries of arms and ammunition to the Franco forces, and the firm of Rowak in Berlin, newly set up to receive Spanish goods, were granted import and export monopolies in German–Spanish trade, 'because, given the needs of the Four-year Plan, there was no other way of ensuring the complete concentration and collection of raw materials and foodstuffs available in Spain and indispensable to the German economy'.[6]

During their first six and a half months of existence the Hisma and Rowak companies succeeded in making large quantities of raw materials—e.g. RM5.25m. worth of wool, as well as iron ore and pyrites—available for German importation. Moreover, Berlin had 60 per cent of the yield of the biggest pyrites and copper-ore mine assigned to it. Anxious to achieve rapid results, Hisma did not shrink from brutal, well-nigh confiscatory means to obtain raw materials. Even though the Spanish Nationalist government was clearly ready to 'give a lot voluntarily for [German] help', this might well change in the future once it discovered that 'through exploitation of its present political and military dependence, it had been compelled to make economic concessions' amounting to a sell-out of its mineral resources.[7] A considerable body of opinion in the Reich therefore called for a contractual regulation of German–Spanish trade in a manner satisfying present German economic interests and ensuring German economic influence in the future—in other words, 'to utilize the present favourable moment so that England, which was well provided with capital, would not take the market away from us at a later stage'. Hitler's instruction to General Faupel, accredited as ambassador to Franco, 'to concern himself particularly with the extension of commercial relations between Germany and Spain' should be seen in that context.[8]

Efforts in that direction, however, failed in the face of opposition on the part of

---

[4] Aviation ministry account of the history of the Condor Legion, Mar. 1940, BA-MA RL 2/v. 3187, fo. 86.

[5] Record of war-economy staff, 11 Sept. 1936, BA-MA Wi I B 2/20.

[6] Bernhardt, head of Hisma, to Canaris, 24 Apr. 1937, quoted from Abendroth, *Hitler*, 125. Cf. Harper, *Economic Policy*, 32 ff.

[7] Remark by Ministerialrat Wucher, ministry of finance, quoted from Abendroth, *Hitler*, 131.

[8] Note by Sabath, foreign ministry, of a remark by Hitler to Gen. Faupel, appointed ambassador to Franco, 27 Nov. 1936, *DGFP*, D. iii. 142.

Franco as well as Göring, though of course for different reasons. The Spanish general refused to have concessions forced upon him while he was under military pressure, when he would be able to negotiate far more favourable terms as a victor. Göring, on the other hand, did not wish to see German–Spanish trade confined within the strait-jacket of a clearing agreement based on equal values of supplies and counter-supplies. In his dual function of *de facto* commander-in-chief of German forces in Spain and of commissioner for the Four-year Plan he was anxious to profit from Franco's military situation and supply position in order to extract from Spain a maximum amount of raw materials and foodstuffs in line with the needs of the Four-year Plan. Application of such an economic policy meant that the powerful position of the ruthless Hisma/Rowak companies must 'under no circumstances be weakened in any way'. Any clearing and trade agreement would 'inevitably . . . impair the position of Rowak/Hisma and hence result in a diminution of raw-material imports from Spain'.[9] Göring's demand won the day. The agreements concluded at governmental level were confined to a supplementary protocol to the German–Spanish trade agreement of 1926,[10] which granted Germany absolute and unlimited most-favoured-nation status, and to three secret protocols with identical contents. The last of these, dating from the summer of 1937, expressed the two parties' intention to achieve the greatest possible expansion of trade between them, taking full account of their respective interests as determined by economic conditions from time to time.

At first glance the statistics may seem to throw doubt on the success of German trade policy *vis-à-vis* Spain between 1936 and 1939: see Table II.VI.I.

TABLE II.VI.I. *German trade with Spain 1932–1939* (RMm.)

	1932	1933	1934	1935	1936	1937	1938	1939
Imports	98.9	86.5	99.7	118.3	97.7	123.4	110.1	118.9
Exports	90.6	85.5	87.5	105.7	69.3	58.7	94.1	67.7

Source: Schieder, 'Spanischer Bürgerkrieg', 178.

The drop in trade in 1936, at the outbreak of Spain's internal conflict, is not surprising—but this was followed by no more than a moderate increase in German imports from Spain, which in 1939 only just managed to regain the level of 1935. If, however, German imports are viewed against those of Spain's other trade partners, it will be found that the Third Reich succeeded in greatly increasing is market share of Spanish exports. By the first half of 1937 it had, by a considerable margin, relegated the USA from first to second place among Spain's customers (Table II.VI.2).

---

[9] Remark by Major von Jagwitz, director of Rowak, quoted from Abendroth, *Hitler*, 129.
[10] Cf. Volkmann, 'Politik und ökonomisches Interesse', 61 ff.

TABLE II.VI.2. *Market shares of selected countries in Spanish exports 1935–1938*

	Jan.–June 1935		Jan.–June 1936		Jan.–June 1937		Jan.–June 1938	
	gold pta. (m.)	%	gold pta. (m.)	%	gold pta. (m.)	%	gold pta. (m.)	%
Germany	9,198	13.1	9,410	10.7	34,394	38.5	38,792	40.7
France	6,167	8.7	12,426	14.1	1,156	1.2	320	0.3
Britain	11,711	16.6	13,672	15.5	7,387	8.2	11,141	11.7
Italy	1,727	2.4	2,933	3.3	3,840	4.3	14,595	15.3
USA	13,986	19.9	15,786	17.9	19,796	22.1	12,858	13.5
Argentina	4,545	6.4	4,590	5.2	2,709	3.0	1,953	2.0

Source: Schieder, 'Spanischer Bürgerkrieg', 181.

An analysis of German imports from Spain by categories of goods and by value clearly shows an orientation towards the priorities laid down by the Four-year Plan (Table II.VI.3). Imports of agricultural produce had substantially declined in favour of industrial raw materials; within the range of agricultural produce such luxury items as wine and citrus fruit had been partially replaced by wool, vegetable oils, and wheat. Hisma actually succeeded in getting vegetable oil—in short supply in Spain itself—released for export, and even in considerable quantities. As a supplier of ores to Germany, Spain maintained the third place in the table, which it occupied before the Civil War—though its share of ore deliveries in terms of value showed a decline (Tables II.VI.3–4). Of major importance were German imports of Spanish pyrites, which, during the period in question, accounted for over 50 per cent of German imports of that raw material (Table II.VI.5).

There is no doubt of the favourable effect which German intervention in Spain had on German rearmament. Just as with a number of south-east European countries and the Baltic states, Germany succeeded in allowing exports to Spain to drop far below imports from that country; in other words, Berlin was deliberately aiming at a negative balance of trade in order to keep exports low in favour of production for rearmament.

In pursuing their plans for the progressive incorporation of a number of European countries in a German-dominated economic community, the National Socialist leaders did not wish to restrict themselves to a mere extension of German–Spanish trade relations. After all, 'obtaining raw materials by purchasing . . . is nothing enduring but merely a hand-to-mouth acquisition of such materials'. In order to safeguard German economic interests in Spain in the long term it was necessary 'to penetrate deeply into the main sources of Spanish wealth . . . in both agriculture and mining'.[11] Although certain initiatives for land acquisition were

---

[11] Report by director of Hisma, 4 Nov. 1937, *DGFP*, D. iii. 501.

TABLE II.IV.3. Spanish exports to Germany 1932–1940[a]

	Fruit		Citrus, tropical fruit		Fish		Wine, must		Skins, hides		Iron ore	
	RMm.	%	RMm.	%	RMm.	%	RMm.	%	RMm.	%	RMm.	%
1932	4.6	4.68	52.3	52.85	1.4	1.43	7.7	7.80	5.3	5.35	7.1	7.15
1933	3.5	4.03	43.6	50.35	1.7	1.57	7.1	8.16	6.1	7.06	5.3	6.08
1934	7.2	7.20	40.9	41.06	1.7	1.66	7.8	7.84	5.6	5.65	6.9	6.98
1935	4.8	4.90	2.1	1.74	5.7	4.78	13.5	11.35	13.2	11.15	8.2	6.89
1936	1.6	1.63	42.7	43.70	1.5	1.53	11.1	11.12	11.1	11.13	6.9	6.92
1937	1.0	0.81	13.6	11.02	4.5	3.64	14.6	11.82	20.7	16.70	13.9	11.26
1938	1.0	0.90	13.4	12.17	5.3	4.81	5.1	4.63	6.1	5.54	30.1	27.33
1939	6.3	5.26	35.5	29.68	2.0	1.67	6.9	5.76	4.4	3.67	18.4	15.38
1940	0.5	2.45	6.6	32.40	0.3	1.47	0.9	4.41	2.9	14.23	0.1	0.49

	Pyrites		Copper		Resin		Wool		Vegetable oils		Wheat		Other	
	RMm.	%	RMm.	%	RMm.	%	RMm.	%	RMm.	%	RMm.	%	RMm.	%
1932	6.3	6.38	1.7	1.70									12.5	12.66
1933	7.5	8.65	0.5	0.55									11.2	13.55
1934	8.8	8.82			1.5	1.51	0.5	0.47	0.5	0.48			18.3	18.33
1935			1.3	1.10	1.7	1.47	1.3	1.12					24.2	20.50
1936			1.2	1.20	2.2	2.20	1.7	1.74					17.7	18.83
1937			4.1	3.32	9.2	7.45	14.0	11.34					27.8	22.57
1938	14.2	12.89			2.3	2.08	2.1	1.90	3.4	3.08	4.5	4.08	22.6	20.59
1939	9.4	7.85			1.0	0.84	4.8	4.01	9.2	7.69	0.8	0.66	20.9	17.53
1940	0.7	3.43			0.2	0.98	1.6	7.85	0.4	1.96	1.0	4.90	5.2	25.43

[a] Excluding Canary Islands.

Source: Schieder, 'Spanischer Bürgerkrieg', 180–1.

TABLE II.VI.4. *Germany's iron-ore suppliers 1932–1939* (% share)

	1932	1933	1934	1935	1936	1937	1938	1939
Sweden	45.1	49.3	56.8	39.1	44.6	44.0	41.0	48.7
France	20.7	22.5	19.5	39.9	37.1	27.8	23.0	13.4
Spain	13.3	8.5	7.6	9.3	5.7	6.7	8.2	5.9
Norway	6.3	5.5	6.4	3.6	2.8	2.4	5.0	5.0
Newfoundland	5.5	4.8	4.1	1.3	0.9	3.9	5.1	3.8
Algeria	4.2	3.7	2.2	1.5	2.8	3.5	3.4	2.6
Greece	2.2	1.7	1.0	1.4	0.9	1.0	1.1	1.1
Luxemburg			1.0	2.6	3.0	7.4	8.0	7.6
Sierra Leone						1.0	2.1	3.1
Others	2.7	4.0	1.4	1.3	2.2	2.3	3.1	8.8

Source: Schieder, 'Spanischer Bürgerkrieg', 177.

TABLE II.VI.5. *Spain's market share of German imports of pyrites 1932–1940* (1,000 t.)

	Total imports	Spanish share	
		1,000 t.	%
1932	650	305	46.9
1933	849	393	46.2
1934	987	532	53.9
1935	1,018	562	55.2
1936	1,042	464	44.5
1937	1,464	835	57.0
1938	1,430	895	62.5
1939	1,120	582	51.9
1940	482	27	5.6

Source: Schieder, 'Spanischer Bürgerkrieg', 178.

considered, they were dropped owing to fear of a land reform foreshadowed by the Spanish government. Towards the end of 1938, however, Germany succeeded, by unscrupulously exploiting the military stalemate towards which the Civil War seemed to be heading, in making deliveries of German arms, on which victory in the war hinged, dependent on Franco's agreement, which was duly given, to German majority participation in four large mining companies.[12]

Even though Hisma succeeded in linking vital enterprises in the Franco-

---

[12] *Note verbale* of the Spanish Nationalist government, 19 Dec. 1938, *DGFP*, D. iii 683–4.

controlled area to the German economy on an ever-increasing scale, Germany's economic ambitions for the long term (beyond the Civil War) were not to be fulfilled in Spain. Following his victory in 1939 Franco sought to normalize relations by reducing German economic influence, and during the Second World War he successfully warded off all German attempts to integrate his country into a European economic system complementary to that of the Third Reich.

2. THE ECONOMIC EFFECTS OF THE ANSCHLUSS

The incorporation of Austria in the Reich, always planned by Hitler, was not only motivated ethnically. It also promised—at least at the moment when it took place—to bring about a not inconsiderable improvement in Germany's economic situation. Finally decided upon from the end of 1937 and implemented in mid-March 1938, the Anschluss must be seen as 'one of the steps in the German leadership's expansion programme which aimed at the establishment of a defensible large-scale European economic sphere'.[13]

Even since the beginning of 1937 Keppler, Hitler's economic adviser and a member of the Four-year Plan organization, had 'concerned himself intensively with Austrian conditions'.[14] In the agricultural sector the country produced milk, butter, and cheese beyond its own requirements and might therefore, at first glance, help fill the corresponding gaps in the Altreich (pre-Anschluss Germany). As for raw materials, it was particularly rich in timber, iron ore, lead, zinc ores, and unused water-power. The Austrian petroleum deposits were also taken into consideration. The Alpine republic had a most efficient, high-quality basic industry and, above all, a processing industry whose capacity, owing to a prolonged recession, was insufficiently utilized and which, given the existence of roughly 400,000 unemployed (largely skilled workers), could be put to use relatively quickly. Austria's unification with the Reich therefore deserved 'special attention from the point of view of the rearmament economy'.[15]

While the economic measures taken after 13 March 1938 were generally designed to make Austria an inseparable part of the Reich economy, German economic policy

---

[13] Schausberger, 'Wirtschaftliche Aspekte', 133. Cf. Messerschmidt, IV.v.7 (a) below.

[14] Kehrl, *Krisenmanager*, 118.

[15] Report of the war-economy staff on the economic situation, 1 Apr. 1938, BA-MA RW 19/86. In the specialized literature the conviction is gaining ground that economic considerations were of especial importance for the annexation of Austria, particularly for its timing. 'Ever since, with the enactment of the Four-year Plan, German economic policy had been clearly aligned to rearmament and hence to autarky, economic aspects were gaining increasing weight in political considerations regarding Austria', according to a study by Butschek, *Österreichische Wirtschaft* (p. 45). This study, prepared at the Austrian Institute for Economic Research, also highlights Austria's economic value to the Reich in 1938: 'Following Austria's union with Germany the National Socialists found an economic situation similar to that which existed in their own country at the time of their seizure of power: a state of disastrous under-utilization of its material and manpower capacities, with a falling trend in prices but a trade balance in equilibrium and some foreign-currency reserves' (ibid. 46); 'The Anschluss meant first of all that 15.5% of Austria's former foreign trade, i.e. that with Germany, now became internal trade, so that the abolition of—substantial—trade barriers was bound to have a considerable "trade-creating" effect' (ibid. 47). The study is graphically illustrated by tabulated statistical material.

was in particular 'primarily designed to incorporate Austria into the sphere of the Four-year Plan as a matter of course'.[16] All steps towards economic integration therefore meant the absorption of Austria's economy into the German rearmament process. Within two days of the German invasion the Four-year Plan came into force in Austria; Göring immediately announced that he would ensure 'the development of the power industry, the extraction of mineral wealth, and the expansion of the principal branches of industry and transport'.[17]

Particular importance was attached to petroleum and iron-ore extraction, both of which increased considerably (Table II.VI.6).

TABLE II.VI.6. *Austrian petroleum and iron-ore production 1937–1939*
(1,000 t.)

	1937	1938	1939
Petroleum	32.9	56.7	144.3
Iron ore	1,880.0	2,660.0	2,971.0

Source: Schausberger, 'Die Bedeutung Österreichs', 62 n. 24.

The economic initiatives developed by Germany led to a kind of belated entrepreneurial boom in Austria, wherein the interests of state and Wehrmacht on the one hand and of business circles on the other converged. In order to adjust what were seen as the slower Austrian economic clocks to the pace of those in Germany, German industry was allowed to bring under its control a major part of Austrian banking and industrial enterprises by way of majority participation or by acquiring whole firms at knock-down prices. In return the National Socialist regime expected an alignment of the economy to the rearmament requirements formulated in Berlin. The new orientation was further guaranteed by a change in the higher echelons in connection with transfers of owership: in the course of that process Austrian 'veteran fighters' of Nazism and numerous men from the Reich moved into key economic positions. At the same time the Hermann Göring works extended its influence to Austria by setting up a gigantic metallurgical plant in Linz and by taking over the management of numerous existing industrial enterprises. Another state-owned concern to gain a foothold in Austria was the Gustloff foundation, which along with IG-Farben controlled extensive areas of chemical (gunpowder) production. Under these conditions the integration of Austrian industry into the direct rearmament process proceeded speedily and with virtually no friction. German investments were needed initially for the mobilization of Austria's economic resources, but the intensive exploitation of economic, transport-geographical, and strategic opportunities resulted in the recovery 'of this financial priming aid within a relatively short period'.[18] At the outbreak of war 245 firms

---

[16] 'Großdeutschland in der Energiewirtschaft', 1224.   [17] Göring, 'Ostmark', 194.
[18] Study by the Reich statistical office, BA R 24/17.

were regarded as rearmament enterprises; they mainly manufactured uniforms, obstacle- and fortification-building machinery, and equipment for the army. Production of superstructures for armoured scouting-cars and of carbines was just beginning, while the establishment of a number of factories for the manufacture of tank- and aircraft-parts and for the production of guns and ammunition of various kinds was imminent.

As Austria's rearmament-linked economic upswing, accelerated by a job-creation programme on similar lines to the German measures of 1933–4, was only able to absorb a certain percentage of Austrian unemployed—and that not immediately—at the end of March 1938 Göring, in view of the increasingly fierce competition for (mostly skilled) manpower in the Altreich, decided to remedy that shortage by the recruiting of Austrians. 'It was unacceptable that in Austria physically fit workers' should remain 'unemployed for prolonged periods' and be drawing 'welfare benefits, while they are urgently needed in the rest of the Reich territory. If, therefore, the Austrian economy is incapable of employing these workers within a foreseeable period of time, employment can take place in the old Reich territory.'[19] When, despite increased wage incentives, it proved impossible to attract a sufficient number of Austrian workers into the Altreich, a 'decree on securing the manpower needed for tasks of special national importance' (22 June 1938) created the basis for mandatory enlistment, resulting, within a short period, in the transfer to Germany of 100,000 Austrian workers, including some 10,000 engineers.

The raw-material stocks and reserves of money and foreign currency found in Austria proved to be so vast that 'the German raw-material and foreign-currency economy' was in a position 'to be continued and maintained in accordance with the existing plan throughout 1938'. According to optimistic estimates, even 'the first half of the Four-year Plan' seemed 'assured in respect of raw materials and foreign currency'.[20] (See Table II.vi.7.)

Added to this was the fact that, following the setting up of a Reichsbank main branch in Vienna, very substantial privately owned amounts of gold and foreign

TABLE II.vi.7. *Austrian gold and foreign-currency reserves taken over by the Reich*

	Schilling (m.)	RMm.
Currency reserves of the Austrian National Bank	460[a]	230
Unminted gold held by the National Bank	296	148
Gold deposited with the Bank of England	80	40
Clearing credits	150	75

[a] Gabriel, 'Österreich', 648, gives 470m.

Source: Schausberger, 'Wirtschaftlicher Anschluß', 255.

[19] *Keesing's Archives* (German edn.) 1938, B 3525.
[20] Report on a Four-year Plan authority conference on economic questions, 19 May 1938, BA R 26 IV/4.

currency began to flow into financial institutions; presumably these were largely made up of gold hoarded within the country and deposits and securities lodged abroad. This flow back into the banks was due partly to regained confidence in the domestic economy, but no doubt mainly to the enactment of obligatory surrender, with the concession of a specially favourable rate of exchange for a short period. While the official rate was 1 Austrian Schilling = RM0.47, gold and foreign-bank deposits as well as securities could be exchanged up to 25 April at the rate of S3 = RM2. Here the minimum total amounts (in Schilling) thought to have been received by the banks:

Gold from within the country	750m.
Foreign bank-accounts	500m.
Foreign securities	500m.
TOTAL	1,750m.

In spite of its small size, Austria earned for Germany fifteen times (at S3 = RM2) or twenty-one times (at S1 = RM0.47) the amount of gold and foreign currency possessed in cash by the Reichsbank. 'It has not, in this respect, come into the Reich empty-handed.'[21] Mention must also be made of the moneys, estimated to be at least S500m., in Austrian giro accounts, banks, and saving-banks; this amount was also transferred to the Reichsbank as early as April 1938, with the result that the bank's giro accounts probably increased by approximately 21.3 per cent.[22]

As regards transport, especially in respect of foreign trade, Germany's position also indisputably improved. The Reich 'now directly [abutted on] the south-east European region, which, as a supplier of raw materials and as a market for manufactures, [represented] its natural hinterland'.[23] Germany now projected 'far into the European south-east with its very great importance for wartime food supplies'.[24] Berlin was firmly resolved to tighten the knot of trade relations with the Danubian states, first tied under the 'New Plan', to such an extent that they would 'in all situations ensure an orderly exchange of goods' on the lines of a developing large-area economy.[25]

Such a policy, however, held out the promise of 'relief for the German raw-material and foreign-currency economy only in the long run'.[26] Until such time as the supplementary economic ties with Germany/Austria were fully established, the Anschluss, in terms of the overall economy, placed a burden on the Reich, consisting primarily in an increased requirement for foodstuff imports. Even though Austrian agriculture—like Austrian industry—was being integrated into the war-economy system, the hoped-for agricultural results failed to materialize. Nevertheless, immediately after the Anschluss the Reich made finance available for

---

[21] Gabriel, 'Österreich', 648–8.

[22] Ibid. 650; id., 'Eingliederung', 422.

[23] Report by the war-economy staff on the economic situation, 1 Apr. 1938, BA-MA RW 19/93.

[24] Study by the Reich statistical office, BA R 24/17.

[25] Göring at a meeting of the general council of the Four-year Plan, 5 Apr. 1938, BA R 26 IV/5.

[26] Minutes of a conference on economic questions chaired by State Secretary Körner, 19 May 1938, BA R 26 IV/4.

construction purposes, for an improvement in rural transport, for the regulation of water-power, and for fertilizer supplies. In addition, a disencumbrance operation was carried out, although this covered only holdings 'in need of disencumbrance', 'capable of disencumbrance', and 'deserving disencumbrance'—in other words, mainly medium-sized and large farming units which could be used to ensure food supplies for the war economy. In view of the fact that the owners involved, in return for the sinking of their debts, were liable to the state with their farmholding, largely in the form of prescribed delivery quotas—which many farms were unable to meet—the measures immediately triggered a flight from the land, resulting in bottlenecks in food supplies.

Hence, the Anschluss resulted in no more than a short-term and localized strengthening of the German economy, so that 'at the beginning of 1939 the situation which emerged was that existing at the beginning of 1938, before Austria's incorporation'.[27] As economic accretion could only produce long-term positive results in a wider territorial framework, the National Socialist leaders were determined now to advance more rapidly along the already chosen road of partial enlargement of living-space, so as to invest the economic gains associated with each step of territorial expansion in new military operations.

3. THE INTEGRATION OF THE SUDETEN REGIONS IN THE GERMAN WAR ECONOMY

In 1938 Berlin's expansionist endeavours, dictated by the dynamics of rearmament and directed towards safeguarding 'major requirements in the event of war', were bound, from a military point of view, to continue to cause 'certain misgivings'. Such a policy, after all, courted the danger of escalation of a conflict for which the Third Reich was still inadequately prepared. In Wehrmacht circles, therefore, given the existing state of rearmament, 'the idea of a large-area economy' was seen as 'perhaps an objective to be striven for' in the more distant future, one whose prerequisite must be comprehensive rearmament. That, however, could only be achieved during a prolonged period of peace, when efforts towards self-sufficiency and the promotion of foreign trade were not mutually exclusive but beneficially complemented each other.[28] However, such reservations about the policy of expansion practised from 1938 onwards no longer had any effect at all on general—and more specifically rearmament—economic, political, or military designs.

Having initially intended to put off the 'settlement of the Czech question' in order 'first to digest Austria',[29] in April 1938 Hitler, utilizing the economic accretion immediately effective after the Anschluss, gave orders to start preparations for 'Fall Grün' (Operation Green), the destruction of Czechoslovakia,

---

[27] Conclusions of a conference of state secretaries, 19 May 1938, BA R 26 IV/4.
[28] Strictly confidential address by Gen. Thomas on war economy and autarky from the point of view of national defence (given to the staff of the Reichsbank), 21 June 1938, BA-MA Wi I F 5/153.
[29] Entry in Jodl's diary, *IMT* xxviii. 372.

on a scale and at a pace allowing for the possibility of international complications. The German economy was entering the phase of immediate war preparations, which, with the country's industrial capacity already overstretched by 12 per cent, called for an even greater focusing on vital war products.[30] The original Four-year Plan was therefore revised in spring of 1938 and in part overtaken by the New War Economy Production Plan, which made production of gunpowder, explosives, war-gases, and light metals, the extraction of mineral oil, and the manufacture of rubber absolute priorities until 1942–3.[31] Drafted in outline by the IG-Farben management, this plan henceforward assured the enterprise of considerable and detrimental influence on economic developments in the Third Reich. This was due not only to the overwhelming importance of the chemical industry within the war economy but also to the personal ties between the state's economic bureaucracy and IG-Farben. On 22 August 1938 the latter's managing director, Krauch, was appointed plenipotentiary (a few months later general plenipotentiary) for the production of mineral oil, unvulcanized rubber, and light metals, as well as gunpowder and explosives, including their feedstocks and ancillary products, and also for the production of chemical weapons. As such he became the most powerful man in the Four-year Plan organization after Göring, the more so as he was also in charge of one of Europe's most important economic research institutes (the economic department of IG-Farben AG).

The production targets laid down in the New War Economy Production Plan (Table II.VI.8*a*, *b*)—also known as the Karinhall or Krauch plan—were not based on the production capacities actually existing in 1938; hence, Germany could only expect to be ready for war after extensive preliminary investment in further production facilities, i.e. only in the long term. In view of the shortage of raw materials and manpower the feasibility of the programme seemed generally in doubt.

Switches to production of items vital for war could only achieve a short-term increase in military striking power, but this the regime intended to apply ruthlessly for the solution of the Czechoslovak question so as to broaden its own economic base. This alone explains the extension, in August 1938, of the New War Economy Production Plan into the 'Schnellplan' (Rapid Plan), under which the rearmament programmes scheduled for completion in 1942–3 were shortened by a year. The National Socialist regime 'deliberately risked the ruin of the German economy in the hope of restoring it by a war conducted as a marauding expedition'.[32]

Germany's rearmament situation did not make it possible—although Hitler would have liked to do this—to solve the Czechoslovak question at a single stroke: i.e. to achieve the incorporation of the Sudeten regions into the Third Reich, the

---

[30] Expert opinion of the war-economy and armaments office on Germany's potential at the outbreak of war, 26 Feb. 1940, BA-Ma Wi I F 5/3442. Cf. *USSBS* ii, arguing, in the light of modern time-and-motion ideas, that German production forces could still have been mobilized on a substantial scale. In point of fact, Speer succeeded during the war in achieving an appreciable increase in performance through standardization and automation.

[31] *Wehrwirtschaftlicher Neuer Erzeugungsplan*, 12 July 1938, BA-MA Wi I F 5/3579.

[32] Bracher, Sauer, and Schulz, *Machtergreifung*, 755.

TABLE II.VI.8(*a*). *Targets of the New War Economy Production Plan*

	Annual capacity in 1938 (1,000 t.)	Annual production target (1,000 t.)	% increase
Mineral oils	24,000	138,000	475
Unvulcanized rubber	5	120	2,300
Aluminium	170	270	59
Magnesium	18	36	100

Source: Petzina, *Autarkiepolitik*, 126–7.

TABLE II.VI.8(*b*). *Targets for gunpowder and explosives*

	Capacity in 1938 (1,000 t./month)	Production target (1,000 t./month)	% increase
Explosives	5.40	17.10	217
Gunpowder	5.00	18.10	262
War-gases	0.92	9.30	911

Source: Petzina, *Autarkiepolitik*, 126–7.

establishment of the Protectorate of Bohemia and Moravia, and the creation of a Slovak state politically and economically dependent on Berlin. Even to back up the negotiations about the detachment of the Sudeten area from the Czechoslovak state it was 'necessary deliberately and ruthlessly to use up foreign-currency holdings and to neglect exports'[33] if Germany demands were to have appropriate weight—backed up if necessary by military threats. German foreign indebtedness in the late summer of 1938 reached a peak that was endangering further imports of raw materials and foodstuffs. The incorporation of the Sudetenland during the second half of the year could not of itself justify such a high economic stake. Admittedly, some important industries, often with spare capacity, fell into German hands, so that, given a large number of unemployed in the region, favourable conditions seemed to exist for relieving the pressure on the German economy. In the raw-material sector the new territory had surpluses of timber as well as rich (and militarily useful) deposits of tungsten and uranium ores, which Germany had so far lacked. Added to these were high-grade lignite deposits, which, unless they were owned by Sudeten Germans, became state property. In terms of quality and quantity they made possible a considerable expansion of mineral oil, Buna, and general chemical production, as well as power generation. In view of these circumstances the

---

[33] Address by Göring to the General Council of the Four-year Plan, 14 Oct. 1938, BA R 25 IV/5.

economy of the Sudeten regions was tied into the Four-year Plan and, in the field of chemicals, into the New War Economy Production Plan as early as the beginning of October 1938.[34] See Table II.VI.9.

TABLE II.VI.9. *Principal industries of the incorporated Sudetenland in 1939*

	Persons employed acquired by Germany	
	No.	% of Czechoslovakia's work-force in the industry
Mining	45,411	37.5
Iron, steel, and metal goods	48,286	33.0
Mechanical engineering	26,485	19.8
Electrical engineering	10,582	23.7
Chemical industry	13,106	32.3
Textile industry	207,400	57.6
Glass industry	41,304	65.0

Source: Barthel, *Politik*, 104.

On the other hand, Sudetenland needed considerable supplies in all other areas of raw materials and in the food sector, so that this territorial gain resulted 'for the moment . . . in a deterioration of the overall economic situation for armament purposes'.[35]

Although Göring had demanded that 'the Sudetenland must be utilized by all possible means',[36] no appreciable progress was achieved in terms of full economic mobilization. As the commissioner for the Four-year Plan admitted with disarming frankness, Germany in the second half of 1938 was 'facing unsuspected difficulties. The tills were empty and the order-books were crammed full for years ahead.' This was not due only to the implementation of the New War Economy Production Plan. Party and state, for instance, continued to require major quantities of material and manpower for building up their image at home and abroad, as indeed also for the construction of the Westwall ordered in May 1938. Efforts were made under the

[34] Reich Centre for Economic Development, *Ausbauplan Sudetendeutschland (Bereich Nordwest Böhmen und Egerland) für Mineralöl, Buna, Chemie einschließlich Vorprodukte und Energie* (Development plan for Sudeten Germany (North-West Bohemia and Eger region) for mineral oil, Buna, chemicals including feedstock, and energy), 15 Oct. 1938, BA-MA Wi I F 3/180.

[35] Report by the armed forces high command on the economic situation, 1 Nov. 1938, BA-MA Wi I F 5/543.

[36] Minutes of a conference in Göring's office, 14 Oct. 1938, quoted from *IMT* xxvii. 163. For another report on the same meeting cf. n. 33 above.

Four-year Plan to postpone projects which were not vital to the war, as well as all social-welfare or wage ambitions. The German Labour Front was warned 'not to make promises to the workers which . . . cannot be kept'.[37] Simultaneously, attempts were made to impose drastic restrictions on the production of consumer goods. Among other things Göring demanded that the engineering industry serving consumer goods should immediately switch to the production of machine-tools and equipment for armaments. Because of excessive use and lack of timely or adequate replacement, industrial plant was showing signs of wear and tear, and there was an acute risk of a general drop in performance. Added to this was the over-extension of the work-force, who often worked a 60-hour week; even in the view of the Wehrmacht this could 'on no account . . . be kept up indefinitely'.[38]

Even though Göring's threat that private enterprise must justify its existence at a difficult time for Germany or else 'he would mercilessly transfer it to the state's economy'[39] was doubtless not meant quite as seriously as it sounded, it was nevertheless an indication of the magnitude of the crisis in the rearmament economy. The slogan of the autumn of 1938, 'Intensified exports to improve the foreign-currency situation', was bound to seem nonsensical alongside the simultaneous demand for 'intensified rearmament'.[40] Thus, the 'export battle', once again announced by Hitler, was lost even before it had begun. Moreover, experts were drawing attention to the decline in foreign orders, atrributing them to 'close links between politics and the economy'. Customers for German exports were clearly worried that the Third Reich might shortly be involved in warlike conflicts and therefore be unable to meet export obligations; in consequence, they were increasingly placing their orders in neutral countries. In addition—as was correctly realized in Berlin—a 'steadily increasing political boycott of German goods'[41] was developing abroad, practised on a growing scale by Britain, Belgium, The Netherlands, and the United States, as well as, unexpectedly, by South American countries, as a reaction to Germany's policy of expansion in general and to the expropriation of Jews in the newly acquired territories in particular.

If the rearmament drive, dictated by foreign-policy considerations, was to be maintained, then the food-supply situation could only be improved on condition 'that Germany can in the long term rely on meeting about 20 per cent of its import requirements from south-east Europe'.[42]

The incorporation of the Sudeten regions was thus expected to pay off only in conjunction with a further extension of Germany's territorial and power-political, and hence also economic, sphere. There had never been any doubt among the National Socialist leadership that 'the peaceful liberation of Sudeten Germany and its

---

[37] Ibid. 161.

[38] Report by the armed forces high command on the economic situation, 1 Jan. 1939, BA-MA W 01-8/47.

[39] Göring at the conference of 14 Oct. 1938, *IMT* xxvii. 161. Cf. n. 33 above.

[40] Göring at the conference of 14 Oct. 1938, *IMT* xxvii. 160. Cf. nn. 33, 36, and 39 above.

[41] Report by the armed forces high command on the economic situation, 1 Feb. 1939, BA-MA W 01-8/47.

[42] Report by the armed forces high command on the economic situation, 8 Feb. 1939, ibid.

annexation to the Reich . . . was but one of the objectives along the road of our nation's life'.[43]

From an economic point of view the annexation of the Sudeten regions generally represented an 'enlargement of the Greater German economic area', with vital importance attaching to 'the existing political and economic dependence of rump Czechoslovakia on the Reich and the resulting increased protection of access to the south-east'.[44]

The loss of the Sudeten regions meant a decisive economic weakening of post-Munich Czechoslovakia, as the level of industrialization in the ceded area was higher than the average for Czechoslovakia as a whole, and indeed higher than in Germany or in Britain. Thus, in the Sudeten regions 51 per cent of all gainfully employed persons worked in the mines and industry, as against a mere 33 per cent in the rest of Czechoslovakia, 40.7 per cent in Germany, and 46 per cent in Britain.[45] The Czechoslovak state, as a result of the separation of the Sudeten regions, lost 69.6 per cent of its glass industry, 40 per cent of its chemical industry, 89.9 per cent of its ceramics industry, 98 per cent of its porcelain industry, 60.5 per cent of its cellulose industry, 68 per cent of its paper industry, and 53.8 per cent of its timber industry. Altogether Prague had to give up 2,317 industrial enterprises, of which 443 were textile plants, while it was left with a mere 3 per cent of its former lignite and 45 per cent of its hard-coal production. Its industry was therefore dependent on coal supplies from Germany and Poland, and was thus exposed to the possibility of extortion.[46]

4. THE PROTECTORATE OF BOHEMIA AND MORAVIA FROM THE STANDPOINT OF THE WAR ECONOMY

Hitler's order on 21 October 1938 to 'finish off rump Czechoslovakia' should be seen against the background of a specific economic situation in the Third Reich, when the demand was raised that the Czechoslovak territories so far left under Czechoslovak sovereignty must 'become German dominions'.[47] Besides, on pure considerations of large-area economy, one could 'not content oneself with the Sudeten German area . . . That was only a partial solution. So the decision to march into Bohemia was taken.'[48]

At the start of 1939 Hitler was at pains to convince a fairly wide circle of the German leadership élite of the need for a step-by-step realization of the party's living-space programme.[49] In a strikingly large number of speeches he emphasized

---

[43] Letter from Göring to the supreme Reich authorities, 15 Oct. 1938, BA-MA Wi I F 5/560.

[44] Expert opinion of the armed forces high command on the war-economy significance of the Sudeten regions, 1 Nov. 1938, BA-MA W 01-8/47.

[45] Polzer, *Wirtschaft*, 12; Volkmann, 'Eingliederung'.

[46] Data of the Czechoslovak statistical office, according to Dress, *Slowakei*, 23.

[47] Göring at the conference of 14 Oct. 1938, *IMT* xxvii. 163 (using the English word 'dominions'). Cf. n. 33 above.

[48] Speech by Hitler to military commanders, 23 Nov. 1939, quoted from *IMT* iii. 195.

[49] Cf. speech to unit commanders of the army, 10 Feb. 1939; speech to the military academy, 11 Mar. 1939, BA NS 11/28.

time and again what he saw as the central problem of the German nation, 'to gain secure control of the sources from which the raw materials which are so essential to its welfare may be obtained'. This German desire was being opposed by 'Jews, democracies, and international forces' which were active also in the remnant of Czechoslovakia. In order to clear the way for the expansion of German living-space towards the east it was necessary to destroy these 'enemies of the German people radically', which was why he had given orders 'to occupy Czechoslovakia militarily within a few days, no later than 15 March'. From that position it would then be possible to integrate Hungary, Romania, and Yugoslavia into the German power-sphere, in order to gain 'unrestricted control of their immense agricultural resources and their wealth of petroleum'.[50]

The invasion of the Czech lands, now proclaimed the Protectorate of Bohemia and Moravia, resulted in an immediate improvement of the German rearmament situation. In the view of top military circles the equipment of the Czechoslovak army and the securing of its war material meant 'an enormous increase in strength'.[51] The great importance attached to the exploitation of Bohemia and Moravia for purposes of rearmament was revealed by the general staff's plans, drawn up at least three months before the invasion, for the confiscation of weapons and military equipment, as well as by the preparations for taking control of Czech armament works. The military war-economy organization for the first time went through its procedure for ensuring German rearmament interests in occupied territories. It was practised with such perfection on this occasion that, while the aggression was still proceeding, major quantities of captured military equipment were being dispatched to Germany. In the event of unexpected international complications the Wehrmacht would have needed these urgently; accordingly 'the Führer . . . could not get a general view of the war material quickly enough, and was continually urging' its accurate recording.[52] In the end the army stores were found sufficient to equip, or complete the equipment of, twenty divisions. The amount of material that fell into German hands is shown in Table II.vi.10. To this must be added all kinds of other military equipment, such as bridge-building, listening, and measuring equipment, searchlights, and motor-vehicles[53] to a total value of RM77m.

Along with the confiscation of the war material found in the country went the take-over of economic installations of military importance, such as power-stations and gasworks, both for the maintenance of production and as a protection against acts of sabotage. The Wehrmacht promptly inspected all armament enterprises and thus gained a quick idea of articles manufactured and of production capacities. At the same time over 200,000 technical drawings and patents fell into German hands. They often proved of considerable importance to the Wehrmacht and to the

---

[50] Report by State Secretary Keppler on a speech by Hitler on 8 Mar. 1939 to leading representatives of the economy, the NSDAP, and the generals, in *Anatomie des Krieges*, 204. Cf. Messerschmidt, IV.v.7 (c) below.

[51] Wagner, *Generalquartiermeister*, 82.

[52] Ibid. 83.

[53] Speech by Hitler, 28 Apr. 1939. Quoted from Domarus, ii. 1156; Mastny, *Czechs*, 66, esp. n. 6.

TABLE II.VI.10. *Military equipment seized in the invasion of Czechoslovakia (1939)*

	According to Hitler	According to Czechoslovak source
Aircraft	1,582	1,231[a]
Anti-aircraft guns	501	
Anti-tank guns		1,966
Field-guns	2,175	2,253
Mortars	785	
Armoured vehicles	469	810
Machine-guns	43,876	57,000
Rifles	1,090,000	630,000
Pistols	114,000	
Infantry ammunition	>1,000m. rounds	
Artillery and gas shells	>3m. rounds	

[a] Plus material for a further 240.

Source: Speech by Hitler, 28 Apr. 1939 (in Domarus, ii. 1156); Mastny, *Czechs*, 66.

German armament industry: Czechoslovakia's armament industry had been extensive and highly developed.[54]

Whatever the exact constitutional link between the Protectorate and the Third Reich, Germany was determined to pursue to the full its 'interests dating back a thousand years, which are not only of a political but also of an economic nature'.[55] The economic autonomy of Bohemia-Moravia, undermined as early as October 1940 by the establishment of a customs union, remained formal and fictitious. In reality all regulations concerning the Protectorate were 'in conformity with the political, military, and economic requirements of the Reich'.[56] In view of the intended wars, both against France and—for the conquest of living-space in the east—against the USSR, this meant not only that 'the war potential of the Protectorate is definitely to be exploited in part or in full, and is to be directed towards mobilization as soon as possible',[57] but also that the entire Czechoslovak economy was to be integrated into the Four-year Plan and the New War Economy Production Plan.

As at the time of the annexation of Austria, so the regime was anxious also, when Prague was occupied, to get possession of Czechoslovak gold and currency reserves. In the summer of 1939, under pressure from the German military authorities, the

[54] Cf. Hummelberger, 'Rüstungsindustrie'.

[55] Speech by Hitler, 28 Apr. 1939, quoted from Baynes, ii. 1621.

[56] Hitler's decree on the Protectorate of Bohemia and Moravia, 16 Mar. 1939, *DGFP*, D. iv. 284.

[57] Account of a conference between Göring and representatives of the armed forces high command and the government, 25 July 1939, *IMT* iii. 170.

Czechoslovak National Bank transferred 809,984 ounces of gold from London to Berlin, in disregard of the British embargo. A year later its gold reserves in Prague were taken 'into safe keeping by the Reichsbank'.[58] Through enforced increases of capital and sales of shares, as well as through the expropriation of Jewish property and Jewish participations, a rapid penetration of banking and industry was accomplished. Bohemia and Moravia were the site of the major part of Czechoslovakia's industries: metallurgy, electrical engineering, and textiles were the most important. Production facilities were predominantly in first-class technological condition, especially in the case of metallurgy, mechanical engineering, and the armament industry. These all had some spare capacity, whose immediate utilization meant a considerable lessening of the load on the overburdened German rearmament economy. The stocks of metal found by the occupying forces were approximately as follows (in tonnes):

Copper	18,500	Lead	3,000	Zinc	8,500
Nickel	1,000	Aluminium	1,500	Tin	320

For this reason it was important that the raw materials found locally should not be moved to Germany. The same applied to available semi-finished goods, which were left to the Protectorate industry for processing. These, however, were not surplus stocks, which might have been transferred to the Altreich, but operating stocks needed for the maintenance of domestic production.

Smelting plants held ore stocks sufficient for ten months.[59] As the Protectorate industry was largely dependent on iron and steel supplies from the Reich, a quota and planning system for iron and steel was immediately introduced in March 1939.[60]

The expansion of German armament production was due mainly to the two biggest armament firms—the Škoda works in Pilsen (Plzeň) and Prague, and the Czechoslovak Arms Works (Zbrojovka) in Brno. An important factor for the German economy had been the voluminous exports of war material, one of the main reasons for Czechoslovakia's usually positive balance of trade. In 1937 Czechoslovakia had held fourth place in the world for exports of war materials. Even though the German authorities' economic intervention in the Protectorate was designed to reorganize 'the production of enterprises to German armament needs',[61] the Four-year Plan nevertheless 'attached outstanding importance, for well-known currency reasons . . . to the maintenance of those exports.'[62] At the very least, provision had to be made to prevent any of the Reich's scarce foreign currency being drawn upon for obtaining raw materials for Bohemia-Moravia. The

[58] Letter from Neurath to Eliáš, chairman of the Protectorate government, 10 June 1940, quoted from Brandes, *Tschechen*, 150.

[59] War-economy inspectorate, Prague, 26 Mar. 1939, BA-MA Wi I F 3/207. Cf. the German production figures in Tables II.IV.16–23 above.

[60] Ordinance of the minister of economic affairs, 18 Mar. 1939, BA-MA Wi I F 3/207.

[61] Kehrl, *Krisenmanager*, 160.

[62] Inspection order No. 3 of the war-economy inspectorate, Prague, 27 Mar. 1939, BA-MA Wi I F 3/207.

Protectorate, like Germany itself, was heavily dependent on foreign raw materials for its extensive exports of manufactured goods. The Wehrmacht, having set up a war-economy inspectorate in Prague immediately after the occupation, 'for the speedily utilization of the Czech lands for rearmament',[63] was therefore obliged to harmonize Czech orders—some of which had already been assigned—with the Four-year Plan. The latter laid down certain export quotas for export-oriented enterprises before making production capacities available to the Wehrmacht. Any foreign armament orders already being worked on had to be completed provided they earned foreign currency. In the late summer of 1939, eventually, control was introduced over all public and nationally important orders in the Protectorate.[64] In this way it was possible 'fully to maintain industrial activity well into the war winter of 1939–40 and to make the placing of the sought-after direct Wehrmacht orders contingent on the firms' ability to meet their raw-material requirements from their own resources'.[65]

As a result of the Third Reich's industrial accretions from the Protectorate and from the incorporation of Austria and the Sudetenland, Germany's share of world industrial production in mid-1939 amounted to 15 per cent. After the United States the Reich therefore held second place in the league table of the world's industrial countries.[66]

As Bohemia-Moravia's free production capacities could not be fully utilized straight away, Germany endeavoured to gain some of the 108,000 registered unemployed for work in the Reich. By mid-April 1939 some 30,000 workers had been enlisted; by the outbreak of the war the figure had risen to 70,000.[67]

There was a somewhat more favourable picture with regard to foodstuffs. The Protectorate had surpluses of the main types of grain, and indeed also of sugar, meat, and animal fats, while it was self-sufficient with regard to potatoes. Overall the territory was able to feed itself.

The creation of the Protectorate of Bohemia and Moravia did not only mean an enhancement of the Third Reich's rearmament potential. National Socialist Germany had inaugurated a new phase of large-area economics. 'European large-area economics used to imply the joint action of several states for common economic objectives and for an increase of their reciprocal exchange of goods on the basis of strict conditions laid down in trade agreements; now this concept has been remoulded for Europe.'[68] The Third Reich had taken the first step from an economy based on complementary trade arrangements with neighbouring states to a policy of economic hegemony.

---

[63] Appendix 1 to Inspection order No. 1 of the war-economy inspectorate, Prague, 22 Mar. 1939, BA-MA Wi I F 3/207.

[64] Record of a conference at the Four-year Plan authority, 8 Aug. 1939, BA-MA RW 29/2.

[65] Geschichte der Rüstungsinspektion Prag (1941), BA-MA RW 22/21.

[66] *Deutschlands wirtschaftliche Lage in der Jahresmitte 1939* (Germany's economic situation in mid-1939), expert opinion of the Reichs-Kredit-Gesellschaft, Berlin. Cf. Barthel, *Politik*, 105.

[67] Cf. Brandes, *Tschechen*, 154–5.

[68] *Protektorat Böhmen und Mähren*, 19.

5. Slovakia's Role in the 'New Economic Order'

With the territorial incorporation of Austria, the Sudetenland, and Bohemia and Moravia the nucleus of the German large-scale economic area, the so-called Greater German Reich, had taken shape. 'This self-contained economic body' could now be 'progressively shaped in whatever way the achievement of supreme efficiency demanded'.[69] The Third Reich therefore left nothing untried to surround its immediate sphere of dominion with a ring of states which were formally sovereign but were in fact politically, and above all economically, controllable from, or better still dependent on, Berlin. One of these was Slovakia. And although Berlin proceeded from the assumption that the Protectorate must 'form a certain economic unit' with the 'ward state' (*Schutzstaat*) of Slovakia, 'especially in the event of a major war',[70] great care was taken to let Bratislava, at least *de jure* and hence in the eyes of the world, keep its freedom of economic action. A customs and currency union with the Reich, initially under discussion, was therefore not implemented, though tariff barriers were abolished for trade with the Protectorate and the Sudetenland. German–Slovak relations were to become the model for close co-operation between the mutually complementary economies of two 'friendly' states. The National Socialist leaders used Slovakia as 'the prospectus offered to the small countries of south-east Europe and particularly to the Slav peoples: this is how independent a small country can be',[71] provided it it did not oppose the economic reorganization of Europe under German direction.

As, in view of the Third Reich's as yet insufficient means of military and political pressure, a 'currency and economic union . . . was feasible for only a few European countries', it was necessary 'in many instances to devise a form of alliance . . . by means of which some of the states could, even without currency union, be economically attached to Germany'.[72] In the case of Slovakia it in fact proved possible, by means of an appropriate system of treaties, to bring the country's economic activity progressively under German control, so that by the time war broke out it was almost totally dominated by Germany. The treaty of protection imposed on the Slovak government (18–23 March 1939) already revealed the limitations of Bratislava's freedom of manœuvre, as it had to conduct its foreign policy (which of course included foreign-trade policy) 'always . . . in close consultation with the German government'.[73] The confidential supplementary protocol forced Slovakia into an economic shot-gun marriage—into indissoluble collaboration in the economic and financial fields in accordance with Germany's general, and particularly rearmament, needs. Slovakia was a predominantly agricultural and forest-cultivating country: the 1938 census revealed the following

---

[69] Ibid.

[70] Friedensburg, 'Rohstoffpotential', 146.

[71] Note by the German minister in Bratislava, 25 June 1940, *DGFP*, D. x. 16.

[72] Minutes of a conference at the ministry of economic affairs on the economic reorganization of Europe, 15 July 1940, quoted from *Weltherrschaft im Visier*, 266.

[73] Treaty of protection between Germany and Slovakia, 18/23 Mar. 1939, *DGFP*, D. vi. 43.

percentage distribution of occupations in the territory of the 'independent' Slovak state.[74]

Agriculture and forestry	57.0
Mining, industry, and crafts	19.8
Commerce and finance	5.3
Communications (railways, post, and others)	4.6
Public service and professions	5.8
Other	7.5

Above all else, then, Slovakia had to help diminish the Greater German Reich's shortage of foodstuffs and animal feed. In consequence, the 'increase and direction of Slovak agricultural production' had to be effected 'with a view to market possibilities in Germany', with particular attention to increasing the breeding of pigs and raising milk production.[75] Slovakia was the first country to have to accept the imposition of a long-term economic plan tailored to the needs of the German raw-material situation: this concerned the sector of timber and forestry. Through this arrangement the Four-year Plan, albeit by an indirect route and in only one economic sector, acquired validity beyond the immediate German sphere of sovereignty. The result of this may be judged from the fact that in 1939 some 83.7 per cent of Slovak timber exports went to the German Reich, where they remedied what was becoming a critical shortage.

Germany's special interest, of course, was focused on Slovakia's mineral wealth. With the help of German advisers and technology this was developed and utilized, and, if not needed to meet Slovakia's own requirements, made available as a matter of priority to the German economy. To ensure that this was done the Four-year Plan assumed control of all mineral prospecting, and hence also plans for extraction, which aimed chiefly at an increase in ore-mining. This was in fact achieved (Table II.VI.11).

Enterprises which did not, in the German view, make optimal use of their mining rights and facilities could forfeit their privileges. Even though, in the words of the bilateral agreement, 'development and direction in industrial production' would be pursued 'with a view to German and Slovak vital interests and market conditions',[76] it was not difficult to guess which of the two would play the dominant role. Altogether German–Slovak trade was based on the principle, already practised under the New Plan, that Germany received agricultural and forestry items as well as raw materials, and in return exported finished and semi-finished goods, as well as capital goods, the latter being so purposefully chosen that they in turn served the satisfaction of German demand. As for trade agreements with third countries, Slovakia was allowed to conclude these 'only after conclusion of the agreements

---

[74] List from Dress, *Slowakei,* 56 n. 1.

[75] Confidential protocol on economic and financial collaboration between the German Reich and the Slovak state, 23 Mar. 1939, *DGFP,* D. vi. 44.

[76] Ibid.

TABLE II.VI.II. *Slovak extraction of minerals 1939–1940* (t.)

	1939	1940
Iron ores	765,897	862,025
Iron slag	17,185	43,622
Iron pyrites	10,184	13,904
Manganese ores	55,580	59,931
Antimony ores	10,907	12,221
Copper ores	123,885	114,252
Mercury ores	1	278
Precious-metal ores	111,430	96,507
Crude oil	16,000	24,458
Salt-pan salt	14,789	5,866
Natural gas[a]	133,331	118,483

[a] m.^{3}

Source: Dress, *Slowakei*, 87 n. 1.

with Germany' and in consultation with the Reich.[77] A trade treaty concluded on 22 June 1939[78] ensured that future consideration would unambiguously and primarily be given to German interests; this was reflected also in the fact that notice of termination of the agreement could not be given by Bratislava.[79] Table II.VI.12 gives a survey of Slovak exports.

By the end of March 1939 the National Socialist regime had assured itself of decisive influence on Slovak financial operations. Bratislava was induced to set up a National Bank, with the Reichsbank participating in its establishment and delegating an adviser to its board, 'who will take part in all important decisions'.[80] Berlin further reserved to itself the right to be consulted on the preparation and implementation of the Slovak budget. Without the consent of the German representative in the Slovak National Bank the Slovak government could not raise any loans.

Within the so-called 'protective zone' (*Schutzzone*), where, as an occupying force, it enjoyed military sovereignty and hence economic usufruct, the Wehrmacht practised direct control over the Slovak economy. But beyond the control which the German forces were entitled to practise over the zone's armament enterprises, which were working for them, there were of course also opportunities for exerting influence on industry in the rest of Slovakia.[81]

In assessing the economic measures associated with the break-up of

[77] Ibid.   [78] *RGBl.* (1939), ii. 860.
[79] Cf. Hoensch, *Slowakei*, 346 n. 52.
[80] Confidential protocol on economic and financial collaboration between the German Reich and the Slovak state, 23 Mar. 1939, *DGFP*, D. vi. 44.
[81] Ibid. vii. 41.

TABLE II.VI.12. *Slovak exports 1939–1943* (Slovak crowns × 1m.)

Export markets	1939	1940	1941	1942	1943
Germany	513	859	920	1,750	2,270
Bohemia & Moravia	1,126	1,382	1,381	1,294	1,507
SUBTOTAL	*1,639*	*2,241*	*2,301*	*3,044*	*3,777*
Italy	21	184	230	575	412
Hungary	67	161	176	249	387
Romania	111	121	74	386	633
Rest of Europe	287	450	410	450	623
Asia	53	18	—	—	—
Africa	2	—	—	—	—
America	17	—	—	—	—
Australia	2	—	—	—	—
TOTAL EXPORTS	2,199	3,175	3,191	4,704	5,832

Source: Dress, *Slowakei*, 108.

Czechoslovakia it may be said that, even before the beginning of the war, the integration of the Sudeten regions, the Protectorate, and Slovakia in an economic union dominated by Germany represented a satisfactory start. 'From the point of the view of the war economy the main advantage accruing to Germany from the new order in Czechoslovak territory was the acquisition of a vigorous and hard-working population and of numerous, often outstanding, processing facilities, especially in industries vital to rearmament.'[82] In addition, 'the situation of both Axis powers' [had] ameliorated because of the economic possibilities which resulted from the transfer to Germany of the great production capacity of Czechoslovakia'. This had contributed 'towards a considerable strengthening of the Axis against the Western powers'.[83]

6. THE INCLUSION OF SOUTH-EAST EUROPE IN GERMANY'S WAR ECONOMY AND LARGE-AREA ECONOMY

In view of the effects of its policy of annexations, after March 1939 the National Socialist regime could no longer entertain the illusion that it alone could 'determine . . . the time and scope of political upheavals in Europe, while avoiding a conflict with a group of powers led by Britain'.[84] Resolved as it was to maintain its

[82] Friedensburg, 'Rohstoffpotential', 155.

[83] Göring at a conference with Mussolini and Ciano, 15 Apr. 1939, *IMT* iii. 170–1.

[84] Progress report by Carl Krauch, general plenipotentiary for special questions of chemical production, to the general council of the Four-year Plan authority, 28 Apr. 1939, quoted from *Anatomie des Krieges*, 211.

expansionist course, it had to contemplate a military escalation on an as yet unpredictable scale. Henceforward the Third Reich had to concern itself not only with its own economic preparedness for war but also with that of its potential allies, among whom it counted the powers of the Anti-Comintern Pact, viz. Italy, Hungary, and Spain, whose dependence on German 'economic support in nearly all areas of requirements . . . was well known'.[85] Germany therefore had to endeavour 'to strengthen its own war potential and that of its allies to such an extent that the coalition could stand up to the efforts of almost the whole of the rest of the world'. Such a task did not seem feasible, even within the Greater German framework with the inclusion of Slovakia.

To this contingency, however, the leaders of the party, government, Wehrmacht, and economy, as well as academic economists, knew the answer. If 'at a given time in a given area the satisfaction of a certain vital need cannot be achieved', then, according to the economic and political doctrine of National Socialism, that need had to be 'met within the range of the political will whose influence radiates out into adjoining areas'.[86] These areas, following the 'solution' of the Czechoslovak question, included primarily south-east Europe. Germany's economic readiness for war could only be achieved through 'the great joint efforts of all allies', above all 'by way of an improved, initially peaceful, enlargement of the economic area to include the Balkans and Spain, so that the raw-material base may meet the needs of the coalition'.[87]

With its foreign-trade policy based on the New Plan and as a result of the close economic ties of the south-east European states with Austria, now part of the Reich, by the end of 1938 Germany enjoyed 'a virtually unchallenged economic and political hegemony in the south-east': it was one of the biggest suppliers of armaments, it had the biggest share in foreign trade, and through its clearing policy it 'held the south-eastern countries firmly in its grip'.[88] Even so, it was now necessary to combine war economy and large-area economic concepts in order to achieve an intensified complementary exchange of goods. After the expansion of the Reich territory by the Ostmark (the 'Eastern March', as Austria was now called), and more especially after the Munich agreement, 'a political development had taken place to create the best foundations for a further evolution of economic relations with the south-east'. The old National Socialist resolve 'to advance through trade agreements to economic alliance' had proved to be realizable.[89]

In detail the Four-year Plan organization envisaged the following measures:

1. establishment of a unified large-scale economic bloc of the four European Anti-Comintern partners, to be joined also by Yugoslavia and Bulgaria;

---

[85] Ibid. 212. [86] Lüdecke, *Sicherung*, 23.

[87] Progress report by Krauch, quoted from *Anatomie des Krieges*, 213–14. Cf. Mitrović, 'Ergänzungswirtschaft'.

[88] Expert opinion of the Osteuropa-Gesellschaft in Vienna, 1942, on the industrial and economic effects of the decline (and growth) of German political influence in south-east Europe since 1938, quoted from *Griff nach Südosteuropa*, 26.

[89] Lecture by T. Frhr. von Wilmowsky on the origin, development, and work of the Mitteleuropäischer Wirtschaftstag (Central European Economic Forum), Nov. 1938, ibid.

2. within this group of states, development and control of the war economy;

3. extension of German influence to Romania, Turkey, and Persia.[90]

The Balkan countries which enjoyed an agricultural surplus would supply the bread- and fodder-grain lacking for Germany's war preparations, and would also meet a large proportion of German meat requirements. Moreover, these states possessed the very raw materials 'which Germany had the greatest need to import':[91] see Table II.VI.13. All the countries of south-east Europe, but especially Romania and Hungary, had deposits of manganese ore for iron and steel production. Their reserves of copper, lead, and bauxite, in particular, were 'if further developed, of major importance to our rearmament situation'.[92] The most important deposits of antimony at the time were in the mountainous Hungarian–Slovak border region. Crude-oil extraction could be greatly increased in Hungary and Romania. Yugoslav chrome ore was extremely important to German high-grade steel manufacture.[93]

Since Germany's industrial capacity (in both equipment and manpower) was fully used up, Berlin considered whether the Balkan countries might be able to build up heavy industries of their own on the basis of their raw materials and manpower. There had to be a guarantee that such industries would place themselves at the service of the German war economy. The question was evidently answered in the affirmative, as 'their inadequate quantities of coking coal . . . enabled the Reich largely to determine the scale of the development of heavy industry in the countries of the south-east'.[94] German expectations of imports therefore largely depended on the extent of German counter-deliveries for the purpose of industrialization, and hence for the extraction of raw materials and for increased local production.

The directives issued by the Four-year Plan authority for German economic policy *vis-à-vis* south-east Europe defined three priority areas. First, there was the safeguarding of mineral-oil supplies on the basis of 'large-area planning to interlink the German development plan with the potential of south-east Europe'.[95] This presupposed not only a rapid increase in Romanian production but also the solution of the problem of transportation to Germany and Italy, by ensuring the availability of the necessary shipping space and by the construction of pipelines. In addition, the planners envisaged the production of synthetic motor-fuel on the basis of Moravian coal in various south-east European countries. Secondly, the Four-year Plan organization aimed at setting up a Buna base in south-east Europe. Finally,

[90] Progress report by Krauch, quoted from *Anatomie des Krieges*, 211.

[91] Schmölders, 'Probleme', 201; secret expert opinion of the Institut für Weltwirtschaft (Institute for World Economics), 'Die Bedeutung der südosteuropäischen Getreidewirtschaft und ihre wehrwirtschaftliche Beurteilung', Apr. 1939, BA-MA RW 19, Anh. 1/572.

[92] Report by Thomas to the foreign ministry, 24 May 1939, BA-MA Wi I F 5/115.

[93] Research paper by A. Kruemmer, commissioned by the war-economy Staff, on the Yugoslav mining industry and its importance to Germany in peace and war, 13 Oct. 1938, BA-MA RW 19, appendix I/115. Cf. Table II.VI.13.

[94] Research paper by the Reichsamt für wehrwirtschaftliche Planung (Reich Office for War Economy Planning), Mar. 1939, on the importance of south-east European raw materials to the German war economy, BA R 7 x/323.

[95] Progress report by Krauch, quoted from *Anatomie des Krieges*, 212.

TABLE II.VI.13. *Principal raw-material resources in south-east Europe* (1,000 t.)

	Bulgaria		Greece		Yugoslavia (Serbia and Croatia)		Romania		Hungary	
	Estimated reserves	Ann. extraction	Estimated reserves	Ann. extraction	Estimated reserves	Ann. extraction	Estimated reserves	Ann. extraction	Estimated reserves	Ann. extraction
Hard coal	140,000	206.0[a]	—	—	45,000	391.0[a]	48,000	257.0[a]	220,000	1,107.0[b]
Brown coal and lignite	3,880,000	2,549.0[a]	≥1,000,000	108.0[b]	c.2,000,000	6,888.2[a]	2,800,000	2,386.0[a]	1,600,000	9,518.0[b]
Crude oil	—	—	—	—	—	1.1[c]	>60,000[d]	5,250.0[e]	—	240.0
Bauxite	—	—	c.60,000	c.180.0[a]	>100,000	c.280.0[a]	≤40,000	10.5[c]	≥250,000	564.0[a]
Copper ores, pyrites, and sulphur ores	>1,200	c.1.0[f]	—	278.8[g]	—	1,063.8[h]	3,500	24.3[i]	>5,500[j]	79.7[k]
Lead and zinc ores	≥3,000	25.0[l]	—	25.2[m]	>9,000	807.0[a]	—	25.6[a]	—	11.9[n]
Chrome ore	—	1.8[b]	—	53.0[c]	—	71.0[a]	2,000	discontinued at end of WWI	—	—
Natural gas[o]	—	—	—	—	—	3,628.1	500–600[p]	1,757,400[a]	—	—

[a] 1940.   [b] 1938.   [c] 1939.   [d] m.³×1,000m.; and < 120m. m.³   [e] 1941.

[f] Copper ores (1938 figure).

[g] Copper ores—3,500 t.; pyrites—244,000 t.; sulphide ores—30,800 t.; sulphur ores—500 t. (1938 figures.)

[h] Copper ores—929,200 t.; pyrites—134,600 t. (1940 figures.)

[i] Copper ores—13,400 t.; pyrites—10,900 t. (1940 figures.)

[j] And < 6.5 m. t.

[k] Pyrites—71,400 t.; pyrites concentrate—8,300 t. (1938 figures.)

[l] Lead ores—15,000 t.; zinc ores—10,000 t. (1938 figures.)

[m] Lead ores—14,900 t.; zinc ores—10,300 t. (1938 figures.)

[n] Lead concentrate—6,700 t.; zinc concentrate—5,200 t. (1938 figures.)

[o] m.³×1m.

[p] t.×1m.

Source: Griff nach Südosteuropa, 12–13.

because of the tight manpower and transport situation in Germany, construction of factories producing light metals was envisaged in Hungary and Yugoslavia.

Ever since 1933–4 Berlin had been working systematically through diplomatic channels for a consolidation and extension of German–Hungarian economic relations; the Anschluss now enabled it to lend effective emphasis to its claim to economic supremacy. After the visit to Budapest by the minister of economic affairs, Funk, in October 1938 German efforts were aimed at gearing Hungary's economic potential to the service of the German war economy by integrating it into the planned large-scale economic area. At the beginning of 1939 a virtual ultimatum was dispatched to the Budapest government 'to adjust Hungarian agriculture . . . to the requirements of the German market to a greater extent than hitherto';[96] in other words, production increases were expected to be focused on the elimination of shortages in the Reich, such as those of fat, wheat, and animal feed. In return, the Berlin rulers promised assistance with the development of Hungarian industry, though they demanded the 'alignment of Hungarian industrial production to German export needs'.[97] In the spring of 1939 the trade agreements between Hungary and the former Austrian state and those between Hungary and the Greater German Reich were brought into line with the recent political and territorial changes. The agreement of 2 March 1939 envisaged the 'reciprocal complementation of the two economies'.[98] Germany henceforward so guided its exports to Hungary that they served the rationalization of agriculture and the intensification of raw-material extraction. As was realized in Hungary itself, the country was to be 'depressed to the level of a raw-material base'.[99] Between 1938 and 1939 there was a decline in Hungary's (already insignificant) exports to Britain and France; exports to the United States even fell from 6 per cent to 3 per cent of the total volume of Hungarian exports. By contrast, trade with the Axis powers increased in importance, mainly as a result of deliberate measures 'designed to bring about the country's organic integration in the new continental European large-area economy'.[100] From 1939 onwards the Third Reich headed the list of buyers of Hungarian goods, and from that date Hungary, for its part, concentrated its exports to a greater extent towards its powerful neighbour.

With the annexation of Austria and the break-up of Czechoslovakia, Hungarian capital fell into German hands; together with German investments this represented in 1939 a German share of more than 50 per cent in Hungary's foreign industrial and mining capital. In more than 100 major enterprises there was a German controlling interest of over 51 per cent. Even before the outbreak of the Second World War the German Reich controlled 'such extensive and ramified investments

[96] German memorandum to the Hungarian government, Feb. 1939, quoted from Ránki, 'Wirtschaftsleben', 239.

[97] Ibid. 240.

[98] Expert opinion of the ministry of economic affairs on the development of German economic relations with foreign countries during the first quarter of 1939, BA-MA Wi VI/122.

[99] Observation by the Hungarian delegation, quoted from Berend and Ránki, *Economic Development*, 284.

[100] Surányi-Unger, 'Ungarische Wehrwirtschaft', 93.

that through them it was able to supervise, and indeed up to a point influence, Hungary's entire economy'.[101]

With the intention of 'extending production in the south-east states and harmonizing it with German needs'[102] the foreign ministry, in conjunction with the Four-year Plan authority, also became quite active in its relations with Bulgaria, and this did not fail to yield results. It was thanks to the policy of the New Plan 'that the Bulgarians had for several years been increasingly orienting themselves in economic matters towards Germany alone'.[103] Subsequently, during the Austrian crisis and the break-up of Czechoslovakia, Berlin succeeded in getting Sofia to increase Bulgarian raw-material exports in return for supplies of military equipment. As German imports had until then consisted primarily of agricultural produce, and as by the end of 1938 these were so large 'that they could no longer be increased to any major extent',[104] imports of industrial raw materials were continually gaining in importance. In order to safeguard them Bulgaria had to accede to the participation of German industrial groups, especially in its lead and zinc-ore mines.[105] Moreover, the Reich granted Bulgaria extensive loans for the intensification of mining and for arms purchases in Germany. In spite of its own growing requirements the Wehrmacht continued to comply readily with Bulgarian requests for war material, especially as this consisted cheifly of ammunition and thus enabled the German forces to get rid of older stock. The continuous credit expansion was generally 'in line . . . with the hoped-for further consolidation of Germany's economic position in the Balkans'.[106]

Although negotiations for an agreement on the promotion of economic relations between Berlin and Bucharest had long been going on, it was only due to massive pressure at the time of the German invasion of rump Czechoslovakia that they came to a conclusion which satisfied the National Socialist regime (23 March 1939). The Romanians initially resisted what Germany had hoped to make the central issue of the bilateral arrangements—'industrial co-operation in a mixed industrial committee'—rightly fearing that 'Germany would deny them the right to control their own industrialization'.[107] The contract which was eventually signed was based on a five-year plan jointly prepared by the two countries, under which Romania was to supply prescribed agricultural products and raw materials, such as mineral oil, while Germany promised to supply the plants and machinery needed for their production and processing. In detail, this is what was envisaged:

[101] Letter from the Hungarian premier dated 1939, quoted from Door, *Politik*, 42.

[102] Expert opinion of the ministry of economic affairs on the development of German economic relations with foreign countries during the first quarter of 1939, BA-MA Wi vi/112.

[103] Memorandum of the foreign ministry, 1 Feb. 1938, quoted from Sohl, 'Kriegsvorbereitungen', 104.

[104] Memorandum by Wiehl, foreign ministry, 15 Nov. 1938, ibid. 108; secret expert opinion of the Institut für Weltwirtschaft on the present state and capacity of Bulgarian cereal farming, Mar. 1939, BA-MA RW, Anh. I/585.

[105] Secret protocol between Germany and Bulgaria, 12 Mar. 1938, quoted from Sohl, 'Kriegsvorbereitungen', 105–6.

[106] Memorandum by Wiehl, 15 Nov. 1938, ibid. 108.

[107] Report from Wohlthat to Göring on his negotiations in Bucharest, 10–23 Mar. 1939, dated 27 Mar. 1939, *DGFP*, D. vi. 165.

1. development and direction of Romanian agriculture towards increased cultivation of animal-feed produce, oleaginous fruit, and fibre-plants;
2. intensification of Romanian lumbering and forestry;
3. accelerated exploitation of Romanian mineral wealth by joint German–Romanian companies;
4. implementation of a grand-scale petroleum programme, likewise by a German–Romanian company;[108]
5. close co-operation between German and Romanian industry with a view to harmonization of German and Romanian foreign-trade interests;
6. German participation in Romanian banks;
7. development of the Romanian transport network and services, largely for the purpose of ensuring speedy and smooth transportation of products and commodities destined for Germany;
8. equipment of the Romanian forces with German weapons (these, given the Third Reich's desperate shortage of foreign currency, were accepted in payment for petroleum).

Bucharest was particularly interested in equipping its armed forces with German aircraft. Quite apart from bypassing the currency problem, this deal had the advantage for Germany that Romania's new weapons and military equipment were in line with German norms and that the country, in consequence, was predestined to become a military ally. Overall the agreement meant 'a decisive step forward in the development of German economic policy in south-eastern Europe; production within our European sphere of influence will be increased with the participation of German capital'.[109] The Third Reich had embarked on the decisive phase of the change-over from world trade to large-area economics. The German–Romanian treaty was regarded as a 'model of modern regulation of economic co-operation between two states within the large-scale economic area'.[110]

In addition to Hungary, Romania, and Bulgaria, Berlin attempted to draw Yugoslavia into its political and economic orbit, i.e. to intervene, on the Romanian model, in the country's economic life in order to align it optimally towards German rearmament requirements. By 1939 Germany had succeeded in guiding an ever-increasing volume of Yugoslav trade towards itself and in moving up to the top place in the list of Yugoslavia's trade partners:[111] see Table II.VI.14.

The method of deliberate indebtedness had also been successfully applied: by importing from Yugoslavia considerably more than it exported to that country, Germany had put Yugoslavia into a relationship of some dependence. Under the clearing procedure Yugoslavia could only use the credit balance in its trade with the Reich for purchasing commodities there, i.e. it more or less had to content itself with what Berlin was able or willing to export. In the now well-tried manner, care

---

[108] On the problems and the significance of German–Romanian oil deals cf. Marguerat, *Le IIIe Reich*.
[109] Report from Wohlthat to Göring, 27 Feb. 1939, *DGFP*, D. v. 407.
[110] Koelble, *Grundzüge*, 63. On the development of German–Romanian economic relations cf. Schwabe, *Wirtschaftsvertrag*.
[111] Cf. Schumann, 'Aspekte', and Table. II.VI.14.

TABLE II.VI.14. *Share of different countries in Yugoslav trade 1926–1940 (%)*

	Germany		Austria		Czechoslovakia		Britain		United States		Italy		France	
	Imp.	Exp.	Imp.	Exp.	Imp.	Exp.	Imp.	Exp.	Imp.	Exp.	Imp.	Exp.	Imp.	Exp.
1926–30	14.2	10.4	18.2	18.9	18.2	9.2	6.0	1.3			12.2	25.8	4.3	3.4
1930	17.5	11.7	16.8	17.7	17.6	8.2	5.9	1.5	4.1	0.8	11.3	28.3	3.9	4.1
1931	19.3	11.3	15.2	15.2	18.2	15.5	6.6	2.0	4.2	1.0	10.3	25.0	4.4	4.0
1932	17.7	11.3	13.4	22.1	15.6	13.2	7.4	2.1	4.4	0.9	12.7	23.1	4.5	2.7
1933	13.2	11.3	16.1	21.7	12.1	10.8	9.7	2.7	5.1	1.9	15.9	21.5	4.2	2.2
1934	13.9	15.4	12.4	16.4	11.7	11.3	9.3	4.7	6.4	4.1	15.5	20.6	5.0	1.3
1935	16.2	18.6	11.9	14.3	14.0	13.4	10.1	5.3	6.2	5.6	10.0	16.7	4.3	1.6
1936	26.7	23.7	10.3	14.6	15.3	12.3	8.5	9.9	6.4	4.9	2.5	3.1	2.5	2.0
1937	32.7	21.7	10.5	13.5	11.3	7.9	6.8	7.4	6.3	5.0	8.4	9.4	1.8	5.4
1938	32.6	35.9	6.9	6.1	10.7	7.9	8.3	9.6	6.1	5.1	9.0	6.4	2.9	1.5
1939	47.6	31.8	—	—	6.5	14.0	5.1	6.7	5.2	5.1	11.7	10.6	2.0	2.5
1940	53.7	36.0	—	—	4.6	10.0	1.9	2.8	4.8	1.0	13.3	14.5	0.4	7.8

Source: Wuescht, *Jugoslawien*, 92.

was taken that the exports earmarked for Yugoslavia served the rationalization of agriculture and, more especially, the development of mining, i.e. Germany's rearmament interests. The National Socialist regime, of course, worked on the assumption that Yugoslavia and the rest of the Balkan countries, because of their low technological level in agriculture and industry, would only be able to mobilize a small part of their economic potential.

Germany's intention to 'tie Yugoslavia ever more firmly to itself' was understood in Belgrade, where efforts were made to consolidate the dominant influence of British and French capital in the Yugoslav economy and, if possible, to stabilize it. But, in the face of the new territorial and political shifts and of the Third Reich's leading position in Yugoslav foreign trade, it was found in 1939 that Yugoslavia had 'already committed itself too deeply for any other economic policy to be pursued *vis-à-vis* Germany . . . without causing upheavals' to the Yugoslav economy.[112] The Belgrade government no longer saw a meaningful alternative to close political and economic collaboration with Hitler's Germany. Although it succeeded in greatly slowing down German capital infiltration before the outbreak of war, it was compelled in the summer of 1939, in return for promised German deliveries of war material, to raise the raw-material and timber quotas which were due to the Reich under existing clearing agreements, to give sympathetic consideration to German 'requests and applications' for 'surveying and exploitation of the raw-material resources, and to . . . grant them as far as possible'.[113]

German foreign-trade policy towards the Balkan states was directed towards intensifying agricultural production and raw-material extraction through German technical equipment and financial participation, and to steer these towards German rearmament needs. Economic relations were governed by the formula: 'expansion of exports by participating in the industrialization of the world'.[114]

In 1937 the Third Reich absorbed 47 per cent of Bulgaria's total exports, 41 per cent of Hungary's, 35 per cent of Yugoslavia's, 32 per cent of Greece's, and 27 per cent of Romania's; these percentages again rose considerably before the outbreak of war (the financial figures are given in Table II.VI.15). As was noted in Germany with some satisfaction, 'this is not just a case of increased exchanges, but the national economies are collaborating with each other—a novelty in trade policy'.[115]

---

[112] Statement by an economist, Jan. 1939, quoted from Wuescht, *Jugoslawien*, 84.

[113] Secret protocol between Germany and Yugoslavia, 5 July 1939, *DGFP*, D. vi. 862. Cf. Schönfeld, 'Rohstoffsicherungspolitik', 221.

[114] This formula was developed by Max Ilgner, member of the IG-Farben board, in an eponymous pamphlet (Jena, 1938).

[115] Kühn, *Verlagerungen*, 22. Cf. Marguerat, *Le IIIe Reich*, 85; and Wendt, 'England', 499 (with lower figures). This division of labour based on foreign-trade arrangements was not to last. 'The significance of the war for the large-area economic development in south-east Europe lies in the fact that it creates the power-political conditions for such co-operation. . . . Not only is a new hegemony arising out of the war, but it represents a phase of large-area economic integration by radically accelerating the necessary reorganization of economic life and enforcing it against all obstacles. What has been left undone must now be made up for within a few years. As a result, the war acquires revolutionary status beyond any other conflict' (Schulmeister, *Werdende Großraumwirtschaft*, 16–17).

TABLE II.vi.15. *German trade with south-east Europe 1933–1940* (RMm.)

	Bulgaria		Greece		Yugoslavia		Romania		Hungary		Total	
	Imports[a]	Exports[b]	Imports[a]	Exports[b]	Imports[a]	Exports[b]	Imports[a]	Exports[b]	Imports[a]	Exports[b]	Imports	Exports
1933	31.3	17.7	53.4	18.7	33.5	33.8	46.1	46.0	34.2	38.1	198.5	154.3
1934	33.7	19.3	55.3	29.3	36.3	31.5	59.0	50.9	63.9	39.6	248.2	170.6
1935	41.4	39.9	58.5	49.1	61.4	36.9	79.9	63.8	77.9	62.9	319.1	252.6
1936	57.6	47.6	68.4	63.5	75.2	77.2	92.3	103.6	93.4	83.0	386.9	374.9
1937	71.8	68.2	76.4	113.1	132.2	134.4	179.5	129.5	114.1	110.5	574.0	555.7
1938	84.3	56.4	93.6	111.1	107.9	118.0	140.4	148.8	109.7	110.0	535.9	544.3
1938[c]	95.7	61.6	101.0	121.2	172.2	144.6	177.8	168.6	186.2	146.4	732.9	642.4
1939	110.0	97.8	92.1	85.5	131.5	181.3	209.5	216.7	222.5	228.7	765.6	810.0
1940	176.8	152.2	93.0	60.3	239.7	317.1	427.1	350.1	207.3	298.3	1,143.9	1,178.0

[a] From.
[b] To.
[c] Within the frontier at the end of 1938.

Source: Griff nach Südosteuropa, 24.

VII. The Third Reich's Economic Readiness for War

1. The Agricultural Supply Balance Sheet in the Large-scale Economic Area

ALTHOUGH the economic domination which Germany had now attained over the countries of south-east Europe had brought the regime a good step nearer to the establishment of its large-scale economic area, the economic strength thus acquired was still not sufficient—with any reasonable hope of success—either for a war of revenge against France, with the risk of British involvement, or for a struggle for living-space in the east, i.e. against the Soviet Union, which was itself conducting mutual-aid negotiations with the Western powers. Foodstuff and animal-feed supplies were by no means assured in the event of a blockade, any more than manpower requirements—which, if only because of the call-up of large numbers for the Wehrmacht, were bound to increase on the outbreak of war. If the rearmament course was to be maintained, an improvement in Germany's economic situation was 'not possible . . . without inroads into foreign states or attacks on the property of others'.[1]

To Hitler the solution of the problem—combining the long-term programme of gaining living-space wth the short-term programme of rearmament—was the conquest of Poland. This he regarded as 'indispensable in securing for Germany Polish supplies of agricultural produce and coal'. If that were achieved, then, in the Fürher's belief, 'Germany would be invincible' and able 'once and for all to settle accounts with its arch-enemy France'.[2]

The rearmament and overall economic situation, of course, would look different if the Western powers were to regard the invasion of Poland as a *casus belli* and, on their part, entangle the Third Reich in military complications. What then were the economic premises which the National Socialist state had ready for that contingency—a contingency which Hitler included in his calculations, even though he did not consider it likely, but which nevertheless occurred?

Before the attack on Poland, and shortly after it, responsible political, military, and economic circles once more examined Germany's economic potential as well as the resources of the states which, since 1933, had been ever more closely linked with the Third Reich, in order, if necessary, to take suitable measures

to make a European group of powers under German leadership blockade-proof. In detail, an analysis was called for of the extent to which that object was attainable either totally or to a high degree, provided the war economy of the region in question . . . was employed to the

---

[1] Hitler to top leaders of the Wehrmacht, 23 May 1939, quoted from Jacobsen, *1939–1945*, 110.
[2] Report of a speech by Hitler to representatives of the economy, the Party, and the generals, 8 Mar. 1939, quoted from *Anatomie des Krieges*, 204. Cf. Messerschmidt, IV.vi.2 below.

maximum, and provided the economy of further states within that region's sphere of influence, such as the Nordic area (Sweden, Norway, Finland, and the Baltic states), was mobilized on a scale necessary and practicable for the war economy.[3]

The result of painstaking analysis of the war-economy situation was inconclusive and called for a different approach. Despite all efforts, since the enactment of the 'New Plan', to safeguard wartime imports by switching foreign trade to European states with secure supply-lines, the hoped-for results had largely failed to materialize. This sobering conclusion was due to the fact that Germany's favoured trade partners, especially in south-east Europe, either did not possess the industrial raw materials and agricultural products needed by the Third Reich in sufficient quantities or else, before the outbreak of the war, were not extracting or producing them on a sufficient scale. Even though imports from south-east Europe were steadily rising during the 1930s, their share of German overall imports still only amounted in 1938 to 9.9 per cent, as against 4.7 per cent in 1933. Hence, in view of the increase in demand resulting from the Four-year Plan, the role played by overseas countries in German imports had inevitably grown again.[4]

1933	45%	1934	41%	1935	38%
1936	40%	1937	44%	1938	46%

In the event of warlike complications with the Western powers, either as a consequence of the German attack on Poland or later in connection with a German preventive strike against France and possibly Britain, the naval blockade which had to be expected was bound to reduce German imports appreciably and restrict them, at best, to the countries and extent shown in Table II.VII.1.

In the event of war, therefore, only some 44.4 per cent of the necessary requirement of imported foodstuffs and 33 per cent of the requirement of imported raw materials could be regarded as relatively secure. These percentages could undoubtedly be stepped up by increasing agricultural yields and extracting larger quantities of raw materials in south-east Europe—which was the aim of the Third Reich's endeavours. On the other hand, it had to be expected that the Western powers would be exerting strong pressure on the neutrals to get them to reduce their peacetime volume of exports to Germany and that they would at least partially succeed in cutting off the supply of raw materials from Belgian and Dutch colonies to their mother countries and thence to Germany—so that ultimately 'considerably less than 33 per cent of the needed raw-material imports' would seem to be assured.[5]

The Berlin rulers nevertheless believed, even before the outbreak of war, that they had found a satisfactory answer at least to the question of wartime food supplies for the civilian population and the Wehrmacht—a question raised much too late during the First World War, and not infrequently dismissed as of secondary

---

[3] Research paper of the Reich office for economic development, 'Möglichkeiten einer Großraumwirtschaft unter deutscher Führung', Part I, July 1939, BA R 25/53.

[4] Expert opinion of Tomberg, of the war-economy and armaments office, end of Jan. 1940: 'Der Außenhandel in den wehrwirtschaftlichen Vorbereitungen Deutschlands vor dem gegenwärtigen Krieg', BA-MA Wi I F 5/1551.   [5] Ibid.

TABLE II.VII.I. *Foreign share of German imports immediately before the war (%)*

	Overall	Foodstuffs	Raw materials
RELIABLE IMPORTS:			
Italy	4.5	6.5	2.9
Czechoslovakia	2.4	1.0	2.6
Hungary, Romania, Yugoslavia, Bulgaria, and Greece	9.9	17.2	5.3
Scandinavia and Finland	11.4	11.2	11.5
Baltic States	1.8	2.2	1.3
Belgium, Holland, and Switzerland	9.1	6.2	7.5
Russia	0.9	0.1	1.9
TOTAL	40.0	44.4	33.0
DEFAULTING OR DOUBTFUL IMPORTS	60.0	55.6	67.0

Source: Expert opinion of Tomberg of the war-economy and armaments office, end of Jan. 1940: 'Der Außenhandel in den wehrwirtschaftlichen Vorbereitungen Deutschlands vor dem gegenwärtigen Krieg', BA-MA Wi I F 5/1551.

importance by those then responsible. Detailed investigations all agreed that Greater Germany would be able to provide 83 or 84 per cent of its own food requirements, and after the absorption of Poland, the Protectorate of Bohemia and Moravia, and Slovakia into the 'Greater German economic bloc' as much as 87 per cent (Table II.VII.2).

As for bread- and fodder-cereals, as well as meat, it was expected that requirements would be safely met by imports from Germany's neighbours, provided that they themselves remained largely unaffected by the war and were able to produce their export surpluses on the same scale as before. Highly problematic, on the other hand, were fat supplies in the event of war. If Germany were to be cut off from the oceans in the course of a war, the shortfall of approximately 50 per cent (referred to earlier) could be reduced, according to official estimates, by no more than 16 per cent. In that event Germany would have to do very largely without oleaginous fruit, animal fats, and whale oil. Only butter imports, mainly from the Baltic countries, were virtually safe from interference, even though the Western powers would be able to cut off Germany's principal suppliers, Holland and Denmark, from imported feeding-stuffs, which in turn would be bound to reduce their butter exports. The five south-east European countries (Hungary, Romania, Bulgaria, Yugoslavia, Greece) were in no position to offset this potential loss. From them the Reich imported only 5 per cent of its fat requirements, including 2.3 per cent from Romania (soya fat) and 1.6 per cent from Hungary. The planners

TABLE II.VII.2. *Food supplies in the Greater German economic area (1939)*

	Population (m.)			Degree of self-sufficiency (%)
	Total	Fed by home-produced foodstuffs	Fed by imported foodstuffs	
Greater Germany:				
Germany (Altreich)	67.50	56.00	11.50	83
Saar	0.84	0.34	0.50	40
Ostmark (Austria)	6.76	5.07	1.69	75
Sudeten region	3.70	2.96	0.74	80
Memel	0.15	0.23[a]	−0.08[b]	c.150[a]
Danzig	0.41	0.28	0.13	c.70
New *Ostgaue* (annexed Polish territory)	7.37	8.03	−0.66	c.109
TOTAL	86.73	72.91	13.82	84
Plus:				
Generalgouvernement (rump Poland)	14.50	14.50	—	c.100
Czech lands	7.10	6.75	0.35	c.95
Slovakia	3.75[c]	3.55	0.20	95
TOTAL GREATER GERMAN ECONOMIC AREA	112.08	97.71	14.37	87

[a] i.e. not only was the population of the territory fed entirely from home-produced foodstuffs, but there was also a surplus: the territory could have fed up to 0.23m. people.
[b] i.e. an export surplus sufficient to feed 0.08m. people.
[c] Provisional figure.

Source: Memorandum of the Institut für Konjunkturforschung (Institute for Cyclical Research) on large-area economics, n.d., BA-MA RW 19, Anh. 1/1147.

therefore estimated wartime fat imports as shown in Table II.VII.3. Dependence on foreign food supplies had greatly diminished compared with 1927, when it still amounted to 35 per cent. However, because of the growth in population and incomes, as well as the shrinkage of agricultural acreage and the drift of an estimated 700,000 to 800,000 rural workers into industry, the degree of food-supply autarky within the territory directly under German rule had not, despite the regime's efforts, significantly increased under the National Socialists: dependence on foreign countries in 1933 was 19 per cent, in 1938 it was 17 per cent, and in 1939 it was 13 per cent. Only on the assumption that the so-called Greater German bloc would form an economic unit with the central European bloc was a 90 per cent level of self-sufficiency assured (96 per cent with the inclusion of the economic potential of the Russian area): see Table II.VII.4. Although one could not proceed from that

TABLE II.vii.3. *German estimates of wartime fat imports*

	Reliable imports		Defaulting or doubtful imports	
	1,000 t.	%	1,000 t.	%
Butter	89	93	7	7
Lard, suet, vegetable oils, fats, margarine, whale oil	159	75	54	25
Oleaginous fruit	74	5	1,571	95

Source: Expert opinion of Tomberg, of the war-economy and armaments office, end of Jan. 1940: 'Der Außenhandel in den wehrwirtschaftlichen Vorbereitungen Deutschlands vor dem gegenwärtigen Krieg', BA-MA Wi I f 5/1551.

premiss at the outbreak of war, the intention was to achieve such a situation in the course of the war.

Amidst the euphoria of large-area politics it was thought entirely possible that 'the production and export potential of the north-east and south-east European group of states would be maintained', and 'a favourable picture of the German food situation' was therefore painted—a situation which, it was confidently believed, could 'not be shaken even by a naval blockade of prolonged duration'.[6]

2. THE RAW-MATERIAL SITUATION

In assessing the success or failure of Germany's raw-material economy only two reliable statements can be made:

1. Considerable production increases were achieved in respect of all important raw materials, especially after 1936. This applied in particular to the chemical industry, and more especially to synthetics. There can be no doubt that German industry achieved performances it had scarcely been thought capable of. Yet although the 'New Plan' and the Four-year Plan had 'made successful provision' for operational economic efficiency in the raw-material sector, this provision, in the view of authoritative Wehrmacht quarters, was 'not sufficient for stabilizing the raw-material situation for a prolonged war'.[7]

2. In many areas the production graphs do not show a sharp upward turn until 1938-9. This suggests that the economic successes of that period have to be seen largely as a result of the territorial and political changes in Europe. This emerges

---

[6] Secret paper by IG-Farben, 'Die Lage der Nahrungs- und Futtermittelversorgung in Deutschland', 1939, BA–MA Wi I/376.

[7] Thomas, *Wehr- und Rüstungswirtschaft*, 146.

TABLE II.VII.4. *Food supplies of the central European economic bloc*

	Population (m.)			Degree of self-sufficiency (%)
	Total	Fed by home-produced foodstuffs	Fed by imported foodstuffs	
CENTRAL EUROPEAN BLOC:				
Greater German economic area	112.1	97.7	14.4	87
Scandinavian economic area	16.7	13.4	3.3	80
Dutch–Belgian economic area	17.0	10.1	6.9	59
Baltic economic area	5.6	6.0[a]	−0.4[a]	107
South-east European economic area	56.9	60.9[b]	−4.0[b]	107
TOTAL	208.3	188.1	20.2	90
Soviet economic area	185.7	188.2[c]	−2.5[c]	101
GRAND TOTAL	394.0	376.3	17.7	96

[a] i.e. the area had a capacity to feed 6m.
[b] i.e. the area had a capacity to feed 60.9m.
[c] i.e. the area had a capacity to feed 188.2m.

Source: Memorandum by the Institut für Konjunkturforschung (Institute for Cyclical Research) on large-area economics, n.d., BA-MA RW 19, Anh. I/1147.

with particular clarity in lignite production, which showed a marked increase only after Austria's incorporation, and subsequently an upward leap following the annexation of the Sudetenland. Iron-ore extraction was intensified by the availability of the former Austrian deposits, and was again vigorously increased after the break-up of Czechoslovakia; 'Germany's 1939 steel output only exceeded that of 1929 because plant in Austria and Czechoslovakia . . . had given her an extra . . . capacity'.[8] The increase in power generation in 1936 can largely be attributed to the reincorporation of the Saar, and that in 1938–9 to the utilization of Austrian hydro-power and Sudetenland lignite.

Yet even within the extended frontiers of the Reich, economic dependence on foreign imports was diminished only slightly and only in certain areas. At the outbreak of war it amounted to roughly one-third of Germany's requirements of raw materials. Consumption of domestic and imported ores, for example, was in a ratio

[8] Milward, *The German Economy at War*, 20.

of 1 to 3. Even allowing for the large volume of German scrap, the necessary import quota for iron ore still amounted to about 45 per cent. Dependence on imports of non-ferrous ores in 1939 was 25 per cent for zinc, 50 per cent for lead, 70 per cent for copper, 90 per cent for tin, 95 per cent for nickel, and 99 per cent for aluminium. For mineral oils it was 65 per cent and for unvulcanized rubber 85 to 90 per cent.[9] If a comparison were to be attempted with 1914, then Germany's degree of self-sufficiency with regard to iron was lower in 1939, due to the lack of the Lorraine ores, and that of mineral oils higher. The need for imports, however, was substantially higher than at the beginning of the First World War: technical development and mechanization had prevented the level of self-sufficiency from rising in spite of considerable increases in production. German imports of vital raw materials are shown in Table II.VII.5.

TABLE II.VII.5. *German imports of raw materials vital to war 1933–1938* (1,000 t.)

	1933	1934	1935	1936	1937	1938
Iron ore	4,572	8,265	14,061	18,469	20,621	21,928
Other ores	2,386	3,071	3,662	4,079	5,622	4,852
Metals	918	1,141	852	895	1,273	2,275
Crude oil	546	623	846	983	1,198	1,326
Fuels and lubricants	2,157	2,535	2,946	3,235	3,109	3,641
Unvulcanized rubber	60	72	74	83	123	109

Source: Expert opinion of Tomberg, of the war-economy and armament office, end of Jan. 1940: 'Der Außenhandel in den wehrwirtschaftlichen Vorbereitungen Deutschlands vor dem gegenwärtigen Krieg', BA-MA Wi I F 5/1551.

Viewing the German raw-material situation in 1939 from the standpoint of large-area economy, one finds that the Axis powers, along with Spain and the Balkan states, as a theoretcally closed economic area were still only able to meet their joint requirements 'incompletely'.[10] Within the area thought of (for the sake of calculations) as consisting of Greater Germany, Slovakia, Hungary, Italy, Spain, and the Balkan countries apart from Greece, the supply situation was favourable only in respect of coal, iron, certain light metals, and mineral oil, and the required quantities even of these 'could not at present be secured in altogether sufficient measure'.[11] Their stockpiling in 1939 was still prevented by cost. Such important raw materials, on the other hand, as most non-ferrous metals, unvulcanized rubber,

---

[9] Cf. Thomas, *Wehr- und Rüstungswirtschaft*, 146; Tomberg's expert opinion, end of Jan. 1940, BA-MA Wi I F 5/1551.
[10] Memorandum of the Institut für Konjunkturforschung (Institute for Cyclical Research) on large-area economics: 'Das Gewerbe im mitteleuropäischen Wirtschaftsraum', BA-MA RW 19, Anh. 1/1147.
[11] Memorandum of the war-economy staff in the armed forces high command on the possibilities of a large-area economy under German leadership, Aug. 1939, quoted from *Weltherrschaft im Visier*, 255.

cotton, and wool were 'arriving only in rather limited quantities or not at all'.[12] It
was expected, however, that in a war of limited duration it would be possible to
purchase and stockpile nickel, tungsten, molybdenum, cobalt, tin, unvulcanized
rubber, asbestos, mica, arsenic, bismuth, antimony, and sillimanite to the value of
RM152m.

But generally it was being realized that 'a blockade-proof war economy ... even
with the greatest effort and in the most favourable circumstances'—i.e. northern
Europe being willing to supply raw materials in a war—could be 'achieved only to a
limited extent':[13] see Table II.VII.6.

TABLE II.VII.6. *German estimates of wartime imports of vital raw materials*

	Reliable imports		Defaulting or doubtful imports	
	1,000 t.	%	1,000 t.	%
Iron ore	12,730	54	10,882	46
Copper	55	15	304	85
Copper ore	272	42	382	58
Lead	11	15	64	85
Lead ore	41	29	100	71
Zinc	43	57	32	43
Zinc ore	16	9	169	91
Tin	4	35	8	65
Nickel	1	28	3	72
Bauxite	900	76	285	24
Crude oil	60	6	1,005	94
Technical oils and fats	83	40	122	60
Fuels and lubricants	569	22	2,072	78
Unvulcanized rubber	4	4	105	96

Source: Expert opinion of Tomberg, of the war-economy and armaments office, end of
Jan. 1940: 'Der Außenhandel in den wehrwirtschaftlichen Vorbereitungen Deutschlands
vor dem gegenwärtigen Krieg', BA-MA Wi I F 5/1551.

The high command of the armed forces therefore demanded that northern Europe
be included in the large-scale economic area, especially for the sake of Scandinavia's
ores and power resources. However, 'complete safeguarding' of a thus enlarged
economic base for Germany at war seemed 'possible only ... with the raw materials
of Russia'.[14] The Four-year Plan authority (the Reich Office for economic

[12] War-economy situation report by the armed forces high command, No. 11, 1 Aug. 1940, BA-MA
RW 4/v. 308.
[13] Ibid.
[14] Research paper of the Reich office for economic development, 'Möglichkeiten einer Großraumwirtschaft unter deutscher Führung', Part I, July 1939, BA R 25/53. Cf. also the secret memorandum by

development) and the high command of the Wehrmacht (its war-economy staff)
agreed that the area could be truly blockade-proof only on the basis of close
economic amalgamation with the USSR.[15] The Wehrmacht revealed itself as a
vigorous champion of safeguarding the large-scale economic area and of economic
co-operation with the Soviet Union. It demanded the adoption of the following
political and economic objectives for peace and war:

Creation and maintenance of a European large-scale economic area which would guarantee
its members' existence in peace and war . . . As far as possible, peaceful penetration and
interlinking of the economy of the large-scale economic area, with the aim of optimal
commercial efficiency for a high standard of living in peacetime and a blockade-proof
situation in war. A policy of alliances which would harness south-east Europe and the
northern region to the service of the coalitiion and enable tolerable relations to be maintained
with Russia . . . Orientation of the entire economy of the large-scale area towards the utmost
economic strengthening of the individual countries, in line with the tasks assigned to each
country in the war.[16]

Fear that the Polish campaign might escalate into a war of uncertain dimension
was probably a major factor in the decision that the resources of the USSR must be
made available to Germany for her conflict with the Western powers before any
extension of 'living-space' beyond Poland. Whereas, ever since 1933, Berlin had
pursued an increasingly restrictive trade policy *vis-à-vis* the USSR, seeing Moscow
as potentially the principal enemy along with France, a noticeable revival of
German–Soviet trade, especially German imports, took place in 1939–40: Table
II.VII.7.

By February 1939, at a time when the first preliminary decisions about the Polish
campaign were being made, the general conditions for an intensification of
commercial exchanges were discussed with the Soviet Union. Although the USSR
was only prepared to supply approximately 50 per cent of the raw-material quotas
wanted by the National Socialist regime, Germany went into the decisive round of
negotiations determined 'for economic as well as political reasons to conclude the
deal with the Russians even if no substantial increase on their last . . . offer . . . can
be achieved'.[17] Since both parties were anxious for a *rapprochement*, a trade and
credit agreement which met the German ambitions was eventually concluded on
19 August 1939: this envisaged supplies worth RM100m. to the German war economy
within the next twelve months. Hitler was convinced that, in the event of French
and British intervention in the impending Polish conflict, 'we need not be afraid of
a blockade', as 'the east will supply us with grain, cattle, coal, lead, zinc'.[18]

---

the Institut für Weltwirtschaft (Institute for World Economics), 'Das russische Wirtschaftspotential und
die Möglichkeit einer Intensivierung der deutsch-russischen Handelsbeziehungen', Sept. 1939, BA-MA
RW 19, Anh. I/701.

[15] Memorandum of the war-economy staff, Aug. 1939, quoted from *Weltherrschaft im Visier*, 255.
[16] Ibid. 257.
[17] Memorandum of the foreign ministry, 15 June 1939, PA Ha.-Pol, Handakten Clodius, *Rußland*, ii.
[18] Hitler's address to commanders-in-chief, 22 Aug. 1939, DGFP, D. vii. 204.

TABLE II.VII.7. *German trade with the USSR 1933–1940*

	Imports from the USSR			Exports to the USSR			Germany's share of USSR's foreign trade (%)	
	RMm.	% of total German imports	USSR's ranking among Germany's suppliers	RMm.	% of total German exports	USSR's ranking among German markets	Imports	Exports
1933	194	4.6	4	282	5.8	5	42.5	18.7
1934	210	4.7	3	63	1.5	20	12.4	23.5
1935	215	5.2	3	39	0.9	27	9.0	18.0
1936	93	2.2	19	126	2.7	13	22.8	8.6
1937	65	1.2	30	117	2.0	19	14.9	6.2
1938	53	0.9	28	34	0.6	35	4.7	6.6
1939	30	0.6	32	31	0.6	35		
1940	391	7.8		216	4.4			

Sources: Puchert, 'Entwicklung', 32; Friedensburg, 'Kriegslieferungen', 333.

Conclusion of the Hitler–Stalin pact met not only the strategic but also the economic demands of Wehrmacht and industry, who believed that, in the event of Germany being cut off from the world market as a result of Britain's entry into the war, there would have to be 'a major increase of exports to the Soviet Union and corresponding imports of Russian raw materials and foodstuffs'.[19] With a comprehensive economic treaty signed in February 1940, providing for a further RM800m. worth of raw materials to be supplied within a period of twelve months, it was expected that 'the British blockade will be decisively weakened by the incoming raw materials'[20]—which was in fact the case. It was largely thanks to the considerable Soviet deliveries to the Third Reich that Germany, though almost completely cut off from world markets after September 1939, displayed such astonishing powers of economic endurance. This was due in particular to militarily indispensable imports of manganese and chrome ore, as well as phosphorus and asbestos, which at the time of the Hitler–Stalin pact accounted for the major part of German supplies in these sectors. Soviet exports of raw materials were by 1940 predominantly focused on the Reich; the proportions of Russian exports received by Germany were as follows:

phosphorus	49.9%	manganese ore	40.7%
asbestos	77.7%	mineral oil	75.2%
chrome ore	62.4%	raw cotton	66.0%

An overview of Soviet supplies to Germany is given in Table II.VII.8.

With a view to the planned 'living-space' war against the Soviet Union[21] the Third Reich restricted its counter-deliveries to a level which was thought just high enough to avoid jeopardizing Soviet supplies to Germany. At the time of the German invasion in 1941 Germany was certainly heavily in debt to the Soviet Union. Data on the magnitude of that debt vary between Russian and German statisticians, which may largely be due to the fluctuating rate of the rouble. Taking a mean figure, it is thought that Berlin paid with German industrial goods, chiefly metal products, machinery, and electrical engineering equipment, for something between 57 and 67 per cent of Soviet supplies; the remaining debt was unpaid.

3. GERMANY'S SUPPLY SITUATION IN 1939 FROM THE WAR-ECONOMY ASPECT

Promising as Germany's war-supply prospects may have seemed in the long term, they could not conceal a multitude of economic problems in 1939. If the economy

---

[19] Kügelgen, 'Deutschland-Rußland', 46.

[20] Memorandum by chairman of German economic delegation, 26 Feb. 1940, *DGFP*, D. viii. 817.

[21] The Third Reich's power-political, racial, and economic intentions *vis-à-vis* the Soviet Union, as here set out, are confirmed in outline in a doctoral thesis suggested and supervised by the present author: Müller, *Tor zur Weltmacht.* This also goes into details of the shaping of economic relations between Berlin and Moscow before the outbreak of the Second World War. What emerges with particular clarity are the specific group-interests of the political-ideological leadership of the Reich, the military, and the representatives of big business'.

TABLE II.vii.8. *Soviet share in German imports 1939–1941* (1,000 t.)

	1939		1940		1941 (1st half)	
	Total	From USSR	Total	From USSR	Total	From USSR
Agricultural and forestry products:						
Rye	133	—	159	82	78	78
Wheat	900	—	672	4	365	189
Barley	382	—	728	697	133	96
Oats	33	—	121	118	190	184
Maize	586	—	507	14	—	—
Pulses	180	11	162	47	—	35
Raw cotton	259	2	120	71	46	30
Flax and tow	238	4	112	14	—	7
Building and commercial timber	2,153	103	3,156	696	1,537	246
Timber for mechanical or chemical processing	1,496	66	1,182	462	523	120
Oil cake and similar	62	—	82	29	—	8
Minerals and raw materials:						
Calcium phosphate	1,025	31	174	129	127	55
Asbestos	18	1	12	8	12	7
Chrome ore	193	—	40	26	4	—
Manganese ore	235	6	119	65	116	75
Mineral oils and residues	4,694	5	1,806	617	816	248
Platinum and platinum metals[a]	3,320	1	2,290	1,474	1,546	1,262
Raw tin	9	—	7	1	1	—
Raw nickel	3	—	5	2	2	1
Copper	144	—	105	7	52	7

[a] Kg.

Source: Friedensburg, 'Kriegslieferungen', 334, 336.

was at all ready for war in 1939, then it was ready only for military operations limited in range and time. Wehrmacht circles were perfectly clear that any prolonged military conflict developing out of the planned attack on Poland could not be survived in the economic situation of 1939. The Wehrmacht's war-economy organization based its supply plans on entirely realistic data. In its view, given the good harvests of 1938 and 1939, as well as the stocks built up with the Reich's last foreign-currency reserves, 'the situation in the foodstuffs sector at the outbreak of war' could be 'described as tolerably favourable'. Bread supplies were thought to be sufficient, following the establishment of considerable stocks. On the other hand, it was necessary to make a cut in wartime fat consumption to 57 per cent of that in peacetime, and to cut meat consumption to 68 per cent.

As for raw-material stocks, it was generally calculated that, unless they were entirely extracted or produced in Germany, they would be sufficient for nine to twelve months in the event of an escalation of the war beyond Poland. Stocks of unvulcanized rubber would meet Wehrmacht and civilian needs for five to six months, assuming a 30 per cent use of Buna, the proportion of which would have to be further increased because foreign currency for the purchase of unvulcanized rubber was virtually exhausted and any supplies of that raw material from overseas were, in any event expected to be cut off by a blockade.

Although aluminium production, predominantly from bauxite imported from south-east Europe, showed a dramatic rate of growth, it still 'fell far below the demands of the Wehrmacht'.[22] Despite increased production, hopes of synthetic mineral-oil output, as envisaged in the Four-year Plan, had proved exaggerated and hence only partially realizable. Demand due to rearmament was growing more rapidly than fuel production. Even so, the Wehrmacht believed itself to be sufficiently equipped for a blitzkrieg against Poland, as it possessed quite considerable stockpiles: see Table II.VII.9.

TABLE II.VII.9. *Mineral-oil supplies of the German Reich (September 1939)*

	Mobilization requirements			Stockpiles
	Total (t./month)	German-produced		
		t./month	% of total	
Motor-fuel	171,000	95,000	55	451,000
Aviation fuel	110,000	41,500	22	492,000
Diesel fuel	142,000	28,000	20	298,000
Heating-oil (navy)	276,000	51,000	19	1,129,000
Engine-oil	32,100	9,950	31	141,000

Source: Kasper, *Erdölgewinnung*, 65.

[22] Thomas, *Wehr- und Rüstungswirtschaft*, 146.

Fuel supplies, in the opinion of competent military circles, offered 'a sound basis for the first few months of war'.[23] Shortages that appeared during the summer of 1939 were due to the instruction to mineral-oil companies and storage centres to build up reserves for the event of full mobilization. This measure seemed justified at a time when supplies of Romanian petroleum—indispensable to the German war economy—presented 'a still unsolved transport problem'.[24] Nor was it possible to dismiss the fact that, as late as the summer of 1939, 80 per cent of Romanian crude-oil extraction and some 90 per cent of the production of finished products was controlled by British–Dutch, French–Belgian, and American groups of companies and banks. This influence was painfully felt by Germany during the first five months of 1939 in a decline of drilling activity by approximately 32 per cent and extraction by 11 per cent compared with the same period in 1938.[25]

In the non-ferrous metal market increasing difficulties appeared in 1939. In this area it was not possible to satisfy even current demand. Stockpiling, regarded 'as an absolute necessity' for 'holding out in a major war over a prolonged period', could 'not be practised at all for the time being' because of the desperate foreign-currency situation.[26] Instead, the Wehrmacht was instructed by an order from Hitler to adjust consumption of non-ferrous metals 'by the most extensive use of substitute materials and an intensified application of research and invention to the amounts produced in Germany itself'.[27] For the first half of 1939 the non-ferrous metal quotas for industry had to be cut to less than 50 per cent of 1938 allocations, which meant that the Wehrmacht had to content itself with 25–55 per cent of its claimed requirements of the principal metals. Only the non-ferrous metals needed for the acceleration of naval construction had an allocation of foreign currency guaranteed by the commissioner for the Four-year Plan in the second quarter of 1939.[28]

At the centre of all efforts connected with raw-material supplies was the stepping-up of coal production: on this depended not only the production of armaments but also, to a considerable extent, Germany's foreign-currency balance. Coal was one of Germany's few surplus commodities which could be exported. In the spring of 1939 all the customary work on preparations for future extraction was halted to enable the manpower to be employed on increasing current production. Moreover, with effect from 1 April 1939 the working day in mining was generally extended from eight hours to eight and three-quarters—a measure which it was hoped would result in an increase in performance of 8.10 per cent per man-shift,[29] following a drop or stagnation in the extraction rate since January. But the extended hours failed to fulfil these expectations. Increased production in April was a mere 2.5 per cent and

---

[23] Ibid. 147

[24] Thomas's report to the foreign ministry, 24 May 1939, BA-MA Wi I F 5/115.

[25] Report by the war-economy staff in the armed forces high command on the economic situation, 1 July 1939, BA-MA RW 19/94.

[26] Thomas's report to the foreign ministry, 24 May 1939, BA-MA Wi I F 5/115.

[27] Report by the war-economy staff in the armed forces high command on the economic situation, 1 Aug. 1939, BA-MA RW 19/94.

[28] Ibid., 1 July 1939.

[29] Ibid., 1 May and 1 June 1939.

in May 3.9 per cent. In the Ruhr, production of hard coal up to the summer of 1939 was as follows (in 1,000 t.):

Jan.	424	May	436
Feb.	419	June	425
Mar.	419	July	420
Apr.	435		

The government therefore found itself compelled to reduce the quantities of coal earmarked for coking, which in turn meant using up stocks at the smelting works, something bound 'in the end to result inevitably in a decline in iron production'.[30] At the same time bottlenecks occurred in supplying bunker coal to German ports, and the aviation ministry made allowances for the situation by temporarily withdrawing its instruction to enterprises working for the air force to hold three months' supplies. Finally, the tight situation in the coal industry was causing increasing nervous strain among the workers, 'because the men are worn out by overtime'. In the opinion of the war-economy staff they were 'in need of breaks and rest' and wanted to be excused attendance at party celebrations and the like.[31]

At the beginning of the Polish campaign there were no production reserves left in coal-mining. Pithead stocks were down to about 15 per cent of monthly requirements, so that, should a prolonged war make the withdrawal of labour necessary for the army, a coal shortage had to be expected by industry and private households—a fear which proved all too justified during the winter of 1939. The call-up of miners and the war-related overburdening of the transport system caused hard-coal production to drop by approximately 10 per cent in September 1939, and by the end of the year by nearly 15 per cent. The shortage of manpower and transport hit lignite-mining to a lesser degree, as, compared with hard coal, it was less labour-intensive and as a rule combined extraction with local processing. Yet even lignite production declined by 6–7 per cent at the outbreak of the war.[32]

Despite an increased demand for power, due to accelerated rearmament on the eve of the Polish campaign, in mid-1939 energy-supply enterprises were permitted to draw coal only to the amount authorized for them in the 1938/9 budget year (April to March). They thus had no alternative but to draw on their stockpiles of hard coal, which in consequence had declined to such an extent by the end of July or beginning of August 'that restriction had already to be introduced in electricity and gas supplies'.[33] This loss of generated power could not be offset even by extending the capacities of lignite-burning stations, which, owing to excessive operation and lack of maintenance, were suffering from serious mechanical damage.

Short-term importation of foodstuffs and animal feed, as well as of raw materials, was faced with general problems resulting from the difficult financial situation into

---

[30] BA-MA RW 19/94, 1 Aug. 1939.

[31] Comprehensive survey by the war-economy staff in the armed forces high command of economic reports by war-economy inspectorates as of 20 Aug. 1939, BA-MA RW 19/68.

[32] Riedel, *Eisen*, 271.

[33] Report by the war-economy staff in the armed forces high command on the economic situation, 1 Aug. 1939, BA-MA RW 19/94.

which the Reich had manœuvred itself by its forced rearmament. The small volume of German exports meant that neither imports from the USSR nor those from any other country could now be offset by the clearing method alone. Germany therefore needed gold and foreign currency to pay for at least a portion of its armament-related imports. In the past it had been able, with its export deals, to earn certain, albeit modest, amounts of foreign currency; after the end of 1938, however, these earnings diminished rapidly and were approaching zero as Germany's policy of expansion had led a number of foreign customers to cancel their orders. The graph of German exports thus reached a low in mid-1938 and, after one more peak, rapidly dropped towards the turn of 1938–9 (Fig. II.vii.1).

At the outbreak of the war nearly all gold and currency reserves had been exhausted. They amounted to approximately RM500m. (including the secret special-purposes fund), 'a sum just about sufficient to finance one-tenth of Germany's peacetime imports'.[34] According to official estimates German deposits abroad, including those in enemy countries, amounted in 1939 to RM1,500m.—a fraction of their value in 1914 (RM25,000m.). But these could only be made liquid with difficulty, and only to the detriment of all economic interests abroad.

Germany's adversaries, in contrast, possessed the gold holdings, dollar accounts, and marketable dollar securities shown in Table II.vii.10. Converted to purchasing power this equalled a total of RM34,000m.

Financing imports by way of foreign borrowing was scarcely possible. For one thing, the financially strong powers were among Germany's potential enemies, and for another, German clearing debts had assumed such proportions that the neutral countries were reluctant to grant the Reich even short-term business loans. At the outbreak of war the country's clearing debts were as follows (in RMm.):[35]

Italy	107	Finland	4	Bulgaria	22
Holland	55	Hungary	41	Greece	17
Switzerland	36	Romania	17	Spain	22
Sweden	3	Yugoslavia	14	Argentina	17

4. OVERSTRETCHED ECONOMIC CAPACITIES

The unsolved problem of delimitation of powers among the state authorities controlling the economy burst into the open in the course of 1939 in a form that threatened to lead to chaos. Some Party and state authorities were still placing large-scale orders regardless of rearmament claims and priorities, which was why, for example, the projects of the inspector-general for urban construction, Speer, remained virtually unaffected by any rearmament-related economic restrictions and why the development of Berlin as an over-sized, ostentatious Reich capital was proceeding practically unchecked. The three Wehrmacht services were competing

---

[34] Expert opinion by the war-economy staff in the armed forces high command, presumably end of 1939/beginning of 1940, BA-MA Wi I f 5/3442.

[35] 'Deutschlands Wehrwirtschaftspotential', BA-MA Wi I f 5/3442.

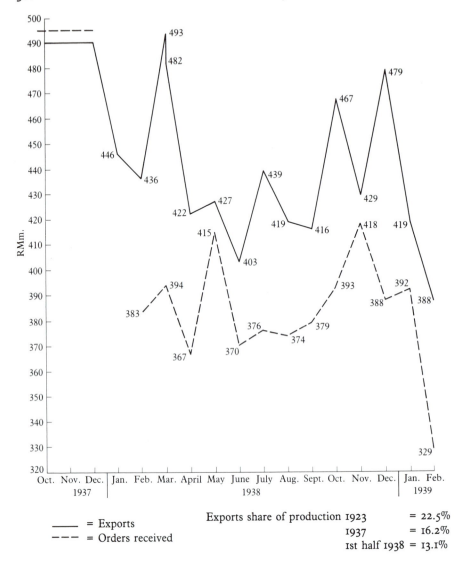

Note: No exact data are available for Dec. 1937–Jan. 1938
Source: cf. Volkmann, 'Außenhandel und Aufrüstung', 99

FIG. II.VII.1 Exports and orders received for the Altreich in 1938

TABLE II.VII.10. *Foreign reserves of gold and dollar-holdings (1939)* ($m.)

	Britain	France	Canada	Colonial territories	Total
Gold holdings	2,000	3,000	215	540	5,755
Dollar accounts	595	315	355	—	1,265
Dollar securities	735	185	500	—	1,420
TOTAL	3,330	3,500	1,070	540	8,440

Source: Federal Reserve Board, Washington, quoted from 'Deutschlands Wehrwirtschafts-potential bei Kriegsausbruch', BA-MA Wi I F 5/3442.

in placing orders and blocking each other inside armament enterprises. The 'smooth flow of economic production' was being 'impeded by an often chaotic placing of orders'. Work was 'started on, to be set aside half-finished because new jobs needed completion'. Too much was being started simultaneously. 'Bottlenecks in production' occurred, and 'less was completed within a given time than might have been completed without those bottlenecks'.[36] That mistaken directives and wastage of raw materials were daily occurrences goes without saying.

To ensure the systematic direction of all labour, with a view to cutting down on economic projects of secondary importance compared with rearmament, in about the middle of 1939 Göring, as commissioner for the Four-year Plan, ordered an examination of all major projects in regard to their political necessity—i.e. their importance to rearmament. But this measure came too late to produce any appreciable results. Manpower shortage thus persisted until the outbreak of war, even though it was increasingly realized 'that the need can only be met by a general examination of projects and by ruthlessly transferring manpower' from overmanned enterprises (which still existed) and industries manufacturing non-rearmament-related products.[37]

The shortage was estimated at approximately one million in 1939; the Hermann Göring concern alone needed 5,000 workers to make full use of its production capacities. The constant flow of labour to better-paying jobs and industries, or to those with better working conditions, was responsible for the fact that mining enterprises of outstanding importance to the Four-year Plan had plant with spare capacity. In consequence, copper extraction at the Mansfeld concern alone had declined by approximately 14 per cent since 1938.[38] Agriculture was no longer able to manage without foreign labour: in mid-1939 it employed approximately 37,000 Italians, 15,000 Yugoslavs, 12,000 Hungarians, 5,000 Bulgarians, 4,000 Dutchmen, over 40,000 Slovaks, and about the same number of workers from Bohemia-

[36] *Völkischer Beobachter*, 23 July 1939.
[37] Report by the war-economy staff in the armed forces high command on the economic situation, 1 May 1939, BA-MA RW 19/94.
[38] 'Deutschlands Wehrwirtschaftspotential bei Kriegsaubruch', BA-MA Wi I F 5/3442.

Moravia.[39] The shortage of agricultural labour had become so much more acute in 1939 that those actually working in agriculture had to achieve considerably higher performances than in past years—in spring sowing, routine farm work, and harvesting. Despite the strict call-up to the Wehrmacht those liable to service could henceforward be given leave for field work or harvest help on farms which they or their parents owned—on full army pay, moreover, and at times even with the loan of horses, motor-cars, and any military personnel attached to them.[40] By 1939 manpower reserves were to be found only by combing out the governmental and party apparatus and by reducing the staff in consumer and small-trade enterprises, where a 'reduction by one-third' was aimed at.[41]

Otherwise the principle of mandatory employment was practised, as a rule through special commissioners for specific branches of production. Owing to the growing number of 'tasks of national importance', the numbers of those directed into compulsory employment rose to such an extent that, in the view of the Wehrmacht's war-economy organization, they were not 'justifiable in the long run, neither economically, nor socially, nor politically':[42] not economically, because a general decline in standard of performance and in output was being observed. Clearly 'the morale and work discipline of compulsorily employed workers left something to be desired'.[43] Moreover, the practice of mandatory employment, which entailed the transfer of employees from one factory or industry to another, at times produced grotesque results: it 'exceeded the bounds of good sense'[44] if, for the implementation of a naval construction programme, qualified skilled workers were withdrawn from enterprises which were themselves subcontractors for the same project.

The frequent separation from their families of those so employed, and their accommodation in primitive conditions, resulted in some political unrest, made worse by the differentials in earnings between different industries and between agriculture and industry generally, differences which might range from RM16 to RM180 per week.[45]

On the eve of the Polish campaign the German economy was beginning to show general symptoms of weariness: there were signs of stagnation and a serious disproportion between orders placed and capacity to fulfil them. According to statements from industry itself, enterprises at the beginning of 1939 suffered from an over-extension of between 10 and 20 per cent, according to the military

[39] Report by the war-economy staff in the armed forces high command on the economic situation, 1 July 1939, BA-MA RW 19/94.

[40] Letter from the armed forces high command to the Four-year Plan commissioner and the Reich authorities responsible for agriculture and manpower employment, 20 Mar. 1939, BA-MA Wi I F 5/2264.

[41] Report by the war-economy staff in the armed forces high command on the economic situation, 1 July 1939, BA-MA RW 19/94.

[42] Ibid., 1 Aug. 1939.

[43] Ibid., 1 July 1939.

[44] Ibid., 1 Aug. 1939.

[45] 'Deutschlands Wehrwirtschaftspotential bei Kriegsausbruch', BA-MA Wi I F 5/3442. On the social and internal situation cf. Wette, I.II.6 above.

significance of the industry concerned.[46] Two measures would have been needed to remedy the situation: first, an extension of capacities, which was not embarked on for lack of raw materials, and second, a replacement, or at least repair, of the machines which had been running at full speed for a number of years (or else a large-scale switch to conveyor-belt production). Although these measures were urgently needed, the rearmament programmes left neither raw materials nor manpower, nor indeed the necessary time, for their implementation. The result was a growing waiting list of orders and a protraction of delivery times, all of which operated against any guarantee of systematic rearmament. The delivery delays, moreover, weakened the competitiveness of German exports in the world market: they obstructed exports, impairing Germany's foreign-currency balance and hence its imports of raw materials and foodstuffs.

German transport had been in grave difficulties ever since the autumn of 1937, by which date all available reserves of the railways, the road-haulage industry, and inland shipping had been fully enlisted in the economic process. The winter of 1938–9 caused serious supply problems, mainly with regard to coal, as navigation found itself paralysed for a considerable period by heavy and protracted frost. The Reichsbahn (state railway system) alone was short of 4,500 engines and 100,000 goods wagons. At the beginning of 1939 industry was compelled to draw on wartime reserves even in areas where this would not have been necessary had there been any regularity in the arrival of supplies. Although Göring concerned himself more directly with transport matters by submitting a five-year re-equipment programme, this project was not declared to be of 'national importance' and was therefore not effectively initiated before the outbreak of the war.[47]

Analysis of these conditions led to the conclusion that, although the German economy in 1939 was 'at a certain peak in terms of work and performance',[48] no further substantial increase of the economic potential was achievable—rather the opposite. 'Because of our restrictions,' Hitler succinctly informed the Wehrmacht leaders, 'our economic situation is such that we can only hold out for a few more years.'[49] The moment for triggering a military conflict in pursuit of the so-called ultimate objective, attainment of world-power status[50] through the expansion of living space, was not yet in sight, but Hitler nevertheless urged 'the creation of the economic prerequisites'.[51] Seeing that 'food supplies and raw materials were secured for a short war, but were insufficient for a long one,[52] then on the well-tested model, the available military economic potential must be employed for the expansion of Germany's territorial (and thus economic) base.

Certainly there was no total mobilization in the economic field in September 1939

---

[46] Cf. 'Deutschlands Wehrwirtschaftspotential bei Kriegsausbruch', BA-MA Wi I F 5/3442; Thomas, *Wehr- und Rüstungswirtschaft*, 147.

[47] Cf. Rohde, 'Eisenbahnverkehrswesen'.

[48] Thomas, *Wehr- und Rüstungswirtschaft*, 147.

[49] Hitler's address to commanders-in-chief, 22 Aug. 1939. *DGFP*, D vii. 201.

[50] Report on address by Hitler to the Wehrmacht leadership, 23 May 1939, quoted from Jacobsen, *1939–1945*, 109.

[51] Ibid. 110.   [52] Thomas, *Wehr- und Rüstungswirtschaft*, 147.

of the kind that would have marked the transition from a preparatory to an actual war economy (from *Wehrwirtschaft* to *Kriegswirtschaft*). Although official pub-lications were at pains to assure the public that 'the German economy, even without special mobilization', was already 'prepared for its war-economy tasks',[53] there was Wehrmacht criticism that 'the economy at the outbreak of the war in 1939 lacked the vitality and strength it had at the outbreak of the 1914 war, being generally under stress owing to many years of rearmament and other major national projects, as well as acute foreign-currency difficulties on account of the food-supply situation'.[54] These observations reflect the desire of the army war-economy administration for in-depth rearmament in view of the possibility of a more protracted conflict. If one views the situation in 1939 from the aspect of economic preparations for a blitzkrieg, then these were adequate, both with regard to foodstuff supplies and to the industrial machine. They were quite certainly adequate on the assumption that trade within the large-scale economic area remained intact. They were adequate also in respect of the efficiency of German industry. By comparison with its potential opponents Germany 'went into the struggle with expanded and modernized capacities, equipped with not inconsiderable stocks of vital raw materials, supported in all key areas by new raw-material industries . . . The chances of industrial superiority therefore existed' —provided always that 'no stronger opponents would join in the struggle and that the war would not go on for too long'.[55]

Comparisons between the war-economy potential and resources of Germany and its allies on the one hand, and those of its enemies on the other, were of course made in foreign countries, especially by *émigrés* who were familiar with the German economic scene. There was general agreement that 'modern war . . . to a much greater degree than the last war . . . would be a battle of machines'.[56] A Swiss study based on the available literature ruled out a successful conduct of the war by Germany on economic grounds alone. It was undisputed that German industry was 'at a very high level' and that 'its engineering output . . . during the past few years had risen vertiginously' and, through its exports, had 'climbed up to the first place among European powers'; German chemical exports were likewise 'the biggest in the world'.[57] Neither the quality of German industrial production nor its advanced rationalization was ignored, nor was there any doubt that German industry was 'as close as possible to total reorientation towards war production', that it was 'in that respect superior to that of any other country', or that 'full industrial mobilization' would be 'achieved faster than anywhere else'. Comparison of Germany's high production figures for steel with those of France or Britain showed that production in these two states had not, at least until 1937, been governed by war-economy requirements but remained 'unchanged within the framework of trade needs'. But the decisive point in a comparison of the relative strength of the war economies was,

---

53 Winschuh, *Wirtschaft*, p. vi.

54 Thomas, *Wehr- und Rüstungswirtschaft*, 145.

55 According to the head of the industry section of the Deutsches Institut für Wirtschaftsforschung, in a manuscript prepared during the war but not published until after 1945: Wagenführ, *Industrie*, 24.

56 'Miles', *Kriegsbereitschaft*, 27.   57 Ibid. 64.

according to this study, that Germany was already working 'all out', that it had got 'hold of every available raw material' and was 'making the maximum use of its industrial capacity', while the reserves of Germany's potential opponents were 'incalculable'.[58] Whereas the two colonial powers were believed to be capable of an enormous increase in their military production process without any excessive strain on their economies, in the case of Germany the question arose 'whether the accelerated introduction of a planned economy would not be accompanied by serious dislocations, and whether the development of a war industry would not, for technical reasons alone, exact a ruinous price in the end'.[59] Moreover, Germany needed considerable imports from abroad, especially from the neutral countries, which, 'as a debtor country with a shaken credit and minimal gold reserves', it would be unable to ensure on a sufficient scale in the long run. France and Britain, by contrast, had at their disposal unimpeded imports from overseas territories.

However, if foreign observers regarded the Third Reich as capable of war only on a limited scale and for a short period of time, this judgement was based not so much on Germany's rearmament or overall economic situation as on the social and political condition of its working people. A brochure widely disseminated in France, Britain, Sweden, and the Netherlands on 'Germany's military strength', asking the key question 'How long can Hitler wage war?', pointed out that 'in the five years of National Socialist rule . . . a considerable deterioration in the standard of living of the German working class' had taken place, with lower real wages and longer working hours than during the world-wide recession.[60] Moreover, consumer goods were in short supply because 'more than two-fifths of production' was 'directly or indirectly channelled into rearmament'.[61] Because of this economic conflict, it was argued, the regime would not succeed in 'generating among the masses the psychological resilience considered necessary by responsible Wehrmacht circles to maintain the fighting spirit of huge armies totalling millions of men'.[62] This was a crucial misjudgement of the attitude of the German people, which, while it did not welcome the war with cheers, saw it through all the way to unconditional surrender.

Today we know how the National Socialist regime tried to solve its war-economy problems—through territorial expansion, through the exploitation of the occupied territories, and eventually through co-ordinated production within the sphere it dominated. This method had been understood within the armed forces from as early as 1933. In that year a first article appeared in the periodical *Deutsche Wehr* on the connection betweem economic and territorial factors and military power. It contained this passage:

Once . . . the conditions are created for the economy to function adequately it becomes the task of the Wehrmacht to enable it to operate with the minimum of interference. For this

[58] Ibid. 65.
[59] Ibid. 66.
[60] Steinberg, *Kriegsstärke*, 175.
[61] Ibid. 176.
[62] Ibid. 347.

purpose . . . the availability of space is a decisive and indispensable prerequisite. It is therefore the task of the Wehrmacht to protect the economy by protecting the space in which it operates. This is the minimum defensive requirement. Any further, offensive intentions depend on reserves of military strength.

Once that strength was established and available it would be necessary, 'on the basis of our military and economic power, which in any case makes an attack a matter of many possibilities, to claim our complete freedom for good or ill. For there is no way of enslaving a nation that has come to realize its strength.'[63]

Postscript (1989)

The findings of this study have meanwhile been confirmed by the eminent Stuttgart economic historian Boelcke. In his book *Kosten* (66–7) he sums up the situation at the beginning of the Second World War as follows:[64]

The German top leadership was aware of the real consequences of the rearmament boom: the shortages of raw materials and manpower, the relative restrictions on the supply of consumer goods, the foreign-trade dilemma, the dangers of wages and price policy, the increasing economic disproportions and friction which slowed down the growth of production, as well as the production bottlenecks. The regime reacted to them with intensified guidance, control, and compulsion. Uneconomic situations had arisen, and ever new uneconomic situations were being created. The system of controls became more rigid and thereby transformed the entire economic order, enforcing a fundamental change of system by suspending the free interplay of market forces. Nevertheless, the danger that the over-extension of productive forces must inevitably lead to an economic catastrophe—as predicted time and again, especially by foreign 'collapse theoreticians', since 1933—did not in fact exist. The boom and full employment were continually maintained by increased public demand. The problem, however, was how the economic engine, already running at full speed in favour of rearmament requirements, could be stepped up to even higher levels of performance, considering that, given the prevailing conditions, it had already been driven close to the limits of a quantitative overall production increase within a short period of time. A halt to rearmament, a brake on the boom, as was occasionally suggested to the leadership, might have opened up alternatives towards new growth and the reduction of economic tensions. But such considerations were diametrically opposed to Hitler's long-term war concepts, to the glittering distant objectives, and were probably unacceptable to others as well. Any radical change of economic direction was therefore out of the question. However, the economic difficulties which had arisen, the increasingly bad news about supply shortages and limits of growth, were probably quite welcome to Hitler as a further weapon in the argument within the various power-groupings in the top leadership, a pretext for convincing waverers that war was inevitable. . . . Yet it would be a mistake to consider that war was the only way to prevent an allegedly imminent 'final economic catastrophe of the regime'.

[63] Steinberger, 'Wirtschaft', 485.

PART III

The Rearmament of the Wehrmacht

Wilhelm Deist

I. The Reichswehr and National Defence

1. The Military-Policy Preconditions

THE traditional picture of the Wehrmacht in the summer of 1939 usually obscures the fact that only a few years earlier the total German armed forces consisted of the 100,000-man army and the navy permitted by the treaty of Versailles. The sudden change from the 'anomaly' of the Reichswehr of the Weimar Republic to the modern Wehrmacht of the Third Reich, fully equipped for a European conflict, was typical of the distorted relationship between armaments and policy which can generally be observed among the great powers of the twentieth century. The causes of this imbalance seem to be very closely linked to the rapid development of technology as well as to the increasing industrialization of production and its complex economic and socio-political effects.[1] In attempting to describe the role of the Wehrmacht in the events and decisions leading to the Second World War, it is important to understand the causes and consequences of this reversal of the relationship between military armaments and purely political factors as a whole in the heartland of central Europe. In this respect it is essential to consider, against the background of ideological continuities and economic developments analysed in the two preceding parts of this volume, the preconditions for comprehensive rearmament created by the Reichswehr of the Weimar Republic before January 1933.

For the Reichswehr, the First World War and its result, the treaty of Versailles, were the points of reference for all actions and planning. The course of the war had shown that the dimensions of violent international conflicts had become even less subject to rational calculation than had earlier been the case. The geographical extent of the fighting, and the mobilization and use of human and material resources, had reached a level which permitted only very limited comparisons with earlier wars. The use of mass armies with millions of soldiers and the *matériel* battles with their far-reaching political, economic, and social preconditions and consequences on the one hand enormously expanded the military's scope of action, but on the other hand they completely changed the conditions for the fulfilment of its tasks. The army and navy, trained and led by their officers, could no longer decide a war alone; the entire nation had become an instrument of warfare. The armed conflict, which had originally been the exclusive domain of the military and decisive for the outcome of a war, could now only be considered part of the total struggle.[2] These developments, presented here only in very general terms, logically necessitated a radical rethinking of the tasks of national defence.

Serious thinking within the Reichswehr about these changed circumstances in the

---

[1] Cf. the pioneering essay by Herzfeld, 'Politik', 255 ff., here 258–9, 269–70.

[2] Cf. Beck's memorandums from the period after his resignation as chief of staff 'Der Anführer im Kriege' and 'Deutschland in einem kommenden Kriege', in Beck, *Studien*, 21 ff., 49 ff.

situation of the armed forces was pushed into the background for years by the shock of the military and political collapse, the revolutionary conditions within Germany, and, finally, the terms of the treaty of Versailles. Only in the years after the Kapp *putsch* was a consolidation of the officer corps and the rest of the army achieved under the dominant influence of Colonel-General Hans von Seeckt, who had become chief of the Heeresleitung (army command). However, this was done on the basis of an extremely reserved attitude towards the republican constitution. Seeckt's bold equation of the Reichswehr with the state[3] was due on the one hand to his orientation towards the values and ideals of the imperial German army; on the other hand it described his programme for the future, for which he sought to train the officers and soldiers of the Reichswehr. He considered the political constitution of republican Germany and the position of the military within it to be 'anomalies' born of military defeat and political collapse and bearing the mark of the treaty of Versailles. In his eyes, therefore, they could only have an interim character. As early as January 1921, Seeckt clearly expressed his view that his task was to train the Reichswehr as a cadre for a larger Wehrmacht, which would no longer be subject to the restrictions of Versailles.[4] For the sake of this goal, and re-establishing Germany's position as a European great power, a development he considered absolutely certain, Seeckt and the rest of the Reichswehr leadership were prepared to resort to illegal measures in violation of the treaty of Versailles, which had the status of a law in Germany, and to cover corresponding actions of subordinates. Seeckt's initiatives in the foreign-policy field, especially the establishment of military co-operation with the Soviet Union, served the same purpose. However, historians now generally agree that, until the beginning of the 1930s, the scope and military importance of the various illegal measures remained relatively small in terms of the personnel and equipment involved.[5]

On the other hand, it could not be denied that the provisions of Versailles limited the structure and strength of the Reichswehr, including the details of its armaments and other equipment of its units; that the Allies of the First World War closely monitored compliance; and that a revision by negotiation, especially of the military parts of the treaty, could not be expected in the foreseeable future. Under these circumstances, was there any military sense at all in trying to maintain a national defence? In any case the Allies had decreed in Article 160 of the treaty that the task of the German army should be limited to 'maintaining order within the territory [of Germany] and control of the frontiers'. In Germany no significant political group was prepared to accept these restrictions and confine the Reichswehr to the character of a police force. This fact should not be forgotten in interpreting subsequent developments. The Reichswehr knew that its claim to be the traditional military instrument for preserving the sovereignty and authority of the state was

---

[3] Wohlfeil, 'Heer und Republik', 136. For a survey of recent literature on the history of the Reichswehr see Geyer, 'Wehrmacht'.

[4] Wohlfeil, 'Heer und Republik', 207–8.

[5] Ibid. 209, 218, 228.

supported by the overwhelming majority of the country and its leading political figures.[6]

Problems resulting from the contradiction between this claim and existing military possibilities were covered up in the first years of the Weimar Republic by more urgent tasks, primarily the maintenance of domestic order. This use of the Reichswehr in situations often bordering on civil war made it an indispensable instrument of the executive power, and the picture of it drawn by contemporaries and historians was formed against this background. Undoubtedly the self-image of its officers and soldiers was strongly influenced by these experiences in the first years of the republic, but the Reichswehr's role as the guardian of domestic order was only partially congruent with the way it saw itself.

After the domestic crisis of 1923, the Reichswehr turned its attention primarily to problems of national defence. The crisis had been overcome with the help of the broad powers granted the chief of the army command by the Reich president, but at the same time the ambitious political goals of the Reichswehr had not been achieved.[7] Seeckt himself announced the new phase with a decree ending the state of emergency on 1 March 1924,[8] in which he stated that the Reichswehr was to 'concern itself exclusively with military tasks'. However, the question was whether, after the experiences of the First World War, an attempt to completely reorganize national defence would make it possible to take the Reichswehr out of politics—Seeckt's announced intention in his decree—or whether such an attempt under the conditions of the treaty of Versailles would not itself inevitably become a major political issue.

Shortly before Seeckt issued his decree, Joachim von Stülpnagel, head of the army operations department (T1) in the Truppenamt ('Troop Office'), which performed the functions of the prohibited general staff in the army command, explained his 'Thoughts on the War of the Future' to officers of the defence ministry in February 1924.[9] They were typical of ideas about the military possibilities of national defence within the Reichswehr leadership at the beginning of the stabilization phase. Stülpnagel's views were based on the conviction that Germany's prospects of surviving and developing as a nation could be secured in the long term only by a new conflict with France. The only question was when and under what conditions this war could and should be fought. In spite of some delusions, especially in his political views, Stülpnagel was very realistic in his assessment of existing military possibilities. He dramatically illustrated the weakness of the Reichswehr for his audience by pointing out that its seven divisions had enough ammunition to fight for only about one hour. Under these circumstances, it was impossible to conduct a war based on the operational experience of the First World War. Stülpnagel believed that the only chance of victory in the event of a military conflict was to pursue a strategy of attrition, in which guerrilla warfare and delaying actions by the population in frontier areas would play the main role. The primary aim would be to

[6] Herzfeld, 'Politik', 264–5.   [7] Cf. Hürten, *Reichswehr*, 34 ff.

[8] Printed in *Offiziere im Bild von Dokumenten*, 236.

[9] Stülpnagel papers, BA-MA N 5/10.

weaken the advancing enemy by constantly disrupting his progress and supply-lines so that the German military leadership would have time to mobilize available human and material resources as far as possible. If they were as successful as they hoped in this effort, the strengthened German army, whose mobility would then be increased by the advantage of internal lines and the possibility of surprise, could risk decisive engagements and even take the offensive. But Stülpnagel was very cautious about the prospects of success in such a 'war of liberation': 'Today and in the foreseeable future fighting a war would only be a heroic gesture', he observed at the conclusion of his talk. He mentioned as a precondition for a favourable outcome not only military intervention by third states but also a successful 'popular uprising', for which he listed a number of requirements that would have subordinated practically all domestic policy to the needs of the war. In 1924 these political preconditions of Stülpnagel's plan were illusory, but his 'Thoughts on the War of the Future' formed the basis and provided an impulse for planning that went far beyond the strictly military sphere.[10]

Stülpnagel's outline of decisive factors and the course of a future war remained well within the scope of public discussion of this question, which centred wholly upon the First World War.[11] In that conflict the very word 'war' had acquired new dimensions. In addition to war in the traditional, military sense, there had been an economic and a propaganda war, whose decisive importance was no longer disputed. The command of mass armies had presented military leaders with serious operational and tactical problems, but the spread of technology and its impact on warfare proved to be even more far-reaching. Individual elements of this fundamental change and their military consequences were discussed extensively in military journals. In view of the paramount role of the armaments industry in the First World War, it is, however, noteworthy that this problem did not receive appropriate attention in the discussion of future warfare. Publications dealing with it appeared only at the beginning of the 1930s, and even then they were concerned primarily with the strategic consequences of the economic preconditions and requirements of modern warfare.[12]

The extensive discussion which took place concerning the Schlieffen plan and the essential elements of the battle of annihilation[13] should be understood against this background of a barely articulated but nevertheless real crisis of the military profession in its function in state and society. On the surface the innumerable studies of the course of miliary events in the summer and autumn of 1914 were concerned with the question of which military decisions should be blamed for the failure of the Schlieffen plan. The intense preoccupation with Schlieffen's ideas was, however intended to prove that in the age of mass armies operational warfare

---

[10] Different aspects of the general problems that the kind of warfare described by Stülpnagel and others presented for the self-image of the Reichswehr officer corps have been analysed in numerous recent publications. Cf. Müller, *Armee*, 11–50; id., 'Reichswehr', 137–51; Geyer, 'Professionals', 77–133; id. 'Dynamics', 100–51.

[11] Cf. Geyer, *Aufrüstung*, 463 ff.

[12] Caspary, *Wirtschafts-Strategie*; Gründel, 'Krise', 209 ff.

[13] Cf. Wallach, *Dogma der Vernichtungsschlacht*; Geyer, *Aufrüstung*, 465.

with the aim of achieving a quick decision was still conceivable and practicable. Such proof seemed to be necessary as especially in this area the First World War, with its change to positional warfare and the inferno of indecisive *matériel* battles, had cast doubt on the qualifications of the military leadership. The war had been decided not by the professional abilities of the commander and his assistants, which were formerly so strongly emphasized, but by superior material and human resources. How serious this problem was felt to be is shown by a question posed by Groener, otherwise one of the most active exponents of Schlieffen's ideas. He concluded his memorandum 'The Importance of the Modern Economy for Strategy' by asking whether the problems of the modern economy did not constitute 'an irresistible force for peace'.[14]

In journals concerned with military history and other military subjects, such thoughts continued to arouse little interest. Authors preferred to concentrate on the search for new strategies suited to war in the age of mass armies and mass production. Few of them saw the strategy of the future in terms of a war of attrition, in which more decisive measures would be expected from the political than from the military leaders. The discussion was dominated by the idea that a war could still be decided by a single battle of annihilation. Again it was Groener who, following Schlieffen, provided an insight into the reasons for this conviction: 'The enormous costs of huge modern armies require a quick decision'.[15] This decision in a short war—the only form still considered acceptable—was to be achieved by highly developed generalship combined with strategic surprise, large-scale encirclements, and the use of modern weapons.[16]

In this regard the question of whether such a war would be fought by mass armies raised by general conscription or by an élite professional army was of secondary importance. More important was the belief of military writers that the proper organization of society and the economy was a precondition for victory even in a short war. The price for maintaining the principle that international conflicts should be decided by a military offensive, even under the changed conditions of modern warfare, was thus the militarization of civilian life and society. This was especially true of preparations for the conversion of industry to the mass production of war equipment and munitions as rapidly as possible. The word 'conversion' actually covered an abundance of far-reaching demands which would inevitably lead to state intervention in the economy even in peacetime. Making provision for a secure supply of raw materials, planning the awarding of contracts, and, finally, influencing the economic and political infrastructures were only a few tasks whose perfect organization in peacetime was a precondition for an effective functioning of the military in the first phase of a war.[17]

---

[14] Printed in *Zeitschrift für Geschichtswissenschaft*, 19 (1971), 1167 ff.

[15] Ibid. 1175; cf. Farrar, 'Short-war Illusion', 39 ff.

[16] On the importance of technology for operational warfare cf. Schwarte, *Krieg der Zukunft*; Justrow, *Feldheer*.

[17] Surprisingly enough, the military did not develop the idea of a blitzkrieg from these premisses (cf. Geyer, *Aufrüstung*, 465); on the other hand, the head of the war-economy staff in the war ministry advocated wars of conquest to support a militarized economy at quite an early stage (ibid. 475 ff.).

It should be noted that the discussion of such considerations and ideas was by no means limited to the Reichswehr and related organizations. In 1926 the transportation minister in the Luther cabinet, Krohne, formulated his position categorically in a memorandum on 'national defence and the armed forces':[18] 'There is absolutely no area which the state should not include in preparing for a future war.' However, Krohne also drew another conclusion from the basic change which had taken place in the concept of national defence since 1918: it was henceforth the responsibility 'not only of the defence ministry but of all ministries under the leadership of the chancellor'. In Krohne's opinion the First World War had limited the function of the armed forces in future conflicts to very specific areas within the general conduct of a war. Although Krohne's organizational ideas were diametrically opposed to the views of the Reichswehr leadership, the latter, interestingly enough, avoided taking a position on this basic question in the following years. It affected the central dogma of military tradition, namely that the protection of the state from foreign danger was the special and exclusive task of the soldier. If, however, modern war forced the nation to mobilize all its material, human, and moral resources for the war effort, a military dictatorship would be necessary for the soldier to fulfil his task. If, on the other hand, he renounced this traditional claim in the interest of a modern form of national defence, his loss of prestige would be accompanied by the bitter recognition that the military had become only one of several state instruments essential to fighting a war.[19]

The discussion about preconditions and forms of future warfare in various German periodicals in the period between the wars, which can only be reviewed in broad outline here, had as its point of reference the experiences of the First World War, but it also included possibilities which modern military technology, such as tanks and aeroplanes, seemed to offer. Interestingly enough, however, the question of the relationship between means and ends, which Clausewitz had considered an essential element in determining the nature of any conflict and which actually made war an instrument of policy, was not even asked.[20] In his memorandum mentioned above on 'The Importance of the Modern Economy for Strategy' Groener indirectly hinted at this problem by explicitly stressing the modern economy as a peace-promoting factor. Generally speaking, however, the war of the future was defined only in terms of the means to be used, in the broadest sense of the word. If any objectives evolved at all, interest centred on proving that they could be achieved militarily. The question of the relationship of the social and economic costs connected with the use of military force, which still involved unpredictable risks, to the desired objectives and their usefulness for the country was not even considered. In Germany even more than in the corresponding literature of the Anglo-Saxon countries, discussion was limited to problems of operational warfare. This was itself simply a result of the fact that war between industrialized states had become so

---

[18] *ADAP*, B. i, No. 172, memorandum dated 18 Mar. 1926.

[19] On the unresolved conflict, illustrated by the whole history of the Reichswehr, between strict professionalism and a claim to overall primacy in the state, cf. Geyer, 'Dynamics', 100–51.

[20] Cf. Geyer, *Aufrüstung*, 463–4, 472; on the remarkable lack of strategic perspectives in German military thinking cf. Deist, 'Strategic Perspectives'.

complex in its preconditions and consequences that many writers could only understand and analyse individual aspects of it.

It cannot be proved conclusively that the theoretical discussion outlined here had any noticeable effect on the basic thinking of the Reichswehr leaders about national defence. In spite of their differences in other respects, however, Stülpnagel, Krohne, and Groener were in complete agreement on one point. Isolated action by the military was a thing of the past; the armed forces could fulfil their tasks only in co-operation with all other executive organs of the state. Their dependence on economic conditions of production was absolute. Finally, they were also dependent on the active support of the population in the broadest sense. Translating this insight into practical action required that the Reichswehr leadership should not only be prepared to co-operate with other state organs but also that they should consciously make use of all possibilities in this direction within the framework of their general objectives.

The second chief of the army command, Colonel-General von Seeckt, dissented from this view; to achieve an internal stabilization of the Reichswehr he had limited such initiatives to a minimum. And in his talk of February 1924 Stülpnagel too had failed to advocate an 'opening' of the Reichswehr towards the republic and society. He had rather made traditional, general demands based on the idea of a garrison state, but nevertheless he became one of the most important members of the so-called 'Fronde' within the defence ministry. This group of officers attempted to understand the concrete realities of the situation in which the army found itself, and was not satisfied with the optimistic but uncertain prospects characteristic of Seeckt's ideas about Germany's future military role. This circle of officers from almost all sections of the Truppenamt, headed by Joachim von Stülpnagel, Bussche-Ippenburg, Blomberg, and Hasse, was not held together by shared political convictions or strategy, but by the common aim of maintaining and improving the military efficiency of the Reichswehr under existing circumstances at home and abroad.[21] In concrete terms, this included various tasks extending from the modernization of equipment to the systematic build-up of the frontier guards and local defence units, the planning and realization of a comprehensive armaments programme, and the new formulation of an active military foreign policy. No progress could be achieved in this area by sweeping demands and repeated appeals to principles, especially during a period of political development that was generally characterized by normalcy and relative stability. The desired aim could only be reached by time-consuming statistical studies, endless negotiations, and exploiting even the smallest advantages. This was not Seeckt's way. For this reason, his dismissal[22] at the beginning of October 1926 and the appointment of Lieutenant-General Wilhelm Heye as his successor marked a turning-point in the history of the Reichswehr. Thereafter, the military policy of the republic developed in new directions and on different levels.

---

[21] Geyer, *Aufrüstung*, 58; Carsten, *Reichswehr* (trans.) 253 ff., interprets this development politically as a 'shift to the left'.
[22] Wohlfeil, 'Heer und Republik', 282 ff.

The statement of Defence Minister Gessler in the cabinet session of 29 November 1926 was symptomatic of this change. In the presence of the chiefs of the army and navy commands and in an atmosphere dominated by vehement Social Democratic criticism of the Reichswehr, he announced that the chief of the army command would provide the cabinet with detailed information about the secret rearmament measures. The cabinet would then have to decide for which of these it could accept responsibility, and the Reichswehr would abide consistently by its decision.[23] In other words, the primacy of political decisions and controls in national defence, the main task of the armed forces, was expressly recognized. A large amount of evidence from the winter of 1926–7 from leading officers of the defence ministry shows that the Reichswehr's abandonment of its previous reserve towards the republic and its institutions was the result of a conviction, born of military necessity, which also affected numerous other areas.[24] The purpose of this co-operation with the civilian executive, begun under Gessler and Heye, was to obtain political support for military personnel and rearmament measures.

In February 1927 the chief of the army command reported to the cabinet of Chancellor Marx on existing secret stocks of weapons as well as the present state and future planning of the frontier guards and local defence units.[25] Heye pointed out that the military considered it 'beneath the dignity of the state' for the Reichswehr to be still dependent on donations from industry and agricultural organizations for national defence. The chancellor and the cabinet indicated that they were certainly not averse to including the costs of illegal armament measures, i.e. those violating the treaty of Versailles, in the ordinary budget. But this could only be done if the funds for that purpose were not subject to the normal review and approval of the Reichstag. With the help of the auditor-general, Friedrich Ernst Saemisch (who had assisted in resolving the scandal caused by the bizarre financial activities of Captain Walter Lohmann),[26] a solution was found in the so-called permanent state secretaries' committee of three representatives from the auditor-general's office, the Reichswehr, and the finance ministry. The committee began its work in connection with the internal resolutions on the budget of 1928.[27] The 'Great Coalition' government under the Social Democrat Hermann Müller, which took office in June 1928, likewise approved the basic decision made a year earlier and accepted responsibility for the secret rearmament measures of the Reichswehr. In October of that year it accepted the recommendations of the state secretaries' committee and expressly approved the armaments planning of the Reichswehr.[28] The real importance of this development was not the amount of money for secret rearmament measures from the budget of the defence ministry, and later from the

---

[23] Carsten, *Reichswehr* (trans.), 265 ff.

[24] Ibid. 257 ff.; it would, however, be a mistake to assume that this change in method signified even a limited change in the political objectives of the Reichswehr leaders. Cf. esp. Bennett, *German Rearmament*, 11 ff.

[25] Carsten, *Reichswehr* (trans.), 250 ff., 266 ff.

[26] Dülffer, *Weimar*, 90 ff.; Rahn, *Reichsmarine*, 214 ff.

[27] Geyer, *Aufrüstung*, 109.

[28] Vogt, *Kabinett Müller II*, i, No. 42, p. 153.

budgets of other ministries, but rather the undermining of the parliamentary system by the use of government decrees. In a matter which was very sensitive at home and abroad, the right and power of the Reichstag to control expenditure were nullified by the concerted action of executive organs.

It is not surprising that resistance to this new policy of the Reichswehr leadership developed within the Reichswehr itself as well as in the civilian executive, not to mention political groups in the Reichstag and the state (Länder) parliaments. The organization of the frontier guard and local defence units was especially controversial. Heye had clearly indicated to the cabinet that the Reichswehr was interested above all in close co-operation with the civilian authorities and that the influence of rightist paramilitary organizations, which had in some respects been dominant until then, would be reduced. This statement undoubtedly made it easier for the cabinet to approve the Reichswehr's defence planning, but it did not guarantee that the Social Democratic government of Prussia would take a similar position. In spite of the support of the central government, the Reichswehr leadership was not able to reach a satisfactory agreement with Prussia beyond a formal statement of basic principles, although the support of the Prussian government was essential to an effective national defence. Prussia refused to agree to mobilization preparations to be achieved by various local defence measures, and the Reichswehr for its part was not in a position to reduce the influence of rightist paramilitary organizations in the frontier guard units to the extent demanded by the Prussian government without endangering the ability of these units to perform their tasks.[29] The resulting tense relations with the Prussian government were to determine the attitude of the Reichswehr towards the so-called 'Prussian coup' of the Papen government on 20 July 1932.[30]

In spite of these difficulties, the new course of the Reichswehr was generally successful. It had made possible the desired escape from political isolation and had enabled the Reichswehr to transfer to the German political leadership its proper responsibility for national defence. Finally, it had created the preconditions for a slow but steady improvement of the desperate armaments situation by including the secret rearmament measures in the ordinary budget.

The success which the Reichswehr leadership had achieved in obtaining the cabinet's approval of these budgetary measures can be understood in its full significance when internal Reichswehr planning is considered. When Blomberg became head of the Truppenamt at the beginning of 1927, the office set itself the ambitious goal of combining all armaments plans of the army in a programme designed to run for several years and to set priorities. After almost two years of preparation, the programme was approved by the chief of the army command on 29 September 1928. The military aims were the guarantee of a first issuing of

---

[29] Ibid. No. 181, pp. 583–4; Carsten, *Reichswehr* (trans.), 355–6; and esp. Bennett, *German Rearmament*, 27 ff.

[30] On the summary deposition of the Social Democratic caretaker government in Prussia and the installation of a Reich commissioner cf. Vogelsang, *Reichswehr*, 235 ff.; Trumpp, *Papen, passim*; Hentschel, *Weimars letzte Monate*, 52 ff.; Bennett, *German Rearmament*, 186 ff.

equipment and ammunition for a sixteen-division army (A-army), the establishing of limited stocks, and measures to improve industrial production capacity in the event of mobilization. The government was prepared to spend approximately RM350m. to realize this plan between 1928–9 and 1932.[31] Compared with the total Reichswehr budget in 1928, viz. RM726.5m. (8.6 per cent of the total government budget), the RM70m. available annually for armaments seemed to be relatively insignificant.[32] However, the somewhat revolutionary element was to be found in the methods used by the army command and the Truppenamt. Even if one considers that the estimates of the navy and the so-called 'air armaments period 1927–31' were not included in the programme,[33] the systematic attempt to achieve specific goals by co-ordinating the endlessly varied and mutually dependent factors of a military armaments programme determined by modern industrial production methods represents a novelty in the history of the German army[34] which can only be compared to the development of the naval construction programme under Tirpitz. That the Reichswehr leadership for its part favoured this attempt was shown by the 'second armaments programme', in which the methods of co-ordination were further improved and which was adopted for another period of several years (1933–8) in 1932.[35]

The fact that the planning was based on periods of several years increased its politically explosive potential. Gessler's successor as defence minister, Wilhelm Groener, assumed office in January 1928 and lent his support to those groups within the Reichswehr that favoured co-operation with the civilian authorities. He obtained cabinet approval for the armaments plan of the army as well as the construction of *Panzerschiff A* (the first pocket battleship), and in the budget consultations of the following years attempted, for good reason and not without considerable success, to persuade the cabinet to accept 1928 as the 'normal year' for budgetary planning.[36] The cabinet's fundamental decision in October 1928 in regard to the armaments programme restricted its own freedom in the following years, with the result that the budget cuts the Reichswehr had to accept during the world depression remained relatively small.

For the leading Reichswehr officers, the new course had been a result of the necessity to develop preconditions for a comprehensive system of national defence within the specific limits imposed by the treaty of Versailles. Thus, this course included from the very beginning a foreign-policy component. After the autumn of 1926 the Reichswehr leadership also demonstrated a readiness to co-operate with the

---

[31] Hansen, *Reichswehr und Industrie*, 119 ff.; Geyer, *Aufrüstung*, 199.

[32] Cf. Rautenberg, *Rüstungspolitik*, appendix, pp. 81–2. The budget of the German army, including that of the ministry itself, amounted to RM513.7m. in 1928.

[33] On the air armaments period 1927–31 cf. Hansen, *Reichswehr und Industrie*, 125 ff.; Völker, 'Entwicklung', 159 ff.

[34] On the activities of the army ordnance office (Heereswaffenamt) and its supplies staff, and the build-up of its cover organization, the Stega (Statistische Gesellschaft), cf. Hansen, *Reichswehr und Industrie*, 64 ff.

[35] Cf. Geyer, 'Rüstungsprogramm'.

[36] Id., *Aufrüstung*, 200–1. Bennett (*German Rearmament*, 75 ff.) points out the domestic political consequences of this military policy, which have not received enough attention.

foreign ministry, especially in relations with Soviet Russia and the League of Nations.[37] The SPD's criticism of Soviet munitions deliveries in the Reichstag in December 1926 put an end to the first phase of German–Soviet military co-operation.[38] The attempts during this phase to have armaments manufactured secretly for Germany in the Soviet Union had not produced any satisfactory results. Now German–Soviet military relations in the field of training were expanded vigorously beyond the pilot training centre which already existed at Lipetsk; the foreign ministry gave its consent and the cabinet its approval.[39] Again the principle of military efficiency and the ultimate responsibility of the chancellor and the cabinet for military policy replaced grandiose political plans and secret military diplomacy. The training of officers in the use of aeroplanes and tanks, the testing of modern equipment, and participation in the development of weapons technology were more important than the production and delivery of artillery ammunition. And in the matter of establishing an attaché service, the Reichswehr under Groener pursued a similar policy.[40]

All ideas and measures for the organization of the military aspects of national defence were regarded by those most directly involved in their realization as stopgaps and temporary improvisations as long as the armed forces of the republic were subject to the military provisions of the treaty of Versailles. In its efforts to achieve a complete revision of these provisions, the Reichswehr could be certain it had the support of a broad majority in the country.

Against this background the expectations of the German side at the opening of the negotiations of the preparatory disarmament commission in Geneva in May 1926 are understandable. In this area too co-operation between the foreign ministry and the defence ministry proved its value. In the latter, special teams were appointed to deal with the various problems.[41] German military representatives participated in the consultations of the sub-committees and obtained insights into the national, economic, and general political preconditions for an international arms agreement. The political aim of the German delegation was the revision of Part V of the treaty of Versailles, but they based their arguments on Germany's moral and legal demand that the other participants disarm as Germany had done. Although the German demands initially received considerable public support, the political goal was not reached. The draft of a convention intended to form the basis for the deliberations of a 'conference on the limitation and reduction of armaments', which was approved by the preparatory disarmament commission on 9 December 1930, contained the stipulation that existing treaty provisions on arms limitations, i.e. the treaty of Versailles among others, would remain in force.

The possible consequences of this setback for Germany were far-reaching. For the Reichswehr a potentially dangerous situation began to develop in which national

---

[37] Geyer, *Aufrüstung*, 121, 149 ff.; Post, *Civil-Military Fabric*.
[38] On Scheidemanm's speech of 16 Dec. 1926 cf. Carsten, *Reichswehr* (trans.), 254 ff.
[39] Völker, 'Entwicklung', 138 ff.; Homze, *Arming*, 9–10, 20 ff.
[40] Kehrig, *Attaché-Dienst*; Geyer, *Aufrüstung*, 173 ff.
[41] Ibid. 125 ff.; Rautenberg, *Rüstungspolitik*, 35 ff.; Messerschmidt, IV.1.4 below.

rearmament in violation of the treaty of Versailles had begun but was not covered by international agreements. The chancellor and the cabinet had indeed assumed responsibility for armaments measures, but they had also created possibilities allowing them to influence and supervise such programmes themselves. If rearmament could not be covered in some way by diplomatic measures, the consensus achieved between German military and political leaders might begin to break down, especially as the cabinet considered the solution of the reparations question to be the most important problem, whereas for the Reichswehr defence policy, and thus rearmament, had absolute priority.

2. THE REICHSWEHR AND REVISIONISM: GROENER'S MILITARY POLICY

Gessler's successor as defence minister, Wilhelm Groener, is usually mentioned in literature on the history of the Reichswehr only as the initiator of the Ebert–Groener alliance of November 1918 and in connection with the prohibition of the Sturmabteilung (SA: Nazi storm troops) in the spring of 1932. The contours of his policies in the four decisive years during which he served as minister, January 1928 to April 1932, remain indistinct and blurred. It is usually overlooked that with Groener a soldier was placed at the head of the defence ministry who, as a result of his various assignments before, during, and after the First World War, was uniquely cognizant of the political, economic, technical, and military problems of warfare and had attempted in numerous writings to analyse the phenomenon of modern war.[42] Despite the generally negative effects of the events of November 1918 on his reputation, his impressive qualifications and familiarity with the military apparatus gave him more authority outside and within the Reichswehr than Gessler had possessed. The main aims of his policy were the energetic continuation and expansion of the co-operation with the executive organs of the central government and the German states begun by Gessler and Heye; expanded armaments planning of the army; and, finally, the successful defence of the naval construction programme in the cabinet and the Reichstag. Groener's importance is, however, due above all to the fact that, in the rearmament phase, he made the first real attempt to make the Reichswehr an integrated military instrument of the general policy of treaty revision as formulated by Stresemann.[43]

Groener's memorandum 'Das Panzerschiff' ('The Pocket Battleship') of November 1928 was the first step in this direction.[44] In it he began by posing the basic question of what tasks the Reichswehr could perform under existing conditions. Only a detailed answer to this question would make it possible to determine adequately the function of the navy in the defence of the country, and then to examine whether the pocket battleship represented a necessary and useful strengthening of Germany's armed forces at that time. However, in practice

---

[42] There is still no biography of Groener. Cf. the contribution by F. Hiller von Gaertringen in *NDB* vii (1966), 111–14, with a list of Groener's main writings.

[43] See Messerschmidt, IV.1.4 below.

[44] Groener papers, BA-MA N 46/147.

German military planning only partially reflected this clear, deductive identification of the tasks of the individual elements of national defence.[45] The armaments programmes of the army and navy which Groener defended in the cabinet in 1928 were hardly co-ordinated and were not based on any unified plan. Groener's ideas in his memorandum and elsewhere, however, leave no doubt that precisely such a governing plan was his goal. He could not ignore the fact that the navy required 30 per cent of the Reichswehr budget and that the decision to build a pocket battleship would tie up considerable defence funds for years.

In order to influence the technical decisions of the army and navy leaders as he desired, Groener needed a military staff which would defend the interests of the armed-forces leadership *vis-à-vis* the army and navy. The Ministeramt (Ministerial Office) was established with expanded authority against the opposition of the chief of the army command at the beginning of March 1929. Its head, Kurt von Schleicher, who had recently been promoted major-general, was to carry out parliamentary-political work and at least attempt the urgently needed co-ordination of armaments measures.[46] It has been pointed out that the complicated planning process, especially in the 'second armaments programme' of the army, severely limited the power of the chief of the army command, and above all the minister himself, to influence decisions and developments.[47] Precisely because of this situation, Groener, who had enough comparable experience as a result of his assignment as chief of the Kriegsamt (war office) in the First World War, had to try to make full use of the remaining possibilities of exerting influence through the Ministeramt. The growing power of the Ministeramt can be traced not only to Schleicher's ambitions but also to the need to strengthen the influence of the defence minister for political and military reasons.

Groener's determination to exercise both his political and military functions as defence minister in his relations with the separate services can be seen still more clearly in another area. In mid-April 1930 he signed a directive on 'Tasks of the Wehrmacht' and sent it to the chiefs of the army and navy commands.[48] It had been drawn up by the Wehrmacht department of the Ministeramt. In it Groener laid down the bounds within which he considered the employment of the Reichswehr possible in the near future and described in detail the military means required. He emphasized that only political considerations were decisive in defining the tasks of the armed forces and that '*definite* prospects of success' were a precondition for the actual employment of the Reichswehr. On these premises he concluded that a 'responsible German government' might 'under certain circumstances decide to offer no military resistance' to a foreign attack, and directed that appropriate preparatory planning (for evacuations, demolition, etc.) should be carried out. The

[45] Cf. Post, *Civil-Military Fabric*, 256 ff.

[46] Wohlfeil, 'Heer und Republik', 121 ff.; Vogelsang, *Reichswehr*, 55 ff.; Carsten, *Reichswehr* (trans.), 296 ff.

[47] Geyer, 'Rüstungsprogramm', 131.

[48] Directive of 16 Apr. 1930, 147/30, W II a, BA-MA PG 34072; draft in Bredow Papers, BA-MA N 97/9. On the interpretation of this directive cf. Geyer, *Aufrüstung*, 213 ff.; Post, *Civil-Military Fabric*, 197 ff.

Reichswehr was only to be used in case of internal disturbances ('Case Pieck'), precisely defined situations requiring emergency action, or especially favourable international situations.

According to Groener's directive, emergency defence situations would exist if attacks by units of a foreign state, whether regular ('Case Pilsudski') or irregular ('Case Korfanty'), threatened to create a *fait accompli*. The Reichswehr was to be used against regular units if the attacking state was 'heavily occupied elsewhere militarily' or if German resistance would 'bring about the intervention of other powers or international authorities'. A favourable political situation was to be exploited if, as a result of pressure by one group of powers, Germany had a chance to improve her military and political position, or if she had the prospect of successfully defending her own neutrality under the same conditions. Finally, the German government might decide of its own accord to deploy the Reichswehr if and when 'a favourable international situation permits us the risk of such a decision'.

But Groener did not limit himself to describing the political conditions for a deployment of the Reichswehr; he also defined the modalities of military action for each of the eventualities mentioned. He distinguished between three basic forms of military action: the use of the standing army, ready to move; the use of this army with reinforcements; and the use of the field army, which would consist of the standing army enlarged threefold (twenty-one divisions) and the frontier guards. The use of the field army was planned only for 'Case Pilsudski' and in the event of a favourable political situation.

In an appendix to his directive Groener formulated comprehensive instructions for improving the combat-readiness of the Reichswehr. He placed particular emphasis on the standing army, the only military force 'immediately available to the government'. He called for a shortening of the period required for the army to be ready to move, the equipment of the army with heavy artillery and other modern weapons, and a general improvement in its training. The basic rule for the field army was that 'plans for organizing new units . . . have to remain within the limits imposed by equipment and supply possibilities'. This was a clear admission that in this area long periods of time would be required, for even the 'second armaments programme', approved at the beginning of 1932, envisaged the first equipping of the twenty-one-division field army and providing it with stocks for six weeks as taking place only by the spring of 1938.[49]

The essential content of Groener's directive is presented in some detail here because it provided an almost classic description of the clearly defined function of the military as an instrument of the political leadership, a great rarity in German military history in the nineteenth and twentieth centuries. Groener's directive also marked the high point of a development since the mid-1920s, in which the Reichswehr leaders had to adopt a more open attitude towards the civilian authorities of the republic and to accept their political control in order to obtain financial and political support for clandestine military measures. As defence

[49] Cf. Geyer, 'Rüstungsprogramm'.

minister, Groener attempted to expand this control by establishing clear objectives for military policy, and, with his precise definition of the purpose of military power, he dealt with one of the key questions of military leadership. Moreover, the appendix to his directive made clear that he intended to use his definition of the circumstances in which the Reichswehr might be used to set priorities in armaments planning. Groener and the Ministeramt under Schleicher drew the logical conclusions from the first sentence of the directive: 'The tasks assigned to the armed forces by the civilian leadership form the basis for their build-up and use.'

The only possible interpretation of Groener's directive is that it was in complete accord with the revisionist policy that had been pursued by all governments of the republic.[50] The security of the supposedly threatened frontiers with Poland was the main concern of the Reichswehr in its actual planning. Here too German leaders had to recognize the importance of a proper functioning of the League of Nations for their security policy, especially with regard to 'Case Pilsudski'. The more ambitious, long-term goals of revisionist policy were also dealt with in the directive. An unprovoked offensive use of the Reichswehr was not excluded, if the risk could be calculated.

If one wishes to determine the internal significance of Groener's directive for the Reichswehr itself, it is necessary to consider the ideas of German military leaders about possibilities of using the Reichswehr as they were expressed in war-games and exercises. In this regard the games, exercises, and studies under Blomberg's direction in the winters of 1927–8 and 1928–9 are especially important.[51] In the exercises the Truppenamt and the army command concerned themselves primarily with the possible forms and course of a war with Poland. The military conclusion was devastating. In the winter war-games of the Truppenamt in 1927–8 a four-month period of tension was supposed to lead to an open military conflict in which the Reichswehr would have to fight under 'downright hopeless conditions'. The exercise of 1928 did not produce better results. The representative of the foreign ministry observed succinctly that a war with Poland could only be waged 'for a short time and with extensive loss of territory'. But Blomberg refused to accept this.[52] Shortly before the fight had to be broken off by the German side because of a shortage of ammunition, he had the League of Nations intervene and force Poland to accept an armistice. Thereupon the Soviet Union was to attack Poland and offer Germany an alliance, which would be gratefully accepted, so that the Reichswehr could conclude the conflict successfully with large-scale attacks! A discussion of this scenario, in which military wishful thinking so obviously determined the assessment of the political situation, is clearly superfluous. On the other hand, it must not be overlooked that the Truppenamt had provided a realistic evaluation of military possibilities and the relative strength of the forces involved.

Thanks to the review of all illegal armament measures and to concrete, long-term armament planning, which was only beginning, it was in fact possible to base the

---

[50] See Messerschmidt, IV.1.4.
[51] Post, *Civil-Military Fabric*, 204 ff.; Geyer, *Aufrüstung*, 188 ff.
[52] Geyer, *Aufrüstung*, 192–3.

war-games to some degree on reliable figures. For this reason there was some weight in the conclusion of the Truppenamt that, on the basis of the level of German armaments on 1 April 1933 (i.e. after the completion of the 'first armaments programme'), the chances of a successful defence against a Polish attack would have significantly improved.

In mid-1928 the German navy had no comparable armaments programme.[53] With some delay compared to the army, the navy had begun preparations for a ship-construction and -replacement plan in 1927. But the decision to build pocket battleships never quite lost the character of an interim solution. The controversy about *Panzerschiff A*, to be followed by three other such vessels, marked the beginning of a long tug of war within and outside the executive branch about these most important projects of naval rearmament.[54] However, the navy command developed its operational ideas almost without regard to the number or kind of ships available. As early as the autumn manœuvres of 1926, the navy was no longer merely concerned with coastal defence. Moreover, its main objective was no longer the protection of German overseas supplies. Instead, it switched to attacks on enemy supply-routes, on the assumption that 'the sea links between an enemy in the west and one in the east' had become 'an important factor in achieving a decision'.[55] In the assumed situation Germany had become involved in a conflict with France as well as Poland, and, in contrast to later manœuvres, Britain and Italy had adopted a benevolent attitude towards France. A year later the navy high command deployed two pocket battleships, which were still in the planning stage, to secure the Baltic in a battle against the combined French and Polish fleets.

The realism of Groener's directive of 16 April 1930 stands in sharp contrast to these military-planning considerations of the army and navy commands. Already in his memorandum on the question of pocket battleships,[56] Groener had clearly stated that 'The idea of a major war has to be ruled out from the very beginning.' He thus indirectly characterized the political combinations and military situations assumed by the navy command as illusory. The political as well as the military preconditions of the navy war-games clearly show that there had been no co-ordination with the army, and that each service apparently assumed that it would be able to fight its own war. Groener attempted to put an end to this absurd spectacle with his uniform directive for both the army and the navy. In his 'pocket battleship' memorandum he had emphasized that even the tasks of such ships should be based on the detailed definition of the function of the navy in the defence of the country. With his directive of 1930 he showed how the navy could be induced to base its operational ideas more on political and military realities.[57]

[53] Dülffer, *Weimar*, 67 ff., 112 ff; Rahn, *Reichsmarine*, 214 ff.

[54] On this subject and the following passage cf. the most recent work by Rahn, *Reichsmarine*, 114 ff.; also Schreiber, 'Reichsmarine', 162 ff., and id., 'Rolle Frankreichs'. Dülffer ('Determinants', 162–3) speaks of a 'status crisis' of the navy in 1928–32.

[55] Cf. Geyer, *Aufrüstung*, 196 ff., esp. n. 27. On the naval war games cf. also Rahn, *Reichsmarine*, 135 ff.   [56] Groener papers, BA-MA N 46/147.

[57] Groener undoubtedly knew that the construction of *Panzerschiff A* made it unsuited for the tasks he described (cf. Salewski, 'England', 165–6). Nevertheless he continued to insist that the navy's primary

The army command and the Truppenamt had made a greater effort to take into account the realities of military power in their war-game of 1927–8. But they too suffered from an unmistakable urge to ignore depressing reality and return to traditional, large-scale warfare, if only in the form of war-games. In the winter war-game of 1927–8 Blomberg ordered an examination of Germany's chances in a two-front war with France allied to Poland, whose forces were supposed to be tied down by the Soviet Union.[58] The results were hardly surprising. Even with the assumed armaments level of 1 April 1933, the Reichswehr was only able to offer a delay, and in the final analysis hopeless resistance. In a memorandum of 26 March 1929, however, Blomberg considered the situation to be 'not so hopeless as it may appear at first'. This optimistic assessment was based on the conviction that 'great states' had never 'endured military rape without military resistance'.[59] In this opinion the head of the Truppenamt flatly rejected the military principles of the defence minister and his Ministeramt. Schleicher, the head of the Ministeramt, had a very low opinion of such ideas of military prestige based on self-deception, which would inevitably end in a national disaster. Indirectly he called upon Blomberg to 'muster the courage . . . to admit that military-political situations can develop in which fighting would be hopeless from the very beginning'. Blomberg did not have the courage, and lost the argument with the defence minister and the Ministeramt. At the end of September 1929 he was replaced as head of the Truppenamt by General Kurt von Hammerstein-Equord.[60] Without a doubt the result of the controversy should be considered a success for the defence minister's viewpoint. However, it did not represent a complete victory, for which consistent political support was necessary.

Under the pressure of circumstances, Groener, who no doubt considered himself a pupil of Schlieffen's, had developed an extraordinarily flexible military policy which had almost nothing in common with the latter's purely operational maxims. The most obvious example of this was his break with traditional ideas and convictions concerning the proper function of the military. This change was not only a result of the restrictions imposed on Germany by the treaty of Versailles; it was also necessitated by the wider meaning given to the term 'national defence' by the First World War. Groener was a strong advocate of the participation of other parts of the executive branch in national defence,[61] but he balanced this enormous

area of activity should be the Baltic Sea. On the adverse reaction of the navy leaders cf. Geyer, *Aufrüstung*, 219 ff., and esp. Schreiber, *Revisionismus*, 54 ff.

[58] Geyer, *Aufrüstung*, 190 ff.; Post, *Civil–Military Fabric*, 215 ff.
[59] Post, *Civil–Military Fabric*, 215 ff., 152 ff.; Geyer, *Aufrüstung*, 192.
[60] Ibid. 207 ff.; Post, *Civil–Military Fabric*, 162 ff. Cf. esp. Geyer, 'Dynamics', 108–9: 'Blomberg turned from professional military analysis to ideology, because he took the problem of German security very seriously . . . but was unable to solve the problem within the context of professional military thinking.' The position taken by Groener and Schleicher was quite different: 'Any appropriate rearmament policy had to increase German military power while maintaining international stability.' This involved walking 'a very narrow line between security and stability on the one hand and armament on the other'. This balance could not be maintained under the double pressure of a domestic political crisis and the requirements of the armament programme.
[61] Cf. Geyer, *Landesverteidigung*, 166 ff.

expansion of military influence with equally strong support for a political definition of the purpose of the military machine. His directive of April 1930 represented an attempt to establish the relationship between political ends and military means, described in such detail by Clausewitz, as the guiding principle of German rearmament from an early stage. This certainly did not mean that Groener considered the permanent role of the armed forces to be that of merely one factor in a defensive security policy; but his basic rule with regard to military support for an expansionist foreign policy was that '*definite* prospects of success' were a precondition for any use of armed force.

3. THE CHANGE IN ARMAMENT POLICY, 1932–1933

The Reichswehr in the spring of 1932 was very different from the Reichswehr under Seeckt at the beginning of the stabilization phase of the republic. Under Groener's leadership the efficiency of the military machine had been greatly improved. A sign of the Reichswehr's political influence was the fact that, without relinquishing his post as defence minister, Groener became minister of the interior in October 1931.[62] Basing its decisions on a modern, comprehensive concept of national defence, the Reichswehr now possessed a realistic plan of action and a middle-term armaments programme; it began to free itself from the restrictions of Versailles.

In comparison to Gessler, Groener made full use of the political and military leadership and supervisory functions of his office and attempted to push through this policy in his relations with the army and navy commands. The precondition for this was continued political stability; but this essential factor was destroyed at the latest in September 1930, by the spectacular success of the National Socialists in the Reichstag elections. At the beginning of October 1930, in a message to his commanders, Groener proudly observed that the Reichswehr leadership had succeeded in 'making the Reichswehr the strongest factor in the state, a factor which cannot be ignored in making political decisions'.[63] He considered this situation a result of the policy the Reichswehr had pursued since 1926–7. It was, however, symptomatic of the situation in Germany that during the Ulm officers' trial in September–October 1930 Groener felt it necessary to use such language to defend his policies. Within the Reichswehr criticism of the policy of co-operation was aimed at its basic precondition, viz. the acceptance of the republic, its institutions, and its parties as political facts.

The trial of the Ulm officers by the Supreme Court at Leipzig and the reaction within the Reichswehr to this event revealed a dangerous disagreement between the leaders of the Reichswehr and the majority of its line officers.[64] Groener felt compelled to refute energetically the charge that the Reichswehr leadership was

---

[62] Vogelsang, *Reichswehr*, 132–3.

[63] Cf. Groener-Geyer, *Groener*, 270 ff.; Carsten, *Reichswehr* (trans.), 322.

[64] On this subject as a whole cf. Bucher, *Reichswehrprozeß*, 122 ff., 143 ff.; Carsten, *Reichswehr* (trans.), 315 ff.

pursuing a 'leftist course' and neglecting the defence of the country. An analysis of opinions prevalent in the officer corps shows that the widespread criticism did not necessarily reflect a rejection of the constitution or the republican form of government.[65] Officers were interested less in the constitution than in the reality of the state. For the typical Reichswehr officer, the state had to have a 'strong', hierarchical structure. Accordingly, the government was expected to give 'national' interests, i.e. the restoration of national sovereignty, absolute priority and to subordinate all other considerations to the goal of freeing Germany from the restrictions of Versailles. This was incompatible with the frequent changes of government resulting from unstable parliamentary coalitions, as well as constant 'party squabbling' in the Reichstag and in public. It was only natural that the officer corps of the Reichswehr judged rightist parties by the same standard as others and frequently expressed sharp disapproval of their behaviour.[66] But there is no doubt that the officer corps as a whole, with its very reactionary view of the proper function of the state, can be included in the conservative, nationalist camp.

Against this background it is not surprising that there was little sympathy in the officer corps for the co-operation policy of the Reichswehr leadership, which necessarily involved acceptance of the compromises essential to maintaining political coalitions. Brüning's government, which was completely dependent on the support of the president and tolerated by the Reichstag, attempted to cope with the political, economic, and social effects of the world economic crisis by relying on the president's power to issue emergency decrees under Article 48 of the Weimar constitution. In doing so the government largely freed itself from parliamentary control but enjoyed, at first, the complete sympathy of the officer corps.[67] But when Brüning found himself forced to prohibit rightist mass movements the situation changed.[68] The institutions of the republic proved less and less able to withstand the attacks of radical movements from the right and left, and many leading officers believed, in spite of their distaste for the rightist paramilitary organizations, that Germany could not do without the 'national substance' found in such mass movements. However, because of the officers' strong basic conservatism, the rise of the National Socialist Party and the unrestrained aggression of the SA became a serious problem for the Reichswehr. The idea of 'taming' the radical movement, advocated by Groener and Schleicher on numerous occasions,[69] had not even been temporarily successful. The outcome of the election of April 1932,[70] which led directly to the fall of Brüning's presidential cabinet, plunged the Reichswehr policy

[65] According to Article I of the 'Professional Duties of the Soldier' (*Berufspflichten des Soldaten*) in the version of 5 Sept. 1930, the soldier owed loyalty to the republican constitution. Cf. Absolon, *Wehrmacht*, i. 172–3.

[66] Cf. Meier-Welcker, 'Briefwechsel', 71 ff.

[67] Ibid., esp. n. 57.

[68] Cf. Wohlfeil, 'Heer und Republik', 289 ff.; Carsten, *Reichswehr* (trans.), 309 ff.; Vogelsang, *Reichswehr*, 113 ff.

[69] Vogelsang, *Reichswehr*, 135 ff.

[70] President von Hindenburg was re-elected in two ballots (23 Mar. and 10 Apr. 1932). State parliament elections took place in Prussia, Bavaria, Württemberg, Hamburg, and Anhalt on 24 Apr. 1932.

pursued by Groener and Schleicher into a serious crisis. As head of the Ministeramt, Schleicher opposed the ban on the SA, which Groener as minister of the interior, and the ministers of the interior of the German states (Länder), considered urgently necessary, and which was supported by Brüning.[71] Schleicher believed that the ban was more and more undermining the basis for a policy in the interests of the Reichswehr as such. The question is whether the change from Groener to Schleicher in the office of defence minister at the end of May 1932 also represented a basic change in Reichswehr policy.

Neither his contemporaries not historians have taken a generally favourable view of Schleicher's political activities.[72] His unusual military career, which led him from one staff department to another and made him a stranger to the rank-and-file soldiers, his role in the forces build-up, his work as head of the Ministeramt, his close association and his break with Groener, and finally his personal relations with Hindenburg's family gave him a reputation of being an *éminence grise*, a 'cardinal *in politicis*', as Groener aptly described him. His belief, shared by Brüning and Groener, that the NSDAP and the SA could be 'tamed' by superior tactics and, in the course of time, integrated into the existing political structure, as well as his politically fatal underestimation of Hitler's will to power and determination to achieve his goals, have greatly contributed to the negative assessment of Schleicher's policies by historians. However, to understand Schleicher as a politician, defence minister, and chancellor, it is necessary to consider the military motives of his actions more than has previously been done. Schleicher was one of the most influential protagonists of the policy of co-operation with the governments of the republic, and played an important role in Groener's by no means unsuccessful attempt to integrate the armaments and deployment planning of the Reichswehr into a comprehensive military policy in line with general revisionist aims.

Schleicher's basic and certainly correct assumption was that the presidential regime as it had developed since 1930 under Brüning was all the more dependent on the president's confidence and support in so far as it lost the support or at least tolerance of a majority in the Reichstag and the country at large. The election of April 1932 had shown that such a majority for Brüning's policies did not exist, and the spring tide of National Socialist successes had by no means ebbed. Groener's attempt as defence minister and minister of the interior to push through and maintain a strict ban on the SA, with the support of Brüning and the Länder but against the intentions of Hindenburg, was incompatible with Schleicher's basic premiss. Because of the close ties between the Reichswehr and the office and person of the president, a Reichswehr policy against Hindenburg was quite inconceivable for Schleicher. The estrangement between Hindenburg and Brüning, which had been growing since the end of 1931, and the conflict between Groener as defence minister and the president caused by the ban on the SA, thus touched a very

---

[71] Vogelsang, *Reichswehr*, 166 ff. Concerning this problem cf. the comprehensive *Staat und NSDAP 1930–1932: Quellen zur Ära Brüning*, with introductory analysis and important new points by G. Schulz.
[72] Cf. Vogelsang, *Schleicher*.

sensitive spot in the Reichswehr's view of itself. Schleicher's break with Groener and his active participation in the fall of Brüning were therefore completely consistent with the basic line of Reichswehr policy.[73]

It is not difficult to recognize in Schleicher's political actions of the following months the attempt to restore the basic conditions for the final success of his policy of 'taming' the National Socialists. With Papen's appointment as chancellor, the executive regained the indispensable support of the president, which made possible new initiatives in the area of practical politics. As the new defence minister, Schleicher played a leading role in developing and formulating the policies of the Papen government.[74] Indeed, military policy increasingly became a dominant factor in government policy in general. This was especially true of foreign policy.

Among the revisionist goals, the Rhineland question and the settlement of the reparations problem had previously been given absolute priority over the demands for a revision of the military provisions of Versailles. After Stresemann had created the political preconditions for ending the Allied occupation of the left bank of the Rhine, Brüning had concentrated on the revision of the parts of the treaty dealing with reparations, together with the Young plan. Papen was able to benefit from Brüning's policy, which had meanwhile had disastrous political consequences within Germany. At the Lausanne conference of June–July 1932 German reparations were reduced to a symbolic sum of RM3,000m. Now demands for military revision received first priority. Whereas Brüning had tried cautiously to obtain the approval of the Western powers for German military wishes in April 1932, such international considerations played no role in the policy of the new defence minister.[75] However, in internal discussions and in his public statements Schleicher demanded from the beginning a much sharper formulation of the German position in the matter of equal rights. His policy concerning this question and towards the Geneva disarmament conference amounted to a change in method; it was also intended to achieve a greater degree of domestic political unity. The German rejection of the conference resolution of 23 July was due to Schleicher's intervention; and the simultaneous announcement that Germany would continue to participate in the conference only if she were granted equality, as well as Schleicher's exploitation of this deliberately provoked controversy in his speeches for propaganda purposes, clearly show its domestic political function. With the Geneva five-power declaration of 11 December 1932 Schleicher achieved international recognition in principle of German equality in armaments, and thus a significant partial revision of Part V of the treaty of Versailles. But he failed

---

[73] Vogelsang, *Reichswehr*, 170 ff.; also Geyer, *Aufrüstung*, 270–1; Sauer, 'Mobilmachung', 35 ff. Bennett (*German Rearmament*, 16 ff., 35 ff., 38 ff., 180 ff.) stresses the political importance of Reichswehr personnel planning for the wartime army, which was less and less able to rely on age-groups that had served in the First World War.

[74] Vogelsang, *Reichswehr*, 209 ff.; Carsten, *Reichswehr* (trans.), 364 ff.; Bennett, *German Rearmament*, 169 ff.; Schildt, *Militärdiktatur*, 50 ff.

[75] On the individual phases of German policy in the disarmament question cf. Deist, 'Abrüstungsfrage', 64 ff.; Salewski, 'Sicherheitspolitik', 121 ff.; Dülffer, *Weimar*, 139 ff., 254 ff.; Rautenberg, *Rüstungspolitik*, 12 ff.; Geyer, *Aufrüstung*, 130 ff., 255 ff.; Messerschmidt, IV.I.4 and IV.II.3 below.

completely in his efforts to create a solid political base among the parties and in the population at large by means of a foreign policy which strongly stressed national interests. The Nazis, and especially Hitler himself, resisted not only Schleicher's policy of 'taming' them but also his attempts to divide the party as a mass movement.[76]

In addition to these domestic factors, the change of method in German foreign policy was due to considerations of armaments policy. In the spring of 1932 the 'second armaments programme', for the period from 1 April 1933 to 31 March 1938, was adopted. At a cost of RM400m.—RM80m. a year—the programme was intended to provide the planned twenty-one-division field army with a first issuing of weapons, equipment, and ammunition as well as minimum stocks for a period of six weeks.[77] In the discussions of the programme every effort had been made to cut the individual requirements drastically and to include a maximum of co-ordinated armaments measures, whose effectiveness had been carefully tested, within the limits imposed by the budget. Inevitably this kind of long-term programme was especially sensitive to changes in economic conditions, affecting the assumptions on which it was based.

For this reason the effects of the world economic crisis soon forced the defence ministry to press the government for more funds in order to protect the second armaments programme. Large armaments firms, such as Borsig (Tegel, Berlin), as well as a number of small companies in central Germany essential to the realization of the armaments plans, found themselves in economic difficulties which threatened their very existence. Like other 'monopoly firms', i.e. those armament manufacturers permitted by the treaty of Versailles, they attempted to overcome their difficulties with the help of the state, specifically by setting high prices for their armament products. From the point of view of the Reichswehr they were able, so to speak, to 'dictate prices'.[78] Their problems were made more difficult by the fact that, for most of them, the ban on arms exports,[79] combined with the relatively low volume of Reichswehr orders, made economically rational production practically impossible. For example, in translating the second armaments programme into concrete procurement plans, the Heereswaffenamt (army ordnance office) had to spend more than half of all available funds for purchases in the form of so-called 'minimum procurement quotas' intended to guarantee a rational use of the capacities of the supplier firms under existing conditions. Above all, these calculations made clear that, at a certain point in the realization of the total programme (in 1935), available funds would not be sufficient to cover the necessary 'minimum procurement quotas'.[80]

In view of this situation the army ordnance office submitted a memorandum calling for a comprehensive reorganization of the armaments industry. Its proposals

[76] On Schleicher's unsuccessful attempt to achieve closer co-operation with Gregor Strasser cf. Vogelsang, *Reichswehr*, 340 ff.; Schildt, *Militärdiktatur*, 116 ff.

[77] Geyer, 'Rüstungsprogramm', 125 ff., esp. 130.

[78] Ibid. 132. On the authorized manufacturers cf. Salewski, *Entwaffnung*, 106 ff.; esp. n. 58.

[79] Hansen, *Reichswehr und Industrie*, 161 ff.

[80] Geyer, 'Rüstungsprogramm', 132 ff., id., *Aufrüstung*, 291 ff.

went far beyond the ideas Groener had presented to the chancellor in mid-April 1932 concerning the participation of the Reichswehr in the government's job-creation programme. Groener had confined himself to financial demands amounting to RM1,000m. for a period of five years. The army ordnance office advocated far-reaching measures in the interest of a limited number of armament firms in order to 'save them from collapse' by specific forms of relief in regard to customs, taxes, credits, and wages, even if these measures were incompatible with previously observed considerations of domestic, foreign, and economic policy.[81] Above all, however, the army ordnance office called for preferential treatment of those firms in the awarding of government contracts and for the repeal of the relevant regulations then in force.

The various statements, proposals, and demands from the defence ministry clearly show that, as a reaction to the worsened economic situation, but also because the Reichswehr leaders had perceived the opportunity presented by the state emergency programmes, their armaments policy was in a state of transition. More than in previous years, armaments questions were at the centre of military policy. It would soon become clear that the limits of the co-operation policy in this area had been reached.

In the spring of 1932 a decisive change also took place in personnel planning for the twenty-one-division field army.[82] As early as 1925 the Heeresorganisationsabteilung (army organization department) had pointed out that there would no longer be a sufficient number of trained men available in the relevant age-group in and after 1931. The Reichswehr sought to relieve this dangerous shortage, which would create difficulties in any mobilization, by introducing a number of improvisations. The build-up of the so-called 'leader army' (Führerheer) and the organization of the frontier guard and local defence units served this purpose.[83] Training outside the regular army, which was carried out within the framework of the frontier guards, local defence units, and air defence, was based on voluntary recruits, most of whom belonged to rightist paramilitary organizations. In 1931 'short training tests' were conducted in all parts of Germany according to uniform guide-lines. The results were positive and the tests were continued in 1932.[84] However, the manpower preconditions for the raising of the twenty-one-division field army could not be fulfilled by spring 1938. The relevant measures were indeed co-ordinated but, for reasons of domestic and foreign policy, could not be carried out with the necessary systematic organization. For the twenty-one-division army, changes in the structure and strength of the existing army were indispensable. But such a plan affected key issues of the treaty of Versailles and thus of foreign policy, even more than did questions of equipment. For years the various aspects of the militia question had

[81] Geyer, 'Rüstungsprogramm', 133, 152 ff.

[82] Geyer, *Aufrüstung*, 293 ff.; Rautenberg, *Rüstungspolitik*, 60–1, 216 ff.; Carsten, *Reichswehr* (trans.), 356 ff.; Dülffer, *Weimar*, 225 ff.

[83] Geyer, *Aufrüstung*, 106 ff. The fitness of age-groups trained before 1918 was declining rapidly. Wohlfeil, 'Heer und Republik', 207 ff.

[84] Rautenberg, *Rüstungspolitik*, 219 ff.

been discussed by politicians and experts.[85] But, in view of the foreign-policy significance of the problem as a whole, definite decisions had been deliberately avoided. Against the background of the comprehensive but also very specific armaments planning described above, however, it could be expected that the Reichswehr leadership would confront the government with specific goals in this equally important question. Only a few weeks after the chief of the army command had approved the second armaments programme, he received a proposal drawn up by the army organization department for the 'new peacetime army'. The aim of this plan was to gradually create the manpower preconditions for raising the twenty-one-division field army by the spring of 1938.[86] The chief of the army command, General von Hammerstein-Equord, supported the plan, but it is doubtful that it received the approval of the defence minister at this time. In any case the cabinet did not discuss it. The German government obviously postponed a decision; they probably still hoped to achieve an international agreement at the disarmament conference.

The conference had opened at the beginning of February 1932 with basic-position statements by the delegations which hardly gave any reason to expect a general understanding.[87] But in March and April there seemed to be a possibility of a Franco-German compromise. Both countries maintained their basic positions, but with the help of the British and Americans a new basis for negotiations was found in the concept of 'equality of treatment'. Neither the German demand for full equality of rights nor the French view that Germany must continue to be bound by Part V of the treaty of Versailles was basically affected by this formula. But at the point the negotiations had reached by the middle of April 1932 it represented a modification of the provisions of Versailles which in principle, though not in its scope, contained all elements envisaged by the Reichswehr for the rearmament phase until February 1938: reorganizing the army by graduated periods of service, supplementing the active army with a militia, and equipping it with modern weapons. The chancellor's attempt at the end of April 1932 to achieve a basic understanding in direct negotiations with the Western powers, including the United States, was unsuccessful. The worsening domestic political crisis in Germany and Brüning's fall prevented a continuation of the talks. The role of the Reichswehr leadership in this diplomatic interlude and their co-operation with the government, which involved putting their own basic demands aside at least temporarily, clearly show that the principle of the subordination of military considerations to the government's revisionist policy, which Groener had advocated so forcefully and effectively, was still valid.[88] In the existing political and military situation international cover for even a minimal improvement in the state of German armaments was in this view more important than a unilateral proclamation of armaments demands and goals, which would only give rise to new risks and whose realization would in any case require several years.

---

[85] Rautenberg, *Rüstungspolitik*, 57 ff.; Geyer, *Landesverteidigung*, 68 ff., 132 ff.
[86] Rautenberg, *Rüstungspolitik*, 216 ff.   [87] Cf. n. 75 above.
[88] Geyer, *Aufrüstung*, 270–1. On the diplomatic negotiations cf. Deist, 'Brüning', 265 ff.

Contrary to external appearances, there was no real change in German military goals when, after Groener's fall, Schleicher, as the new defence minister, began to present his uncompromising demands in cabinet meetings, to proclaim them for domestic propaganda purposes, and to make them a central theme of German foreign policy. The decision on the reorganization and expansion of the 100,000-man army, which had only been postponed in March, was submitted to the cabinet and approved at the beginning of November.[89] This programme—which presumably was the reason for the acceptance of a larger number of additional officer candidates as early as 1 October 1932, and for the reduction of the service time of additional soldiers taken into the army to three years—provided for the formation of the 'new peacetime army' consisting of the active professional army and a 'militia'. The professional army of 100,000 men was to be increased to 144,000 in various phases by 31 March 1938. In addition it was planned to recruit 85,000 men each year, beginning on 1 April 1934, whose active service would be limited to a short three-month training period and four or five short reserve exercises. In this way the personnel requirements of the twenty-one-division field army could be covered by the spring of 1938. The strength of such an army was estimated at 570,000 men.

However, Schleicher's methods of carrying out specific rearmament measures differed appreciably from those Groener had used. Under the pressure of domestic political conditions and the economic realities of armaments production, Germany's disposition to withdraw from the international security system for reasons of military policy grew stronger. Schleicher did maintain the principle of international cover for German rearmament measures, but there was now an alternative. During the Lausanne conference Papen and Schleicher had attempted to reach a bilateral arms agreement with France. Not the least important reason for the failure of this attempt was Papen's dilettantism. At the end of 1932 and the beginning of 1933, shortly after the five-power declaration on the question of equal rights, Schleicher seems to have made a second attempt.[90] The methods of German military policy began to change on the international level.

In domestic politics the influence and decisive involvement of the Reichswehr also increased. The deposition of the Social Democratic caretaker government of Prussia and the installation of a Reich commissioner on 20 July 1932 were not, it is true, the result of any initiative on the part of the defence minister, but Schleicher fully approved of and actively supported the political coup.[91] In view of the long conflict with the Prussian government about the build-up and organization of the frontier guards and local defence units, which had been settled only superficially and with difficulty, the complete subordination of this state (Land), which was of decisive importance in any military planning, to the national executive was definitely in the interest of the Reichswehr.

---

[89] Rautenberg, *Rüstungspolitik*, 216.

[90] On the Franco-German contacts cf. Rautenberg, *Rüstungspolitik*, 62 ff.; Geyer, *Aufrüstung*, 298 ff.

[91] Vogelsang, *Reichswehr*, 238 ff.; Carsten, *Reichswehr* (trans.), 368 ff., cf. also Trumpp, *Papen*, 36 ff., 128 ff.

Schleicher's attitude towards the National Socialist movement and its leaders has been the subject of numerous, sometimes controversial, interpretations. Most of them agree that the general at first underestimated the political strength of the National Socialists and Hitler's own will to power, but that in the summer of 1932 he recognized the absolute nature of Hitler's ambition and took appropriate steps.[92] He was not prepared to give in to the pressure from Hitler and his party. However, the idea of mobilizing all loyal republican groups to counter the extremists on the left and the right was far from his intention, quite apart from the question of whether such groups could still have been mobilized at all for this purpose. For general foreign policy as well as for military reasons Schleicher rejected the idea of turning the state over to the militant nationalists of the NSDAP. He believed that the confidence of the president and the help of the Reichswehr and other executive organs would enable him to overcome the danger. Schleicher tried to broaden this narrow political base by using the state to organize certain groups of the population and society. The 'Reich institute for the training of young people' under the retired General Edwin von Stülpnagel, the appointment of a Reich commissioner for voluntary-labour service, and the repeated attempts to subject the paramilitary units to military control in the frontier guards are the best known examples of this policy, which was in many respects successful.[93]

All of Schleicher's initiatives were aimed at giving the government a new, primarily extra-parliamentary base of support. In these efforts he was, as chancellor and defence minister, dependent on the Reichswehr and its officer corps. The Ministeramt under Major-General Ferdinand von Bredow displayed intense political activity. Men enjoying the confidence of Schleicher and the defence ministry were appointed to key positions in the civilian executive apparatus, and even the army rank and file were not excluded from political tasks whose direction Schleicher had entrusted to the Reichswehr. Compared to the years when Groener had been head of the Reichswehr, not only had its political activity greatly increased under Schleicher, but the political sphere in which this activity developed had expanded considerably.[94] We need not enquire here whether Schleicher viewed this expansion of the army's role as part of a long-term programme or as an emergency solution. In any case the decisive participation of the Reichswehr in the shaping of foreign and domestic policy, especially in the broad areas of propaganda, youth programmes of all kinds, finance, and economic policy, was in complete accordance with ideas about a war of the future based on the experiences of the First World War. In this view the state and all aspects of public life had to be organized on a military basis. If one considers Schleicher's political activity in 1932–3 from this perspective, Germany was already on the way to becoming a garrison state.

In January 1933 Schleicher's experiment broke down because his policies lacked

---

[92] Vogelsang, *Schleicher*, 76 ff.; id., *Reichswehr*, 256 ff.; Carsten, *Reichswehr* (trans.), 371 ff.; Sauer, 'Mobilmachung', 37 ff.

[93] On the Reich Institute cf. Vogelsang, *Reichswehr*, 285–6.; Rautenberg, *Rüstungspolitik*, 239 ff.; Geyer, *Aufrüstung*, 295–6.

[94] Geyer, *Aufrüstung*, 284–5, 303–4, 307 ff.; Carsten, *Reichswehr* (trans.), 388–9.

3. Change in Policy, 1932–1933

the support of key political and social groups. With the Reichswehr alone Schleicher could not overcome this weakness, especially as he encountered increasing criticism within the officer corps because of his mixing of political and military matters. This criticism was directed not against the main foreign and domestic aspects of his military programme, but against the methods he used to carry it out[95]—above all, the increasingly frequent use of the Reichswehr for political tasks. For this reason the appointment of Hitler as chancellor and Blomberg as defence minister, which released the military from responsibility for the total political situation in the country, appeared to many officers as in some degree a return to normal conditions, which they had long desired.[96]

The appointment of Blomberg as defence minister on 30 January 1933 took place under unusual circumstances. His swearing-in in advance of the rest of the cabinet demonstrated the importance attached to the armed forces by persons around the president and Papen, as a stabilizing factor for the 'national government'. Although Hitler, for obvious reasons, had originally wanted to appoint one of his party comrades to the post of defence minister, he too found Blomberg's appointment quite acceptable, as he had already established satisfactory contacts with the general and his chief of staff, Colonel Walther von Reichenau. The co-operation between Hitler and Blomberg was based on an agreement which played a major role in all future developments in foreign and domestic policy. The break with Schleicher's methods lay in Blomberg's undertaking, which he reaffirmed at the cabinet meeting on 30 January, to renounce the right previously claimed and exercised by the Reichswehr to ensure order in domestic affairs.[97] In its relations with a cabinet of 'national concentration', this renunciation accurately reflected the Reichswehr's view of its proper political role. For Hitler, Blomberg's promise was a precondition for his planned radical changes in political conditions within Germany. As a quid pro quo, Hitler recognized the Reichswehr in its existing structure as the 'most important institution of the state',[98] thus dissociating himself from the plans and hopes of some of his followers to turn the armed forces into an instrument of Nazi rule with the help of the SA. Most important, however, was his affirmation, in a talk to the Reichswehr leadership, of his intention to carry out comprehensive rearmament as a means towards the realization of his political programme. This conformity between Hitler's goals and those of the military leaders was one of the main guarantees of the stability of the regime in the following years. For the Reichswehr this 'alliance' represented primarily a domestic guarantee of its unchanged military and armament objectives. The Hitler–Blomberg 'alliance' was therefore based on common basic interests of both sides, and this fact was the source of its strength and durability.

For the Reichswehr leadership Hitler's promise to promote rearmament in every

---

[95] Geyer, *Aufrüstung*, 307 ff.
[96] Carsten, *Reichswehr* (trans.), 390 ff.; Vogelsang, *Reichswehr*, 397 ff.
[97] Wollstein, *Revisionismus*, 23 ff.; Carsten, *Reichswehr* (trans.), 397 ff.; Vogelsang, *Reichswehr*, 397 ff.; *Regierung Hitler*, pt. i, vol. i, No. i, p. 3; Bennett, *German Rearmament*, 320–1.
[98] Vogelsang, 'Dokumente', 434–5 (Liebmann's notes of 3 Feb. 1933).

possible way meant, in concrete terms, that funding for the second armaments programme was guaranteed and that additional funds might even make it possible to accelerate the programme.[99] Blomberg, who till then had been the chief Reichswehr delegate at the Geneva disarmament conference, was aware that this was only one aspect of the problem. As long as the treaty of Versailles remained in force, German armaments would continue to be to a very large extent a foreign-policy matter. Groener and Schleicher had taken this fact into account in their defence planning, along with the complications arising from Germany's geographical position in the middle of Europe. The question was whether the change of government would produce any variation in the assessment of this situation.

Barely three weeks after the Hitler government had taken office, its reaction to a French proposal at Geneva gave an indication of its ideas concerning the need to obtain foreign-policy cover for German rearmament.[100] On 17 February the French aviation minister, Pierre Cot, had presented a plan intended to achieve agreement in the long-disputed security problem through a standardization of the structure of European armies. The French initiative was noteworthy above all because it contained no specific proposals on a number of important questions. This seemed to leave room for negotiation, and the head of the German delegation at Geneva, Ambassador Rudolf Nadolny, even spoke of the conference having reached a turning-point.

Blomberg, however, stated his own views, which clearly expressed the new German course in armaments policy, even before the foreign ministry had expressed its opinion. In a directive to the German delegation[101] he formulated a number of 'preliminary questions' to which satisfactory answers were required before the idea of a standardization of armies could be discussed. In these preliminary questions all the earlier, most difficult disarmament problems were deliberately pushed into the foreground. It was clearly Blomberg's intention to prevent any foreign control whatever of German rearmament. The foreign minister, Konstantin von Neurath, who considered the French and German foreign-policy goals incompatible, supported Blomberg's views. The two ministers do not seem to have been alarmed by the prospect that the Geneva conference would break down and Germany become increasingly isolated. It was typical of the new situation, moreover, that this political decision was taken at ministerial level without the chancellor himself being consulted. When, in the presence of Neurath and Blomberg, a member of the delegation reported to Hitler in mid-March 1933 on developments at the conference, it turned out that the chancellor wished after all to take advantage of the French proposal and preferred a 'positive conclusion' of the conference to 'rearmament without the sanction of a treaty'.[102] However, his

[99] Geyer, 'Rüstungsprogramm', 134–5, 156 ff.

[100] The best summary of this episode can be found in Wollstein, *Revisionismus*, 45 ff. Cf. also Messerschmidt, IV.II.3 below; Bennett, *German Rearmament*, 307 ff., 449 ff.

[101] *DGFP*, c. i, No. 26.

[102] Ibid., No. 94. On Hitler's attitude cf. Carr, 'Rüstung', 437–8.

directive did not prevent the two ministers from instructing the delegation in Geneva to continue to follow strictly the policy guidelines they had issued.[103]

This strange episode is characteristic of the first phase of Nazi rule and illustrates the very strong position of the defence minister in his 'alliance' with the chancellor. Hitler himself was convinced that the rearmament he so strongly supported was incompatible with any kind of arms convention in the long term; but in the initial phase of the remilitarization (*Wiederwehrhaftmachung*) of the German people he wished as far as possible to avoid diplomatic isolation or sanctions, even if they were only political or economic, by skilful manœuvring. Therefore in mid-May he overruled his foreign and defence ministers, who almost openly advocated withdrawal from the disarmament conference, and chose not direct confrontation but a policy of deception, the first high point of which took the form of his 'peace speech' in the Reichstag on 17 May.[104] This tactic was continued until the beginning of October.[105] Then, however, numerous signs indicated that the British mediation proposal which was to be presented to the disarmament conference in mid-October would not improve Germany's position in the first phase of the agreement under discussion, but would instead involve a system of arms control. From this point on Hitler was determined to break openly with the international system,[106] although he had told Neurath only a few days earlier that 'it would be desirable in any case to conclude a disarmament convention even if not all our wishes were fulfilled by it', and that it would be wrong 'to ask for more than we are able for technical, financial, and political reasons actually to procure in the next few years'.[107] The German government's statement of 14 October 1933, and its withdrawal from the League of Nations and the disarmament conference, marked its final break with the system of collective security, which had previously been an essential element of German revisionist policy.

If one attempts at this point to summarize developments in the field of national defence and its main principles from Groener to Blomberg, the key is no doubt to be found in the difference of basic outlook between successive ministers. Groener defined national defence in political categories; for him its tasks were determined by political factors. Military potential was an important but integrated instrument of the general revisionist policy. The most succinct expression of this view was Groener's directive of April 1930 on the 'Tasks of the Wehrmacht'. His military and armaments policy remained within the multilateral security system as it had developed since 1919. Under the pressure of domestic political conditions, but also because of the effect of economic factors on armaments, this policy changed considerably under Schleicher, although the military goals remained the same. Schleicher was the first to attempt a revision of the military provisions of the treaty

[103] *DGFP*, c. i, No. 106.

[104] Cf. Messerschmidt, Part IV below; Wollstein, *Revisionismus*, 96 ff.

[105] On the German attitude towards the MacDonald plan and the four-power pact cf. esp. Wollstein, *Revisionismus*, 64 ff., 147 ff., 181 ff.; Messerschmidt, IV.II.3 below.

[106] Wollstein, *Revisionismus*, 190 ff.

[107] Ibid. 187; quotation from *DGFP*, c. i, No. 475.

of Versailles through bilateral negotiations. To Blomberg, finally, the conditions which had previously been accepted as the basic framework determining German military and armaments policy no longer seemed valid. As head of the Truppenamt he had already rejected the logical military conclusions of Groener's policy and indicated that, for him, national defence was a purely military matter. After the experience of the First World War, this was a remarkable narrowing of the military horizon; it was to have profound consequences, and can be considered a precondition for the Hitler–Blomberg 'alliance' and the years of basically smooth co-operation between the Reichswehr and the Nazi regime.[108] In 1933 Groener's remark in his directive of April 1930 that the Reichswehr leadership should not even think about a 'major war' because of the completely inadequate state of Germany's armaments was still valid. It was typical of the new line in military policy that in spite of the weakness of the Reichswehr, which was even more serious in the first phase of rearmament, Blomberg was decidedly in favour of unilateral rearmament without diplomatic protection. In contrast, the 'Austrian corporal' was much more realistic in his assessment of Germany's international situation. Blomberg's attitude was certainly an expression of a professionalism which had become an ideology; on the other hand it also reflected his conviction that under National Socialism Germany had made great progress towards remilitarization and that popular support for the armed forces had become much stronger. The possibility must not be forgotten that, in the actual situation of October 1933, the accelerated second armaments programme and the conditions it created in regard to armament policy may have put the German government under a certain compulsion to act. With Germany's withdrawal from the disarmament conference and from the League of Nations, which Blomberg had advocated and prepared, the principles of Groener's national defence policy were definitely abandoned. They had been characterized by regard for political factors and commitment to a system of collective security. The way was now clear for the adventure of unrestricted rearmament.

[108] On Blomberg's ideas cf. Geyer, *Aufrüstung*, 207 ff., 312 ff.

II. The Rearmament of the Individual Services, 1933–1939

1. THE POSITION IN THE SPRING OF 1933

THE new orientation of Polish foreign policy under Marshal Pilsudski revealed immediately the potentially fatal risks for Germany which were involved in Blomberg's policy, based solely as it was on military strength. Pilsudski's abandonment of the security system based on Versailles, which had been evident since the beginning of the 1930s, and his attempt to reach an understanding with Germany through a calculated combination of pressure and readiness to negotiate, found expression in March 1933 in the temporary occupation of the Westerplatte peninsula in the territory of the free city of Danzig.[1] This demonstration was probably the reason for Blomberg's directive to Hammerstein, the chief of the army command, and Adam, the head of the Truppenamt, to undertake a study of Germany's situation between its eastern and western neighbours and its military possibilities in the event of a conflict. Hammerstein's and Adam's statements in this regard were especially important because their assessment of the situation necessarily involved critical examination of the basic military assumptions of Blomberg's policy. In his memorandum, Adam bluntly described the situation as hopeless.[2]

Trained reserves, officers, sufficient equipment, and modern weapons were lacking for the twenty-one-division field army. Most important, however, was the fact that, in Adam's opinion, available ammunition was sufficient for only fourteen days of fighting. He did consider that Polish advances on Berlin might be repelled, but Germany would be able to resist only for a limited time. In the event of a Czechoslovak or, still worse, French intervention, the initiative would have to be left completely to the enemy. In that case the Reichswehr would only be able, in Adam's words, to 'administer pinpricks here and there'. The Truppenamt concluded that everything must be done to avoid military confrontations, 'even at the price of diplomatic defeats'. In urging such a policy Adam was aware of the special diplomatic risks of a cautious but systematic rearmament involving constant violation of the treaty of Versailles, which was still legally in force. Precisely for this reason he warned against 'fanfares which could unnecessarily provoke the enemy and intoxicate our own people'. If one considers Adam's position from a political point of view, it contains early, sharp criticism of the policy pursued by the defence minister towards the disarmament conference in 1933. At the same time, his memorandum clearly describes the armaments situation of the Reichswehr before the adoption of the extraordinary measures to accelerate rearmament.

[1] Wollstein, *Revisionismus*, 125 ff.
[2] StA Nürnberg, X VDB (d), Krupp, No. 26, pp. 25–32; Adam's affidavit of 5 Mar. 1948. Hammerstein's memorandum has not survived.

Adam wrote his pessimistic assessment at a time when, unaffected by day-to-day politics, the modest rearmament programme of the Reichswehr was entering a new phase. In the personnel area a new goal had been set with the plan of November 1932 for 'reorganizing the peacetime army'.[3] The strengthening of the active army and the training of militia-type 'supplementary reservists' were intended to create the basis for raising a wartime army of twenty-one divisions by the spring of 1938 and to overcome the lack of trained reserves, which was considered especially serious and could not be eliminated even by using the paramilitary organizations. In his internal memorandum for the defence minister Adam observed: 'We must not suppose that training in the paramilitary organizations, which provide most of our volunteers, is much more than playing at soldiers.' In accordance with this line of thought, it was clearly stated in the reorganization plan of November 1932 that the training of the supplementary reservists was to take place 'within the framework of the professional army', i.e. 'with the troops and not alongside them'.[4]

From Adam's memorandum it is also clear that the long years of effort by the Reichswehr command to organize the frontier guard units, above all in the eastern part of Germany, had not produced any satisfactory military results. Adam described the existing frontier guard units as 'various groups of more or less willing fighters bound to a particular location.' Unlike the supplementary reservists, the frontier guard units were to be trained outside the Reichswehr in battalions to be created for the purpose. It was planned to provide two weeks of training annually for at least 80,000 men in the eastern frontier guard units.[5] The western frontier area remained unaffected by such measures; the risk of French sanctions against violations of the provisions of Versailles concerning the demilitarized zone seemed too great. The zone was likewise not included in the accelerated build-up of a replacement system under the reorganization plan of November 1932.[6] In March 1933, when the head of the Truppenamt wrote his assessment, none of the many measures of the reorganization plan of November 1932 had been carried out. The Reichswehr as a whole had at this time only slightly exceeded the personnel strength prescribed by the treaty of Versailles.

In the area of material armaments, on the other hand, the picture was somewhat more favourable. Although Adam correctly observed that neither sufficient ammunition nor modern weapons, especially tanks and aeroplanes, were available, the 'first armaments programme', which ended in the spring of 1933, and the already completed technical, organizational, and financial preparations for the 'second armaments programme', had created a solid foundation for accelerating rearmament at any time by allocating additional funds, and had produced their first concrete results.[7] Most important was the fact that detailed, carefully examined planning for special areas and for material armaments in general had been completed. For example, whether the second motorization programme could be

[3] Cf. Rautenberg, *Rüstungspolitik*, 216 ff.; id., 'Dokumente', 103 ff., and the file BA-MA RH 15/v.287.
[4] Cf. also Rautenberg, *Rüstungspolitik*, 60 ff.
[5] Ibid. 220 ff.   [6] Ibid. 235 ff.
[7] Geyer, 'Rüstungsprogramm', 134 ff.

started at the beginning of the second rearmament period (1933–8) depended only on the availability of funds.[8] This form of co-ordinated, systematic internal army planning, which had been carried on intensively since 1926–7, was one of the preconditions for the rapid, astonishingly smooth progress of rearmament in 1933–6.

The complete prohibition of German military aviation in the treaty of Versailles sharply restricted the Reichswehr leadership's room for manœuvre in that area. By transferring aircraft production abroad, co-operating closely with enterprises involved in civil aviation, especially Lufthansa, and finally by training officers as pilots and observers in friendly foreign countries, the Reichswehr leaders were able to keep up with the latest technical developments and obtain all desired test results.[9] This knowledge was translated into concrete planning for the first time in the preparations for the second armaments programme. A directive of 28 July 1932 provided only for the establishment of training units in 1933–4.[10] German civil aviation still provided more or less adequate camouflage for these units, but not for the twenty-two squadrons with about 200 aeroplanes which, according to the directive, were to be at the disposal of the German command in 1937. This clearly shows that a fundamental revision of the military provisions of Versailles was, so to speak, included in the second armaments programme and the reorganization plan. In the spring of 1933 the number of aeroplanes fit for action was, however, very small. In his memorandum Adam noted laconically: 'The air force (*Fliegerwaffe*) is at the very outset of its development.'

Still, Adam did mention the new service branch in his memorandum and thus underscored its importance in warfare. This was in contrast to the navy, which received more than a quarter of the total Reichswehr budget[11] but which Adam did not even mention in connection with the defence or surrender of East Prussia in the event of a Polish attack. This is further evidence of the already mentioned lack of co-ordination in operational planning and in the armaments programmes of the army and the navy.

The naval armaments situation was fundamentally different from that of the army in that the navy's 13,900 non-commissioned officers and men and its 1,100 officers[12] did not even have the ships permitted Germany by the treaty of Versailles. The limit had almost been reached for the lighter ships, such as cruisers and torpedo-boats, but the replacement of the obsolete battleships of the Tirpitz era with modern pocket battleships of the Deutschland class had only just begun.[13] Under the treaty of Versailles, Germany was allowed to have six of these 10,000-ton ships in service, but only three had been ordered, and none finished.[14] This explains in

---

[8] Barthel, *Heeresmotorisierung*, 183 ff.

[9] On German air armaments before Jan. 1933 cf. Völker, 'Entwicklung', 123 ff.; Homze, *Arming*, 1 ff.; Rautenberg, *Rüstungspolitik*, 317 ff.; Petersen, *Hitler–Mussolini*, 271 (training of German pilots in Italy).

[10] Rautenberg, *Rüstungspolitik*, appendix, 88.

[11] For a survey of the development of the Reichswehr budget see ibid. 81–2.

[12] Cf. Dülffer, *Weimar*, 232.

[13] Cf. Giese, *Marine*, 21 ff.

[14] Cf. the list of construction dates by J. Rohwer in Dülffer, *Weimar*, 570 ff.

part the almost exclusive interest of the navy leaders in heavy ships and related problems in the years after 1928. A modification of this tendency was reflected in the naval reorganization programme approved by the defence minister on 15 November 1932. In accord with the army reorganization plan, every advantage was to be taken of the possibilities offered by the treaty of Versailles until the spring of 1938, but in addition an aircraft-carrier and a first series of submarines were to be put into service and naval aviation units organized. These planning goals encountered criticism within the navy from officers who complained that better use should be made of the 'opportunity to satisfy our most urgent requirements after years of being hobbled'.[15] But the reorganization plan increased the enlisted strength of the navy and the number of its officer positions, without which more ambitious goals would not have been conceivable. The special emphasis it placed on the development of submarines and naval aviation units formed a counterweight to the excessive influence of the strategic traditions of the Tirpitz era.

The above survey shows that in the spring of 1933 the intention, for military and political reasons, to strengthen the Reichswehr beyond the limits of the treaty of Versailles had assumed, with differing intensity in the army and navy, the form of comprehensive and systematic programmes and had already produced its first, modest results.[16] The armaments programme began to develop its own momentum. Above all, however, the long-term, complex nature of the programme was so flexible that increased funds would make it possible to achieve the armaments goals much more rapidly than originally planned.

2. THE REARMAMENT OF THE ARMY

(a) The 'December Programme' of 1933

The assumption of power by the National Socialists at the end of January 1933 created new, extraordinarily favourable conditions for the realization of the Reichswehr's armaments plans. The special position of the defence minister in the Hitler cabinet, the Hitler–Blomberg 'alliance',[17] and the intensive efforts of the new chancellor to win the loyalty of the Reichswehr were unprecedented in the short history of the Weimar Republic.

Hitler's talk to representatives of the Reichswehr in the house of the chief of the army command on 3 February 1933 may have been intended for effect, but it also

---

[15] Dülffer, *Weimar*, 231 ff.

[16] Bennett and Geyer have emphasized the disproportion between the military results and the foreign and domestic political effects and actual consequences of Reichswehr armaments policy, especially in 1931–2. Cf. Bennett, *German Rearmament*, esp. 301 ff., 506 ff.; Geyer, 'Professionals', 77–133; id., 'Dynamics', 100–51.

[17] Cf. Sauer, 'Mobilmachung', 41 ff.; Wollstein, *Revisionismus*, 23 ff. The term used by Müller (*Armee*, 31), 'Entente', implies, however, a degree of independence on the part of the groups involved which at least the Reichswehr did not possess in Jan. 1933, even with regard to the objectives that armaments planning was intended to achieve. Cf. also Hüttenberger's remarks in 'Polykratie', 423. Hüttenberger describes the relationship among the ruling groups as a 'pact' which varied from time to time. Many examples to support his thesis can be found in relations between the Wehrmacht or particular armed services and competing power-centres.

clearly showed the change in the basic conditions under which future questions involving the armed forces and armaments policy would be decided. At the very beginning of his talk Hitler announced that 'regaining political power' would be the sole aim of his policy, this depended on a complete 'transformation' of domestic political conditions, the introduction of a 'strict, authoritarian leadership of the state', and initiatives in the area of economic policy, as well as the strengthening of Germany's 'military determination' (*Wehrwille*) by every means.[18] Using various examples, Hitler explained to the generals his programme for remilitarization (*Wiederwehrhaftmachung*) and promised to overcome politically motivated resistance to the military organization of national defence, against which the Reichswehr had previously found itself helpless. His programme of remilitarization formed the solid basis for co-operation between the Reichswehr and the National Socialist movement. Blomberg spoke of the cabinet being 'the expression of a broad national will and the realization of what many of our best people have been striving for for years'.[19] For the first time it seemed possible to take the main lesson of the First World War into account on a large scale in defence planning—viz. the need to organize the nation and its human and material resources as a precondition for any armed confrontation between industrialized states. Hitler's view that success at the disarmament negotiations in Geneva would be 'pointless' if 'the nation' did not have 'the will to rearm' succinctly expressed this policy.

However, Hitler was very cautious about announcing specific armament measures. He described the reintroduction of general conscription as an obvious, natural goal, but did not set any time for achieving it. Blomberg, too, warned his commanders against 'excessive hopes and expectations'. The 'scope of what we want to and can achieve at first' was, he said, very modest. The caution of the chancellor and the defence minister was understandable in view of the uncertain foreign and domestic situation at the beginning of February 1933. For the generals it was decisive that both Hitler and Blomberg had indicated their intention to broaden and strengthen support for the Reichswehr in the population and to transform the professional army into an army based on general conscription. The assertion of the newly appointed chief of the Ministeramt, Colonel von Reichenau, in early February of 1933 that the Wehrmacht had never been 'more identical with the state' was certainly premature; but it did describe perfectly the goal the generals hoped to achieve and for which, as would become clear, they were prepared to pay a high price—the subservience of the armed forces to the policy of *Gleichschaltung*, i.e. the complete subordination of German society to National Socialist programmes and purposes.[20]

The army reorganization plan of November 1932 and the second armaments programme were of decisive importance for the armament measures of 1933. A considerable acceleration of the programme became evident as early as the

[18] Vogelsang, 'Dokumente', 434 ff.; cf. also Dülffer, *Weimar*, 237 ff., and Irving, *War Path*, 32 ff. Cf. Wette, I.II.3 and 4 above; Volkmann, II.II.I above, and Messerschmidt, IV.I.2 and 4 below.

[19] At the commanders' conference on 3 Feb. 1933: cf. Vogelsang, 'Dokumente', 432.

[20] Cf. Sauer, 'Mobilmachung', 49 ff., esp. 53.

beginning of February, following the release of additional funds.[21] It could not be expected that the size of the army could likewise be increased, because the raising of new units on a large scale could not be concealed. The limits of what was considered possible were determined by assessments of the scope of Germany's freedom of action in foreign policy. For example, the reorganization plan provided for the removal of limitations on the personnel strength of units and above all the raising, or inclusion in the budget, of new artillery, anti-aircraft, and signals units. These measures increased the personnel strength of the army by about 14,000 men.[22] In violation of the treaty of Versailles, the new volunteers inducted into the army were to enlist for only three years. The organization of the replacement system and the corresponding agencies was begun.[23] For these tasks three sub-district offices were established in each of the seven military districts. In addition to the considerable increase in the strength of the active army, the reorganization plan for 1933 had a second major aim: intensifying the training of the frontier guard units. For this purpose it was planned to form nine frontier guard training battalions, which, in co-operation with instructors from the individual services, would prepare the frontier guards in two-week training courses. The National Socialist assumption of power hardly changed the basic features of this modest programme. Only the total number of new enlistments seems to have increased significantly, by more than half again over the planned number.[24]

The continuity and momentum of the systematic armament planning of the Reichswehr initiated in 1926–7 was evident in the carrying out of the first part of the reorganization plan of November 1932. More or less unaffected by domestic political and economic shocks and radical changes, the decisive step to expand the peacetime army was taken with the measures of 1933. The provisions of the treaty of Versailles anchored in German law were circumvented and in effect annulled. In spite of the elaborate system of concealment and camouflage, difficulties in relations with other countries were inevitable. From this point of view the reasons for Blomberg's consistent rejection of a multilateral armaments convention become clearer, and the facts and necessities behind Hitler's first foreign-policy coup become visible.

The programme of remilitarization which Hitler presented to the Reichswehr generals at the beginning of February produced results in the first phase of the Reichswehr's 'reorganization' which, while of widely varying significance in themselves, were as a whole extremely important for future developments. In this regard the most significant factor was the dominant influence of the NSDAP in the

---

[21] Geyer, 'Rüstungsprogramm', 134 ff.; Dülffer, *Weimar*, 239 ff.; on Hitler's initiatives in economic policy cf. Volkmann, II.III.1 above. On the early decisions about the financing of rearmament cf. Bennett, *German Rearmament*, 338 ff.; Geyer, 'Professionals', 121, and above all *Regierung Hitler*, i. 1, No. 17, pp. 50–1; No. 19, pp. 61–2; No. 67, pp. 237–8; No. 86, pp. 290–1; No. 87, pp. 291–2; No. 90, pp. 299 ff.; No. 97, pp. 336 ff. These documents clearly show the fundamental importance of the German government's decision of 4 Apr. 1933.

[22] Rautenberg, *Rüstungspolitik*, 217; id., 'Dokumente', 135 n. 142.

[23] For this and the following passage cf. Rautenberg, *Rüstungspolitik*, 220 ff., 235 ff.

[24] Rautenberg, 'Dokumente', 107 and 135 n. 142; according to Rautenberg a total of 22,000 instead of 14,000 men were taken into the frontier guard troops.

media and in shaping public opinion. The media were placed at the service of remilitarization at all levels and in every conceivable area.[25] A number of changes intended to restore tradition within the Reichswehr seem less important than the party's vehement and intensive indoctrination, but, given the tradition-bound mentality of the officer corps, these measures also contributed significantly to the strengthening of the army's self-confidence.[26]

Much more significant, however, was the establishment of a Reichsverteidigungsrat (Reich defence council) by a decision of the cabinet at the beginning of April 1933. The council consisted of six Reich ministers under the chancellor's chairmanship, with the defence minister as his permanent representative. Its main task was to co-ordinate at all levels of the executive all preparatory measures necessary for defence. More important than the council itself, which only met at full strength for an initial organizing session, was the Reich defence committee it set up, in which lower-ranking representatives of the ministries did the actual work.[27] Contrary to appearances, it can be assumed that this large-scale attempt to translate political, economic, and military demands for optimum preparations for war into co-ordinated executive measures was at least effective in some fields. In their organization the council and the committee were in complete accordance with the national defence plans developed by the Reichswehr, which was in overall charge.

In 1933 the remilitarization of the nation was pushed forward with great energy, above all by the integration of the paramilitary organizations into the national defence establishment. In this respect the SA became an indispensable instrument of military policy for Hitler as well as for the Reichswehr, whose leaders considered it primarily a reservoir of urgently needed reservists. For them the SA was the accepted instrument of remilitarization. No other institution seemed better suited to create the necessary attitude on the part of the general population which Hitler had described at length in his talk to the generals on 3 February 1933. In the first months of National Socialist rule the SA assumed functions which permitted the Reichswehr to preserve the fiction of its own aloofness from domestic political conflicts. But the SA's indispensability also created very real dangers. Under Ernst Röhm and as a result of the gradual absorption of the Stahlhelm, it became the numerically strongest, most tightly structured organization of the regime in 1933.[28] Because of this power Röhm and the other SA leaders developed political and

---

[25] Cf. Wette, I.II.2 and 4 and III.I above.

[26] Especially the reintroduction of the black, white, and red colours and cockades (12–14 Mar. 1933) and the system of courts martial (12 May 1933), as well as the appointment of Blomberg as defence minister and commander of the entire Wehrmacht (27 Apr. 1933). Cf. Absolon, *Wehrmacht*, ii. 475 ff. It should be noted that as early as 10 July provision was made in a separate appendix to the Reich concordat of 20 July 1933 for the possibility of 'a reorganization of the present German military system in the direction of introducing general conscription'. Cf. Rautenberg, *Rüstungspolitik*, 438, annex 24*b*.

[27] Meinck, 'Reichsverteidigungsrat', 411 ff.; Absolon, *Wehrmacht*, ii. 483–4. There is still no critical study of the activities of the committee and especially the subcommittees it established until the outbreak of war.

[28] Cf. Sauer, 'Mobilmachung', 234 ff.; Bennecke, *Hitler*, 212 ff. Bennecke also provides data on the strength of the SA in 1933–5; additional data in Sauer, 'Mobilmachung', 223, 268, and Kater, 'Soziologie der SA', 799.

military ambitions which were bound to involve them in a conflict with Hitler as well as with the Reichswehr leadership. Given the millions of people still unemployed in Germany in the autumn and winter of 1933 and the ambition of the SA leaders, there was strong popular support for the view that the National Socialist revolution had not yet achieved its aim and that the last obstacles could be overcome only with the help of the SA, its sole armed organization.[29]

For this reason the SA presented a dangerous threat to Hitler, who at the beginning of July 1933 had already declared that the National Socialist revolution had attained its goals.[30] In the power-struggle behind the scenes between Hitler and Röhm, which came to a bloody end on 30 June 1934, armaments policy played a central role. By withdrawing from the disarmament conference and the League of Nations in mid-October 1933, and having his policy sanctioned by a resounding plebiscite and new Reichstag elections on 12 November, Hitler was able to expand and consolidate his power against Röhm.[31]

At times the position of the Reichswehr in regard to the SA was very precarious. The army had little with which it could effectively oppose the self-confidence of the SA, the closeness of its leaders to the regime's centre of power, and its claim to be the National Socialist alternative to the Reichswehr itself. Blomberg's expressions of loyalty at every opportunity, which went far beyond routine professions of faith in the party and the National Socialist state, and his appeals to the officer corps to support the National Socialist movement without question, are especially revealing when considered in this light.[32] Because of the shared ideology, the power-political situation, and finally the military necessity of maintaining the ability of the frontier guard units to perform their tasks, the Reichswehr leaders were dependent on co-operation with the SA. In the conflict between the two organizations, Blomberg and Reichenau were solely concerned with preserving the position of the Reichswehr as the only military instrument of national defence, and with convincing Hitler that it was essential to the rearmament already in progress. For this reason they were prepared, for instance, to renounce their dominant influence in the pre-military training programme initiated by Schleicher, the 'Reich Institute for the training of young people', and the voluntary-labour service.[33] At first the Reichswehr supported the SA in all matters of military training. This became clear after Hitler had instructed the SA on 12 July 1933 to train 250,000 officers and men within a year to serve as a reserve for the army in the event of war.[34] This order could only be carried out in co-operation with the Reichswehr, which sent special teams of instructors to SA camps.[35]

[29] Cf. esp. Sauer, 'Mobilmachung', 255 ff., and Müller, *Heer*, 88 ff.
[30] Müller, *Heer*, 89–90 (speeches of 1 and 6 July 1933); cf. also Domarus, i. 286–7; Baynes, i. 483–4, 553–4.
[31] Cf. Wollstein, *Revisionismus*, 203 ff., esp. 206.
[32] Cf. esp. Müller, *Heer*, 49 ff., 91 ff.
[33] Sauer, 'Mobilmachung', 266 ff.; Rautenberg, *Rüstungspolitik*, 241 ff.; id., 'Dokumente', 108 ff.
[34] Absolon, *Wehrmacht*, ii. 487. On the details of the agreements between the Reichswehr and the SA in June–July 1933 cf. also Bennett, *German Rearmament*, 346 ff.
[35] Cf. Meier-Welcker, 'Briefwechsel', 89 ff.; Rautenberg, 'Dokumente', 133 nn. 118–19.

In this way the Reichswehr leaders were indeed able to increase their influence on the chief of the SA training organization, but by their assistance they were, indirectly and against their own interests, supporting Röhm in his ultimate intention to supplant the Reichswehr with his own organization.[36] Moreover, the extended training activities in the Reichswehr itself, in addition to the army responsibility for training the frontier guards and now also the personnel at SA camps, impaired to an unacceptable degree the efficiency of the military machine.[37] The training capacity of the Reichswehr was at full stretch and was being used to a considerable degree to help an organization which threatened the existence of the Reichswehr itself. In this situation the Reichswehr had to concentrate all its energy on expanding its own base by exploiting every possibility of material and personnel rearmament. Hence, the relatively long-term armament planning of 1932 no longer answered to the military and domestic requirements of autumn 1933.

The international situation had also changed in a way favourable to an accelerated armament programme. After Germany's withdrawal from the League of Nations and the disarmament conference in mid-October 1933, Britain and France had taken no concerted action. Both governments had acquiesced in the breach of the military provisions of the treaty of Versailles.[38] Meeting no determined opposition in the form of sanctions, Hitler used the opportunities presented by bilateral talks and declared his basic willingness to negotiate and compromise; he held out hope of possible solutions and demanded, as the core of his offer to negotiate, a German army of 300,000 men with a one-year period of service.[39]

Against this background, and in the absence of any effective Western resistance, the decision was taken in December 1933 to create a peacetime army of 300,000 men.[40] As late as the end of November the Truppenamt had given orders to carry out the measures that had been scheduled for 1934 in the reorganization plan of 1932. In mid-December a development began in the defence ministry which can only be described as hectic. On 14 December the Truppenamt submitted a memorandum from the organization department on the 'build-up of the future peacetime army', which had already been approved by the defence minister (see Table III.II.3, p. 446 below). Only four days later the chief of the Truppenamt, Lt.-General Ludwig Beck, signed the basic directive to create the new peacetime army;

[36] Cf. Sauer, 'Mobilmachung', 274–5; Müller, *Heer*, 94–5; Absolon, *Wehrmacht*, ii. 493 ff. (6 Nov., 1 Dec. 1933).

[37] Rautenberg (*Rüstungspolitik*, 224–5) attempts to provide figures for the demands made on the Reichswehr by the various training measures at the beginning of the summer of 1933; according to this estimate 60% of young regimental officers were engaged in these tasks, even though the SA camps are not covered by the figures. On transfers to the Luftwaffe cf. Rautenberg, 'Dokumente', 125 n. 213.

[38] On 24 Nov. 1933 Sir John Simon expressed the British view in these words: 'The choice is between limited rearmament on the one hand and unlimited rearmament on the other.' Cf. Meinck, *Aufrüstung*, 63, and Rautenberg, 'Dokumente', 104 ff.

[39] Cf. Messerschmidt, IV.III.2 below, and Wollstein, *Revisionismus*, 229 ff. On Hitler's diplomatic initiatives cf. Bennett, *German Rearmament*, 491 ff., 502 ff.

[40] On the planning decisions of the Reichswehr leaders in Dec. 1933 cf. Geyer, *Aufrüstung*, 329 ff.; the comprehensive article by Rautenberg, 'Dokumente', 110 ff., and Bennett, *German Rearmament*, 496 ff. Cf. also Müller, *Beck-Studien*, Document No. 9 (memorandum of 14 Dec. 1933); also printed in *Regierung Hitler*, ii. 2, No. 273, pp. 1032 ff.

at the same time the German government published its memorandum on disarmament and equal rights. Finally, a commanders' conference was convened on 20–1 December in Berlin at which Blomberg, Beck, and other senior officers explained the aims and details of the plan. Before the end of December numerous orders were issued to ensure that the build-up could actually begin on 1 April 1934.[41] No reliable information is available about the reasons for this very unusual procedure, but it can be assumed that in this way Blomberg and Reichenau also wanted to strengthen their position in their conflict with Röhm.

The programme of the Reichswehr leadership envisaged the creation of a twenty-one-division peacetime army during the next four years, i.e. by the end of March 1938, and was concerned only with the personnel side of the problem. The basis of planning was the introduction of the one-year period of service, which the Reichswehr leaders expected would be laid down by a general law on conscription not later than the autumn of 1934; therefore volunteers with a one-and-a-half year period of service were still to be inducted on 1 April 1934. The organizational problems involved in tripling the size of the army were to be mastered with the help of the replacement system already established in the twenty-one Wehrgaue (military subdistricts). Beck and the organization department considered 7 per cent to be the desirable proportion of officers in the army as a whole. Nevertheless, they believed that the build-up of the peacetime army could be carried out with an officer strength of only 3 per cent. But even the 9,000 officers this would involve could not be found for the first phase of the build-up in 1934–5, although existing possibilities were fully exploited. The use of retired officers, local defence and police officers, and reliable NCOs, as well as a shortening of the training period for officers, was intended in the view of the personnel office to guarantee at least that the level of officers would reach 4 per cent by 1940.

The military goal of the 'December programme' was clearly formulated in the organization department's memorandum. The wartime army, to be mobilized from the peacetime army, was to be able to fight 'a defensive war on several fronts with some prospect of success'. The significance of this formulation becomes clear when it is compared with earlier definitions of military goals in the event of a conflict, such as Groener's 'Tasks of the Wehrmacht'. Groener had mentioned '*definite* prospects of success' as a precondition for the use of the Reichswehr and stressed that, in view of Germany's relative weakness, the 'idea of a major war' could not even be considered.[42] But precisely that idea formed the centre of Beck's armament programme. Was a defensive war on several fronts conceivable without conscription, or without the industrial potential of the Ruhr and military control of the Rhine valley? These questions were not discussed in December 1933, but all officers involved knew from earlier Reichswehr planning that without these preconditions a defensive war against France could not be waged with 'some prospect of success'. Only when these conditions were met would it be possible to expect the sixty-three-division wartime army to be able to fulfil its prescribed tasks.

41 Cf. Rautenberg, 'Dokumente', 114.
42 Cf. III.II.2 above.

This shows that Hitler's spectacular March actions—the introduction of general conscription in 1935 and the occupation of the Rhineland in 1936—were necessitated by the military planning and goals of 1933, even though the timing of these actions was determined by other factors.

The unusual haste with which the programme was planned and the first steps taken to carry it out in the second half of December suggest that it had not only military but also political goals. The defence minister stated the domestic political motives behind the programme very clearly at the commanders' conference in Berlin on 20 December 1933.[43] After a brief survey of the chief points of the military planning he discussed 'two main difficulties' which had developed 'in the defence question': the 'settling of the frontier guard problem' and 'the efforts of the SA to form a Wehrmacht of its own'. The December programme of the Reichswehr was intended to remove these difficulties. The training of volunteers in the frontier guards by special training battalions and instructor groups of the various arms of the service, which had only begun in the spring of 1933, was ended on 31 March 1934, when the battalions were integrated into the new peacetime army.[44] The Reichswehr training detachments were also recalled from the SA camps in March.[45] Because of the acute shortage of officers, the Reichswehr leadership considered such training to be an unjustifiable dispersal of resources. Moreover, by concentrating on its own build-up the Reichswehr would deprive its dangerous rival of important prerequisites for any claim to military power.

In spite of its strong domestic political components, the December programme was primarily a contribution to the realization of Hitler's proclaimed goal of 'regaining political power'. Hardly a year after the chancellor had explained his aims to the Reichswehr leaders, specific, far-reaching rearmament measures began to give real meaning to the original rhetoric about 'remilitarization'. At a commanders' conference on 2 February 1934 Blomberg formulated the further 'thoughts of the Reich chancellor' as 'securing peace for a number of years so that the reconstruction of Germany and the reorganization and build-up of the Wehrmacht' could be carried out. There was 'no intention then to attack anyone', but 'Germany should be able to play a more active role in important questions of international politics.'[46] However, the military objectives of the programme might create requirements in the field of foreign affairs which, while corresponding to the general direction of Hitler's policy, would necessarily determine future decisions to a greater degree than would otherwise have been the case. Militarily, the December programme completely dislocated the co-ordination of personnel and material armaments planning achieved in 1932. The 'second armaments programme', which was to be carried out as rapidly as possible, could be used to equip the twenty-one-division peacetime army, but there was no comparable programme for guaranteeing

---

[43] Cf. Rautenberg, 'Dokumente', 119–20.

[44] Ibid. 130 ff. (nn. 66, 117, 118, 119, 124); IfZ Archives, ED 1, vol. i, Liebmann's notes on the commanders' conference of 2 Feb. 1934.

[45] IfZ Archives, ED 1., vol i, Liebmann's notes on the commanders' conference of 2 Feb. 1934; Meier-Welcker, 'Briefwechsel', 93 ff., esp. n. 136.

[46] IfZ Archives, ED 1, vol i, Liebmann's notes of 2 Feb. 1934.

equipment and supplies for the sixty-three-division wartime army. This lack of co-ordination between the two components was typical of German rearmament as a whole after 1933.

(b) Implementing the 'December Programme'

At the commanders' conference on 20–1 December 1933 Lieutenant-General Beck had stated that the most rapid part of the build-up would be in the first two years of the four-year programme, 'because in these years the efficiency of the army' would 'still be greater'; after the 'first dilution' the reorganization would proceed more slowly.[47] In fact the first phase of the 'expansion' of the army in 1934 with the important deadlines of 1 April and 1 October, was completed without significant problems. The organizational foundation had already been laid by the creation of military subdistricts and recruiting offices in 1933. The legal basis was created by the unpublished law of 21 December 1933 on the 'length of service in the Wehrmacht'.[48] By the autumn of 1934 the strength of the army rose to about 250,000 men.[49]

In the spring of 1934 the Reichswehr leaders were even more occupied with the increasingly serious conflict with the SA than with the expansion of the army. This conflict was the main topic at both commanders' conferences in February.[50] Although Hitler had often declared himself against Röhm's demands and views on military policy, and had decided in favour of the traditional plan advocated by the Reichswehr leaders for the build-up of the armed forces, Röhm refused to change his position.[51] At the beginning of 1934 Blomberg thought it would still be possible to come to a satisfactory agreement with the SA. His closest co-worker, the chief of the Wehrmacht office, Major-General von Reichenau, was more sceptical and did not try to avoid a confrontation. After March 1934 it can be seen that the military leaders were beginning to prepare for a possible violent clash with the SA and were co-operating in this respect with the 'political alarm squads' (*politische Bereitschaften*) of Himmler's SS and SD.[52] When Hitler decided to carry out a preventive elimination of the SA leadership on 30 June, the army was on alert. By providing transportation, weapons, ammunition, and lodging, the military leaders ensured that the SS units would be able to carry out the mission Hitler had assigned to them. Preparations were made for the use of the army itself. For the Reichswehr the murder of Röhm removed a dangerous rival for the position of 'sole bearer of arms' in the state. However, it was not able to consolidate its own position within

[47] Cf. Rautenberg, 'Dokumente', 121 n. 143.

[48] Ibid. 132 n. 113.

[49] Cf. Schottelius and Caspar, 'Organisation des Heeres', 296–7; Rautenberg, 'Dokumente', 114–15. In contrast to the thorough research into the organization of the army (cf. Tessin, *Verbände und Truppen*) only approximate figures can be given for its growth size.

[50] IfZ Archives, ED 1, vol. i, Liebmann's record of the conferences of 2–3 Feb. 1934.

[51] Cf. Sauer, 'Mobilmachung', 324 ff.; Müller, *Heer*, 95 ff.; Salewski, 'Bewaffnete Macht', 60 ff.

[52] On the form and extent of this co-operation cf. Müller, 'Reichswehr', 107 ff. On the Röhm affair cf. esp. Müller, *Heer*, 125 ff.; Bracher, *Dictatorship*, 238 ff.; Kern, *Innere Funktion*, 50 ff.; Wette, I.III.4 above. On the importance of the conflict for the relationship between the Wehrmacht and National Socialism cf. III.II.2(*a*) above and III.III.3 below.

the regime to a corresponding degree, for it was Himmler's SS, and not the Reichswehr, that had proved indispensable to Hitler on that occasion.

The connection between the first phase of rearmament and the struggle for positions of domestic power can also be seen in the controversy over the accelerated implementation of the December programme in mid-May 1934. From a statement by the chief of the Truppenamt on 20 May[53] it is clear that Hitler had suggested or demanded that the build-up of the 300,000-man army be completed by 1 April 1935, and the Allgemeines Heeresamt (general army office) under Colonel Fromm had even proposed that the organizational framework for the projected peacetime army should be ready to its full extent as early as 1 October 1934. In his rejection of this suggestion Beck touched upon the domestic political aspect of the problem and observed that 'the conflict with the SA (and the SS!) could not be settled' with such an 'improvised instrument of state power.' This problem would have to be solved 'in another way'. Beck did not say how this was to be done; for him it was important that the 'authority of the state as such' be restored. Beck's view was an example of the basic misunderstanding, on the part of German conservatives, of the function of the state for the National Socialist leaders and above all of their methods of rule.

Apart from this domestic political aspect, the controversy between Beck and Fromm reflected a general problem of German rearmament as a whole between 1933 and 1939. Beck's statement contained the sentence: 'In my opinion this is the least effective way to make up for our failure to play the rearmament card immediately on 14 October 1933.' His basic assumption was that only by means of a long-term, openly proclaimed rearmament, which must not be reduced to an object of political tactics, could an adequate instrument be created to meet the requirements of a great-power policy in Europe with emphasis on military factors, taking into account Germany's geographical situation and the experience of the First World War. Of course Beck also wanted to build up the 'new peacetime army as rapidly as possible' but on a militarily responsible, 'healthy foundation', as he wrote in the Truppenamt memorandum of 14 December 1933. He was referring to the necessity of solid training for enlisted men and even more for officers, and of taking the requirements of an actual war as the standard by which all measures should be judged. He did not want the expansion of the peacetime army to become an end in itself; its main purpose should be to 'provide trained men for the wartime army'.[54]

For this reason Beck pressed for the earliest possible reintroduction of general conscription and called the 'quickly raised 300,000-man army . . . a premature birth'.[55] This tendency in military thinking and planning was strongly represented above all in the Truppenamt, and included among its supporters the chief of the army command, Freiherr von Fritsch. Paradoxically, the constant efforts of its

[53] Beck Papers, BA-MA N 28/1. Cf. esp. Müller, *Beck-Studien*, 142 ff. Müller emphasizes the domestic political motives of Beck's intervention. I should like to thank Klaus-Jürgen Müller (Hamburg), who permitted me to see the manuscript of his study before it was printed. Independently, we have reached very similar conclusions; where our interpretations differ, this will be noted.

[54] Quoted from memorandum of 14 Dec. 1933; cf. Rautenberg, 'Dokumente', 115.

[55] Quoted from Beck's statement of 20 May 1934 in Müller, *Beck-Studien*, Document No. 11.

advocates to add measures they considered militarily necessary to the improvisations of the politically motivated process of rearmament became themselves an
accelerating factor.

Colonel Fromm represented another group of officers, who, in spite of all
differences in their methods, were allied with the circle around Beck in their
unquestioning acceptance of common military and political objectives. As chief of
the general army office, Fromm was responsible for carrying out planning
decisions. He also directed the budget department, the replacement system, and,
among other things, the quartermaster inspectorate, which was in charge of the
production, storage, and distribution of weapons, equipment and ammunition.[56]
This incomplete description of his tasks clearly shows why, in this area, the
organizational aspect of rearmament was of special importance. From this point of
view it was completely consistent to take the projected goal as the point of reference
for the organizational basis of rearmament from the very beginning. For this reason
Fromm suggested deploying twenty-one divisions of the peacetime army as
framework units as early as October 1934 . This was organizationally more effective
and easier to manage than a phased build-up, but it was incompatible with Beck's
ideas. Whereas Beck rejected Hitler's politically motivated demands on grounds of
military effectiveness, Fromm saw in them a chance to carry out rearmament under
optimal organizational conditions. This disagreement within the military leadership
was important because the defence minister, who in December 1933 had expressly
rejected improvisations in the build-up of the 300,000-man army, attached less
significance to the arguments of the chiefs of the army command and the
Truppenamt than to the chancellor's political intentions.[57] This explains the rapid
pace and scope of German rearmament in the years from 1933 to 1937–8. The
acceleration was a consequence of political demands, a highly developed
organizational ability to manage them, the military goals of the December
programme, and the resulting military 'necessities'.

It is only necessary to remember Groener's directive of April 1930 on the 'Tasks
of the Wehrmacht' to understand the fundamental change that had taken place in
German military policy since then. Blomberg's perspective, which was limited to
the development of military power, has already been described.[58] For Beck too
rebuilding German military strength was a fundamental demand which permitted
no discussion. He especially saw in the development of such strength the main
precondition for re-establishing Germany as a European great power and achieving
related political goals. Strongly influenced by the experience of the First World
War, he was much more aware than Blomberg of the importance of European
alliances; but he still thought that the intention to rearm should have been
proclaimed openly at the time of Germany's withdrawal from the disarmament
conference, regardless of international public opinion. While he preferred a slower

---

[56] Cf. Schottelius and Caspar, 'Organisation des Heeres', 333–4. Until 1934 the general army office
(Allgemeines Heeresamt) was styled the 'Wehramt' of the army command.
[57] Rautenberg, 'Dokumente', 119. On Hitler's demand cf. Geyer, 'Militär', 260, and Robertson, *Pre-
war Policy*, 33–4.
[58] Cf. the concluding paragraphs of III.1.2 and 3 above.

pace for military reasons, his perspective too was limited to the purely military problems involved.[59] Only later, after his resignation as chief of the general staff, did his view expand to consider the broader implications of modern warfare.

This limited perspective is all the more surprising as the military decision-makers—the defence minister, the chief of the army command, and the head of the Truppenamt—had at their disposal organizations and information which enabled them to understand the preconditions and consequences of a rearmament reflecting their military demands. In addition to the Reich defence council and the Reich defence committee, mention should be made of the Heereswaffenamt (Army ordnance office), which had acquired a wide knowledge of the economic basis of modern armaments through planning and carrying out the two armament programmes. On 9 May 1934, barely two weeks before Beck rejected the idea of accelerating the build-up of the 300,000-man army, the head of this office, Major-General Liese, gave a very detailed talk on the material armaments situation to the Reichswehr commanders.[60] After a brief historical introduction, Liese illustrated the importance of the material factor in the build-up of the wartime army with a dramatic truism: 'A Wehrmacht which has to lay down its weapons after six or eight weeks because of a complete lack of ammunition or fuel is neither a usable instrument in the hands of its commander nor a power factor in the hands of the statesman who wants to conduct foreign policy.'

This example was not pure fantasy. In the judgement of the army ordnance office it was an accurate description of the armaments and supply situation of the twenty-one-division wartime army at the end of 1934. At that time 'the most essential equipment for a first issuing and stocks for six weeks' were available for the wartime army. In and after the third month of a war, however, deliveries would be completely inadequate, comprising in the case of ammunition only a small percentage of requirements. The twenty-one-division wartime army represented Reichswehr planning before Hitler came to power. As to the armaments target since December 1933, Liese explained that for the sixty-three-division wartime army too a first issue of equipment and supplies for six weeks would be available by 1938. But material rearmament could keep pace with the personnel build-up of the army only if large funds were provided. And the start of weapons and equipment production sufficient for a war could only be more or less guaranteed if considerable sums were made available for factories and continuous procurement orders to industry. There was still a serious bottleneck with all kinds of munitions: possible war production amounted to only 50 per cent of probable requirements. Liese only touched briefly on the question of supplying the sixty-three-division wartime army with the necessary fuel. While he sketched a relatively hopeful picture of the level of armaments to be achieved by 1938, in contrast to the catastrophic situation in many respects in 1934, he was able to do so only on the assumption that industrial

---

[59] Cf. Geyer, *Aufrüstung*, 373 ff.; Müller, *Beck-Studien, passim.*

[60] H. Wa.A. No. 875/34, g.Kdos. WiJ of 9 May 1934, BA-MA Wi/I F 5/1638. The following quotations are taken from this document. Cf. also the documentation in Nuss and Sperling, 'Rüstungskonzeption', 203 ff. On an additional armaments-economy initiative of the army ordnance office in these months cf. III.III.2 below, esp. n. 7.

production possibilities would be fully used and not restricted for financial reasons or by a shortage of raw materials. From his address it was also clear that, because of the complexity of industrial production processes, any programme change would present the procurement agencies with enormous additional difficulties in their planning and supervisory functions. In this area improvisation seemed less desirable than elsewhere; it would inevitably lead to price increases and uneconomical production methods. Liese therefore called for the 'planning of procurement programmes running for several years in order to guarantee the most continuous possible use of industrial capacities'.

Liese's talk to the commanders had been 'ordered' by the head of the Truppenamt in February 1934. Its importance was emphasized by the fact that Hitler called for a copy of the text and Röhm also informed himself about it.[61] One motive for the interest of Beck and the chief of the army command, who probably saw to it that Hitler and Röhm were informed, may have been to warn Hitler in this way against pursuing a risky foreign policy and to confront him with the enormous financial demands of rearmament. Liese himself probably had an additional purpose in giving his talk. Its entire plan and wording were intended to show the Reichswehr leaders the decisive importance of the material factor in rearmament and in the ability of the peacetime and wartime army to function, as well as in operational planning, and to persuade them to give this factor appropriate consideration in all their planning decisions. However, his efforts were in vain. Beck's reply to Hitler's demand and to Fromm's proposal that the period for creating the twenty-one-division peacetime army be drastically shortened[62] shows that the fundamental requirements mentioned by Liese played only a marginal role in the thinking of the later chief of the general staff. In Beck's eight-page, handwritten memorandum there was not one word about the effects of the proposal on the current armaments situation or on armaments planning. For Beck the armaments economy aspects of the build-up were certainly interesting and could be used to support military demands, but they played no role in his thinking and actions in his own area. This example shows that even the army leaders were not able to understand and evaluate the importance for warfare of the individual components of the armament programmes in the broad sense, although this was basically the main purpose of all their activity. This fact had already become evident in the December programme. Now that the programme was being carried out, there was no co-ordination among the organizers of material rearmament, the personnel build-up, and the plans to actually use the army, although this would certainly have been possible in accordance with the comprehensive idea of national defence which the Reichswehr had itself developed. Because of this, and not only because of Hitler's interference, decisions affecting the whole rearmament of the army acquired the character of temporary, partial solutions.

---

[61] Cf. Rautenberg, *Rüstungspolitik*, 435 n. 4.
[62] Cf. III.11.2 (*b*), text to nn. 53–4 above.

(c) From the Introduction of General Conscription to the Occupation of the Rhineland

The most important foreign-policy event at the beginning of 1935 was the plebiscite in the Saar. Ninety per cent of the population of that area voted for its return to Germany, which accordingly took place on 1 March. On direct orders from Hitler or as a result of urging by the foreign ministry, great caution had been observed with regard to a number of armament plans in the autumn and winter of 1934 to avoid endangering the political outcome.[63] It was now to be expected that the success in the Saar would cause the political leadership, i.e. Hitler, to re-emphasize the rearmament plans of the services and thus again start the acceleration process driven by political, military-organizational, and operational considerations.

In November 1934 the disarmament conference, which had been continuing its shadowy existence in Geneva, had adjourned with the intention of making another attempt to achieve an international limitation of armaments after the Saar question had been settled.[64] Although Hitler was only interested in bilateral arms agreements, the foreign and defence ministries began to consider the minimum demands which, in the view of the German government, would have to be included in an arms convention. In this connection the Truppenamt of the army command produced a memorandum dated 6 March 1935 in which Beck summed up the demands that seemed to him necessary to provide 'at least a minimum guarantee of the security of our living-space'.[65] Like Blomberg, he took as his point of reference a concept of security defined in purely military terms and based on a traditional understanding of power politics with a strong military accent. He shut his eyes to the fact that the one-sided German rearmament which he supported (complaining only that it was not rapid enough) had itself become a factor threatening Germany's security. Misjudging the international political situation, he believed that he could justify an expansion of German armament plans with the argument that other countries had 'rearmed to a very high level' in 1934.[66]

The military demands presented by the Truppenamt in the memorandum corresponded to the armaments objective announced by Hitler ten days later, on 16 March 1935, in connection with the reintroduction of general conscription. For Beck the main question was what strength the peacetime army would have to

---

[63] e.g. with regard to the submarine construction of the navy, cf. Robertson, *Pre-war Policy*, 45–6; Dülffer, *Weimar*, 252–3, 293. The reservations of the foreign ministry concerned above all the build-up and expansion of the reinforced frontier surveillance service in the demilitarized zone. Cf. *DGFP*, c. ii, No. 452 (16 May 1933); i, No. 490 (11 Oct. 1933); ii, No. 366 (29 Mar. 1934); iii, No. 2 (14 June 1934); iii, No. 369 (1 Dec. 1934).

[64] Cf. Rautenberg, *Rüstungspolitik*, 292.

[65] TA, No. 205/35, g.Kdos., BA-MA RH 2/v. 1022. Printed in Müller, *Beck-Studien*, Document No. 24; also the memorandum of T 2 of 27 Mar. 1935 (Document No. 25).

[66] Müller (*Beck-Studien*, 142 ff.) comes to the same conclusion in a thorough analysis of Beck's contacts with the state secretary of the foreign ministry, Bülow. On the general problem of the relationship between rearmament and security cf. esp. Michael Geyer's introduction to his definitive study *Aufrüstung*, 1–15, and the final chapter, 'Determinanten militärischer Unsicherheit', ibid. 489–505. Cf. also id., 'Dynamics', 100 ff. The relationship between the military-political objective and Beck's demands regarding the shaping of German foreign policy is generally reminiscent of Tirpitz's naval policy.

achieve to enable the wartime army, which was to be mobilized from it, to fight a war on several fronts 'with some prospect of success', in the words of the December programme of 1933. In his very detailed calculations important emphasis was given to the fact that a relatively large number of combat-ready divisions (nine or ten) had to be available to counter a French attack because of the geographical conditions of the demilitarized zone east of the Rhine and the feared high mobility of the French army. Therefore these divisions could not be used as cadres for new formations. Thus, the twenty-one-division peacetime army planned in December 1933 was no longer adequate to serve as a base for the wartime army, whose strength under these conditions was estimated by the Truppenamt at sixty-three infantry, three cavalry, and three armoured divisions. The chief of the army command, General von Fritsch, approved the conclusions of the study and stated the desired armaments goal more precisely by advocating an enlargement of the peacetime army to 'thirty to thirty-six divisions,' depending on 'available material and personnel'.[67]

Hitler's proclamation of 16 March 1935 with the promulgation of the 'law on the organization of the Wehrmacht', in which the strength of the peacetime army was set at thirty-six divisions (the navy and the Luftwaffe were not mentioned in the law),[68] was therefore no surprise to the military leaders.[69] Hitler merely stated publicly the planning goal set by the military, as was also the case with the reintroduction of general conscription announced at the same time. The increases in the size of the army in 1933 and 1934 had been achieved with volunteers, who had enlisted for different periods. The military leaders always regarded this form of recruiting as an unsatisfactory, interim solution. As early as December 1933 Beck had demanded the introduction of general conscription in the autumn of 1934.[70] In October 1934 he emphatically repeated this demand and expressed to commanders of the Reichswehr his hope that the 'defence bill with general conscription' would 'come into force on 1 October 1935'.[71] In proclaiming the restoration of German military sovereignty in March 1935 and the introduction of general conscription with a one-year period of service on 1 October of that year, Hitler was thus keeping the promise he had made to Reichswehr generals as early as the beginning of February 1933; this had been made possible in terms of foreign policy by the return of the Saar to Germany. The chief of the army command stressed the logical consistency of this measure when he told the Reichswehr commanders on 24 April 1935[72] that the 'proclamation' could have been 'less dramatic' but that 'in some form it was inevitable', as 'a further development of the army without conscription was not possible, and secret conscription' could be carried out 'only to a limited extent'.

[67] Müller, *Beck-Studien*, 142 ff., Fritsch's statement of 11 Mar. 1935. At first Fritsch even advocated a peacetime army of 36–40 divisions. Cf. ibid. 191 ff.; Schottelius and Caspar, 'Organisation des Heeres', 300–1.

[68] Cf. Domarus, i. 491 ff.; Baynes, ii. 1208 ff.

[69] Müller, *Heer*, 208–9. For another point of view cf. Hossbach, *Wehrmacht*, 81 ff., in conjunction with Foerster, *Beck*, 34.

[70] Rautenberg, 'Dokumente', 121.

[71] IfZ Archives, ED 1, vol. i, Liebmann's record of the commanders' conference of 9 Oct. 1934.

[72] Ibid.; cf. also Müller, *Heer*, 209. Among the military leaders only Blomberg actually showed any 'signs of reluctance' (ibid.) on 15 Mar. 1935.

Hitler's proclamation was therefore the expression of a consensus on military objectives between the German generals and the political leadership. In the planning decisions which now became necessary the conflict arose anew within the army command as to how and within what period the goal of a thirty-six-division peacetime army should be achieved. For the Truppenamt deployment problems were the most important concern; for the operations department strengthening the divisions on the eastern frontier of the demilitarized zone had the highest priority. Beck's statement of 21 March 1935 on this particular question shows how he thought the build-up of the thirty-six-division army should be carried out. He continued to advocate the complete and uninterrupted build-up of the twenty-one-division army, which was to be strengthened by the continuous creation of new, as it were 'supernumerary', units from which 'new divisions and corps could for the most part be formed'.[73] A short time later he received the views of the chief of the general army office, Colonel Fromm. As he had done in 1934, Fromm urged the immediate build-up of a thirty-six-division army for organizational reasons. But now he based his opinion primarily on political arguments:[74] 'The most important thing is that we have thirty-six divisions *in reality* as soon as possible. The Führer's words and the law of 16 March will lose their credibility if the whole world knows, for years ahead, that we have fewer than thirty-six divisions.' Fromm's suggestion was not without support in the Truppenamt. Beck himself found it difficult to maintain his original position and suggested—assuming a relatively calm international situation—the expansion of the army in the autumn of 1935 to, at first, twenty-four divisions; he even considered an expansion to twenty-seven or twenty-eight divisions by the autumn of 1935 feasible in the event of a worsening of the international situation.[75] In agreement with Beck, the chief of the army command finally decided on 2 April 1935 that a twenty-four division army should be formed by the organization deadline of the autumn.[76]

This consensus-building process and the decision within the army command would not be worth mentioning if they did not provide an excellent illustration of the structural elements of German rearmament. It should be noted again that there is no evidence whatever of military or political opposition to Hitler's rearmament goals; nor was such opposition to be expected, as his specific statements were based on the military planning or in general agreement with it. It was probably more typical that the military tended to interpret the target figures expansively once they had been set. For example, Fromm maintained that the figure of thirty-six divisions in the law of 16 March could only mean infantry divisions, and that existing cavalry divisions as well as the armoured divisions being formed should be added to that number. It is also noteworthy that conflicting viewpoints within the army command were increasingly defended with political arguments. In this respect the ideas of the Truppenamt, i.e. Beck, are revealing. He wanted to react to the worsening

---

[73] Beck's final remarks regarding the statement by T 1 (the army department of the Truppenamt) on the 'intended reorganization of the peacetime army', BA-MA RH 2/v. 1017.

[74] AHA, 'Vortragsnotizen Chef HL', 22 Mar. 1935, BA-MA RH 2/v. 1017.

[75] TA, T 2, 'Vortragsnotizen', 21 Mar. 1935, BA-MA RH 2/v. 1017.

[76] TA, No. 1140/35, g.Kdos., 2 Apr. 1935, BA-MA RH 2/v. 1018.

international situation, caused primarily by German rearmament, with a new acceleration of armament programmes. In doing so he accepted a reduction of the operational readiness of the army, overlooking that such a measure would considerably increase political tensions but not achieve a corresponding improvement of Germany's military starting position. For the military leaders there was no alternative to rearmament. Finally, the discussion was ended by a decision of the chief of the army command. There is no evidence of massive influence from Hitler or Blomberg, an indication that the military leaders enjoyed greater freedom in making their decisions than is even now often assumed.[77]

The decision of the chief of the army command to create a twenty-four-division army by the autumn of 1935 must be understood as an *ad hoc* response to special circumstances in the spring of that year. In March 1935 the Reichswehr leaders had twenty-one divisions at their disposal, which, however, had not yet reached their full personnel and material strength. About 280,000 men were under arms, but of the 189 infantry battalions planned for the final twenty-one-division army only 109 had actually been formed. The two armoured battalions had only twelve tanks between them.[78] According to the original planning a further step towards filling out the ranks was to be taken in the autumn of 1935 and would be followed by a consolidation phase in the autumn of 1936; the fully trained twenty-one-division peacetime army was to be ready for action in the spring of 1938, although planning for its expansion into a wartime army was still causing personnel and material difficulties.

The creation of three additional infantry divisions, planned for the autumn of 1935, was the first step towards the new goal of a thirty-six-division peacetime army. This step was made possible by taking over about 56,000 men of the Landespolizei (state-police units) quartered in barracks.[79] Since the autumn of 1933 these units had increasingly assumed the character of military formations. Their training was organized and supervised by the Truppenamt of the army command. The 'law on the reconstruction of the Reich' of 30 January 1934 transferred the police authority of the individual states to the central government, and the Reich minister of the interior assumed command of their police units. On 8 February 1934 a decree from Blomberg as minister of defence placed them under the army command in the event of war. Their open transfer to the Wehrmacht was begun by Hitler's directive of 31 January 1935, which ordered that preparations be made for their integration on 1 April 1935. This was carried out in several stages. Only in a few cases were police formations of battalion size taken into the army as complete units. Three such units, forming the state-police group 'General Göring', were taken over by the Luftwaffe as the regiment bearing the same name on 1 October 1935.[80] (As minister-president

---

[77] Cf. Rautenberg, *Rüstungspolitik*, 313 ff.; Hüttenberger, 'Polykratie', 425; it should also be noted that through general conscription the Wehrmacht was able to control a not insignificant part of the population: cf. ibid. 437 ff.   [78] Cf. Rautenberg, *Rüstungspolitik*, 312–13 and annex, 94–5.
[79] On the development of police units quartered in barracks in Baden, Bavaria, Hamburg, Prussia, Saxony, and Württemberg, and their transfer to the Wehrmacht, cf. Absolon, *Wehrmacht*, iii. 31 ff.; Tessin, *Verbände und Truppen*, 459 ff.; Schottelius and Caspar, 'Organisation des Heeres', 301–2.
[80] Cf. Stumpf, 'Luftwaffe', 860 ff.

of Prussia, Göring had long sought to obtain command authority over the Prussian state police as part of his power-base.) State-police formations in the demilitarized zone were not affected by these measures; only individual units were taken out of the zone and integrated into the army in the autumn of 1935. The integration of the state-police forces into the army, which brought it a significant qualitative increase in experienced non-commissioned officers and enlisted men, was formally concluded by the order of the day of the army commander-in-chief on 1 August 1935.

In the autumn of 1935, with the new units, the strength of the army rose to about 400,000 men in twenty-four infantry, three armoured, and two cavalry divisions, as well as one cavalry and one mountain brigade.[81] In only two and a half years the army had increased its personnel strength fourfold. But figures from the spring of 1935 clearly show that material rearmament had not kept up with this pace, and the responsible leaders were well aware that the quality of the military machine had inevitably suffered as a result of this rapid expansion.

The decision of 2 April 1935 represented an interim solution for the build-up of the thirty-six-division peacetime army, which Hitler had set as the rearmament goal. Longer-term thinking and planning began at the end of April and was provisionally concluded in July. This preliminary quality was the most typical characteristic of the plans involved. A first suggestion from the Truppenamt at the end of April described the final goal as the build-up of a peacetime army of thirty-three infantry and three armoured divisions.[82] Interestingly enough, however, only the targets for 1936 and 1937 were presented in detail. The army was scheduled to reach a strength of twenty-nine infantry and three armoured divisions, plus a mountain and a cavalry brigade, by the autumn of 1937. The departure from the four-year cycle of all previous plans was a first sign that the hectic pace of short-term decisions was now also beginning to affect the army command. Nevertheless, the chief of the army command, Fritsch, insisted that a plan be presented for the complete build-up of the thirty-six division army, including an analysis of its financial and personnel, but not its material, consequences.

At the end of June the army general staff[83] worked out a proposal to be discussed internally with the army personnel office and the general army office for the build-up of an army of thirty-three infantry and three armoured divisions as well as one mountain and one cavalry brigade, by 1 October 1939 (see Table III.ii.3, col. 2,

---

[81] Cf. Schottelius and Caspar, 'Organisation des Heeres', 302–3. On the following cf. Rautenberg, *Rüstungspolitik*, appendix, p. 94 (list of 5 Mar. 1935).

[82] TA, No. 1332/35, g.Kdos., undated, BA-MA RH 2/v. 1018. Against Müller's view (*Beck-Studien*, 198 ff.), it should be emphasized that the decision of the chief of the army command of 2 Apr. 1935 only affected the autumn deployment in 1935; long-term armament planning began only at the end of Apr. 1935.

[83] After the promulgation of the defence law on 21 May numerous new designations were introduced in June–July 1935. The Reichswehr became the Wehrmacht; the Reichswehrminister (minister of defence) the Reichskriegsminister (war minister); the three armed services were placed under commanders-in-chief (Oberbefehlshaber) with their high commands (Oberkommandos). The Truppenamt was henceforth openly referred to as the (army) general staff. Cf. Schottelius and Caspar, 'Organisation des Heeres', 299; Absolon, *Wehrmacht*, iii. 9, 22, 38.

p. 446 below). By then the army was to have a total strength of 695,000 men. Compared to the April planning, only small changes were made for 1936 and 1937. Apart from the extension of the plan until 1939, the return to the usual four-year cycle, it is interesting that for the first time concrete figures were provided about the wartime army to be formed from the peacetime army. The general staff assumed that the wartime army of twenty-eight divisions on 1 April 1936 would grow to thirty-five in 1937, forty-two in 1938, forty-nine in 1939, fifty-six in 1940, and would reach sixty-three divisions only in 1941.[84] According to the planning of December 1933 the wartime army was to achieve that strength as early as the spring of 1938. The clear change from the original plan was probably due to the one-year delay in the reintroduction of general conscription and the intention to station a large number of divisions near the western frontier, which meant that they could no longer be used to organize divisions consisting largely of reservists.

Although it was certainly remarkable that the army ordnance office had not even been consulted in working out the draft plan—a continuation of the policy of disregarding material factors in armament planning—the limits of the human resources available for rearmament now became apparent for the first time. The head of the army personnel office, General von Schwedler, emphatically rejected 'any increase of any kind in the size of the army for 1936'.[85] The essence of Schwedler's argument was that as a result of the use of non-commissioned, inactive reserve, and police officers and the deployment of numerous new units, there could 'no longer be any talk of an officer corps in the true sense of the word'. The significance of this categorical veto can only be understood if one compares the situation described by Schwedler with the guide-lines for the selection and training of future Reichswehr officers, introduced by Seeckt and in force until 1932–3. All leading officers of the Reichswehr and the Wehrmacht, especially Fritsch and Beck, felt deeply bound to this tradition. They were, however, aware that any form of forced rearmament would necessarily result in a decline in the quality of the officer corps and its numbers in relation to total personnel strength. The question was at what point such a decline and its effects on the troops would become unacceptable. In Schwedler's opinion this point had already been reached, or even passed. In December 1933 Beck had assumed that the officer corps would constitute 7 per cent of total army strength. For the first phase of the build-up he was prepared to accept 3 per cent.[86] With the autumn deployment of 1935 the proportion of active officers fell to 1.7 per cent, or 2.4 per cent including Ergänzungs- or E-Offiziere (supplementary reserve officers).[87]

Schwedler justified his veto by the disturbing quantitative bottlenecks as well as the accompanying loss of quality. The Reichswehr officer corps, with its shared conventions and training, was losing more and more of its homogeneity, and this

[84] TA, No. 1800/35, g.Kdos., 24 June 1935, BA-MA RH 2/v. 1019.

[85] PA, No. 450/35, g.Kdos., 15 June 1935, BA-MA RH 2/v. 1019. On the following cf. esp. Model, *Generalstabsoffizier*, 21 ff. (main parts 1 and 2).

[86] Cf. III.II.2 (*a*) above.

[87] Cf. the figures on the strength of the officer corps in Absolon, *Wehrmacht*, iii. 162, in conjunction with the army strength mentioned in III.II.2 (*c*) above.

process was accelerated by the increasingly frequent measures to expand the army. On 1 October 1933 the officer corps consisted of 3,800 officers; two years later, on 15 October 1935, the figure was 6,553, an increase of 72 per cent. This had been achieved only by the use of groups previously outside the corps, above all officers of local defence units, who were taken over as active officers by the Reichswehr and formed the so-called supplementary officer corps after March 1935.[88] On 1 November 1935 this corps contained 3,073 officers. However, most of them were in the older age-groups, which placed limits on their reactivation. The same was true of the large number of former officers outside the corps. The situation was more favourable concerning the taking over of officers of the state-police forces in the summer of 1935. According to the head of the army personnel office, about 1,200 police officers were taken over with the consent of the defence minister. Finally, as early as December 1933 Blomberg had mentioned experienced non-commissioned officers as a possible source of new officers. In 1934 about 400 NCOs were promoted to officer rank.[89] These makeshift measures naturally reduced the homogeneity of the officer corps, but in the opinion of the head of the army personnel office they were necessary to cope with a temporary emergency situation. His objection was rather to the reduced officer training and excessive demands, especially on lower-ranking officers, which accompanied the increases in the size of the army and inevitably had adverse effects on their further training and education. For this reason he suggested[90] carrying out the build-up of the thirty six-division peacetime army in two instead of four stages. This meant concentrating the new deployments and expansions in the autumn of 1937 and 1939, with the aim of achieving 'greater continuity' and soundness in the build-up. In this way it would again be possible for regimental commanders 'to weld their officers together and train them . . . for the newly organized units'.

The objections of the army personnel office caused some concern in the general staff, which was expressed in comments by individual departments. The chief of the general staff, General Beck, also felt compelled to state his position.[91] He pointed out that Hilter had 'often clearly expressed his intention to hold to the number of 12 corps commands, 33 + 3 divisions'. Typically, Beck referred again to the operational goals of the December programme of 1933 to justify the build-up of the planned peacetime army. The wartime army to be mobilized from it was intended to guarantee that Germany would be able to fight a 'war on several fronts with some prospect of success'. In 1934 'the extremely serious international situation in particular' had made it necessary 'to shelve plans to create conditions for a gradual build-up of the new peacetime army with the greatest possible emphasis on quality, and to aim instead at a build-up permitting rapid mobilization'. This state of affairs had not changed. On the contrary, Germany's position had 'become increasingly

---

[88] Cf. Absolon, *Wehrmacht*, ii. 57–8; iii. 219–20, 329 ff. On the establishment of the E-Officer Corps cf. also Schottelius and Caspar, 'Organization des Heeres', 369.

[89] Rautenberg, 'Dokumente', 120 n. 123.

[90] Cf. Schwedler's new statement, PA, No. 493/35, g.Kdos., 3 July 1935, BA-MA RH 2/v. 1019.

[91] Handwritten statement of 9 July 1935, BA-MA RH 2/v. 1019. The statements of the various departments are in the same file.

dangerous since then'. The 'unstable political situation in Europe' meant, in Beck's opinion, that 'greater demands were made and had to be met' regarding the pace and extent of the army build-up 'in a direction not always completely satisfactory to the general staff'. Political conditions, plus the fact that the annual new deployments made possible the induction and training of the maximum number of persons liable for military service, and thus an increase in the number of units ready for action, constituted in Beck's view the most important reason for continuing the build-up of the army 'as rapidly and continuously as possible'. He did not deal to any extent with the arguments of the army personnel office, but was content to remark that the procedure it had suggested would not lead to an improvement in the number of officers. His paper contained no ideas about how the quality of future officers could be improved. He had taken his stand on this question in 1934, when he decided to carry out the personnel build-up in such a way as to bring the army to full planned strength as soon as possible. Under the pressure of his own military goals and his judgement of the international situation, which itself was influenced by military considerations, Beck pushed for a continuation of high-pressure rearmament but did not even consider its material aspects.

The extent to which the high command was dominated by the idea of fully exploiting the potential represented by the number of men liable for military service for the build-up of the wartime army can be clearly seen in a draft of the general army office on the personnel situation for the build-up period 1936–9. A comparison of the strengths of the different age-groups and personnel requirements of the Wehrmacht showed that, with a one-year period of service and a fitness rate of 70 per cent, it would no longer be possible to completely cover manpower needs as early as 1938. The organization department of the general staff therefore came to the conclusion that 'a change to a two-year period of service . . . after the autumn of 1938', in which all men available for military service could receive their training only through service in supplementary units, seemed advisable.[92] In other respects, however, the draft of the general army office showed a clear preference for a one-year period of service, which alone guaranteed that it would be possible to achieve the projected wartime strength as early as the spring of 1940 or 1941.

After the introduction of general conscription the supplementary reserve units of the army, which had been planned since the autumn of 1934, were used to train the so-called 'blank age-groups'—men born between 1901 and 1913 and previously not affected by conscription—at first on a voluntary basis in two-month courses. For the autumn of 1935 an authorized strength of 121,000 men was planned for this 'Ergänzungsheer' (supplementary reserve army). The general staff urged that persons liable for military service who could not be taken into the active army should also be trained in the supplementary reserve units. Here too the aim was clearly to increase the number of men available for mobilization in every conceivable way.[93]

---

[92] Draft of the general army office, AHA, No. 3400/35, g.Kdos., 19 July 1935, and comment by the organization department of 20 July 1935, BA-MA RH 2/v. 1014; cf. III.II.2 (*d*) below.
[93] Cf. Mueller-Hillebrand, *Heer*, i. 32 ff.; Rautenberg, *Rüstungspolitik*, 229.

The planning of the general staff was the subject of a conference in the office of the commander-in-chief of the army on 10 July 1935, in which the chiefs of the army personnel office and the general army office also participated.[94] Fritsch requested some additional information; such as details on the numbers of officers and the costs of the build-up programme.

The revised draft of 19 July 1935[95] clearly shows that the reservations of the chief of the army personnel office had not been accepted. The plan of the general staff for the build-up of a thirty-six-division army with a strength of almost 700,000 men by 1 October 1939 was not changed. It seemed indeed to represent the limits of what was possible. But Fritsch made no decision. In mid-August 1935 the organization department of the general staff noted that a decision, at least on the army build-up for 1936 and 1937, was urgently necessary, as otherwise the army would fall behind the navy and the Luftwaffe in placing orders. A further note indicated that the commander-in-chief supported the planning but that the war minister was evidently not prepared to make a decision. On 9 September the chief of the general staff instructed the offices concerned with the army high command to begin preparations for the army build-up in 1936 on the basis of the July planning.[96] But this did not mean that a final decision had been taken. In the winter of 1935–6 there were no clear and detailed ideas about the short- or medium-term goals of the army build-up, as can be seen in the remark of the head of the army personnel office of 13 December 1935[97] that 'a considerable number of new demands are made almost every month'. Schwedler declared openly that he was no longer prepared to comply with 'wishes and orders concerning the creation of new units' because 'we would be ordering an army build-up on a very shaky basis, yet one which would be even greater than that of another service'. For the time being Schwedler's protest remained without any effect, as Blomberg reserved the decision on the pace and extent of further rearmament for himself.

The war minister's hesitation in approving long-term armament planning for the army[98] was probably connected with the problem of the demilitarized zone. For the defence economy as well as for military operational reasons the re-establishment of German military sovereignty in that area was becoming an increasingly urgent necessity. The discussion of the build-up of the thirty-six-division army in the spring of 1935 had made clear the special difficulties created by the existence of the zone in planning any defence against a French attack. The early establishment of a line along the Rhine in the event of a conflict was considered essential for even a temporarily successful defence. In February 1936, after detailed studies, the general staff came to the conclusion that troop units stationed east of the zone could not be

---

[94] Handwritten note on a report of the organization department of the general staff of 10 July 1935, BA-MA RH 2/v. 1019.

[95] Generalstab des Heeres, 2. Abt., No. 1900/35, g.Kdos., 19 July 1935, BA-MA RH 2/v. 1019.

[96] Report of 15 Aug. 1935; note of 19 Aug.; order of 9 Sept. 1935, BA-MA RH 2/v. 1019. Müller (*Beck-Studien*, 203 ff. and document 34) assumes that a decision was made on armaments planning as early as June 1935. This is not the case.

[97] BA-MA RH 2/v. 1020.

[98] The navy and the Luftwaffe were not affected. Cf. III.II.3 (*b*) and 4 (*a*) below.

transported by train to their planned areas of action in the assumed time available. The belief that the French army possessed a high degree of mobility was not questioned.[99] For these reasons the zone was considered an almost insurmountable obstacle to achieving the strategic goals already set in December 1933.

In the years before 1936 various attempts were made to overcome these difficulties. In 1929, as head of the Truppenamt, Blomberg had urged without success that units similar to the frontier guard units in the east be organized for the western part of Germany.[100] As defence minister in and after November 1933 he supported the formation of a Grenzsicherungsdienst (frontier security service) against the opposition of the foreign ministry. In 1934, with the help of civilian administrative agencies, the service was created as the Verstärkter Grenzaufsichtsdienst (VGAD: Reinforced Frontier Surveillance Service). Under the supervision of the Truppenamt, the tasks of the VGAD were entrusted primarily to personnel from the customs service, the Landespolizei (state police) within the demilitarized zone, and the paramilitary organizations.[101] The military effectiveness of this service was, however, limited, as the strict secrecy and camouflage, on which the foreign ministry insisted for political reasons and which the military leaders accepted, prevented intensive training of its members.

The date of Hitler's decision to occupy the demilitarized zone was, it is true, not determined by the military and defence-economy aspects of the problem, of which, however, he was undoubtedly aware.[102] The favourable international situation, and possibly general domestic motives, as the subsequent Reichstag election indicates, probably influenced his decision. But his action was a logical step on the way to 'regaining political power'; the occupation of the Rhineland greatly improved the ability of the armed forces to act, and Hitler knew that his political goals could not be achieved without their help.

With the occupation of the Rhineland on 7 March 1936 the Wehrmacht, for the first time since the National Socialist assumption of power, acted as the instrument of a political decision which, from Germany's point of view, involved considerable international risks. The possibility could not be excluded that France would react to the breach of the last remaining military provisions of Versailles and Locarno by intervening militarily and perhaps occupying the left bank of the Rhine. Since Germany's withdrawal from the disarmament conference and the League of Nations in October 1933, Blomberg had given the Wehrmacht orders for defensive purposes, which essentially involved the early evacuation of threatened areas and the use of delaying tactics to stave off defeat.[103] The military leaders were informed of Hitler's intentions several weeks before his so-called 'surprise coup', and so it was

---

[99] Generalstab des Heeres, 5. Abt., No. 378/36, g.Kdos., 14 Feb. 1936, BA-MA II H 593/3. Cf. also Geyer, 'Militär', 254.

[100] Cf. details in Geyer, *Aufrüstung*, 210 ff., 336 ff., 381 ff.

[101] Cf. Mueller-Hillebrand, *Heer*, i. 58; Geyer, 'Militär', 253; Rautenberg, *Rüstungspolitik*, 225 ff. Cf. also the account in Müller, *Beck-Studien*, 214 ff.

[102] Messerschmidt, IV.v.1 below; Funke. '7 März 1936', 277–8; Robertson, *Pre-war Policy*, 66 ff.

[103] *IMT* xxxiv. 488 ff.; for an interpretation cf. Geyer, *Aufrüstung*, 373 ff.; cf. also III.III.4, text to nn. 85–7 below.

not an improvised military action.[104] In issuing the necessary orders Blomberg and Fritsch[105] took the danger of international complications into consideration to the extent that only three battalions were to advance far beyond the Rhine to the cities of Aachen, Trier, and Saarbrücken, while most of the units involved were to occupy garrisons on the right bank of the Rhine and establish bridgeheads at key points. After the political provocation every effort was made to prevent a military reaction. However, the widespread belief that the three infantry battalions would have been withdrawn without a fight if France had intervened militarily is altogether unfounded. Their orders were in fact to co-operate with the VGAD and use prepared obstacle- and defence-zones to resist the enemy. The aim of the military leaders was in any case to occupy the Roer–Rhine–Black Forest line. This was indicated by the extensive measures taken for the possible removal or destruction of anything that might be useful to French forces, so as to impede or even prevent the establishing of French bridgeheads on the right bank in the event of a rapid French reaction. But the genuinely feared French reaction did not take place; the young Wehrmacht had passed its first test without being exposed to combat.

With the occupation of the Rhineland the last restrictions on German military sovereignty under the treaty of Versailles were removed. All persons liable for military service in the Rhineland were now available to the Wehrmacht, which also now had a very strong defensive position along the Rhine. Most significant, however, was the fact that the most important centres of the German armaments industry were no longer as exposed to foreign attack as they had been since 1919. The events of March 1936 fulfilled the preconditions for the armaments goal on which the December programme was based. The introduction of general conscription in 1935 and the restoration of German military sovereignty in the west decisively improved the possibility of achieving Beck's goal of being able to fight 'a defensive war on several fronts with some prospect of success'. The spring of 1936 also opened new possibilities for further armament planning. Compared with the original ideas of the Truppenamt, the pace and scope had been increased considerably, most recently by the programme for the next several years worked out in the summer of 1935. Military requirements and considerations were among the most important reasons for the increases. Blomberg's hesitation in approving this programme was in fact due to his expectation that German military sovereignty in the west would be restored in the foreseeable future; it was also due to military considerations and developments which, together with the changed political and armaments-economy situation, offered a new possibility of again setting higher qualitative and quantitative goals.

The military considerations involved the problem of the future use of the three armoured divisions created on 15 October 1935. The order establishing them represented the temporary conclusion of a development which illustrated in

[104] Braubach, *Einmarsch*, 12 ff.
[105] For details cf. Watt, '*German Plans*', 193 ff. On Blomberg's hesitant attitude on the day of the occupation cf. also Messerschmidt, IV.v.1 below. On the French military reaction cf. Michalon and Vernet, 'L'armée française'.

exemplary fashion the effects of Versailles on the thinking and actions of German military leaders.[106] The provisions of the treaty had forced the Reichswehr leaders to consider how to achieve the greatest possible military efficiency with the smallest possible investment of material and personnel. This necessitated the creation of units with a high degree of mobility, as short-term successes seemed possible only by surprising the enemy. Mobility to achieve surprise was, however, only possible if, in addition to the railways, motor-vehicles were used. This fact was reflected in the motorization programme of the Reichswehr leaders on the one hand and in Guderian's idea of operational, independent armoured units on the other.[107] Guderian was a typical representative of a small group of officers who had developed forms of combat with mechanized units and formations in the course of their work on road transport in the 1920s. As a result of this development the 'inspectorate of motorized transport troops' (MT troops) became the 'office of the commander of mechanized combat forces.'[108] Important events in this process were the establishment of a training centre for the use of armoured vehicles near Kazan in the Soviet Union in the mid-1920s, and the field exercises promoted and carried out with particular vigour in and after 1932 by the inspector of the MT troops at that time, Major-General Lutz, and his chief of staff, Lieutenant-Colonel Guderian.[109]

Although these exercises demonstrated the great possibilities of motorized and mechanized units, there was strong opposition to the idea Guderian had developed since 1929 of armoured divisions as the most important operational units of a future army. Criticism of this idea was not based primarily, as might have been expected, on technical, economic, and financial difficulties connected with the build-up of this modern service-arm, but followed rather the deeply rooted, traditional lines of military thinking. The cavalry, feeling its existence threatened, resisted the take-over of its functions by motorized units. But even in leading military circles, in which the purpose of Guderian's idea—regaining freedom of operational warfare—was accepted, there was a certain fear of the far-reaching consequences it would have for the organization of the army as a whole.

Help from the outside was necessary to overcome this resistance. As early as February 1933, at the opening of the automobile show, Hitler had indicated that his attitude towards motorization was quite positive. His announcement, in a speech on 1 May 1933, of his intention to begin construction of a motorway system underlined his interest in a more spectacular fashion.[110] The officers promoted to leading positions in the Reichswehr in 1933—Blomberg, Reichenau, and even Fritsch—were known for their receptiveness to unconventional ideas. According to the report of a member of the inspectorate of MT troops, the build-up of three

[106] Cf. Deist, 'De Gaulle et Guderian', 47 ff.

[107] The abundant literature on Guderian and the development of the German armoured units is used and discussed in the most recent biographies: Macksey, *Guderian*, and esp. Walde, *Guderian*.

[108] Nehring, *Panzerwaffe*, 78–9.

[109] Cf. the relevant reports in Nehring, *Panzerwaffe*, 67 ff. and in Guderian, *Panzer Leader*, 28–9.

[110] Cf. Domarus, i. 208–9 (11 Feb. 1933), 263 (1 May 1933); Baynes, i. 838 (1 May 1933); also Irving, *War Path*, 22–3, and Volkmann, II.III.1 above.

armoured divisions in the autumn of 1934 was begun as a result of direct intervention in the previous February by the defence minister and the chief of the Wehrmacht office.[111] Only personnel of the seven motorized units of the Reichswehr were available, together with normal caterpillar tractors and chassis of the future Tank I; but the basic decision to form armoured divisions as Guderian wanted them had been made and the organizational framework created. With the start of mass production of the Tank I—a 5.5-ton armoured vehicle with two machine-guns—in the winter of 1934–5[112] it was possible to equip the basic units, although inadequately, with the necessary vehicles in the course of 1935.

In the summer of that year the still controversial type of modern, highly mechanized fighting unit advocated by Guderian passed its first test. At a demonstration of new weapons organized by the army ordnance office at the military training area of Kummersdorf on 11 July Guderian had the opportunity to show Hitler several of the motorized elements of the new armoured divisions.[113] Hitler was enthusiastic and welcomed the plan Guderian outlined to him in the presence of the commander-in-chief of the army. A month later, at the instance of the inspectorate of mechanized combat forces, a four-week exercise with a 'practice armoured division' took place at the training area of Munsterlager under the command of Lieutenant-General von Weichs.[114] Its purpose was to demonstrate the possibilities of commanding large, rapidly moving armoured units in battle as well as in co-operation with the infantry and artillery. This exercise too was conducted in the presence of the commander-in-chief of the army, who helped the new armoured units achieve widespread recognition by inserting a specific 'problem' which they mastered without difficulty. The successful demonstrations at Kummersdorf and Munsterlager, which offered a way to avoid the *matériel* battles and positional warfare of the First World War, had effects of very different kinds on the plan for the overall structure of the army.

The reaction of the commander-in-chief of the army to the decisive success of the new armoured weapon was to order a study of the possibilities of an anti-tank defence through offence. In his opinion the tank itself represented the best defence against armoured attacks.[115] This was also the view of the inspector of mechanized combat forces, who had observed at the final conference at Munsterlager that the 'best defence was to produce even more tanks'.[116] There was opposition from several quarters. The head of the training department of the army general staff, Colonel Hans Reinhardt, doubted that the army would ever be able to afford enough tanks for an adequate defence. He was completely under the impression of the demoralizing effect of concentrated tank attacks on infantry units during the

[111] Nehring, *Panzerwaffe*, 78.
[112] Senger and Etterlin, *Kampfpanzer*, 55 ff.
[113] Cf. Guderian, *Panzer Leader*, 29–30 (with a mistaken date-reference to 1933).
[114] Cf. Nehring, *Panzerwaffe*, 88–9; Guderian, *Panzer Leader*, 35–6.
[115] From the statement of the army ordnance office (Bb., No. 431/35, g.Kdos, 30 Oct. 1935, BA-MA II H 630.
[116] From the statement of the head of department 4 of the army general staff, No. 1290/35, g.Kdos, 4 Sept. 1935, BA-MA II H 630.

exercise. He argued that the infantry soldier had to be convinced of the possibility of a successful defence against tanks by being given proper equipment and intensive, realistic training.[117]

Fritsch's concept of 'offensive defence' presented new perspectives for the army general staff. For them 'mobile combat' and delaying actions had always been necessities resulting from the limitations on their own forces. The successful demonstrations of the armoured units had exceeded all expectations and greatly expanded the possibilities of mobile warfare. The concept of 'offensive defence' seemed to make possible an operational breakthrough in the form of offensive encirclements. This internal development coincided with a stagnation in the general planning for the army build-up. The urgent decision on the units to be organized in the autumn of 1936 had not yet been taken. The extension of German military sovereignty to the demilitarized zone was considered to be only a matter of time; Blomberg was already taking various measures to prepare for it. Generally the situation was still open, and there was thus an excellent opportunity to integrate the organizational and operational problems presented by the tank into the planning of the total structure of the new army. This was done under the revealing heading 'Increasing the Offensive Power of the Army', which marked the start of a new expansion and acceleration of rearmament, this time for military reasons and not because of the oft-mentioned pressure from Hitler. Rather, the chancellor's political plans were effectively supported by the professional judgement of the military leaders.[118]

The high point of the discussion about 'Increasing the Offensive Power of the Army', which continued until the summer of 1936, was Beck's memorandum of 30 December 1935 for the commander-in-chief of the army, which determined the direction and set the standards of the debate from the very beginning.[119] Beck first rejected possible assumptions that the intended increase in offensive capacity was connected with new objectives concerning the build-up of the army. The aim formulated in the December programme of 1933, according to which the mobilized wartime army should be able to fight a defensive war on several fronts with some prospect of success, was still valid. The increase in offensive capacity was justified on the principle that 'the strategic defence' would 'only be successful if it is also conducted in the form of attack'. The term 'strategic defence', however, expressed the new interpretation given to the objectives of 1933 as a result of changed circumstances. The army general staff could now afford to think in broader terms and continue the ideas of Moltke and Schlieffen, whose plans for a war on several fronts could also be described as defence through offence. This change of

---

[117] The head of the army ordnance office likewise did not share the view that armour was the best defence against armour; he recommended an improvement and further development of available anti-tank guns. Cf. n. 121 below.

[118] Geyer ('Professionals', 77 ff.) has emphasized the political significance of the change in the self-image of the officer corps to that of a 'professional managerial élite'.

[119] O.Qu., 1/2. Abt., No. 26 55/33, g.Kdos., 30 Dec. 1935, BA-MA II H 662. Cf. also Müller, *Beck-Studien*, 206 ff., referring to the French motorization programme as an additional factor, and the documents 37 and 39 printed there (memorandums of 30 Dec. 1935 and 30 Jan. 1936).

perspective was clearly due to the convincing demonstration of the possibilities offered by the new armoured units.

The extent to which the general staff was dominated by this idea can be seen in the measures Beck suggested to improve the offensive capacity of the army. Previous planning had provided for three armoured brigades with the infantry in addition to the three brigades of the three armoured divisions. Beck now considered it realistic and necessary that every corps of the peacetime army should have an armoured brigade (four armoured units), which amounted to doubling the previous number of armoured brigades.[120] More important than the numerical planning was the use to which Beck wanted to put the armoured formations. He listed three main tasks for them: (1) support of infantry attacks ('inf. Tank'); (2) anti-tank defence; and (3) 'independent operational use together with other motorized forces (at present armoured division)'.

Beck devoted special attention to the third task. He noted that a frontal attack without tanks against an equally strong and well-trained enemy 'could hardly be successful'. Only the use of armoured divisions could be considered in the case of 'more ambitious targets', but the composition of the existing divisions needed to be re-examined. The memorandum gives the general impression that Beck and Guderian agreed in all important points on the use of armoured units. However, Beck preferred greater organizational flexibility. In addition to the armoured brigades, which were to be organized independently of the existing armoured divisions, he called for the creation of motorized infantry regiments which could be combined to form operational combat formations as circumstances required, and were intended to take over the tasks of the armoured divisions. At the same time he thought these motorized infantry regiments might form the basis for 'light divisions' to be organized later. While Guderian thought exclusively in terms of creating more armoured divisions, Beck realized the possibility of increasing the offensive capacity of the army as a whole by additional or partial motorization of more infantry divisions.[121]

Beck's plans amounted to a far-reaching restructuring of the army. He remained within the limits of the thirty-six-division army (33 + 3) planned earlier, but he wanted to provide the military leaders with motorized and mechanized combat units for offensive operations with more ambitious targets by the end of the build-up phase in 1939–40. In the event of war these units would amount to more than a third of the peacetime divisions. This would create completely new military preconditions for 'strategic defence' in a war on several fronts. With the organization of its three armoured divisions the German army had already left the

---

[120] This meant 12 armoured brigades for the 12 army corps of the peacetime army; in addition there were the 3 armoured brigades of the 3 armoured divisions.

[121] On this controversy cf. also Senff, *Panzerwaffe*, 18 ff., and Cooper, *German Army*, 143 ff. (already out of date). It is quite clear from Beck's remarks that he was favourable to the latest developments, if only because of the new operational possibilities they offered. Cf. the corresponding development in the navy, where the decision to build pocket battleships meant abandoning the old Tirpitz *idée fixe* of a decisive battle in the North Sea: Gemzell, *Organization, passim*.

armed forces of neighbouring countries far behind. Beck's programme was well suited to increase this advantage considerably.

Further discussions within the army high command showed the balanced quality and breadth appropriate to its goal on which the plan of the general staff was based. Beck emphatically rejected the suggestion of the inspectorate of mechanized combat forces that Tank I be used to provide 57 per cent of the vehicles for operational armoured units, precisely because he was convinced of the latter's special importance. He demanded that these units be equipped with heavier models still being developed, and especially with armour-piercing weapons.[122] Compared with these well-founded, forward-looking demands, the disputes about the composition of the armoured divisions, which gave Beck and the general staff the reputation of being basically opposed to Guderian's ideas, were insignificant.

On the other hand, the general staff had to deal with some very conservative tendencies. For example, the chief of the general army office, Colonel Fromm, was of the opinion that the 'over-refinement of weapons and the fear of blood' led to 'tactical degeneration'.[123] Fromm was also a determined opponent of the existing armoured divisions. He believed that the main function of tanks should be to support infantry attacks. In other respects, however, he clearly recognized the advantages of the motorization and mechanization of combat units, and his criticism of Beck's ideas of partially motorized infantry divisions was convincing. After several intermediate stages this opposition led to the plan for 'light divisions', which were organized from the summer of 1936 onwards.

The 'Considerations on Increasing the Offensive Power of the Army' had not yet been translated into a concrete, comprehensive, realizable armaments plan, but Beck had already indicated that neither financial nor economic difficulties would prevent him from pursuing the right military planning objectives. When the head of the general army office expressed his doubts that the army could afford forty-eight armoured units, Beck firmly rejected any reduction for financial reasons. And in a statement on the equipment and organization of the projected armoured units he demanded that German military planners 'free' themselves 'from the still limited armament possibilities. The tasks given the armoured units by the leaders were the most important factor in achieving the final goal'.[124] This blithe disregard of the economic foundation vital to all armament programmes showed again how futile had been the efforts of the head of the army ordnance office in May 1934 to make clear to the military leaders the importance of balancing material and personnel factors, as well as to persuade them to give due weight to 'actual possibilities' in their arms planning.[125]

Two years after the decision to create a twenty-one-division army, the process of rearmament had reached a new level with the 'Considerations on Increasing the

[122] Statement of the chief of the general staff (O.Qu., 1/2. Abt., No. 15/36, g.Kdos.) on 9 Jan. 1936, BA-MA II H 662.

[123] AHA, No. 5000/35, g.Kdos., 22 Jan. 1936, BA-MA II H 662; cf. Beck's rebuttal (O.Qu., 1/2 Abt., No. 162/36, g.Kdos.) of 30 Jan. 1936, BA-MA II H 662.

[124] O.Qu., 1/2 Abt., No. 15/36, g.Kdos., 9 Jan. 1936, BA-MA II H 662.

[125] Cf. III.II.2 (*b*) above, text to nn. 60–3.

Offensive Power of the Army'. The conventional divisions in their respective stages of build-up could still not be considered full combat units. The development of the wartime army to its projected size had hardly begun when, primarily for military reasons, a new planning phase was started which was largely to change the basic structure of the army.

(*d*) *Planning in the Summer of 1936 and its Realization up to the Outbreak of War*

In spite of the detailed planning in the summer of 1935, the question of the units to be organized in the autumn of 1936 was left open for some months.[126] In December the general staff clearly expressed its desire for an acceleration of the army build-up far beyond that called for by the total plan. At the end of December, Beck advocated the creation of the planned thirty-three infantry divisions as early as 1 October 1936, whereas six months earlier this goal had been set for 1 October 1939.[127] In the first organization order for the autumn deadline, issued on 12 January 1936, this suggestion was only partially accepted. 'Only' thirty-two, and not thirty-three, divisions were to be created. Compared with the planning of the summer of 1935, which had envisaged a total of twenty-eight divisions by the autumn of 1936, the increase was striking. It was typical of the unclear ideas within the military leadership that a few days later a new variant of the general build-up plan was submitted which envisaged the organization of the thirty-third infantry division only in the autumn of 1939, but had as its goal a significant increase in the number of combat formations to be available by then, as compared with the plans of the summer of 1935.[128]

These changing goals reflected the still unclear situation in the west and the new possibilities resulting from the lively discussion in progress at that time concerning an increase in the offensive power of the army. It is not surprising, then, that after the occupation of the Rhineland the first organization order creating the new units was revised by a second one of 1 April 1936.[129] The only surprise was the scope of the new units ordered for 5 October 1936. The army general staff had previously assumed that the figure of thirty-six divisions mentioned by Hitler on 16 March 1935 included the armoured divisions. But Colonel Fromm's interpretation of the spring of 1935, according to which it represented only the infantry divisions, was now accepted. The order of 1 April stated that the army was to consist of thirty-six infantry and three armoured divisions, a mountain division, and a cavalry brigade—a total of forty-one division-level formations (*Divisionsverbände*)—by the autumn of 1936. Compared to the level in the autumn of 1935, this represented a 50 per cent increase in infantry divisions, from twenty-four to thirty-six. In the autumn of 1936 the army reached a strength of about 520,000 men. In the former

[126] Cf. III.II.2 (*c*) above, text to nn. 95–6.

[127] Müller, *Beck-Studien*, Beck's statement in his memorandum of 30 Dec. 1935 (cf. n. 119 above); cf. also the suggestion by the second department of 11 Dec. 1935, BA-MA RH 2/v. 1020.

[128] Cf. Schottelius and Caspar, 'Organisation des Heeres', 303–4.

[129] O.Qu. 1/2 Abt., No. 500/36, geh., 1 Apr. 1936, BA-MA H 1/120; cf. also Schottelius and Caspar, 'Organisation des Heeres', 304–5 (also for the following strength figures).

demilitarized zone the organization of new units was still carried out with certain precautions.

The order of 1 April 1936 completely overturned the plans of summer 1935 for a medium-term build-up. The changed political and military situation in the spring of 1936, on which it was based, forced the army high command to make a new attempt to set certain goals for the future development of the army. These objectives were intended to serve as a basis for detailed planning and to make possible the urgently required long-term measures. At a conference on 8 June 1936 in the office of the commander-in-chief of the army, General von Fritsch, about the course and results of which no documents are available, corresponding goals were set, and the general staff, as well as the offices of the army high command, were ordered to start detailed planning.

A few days later, on 12 June, the chief of the general staff submitted specific figures on the strength of the future peacetime and wartime armies, as well as the build-up stages to be carried out each year.[130] According to these figures the complete peacetime army was to consist of thirty-six infantry divisions (among them four fully motorized formations), three armoured divisions, three light divisions, a mountain division, and a cavalry brigade. In addition there would be strong army and corps troop formations, e.g. thirteen heavy and three light artillery regiments as well as thirteen armoured brigades of four armoured units each. The general staff calculated the total personnel strength of the army, including unarmed auxiliary personnel, at 793,410 men, of whom 33,943 were officers. The wartime army, whose build-up was to be greatly accelerated by various measures after the summer of 1936, reached a strength of 2,680,936 men in the mobilization year 1937/8 according to the statistics of the general staff. In the mobilization year 1940/1, when the build-up was to be essentially completed, the field army would, according to the plans, consist of seventy-two infantry, three armoured, three light, and twenty-one militia divisions, as well as one cavalry and two mountain brigades. The personnel strength of the wartime army would reach 3,612,673 men after October 1940. Although Beck did not expressly mention it, it was clear from the plan of the individual build-up phases that, with the exception of a large number of heavy motorized artillery and armoured units, the formation of the peacetime and wartime armies was to be concluded by the autumn of 1939. Beck pointed out, however, that the build-up largely depended on the 'availability of the necessary materials, including sufficient supplies'. This was a view he had flatly rejected only a few months before. Compared with the December programme of 1933 and the planning of the summer of 1935, the figures, especially for the wartime army, seem at first glance to have been quite in accord with previous planning. The seventy-two divisions represented the upper limit Beck had considered necessary as early as March 1935. The important difference was in the additional militia divisions now

---

[130] Generalstab des Heeres, 2. Abt., No. 929/36, g.Kdos., 12 June 1936, BA-MA RH 2/v. 1021. From this document it is clear that the date of the conference was 8 June 1936. On the armaments planning in the summer of 1936 cf. also Müller, *Beck-Studien*, 218 ff. Müller's analysis differs in some details from the one presented here. For example, he attributes too much importance to the general staff's proposal of 12 June 1936; however, our interpretations agree.

available and the greatly expanded army and corps troops, which increased the strength of the planned wartime army to 102 division formations. In 1914 the German wartime army had consisted of eighty-seven divisions and forty-four militia brigades; its strength of 2,147,000 in 1914 was less than that now projected for October 1940.[131] Was it really only the political pressure from Hitler after the successful occupation of the Rhineland that forced the military leaders to try to outdo, in little more than seven years, what the imperial army had achieved after an uninterrupted development of more than four decades?

The problems presented by these planned figures can be understood if one remembers Liese's observations of 1934 or the objections of General von Schwedler to the planning ideas of the general staff in the summer of 1935. In the summer of 1936 Schwedler seems to have abandoned his opposition. According to a letter from the organization department to the central department of the general staff dated 24 June 1936, in 1941 the peacetime army would have a calculated authorized strength of approximately 33,950 officers and an effective strength of 20,800, assuming that there were no discharges and that the number of 'forced departures' would be minimal.[132] Under normal circumstances the calculated shortfall of 13,150 officers could be completely eliminated only in 1950. For this reason the general staff requested that the possibility be considered of promoting more non-commissioned officers to officer rank, drastically increasing the yearly quota of officer cadets, recalling more reserve officers to active duty, and reactivating more former officers. In December 1933 Beck had considered 7 per cent of total personnel strength as the final goal for officers. In 1936 the figure with regard to active officers was barely 1.6 per cent, 2.6 per cent including supplementary reserve officers.[133] In 1941 the figure, including supplementary reserve officers, would still be at the level of 1936. Beck seemed prepared to accept this situation, however. Referring to the imperial army of 1914 in the build-up plan, which was completely irrelevant, he claimed that 'requirements for peace and war' would be 'more or less adequately covered' when 'three-fifths of the total strength' were 'present in the active army'.[134] This corresponded approximately to the figure of 2.6 per cent. The principle of 7 per cent was thus abandoned. The military leaders were aware that the general decline of quality would only be made worse by the proposed measures, but, as was pointed out in the letter from the organization department, the 'pressure of the moment' made them necessary. What was this 'pressure of the moment' which forced Beck to assume responsibility for a development clearly incompatible with his basic military principles? He still viewed the international situation pessimistically and was aware that Germany's isolation was primarily due to the nature and manner of National Socialist actions. But he shut his eyes to the foreign-policy consequences of rearmament, and thus fell a victim to the circular argument that the threat of isolation could only be met by a further acceleration of the arms programme.

[131] In 1914 the population of Germany was 67.8m.; in 1933 the figure was 66m., and in 1939 69.3m.

[132] Letter No. 983/36, g.Kdos., 24 June 1936, BA-MA RH 2/v. 1015.

[133] On Beck's opinion in December 1933 cf. III.II.2 (*a*) above; on the strength of the officer corps on 6 Oct. 1936 cf. Absolon, *Wehrmacht*, iii. 162. On the auxiliary officer corps cf. III.II.2 (*c*) above.

[134] Cf. n. 130 above.

Moreover, he was probably not entirely unaffected by the fascinating possibilities of a rearmament involving the task of conducting a 'strategic defence' in a European war on several fronts.

In response to a directive from the commander-in-chief of the army, the general army office, in co-operation with other departments of the high command, took over the detailed planning on the basis of the plan submitted by the general staff. For example, the question of how many uniforms had to be available for which units at what time had to be answered. The financial and economic consequences resulting from calculations of ammunition, weapons, and equipment often assumed enormous dimensions, e.g. in regard to heavy artillery and tanks, which made a revision of military objectives seem possible.

The head of the general army office, Major-General Fromm, submitted the impressive figures to the commander-in-chief of the army with a letter on 1 August 1936 (see Table III.II.3, col. 3, p. 446 below).[135] Fromm's presentation showed much more clearly than the build-up plan of the general staff that the purpose of the commander in chief's order was to have the peacetime and wartime armies ready for combat at the planned strength by 1 October 1939. Fromm pointed out that this requirement would lead to 'serious difficulties . . . in the area of tanks and munitions deliveries, fulfilling lorry mobilization requirements, and in the unclear future situation with regard to raw materials, machines, and skilled workers'. He concluded that 'the creation and supplying of the planned army in peace and war' could be achieved 'purely theoretically' if the necessary funds and foreign exchange were made available 'in time'. But it was precisely that that was not certain. The estimated financial requirements for the period 1937–45 are shown in Table III.II.1.[136]

Fromm's figures for these nine budget years show the dimensions of the 'August programme' of the army high command. Compared with the planning in the summer of 1935, which itself had envisaged a doubling of the 300,000-man army of the December programme of 1933, financing requirements were almost doubled again.

And Fromm's figures did not include additional bill-of-exchange costs or the fact that 'the mobilization capacity of the armaments industry would have to be maintained from 1940 onwards by large, fixed minimum-procurement orders *without any real need*'. The question of minimum-procurement quotas had already worried the planners of the second armaments programme in the spring and summer of 1932 and caused them to make far-reaching demands.[137] According to the calculations of the army ordnance office these costs would exceed those for the maintenance of the peacetime army after 1942, as shown in Table III.II.2.

Such figures implied facts that could not have seemed very sensible even to the

[135] AHA, No. 1790/36, g.Kdos., 1 Aug. 1936, BA-MA RH 15/70.
[136] According to Fromm's information, in addition to the new requirements there were 'bill-of-exchange costs' (*Wechselunkosten*), which he did not define precisely, up to RM700m. annually.
[137] Cf. III.I.3. above, text to n. 78. As indicated, the minimum-procurement quotas were intended to maintain production capacity of the armaments industry at a level which would guarantee the fastest possible conversion to planned war production in the event of mobilization.

TABLE III.II.I. *Estimated financial requirements for army armaments 1937–1945 (RMI,000m.)*

	1937	1938	1939	1940	1941	1942	1943	1944	1945
Previous requirement (summer planning 1935)	3.575	3.675	3.859	3.439	2.584	2.584	2.584	2.584	2.584
New requirement	8.882	8.979	8.858	4.669	4.294	3.499	3.469	3.469	3.169

Source: AHA, No. 1790/36 g.Kdos., 1 Aug. 1936, BA-MA RH 15/70.

TABLE III.II.2. *German army ordnance office calculations of armament costs against minimum procurement costs 1940–1945* (RM1,000m.)

	1940	1941	1942	1943	1944	1945
Requirement (general army office)	4.669	4.294	3.499	3.469	3.469	3.169
Costs of minimum procurement	2.900	3.325	3.750	4.175	4.600	4.600
TOTAL	7.569	7.619	7.249	7.644	8.069	7.769

Source: AHA, No. 1790/36 g.Kdos. (1 Aug. 1936), BA-MA RH 15/70.

military planners. For example, it was clear that, solely because of the minimum-procurement quotas, an annual increase of 36,000 machine-guns had to be expected, although these could not possibly be used. Examples from ammunition production showed even more clearly that to maintain combat readiness, the need for which neither Fritsch nor Beck nor Fromm questioned or explained in greater detail, would have militarily unacceptable consequences.[138]

In view of the high financing requirements, the general staff suggested in September 1936 that the formation of the seventy-two-division wartime army be completed only on 1 April 1942, the build-up of armoured brigades be concentrated in 1940–1, and planned provision of equipment be made later. This would have reduced the required expenditure considerably and distributed it more evenly over the years 1937–41. The questions of foreign exchange and raw materials, and the problem of minimum-procurement quotas, were not even addressed in this variation of the original plan, and could hardly be affected by the results achieved.[139]

The facts and figures presented by the general army office inevitably confronted the military leaders—Blomberg, Fritsch, Beck, and the heads of departments in the army command—with the question of the purpose of their actions. Rearmament planning had reached a decisive point. The head of the general army office, Major-General Fromm, formulated the central military question resulting from the programme clearly for his commander-in-chief: 'Following the rearmament period the Wehrmacht must either be used in combat very soon, or the situation must be alleviated by reducing the required level of war-readiness.' Before a final proposal could be worked out, Fromm continued, Fritsch would have to ask the war minister to clarify the foreign-exchange and raw-materials situation and the possibility of a large-scale export offensive in and after 1940 so as to reduce the burden of the minimum-procurement quotas. Above all, however, he must find out whether

---

[138] Cf. annex II to the draft of 1 Aug. 1936, AHA, No. 1790/36, g.Kdos., 1 Aug. 1936, BA-MA RH 15/70.
[139] Cf. the undated draft of the general army office, AHA, No. 1890/36, g.Kdos., Sept. 1936, BA-MA RH 15/70.

it 'was definitely intended to commit the Wehrmacht to action at some already determined time'.

Fromm never received a clear answer to this crucial question, and Fritsch disregarded the suggestions of the general staff to cut the programme and extend the period for its realization. Rather, the decisions in the second half of 1936 leave no doubt that, from that point on, the rearmament of the army followed the original August programme.

What political goal did this forced rearmament serve? One may be tempted to interpret the August programme as the decisive change from defensive to offensive armaments, to an aggressive war policy set for 1939–40. A survey of German rearmament after 1933 shows, however, that the August programme marked only a further step in the acceleration of its momentum. The political aim of armament planning was in agreement with the programme Hitler had explained to the Reichswehr generals at the beginning of February 1933, the central point of which for the military leaders was the restoration of Germany's position as a European great power, an objective that had guided the actions and planning of the Reichswehr ever since 1919. After the preconditions had been created, this goal expanded to include traditional ideas of an active military great-power policy in Europe, a policy in which the instrument of war would play its traditional role. The August programme was, therefore, an example of the continuity of German military thinking and planning. The economic consequences of rearmament, the enormous, continuous financial burden and possible effects on society, were of only very secondary importance for the military leadership. The August programme, at all events, represented a qualifying of Blomberg's claim at the beginning of February 1934 that Hitler had no intention 'of attacking anyone' after the completion of the rearmament programme. German armament planning was now based on the assumption of military aggression.

On 12 October 1936 Fritsch submitted the build-up plan of the army high command to Blomberg.[140] It began with the sentence: 'In accordance with the Führer's orders, a powerful army is to be created in the shortest possible time.' Although this general statement indeed reflected Hitler's ideas, it was the military leaders who converted them into a timetable. Fritsch assured Blomberg that 'the army high command would be able to fulfil the most important parts of this task by 1 October 1939'. Studies had shown, he said, that a peacetime army of 830,000 men and a field army of 2,421,000 could be created by then.[141] A comparison of the estimated costs of the programme clearly shows that it was based largely on the general army office draft of 1 August. All of the data used were the same.

Fritsch also took up the question of officer requirements. He estimated that about 140,000 officers would be necessary (3.1 per cent) for a wartime army of over 4.5 million men. However, under existing provisions the actual figure would amount to

---

[140] AHA, No. 2300/36, g.Kdos., 12 Oct. 1936, BA-MA RH 15/70.

[141] Fritsch estimated the total strength of the wartime army at 4.620m., including the replacement army. This figure was far higher than that given by Beck in June. Cf. text to nn. 129 and 130 above.

less than half of that on 1 October 1939. To alleviate this disastrous shortfall Fritsch suggested the measures already proposed by the general staff in June.

Fritsch mentioned Fromm's fundamental questions only in passing. He described the already serious difficulties in supplying the army with munitions and vehicles of all kinds as if the army could overcome them by itself. Only in a few places did he show an awareness of the dependence of military planning on political and economic factors, e.g. when he remarked that the 'fuel and rubber situation' seemed satisfactory provided 'the economy could be slowed down somewhat'. There was 'no doubt that this could be done after the completion of the Führer's Four-year Plan'. Among the military leaders, as elsewhere, professions of faith in Hitler replaced objective discussion very early. The problem of raw materials and foreign currency was simply pushed into Blomberg's area of responsibility, as it was after all the 'special task' of the war-economy staff, which was directly subordinate to the war minister. In the all-important question of minimum procurement quotas, Fritsch took the position that 'the large capacity that industry will achieve by [1940] will require large funds to continue procurement orders in the absence of any significant Wehrmacht requirements. Of course it is impossible to overcome the difficulties in this way; it is absolutely essential to find other ways.'

Surely there are few documents that so clearly express the reluctance or refusal of the military leaders at that time to face the consequences of their actions for the armed forces that were their responsibility. They concerned themselves primarily with the great goal of military policy, the build-up of an army capable of a 'strategic defence' as an instrument of an active great-power policy in Europe. Fritsch avoided facing the effects of this objective in his own area of responsibility and simply claimed that it was not his province. In view of this attitude it may seem strange that Fritsch, after he had requested the approval of the defence minister for the build-up plan, emphatically demanded that the necessary funds be included in the budget and that the annual allocation of the total sum be placed at his disposal. His surprising justification was that only in this way could 'proper and economically efficient' work be guaranteed. This was another example of how convenient it was for the military leaders to confine themselves to their own narrowly defined areas and concentrate on current tasks; economic efficiency was only important when it involved the use of funds allocated for those areas. Looking beyond the confines of their own departments involved a dangerous and exhausting conflict with obstacles involving great risks to themselves and only limited possibilities of success. At any rate Fritsch did not take advantage of this slight opportunity. At the beginning of December 1936 he declared the build-up plan the 'basis of all further measures' and empowered the army ordnance office to conclude long-term delivery agreements for total requirements of weapons and ammunition, calculated within the framework of the general plan.[142]

On 10 October 1936, shortly before Fritsch forwarded the suggestions of the high command for a further build-up of the army to the commander-in-chief of the

---

[142] Note of 7 Dec. 1936 recording conference with the commander-in-chief of the army on Saturday, 6 Dec. 1936 at 11 a.m., BA-MA RH 15/70. Cf. also Geyer, 'Militär', 264–5.

Wehrmacht, the army ordnance office submitted its ideas for an 'economically acceptable' planning of rearmament, which, however, had no influence on Fritsch's basic decision.[143] General Liese strongly supported Fromm's view that the 'hundred per cent realization of the build-up plan' seemed 'irresponsible' if there were no 'firm intention' to 'commit the Wehrmacht to action at some already determined time'. Liese presented proposals which primarily involved a reduction of required monthly supplies in case the decision should be taken to slow down the programme. He also believed that he could reduce the harmful effects of the minimum-procurement quotas by placing a legal obligation on ammunitions factories, the main problem area, to use the munitions orders they received so as to train their entire work-force. To guarantee this continuous training, which was to be carried out in stages of six months, Liese considered it necessary to suspend the workers' freedom of movement for the duration of the training period, and recommended that they be placed in a special category so that they could immediately be released from military service to work in their factories in the event of mobilization. These ideas are interesting because in the course of further developments the military leadership, i.e. Fritsch, on the one hand held to the principle of a complete realization of the original programme, but on the other hand accepted several of Liese's suggestions to reduce the costs. This was true not only of the early restrictions on the freedom of movement of workers in armaments factories[144] but also of Liese's recommendations to place large orders running for several years for projected total requirements, so as to motivate industry to bear the necessary investment costs itself.[145]

Fritsch's decision of 6 December 1936 started the last comprehensive armaments plan before the outbreak of war. After the programmes of December 1933 and the summer of 1935, this last programme marked the beginning of planning for an army capable of a strategic offensive, which had been made possible by the restoration of full German military sovereignty after the occupation of the Rhineland. The quantitative point of reference for the planning was the imperial army before the First World War; the qualitative basis was provided by the intensive debate on 'increasing the offensive power' of the army, with its purely military criteria. A further characteristic of the planning was the short-term nature of its deadlines. In barely three years not only the peacetime army, whose formations had been increased again by almost 50 per cent in October 1936, but also a gigantic wartime army, which had previously not received much attention, was to be fully equipped and ready for combat. So strong was the emphasis on meeting deadlines that serious military shortages, especially of officers, were accepted, quite apart from the financial consequences and those in the armaments industry. If one accepts Fritsch's statement in his letter to Blomberg of 12 October 1936 that Hitler wanted 'a powerful army in the shortest possible time', i.e. without setting a specific

---

[143] Wa.A., No. 1232/36, g.Kdos., 10 Oct. 1936, BA-MA RH 2/v. 240.
[144] Mason, *Arbeiterklasse*, 100 ff., 150 ff., 666 ff.
[145] Relevant material is in the file BA-MA RH 15/70.

TABLE III.11.3. *Data on German armaments planning 1938-1939*

	Memorandum of the Truppenamt of 14 Dec. 1933: build-up of a 21-div. army by 1 Apr. 1938[a]	Proposal of the general staff of 19 July 1935: build-up of a 36-div. army by 1 Oct. 1939[b]	Armaments plan of the general army office of 1 Aug. 1936: build-up of the peace and wartime army by 1 Oct. 1939[c]
A. *Higher commands*			
Group commands	3	4	4
General (corps) commands	8	12	13
Cavalry command	1	1	
Armoured corps command			1
Reconnaissance forces command			1
B. *Formations* (Verbände)			
Infantry divisions	21	33	32
Infantry divisions (mot.)			4
Mountain division			1
Mountain brigade		1	
Cavalry divisions	3		
Cavalry brigade	1	1	1
Armoured divisions		3	3
Armoured formation	1		
Light divisions	1		3
C. Strength of the peacetime army	300,000	693,580	830,000
whereof corps and army troops	c.50,000	129,020	
D. Strength of the wartime army	63 divisions		4,620,000
Number of field army divisions in the wartime army	33 divisions	54 div. formations	102 div. formations

[a] Text in Müller, *Beck-Studien*, doc. No. 9, pp. 339-44.
[b] Generalstab des Heeres, 2. Abt. No. 1900/35 g.Kdos., BA-MA RH 2/v. 1019.
[c] AHA, No. 1790/36 g.Kdos., BA-MA RH 15/70.

deadline, it can be assumed that the date was set by the military leaders themselves, in particular by the war minister, von Blomberg.

However, the real significance of the August programme can be understood only if its internal preconditions, considerations, and goals are seen, analysed, and interpreted in relation to the total process of rearmament, which was not confined to strictly military areas. Although economic and political factors played a progressively smaller role in military planning, this does not mean that they became less important in reality. On the contrary, in detailed studies of National Socialist economic policy it has been shown that from the very beginning armament–economy factors increasingly determined the goals and methods of economic policy.[146] The first high point of this development was reached in 1936. In his memorandum on the Four-year Plan[147] Hitler clearly stated his intention to place the entire economy fully in the service of rearmament. The connection between the military and the economic programme of the summer of 1936 has not yet been examined closely, but the parallel nature of these developments is striking and indicates that both were the results of a decision made in the spring. At the beginning of April Hitler instructed Göring to examine possibilities for improving the raw-materials and foreign-currency situation; a month later the raw-materials and foreign-currency staff began its work.[148] Blomberg and the war ministry played a decisive role in all consultations and decisions in this area. Although he was fully aware of the strained economic situation, Blomberg directed the commander-in-chief of the army to draw up a comprehensive build-up plan at the end of May or the beginning of June. In August a draft was accordingly submitted. At the end of August, in a letter to Göring, Blomberg suggested a discussion by the raw-materials and foreign-currency staff of the future costs of rearmament, and mentioned figures which corresponded approximately to those of the build-up plan.[149] Given Blomberg's known preoccupation with the economic aspects of rearmament since April, it can be assumed that he mentioned this subject to Hitler. This assumption is supported by Schacht's dramatic demand that Blomberg should persuade Hitler at the last minute not to proclaim his economic programme at the NSDAP party rally. Blomberg refused because he hoped that the measures Hitler had announced in his memorandum (with which Blomberg was familiar) would overcome all difficulties.[150]

Although these circumstances show that Blomberg was concerned equally with the economic and military aspects of rearmament, there is no evidence of co-ordinated planning. It is, however, certain that, after the restoration of military sovereignty in the spring of 1936, armaments policy was placed on a new basis with the introduction of the August programme of the high command together with

---

[146] Cf. the general description in Carr, 'Rüstung', 440 ff; Volkmann in Part II above.

[147] Cf. Treue, 'Hitlers Denkschrift': trans. of memorandum in *Documents on Nazism, 1919–1945,* 401–8.

[148] Cf. Volkmann in Part II above.

[149] Blomberg's letter to Göring of 31 Aug. 1936, *IMT* xxvii. 150 ff.

[150] Note by Col. Thomas of 2 Sept, 1936, ibid. 153–4; Treue, 'Hitlers Denkschrift', 195; Volkmann in Part II above.

Hitler's Four-year Plan. Hitler's demand at the conclusion of his memorandum on the Four-year Plan that 'the German armed forces must be operational within four years' and 'the German economy must be fit for war' in four years[151] was not merely a rhetorical phrase but a concrete directive which the army had already taken into consideration in its planning. The mobilization phase for the peacetime and wartime armies planned for 1 October 1939 began on 1 April 1940.

Hitler's action in increasing the service period under general conscription from one to two years on 24 August 1936 seems at first to be incompatible with this picture of unrestrained rearmament.[152] This measure is usually interpreted as having had a retarding effect on the pace of rearmament and as reflecting the principles which the military leaders, especially Fritsch, considered necessary to improve the quality of training and the army build-up.[153] It must be noted, however, that the extension of the period of service had been only a fringe issue in planning since 1933. As has been shown, because of the goals the military had been given or had set for itself, solid training was not considered especially important.

Fritsch expressed his opinion about the length of the period of service at a commanders' conference in January 1935.[154] He explained that the two-year period of service was the desired goal but that 'for foreign-policy and technical reasons' it could not be realized 'within the present army build-up'. At that time he still thought that it would be possible after the size of the army had been doubled. In March 1935 he strongly advocated a two-year period of service for military reasons, adding that, with a one-year period, 'the political leadership could only afford to become involved in a military conflict in the short time between mid-summer and the end of September'.[155] But he made no suggestions about when the two-year period of service should be introduced. In addition, he encountered opposition from Beck, who considered effective measures for the quick formation of reserves to be more important.

Basing its position on a statistical survey of manpower requirements and availability by the general army office, the organization department of the general staff noted in July 1935 that from 1938-9 onwards a change to a two-year period of service would be necessary because it would not be possible to cover military manpower requirements with a one-year period.[156] Thus, not quality but only considerations of quantity were decisive. This was also the basis of the decision of August 1936. Problems encountered during this autumn deployment of 1936 were

---

[151] Treue, 'Hitlers Denkschrift', 210 (trans., 408). Dülffer's remark in 'Beginn des Kriegs', 463, that 'repeated demands of the German dictator to accelerate or expand certain armaments measures as well as the Four-year Plan resulted *primarily* from the armaments competition of other countries' (my italics) seems incorrect. This can, however, be considered an *additional* factor from 1937-8 onwards. The treatment of Fromm's inquiry shows that a slowing-up of rearmament was never seriously considered (ibid. 464).

[152] Domarus, i. 635; Baynes, ii. 1327.

[153] e.g. Foerster, *Beck*, 34.

[154] IfZ Archives, ED 1, vol. i. Liebmann's record of the conference on 12 Jan. 1935.

[155] Müller, *Beck-Studien*, 193 ff. Fritsch was referring to the level of training of the troops.

[156] Cf. the draft by the general army office, AHA, No. 3400/35, g.Kdos., 19 July 1935, and comment by the organization department of 20 July, BA-MA RH 2/v. 1014.

probably the main factor in the early introduction of a two-year period of service. The high level of training of the 100,000-man army had made it possible to absorb a threefold increase in the number of division formations in accordance with the December programme of 1933. But now the army faced another great expansion, from twenty-four to thirty-six divisions, and motorization and mechanization also presented special problems. In view of the decline in the quality of the army, the oft-mentioned 'watering down', such an increase based on a one-year period of service represented an unacceptable burden. With the introduction of the two-year period of service the situation improved considerably because, in addition to the career soldiers, a fully trained age-group of conscripts was now available for new tasks and the induction of a new group of recruits. Thus, the introduction of a two-year period of service was quite in accordance with the acceleration of rearmament since the spring of 1936.

The further build-up of the army in the years 1937–9 was carried out essentially according to the basic guidelines of the August programme. An important factor was the decision of the commander-in-chief of the army in December 1936 to award supply contracts running for several years on the basis of that programme.[157] At first glance it seems striking that the planning figures agree almost completely with the quantitative results of the build-up in the autumn of 1939. According to plan, the field army was to consist of a total of 102 division formations on 1 October 1939, and in fact at the outbreak of war 103 were mobilized.[158] But, in view of the annexation of Austria and the Sudeten areas, it would clearly be a mistake to conclude that this fact points to a consistent, planned development. The opposite was true. As early as 1937 the raw-materials situation had become the decisive factor in further rearmament, and necessitating constant changes in planning and a slowing of the pace of rearmament. The military actions against Austria and Czechoslovakia, while causing additional problems, greatly facilitated the expansion of the reservoir of available manpower and the German industrial base and provided valuable organizational experience. In contrast to the build-up phase of 1933–6, the military now began to concentrate more on operational planning and command organization; questions of armaments planning were pushed into the background. The August programme was the final plan in this latter area.

With the exception of a 'light brigade' organized in the autumn of 1937, no new division-level formations were created.[159] The idea of light divisions was a result of the debate on 'increasing offensive power' in the spring of 1936. These units, of which four were organized by the beginning of the war, were intended to take over the tasks of the earlier army cavalry: primarily long-range reconnaissance, securing wide gaps in the front, and protecting open flanks. In the view of the general staff they were supposed to be very 'fast and mobile units' with considerable 'defensive ability'.[160] The most important other build-up measure carried out in 1937 was the

---

[157] Cf. BA-MA RH 15/70.

[158] Mueller-Hillebrand, *Heer*, i. 68; cf. also Schottelius and Caspar, 'Organisation des Heeres', 312 ff., 366 ff.   [159] Schottelius and Caspar, 'Organisation des Heeres', 308.

[160] Generalstab des Heeres, 2. Abt., No. 223/36, g.Kdos., 6 Feb. 1936, BA-MA II H 662.

motorization of four infantry divisions. Most units had not yet reached their full personnel and material strength, but compared with 1936 the shortfalls, especially in the infantry and artillery, had been considerably reduced. After three years of continuous creation of new units, the structure of the army had changed profoundly; 1937 brought a short consolidation period.

Since the autumn of 1936 the organizational expansion of the wartime army had been pushed forward with increased vigour. In the autumn of 1937 large numbers of reservists were discharged from the peacetime army for the first time since the introduction of general conscription, thus creating eight reserve divisions which could be mobilized in the event of war. A further measure to strengthen the wartime army affected the frontier guard units on the eastern border and the reinforced frontier surveillance service in the west. In the autumn of 1936, on the initiative of Colonel von Manstein, the assistant chief of staff (operations), the organization of the frontier guards planned for wartime was adjusted to the changed conditions. Because of the increased strength of the peacetime army, the need for frontier units stationed in fixed locations had largely disappeared. To protect the frontiers, a so-called 'frontier police force' was organized, also with permanent locations but with significantly reduced personnel and equipment. It was planned to form a total of twenty-one militia divisions in the event of mobilization by using the material thus made available from the frontier guard units in the east, the active army, and persons born in or before 1900 who had already been conscripted during the First World War. This increased the size of the wartime army in the mobilization period 1937/8 to a total of seventy-one division formations,[161] a strength which Beck had described as the final goal of the army build-up in 1935.

German territorial expansion in 1938 and the establishment of the Protectorate of Bohemia and Moravia in March 1939 also affected the army build-up. On 10 March 1938 Hitler, who had assumed the position of commander-in-chief of the Wehrmacht after the Blomberg–Fritsch crisis, unexpectedly ordered the partial mobilization of the units earmarked for action against Austria in the seventh and thirteenth military districts. The invasion of Austria by these units on 12 March revealed organizational weaknesses in the mobilization and the motorized formations which were largely remedied before the outbreak of war in 1939.[162] In addition to this valuable experience, the integration of the Austrian army itself represented a considerable increase in the strength of the Wehrmacht. In the course of 1938 a total of two infantry and two mountain divisions, one armoured, and one light division could be re-created. About 60,000 Austrian soldiers were taken into the Wehrmacht. Of a total figure of about 3,100 Austrian officers, approximately 1,600 were integrated into the German officer corps.[163]

---

[161] On the build-up of the wartime army cf. Mueller-Hillebrand, *Heer*, i. 57 ff.; Schottelius and Caspar, 'Organisation des Heeres', 305–6, 386 ff.; Manstein, *Soldatenleben*, 250–1.

[162] Murray, *Change*, 338 ff.; also id., 'German Response', 285–98, using the retrospective reports (*Erfahrungsberichte*) of several units participating in the military actions in 1938–9. Cf. also Guderian, *Panzer Leader*, 49–50; Manstein, *Soldatenleben*, 323 ff.; Görlitz, *Keitel*, 178 ff.; Thomas, *Wehr- und Rüstungswirtschaft*, 125 ff.; Mueller-Hillebrand, *Heer*, i. 62–3.

[163] Mueller-Hillebrand, *Heer*, i. 30, 36; Schottelius and Caspar, 'Organisation des Heeres', 309–10; Manstein, *Soldatenleben*, 326 ff.; Gschaider, *Bundesheer, passim*; cf. also Volkmann in Part II above.

The worsening relations between Germany and Czechoslovakia, which had been obvious since May 1938 at the latest,[164] led to the German annexation of the Sudetenland at the beginning of October. In this case there was no partial mobilization. The new areas were organized militarily as parts of contiguous military districts. In addition, a new infantry division and a new armoured division were created.[165] However, the occupation of the remainder of Czechoslovakia in March 1939 was much more important for the armaments situation. The decisive significance of the industrial capacity, raw materials, and foreign-currency reserves of the newly occupied areas for the continuation of German armaments plans according to the Four-year Plan has been described elsewhere.[166] The high-quality weapons, ammunition, and equipment found in Czechoslovakia were most welcome in the context of the programme of August 1936. The booty, which Hitler described in detail in his speech to the Reichstag on 28 April 1939,[167] made it easier to achieve the goal of the August programme concerning the build-up of stocks of weapons and equipment for fifteen infantry divisions (equipment divisions). The armoured units also profited from the booty and the further use of Czechoslovak industrial capacity. In the campaign against France three German armoured divisions were equipped with Czechoslovak vehicles.[168]

These data should not, however, be allowed to obscure the fact that German rearmament was generally determined, after 1937 at the latest, by economic factors which the chief of the army ordnance office had warned of as early as May 1934.[169] The economic limits to large-scale rearmament had hardly been noticeable in the first years of the Third Reich. Shortages of one kind or another in the still expanding armaments industry could be traced to a number of causes. After 1936 this situation changed completely. Hitler's announcement of the Four-year Plan was only the expression of an increasingly serious economic crisis. Nevertheless, the army's August programme was conceived almost at the same time without any consideration of economic facts. This conflict between military requirements and economic realities determined the pace and scope of rearmament from 1936 to 1939. Here we can only point out that the confusion was greatly intensified by open or behind-the-scenes conflicts among the services, not for more or fewer divisions, brigades, or battalions, but for tons of the increasingly scarce raw materials.

Barely four weeks after the commander-in-chief of the army had approved the August programme in 1936, he received a report from the army ordnance office at the beginning of November informing him that the copper requirements of the army could only be met by half. General Liese pointed out that this meant that the munitions industry could only operate at half capacity.[170] As a result, the general

---

[164] Cf. Messerschmidt, Part IV below.

[165] Zorach, 'Fortifications', 81 ff.; Schottelius and Caspar, 'Organisation des Heeres', 310–11.

[166] Cf. Volkmann in Part II above; Thomas, *Wehr- und Rüstungswirtschaft*, 129 ff.

[167] Domarus, ii. 1156. Cf. also Volkmann, II.vi.4 above.

[168] Cf. Hummelberger, 'Rüstungsindustrie, 308 ff., esp. n. 13; Murray, *Change*, 290 ff.

[169] Cf. III.ii.2 (*b*) above, text to n. 60. On the development of the defence economy as a whole, cf. Volkmann in Part II above.

[170] Chef des Heereswaffenamtes, No. 1392/36, g.Kdos, 10 Nov. 1936, BA-MA RH 2/v. 240. Cf. also the comment by the army ordnance office of 10 Oct. 1936, Wa.A., No. 1232/36, g.Kdos., BA-MA RH 2/v. 240.

allocation system for non-ferrous metals was introduced on 1 January 1937, largely at the urging of the army. But this measure was completely inadequate to meet the army's requirements in the long term.[171] On 10 February 1939 the commander-in-chief informed the chancellor that it was virtually certain that a large part of the ammunition produced in 1939 would 'be delivered at first without guide rings and fuses', as the necessary copper was not available.[172]

The difficulties were not limited to the general scarcity of non-ferrous metals. At the end of 1936 and the beginning of 1937 a severe shortage of raw steel necessitated the introduction of an allocation system for steel and iron in May 1937. But this system too did not lead to any lasting improvement.[173] In long memorandums the army ordnance office demonstrated that delivery delays, rivalry with other services, and priority deliveries for state and party building projects had kept the army from receiving the quantities allocated to it and that its allocations were constantly being reduced.[174] After May 1938, when Hitler ordered the immediate, large-scale expansion of the fortifications in the west regardless of the economic situation and especially of available quantities of iron and steel, the struggle for strategically important materials became even more intense. Allocations for the army did improve slightly, but remained far below requirements necessitated by Hitler's order. The quantity allotted to the army in 1939 was only slightly larger than that of 1938. In addition, serious delays in delivery still made it impossible to supply the army with weapons, equipment, and ammunition according to plan. In February 1939 the commander-in-chief of the army found it necessary to explain to Hitler in a long report the importance of bar steel for the production of armaments, especially carbines, machine-guns, and light infantry artillery, as the economics minister had suddenly frozen all orders for such steel and thin sheet metal in December 1938 because of the flood of such orders.[175] Brauchitsch was especially angry that this did not apply to orders placed by his rival, the navy, which was expressly exempted.

A number of other examples could be mentioned. They clearly show that the army build-up in 1936–9 was based on a comprehensive programme determined by military criteria. Its realization was, however, dominated by often abruptly changing factors in the defence economy. The offices in the army high command and the general staff constantly tried to adjust the plans for the military build-up to the changing situation in the defence economy, but their efforts did not progress beyond the drafting stage. In mid-February and at the beginning of March 1937 the general staff and the general army office drew the logical conclusion from the raw-

---

[171] On the actual administrative efforts to overcome the raw-material shortages with the help of quotas cf. the detailed study by Sarholz, *Auswirkungen*. Geyer ('Rüstungsbeschleunigung', 129, 135–6, 161 ff., 174–5) provides additional information on the situation with regard to non-ferrous metals.

[172] Oberbefehlshaber des Heeres, No. 64/39 g.Kdos, 10 Feb. 1939, BA-MA III H 98/4.

[173] Cf. Thomas, *Wehr- und Rüstungswirtschaft*, 120 ff.; Volkmann, II.v.5 above.

[174] Cf. here and in the following passage the file BA-MA III H 98/1–5. On the course, causes, and very complicated effects of the crisis of the defence economy in 1938 cf. the definitive analysis by Geyer, 'Rüstungsbeschleunigung', 121 ff. Geyer considers that it was also a crisis of the system, which was overcome in a manner appropriate to it only with the proclamation of total war. Cf. also Sarholz, *Auswirkungen*, 300 ff.

[175] Cf. Oberbefehlshaber des Heeres, No. 64/39, g.Kdos., 10 Feb. 1939, BA-MA III H 98/4.

materials shortage. The general army office observed that the peace and wartime armies planned in August 1936 could only be fully ready on 1 April 1941, a delay of one and a half years. The shortage of raw materials had a much more serious effect on the production of ammunition and equipment, with delays of between two and a half and three years. In the view of the military leaders this constituted a serious threat to the goal of creating a powerful, combat-ready army. General Fromm calculated that on 1 April 1939 it would be possible to produce ammunition supplies for twenty days of fighting. At the same time investment in factories to guarantee prompt production of new supplies had to be reduced to the point that monthly ammunition production sufficient for a first supplying of the field army would be reached only on 1 April 1942. The outbreak of a war between the two dates could easily lead to a situation in which the army would soon find itself facing the enemy without ammunition.[176]

In these circumstances one might have expected that the army high command would take the initiative in extending the period for the realization of the August programme and for carrying it out in such a way that, although the army would then necessarily be smaller, its striking power and combat-readiness would be guaranteed in every phase of the build-up. But the opposite was the case.

In mid-December 1937, a few weeks after the conference of 5 November, Beck, acting for Fritsch, sent Blomberg a letter in which he said that the army leadership had decided, in spite of all difficulties, to 'complete the peacetime build-up for 1938'.[177] But, he added, this must not 'conceal the internal weaknesses of the army, which exists only as an organizational framework'. As justification for the decision Beck added that the important thing was 'to expand training possibilities as much as possible and thus create significant reserves'. For this reason the army leaders were prepared to accept certain delays, e.g. the fact that, until the winter of 1938–9, it would only be possible to train motorized troops because of the lack of vehicles; not until 1 April 1939 would they reach their marching-out strength. Supplies of some kinds of ammunition were sufficient for only fifteen days of combat. The effects of the raw-materials shortage on the use of industrial capacity were considered especially serious. In the cases mentioned the use of capacity was under 50 per cent, which reduced the required capacity for early mobilization even more. With regard to the intended military action against Austria and Czechoslovakia even before the conclusion of the build-up, which Hitler had mentioned at the conference of 5 November, Beck pointed out at the end of his letter that 'during the winter of 1938–9 the whole army' would not 'be ready for combat' and that 'even later serious limitations' were 'to be expected'. On the other hand, the reorganization of the armaments programme announced in the letter certainly reflected the timetable announced by Hitler on 5 November; Beck stated at the beginning that by 1 April 1943 the full wartime army would be ready. Fromm's disturbing question of 1936 as to whether maintaining the army at a level of maximum combat-readiness was

[176] AHA, No. 567/37, g.Kdos., 11 Mar. 1937, BA-MA III H 98/1.
[177] Oberkommando des Heeres, No. 2798/37, g.Kdos., 14 Dec. 1937, BA-MA III H 98/2. On the conference of 5 Nov. 1937 cf. III.III.4 below.

economically acceptable was no longer relevant, as Hitler had announced his intention to begin his war to expand German living-space from 1943 at the latest, and the military leaders acted accordingly.

The political events of 1938 also made this interim planning within the framework of the August programme obsolete. With the new units organized in Austria and the Sudeten German areas, as well as the doubling of the replacement army,[178] the figures planned in the August programme were exceeded for the first time. As a memorandum of 15 April 1939 shows, Hitler's demands for even more armaments in certain areas, e.g. for the Westwall and the Luftwaffe,[179] resulted in a situation in which the field army was without supplies of weapons and equipment, thirty-four infantry divisions were only partially provided with necessary weapons and equipment, the replacement army had only 10 per cent of the necessary rifles and machine-guns, and total stocks of ammunition fell to a level sufficient for fifteen days of fighting.[180] This unacceptable situation was tolerated only because of expectations of a larger allocation of steel. But this hope proved to be unfounded, and the shortage of bar steel mentioned above made the situation temporarily worse.

The memorandum of 15 April 1939, written in preparation for a report by the commander-in-chief to Hitler, shows how dramatically the army high command viewed the problem from a politico-military point of view:

> The present situation resulting from the shortage of bar steel is similar in certain respects to that before the First World War. At that time the creation of the three army corps, which were not available in the first year of the war to bring about a quick decision, was not possible because parliament refused the necessary funds. Today the army is being denied the necessary quantities of bar steel to equip itself with modern offensive weapons. The consequences could be similar to those of 1914.

The German army at the outbreak of war in 1939 was among those equipped with the most modern weapons in the world; this was the result of a continuous development since 1925–6, which, especially in the area of weapons technology, would not have been possible without the theoretical and practical development work of the Reichswehr under the Weimar Republic. The high point of organizational planning was the August programme of 1936, which had already been exceeded in terms of personnel and the number of active units by 1 September 1939, although the corresponding equipment and weapons were not available at that time. The plan called for a field army with a strength of 2,421,000 men; in fact the strength of the army rose to 2,758,000 by 1 September 1939. Instead of forty-four division formations of the active army there were fifty-three large units: thirty-five infantry, three mountain, six armoured, and four light divisions, as well as four motorized infantry divisions and one cavalry brigade. The 103 mobilized formations in 1939 corresponded almost exactly to the number projected in 1936, viz. 102.[181] Compared with earlier plans, the mobilization organization had been greatly refined.

---

[178] Cf. Schottelius and Caspar, 'Organisation des Heeres', 388.

[179] Cf. III.II.4 (*b*) and III.III.4 below.

[180] AHA, No. 1220/39, g.Kdos., 15 Apr. 1939, BA-MA III H 98/5.

[181] Mueller-Hillebrand, *Heer*, i. 65 ff.; Schottelius and Caspar, 'Organisation des Heeres', 312 ff., 387 ff.

2. Army: Plans and Realization, 1936-1939

The mobilization of the European armies in 1914 had proved extremely dangerous in its political effects. The proclamation of full mobilization had been almost synonymous with the start of hostilities and had left no further room for political or diplomatic efforts. This automatic element had been especially disadvantageous to Germany. For this reason, new forms of mobilization were developed between the wars, though still with the object of rapidly converting the peacetime army into the wartime army; transporting its mobile part, the field army, to planned deployment areas, and starting the supply programme for the whole wartime army as quickly as possible. Clearly the detailed measures involved in this task affected numerous areas of public and economic life. For this reason a systematic co-ordination and avoidance of possible damaging effects were extremely important in maximizing the nation's readiness for war. Since the reintroduction of general conscription, preparations for mobilization had been resumed and an 'army mobilization plan' drawn up. Through a system with various stages it was possible to carry out a mobilization with or without a public announcement and even to limit it to certain regions, as the example of Austria had shown. The rapidity with which mobilization could be carried out was based on solid planning, guaranteed by annual re-examination of all individual measures, and on the capacity and flexibility of the railway system. In addition, a special procedure had been developed to form the field army from the peacetime army. The infantry divisions in the field army were divided into four different categories ('waves', *Wellen*). The thirty-five divisions of the first category had in peacetime 78 per cent active-duty personnel with very few reservists. In contrast, the sixteen divisions of the second category had only 6 per cent active-duty personnel; 83 per cent of their soldiers were Wehrmacht reservists with at least nine months of training. The twenty divisions of the third category were composed primarily of reservists from the supplementary reserve units of the army and of men required to serve in the militia, some of whom had completed their training before 1918. Finally, the fourteen divisions of the fourth category had 21 per cent Wehrmacht reservists, but contained primarily supplementary units and reservists from such units.[182]

In the summer of 1939 the military leadership described the army as not being ready for a war, and this judgement is repeated in all relevant military memoirs.[183] It is true that the infantry divisions of the first wave had not reached their full strength; the training and above all the equipment of other large units had not reached a satisfactory level. Moreover, the state of the transportation system was not yet up to military requirements.[184] But the judgement was determined by the standard applied; the military leaders used the criteria provided by the August programme. Measured by these standards the authorized requirements had not been met as regards equipment, stocks, and above all the conversion of factories to help meet the need for prompt and sufficient supplies.

[182] Cf. Mueller-Hillebrand, *Heer*, i. 47–57, 68 ff.; Schottelius and Caspar, 'Organisation des Heeres', 387 ff.

[183] Cf. Müller, *Heer*, 407 ff., esp. the reaction to Hitler's speech of 22 Aug. 1939 (409 ff.); Breit, *Generale*, 185 ff. Cf. also many interesting details in Cooper, *German Army*.

[184] Rohde, *Wehrmachttransportwesen*, 37 ff.

The comparison with the situation before the First World War in the memorandum of 15 April 1939 shows clearly that Blomberg, Fritsch, and Beck based their old-fashioned armament planning, with its primarily military criteria, on inadequate premisses. Nowadays it was not a matter of battalions, divisions, and army corps, but of bar steel and the realities of the defence economy; these had been recognized by defence planners under the republic as the basis of any armaments programme, only to be neglected after 1933 in the euphoria over the possibilities created by Hitler for an apparently unlimited rearmament. Groener's principle in his directive of April 1930, which had been accepted only reluctantly by other military leaders at the time, that the tasks of the Wehrmacht should be defined strictly by political criteria, had now become reality. Hitler's political will and decisions replaced the independence of the army, which had been so jealously guarded. In this way rearmament proved to be the most important factor in the integration of the army into the National Socialist system of power.[185]

3. NAVAL REARMAMENT

(a) Armament Objectives of the Navy

Like the rearmament of the army, that of the navy in 1933–9 also had as its starting-point the armaments programmes of the Weimar Republic, the final version of which was the 'reorganization plan' of November 1932.[186] The measures planned for the navy in 1933 also involved violations of the limits imposed by the treaty of Versailles; but, unlike those envisaged for the army, they were sufficiently small to be kept secret. This was especially true of the skeleton organizations for submarines and naval aviation, as well as the relatively small increase in the number of officers and men (fifty additional officer cadets and 1,400 non-commissioned officers and men). The construction of an aircraft-carrier, the commissioning of the first submarines, and the expansion of naval aviation were planned for later.[187] Unlike army planning, which was carried on precipitately after December 1933, naval rearmament began much later. But it also profited from the abundant funds available after February 1933, which were largely used for purchasing weapons and ammunition and for coastal defence and harbour construction.[188]

In the end, however, the pace and extent of the naval build-up assumed forms quite comparable to those of the army. For example, the personnel strength (officers, non-commissioned officers, and men) rose from 15,000 in November of 1932 to 16,450 in 1933 and a total of 78,892 by the start of the war, a fivefold increase in barely seven years.[189] However, the problem of officer replacements did not lead

---

[185] Cf. III.III.2 and 3 below.   [186] Cf. III.I.3 above.

[187] For the specific dates of the reorganization measures envisaged for 1933 cf. Dülffer, *Weimar*, 565–6. On the foreign contacts of the navy, esp. in order to promote submarine construction, cf. ibid. 71 ff. and the literature cited.

[188] Ibid. 241 ff.

[189] Güth, 'Organisation der Kriegsmarine', 405, 439, 444. Cf. also the figures, including civil servants and employees, in *IMT* xxxv. 571 (report of Fleet Paymaster Thiele on 12 July 1944 on the development of the navy budget from 1930 to 1939).

to the same serious situation as in the army. Requirements were met by shortening the training period and raising the annual number of cadets accepted for officer training. In November 1932 the navy had 1,100 officers, and on 31 August 1939 there were 4,992 of all specialities.[190] The annual expenditure figures in Table III.11.4 provide a clear picture of the naval build-up. Compared with 1932, the figure for 1939 represented a more than twelvefold increase in funds. This rate of increase far exceeded even that of the Tirpitz naval construction programme before the First World War.[191]

TABLE III.11.4. *German annual expenditure on the navy* (1932–1939)

	Total budget (RMm.)	Ship construction	
		RMm.	% of total
1932	187.4	49.6	26.5
1933	311.8	76.1	24.4
1934	496.5	172.3	34.7
1935	695.1	287.0	41.3
1936	1,160.7	561.3	48.4
1937	1,478.5	603.1	40.8
1938	1,756.3	458.8	26.1
1939	2,389.9	545.1	22.8

Source: Dülffer, *Weimar*, 563.

The short-term nature of this development presents special difficulties in any attempt to provide a balanced analysis. The build-up of the imperial navy extended over more than a quarter of a century, which makes it easier to determine and describe the changing political and military factors involved, as well as the consequences of that expansion. In contrast, the Raeder programme was compressed into a period of a few years. However, this fact shows the almost insurmountable problems with which Raeder and the navy leadership were confronted in the years 1933–9. Tirpitz himself had repeatedly pointed out that the build-up of a fleet could not be carried out from one day to the next, but rather required decades. Raeder shared this opinion and emphasized the necessity of long-range naval planning in his first talk with Hitler.[192] An extreme example was the

---

[190] Güth, 'Organisation der Kriegsmarine', 415, 439.

[191] Cf. table xiv in Witt, *Finanzpolitik*, 380–1.

[192] On 25 Dec. 1905 Tirpitz wrote to Prince Heinrich of Prussia: 'One can no doubt raise armies overnight, as Scharnhorst and Gambetta did, but it takes a generation to build up a fleet with the necessary bases and reserves': cf. Berghahn, *Tirpitz-Plan*, 183. And Raeder told Hitler in Mar. 1933: 'Navy build-up: twenty years in advance. Not for today, but the total situation'; cf. Salewski, 'Marineleitung', 154.

pocket battleship *Deutschland*, whose development and construction extended over more than a decade from the first designs in the construction department of the navy high command to its commissioning on 1 April 1933.[193] The history of the *Deutschland* also illustrates the difficulties builders, engineers, shipyards, and numerous suppliers still faced in the 1930s. The problems began with the often wearisome process of combining military, design, and technical factors in the planning of a warship intended for certain tasks, and continued in the shipyards, which after years of inactivity suddenly had to deal with the special problems involved in warship construction. They needed much time to acquire the necessary experience. The Deutsche Werke in Kiel took five years to build the heavy cruiser *Blücher*, from the awarding of the contract to the commissioning; three and a half years for the light cruiser *Karlsruhe*, and almost three years for the first Type 34 destroyers.[194] These factors must also be considered in judging the actual results of the naval build-up by 1939.

Because of the short peacetime naval build-up and the basic complexity and long-term nature of naval armaments programmes, an interpretation of the extremely rapid growth of the German navy in this period must take as its main point of reference the general objectives of naval planning and not the details of the innumerable planning documents or their realization. It has already been pointed out that Raeder and the navy leadership did not accept the task Groener had set them of protecting the important sea routes in the Baltic, and concentrated their planning for the future more and more on the North Sea and even the Atlantic.[195] In Hitler a political leader became chancellor who, in his writings as well as his speeches, made no secret of his rejection of Tirpitz's naval policy, did not believe in a 'maritime' orientation, and evidently was quite prepared to accept only a 'coastal navy' in order to achieve an understanding with Great Britain. For Raeder and the other leading naval officers this was a completely unbearable thought.[196] The development of relations between the chief of the navy command and the new military and political leaders was therefore of decisive importance for the future course of naval policy. At best Neurath and Blomberg were favourably disposed towards the navy, but it had to be assumed that Blomberg would attempt to give greater priority to the rearmament of the army, which indeed the navy had never challenged. And Göring, who in addition to occupying numerous influential party and state positions had been appointed Reich commissioner for aviation, soon proved to be a powerful rival of the navy.

The first known conversation between Hitler and Raeder, which probably took place at the beginning of April 1933, must be seen against this background. Raeder had specific reasons for seeking a meeting with Hitler, namely to discuss measures against certain dangers resulting from the plan put forward by the British prime

---

[193] Sandhofer, 'Panzerschiff "A"', 35 ff.

[194] Cf. the table of construction dates by J. Rohwer in Dülffer, *Weimar*, 570 ff. The *Karlsruhe* was the third ship of the series, but the first cruiser built by Deutsche Werke.

[195] Cf. III.1.2 above, text to n. 55. On the war games of the early 1930s cf. Gemzell, *Raeder*, 31 ff., 42 ff.; also Schreiber, *Revisionismus* 87 ff.; id., 'Rolle Frankreichs'.

[196] Salewski, 'Marineleitung', 121 ff.; Dülffer, *Weimar*, 204 ff.

minister MacDonald at the disarmament conference, but in addition he probably sought the meeting to inform the chancellor about the military and political elements of the naval build-up and to win his support for the navy's goals.[197] The conversation cannot be reconstructed on the basis of Raeder's memorandum. In addition to an abundance of diplomatic and technical details, which very probably aroused Hitler's interest, Raeder clearly described the provisional aims of the naval construction programme, which seemed to be quite modest. He expressed his satisfaction with the number of ships permitted by the treaty of Versailles, although he later mentioned the necessity of building submarines and an aircraft-carrier, which were essential parts of the reorganization plan. His main aim was to achieve freedom of action in accordance with the claim for 'equal rights' that Germany had advanced in 1932. This led to a demand that the new pocket battleship 'D' planned for 1934 should have a tonnage and guns which would make it a match for the corresponding new French ship, the *Dunkerque*. Especially noteworthy were Raeder's political arguments at the beginning and end of his memorandum; the brief summary of broader perspectives was probably not unintentional. Raeder was aware that Hitler had rejected an acceleration of naval construction primarily because of its probable consequences for his policy towards Britain. For this reason Raeder declared at the start of the conversation that there could be no question of the 'navy ever regarding Britain as an enemy'.[198] His memorandum concluded with the single, underlined term 'eligibility as an ally' (*Bündnisfähigkeit*). He thus showed that he was a good pupil of his former superior Tirpitz—a master of political tactics—and attempted in this way to make the naval build-up appear as a harmless and even desirable component of Hitler's continental policy.

Although Raeder does not seem to have won Hitler's support for the 'cause of the navy' with his presentation, he was able to convince the chancellor of its value as a political instrument. In any case Hitler's speeches in Kiel and Wilhelmshaven show that he had changed his original position.[199] And in September 1933 Raeder was able to tell a group of naval officers: 'The chancellor very often mentions the importance of the naval build-up and is completely convinced of the significance of the navy as a factor in possible alliances and in projecting power.'[200] Raeder's skilfully established relations with Hitler (nothing similar seemed to have been attempted by Hammerstein or Fritsch) had positive but also negative effects on the further naval build-up.

For the navy as well as the army the period from 30 January until the end of 1933 was dominated by the uncertainty about developments at the disarmament conference and armament restrictions that might be expected from it. At the beginning of 1934, however, there was a marked acceleration in warship construction; in January contracts were awarded for two pocket battleships with

---

[197] Salewski, 'Marineleitung', 125 ff., 153 ff. (facsimile); Dülffer, *Weimar*, 244 ff.

[198] Dülffer's argument (*Weimar*, 245), which attributes this statement to Hitler, is unconvincing for reasons of both form and content; cf. also Salewski, 'Marineleitung', 126.

[199] Dülffer, *Weimar*, 248–9.

[200] Ibid. 249.

considerably increased tonnage ('D' and 'E') and for four destroyers with a tonnage more than double the Versailles limit; the preparations for submarine construction were continued.[201]

The stimulating effect on the naval leadership of an armaments policy increasingly freed from foreign-policy restrictions was evident in the fact that in March 1934 a new ship-replacement plan was drawn up and submitted to the chief of the navy high command which, in accordance with Raeder's wishes, disregarded international obligations and considered only Germany's needs. This plan envisaged the construction of eight pocket battleships, three aircraft-carriers, eighteen cruisers, forty-eight destroyers, and a total of seventy-two submarines; it was to be completed by 1949.[202] Orders were placed for the heavy cruisers *Blücher* and *Admiral Hipper*, as well as an additional five destroyers, in the autumn of 1934. This plan marked the final, clear break with the 'Versailles fleet'. Not only the tonnage of the individual ships, as Raeder had explained to Hitler a year earlier, but also the size of the future fleet was determined solely by Germany's needs.[203]

The fundamental importance of this decision is usually overshadowed by the endless arguments, decisions, and counter-decisions within the navy leadership, or between it and the foreign ministry or Hitler, about the size, armament, construction starts, and other details of build-up planning. It is not necessary to consider them here. It is more important to determine the military-policy objective of the plan of March 1934, only a small part of which was realized before the outbreak of war in spite of all attempts to accelerate its progress. A first indication was provided by the head of the 'group for naval conferences' in the navy command, Admiral von Freyberg-Eisenberg-Allmendingen, for many years the German naval representative at the Geneva disarmament conference. In connection with preparatory discussions for a possible German participation in the London naval conference planned for 1935, he told a representative of the foreign ministry at the beginning of February 1934 that the navy command was thinking about 'parity' with France.[204] In mid-February the head of the Marinekommandoamt (navy command office), Rear Admiral Groos, formulated this principle succinctly for the purpose of this naval construction plan: '(1) qualitative equality of rights, (2) quantitative equality with France and Italy, (3) short transitional periods pending equality.'[205] Finally, at the end of May or the beginning of June 1934 Raeder went beyond the March planning and directed all departments concerned to 'use the figure of one-third of the British tonnage as the standard for settling the strength of the German fleet'.[206] A little later this figure was changed to 35 per cent because it

---

[201] Dülffer, *Weimar*, 250 ff.; Salewski, 'Marineleitung', 132 ff. The pocket battleships involved were the *Scharnhorst* and the *Gneisenau*, which at first had a planned displacement of 18,000 t.

[202] Dülffer, *Weimar*, 566. On 1 Apr. 1934 the fleet consisted of the following ships built after the First World War: 1 pocket battleship (the *Deutschland*), 5 light cruisers (the *Emden, Königsberg, Karlsruhe, Köln*, and *Leipzig*), 12 torpedo-boats, 8 minesweepers, and 8 patrol boats; training ships, escort boats, etc. are not included. For the level of armaments in 1939 cf. III.II.3 (*c*) below.

[203] Dülffer, *Weimar*, 251 ff., 566; Salewski, 'Marineleitung', 133 ff.

[204] Salewski, *Seekriegsleitung*, i. 8.

[205] Dülffer, *Weimar*, 275.

[206] Salewski, *Seekriegsleitung*, i. 13.

corresponded exactly to the principle of 'parity' with France according to the Washington treaty of 1922.[207] However, officers in the navy command quickly came to the conclusion that the 35 per cent formula would not guarantee 'parity' with France, especially in regard to cruisers.[208] Accordingly, Groos demanded that 'For cruisers, destroyers, and submarines a different proportional figure must be set.' Raeder therefore ordered a new calculation based on a figure of 50 per cent. The results were satisfactory and were available in mid-June; the principle of parity with France was guaranteed by a relative strength of 1 to 2 compared with the British fleet.

This military calculation was combined with political considerations which Raeder had already summed up in the phrase 'eligibility as an ally' in his meeting with Hitler. In a conversation with the British naval attaché at the end of November 1933 he defined this idea more precisely:[209]

I could imagine that . . . a German fleet of a certain size, perhaps a squadron of large ships, could be very helpful for Britain. Given the quantitative equilibrium between the British and the American fleets, such a German squadron might be considered a political advantage for Britain, assuming good relations between Britain and Germany.

Within the navy command office itself there were doubts as to whether the 'British would find this argument very convincing'.[210] Raeder's idea of a common political or even military front against the United States had no chance of being understood by British political and military leaders. It was in fact a grotesque idea in view of the international situation at the end of 1933 and the beginning of 1934. But for the sake of the greater goal, hesitant expressions of doubt were pushed aside with such rhetorical phrases as: 'The world-power position of nations is identical with their ranking as sea powers.'[211]

It is clear that Raeder and the navy leadership considered a qualitative and quantitative parity with France to be the provisional goal of German fleet construction, and that they began to work towards the realization of this goal very early. The parity they sought was not only intended to prevent the French fleet from entering the Baltic in the event of war, but also to enable Germany to disrupt French communications in the Atlantic[212] and possibly the Mediterranean—areas in which Britain had a vital interest—with a strength equal to half that of the British fleet. The goal of parity with France was set and made binding in a situation in which Germany had withdrawn from the collective security system of the League of Nations, had begun a large army build-up, and was in the process of creating a

---

[207] On the international agreements after the First World War cf. Dülffer, *Weimar*, 130 ff. The Washington treaty had set ratios for the fleets of the USA, Britain, Japan, France, and Italy at 5 : 5 : 3 : 1.75 : 1.75.
[208] Ibid. 283 ff.; Salewski, *Seekriegsleitung*, i. 10; id., 'Marineleitung', 138–9.
[209] Salewski 'Marineleitung', 131.
[210] Id., *Seekriegsleitung*, i. 10.
[211] Memorandum of mid-June 1934; cf. ibid. 8; id., 'Marineleitung', 139.
[212] Salewski, 'Marineleitung', 136–7.

Luftwaffe which would threaten the security especially of Britain and France. Nevertheless the navy leadership continued to cling to the illusion that an agreement with Britain was a precondition for any naval policy and especially for one based on the demand for parity with France. One interpretation of this policy sums it up as follows:[213] 'The naval armaments programme was to be planned and carried out in such a way as to achieve the strategic purpose without calling in question its political preconditions'. This is a case in which the view of the navy leaders influenced their interpreter, for the 'strategic purpose', parity, was conceived without regard to political preconditions. Indeed, it showed a misunderstanding of the simplest political relationships. Whereas the Truppenamt, later the general staff, had always based its planning on the worst possible case and had even exaggerated in that direction, in this decisive point of its armaments planning the navy indulged in wishful thinking that cannot be explained even by Hitler's peace speeches. The historical roots of this thinking are clearly to be found in the Tirpitz tradition. A naval officer's criticism of Tirpitz's plans in February 1894, in the form of an analysis of the origin and significance of the term 'a fleet worthy of an alliance' (*allianzkräftig*) can also be applied to Raeder and the navy command under Hitler.[214] Raeder's phrase about 'eligibility' was a congenial but, in the final analysis, empty expression; its main motive was the wish to live up to the traditions of the navy and make it again an important national and international power factor. As was the case in the rearmament of the army, Hitler's will alone did not determine the extent of the naval armament programme. Even more than in the army, in the navy military considerations led to a significant expansion and acceleration of armament planning.

(b) Armament Goals and the Anglo-German Naval Agreement

The further development of naval planning was determined by the agreement concluded with Britain in June 1935. Previous discussions involving Hitler, the foreign ministry, and the navy command concerning international limitations on German naval strength had been conducted with varying intensity, with an eye to the international naval conference expected in 1935 as well as to a bilateral Anglo-German agreement. In accordance with Neurath's wishes it was decided on 22 June 1934, at a meeting at which Hitler, Neurath, Blomberg, and Raeder were present,[215] not to participate in an international conference. The project of an understanding with Britain, which corresponded to Hitler's tactical and political calculations, was thus given priority.

Raeder, however, used the opportunity presented by this top-level conference to submit the suggestions he had worked out since March for the naval build-up. 'Parity' with France was again the main goal, and it can be assumed that Raeder also

---

[213] Salewski, *Seekriegsleitung*, i. 9. For a different view cf. Schreiber, 'Kontinuität', 121 ff.

[214] Deist, *Flottenpolitik*, 45. In Feb. 1894 Curt von Maltzahn wrote that neither the chancellor nor the foreign ministry, but only the navy high command, demanded 'a fleet worthy of an alliance'; he concluded that not the 'alliance' but rather the 'fleet' was the real reason for this demand.

[215] Dülffer, *Weimar*, 286 ff.; Salewski, *Seekriegsleitung*, i. 14–15; id., 'Marineleitung', 138 ff.

argued for the 50 per cent solution worked out a few days before in the navy command office. However, he could not obtain a decision. It is probable that he encountered opposition from Neurath and Blomberg. It shows Raeder's persistence and his identification with the maximum programme of the navy that a few days later, on 27 June 1934, he took advantage of a report by the commanding officer of the light cruiser *Karlsruhe*, on return from a foreign tour, to discuss basic questions with Hitler again. In addition to the discussion of a number of routine matters, he was able to obtain Hitler's consent to a drastic increase in the tonnage of the already ordered pocket battleships 'D' and 'E' as well as to an increase in the size of their guns.[216] This fact was supposed to be kept as secret as the programme of submarine construction.

The most important topic of further armaments planning was contained in a single line of Raeder's notes on the main points of the conversation: 'Development of fl[eet] later perhaps against B[ritain]', and 'Maintain tradition. I: from 1936 on large ships with 35 cm. If money, yes. Alliance 1899. Situation of 1914?' There has been much discussion about the meaning of these words because they do not fit into the picture of the overall development of the German navy in the Third Reich, based on memoir literature and early historical interpretations. If one considers them in connection with the parity with France the navy command had been demanding for months, and its effects on relations with Britain, which were probably also discussed at the conference of 22 June, there is no doubt that, if only for a brief moment, Raeder admitted to himself the consequences of the naval policy he was pursuing. Of course his plans assumed a long, peaceful development, for naval construction was necessarily a long-term matter. But, he probably asked rhetorically, would an alliance with Britain in 1899 have prevented the First World War? As he was attached to Tirpitz's ideas, his answer to this question must have been negative. Consequently, the fleet had to be prepared for possible later action against Britain 'with some prospect of success', to use Beck's phrase. This was the reason for the demand for parity with France and for large ships with 35-cm. guns as soon as possible. Of course Raeder kept such visions of the future to himself; they were not discussed by leading naval officers, at least not at this time. Tirpitz had followed a similar strategy for more than a decade, but Hitler was not William II. He had his own plans and treated the navy as one instrument of power among others. In his skilful efforts to protect and promote the interests of the navy against the competing institutions of the executive by direct contacts with the chancellor, Raeder failed to see the basic contradiction between his own necessarily long-term armament planning and Hitler's primarily tactical, short-term political decisions. This explains the unpleasant awakening he experienced when Hitler switched to an anti-British policy too early to suit the navy.

The decisions of Raeder and the navy command in the winter of 1934–5 confirm this interpretation of events in the summer of 1934. The first result of Raeder's conversation with Hitler was the interruption, ordered on 15 July 1934, of work on

---

[216] On the following passage cf. Salewski, 'Marineleitung', 140 ff., 156; Dülffer, *Weimar*, 288 ff. The pocket battleships 'D' and 'E' later received the names *Gneisenau* and *Scharnhorst*.

the pocket battleships 'D' and 'E'. In spite of considerable difficulties which were entailed, the construction specifications were changed again. The ships were now to have a displacement of over 30,000 tons and a main armament of nine 28-cm. guns. At the beginning of July the construction department also received the order to prepare plans for the 'first battleship' (*Großkampfschiff*—i.e. the replacement ship 'F') in such a way that construction could be started on 1 April 1936.[217] Finally, the decision to build the first two heavy cruisers was taken; the contracts were awarded to shipyards in Kiel and Hamburg on 30 October 1934.

These internal directives were issued at a time when the prospects of diplomatic cover for a naval construction programme based on Hitler's and Raeder's wishes had seriously deteriorated. The Röhm affair and its consequences, as well as developments in Austria, had increased Germany's isolation and provoked reactions from Britain and France which seemed to indicate that German rearmament would not be tolerated. Therefore Hitler waited until November to make another attempt to discuss armaments questions with Great Britain. His talk on 27 November with Sir Eric Phipps, the ambassador in Berlin, is generally regarded as the beginning of the lengthy negotiations that led to the Anglo-German naval agreement of 15 June 1935.[218] It is not necessary to discuss here the political motives which caused Britain to conclude the agreement despite her awareness of the trend of German military policy.[219] The German motives were tactical from the very beginning. For Hitler every breach in Germany's isolation meant additional security for his decisions on army and Luftwaffe armaments, which were to be made in the spring of 1935 after the return of the Saar to Germany and whose consequences it would not be possible to conceal. But the programmatic aspects of Hitler's policy towards Britain, and especially the time-frame of the planning and carrying out of the naval build-up, permitted temporary compromises. In view of the decisions already made on ship construction, Hitler's opinion, repeatedly expressed during the negotiations, that the tasks of the German fleet lay primarily in the Baltic clearly showed his tactical intentions. The thinking of the navy leaders was also based on this tactical plan. Raeder assured the British at every opportunity that German fleet construction was not directed against Britain, but in contrast to Hitler, who publicly stressed the finality of the 35 per cent figure, he insisted that the agreement should be concluded for 'as short a period as possible (about five years) . . . especially as we can reach 35 per cent of the British tonnage in considerably less than ten years'.[220]

In mid-January the navy command noted with satisfaction that Hitler had 'recently stressed again that, in view of the strong pressure that can be expected from Britain and France after the Saar plebiscite, it is necessary to accelerate important armament plans even more than has been done up to now to achieve the . . . highest possible level by the time any negotiations take place'.[221] The navy

---

[217] Dülffer, *Weimar*, 294–5; Salewski, 'Marineleitung', 147. Salewski's view that in the years after 1933 the navy was in a primarily 'theoretical' planning phase ('England', 174 ff.) is not convincing.

[218] *DGFP*, c. iii, No. 358.

[219] On the naval agreement cf. Dülffer, *Weimar*, 338 ff., and Wiggershaus, *Flottenvertrag*. On the political significance of the agreement cf. Messerschmidt, IV.iii.2 below.

[220] Salewski, 'Marineleitung', 148.

[221] Dülffer, *Weimar*, 303–4.

leaders reacted to the general directive by awarding contracts for several additional destroyers and ordering the assembly of the first submarines, which had already been ordered in January 1934. Moreover, Raeder ordered that the date for the start of construction of the first aircraft-carrier be moved up to 1 April 1935, although no decisions had yet been taken as to its most important construction specifications.[222] More significant than these measures, in the spring of 1935, was no doubt the elimination of previous qualitative restrictions on ship construction on Hitler's initiative, a possibility that had also figured in the thinking of the navy leaders. Under the impression of the favourable development of the Anglo-German negotiations from his point of view, Hitler seemed to be ready to increase the tonnage and armaments of the pocket battleships 'D' and 'E' again, and ordered that the possibility be examined of increasing the size of the main guns of the new ship 'F' to 38 cm. The navy command did not change the decision to arm the ship with 35-cm. guns, but in the summer of 1935 they began the planning of infrastructure measures, e.g. floating docks, which far exceeded the size required by the first battleship ('F'), for which the contract was awarded in November 1935.[223]

The Anglo-German naval agreement of 18 June 1935 did not, therefore, represent a renunciation by the navy of its long-term goals. German political and military leaders did not consider it 'definitive', but rather as a 'provisional' settlement of the relative strength of German and British naval forces. 'In this respect the agreement of 1935 was only a form of camouflage, a diplomatic deception, and thus reflected Hitler's foreign-policy programme and Raeder's ideas about the future of the navy'.[224] It was decisive that, in the course of the preparatory talks in 1934–5, Raeder became convinced that the continental orientation of Hitler's political plans was quite compatible with the ambitious traditional naval goals concealed behind the phrase 'parity with France'.

In addition to the favourable prospects it opened for the navy, the agreement also represented an important immediate success. Apart from the enormous increase in prestige for Hitler, the framework guaranteed by the agreement permitted the navy greatly to expand its armaments programme. Instead of the approximately 144,000 tons permitted by the treaty of Versailles, it was now given a limit of 520,000 tons for warship construction,[225] a figure whose rapid realization would exceed the capacity of German shipyards. In April 1935 the negative side of the acceleration of rearmament constantly demanded by Hitler became evident for the first time. In a position paper the navy command pointed out that

an acceleration of the construction of pocket battleships, cruisers, destroyers, support ships, patrol boats, minesweepers, and aircraft-carriers is not possible, as construction periods cannot be shortened any more, the shipyards are operating at full capacity, and all available skilled workers are fully employed. . . . German shipyards cannot accept orders for additional ships until further notice.[226]

[222] Ibid. 304.
[223] Ibid. 313–14, 383. On the removal of qualitative restrictions cf. Salewski, 'Marineleitung', 146 ff.
[224] Salewski, 'Marineleitung', 149.
[225] Dülffer, *Weimar*, 348. Gemzell (*Raeder*, 42 n. 42) mentions a different figure (approx. 420,000 t.).
[226] Dülffer, *Weimar*, 315. It should be noted that, in spite of the greater construction activity, the fleet

The volume and pace of naval construction achieved since 1933 could not be more clearly described; the negotiations for an agreement with Great Britain had only functioned as a catalyst.

The reference to the limited capacity of German shipyards touched on a subject common to all three services. For the navy, as for the army and Luftwaffe, economic factors had a stronger effect on developments in the following years than did its own objectives and the further negotiations with Britain on the realization and application of the 35 per cent rule.

In the Anglo-German agreement an exception had been made for one category of ships, the submarine. In principle, parity in submarine tonnage had been agreed upon, but for the time being Germany agreed to build only 45 per cent of British tonnage. Since the First World War and the successes of German submarines against vital British sea links, the submarine had been the preferred weapon of the weaker naval power. For this reason Britain had never placed particular emphasis on the construction of a large submarine fleet of her own, and had concentrated on developing anti-submarine defences. Because of technical developments in that area—and international agreements limiting the use of submarines in wartime—the opinion prevailed in the leading circles of all great navies in the mid-1930s that the submarine had completely lost the role it had achieved in the First World War as one of the most effective instruments of naval warfare. Such views were to be found in Germany too, and even in the navy leadership they exercised some influence within the framework of the Tirpitz tradition, although the navy command had done everything possible since the signing of the treaty of Versailles to circumvent the prohibition on submarines for Germany.[227] As a result of its efforts thirty-six submarines of various types with a total displacement of about 14,500 tons had been ordered by the time the Anglo-German agreement was concluded. This figure amounted to two-thirds of the 22,000 tons permitted under the 45 per cent rule. Compared with the planning of March 1934, which envisaged a fleet of seventy-two submarines with a total displacement of 31,200 tons, the 45 per cent rule represented a considerable reduction.[228]

However, until the autumn of 1936 and later the submarine policy of the navy high command was determined not so much by the tonnage question as by internal discussion about the military role of the submarine. In the autumn of 1935 Captain Dönitz became commander of the first submarine flotilla, *Weddigen*; a year later he was appointed commander of submarines (Führer der U-Boote, or FdU) and entrusted with the development of principles for their wartime use and guidelines for training. He repeatedly expressed the opinion that it would be the main task of submarines in a future war to mass 'near enemy ports and concentration-points of enemy shipping'[229] to achieve the greatest possible effect. As he did not at first

grew only very slowly, Compared with its size on 1 Apr. 1934 (cf. n. 202 above), by 1 June 1935 it had increased by only 1 pocket battleship (*Admiral Scheer*), 8 minesweepers, and 4 patrol-boats. The first submarine was commissioned on 29 June 1935.

[227] Cf. Salewski, *Seekriegsleitung*, i. 21 ff.; Dülffer, *Weimar*, 386; Gemzell, *Organization*, 289 ff.

[228] Cf. Gemzell, *Organization*, 575; Salewski, *Seekriegsleitung*, i. 24.

[229] From Dönitz's memorandum of 21 Sept. 1935. Cf. Dülffer, *Weimar*, 387; also Dönitz, *Zehn Jahre*, 14 ff., 29 ff.

consider the possibility of a war with Britain, he, like most other officers concerned, regarded a submarine war against enemy trade as a matter of secondary importance. His intention was to use submarines primarily against the French fleet and troop transports, especially in the Mediterranean. His main tactic was the massed attack; for this reason he urged that future construction should concentrate essentially on one type of long-range submarine of 750 tons. Although the high command was not basically opposed to Dönitz's views, it did consider the construction of larger and more powerful submarines for possible use in the eastern Mediterranean and the Atlantic.[230] In general German submarine-construction policy remained unclear and without definite direction. After extensive discussions in 1936, Raeder decided at the end of October to accept a compromise by ordering the construction of seven submarines of the type Dönitz favoured and four larger ones (IX A, 1,032 tons).[231] In an order of 11 November the high command directed that the expansion of the submarine fleet was to be put in hand 'and completed with great speed and energy'. But in spite of the priority given to all orders for submarines, the additional contracts made possible by British submarine construction and awarded in 1937 show the same indecisiveness in planning.[232] For surface ships decisions had already been made in the winter of 1934–5 which were incompatible with the Anglo-German agreement.[233] There is no evidence of a comparable consistency based on clearly defined goals in the area of submarine construction. Nothing better illustrates this situation than the fact that, in 1937, submarine construction actually benefited from the economic difficulties affecting the warship programme. In June and July contracts were awarded for eight submarines of the smallest type because, unexpectedly, shipyard capacity became available.[234] In this case construction policy was determined neither by military nor by political calculations, but by economic possibilities—a foretaste of developments in coming years.

After the new year 1936–7 new possibilities presented themselves for the navy within the framework of the Anglo-German agreement. These were the result of the unsuccessful British attempt to preserve the quantitative and qualitative limitations of the Washington and London treaties affecting the great sea powers in a new, modified agreement. In spite of the intensive efforts of the British government, the naval conference which met in London from 9 December 1935 to 21 March 1936 had failed because of Japanese demands. Subsequent British attempts to prevent the expected naval arms race by an understanding on certain qualitative restrictions had also been unsuccessful. As was to be expected, the German government, which was included in these negotiations, clearly showed its lack of interest in an effective

---

[230] For submarines too tonnage is always given here as standard displacement; cf. the table by J. Rohwer in Dülffer, *Weimar*, 570 ff. On the submarine question cf. ibid. 386.; Salewski, *Seekriegsleitung*, i. 22 ff.

[231] Salewski, *Seekriegsleitung*, i. 28. The data cited should be corrected according to Dülffer, *Weimar*, 389 and 576. The first contract for four submarines of the type IX A had already been awarded at the end of July 1936.

[232] Cf. Dülffer, *Weimar*, 576–7. According to Dülffer contracts were awarded for 8 750-t., 5 1,050-t., and 8 290-t. submarines in 1937.

[233] Dülffer, *Weimar*, 313–14, 383. On the removal of the qualitative restrictions on ship construction cf. Salewski, 'Marineleitung', 146 ff.

[234] Dülffer, *Weimar*, 389. The submarines were of the type II c (290 t.)

international agreement. The lack of results in spite of all their efforts caused the British government to consider strengthening their own navy, thus automatically expanding the limits on German naval armaments under the 35 per cent rule.[235] When, therefore, the British delegate informed Ribbentrop in December 1936 that Britain would begin construction of five battleships in the coming year, this news necessarily had a stimulating effect on German naval planning. As early as the beginning of January 1937 Raeder ordered preparations for awarding the contracts for two additional battleships, whose displacement and armaments far exceeded previous limits. The planning of the navy high command for the coming years gives one the general impression that all restrictions had been deliberately pushed aside. A few months after Raeder's order of January 1937 the number of planned new battleships was raised from two to four and finally to six. The dimensions of the ships and the projected construction pace also increased. For many reasons, however, these ideas did not yet assume the form of concrete plans, and so there was not always a consistent, logical relationship between the individual projects. Finally, on 21 December 1937 Raeder approved a programme which not only envisaged the construction of six battleships but also added two more aircraft-carriers to the two already being built.[236] The technical shipyard department calculated on the basis of this plan that the navy would have 365 ships by 1944, which compared favourably with the 324 ships of the imperial navy in 1914. But for the time being the approval of the plan was not followed by the awarding of any contracts to shipyards; indeed, in 1937 not a single contract was awarded for large ships or even destroyers.

Compared with these grandiose plans, the fleet actually available to the German government as an instrument of military power was still quite modest in 1937. In 1933 it had consisted of the new pocket battleship *Deutschland*, the pre-1914 battleships (the *Schlesien*, the *Schleswig-Holstein*, and the *Hannover*), five light cruisers built in the late 1920s (the *Emden*, the *Königsberg*, the *Karlsruhe*, the *Köln*, and the *Leipzig*), twelve torpedo-boats, and a large number of smaller ships. By the end of 1937 the situation had improved to the point that almost all warships available were more modern. But the number of larger ships had declined. The fleet consisted of three pocket battleships, six light cruisers, seven destroyers, and twelve torpedo-boats.[237] The construction plan of 1937 must be understood against this background. Compared with the situation in 1933, the gap between plan and reality had become even larger.

The development of the submarine fleet and ship construction as a whole contrasts sharply with the basically long-term nature of naval armaments policy, which called for systematic planning. This situation was caused by two main factors. On the one hand, the relative stagnation of naval construction and specific planning was a result of the crisis in the defence economy in 1937, which led to

---

[235] Dülffer, *Weimar*, 402 ff.; Salewski, *Seekriegsleitung*, i. 38–9.

[236] Salewski, *Seekriegsleitung*, i. 39; Dülffer, *Weimar*, 455; Gemzell, *Raeder*, 83. Contracts for the aircraft carriers 'A' (*Graf Zeppelin*) and 'B' had already been awarded on 16 Nov. 1935. These ships had a displacement of 23,000 t. each; only 'B' was launched (8 Dec. 1938).

[237] Cf. nn. 202 and 226 above and the diagram in Güth, *Marine*, 157.

drastic reductions of quotas of raw materials and considerable difficulties in naval construction. On the other hand, achieving parity with France, which had been the main German goal since the beginning of the 1930s, had been overtaken by events. The more the decisions made in the winter of 1934–5 were carried out, and the more clearly the 'provisional' nature of the Anglo-German agreement began to affect planning and concrete armament measures, the more inescapable the question of future relations with Britain became. The taboo which had prevented discussion of a new confrontation with British sea power since the end of the First World War began to weaken. Raeder himself had taken the initiative in his talk with Hitler in June 1934 when he mentioned that the fleet could possibly be developed later for use against Britain. This meant that the goal of parity with France no longer had clear priority. After the conclusion of the Anglo-German agreement it gradually ceased to be one of the navy's major demands. When the news of British rearmament measures at the end of 1936 provided the impulse for new German planning, its scale could no longer be justified by the demand for parity. A new formula was necessary, but it was not developed at first, for that would have required the admission of the unthinkable, the possibility of a conflict with Britain.

The taboo against mentioning such a possibility reflected the assumption of benevolent British neutrality in the operational planning of the navy. It was significant and typical of new developments within the navy that this dogma largely lost its binding force in 1937. After a preliminary internal study the question of a naval war with Britain was discussed extensively within the naval air staff and among the highest-ranking commanders in the summer of 1937.[238] The fact itself is more important here than the details or the general tendency of these deliberations. The anti-British element of German naval ideology, dating back to Tirpitz, assumed an increasingly prominent role and prepared the way within the navy for the open change of course against Britain[239]—a change that was realized on the political level with the conference of 5 November 1937 and developments following the crisis of May 1938. This gave naval planning a new, comprehensive goal after the lack of certainty in this respect in previous years.

The reorientation of naval programmes was carried out at a time when armament measures in general, and especially ship construction, were beset by acute difficulties. In addition to technical problems (e.g. in the development of large engines) and the increasingly serious shortage of skilled workers, inadequate deliveries of steel and non-ferrous metals for the shipyards were a prime cause of the widening gap between planning goals and results. The seriousness of the problems in ship construction can be seen in a list prepared for Raeder of delays between March and August 1937 for all warships under construction.[240] Taking the

---

[238] Cf. Salewski, *Seekriegsleitung*, i. 20 ff., esp. 30 ff. It was quite typical that, at the same time, a broad discussion began within the navy leadership on the question of bases for a war in the Atlantic; cf. Gemzell, *Raeder*, 45 ff., 49 ff., 58 ff., 97 ff., 113 ff.; id., *Organization*, 278 ff., 282 ff.; Dülffer, 'Determinants', 154 ff.

[239] Cf. Schreiber, 'Reichsmarine', 159 ff.; id., *Revisionismus*, 109 ff.; id., 'Kontinuität', 123 ff.

[240] On war-economy developments in areas affecting the navy cf. Dülffer, *Weimar*, 425 ff., esp. 433 ff. On construction delays, ibid. 446, 568–9.

completion dates effective in March 1937 as a point of reference, the list showed
delays of up to eight months for bigger warships; the aircraft-carrier 'A' was even
found to be a year behind schedule. Delays for all ships, including torpedo-boats,
since the start of construction were between three and twenty-two months, with an
average of, if anything, over twelve months. In view of this situation an expansion
and acceleration of the construction programme, as had been envisaged earlier in
1937, had to be considered illusory. If Raeder wanted to maintain the aims of his
naval policy, he had to give absolute priority to the struggle for adequate steel and
copper allotments and sufficient deliveries to the shipyards of special sheet metal for
submarines. Raeder accepted this objective and, in a letter of 25 October 1937,
urged Blomberg to obtain an immediate decision from Hitler on the naval
armaments programme.[241] This problem was also discussed at the conference
attended by Hitler, Foreign Minister von Neurath, and the leading officers of
the Wehrmacht on 5 November 1937, recorded in the well-known 'Hossbach
memorandum'. According to this, Raeder did not express any opinion concerning
Hitler's policy of solving the 'German question' by force no later than 1943–5; nor
did he join Blomberg and Fritsch in contesting Hitler's views on the probable
attitude of Britain and France to German action against Austria and Czechoslovakia. He was more interested in the second part of the conference, about which
Colonel Hossbach did not take any notes and in which the continuation of
rearmament was discussed. In this area Raeder was able to have his way; the navy
was granted a monthly steel allocation of 74,000 tons instead of the previous 45,000
tons. This permitted the realization of the armaments programme based on the
decisions of 1935.

In Raeder's eyes the decision on armaments policy, the picture drawn by Hitler of
the European power-constellation, his goals and suggested solutions, were a confirmation of the previous policy of naval build-up. Hitler had recognized that the
economic goal of complete autarky could not be achieved in the foreseeable future.
Germany would remain dependent on imports from overseas, and the protection of
the necessary sea links was the traditional and undisputed task of the navy. Hitler's
extensive discussion of the British reaction to German expansion in east central
Europe, and the criticism from the army leaders on this very point, necessarily
strengthened Raeder's conviction, which he had already expressed in 1934, that
naval construction later might have to be directed against Britain. Although Hitler
insisted on his belief that Britain would not intervene in a conflict involving
Germany against Czechoslovakia and Austria, even he could no longer completely
rule this out as a 'worst case'. For Raeder the increasing signs of Hitler's turning
against Britain were of the utmost significance, although the latter's overall aims
were still essentially continental. The change in Hitler's plans confirmed and

---

[241] Dülffer (*Weimar*, 446 ff.) was the first to point out the war economy background of the conference
of 5 Nov. 1937; cf. now also Sarholz (*Auswirkungen*, 248 ff.), discussing the detailed preparations of the
high commands of the Wehrmacht services for the defence economy conference. See also Schreiber,
Revisionismus, III ff. On the conference of 5 Nov. 1937 cf. also III.II.2 (*d*) above (the army), III.II.4 (*b*)
below (the Luftwaffe), and III.III.4 below.

strengthened the anti-British elements which had long been part of Raeder's own policy. Thus, the conference of 5 November 1937 had more important consequences for the navy than the approval of the desired monthly steel allocation. Before the end of November, Raeder ordered a study of the possibilities of expanding the programme of submarine construction.[242] This is rightly considered to have been a preparatory measure for a possible conflict with Britain. The results of the study, which were available by mid-January 1938, showed that the shipyards building submarines were not able to accept any new orders. Other shipyards demanded the allocation of additional workers before accepting such orders. It became clear that there could be no question of expanding the programme of submarine construction before the spring of 1939.[243]

Raeder's approval of the construction programme of 21 December 1937 was no doubt also strongly influenced by the prospects Hitler had outlined at the conference of 5 November. But, as with the submarine problem, the gap between planning and reality was becoming wider and wider. The navy had been promised a monthly allocation of 74,000 tons of steel in November 1937, but apparently it was not able to use such a quantity. For April and May 1938 it requested only 53,000 tons, and in June 71,000 tons, which was still below its own minimum estimated requirements.[244] This situation was certainly the result of many different factors. But the facts mentioned above give the impression that, in addition to the shortage of workers, the lack of co-ordination of armament measures by the controlling agencies of the navy and the 'war economy' as a whole was responsible for these conditions.

The development of the navy in the three years after the negotiations leading to the Anglo-German agreement presents a picture in some respects confusing and contradictory. The important decisions on warship construction were changed several times and were not based on a detailed, structurally well-thought-out plan. They were rather the results of the adaptation of traditional naval thinking and planning to prevailing national and international political conditions. Raeder's decisions on ship construction consequently lacked a long-term perspective. Moreover, the concrete armament measures suffered from the effects of Versailles on ship design and actual building. In addition, warship construction was affected more than other armament plans by the general crisis of the defence economy, which made a consistent policy in this area difficult and in some respects impossible.

The serious shortages at both levels of armament policy had a cumulative effect, and this fact again clearly shows the importance of the lack of clear objectives until 1938. The gradual realization, over a period of four years, that the demand for parity with France and the operational plans based on it made a political and strategic confrontation with Britain inevitable can be explained in the final analysis only in psychological terms. Just as the trauma of November 1918 dominated the thinking

---

[242] Within the framework of the 100% rule for this ship category in the Anglo-German agreement.

[243] Salewski, *Seekriegsleitung*, i. 37–8; Dülffer, *Weimar*, 452 ff.

[244] Dülffer, *Weimar*, 458 ff.

of the navy until long after the Second World War,[245] the generally accepted maxim that Britain must be excluded from any possible coalition against Germany—itself a result of the experience of the Tirpitz era and the First World War, but also of the weakness of the German navy in the Weimar period—prevented the navy leaders from understanding the consequences of their own actions. Raeder himself, who was undoubtedly aware of the temporary nature of this maxim, is the best example of this fact and of the pronounced service particularism which only made worse the serious lack of realism in German naval policy. The stages by which clarity was achieved, as well as the delaying elements, have been described above. The strength of autistic thinking in the navy leadership is shown by the fact that Raeder waited for six months after the conference of 5 November 1937, at which a confrontation with Britain was mentioned as a real possibility, before discussing it with a larger group of naval officers.[246] But an initiative from Hitler was necessary to induce the navy command to draw the logical conclusion from this situation.

(c) The 'Z-plan' Fleet against Britain

The crisis resulting from the partial Czechoslovak mobilization of 20–1 May 1938[247] caused Hitler to set new priorities for the naval construction programme also. On 24 May his naval adjutant, Lieutenant-Commander von Puttkamer, sent the navy commander-in-chief a list of points to be discussed at a high-level conference of military leaders and the foreign ministry, scheduled for the end of May. The list clearly showed Hitler's intentions.[248] He was mainly concerned about accelerating the construction of battleships and expanding the submarine fleet up to full planned strength as rapidly as possible. At the conference at the navy high command some of Hitler's demands were criticized; for example, the suggested changes in the armament of the battleships *Scharnhorst* and *Gneisenau* were rejected. But under the impression of Raeder's statement that Hitler now expected Britain and France to be on the enemy side in the event of a conflict, the participants attempted to make the almost impossible seem possible. And Raeder himself did not seem prepared to convey to Hitler unwelcome suggestions from his subordinates attending the conference, viz. that ambitious state and Party programmes should be reduced to achieve the desired acceleration of rearmament.

There is no information concerning any specific decisions on naval rearmament at the chancellor's conference of top military leaders on 28 May 1938. However, the indirect consequences of Puttkamer's inquiry and Hitler's address,[249] which left no doubt as to his determination to settle the 'German question' by force, meant that, for Raeder and other officers of the Navy High Command, discussion of an Anglo-

---

[245] Cf. Salewski, 'Selbstverständnis', 69 ff.; id.; 'Schlachtschiffe', 53 ff. Salewski exaggerates the effect of Hitler's policy towards Britain on the armament policy of the navy in 'England', 177.

[246] Dülffer, *Weimar*, 461 ff. (final discussion of the war games of 1937–8 on 12 Apr. 1938 in Kiel). On the change to a policy against Britain cf. above all Schreiber. 'Kontinuität', 101 ff., and id., 'Strategisches Lagebild', 175 ff.

[247] Cf. III.II.2 (d) above; III.II.4 (b), III.III.4, and IV.V.7 (b) below.

[248] Cf. Salewski, *Seekriegsleitung*, i. 41 ff.; Dülffer, *Weimar*, 468 ff.; Gemzell, *Raeder*, 79 ff.

[249] Cf. Domarus, i. 868 ff.

German naval confrontation, a forbidden subject since the end of the First World War, was now permitted again. The logical steps in regard to strategy and ship construction were discussed and taken, at first cautiously and with restraint and then with astonishing speed, within the next six months. In June 1938 Raeder instructed Commander Heye of the operations department of the naval war staff to prepare a memorandum on the possibility of 'conducting a naval war against Britain and the resulting requirements for strategic objectives and the build-up of the navy'.[250]

It should be noted that this order provoked the first politically motivated criticism from within the navy leadership of the attack on Czechoslovakia which Hitler had been planning since the end of May. Heye opposed an over-hasty, risky action, which could only endanger 'the great goals' Germany had set for herself and would result in 'encirclement' by the stronger enemy coalition. The chief of staff of the naval war staff, Vice-Admiral Guse, supported Heye and recommended that Raeder, together with the commander-in-chief of the army, should make clear to Hitler the high risks and possible consequences. But Raeder, who was never able to free himself from narrow departmental thinking, refused to follow the urging of his subordinates and abandon his reserve. He said nothing in this regard to Hitler, as he had said nothing on 5 November 1937.[251]

The first draft of Heye's memorandum on the possibility of conducting a naval war against Britain was submitted in August 1938.[252] Heye assumed that, in a war with Britain, Germany would not be able to protect her own imports from overseas and that the navy would never have the strength to overcome a British blockade for any significant length of time. Therefore the objective of such a war could only be to disrupt British overseas trade. This definition of the strategic objective affected the composition of the fleet. Heye and Vice-Admiral Guse favoured a cruiser war and thus the construction of fast pocket battleships with great cruising range, small cruisers, and submarines. In this connection Heye stressed that to be successful a war against British trade could not be restricted to the massive use of submarines. If one considers the emphasis placed on the construction of bigger ships after 1934 and the interest with which Hitler himself followed and influenced the battleship construction programme in those years, the course advocated by Heye and Guse can correctly be termed an alternative plan with, however, poor chances of being realized. For this reason Heye, who was probably aware that many of his superiors did not share his opinions, treated the question of the future use of battleships very cautiously and, in the end, evasively. On the one hand, he conceded that they would have a protective function in the North Sea and be used to support the cruiser war in the Atlantic. But on the other hand he also demanded for such tasks a new type of battleship and saw its main function in a war with France as fighting the French

---

[250] Cf. Salewski, *Seekriegsleitung*, i. 44 ff.; Dülffer, *Weimar*, 475.

[251] Guse and Heye acted in agreement with the chief of the general staff. Cf. Gemzell, *Raeder*, 169 ff.; Dülffer, *Weimar*, 475–6; cf. also III.iii.4 below.

[252] On the memorandum cf. Salewski, *Seekriegsleitung*, i. 45 ff.; Dülffer, *Weimar*, 476 ff. The final version of the memorandum is printed in Salewski, *Seekriegsleitung*, iii. 28 ff.

battle fleet. The assignment of these tasks in a memorandum concerned with the conduct of a naval war against Britain shows Heye's uncertainty about the specific role of battleships in his plan for a cruiser war. Although this followed logically from the given premises, the weak point of the memorandum was evident in the question of how a cruiser war in distant oceans could be supported in view of the decisive geographical facts which Germany had to take into account. Even assuming that at the outbreak of a war all ships suitable for cruiser warfare were in the Atlantic and could be supported in the short term by supply ships, this form of war against British trade would be over in three months at the latest. As a solution Heye recommended the acquisition of bases or extending German control of the coast, especially the occupation of the French coast of the Channel as far as Brest.

The planning committee appointed by Raeder in mid-August in connection with Heye's memorandum was given the task of working out a *'uniform view* of strategic principles for the overall build-up of the navy'. It concerned itself first with the highly political question of bases, but was naturally unable to produce more than a list of wishes in order of priority.[253] The chief of staff of the naval war staff prevented any further discussion with his remark that the committee should base its planning on 'present geographical conditions'. As Raeder himself did not demand a clarification of this political precondition of the strategic plan, it did not acquire the clear outlines which would have made it, as a whole or in its various parts, a point of reference for future planning.

As was to be expected, the committee's discussions concentrated on the tasks of battleships within the basic plan for cruiser warfare, which had been approved in principle. The majority of members strongly supported the retention of a strong battle fleet but could not refute Heye's arguments that battleships as a rule had no essential function in a cruiser war in the Atlantic. However, they were also not able to accept Heye's plan, which sought to restrict the use of battleships primarily to the improbable case of an isolated Franco-German conflict. This resulted in a paradoxical situation in which the chief of staff of the naval war staff concluded at the end of the discussion that all participants agreed that battleships were necessary, but that no consensus regarding their use could be achieved for the time being.[254] The committee did, however, develop precise recommendations concerning the additional types of ships necessary for a cruiser war. Such a war against British trade was to be conducted essentially by pocket battleships of about 19,000 tons supported by light cruisers (Type M, about 7,800 tons) and destroyers. Neither the submarine question nor the problem of air support was discussed in detail, nor were experts consulted for advice on these matters.

On Raeder's orders only the commander-in-chief of the fleet, Admiral Carls, and his successor, Admiral Boehm, were given the opportunity to submit their views. They too supported the basic ideas of Heye's memorandum, made suggestions on

[253] Cf. Salewski, *Seekriegsleitung*, i. 51 ff.; Dülffer, *Weimar*, 481 ff.; Gemzell, *Raeder*, 84 ff. The first session of the committee took place on 23 Sept. 1938. On the problem of bases cf. n. 238 above. On the following passages cf. also Schreiber, *Revisionismus*, 122 ff.. 135 ff.; id., 'Kontinuität', 124 ff.
[254] Cf. Salewski, *Seekriegsleitung*, i. 48-9, 52 ff.; Dülffer, *Weimar*, 482 ff.

individual questions, and thus strongly influenced the final decisions on the specific types of ships suggested by the committee.[255] Carls also took advantage of the opportunity to repeat ideas about world power based on naval strength which had influenced the navy's thinking since the turn of the century:

If, in accordance with the will of the Führer, Germany is to achieve a firm world-power position, it will need, in addition to sufficient colonies, secure sea routes and access to the high seas . . . A war against Britain means a war against the Empire, against France, probably also against Russia and a number of countries overseas, in other words against one-half or two-thirds of the whole world.[256]

But Carls was not content to describe such grandiose ideas; he also believed he could show a way to achieve success and recommended that the war be thoroughly prepared economically, politically, and militarily. He called for the conquest of the French Atlantic coast, Holland, and Denmark in order to expand Germany's base for naval operations, and suggested the rapid construction of a powerful home fleet whose area of operations should include the ocean west of Britain. In addition he proposed the construction of a high-seas fleet comprising four separate task-forces, each consisting of a battle cruiser, a heavy cruiser, and aircraft-carriers, as well as destroyers, submarines, and supply ships, and each able to operate independently in the oceans of the world. This was certainly an alternative to Heye's comparatively modest plans, but it was completely unrealistic and betrayed a degree of self-delusion astonishing for a military leader in a position of great responsibility. Carls's ideas are clear proof of the continued influence of the Tirpitz tradition and the mentality of those to whom the Anglo-German agreement with its 35 per cent rule, and the demand for parity with France, were only temporary arrangements. To these officers, the change to a policy openly directed against Britain in the spring of 1938 came as shock only in the sense that it was announced at the wrong time, before the navy's armament programme had been completed.[257]

In the final analysis these apocalyptic visions had no effect on the work of the planning committee. Its members had been instructed to develop a coherent plan by mid-October for conducting a naval war against Britain and for the necessary fleet. For this reason they worked under a certain pressure, which did not permit adequate discussion and a balanced report on the complex problems involved. In view of these factors, it is not surprising that Heye's basic ideas were included in the final memorandum with only slight modifications. The report of the committee to Raeder on 31 October was based on the memorandum. The committee had agreed on a construction plan for a 'provisional target' of ten battleships, fifteen pocket battleships, five heavy, twenty-four light, and thirty-six small cruisers, eight aircraft-carriers, and 249 submarines.[258] The construction possibilities until 1942–3 had been examined for only a small number of the new ships. In accordance with

---

[255] Dülffer, *Weimar*, 486 ff.; Salewski, *Seekriegsleitung*, i. 55–6; Gemzell, *Raeder*, 87 ff. On an additional memorandum by Carls cf. Gemzell, *Raeder*, 97 ff.

[256] Dülffer, *Weimar*, 486–7 ff.

[257] Cf. Schreiber, 'Reichsmarine', 175–6.

[258] Cf. Salewski, *Seekriegsleitung*, iii, 62–3; Gemzell, *Raeder*, 92 ff.

Hitler's ideas at the end of May 1938, which were the basis of all planning, concrete naval armament measures were to be accelerated. Hitler wanted ships, not plans. Therefore the committee had suggested the construction of two battleships and four pocket battleships; one variant of this plan envisaged completing the pocket battleships as early as 1 December 1942 and postponing the construction of the battleships until 1945.[259]

This alternative plan reflected the conclusions of a conference at the navy high command on 19 August 1938. At the conference Raeder had blamed the armament firms for the continuing construction delays, and at the same time announced the acceleration and expansion of the previous construction programme (the 35 per cent fleet plus six battleships). Already at this time he based his arguments on the conclusions of Heye's study. In addition to the battleships, the construction of battle cruisers and pocket battleships was discussed, and Raeder even considered that four of the additional battleships of the H type might be dropped to make possible the construction of fast battle cruisers and pocket battleships for service in the Atlantic. A number of construction proposals were then worked out in August and September 1938, all involving a combination of battleships and pocket battleships.[260] The question which type of ship should be given priority was still undecided when the conclusions of the planning committee and the parallel construction planning of the high command were presented to the commander-in-chief at the conference of 31 October.

The conference was called to help prepare Raeder's report to Hitler on future naval construction programmes, which was presented on 1 November 1938. At the conference with his advisers Raeder seems to have expressed his preference for pocket battleships; he approved the proposal to construct four such ships and two battleships by mid-1944. This supports the conclusion that, after the preparatory work by Heye and the planning committee, the navy leadership decided to conduct a cruiser war against Britain in the Atlantic with battleships and pocket battleships. Because of the time required for the build-up of the fleet recommended by the committee, which had itself been described as only a 'provisional target', even a man like Raeder, whose mental horizon was largely limited to matters concerning the navy, must have had doubts that naval armaments could keep pace with political developments after the events of September and October 1938 and Hitler's directive of 21 October announcing his intention to 'finish off the remainder of Czechoslovakia'.[261] Considered from this perspective, long-term planning lost much of its fascination, whereas problems such as the rational use of shipyard capacity and the struggle for raw-material allocations and skilled workers again became more important.

There are no records of Raeder's report to Hitler and its results. On 7 November, however, Raeder sent the chief of the Wehrmacht high command, Keitel, a letter from which it is clear that Hitler had not only described the realization of the

[259] On the variants of the plan cf. Salewski, *Seekriegsleitung*, i, 57; Dülffer, *Weimar*, 492.
[260] Dülffer, *Weimar*, 478 ff.
[261] Cf. III.III.4 below, text to nn. 97–100.

previous programme as especially urgent but had also approved the inclusion of additional types of ships, i.e. pocket battleships. Raeder urged Keitel to order that priority be given to supplying all firms producing armaments for the navy with raw materials and sufficient workers. He demanded openly that the naval construction programme be given priority over the programmes of the other services, on the same footing as the all-important export orders. Keitel complied with this demand at first by instructing the commanders-in-chief to submit detailed versions of their armaments programmes, as Hitler had decided to 'spread the total rearmament of the Wehrmacht over several years according to uniform criteria and urgency'.[262] The struggle for shares of the total economic potential for armaments purposes approached a new climax. In the naval war staff the fear arose that Hitler might find it necessary to 'temporarily entrust tasks to other services (e.g. the Luftwaffe) which, by their very nature, can only be fulfilled by the navy'. Again the navy leadership came under pressure to find ways and means to achieve the greatest possible acceleration of the ship construction programme. A study of 17 November by the naval war staff came to the conclusion that this could only be accomplished if 'priority is given to creating forces suited to conducting an independent war at sea'. This meant that the submarine construction programme had to be completed and eight of the twelve planned pocket battleships, as well as eighteen of the twenty-four planned light cruisers, built by 1943.[263] The battleships and aircraft-carriers with their extremely long construction periods were, on the other hand, pushed into the background. But Hitler had long indicated that he intended to insist on accelerating the construction of the planned six H-type battleships. The question was, therefore, whether Raeder would be able to persuade Hitler of the prospects of successful cruiser warfare against Britain and the need for a corresponding programme of ship construction.

At the end of November another meeting took place between Raeder and Hitler, which ended with Raeder tendering his resignation.[264] According to him Hitler had 'criticized everything we are building and planning in a disparaging way'. From the plan subsequently worked out by the high command, and especially the so-called 'Z plan', it is clear that Raeder had not been able to persuade Hitler to give priority to the construction of pocket battleships. Hitler had not accepted the cruiser-warfare strategy worked out by Heye and supported by Raeder, and had insisted on accelerating the construction of battleships. Although he was at pains to normalize his personal relations with Raeder in the days thereafter, he refused to change his mind on this point.

At the beginning of December Rear-Admiral Fuchs, the head of the fleet department, submitted two construction plans, 'X' and 'Y', in which he attempted to find a way to proceed simultaneously with the construction of battleships and pocket battleships. But, following a further conversation with Hitler on 9 December, Raeder found it necessary to order that the completion of four

[262] Dülffer, *Weimar*, 492–3, 495.
[263] Ibid. 493–4.
[264] Ibid. 496.

battleships and four pocket battleships be planned for the end of 1943. This decision, which meant an enormous acceleration compared with plans 'X' and 'Y', formed the basis of the alternative construction plan 'Z', the later 'Z plan'. When Raeder finally submitted this plan to Hitler on 17 January 1939, however, Hitler rejected it too as insufficient and ordered the construction of six battleships by 1944.[265]

All discussions within the navy high command had come to the conclusion that Hitler's order could only be carried out if a much larger share of total armaments-industry potential were devoted to naval projects. And Raeder seized this opportunity; as a result of Hitler's insistence on the accelerated construction of six battleships, his request to Keitel in November 1938 that naval armaments be given priority received the necessary support. As early as December he was able to obtain a reduction of commercial ship construction in favour of the navy. Now he demanded that 'priority over all other government and export orders be given to deliveries for the navy by industries directly or indirectly connected with the ship-construction programme'. On 27 January 1939 Hitler signed the necessary directive, to which Göring, the commander-in-chief of the Luftwaffe and commissioner for the Four-year Plan, agreed after Raeder had renounced the independent development of naval aviation units.[266] Hitler's decision represented a success for the navy leadership—which, however, as soon became clear, was very short-lived. The acceleration of battleship construction by all possible means was indeed compatible with the navy's own plan for a war against Britain, but the basic strategic ideas of that plan had never reached the stage of final clarity about the proper ships for the necessary fleet. Hitler's stubborn insistence on the construction of battleships in connection with his directive of 27 January seemed, as in the Tirpitz era, to open the way to the build-up of a fleet embodying Germany's claim to be a sea power and thus, in the navy's view, a world power.

As early as 23 January Raeder had appointed the head of the fleet department, Rear-Admiral Fuchs, to be his special representative for the battleship programme. In an astonishingly short time the contracts for the battleships 'H' and 'N' were awarded, large-scale material deliveries started, and construction began. But there were delays. Deliveries of non-ferrous metals and bar steel were insufficient, and the problem of obtaining enough workers was even more serious. As early as the autumn of 1938 the personnel problem could only be solved, to some extent, by compulsory service, which had been introduced in July of that year. But because of the general labour shortage, requirements for the battleship programme for 1939 could not be met even in this way. After Hitler's directive of 27 January, co-operation with the other services was impaired. In addition, the housing situation of the shipyard workers and the extra pay for compulsory workers led at times to very poor morale in the work-force and fears of possible unrest.[267]

[265] Dülffer, *Weimar*, 497 ff.; Salewski, *Seekriegsleitung*, i. 58–9.

[266] Salewski, *Seekriegsleitung*, i, 58, 253; Dülffer, *Weimar*, 499 ff., esp. 502.

[267] Dülffer, *Weimar*, 501, 504 ff.; Salewski, *Seekriegsleitung*, i. 61 ff. For the battleships 'H' and 'J' with a displacement of 56,200 t. each, contracts were awarded on 14 Apr. 1939. The keels were laid on 15 July and 15 Aug. 1939. Contracts for the battleships 'K', 'L', 'M', and 'N' were awarded on 25 May 1939, but the keels were never laid.

In addition to the construction of battleships, whose number Hitler had raised from the four envisaged in the alternative plan 'Z' to six, the 'Z plan' included the construction of four pocket battleships by the end of 1943. But this had to be changed as early as June 1939, when the intention to arm the battleships *Scharnhorst* and *Gneisenau* with larger guns was abandoned, which meant that the already ordered 38-cm. guns became available for other uses. Although he encountered opposition in the navy high command, Raeder decided in this situation to build three battle cruisers of 32,000 tons each, for which contracts were awarded in August 1939.[268] For armament-organizational reasons the 'Z plan' was thus reduced to a torso even before the outbreak of war put an abrupt end to the construction of heavy ships. One searches in vain for a guiding principle in the German naval construction programme at this time.

The enormous increase in naval armaments in 1939 suffered not only from war-economic and programmatic weaknesses; its base, Hitler's directive of 27 January, turned out to be not very solid. The other services felt discriminated against, as they were under considerable pressure to achieve their own armament programmes. For this reason they opposed the preferential treatment given the navy. Göring in particular indicated on various occasions that he was not prepared to accept Hitler's decision as final. But his first attempt to persuade Hitler to change it, in May 1939, was unsuccessful. In agreement with Göring, General Thomas, the head of the war economy staff, also tried to get Hitler to change his mind. At the end of June he tried to induce his superior, General Keitel, to attempt to influence Hitler in this matter. He was able to obtain an order to study the negative effects of the January directive on the industries concerned. At the end of August Göring and Thomas undertook a new initiative. Göring persuaded Hitler to give the same priority to air-force programmes that had been given to those of the navy.[269] This represented a breach that could be widened and which decisively weakened the navy's privileged position. The directive of 27 January thus represented only a short-lived victory for the navy in the inter-service struggle for armament resources. This situation would sooner or later create difficulties for the realization of the 'Z plan'.

An additional problem should be mentioned which shows the Utopian character of the 'Z plan' much more clearly. According to an estimate of 31 December 1938 by the department of war economy in the navy high command, the fuel-oil mobilization requirements for the 'Z-plan' fleet amounted to 6 million tons and the corresponding diesel-oil requirements to 2 million. In 1938 total German consumption of mineral-oil products reached 6,150,000 tons, of which only 2,400,000 were produced domestically. The aim of naval planning was to be able to fight a war for twelve months with the completed 'Z-plan' fleet. Fuel requirements were to be met by advance storage of fuel and increasing the allocated share of domestic production. The navy planned to build storage tanks with a total capacity of ten million cubic metres by 1945. These plans did not, of course, take into consideration the demands and requirements of the other two services.[270]

---

[268] Dülffer, *Weimar*, 503–4. The construction designations for the battle cruisers were 'O', 'P', and 'Q'.   [269] Ibid. 510–11.

[270] Meier-Dörnberg, *Ölversorgung*, 29–30. On the oil supply of the navy cf. also Rasch,

When Britain declared war on Germany on 3 September 1939, Raeder assessed the results of more than six years of naval rearmament:

As far as the navy is concerned, it is of course by no means ready for the big war against Britain in the autumn of 1939 . . . The surface ships are so few and so weak compared with the British fleet that, even if fully committed, they would only be able to show that they know how to die with honour and are resolved in this way to lay the foundation for a new build-up later'.[271]

Indeed, at the outbreak of war the navy had only two battleships, two pocket battleships, one heavy and six light cruisers, twenty-one destroyers, twelve torpedo boats, and fifty-seven submarines.[272]

Raeder's resigned assessment of the situation reflected the results of an armaments policy which had been frustrated by the tension between the long periods of time required for a naval build-up and short-term political decisions. For many years the negative aspects of this fundamental dilemma, which Tirpitz had also once faced, were made more serious by the unclear, contradictory goals of German naval policy, which were themselves consequences of the shock of the defeat suffered by the imperial navy in the First World War. Raeder, who was particularly aware of the position of the navy in relation to the other services—itself a result of the complexity and long-term nature of naval construction—had attempted, as had his mentor Tirpitz, to compensate for this weakness by establishing direct contact with the political leadership of the country. In this way he was able to obtain a certain special position for the navy; in his eyes this was justified by its far-reaching political significance. But he could not prevent political decisions from playing an increasingly important role in the naval construction programme as a direct result of that position. Raeder's remarks[273] in his memorandum of 3 September 1939, which are reminiscent of the plan to engage the high seas fleet in battle in October 1918, clearly show the extent of his mortification over the failure to achieve his political and strategic goals as well as to realize his own professional ambitions.

4. THE BUILD-UP OF THE LUFTWAFFE

More than the rearmament of the army and the navy, the spectacular development of the Luftwaffe in the six years from 1933 until the outbreak of the war aroused the boundless admiration as well as the dark forebodings of contemporaries. Even today the inventions and brilliant technical achievements of those years in the area of

---

'Mineralölpolitik', 71 ff. On similar Utopian planning of the Luftwaffe cf. III.II.4 below, also Volkmann, II.v.5 above.

[271] *Lagevorträge*, 20–1.

[272] Cf. nn. 203 and 227, also III.II.3 (*b*) above. The number of ships envisaged in the reorganization plan of 15 Nov. 1932 for 1938 had been exceeded only in destroyers, torpedo-boats, and submarines (Dülffer, *Weimar*, 565). For the organizational structure of the navy leadership on the eve of the war cf. Fig. III.III.1c below (p. 519).

[273] Deist, 'Rebellion', 341 ff.

aircraft and rocket construction are still surrounded by myths which lend the brief history of the Luftwaffe a special glory, in spite of its ultimate failure. The change from the biplane to the first jet fighter in the world, from the three 'aerial advertising squadrons' of 1933 to the 4,093 front-line aircraft at the beginning of the war was indeed without parallel in the short history of military aviation. It inevitably reminds one of the German fleet programme under William II and Admiral von Tirpitz between 1897 and 1914, but not of the work of Tirpitz's epigone Raeder. Above all, the immediate secondary effects of the fleet and the Luftwaffe, both of them eminently the products of modern industrial technology, were very similar. In both cases fascination with new possibilities opened up by a new weapon combined with a nationalistic claim to great-power status to produce an awareness of power that led to quite similar consequences in foreign policy. The diplomatic, political, and military reaction of Britain to the perceived threat of the German naval and later the Luftwaffe build-up demonstrates this fact with startling clarity. But this similarity probably did not extend to the political and military motives behind the Luftwaffe build-up. Moreover, it must be asked whether this build-up did not differ fundamentally from the imperial fleet construction programme of the turn of the century, because of its greater dependence on technology and the resulting planning and economic problems. Nevertheless, the similarity, which was also noticed by contemporaries, may provide better insights into the political and military problems involved in the Luftwaffe build-up.

(a) The 'Risk Luftwaffe', 1933–1936

The ideas developed within the framework of general Reichswehr planning concerning the future creation of an air arm have already been mentioned.[274] Essentially they envisaged the use of air power to support the army and navy. Specific organizational and technical as well as personnel and material measures, some of which were very significant, had already been taken in accordance with this objective. The appointment of Göring as Reich commissioner for aviation on 30 January 1933 and of Erhard Milch as state secretary in Göring's Reichskommissariat seemed to mark a basic change in this area. Immediately after his appointment Milch indicated that the Reichskommissariat should be considered only an interim stage on the way to a Reich aviation ministry, which would be responsible for all areas of civil and military aviation.[275] When this ministry was created by a decision of the president and a decree of Defence Minister von Blomberg on 10 May 1933, it represented more than a centralization of all branches of aviation.[276] Göring's influence within the Party and his many positions and tasks

---

[274] Cf. III.II.I above. In addition to the literature cited in the following notes cf. Köhler and Hummel, 'Organisation der Luftwaffe', 501 ff., for all questions concerning the development of the Luftwaffe until 1939.

[275] Völker, *Entwicklung*, 201–2.

[276] Völker, *Dokumente*, No. 41, pp. 131 ff. Cf. also *Regierung Hitler*, i. 1, No. 5, p. 15 ('Reichskommissariat für Luftfahrt'); No. 22, p. 81 ('Nachtragshaushalt 1932 für Reichskommissar für Luftfahrt'); No. 25, pp. 99–100 ('Reichshaushalt für den Reichskommissar für Luftfahrt'); No. 115, p. 417 ('Umbildung des Reichskommissariats für Luftfahrt'); ii. (Boppard, 1983), No. 274, pp. 1045–6 (draft of a law on the Reich aviation administration).

in the government meant that the status of the Luftwaffe as an independent service within the Wehrmacht was secured once and for all without the loss of time and energy connected with similar developments in other countries. The army and especially the navy did not accept this drastic limitation of their authority over air units without resistance. They attempted to regain the lost ground, but all their efforts failed because the most important man in the Nazi movement after Hitler had set himself the task of creating an independent Luftwaffe as an appropriate expression of Germany's claim to be a great power.[277] Of course the status of an independent service also offered new possibilities in setting and planning armament targets.

Milch, who was the driving force behind the planning and realization of the Luftwaffe armament programme until the end of 1936, concerned himself after April 1933 at the latest with drafting a new arms plan for the service. In May he received a memorandum from the Lufthansa director Dr Robert Knauss on 'The German Air Fleet',[278] containing ideas with which he declared his 'complete' agreement. As this memorandum received Milch's approval, it can be considered the earliest authoritative statement reflecting the views of the air ministry chiefs on the basic principles of air warfare.

Knauss's basic assumption was that the goal of the 'national government' was to 're-establish Germany's position as a great power in Europe', and that this goal could only be reached by a rearmament that would at least permit Germany to fight a 'two-front war against France and Poland with prospects of success'. In Knauss's opinion, there was no more effective means than the creation of a strong air force to shorten the 'critical period' required for the realization of this aim. For him 'the most important feature of the Luftwaffe as an independent service was the 'long-range, operationally mobile striking power of its bombers'. This 'would greatly increase the risk for any conceivable enemy in a war' and would reduce the danger of a preventive attack against a Germany that was regaining its strength. The striking feature of this plan for a 'risk Luftwaffe'[279] was not only its revival of Tirpitz's military theory, but primarily that it closely followed Hitler's views in his talk to the Reichswehr leaders on 3 February 1933.

The most important factor in determining the effect of the memorandum was probably that Knauss was not content to present his suggestion for a 'risk Luftwaffe' and embellish it with ideas of the Italian aerial warfare theoretician Douhet. He described in detail the operational possibilities as well as the tactical and organizational principles and requirements for the aeroplanes to be produced, and argued that they were quite achievable. This gave his programme clarity, coherence, and persuasiveness.

[277] Völker, *Entwicklung*, 204 ff.; Salewski, *Seekriegsleitung*, i. 251–2; Irving, *Rise and Fall*, 30 ff.

[278] Heimann and Schunke, 'Denkschrift', 72 ff. On Knauss cf. Rautenberg and Wiggerhaus, 'Himmeroder Denkschrift', 189; on the memorandum cf. Boog, *Luftwaffenführung*, 153–4.

[279] The term itself does not appear in the memorandum. Cf. Boog, *Luftwaffenführung*, 154 ff. On the Italian General Giulio Douhet, mentioned again below, cf. his main work *Il dominio dell'aria* (Command of the Air) (1921), translated into German in 1935 (English in 1941); also Köhler and Hummel, 'Organisation der Luftwaffe', 558–9.

Specifically, Knauss proposed the rapid, secret creation of a force of about 390 four-engine bombers supported by ten air reconnaissance squadrons. He believed it would be possible 'to prepare the necessary personnel and material measures by using the army aviation units and the Lufthansa organization in such a way that they could be combined to form an air force in a surprisingly short time'. He was convinced that such a highly mobile, operational military instrument would give Germany decisive advantages in a possible conflict with France and Poland, but more important in his view was the expected deterrent effect of the 'risk Luftwaffe'. To achieve his military objectives, Knauss argued forcefully for an armament policy with clear priorities. 'Equal rearmament in all areas' would lead to a 'waste of energy' and increase the danger of a preventive attack. In the risk phase of German rearmament, the rapid creation of five army divisions or the construction of two pocket battleships would only slightly change the balance of military power in Europe. This argument was directed primarily against the known construction plans of the navy. Knauss explicitly rejected the Tirpitz policy and, in the interest of national defence, assigned the navy only a defensive function in the North Sea and the Baltic. He explained that the funds required for the construction of two pocket battleships would be sufficient to build an air fleet of 400 large bombers, which would 'secure Germany's air superiority in central Europe within a few years'. But within the air programme too Knauss demanded clear priorities. Especially striking was his rejection of any operational function for fighter aircraft and his description of them as only support weapons for the army and the navy. For him the only important goal was the creation of a bomber fleet and the attached reconnaissance squadrons. He concluded his arguments for a 'risk Luftwaffe' and its great importance for the success of general rearmament by pointing out that in Italy and France the idea of independent, operational air warfare had many supporters, and that especially the new French minister of aviation, Pierre Cot, had already taken the first steps in this direction. Any delay would therefore reduce the 'lead Germany can gain today, perhaps for a decade, by creating an air fleet', and 'precisely that decade would be decisive'. Knauss professed himself optimistic, for the 'enormous dynamism of the national government' and the 'leadership qualities of the first German minister of aviation' were the best guarantee that the 'life-or-death decision' regarding the Luftwaffe build-up would be made quickly and that all resistance to carrying it out would be overcome.

In spite of Milch's agreement, the effect of Knauss's memorandum on the armament planning of the Luftwaffe cannot be precisely determined. On Milch's orders the responsible departments of the newly founded ministry of aviation had been studying the possibilities of a first, large-scale aircraft procurement programme since the beginning of May. His suggested objective of 1,000 aeroplanes for the first build-up phase in 1933–4 proved to be somewhat unrealistic at first because of the small capacity of the German aircraft industry.[280] As early as June 1933 preparations had reached a point at which Milch and the head of the

---

[280] Homze, *Arming*, 74; Irving, *Rise and Fall*, 32.

Ministeramt in the defence ministry, Colonel von Reichenau, were able to agree on a provisional armament programme, which was approved by Göring and Blomberg around the end of the month. This envisaged the creation of an air fleet of about 600 aeroplanes in fifty-one squadrons by the autumn of 1935.[281] In contrast to all previous air armament programmes, this one was characterized by a strong emphasis on bomber squadrons. The backbone of the air fleet was to be twenty-seven bomber squadrons in nine groups. This programme, which was changed slightly in August and September, was only partially compatible with Knauss's ideas, for neither did the air fleet consist of the uniform type of heavily armed bomber he wanted, nor was it to be as large as he had recommended. Nevertheless, about 250 bombers were to be available for combat by the autumn of 1935. Without setting a date for achieving his target, Knauss had demanded a fleet of about 400. On the other hand, the basic features of the programme clearly reflected the idea of the 'risk Luftwaffe'. The bomber groups were to form the core of the future Luftwaffe and assume the political and military deterrence functions Knauss had assigned to them.

And although the Luftwaffe created on the basis of this programme was indeed inadequate, it fulfilled its political tasks from the very beginning far better than Knauss had demanded. His air fleet had been conceived primarily as a weapon against Germany's continental neighbours, especially France and Poland. Paradoxically, however, it produced the strongest political reaction in Britain, a country Knauss had not mentioned at all in his memorandum and which could not be seriously threatened by the aircraft of the first German armament programme. The first signs of public concern in Britain about the Luftwaffe build-up could be observed as early as the summer of 1933.[282] This concern was intensified by developments in Germany and by the German withdrawal from the League of Nations and the disarmament conference. The threat from the air and the graphic description of all its possible aspects soon became a constant subject in the British media. Baldwin's statement in the House of Commons on 30 July 1934 that, in view of the developments in military aviation, Britain's line of defence was no longer the cliffs of Dover but the Rhine marked the first high point of this general anxiety.[283] Compared with other European air forces, the German Luftwaffe was still weak at the end of 1934; its number of usable, front-line aeroplanes is estimated at about 600.[284] This modest force had, however, created a situation which permitted Hitler to negotiate with Britain about an air pact.[285] In the first phase of its build-up, which at least bore some similarity to Knauss's principles, the Luftwaffe had fulfilled its intended purpose. There is no evidence of how the air force leaders reacted to this overestimation of their capabilities or what conclusions they drew.

---

[281] Irving, *Rise and Fall*, 33; Homze, *Arming*, 74–5; Völker, *Entwicklung*, 212–13; Rautenberg, *Rüstungspolitik*, appendix, pp. 89–90.

[282] Irving, *Rise and Fall*, 38.

[283] Howard, *Commitment*, 110; *Schulthess*, *1934*, 364 ff. (House of Commons debate of 28 Nov. 1934); cf. Messerschmidt. IV.III.2 below.

[284] Irving, *Rise and Fall*, 42; Völker, *Luftwaffe*, 57 ff.; Rautenberg, *Rüstungspolitik*, appendix, p. 91.

[285] Cf. Messerschmidt, IV.III.2 below.

But it is improbable that they were completely unaffected by the public debate. It is rather more likely that, in contrast to the starting situation Knauss had described, Britain began to assume an increasingly important role in the thinking of the Luftwaffe leaders. At first it was not, of course, included in their operational planning, but it was regarded more and more as a competitor and a standard by which the Germans measured their own accomplishments. Thus, the political effects of the 'risk Luftwaffe' were much more far-reaching than originally intended and opened up possibilities beyond the first, limited objectives.

Knauss had written his memorandum at a time when the first organizational decisions for the build-up of an independent service had been taken, but the personnel and material decisions were still open. The ministry of aviation created by Blomberg's decree of 10 May 1933 was composed of Göring's Reichs-kommissariat and the recently organized Luftschutzamt (air-defence office) of the defence ministry, with responsibility for 'aviation and air defence of the army and navy'.[286] The scale of German efforts in this initial phase can be judged by the fact that at the beginning of June 1933 the staff of the ministry consisted of only seventy-six active and retired officers.[287] Moreover, as a result of the long years of intensive preparation by the army and navy, the state secretary in the air ministry was also in charge of the first flying units camouflaged as 'aerial advertising squadrons': i.e. the flying school command organized in February 1933, which was responsible for the military departments of the civilian schools in Brunswick, Jüterborg, Schleißheim, Warnemünde, and Würzburg, as well as the German military aviation centre at Lipetsk in the Soviet Union.[288] These institutions formed the essential organizational foundation for the Luftwaffe build-up. On the whole, probably only a relatively small number of people were involved in German military aviation in the summer of 1933. Under the provisions of the treaty of Versailles, which were still in force, an expansion of the Luftwaffe seemed possible only if all executive organs of the state, especially the Reichswehr and the transportation ministry, actively supported the new service.

At the commanders' conference following the inauguration of the ministry of aviation, Blomberg took the opportunity to emphasize that the 'flying officer corps' should be an 'élite corps' imbued with 'an intensely aggressive spirit'; its 'preferential treatment in all areas' was necessary and should be accepted by the other services. After they had been prepared for the new situation in this way and concrete planning had begun in the ministry of aviation, Blomberg informed his commanders at the beginning of October 1933 how far the army and navy were expected to contribute to the personnel build-up of the Luftwaffe.[289] According to his figures 228 officers up to the rank of colonel had already been transferred to the Luftwaffe; an additional seventy were to follow by January 1934. About 1,600

---

[286] Völker, *Dokumente*, Nos. 35, 36, 41, pp. 117 ff.

[287] Völker, *Luftwaffe*, 229–30.

[288] Ibid. 13.

[289] IfZ Archives, ED 1, vol. i, Liebmann's record of the commanders' conferences of 1 June and 3 Oct. 1933.

non-commissioned officers and men had also been transferred. For reasons of secrecy the Luftwaffe continued to be dependent on the support of the army and navy in the following years. After 1934 it took over its own recruiting, but its personnel were still trained in units and schools of the other two services until 1935.[290] According to Blomberg an additional 450 officers were to be transferred to the Luftwaffe by 1 April 1934; in the following years the Luftwaffe would itself have to recruit 700 officer cadets each year. Blomberg stressed that nothing would be more short-sighted than the transfer of poorly qualified personnel to the Luftwaffe; it needed rather 'the best of the best'. At subsequent commanders' conferences Blomberg continued to support energetically the wishes of the Luftwaffe in personnel questions and did not exclude compulsory transfers. The transfers to the Luftwaffe from the army and navy continued in the following years; in a survey of personnel requirements in December 1938, a result of Hitler's armament demands, the transfer of army officers was taken for granted.[291] A large number of young civilian pilots also joined the Luftwaffe officer corps at the beginning of 1934; so, after 1 April 1935, did officers of the flak artillery, the air signals corps, and the local defence units, the later supplementary reserve officers.

This incomplete survey clearly shows the difficult problems facing the Luftwaffe personnel office created on 1 October 1933, which had the task of forming a uniform officer corps under difficult conditions on the model of the other two services in the first phase of the secret build-up. From 1 June 1933 onwards the personnel system of the Luftwaffe was under the direction of Colonel Stumpff of the old army (Reichsheer), who became chief of the Luftwaffe general staff in June 1937. The difficult problems he faced can be better understood if one remembers the emphatic, gloomy warnings of the chief of the army personnel office in the summer and winter of 1935 against a new, accelerated expansion of the army.[292] In addition to the necessity of forming the very difficult groups from varied professional backgrounds and experience in the other services and branches of the Luftwaffe into a uniform officer corps, Stumpff was confronted with the problem of familiarizing the new officers with the complex technology of their weapons, as competent leadership at all levels was impossible without such knowledge. Both these tasks, the formation of the officer corps and familiarization with the new technology, could be fulfilled, if at all, only in a lengthy process. The rapid, even over-hasty build-up between 1933 and 1939 created the worst possible conditions for such a development.[293] The figures on the growth of the officer corps and personnel strength provide an impressive picture of the difficulties to be overcome. When camouflage measures were abandoned in the spring of 1935, the officer corps consisted

[290] Völker, *Luftwaffe*, 52 ff.

[291] On Blomberg's efforts cf. IfZ Archives, ED 1, vol. i, Liebmann's record of the commanders' conferences of 2 Feb. and 27 Feb. 1934. In the comment by the army personnel office of 15 June 1935 cited in n. 85 above (PA, No. 450/35, g.Kdos., 15 June 1935, BA-MA RH 2/v. 1019), the head of that office assumed that until 1939 the number of officers transferred to the Luftwaffe annually would be about 500. Cf. the survey by the Luftwaffe personnel office of 5 Dec. 1938 in Völker, *Dokumente*, No. 135, pp. 298 ff.

[292] Cf. III.II.2 (c), text to nn. 85 ff. above.

[293] Cf. Boog, 'Offizierkorps der Luftwaffe'; Völker, *Luftwaffe*, 52 ff., 121 ff.

of 900 flying and 200 flak officers commanding about 17,000 non-commissioned officers and men. Two and a half years later, at the end of 1937, the size of the officer corps had increased fivefold: in the three branches of the Luftwaffe there were slightly more than 6,000 officers. By August 1939 the corps had grown to more than 15,000 officers; the number of NCOs and men had risen to 370,000.[294] Thus, after March 1935 the officer corps grew thirteenfold in barely four and a half years. In view of the fact that, unlike the army, the Luftwaffe officer corps did not have a relatively broad, homogeneous base, it was probably lacking in the coherence necessary for the performance of its military functions. A particularly serious shortcoming was the fact that the entire senior officer corps of the Luftwaffe consisted of former army officers, who at first viewed the far-reaching posibilities of independent air warfare with scepticism and, above all, possessed no experience in commanding large air units. This problem was caused by the nature of the Luftwaffe build-up and could not be overcome before the outbreak of war. It is interesting that Dr Knauss, a director of Lufthansa, did not mention the personnel problems connected with the 'risk Luftwaffe' at all in his memorandum.

In addition to these weaknesses in personnel, which were in the final analysis unavoidable, the material build-up also led to enormous problems. As a result of discussions in the ministry of aviation and with the other two Wehrmacht services, Milch's initial ideas of May 1933 assumed a form sufficiently concrete to make it possible to lay down the programme for the first organization period, 1934, in a directive of 12 July 1933.[295] According to this programme a total of twenty-six squadrons were to be created as unit formations after 1 July 1934, but they were to be aligned with institutions of civil aviation 'to preserve secrecy as far as possible'. The ten planned bomber squadrons, which were to be supported by seven reconnaissance and seven fighter squadrons, were the centre of the programme. Six weeks later, on 28 August, Milch signed the programme for the second build-up period, 1935. This programme envisaged the creation by 1 October 1935 of an additional twenty-nine squadrons as combat formations, of which seventeen were described as bomber squadrons, with only eight reconnaissance and four fighter squadrons. The number of aircraft delivered by the end of 1934 shows that the industry fulfilled its obligations according to the programme. At the end of 1934 the air units disposed of 270 bombers, ninety-nine single-seat fighters, and 303 reconnaissance aircraft; a much larger number, about 1,300 aircraft, were used for training and other purposes.[296]

This achievement of the German aircraft industry, which had been seriously affected by the economic crisis, was indeed impressive. At the end of January 1933 the producers of airframes and motors belonging to the Reich association of the aircraft industry employed scarcely more than 4,000 workers.[297] The achievements of the most important producers—Junkers in Dessau, Heinkel in Warnemünde,

---

[294] Völker, *Luftwaffe*, 56, 125, 183.
[295] Völker, *Dokumente*, No. 80, pp. 194–5.
[296] Ibid., No. 82, pp. 197–8; id., *Luftwaffe*, 57; Rautenberg, *Rüstungspolitik*, appendix, p. 91.
[297] Völker, *Luftwaffe*, 24; Irving, *Rise and Fall*, 34; Homze, *Arming*, 73.

Dornier in Friedrichshafen, and the Bayerische Flugzeugwerke in Augsburg—in the area of aircraft development were significant, but their production capacity was limited because of the economic crisis and the special financial problems of their industry. State Secretary Milch, the head of the ministry of aviation under Göring, was himself a former Lufthansa director, thoroughly familiar with conditions in the industry and able to evaluate its potential contribution to the armament programmes. A precondition for the build-up of an air force comparable to those of other European powers was, in addition to considerable funds for the expansion of production, above all the rationalization of the industry. At the beginning of June 1933 a ministerial conference took place under Hitler's chairmanship at which Schacht explained his plan to finance job-creation and rearmament, and thus the expansion of the aircraft industry, by means of the famous 'Mefo' bills.[298] In the same month the head of the administrative department of the ministry of aviation, Colonel Kesselring, was sent to Ernst Heinkel at Warnemünde to persuade him to build a new factory near Rostock with a starting labour force of 3,000 workers. Kesselring was successful.[299] The result of the ministry's initiative, which affected the whole industry, was a sharp and continuous rise in the number of persons employed in aircraft production. The figure rose from about 4,000 in January 1933 to 16,870 at the beginning of 1934 and 59,600 on 1 April 1935. A year later it reached 110,600; on 1 April 1937 it was about 167,200, and on 1 October 1938, 204,100 people were working in the aircraft industry, not including those employed by companies providing equipment and repairs.[300] The labour force in the industry as a whole had thus increased fiftyfold in five and a half years.

The rationalization of production was also carried out on the initiative of the aviation ministry. The best-known example in this area was the Junkers firm. In Dessau Junkers was able to produce only eighteen Junkers 52 aircraft per annum before 1933, if at the same time no other models were produced. After the removal of the founder of the company, Professor Hugo Junkers—due to an inextricable mixture of personal, political, and financial motives of rival groups within the company and the ministry of aviation—Milch informed Klaus Junkers in August 1933 about the ministry's armament plans, which called for the purchase of 179 Junkers 52s in 1934 alone. Such an order could only be filled if production methods were radically changed. With the decisive help of one of their directors, Koppenberg, Junkers developed the so-called 'ABC programme' in the following months, under which mass production of the Junkers 52 was begun around the end of the year. In this programme a number of small firms supervised by Junkers produced individual parts. Only the final assembly of the aircraft was done in the factory at Dessau. This represented a decisive step in the efficient organization of supply firms and at the same time marked the beginning of co-operation among the aircraft producers, who until then had jealously guarded their independence. The way was thus open for the introduction of licensing, which acquired increasing

---

[298] Irving, *Rise and Fall*, 32; cf. also Volkmann, II.III.3 above.
[299] Irving, *Rise and Fall*, 34; Heinkel, *Leben*, 245 ff.
[300] Homze, *Arming*, 78-9, 93, 184 ff.

significance in the following years. Between 1933 and 1945 a total of 17,552 Junkers aircraft were built under licence by other firms. The expansion of production under licence was also a consequence of the fact that as early as 1933 the clear prospect of a boom and higher profits in the aircraft industry attracted a growing number of firms.[301]

In this way Secretary Milch and the technical office of the ministry of aviation under Colonel Wimmer, working in close co-operation with the producers, laid the foundations for the Luftwaffe build-up in a surprisingly short time. The mobilization exercise planned by Milch and Wimmer from the beginning of 1935, and conducted between October and December of that year, in the Arado plant in Brandenburg can be considered a test of the success of this method. In eighteen weeks monthly production rose from twenty to 120 aircraft, the size of the factory was nearly doubled, and the labour force tripled. Although this demonstration of efficiency was convincing, it also revealed weaknesses in the production process which the ministry could only partially overcome on its own. The availability of raw materials and above all machine-tools turned out to be unsatisfactory. It was considered less serious that the lodging of extra workers in barracks had a negative effect on productivity and that difficulties arose in one case in starting production under licence.[302]

The Arado experiment proved that the industrial basis for the Luftwaffe build-up had been created in a surprisingly short time. The question was, however, what the dimensions and technical requirements of such a build-up should be. Milch's programme of 12 July and 28 August 1933 for the first and second build-up periods, 1934 and 1935, had placed the main emphasis on the creation of bomber formations, as Knauss had wanted, but the aircraft planned for these formations did not meet his technical performance standards, nor was the preference given to bombers based on a general consensus of all departments concerned. The Truppenamt of the army command was quite prepared to acknowledge the importance of a bomber fleet for the conduct of a future war, but rejected Knauss's arguments in this regard as completely one-sided and pointed out that, in the future, wars would still be won by the co-operation of all services. Finally, in a directive of 16 August 1933, Blomberg explained that no build-up of a 'strategic Luftwaffe' was planned. The objective was rather to create an 'operational' Luftwaffe that—either independently and supported by squadrons of long-range reconnaissance aircraft, or in co-operation with the army and navy—would take over operational functions within the framework of a total strategy in the event of a war on several fronts against Poland, France, Belgium, and Czechoslovakia. Moreover, Blomberg indicated that the army and navy would still have their own air units.[303]

Within the framework of such an operational air fleet, the bomber formations

---

[301] Ibid. 62 ff.; Irving, *Rise and Fall*, 34, 39, 403 n. 92.

[302] Homze, *Arming*, 115–16.

[303] Cf. the comments of the operations department of the Truppenamt of 28 June 1933 on Knauss's memorandum in Rautenberg, *Rüstungspolitik*, 321 ff., and Blomberg's directive, ibid.; also ibid., appendix, 89–90, and Völker, *Dokumente*, Nos. 182–3, pp. 428–9. On the use of the term 'operational Luftwaffe' cf. Köhler, 'Operativer Luftkrieg', 265 ff.

Knauss had described still had a special deterrent function. However, in the winter of 1933–4 a Wehrmacht war game suggested by the operations department of the Truppenamt showed that the bomber fleet alone could not eliminate hostile air forces quickly enough, and that Germany's exposed position urgently required a strong air defence in the form of fighter units and flak artillery.[304]

In the programme he had signed on 28 August 1933 for the second build-up period, 1935, Milch announced an additional programme for 'total armaments plan for 1934–8', which would have to take into account 'the requirements of national defence and the technical possibilities'.[305] The organizational, personnel, and industrial conditions for this programme had been created by the beginning of 1934, and the military tasks of the Luftwaffe had been clarified by the Wehrmacht war game. The aircraft procurement programme of 1 July 1934 was based on these conditions and represented a continuation of a revised purchase programme of January 1934 for the first and second phases of the build-up. The 'July programme' of 1934 was the first long-term programme for the Luftwaffe and envisaged the purchase of 17,015 aircraft of all kinds by 31 March 1938.[306] The importance of this programme is shown by the fact that, at Hitler's request, Göring and Milch reported to him on it at the end of July. Milch, whom Hitler evidently valued as an expert and man of ideas, was able in the end to resist Hitler's demands to increase and accelerate the Luftwaffe build-up. At the end of August 1934 Hitler approved a cost estimate for the programme, amounting to RM10,500m.[307] This clearly showed the special position of the Luftwaffe in relation to the other two services. It was not Blomberg, the defence minister, who presented the financial requirements of an integrated Wehrmacht armaments programme; instead Göring, as the second man in the state, was able to advance the interests of his own service with only an informal agreement with Blomberg.

Of the enormous number of aircraft in the July programme only 6,671 were to be combat aeroplanes. They consisted of the following types:[308]

Fighters	2,225
Bombers	2,188
Dive-bombers	699
Reconnaissance aircraft	1,559

The proportion of combat to training aircraft reflected the awareness of the Luftwaffe leadership that the consolidation of the service would be the most important objective in the coming years and that therefore the main emphasis should be placed on training in all areas. The surprisingly large number of fighters was a result of the Wehrmacht war game in the winter of 1933–4, which had led to a strengthening of the air defence components of the total programme. The

---

[304] Völker, *Dokumente*, No. 184, pp. 429–30; Rautenberg, *Rüstungspolitik*, 325.

[305] Völker, *Dokumente*, No. 82, pp. 197–8.

[306] Völker, *Luftwaffe*, 56–7; Rautenberg, *Rüstungspolitik*, 325–6, appendix, p. 91; Homze, *Arming*, 79 ff.; Overy, 'Production Plans', 779–80.

[307] Irving, *Rise and Fall*, 42.

[308] Overy, 'Production Plans', 780.

programme itself was based on the plan for an operational Luftwaffe as Blomberg had described it in his directive of August 1933.

In the first phase of its realization a total of 3,021 aircraft were to be delivered to the Luftwaffe by 30 September 1935; more than half of them were to be used for training. To achieve this objective, it was planned to increase monthly aircraft production from seventy-two in January 1934 to 293 in July 1935. Thus, the industry was expected to quadruple its production in a relatively short time. At the end of December 1934 1,959 aircraft had already been delivered; the shortfall compared with the plan figure was only 6 per cent. This was indeed an impressive accomplishment; the planning figures of the ministry of aviation and existing production capacity were almost identical.[309]

For a long time at home and abroad, the certain result of the Saar plebiscite in January 1935 had been considered an event which Hitler would use for new foreign-policy and armament initiatives.[310] On 26 February, even before the final re-integration of the Saar on 1 March and the proclamation of general conscription in Germany on 16 March, Blomberg had ordered the gradual removal of the camouflage measures for the Luftwaffe. In an interview on 10 March Göring emphasized its purely defensive character, while Hitler told the British foreign secretary on 25 March that the Luftwaffe had already reached the strength of the Royal Air Force! This was in accord with instructions put out by the Wehrmacht office, probably not without Blomberg's approval, that it was important to give other countries the impression that Germany now had a strong Wehrmacht capable of fulfilling its tasks even under difficult conditions.[311] For the Luftwaffe, which at this time had about 2,500 aircraft, of which 800 could be used in combat in the event of war,[312] this marked the beginning of a new phase in its political function as a 'risk Luftwaffe'.

In his directive of 28 August 1933 Milch had stated two conditions for the overall programme in 1934–8: on the one hand it must provide an adequate national defence, and on the other it must make use of possibilities provided by technology. The astonishing fulfilment of planning goals combined with the obvious deterrent effect on other countries, however achieved, demonstrated convincingly that the Luftwaffe met the requirements of national defence in these years. But to what extent did the total programme take into account technical possibilities? The 270 bombers delivered by the end of 1934 were Junkers 52s and Dornier 11s; the ninety-nine single-seat fighters were Arado 64 and 65 biplanes. In the service and in the ministry of aviation there was complete agreement that these models were technically obsolete. Milch was well aware of this situation; he had rejected Hitler's demand to increase production still further with the argument that it would result in too many obsolete aircraft. Major von Richthofen, the head of development in

[309] Homze, *Arming*, 93; Völker, *Luftwaffe*, 57.

[310] Cf. III.ii.2 (*c*) and III.ii.3 (*b*) above.

[311] Völker, *Luftwaffe*, 68 ff. On the measures taken to conceal German rearmament cf. also Whaley, 'Covert Rearmament', 3 ff.

[312] Völker, *Luftwaffe*, 57–8; Irving, *Rise and Fall*, 45.

the technical office of the ministry of aviation, expressed the guiding principle of this first phase succinctly in August 1934:[313] 'An aircraft of limited usefulness available now is better than none at all.' The new models, especially the medium-range bombers such as the Dornier 17, the Heinkel 111, and the Junkers 86, as well as the Junkers 86 dive-bomber, were already being developed. But the question was when they would be ready for mass production after the lengthy process of development and testing. Moreover, there was a serious problem in the development and production of aircraft engines. Only Junkers had been involved continuously in their further development in the 1920s. Daimler-Benz and BMW (Bayerische Motorenwerke) had no previous experience in this area. The use of funds from the ministry of aviation, which had been so successful in the build-up of the airframe industry, was of only limited effectiveness in this case. Of course the expansion of capacity was supported as far as possible, but Richthofen's demand at a conference with the producers of aircraft motors on 20–1 September 1934 that the time required for the development of a new motor be reduced from five or six to two years simply ignored reality.[314]

The objective of equipping the Luftwaffe units with new and better aircraft, for which Milch and the technical office had been striving since 1934 at the latest, clearly was not reached as planned. The development and testing of models and motors, and their mass production, were a process which could be directed and planned only to a limited extent. The previous planning of the ministry of aviation had promoted the production of aircraft which it knew would be obsolete in a short time, not only in the interest of national defence but also because an efficient aircraft industry could only be created in that way. After the first measurable success had been achieved at the end of 1934 and the beginning of 1935, re-equipping could be carried out only gradually, in order to avoid having to close factories until the new models were ready for mass production. The many supplementary programmes of 1935 and the first half of 1936 must be understood against this background. In January and October 1935 Milch approved procurement and delivery plans that went beyond the July programme of 1934 and were intended, e.g. in the case of bombers, to permit the discontinuation of the old models and increased production of new ones, such as the Heinkel 111, the Dornier 17, and the Junkers 86.[315] Pressure from Hitler and Göring in setting constantly increased production requirements probably also played a significant role. Although the re-equipping process required much more time and was actually carried out only in 1937, planning remained astonishingly flexible until the summer of 1936. For example, production of the Junker 52, which had been considered a stop-gap solution from the very beginning, was continued until the new bomber models could be put into mass production. The Junkers 52 later became the most important transport aircraft of the Luftwaffe.

---

[313] Völker, Luftwaffe, 58.
[314] Ibid. 58–9; on the engine question cf. Homze, Arming, 82 ff. On Richthofen's demands cf. ibid. 84.
[315] Ibid. 103 ff. On the change in 1937 cf. Völker, Luftwaffe, 131 ff., and Murray, 'German Air Power', 110.

The flexibility in planning, however, clearly went along with uncertainty as to the technical and military requirements for the individual types of aircraft, and this had a lasting, negative effect on the development process. This effect had already become obvious in the development of a new two-engine horizontal bomber[316] and would also be the fate of the four-engine strategic bomber. The aviation officers of the Reichswehr had already worked on this project. Colonel Wever, the head of the Luftkommandoamt (air command office), who had concerned himself intensively with the problems of air warfare, quickly recognized its importance. As early as May 1934 a development contract was awarded to Junkers and Dornier. The bomber was to be ready for mass production as early as 1938, but before the test flights of the Junkers 89 and the Dornier 19 had taken place doubts were expressed as to whether they had adequate speed and range. The motor problem also played a decisive role. On 17 April 1936 Wever approved guidelines for the further development of the strategic bomber. The existing prototypes could not meet the new requirements.[317] The result was that, after Wever's death on 3 June 1936, development of the bomber was delayed even further and finally dropped from the general development programme. The reasons for this decision and its consequences cannot be determined with adequate clarity. It is as difficult to answer the question whether Germany had the economic means to build a large strategic air fleet as it is to determine whether the engine question was decisive. Undoubtedly, however, Wever's death and the subsequent far-reaching personnel changes in the ministry of aviation led to the decision being made, as it were, incidentally, in a manner not appropriate to the importance of the question.[318]

Wever's death marked the end of a significant period in the build-up of the Luftwaffe. The years 1933–6 were characterized by the work of a number of competent officers as heads of the offices in the ministry of aviation, which was directed less by Göring than by Milch. The available evidence indicates that Milch and the colonels Wever, Wimmer, Kesselring, and Stumpff developed a close working relationship with clear objectives; they showed considerable foresight in laying the foundation for the build-up of the Luftwaffe in the following years, during which the leadership of the ministry underwent decisive change. In addition to the successful development of the aircraft industry, which was due essentially to the initiative of Milch, Wimmer, and Kesselring, above all Wever had thought out and defined the military function of the Luftwaffe in its enlarged form. As an army general staff officer and former head of the training department of the Truppenamt, he had mastered the new problems surprisingly quickly and, like Milch, had recognized the strategic and operational possibilities of air warfare with the help of a bomber fleet as described by Knauss in his memorandum. At the same time, however, he had rejected as dangerous the one-sidedness of Douhet's ideas. Typical of all armament programmes for which he was even partly responsible was the

---

[316] Homze, *Arming*, 120–1.

[317] Irving, *Rise and Fall*, 46–7; Homze, *Arming*, 121 ff.; Völker, *Luftwaffe*, 132–3.

[318] However, this did not mean the end of demands for a 4-engine bomber for the Luftwaffe or plans to develop one, as the varied history of the Heinkel 177 shows (Kens and Nowarra, *Flugzeuge*, 292 ff.).

priority given to the bomber. This was also true of the July programme of 1934, if the planned numbers of horizontal and dive-bombers are added together. As a result of the Wehrmacht war-game of 1933–4, Wever did place more emphasis on air defence, but it should not be forgotten that the strategic bomber was developed on his initiative, and one can only speculate about what solution he would have chosen after the decision of 17 April 1936.

Wever expressed his opinions succinctly in Luftwaffe regulation 16 on 'Air Warfare', issued in 1936, which marked the change from a purely 'risk Luftwaffe' designed to protect Germany until rearmament was completed.[319] This document reflected the conviction that the first and only decisive task of the Luftwaffe was to conduct an offensive against the very broadly defined 'fighting ability of the enemy' and the 'adversary's will to resist'. From these general functions Wever deduced three main tasks: (1) 'the war against the enemy air force'; (2) direct support of the operations of the army and the navy; and finally (3) the 'war against the sources of strength of the enemy forces' and the disrupting of the 'flow of strength' from these sources to the front. The Luftwaffe could attack 'the hostile nation' at the most sensitive point, at its 'roots', as Wever expressed it elsewhere. In its own eyes the Luftwaffe had already developed far beyond the role of a mere support weapon for the army and navy. The regulation covered all elements of modern air warfare. The variety of possible uses for the Luftwaffe led to the conclusion that air warfare was conceivable only within the framework of the general conduct of a war: 'The politico-military leadership must, therefore, continue to determine the aims of air warfare' (point 12). A slight uncertainty, however, remained in the attempt to define more precisely the co-operation with the army and navy. If one compares these thoughts on air warfare with the views of the leaders of the other two services, it is clear that, in contrast to his counterparts in the army and navy, Wever had retained an overall view and had shown how the Luftwaffe could act independently as well as together with the other services.

The Luftwaffe build-up in the years 1933–6 was a period of comprehensive and cautious planning in which the Luftwaffe leaders tried to take into account the political, military, and technical-industrial factors involved in armaments programmes, although the difficulties and weaknesses, above all in personnel build-up and training, were obvious. These very energetic and successful efforts were reminiscent of the naval build-up before the First World War, and differed strikingly from the narrow perspectives under which the armament programmes of the other two branches of the Wehrmacht were carried out.

(b) *Luftwaffe Armament, 1936–1939*

Immediately after Wever's death, Göring made two personnel decisions which marked the beginning of the end of the previously uniform and effective Luftwaffe leadership structure. Wever's successor as head of the Luftwaffe command office was the previous head of the Luftwaffe administrative office, Lieutenant-General

---

[319] Völker, *Dokumente*, No. 200, pp. 466 ff. On the German plans for an air war cf. esp. Maier, 'Aufbau der Luftwaffe'; Boog, *Luftwaffenführung*, 164 ff., 631 ff.; Maier, 'Total War', 210 ff.

Albert Kesselring. The fighter pilot and stunt flyer Ernst Udet replaced General Wimmer as head of the technical office. Kesselring was considered an organization expert, but he was probably not a good choice as head of the general staff. Udet had let himself be persuaded to join the Luftwaffe after 1933. Before becoming head of the technical office he was inspector of fighter and dive-bomber pilots, with the rank of colonel. He possessed abundant flying experience but not the technical and organizational abilities his new position required. Both personnel changes had far-reaching consequences for the planning and realization of the Luftwaffe armaments programme, but their negative effects were aggravated by the frequent changes in the command structure, at least until 1939. This problem has already been examined in detail in the relevant literature.[320] Kesselring was replaced by General Stumpff after only a year as chief of the general staff. Stumpff in turn was followed by Colonel Jeschonnek at the beginning of 1939. The changes in the leadership were accompanied by organizational changes. The creation of new positions was combined with the open or concealed limitation of the authority of those already existing and an expansion of the total organization. To some degree this may have been a 'natural' development, but the more active role assumed by the commander-in-chief of the Luftwaffe, Göring, was indeed a new element.

Although the build-up of the Luftwaffe in the manner in which it took place before 1936 would not have been conceivable without Göring's position and prestige, he seems to have participated relatively little in the actual decision-making. Milch, Wever, Wimmer, and their colleagues essentially determined the course of Luftwaffe rearmament. There were numerous indications that Göring considered Milch's dominant role as an encroachment on his own authority as commander-in-chief. After 1934 the tension between the minister and his state secretary increased.[321] Milch was not consulted about the appointments of Kesselring and Udet, which made clear Göring's intention to take a more active part in the development of 'his' Luftwaffe. He was aided by the fact that in the armament economy instruments of power were available to him that were of decisive importance for the further build-up of the Luftwaffe. Milch's attempts to defend his position were unsuccessful, with the result that his authority and functions were constantly reduced.[322] This conflict coloured by personal factors would have been unimportant if a leadership structure conducive to efficient decision-making had replaced the earlier one. But this was not the case. Göring established a special Ministeramt; the Luftwaffe general staff greatly strengthened its position; new offices and areas of responsibility were created; and, finally, in May 1938 Udet divided his office into thirteen departments, with each department head having direct access to him. Gradually Milch's ability to keep track of all developments in

---

[320] On organizational questions cf. above all Völker, *Luftwaffe*, 75 ff., 166 ff.; on personnel decisions also Irving, *Rise and Fall*, 47, 50–1, 54–5; Homze, *Arming*, 233 ff.; Boog, *Luftwaffenführung*, 37 ff.

[321] e.g. Irving, *Rise and Fall*, 42–3. The most recent Göring biographies deal only in passing with his function as pre-war commander-in-chief of the Luftwaffe. Cf. Martens, *Göring*, 25 ff., and Kube, *Pour le mérite*, 48 ff.

[322] Irving, *Rise and Fall*, 50–1.

his office was inevitably lost, and decisions were not made by responsible but rather by subordinate persons.[323]

These changes in the senior leadership structure of the Luftwaffe were made during a period in which the introduction of new aircraft and equipment, with all its accompanying difficulties, was being carried out; production was suffering from the general shortage of raw materials, and, finally, Britain—whose reaction to the German build-up had been clear from the very beginning—was increasingly considered a potential enemy in Luftwaffe operational planning.

It has already been mentioned that, while the necessity of equipping the Luftwaffe with aeroplanes of the second generation had been realized in 1934, this could be fully carried out only in 1937. By then, however, the ministry was already considering a second phase, in which the bombers being introduced—the Heinkel 111 and the Dornier 17, or even the Messerschmitt 109, a fighter—would be replaced by more modern aircraft. This new change was to be started as early as 1939 and more or less concluded by 1940.[324] As the aircraft and the technology involved were becoming increasingly sophisticated and their mass production thus very susceptible to disruption, the choice of new models was an extremely risky process. In order to reduce this risk, Udet wanted to promote the 'principle of the military airframe and the military aircraft engine'.[325] He defined 'military airframe' as 'a usable frame that is so produced from the very beginning that it can be assembled by untrained or quickly trained workers like a Meccano toy'. A 'military aircraft engine' was one that required 'almost no maintenance and is free of everything that could cause new mechanical problems'. Udet's objective was to develop 'a few uncomplicated models' that, 'with little time and effort, could be produced in durable, easily maintained versions in the quantities necessary for the front'. These were undoubtedly ideals that had little relation to reality. The idea of a uniform military airframe and engine was—in view of the different tasks of the various kinds of aircraft, the fact that their very variety promised to make the Luftwaffe the military instrument of the future, and the accelerating pace of technical development—a completely inadequate approach to military technology. It was, however, urgently necessary to reduce the number of aircraft types. The Heinkel firm was producing only one of its development projects in large numbers, but was also working on ten additional models.[326] The financial and material investment and the number of workers involved were out of all proportion to the result. Udet demanded simple, durable aircraft but was apparently unaware that such perfected technical products are usually the result of intensive development and, above all, testing. The time this would require was, however, the last thing the ministry of aviation could give the industry. Under these circumstances the second phase of

---

[323] Homze, *Arming*, 234 ff.; Overy, 'Production Plans', 789. On the organization of the Luftwaffe command immediately after the outbreak of war cf. Fig. III.III.1 D below (p. 519) and the comprehensive account in Boog, *Luftwaffenführung*, 215 ff.

[324] Homze, *Arming*, 156-7; Völker, *Luftwaffe*, 132 ff.

[325] Cf. Udet's report at the commanders' conference on 6 Oct. 1936, BA-MA RL 3/55.

[326] Homze, *Arming*, 212-13.

converting to new aircraft and the unavoidable reduction of the number of models became a very unpredictable enterprise.

The development of the two-engine Junkers 86 horizontal bomber provides a good example of the conflict between Udet's principles and reality. This aeroplane seemed to fulfil many of Udet's requirements and was already in mass production in the autumn of 1936.[327] In May and April 1937 it became clear that the aircraft was inadequate in many respects. But if mass production were stopped, this would involve the high cost of scrapping 162 aeroplanes in various stages of construction and at least temporary unemployment for 2,100 workers. Retooling for the production of another kind of aircraft would have required eight to nine months. In this particular case another solution was found, but the example illustrates the consequences that could be expected from a wrong decision.[328] It also shows that decisions about the kinds of aeroplane to be produced could only be made after careful consideration of the choice of engines. In the autumn of 1936 the development of German aircraft engines had reached a certain stable level. In the opinion of the technical office, a large number of motors from Junkers, Daimler-Benz, and BMW could now be put into mass production. However, the test results for the air-cooled engine were still not completely satisfactory.[329] For this reason interim solutions were developed whose effects on mass production and the equipment necessary for it had to be considered. These few remarks clearly show that the arming of the Luftwaffe, the most modern technical military instrument of its time, set in motion a very complicated, extremely sensitive process of development, testing, and production that could be effectively controlled only by adequate planning agencies. Even the boastful Göring and the well-intentioned but incompetent Udet could not change these facts.

In 1938, when the Luftwaffe leaders began to realize that Britain should be considered a possible enemy, an aircraft had to be found or developed for an air war against the island, as neither the Heinkel 111 nor the Dornier 17 had the range or the bomb load for such a task. Thus began the story of the Junker 88, which was developed as a fast bomber in accordance with the specifications of the air command office and the technical office in 1936, tested in the summer of 1937, and incorporated into production planning in the spring of 1938.[330] When the Junkers 88 was considered and finally designated as the successor to the Heinkel 111 and the Dornier 17, the military raised their requirements for the aircraft. The most far-reaching demand of the general staff, which Udet supported, was that the fast bomber should not only be able to carry two tons of bombs 3,200 kilometres, but that it should also be able to bomb its target by diving. There was no question that,

[327] At the commanders' conference mentioned in n. 325 above, Udet had praised the ease with which this aircraft could be maintained and repaired and the lack of problems in its production.

[328] Homze, *Arming*, 103 ff., 129, 152–3. In this case most of the 162 aircraft were delivered to the Luftwaffe unchanged, others were equipped with a different type of engine, and the rest exported or scrapped.

[329] Ibid. 159 ff.

[330] On the following passage cf. ibid. 163 ff.; Irving, *Rise and Fall*, 65; Völker, *Luftwaffe*, 190; and the extensive analysis by Boog, *Luftwaffenführung*, 53 ff.

with the bomb-sights available at the time, this form of bombing was more effective and economical than area bombing. Udet himself had supported the idea of dive-bombing since the beginning of the 1930s, and it had been tested in combat by the Condor Legion in Spain.[331] Since then, however, it had become almost an obsession. These military demands had an extremely adverse effect on the flight characteristics of the Junkers 88. Its weight rose from seven to twelve tons, and its speed fell from almost 500 kilometres an hour to barely 300. The claim that 250,000 changes were made in its construction may be exaggerated; but only eighteen of Göring's 'wonder bombers', for whose accelerated production the Junkers general director Koppenberg had received all necessary authority from Göring personally at the end of September 1938, had been delivered a year later. In May 1938 the planning of the technical office had called for the delivery of 1,060 Junkers 88s as early as March 1940 and for stopping production of the Heinkel 111 and the Dornier 17 in October 1939. The complexities of development, testing, and production confronted the planners in the ministry of aviation with tasks of a magnitude for which there were hardly any precedents in the military or civil sphere. If, during this difficult process, such extensive changes, which were moreover completely alien to the original design and purpose of an aircraft, were demanded and accepted, the result could only be negative, as was the case with the Junkers 88 and the Messerschmitt 210.

It is hardly necessary to point out that these weaknesses, and in some cases the failure to master advanced technology, inevitably affected production and productivity. After the comprehensive armaments plan of July 1934 there were a total of fourteen aircraft procurement plans before the outbreak of the war, some of them with several variations. The length of these programmes varied. Changes in the political and economic situation, as well as difficulties with individual aircraft prototypes, led to new procurement programmes that overlapped in many respects, which makes comparisons difficult. For the period 1937–9 annual production has been calculated according to the various procurement plans (Table III.II.5). The most striking feature of these figures is not so much the discrepancy between planned goals and reality, but rather the decline of production in 1938. This becomes even clearer if one considers the rise in production from 1934 to 1936. According to the sources cited in Table III.II.5, the figures for aircraft of all kinds were as follows:

	Estimate 1	*Estimate 2*
1934	1, 968	1, 817
1935	3, 183	3, 307
1946	5, 112	5, 248

This shows that in the most important area of Luftwaffe armament the years 1937

---

[331] Cf. Irving, *Rise and Fall*, 49–50. On the use of the Luftwaffe to support Franco cf. Maier, *Guernica*; on the plans and reaction of the navy cf. Schreiber, *Revisionismus*, 100 ff.

TABLE III.II.5 *German annual aircraft production 1937–1939*

	Planned Production		Actual Production	
	Plan	No.	Est. 1	Est. 2
1937	4	6,843	5,606	5,749
	4–5	5,767		
	5–6	5,711		
1938	6	5,800	5,235	5,316
	7	6,021		
	7–8	6,154		
1939	8	9,957	8,295	7,582
	10	8,299		
	10–11	8,619		

Sources: (PLANS) Overy, 'Production Plans', 781 (cf. also Homze, *Arming*, 102 ff., 149 ff., 222 ff.); (ESTIMATES) Homze, *Arming*, 159 (Est. 1 from US Strategic Bombing Survey; Est. 2 from engineer E. Hertel, technical director of Heinkel).

and 1938 were marked by a stagnation, some of whose causes have already been mentioned.

In addition to the problems resulting from the change to more modern aircraft, the decline in production was due above all to the general scarcity of raw materials after 1936, which also affected the Luftwaffe. At a conference on 2 December 1936, called because of the tense international situation (Spain), Göring proclaimed that after the beginning of 1937 'all factories of the aircraft industry should operate at a mobilization level'[332] and declared that financial considerations should play no part. But only a few days later, on 25 December, the technical office had to set priorities for individual aircraft types because of shortage of raw materials for the factories; this endangered the entire procurement programme. In January 1937 it became clear that the shortage of iron and steel was also having an adverse effect on the further expansion of the aircraft industry.[333] In 1937 the Luftwaffe, like the army and navy, was seriously affected by the problem of securing regular and adequate deliveries of raw materials. This problem had not been solved by the introduction of a quota system. The fact that the commander-in-chief of the Luftwaffe was also Hitler's commissioner for the Four-year Plan undoubtedly made many things easier, but it could not shield the Luftwaffe from the effects of the general crisis. Only a third of its steel requirements could be met. On 30 October 1937, in a report to his commander-in-chief, Milch observed that the steel shortage had already led to serious delays in the expansion of the aircraft industry and the aerial-defence programme and would continue to cause difficulties in future.[334] The struggle for

[332] *IMT* xxxii. 334 ff.
[333] Homze, *Arming*, III, 144–5.
[334] Ibid. 145; Irving, *Rise and Fall*, 57.

raw-material allocations was waged by all three Wehrmacht services with the same dogged determination, but in the Luftwaffe the crisis coincided with the many uncertainties associated with the change of the bomber fleet to the Junkers 86, the Heinkel 111, and the Dornier 17, as well as with the difficulties involved in the introduction of the Messerschmitt 109. This special combination of factors in the Luftwaffe armament programme was probably not the least important reason for the subsequent increase in the number of fighters at the expense of the bombers in production plans.[335]

In the summer of 1938 Göring tried to overcome the stagnation in aircraft production by, among other things, a direct appeal to the manufacturers. His speech of 8 July was a notable mixture of recognition of the industry's accomplishments and threats against any deviation from the prescribed general line, combined with a pessimistic analysis of the political situation.[336] On 14 October 1938, after the Munich agreement had been signed—which Hitler regarded as a defeat—Göring announced in his orders a 'gigantic' armaments programme, in particular a fivefold increase in the size of the Luftwaffe.[337] At the same time the armaments programmes of the navy and the army were to be accelerated, exports increased, workers used more efficiently, and many other improvements made. Göring proclaimed practically the general mobilization of economic resources. But he said nothing or resorted to vague, general statements when explaining how these plans were to be carried out. In the Luftwaffe high command this announcement led to a burst of frenetic activity. At the end of October the general staff submitted a programme based on Göring's demands; it envisaged an expansion of the Luftwaffe to about 19,000 front and reserve aircraft, as well as 500 aeroplanes for carriers and other ships, by the spring of 1942.[338] Of course this 'gigantic' programme did not change the material facts of the German armaments situation at that point. To keep this Luftwaffe ready for action for a period of some length in a war which it was assumed would break out in 1941, such huge quantities of fuel would have been required that it would have been necessary to import 85 per cent of the known world production at that time to fill the storage tanks—although these had still not been built.[339] Moreover, the iron and steel situation, though it had improved slightly compared to 1937, made such a programme impossible, especially after Hitler had granted the navy unrestricted priority for its armaments projects at the end of January 1939. But these facts did not prevent the officers responsible for the plan in the ministry of aviation from drafting a new procurement programme in January and April 1939, whose monthly figures obviously bore no relation to the production situation of the industry but were still below the corresponding figures of the August programme of 1938. The fact that, in contrast to other European countries, monthly aircraft production in Germany did not rise but fell even in planning after

[335] Overy, 'Production Plans', 783 ff.
[336] *IMT* xxxviii. 375 ff.; Homze, *Arming*, 157–8.
[337] *IMT* xxvii. 160 ff.
[338] Völker, *Dokumente*, No. 89, pp. 211–12; Homze, *Arming*, 222 ff.; Overy, 'Production Plans', 782–3, 787 ff.; Irving, *Rise and Fall*, 67.
[339] Irving, *Rise and Fall*, 67; Völker, *Luftwaffe*, 138; Homze, *Arming*, 223; cf. Volkmann, IV.v.5 above.

the Munich conference showed that the economic limits of rearmament had been reached.[340] The grandiose programmes increasingly became plans for the future.

The various procurement programmes, which all remained drafts, including the 'concentrated procurement programme'[341] of August 1939, had no more significance for the period before the outbreak of the war. The intentions and goals they expressed are of little interest in view of the actual production conditions. The really decisive question was whether the privileged position of the navy in the armament economy could be eliminated, which would make skilled workers and raw materials available as the procurement programme had intended. Göring's more or less successful efforts in this regard in co-operation with the head of the war-economy staff, Major-General Thomas, have already been mentioned.[342]

As commander-in-chief of the Luftwaffe, Göring had other means to convince the commander-in-chief of the Wehrmacht of the importance of that service for the conduct of a future war, and to induce him to issue appropriate war-economy directives. For this purpose it was probably Milch who took the initiative in arranging a demonstration of modern developments in all fields of military aviation for Hitler at Rechlin on 3 July 1939, at which everything was shown that could possibly make a good impression—from the pressurized cabin to a radar system, a 3-cm. aircraft cannon, and a model of the Messerschmitt 262.[343] The demonstration possibly caused Hitler to overestimate the striking power and technological superiority of the Luftwaffe, and thus affected developments far beyond its intended purpose (which itself was not achieved). In this way armament projects became instruments in the struggle among the Wehrmacht services for a share of the available resources of the war economy.

The question remains as to the military objectives of the Luftwaffe in this struggle, in which it obviously used all available means to achieve its goals.

In the years before 1936 and, finally, with the sending of the Condor Legion to Spain, the Luftwaffe had fulfilled its initial political task. But what was its own estimation of its military possibilities? Was the politically successful 'risk Luftwaffe' also able to fulfil the military expectations of its creators? Knauss had planned his air force for a two-front European war with Poland and France; and this situation, with Czechoslovakia replacing Poland, also formed the basis of the 'Wehrmacht study 1935–6'. After this war-game, based on the relative strength of the various countries on 1 April 1936, the leaders of the Luftwaffe had to conclude that German air armaments were 'completely inadequate'. It was true that, during the game, the Luftwaffe had been able to fulfil its tasks as far as Czechoslovakia was concerned, but, in the opinion of the air command office under Wever, it would inevitably have been defeated by the much stronger French air force in the long term.[344] Therefore the objective of the Luftwaffe had to be to improve its

[340] Overy, 'Production Plans', 787–8, 795 ff.

[341] Ibid. 780 ff.; Homze, *Arming*, 226 ff.; Irving, *Rise and Fall*, 74–5; Köhler and Hummel, 'Organisation der Luftwaffe', 562 ff.

[342] Cf. the last three paragraphs of III.ii.3 (c) above.

[343] Irving, *Rise and Fall*, 73 ff.; Homze, *Arming*, 248–9; Boog, *Luftwaffenführung*, 44 ff.

[344] Völker, *Dokumente*, No. 196, pp. 449–50.

organizational, personnel, and material effectiveness in the following years. Reports from the field, and the appointment of an 'inspector of flight safety and equipment' in February 1936, showed the not surprising weaknesses resulting from the over-hasty Luftwaffe build-up.[345] In October 1936 the director of operations in the air command office, Major Deichmann, gave a lecture on the 'principles of operational aerial warfare' which indicated that, in addition to direct support of the army and navy, the Luftwaffe was working on the development of tactics against the 'sources of strength' of enemy forces and the 'will to resist' of the enemy population, quite in accordance with the guidelines of Luftwaffe regulation 16. The lecture also showed, however, that in the area of operational thinking there was still a significant lack of clarity and that systematic work on the relevant problems had only begun. Deichmann, who introduced his listeners to the complexity of target planning necessary for operational air warfare with convincing examples, explained with refreshing clarity[346] that 'most officers who concern themselves with the question of conducting an operational air war are of the opinion that it is only necessary to destroy as many of the enemy's factories as possible. The side that can do this first wins the war.' The urgent need to intensify training at all levels and to expand the infrastructure, especially the so-called 'E air-bases' planned as alternative bases in the event of war, was generally recognized.[347] However, this consolidation was slowed down and made considerably more difficult by the change to new aircraft, which required all the Luftwaffe's attention in 1937. Only after it was completed and the necessary qualitative improvement of the material, infrastructure, and training achieved did there seem to be a chance that the Luftwaffe would be able to fulfil its tasks in a European war on several fronts.

But at the same time developments began that led to a significant expansion of the Luftwaffe's military objectives. At the conference on 5 November 1937 Hitler explained his programme of conquest and stated his conviction that Britain would 'stand aside' and that 'military action by France against Germany' was improbable; but this judgement of the political situation was opposed by Neurath, Blomberg, and Fritsch. Their criticism seemed to impress even Göring, for he recommended ending the 'Spanish enterprise', probably in order to concentrate available forces in Germany for the intended operations, or for fear that the German military presence in Spain could led to a confrontation with the Western powers at the time of the intended expansion to the east and south-east. In any case, the Luftwaffe leaders could no longer exclude the possibility of a confrontation with Britain.

In the area of armaments this led to a decision by the technical office (Udet) in December 1937 to choose the Junkers 88 as a fast bomber and the successor to the Heinkel 111, and at the same time to require that it be able to serve as a dive-bomber. The first Junker 88 thus modified made its maiden flight on 18 June 1938. A month earlier the technical office had already planned to start mass production after

---

[345] Völker, *Dokumente*, No. 46, pp. 137 ff.; No. 173, pp. 413 ff.; No. 176, p. 420.
[346] Ibid., No. 198, pp. 454 ff.
[347] Völker, *Luftwaffe*, 105–6; Irving, *Rise and Fall*, 47.

November 1938.[348] This procedure, like the subsequent development of the Junkers 88 programme, can only be described as the corruption of the technical and industrial development and planning process by the new military objectives.

The 'advanced orientation' of 18 February 1938 by the chief of the general staff about the plans for air warfare in the west has come to be regarded as the earliest evidence of this change on the operational level.[349] In it the air-bases in eastern England, London with its docks and armaments factories, and the Channel ports were designated operational targets. On 4 May 1938 a discussion took place between the director of operations in the Luftwaffe general staff, Lieutenant-Colonel Jeschonnek, and Commander Heye of the operations department of the naval war staff.[350] From the record of this meeting it is clear that the Luftwaffe command was thinking of occupying Holland and Belgium to use those countries as bases for an air war against Britain and for a 'strategic surprise attack' on the British fleet. Jeschonnek also hoped that Italy's entry into the war would make it easier to attack Britain. On the whole these were vague aims; they were given concrete form only in the memorandum of the commander of the second Luftwaffe group command, General Felmy, on 22 September 1938 and in the plan game he directed in May 1939.[351] Felmy's sober observations on the still unsolved problems of conducting an operational air war across the sea and the inadequate training of air crews for the special conditions of a war against Britain, quite apart from the insufficient penetrative ability of the available bombers, pointed to the inevitable conclusion that the Luftwaffe could not carry out its new tasks. Even the planned mass production of the Junkers 88 could not have altered this position for a considerable time.

In August 1939 the Luftwaffe leaders had a total of 302 combat-ready squadrons at their disposal, most of which were organized in twenty-one groups.[352] More than 90 per cent of the 4,093 front-line aircraft available on 1 September 1939 were described as ready for action. Measured by Knauss's standards of 1933, there were 613 reconnaissance aircraft, a bomber fleet of 1,542 aeroplanes (including 366 dive-bombers), and a total of 771 fighters, to which, however, 313 more heavily armed Messerschmitt 109 'destroyers' can be added.[353] Thus, the proportions had shifted:

---

[348] Homze, *Arming*, 156–7, 163–4; Kens and Nowarra, *Flugzeuge*, 365. Cf. also nn. 330–1 above.

[349] Gundelach, 'Gedanken', 33; cf. also Gemzell, *Raeder*, 178 ff.; also Schreiber, 'Strategisches Lagebild', 175 ff.

[350] RML u. ObdL Genstb., i. Abt.; No. 144/38, g.Kdos., 20 May 1938, BA-MA PG/33272, Case GE 1165.

[351] Gundelach, 'Gedanken', 35 ff.; Völker, *Dokumente*, No. 199, pp. 460 ff.; Völker, *Luftwaffe*, 159 ff.; on the state of German air armaments and the level of readiness for action and combat-readiness of the Luftwaffe in the autumn of 1938 cf. esp. Murray, 'German Air Power', 107 ff. On the development of the Luftwaffe's operational plans—in which the element of an independent air war against the enemy's 'sources of strength' and 'will to resist' became increasingly important under the impression of political developments in 1938–9—cf. Maier, 'Aufbau der Luftwaffe'; also id.; 'Total War', 210 ff.

[352] Völker, *Luftwaffe*, 174–5.

[353] For an exact list, in which further possibilities of use are also given with corresponding figures, cf. ibid. 188 ff. On the changing tasks of individual types of aircraft cf. the data in Kens and Nowarra, *Flugzeuge*. Different figures are given in Köhler and Hummel, 'Organisation der Luftwaffe', 570–1.

air defence had been greatly strengthened compared with earlier armaments programmmes. Within the framework of total Luftwaffe armaments this preponderance was increased by the fact that the flak artillery with its twenty-one regiments was not only very well equipped with weapons but also had at its disposal nearly a third (107,000) of the total personnel (373,000) of the Luftwaffe in the summer of 1939. At the outbreak of war about 2,600 heavy anti-aircraft guns (88 mm.) as well as 6,700 medium-size and small guns (37 and 20 mm.) were available for defence against enemy air attack.[354]

The fact that in the course of its development the Luftwaffe had abandoned Knauss's ideas (which had never been binding), as well as those of the first armaments programmes, was due to Wever's influence. As head of the air command office he had placed more emphasis on co-operation with the other two Wehrmacht services. But it was also undoubtedly due to the technical and industrial conditions of Luftwaffe armaments programmes after 1936.

In view of the stagnation of aircraft production in 1937 and 1938 it would have seemed logical to eliminate first the many cause of the crisis as far as possible, with the exception of the raw-materials shortage, which could not be changed. The opposite was done. At the end of 1936 Göring demanded that the aircraft industry produce on a 'mobilization basis', and in the autumn of 1938 Hitler ordered a fivefold increase in the size of the Luftwaffe. This method of overcoming crises by excessive demands inevitably failed or produced largely adverse results in such a complicated matter as the Luftwaffe build-up. Politically motivated armament demands did not change the fact that the Luftwaffe only had two months' supply of fuel at the outbreak of the war. In addition the Luftwaffe was confronted with a new enemy: Britain.

International political developments, in which the Luftwaffe itself played a major role in the first years of the Third Reich, had caught up with it by the outbreak of the war. In an astonishingly short time the preconditions had been created for the Luftwaffe to fulfil its main task of waging an operational air war in the event of a European war on several fronts. However, the international consequences of German rearmament, especially of the Luftwaffe build-up, led to it being given a new mission which it had neither the leadership nor the weapons technology to carry out. The 'risk Luftwaffe' had itself created a political risk which it could not overcome militarily.

[354] Völker, *Luftwaffe*, 176 ff., 183, 193–4.

III. The Wehrmacht of the Third Reich

1. REARMAMENT AND THE EXPANSION OF THE SERVICES

IN February 1933 Hitler had described the build-up of the Wehrmacht as the most important precondition for re-establishing Germany's position as a great power. And in fact German rearmament in the following years became the most important and constant factor among the many different causes of the rapid and radical change in the European balance of power. More especially, in other countries it was considered a planned, purposive, uniform process, and this was not the least significant reason for its political effects, which were supported by propaganda. Because of Hitler's enormous power, his declaration to the Reichstag on 1 September 1939 that he had 'worked for over six years to build up the German Wehrmacht'[1] was regarded as a confirmation of this belief.

Nevertheless, the present survey of the individual stages of German rearmament has shown that the arming of the Wehrmacht as a whole was anything but planned and orderly. Rather, it was essentially an uncoordinated expansion of the individual services. There was no Wehrmacht armament programme as such. As far as can be seen, the services made their basic decisions without consulting or even conferring with each other. This was true of the army programmes of December 1933 and August 1936, the decisions on ship construction in the spring of 1935, and the planning of the navy in the autumn of 1938, as well as the first long-term aircraft procurement programme of the Luftwaffe of July 1934 and the programmes of the autumn and winter of 1938.

At first glance one is tempted to attribute this lack of co-ordination solely to the much-discussed but unresolved problem of the Wehrmacht senior command structure and the inadequate organizational authority of the defence (war) minister and commander-in-chief of the Wehrmacht. Undoubtedly this state of affairs was unsatisfactory and greatly strengthened the traditional tendency of the individual services to pursue their own objectives. But this explanation overlooks a deeper problem. The Reichswehr leaders under the Weimar Republic had learnt from the preparation of two armament programmes and related special programmes that the planning and goal-oriented co-ordination of material armament measures were a time-consuming and expensive process. Blomberg himself had participated in this work. The experiment, from which the navy typically had abstained, had been carried out under the pressure of special political conditions and limited funds. From 1933 onwards this pressure diminished considerably, permitting the military leaders in December of that year to plan an expansion of the army without any consideration of war-economy factors and related consequences. This clearly showed that they did not regard the modern armament planning achieved in the

[1] Domarus, ii. 1315. Salewski, 'Bewaffnete Macht', does not discuss the problems connected with the 'Wehrmacht' concept.

earlier programmes, which had been based on the experience of the First World War, as a guide and procedure to be extended to all services of the Wehrmacht. As the economic basis of armaments common to all the services did not receive sufficient attention for this reason, their traditional self-centred thinking, which had always been very pronounced in the navy, became even stronger. The Luftwaffe quickly followed this example, although it had paid the most attention to economic factors in its plans at the beginning of rearmament. Thus, the expansion of the individual services was a result not only of unsolved organizational problems but also of the inability of the military leaders to comprehend adequately the radically changed relationship between armaments and the economy since the First World War.

The increasing independence of the individual services was strengthened by another factor. Defence Minister Groener had begun his directive on the 'Tasks of the Wehrmacht' with this sentence:[2] 'The basis of the build-up and use of the armed forces is determined by the tasks set for them by the responsible political leaders.' For the Wehrmacht of the Third Reich such political directives could only come from Hitler himself, although Blomberg is said to have attempted to pursue a policy of his own, with Hindenburg's support, in the first months of 1933. But, as far as is known, apart from occasional, very general statements, Hitler never issued a directive encompassing all Wehrmacht armaments and prescribing some limitation of objectives, which would have called for at least a loose co-ordination of armament programmes of the individual services, before the outbreak of the war. Instead, all available evidence indicates that his participation was confined to making decisions in each case solely on the basis of factors important for the service concerned. The development of naval armaments is the most striking example. In addition, by constantly demanding acceleration of the armament programmes of the services on the one hand and setting up new institutions important for the defence economy on the other,[3] Hitler greatly intensified competition among the services. How little their expansion was related to the unsolved problem of the senior command structure is shown by the fact that Hitler did not change the decision-making procedure in armament questions after assuming direct command of the Wehrmacht at the beginning of February 1938. On the contrary, the competition among the services was intensified by new demands.

Under Groener's directive the 'build-up and use of the armed forces' was determined by the defined task. For different reasons Hitler and Blomberg did not follow this precedent. It was typical of the limited outlook of the military leaders after 1933, of which we have seen many examples, that the unity of the Wehrmacht was only expressed in the directives on uniform war preparations issued by the Wehrmacht office or the Wehrmacht high command in and after 1936. These directives dealt not with the very complex process of the build-up of the

---

    [2] Cf. III.i.2 above.
    [3] Cf. Volkmann, in Part II above. Dülffer, 'Beginn des Krieges', 456–7, also stresses the importance of Hitler's forcing the pace. Keitel failed in Nov. 1938 to induce Hitler to make the appropriate decisions: cf. III.ii.3 (c) above and the study by Geyer, 'Rüstungsbeschleunigung', 121 ff.

Wehrmacht, but merely with guide-lines for its use. This was still the real and almost exclusive domain of military thinking, as it had been during the First World War.

If one looks for common features in the rearmament of the three branches of the Wehrmacht, an institution comes to mind which, unlike the isolated programmes of the army, the navy, and the Luftwaffe, vigorously advocated a co-ordination of armament measures: the war-economy staff of Colonel (later Major-General) Thomas.[4] It had developed from the supply staff of the army ordnance office and played a key role in the organization of the first two armament programmes. In November 1934 it was integrated under an altered name as a department into the Wehrmacht office. Thomas, who since his transfer to the army ordnance office in 1928 had concentrated on the economic aspects of preparing and waging wars, attempted, together with other officers of the ordnance office, to put into practice the often cited 'lesson' of the First World War, that economic warfare was as important as the traditional armed conflict. If the economic resources of a nation had in fact become a decisive element in the conduct of a war, they ought to be systematically inventoried and their use in the event of war prepared as comprehensively and effectively as possible, and peacetime rearmament ought to be integrated into this system of economic war preparations.[5] But the complexity of economic processes and industrial-technical production presented many formidable obstacles to the realization of these ideas, which Thomas and his co-workers tirelessly promoted in memorandums and talks. Nevertheless, these inherent difficulties were not responsible for the fact that economic war preparations and rearmament were not organized and carried out according to 'war-economy' criteria; the primary reason was the refusal of the services to subordinate their own armament programmes to the guide-lines and directives of a single Wehrmacht office. Thus, the war-economy staff was limited from the very beginning to a consulting and, as far as possible, mediating function; it was never able to exercise any important influence on key decisions. The staff and its economic officers in the military districts represented the interests of the Wehrmacht in relations with industry. And because of its uncertain authority, relations with organizations and agencies outside the Wehrmacht involved in war-economy matters were extremely complicated.[6] As a result the influence on development of the only agency that attempted to achieve a co-ordination of Wehrmacht armaments programmes must be described as very limited.

The expanded authority of the army ordnance office in the development and procurement of individual armaments items for the other two services did not change the fact that the rearmament of the Wehrmacht was a domain of its

---

[4] Cf. Thomas, *Wehr- und Rüstungswirtschaft*, esp. pt. 1.

[5] On the resulting controversy, as between rearmament in depth and a broad, general rearmament, cf. Volkmann, II.v.1, 6 above; also the Conclusions to the present volume. On the 'blitzkrieg', a product of later ideas, cf. Carr, 'Rüstung', 445 ff.; Salewski, 'Bewaffnete Macht', 143–4; and Cooper, *German Army*, 113 ff.

[6] Especially relations with the president of the Reichsbank, Schacht, in his capacity as plenipotentiary for the war economy. Cf. Volkmann, II.II.5 above.

individual branches. The occasional conferences among their representatives did not lead to any co-ordination of the innumerable armament claims.[7] In spite of his official authority, Blomberg was not able to assert himself against Göring and Raeder and seems to have given up the attempt at a very early stage. The only feature the armament programmes of the Wehrmacht services seem to have had in common was Hitler's approval. As we have seen, he himself exercised no co-ordinating influence.

The dimensions and structure of the rearmament of the Wehrmacht as a whole were thus determined solely by the programmes of the individual services, whose objectives were in turn dominated by their respective, divergent ideas concerning the conduct of a European war on two or more fronts. Moreover, the dimensions of the programmes were constantly expanded by Hitler's demands that they be speeded up. The only limiting factors in an otherwise unrestrained rearmament were the serious shortage of militarily important raw materials, beginning in the second half of 1936, which finally forced the introduction of allotment quotas, the general economic bottlenecks after 1937, and the financial difficulties after the end of the Mefo-bills system in the spring of 1938. Hitler had not, as he claimed in the Reichstag on 1 September 1939, worked for six years building up the Wehrmacht. Rather, as chancellor and as supreme commander, he had neglected the idea of the Wehrmacht as a unified force and done his best to promote an uncoordinated expansion of the individual services.

This fact is also relevant to the analysis of Hitler's foreign policy, in ways which cannot be discussed here.[8] Even taking for granted that Hitler's foreign-policy objectives were based on ideological considerations, and that he pursued these goals in a fairly systematic manner, it cannot be overlooked that the rearmament of the Wehrmacht, which he rightly described as the most important precondition for his policy, was carried out without any recognizable overall planning determined by political aims. In addition to this political aspect of the manner in which the Wehrmacht was built up, there were the related military problems.

2. DISPUTES ABOUT THE STRUCTURE OF THE TOP-LEVEL COMMAND

As defence minister, Groener, who under the law of 23 March 1921 commanded the entire Reichswehr under the president as supreme commander, had given the services clear guide-lines for their further build-up and possible use with his directive of 16 April 1930. For this purpose he had made use of his Ministeramt, which as a military staff had the task of giving concrete form to his legal authority

---

[7] There is no adequate proof that Blomberg had a co-ordinating function in the armaments sector, as Dülffer postulates ('Beginn des Krieges', 452). Dülffer concentrates on the operational sector. In the economic committees Blomberg and Thomas did strongly support the general demands of the Wehrmacht, which, however, were uncoordinated. Cf. Thomas's memorandum 'Umbau des Heeres und Wirtschaftslage' of 20 June 1934, submitted through Blomberg to Hitler: text in Barthel, 'Rüstungswirtschaftliche Forderungen'. On this subject as a whole cf. Volkmann, II.v.2 above.

[8] Cf. concluding paragraphs of Messerschmidt, IV.vi.4 below, and Conclusions to the present volume.

not only to represent the Reichswehr politically but also to command it militarily. This attempt to achieve a co-ordinated direction of national defence failed primarily because of the collapse of the political base on which Groener had relied for support. In contrast, Blomberg's position was made much more favourable by the circumstances under which he was appointed defence minister. His strong position in the new cabinet, based not only on the support of the president but also on the Hitler–Blomberg 'alliance', seemed to offer a good chance to achieve a uniform leadership of the Wehrmacht in the build-up just beginning. In the first months after the National Socialists came to power, Blomberg's position was still further strengthened. By a cabinet decision of 4 April he was appointed permanent representative of the chancellor for all questions of national defence in the newly formed Reich defence council. This gave him the decisive voice in all organizational matters concerning the mobilization of the nation and its human, material, and moral resources in preparation for war. Finally, at the end of the month he was appointed defence minister and commander-in-chief of the Wehrmacht.[9] Although the appointment, which was not publicly announced, was only a formal confirmation of the authority given him within the framework of the defence council, the designation 'commander-in-chief of the Wehrmacht' opened up new possibilities. For the first time in the history of the Reichswehr the minister had all the authority necessary for a comprehensive organization of national defence, and for the first time this task had been given to a general on the active list, who was qualified for this highest military position by virtue of his experience as head of the Truppenamt. However, this development radically affected the argument, which had been going on for years, about the senior command structure.

In mid-October 1933 Blomberg instructed the Truppenamt to work out appropriate proposals, which were submitted at the end of the year.[10] They were intended to provide a form of organization suitable for peace and war, so that 'the chain of command . . . should accustom itself in peacetime' to function as it was meant to do in war conditions.[11] This principle reflected the widespread conviction in the officer corps that the change from peace to a state of war would be smooth and rapid and that, especially given Germany's strategic and economic situation, the opening phase of a war would be decisive. The greatest possible concentration of military power at the beginning of a war was therefore an urgent necessity. But as early as January 1934, in the discussion primarily within the army, clear distinctions were made between the functions of the military institutions in peace and in war.[12] In the further course of the debate the problem was reduced to the question of

---

[9] Cf. Absolon, *Wehrmacht*, i. 233–4, ii. 478, 450; Meinck, *Aufrüstung*, 101 ff., esp. 113 ff.; Müller, *Heer*, 216 ff.; Rautenberg, *Rüstungspolitik*, 322 ff.

[10] Cf. Rautenberg, *Rüstungspolitik*, 334 ff.; Müller, *Heer*, 622 ff.; id., *Beck-Studien*, Document No. 10 (memorandum of 15 Jan. 1934).

[11] From the position paper of the organization department of the Truppenamt (7 Dec. 1933): Müller, *Heer*, 622.

[12] Cf. Beck's memorandum of 15 Jan. 1934. At the beginning of his memorandum Beck wrote 'The senior command structure in peacetime must as far as possible be adjusted to the wartime organization from the very beginning', but he still considered important changes necessary in wartime; cf. also Rautenberg, *Rüstungspolitik*, 336 ff.

which institutions, with what authority, within the military apparatus would be responsible for the *operational* command of the Wehrmacht in wartime. This only took into account one aspect of modern warfare. Viewed from this perspective, the controversy loses much of the political and military significance attributed to it in the relevant historical literature.

In his capacity as defence minister and commander-in-chief of the Wehrmacht, Blomberg undoubtedly tried in 1933–8 to continue and expand the policy of an integrated command pursued by Groener and Schleicher. In view of the scale of rearmament in the Wehrmacht services, the resulting problems in the war economy, and the general organizational preparations for war within the framework of the defence committee, Blomberg was confronted with an enormous task. To prepare and deal with the innumerable decisions he had to make in his expanding area of responsibility, he had only the Ministeramt established by Schleicher. As head of this office he appointed Colonel Walther von Reichenau, who had already served under him as chief of staff in the first military district (East Prussia) and was known to be an enthusiastic advocate of an integrated Wehrmacht command. In his first year Reichenau seems to have concerned himself primarily with defending the independence of the armed forces in the National Socialist state; there is only occasional evidence of his having defended the interests of the Wehrmacht as a whole against the individual services.[13] Blomberg, on the other hand, defended those interests in the context of the disarmament conference and *vis-à-vis* the individual services in armaments as well as operational questions.[14] But it became clear that the Ministeramt did not have the personnel or other resources for this task. The responsibility for representing the defence minister in the Reich defence committee and for dealing with operational questions had to be transferred to the Truppenamt.[15] Only in February 1934 was the Ministeramt renamed the Wehrmacht office to indicate its future functions, and within it an 'Abteilung Landesverteidigung' (department of national defence) was created which, as Blomberg explained at a commanders' conference, was intended to be the nucleus of a Wehrmacht general staff. A special 'school of the Wehrmacht general staff' was also to be established. In the autumn of 1934 the Wehrmacht office assumed the chairmanship of the Reich defence committee, and on 1 November the office was expanded to include a new agency, the war-economy and armaments office under Colonel Thomas, to co-ordinate armament plans for the three services.[16] The expansion of this agency, the only one directly responsible to Blomberg, was clearly

---

[13] On Reichenau cf. Müller, *Heer*, 53 ff.; 217; Meinck, *Aufrüstung*, 114–15; Rautenberg, *Rüstungspolitik*, 337. Reichenau seems to have concerned himself more closely only with the armaments programme of the Luftwaffe. Cf. Rautenberg, *Rüstungspolitik*, 321–2.

[14] Cf. III.i.3, text to nn. 102–8; III.ii.2 (*a*), text to nn. 39 ff., above.

[15] Cf. Absolon, *Wehrmacht*, ii. 478 (4 Apr. 1938); Geyer, *Aufrüstung*, 362 ff., 372 ff.; Dülffer, *Weimar*, 317 n. 75.

[16] IfZ Archives Ed 1, vol. i, Liebmann's records of the commanders' conference of 2–3 Feb. 1934; Absolon, *Wehrmacht*, ii, 499, iii. 412; Meinck, 'Der Reichsverteidigungsrat', 413; Mueller-Hillebrand, *Heer*, i. 103; Meinck, *Aufrüstung*, 114 ff.; Thomas, *Wehr- und Rüstungswirtschaft*, 63–4; and the comprehensive description in Schottelius and Caspar, 'Organisation des Heeres', 319 ff. On the establishment and importance of the Wehrmacht academy created in the autumn of 1935 cf. Model, *Generalstabsoffizier*, 105 ff.

intended to enable him to exert his authority in directives and guide-lines for a general organizational preparation of the civil executive power and the nation for war, for the co-ordination of the rearmament of the individual services and the necessary economic measures, and for the preparation of future operational warfare. In brief, the Wehrmacht office was intended to take over the central function of directing all these measures.

It is known that the army, especially Fritsch and Beck, vigorously opposed this solution of the problem of the senior command structure and advanced arguments which went far beyond the internal military controversy. What were the chances of success of Blomberg's plan for an integrated Wehrmacht command? In his talk to the Reichswehr leaders on 3 February 1933 Hitler had pointed out that in Germany's relations with other countries 'the most dangerous period' would be that required for the 'build-up of the Wehrmacht'. Apart from the need to secure adequate domestic support, it was therefore the most important task of the commander-in-chief of the Wehrmacht to adjust the rearmament programmes of the three services so that they could be realized despite economic and financial uncertainties. The Luftwaffe programme of June 1933 seems to have met these criteria; the build-up of the twenty-one-division peacetime army decided upon in December of that year represented more a contravention of them, as it disregarded the economic aspects of rearmament.[17] However, insurmountable difficulties of co-ordination became clear not primarily in the planning of this first step of rearmament, but in its realization. The ordnance offices of the individual services insisted on carrying out their armament plans independently of each other. The inter-service co-operation important for the armaments economy was neglected; the competing 'consumers' negotiated their own industrial contracts separately. From the beginning of 1934 the head of the army ordnance office and his economic staff attempted repeatedly, with the support of the chief of the army command, to secure an agreement that the procurement of arms for the three branches of the Wehrmacht should be co-ordinated and organized by a central agency authorized to issue the necessary directives, but these efforts met with no success.[18] Their only result was the establishment, mentioned above, of the war-economy and armaments office in November 1934 under Colonel Thomas as a new department of the Wehrmacht office. But this office was unable to exert any significant influence on armament decisions and the way they were carried out.

The resistance to a uniform organization of Wehrmacht armament programmes came especially from the youngest service, the Luftwaffe, under its state secretary, General Milch. After he had secured adequate funds for armaments in close co-operation with Schacht and had succeeded in expanding the industrial base of aircraft production, Milch was able to resist all attempts by the Wehrmacht and army leaders to penetrate his domain, and was even able to expand it. He obtained Hitler's personal approval for the long-term programme of July 1934. The commander-in-chief of the Wehrmacht seems to have played second fiddle in this matter.[19]

[17] Cf. III.II.2 (a), (b); III.II.4 (a), at nn. 281 ff., above.
[18] Cf. Thomas, *Wehr- and Rüstungswirtschaft*, 62–3.
[19] Cf. III.II.4 (a), at n. 303, above.

The navy followed the same course as the Luftwaffe and insisted on independently carrying out its own measures. As chief of the navy command, Raeder sought and established contact with Hitler from the very beginning in the interest of his own armament plans. At the end of June 1934 he bypassed Blomberg and obtained Hitler's approval for important changes in the planning of ship construction.[20] The net result of these developments was that Blomberg's attempt as commander-in-chief of the Wehrmacht to organize and define the build-up and expansion of the armed forces within the framework of his own authority failed as early as the autumn of 1934.

Blomberg's difficult position in relation to Göring, who was far more powerful politically, is not in itself an adequate explanation of this failure. Next to the consolidation of the regime at home, rearmament was given absolute priority within the framework of Hitler's policies; consequently, intervention on his part to achieve a co-ordinated rearmament of the Wehrmacht would certainly have been conceivable.[21] But he did not intervene—quite the contrary. Did Blomberg really try to win Hitler's support? Or did he consider the ideological indoctrination of the Wehrmacht with National Socialist views more important? If Hitler was ever confronted with these basic problems, what motives were decisive for his obvious support of the independent armament programmes of the individual services? In the present state of research we cannot answer these questions. We can only observe that in this most important area for the conduct of future wars, the Wehrmacht idea suffered its first and, in the final analysis, decisive defeat.

In addition to Blomberg's attempt to establish a common foundation for rearmament, and his work in the Reich defence committee to achieve a general preparation of the nation for war, Blomberg's plan to direct preparations of the services by means of a Wehrmacht general staff represented a third area in which he intended to realize the idea of defence co-ordination. In October 1933 he still had to make use of the Truppenamt of the army command for this purpose, but shortly after he announced his intention at the beginning of February 1934, the relevant order to the Truppenamt was cancelled.[22] According to available evidence, the Wehrmacht office and its department of national defence took over this operational responsibility for the first time in the spring of 1935. On Blomberg's orders, Reichenau instructed the individual services at the end of March 1935 to send him documents and information on the time required for mobilization, as well as their deployment and operational plans in the event of a Franco-Italian attack. It was assumed that Czechoslovakia would not join in such an attack at the outset; it was expected to intervene later, however, and a surprise attack to eliminate the 'Russo-Czech air-base' (i.e. the Czechoslovak state) was to be considered in operational planning for such an eventuality.[23] On 12 April 1935 a conference attended by

---

[20] Cf. III.II.3 (*a*) above.

[21] Cf. Rautenberg's remarks, *Rüstungspolitik*, 338 ff. Attempts at an explanation based on Blomberg's personal inadequacies are not convincing; there is still no adequate biography of Blomberg. On the role of the special representatives in the armament economy cf. Volkmann, II.v.2 above.

[22] Dülffer, *Weimar*, 317 n. 75.

[23] *DGFP*, c. iii, Nos. 540, 568.

Hitler, Blomberg, and the commanders-in-chief of the three services was held to discuss the Wehrmacht build-up. On this occasion the tense international situation and its military implications were probably also analysed. One result of this conference was Blomberg's much-discussed directive to continue preparations for a surprise attack on Czechoslovakia, which has become known under the code-name 'Training' (*Schulung*) and which became completely detached from the context, assumed by Reichenau, of a Franco-Italian combination against Germany.[24]

Significantly, it was this directive of Blomberg's which gave rise to the dispute about the senior command structure of the Wehrmacht, which lasted until 1938 and broke out again during the war. To appreciate the actual scope of this controversy it is necessary to emphasize that only one branch of the Wehrmacht, the army, was deeply involved in it; that the other two services only occasionally showed an interest; and that it was almost exclusively concerned with the question of the institutional form of the operational command of the Wehrmacht in wartime. It did not affect the decisive question of the build-up period, the Wehrmacht armament programme. Finally, it should be remembered that Hitler, who assumed command of the Wehrmacht after Hindenburg's death and, by the defence law of 21 May 1935, was the 'supreme commander (Oberster Befehlshaber) of the German Wehrmacht', was confronted with the controversy for the first time as an incidental consequence of the Blomberg–Fritsch crisis at the beginning of 1938, when he promptly ruled against the army. Against this background the conflict between the army high command and the Wehrmacht office or the Wehrmacht high command appears primarily as a not unusual conflict of authority about a subject of only relative importance for the build-up of the Wehrmacht and the comprehensive organization of the nation for war. Specifically, it involved the question of how much influence the commander-in-chief of the army and his general staff should have on the command of the Wehrmacht in wartime, since uniform leadership was recognized by all sides to be an absolute necessity.

The problem had been discussed many times in the Truppenamt, the last occasion being at the turn of 1933–4, but no practical results or even a consensus on principles of a future solution had been achieved.[25] Blomberg's directive of 2 May 1935, drafted in the department of national defence of the Wehrmacht office, completely changed the basis of this discussion. There was now a Wehrmacht leadership with broad authority which did not share the ideas of the army leaders or their image of themselves and their service. On 3 May Beck, as chief of the Truppenamt, submitted his comments to the chief of the army high command. In a biting criticism of the directive he cast doubt on its military-policy assumptions, questioned the competence of the Wehrmacht leaders, and threatened to resign if they actually intended to begin practical war preparations on the proposed basis.[26] In terms of personnel policy, Beck's step, which was very probably supported by

---

[24] *IMT* xxxiv. 485–6. Robertson, *Pre-war Policy*, 60, 89–90; Müller, *Heer*, 211 ff.; Dülffer, *Weimar*, 318–19; Geyer, *Aufrüstung*, 417 ff. For an interpretation of Beck's attitude cf. esp. Müller, *Beck-Studien*, 225 ff. and Documents Nos. 28–30.

[25] Cf. III.III.2 above.

[26] Foerster, *Beck*, 58 ff.; Müller, *Heer*, 211 ff.; Geyer, *Aufrüstung*, 421 ff.

Fritsch, seems to have been initially successful. In June 1935 a man in whom the army, and especially Beck, had confidence took over the direction of the department of national defence in the Wehrmacht office: Colonel Alfred Jodl replaced Colonel von Vietinghoff, who had been responsible for the directive of 2 May. In autumn of that year the position of chief of the Wehrmacht office became vacant, and in this case too the commander-in-chief of the army had taken the necessary measures in time and was able to push through his candidate, the organization expert Keitel, against Blomberg's wishes.[27] Blomberg's intention to create a general staff in the Wehrmacht office seemed to be blocked by these two personnel decisions. But Fritsch and Beck were soon to realize that they had only achieved a Pyrrhic victory, as Keitel and Jodl proved to be determined and, finally, also ideological champions of an integrated operational command.[28] They succeeded in forcing through their own institutional settlement of the conflict.

The main points of the arguments advanced in memorandums by the army leaders in December 1935 and August 1937 can be easily summarized.[29] Beck and Fritsch claimed that the national defence department of the Wehrmacht office was not in a position to understand and judge the complex command problems of the three services, if only because it lacked the necessary establishment. The Wehrmacht office's function of advising the commander-in-chief of the Wehrmacht in matters of military command, ministerial tasks, and the 'organization of the fighting nation', they declared, exceeded its abilities, and, by attempting to take the place of competent advisers (the commanders-in-chief of the three services), the office was actually becoming an immediate danger. The army representatives assumed in their counter-proposals that, in any conceivable military conflict in which Germany might be involved, the army would have to bear the brunt of the fighting. This led logically to the demand that the commander-in-chief of the army and his general staff should be the first advisers of the commander-in-chief of the Wehrmacht in all important questions on the general conduct of a war. In August 1937 Fritsch formulated this demand as 'achieving complete agreement between the operational conduct of a war as a whole and the command of the army, by entrusting the commander-in-chief of the army with the formulation of all proposals for the total conduct of a war'. In December 1935 Beck had gone much further. He had considered the 'participation of the commander-in-chief of the army necessary in all important questions of national defence or war preparations, even in the cabinet or the Führer's office'. He repeated this demand, which constituted a claim to considerable influence in political decisions, in the conflicts in the spring of 1938 after Fritsch and Blomberg had been dismissed.[30]

---

[27] Meinck, *Aufrüstung*, 116, 221 n. 97; Dülffer, *Weimar*, 318 n. 80. On Jodl's qualifications cf. Müller, *Heer*, 240 n. 170. On Keitel's appointment cf. Görlitz, *Keitel*, 78 ff.

[28] Müller, *Heer*, 219 ff.

[29] Beck's memorandum of 9 Dec. 1935, 'Der Oberbefehlshaber des Heeres und sein 1. Berater, BA-MA N 28/2, text in Müller, *Beck-Studien*, Document No. 36 (for interpretations cf. Meinck, *Aufrüstung*, 121 ff., and Müller, *Heer*, 229 ff.); Fritsch's memorandum of Aug. 1937, 'Wehrmachtspitzengliederung und Führung der Wehrmacht im Kriege', is printed in Görlitz, *Keitel*, 123 ff.; cf. also Manstein, *Soldatenleben*, 289 ff. (for interpretations cf. Müller, *Heer*, 238 ff., and Düffler, 'Überlegungen', 146-7).

[30] Beck's political views in relation to the dispute about the senior command structure (cf. Müller,

At the beginning of September 1937 Blomberg flatly rejected the ideas and organizational suggestions of the commander-in-chief of the army.[31] However, it probably provided a certain satisfaction for the army high command that Blomberg entrusted them with the planning and execution of the first Wehrmacht manœuvre on 20–6 September 1937, on the ground that such a task would overtax the limited resources of the national defence department of the Wehrmacht office.[32] Although this conformed to the basic ideas of the army command, it became clear in day-to-day work that the aims and ideas of the Wehrmacht office had not changed. On the contrary, its expansive tendencies were unmistakable.[33] Ideological factors also played a role, though not a decisive one. Contrary to the expectations of Fritsch and Beck, Keitel and Jodl became not only enthusiastic advocates of an integrated Wehrmacht command, but also loyal and, in the end, uncritical followers of Hitler, whose foreign policy Fritsch and Beck opposed as representatives of the army high command because they considered the risks involved too high.

At the end of January 1938, when Hitler dismissed the commander-in-chief of the Wehrmacht as well as the commander-in-chief of the army, for a brief moment the question of the senior command structure remained open. But two important points rapidly became clear. In principle the three services did not question the need for a unified Wehrmacht command as it had existed until then; while Hitler on 26 January had rejected the idea of appointing Göring war minister, and had told Keitel on 27 January that he supported the idea of a 'single, unified Wehrmacht command'.[34] However, the personnel and institutional forms it was to take remained unclear for the time being. On 26 January Hitler had implied that he would temporarily take over Blomberg's functions and therefore work closely with the Wehrmacht office, but all interested groups attempted to achieve their own objectives in the vacuum that had been created at the highest levels of the Wehrmacht and the army. Hitler's prompt decision had put paid to Göring's ambition to add the war ministry to his list of party and state positions. It is uncertain whether concrete ideas about the future command structure of the Wehrmacht were an important factor in Göring's active role in preparing and initiating the Blomberg–Fritsch crisis.[35] After Hitler's decision, Göring's influence (as Luftwaffe chief) on the institutional solution of the Wehrmacht command problem remained decisive. On the other hand, several attempts by the army high command, especially Beck, to take advantage of the new situation to push through revised versions of the ideas Fritsch had presented in August 1937 were

'Staat und Politik', 607 ff.) do not alter the fact that it was essentially an internal organizational problem of the military and was regarded as such. Considering the power relationships in the National Socialist regime, its organizational forms, and the expansion of the Wehrmacht services, Beck's political plans showed a remarkable lack of realism.

[31] Görlitz, *Keitel*, 142.
[32] Müller, *Heer*, 323 n. 125.
[33] Cf. the controversies about the introduction of Wehrmacht commanders, *IMT* xxviii. 350, 354–5 (Jodl's diary); Müller, *Heer*, 231–2. In Oct. 1937 the department 'Wehrmacht communications' was created in the Wehrmacht office: Mueller-Hillebrand, *Heer*, i. 110.
[34] *IMT* xxviii. 356 ff. (Jodl's diary); Müller, *Heer*, 256 ff.
[35] Müller, *Heer*, 256–7.

unsuccessful. The commander-in-chief of the navy, Raeder, was very reserved and seemed mainly interested in preventing solutions that would have reduced the navy's independence.[36] Under these circumstances the real moving force was the Wehrmacht office, whose chief had become Hitler's confidential military adviser. Keitel and the head of the department of national defence, Jodl, not only strongly influenced Hitler's personnel and organizational decisions of 4 February 1938, but actually prepared them in detail.

The most important change resulting from the decree of 4 February was that Hitler himself took over command of the entire Wehrmacht.[37] The loyalty of the commanders-in-chief of the individual services was thus more closely bound to the person of the 'Führer and chancellor'. Hitler's military staff consisted of the former Wehrmacht office as the Wehrmacht high command, whose head now assumed the functions of the war minister. The unity of the Wehrmacht command was thus guaranteed and significantly strengthened at the top. The importance of the Wehrmacht office was greatly increased by its being made directly responsible to Hitler, although the term 'Wehrmacht high command' is misleading. The office was still not a central command with corresponding authority. Nevertheless, it did represent an important step in the direction of a Wehrmacht general staff, the objective Blomberg had announced as early as 1934. An indication of this tendency was the transfer of the military functions of the former Wehrmacht office to the newly formed 'Amtsgruppe Führungsstab' (operations staff group) in the Wehrmacht high command.

In the following months, however, the conflict about claims to military leadership broke out anew. By laying down that 'the Wehrmacht high command' was 'responsible in peacetime for the uniform preparation of the defence of the country in all areas' Hitler himself had left open the question of the senior command structure in wartime. The army high command—mainly Beck, supported by Manstein—took advantage of this opportunity to submit a new memorandum on 7 March 1938 which in its basic principles hardly differed from Fritsch's memorandum of August 1937. It was also sent to the commanders-in-chief of the navy and the Luftwaffe, but did not receive the expected support. Instead, Göring informed Keitel that there 'could be no question whatever' of the solution proposed by the army and that he would support the Wehrmacht high command.[38] Keitel and Jodl studied the army memorandum carefully. In a note of 22 March 1938 the opposing points of view were compared; the army high command seems to have been given the opportunity afterwards to formulate several points more precisely. Thereupon the head of the Wehrmacht high command, Keitel, stated his views on all related questions in a lengthy memorandum of 19 April 1938, 'Warfare as an Organizational Problem'.[39] It can be assumed that this memorandum was submitted

---

[36] Dülffer, 'Überlegungen', 147 ff.; Müller, *Heer*, 289 ff.

[37] Printed in Absolon, *Wehrmacht*, iii. 500–1. Cf. also Mueller-Hillebrand, *Heer*, i. 113; Müller, *Heer*, 291–2, 641 (Document No. 35, Keitel's organizational decree of 7 Feb. 1938); a different interpretation in Cooper, *German Army*, 84 ff.

[38] Cf. Dülffer, 'Überlegungen', 149 ff.; 160 ff.; *IMT* xxviii. 370 (Göring's comment); *Heeresadjutant bei Hitler*, 29 (with the certainly wrong date of 2 Aug. 1938).

[39] Görlitz, *Keitel*, 143 ff. (note of 22 Mar. 1938), 154 ff. (memorandum of 19 Apr. 1938).

to Hitler and received his approval before being sent to the commanders of the Wehrmacht services.

Hitler, who at the time was primarily concerned with the Austrian and Czechoslovak questions, probably did not pay much attention to the controversy. After his basic decision of 4 February, he seems to have been more inclined to win the support of the commanders-in-chief for the new 'Wehrmacht high command solution' by making tactical concessions. For example, on 25 February he raised the rank of the new commander-in-chief of the army to that of a minister, and on 2 March transferred to the commanders-in-chief some functions previously exercised by the war minister.[40] But according to Keitel, Hitler considered the army memorandum, which Brauchitsch handed to him on 7 March, as a personal attack.[41] This reaction meant that the army had suffered a setback in an important preliminary decision. Keitel's memorandum marked the final rejection of the army's ideas. Finally, at the end of May Hitler issued a decree in which the responsibilities of the Wehrmacht high command were defined more precisely in accordance with the views of Keitel and Jodl.[42]

In the struggle for a unified Wehrmacht command, in the particular area of preparations for operational warfare, the objective Blomberg had pursued since 1934 had thus been accepted in principle by the outbreak of the war; this, however, was not the result of a compromise on basic positions but rather of Hitler's assuming direct command of the Wehrmacht. The head of the Wehrmacht high command, in his memorandum of 19 April 1938, had presented convincing arguments for a central, comprehensive organization of the Wehrmacht and the nation for war purposes, basing his opinions on views of warfare that clearly reflected those developed by the Reichswehr in the late 1920s. However, a comparison of the principles involved with the actual results of the controversy about the senior command structure clearly shows that his success was relatively insignificant. Neither the problem of organizational measures for the 'co-ordination of the propaganda and economic war to support the military struggle' nor the problem of 'the organization of the nation in arms' had been resolved satisfactorily from a military point of view. In addition, the reason for the success was at the same time its weakness. In a masterly fashion Hitler had succeeded in making all power, including military power, dependent on himself. However, in the necessary delegation of tasks and functions he preferred to create competing centres of power, thus preventing any attempt to achieve a systematic co-ordination and structuring of areas of responsibility.[43] His personal assumption of direct command of the Wehrmacht, and the 'Wehrmacht high command solution', did not guarantee a

---

[40] Dülffer, 'Überlegungen', 150. On the organizational structure of the military command at the beginning of the war cf. Fig. III.III.1.

[41] Görlitz, *Keitel*, 184.

[42] Dülffer, 'Überlegungen', 154 ff.

[43] The picture drawn by Hüttenberger ('Polykratie', 423 ff.) of power-relationships in the Third Reich is confirmed by developments in the military sphere, an area that Hüttenberger himself neglects. However, it must be noted that Hitler's position was far more powerful than those of the competing power-centres; the term 'polycracy' can therefore be misleading. Cf. Haffner's remarks (*Meaning of Hitler*, 43 ff.) about the 'destruction of the state' by Hitler.

A.

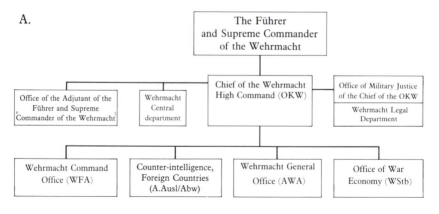

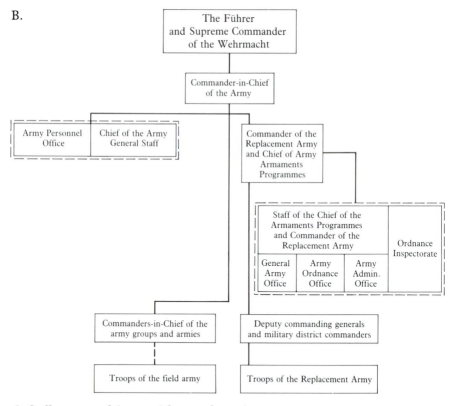

B.

A. Staff structure of the armed forces, 1 September 1939
B. Command structure of the army, 1 September 1939
C. Command structure of the navy, 1 June 1939
D. Command structure of the Luftwaffe, 2 (5) October 1939

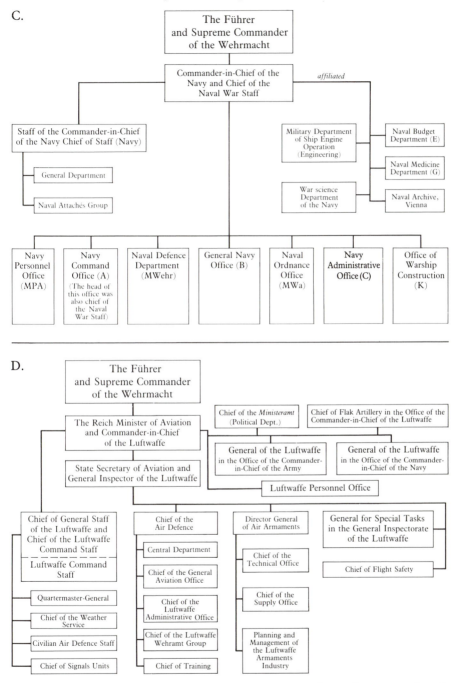

Sources: (A–C) compiled by Dr Klink; (D) compiled by Dr Boog (from 2 documents, of 2 and 5 Oct. 1939)

FIG. III.III.I. Command structure of the services, 1939

unified command organization of the Wehrmacht in wartime, nor did it mean that war preparations would be systematically co-ordinated, as was obvious in the area of Wehrmacht armaments.

3. THE *GLEICHSCHALTUNG* OF THE ARMED FORCES

Thus, as far as the Wehrmacht was concerned, the Blomberg–Fritsch crisis[44] did not lead to a 'concentration and strengthening of the political, economic, and military power of the Reich', as was claimed in the press release on the cabinet meeting of 5 February 1938.[45] More to the point was Hitler's categorical statement to the Reichstag on 20 February that there was in Germany 'no problem of . . . the relation between the National Socialist Party and the National Socialist armed forces', and that the latter were 'devoted to the National Socialist state in blind loyalty and obedience'.[46] This ideological unity of party, state, and Wehrmacht postulated by Hitler in conjunction with the new organization of the Wehrmacht command did not leave any room for the ideas advocated in different ways by Blomberg and Fritsch of an independent role for the armed forces in the National Socialist state. The tensions between the party, its organizations, and the state on the one hand and the armed forces on the other were resolved by the complete subordination of the latter to the purposes and aims of the former. This was the real significance of the Blomberg–Fritsch crisis.

At the beginning of February 1933 Blomberg had summed up his intentions in a talk to Reichswehr commanders. He considered it his task to maintain the Reichswehr as an 'instrument of power above party politics, to underpin the Wehrmacht by making the population fit to fight (*wehrhaft*)', and 'to build up the Wehrmacht with all possible means to make it a usable instrument for preserving national security'.[47] The idea of the army being 'above politics', which Blomberg deliberately emphasized in the changing situation of February 1933, not only reflected a traditional position but was also intended, in conjunction with the aim of making the population battle-ready, to express the attitude of the military leaders towards the new political forces outside the executive. The army's duty to remain 'above politics' also implied maintaining a clearly reserved attitude towards the dominant political party, the NSDAP. In Blomberg's opinion, abandoning this position would mean a 'decline to the level of a party army (*Parteitruppe*)' and destroy the foundations on which the Reichswehr had been built up. This ingrained

---

[44] Historians have still not arrived at a clear account of the background and above all the individual phases of the Blomberg scandal, the Fritsch crisis, and the plot as a whole. Cf. Müller, *Heer*, 255 ff.; Deutsch, *Conspiracy, passim*; Reynolds, *Treason*, 121 ff.; and the informative review of the German version of Deutsch's book by Peter Hoffmann in *MGM* 20 (1976), 196 ff. Salewski provides many details in 'Bewaffnete Macht', 193 ff. There is general agreement that the crisis was connected with the conference of 5 Nov. 1937 and the generals' disagreement with Hitler's assessment of the situation, also Himmler's drive to expand his own power and Göring's ambition to become war minister. Cf. Irving, *War Path*, 4 ff.

[45] Domarus, i. 786.

[46] Ibid. 796–7; Baynes, i. 451 (incomplete).

[47] Commanders' conference of 3 Feb. 1933. Cf. Vogelsang, 'Dokumente', 433.

attitude became difficult for the military leaders to maintain when, in the summer of 1933, it became clear that in future the state would be controlled not by several but by only one, totalitarian party. Remaining above politics in a one-party state was not only a logical, but also a political impossibility. For this reason Blomberg abandoned his earlier attitude as early as the beginning of March 1933 and called upon his commanders to 'support the national revolution' without reservation.[48] Moreover, he lost no opportunity to point out that the leaders of the NSDAP deserved the confidence of the Reichswehr, as they represented the best traditions of Germany's past and took those traditions as guide-lines for their actions.[49] The domestic and foreign-policy decisions of Hitler's government in 1933 supported Blomberg's assertions. In spite of their sceptical attitude towards the party and their criticism of NSDAP political forms and methods, the officer corps could not maintain the reserve implied by the principle of remaining 'above politics' towards a movement whose domestic and foreign-policy goals largely agreed with the national traditions embodied in the Reichswehr itself. The 'partial identity of aims'[50] required a new definition of the relationship between the armed forces and the state.

In his speech on the anniversary of his coming to power, Hitler himself coined the expression that the state was 'supported by two pillars', politically by the 'national community' (*Volksgemeinschaft*) organized in the National Socialist movement, and militarily by the Wehrmacht.[51] This two-pillar theory, whereby Hitler also declared the Wehrmacht to be the 'sole bearer of arms' in the state, agreed completely with the ideas of the Reichswehr leaders and the officer corps in general. It implied the recognition of the independence of the armed forces within the state, and also seemed to accept the military's claim to a decisive influence in political matters. But the symbolism of the two pillars also expressed the competitive element in the relationship between the military and the Party and its organizations as the 'sole embodiment of the political will of the nation'. As Hitler was not only the head of state but also the undisputed leader of a totalitarian political movement, it was inevitable that sooner or later the armed forces would come to be regarded no longer as part of the foundation of the state but rather as merely its instrument, and would thus forfeit the special degree of influence and independence on which the two-pillar theory was based. This point was reached in 1938. Thereafter, the armed forces constituted a 'National Socialist Wehrmacht' with Adolf Hitler as its commander-in-chief.

The political history of the Wehrmacht in 1933–9 is usually described against the background of the important political role played by the Reichswehr in the Weimar Republic. But it should not be overlooked that the special circumstances under which the Reichswehr had been an important factor in German domestic politics disappeared more or less rapidly after 1933. Above all, within little more than two

---

[48] IfZ Archives Ed 1, vol. i, Liebmann's record of the commanders' conference of 1 Mar. 1933.

[49] On Blomberg's attitude towards Hitler and the Nazi movement cf. Müller, *Heer*, 49 ff., 61 ff.; also the inadequate analysis in Cooper, *German Army*, 20 ff.

[50] Messerschmidt, *Wehrmacht*, 1 and *passim*.

[51] Müller, *Heer*, 67.

years the military leaders and the entire officer corps were freed from all the domestic- and foreign-policy restrictions that had prevented them from performing their military functions before 30 January 1933. Concentration on a rapidly increasing number of military tasks led to a decline in political activity within the Reichswehr and also in its domestic political influence.

In January 1934, when Hitler formulated his two-pillar theory, the Reichswehr was still an important factor in domestic politics and even necessary for the stability of the regime, as Röhm's SA threatened not only the position of the military but also, implicitly, that of the party itself. In the eyes of the Reichswehr developments from the 'seizure of power' until the Röhm affair at the end of June and the beginning of July 1934 confirmed the wisdom and success of the political course pursued by Blomberg and especially Reichenau. The Reichswehr's ideological acceptance of the new regime—which the officer corps generally found quite easy, since it emphasized their own strongly national and military traditions and convictions—had been rewarded, as they saw it, with the elimination of their dangerous rival for the position of 'sole bearer of arms' within the state.

Blomberg had not only vigorously promoted the 'opening' of the Reichswehr towards the National Socialist regime[52] in speeches and articles; he had also taken appropriate measures, ranging from permission for the Reichswehr music corps to play hallowed National Socialist tunes to acceptance of the 'Aryan clause' for the Reichswehr.[53] To this last measure may be added the Reichswehr's active participation in the elimination of its rival Röhm and his SA, its unprotesting acceptance of the murders on that occasion of Generals Schleicher and Bredow,[54] the constantly intensified 'national political indoctrination courses' at all levels, and above all the administering of the Wehrmacht oath of loyalty to the person of Adolf Hitler, the 'Führer of the German Reich and nation', on the day of Hindenburg's death—a measure taken on the initiative of Blomberg and Reichenau.[55] With all these developments, the process of 'adjustment' and 'opening up' amounted to an almost complete ideological integration of the Wehrmacht into the National Socialist regime. Blomberg consistently promoted what he called 'this *Gleichschaltung* with the National Socialist philosophy'[56] until his dismissal at the end of January 1938. He refused to be deterred either by frequent conflicts with individual groups within the party or by the end of the Wehrmacht's status as 'sole bearer of arms' when Hitler sanctioned the creation of three armed SS regiments.[57]

Blomberg and the head of the Wehrmacht office, Reichenau, based their policies on the assumption that the rearming of the Wehrmacht, together with the comprehensive organization of the nation for war, directed and supervised by the

[52] Müller, *Heer*, 71 ff. Blomberg thus created an essential precondition for the penetration process defined by Hüttenberger ('Polykratie', 427).

[53] Müller, *Heer*, 68, 78.

[54] On the Röhm affair cf. III.II.2 (b) above.

[55] Müller, *Heer*, 134 ff., Salewski, 'Bewaffnete Macht', 53, 81 ff.; cf. Blomberg's announcement at the ministerial conference on 1 Aug. 1934, in *Regierung Hitler*, ii, No. 382, p. 1385.

[56] Blomberg at a commanders' conference on 12 Jan. 1935; cf. Müller, *Heer*, 167.

[57] Höhne, *Order*, 439 ff.; Müller, *Heer*, 147–8.

military leaders, which the experience of the First World War had shown to be necessary, and, finally, the conduct of the armed conflict itself, were only conceivable and feasible if the Wehrmacht enjoyed a firm base of support in the state and the population. Then the military leaders would be able to exercise influence commensurate with their responsibility for the defence of the nation in a conflict. However, this plan failed quite early within the Wehrmacht itself, as the individual services resisted the control of the Wehrmacht leaders in major areas. The same was true of important parts of the state executive. Blomberg's influence on Hitler is difficult to assess precisely; it undoubtedly declined with the increasing stability of the regime and the growing significance of economic factors in armament programmes. Reichenau concerned himself much more than Blomberg with the political interests of the Wehrmacht and attempted with great tactical skill to defend them against the Party and its organizations. His removal in the autumn of 1935 and the appointment of Keitel as his successor contributed to the fact that the integration of the Wehrmacht into the National Socialist state did not give it the decisive influence its leaders had originally expected.

Particular aspects of the political activities of the Wehrmacht leaders were watched critically by the staffs of the individual services. Because of the importance of the army in the Reichswehr and the Wehrmacht, reactions within it have been examined in detail, whereas the navy and the Luftwaffe have received little attention in this regard.[58] In summary it can be said that the criticism was directed less at the general direction of Blomberg's policies than at the methods used to carry them out. In many respects the army, the navy, and the Luftwaffe were all of the opinion that Blomberg was over-hasty in pursuing his policy of 'opening' the Wehrmacht to the National Socialist movement, its ideology and values, by issuing one decree after another without considering all the consequences. Even Hitler thought he occasionally forced the pace too much in the political reorientation of the Wehrmacht.[59] The staffs of the individual services preferred a more leisurely approach and concentrated on establishing institutional safeguards against excessive influence by the party or its organizations. Fritsch and Raeder in particular placed great value on preserving their freedom of action in personnel matters, and based their decisions in this area more than did the Wehrmacht high command on traditional values and standards of behaviour. But Fritsch too was convinced that 'the foundation of the modern army must be National Socialist',[60] and Raeder declared in a speech in March 1939 that the 'Wehrmacht and the Party have become an indivisible whole in attitude and spirit'.[61] Thus, in principle Fritsch and

[58] On the army cf. Müller, *Heer, passim*, and Messerschmidt, *Wehrmacht, passim*, with evidence of reactions in the navy and the Luftwaffe (9, 46–7, 60–1, 78, 140 ff., 184 ff.); cf. Schreiber, 'Reichsmarine', 11.

[59] Messerschmidt, *Wehrmacht*, 210 n. 746; cf. *Heeresadjutant bei Hitler*, 20.

[60] Müller, *Heer*, 143.

[61] Messerschmidt, *Wehrmacht*, 78–9. Cf. Hitler's speeches of 18 Jan. 1939 (to lieutenants finishing their training in 1938, cf. Domarus, ii. 1039) and 10 Feb. 1939 (to army commanders, cf. Domarus, ii. 1075). For the interpretation cf. Thies, *Architekt*, 112 ff., and Schreiber, *Revisionismus*, 272–3, and the reaction in the small circle of officers opposed to the regime (Groscurth, *Tagebücher*, 166 ff.). The complete speech of 10 Feb. 1939 is printed in *Hitlers Städte*, 290 ff.

Raeder approved the policy towards National Socialism which Blomberg had been pursuing so consistently since 1933; their criticism was limited to the methods used and to the extent of the integration sought.

The fact remained that tension between the Wehrmacht and the National Socialist organizations was reduced only temporarily after the elimination of the SA and finally led to the Blomberg–Fritsch crisis. This was because Hitler believed that complete freedom to dispose of all military forces as he saw fit was a more important precondition for his expansion plans than ideological conformity on the part of the Wehrmacht. In this regard he distrusted the corps of senior officers, all of whom were marked by the Reichswehr spirit. In April 1938 he declared that the great majority of the generals had rejected him, and in September 1939 he observed even more pointedly that 'the spirit of the 100,000-man army' would be overcome only when all candidates for the officer corps were recruited from the Hitler Youth.[62] The above-quoted statement in his Reichstag speech of 20 February 1938 that the Wehrmacht was 'devoted to the National Socialist state in blind loyalty and obedience' was thus more of a wish than an accurate description of the existing situation. In addition to the not unfounded expectation that the ideological indoctrination of the Wehrmacht could be achieved more quickly with younger officers, Hitler also planned to realize this objective with the help of Heinrich Himmler's Verfügungstruppe (SS special-duty force), whose strength had risen to about 18,000 by the outbreak of the war.[63]

On 30 June 1934 the SS-Leibstandarte (bodyguard regiment) 'Adolf Hitler', organized in the summer of 1933, had performed invaluable services for Hitler in his precarious situation between the SA and the Reichswehr. On the same day Hitler rewarded this unit by ordering that in future it should be organized as an independent regiment equipped with modern weapons and outside the Reichswehr.[64] A few days later the SS was made directly responsible to Hitler. Thus, at the very moment of its victory over the SA the Reichswehr was confronted with the fact that, as a result of a specific decision by Hitler, it had again been deprived of its position as 'sole bearer of arms' of the nation.

The reactions to this event of the defence minister and the army command throw a revealing light on the causes of the diverse conflicts between these top-level military institutions. Blomberg accepted Hitler's decision immediately and without reservation, and informed the Reichswehr commanders that the SS would be organized and equipped in division strength but would consist of three independent

---

[62] Cf. Messerschmidt, *Wehrmacht*, 210 n. 746; *Heeresadjutant bei Hitler*, 20.

[63] On the development of the SS special-duty force (Verfügungstruppe) cf. Höhne, *Order*, 436 ff., 456. Höhne gives the strength of these troops at the start of the war as about 18,000 men; Hitler's decree of 18 May 1939 set 20,000 as the final goal (cf. Klietmann, *Waffen-SS*, 32 ff.). The Totenkopf (Death's Head) units were additionally part of the SS military formations; at the beginning of the war they were organized in 5 Standarten (regiments). No reliable figures are available on their strength, which, however, was probably about 10,000. Cf. Höhne, *Order*, 455; Buchheim, 'SS', 195; Klietmann, *Waffen-SS*, 345 ff. On the Waffen-SS (armed SS) cf. Wegner's comprehensive survey of the relevant literature ('Garde', 210 ff.), covering many different aspects, also his standard work *Hitlers politische Soldaten*, 290 ff., and id., 'Honour', 220 ff.

[64] Müller, *Heer*, 147.

regiments.[65] His motives for so doing are not absolutely clear, but it seems certain that he never considered opposing Hitler. The army command, which had recognized the function of the SS as a party army from the very beginning and had taken warning from its experiences with the SA, of course had to accept Hitler's and Blomberg's decisions and orders; but, in accordance with its self-protective policy, it did everything in the following months and years to limit the influence of its new rival. Beck, who concerned himself intensively with this matter, was able in stubborn, time-consuming negotiations to expand the influence of the army command on the training of the SS units. He made the army's power of inspection into an effective instrument of supervision and, in co-operation with Fritsch, was able to block plans to equip the SS units with artillery.[66] In revenge for this restrictive tactic adopted by the army command, Himmler organized a thoroughgoing slander campaign against the army with the help of his Sicherheitsdienst (SD: security service), which was ended temporarily to the satisfaction and relief of the Reichswehr by Hitler's speech at the 'rally of German leaders' (Kundgebung der deutschen Führerschaft) on 3 January 1935.[67]

A month later, however, Hitler issued a decree that showed his great tactical skill and persistence in pursuing his objectives. The SS units were placed under the command of the defence minister in peacetime to be prepared for service in war. This was a concession to the army command. But at the same time Hitler ordered that, in the event of war, the SS formations would be integrated into the army as divisions.[68] This blocked Beck's intention to dissolve the SS units as such in wartime. The feud between Beck and Himmler continued over how Hitler's decision should be carried out. Both sides regarded it as only a temporary solution. The conflict acquired a new dimension as a result of Himmler's appointment as chief of the German police on 17 June 1936. In principle Beck supported the central organization of police forces, as he hoped this would divert Himmler's attention from military matters. But in November 1937, when Himmler ordered the appointment of a 'senior SS and police Führer' in every military district for mobilization purposes, Beck recognized the danger to uniform mobilization planning by the Wehrmacht, in this case its district commanders.[69] By concentrating the police forces in his hands, Himmler was able to circumvent Beck's previously successful efforts to shield the army from the demands of the SS units.

Finally, in January 1938, when Himmler made a second, this time successful, attempt to organize the downfall of the commander-in-chief of the army, it became

---

[65] Ibid. 147–8; Reynolds, *Treason*, 56.

[66] Müller, *Heer*, 148 ff.; Reynolds, *Treason*, 56 ff, offers interesting material on this phase of the controversy.

[67] On this crisis cf. above all the detailed description in Müller, *Heer*, 154 ff.; Reynolds, *Treason*, 62; Domarus, i. 468 ff.

[68] On Hitler's decree of 2 Feb. 1935 cf. Müller, *Heer*, 151 ff.; Reynolds, *Treason*, 63. Part of the decree is printed in Klietmann, *Waffen-SS*, 20.

[69] Cf. Buchheim, 'SS', 55 ff., 133 ff. (text of decree of 13 Nov. 1937); Reynolds, *Treason*, 67. Hüttenberger, 'Polykratie', 436, stresses the consolidation and increasing power of the SS, the SD, and the Gestapo after 1936.

clear that, compared to the situation in January 1935, the Wehrmacht had lost much of its political influence and the army officer corps much of its homogeneity. Blomberg's policy of preserving the decisive influence of the Wehrmacht through its ideological integration with the regime, and the army policy of preventing the penetration of the military establishment by National Socialist organizations, especially the SS, had failed. This was clearly shown by the conditions under which General von Brauchitsch became Fritsch's successor[70] and by Hitler's decree of 17 August 1938, which completely changed the status of the SS military units.[71] The Verfügungstruppe was placed under Himmler's sole command (as Reichsführer SS) in peacetime, and all limitations on the strength of the SS military units were removed. The 'Party army', which the officer corps of all three Wehrmacht services had always considered a denial of all military tradition, was now advancing and expanding. At a time when the ideological unity of the Wehrmacht based on loyalty to Hitler had been largely achieved as a result of Blomberg's policies, when Hitler's foreign-policy successes had reached new heights in the annexation of Austria, and when the homogeneity of the officer corps had been largely undermined by the process of rearmament, Hitler in his political capacity indicated that he considered the subordination of the armed forces to the National Socialist regime by no means completed. In Himmler's later plans the Verfügungstruppe represented the core of a future Wehrmacht in which, in line with Hitler's intentions, responsible military behaviour would give way to 'blind loyalty and blind obedience'.

4. HITLER AND THE OPERATIONAL PLANNING OF THE WEHRMACHT

A month before Hitler's SS decree, on 16 July 1938, the chief of the army general staff, General Beck, had described in trenchant language the exact opposite of the kind of soldier Hitler desired, in notes for a report to his commander-in-chief: 'In the judgement of history these [military] leaders will have blood on their hands if they do not act in accordance with their professional and political knowledge and conscience. Their soldierly obedience ends when their knowledge, their conscience, and their sense of responsibility forbid them to carry out an order.'[72]

With Beck's memorandums of July 1938 the long-standing dispute about the senior command structure and the relationship between the armed forces and the National Socialist regime was placed on a new level in the context of the Blomberg–Fritsch crisis and Hitler's clear formulation of his warlike intentions. Beck still believed that the problem was to free Hitler, the responsible statesman, from the influence of 'radical' forces that were strengthening or at least obsequiously supporting his resolve to 'smash Czechoslovakia by a military

[70] On Brauchitsch's 'capitulation' to Hitler cf. Müller, *Heer,* 262 ff., 268–9; Messerschmidt, *Wehrmacht,* 210 ff.; Reynolds, *Treason,* 132, 137.

[71] Partial text in Klietmann, *Waffen-SS,* 26 ff.; cf. Höhne, *Order,* 448 ff.; Buchheim in *Anatomy,* 262 ff.; Müller, *Heer,* 345–6; *Heeresadjutant bei Hitler,* 15, 18–19, 41.

[72] Note of 16 July 1938: Müller, *Heer,* 321; Reynolds, *Treason,* 148 ff., 157 ff. On Beck's memorandums in the summer of 1938 cf. Müller *Heer,* 300 ff.; id., *Beck-Studien,* 272 ff. and Documents Nos. 44–54.

operation in the foreseeable future'.[73] As in Beck's responsible judgement the political and military consequences of such an operation at the time for which it was planned would inevitably lead to a disaster for Germany, he considered that the limits of soldierly obedience had been reached. He not only informed Brauchitsch of his intention to resign if it proved impossible to persuade Hitler to change his mind; he also urged that, because 'unusual times require unusual deeds', the generals should act together and threaten to resign collectively to force Hitler to abandon his war plans. If this plan were successful, a conflict with the 'radical' forces in the party and the state, especially the SS, would be inevitable. Beck was not deterred by this prospect in his assessment of the military and political situation. The essence of his ideas[74] was to win this conflict with the help of the Wehrmacht 'for the Führer' in order to reform the Third Reich. He completely rejected any idea of a *putsch*, a plot against Hitler or the National Socialist regime as such.

Beck's initiative, which was downright revolutionary for a chief of the German general staff, ended with his unspectacular resignation on 21 August 1938, under conditions he obediently fulfilled.[75] The course of events and the reasons for the failure of his plan have often been described and discussed. The refusal of the commander-in-chief of the army to accept the arguments of his chief of staff, the half-hearted support of Beck's views by the group commanders and commanding generals assembled in Berlin on 4 August 1938, and finally Hitler's vigorous counter-measures forced Beck to abandon his position.[76] With the majority of his contemporaries Beck shared the belief that there was a difference between Hitler and the 'radical' forces around him. This illusion was the result of the 'partial identity of aims' that had bound the military leaders, as well as representatives of other groups and classes of the population, to the National Socialist regime since 1933, and which finally made their ideological assimilation an easy matter.

The hesitation and inactivity of the generals was, however, not so much due to the conclusions Beck drew from his erroneous belief, but rather to his general judgement of the military and political situation. Brauchitsch and the other generals completely agreed with him that the Wehrmacht was not then able to fight a European war and that a world war would mean the end of Germany.[77] But they did not share his conviction that the conflict with Czechoslovakia would inevitably lead to a confrontation with the Western powers. There were military and political reasons for their position. They did not deny the possibility of such a confrontation, which Hitler himself had admitted in his directive of 30 May 1938 for the 'two-front war with the main area of concentration in the south-east'.[78] But in this question

[73] From the directive of 30 May 1938, *IMT* xxv. 434.

[74] On the note of 19 July 1938 cf. Foerster, *Beck*, 124 ff.; Müller, *Heer*, 326 ff.; Reynolds, *Treason*, 160 ff.; Müller, *Beck-Studien*, 304 ff.

[75] Müller, *Heer*, 339 ff.; Reynolds, *Treason*, 167 ff.

[76] On the conversations on 4 Aug. and Hitler's statements to the generals on 10 and 14 Aug. 1938 cf. Müller, *Heer*, 333 ff., 338 ff.

[77] Cf. the statement by Freiherr von Weichs on the results of the conversation of 4 Aug. 1938, ibid. 335. [78] See *IMT* xxv. 434.

they had more confidence in the chancellor's political judgement than in that of the chief of the general staff. Since 1933 Hitler had demonstrated such political skill that doubt in his judgement was possible only from a position of fundamental opposition.

In any case Hitler was convinced, and made every effort to convince his generals, that neither France nor Britain was able and prepared to risk a conflict with Germany because of Czechoslovakia. However, in his directive of 30 May he had described as the assumption on which his political assessment was based 'the ability of the Wehrmacht to create a situation within the first two or three days that would make clear to interventionist enemy states the hopelessness of Czechoslovakia's military position'. The weakness of Beck's arguments lay in his estimation of this ability. Studies by the general staff came to the conclusion that the Wehrmacht would be able to subdue the Czechoslovak forces in a relatively short time, in any case far less than the three weeks Beck had estimated at the beginning of June.[79] Thus, the basis of his military arguments, his ability to make an objective military judgement of the situation, was shaken. Although his assessment of the European consequences of a conflict between Germany and Czechoslovakia later turned out to be quite accurate, Beck's credibility and ability to convince the commanders and general staff officers began to decline from the moment when his military judgement of the situation proved to be incorrect. Finding his position intolerable, he took the only logical course in requesting to be relieved of his post as chief of the general staff.

Beck's resignation four days after Hitler's SS decree marked the complete failure of the policy of protecting the army from the Party and its organizations. Beck's conflict with Hitler's policy of war was a manifestation of the unresolvable dilemma of a military opposition whose members had destroyed the basis of their own actions as a result of the 'partial identity of aims'—in this case their continued pursuit of a militarily and politically aggressive great-power policy and their support of unrestrained rearmament. Moreover, Beck's defeat had the effect that in the military leaders' own special area, viz. comprehensive operational war preparations, the interference of the new commander-in-chief of the Wehrmacht, Hitler, increased and became completely dominant. In operational planning the complete subordination of the Wehrmacht to Hitler's will proceeded rapidly and with little friction between Beck's resignation and the outbreak of war in September 1939.

The first 'Directive for the Uniform War Preparations of the Wehrmacht', which has been mentioned several times above, was issued by the war minister and commander-in-chief of the Wehrmacht on 24 June 1937.[80] It went into effect on 1

---

[79] Cf. Müller, *Heer*, 314, 336; Reynolds, *Treason*, 154. On the Czechoslovak defences cf. Zorach, 'Fortifications', 81 ff.; on the military technical factors cf. the thorough and convincing analysis by Müller, *Beck-Studien*, 298 ff.; id., 'Militärpolitik', 333 ff., and 'Militärpolitische Konzeptionen', 159 ff.

[80] *IMT* xxxiv. 734 ff. For interpretations cf. Meinck, *Aufrüstung*, 127 ff.,; Robertson, *Pre-war Policy*, 90 ff.; Müller, *Heer*, 211, 236 ff.; Dülffer, 'Weisungen', 651; Geyer, *Aufrüstung*, 429 ff. A comprehensive interpretation from Beck's point of view is in Müller, *Beck-Studien*, 243 ff., which clearly shows the lack of realism in his plan (reminiscent of Tirpitz) for an 'active military policy of [treaty] revision while avoiding a major war'. Cooper's interpretation (*German Army*, 49 ff.) is completely inadequate.

July 1937 and replaced a directive of June 1936, no copies of which have been found. In the 'general guide-lines' (part 1), which preceded the 'description of the preconditions, tasks, and targets in a probable war' (part 2) and the 'procedural suggestions for certain special preparations' (part 3), it was stated that because of the general international situation Germany 'had no reason to expect an attack by any other country'; and Germany herself did not intend to 'start a European war'. Nevertheless, it was necessary that the Wehrmacht should always be 'ready for war', able to 'repel attacks at any time' and 'to militarily exploit favourable political opportunities'. The directive described only two probable types of war: a two-front war with a concentration of the fighting in the west (Deployment 'Red') and a two-front war with a concentration of the fighting in the south-east (Deployment 'Green'). In 'Case Red' the directive envisaged a purely defensive war against France, holding the Rhine–Black Forest line against the expected French offensive. 'Case Green' was a variation of 'Red' in which the Soviet Union and Czechoslovakia were expected to assume a 'hostile posture'. 'Case Green' was intended to forestall an 'imminent attack' by a superior coalition consisting of France, Czechoslovakia, and the Soviet Union, by carrying out a 'surprise attack on Czechoslovakia'. The 'purpose and objective' of this attack would be to 'smash' the Czechoslovak armed forces and occupy Bohemia and Moravia—but not Slovakia—in order to eliminate the 'Czechoslovak threat in the east' for the duration of the war and thus concentrate on the 'war in the west'.

The third part of the directive listed the special cases which were to be 'reviewed' only within the high commands of the individual services.[81] Among these were plans for intervention in Austria in the event of a restoration of the Habsburg monarchy (Special Case 'Otto') and preparations for the possibility of a military confrontation with 'red' Spain (Special Case 'Richard'). Of particular interest was the special case 'Extension of Red/Green', in which a possible worsening of the military starting-position of cases 'Red' and 'Green' was to be considered. Here it was assumed that Britain, Poland, and Lithuania would join the enemy coalition individually or jointly. 'This would make our military situation unacceptable, even hopeless. The political leadership will therefore do everything possible to keep these countries, especially Britain and Poland, neutral.'

If one compares this directive with Groener's 'Tasks of the Wehrmacht' seven years earlier,[82] the radical change becomes impressively clear. German military policy was no longer based on 'self-defence' in an emergency or on using the Wehrmacht to take advantage of a favourable situation within the framework of the collective security system, regarded as a guarantee of Germany's existence. Instead, planning concentrated on the problem of a European war on several fronts, in which Germany would not limit itself to defensive measures. Groener had demanded '*definite* prospects of success' as a precondition for a possible use of the Reichswehr, and had especially stressed aspects and requirements of the armaments economy in outlining its tasks and operational plans. No trace of this was to be

[81] Cf. Görlitz, *Keitel*, 95; the formula suggests a compromise.
[82] Cf. III.I.2, at n. 48 above.

found in Blomberg's directive, which was rather an expression of 'purely instrumental, technical thinking usable at any time for any purpose,'[83] a conception that had been alien to Groener.

'Case Red' had its precursor in Blomberg's directive of 25 October 1933,[84] and for 'Case Green' Blomberg had already ordered an operational study under the cover name 'Training' (*Schulung*) at the beginning of May 1935.[85] The reaction of the commander-in-chief and the army general staff to the directives from Blomberg and his Wehrmacht office has been examined in detail many times. The army leaders' criticism at that time was basically not directed at the military and political objectives expressed in the directives. But Fritsch and Beck did object to what they regarded as the completely inadequate consideration given to Germany's military and armaments situation in 'Training' and 'Otto'. However, their sharpest attacks were aimed at the Wehrmacht office and its growing authority. Beck protested with good reason against 'Training'. There was no such criticism of 'Case Green', most probably because it was part of a European war on several fronts, which Beck expected in any case. As Special Case 'Otto' did not agree with these well-founded expectations, he did not cause the general staff to make the necessary plans, but he energetically took charge of the planning himself when Hitler ordered him to prepare the annexation of Austria in March 1938.[86] Nothing shows more clearly the nature of the institutional conflict than the fact that the army leaders reacted to the operational directive of June 1937 with their memorandum of August 1937 on the senior command structure and the command of the Wehrmacht in wartime.[87]

Hitler's statements at the conference with Blomberg, Neurath, and the commanders-in-chief of the three services[88] on 5 November 1937 changed the basis of Wehrmacht operational planning in one important respect. Previous planning, of which the directive of 24 June 1937 was a good example, had concerned itself in a traditional way with solving the military problem of a two-front war. The political framework was based essentially on the conditions created by the treaty of Versailles and other treaties ending the First World War. German operational planning certainly contained offensive elements in a general revisionist sense, but a clear political objective had hitherto been lacking. This was provided by Hitler's statement of 5 November 1937 that the 'goal of German policy' was 'the protection and preservation of the national substance (*Volksmasse*) and its increase' and that therefore the main issue was the 'problem of space', which could only be solved 'by

---

[83] Müller, *Heer*, 237.

[84] *IMT* xxxiv, 488 ff.; cf. Robertson, *Pre-war Policy*, 26; Geyer, *Aufrüstung*, 362; III.II.2 (*c*) above.

[85] Cf. III.III.2, at n. 24 above.

[86] Müller, *Heer*, 236 ff.; cf. id., *Beck-Studien*, Document No. 41, and Irving's description in *War Path*, 82 ff.

[87] On the navy's reaction to the operational instructions of the Wehrmacht command cf. esp Gemzell, *Raeder*, 45 ff., 58 ff., 113 ff.; id., *Organization*, 278 ff., 285 ff. The reaction of the Luftwaffe can hardly be determined. Cf. Völker, *Luftwaffe*, 71 ff.; III.II.4 (*b*) above.

[88] On the conference of 5 Nov. 1937 cf. esp. Messerschmidt, IV.v.5 below, and the abundant literature cited in the notes there; Carr, 'Rüstung', 438 ff.; and the earlier work by Meinck, *Aufrüstung*, 173 ff. On the reaction of the military cf. Müller, *Heer*, 243 ff., and Reynolds, *Treason*, 115 ff. On the background of the conference and the armaments-economy factors involved cf. III.II.3 (*b*) above.

force' and 'never without risk'. In concrete terms Hitler did not go beyond the territorial aims described in cases 'Green' and 'Otto', but he indicated that they were only the first steps on the way to a 'total solution'. The routine work of the general staff came increasingly under the dynamic influence and pressure of his political will. For Hitler the only remaining questions were when and how his objectives should be reached. He reserved the answers to these questions for himself. Beck, who did not understand the full dimensions of Hitler's projected expansion of German 'living-space', and who in his memorandum of 12 November 1937 strongly condemned the proposed actions against Czechoslovakia and Austria[89] because he feared their military and political consequences, was the first to be confronted, in March 1938, with Hitler's determination to decide the time and form of the military operations himself. In the summer of that year Beck failed in his attempt to change Hitler's aims or even to modify details of his plans.

The head of the department of national defence in the Wehrmacht office, Colonel Jodl, took the initiative in translating the new political objectives into military directives. After advance notification by the war minister, the part of the directive of 24 June 1937 dealing with 'Case Green' was replaced by a new version of 21 December 1937.[90] According to this, 'when Germany has achieved complete preparedness for war in all fields, the military conditions will have been created for an offensive war against Czechoslovakia, so that the solution of the problem of living-space can be carried to a victorious end even if one or other of the great powers intervenes against us'. This was a very narrow interpretation of Hitler's statements, for he did not consider the 'smashing' of Czechoslovakia anything like a solution of the 'living-space' problem, and the phrase about 'complete preparedness for war in all fields' could be interpreted very broadly. The new version greatly strengthened the offensive, aggressive elements in the directive of June 1937, which, however, was maintained as a whole.

As a result of the Blomberg–Fritsch crisis, the related institutional changes, and the annexation of Austria, Hitler's role in operational planning became even more important. On 21 April 1938 the head of the Wehrmacht high command was ordered to produce a new version of 'Case Green', as the version of 21 December 1937 no longer reflected Hitler's intentions. From the notes of the conference on 21 April it is clear that Hitler preferred a 'lightning-like operation following an incident', and had already developed very specific ideas about how the military action should be carried out.[91] Strangely enough, Keitel submitted the draft of the new version to Hitler only on 20 May. In an accompanying letter he stressed that new 'strategic directives' must be issued to go into effect on 1 October 1938 for the mobilization

---

[89] Müller, *Heer*, 249 ff.; Reynolds, *Treason*, 117 ff. Cf. esp. the thorough and convincing analysis by Müller, *Beck-Studien*, 248 ff. and Document No. 43; for another interpretation cf. Salewski, 'Bewaffnete Macht', 190 ff.

[90] Müller, *Heer*, 246–7; Dülffer, 'Weisungen', 651–2. The text of the directive of 7 Dec. 1937 is in *IMT* xxxiv. 745 ff.; the directive of 21 Dec. 1937 is in *DGFP*, D. vii. 635 ff. In the quoted passages the directive certainly reflected Beck's plans. Cf. Müller, *Beck-Studien*, 261 ff., and Messerschmidt, IV.v.5, at nn. 122–5 below.

[91] *IMT* xxv. 415 ff.; Dülffer, 'Weisungen', 665, 705; Görlitz, *Keitel*, 182–3; Robertson, *Pre-war Policy*, 121; Müller, *Heer*, 300 ff.; Reynolds, *Treason*, 148 ff.; *Heeresadjutant bei Hitler*, 27–8, 33.

year 1938/9, and that the new version for the interim took into account the changes in the strategic situation created by the annexation of Austria.[92] The intention of the Wehrmacht high command behind this statement was probably, as it had been a year earlier in June, to issue a comprehensive directive for the 'uniform' war preparations of the Wehrmacht. But Hitler's concentration on the Czechoslovak question frustrated this plan. The comprehensive directive remained only a draft. Under the pressure of Hitler's influence, Wehrmacht operational planning came to consist of directives for particular current tasks. The instrumentalization of the Wehrmacht, its *Gleichschaltung*, thus already affected operational war preparations at this point.

After his talk with Keitel on 21 April 1938 and the partial Czechoslovak mobilization of 20 May, which he regarded as a provocation, Hitler concerned himself for months with military preparations for a forcible solution to the 'Czech question' and with the construction of a belt of defensive fortifications against France and Belgium. In both cases he acted as chancellor and commander-in-chief of the Wehrmacht in such a way as to disrupt the previous command structure. Not only did he order the 'general inspector of the German road system', Fritz Todt, to carry out the construction of the 'West Wall', but he also ordered the Reich labour service and troops stationed in the west to be used for that purpose, and himself dictated a long, detailed 'Memorandum on the Question of our Fortifications', which he sent to the high commands of the Wehrmacht and the three services. The responsible department of the army general staff, the inspector of engineers and fortresses, and the army command as a whole played only a subordinate role in this plan and finally incurred Hitler's anger because of their reservations and criticism. Hitler did not consider the additional demands this project would place on the labour market and the transport system, or the increased raw-materials requirements, nor were they discussed with the responsible agencies or persons, especially Göring.[93] The sole determining factor remained the political decision to 'smash' Czechoslovakia.

On 28 May Hitler personally informed the commander-in-chief of the army of this decision at a meeting of representatives of the Wehrmacht, the Party, and the state in the Reich chancellery. At this meeting he also left no doubt that he would not be deterred from carrying out his decision by the threat of a conflict with the Western powers.[94] Two days later he signed the new version of the directive for 'Case Green', which, compared with Keitel's draft of 20 May, had been given a considerably more aggressive tone.[95] It began with the notorious sentence 'It is my

---

[92] *IMT* xxv. 422 ff.; Müller, *Heer*, 307–8; Dülffer, 'Weisungen', 705. There is no evidence that the drafts of 18 June and 7 July 1938 (*IMT* xxv. 445 ff.; Dülffer, 'Weisungen', 706–7) were issued as directives; they are not referred to in later directives.

[93] On the fortifications programme in the west cf. Görlitz, *Keitel*, 184 ff., 193 ff.; *IMT* xxv. 429, 432, 443; Förster, *Befestigungswesen*, 45 ff., 113, 123 ff. (Hitler's memorandum); Leeb, *Tagebuchaufzeichnungen*, 49, 462 ff.; *Heeresadjutant bei Hitler*, 26 ff., 32–3; Mason, *Arbeiterklasse*, 106–7, 152 ff.; Dülffer, 'Beginn des Krieges', 457, 470; and, with important new material, Irving, *War Path*, 117 ff., 155 ff., 207, 227.

[94] Müller, *Heer*, 307–8; Reynolds, *Treason*, 151.

[95] *IMT* xxv. 433 ff.; Dülffer, 'Weisungen', 706.

unalterable decision to smash Czechoslovakia by military action in the foreseeable future.' The Wehrmacht was instructed to 'make the necessary preparations immediately'. And Hitler did not confine himself to issuing these general instructions, but participated closely in the actual preparations. He not only informed himself about the condition of the Czechoslovak fortifications, the troops manning them, and the equipment of the Czechoslovak army, but also concerned himself with the German forces to be used in the operation and formed his own conclusions. When the new chief of the army general staff, General Halder, explained the operational plan to him at the end of August, according to which a co-ordinated offensive from Silesia and Austria was to prevent a withdrawal of the Czechoslovak army from Bohemia and Moravia, Hitler confined his criticism to individual points; but it soon became clear that he did not share the opinion of his chief of staff regarding the use of motorized forces, especially armoured divisions. He demanded that they be concentrated in the Tenth Army, which was to advance from northern Bavaria against Pilsen and Prague. In two dramatic discussions with Brauchitsch and Halder at the beginning of September 1938, Hitler overrode their objections.[96] Thus, the army general staff itself was reduced to a mere instrument for carrying out his will.

Munich deprived Hitler of the military triumph on which he had been concentrating all his energies for months, and the result finally achieved did not satisfy him. The day after the occupation of the Sudeten areas he sent Keitel a number of questions through his Wehrmacht adjutant Schmundt that clearly showed he was already thinking about the occupation of all of Bohemia and Moravia. Ten days later he issued a directive to the Wehrmacht services which referred to 'finishing off the rest of Czechoslovakia' as a task for which the army and the Luftwaffe must be prepared at any time.[97] In a supplementary directive of 17 December 1938 he ordered that the plan, which was to be carried out as a surprise attack and without special mobilization measures, should appear to the outside world as a mere 'pacification'.[98] Preparations were to be made accordingly, and the operation of 15 March 1939 was actually carried out in this fashion.

In the directive of 21 October 1938 the Wehrmacht high command had made another attempt to advance the ideas of the directive of June 1937 concerning uniform war preparations. The first sentence read: 'I shall define the future tasks of the Wehrmacht and the necessary preparations for conducting a war in a further directive.' But for the time being this was not done. The first point of the directive dealt in some detail with the general task of 'securing the frontiers' and 'protection against surprise air attacks', but the following parts were concerned only with individual operations such as 'finishing off the rest of Czechoslovakia' and 'occupying Memel'.[99] A month later a supplement dealt with another possible operation, the 'surprise occupation of Danzig'.[100]

---

[96] *IMT* xxv. 426 ff.; Görlitz, *Keitel*, 190–1; *Heeresadjutant bei Hitler*, 36–7; Irving, *War Path*, 133 ff.; Murray, *Change*, 225 ff.

[97] *IMT* xxv 520 ff., xxxiv. 477 ff.; Dülffer, 'Weisungen', 707 ff.   [98] *IMT* xxxiv. 483–4.

[99] A directive had already been issued for this on 18 Mar. 1938 (*DGFP*, D. vii. 639 ff.), and was now reconfirmed.   [100] Directive of 24 Nov. 1938, *IMT* xxxiv. 481 ff.; Dülffer, 'Weisungen', 709.

Compared with the directive of June 1937, which had provided instructions on the tasks of the entire German armed forces for certain situations of political conflict and had given the services clear orders forming parts of an overall plan, Wehrmacht planning after the spring of 1938 was determined more and more by Hitler's short-term political intentions. For example, no uniform directives were issued for all parts of the Wehrmacht concerning the necessary staff planning for conflicts with France and/or Britain, which Hitler indicated that he considered quite possible. The situation resembled that in the armaments sector; there was less of an effective Wehrmacht command than ever.

On 25 March 1939, after the occupation of Bohemia and Moravia on 15 March and the Memel district on the 23rd, Hitler explained his future intentions to the commander-in-chief of the army, Brauchitsch, for the first time in concrete terms.[101] He first said that he did not want to solve the Danzig problem by force and thus drive Poland into Britain's arms, but he did not exclude the possibility of a *fait accompli*. Then he turned to the 'Polish question', which he was not thinking of solving 'for the time being' but the solution of which should now be studied by the general staff. If there were a conflict, Poland would have to be 'so completely crushed' that she would not 'have to be considered as a political factor in the coming decades'. The German frontier would then be pushed far to the east. Hitler did not intend to advance into the Ukraine, but the establishment of a separate Ukrainian state could be envisaged. Thus, the defeat of Poland and the annexation of substantial parts of the Polish state were Hitler's next territorial goals.

According to Keitel, Hitler had closely studied the military situation *vis-à-vis* Poland in connection with the directive of 24 November 1938 on the occupation of Danzig, and had expressed himself in a contemptuous fashion about the fortifications there.[102] But for the military leaders a new stage in Hitler's expansion policy was reached only with his order to Brauchitsch to have the general staff study what later became 'Case White'.

It was typical of Hitler's disregard of formal divisions of responsibility, here as in other areas, that at first his own military staff, the Wehrmacht high command, was not informed of the new order. But a preparation of 'Case White' only made sense if the other two Wehrmacht services participated. For this reason Keitel tried to reverse this dangerous precedent for the Wehrmacht high command as soon as possible after hearing of Hitler's 'expression of will'. At the same time he tried to co-ordinate the operational planning of the armed services by means of a comprehensive directive. In his letter on 3 April he announced his intention to issue a 'directive for uniform war preparations of the Wehrmacht for 1939–40' and tried in this way to uphold the principles of the directive of June 1937.[103] But he was only able to send part of the promised directive, namely 'Case White'; the other parts were to follow later.

---

[101] *IMT* xxxviii. 274 ff.; Dülffer, 'Weisungen', 710; Müller, *Heer*, 390–1. On political and diplomatic developments in regard to Poland cf. Messerschmidt, IV.vi.2 and 4 below.

[102] Görlitz, *Keitel*, 196–7; Müller, *Heer*, 382–3.

[103] Dülffer, 'Weisungen', 710 ff.; Müller, *Heer*, 391 ff.; *IMT* xxxiv. 380 ff.

The description of the political preconditions and objectives, like the section on military conclusions and the tasks of the Wehrmacht, was, it is supposed, dictated by Hitler himself.[104] It was couched in somewhat veiled language: the guiding principle of Germany's relations with Poland was still to 'avoid all disturbances'. But if Poland assumed a threatening attitude, a 'final settling of accounts' could become necessary. In that case it would be the task of the political leaders to isolate Poland and limit the war to that country. 'Case White' should therefore by no means be considered the 'precondition of a military showdown with our enemies in the West', whose hostility still determined the 'dominant objectives in the build-up of the Wehrmacht'. The task of the Wehrmacht in 'Case White' would be to 'annihilate the Polish forces'. For this purpose preparations for an 'initial surprise attack' were to be made. Keitel also informed the commanders-in-chief that preparations were to be made in such a way that, from 1 September 1939 onwards, 'Case White' could be put into effect at any time. Although the tasks of the branches of the Wehrmacht were described in some detail in the directive, Keitel demanded that the individual services submit their 'intentions' by 1 May.[105]

The services received further sections of the directive with a letter of 13 April. These dealt with 'securing Germany's frontiers and protection against surprise air attacks' (section I)[106] and the 'occupation of Danzig' (section III).[107] Both parts were based on the directives of 21 October and 24 November 1938, but some sections were more detailed. In addition, 'instructions concerning command authority in East Prussia in the event of hostilities' were sent as section IV; their precursor was to be found in an order of 27 September 1938.[108] Finally, on 10 May the three high commands received sections V, defining the operations areas of the army,[109] and VI, 'instructions for the war against the enemy's economy and the protection of the German economy'.[110] 'Special instructions' for sections I–III were issued one day later by the Wehrmacht high command.[111]

Thus, in barely one and a half months a thick bundle of directives intended to guarantee co-ordinated action by the Wehrmacht services had been issued. This underlined the claim of the Wehrmacht high command to be the central command institution of the Wehrmacht, and seemed to make it far more than the mere staff of the Wehrmacht commander-in-chief. But Hitler's sentence in his letter of 11 April was still valid: the 'future tasks' of the Wehrmacht would be defined in a special directive; the individual directives represented, so to speak, only a temporary solution. And indeed they dealt with only one of the possible conflicts, the imminent clash with Poland. Deployment 'Red', which had still been in the foreground in the directive of June 1937, had already been replaced in that position

---

[104] Dülffer, 'Weisungen', 711.
[105] *IMT* xxxiv, 381.
[106] Ibid. 382–4.
[107] Ibid. 397–8.
[108] Ibid. 400–2.
[109] Ibid. 402.
[110] Ibid. 403–8.
[111] Ibid. 384–7, 392–6, 398–400. Cf. also Raeder's directive for 'Case White' of 16 May 1939, ibid. 428–42.

by 'Green' in a supplement of 7 December 1937. In the directives of the spring of 1939 'Case Red' was no longer mentioned. The possibility of a conflict with France was only touched upon under the heading 'frontier security West'. The same was true of the special 'Case Red/Green', although the navy and the Luftwaffe had been working intensively on the problems involved in a war against Britain since 1938.[112]

This fact is all the more astonishing as Hitler had conceded the possibility of a war with the Western powers at a conference with his senior commanders and their closest advisers on 23 May 1939.[113] If one accepts Schmundt's notes, which were written later, on this point, Hitler even considered the conflict with Poland a relatively unimportant issue. His thoughts were concentrated on the unavoidable conflict with Britain, the 'motive force of opposition to Germany'. If Poland could not be isolated 'it would be better to attack the West and finish off Poland at the same time'. For that possibility Hitler outlined very specific military objectives, such as the occupation of Holland and the capture of Belgian air-bases. If, however, Poland could be isolated from her former friends, Hitler was determined to attack her 'at the first opportunity'. Then it would be possible to plan the war against Britain, which would have to be carefully prepared, for the period 1940–5. Accordingly, the target date for the completion of the arms programme was to be 1943–4. However, no operational planning was begun in the Wehrmacht for this possible conflict Hitler had outlined in such detail, as would normally have been the task of the staffs of the Wehrmacht services. This fact shows the complete subordination of the Wehrmacht to Hitler's will, the sole determining factor. The Wehrmacht had lost its once jealously guarded independence even in the area of operational planning, and did not even fulfil its task of advance planning for a conflict which the political leadership described as possible.

Hitler's failure to issue direct orders was due to his conviction that, in spite of all their statements to the contrary, the Western powers would not actively oppose a German attack on Poland. He was also aware that the army, navy, and Luftwaffe commands, and even the Wehrmacht high command, were more than sceptical about Germany's chances and prospects in a war with the Western powers. How much this silent opposition of the military leaders disturbed him can be seen in his speeches at the Berghof to the Wehrmacht generals on 14 and 22 August 1939.[114] He informed his listeners in uncompromising terms that he had decided to crush Poland, and explained the political and ideological reasons for his decision. In addition, he obviously placed great value on convincing the military leaders that the Western powers would not intervene. His strongest argument in this respect was that negotiations for a non-aggression treaty between Germany and the Soviet Union were almost concluded. Many officers no doubt found this convincing, but the signing of the Anglo-Polish alliance on 25 August left no doubt about British

---

[112] Cf. III.II.2 (*d*), at nn. 177–85, and III.II.4 (*b*), at nn. 349–51 above.

[113] *IMT* xxxvii. 547 ff.; Müller, *Heer*, 397; Dülffer, 'Weisungen', 712–13.

[114] On Hitler's speech of 14 Aug. cf. Halder, *Diary*, i. 6 ff.; *DGFP*, D. vii. 551. On Hitler's speech of 22 Aug. 1939 cf. Halder, *Diary*, i. 20; Müller, *Heer*, 409 ff.; Baumgart, 'Ansprache Hitlers', 120 ff.; *Heeresadjutant bei Hitler*, 58–9. On both speeches Domarus, ii. 1229 ff.

determination to oppose further German expansion. This created immense difficulties for Hitler's planning, as no general staff preparations had been made for such an eventuality. This explains the paradox that 'Directive No. 1' for the conduct of the war, which Hitler signed on 31 August 1939, dealt in greater detail with the unexpected conflict with the Western powers than with the war against Poland, for which, because of the thorough preparations, only two short sections were necessary.[115] In this respect the operational planning of the Wehrmacht faithfully reflected Hitler's political miscalculation.

5. ARMAMENT POLICY AND WAR

German rearmament was the major factor in the rapid and radical change in the European power-constellation between 1933 and 1939. The development led from one 'anomaly' to another, from the 100,000-man army of the republic to the Wehrmacht of the Third Reich, poised for aggression and superior to all other European armies. The planning and efforts of the Reichswehr had concentrated on securing the defence of the country by both military and political means. Maintaining the sovereignty of the state in a conflict seemed possible only within the existing collective security system, which was also considered indispensable for achieving a revision of the treaty of Versailles. Armaments policy was thus one component of a total policy whose aims were security and revision. Blomberg's appointment as defence minister marked the end of this phase. For him national defence was an end to be safeguarded solely by military means; he rejected the idea of securing it politically by a multilateral treaty system, and even viewed bilateral arms agreements with scepticism. This tended to make German armaments policy from the very beginning much more an end in itself than it had been under Groener or even Schleicher. At first this development had nothing to do with Hitler's ideas or directives. Germany's withdrawal from the system of collective security thus had at least two causes: Blomberg's views on military policy, and Hitler's general political aims.

One result of this rapid development, which reached its first high point in the German withdrawal from the League of Nations and the disarmament conference, was that Germany became completely dependent for its security on the Reichswehr, which had neither the personnel nor the equipment for this task. It is therefore not surprising that German military leaders felt their country to be even more threatened than it had been since 1918, and that an accelerated rearmament far beyond previously accepted limits seemed justified and even the only possible alternative. Not the least important factor in the plan for a 'risk Luftwaffe' and the 'December programme' of the army command for the creation of a sixty-three division wartime army was the military policy Blomberg had been pursuing since 1929. The non-aggression treaty of January 1934 with Poland did not diminish these fears, but rather concentrated the attention of the military on what they considered to be the imminent danger of a Franco-Czechoslovak attack. In March 1935 Beck

[115] Cf. *IMT* xxxiv. 456 ff.

defended the new drastic increase in German armaments demands by pointing to the 'alarming' armament measures taken by Germany's neighbours in 1934—which, however, at least in the case of France, were of no real significance. Before January 1933 no vigorous defence measures had been undertaken in the western part of Germany because Groener and Schleicher had been convinced that there was no rational alternative to the Locarno treaty as a guarantee of the western frontiers. Blomberg's decision to abandon this political component of German defence planning opened the way for an unlimited rearmament, whose goal became less and less the guarantee of a military security that was in any case largely fictitious, and more and more the re-establishment of German military supremacy in Europe. Participation in a collective security system, incomplete as it had been, was replaced by a military and armaments policy determined by a varying number of 'cases' involving possible conflicts with other states. The forces resulting from this development can be seen in Hitler's 'March operations' in 1935 and 1936, as well as the conflict-oriented, aggressive armaments planning of the summer of 1936.

In view of this situation the question arises as to how far the rearmament process influenced Hitler's policies and decisions; at first it was largely a military matter, but over the years it came to dominate more and more areas of the state apparatus and the economy. This cardinal question is too large to be answered here. An answer would, however, have to take into account the fact that political realities in Germany before the outbreak of the Second World War were strongly influenced by the effects of military rearmament. The precarious economic situation, the collapse of state finances and the resulting inflationary tendencies, the organization of labour by the state and the related socio-political problems, as well as the total effect of these factors in potentially threatening the domestic basis of the regime, cannot be overlooked in any analysis of Hitler's policy of aggression at least from 1936 onwards. On 3 February 1933 Hitler had described the build-up of the Wehrmacht, in other words rearmament, as the most important precondition for 'regaining political power'. In 1939 the possibility could not be excluded that the carrying out of this programme was endangering the actual goal.

This state of affairs was not only a result of Hitler's political directives and Blomberg's military policy; it was also due to the uncoordinated armament programmes of the individual services. The army, navy, and Luftwaffe each developed a different momentum which, because of the lack of effective political and military controls in accordance with an integrated programme, contributed to the excessive growth of armaments and war-economy activities in 1938–9. In the army Fritsch and Beck defended their conviction that any conflict affecting Germany would develop into a European war on several fronts, and that the only chance of success in such a war would be a 'strategic defence', i.e. to take the offensive. This led to constantly expanding armament programmes. As a result of this strategic plan the army was transformed after 1933 from a completely inadequate instrument of defence into a power factor designed for an offensive war and capable of aggressive action at the command of the military and political leaders. In the navy, by contrast, the strategic plan did not play a decisive role as an accelerating factor. The navy had its own political and ideological objectives, rooted in a strong tradition which gave the build-up of the fleet its own momentum. The navy's objectives were characterized by the desire to be again one of the great sea powers and to demonstrate its ability to fight a war at sea, and by the almost inevitable, yet initially taboo, confrontation with Britain that these goals would involve. This gave a peculiar arrogance to the navy's armament planning as a whole, rather than to its specific measures. Finally, at the latest after the German government had openly admitted its existence in March 1935, the Luftwaffe was under constant pressure to succeed because of its use as a propaganda instrument at home and abroad. However, its ability to carry out its military task proved increasingly incompatible with the technical and industrial production conditions of a weapons system which claimed to be a symbol of scientific and technical progress. These conditions had a braking effect on the Luftwaffe's development in general. The military result of its armament programme was influenced less by strategic-operational or ideological factors than by the constant necessity to modernize, and by its leaders' ability to translate scientific and technical progress into planning compatible with projected military goals and conditions of industrial production. This was not the least important factor determining the success or failure of Luftwaffe armament programmes.

The reference to the political effects of rearmament and the determining factors in the unrestrained expansion of the three services should not divert attention from the question of the political and military function of the Wehrmacht build-up between 1933 and 1939. In his directive of April 1930 Groener had attempted to define clearly the military functions of the armed forces within a concept of national defence determined by political objectives. He demanded that the use of military force be proportional to its political purpose. 'Definite prospects of success' were for him the precondition for any use of military force. This line of military-political thinking, which was criticized even in the operational planning of the Reichswehr command, was completely reversed after 1933. Hitler's political convictions were based on social Darwinism: in his opinion force, struggle, and war determined the 'order' of relations among states, nations, and races. The aims of his policy based on these principles were, in their basic tendencies, unlimited. They thus excluded Groener's principle that the build-up and use of the Wehrmacht should be determined by political objectives. But German military thinking, too, was at variance with Groener's maxim, in the tradition of Clausewitz, that the build-up of the Wehrmacht must be based on an acceptable relationship between ends and means. In the staffs of the Wehrmacht services this principle was no longer so much as mentioned; nor did it receive much attention in literature and articles dealing with the First World War. Most discussions were not about war as such, but about how it should be fought. This was due to the lesson of 1914–18 that war between industrialized states was no longer a purely military matter and that the domain of the military should henceforth be limited to 'armed combat'. Against this background and because of the lack of political objectives and controls, the ineffectiveness of all efforts to achieve co-ordination of 'uniform war preparations' is understandable. Thus, the expansion of the individual branches of the Wehrmacht, with its ultimately catastrophic political and military consequences, was also an expression of the unresolved political and social-identity crisis of the military leaders. Their tendency to concentrate on technical and tactical questions of their own services implied a renunciation of responsibility in the larger question of the means and ends of military policy, a responsibility of which many were no longer aware. But this tendency also implied the self-degradation of the senior officers to mere recipients of orders. In this way the Wehrmacht became an instrument in the hands of the dictator. Beck's appeal to the military leaders' sense of responsibility *to the nation* in view of the danger of a European war failed because, for ideological and political but also military reasons, in most cases the ethical principles which would have been necessary to induce commanders to break their military oath of obedience and accept the responsibility Beck required of them no longer formed a significant part of their mental make-up. Instead, they were prepared only to accept responsibility for individual acts in the conduct of a war. Thus, the military leaders were already disposed to give Hitler the 'blind obedience' he demanded.

PART IV

Foreign Policy and Preparation for War

Manfred Messerschmidt

I. Hitler's 'Programme' and the Problem of Continuity in German Foreign Policy

1. THE FUNCTION OF WAR IN HITLER'S 'PROGRAMME'

IT is generally assumed today that when Hitler became chancellor in 1933 he already had a clear conception of the foreign policy he intended to pursue.[1] This does not necessarily mean that foreign relations developed according to plan from 1933 onwards. Some analyses of the National Socialist system, which see it in terms of the 'parasitic erosion of a traditionally authoritarian state',[2] even question the existence of a systematic foreign policy. According to the so-called 'agent theory', Hitler was no more than a puppet of capitalism. In the present study we shall investigate whether German foreign policy after 1933 was at least inspired by a programme, even if it did not always conform to it.

One preliminary remark seems desirable. The evolution of Hitler's policy, which began with outlining a set of aims that had no chance of immediate realization, which continued with his first experience of directing foreign affairs, and which culminated in the unleashing of the war, coincided from time to time with revisionist demands of the old type. Continuity in foreign policy figured among the assurances proffered by him from 1933 onwards. However, these common features of the old and the new policy were only transitional phases as far as Hitler was concerned. What was actually new, as will appear from the present volume, was the unprecedented speed at which national resources were devoured in order to prepare Germany, materially and psychologically, for war. Speed became a principle in itself, a principle which was dictated by a new objective but at the same time reacted upon it.

The ruthless over-exploitation of the country's economic resources, together with certain achievements in the international field, was intended to prepare for a war

[1] Kuhn, *Programm*, 11. Trevor-Roper, 'Kriegsziele', is an important early work. Also important are Hillgruber, *Germany*; Hildebrand, *Foreign Policy*; Jäckel, *Hitlers Weltanschauung*, 29 ff.; Fest, *Hitler* (trans.), 213 ff. These and other authors take Hitler's programme seriously; they see in it a continuity extending to the war years, and oppose the 'underrating' of Hitler by such authors as Namier and Taylor, who question the programmatic nature of his foreign policy.

[2] Mommsen, *Beamtentum*, 13; Broszat, *The Hitler State*. These authors' analyses of the power structure lay stress on the 'polycracy' of different departments and authorities, and diagnose a structural pluralism in the National Socialist state. On the strength of such views, doubt has been cast on the idea of a monolithic foreign policy conducted according to a programme. Jacobsen in *Außenpolitik* holds to the view of a systematic policy on Hitler's part, whereas Broszat (cf. e.g. 'Soziale Motivation') speaks in terms of a basically aimless movement and a system prone to impulsive action. Mommsen doubts even the existence of a specific foreign-policy system: cf. p. 183 of his review of Jacobsen's *Außenpolitik*, also Mommsen, 'Nationalsozialismus'. In his view Nazi foreign policy was, formally speaking, an 'external projection of domestic policy', while its content was bounded by the horizon of 'objectless expansion'; the regime's technique was one of 'rule by state of emergency'. For a summary of the present state of research see Michalka, 'Außenpolitik'; and, for the nature of the system after 1933 also Hüttenberger, 'Polykratie'.

that could be won quickly with the means thus created. A premature war, or a war on two fronts against major powers, was bound to disturb and even endanger this highly precarious harmony of economic and war-directed policy. Paradoxically, only the war itself could bring about the optimum conditions for waging it, viz. autarky and an enlarged economic area (*Lebensraum*). Working towards this aim, Hitler had to make his policy acceptable to those whom he desired as partners, while perforce taking certain steps which might involve danger. His foreign policy required him to assume this pioneering function. He had to appear more rational than the ends he had set himself. His policy had to be one which Europe in the 1930s would tolerate, although the National Socialist vision of the future as a whole was such as to arouse the deepest suspicion. His policy was in the service of a system that was so over-extended, materially and ideologically, as to be headed for self-destruction unless Europe could be made to conform to Hitler's design. Hitler's foreign-policy 'programme' is distinguishable from that of the NSDAP.[3] It does not form a cut-and-dried system in itself; but Hitler's ideas on foreign policy rested on certain 'pillars of his world-view',[4] which we should now briefly describe.

Hitler's idea of the function of war in a nation's history can be inferred from his general view of foreign affairs, and is perhaps the clearest way of illustrating his departure from the revisionist viewpoint which he originally espoused. By the time he was writing *Mein Kampf*, if not earlier still, he had already ceased to differentiate between the political strategies of the republican government, the foreign ministry, and the Reichswehr leadership,[5] and had ceased to limit his objectives to those of the Pan-Germanists[6] and the extreme revisionists. The German people's future as he saw it went far beyond the rectification of the treaty of Versailles, the incorporation of Austria or the Sudetenland—objectives which, the diplomats and military leaders believed, might either be attained by negotiation or might, in part at least, be achievable only by force of arms.

In *Mein Kampf* and more fully in his 'second book',[7] Hitler expounded a different relationship between political aims and war. The mixture in his ideology of heterogeneous elements of all kinds is so singular[8] that it is far more convincing from a scientific point of view to speak of Hitler's foreign policy than of a National Socialist one. Its basic axiom is that 'self-preservation and continuance' are the chief motive for the actions of a healthy nation, directed towards securing a livelihood for its growing population. Since there is not enough space on earth for all nations, the possibilities of expansion are limited. The 'logical consequence' of this, to Hitler, self-evident proposition is 'a struggle in all its forms . . . for the satisfaction of the instinct for self-preservation'. Since politics must always be 'the struggle of a nation

---

[3] For Hitler's opinion of programmes see Fest, *Hitler* (trans.), 205–6.

[4] 'Konstanten seines Weltbildes': Fest, *Hitler*, 296 in the original (=trans., 206).

[5] On the development of Hitler's foreign-policy aims see Kuhn, *Programm*, 3 ff. Details of differences between the civil and military strategies in Hillgruber, *Germany*, and id., *Großmachtpolitik*, 25 ff.

[6] For the influence of Pan-German ideas on Hitler while still a student see Maser, *Hitler*, 155 ff.

[7] Of 1928; published as *Hitlers zweites Buch*, 1961; trans. as *Hitler's Secret Book* (New York, 1961) (cited below as *Secret Book*).

[8] Described in detail in Fest, *Hitler*, and Maser, *Hitler*.

for its existence', which is inescapably a matter of life and death, such ideas as the alternative between peace and war 'immediately sink into nothingness'.[9]

Hitler was capable, as he showed during the first years after the seizure of power, of concealing his intentions by aiming at temporary, partial objectives and using deceptively reasonable language; but at no time did he inwardly accept a state of affairs that presupposed long-term peaceful coexistence among nations. It seemed to him impossible, as a matter of principle, that peoples and states could live together and satisfy their material needs by economic exchanges; the necessary basis of life, in his view, was not trade but warfare.

According to Hitler's formulation of his ideas in 1928, the dangers of a 'fundamentally peaceful' policy and of war that 'becomes a permanent phenomenon' are basic reasons why it is necessary to engage in a supreme conflict for living-space and hegemony. Germany's 1914 frontiers must no longer be the object of her foreign policy.[10] Even the 'bourgeois proposals' of the annexationists in the First World War fell far short of a real territorial policy. The monarchy, the capitalists, the bourgeoisie and the liberals had not understood the point of that' war. The appointment of unemployed German princes to govern buffer states on the eastern border, the conquest of the mines of Longwy and Briey or Belgian fortifications on the Meuse—none of this remotely sufficed to justify the greatest blood-letting of all time. The only war aim, in Hitler's opinion, that would have been worthy of Germany's sacrifice would have been the acquisition of 'so and so many hundred thousand square kilometres' of land for colonization.

Hitler's 'second book' was written to indicate that he felt called on to correct the past errors of German policy and its lack of adequate war aims. Whenever he spoke of political objectives in general he had in mind future foreign policy and expansion eastward, into Russia—a territorial policy of this kind could not be carried out 'in the Cameroons, for instance'.

Hitler's views on race and the connection between racial purity, vital energy, and culture took shape at a very early stage and determined his objectives in the field of foreign affairs. The German people, divided by blood into 'superior and inferior racial elements', was threatened by special dangers. Only exceptional efforts could compensate for the 'dubious aspects of our racial composition (*Volkskörper*)'. German policy in the past, the misconceived aims pursued in the First World War, the revisionist policy of the Weimar Republic, and indeed that republic itself, had increased these dangers. The German people was in danger of gradually losing its 'blood-value' (*Blutswert*), the sense of individuality and the urge for self-preservation. How could this be averted? Hitler's 'second book' spoke of the dangers of a 'peaceful economic policy'. Germany's population could shortly increase to a level which bore no relation to the economic yield of her territory. Reliance on economic principles would rob the nation of those very virtues and

---

[9] *Secret Book*, 47–8; Wette, I.1.2 above.

[10] Hitler began after 1918 as a radical revisionist, calling for the abolition of the treaty of Versailles and, as a principal aim, the restoration of Germany's 1914 frontiers. See in more detail Schubert, *Anfänge*; Dickmann, 'Machtwille'; Jäckel, *Hitlers Weltanschauung*, 31–2.

qualities 'by which alone, in the last resort, peoples and states can maintain their existence on this earth'. Urban agglomerations would become mere places of employment and no longer centres of culture. These 'abscesses in the body of the nation' were breeding vices and disease of all kinds; they were hotbeds of bastardization. A nation could only exist if its population and territory bore a certain healthy relation to each other. Population figures would increase; the earth's area was limited; therefore there must be a battle for living-space. Such was the war Hitler envisaged.

War itself, on the other hand, and especially war as a permanent phenomenon, was in his view a danger to racial values. Being a process of racial selection, it led to the 'preferential destruction of a nation's best elements': heroes fell in battle, criminals remained alive. War must never be regarded as an end in itself, only as a means of life; but for this purpose it demanded an extreme sacrifice in terms of blood—a sacrifice which would be made good in peacetime. Compared to the consequences of a basically peaceful policy, namely birth restriction and emigration, the utmost sacrifices that could be made in war were infinitesimal. The cruellest war was that which people believed to be the most peaceful, viz. economic competition, which brought casualties far exceeding those of the First World War. 'War at most kills off a fragment of the present, economic warfare murders the future.'[11]

The war for living-space called for a basic attitude on the people's part, beyond the ken of democracy and the parliamentary system. It was not sufficient to prepare for war in terms of military technology alone. Those who did this could expect only transient successes; the future would not be theirs. The only way to secure the future 'almost as by law' was by means of the thoroughgoing inner training and education of a people.[12]

It is a mistake to suppose that these ideas of Hitler's were no more than general reflections of a purely abstract nature; nor should we overlook their affinity with the 'philosophy of war' that became widespread after 1918.[13] Hitler's ideas and foreign-policy objectives, as his later statements show, combined to form a thoroughly effective basis of political action. In his very first exposé of general policy to the army and navy commanders on 3 February 1933 he defined his basic political views and aims in terms of his reflections and formulations up to that time. Two principles were closely linked: the nation must be made to realize 'that we can be saved only by fighting, and that every other thought must give way to this', and the solution was to conquer fresh living-space in the east. It would be the Party's task to concentrate the nation's thoughts, especially those of its young people, on war, to strengthen its fighting spirit and save it from being 'poisoned' by pacifism, Marxism, and Bolshevism. Once the planned conscript army had been brought into line politically, it was for the Party to create an ideologically trained reserve which would be a reliable instrument of Hitler's foreign policy: 'perhaps fighting for new

[11] *Secret Book*, 49.
[12] Ibid. 32.
[13] Cf. Wette, I.1.3 (c) above.

export outlets, perhaps—and better, no doubt—conquering fresh living-space in the east and Germanizing it ruthlessly.'[14] The role of the armed forces in preparing for war was to be, from the beginning, a 'non-political' one. This was a double-edged hint, referring not only to war preparations as such but to any claim on the army's part to a say in home affairs—a role which it had usurped to a considerable degree, especially during General von Schleicher's tenure of the defence ministry.

In preparation for a future war to secure living-space and hegemony in Europe, Hitler's requirements included firm Party control of home affairs, a powerful military force (but not necessarily one 'fully prepared for war', since an army was 'never ready' and a statesman who waited for it to be so would never get anywhere)[15]—and the will to take ruthless action, to crush the adversary and keep him down for a long period. Above all there must never be another 1918, a collapse of the home front and a stab in the army's back. The Party's 'educational work' during the period of preparation for war would consist in getting rid of the 'dubious' political heritage left by the monarchy and parliamentary democracy, thus countering any centrifugal tendencies that might be inherent in the 'different racial nuclei' of the German people.

2. BASIC OBJECTIVES

Hitler's idea of a war which would demand a supreme sacrifice in blood but which alone could safeguard the nation's future in the long run was not a mere fancy but can be regarded as the lodestar of his foreign policy. He kept it in view through all the changes of direction occasioned by day-to-day events, the reactions of the major powers, and Britain's attempts to establish a peaceful international order. Before his accession to power he already had a mental picture of how the war was to be brought about.

The basic feature of his design can be found in *Mein Kampf* (1924),[16] where he described the steps in foreign policy that would be necessary as a preliminary to conquering living-space in the east. Previously his ideas had centred on a war of revenge against France: 'Our enemy is across the Rhine, not in Italy or elsewhere.'[17] A war for the complete revision of the treaty of Versailles seemed to him the principal short-term objective, designed to put an end to French hegemony in Europe. Franco-Italian rivalry could be exploited to this end. The idea of a closer link between Germany and Italy made its appearance around 1920 and remained an important factor in Hitler's calculations.[18] For its sake he was prepared to sacrifice the south Tyrol[19] as the precondition of an effective policy towards France. Those

[14] Hitler's statement to army and navy commanders on 3 Feb. 1933, record by Liebmann; text in Vogelsang, 'Dokumente', 434–5.
[15] Draft of Hitler's order of the day, WFA Chef, dated 19 Oct. 1938, BA-MA RW 4/v. 35.
[16] Jäckel, *Hitlers Weltanschauung*, 37; Kuhn, *Programm*.
[17] Phelps, 'Hitler', 305.
[18] See the remark (also cited by Jäckel, *Hitlers Weltanschauung*, 33) in a letter of 4 Dec. 1932 to General von Reichenau, in Vogelsang, 'Hitlers Brief an Reichenau', 433.
[19] Schubert, *Anfänge*, 77.

who, contrariwise, made the south Tyrol the corner-stone of German policy and therefore adopted an anti-Italian standpoint were, in his view, 'destroying the last hopes of a German resurgence'.[20]

There were three reasons, in Hitler's view, why Fascist Italy was important to National Socialist foreign policy. In the first place, like Germany, Italy had to pursue a policy of expansion to safeguard her existence, and was bound therefore to challenge the post-war security system. This evolution of Italian policy was important above all because it would break up the wartime coalition. In Hitler's view Italo-French antagonism must 'increasingly deepen and one day end in an overt struggle. Whether she likes it or not, Italy will have to fight for her state's existence and future against France, just as Germany herself will.'[21] Italy thus appeared as the first potential ally among the victors of 1918. 'Without this alliance signifying an immediate war for Germany, for which we are not equipped militarily,'[22] he believed that the Fascist regime and its pursuits of a racial (*völkisch*) foreign policy, in which he saw no ground for conflict with German national interests, would be a decisive factor in safeguarding the consolidation of National Socialist rule and a future National Socialist foreign policy. It was also not good for Italy 'for Fascism to exist isolated in Europe as an idea. Either the philosophy from which it stems is generalized or Italy will once again succumb to the general ideas of another Europe.'[23] Hitler envisaged the link with Fascist Italy as forming the nucleus of a new Europe, capable of arresting the process whereby the European democracies would otherwise fall victim, one by one, to 'Jewish–Marxist Bolshevism'.[24] Such ideas already went far beyond Hitler's original revisionist outlook, which had represented France as the chief enemy.

Hitler believed that a solution could be found to the problem of the Anschluss, which at that time was generally regarded as the decisive obstacle to a German–Italian *rapprochement*. He was eventually proved right in this, though for reasons different from those he envisaged in the 1920s. In 1923 he still believed that Italy would consent to the Anschluss in return for the abandonment of German claims to the south Tyrol;[25] but at the time of his 'second book' he saw the key to a solution in the state of tension between Italy and France. Italy, he argued, could not afford to let the non-viable state of Austria gravitate into the French sphere, and therefore she must be in favour of Austrian union with Germany.[26] On both political and military grounds it was in Italy's interest to regard the prohibition of the Anschluss as of no effect.

These arguments illustrate the way in which Hitler, seeking for potential allies, was apt to treat hypotheses as political realities, skilfully entwining and identifying the supposed interests of other powers with his own ambitions.

The same can be said in regard to Great Britain, to which Hitler assigned a special

[20] *Secret Book*, 2; Pese, 'Hitler'.

[21] *Secret Book*, 173. On German–Italian relations in general see Petersen, *Hitler–Mussolini*, here esp. 55 ff.

[22] *Secret Book*, 207.   [23] Ibid. 208.

[24] Ibid.   [25] Schubert, *Anfänge*, 77.

[26] *Secret Book*, 196–8; Petersen, *Hitler–Mussolini*, 63–4.

role in the context of *Lebensraum*. In *Mein Kampf* he still took serious account of Britain's policy of maintaining a balance of power on the Continent; in his 'second book' he moved on to a different viewpoint. In 1924–5 he still saw Britain's objectives as preventing the hegemony of any one power in Europe, i.e. not allowing any European country to assume the status of a world power, but in 1928 he qualified this in a characteristic manner. Britain, he argued, had never objected to military powers so long as they confined their aims to the Continent; she only felt challenged when they threatened her maritime or commercial interests. For this view of history Hitler invoked the examples of Spain, Holland, and Wilhelmine Germany. Frederick the Great's Prussia was a converse example: a continental power of the first rank, but which occasioned no alarm whatever to Britain. Significantly, the argument takes no account of Napoleon with his plans for continental hegemony. Where Hitler mentions the British policy of continental equilibrium at all, he contends that 'Napoleonic France viewed her continental policy only as a springboard for greater, altogether non-Continental aims.'[27]

Hitler's argument was based on the assumption of a logical division of interests between Britain as a maritime world power and the continental military power of Germany, preparing to seek her living-space in the east. This was perhaps his gravest political miscalculation, dominating his choice of objectives until 1940. He spoke of Germany concentrating all her forces in order to conquer sufficient living-space in the east for the next hundred years: neither for Britain nor Italy should this be a reason 'to keep up the enmity of the [First] World War'.[28] It seemed to him almost a foregone conclusion that France, the Soviet Union, and the United States would oppose British interests, and that Britain was thus the natural ally of Germany and Italy. Any doubts were only due to the influence of 'world Jewry' in Britain; but they did not destroy his confidence that 'If Germany adopts a fundamentally new political orientation which no longer contradicts England's sea and trade interests but spends itself in continental aims, there is no longer any logical ground for England's enmity, which would then be just hostility for hostility's sake [!]'[29] Together with his remarks about British motivation in the Napoleonic wars, this suggests that from 1928 onwards Hitler envisaged a policy of expansion on the Continent only; according to his conception of British policy there was no reason then to fear a collision with her imperial and maritime interests, indeed such a thing would be inconceivable.

Can it be supposed that Hitler did not realize what he was implicitly expecting of Britain? Apart from the question of racial ideology, which could be expected to place a strain on relations between Germany and the English-speaking world, he surely realized that, as a matter of world policy, Germany could not establish and consolidate her rule over European Russia without British acquiescence. As he put it clearly in *Mein Kampf*: 'What England has always desired, and will continue to desire, is to prevent any one continental power in Europe from attaining a position

---

[27] *Secret Book*, 150. For a general view of the initial years see Vaïsse, *Sécurité d'abord*.
[28] Ibid. 145.
[29] Ibid. 157–8.

of world importance. Therefore England wishes to maintain a definite equilibrium of forces among the European states; for this equilibrium seems a necessary condition of England's world hegemony.'[30] Can he have completely repressed this awareness by 1928?

In Hitler's assessment of the degree to which German foreign policy would be tolerated in Europe, it was clearly vital to know whether her attempts to achieve continental hegemony might not in certain circumstances be 'misinterpreted' as bids for world power. He sought to prevent this by such methods as temporarily waiving German claims to colonies or to an overseas policy, and putting forward his desiderata in piecemeal fashion. It seems very doubtful that, when it came to continental expansion, he can have failed to perceive any possible clash between German and Anglo-American interests,[31] especially as in his view German domination of continental Europe would of itself furnish the necessary basis for world-power status.[32]

Historians generally consider that an attempt to extend German power beyond the Continent marked the beginning of a final contest with the United States for world mastery.[33] No direct reference to such an idea, however, can be found in Hitler's programmatic writings. They present the United States as an economic factor of unique magnitude, a power marked out for future hegemony by its racial quality (*Volkswert*) and the size of its territory, and a far stronger state, in Hitler's opinion, than the USSR. But his ideas on how to confront this self-sufficient world power were for the most part defensive in tone. For the time being he saw no power—least of all a united Europe—that was capable of challenging America. Once the United States had completed its 'internal colonization', its 'activist urge' would be directed outwards. In Hitler's view the only state that could in future stand up to the Americans would be one 'which has understood how to enhance the racial value of its people and endow it with the most appropriate political structure, by the nature of its inner life and the direction of its foreign policy'.[34] In the context of Hitler's ideas on foreign affairs in the late 1920s, and from the systematic point of view, these remarks do not unequivocally suggest a planned series of aggressive steps. They sound more defensive than offensive, and in any case seem to relate to distant eventualities. The very first precondition, that of enhancing Germany's 'racial quality', is itself too uncertain and scarcely to be related to a time-scale. The idea that Germany would be on the defensive in a future showdown with America is emphasized by a passage in the concluding section of the 'second book', which speaks of 'a new association of nations . . . which could stand up to the threatened overwhelming of the world by the American Union', and argues that 'English world

---

[30] Hitler, *Mein Kampf* (trans.), ch. XIII, pp. 503 ff.

[31] Hillgruber, *Germany*, 52. Against such an underestimate see also Jäckel, *Hitlers Weltanschauung*, 50.

[32] Cf. also Hillgruber, *Germany*, 52-3.

[33] Ibid.; Hildebrand, *Foreign Policy*, 21.

[34] *Secret Book*, 106-7. Thies, 'Hitler in Offenburg', 303, sees this as evidence of an intention to dominate the world. More pertinent, it would seem, is the reference to a passage in Hitler's Erlanger speech of 13 Nov. 1930, ibid.

rule inflicts less hardship on present-day nations than the emergence of an American world rule.'[35] Apart from such reflections on future world politics and power-relationships, there are references in Hitler's writings to the missionary role, envisaged on a world basis, of the 'best of humanity' or the 'superior race'; such passages are in unresolved contradiction to those that speak of a racial (*völkisch*) state. The missionary role, however, related to the 'most distant future'; meanwhile a process of racial selective breeding must be instituted and maintained so as to produce the 'master race' (*Herrenvolk*) of the future. This series of pictures and 'visions' may fairly be regarded as belonging to the world of myth, as distinguished from Hitler's more specifically historical ideas concerning world power. His 'mythical' imaginings are only very indirectly related to his 'programme', considered as a system of foreign-policy objectives for the medium and longer term.[36]

Thus, Hitler's main writings do not furnish any unambiguous answer as to whether his programme embodied any plans for world domination. However, his ideas went on developing after 1933. At that date any idea of world domination clearly played no specific part in determining the course of his foreign policy. The furthest objective to which references were made by the Führer and his circle was that of *Lebensraum* in the east, though admittedly unchallenged possession of this would have made Germany a world power.

What place did Hitler assign to the Soviet Union in his design for foreign policy? According to Hitler's 'second book', Bismarck was able to conclude an alliance with Russia because that country was governed in his day by a non-Slav, Germanic upper stratum. This had been destroyed by the war and revolution, and now Russia was dominated by 'world Jewry'. An alliance with the Soviet Union was only thinkable if Moscow were to shake off 'Jewish-capitalist rule' and establish a national anti-capitalist form of Communism. But an alliance, even if conceivable in theory, was still impossible because of the deep-seated Slav hostility to Germany. Bourgeois German 'politicals' who believed in such an alliance understood nothing of the 'psyche of the Slavic folk-soul'.[37] In any case, from the military point of view—'and there is no such thing as an alliance without the idea of war'—such a link would not only be ineffective but dangerous for Germany. Germany, allied with Russia, would become a historic battlefield. Russian help could only arrive when it was too late. It was in fact 'quite improbable' that Russia could overcome Poland; meanwhile 'Germany would be exposed to the concentrated attacks of all Western Europe', with the result that 'French national chauvinism, under the protection of a new world coalition, could come much closer to fulfilling its ultimate war aim.'

---

[35] *Secret Book*, 209.

[36] Hitler's architectural megalomania is probably not directly relevant here. The discussion as to his long-term aims is still open. Close connections are perceived by Thies, *Architekt*, 31–2, 62–3; Weinberg, *Foreign Policy*, 7; Hildebrand, *Foreign Policy*, 21; Hillgruber, *Germany*, 52–3. More reserve is expressed by Jäckel, *Hitlers Weltanschauung*, and Carr, *Arms*, 7: 'Eastward expansion remained the ultimate rationale of Hitler's whole policy.' Often quoted in this connection: Speer, *Inside the Third Reich*, e.g. 73 ff., 80, 148, 152 ff., 160; *Mein Kampf* (trans.), e.g. 322, 339, 522 ff.

[37] *Secret Book*, 134–5.

On the strength of this seemingly superficial argument, which none the less decisively affected his future foreign policy, Hitler regarded the inherent impossibility of a German–Russian association as a stroke of historical good fortune:

For the future an alliance with Russia has no sense for Germany, either from the viewpoint of sober expediency or from that of human affinity. On the contrary, it is fortunate that the situation has developed in just this way, breaking a spell which would have prevented us from seeking the goal of German foreign policy where it solely and exclusively can lie: territory in the east.[38]

In 1920 Hitler had declared that an alliance with Russia might be possible if Jewish influence were eliminated[39]—an argument that suited his radical revisionist attitude at that time. In 1925, however, when he had adopted the concept of *Lebensraum*, Russia no longer figured as a potential asset in foreign affairs but only as an object of German expansionism, to be implemented by means of a resolute foreign policy with, it was assumed, the support of Britain.

From the time of his 'second book' in 1928 Hitler's concept of foreign policy finally moved away from that of mere revisionism: the only worthwhile object of a future war would be to conquer space in Russia. The settling of accounts with France, while still regarded as inevitable, no longer had anything to do with frontiers or revenge, but was simply a matter of eliminating Germany's most dangerous enemy as a prelude to the struggle in the east. France would always be on the side of Germany's adversaries. French continental ambitions, intended 'to serve the fulfilment of greater world-political aims', were for Germany 'a question of life and death'.[40] But a contest that had no aim beyond bringing France to subjection would be 'ineffectual as regards the main purpose'. It could only serve that purpose if it were intended to cover Germany's rear while she conquered living-space in the east: in other words, it is assumed 'that Germany sees in the suppression of France nothing more than a means which will make it possible for our people finally to expand in another quarter'.[41]

The military problem, in Hitler's view, consisted in eliminating France; for the 'colossal empire in the east' was 'ripe for dissolution'.[42] Hence, Germany's foreign policy must be concentrated on Italy and Britain.

The contradictions in Hitler's survey of foreign affairs are partly to be explained by the fact that various groups both in and outside the Party had to be convinced simultaneously. As a constant element we may discern a complex of assumptions and beliefs concerned with racial ideology, which were to determine his subsequent foreign policy together with considerations of power politics and often purely tactical motives. All these factors are not always clearly articulated. Even in the circle of his closest associates, Hitler was seldom at pains to achieve a congruity of

---

[38] *Secret Book*, 139.
[39] Phelps, 'Hitler', 308; also Jäckel, *Hitlers Weltanschauung*, 35.
[40] *Secret Book*, 129.
[41] Hitler, *Mein Kampf* (trans.), ch. xv, p. 549.
[42] Ibid., ch. xiv, p. 533. The first German edition referred rhetorically to the Persian empire. Cf. Jäckel, *Hitlers Weltanschauung*, 45 n. 32.

views: it was sufficient for him to rough out a programme that could be adhered to. The racial ideology that governed his thinking in foreign affairs may be paraphrased as follows.

The task of National Socialism was to enhance the biological quality of the 'racially disrupted' German people. According to Hitler this disruption (*Zerrissenheit*) showed itself in a weakening of the instincts and qualities necessary in the struggle for life. The basic doctrine that Hitler sought to express in various interchangeable terms—racial value, folk-value, blood-value—should not be dismissed as unimportant merely because it is founded on premises that will not hold water scientifically. Its 'negative side' is especially relevant to the consideration of Hitler's ideas on foreign policy. As regards the positive application of racial theory to foreign affairs, Hitler's ideas differed from those of other leading Party members, with important results, for instance, as regards Italy and Scandinavia; but they agreed, negatively, as regards the 'Jewish-parasitic' element which threatened to undermine the racial quality and 'blood-value' of all healthy peoples. This view is succinctly expressed in the conclusion to the 'second book'. The Jewish people, itself incapable of creating a territorial state, needs for its own existence the creative power of other nations. The Jew's ultimate goal is 'the denationalization, the promiscuous bastardization of other peoples . . . the extirpation of the *völkisch* intelligentsia and its replacement by the members of his own people'. The Jews were fighting a world-wide battle to bring about 'bloody Bolshevization' and their own domination over mankind.

In Hitler's eyes Jewish rule and Bolshevism were identical. In Russia the 'Slav race instinct' had helped Jewry to exterminate the 'former non-Russian upper stratum'; the country was now ruled by Jews,[43] whose auxiliaries in other countries were 'Marxism, democracy, and the so-called Christian Centre'.[44] The Jews had won the battle in Russia and also in France, where they had achieved a community of interests with national chauvinism. In Britain the decision was still uncertain, while 'the bitterest struggle for the victory of Jewry at the present time' was being waged in Germany.

These views, with variations to suit altering circumstances, were reflected in Hitler's political outlook to the very end, with the cast-iron certainty of axioms. It is thus right to speak of a 'mixture of racial and power-political motives' in Hitler's conception of foreign policy.[45] The question is how the two elements were combined. There was in fact a basic incongruity in Hitler's views. On the very points where he claimed to be more logical and far-seeing than official German policy before and after the First World War, his argument rested on unfounded statements and assumptions. His picture of Russia was artificial and arbitrary; true, the internal and military strength of the 'colossus' was underrated in the West as well as by Hitler, but he compounded this error with his diagnosis of racial and biological weakness. His view of Britain was ambivalent, containing elements both

[43] *Secret Book*, 138.
[44] Ibid. 215.
[45] Hildebrand, *Foreign Policy*, 21.

of falsehood and of truth; it became untrustworthy when he sought to reconcile British interests with the fight for *Lebensraum* in the east which, according to him, was essential to Germany's political and racial future.

How could such a combination of misjudgement and ideological dogma enter the realm of practical policies? The question can only be answered by taking into account the co-operation of the German economy, the army, the Party, and the state apparatus in rearming Germany, and the inability of the great powers to pursue a determined policy towards her. It is also to be noted that Hitler prevented the Party from being distracted by 'secondary conceptions' of the issues at stake, and that he made skilful use of revisionist initiatives dating from the Weimar period, adopting them and allowing them to remain effective in so far as they served his own aims, albeit incompletely.

A brief survey of these aspects will help to explain Hitler's foreign policy from 1933 onwards.

3. SECONDARY CONCEPTIONS

After the accession to power, the basic ideas of other Nazi leaders concerning foreign policy never came into serious competition with Hitler's plans.

In the 1920s there was a competing 'socialist' line of thought that was incompatible with Hitler's aims and also with the imperialist notions of the group associated with Ritter von Epp,[46] president of the League of Colonial Fighters and afterwards Reich governor of Bavaria. The socialist approach, represented chiefly by the brothers Gregor and Otto Strasser and the association of north-west German gauleiters,[47] was ineffectual after 1930 and gained no influence over Hitler. After various changes of direction this 'left-wing' group gave up the idea of colonial claims,[48] emphasizing its sympathy for oppressed peoples and opposition to the Western 'plutocracies'. As far as the East was concerned, it stood for co-operation with the Soviet Union.

For a time after 1933, a group of 'blood-and-soil' theoreticians headed by Walter Darré[49] took a strong line against colonial imperialism and advocated a *rapprochement* with Britain as a basis for eastward expansion; they proposed to colonize broad areas of Russia in order to provide the German people with a secure and permanent racial base. This programme certainly tended to support Hitler's ideas, though the latter were much more influenced by power policies. Of far greater importance within the Party, however, were advocates of imperialist ideas of the pre-1914 type, the chief of whom was Hermann Göring. Ribbentrop is also to be mentioned here. The importance of this school of thought was that they were able to integrate the aims and hopes of conservative groups, not least in the Reichswehr

---

[46] Hildebrand, *Foreign Policy*, 14–15. For ideas of foreign policy in the first days of the NSDAP see Schubert, *Anfänge*.

[47] See further Schildt, *Arbeitsgemeinschaft*, and Kühnl, *Nationalsozialistische Linke*.

[48] The 'Bamberg programme' of Nov. 1926 also demanded colonial territory in Central Africa: see Kühnl, 'Strasser-Programm'.

[49] Hildebrand, *Foreign Policy*, 18; Gies, *Darré*.

and the economy, into the spectrum of foreign policy after 1933. But their ideas were only effective when they were compatible with Hitler's basic aims or when he found them useful for camouflage purposes.

Alfred Rosenberg, as 'foreign minister designate', was entrusted with the task of setting up the Außenpolitisches Amt (foreign-policy office) of the NSDAP;[50] he certainly influenced Hitler's view of Russia, but scarcely counted in day-to-day foreign policy. His directorship of the Außenpolitisches Amt and his 'cultural policy' did not enable him to control or intensify activity in the field of foreign policy or international law. Hitler in his *Table Talk* subsequently claimed that he had read only a small part of the *Mythus*; but much of what it had to say on foreign affairs actually coincided with his views, as did passages in Rosenberg's work of 1927, *Der Zukunftsweg einer deutschen Außenpolitik*. This spoke of *Lebensraum* in the east; France and Poland were designated as enemies; Italy, a suitable ally for Germany, should seek her future in North Africa and the Adriatic. Germany, the 'central power' on the Continent, should ally herself with Britain, which, like Italy, offered no obstacle to German ambitions.[51] While Hitler's racial ideas were closely linked with expansionist ambitions, mostly from the negative point of view that the parasitic force of 'world Jewry' presented a threat to racial health, Rosenberg argued for a symbiosis of state systems on a racial basis which would ensure the world-wide domination of the white race.[52] As a specific possibility the 'ideologist in chief' envisaged that Germany, dominating the Continent, would form a close association with Britain and Scandinavia. This 'Nordic' Europe was in his eyes the organic theme of the future, as opposed to a chaotic system of 'world jurisdiction' (the League of Nations) or the 'confusion of forms' in consequence of democratic-Marxist world policy. A plan was developed by the Außenpolitisches Amt for a 'German–Scandinavian bloc', to be prepared for by ideological infiltration or 'cultural work'; this had no basis in practical reality, and came to nothing. Rosenberg's theoretical notion of foreign policy was close to the views of the *völkisch*-nationalist opponents of the conventional Weimar revisionists. The main difference between him and Hitler lay in the scale of their radical expansionist objectives in the east. Rosenberg advocated an alliance between Berlin and Kiev: traditional Russia was to be dismembered, but not swallowed up in its entirety. Rosenberg's ideas were discussed by theorists and experts in international law,[53] but had next to no influence on actual policy.

4. HITLER AND THE LAST PHASE OF WEIMAR REVISIONISM

The dominant aim of all important groups in the Weimar Republic was to do away with the treaty of Versailles. Some pressed impatiently for total revision, others

---

[50] Jacobsen, *Außenpolitik*, 45 ff.; for Rosenberg's position in the Party cf. also Bollmus, *Amt Rosenberg*.

[51] Rosenberg, *Mythus*, 642; Jacobsen, *Außenpolitik*, 52.

[52] *Mythus*, 675, on racial theory and Rosenberg's political ideas. On the Scandinavian policy of the Third Reich see also Loock, 'Nordeuropa', and Stegemann in vol. ii of the present work.

[53] Messerschmidt, 'Revision', 64 ff.

advocated a step-by-step procedure; the latter included those stigmatized by the Nazis as 'fulfilment politicians'.[54] Of the three basic revisionist demands—financial, military, and territorial—the first was practically met by the conference of Lausanne in 1932. The territorial demands, over and above the recovery of areas ceded in and after 1919, included the Anschluss with Austria (together with south Tyrol) and the Sudetenland. These demands were viewed by Hitler with a critical eye. They could not be aims in themselves, since they involved the risk that the Allies of the First World War would again close ranks against Germany. Thus, the foreign ministry and the army leaders, together with a practically united phalanx of party politicians, were pursuing territorial objectives that Hitler regarded as unwise and anachronistic. To the parties of the right it was of especial importance that the Locarno treaty had barred the way to the west; the question of the eastern frontier, on the other hand, was regarded as an open one even by parties loyal to the republic, such as Stresemann's Deutsche Volkspartei (DVP). For these parties the recovery of the territories lost to Poland and Lithuania remained on the agenda, as did the Anschluss. Stresemann, as chancellor and foreign minister of the republic, aimed to bring about the status quo ante as far as Poland was concerned, and would not accept a special solution for Danzig alone.[55]

The key question as regards territorial revision was how to achieve it—by military force or economic pressure? Stresemann believed that the latter policy, and especially a 'customs war' with Poland, offered great opportunities, not only for frontier revision. In his opinion Germany could recover her position as a great power by means of economic pressure and reducing smaller states to a dependent role.[56] Thus, the architect of Locarno also thought in terms of power politics. Self-limitation in the west[57] was in his view the presupposition of a revisionist policy in the east, and as regards the eastern frontier he took care to give no promise of abstaining from military action.[58]

In December 1925 Stresemann thought it necessary to assure the umbrella organization, in Berlin, of former inhabitants of the eastern provinces (Arbeitsge-meinschaft Deutscher Landsmannschaften) that the German government had informed the Polish foreign minister that it refused to rule out a recourse to war; Germany's entry into the League of Nations did not preclude her making war either. Even as regards the western frontier the treaties did not signify 'the eternal maintenance of the status quo'. At present, Stresemann went on, Germany's

---

[54] Cf. summary in Bloch, *Hitler*, 7 ff., including reference to the Centre politician Erzberger; also Wirth, *Reden während der Kanzlerschaft*.

[55] Broszat, *Polenpolitik*, 170 ff.; also Korbel, *Poland*, 68 ff., 110 ff.

[56] Key documents on Stresemann's foreign policy include his letter of 7 Sept. 1925 to the former crown prince in Stresemann, *Diaries*, ii. 503–5; speech in Berlin to the Arbeitsgemeinschaft Deutscher Landsmannschaften, 14 Dec. 1925, in *ADAP*, B. i. 727 ff.; Hillgruber, *Großmachtpolitik*, 26–7; Maxelon, *Stresemann*.

[57] In the conversation at Thoiry on 17 Sept. 1926 which marked the peak of Franco-German understanding in the Weimar period, Stresemann also told Briand that Eupen and Malmédy must revert to Germany some day. On this conversation see Sieburg, 'Das Gespräch zu Thoiry 1926'; also *ADAP*, B. i, pt. 2, minute of conversation between Briand and Stresemann, No. 88, pp. 188 ff.

[58] For the opposition to Stresemann's western policy see Walsdorff, *Westorientierung*, 105–6.

strength and her one powerful weapon in foreign affairs consisted in her 'economic position as a consumer country' and as a 'large-scale debtor *vis-à-vis* other countries'. But he made no doubt that the principal means of a future foreign policy would be 'material strength, an army and a navy'. Germany, as a debtor nation in the 1920s, could not hope to achieve such aims as he had indicated to the crown prince a few weeks earlier: 'the recovery of Danzig, the Polish Corridor and a frontier rectification in Upper Silesia, the Anschluss and the return of our colonies'. Earlier still, in January 1925, Stresemann had defined as the object of 'German hopes' a state that would include all branches of the German nation living in the area of German habitation in central Europe, an aim that could not be achieved 'without placing some members of other nations under German sovereignty along with our compatriots'.[59]

All attempts under the republic to isolate Poland and deprive her of a substantial guarantee were aimed not only at keeping the frontier question open but also at preventing a Russo-Polish *rapprochement* that would relieve Poland of anxiety in the east. The foreign ministry regarded the eastern frontier beyond Poland as 'open'.[60] But after Pilsudski's *coup d'état* in 1926 Stresemann and the foreign ministry realized that Schacht's strategy of using financial pressure to solve the frontier problem was a failure. Poland's international status was enhanced; quick solutions in the east were no longer to be expected.

This meant, however, that Germany's basic attitude towards Poland was once again dominated by the military aspect, calling for long-term preparation and an acceptable solution of the armaments question. The Truppenamt, the *de facto* general staff of the Reichswehr, set forth its objectives in a memorandum of March 1926.[61] This called for the recovery of full sovereignty and complete integration of the territory at present separated from Germany: i.e., the liberation of the Rhineland and the Saar district, elimination of the Corridor and recovery of Polish Upper Silesia, incorporation of German Austria, and abolition of the demilitarized zone. These aims necessarily involved conflict with France, Belgium, Poland, Czechoslovakia, and finally Italy. Hence, the main object of German disarmament policy must be to 'deprive France of her dominant military power'; Poland must next be disarmed, then the other states in question. The skilful differentiation of German disarmament demands was seen by the Truppenamt as a means of achieving its interests. Concessions could readily be offered to some countries, e.g. Russia, Yugoslavia, Romania, and even Italy. There was 'for the time being no special interest' in British disarmament. The first priority was German rearmament

---

[59] Quoted in Ruge, *Deutschland*, 530–1. Dirksen's minute of 24 Apr. 1925: excerpt in Walsdorff, *Westorientierung*, 100.

[60] Dirksen opposed the suggestion by Köster, German minister in Riga, that the Baltic States should be guaranteed by Germany in order to prevent their moving closer to the 'Franco-Polish combination'; as regards Lithuania, there could be no question of such a guarantee. The foreign ministry also refused to consider a non-aggression pact. See also Ruge, *Deutschland*, 282, 531, citing a memorandum from the ministry to the president as regards a free hand in the east: ZStA, Büro des Reichspräsidenten, No. 697/1, Bl. 18.

[61] Memorandum of 6 Mar. 1926 from Col. von Stülpnagel to Legation Counsellor von Bülow, *ADAP*, B. i. 341 ff.

by land and in the air. The disarmament of Britain and 'other continents' might be the subject of concessions 'for the present, until such time as Germany's vital aims are attained'. Politically, Germany's next objective should be to recover her status in Europe, and 'much later' that of a world power.

The army command wished priorities to be fixed for land and air rearmament as a basis for a foreign policy attuned to Germany's vital interests. In their view armaments would be the most important lever of German foreign policy in the late 1920s and early 1930s. The concept of 'disarmament' related only to France and her allies. In the disarmament negotiations the demand for 'equal rights' (*Gleichberechtigung*) was simply intended to hold open the possibility of German rearmament. 'The question whether Geneva or Versailles is to be decisive for the state of German armaments' would be the most difficult for the country's diplomatic and military representatives, but was also the one whose consequences would be 'the most far-reaching in all directions'.[62] The strategic aim of the army leaders was that the negotiations should break down, but not on the issue of German demands: this was what made the task such a delicate one.

The development continued beyond Stresemann's time.[63] The phase of a policy of understanding, in which nationalist aims took second place, came to an end. Its object had been to evade rather than challenge the position of France, which was regarded without question as the obstacle to a rapid recovery of Germany's great-power status. Under Schleicher the army command gained greater influence over foreign policy. The world economic crisis seemed to offer opportunities for shaking off the Versailles restrictions on armaments.[64] The army leaders continued to regard France as the major obstacle to German interests. As early as 1924–5 Colonel Joachim von Stülpnagel of the Truppenamt had envisaged 'in foreseeable time' a war to liberate Germany from 'the Versailles treaty and the French rabble in the Rhineland'.[65]

There is a suggestion here of a revival of the system of dual control under the monarch which had such pernicious effects in Germany before and during the First World War. Highly placed military men assumed as a matter of course that they were competent in foreign affairs. Certainly some 'politicians' in the army took a more flexible line on political matters than their purely military colleagues, though no sharp line can be drawn in this matter. Thus, a ministry memorandum of 1930 on the 'Tasks of the Wehrmacht' mentioned as natural aims that of territorial revision 'when the political situation is favourable' and the restoration of Germany as a great power.[66]

---

[62] *ADAP*, b. i. 347.

[63] Bloch, *Hitler*, 13; Gatzke, *Stresemann*. On the contrast between 'equal rights' and the 'parity' of armaments subsequently demanded by the Reichswehr see Rautenberg, *Rüstungspolitik*, 36, 40.

[64] Hillgruber, *Großmachtpolitik*, 28–9.

[65] Stülpnagel to Truppenamt No. 270/24 T II b, in Stülpnagel papers, BA-MA n 5/20. These military theoreticians envisaged the next conflict as a 'total, scorched-earth war'. For Stülpnagel's drafts for a concluding discussion of the war games in 1924 and 1925 see ibid. and Geyer, 'Militär', 242.

[66] Quoted in Geyer, 'Militär', 242. The draft was by Lt.-Col. von Bredow; von Bredow papers, BA-MA n 97/9; cf. also Post, *Civil–Military Fabric*, 232–3, and Deist, III.1.2 above.

The growing influence of the military in foreign affairs has rightly been seen as helping to pave the way for Hitler.[67] It is thus of some interest to examine how far the long-term aims of Schleicher's confidant Stülpnagel coincided with Hitler's, and how far they differed. A policy of rearmament by land and in the air, directed mainly against France, was certainly in accordance with Hitler's basic idea. But while Hitler regarded the elimination of France as a preliminary to turning eastward, Stülpnagel, who was probably representative of the army leaders in this, held that once France had ceased to oppose German recovery, Germany would thereby have regained her position as a great power. 'On the basis of a firm position in Europe, after a new settlement of the Franco-German question by peaceful or warlike means' it would then be possible to embark on a struggle for raw materials and markets, which would bring Germany into competition with the 'Anglo-American power-sphere' and thus require adequate naval armaments. This laid far more emphasis on rivalry with Britain than did Hitler's plan, though it was equally optimistic as regards Britain's attitude towards German hegemony on the Continent. As regards Italy, the army leaders were prepared to make concessions; they did not give special consideration to the effect of the Anschluss demand on German–Italian relations. Russia, which the defence ministry considered almost exclusively from the standpoint of power politics, was seen by Hitler in a completely new perspective; but this difference was not of decisive importance during the transitional period, pending Germany's achievement of 'political power'. The Reichswehr's immediate goal of rearmament on land and in the air was well suited to Hitler's programme, as were the suggested negotiating tactics at Geneva.

The foreign ministry differed somewhat from the military in their assessment of the importance of the arms question. Under Stresemann's successors the higher officials of the ministry were able to exert more influence on policy,[68] and the disarmament issue was helpful to them as an occasion for fresh initiatives, but they did not ascribe to it the same absolute priority as did the generals. Under Brüning's chancellorship especially, economic questions once again occupied the centre of the stage,[69] in close connection with the world-wide depression.

At this time State Secretary von Bülow conceived the idea of a German–Austrian customs union as a step towards the Anschluss and a means of exerting decisive influence in south-eastern Europe.[70] This attempt failed, but it bore witness to the confidence with which earlier ideas of 'Mitteleuropa' were being revived, in deliberate opposition to Briand's conception of a pan-European federation. The Brüning cabinet saw the issue as a clash between German and French national interests. While the government's great-power policy was essentially based on economic and financial considerations, it naturally had the effect of boosting the Reichswehr's demand for military parity. The new alliance between the foreign and defence ministries under Neurath and Schleicher scored an important success with

---

[67] Hillgruber, *Großmachtpolitik*, 28–9.
[68] Cf. Lipgens, 'Einigungsidee', 329 ff.
[69] Conze, 'Regierung Brüning', 233 ff.; Hillgruber, *Großmachtpolitik*, 29.
[70] Bloch, *Hitler*, 16; Bennet, *Diplomacy*, 78 ff.

the five-power declaration of 11 December 1932 on equal rights and disarmament; after Hitler became chancellor, General von Blomberg and his chief of staff Reichenau treated this declaration as the starting-point for a final break-through to freedom in arms matters.

In the generals' view, rearmament was the most important weapon of German policy.[71] Their secret military preparations and their ideas on foreign policy both impelled them to take this view. On the other hand General Groener, the defence minister from 1928 to 1932, endeavoured to strike a just balance between rearmament and foreign policy. He thought it possible to improve Germany's external situation by negotiation, until such time as the republic should be strong enough to bring about frontier revision by force of arms.[72] By the beginning of 1932 at latest the Reichswehr had defined its position with regard to the disarmament talks at Geneva in the sense that freedom to rearm was a possibility that must be kept open at all costs.[73] Schleicher used his growing influence in order to bring the foreign ministry into line with the general's views.

On 23 January 1932 the Chef der Heeresleitung (head of the army command) approved the second armaments programme.[74] What might appear superficially to be a 'battle of figures' between departments actually involved basic questions concerning the aim and methods of German foreign policy.[75] This can be clearly seen from Schleicher's opposition to the negotiating position of Ambassador Nadolny at Geneva, who was working for an arms moratorium.[76] Schleicher underlined the Reichswehr's misgivings with the statement that 'the interests of the armed forces' called for the breaking-off of negotiations, 'which must then . . . necessarily lead to an expansion of our forces'.[77] In other words, it was in the Reichswehr's interest to carry on with the second programme and either obtain treaty cover for doing so or allow the conference to break up with all the consequences that would have for Germany's international position.

The Reichswehr policy was a difficult one to modify, based as it was on a single-minded military pursuit of great-power status.[78] The world depression had brought about a more fluid international situation, but the possibilities of politically exploiting this were envisaged almost exclusively from the arms angle. However, as has been rightly pointed out, the European order was bound to be transformed, not only—as at a later stage—by territorial revision with the aid of a military instrument

---

[71] For details of the aims of individual Reichswehr leaders see Rautenberg, *Rüstungspolitik*, 36 ff.

[72] Geyer, 'Militär', 242; also Post, *Civil–Military Fabric*, and Deist, III.1.3 above.

[73] Rautenberg, *Rüstungspolitik*, 40.

[74] See Geyer, 'Militär', and Rautenberg, *Rüstungspolitik*, 381, with reference to a memorandum of the beginning of 1932, 'Ziele und Wege Deutschlands auf der Abrüstungskonferenz', Schleicher papers, BA-MA N 42/34; see Deist, III.1.3 above.

[75] Rautenberg, *Rüstungspolitik*, 45, describes the contrast by the formula that the defence ministry demanded the theoretical maximum while the foreign ministry limited itself to minimum figures based on reality.

[76] Nadolny sought disarmament on the basis of 'equal rights': see Nadolny, *Beitrag*, 120 and *passim*.

[77] Rautenberg, *Rüstungspolitik*, 44; Deist, 'Schleicher', 167; Vogelsang, *Reichswehr*, 222 ff.; also IV.II.1 below.

[78] On this consistency see also Volkmann in Part II and Deist in Part III above.

created for the purpose of achieving this in accordance with German wishes; the transformation was already brought about by the revision of the military terms of the treaty of Versailles itself. The 'fact of a developing military power'[79] had its own weight in the European scales, as the strength of French resistance showed very clearly. The determination with which Germany none the less pursued total revision, expressly as a 'means' of foreign policy, makes it difficult to pinpoint changes in that policy immediately after Hitler's accession to power. His programme for the time being was couched in very general terms and could accommodate the various aspects of foreign and rearmament policy. He let it be seen that he intended to speed up the arms programme at an early date, but, within the framework of 'rebuilding Germany's military capability', directed his immediate attention more to domestic and propaganda tasks.

In a long-term view, this domestic policy created conditions for an expansive foreign policy. The reorientation of the German national spirit (*Volkstum*)[80] was to extend to foreign affairs also. A clear, stable foreign policy would, in Hitler's view, take shape of its own accord once the German people became aware of the vast territorial opportunities in the east. But an account of the actual development after 1933 must not lose sight of the interrelation between foreign and domestic goals. Nazi domestic policy was not an 'end in itself'—nor, however, was it solely devoted to 'creating a particular basis for foreign policy'.[81] Combined with a foreign policy adjusted to circumstances, it was intended to launch the German people in the direction of fresh objectives. In this connection the process of remilitarizing Germany by way of political education ran ahead of the conduct of foreign policy, which had to be adjusted to circumstances and to the interests of the major powers; this created difficulties rather than advantages. Hitler's domestic policy, designed 'to awaken the energies and talents of the nation' and concentrate its political will on the struggle for life, was associated from the beginning with methods and consequences that aroused alarm in foreign countries and, for this reason, were officially dismissed by the foreign ministry as transitional phenomena without importance. For the time being Hitler did not aspire to any foreign policy that was more than a means of making possible the undisturbed transformation of the internal political order and ensuring the material basis for rearmament. This was, among other things, the true reason for transforming, unobtrusively at this stage, the organization and method of foreign policy.

Yet it was not short-term aims in the narrow sense that Hitler expounded to the Reichswehr commanders on 3 February 1933.[82] His plans in themselves involved a dramatic stepping-up of revisionist aims on the basis of a 'clean sweep' in home affairs, and especially in the field of political education. 'A complete reversal of present political conditions. . . . No toleration of activity by any school of thought that opposes our aim. . . . Radical extermination of Marxism. Young people, and

---

[79] Geyer, 'Militär', 240.

[80] *Secret Book*, 210.

[81] Wollstein, *Revisionismus*, I, sees these possibilities as a frame of reference for possible interpretations; see also Wette, I.II.4 above.

[82] Vogelsang, 'Dokumente'.

the whole nation, to be taught that only battle can save us. . . . Use of all means to toughen young people and strengthen their fighting spirit. . . . A strictly authoritarian political system.' This concept could easily be adapted to increased activity in foreign affairs as the country became stronger in itself and as rearmament got under way. From the programmatic point of view it clearly performed a bridging function as far as foreign policy was concerned. While Hitler's remarks on domestic and economic affairs (settlement policy, rescue of the peasantry) were repetitions of principles laid down in *Mein Kampf* and the 'second book', those on foreign policy formulated tactical and strategic aims but did not embody the full programme expressed in those writings. What tactics could be pursued pending achievement of the strategic aim of political power? By 'political power' Hitler meant here the attainment of military and political freedom of action for continental enterprises. The principal aim meanwhile was to build up the Wehrmacht, acquire allies, and combat the Versailles system. The 'conquering of new living-space in the east' was—probably by design—indicated as no more than a possibility. For Hitler there was only one factor of uncertainty at this stage, namely France. It would be seen whether France had any statesmen: if she did, she would allow Germany no time to recover. For the time being, German policy could allow this topic to follow its old course. Revisionist aims could still be pursued. The disarmament negotiations could continue with the objective of equal rights in view, i.e. the unrestricted right to rearm.

For Hitler this distinction of tactics and strategy had the advantage of camouflaging his long-term aims. The German diplomats could imagine that they were still in charge; the generals were gratified by the assurance that they would enjoy a monopoly of arms-bearing within the state and were impressed by Hitler's resolve to reintroduce conscription. As far as foreign relations were concerned, the plan enabled Hitler to protest his peaceful intentions at all times, and to maintain his predecessors' line of representing France as blocking the way to a peaceful Europe.

The most skilful move in this game—in itself not a complicated one, and largely dictated by circumstances—was, while aiming at familiar short-term objectives, to involve leading bourgeois-conservative circles in preparing the way for more distant aims. For many such people these objectives raised doubtful issues of conscience, as historico-political habits of thought stood in the way of a sober intellectual and moral assessment of the situation.

This brings us to the question of continuity, which remains to be examined. For foreign ministry officials and for the military, among others, this problem was not merely one of the continued validity and influence of certain mental attitudes. The connection between domestic and foreign policy, the clean sweep in home affairs, the emergency laws and measures designed to destroy all forms of opposition, the concentration of state power in a 'strictly authoritarian' government, the branding of democracy as a 'cancerous growth'—all this raised the question of the motives and purpose of foreign policy. Hitler's plan at the beginning of February 1933, while only the tip of an iceberg, recognizably called in question the foundations of home and foreign policy as they had hitherto existed. It was no longer merely a question of power politics: the mental categories of the extermination and destruction of 'enemies' came in sight. That these categories were repressed by the government, the army, the economy, and the administration is part of the complex problem of the continuity of German political attitudes in the transition to National Socialist rule.

5. CONTINUITY OF FOREIGN POLICY?

The 'foreign policy' of the first few months, the chief objective of which was to achieve rearmament through the disarmament negotiations, was handled by the foreign ministry. The conservative revisionism of its leading officials provided cover for the transformation that was taking place in internal affairs. In particular the fact that Neurath and Bülow, the minister and the state secretary, remained in office served, both at home and abroad, to palliate the assumption of power by the National Socialists. From this point of view foreign policy and its propaganda aspects must be seen as functions of an all-round policy, the ultimate aims of which were not yet fully clear to the ministry itself, precisely because of the partial similarity between Hitler's designs and its own power-political approach.[83]

On questions of timing and emphasis, priority for armaments or the reparations question, the Reichswehr and foreign ministry differed from time to time; but they agreed as to the aim, viz. German hegemony in Europe and a future world role for the Reich. These objectives fitted without difficulty into Hitler's aims as formulated in 1933. However Hitler's 'programme' may be seen as the mainspring of German war policy, there remained an accompaniment of national-conservative and economic-imperialist aims. Their origin in the imperial period, as far back even as Bismarck, has from time to time been emphasized or adduced for interpretative purposes. As a result of such investigation it can be said that the formulators of German foreign policy in the foreign ministry, the Reichswehr, and the conservative-bourgeois parties began at the point where matters had been left before and during the First World War.

The sense of having been unjustly dealt with in the peace treaty became a widespread political conviction in Germany. Revisionist arguments and propaganda had so strong a uniting effect that the concept of a great-power policy making use of Germany's remaining potential assets found acceptance in almost every quarter.

The question as to who was empowered to take foreign-policy decisions after 1933 is perhaps still more important than the continued influence of great-power and world-power concepts, which was less sensational among the generation that had lived through the transition from the Wilhelmine era to the post-war period. That generation had known the time when Germany was the chief power on the

---

[83] On foreign policy in the initial phase see Jacobsen, *Außenpolitik* and id., 'Rolle Deutschlands'. Bloch, *Hitler*, p. 22, notes that the seizure of power 'did not immediately signify any radical breach with the foreign policy of the preceding years'. See also Bracher, 'Anfangsstadium'.

Continent; it was convinced that she must and would recover that role. But who was to take the necessary decisions?

Scholars agree that the bureaucracy of the foreign ministry possessed considerable freedom of action after Hitler's accession to power. It can also be seen that the ministry relied to some extent on the new Reichswehr leaders. In the first weeks after 30 January 1933 the ministry successfully applied negotiating tactics at the Geneva disarmament conference that went beyond Hitler's ideas; but can this be taken as signifying that it was firmly in charge of foreign affairs? The ministry certainly overrated its own strength when, enjoying the support of the Reich president and the senior Reichswehr officers, it believed itself to be relatively independent.

A survey of German foreign policy in the years preceding the Second World War will show that in the initial phase the 'independence' of the foreign ministry went beyond mere diplomatic nuances; but its freedom of action can only be adequately assessed against the background of Hitler's ideas and aims. As long as Hitler was chiefly concerned with consolidating his rule at home, he needed a phase of 'normality' in foreign affairs, which could be most plausibly assured by officials whose names were familiar in foreign countries. Neurath, Bülow, and the others seem privately to have felt some scepticism as to the possibility of continuing the previous foreign policy, but they represented it to the outside world as a certainty.

The individuals in question differed widely in their awareness of events, background experience, and political motivation. Neurath, who had been foreign minister in Papen's cabinet, had a reserved attitude towards the republic. His experience as ambassador in Rome may have given him the impression that the German revolution, like the Italian one, could be 'tamed' as far as home affairs were concerned. In foreign affairs he overrated the strength of his position as Hindenburg's *homme de confiance*. However, the deciding factor that induced him to stay in office was probably the complex of ideas on military and power politics that caused him, believing as he did in the recovery of former positions of power, to advocate a policy which placed rearmament in the forefront of its objectives. Bernhard Wilhelm von Bülow, the state secretary since 1930, had previously resigned from the service as a protest against Versailles. He was at least as strong a devotee of treaty revision and equal rights for Germany as was von Neurath; like his chief, he believed in making Germany a great power once again by building up fresh economic and then military strength.

Like the soldiers, the officials of the foreign ministry were not unduly disturbed by the Nazi seizure of power, or filled with pessimism as to Germany's future. As experts, they were understandably anxious lest they should lose influence or be replaced by amateurs. Bülow even addressed a circular to heads of missions on 30 January 1933,[84] intended to calm their fears and instructing them to take a reassuring line in conversation. Its revealing combination of self-deception and 'cover-up' throws an interesting light on the ministry's attitude towards Hitler.[85]

---

[84] *DGFP*, c. i, No. 1.
[85] Wollstein, *Revisionismus*, 29–30; id., 'Denkschrift'. On Bülow cf. also Jacobsen, *Außenpolitik*, 33.

Clearer still, perhaps, is the mixture of independent-mindedness and adaptability on the part of the future state secretary, Ernst von Weizsäcker. At the outset of the 'revolution', when he was minister in Oslo, he felt a stronger sense of insecurity than Neurath or Bülow. His sceptical attitude towards the new regime and the National Socialist movement made him wonder whether it was possible to 'go along with it',[86] and how far 'that part of the bureaucracy which is still intact' could retain 'the necessary influence'. Like others, he was reassured by the fact that Neurath and Bülow were remaining in office, which even seemed to him a 'guarantee of reasonableness'.[87] In March he already believed that the second stage of the revolution might take a 'constructive' turn, and in August 1933 he felt that all members of the foreign service who were then abroad should visit Germany for a time, as otherwise they would 'not understand what is going on here, and the opportunities it gives us *vis-à-vis* foreign governments'.[88] Hitler had, it appears, made a 'metaphysical' impression on him. Evidently by March the ministry's initial fears of major personnel changes and 'experiments' in foreign affairs had already been dissipated.

Weizsäcker was in charge of the personnel department of the ministry for a time in the summer of 1933, and in the middle of July—no doubt partly in order to ward off external pressure—he made it his first objective 'to see that the gates of Party membership were once more thrown open to members of the foreign service'.[89] He believed that almost all of them would take advantage of this. To this day we do not know precisely how many foreign-service officers were Party members,[90] but, roughly speaking, out of ninety-two senior officials about a third had joined the Party by 1937; seven had done so before 1933. As in the rest of the administration and public life, it was mainly opportunists and careerists who joined after the 'seizure of power'. However, the process as a whole is of interest as affecting the problem of continuity in the personal sphere. Even the degree of *rapprochement* represented by passive Party membership helped to smooth over differences of view, or at any rate made it difficult to adopt an attitude of detachment. Hence, it was more important than is sometimes supposed when high honorary rank in the SS was subsequently bestowed on persons who were not typical representatives of the Party élite, such as Neurath and Weizsäcker—to mention the most outstanding.[91] Although it is impossible to obtain a clear picture of the background to transfers and dismissals, it can be said that out of nearly ninety senior officials only a small percentage were relieved of their posts on political grounds.[92]

The ministry's anxiety lest its specialized diplomatic work should be nullified by unskilful action reflected reservations that Hitler's initial moderation was calculated to dispel. At the outset he gave priority to rearmament in his foreign policy, just as

[86] *Weizsäcker-Papiere*, 60.
[87] Ibid. 69.
[88] Ibid. 75.
[89] Ibid. 74.
[90] Jacobsen, *Außenpolitik*, 28, and the estimates in Seabury, *Wilhelmstrasse*, 103.
[91] Jacobsen, *Außenpolitik*, 28.
[92] Jacobsen, ibid. 25, estimates '6% at most'.

Papen and Schleicher had done, and this appeared to guarantee a continuation of the previous line.

The diplomats, like the soldiers and other 'leading groups', were prone to think, in and after 1933, that the Führer, in his capacity as chancellor, must necessarily move closer to their idea of the state. Many felt that for them to carry on at their posts was a positive precondition of national and political continuity.

This attitude became pernicious as soon as it was clear that it entailed conscious approval, or at any rate acceptance, of the new order in domestic affairs. The ambassador in Washington, von Prittwitz und Gaffron, was the only one among the top diplomats who found the price of continuity impossible to reconcile with his conscience. In a letter to Neurath[93] he made clear that his political views were rooted in a liberal conception of the state and in the 'basic principles of republican Germany', hence in ideas that were condemned by leading members of the new government. Foreign ministry officials in Germany were even better able than Prittwitz in the United States to perceive the truth of his assessment.

The problem of continuity is thus not only to be seen in the fact that the 'old élite' wished to be able to carry on its policies in foreign affairs, but also that this expectation seemed sensible and politically realizable even if hope were abandoned of preserving the liberal regime based on the rule of law, which was admittedly shaken by crises and already half dismantled before the Party's assumption of power.

Revisionist aims in foreign policy were also part of the National Socialist programme.[94] This aimed at the full implementation of the principle of the national state, but seemed at the same time to accept an 'apparent self-limitation'.[95] From the last third of the nineteenth century onwards the leading circles of Prussian Germany had made the Reich participate in the imperialist race without allowing liberal-democratic forces a share in the process of political decision. This meant that foreign policy and defence policy, in particular, were excluded from parliamentary control, and that Germans grew accustomed to a state superstructure manifesting itself primarily in these two fields. This conditioning of public opinion was supported by a political and demagogic strategy which, from Bismarck's time onwards, skilfully exploited domestic and foreign aims, intentions, and 'necessities'.[96]

The Weimar parliamentary system had to live with this democratic deficiency in society at large and in political parties—a deficiency due not only to the lack of relevant experience but to deeply rooted habits of thought and action. Thus, it has rightly been said that the character of the German parties was 'governed by the notion of an authoritarian state'.[97] Hitler, immediately after the seizure of power, expressed a number of principles and aims that could be welcomed as entirely

---

[93] Letter of 11 Mar. 1933: *ADAP*, b. i. 1, No. 75, pp. 145–6.

[94] Feder, *Programm.*

[95] Bracher, 'Stufen der Machtergreifung', 221.

[96] Survey of literature in Messerschmidt, *Militär und Politik*. See also Wette in Part I above.

[97] Bracher, 'Stufen der Machtergreifung', 32. On the whole problem see also Weber, 'Parlament und Regierung', 184, and Wette, I.1.5 above.

familiar by members of his government. As the Reichswehr leaders renounced the right to a voice in internal affairs out of inner assent to 'national renovation' and for the sake of achieving more rapid rearmament, so the foreign ministry could accept the new system on the basis that 'there was at present no idea of a spectacular new departure in the field of foreign affairs'.[98] There were, however, perceptible signs that the emphasis might be changed.

Leading conservatives intended to work to restore Germany's position as a great power and to create a suitable military instrument for the purpose. In 1936–7 it became clearer to them that Hitler's intention went further. He wished to bring about a much more rapid change in the European balance of power; and he was readier to accept the idea of war than were the bureaucracy and the military, who—bearing in mind the war of attrition in 1914–18—wanted first to create a substantial defence force, with reserves and adequate supplies. Hitler had a different picture of war: it meant effecting decisions by rapid blows, playing adversaries off against each other, perhaps using them alternately to cover his rear—all with the object of rapidly achieving a position from which he could start the war for *Lebensraum* in the east.

If the matter is closely examined, Hitler and the conservative leaders can be seen to have differed in various ways in their foreign objectives and notions of procedure, especially in the matter of armaments. But Hitler was able to leave these differences unsettled for a relatively long time. When he brought them into the open and showed himself to be resolved on war, he was as a rule met with the argument 'Not yet'. Hence, it is not profitable to go into the differences in detail. In foreign affairs the incomplete accordance of aims proved to be no disadvantage to Hitler. On the contrary, for years action proceeded in parallel, and later, especially from 1938 onwards, the missing degree of congruence was reflected only in ineffectual steps.

[98] See in detail Wollstein, *Revisionismus*, 18 ff.

II. The Great Powers and the Aspiring Great Power

1. Freedom of Manœuvre after the Seizure of Power

HITLER'S seizure of power and the *Gleichschaltung* (forcible co-ordination) which followed on the home front was from the beginning more than an event in domestic politics. Its effects on neighbouring countries were hard to estimate, but on the whole the consequences of the world depression were fairly favourable to the assertion of German independence. American isolationism had received a stimulus, while Britain was deeply involved in her own problems. The democratic governments were hard put to it to justify expenditure on armaments to their own peoples. At this time the international security system of the League of Nations ran into great difficulties. Readiness to rely on it was visibly diminishing. Japan, the first great power to break out of the system, invaded China in 1932 and conquered Manchuria without fear of incurring serious sanctions from the League. Her condemnation by the latter was an empty gesture, to which she reacted by withdrawing from the collective security system.

Until 1933 Germany's attempts to manœuvre her way back into the ranks of the great powers took place within the post-war system, which had not yet been openly challenged. From the beginning Hitler set his sights on the abolition of that system, while continuing to speak a basically pacific language. He pressed on with rearmament under the slogan of 'equal rights', and endeavoured to undermine collective security with bilateral arrangements, This method has been described as a 'grandiose self-belittling strategy',[1] as 'covert preparation for aggression',[2] and as a prelude to expansionism under the guise of traditional revisionist demands.[3] In Hitler's view, which was also that of the army leaders and the foreign minister, rearmament was no longer compatible with multilateral treaties and a European security system: in future Germany must be able to fix her own timetable. In any case international peace-keeping arrangements were contrary to Hitler's principles. None the less, throughout 1933 and into 1934 the debate among European statesmen was dominated by the theme of disarmament, the League of Nations, and methods of international control. Britain's commitment, in particular, was inescapable. The climate thus created in Europe was far from congenial to Germany's middle-term policy of expansion and aggression. It was therefore her aim to destroy the existing system, which was in any case ineffectual, without being branded as a disturber of

[1] Jacobsen, *Außenpolitik*, 328.
[2] Ibid. 391 ff.
[3] Hildebrand, *Foreign Policy*, 24. This was a strategy that Hitler did not actually need to invent. Papen and Bülow were to tread this path in 1932, and even proposed general-staff contacts to the French: see n. 55 below, and cf. *DDF*[1] i. 71, confidential note of a conversation between Bülow and de Laboulaye on 18 June 1932. Instead of 'equal rights' Bülow preferred to speak of 'equal treatment'.

the peace. Caution and skill were necessary in order to get through the dangerous period until German rearmament was accomplished. The military and political leaders did not differ from Hitler on this point, and they favoured his policy on economic grounds, seeing a connection between rearmament and the possibility of an economic upturn.[4]

This approach to foreign relations was hampered by the domestic methods used to carry out the National Socialist policy of remilitarization. The persecution of Communists, democrats, and Jews, and the *Gleichschaltung* of parties and organizations, were noted in foreign countries and not regarded as merely Germany's own affair.

None the less, internal and external conditions were not unfavourable to Germany's middle-term chances of making a bid for hegemony in Europe. On the home front, the consensus over immediate objectives encouraged co-operation from conservative leaders in the business world, the army, and the foreign service. The process of consolidating power in home affairs could continue undisturbed. An economic potential, unaffected structurally by the peace treaty, was available for the purpose of recovery and rearmament.[5] After 1933 that potential could be developed still further without arousing apprehensions on any important scale, particularly in Britain—a contrast to the situation before the First World War.[6] The powers remained lookers-on, though changes in their attitude to Germany could be perceived after 1933.

The most significant change was in Britain, where the military took a realistic view of the danger to be expected from Germany, in accordance with the British principle of holding an even balance on the Continent.[7] They estimated, no later than 1933, that a great-power Germany under Hitler, which let it be seen that it was opposed to a policy of accommodation, would in future rank as Britain's prime enemy.[8] In October 1933 the chiefs of staff expressed the view that as soon as Germany felt strong enough she would start an aggressive war in the east, combined if necessary with a defensive war in the west. Britain might expect to have to take military action in the next three to five years.

This did not mean that Britain intended to increase her commitment in Europe or had any idea of giving France the guarantee against Germany which she had desired since Versailles; but it marked the beginning of a process of rethinking, though for a

---

[4] Hildebrand, *Foreign Policy*, 27; Turner, 'Monopolkapitalisten'; cf. Volkmann, II.III.1 above.

[5] Hildebrand, *Foreign Policy*, 9.

[6] Kennedy, 'Splendid Isolation', 161.

[7] See esp. Chiefs of Staff Annual Review of Defence Policy, 12 Oct. 1933, PRO COS 310, Cab 53/23; also Howard, *Commitment*, 104. The Annual Review stated that 'Germany is not only starting to rearm, but . . . she will continue this process until within a few years hence she will again have to be reckoned as a formidable military power.'

[8] Gibbs, *Strategy*, i. 94. Gibbs refers to the report of the defence requirements subcommittee of the committee on imperial defence, dated 28 Feb. 1934 and reporting a meeting of 14 Nov. 1933. Members of the subcommittee were Hankey (chairman), Warren Fisher, Vansittart, and the three chiefs of staff. The report described Germany as the principal opponent 'against whom all our long-range defence policy must be directed'. Gibbs observes: 'Already, in effect, Germany headed the list of Britain's potential enemies, and nothing seriously affected her position there before war broke out in Sept. 1939.'

long time it was overshadowed by the predominantly economic aspects of British policy. Britain recovered from the world depression faster than other countries in 1933–5, and it was logical for economic factors to continue to play a major role in her foreign policy.[9] While noting the far-sighted analysis by the British military leaders and the civilians represented on the defence requirements committee, one must bear in mind that all political groups in Britain regarded war as a last resort, a contingency which was bound to affect a trading nation like Britain more severely than any other country; moreover, conservative circles believed that it would bring about an unforeseeable degree of undesirable social change. Hence, clearly though the German danger was perceived, Britain remained an advocate of collective security.

An additional factor was the British public's dislike of war and warlike preparations, and the survival of the imperialist way of thinking, according to which British foreign policy and strategy were centred in the Empire and not in Europe. It was with little effect that Sir H. Rumbold, the ambassador in Berlin, reported that 'the spirit of Weimar had yielded to the spirit of Potsdam'.[10] Europe's problems could, it was believed, be solved within the framework of the League of Nations; and the League of Nations or some other system of collective security seemed—though not to the chief of staff or the committee of imperial defence—to make it unnecessary to maintain a strong system of armaments.[11] In consequence of this, and in view of the deficiency of defence preparations, the idea of collective security soon became more or less the chief abiding principle of British policy and a basic feature of appeasement. In the long term it acted as a decisive counter to Hitler's plans, as it was made a touchstone of the sincerity of German professions and a standard against which the intentions of Germany's bilateral policy could be judged. But in the first years after 1933 the principle of collective security was still no great obstacle to Hitler, as the British concept could be opposed by that of equal rights for Germany, a principle which found acceptance particularly in London. British attitudes were still conditioned by memories of the carnage of the First World War and the loss of British trade. Pacifist ideas had much influence, and there was a predominant desire to be free of continental commitments and on no account get involved in another arms race. Even after the 'ten-year rule',[12] which had been reinforced in 1928 and which laid down that Britain need not expect a major war within the next ten years, was abolished in March 1932 at the instance of the chiefs of staff, it was more than a year before a policy of systematic opposition to Hitler could be introduced. Any attempt to get more involved on the Continent would have met with criticism and indeed opposition from the Dominions, who had already objected to the Locarno treaty, and who firmly rejected the idea of any

---

[9] Middlemas, *Diplomacy*, 12 ff.

[10] Kennedy, 'Splendid Isolation', 162; Gilbert, *Rumbold*, 374.

[11] Even Hankey, the influential secretary of the cabinet and the CID, did not himself believe in the need, but he wanted to turn the rearmament effort to the benefit of the Empire.

[12] Howard, *Commitment*, 89–90; Gibbs, *Strategy*, i. 55 ff., on the development of the ten-year rule; Roskill, *Hankey*, vols. i and ii; also Dennis, *Decision*; Higham, *Armed Forces*; and Johnson, *Defence*; cf. the survey of literature in Schmidt, 'Strategie und Außenpolitik'.

British obligation, for instance by way of an alliance with France, to oppose German expansionist attempts.[13]

This background must be borne in mind with reference to British criticism of the National Socialist measures that followed the seizure of power.[14] However, the effect of those measures, and of German rearmament coupled with the evident impossibility of Franco-German reconciliation, was to give a stimulus to Britain's traditional balance-of-power policy. In March–April 1934 ministers debated whether Britain should be prepared to go to war to defend Holland,[15] as had been proposed by the defence requirements committee, in particular by Sir R. Vansittart, permanent under-secretary at the foreign office, and Sir Warren Fisher, head of the civil service. The chiefs of staff pointed out the importance of such a decision to Belgium.[16] The premier, MacDonald, was impressed, but the chancellor of the exchequer, Neville Chamberlain, raised financial and psychological objections which defeated the proposal. In August 1933 Vansittart already foresaw the danger that Germany would annex Austria and attack Poland and France, perhaps also Britain, if she were not compelled to cease rearming.[17] The drastic Nazi measures on the home front intensified such fears. Above all the persecution of the Jews shocked British opinion, casting a dark shadow over Germany's reputation.[18] Rumbold lost no time in pointing this out to Hitler and warning him of the adverse effects it would have on Britain's attitude towards treaty revision.[19]

At this early stage of Hitler's rule it is basically unimportant that even far-seeing British political and military leaders did not perceive the main thrust of Hitler's programme, viz. a war for 'living-space' in the east.[20] Their estimate of his policy, above all the consequences of German rearmament, was much more realistic than Hitler's ideas concerning Britain's future attitude towards Germany. True, it was a long time before leading British circles agreed on a policy reflecting their understanding of the position. The cabinet, the armed forces, and the foreign office did not see eye to eye. But from the outset there was no chance whatever of Britain playing the role Hitler designed for her. His protestations of peace were taken at their true value, though for some time to come Germany's 'equal-rights strategy' found acceptance in many circles, while France was an object of mistrust.[21] The

---

[13] For the Dominions' attitude after 1933 see also Howard, *Commitment*, 99–100.

[14] Simon endeavoured to exploit this state of mind in Britain to gain approval for the British disarmament plan. He observed to Nadolny in Geneva on 16 Mar. 1933 that 'Feeling toward Germany in England as well as America had been increasingly favourable until recently. This had unfortunately changed in the past several weeks as a result of internal events in Germany' (*DGFP*, c. i. 169).

[15] Cabinet disarmament committee debates on European security, Mar.–Apr. 1934, PRO Cab 27/506.

[16] On the question of the defence of Holland and Belgium see Middlemas, *Diplomacy*, 18; Howard, *Commitment*, 108–9.

[17] *DBFP*² v, No. 371.

[18] Events in Germany were criticized in Commons debates. Simon informed Hoesch, the German ambassador, that 'it was an undeniable fact that Germany had lost a great deal of sympathy in England during the past weeks' (*DGFP*, c. i. 351–2).

[19] Conversation between Rumbold and Hitler, with Neurath present, on 11 May 1933; Neurath's record in *DGFP*, c. i. 404–6; Rumbold's report in *DBFP*² v, No. 139.

[20] Hildebrand points this out in *Foreign Policy*, 25, referring to Vansittart's analysis of 7 Apr. 1934, *DBFP*² vi, appendix III, pp. 975 ff.

[21] See e.g. Eden, *Facing the Dictators*, 186; also Bloch, *Hitler*, 26.

British leaders well knew which power they might one day have to use force against. The object of British policy was to postpone that day if it could not be averted. German–French relations were seen to be the root of the problem, and disarmament seemed an important key to its solution. If Franco-German antagonism could be resolved in that area it would be a major step towards peace. Thus, disarmament problems were the main issue in the three-cornered argument between London, Paris and Berlin, but the idea of gaining time played a major part. And it was Hitler's great good fortune that British optimism won the day over French pessimism.

France viewed the new regime in Germany with great concern and scepticism. Her fears were excited above all by the wave of terror in Germany itself and in the frontier area by members of the Sturmabteilung (SA: storm troops).[22] Events of this sort added fuel to the French demand that German rearmament should be checked.[23] Alarm was intensified by rumours of the conclusion, in 1932, of a secret treaty between Germany, Italy, and Hungary.[24] Fears of what Germany might do next added to French anxiety. 'Suspicion of a Fascist alliance'[25] long remained alive in France, even after the German *démenti*. It is not too much to say that France's basic psychological attitude towards Germany underwent a change. France had always seen conquered Germany as a potential danger, despite or because of the treaty of Versailles, not least because the United States and Britain had refused France the guarantee she asked for; but now the threat seemed to become more and more overt. Nazi activities in the Saar region were the subject of a warning to the German ambassador in Paris from French Radical Socialist deputies, who attributed the concern of the French public to Germany's policy towards the Jews.[26] The main anxiety, however, related to south-eastern Europe, where a German–Italian–Hungarian line-up might have dislocated France's alliance system—the 'Little Entente' of Czechoslovakia, Yugoslavia, and Romania, created in 1920–1 and reinforced in 1934, on France's initiative, by the 'Balkan Entente' of Greece, Yugoslavia, Romania, and Turkey.

Basically France felt threatened by the German policy of remilitarization, which in the nature of things had to be chiefly directed against the uncompromising defender of the Versailles system.[27] French statesmen perceived the threat to her position as the strongest military power on the Continent. This prospect, and uncertainty as to the true nature of the governing forces in Germany, were the chief problems confronting France after 30 January 1933: not as an abstract question of primacy, but on vital grounds of security. A stronger Germany could nullify the

---

[22] Köster, the German ambassador in Paris, reported on 10 Mar. 1933 on French press accounts of the occupation by National Socialists of a barracks in Kehl, in the demilitarized zone: *DGFP*, c. i, No. 69, p. 134. This incident was also the subject of a conversation between Neurath and François-Poncet on 14 Mar.

[23] See Bülow's record of 18 Feb. 1933 of a conversation with François-Poncet, in which the latter referred to France's anxiety over forecasts of foreign policy in the German press: *DGFP*, c. i. 49–52.

[24] Bloch, *Hitler*, 29–30.

[25] Petersen, *Hitler–Mussolini*, 122.

[26] Köster to Bülow, 5 Apr. 1933: *DGFP*, c. i. 250–2.

[27] Knipping, 'Frankreich', 619.

French system of alliances; above all it could not be held in check by diplomatic means alone. Instead the Third Republic would have to make strong efforts of its own, for which there was much less enthusiasm in France than in Germany, which was already bent on large-scale rearmament.

Italian reactions to Hitler's seizure of power constituted the major exception among the great powers. Press comment was mainly favourable, even warmly so. Hitler's association with 'nationalist forces and defence organizations' was welcomed, and there were references to a 'decisive turning-point in modern German history'. The press also emphasized that Hitler was 'following in the footsteps' of Fascism.[28] The German ambassador's reports at this initial stage could not be other than welcome in Berlin. The Italian press declared openly what France most feared: Hitler's seizure of power meant the end of Versailles, a new Europe was being born, a Europe, as one writer put it, 'in accord with the basic principles of Fascism'. Such expressions were eagerly publicized by the party press in Germany.[29]

Mussolini spoke of the possibility of a 'closely associated' policy between Germany and Italy, indicating that disarmament, the world economic conference, and south-eastern Europe might be suitable areas of co-operation, as the two countries' interests there were closely allied. He clearly over-estimated the conservative influence on Hitler's government, as did contemporaries both in and outside Germany. He even supposed that Hindenburg was the chief prop of the regime.[30] His comment also implied that there were still important areas of disagreement between Italy and Germany. Neither the German nor the Italian foreign ministry wanted a *rapprochement* proclaimed from the house-tops. Mussolini evaded Hitler's desire—shared by virtually no one else—that the German dictator should visit Rome.[31] The Italian leader evidently misjudged the position when he thought the National Socialist leader would encounter stronger international opposition than had Fascism in Italy,[32] so that the regime would take many years to win through completely. The election of 5 March 1933 proved him mistaken. The consolidation of National Socialism was warmly welcomed in Italy, but it was made clear that the credit for its intellectual and political foundations belonged to the pioneer regime in southern Europe. From that time onwards 'a battle was waged, half in secret, over the right of primogeniture'.[33] Much more awkward, however, were the continuing conflicts of actual interest, which stood in the way of a joint foreign policy in the spirit of the two powers' rhetorical protestations. Mussolini at any rate was not prepared simply to forget about the bone of contention *par excellence*, the union of Austria with the Reich. What was inevitable should at least be postponed as long as possible. Italy was conscious of the

[28] References in Peterson, *Hitler-Mussolini*, 114.
[29] e.g. the *Völkischer Beobachter* (cf. Petersen, *Hitler-Mussolini*, 155). Hitler received representatives of the Italian press as early as 2 Feb. 1933, which made a great impression in Italy: ibid. 116.
[30] *DGFP*, c. i. 25.
[31] Various references in Petersen, *Hitler-Mussolini*, 123-4.
[32] Ibid. 126.
[33] Ibid. 129.

connection between the Anschluss and the south Tyrol, and experience led her to take a view of these questions different from that adopted by Hitler in his writings. As early as the beginning of February, Mussolini expressed the desire that Hitler would not raise the question of the Anschluss.[34]

Italy's policy towards Germany after the seizure of power must be seen as a complex of ideological and national, power-political motives. There is much truth in the view that 'German National Socialism in the wilderness was more agreeable to Signor Mussolini than German National Socialism in the saddle'.[35] Differences between the two brands of Fascism can also not be overlooked. There was no question of a solid ideological basis for a joint foreign policy of expansion.

In the United States the Weimar Republic had enjoyed increasing sympathy once wartime hostility began to die down. This process was aided by a mood of growing disillusion with the Allies of the First World War, especially France, due in large measure to the Europeans' reluctance to repay war debts. Between the United States and Germany there were virtually no important causes of disagreement.[36] America's readiness to give the young republic a fair chance was noted and appreciated by influential German circles. The success of German foreign policy was due in part to the American attitude. The way to increased independence in economic matters and hence in foreign relations led through the United States. German revisionist policy was based to an important extent on economic co-operation with the Americans, who for their part saw such co-operation as conducing to European stability.[37]

The 'stabilization of Europe' was an objective incompatible with American isolation after 1918. American economic policy was largely identical with 'reconstruction policy' in Europe.[38] It was of course not intended to stabilize Europe for the latter's own sake, but was a matter of national self-interest in the broadest sense. However, despite the Kellogg pact and the Stimson doctrine, American self-interest shrank from active participation in the collective-security system,[39] since the primary concern was to preserve America's freedom of action. This afforded a further opportunity to the German revisionist campaign. If America had put its whole weight behind the League of Nations, France could have afforded to treat Germany with greater leniency; she would not have had to take such an individual line, and would have lost less sympathy in the Anglo-Saxon countries. In any case, a sizeable amount of America's trade was directed to the Far East and Latin America; and at the outset Japanese expansion aroused more interest than Germany.

None the less, America did not look on with unconcern at the events that led to Hitler's assuming the chancellorship. Germany was seen in America as a bulwark

---

[34] *Allianz Hitler–Horthy–Mussolini*, No. 2; Petersen, *Hitler–Mussolini*, 131.

[35] Toynbee in *Survey of International Affairs, 1933*, 198–9; Petersen, *Hitler–Mussolini*, 129

[36] On German–American relations in the Weimar period see the brief survey in Weinberg, *Foreign Policy*, 132 ff.; Adler, 'War-guilt Question'.

[37] On the first stages see Krüger, *Reparationen*, and Link, *Stabilisierungspolitik*.

[38] Costigliola, *Financial Stabilization*; Williams, 'Isolationism'.

[39] Angermann, 'Lage', 116–17.

against Bolshevism. The growth of radical influence at both ends of the political spectrum aroused anxiety.[40] Very soon after the Nazi revolution Prittwitz, the ambassador in Washington, warned his government that internal events in Germany were likely to affect American attitudes.[41] This was true above all of the anti-Jewish measures, but alarm was also caused by the rearmament drive,[42] which clearly conflicted with Germany's economic and financial policy *vis-à-vis* American creditors. Schacht's policy gave Americans the impression that the object of his manœuvres was to make them help pay for German rearmament. There were also other fields of conflict in economic matters. As a result, and despite constant protestations of good intentions from Berlin, the latter forfeited much of America's confidence within a short time of Hitler's accession to power. The foreign ministry did its best to preserve friendly contacts in the United States, but to little avail.[43] This phase of German policy comes under the heading of 'cover-up' strategy on the part of the foreign ministry in the initial period of National Socialist rule.[44] After 30 January 1933 the European great powers and the United States were faced with the unpleasant question whether Hitler's Germany had brought a new spirit into foreign affairs. Various answers were given to this question, but all were aware that new developments must be expected.

Concentration on the restoration of Germany's military capability led to her withdrawing from the intentional economic system and pursuing a policy of autarky. This limited the scope of her foreign policy in the areas traditionally concerned with peaceful international exchanges, which had created a multiplicity of links and kept alive an interest in reciprocity.

Germany's relations with the Soviet Union and Poland had always been to a large extent a politico-strategic reflection of French security policy after Versailles. Neurath and Bülow, and the army leaders, saw no reason for a radical change of course. Towards the Soviet Union, the foreign ministry pursued an especially intensive policy of playing down any question of a German threat. Even before 1933 Berlin had felt obliged to take especial care of its relations with Moscow, though it also did not hesitate to impress on the Western powers its mistrust of Bolshevism and to draw conclusions from this as to Germany's need for security. After the Rapallo treaty of 1922 and the Berlin treaty of 1926, in which Germany promised neutrality if the Soviet Union were involved in a defensive war, German–Soviet relations were kept as free as possible from any basic conflict arising from differences of social, political, and economic structure. However, relations were to some extent unstable owing to Germany's dependence on the victors of 1918, which from time to time appeared in Moscow to present the danger of a Western bloc forming against the Soviet Union. This aspect was at its clearest during the

[40] Important literature includes Link, *Stabilisierungspolitik*; Frye, *Nazi Germany*; Crompton, *Swastika and Eagle*; Schröder, *Deutschland*.

[41] *DGFP*, B. i. 334.

[42] Leuchtenburg, *Roosevelt*, 210 ff.

[43] Esp. Schröder, *Deutschland*, and id., 'Das Dritte Reich', 340 ff.; also Deist, 'Aufrüstung in amerikanischer Sicht'.

[44] See also Bracher, 'Anfangsstadium', 74.

chancellorships of Brüning and Papen. But even earlier a kind of 'concertina effect' was repeatedly observable in German–Russian relations: whenever German revisionist policy led to diplomatic negotiations with the Western powers, Russian suspicions were aroused and had to be assuaged until the next time.[45]

From time to time relations rose from a 'trough' of this kind to a new peak, such as the Rapallo and Berlin treaties. On the occasion of the Young Plan negotiations and the evacuation of the Rhineland, Germany and Russia again assured each other of the validity of the Rapallo treaty and the need for good relations. The chief advantage for Germany was that the Soviet Union adopted a benevolent attitude towards her claims in the disarmament negotiations;[46] co-operation in military matters was throughout an important feature of relations between the two countries.

From 1931 onwards, however, Russian policy sought to adopt a fresh course. There was talk of 'reinsurance' against Germany in the form of contacts with Poland and France, the very powers whose attitude had so far afforded the strongest reason for German–Russian *rapprochement*. Russia's problems in the Far East, and her economic difficulties, played an important part in the developments that finally led to her concluding non-aggression treaties with those countries; so did Brüning's strategy of using the world economic crisis as a means of finally shaking off Germany's obligations in regard to reparations, and thus paving the way for her recovery of great-power status. Brüning's policy stood in the way of an economic underpinning of German–Russian relations, which the Soviet Union made intensive efforts to secure in 1931–2.[47]

The Soviet Union realized that the object of Germany's policy concerning reparations, which Russia so often supported, was to re-establish Germany as a great power. She wished to have good relations with that power, but, as in the 1920s, was still afraid that Germany might transfer her friendship to the Western powers.[48] An immediate danger of this seemed to lie in Papen's plans for a defensive continental bloc excluding the Soviet Union. Aware of the German offer to the Western powers,[49] Moscow felt that its fears were confirmed and that it must adopt a different course.

Schleicher, however, reverted to a more pro-Russian policy, both in economic and in military matters. He was able to restore co-operation with the Red Army in

---

[45] The history of German–Soviet relations is analysed, so far as access to the sources permits, in Weingartner, *Stalin*, and Niclauss, *Sowjetunion*. Recently, for the first phase after 1933, see Wollstein, *Revisionismus*, and Allard, *Stalin*. The latter refers (32 ff.) to Stalin's change of attitude after the Röhm affair (30 June 1934), when he saw Hitler in a new light; also Hildebrand, *Das Deutsche Reich*. Papen's attempt at a *rapprochement* with France, which was rejected by the Herriot government, was accompanied by side-thrusts at Moscow: see Bülow's remarks to de Laboulaye on 2 June 1932, *DDF*[1] i. No. 46, annex III, p. 72.

[46] Weingartner, *Stalin*, 16, has drawn attention to the parallel between the oscillations in German–Russian relations in 1929–30 and in the period of the Locarno and Berlin treaties.

[47] Niclauss, *Sowjetunion*, 43 ff.; Wollstein, *Revisionismus*, 102 ff.

[48] Cf. e.g. the official view of GDR historians on the Locarno treaty: 'The Locarno agreements, the conclusion of which was greeted with the high-flown rhetoric of peace, marked an important step on the way towards enrolling Germany in an international anti-Soviet coalition' (Ruge, *Deutschland*, 282).

[49] On the whole subject see Weingartner, *Stalin*, 139 ff.; Niclauss, *Sowjetunion*, 59 ff.; Wollstein, *Revisionismus*, 40.

Russia to its old level, although here too the Russians had shown signs of withdrawal.[50] Neurath, initially, continued to pursue Schleicher's line. Russia's increased eligibility as an ally was a challenge to German interests, and Neurath accordingly worked for a policy of depending on the Soviet Union for support.[51] The Soviet Union for its part showed interest in lifting German–Soviet relations out of their state of stagnation. Such was the situation as Hitler found it.

On the very day of Hitler's assumption of power, 'in view of the foreign comments so far', the state secretary in the foreign ministry issued a circular telegram to all posts (as we have seen) instructing them 'to exert a calming influence'. This first important document of the ministry's 'protective' policy was aimed, not least, at reassuring the Soviet Union. Germany, it stated, 'would continue to avoid making her attitude towards other countries dependent upon the tenets (*Maximen*) of whatever government happened to be in office at the time'.[52] This formula, alluding to the Nationalist Socialist party's anti-Communism while minimizing its importance as far as foreign affairs were concerned, was bound to be appreciated in Moscow. To the Soviet leaders it was in any case hardly thinkable that German policy would be systematically directed against the Soviet Union as well as against France. They therefore felt safe in assuming that, in spite of all Germany's internal anti-Communist measures, France would continue to be her main enemy: this seemed indeed to be publicly confirmed by National Socialist propaganda against France in the matter of disarmament.[53] The Soviet leaders' view was partly accounted for by their overestimation of the role played by the Reichswehr and traditional governing circles in Germany after Hitler's accession to power. At the same time, with a view to a more elastic foreign policy, they did not wish to break off contact with France, and this caused fresh problems for the German foreign ministry. From time to time, especially during the persecution of Communists after the Reichstag fire, relations were embarrassed by internal events in Germany, which however did not as yet lead to an estrangement from the USSR.[54]

Poland was the chief object to the foreign ministry's territorial designs, in accordance with the general thrust of Weimar revisionism. The Reichswehr's rearmament plans were based on the idea of building up a defensive potential against the Franco-Polish combination, with the eventual object of enforcing territorial changes in the east. In February 1933 Neurath rejected plans, which emanated chiefly from French business circles and had been previously considered by Papen, for economic and political co-operation between Germany, France, and

---

[50] Weingartner, *Stalin*, 182 ff.; Niclauss, *Sowjetunion*, 70 ff.; Wollstein, *Revisionismus*, 104–5.

[51] Wollstein, *Revisionismus*, 105.

[52] *DGFP*, c. i. 1–2.

[53] Weingartner, *Stalin*, 45–6.

[54] Thus, it has been suggested that Litvinov's complaints, in his conversation with Neurath on 1 Mar. 1933, also had the tactical object of securing assurances about German policy towards Russia: Niclauss, *Sowjetunion*, 96; Wollstein, *Revisionismus*, 112. In any case Litvinov's concern shows that German internal policy was regarded in Russia as a barometer of German–Soviet relations. Neurath was aware that there might be a tactical element in Litvinov's statements: see his despatch to Moscow of 22 Feb., *DGFP*, c. i. 71.

Poland. The object, as shown by several records of conversations, was no less than a European peace order centred on a Franco-German nucleus[55] and involving a revision of the German–Polish frontier, with a land link to east Prussia, the return of Danzig to Germany, and adjustments in Upper Silesia. Hitler was not informed of these conversations.[56] Neurath's guiding principle was to let time work in Germany's favour; he thought it too early for a settlement, as the world was insufficiently convinced of the justice of Germany's revisionist claims. 'We must always bear in mind that the revision of the eastern frontier is an indivisible problem and that there will be only one more partition of Poland';[57] that partition must therefore be on a basis that Germany could accept in principle. As such a solution could not be obtained with French support, Neurath regarded an arrangement with France and Poland as out of the question. 'A German–French guarantee of Poland's Eastern frontier can *never* be considered.' A further approach from Daladier's government in March 1933 failed for the same reason.

2. PROVISIONAL CHARACTER OF THE EUROPEAN ORDER

The foreign ministry was working for a European balance of power, but only a temporary one. Peace and security were not sought as an end in themselves, but as a precondition of the recovery of German strength, after which some change could be injected into the rigid European situation.

Together with the territorial problems already mentioned, Neurath's preoccupations included disarmament and security. In the foreign ministry's view the key to Germany's attitude over disarmament depended on whether the eventual solution would enable her to build up a potential such that territorial problems could if necessary be solved by force. The foreign minister considered 'a disarmament agreement between Germany, Belgium, France, and Poland . . . neither desirable nor practicable', not least because France would seek to include Czechoslovakia, and Germany would then have to demand the participation of the Locarno powers, including Italy. This would have had the effect of 'freezing' the new security system and Germany's eastern frontier, albeit in an improved form.

This attitude to the question of a European security system makes clear the true basis for the early agreement between the foreign ministry and Hitler as to the conduct of foreign policy: viz., that any security system in Europe would be an obstacle to German expansion. Neurath's approach was clearly reflected in a memorandum of March 1933 by State Secretary von Bülow.[58] He too thought it inadvisable to press for a general revision of Versailles, which might take the form

---

[55] Wollstein, *Revisionismus*, 40–1; *DDF*[1] i, No. 46, pp. 68 ff. Records of conversations also in *DGFP*, c. i. 2 ff. Papen had already put such ideas to the French at the Lausanne conference in June 1932. For a survey of attempts from the industrial world to arrive at a German–French understanding see Bariéty and Bloch, 'Tentative'; L'Huillier, *Dialogues franco-allemands*.

[56] Wollstein, *Revisionismus*, 42.

[57] Neurath's letter to Papen of 9 Feb. 1933, *DGFP*, c. i. 38 ff.

[58] Wollstein, 'Denkschrift'; see also interpretation of the memorandum in Krüger and Hahn, 'Loyalitätskonflikt'.

of a compromise with a less than satisfactory result for Germany. It was preferable to proceed by separate steps, awaiting the favourable moment for each. Above all, the question of frontier revision should only be broached when Germany was 'sufficiently consolidated from the military, financial, and economic points of view'. Till then, the right course was to rely on propaganda use of the 'Wilson points'. By this Bülow of course meant only those of the points announced by Wilson on 8 January 1918 which lent themselves to German propaganda, especially universal disarmament and an impartial settlement of the colonial question. Meanwhile heavy financial sacrifices were necessary in order to maintain and strengthen the German element in the ceded territories. Like Neurath, Bülow held that there would only be one more partition of Poland, and on that occasion 'it should be Germany's aim to recover all the Polish territories concerned'. Other frontier problems (the Memel and Hultschin districts) were not to be broached before the German–Polish frontier was settled, since otherwise Lithuania, Czechoslovakia, and the Little Entente might interest themselves in the question of Poland. Bülow also recommended that frontier problems with France, Belgium, and Denmark should be left alone for the time being. 'We have no interest at present in reviving the question of Alsace-Lorraine.' Not only this remark—making the Locarno treaty a purely provisional arrangement—but also Bülow's observation that it was undesirable to demand the return of colonies 'prematurely', or to take active steps 'just now' to bring about the Anschluss, shows clearly enough what Germany's aims were to be once she had regained great-power status. These aims were quite compatible with the ministry's fear lest Hitler should endanger everything by over-hasty action.

Neurath and Bülow envisaged treaty revision by stages, beginning with Poland. They wished to avoid clashes in foreign affairs in any direction until such time as Germany should again be militarily strong. Above all, in their opinion, it was vital to avoid military risks 'to which we are unequal at present'. 'Peace and quiet' was therefore to be the watchword in every quarter, with the sole exception of Poland. A certain degree of German–Polish tension must be kept up, though not so much as to provoke the Poles to a preventive war. This was to keep the world interested in Germany's revisionist claims and to harass the Poles politically and economically. The ultimate objective in the eyes of the state secretary was a powerful Germany dominating the Continent, its economic influence being mainly in the south-east; it would be supported by the Soviet Union, established once again in Africa and pushing its way into the world market.

Even before Hitler embarked on a bilateral policy deliberately aimed against the collective-security system, the senior members of the foreign ministry made it clear that they regarded the existing European order as provisional. They only differed from Hitler as to the time required for change. Not peace, but the avoidance of premature conflict, should, in their view, be the objective of German political strategy in Europe. This would be best achieved, they thought, by a combination of economic and armaments policy. Germany should also work for better world economic conditions, the importance of which was envisaged from a typically imperialist point of view. It was a question of colonies, old and new, the opening up of new areas to improve Germany's basic position, combating over-population and scarcity of raw materials, preventing the industrialization of agrarian countries—in short, a classical imperialist-capitalist programme, basically divergent from Hitler's own. But till then, and until Germany's recovered strength had been consolidated in all fields, there was to be a kind of truce in foreign affairs, or else a series of bilateral or multilateral arrangements 'without any formal agreement', so as to provide a breathing-space of several years. Germany—so Bülow explained in the memorandum summing up the views of the ministry at top level at the beginning of Hitler's rule—might declare that once the question of disarmament was settled she would concern herself first and foremost with economic and financial questions. This might make it possible to drive a wedge between the powers and break up the front 'that at present unites most European states, as a reaction to the new regime'.

The foreign ministry at this time saw their conception of foreign policy as endangered by Hitler, not as far as ultimate objectives were concerned, but more as regards the choice of methods and timetable. They warned against 'the over-hasty advancing of foreign-policy demands' and provocative manifestations by associations 'closely connected with the government'. They advised that all government statements on foreign policy should be co-odinated so that, in particular, relations with Britain, Italy, Russia, France, and the United States might be conducted cautiously and in accordance with Germany's essential aims. Bülow considered that an arms race with France was excluded for the foreseeable future. Apart from this he pointed to the need to carry out the re-equipment of German forces 'comparatively slowly', so as to avoid upsets in foreign relations.

But Bülow's and Neurath's lack of respect for Germany's obligations under Locarno, and their reluctance to enter into new, permanent international agreements which might not be wholly advantageous, were similar to positions adopted at that time by Hitler and the army leaders.

After the settlement of the reparations problem and the five-power declaration of 11 December 1932 on disarmament, the foreign ministry assumed that the revisionist policy would continue to be conducted by stages, and wished to apply the same strategy to territorial questions. As long as membership of the League of Nations could be of use it was advisable to remain in the organization, so as not to leave the field to France or incur other disadvantages. This was far from a positive estimation of the value of the League to Germany: Bülow recommended withdrawal as soon as it should appear 'basically advantageous'.

Neurath presented Bülow's views at a cabinet meeting on 7 April 1933.[59] Hitler did not dissent, although they were clearly at variance with his programme, not so much in the analysis of the situation as in the recommendations concerning long-term policy. But Hitler's own activity in foreign affairs, which soon made itself felt, showed clear differences as to timing and method. Any impression left by the cabinet meeting that the ministry was determining the course and emphasis of German foreign policy soon disappeared. It was characteristic of this that Hitler turned his attention first to the very point which the ministry regarded as outside

[59] Wollstein, 'Denkschrift', 77; record of cabinet meeting of 7 Apr. 1933, *DGFP*, c. i. 255–60.

the field of discussion for the time being, namely Poland. There could have been no clearer indication of his low opinion of the ministry's programme. This was much more than a departure from the 'hackneyed anti-Polish definition of German interests by the foreign ministry and the army':[60] it was an antithesis to the ministry's whole strategy during the phase of clandestine rearmament.

3. THE STRATEGY OF REARMAMENT

The five-power declaration of 11 December 1932 laid down as a major principle 'the grant to Germany, and to the other powers disarmed by treaty, of equality of rights in a system which would provide security for all nations'.[61] This principle, given the British attitude, weakened France's position from the outset. But German rearmament strategy involved more than merely exploiting dissensions among the Western powers. The differences of view between the foreign ministry and the army leaders were not of decisive importance after Hitler's accession to power. Neurath soon rallied to Blomberg's view, and German 'disarmament' policy was now directed towards unrestricted rearmament. The Reichswehr programmes were bound to provoke France in the first instance, and German rearmament policy, the directest form of preparation for war, thus came up primarily against the Western powers. Thus, the various proposals for pacts and disarmament that emanated from Britain, Italy, and France were primarily of concern to relations between Berlin, London, and Paris.

Germany's position in all the complicated negotiations had the strength of simplicity. Her representatives spoke of equal rights and desire for peace, while aiming to achieve a position of military strength in order to force the pace of revision and attain hegemony in Europe.

The foreign ministry blocked the proposals of the Western powers with support from the new Reichswehr leaders, Blomberg and Reichenau, while Hitler's immediate ideas of tactics were much more cautious. Thus, the impression was once more given that it was still the ministry that determined policy. The successive Western initiatives were: the offer by Daladier's government on 4 February 1933 for a Franco-German pact of mutual assistance, taking into account Germany's wish to re-equip her forces;[62] the 'Cot plan' of mid-February for the standardization of land forces; the 'MacDonald plan' put forward by the British government in mid-March; and the Italian four-power project.

The French proposals were not far removed from German ideas of 1932, when Schleicher, with the foreign ministry's full support, aimed to secure equality of rights in respect of a German defence force[63] of the kind envisaged by the Cot plan. The latter was well calculated to meet the German desire for equal rights. The foreign ministry, however, viewed German–French relations in a different light.

---

[60] Dülffer, 'Decision-making Process', 201–2.
[61] *Documents on International Affairs, 1932*, 233.
[62] Neurath's record, dated 6 Feb., of conversation with François-Poncet on 4 Feb., *DGFP*, c. i. 20–1.
[63] Cf. Wollstein, *Revisionismus*, 43 ff.

Neurath saw Poland and France as the great obstacles to an active revisionist policy, which could no longer be overcome by accommodating gestures. The foreign minister had in mind a radical settlement of the Polish question to which there was no chance of the French agreeing. He rejected France's offer of a pact of mutual assistance without even discussing it with Hitler.

On 15 February 1933 Neurath instructed Nadolny, head of the German delegation at Geneva, that if the conference broke down it must be seen as due to 'the lack of an intention to disarm on the part of France'.[64] He evaded the Cot plan in concert with Blomberg, who saw to it that the German delegation was instructed to avoid a vote on the plan. Discussion was to be stalled off and eventually made impossible by means of a lengthy set of preliminary questions. The new Reichswehr minister was determined to push on with rearmament. From his own angle his initiative was as anti-French as the political strategy of Neurath and Bülow. The foreign ministry adopted the military view, which was embodied in the instructions to Geneva.[65] When the conference adopted the basic idea of the Cot plan as a basis for a new European security system,[66] Germany under her new leadership—even though Hitler had not yet directly intervened—already had one foot outside the system. Hitler, at the time, was still fully occupied with domestic problems. He wished to avoid being isolated at Geneva, and thought it a mistake to sabotage a positive solution that would be better than rearmament unsanctioned by any treaty.[67] He even went further by indicating that there was no objection to meeting the French proposal with flexible tactics. In certain, more precise, circumstances it might even be possible to accept it in principle. The military head of the disarmament delegation at once took action to counter this policy: a few days later, Neurath instructed Nadolny to regard the memorandum embodying Hitler's directive as 'non-existent'.[68]

Were there, in February and March 1933, two opposite strategies towards France, one represented by the foreign ministry and the army leaders and the other by Hitler? The question seems justified, since attention has recently been drawn to changes in Hitler's ideas about France in or around 1931.[69] His new attitude differed from that set out in *Mein Kampf* and the *Secret Book* inasmuch as he no longer thought it absolutely necessary to defeat France as a preliminary to expanding eastward. He expressed this view in May and June 1931 to Richard Breiting, editor of the *Leipziger Neueste Nachrichten*,[70] when he spoke in terms of a preliminary arrangement with Britain and France and a four-power plan for Europe, whereby

---

[64] *DGFP*, c. i. 42–4.

[65] Blomberg's directive of 19 Feb. 1933, ibid. 56–7; Wollstein, *Revisionismus*, 46 ff. On the Cot plan see Deist, III.1.3 above.

[66] League of Nations, series B, ii. 303.

[67] Wollstein, *Revisionismus*, 48. Freiherr von Rheinbaben's record of Hitler's directive of 15 Mar. 1933 is contained in Nadolny's telegram to Neurath of 17 Mar.: *DGFP*, c. i. 175–6.

[68] Telegram of 22 Mar., *DGFP*, c. i. 192. For the comments of General Schönheinz, military head of the delegation, on 18 Mar. see ibid. 192.

[69] Knipping, 'Frankreich', 616 ff.

[70] Calic, *Ohne Maske*. On the disputed value of the source see Wiggershaus's review of Calic in *Der Spiegel* (1972), 37: 62 ff.

France would give up her 'policy of encirclement' and play a 'proper part' in Western Europe.[71] He envisaged that once in power he would extend a hand to the two Western powers, counting on their understanding that he must lead a crusade against Bolshevism. What did it matter to Britain and France 'who governed Russia tomorrow'?[72]

This was a clear departure from the idea of irreconcilable Franco-German hostility. How far it governed Hitler's policy down to 1940 is difficult to judge. Did he think that France was more and more losing her position as the leading military power on the Continent and was no longer to be looked on as a dangerous adversary?[73] Or did he believe that France (like Britain in his opinion) would raise no objection to Germany dominating Eastern Europe so long as Germany left her alone in Western Europe and did not interfere with her colonies? These questions cannot be answered with complete certainty; but in the first phase of his rule Hitler undoubtedly displayed a flexible attitude towards France. At the same time it was an open question whether this optimistic view of France's attitude towards his plans for hegemony was justified by the facts. His picture of France was clouded by this uncertainty.[74] It may explain his readiness to compromise over disarmament in February–March 1933, although he had a more far-reaching aim in view than the army leaders. In the Breiting conversations he also showed a much more optimistic estimate of the German economy and the rate of rearmament that it would allow. While Neurath and Bülow thought it would take at least five years to build up an armed force equal to that of Poland, Hitler maintained that Germany with her 20 million workers and high technological standard would be able to make 'a financial effort of four or five years to achieve a degree of military power that will put an end to the Versailles system, so that in that length of time the German people can be assured of living-space and enabled to occupy a place on the Continent such as is due to it on racial and historical grounds'.[75]

Hitler's aim was to create an outlet for this potential in a more ambitious fashion than by tinkering with separate territorial issues. For this purpose he wished to see a European order that would provide scope for a corresponding strategy. In the first instance it might suffice to exercise indirect control over the countries between Germany and the Soviet Union—a 'military protectorate'[76] which might, he thought, be acceptable to France under certain conditions. At any rate he did not think it necessary to assume such complete intransigence on France's part as did Neurath with his thoughts of a last, once-and-for-all partition of Poland. Hitler's concern for the process, still in its initial stage, of restoring Germany's position as a great power, together with his ideas of foreign policy that rested so largely on wishful thinking, may account for the fact that he showed less impatience for rearmament at the outset than did Neurath and Blomberg—though, so long as the

[71] Calic, *Ohne Maske*, 92–3.
[72] Ibid. 100–1.
[73] Scheler, *Beziehungen*, 16.
[74] Knipping, 'Frankreich', 617, with reference to the 'ambivalence of two basic objectives'.
[75] Calic, *Ohne Maske*, 78–9.
[76] Ibid. 77.

latter's calculations proved successful, they had no reason to fear trouble with Hitler. The foreign ministry and the Reichswehr refused to be party to an effective security system that would have impeded their plans for rearmament and territorial aims. Hitler hoped for a new political order that would give Germany a free hand to defend Europe against Bolshevism, an aim desired by all. In this connection the thought chiefly of Britain and Italy. It can thus be said that in the initial months Hitler's foreign policy had no need of being 'tamed' by the conservative forces in his government;[77] for the time being, Blomberg and Neurath conducted policy at a much brisker pace.

This was also the case with Germany's reaction to the British and Italian proposals. At the outset Hitler's influence was underrated by many of the British leaders[78]—consistently enough, as it was hard to perceive from outside which of the forces in Germany had the main interest in blocking the MacDonald plan.

The British were themselves divided as to the advisability of the plan. Among the motives that prevailed were reasons of economic policy, some uncertainty as to the respective competence of different German leaders, and the realization that, if the Geneva talks failed, Germany could no longer be prevented from rearming to her heart's content.[79] Lord Lothian believed that fair treatment for Germany was the only way to 'reform' the Nazi regime.[80]

The French, after the failure of their proposal, saw no further way of coming to terms with Germany; instead they pursued a course that would make Germany clearly responsible for the collapse of the conference. Daladier saw co-operation with the United States and Britain as the only way of stabilizing Europe.

The advocates, at this time, of 'appeasement'—MacDonald, Simon (the foreign secretary), and Eden—were no less pessimistic as to Europe's future. If the disarmament conference broke down on account of Franco-German antagonism, Germany would rearm; she would gain international sympathy, and the upshot would be a second European war.[81]

The MacDonald plan was of no interest to the Reichswehr leaders. Two hundred thousand soldiers each for Germany, France, and Poland, complete equality of rights in the arms sphere only after a transitional phase—all this was quite unacceptable to Blomberg.[82] The plan might have fitted in with the general ideas of Bülow and Neurath in March 1933, involving long-term rearmament, but it contained other, less welcome elements, such as a clause on the avoidance of war and a decisive disparity as regards air forces.

---

[77] Hillgruber, 'Kontinuität', 31.

[78] Wendt, *München*.

[79] Brief summary in Wollstein, *Revisionismus*, 50–63; Gilbert, *Roots*. On Anglo-German trade relations, esp. the effect of economic predictions on the attitude adopted towards the Hitler government, see Wendt, *Economic Appeasement*, 73 ff.

[80] Gibbs, *Strategy*, i. 83; Butler, *Lord Lothian*, 197.

[81] *DBFP*[2] iv. 299.

[82] For details of the plan see League of Nations, *Conference for the Reduction and Limitation of Armaments, Draft Convention*, 2–16; also Schwendemann, *Abrüstung*, ii. 60 ff. On the differing assessments by the foreign ministry and the army see Rautenberg, *Rüstungspolitik*, 99–100, and Deist, III.1.3 above.

The conservatives among the German leaders wanted good relations with Britain, but relied chiefly on exploiting favourable trends in British public opinion, together with a show of amenability in certain minor matters;[83] they also did their best to mislead the British as to conditions in Germany and the balance of power among the leaders.[84]

Their efforts failed. The British proposal gathered support in Geneva. At the German cabinet meeting on 12 May Neurath advised withdrawing from the conference; Blomberg was for remaining at Geneva but taking no part in the negotiations. Between them the two ministers put Hitler in a position where he was obliged to break the log-jam by a major political speech. Neurath, despairing of success at Geneva, expressly asked the chancellor to do so.[85] Thus, on a key question connected closely with preparations for his expansionist designs, Hitler for the first time made clear to the conservatives who had hitherto conducted foreign and military policy that it was time for a change of method. 'The German people', he declared to his ministers, 'are united on the disarmament question. This unity must be demonstrated to the world.' Rearmament 'by normal means' was not possible. 'Geneva [was] not the suitable forum' for replying to foreign machinations.[86] Hitler put the new tactics into effect a few days later, in the so-called 'peace speech' of 17 May 1933.[87] The new methods that the foreign ministry had feared all along—the new style, the hustling, and so on—were now displayed and were seen to be effective.[88] Germany's foreign policy was predicated on her withdrawal from the collective security system. For some time her continued membership of the League had been merely a tactical device to avoid leaving the field to France or upsetting the British. From now on the threat of withdrawal was to be used, still more plainly than before, as a means of pressure. It must be made clear, Hitler declared, that 'Germany's further remaining in the League had been made exceedingly doubtful by the actions of our opponents'.[89]

The 'peace speech' of 17 May 1933 has rightly been described as one of Hitler's masterpieces of propaganda at this period.[90] The arguments were not new, nor was the discrepancy between his real plans and his loud assurances of being willing to disarm completely if other powers would do likewise. What was new was the use of the parliamentary rostrum for a demagogic exercise in foreign policy. The appeal was directed chiefly to Britain, whom Hitler regarded as the foreign power likely to give him most help in pursuing his plans of eastward expansion.

---

[83] e.g. the extension of the creditors' moratorium of 17 Feb. 1933, which gave the impression abroad that Germany would co-operate loyally in the solution of international financial problems and that her policy would not be governed by National Socialist slogans; cf. Wendt, *Economic Appeasement*, 91 ff.

[84] Neurath and the German ambassador in London consistently pursued a policy of playing down the Nazi threat; this at times hoodwinked both the foreign office and the embassy in Berlin. Cf. Wollstein, *Revisionismus*, 58–9.

[85] Record of ministers' meeting of 12 May 1933, *DGFP*, c. i. 409 ff.

[86] Ibid.

[87] Baynes, ii. 1041–58.

[88] Meinck, *Aufrüstung*, 31, also cites the 'peace speech' in this context.

[89] Record of ministers' meeting of 12 May 1933, *DGFP*, c. i. 411.

[90] Bullock, *Hitler*, 321.

The appeal of this speech,[91] both to a domestic and to a foreign audience, should not be underrated: it captured the agreement of this Social Democrats, and won sympathy abroad with its emphasis on Hitler's peaceable intentions, its skilful appeal to a sense of justice, and the adroit use of Italian and American proposals. Its real purpose, however, was to conceal from the world Germany's intention to rearm, rapidly and without restraint, for expansionist aims, and to forestall any criticism of her withdrawal from the disarmament conference and the League of Nations. The culmination of duplicity was the statement that 'Germany is at any time willing to undertake further obligations in regard to international security, if all the other nations are ready on their side to do the same.'

Hitler was to make similar 'offers' at future times of crisis. The peace speech marked the beginning of the great campaign of dissembling Germany's intentions. In addition it put the world on notice that it was Hitler who would in future determine Germany's foreign policy. Although still apprehensive of possible intervention by the Western Allies, in the matter of armaments Hitler was no longer opposed to a more vigorous policy on the part of the foreign ministry and the army leaders.[92]

Mussolini's proposal for a four-power pact was intended, like Hitler's strategy, to replace the security system based on the League. He aimed to use the establishment of the National Socialist regime to bring about a new concert of great-power interests that would avert the dangers to Austria and Italy inherent in German revisionism.[93] It was in Italy's interest to divert revisionist claims from Austria and the south Tyrol to other areas, in particular the German–Polish frontier. In this way Mussolini could present himself to the Western powers as a mediator. He sought to avoid giving the impression of an Italo-German line-up or a close ideological affinity between the two regimes.

This aspect of Mussolini's political strategy was especially important in relation to Britain, in whose appeasement policy Italy played a considerable role.[94] Its importance could be greater or less according to the scope of long-term British aims. In the next few years it was still a matter of debate in London whether the object should be merely to exercise a moderating influence on Hitler through Mussolini, or whether the 'little dictator', Mussolini, should gradually be prised away from the greater one; the latter was the view of Sir R. Vansittart, probably the most consistent opponent of Germany in the foreign office.[95]

[91] Baynes, ii. 1041 ff.

[92] Hillgruber, 'Kontinuität', 31–2, considers that Hitler exercised a restraining function of this kind as late as Sept. 1933; cf. Deist, III.1.3 above.

[93] On the strategy of the four-power pact see Petersen, *Hitler–Mussolini*, 137 ff. The plan created difficult problems for France, as it provoked 'an outburst of indignation' in the capitals of the Little Entente. France's Eastern allies feared they would have to foot the bill for the Western settlement. Prague and Warsaw brought pressure to bear on Paris, which was able to avoid unpleasant consequences thanks to the Quai d'Orsay's success in diluting the whole project. Cf. Poidevin and Bariéty, *Relations franco-allemandes*, 288 ff.

[94] Mussolini's idea of a four-power pact has been interpreted as an attempt to preserve his distance from all the great powers—a strategic retreat in order to gain freedom of movement. Cf. Quaroni, *Diplomatengepäck*, 175; Petersen, *Hitler–Mussolini*, 140–1.

[95] For details of the Vansittart–Churchill circle see Aigner, *Ringen*, 141–74.

Mussolini's initiative was psychologically well calculated to fit in with Hitler's plans. The Italian dictator seemed to divine the needs of the National Socialist regime. His arguments found much more favour with Hitler than with the foreign ministry; they were entirely in accord with Hitler's early ideas on the importance of Germany and Italy joining hands. Apart from the tactical advantage of blocking the British plan, Hitler's reaction was one of heartfelt assent.[96] The foreign ministry, however, took an entirely different view. Neurath firmly believed that a four-power pact must serve the purpose of releasing Germany from her obligations under the peace treaty and League of Nations procedure. The primary aim should be the recognition by the powers that the peace treaties were obsolete and that after another five years Germany should be subject to no further restrictions in the matter of equal rights.[97] In April the foreign ministry made some last attempts to render the four-power pact ineffectual or prevent its coming about;[98] thereafter the negotiations were pursued through other channels.

In the face of Mussolini's personal appeals to Hitler, Neurath was only able to hold out for a short time.[99] Hitler hesitated at first to commit himself for years ahead, but the decisive argument was finally contributed by Blomberg, who on this point parted company with the foreign ministry. To the army leaders the problem was relatively straightforward: rearmament must go on, and the disarmament talks would not afford the necessary freedom of action, nor would Mussolini's plan. It therefore seemed advisable for the present to accept the latter without making further conditions. The pact did not commit Germany to anything, but it might provide a breathing-space for rearmament. The important point was that rearmament could take place 'in a quiet international atmosphere'.[100] The foreign ministry was outflanked by Hitler, Blomberg, and Göring.[101] Hitler entered into an agreement that could act as a cover for his rearmament plans; it was a step in a policy of shaking off international obligations, which was in future to be pursued by one coup after another. The pact was signed on 15 July, but never entered into force owing to Germany's withdrawal from the League of Nations.

The disarmament talks in Geneva continued. Britain and France insisted that Germany should only be allowed to start rearming after a trial period and to a

---

[96] e.g. the reference in the 'peace speech' to the 'apt and far-sighted plan of the head of the Italian government' (Baynes, ii. 1055). Text of Mussolini's proposal in *DGFP*, c. i. 162.

[97] Bülow to Hassell, 15 Mar. 1933, *DGFP*, c, i. 168–9; Neurath to Hassell, 5 Apr. 1933, ibid. i. 248 ff. The German counter-draft, taking account of French proposals, also endeavoured to save the principle of revision. *DGFP*, c. i. 377–8. see also Petersen, *Hitler–Mussolini*, 170–1.

[98] Petersen, *Hitler–Mussolini*, 170 ff.

[99] Ibid. 172–4; *DGFP*, c. i. 482; Aloisi, *Journal*, 30 May 1933.

[100] Liebmann record, quoted from Meinck, *Aufrüstung*, 31. See also Petersen, *Hitler–Mussolini*, 173, on Blomberg's arguments put to Hitler on 30 May, with reference to Cerutti's statements in *Rivista di studi internazionali* (Jan.–June 1946).

[101] Petersen, *Hitler–Mussolini*, 174; Neurath's record of conversation with Göring on 22 May, *DGFP*, c. i. 478–9. Göring had been acting as Hitler's emissary in Rome. His general attitude was to be less concerned with details, and evidently he was not impressed by Neurath's comment that the amendment of the draft had made it 'entirely worthless for us'. The main thing, in Göring's view, was that 'through the treaty we had to deal with only a small body of four'. On the history of the treaty see Jarausch, *Four Power Pact*.

limited extent. Other French demands were unsuccessful, e.g. that Britain should take part in sanctions in the event of Germany violating the treaty or evading arms controls. The British view was that even German military measures in the Rhineland should as far as possible not be treated as a breach of the Locarno treaty.[102]

Although London and Paris were agreed on the need for a trial period, they differed basically as to the proper way to treat Germany. However, the political and military leaders of the two countries did not differ fundamentally in their estimate of the danger from Germany.

Sir J. Simon's proposals for action in the event of Germany violating her disarmament obligations were very cautiously formulated, and virtually ruled out an occupation of German territory.[103] Britain did not wish to be responsible for any guarantees that might involve her in continental commitments.[104] The British thought that Hitler's tactical position was a strong one, because he had nothing to lose.[105] The Americans too were against sanctions.

On 4 October Hitler and Blomberg decided to refuse to negotiate over fresh proposals, without of course letting it appear that the conference had broken down on account of German demands. Blomberg was in favour of sticking to the 'original question', i.e. demanding by ultimatum the disarmament of the other powers; then, if Germany were denied equality of rights, she should walk out of the conference and announce her withdrawal from the League of Nations. Hitler envisaged making another major speech, an appeal to world opinion.[106] Bülow's telegrams to Rome, London, and Washington toned down the policy so as to make it appear that the German demands were not in the nature of an ultimatum.[107] But on 6 October instructions went to the delegation in Geneva[108] that the latest British proposal was to be 'branded' as no more than an attempt by the highly armed states to avoid disarming. The delegation was to refuse to discuss such proposals, and to indicate that they were likely to result in Germany withdrawing from the conference and the League of Nations. 'The chancellor reserves for himself the decision concerning the carrying out of this intimation.'

For the time being Hitler seemed prepared not to demand more in the way of armaments than Germany could actually manage, for technical, financial, and political reasons, to procure in the next few years.[109] To Neurath's question 'whether a disarmament convention was to be concluded or whether the negotiations were to be delayed or broken off', he replied that 'it would be desirable in any case to conclude a convention, even if not all our wishes were fulfilled by it'.

This statement is to be evaluated in the light of Hitler's general attitude to treaties

---

[102] *DBFP*² v, No. 413; Bloch, *Hitler*, 45.
[103] Foreign office memorandum for the cabinet, 30 May 1933, PRO Cab 24/241, fos. 220 ff.
[104] Cf. Cowling, *Impact*, 64 ff.; *DBFP*² v, Nos. 399–403, e.g. Simon to the French ambassador in London on 21 Sept. 1933.
[105] See the penetrating analysis in Cowling, *Impact*, 66.
[106] Bülow's record of 4 Oct. 1933, *DGFP*, c. i. 887.
[107] Telegram of 4 Oct. 1933, ibid. 888–9.
[108] Ibid. 892–3.
[109] Thus to Neurath on 30 Sept. 1933, ibid. 882.

and, in the present case, the fact that his loyalty to the proposed treaty was from the beginning dependent on the speed with which Germany could rearm. When Simon on 14 October presented the new Anglo-French–American disarmament proposals at Geneva, Berlin announced that Germany was withdrawing from the League and the conference. Hitler then delivered the speech he had comtemplated. The dissolution of the Reichstag and fresh elections were intended to show the world that the German people 'identified itself with the peace policy of the Reich government', and, together with the broadcast speech, would 'capture the attention of the world in a manner quite different from the past'.[110]

Thus, Germany's rejection of the international obligations of the collective-security system was accomplished. But Hitler's strong tactical position deceived no one as to the real motives of National Socialist Germany. It was clear to the great powers what Hitler was aiming at with the series of bilateral agreements on which he now embarked. Hitler himself explained more clearly than the most elaborate enquiries could have done in what way his foreign policy differed from that of establishing a peaceful order under the League of Nations: 'It will be a service to the world if the League of Nations, the establishment of which was in the last analysis only designed as a measure directed against Germany, is gradually rendered inactive by demonstrating its inability to solve the problems submitted to it.'[111]

[110] Record by Thomsen of ministers' meeting of 13–14 Oct. 1933, ibid. 922 ff.
[111] Ibid.

III. Bilateral Foreign Policy

1. The New Approach

GERMANY's abandonment of the international collective-security system made no lasting impression on her neighbours. France, despite the fall of the Daladier government, did not rouse herself to take any energetic steps, as was for a time feared in Berlin.[1] Britain and Italy saw no cause to intervene. Even the French military did not consider action against Germany, which would have had to be taken by France alone. In the poll of 12 November 1933 Hitler obtained 92 per cent of votes, thus arousing 'world attention' and obtaining the necessary basis of confidence in his policy.

This success, in what were thought to be extremely risky circumstances, was the decisive event in foreign affairs in the first year of Hitler's regime. The lessons it taught were used repeatedly in the ensuing stages of preparation for war. Psychologically, it led to an underestimation of the European great powers, especially their potential will to resist, and an overestimation of Germany's own strength. At the moment of withdrawal from the League of Nations, Hitler stood practically isolated in Europe. At the meeting of ministers on 17 October he was able to say that the critical moment was probably past and that all had gone according to plan.[2]

The repudiation of the principle of collective security did not, of course, in itself make Germany free to pursue a policy of expansion by force, in accordance with the various ideas of her leaders. The international peace-keeping system had to be replaced either by the Neurath–Bülow policy (directed in the first place against Poland, and involving long-term rearmament and strengthening of the economy) or by a new strategy of Hitler's. There is no direct evidence concerning Hitler's reasons for rejecting the foreign ministry's objectives. Probably the latter's programme seemed to him too time-consuming, and the aspect of economic imperialism was in conflict with his own philosophy.

The time factor must probably be regarded as an essential aspect of Hitler's bilateral strategy. He wanted to gain time to create a situation that would make possible an early use of military power. Prestige was also a consideration. From both the domestic and foreign point of view, the Concordat signed on 20 July 1933 was well calculated to serve his purpose.

(a) Poland

The first opportunity for a striking move in bilateral policy, designed to afford cover for further steps and eventually prepare for eastward expansion, presented itself in relation to Poland. Under Pilsudski's 'dictatorship' Polish ruling circles

---

[1] On 25 Oct. 1933 Blomberg issued instructions in case of invasion: see Bloch, *Hitler*, 48; Holldack, *Hintergründe*, 281 ff.; Meinck, *Aufrüstung*, 50; *IMT* xxxiv. 487 ff., and summary in *DGFP*, c. ii, No. 26.
[2] *DGFP*, c. ii, No. 9, p. 11.

realized that the Versailles system offered them doubtful protection if ever Germany and Soviet Russia should regain the status of great powers, as they effectively did in 1932–3.[3] However, Poland's change of policy was displayed as early as 1930 in an offensive attitude towards Germany; this was followed in July 1932 by a non-aggression pact with the Soviet Union, though for various reasons the pact provided no basis for an alliance. The Poles attempted to sound out Germany by combining a show of strength with readiness to negotiate. In the summer of 1933 they wished at all costs to avert the danger of German revisionism being deflected against Poland as a result of the negotiations for a four-power pact—an aim which Mussolini had in view and which the Western powers shared to some extent at least. In addition, the Poles were concerned by the prospect of forfeiting their half-achieved great-power status.

In Hitler the Polish leaders had to do with a negotiator for whom the revisionist aims of Weimar were not an end in themselves. In the context of his plans for *Lebensraum* in Russia, Poland was emphatically a variable quantity. He was not wedded to a particular timetable or succession of steps as far as his plan for Poland was concerned. Poland might play the part of an accomplice or a victim—Hitler's choice was still open and depended on circumstances in regard to which he wished to retain a free hand, subject to his one paramount purpose.

Given the German boycott of the collective-security system and the isolation that was bound to ensue, it became Poland's important role to be Hitler's first partner in the process of advancing by bilateral agreements, one stage at a time. The *rapprochement* was of the greatest immediate value and, as far as Hitler was concerned, precluded nothing in the future. In a series of contacts with the Polish ambassador in Berlin between May 1933 and January 1934 he effected a complete reorientation of German policy towards Poland. The foreign ministry, traditionally hostile to any arrangement with Poland, was forced to acknowledge the dangers of the Reich's external situation and co-operate in a policy of accommodation which it regarded as temporary. The groups that were fundamentally hostile to the German–Polish agreement were unable to stand in the way. Bülow emphasized its value in present circumstances, but wished to hold open the option for a future change of course. In effect his attitude, apart from Hitler's anti-Soviet angle, was favourable to the agreement, though probably for tactical purposes only.[4] Hitler presented himself to the world as one ready to compromise and anxious to put an end to German–Polish hostility. An alteration of the frontier was a matter to be broached later on, by peaceful means. The Soviet Union was represented as the great danger to Europe.

Hilter seeemed to be choosing his words with especial significance when he declared that Germany recognized Poland's historic right to exist and to grow stronger.[5] He also acknowledged Poland's claim to compensation for the weakening of her position as a result of Germany's withdrawal from the League of Nations.

---

[3] For Pilsudski's views see Dziewanowski, *Pilsudski*; for the switch in Polish policy, Rickhoff, *German–Polish Relations*; literature cited in Wollstein, 'Politik'.

[4] Wollstein, *Revisionismus*, 282.

[5] In a conversation on 13 July 1933, not preserved in the German records; see also Wollstein, 'Politik',

Promises to abstain from the use of force, and assurances that he had no desire to Germanize other peoples, were part of his repertoire at all times and had their effect on this occasion also; as regards Danzig, the i's were dotted by the new president of the city's senate, Hermann Rauschning. In the autumn of 1933 agreement was reached at Geneva to call off press campaigns on either side, and in November a communiqué was issued outlining the substance of the German–Polish exchanges.[6] On the basis of the renunciation of force, the parties agreed to resolve tension by bilateral means and to co-ordinate their interests in the future.

The Poles believed that by this means they could neutralize the dangerous revisionists among the German leaders; in fact they overestimated the influence of the conservative ruling classes in Germany as much as did their British and French opposite numbers. The German foreign ministry and the army leaders had tried in vain to arrest the course of events. They continued to be anti-Polish in the traditional revisionist sense.[7] To gain time they attempted to mislead the Poles by demanding a free hand in the west, but Pilsudski played the French card more skilfully and thus brought about some movement in the interplay of forces.[8] The German side was finally obliged to move fast, as it was desired to anticipate Polish proposals with definitions, as precise as possible, of the concept of 'aggression'.[9]

The ten-year non-aggression pact of 26 January 1934 made a decisive breach in Germany's isolation.[10] Poland under Pilsudski had had definite thoughts of moving against Nazi Germany on tactical grounds, which might have brought about a chain reaction if there had been equally adventurous spirits in charge in Paris. Hitler's treaty removed a danger of intervention that had given great anxiety to Weimar politicians. But had anything more been achieved than a breach in the wall of isolation? A basis for concerted policy against the Soviet Union, for instance? Or even a securing of Germany's rear to enable her to deal a few 'short, sharp blows' against France (Britain being supposed neutral), and then turn back to conquer *Lebensraum* in the east?[11]

These possibilities lay too far ahead. They depended on conditions that were not and could not be fulfilled—British neutrality among them. Precisely because no role was assigned to Poland in the 'basic plan' as it appears from Hitler's programmatic writings, such considerations must remain purely speculative; the more so as the treaty expressly safeguarded the Franco-Polish alliance, which public opinion and

---

[6] Following the conversation between Hitler and Lipski on 15 Nov. 1933; recorded by Ministerialdirektor Meyer, *DGFP*, c. ii, No. 69; text of communiqué ibid.

[7] *DGFP*, c. ii, No. 77; Bloch, *Hitler*, 51.

[8] On the question of the discussions with France concerning a preventive war see Roos, *Polen*, 114 ff.

[9] Wollstein, *Revisionismus*, 272.

[10] Roos, *Polen*; Gasiorowski, 'Non-aggression Pact'; Korbel, *Poland*. Poidevin and Bariéty, *Relations franco-allemandes*, 290, speak of the 'French system' beginning to disintegrate: Franco-Polish relations were no longer as friendly as they had been. Poland saw in the four-power plan a danger that she would be deserted by France. Hitler exploited a 'tactically favourable situation'. Cf. Young, *In Command of France*.

[11] Thus Hildebrand, *Foreign Policy*, 33, referring to Hitler's statements to senior Reichswehr officers a few weeks after the conclusion of the non-aggression pact with Poland, and to Hitler's 'basic plan'. Hitler's statements are as recorded by Field Marshal von Weichs, IfZ 182, fos. 8 ff.; Hillgruber, 'Quellen', 118.

much of the officers' corps in Poland had no wish to give up. The Poles did not want to take this bilateral step at the expense of their other external safeguards, or to expose themselves wholly to Germany's embrace,[12] especially as the treaty excluded the possibility of frontier revision only in a provisional manner.

The treaty was advantageous to Germany *vis-à-vis* France, however her relations with the latter might develop. Whatever attitude Paris might take towards Germany's eastward expansion, the German–Polish *rapprochement* enabled Hitler to go forward with greater confidence. The Franco-Polish alliance was devalued. Poland was reduced, more or less involuntarily, to the unpopular role of Hitler's advance guard. But the decisive condition for the success of Germany's bilateral policy was the half-hearted attitude of France, which probably first led Poland to pursue the course she did. At the same time it should be noted that by prolonging the Polish–Soviet non-aggression pact in May 1934 the Poles in some degree opposed a counterweight to their agreement with Hitler.

Hitler's motives are still a matter of controversy.[13] The immediate consequence of Germany's policy of using bilateral agreements to overcome her isolation and cover her rearmament was to increase concern on the part of France and the Soviet Union and bring them closer together, despite the hesitations of both sides. France proposed an alliance to Moscow as early as the end of October 1933, but refused to enter into a general alliance as proposed by the Russians at the end of 1933.

Even in Italy, where the removal of a potential source of unrest was welcomed in itself, there was alarm lest Germany might now turn her attention more vigorously towards Austria and south-east Europe; in Poland the same possibility was envisaged, in this case with relief.[14]

Hitler's policy now prevailed without dispute as regards both Poland and the Soviet Union. Neurath adapted to it without difficulty. Bülow was much more reserved, but could only exert a tactical influence in day-to-day matters. Control of foreign policy was more and more in Hitler's hands. In the east a solution had been found on which a systematic policy might one day be constructed.

(b) The Role of France

What chances were there in the West for a bilateral policy that might gain some leeway for rearmament and, if possible, secure Germany's rear as well? Compared to France, no other European power had so much security to risk by entering into bilateral ties with Hitler's Germany, or had to discard so many apprehensions and assumptions that had hitherto been regarded as self-evident. France, the strongest military power on the Continent, figured in Hitler's scheme of things as a risk factor inhibiting action against the Soviet Union. Her first reactions to the Nazi seizure of power offered little prospect of the accommodating attitude that Hitler, quite recently, had still thought conceivable on her part. The German military were afraid of France's strength, and she therefore had to be treated with especial care.

---

[12] Lipski, *Diplomat*, 96; Wollstein, *Revisionismus*, 272.
[13] Roos, *Polen*, 129.
[14] Cf. Petersen, *Hitler–Mussolini*, 302; *DDF*[1] v, No. 328, pp. 621–5.

From 1934 to 1936 Hitler was profuse in reassuring statements. Each successive move to throw off the restrictions of Versailles was accompanied by peaceful gestures; but he evaded any serious commitment. Certainly he wanted a change of atmosphere; nothing could be more useful to his policy. He avoided challenging France in ways that would have been counter-productive, given the ratio of strength. Thus, he forbade the development of a National Socialist movement in Alsace.[15] At the same time he pursued a policy of isolating France, above all by cultivating relations with Britain, Italy, and Poland. After each German move against the Versailles system France found herself in a situation where she must intervene single-handed or be condemned to do nothing.

How did Hitler seek to use the situation for his own ends? The German rearmament programme called for an army 300,000 strong as a basis. Hitler wished to secure this aim by offers to France and Britain which would have partly legitimized Germany's clandestine rearmament and excluded any effective control. In secret conversations France was offered political concessions in return: an all-time renunciation of Alsace-Lorraine, and security guarantees. Hitler enlarged on these prospects, but Paul-Boncour, the French foreign minister, rejected a bilateral agreement on the basis of the German proposals,[16] pointing out that arms questions involved European and not merely bilateral interests. This line, if accompanied by effective sanctions, might still have thwarted Hitler's plans from 1934 onwards. No other serious obstacle was in sight. After France finally called off the bilateral talks in April of that year,[17] Hitler again turned more firmly towards Britain. France was not to be won over in the middle or the long term; would she be amenable to an indirect approach through her British ally?

2. BRITAIN'S KEY POSITION AND THE NAVAL TREATY

The importance of Britain and the function assigned to her in Hitler's 'programme' cannot be reduced to a single formula. During the phase of striving for continental hegemony he saw Britain as a power factor whose attitude would be decisive for his chances of successful eastward expansion. In the fight for *Lebensraum* and the destruction of 'Jewish Bolshevism' he did not want to incur the risk of a war on two fronts. He believed—or at any rate his writings can be so interpreted—in the possibility of an Anglo-German consensus based, provisionally at all events, on a delimitation of continental and world-wide interests, political and economic. This raises the question whether Hitler attributed to Britain a programmatic significance in the period preparatory to eastward expansion, while German supremacy on the Continent was being consolidated. Scholars differ in their assessment of this point.[18]

To an observer at the present time, the answer lies in the power-political spectrum of the 1930s. Since Hitler underrated the Soviet Union and regarded France as

---

[15] Domarus, i. 476. General survey in Kettenacker, *NS-Volkstumspolitik*.
[16] Note of 1 Jan. 1934; Schwendemann, *Abrüstung*, ii, appendix 32; *DDF*[1] v, No. 182, pp. 383–8.
[17] Note of 17 Apr. 1934, Schwendemann, *Abrüstung*, ii, appendix 43.
[18] Henke, 'England-Konzeption'; Hillgruber, 'England'.

a satellite of Britain, the latter was in his eyes the primary obstacle to German hegemony. Britain held the key to Germany's success, but it does not necessarily follow that a role was assigned to her in a cut-and-dried programme.[19] The years after 1933 were the testing time for Hitler's earlier prognoses of British reactions to Germany's bid for hegemony. How did they affect the idea of partnership with Britain based on the temporary shelving of Germany's world-power ambitions and the supposed interest of both countries in combating the 'world-wide Jewish-Bolshevik enemy'? How did matters stand with the 'racially valuable elements' in Britain which Hitler regarded as a substantial counter to Jewish influence? A partnership with Britain as the superstructure of a power-political arrangement and a shared racial and ideological background, among the aristocracy at least—this was and remained a chimera. But even in Hitler's own imagination the idea of an alliance had one decisive weakness. As is known, he hoped to tempt Britain by guaranteeing the British Empire, an offer which had no effect whatever on British calculations.

The principle of the balance of power was a much more realistic basis of political and strategic expectations. No one in British ruling circles was prepared to look on calmly as Hitler built up a position of military and strategic hegemony on the Continent, which he could then use in any way he felt inclined.

In his conception of Germany as a world power Hitler thought in terms of long periods.[20] At some stage there would be a show-down with the Anglo-Saxon powers over colonies and sea-power; possibly Britain, out of rivalry with the Americans, might find herself on Germany's side and dependent on a strong Germany. This was not a sound basis for a lasting German–British arrangement. And, just as Hitler was at fault in his estimation of British strategy, especially the effect of continental decisions on British security needs, so too he miscalculated the effects of his own policy towards Britain. His behaviour in the disarmament negotiations and his withdrawal from the League of Nations were regarded in Britain as portents of German rearmament in accordance with a programme of expansion and war in the measurable future. There was thus little reason for Hitler to suppose that his policy would succeed in manœuvring Britain in the direction he desired. Did he not himself have occasional doubts of achieving this? There is a record of his statements to senior army officers in 1934; he seems then to have intended, if his plans for an alliance should fail, to clear the way for his eastern policy by one or two swift blows in the west.[21] Even if he thought the non-aggression pact with Poland, concluded a few weeks earlier, left him free to eliminate France provided Britain stood aside, his reasoning was highly precarious and based on a completely false estimation of

[19] Henke's statement, 'England-Konzeption', 585, that it can be shown that 'Hitler's idea of Britain was subordinated to a higher overall programme' may be accepted as a sufficiently elastic 'definition'; 'subordination' at any rate admits of a certain detachment from the inevitabilities associated with such terms as 'axiomatic' and 'programmatic'.

[20] *Secret Book*, 145; also Hildebrand, *Reich*, 279; Hillgruber, 'England', 71–2; Henke, 'England-Konzeption', 589.

[21] Record by Maximilian (afterwards Field Marshal) von Weichs, 'Zeugenschrifttum', IfZ 182, fos. 8 ff.; Hillgruber, 'Quellen', 118; see also O'Neill, *German Army*, 40 ff.; Hildebrand, *Reich*, 460 n. 58, 570–1; id., *Foreign Policy*, 33.

Britain's security interests. However, after all his statements about *Lebensraum* and the importance of war to future generations, it was consistent for him to make early preparations for turning eastward; for the Soviet Union was and remained the intended prize of a decisive military conflict. If Britain should thwart Germany's efforts to achieve hegemony, there would be no alternative but to remove the obstacle by aiming the necessary 'short, swift blows' at Britain as well as France. But for the time being Hitler did not consider himself to be faced with this choice. His statements did not as yet prescribe any sequence of actions. His estimate of Soviet power itself throws doubt on the idea that the 'programmatic' war in the east must be preceded by a 'limited conflict' in the west; for in the 1930s such a conflict was considered a far riskier undertaking from the military point of view. Hence, Hitler's words were probably aimed at his military audience rather than intended as part of a middle-term policy. Even if he did not regard an understanding with Britain as a '*sine qua non* of his programme of eastward expansion',[22] it did not follow that he must necessarily fight a war with Britain before embarking on the war in the east. Hitler's constant concern with Britain's attitude, up to the very moment of war, shows that he believed it possible to achieve his object in the east even if he could not count on a true partnership or alliance with Britain.

But in fact he could not rely on British acquiescence either. Britain showed compliance with regard to a decision that signified German supremacy on the Continent, but this did not mean she was prepared for a general compromise. In 1933–4 the British cabinet and its closest advisers already saw Hitler as the adversary who was to confront them in 1939. As a British historian has aptly put it, 'In the first six months of 1934 almost everything that was to be said about Hitler in the next six years was said for the first time.'[23]

After quitting the disarmament conference and the League of Nations, Hitler sought an understanding with Britain in which Germany would gain more than she gave. In the first place, she would rearm openly with British approval. Not the disarmament of other powers, but German rearmament—as the army leaders had long desired—was henceforth the avowed watchword. Hitler formulated, with some caution at first, the basis on which he hoped to reach agreement with Britain. In a conversation with the British ambassador on 24 October 1933, ten days after withdrawal from the League of Nations, he 'offered' a German army of 300,000 equipped with defensive weapons only.[24] His promptitude shows clearly that the initiative in foreign affairs had now been taken decisively out of the hands of the Wilhelmstrasse. On the other hand, we may assume that his move had the support in principle of the army leaders, for his 'offer' corresponded very closely to the 'December programme' formulated a few weeks later by the Reichswehr.[25] For Hitler, it was no more than a feeler, in line with his policy of 'not asking for more than we can ourselves manage'. He seems to have believed, however, that an

[22] Henke, 'England-Konzeption', 591.

[23] Cowling, *Impact*, 67.

[24] Kuhn, *Programm*, 146; Neurath's record of conversation between Hitler and Phipps, 24 Oct. 1933, in *DGFP*, c. ii, No. 24.

[25] Rautenberg, 'Dokumente'; cf. Deist, III.II.2 (*a*) above.

alliance or even 'friendship' with Britain could be erected on this basis. In November–December 1933 he evidently hoped to be able to press forward to a triangular relationship between Berlin, London, and Rome. Anglo-French relations, he thought, were so uneasy that Britain must actually be looking for new partners. In these initiatives the foreign ministry and even the army leaders were little more than onlookers, although Hitler and Blomberg basically saw eye to eye in rearmament matters. Bülow as state secretary could do no more than try, through Germany's ambassadors abroad, to damp down reactions to Hitler's independent policy.[26]

Association with Britain and Italy on the lines of the proposals put forward in several conversations with Sir E. Phipps, the British ambassador, would have been the most expeditious way of putting into effect Hitler's basic ideas as expressed in his writings. By the end of 1933 France would already have been isolated and dependent on a combination of British and German power. Freedom for Britain to rearm at sea and in the air—Hitler, as is known, impressed the ambassador by urging that the British navy and air force should be strengthened—would not have been a serious obstacle to Germany soon becoming the dominant continental power: thus, the vision of Germany enjoying a free hand in Europe would have been brought into the realm of practical politics.[27]

However, this first over-hasty attempt to secure a British alliance did not succeed.[28] Britain, with Mussolini's support, did produce counter-proposals which went a long way to meet the German desire for rearmament, except in the air;[29] but the foreign office, for the sake of French security, stipulated that Germany should not attain equality of rights for another ten years. Hitler's reaction was flexible, but basically his plan for Britain was not well served by an arrangement that preserved features of international control, with Britain and Italy, his two desired allies, acting in the name of an international security system. France's prompt rejection of his proposals was actually to Hitler's advantage, since his initiative was aimed at Britain and was intended to drive a wedge between the two Western powers.[30] It was also pointed out in Britain that parity with France would give Germany decisive influence in Austria and Czechoslovakia. For this and other reasons Britain was obliged to consider France's interests and take seriously her need for security. However, French demands for the control and supervision of German rearmament were regarded in London as unreasonable.[31]

In April–May 1934 Britain inclined towards a solution that would have

---

[26] Kuhn, *Programm*, 147; Bülow's telegram of 26 Oct. 1933 to London embassy, *DGFP*, c. ii, No. 29.

[27] Hitler's reply to Phipps on 11 Dec. 1933, *DGFP*, c. ii, No. 117.

[28] *DBFP*[2] vi, Nos. 108, 190 and Nos. 141, 259 (8 and 20 Dec. 1933); see also *DGFP*, c. ii, Nos. 111, 117, 141; Kuhn, *Programm*, 140–1.

[29] British memorandum of 25 Jan. 1934, communicated to the powers on the 29th. According to this, Germany was to be allowed an army of 200,000–300,000 men and also light tanks. Britain would even agree to a military air force if the disarmament commission did not reach a decision for the abolition of such forces within two years. The SA and the SS were not to be counted. Cf. Bloch, *Hitler*, 57, and *DBFP*[2] vi, No. 206.

[30] Thus the probably correct interpretation in Kuhn, *Programm*, 149.

[31] Cowling, *Impact*, 68.

completely upset Hitler's plans. It was clear by then that German and French aims were irreconcilable. Accordingly, the British would have liked to see a world-wide security system based on regional pacts, supplementing the general obligations of members of the League of Nations; there was also a proposal for sanctions, especially economic ones, that could be applied in concert with the United States.

Anglo-German relations, from the point of view of Britain's position in the Empire, were part of an equilibrium based on Britain's maritime supremacy but also on collective security. Britain could not afford, financially, to defend the Empire single-handed. The situation within the Empire made it unlikely that its members would pool their efforts. London therefore had to put its trust in collective security—an international political system which required bringing up to date but which in the last resort was based on Versailles, Locarno, the Washington naval treaty, and the League of Nations. The alternative was to enter into closer relations with Germany in Europe, and this would have meant sacrificing security in every other respect.

By his determination to induce Britain, as Germany's partner, to pursue a policy in Germany's interest, Hitler pushed her into a key position that finally wrecked his timetable. The idea that the security of the Empire could be guaranteed by means of an agreement with a dominant European power was Hitler's and perhaps his alone. At all events it was unthinkable to British statesmen, and no basis for an alliance. On the contrary, in the summer of 1934 Whitehall based its policy on the belief that the peace of Europe and the existence of the Empire might be exposed to the same threat as in 1914. An alteration of the status quo in Europe—or, of course, in Asia—did not suit London's book, while for Hitler it was the essential preliminary to carrying out his intentions. Thus, as early as 1933–4, short- and long-term considerations in London and Berlin, not to mention traditional tenets of foreign policy, pointed to confrontation and not co-operation. British concessions in the ensuing years were always a matter of tactics, not of principle. Even Neville Chamberlain, as chancellor of the exchequer, was convinced in 1933 by the conclusion of the chiefs of staff report that Germany was rearming on a scale that would make war probable in a few years' time,[32] and held that the nation's financial worries were no longer more acute than its military ones.[33] None the less, financial considerations played their part in the appeasement policy. The full realization by the military of Britain's strategic necessities, and the refusal of Chamberlain and others to draw the proper financial conclusions, must be regarded as the background and partial explanation of certain successful moves by Hitler, who initially saw them as stages on the road to continental hegemony.

At this time Hitler still believed in the possibility of combining eastward expansion on racial grounds with an Anglo-German share-out of interests on a power basis. The persecution of Jews in Germany aroused strong criticism in Britain, but was for the most part looked on as an internal German affair. It did not

---

[32] Chiefs of Staff Annual Review of Defence Policy, 12 Oct. 1933, PRO COS 310, Cab 53/23; Howard, *Commitment*, 104–5.

[33] Howard, *Commitment*, 104.

prevent numerous statesmen, journalists, and figures in public life—mostly conservatives—from visiting Hitler and conveying their impressions to the British public, mostly in favourable terms.[34] Perhaps Hitler may even have hoped, given time, to convince the British of the rightness of his racial dogmas.

But the impossibility of combining ideology and power politics[35] was not the only reason why Hitler's dream of an alliance with Britain proved illusory. His political ambitions were in themselves quite sufficient to make Britain his adversary. Perhaps the British attitude was not based on a full realization of the danger Hitler presented;[36] but who in Europe in the mid-1930s seriously believed that a great power could base its foreign policy on racial ideology? Certainly the German foreign ministry had no such idea. Hitler's skill in dealing with Britain consisted of achieving a bilateral agreement on the basis of traditional foreign-policy considerations: this was the case over disarmament, and also in the negotiations for a four-power pact.

As regards rearmament, with the British memorandum of January 1934 the theme of Anglo-German talks shifted to that of the air force. This was of crucial importance to Britain—Baldwin in the previous November had said that the RAF could no longer remain in a state of inferiority to other powers—and was therefore an especially critical point for German rearmament. The chiefs of staff had pointed out that reinforcement of the RAF was particularly urgent and was also financially feasible. In a situation where Britain could afford to confront either Germany or Japan but not both, she gave her primary attention to defence against air attack, which seemed to be the main threat to British security. For this reason the topic was a particularly delicate one.

In February 1934 Ribbentrop and Hitler tried to induce Phipps and A. Eden,[37] the lord privy seal, to look kindly on the early creation of a German air force, by pointing out France's air strength and invoking the doctrine of the balance of power. Soon afterwards, in April 1934, Ribbentrop was appointed commissioner for disarmament. Hitler's object in the talks was to evade the British proposal of January, which would have delayed German air armament by at least two years. The Germans also offered to disarm the SA and SS and place them under supervision, a proposal which impressed Eden.[38] But in the second conversation between Eden and Hitler[39] it appeared evident that the German offer—supplemented by an undertaking, if Germany's army was fixed at 300,000 men, to reduce the police force by 50,000—was to attempt to prise Britain away from France, to undermine the European security system, and to bring about a German–British–Italian combination. The Germans even asked for an air force up to 30 per cent as large as that of the neighbouring countries, or a maximum of 50

[34] See e.g. Henke, *England*, 32–3; also Gilbert and Gott, *Appeasers*, 41 ff.

[35] Hildebrand, *Foreign Policy*, 33–4.

[36] Thus in effect Hildebrand, ibid.

[37] Record of conversation between Hitler and Eden on 20 Feb. 1934, *DGFP*, c. ii, No. 117.

[38] Eden, *Dictators*, 74, 86.

[39] On 21 Feb. 1934: *DBFP*² vi, No. 305, pp. 463–4; *DGFP*, c. ii, No. 273. On these plans cf. Deist, III.ii.2 (*b*) above.

per cent of the French figure. The offer to demilitarize the SA, which made such an impression on Britain, no longer had any meaning, as the Reichswehr was determined to cease placing its training facilities at the SA's disposal: the latter was taken seriously as a rival force. The breach between the army and the SA was completed in March 1934; with the December rearmament plan Hitler had definitely opted for the Reichswehr and ruled out all ideas of a revolutionary militia. Röhm's SA was already earmarked for destruction when the illusory 'concession' was offered to Eden.

Considering Britain's financial straits and the strategic ideas of its leaders, Hitler's attempt to use the air force talks as a means to a British alliance must be regarded as altogether misguided. A German air force was precisely what the British feared. Germany was coming more and more into view as a potential enemy. However, the DRC (Defence Requirements Committee) did not secure acceptance of its report of February 1934,[40] which included the recommendation that an expeditionary force be created for the defence of Holland, so as to prevent Germany from occupying air-bases on the coast facing Britain. However, the cabinet accepted the proposals in the first programme to remedy the chief deficiencies, involving an increase from 52 to 82 squadrons. The army and navy had to accept substantial cuts.[41] In deciding to step up air armament the cabinet took account of British public opinion, which was overwhelmingly opposed to any continental commitment. The logic of the strategic argument was, however, that Britain could only ensure her security and implement her own guarantees if she was prepared to defend the territories of the Low Countries. In any case, Baldwin was convinced by the chiefs of staff. His statement of June 1934 that Britain's frontier was now on the Rhine[42] was based on the warnings and advice of the military. He saw it as his duty to enlighten the British public accordingly.[43] All these calculations clearly reflect awareness of the threat presented to Britain by modern air warfare.

Hitler, Ribbentrop, and Rosenberg, however, believed that by proposing air parity between France and Britain they could sow discord between the Western powers, thus making possible German rearmament in the air and closer Anglo-German links. This was the concealed object of the proposals put by Ribbentrop to Simon and Eden on 10 May 1934. Stress was laid on the modesty of the German claim to 'only' 50 per cent of British or French strength; but nothing was offered beyond what Britain could have achieved by her own decision. There was also no logical basis for the German belief that France would regard British rearmament in the air as such a threat that it would overshadow her fears of Germany.[44]

[40] Gibbs, *Rearmament Policy*, 93 ff.

[41] Howard, *Commitment*, 104 ff.; Gibbs, *Rearmament Policy*, 102 ff. It must be noted, however, that the 52 squadrons planned in 1923 were by no means all in being in 1934. Knowledge of secret German rearmament brought an abrupt change after 1934. Cf. Hyde, *British Air Policy*, 492 ff.

[42] Howard, *Commitment*, 108.

[43] *HC Deb.*[5] 292: 2339, 30 July 1934: 'When you think of the defence of England you no longer think of the chalk cliffs of Dover; you think of the Rhine. That is where our frontier lies.'

[44] See Rosenberg's memorandum of 12 May 1934, 'England und Deutschland' (PS-049), repr. in Rosenberg, *Tagebuch*, 163 ff.; also Kuhn, *Programm*, 154–5; *DGFP*, c. ii. No. 443. For German air rearmament cf. Deist, III.II.4 above.

Before the naval treaty of 1935 gave fresh sustenance to the idea of an Anglo-German alliance, its bankruptcy had become obvious. The main features of German internal politics—the Röhm crisis with its brutal denouement, the treatment of the Jews and churches, the persecution of political opponents, and the ill-treatment of political prisoners, all combined to reduce Germany's eligibility as an ally. Moreover, her role in the Austrian crisis of July 1934 was seen as a clear attack on Austria's independence, such as Britain, France, and Italy were not prepared to tolerate, as they had indicated in the previous February.[45] The stiffening of Italy's attitude was especially ominous for Hitler's hopes of a European alliance.

Thus, the naval agreement of 1935 was of 'programmatic' importance to Hitler, and was fully in accord with his ideas of the 1920s as to the correct policy towards Britain. But the developments leading up to it were also an indication that this policy was not the only possible one from the point of view of achieving German hegemony in Europe. Hitler's naval policy as a factor in his policy of alliance-seeking was at variance with the rearmament targets for the German army and air force. On 9 March 1935 Hitler dramatically introduced into the naval talks the disclosure that Germany once again possessed an air force,[46] and on 16 March he announced the introduction of conscription and the increase of the army to thirty-six divisions. The violation of the treaty of Versailles, of which Germany's neighbours had long been aware, was thus openly admitted. Negotiations with Germany could in future be bilateral only. At the end of January 1935 Hitler explained to Lord Lothian the idea of an Anglo-German *rapprochement* in a new and characteristic form, by suggesting that Britain and Germany should announce that they would punish any country that might disturb the peace in future.[47] Clearly he no longer thought it a practical possibility that anyone would punish a German breach of the peace: the 'danger zone' of German rearmament was, in his judgement, already past.

Hitler was to undermine his own basic policy towards Britain by his repeated *coups de théâtre* and unilateral moves, but in 1935 he did not yet see the contradiction between his actions and the desired aim. His offer of a 100:35 ratio of naval strength was made in the hope of reaching an accommodation; but the increasing scale of German rearmament on land and in the air afforded the material basis for a policy of hegemony regardless of Britain. Not until 1937 did it become quite clear that he possessed the political will to 'go it alone' in this fashion if necessary. But a study of his economic, rearmament, and foreign policy indicates that the process of enabling Germany to stand alone was initiated as early as 1935,[48] though it did not continue without a break. Ribbentrop was sent as ambassador in the summer of 1936 to improve relations with Britain, though with increased emphasis on German demands and demonstrations of strength. If Britain wished to co-operate, well and good, but otherwise she must be compelled.

[45] See note of 17 Feb. 1934 in *Dokumente der deutschen Politik*, iv, No. 52; Petersen, *Hitler–Mussolini*, 292 ff., esp. on Italy's role.
[46] Domarus, i. 489; Kuhn, *Programm*, 160; Wiggershaus, 'Enttarnung'.
[47] Kuhn, *Programm*, 159, after Butler, *Lord Lothian*, 330–7.
[48] Details in Hildebrand, *Reich*, 464; Henke, *England*, 35 ff.

Simon, the foreign secretary, visited Berlin with Eden at the end of March 1935, when the naval treaty was in preparation and when Hitler had made his surprise announcement about conscription and the air force. The visitors made it clear that Britain was not prepared to enter into bilateral links with Germany at the expense of collective security.[49] Hitler evaded the proposal for an Eastern pact; Britain was not willing to desert France. The talks confirmed Hitler in his view that Britain was best dealt with from a posture of strength, not merely respect or admiration. He believed that the naval negotiations would not have got going but for his bluffing statement that Germany had already achieved air parity with Britain.[50]

Hitler certainly impressed and misled the British by his abrupt negotiating tactics, alternately stalling for time and springing surprises such as the announcement that the U-boat programme was under way.[51] He was, however, disappointed in his aim of using the naval agreement as a means to a defensive and offensive alliance, a long-term division of interests between the naval world power and the future ruler of the Continent.[52] The treaty met German wishes by fixing the ratio strength at 100:35 and allowing greater freedom as regards U-boat construction. British interests were served by the agreement that naval strength should be measured according to classes of ships, and that Germany would adhere to the prescribed ratio irrespective of the naval armaments of third powers. The treaty contained more 'international' elements than Hitler was willing to admit. While he was thinking in terms of preparing the way for an association with Britain, the latter was mainly concerned with international aspects. The treaty in itself did nothing to promote the idea of an alliance or any other, more distant ambitions on Hitler's part.

By signing the naval treaty of 18 June Britain broke up the Stresa front, but she did not abandon European or French interests. Hitler was disappointed in his hope that the treaty would provide the impetus for an Anglo-German alliance. Indeed, the effective end of his 'alliance policy' dates from this time. The German naval leaders accepted the treaty only because it obviated naval rivalry for the time being and they were in any case unable to build more ships during the next few years;[53] moreover, the treaty acknowledged Germany's equal rights and rescued her from the isolation of March–April 1935. The navy did not see the treaty as part of the preparation of a war for hegemony, but as the means of carrying out their short-term construction programme.

[49] Full German record in *DGFP*, c. iii, No. 555, pp. 1043–80.

[50] On the negotiating tactics and the exclusion, to a large extent, of the foreign ministry (which, as represented by Bülow, had divergent ideas) see also Jacobsen, *Außenpolitik*, 413 ff.; Kuhn, *Programm*, 166 ff.

[51] Various British reactions to the German announcement in *DGFP*, c. iv, Nos. 1, 52, 54, 55, 58, 59. On the background to the naval treaty also Hauser, *England*, i. 120 ff.

[52] Cf. Hitler's instructions to the German delegation in Kordt, *Wilhelmstraße*, 100; Kuhn, *Programm*, 168; also Hitler's address to members of the delegation after the conclusion of the first phase of negotiations on 13 June: Kordt, *Wilhelmstraße*, 109.

[53] Jacobsen, *Außenpolitik*, 415–16; Salewski, *Seekriegsleitung*, i. 8 ff.; Wiggershaus, *Flottenvertrag*, 347; Raeder's message to the corps of officers, *IMT* xli, Doc. Raeder—12; Bensel, *Deutsche Flottenpolitik*, 30; Deist, III.II.3 (*b*) above.

The British navy saw the agreement differently, as a means of achieving a satisfactory balance in Europe without overstraining British resources in the light of imperial commitments.[54] The treaty, to them, was an effect of the German challenge, and did not reflect any desire for closer relations with Germany. Without a treaty, it was argued, Germany could be much more troublesome than she was. Her capacity was more or less correctly estimated, viz. that she would not be able to build up to the treaty limits until the 1940s. Without a treaty, however, Germany could have set whatever rearmament targets she liked.[55] The treaty itself did not put an end to Britain's worries. By liberating Germany from the Versailles restrictions it compelled the British navy to realize that the one-power standard, even as updated in 1932, must give way to a two-power standard.[56] It was no more than consistent with this that the DRC in November 1935 called for a Far Eastern fleet that could stand up to Japan and for a fleet in European waters that was at least a match for Germany's.[57] The strength of the navy was the most critical aspect of British overall strategy from the mid-1930s onwards. The RAF was expected to be used mainly in Europe, the army overseas, but the navy was required world-wide. Hence, the hope of keeping Italy neutral, and if possible 'positively friendly', was a vital element in British foreign policy up to the outbreak of war. Similar considerations were advanced as regards Japan.[58] The naval treaty with Germany was concluded for financial and strategic reasons; on this ground Britain accepted the odium, immediately after Stresa, of enhancing the prestige of Nazi Germany and disrupting the treaty of Versailles. The European powers, from the USSR to France, were not sparing in their criticism.[59] Eden admitted the legal case, but maintained that on practical grounds no British government could have acted otherwise.[60]

In principle British policy was still multilateral, and opposed Hitler's attempt to use bilateral arrangements to prepare for a war of hegemony.[61] British strategy was

[54] Howard, *Commitment*, 103, and Cab. P. 218 (36): 'The greater our commitments to Europe, the less will be our ability to secure our Empire and its communications', quoted ibid. Cf. also Best, 'Anglo-German Naval Agreement', 68–85. Best considers (p. 77) that the decisive part on the British side was played by the Admiralty, which clearly saw the problem from the point of view of naval limitation and the possibility of deploying greater strength in the Far East. Further light is thrown on the British attitude by Watt, 'Anglo-German Naval Agreement'. The background of British political and especially financial considerations is treated fully in Peden, *British Rearmament*. Best points out (pp. 77, 83) that the lack of opposition by Vansittart and Warren Fisher was due to their interest in strengthening the army and air force for a continental commitment against Germany. The strongest opposition evidently came from Simon: cf. Gibbs, *Grand Strategy*, 166. But scarcely anyone took a firm stand against the Admiralty, which used the treaty to put pressure on the government to regain the two-power standard: cf. also Kennedy, *Rise and Fall of British Naval Mastery*, 289.

[55] Wiggershaus, *Flottenvertag*, 347 ff.

[56] Gibbs, *Strategy*, i. 333 ff.: the two-power standard related expressly to Japan and Germany.

[57] Ibid. 340: 'adequate to counter Germany with a sufficient margin'.   [58] Ibid. 378 ff.

[59] e.g. Litvinov to Chilston (British ambassador) on 20 June 1935, to the effect that Hitler had won a great diplomatic victory, marking the end of Anglo-French co-operation (*DBFP*[2] xiii, No. 359, p. 442), and Laval to Eden on 21 June (ibid., No. 363, pp. 447–8).   [60] *DBFP*[2] xiii, No. 363, p. 447.

[61] Thus e.g. Hildebrand, *Foreign Policy*, 39. But it is also to be noted that Britain was by this time considering large-scale rearmament. An overall plan was submitted by a subcommittee of the CID at the end of 1935: see Parker, *British Rearmament*. The text is in the PRO: CID, Defence Requirement Sub-Committee, Programmes of the Defence Services, Third Report, CAB 4/24.

aimed at reconciling imperial defence needs with the looming danger in Europe, but there was no thought of an arrangement such as Hitler desired. The course of events prevented Hitler from telling his military leaders in good time what sort of war they should prepare for. Many possibilities remained open. Problems could not be defined and dealt with in isolation, because Britain would not play her part and left Hitler uncertain of her intentions. Later there was talk in the British cabinet of 'keeping Hitler guessing'. In fact he had no alternative but to plan for several eventualities and to leave unknown quantities in his calculations; these affected, not least, the German rearmament programme and led to the strains that became evident from 1936 onwards.

IV. Chances of Hegemony: Stresa and the Break-up of European Solidarity

IN 1934-5 Hitler, with his bilateral foreign policy—supplemented by an economic policy aimed at hegemony, especially in relation to south-east Europe—entered a field of power politics in which he enjoyed considerable freedom of action. German rearmament encountered no determined resistance. True, the announcement of Germany's military sovereignty (*Wehrhoheit*) elicited a demonstration by Britain, France, and Italy: the three heads of government, meeting at Stresa, issued a declaration sharply condemning the German action. The 'Stresa front' proved fragile, however, as can well be understood in view of its background and subsequent events.

The reaction to Germany's abandonment of the collective-security system reflected the diverging national interests of the victors of 1918. Effective common action was prevented by their fears of incurring isolation or sacrificing themselves for one another's interests. There was no question, for instance, of transforming the Locarno treaty, in response to Germany's move, into an alliance between Britain, France, and Belgium.[1]

Similarly, the National Socialist policy towards Austria, which aimed at rapid successes in 1933 and again in 1934, did not have the effect of transforming the national egoisms of Germany's neighbours into a lasting anti-German front. However, Hitler realized that he did not yet possess a broad enough base from which to take unilateral steps against the international order. In July 1933 there appeared to be a possibility of Italy and the Western powers intervening against the Austrian Nazis under Theo Habicht, who enjoyed Hitler's support in a subversive policy which has been described as an attempt to 'export the *Machtergreifung*' (the 'seizure of power' in Germany in January 1933).

In February 1934, following Austrian accusations against Germany, the governments of Britain, France, and Italy issued a declaration affirming their belief in the necessity of maintaining Austria's independence.[2] Hitler's meeting with Mussolini in June 1934 brought him no further towards his goal. Mussolini listened but offered no encouragement, and it was recorded that an Austro-German union was 'not under discussion'. Hitler declared, in accordance with his programme, that Austria would not be an obstacle to the development of Italo-German relations; meanwhile he played down all his specific demands. Agreement on the fate of

---

[1] Cowling, *Impact*, 67. In London the chief supporters of the 'Stresa front' were Eden, parliamentary under-secretary of state in the foreign office, and Vansittart, permanent under-secretary. This policy was, however, scarcely based on 'settled principles' agreed by the cabinet, as stated by Best, 'Anglo-German Naval Agreement', 72. Chamberlain, Hankey, and others were not convinced.

[2] Text of declaration published on 17 Feb.: *Survey of International Affairs, 1934*, 455; see also Petersen, *Hitler-Mussolini*, 299. For the German reaction to the proposed declaration see Bülow's telegram of 16 Feb. to the London embassy, *DGFP*, c. ii, No. 261.

Chancellor Dollfuss was not reached. The conduct of foreign policy on *Machtergreifung* lines proved to be an illusion as far as Austria was concerned.

The attempted Nazi *putsch* in Vienna on 25 July 1934, which was evidently not master-minded by Hitler, did not lead to any permanent combination being formed against him. Some Italian divisions were mobilized as a demonstration; Mussolini uttered threats from the Brenner. Nothing else happened except for some chilling of relations between Berlin and Rome. Germany's determination to bring about the Anschluss sooner or later was more effectual than great-power gestures. Berlin's reply of 1 February 1934 to the complaints of Dollfuss's government, which were backed by Italy, indicated the line that was to be followed: it was not a dispute between two states, but a matter of opposition by the Austrian government to 'a historical movement of the whole German people'.[3]

Hitler and the foreign ministry did not differ over the Anschluss as such, but only in respect of methods and timing, and especially their estimation of Italy's future role. The foreign ministry regarded with suspicion the Rome protocols signed by Italy, Austria, and Hungary in March 1934. These provided for closer economic co-operation and consultation in foreign affairs, and from Italy's point of view they were aimed at strengthening Austria. The Hungarians, on the other hand, were at pains to avoid any anti-German implication, and let it be known in Berlin that they had not committed themselves to the maintenance of Austrian independence. If this group of states had joined forces with the Little Entente and also France—Britain in any case would have been in sympathy—Germany's road to hegemony might have been seriously obstructed; but the necessary strength and motivation were lacking. Only for the time being did Germany's rulers regard the Anschluss as 'not under discussion'.[4] Hitler was obliged to plan more patiently, and to take up a position closer to that of the foreign ministry. A halt was called to the activities of the Austrian Nazis, and their organization was officially separated from that in Germany. Papen was sent as ambassador to Vienna with fresh instructions,[5] and a waiting game began. Mussolini was unable to achieve an Anglo-Franco-Italian guarantee of Austria, and did not dare take on the role single-handed. France wanted a non-intervention agreement of all Austria's neighbours or even a League of Nations guarantee, which was not in Italy's interest; and the British could not be got to do more than reaffirm the February declaration.

During the dramatic events in Vienna in the spring of 1934 Cerruti, the Italian ambassador in Berlin, who believed that Germany would absorb Austria in the foreseeable future, warned that her doing so would lead to the break-up of Czechoslovakia: 'In a few years Germany will form a compact bloc of 80 millions in the centre of Europe.'[6] Many other warnings and fears were expressed at this time.

---

[3] Petersen, *Hitler-Mussolini*, 298. Text of Austrian complaint of 17 Jan. 1934: *DGFP*, c. ii, No. 188, annex. The German reply was published in part; English trans. in *DBFP*[2] iv, No. 259, annex.

[4] This formula (replacing the Italian wording 'out of the question') appears in the agreed record of the Hitler–Mussolini conversation in mid-June 1934: *DGFP*, c. iii, No. 7; Petersen, *Hitler-Mussolini*, 350.

[5] Hitler's directive to Papen, 26 July 1934: *DGFP*, c. iii, No. 123, p. 252.

[6] Quoted from Petersen, *Hitler–Mussolini*, 296. Barthou in particular wanted to exploit German–Italian tensions and bring Italy firmly on to France's side: see Poidevin and Bariéty, *Relations franco-*

Hitler, when offering bilateral arms agreements to Britain and France, had let it be known that he meant Germany to expand at the Soviet Union's expense. Thus, it was more than mere speculation to assert that German rearmament was not purely defensive. That being so, how was it that Germany was allowed to achieve effective continental hegemony in so short a time?

Even grave political mistakes on Hitler's part were reduced to insignificance by the lack of co-operation among the great powers. Italy went so far as to put out new feelers in October 1934; but Mussolini insisted on the recognition of Austrian independence, and Berlin could afford to pay no attention. On this point there was full agreement between Hitler and the foreign ministry. Hassell (the ambassador in Rome) and Papen advised their government to grasp the outstretched hand, but in vain; Italy was thrown back towards France, and the two countries very soon came to terms. When agreement was reached in Janaury 1935 concerning North Africa and Abyssinia, it seemed that a stable and lasting settlement had been reached and that 'Italy had finally joined the ranks of the anti-revisionist powers'.[7] The Italo-French agreements contained an unambiguous safeguard against Germany. As regards Austria, a non-intervention agreement by her neighbours was after all to be envisaged, in accordance with French wishes. There were to be consultations about 'measures to be taken' if Germany should take unilateral action with regard to armaments, and also military talks for the purpose of joint action against Germany. Mussolini was in a hurry to conclude the agreement, believing it gave him a free hand in Abyssinia: he wished to create a *fait accompli* in Africa before there could be any increase in Germany's strength which might affect the Austrian situation.

Was this not a repetition of the 1916–18 line-up against Germany, with a group of powers engaging in specific talks for military action against Hitler? The Soviet Union, deeming itself rebuffed by Hitler, had also joined the anti-revisionist powers. In January 1935 it was open to question whether there was any chance at all for German hegemony in Europe. Germany had given up the attempt to bring about the Anschluss by revolutionary means; the major powers were concerned with the security of south-east Europe and with curbing German rearmament. But it soon appeared that there was no anti-revisionist 'camp' worthy of the name. Here lay Hitler's opportunity, which he seized with determination.

The introduction of conscription and the announcement of 'defence sovereignty'—clear violations of the treaty of Versailles—had led to the formation of the 'Stresa front', which looked threatening but produced no more than protests and declarations, the most vehement from Italy. But by March 1935 the signals from Rome were not of determination but rather of disappointment and hysteria. Military preparations against Abyssinia were under way; might they not be hampered and nullified by European obligations? Mussolini began to be fearful of the consequences of German rearmament, which was now unconcealed. He

---

allemandes, 291. On the outlook in France cf. also Duroselle, *Décadence*, and contributions to the Franco-German historians' symposium in Paris, 1977, published in *La France et l'Allemagne 1932–1936*.

[7] Ibid. 378; see *Survey of International Affairs, 1935*, i. 91–118, and, for further literature, Baer, *Italian-Ethiopian War*, and Laurens, *France*.

indicated that Italy would not in future recognize *de facto* situations brought about unilaterally by Germany.[8] Increased German pressure on Austria was feared, and France was warned of a possible violation of the demilitarized zone; more, it was suspected that Germany might take advantage of Italy's involvement in East Africa to bring about the Anschluss. From time to time the Italian hysteria took on an aggressive tone which was not without effect in Berlin. Blomberg took it for granted that Italy would support France in the event of a Franco-German war.[9]

During the preliminary stage of the Stresa conference it appeared to the German ambassadors in Paris and Rome that a firm anti-German coalition was being formed, a new *entente cordiale*. Hassell sent dramatic appeals to Berlin. But the British, French, and Italian prime ministers who met at Stresa from 11 to 14 April 1935 did not create a united front. The German danger was averted for the time being, but the Duce was mistaken in thinking that a threat of force was sufficient to bring Germany to heel. Italy herself was vulnerable; Mussolini at Stresa was at pains to secure cover for his impending operations in Abyssinia. Not least on this account, he believed that all his links with Germany were now severed and that Italy was, once and for all, on the side of the Western powers.[10]

The final declaration of the three powers was not such as to frighten Hitler. Even in the foreign ministry scarcely anyone was much impressed. Berlin would have been much more alarmed by a disclosure of the secret Franco-Italian military talks, which envisaged joint action in the event of a German move against Austria, and which led to a reduction of forces on the common frontier, so that more troops were available against Germany.[11] In February, when Laval and Flandin visited London, the British cabinet agreed to a mutual guarantee against air attack and proposed a declaration on the independence of Belgium.

What was left of the Stresa front? In the spring of 1935 a diplomatic basis existed for the effective isolation of Germany. German rearmament and the attempt to bring about the Anschluss by revolutionary means had caused general alarm in Europe. But Italy's imperialist venture was degenerating into crass egotism. Laval, Eden, and Litvinov tried in vain to deter Mussolini from his Abyssinian designs, so as not to compromise his power to intervene in Austria. Mussolini, however, retorted that Austria was a European affair; Italy did not want to be tied down to a sentinel's post on the Brenner. Meanwhile, the British for their own sakes were conniving at Hitler's armament plans and turning their back on Stresa. In February Vansittart noted with resignation that Mussolini's preparations would endanger Anglo-Italian co-operation at Geneva, which had been a key to European peace. The dispute between Britain and Italy over Abyssinia opened a breach in the anti-Hitler front, such as could never have entered into Germany's calculations. Here was a first-class opportunity for a fresh German attempt to dominate the Continent.

Another stroke of luck for Germany was that Britain was able to ensure that the

---

[8] *DGFT*, c. iii, No. 550, 21 Mar. 1935.
[9] Reichenau to commanders-in-chief, 30 Mar. 1935; *DGFP*, c. iii, No. 568.
[10] Petersen, *Hitler–Mussolini*, 400, and Aloisi, *Journal*, entry of 4 May 1935.
[11] Petersen, *Hitler–Mussolini*, 401–2.

Franco-Russian alliance, which it regarded with misgiving, did not become the nucleus of an effective anti-German grouping. In France it was increasingly being debated whether decisions of principle could be taken in a sense contrary to British policy. It is generally agreed today that Louis Barthou, the foreign minister assassinated in October 1934, would have had the strength to do so.[12] The Franco-Soviet proposal, put forward at Geneva in May 1934, for an East European pact of mutual assistance between Germany, Poland, the Soviet Union, Czechoslovakia, and the Baltic States was primarily intended to serve French interests. France herself wished to remain outside this 'Eastern Locarno' but to undertake the commitments of a member *vis-à-vis* the Soviet Union, if the latter would similarly accept the Western Locarno obligations. If Germany rejected the plan, Barthou thought this would afford grounds for restricting her freedom for the time being. But for this very reason the British were lukewarm about the plan;[13] in their view, in its first version it was too much like an anti-German alliance. The British sought to tone down this tendency and emphasize the aspects of security and equal rights. Their object was to revive the negotiations for general disarmament, and they succeeded in winning over the French and Italians for that purpose;[14] but Germany and Poland continued to reject the plan. However, as early as August 1934 Phipps, the ambassador in Berlin, doubted the relevance of the Eastern pact project, which he thought very unlikely to be realized.[15] France was unable to make good use of the Franco-Soviet pact of mutual assistance which she concluded as a *pis aller* on 2 May 1935. Pierre Laval, the foreign minister, tried to make it more or less ineffective, and refused to sign the military convention which was its logical completion. But the subsequent Popular Front government also did nothing to activate the treaty.[16] In May 1935 the Soviet Union reinforced it by a pact of mutual assistance with

[12] Cf. Duroselle, 'Milieux gouvernementaux'.

[13] Gibbs, *Strategy*, i. 134. For the Eastern Locarno proposal see also Scott, *Alliance*, 171 ff. Barthou's main object was to curb Hitler's activity by involving the Soviet Union in European politics. He also wanted to open the eyes of the Poles; if Germany refused to join an Eastern pact it would make manifest the 'emptiness of the German–Polish non-aggression treaty': thus Poidevin and Bariéty, *Relations franco-allemandes*, 291. A Russo-Polish *rapprochement*, moreover, could certainly have thwarted Hitler's plans. Barthou's policy offered the most effective means of countering Hitler's political strategy up to 1939. Britain supported the plan in the hope of influencing France's attitude over the arms question. Barthou indeed was apparently prepared to be more flexible over this: cf. Manne, 'Foreign Office', 725–55 (here 728). Barthou and the foreign office were basically pursuing quite different aims *vis-à-vis* Germany and the Soviet Union; Vansittart, however, agreed with Barthou that an Anglo-Soviet *rapprochement* would offer a possibility of stopping Hitler. Manne (p. 729) refers to the British 'fear of Rapallo', which was reawakened by the Röhm *putsch*: many British observers thought the Reichswehr and Junkers were gaining the upper hand once more, and that this portended 'a return to the Rapallo line'. Vansittart wrote: 'If we try to keep France and Russia apart now, we may—since Germany is now going towards the Right and the militarists—find the Germans resuming their old policy of working with Russia' (minute of 5 July 1934, quoted by Manne, p. 729).

[14] PRO Cabinet Papers 188 (34), quoted from Gibbs, *Strategy*, i. 134–5.

[15] 'To bind Germany and her rulers by an Eastern Pact of mutual assistance would seem highly desirable; but, pact or no pact, it appears essential for Europe, whilst careful to avoid giving Germany any just cause for complaint, to remain watchful, strong and as united as possible' (*DGFP*[2] xii, No. 5, Phipps to Sir John Simon, 8 Aug. 1934).

[16] The advantages of the treaty for France are stressed in the GDR work *Deutschland im zweiten Weltkrieg*, i. 97–8; see n. 12 above.

Czechoslovakia, but Prague devalued this by the proviso that its obligations would only come into effect it the victim of aggression was also aided by France.

After Stresa there existed, on paper, safeguards against German revisionism, but the conflict of aims between the Italo-French and Franco-Soviet groupings could only be concealed with difficulty. In Germany any development on the lines of an Eastern Locarno was contrary to the ideas of all concerned with foreign policy. It would have blocked what had been German aims since Weimar days, and was quite incompatible with Hitler's programme. Its failure was especially relevant to German–Soviet relations.

The Soviet Union had probably only consented to join in the initiative for an Eastern Locarno because Germany had failed to respond to bilateral Soviet approaches. For instance, in the spring of 1934 Hitler rejected the Soviet plan for a pact guaranteeing the security and inviolability of the Baltic States, and in so doing made it clear that Germany was not interested in furthering stability and security in the East. Hitler's attitude to the Eastern Locarno project could only be interpreted as a consistent pursuit of his ambitions. In June 1934 Neurath indicated to Litvinov, the commissar for foreign affairs, that Germany would conclude only bilateral non-aggression pacts and refused to be drawn into a pact system.[17] He mentioned ideological differences and intimated that there was no prospect of a general agreement. Hitler was not informed of this strategy till some weeks later, when he expressed approval of it.[18] Despite Germany's relatively weak position between the major powers to the west and east, Berlin held firmly to the policy of keeping a free hand *vis-à-vis* her eastern neighbours. Nor was Hitler moved by Moscow's announced intention of concluding a pact with France if the Eastern Locarno project failed. Again, Germany mobilized the Stresa front against herself by the announcement of universal conscription; yet her self-sought isolation did not do any lasting harm. The divergent interests of her neighbours to the west, east, and south were apparently such as to justify the calculation that it was possible to conclude alliances according to the needs of a rapidly rearming Germany so as to facilitate her subsequent territorial expansion. Even the Franco-Soviet pact contained clauses that prevented its being a guarantee of security for the Soviet Union, linked as it was with the machinery of the League of Nations and with the Western Locarno treaty. Moscow was sceptical of French assurances from the beginning, especially as the promised general staff talks did not materialize.

France and the Soviet Union did not succeed in enlisting British support; the visit of Simon and Eden to Berlin on 25–6 March 1935 had been an awkward background to the Stresa front in April. The British attitude must be regarded as the chief reason why nothing was done to check Germany's intensive rearmament despite the evident threat it presented to Europe's future. In the face of massive criticism of the government's rearmament measures, for instance by Churchill in the Commons debate at the end of 1934, Britain's attitude towards Germany was based on three main considerations, the first of which was something of a preconceived idea: (1) the

---

[17] Neurath's record of conversation on 13 June 1934, *DGFP*, c. ii, No. 504.
[18] Conversation between Hitler and Neurath, 17 July 1934, DGFP, c. iii, No. 93.

French-style policy of reparations was a failure; (2) Germany must be brought back into the collective-security system; (3) this was only conceivable if the fact of her clandestine rearmament was accepted. It was too late to patch up the damage to Versailles; in future the principle of equal rights for Germany must prevail. This alone would create an atmosphere enabling Germany to take part in constructive measures to safeguard international peace.[19] The alternative was a new arms race, since no power was prepared to put a stop to German rearmament.

Had Germany been concerned solely with equality of rights, it would have been hard to devise a fairer, more reasonable policy. With Hitler as an adversary, however, it was a diminution of Britain's political weight to accept Germany's 'secret' rearmament without at once embarking on a vigorous arms programme of her own. The government's admission to Parliament that they had certain knowledge of German rearmament but could not at that time say what was being, or would be, done to counter it confirmed Hitler in his policy of 'remilitarizing' Germany and creating political conditions for the use of the highly up-to-date military instrument that he was rapidly forging for himself.

Such was the policy with which Britain, after the events of 1934, began a year that was to be full of crises and decisive for the arms question. Britain partially imposed her policy on Laval. The Western powers were already under pressure of time: they did not want to delay making fresh proposals until Hitler was fortified by the result of the Saar plebiscite, which was expected to be strongly in Germany's favour. But Britain offered the French no more than assurances that were primarily in her own interest: a possible declaration on Belgian independence, a statement of continued British interest in the demilitarization of the Rhineland, and a proposal concerning the safeguarding of Austrian independence. This, and no more, was the basis for the Stresa front, and it was not reinforced thereafter. The British cabinet turned down some further proposals of Laval's: in line with public opinion, they rejected the idea of giving 'teeth' to Locarno. They would not hear of undertaking that Britain would react at once with all her strength to a violation of Belgian neutrality, or of conducting staff talks with Belgium and France.[20] Britain hoped Germany would return to the League of Nations; she wanted peace, Hitler was bent on war. Britain saw the danger, but still thought that by means of a discriminating policy Hitler might be tamed and the peace of Europe preserved.

Although Neurath and Hitler had virtually provoked the Soviet Union to reverse its foreign policy, even this did not bring about an alliance capable of holding Hitler in check. One reason was that Stalin was basically unwilling to abandon the wait-and-see policy that he had adhered to since the 1920s.[21] Just as Hitler intended to rearm and prepare the German nation for war before embarking on an aggressive foreign policy, so the Soviet leaders wished for a period of quiet in foreign affairs while they strengthened their country economically and militarily. From the point of view of Communist theory, the most obvious way to achieve this was to keep

---

[19] See Gibbs, *Strategy* i. 141 ff. [20] Ibid. 146–7.
[21] Cf. e.g. Stalin's statement to the central committee of the CPSU on 19 Jan. 1925, in Stalin, *Works*, vii. 11–14.

alive the differences between the chief European powers. At all costs they must prevent a ganging-up of the 'imperialist' capitalist powers in a new war of intervention against the Soviet Union. Fot this purpose, the method that had proved its reliability was that of exploiting the opposition between the victors of 1918 and the revisionist powers, especially Germany.

Since Hitler's accession to power, Germany's foreign policy in its revisionist guise appeared still to present opportunities for a continuation of the Rapallo policy; but Moscow nevertheless felt some anxiety. The Berlin treaty of 1926 was prolonged in May 1933, and this appeared to confirm the assurances offered by German diplomacy that the persecution of German Communists in no way invalidated the government's desire for close relations with the Soviet Union. But Hitler soon gave matters a different slant. Germany's withdrawal from the League of Nations was accompanied by so clear an intention to rearm that the Soviet government could hardly regard it as a propitious sign, however much they might welcome the exacerbation of Franco-German relations which resulted. The German–Polish non-aggression pact placed a still greater strain on relations between Berlin and Moscow. At first Stalin evidently believed that the German military might be aiming at a war of revenge against the victors of 1918; but the suppression of the SA in June 1934 seems to have opened his eyes to Hitler's intentions and caused him to take the *Lebensraum* programme seriously.[22] For that reason he tried to bring about conditions that would induce Hitler to accept a division of interests in line with Soviet strategy; a *rapprochement* with Moscow would divert German energies westward. But Hitler would not play the part designed for him.

In the spring of 1934 it became clear that conservative circles in the foreign ministry, the army, and the business world no longer dictated the main lines of German policy. As regards the Soviet Union, Neurath had dissociated himself from this group and, in effect, frustrated the efforts of Nadolny, the ambassador in Moscow, to improve relations. Even Bülow, the state secretary, in vain put forward new ideas for a more positive policy towards Russia. On the occasion of the proposal for a Baltic Pact a memorandum drawn up on his instructions pointed out the importance of the USSR securing Germany's flank, which could not be done by Poland. But Neurath did not submit the memorandum to Hitler and merely opposed the pact. The Russians waited for a sign from Berlin, but none came. Neurath, it had been maintained, took a more 'ideological' line than Hitler at this turning-point in German–Soviet relations.[23] Nadolny went into retirement.[24] Neurath's policy of playing down ideological differences took on a more anti-Soviet tone; he turned the tables by suggesting that the cooling of relations was due to Soviet hostility towards Nazism,[25] whereas the contrary was the case. In effect,

---

[22] See e.g. Hilger, *Allies*, 259–60; Lange, *Hitlers unbeachtete Maximen*, 151 ff. On Soviet foreign policy in general see *Osteuropa-Handbuch, Sowjetunion. Außenpolitik 1917–1955*; also the Soviet *Geschichte des zweiten Weltkrieges 1939–1945*, i; there is a brief survey in Kuhn, 'Deutschland'. On the significance of the events of 30 June 1934 see Allard, *Stalin*, 29–30.

[23] Niclauss, *Sowjetunion*, 175.   [24] On Nadolny's efforts see his *Beitrag*, 166–7.

[25] Niclauss, *Sowjetunion*, 172.

Neurath simply conformed to Hitler's policy as inaugurated by the German–Polish agreement, the purpose of which was to ensure freedom of movement in the east.

The Russians for their part were faced by the problem of revising their theory of Fascism. Since co-operation with France, in particular, was on the *tapis*, the object was to attract socialists, social democrats, and left-wing bourgeois groups to the respective Communist parties: Popular Front tactics might be found useful as a means of pressure on Hitler. In this connection Stalin had in mind not only France but also Spain, Britain, and smaller states. Even the Soviet attitude to the German social democrats underwent a change. The Soviet entry into the League of Nations in September 1934 was also a reason to draw stricter lines against Fascism. This task was undertaken by the Seventh World Congress of the Comintern in 1935. Thus, the ideological fronts on both sides were clearly defined before the first clash, in Spain, of the international forces of Fascism and Communism. In the Soviet view, the inauguration of an openly terroristic dictatorship by the bourgeoisie of the Fascist states constituted a particularly dangerous and aggressive form of capitalism.

In this way the strategy of exploiting differences among capitalist states took on an important new ideological dimension. Sharp and frequent criticism of Hitler's aims and the speed of German rearmament was publicly expressed in the Soviet Union.[26] In Berlin such utterances were described as 'malicious poisoning of the wells'.[27] Count von der Schulenburg, the new German ambassador, spoke of 'marked hostility to Germany'[28] and reported that Germany was 'at present being portrayed in the Soviet Union as the sole enemy and threat to peace'; even in regard to Japan there was talk of Moscow coming to some understanding. However, Stalin's manœuvres were not one-sided. The *rapprochement* with France was still intended to isolate Hitler and cause him to revise his strategy. Stalin accordingly kept the door ajar and would have welcomed an accommodation with Hitler. As Nadolny observed, Stalin's public attitude was less hostile to Germany than Litvinov's.[29] Germany's first overt rearmament in 1935 aroused Stalin's anxiety as to its likely purpose; a German–Japanese combination seemed a threatening possibility. Such Soviet fears can be inferred from the conversations between Eden and Litvinov in Moscow in March 1935.

In Germany, however, a propaganda campaign was deliberately aimed at exacerbating the differences of ideology,[30] which precluded any resumption of

---

[26] The German military attaché reported statements of this kind by Tukhachevsky, deputy commissar for defence, in *Pravda*, 31 Mar. 1935: WA (Ausl.), BA-MA RW 5/v. 461.

[27] Bülow, ibid. (the Reich defence minister concurring).

[28] Report of 1 Apr. 1935, ibid. (copy).

[29] Telegram of 29 Jan. 1934 from Nadolny to foreign ministry: *DGFP*, c. ii, No. 227, pp. 435–6. Vansittart's fears would have been justified if Bülow and Nadolny had been directing German policy. The prevalent view in the foreign office was that of Sir O. Sargent, the under-secretary in charge of central department. He was against the proposed Eastern pact and feared that a Franco-Russian alliance would be a major obstacle to British policy towards Germany: cf. Manne, 'Foreign Office', 737 ff. The cabinet endorsed the views put forward by Sargent in a memorandum of 7 Feb. 1935 (*DBFP*[2] xii, No. 428). This argued that a Franco-Russian alliance would split Europe into two camps as before 1914; Britain should therefore do her best to discourage it.

[30] Wette, I.II.3 above. Eden's visit to Moscow in Mar. 1935 marked the nearest approach to an Anglo-Soviet *rapprochement*. However, the cabinet had previously decided that Simon, the foreign minister,

German–Soviet co-operation on a conservative revisionist basis. It might therefore seem that Germany was to a large extent isolated and that there was every chance of a lasting association between the Western powers and the Soviet Union. But the anti-German solidarity did not last long. Even between the Soviet Union and France under its Popular Front government there was at no time any underlying harmony based on mutual confidence. As for the British government, it was their policy to prevent the formation of hostile blocs in Europe, which could only lead to conflict; instead, they sought to revive the collective-security system.

The Soviet government did not regard its security problem as solved. Stalin could not judge which would be the first target of German expansionism. He tried repeatedly to renew contact with Germany, but met with no response. Hitler turned a deaf ear; it made no difference to him that the Red Army once again showed interest in improving German–Soviet relations,[31] or that it depended largely on Berlin whether the Franco-Soviet treaty was effective or not. Russian officials emphasized that ideological differences need not prevent practical co-operation; countries with mutual economic interests must surely find a political *modus vivendi*. In January 1937 the Soviet government proposed negotiations for the improvement of relations and for peace in general. Neurath and Hitler showed no interest. It must be noted, however, that despite the war of ideology and propaganda, for reasons of strategy and security Moscow was careful to leave the door open for negotiations at all times, and Hitler for his part never quite closed it either. The Hitler–Stalin pact of 1939 was less of a 'bolt from the blue' than is often imagined.

and Eden should first go to Berlin; Simon did not follow on to Moscow, so as to avoid exaggerating the importance of the visit. Up till 1939 the priority of policy towards Germany remained unaltered: cf. Manne, 'Foreign Office', 734. An important statement of the British position is the Sargent–Wigram memorandum 'Britain, France and Germany', dated 21 Nov. 1935 (*DBPF*[2] xv, appendix 1), arguing that 'coming to terms with Germany' was the only realistic policy.

[31] Niclauss, *Sowjetunion*, 189. For further approaches see Allard, *Stalin*, 52 ff.

V. The Road to War, 1936–1938

1. THE REOCCUPATION OF THE RHINELAND

ON 7 March 1936 German troops moved into the demilitarized area on both sides of the Rhine. This made possible a rapid restoration of the military balance with France, and was also an important basis for Germany's future eastern policy. Peaceful protestations and carefully planned, illusory offers were now put into operation by a skilful propaganda machine. Europe looked on; nobody took action.

Hitler afterwards declared that 'The 48 hours after the march into the Rhineland were the most nerve-racking (*aufregend*) in my life'.[1] Calculated though his action may have been, was there not also an element of impatience and a desire to enhance his prestige within Germany? The foreign ministry was of that opinion. The ambassador in Rome thought the risk too great in proportion to the likelihood of success.[2] While the troops were still marching in, Blomberg was alarmed by a warning telegram from the military attaché in London. To avert countermeasures by the Western powers he proposed to re-evacuate Aachen, Trier, and Saarbrücken, but this merely caused Hitler to regard him as a minister lacking in nerve.[3]

With hindsight it appears that the professional diplomats were wrong: Hitler was shrewder than they in realizing that the Stresa front had crumbled and that the Western powers were incapable of action. If Hitler really needed a success on the home front—if he wished to show the masses, by a stroke of foreign policy, that he was a genuine 'leader'—it was easy to do so on this occasion. The risk factor no doubt appeared considerable, but was objectively small and was outweighed by Hitler's psychological victory. The ensuing plebiscite brought him a triumphant 99 per cent of votes.

During the days and weeks before 7 March the French government was in a state of uncertainty. Contradictory reports were received as to German intentions. On the 6th François-Poncet reported that it was still not clear 'who had been victorious in the discussions of the last few days, the men of moderation or the advocates of force'; but in his opinion all power was centred in Hitler, who was 'capable of abrupt decisions'.[4] None of the French parties advocated a decisive stand; in general, there was little to choose between the foreign policy of the 'moderates' and that of the Popular Front.[5] Albert Sarraut's caretaker government was incapable of determination. On 9 March it was resolved not to take military measures against Hitler's violation of the treaty, but to appeal to the League of Nations.

---

[1] Schmidt, *Interpreter*, 41.

[2] On the reoccupation of the Rhineland see Robertson, 'Wiederbesetzung'; Jacobsen, *Außenpolitik*, 416 ff.

[3] Hossbach, *Wehrmacht*, 84–5; also Deist, III.II.2 (*c*) above.

[4] Duroselle, 'Milieux gouvernementaux'; see also François-Poncet to Flandin, 6 Mar. 1936, *DDF*[2] i, No. 265.

[5] Duroselle, 'Milieux gouvernementaux'. On the French attitude cf. also Adamthwaite, *France*.

It was for Britain to play the decisive role between Germany, France, and Italy. Her attitude also determined Hitler's policy during the subsequent period. On the particular question of the demilitarized zone the cabinet's position was still what it had been at the beginning of 1935, when Simon failed to obtain agreement that Britain should declare her 'vital interest' in the demilitarization of the Rhineland in order to induce France to come to terms with Germany on the arms question. Thus, the Rhineland was not deemed to be a vital British interest.

On the basis of sober reports from the ambassador in Berlin it was expected in London that Hitler would tackle the Rhineland problem as soon as a favourable opportunity offered. Eden obtained reports from the committee of imperial defence on the strategic importance of continued demilitarization from the French, Belgian, and British points of view.[6] But although the army staff rated it much higher than did the RAF, the cabinet drew no conclusion from this. It was concerned at the same time with a general review of British policy towards the German danger, based on a memorandum by Eden arguing that Britain must continue to rearm so as to be prepared for all eventualities. At the same time it was to be considered whether there was a possibility of reaching some *modus vivendi* with Germany.[7]

Britain wished to come to an arrangement with Germany consistent with honour and security. In February 1936 Eden advised the cabinet that no talks should be held with the French government as to what Britain would do 'in the hypothetical case of a violation of the demilitarized zone'.[8] The zone had been created for the sake of French and Belgian security, and it was for those governments to consider what price they would pay for its continuance. They would no doubt be very pleased, Eden said, if Britain would take the decision for them. In any case he thought it unlikely that France would attack Germany merely in order to maintain demilitarization. It seemed wiser to negotiate with Germany over the renunciation of rights at a time when those rights still had some value. On the eve of the German action the cabinet was of the clear opinion that neither London nor Paris was capable of taking effective military measures if Germany should violate the Locarno treaty.

Thus, Hitler secured a cheap success—cheap in price, but of enormous effect. The change in the international situation, political and military, was of even greater importance than his triumph at home. The demilitarized Rhineland was an unknown quantity in the strategic calculations of the German arms programme. According to the role assigned to France in the phase of German expansion, it was either to be regarded as a deployment area or as a security zone, in any case essential to the military organization of the Reich. Army leaders such as Fritsch were in principle favourable to extending full German sovereignty over the area, but they estimated the risk much more highly than Hitler did.[9]

Hitler, it appears, intended to take the step no later than the spring of 1937.[10]

[6] Gibbs, *Strategy*, i. 230–1.
[7] PRO Cabinet Papers 13 (36), pp. 1–2; Gibbs, *Strategy*, i. 231.
[8] Gibbs, *Strategy*, i. 233: 'in the hypothetical case of a violation of the demilitarized zone'.
[9] Hossbach, *Wehrmacht*, 83–4; Deist, III.II.2 (c) above.
[10] Hassell's record of conversation with Hitler, 14 Feb. 1936, *DGFP*, c. iv, No. 564, pp. 1142 ff.; Hossbach, *Wehrmacht*, 97, also Braubach, *Einmarsch*.

Then suddenly the spring of 1936 seemed a favourable time politically for two reasons: the growing estrangement between Italy and the Western powers owing to the former's Abyssinian adventure, and the ratification of the Franco-Soviet pact, of which neither Italy nor Britain approved. Poland too was looking for a fresh orientation. The French security system, in which she was an important factor, had little attraction left for her. At all events Germany received assurances from the Poles that they would not react to the remilitarization of the Rhineland. French pressure was no longer effectual.[11] Thus, Poland came of her own accord to cover Germany's rear in a way that the foreign ministry's policy could hardly have brought about.

Hitler's political calculation over the Rhineland combined the instant exploitation of current possibilities with long-term objectives; the manœuvre was also intended to draw Italy closer to Germany.[12]

In Hitler's opinion too, the operation would have been less risky in 1937. Germany would be stronger, and Russia perhaps involved in a conflict with Japan. The reoccupation of the Rhineland could be combined with a general move to abolish Germany's Locarno obligations, especially if Mussolini could be persuaded to come forward and denounce that treaty on the ground that its provisions were falsified by the inclusion of Russia. Getting rid of Locarno must be regarded as an important additional aim of Hitler's in reoccupying the Rhineland—so important to him that he was prepared to go ahead without Mussolini. When the German ambassador in Rome reported Mussolini's misgivings, Hitler showed his hand a little further. Given the situation of their two states, Fascist and National Socialist, surrounded by democracies 'infected with Bolshevism', passivity did not pay in the long run: the best strategy was to attack. The Franco-Soviet pact was to be the ostensible ground. However, so that the other side could not accuse Germany of aggression, Hitler intended to make a whole string of offers that were not meant seriously; if they had been, they would have involved the very 'passivity' that he considered wrong in principle.

The offers comprised:

1. continuance of the demilitarized zone—but extended to the French side also;
2. a three-power pact to safeguard Dutch and Belgian territory;
3. a three-power air pact in the west;
4. a long-term non-aggression pact with Russia;
5. revival of the basic idea of the four-power pact.

There was something for everyone here, in particular Britain and France. Even Locarno, which Hitler had just torpedoed, was to be revived in principle.[13] Acceptance of this 'offer' would have devalued the Franco-Soviet pact, just

---

[11] Sawka, 'Franco-Polish Alliance'; Wollstein, 'Politik', 802; Funke, *Sanktionen*, with review of German policy during the Rhineland crisis.

[12] Conversation with Hassell on 14 Feb. 1936, *DGFP*, c. iv, No. 564, pp. 1142 ff.

[13] Hassell's record of 20 Feb. 1936, ibid., No. 575, pp. 1163 ff. The substance of these points was repeated in Hitler's 'peace speech' of 7 Mar. 1936: *Völkischer Beobachter*, 8 Mar. 1936, and Baynes, ii. 1271 ff. On the 'peace speech' and its function see Emmerson, *Rhineland Crisis*, 150 ff. For the Western powers' reactions to Hitler's proposals see *DBFP*² xvi, Nos. 48, 63, 144.

concluded, and destroyed France's credibility. Clearly she could on no account accept it, and so it fell to the ground. If France had accepted, it would in principle have been to the advantage of Hitler's plans in the east, by enabling him to concentrate his efforts in that direction. In this sense it was far from being an invitation to a policy of peace.

Hitler's policy of 'doing away with Locarno' went far beyond the mere restoration of sovereignty in the Rhineland, which was how the German military had understood his decision. The problem, not only of the western frontier but of the connection between future policy in the west and in the east, was raised to a new level.

This revolution in the international situation, for which Hitler had chosen the spring of 1936 as the right 'psychological moment', improved Germany's military position but weakened her politically. Even if one is not inclined to argue from the basis of Hitler's 'programme', it must be wondered how a power that was not yet 'adequately' prepared militarily can have seen advantage in denouncing a security system with treaty guarantees of peaceful coexistence at a time when her most powerful neighbours, or those who were potentially such, appeared to be combining against her in response to a threat which they already felt.

Hitler, however, did not believe that a firm coalition was capable of being formed against his policy, which was aimed at association with Italy and Britain. A Russo-French alliance was, if anything, calculated to further his plans. He also underrated both France and the Soviet Union. The former, he believed, was 'distracted by her own problems' (*innerlich zerfahren*), and in both France and Britain there was, to Germany's advantage, 'strong opposition to the Russian pact'.[14] His declarations and assurances were intended, without any scruple, to take the utmost advantage of the psychological aspects of a given situation. Thus, as late as 21 February 1936 he spoke to the French journalist Bertrand de Jouvenel of Germany's peaceful intentions and the absurdity of the hereditary enmity between her and France. This prompted the French government to take soundings on 3 March through François-Poncet, who enquired what proposals Hitler had for improving Franco-German relations. Hitler riposted that the imminent signature of the Franco-Soviet pact was 'a great impediment to the improvement in Franco-German relations for which he was striving'.[15] At the same time as this conversation a full programme had been worked out for the Rhineland coup, complete with rhetorical assurances and bogus offers. Neurath, the foreign minister, had reservations, especially on the ground that 'the speeding-up was not worth the risk', but did not interfere at the decisive moment.[16]

The soundings of the Stresa powers soon indicated to what extent the Abyssinian and Rhineland operations relieved pressure on Germany and Italy respectively. Many observers noted the diversionary effect of the Rhineland occupation.[17]

---

[14] *DGFP*, c. iv, No. 564, p. 1119.
[15] Neurath's record of conversation with François-Poncet on 3 Mar. 1936, ibid., No. 604, p. 1220.
[16] Hassell's record of 20 Feb. 1936, ibid., No. 575, pp. 1163–6.
[17] Petersen, *Hitler–Mussolini*, 477.

Neurath himself pointed this out to the Italians and expressed the hope that they would not exploit the situation against Germany.[18] Mussolini had been completely surprised by the timing, at all events, of the German move, the more so as on 22 February he had had a long conversation with Hassell on the international situation, the Franco-Soviet pact, sanctions, Locarno, and the League of Nations, at which they had appeared to be in far-reaching agreement.[19] The Duce was especially vexed at Hitler's suggestion to the Western powers that Germany might re-enter the League of Nations, as it devalued his own threat to defy sanctions by walking out of the League. Rome seemed to believe that Germany was reorienting her policy.[20] Despite Mussolini's promise on 22 February that he would not be a party to any Anglo-French action on account of 'an alleged breach of the Locarno treaty by Germany'—a promise which he repeated on 9 March[21]—on the 19th Italy joined in the condemnation of Germany's action by the League Council. Only German protests caused Mussolini to change course and put a stop to the policy of his foreign ministry, on which French hopes had been based.

On 8 March Eden proposed to the cabinet that Britain should negotiate with Germany on the basis of the existing situation: he had in mind particularly an air pact. Hitler's methods were not approved, but had he not seized what the powers had already been prepared to grant him? The cabinet admitted the logic of this. They also agreed that Britain should persuade France to refrain from military action, and that no resolution by the League Council should be allowed to serve as a pretext for French intervention.[22]

The reactions of the Locarno powers were violent in words only. The demands made on Germany on 19 March were rejected in Berlin. Germany was not disposed to allow the matter to be decided by the Court of International Justice, or to agree that an international force might be admitted to the zone pending negotiations as to its future and as to a general European agreement.

The Stresa front was broken, the Versailles treaty largely invalidated. Locarno had proved an inadequate safeguard against a policy which skilfully exploited the conflicts of interest among the European powers. Above all, France's inability to take decisive action visibly enhanced Hitler's prestige in Europe and the world. Belgium pulled out of her alliance with France. Poland, which had hesitated during the crisis, was now more dependent on Germany than she had been before, yet of decidedly less importance to Hitler.

Italy too now moved more decisively in Hitler's direction. Mussolini saw Britain

---

[18] Ibid.; Neurath to Hassell, 8 Mar. 1936, *DGFP*, c. v, No. 26.

[19] Report from Hassell to foreign ministry, *DGFP*, c. iv, No. 579, pp. 1172 ff.

[20] Mussolini's motives and strategy are still not fully clear: see Petersen, *Hitler-Mussolini*, 475.

[21] Hassell to foreign ministry, *DGFP*, c. iv, No. 579, pp. 1172 ff; and Peterson, *Hitler-Mussolini*, 477.

[22] Quotations from the Eden memorandum of 8 Mar. in Gibbs, *Strategy*, i. 239–40; full text in *DBFP*[2] xvi, No. 48. On the air pact see Eden to Baldwin, 8 Mar. 1936, ibid., No. 50. Eden no doubt realized that a different offer would be required from that which Hitler had rejected in Dec. 1935 on account of the Franco-Soviet pact. Hitler used the Franco-Russian alliance as a well-tried means of pressure, confirming the fears of its British opponents. For the Hitler–Phipps conversation on 13 Dec. 1935 see *DBFP* xv, No. 383, Phipps to Haase, 16 Dec. Hitler wanted a special agreement between Britain and Germany, 'the two great Germanic peoples': cf. also Manne, 'Foreign Office', 725–55 (here 742).

as the chief opponent of his imperialist policy. He now proposed to Hitler that Germany and Italy should co-ordinate their action in matters relating to Locarno.[23] True, he also offered assurances to the other side on condition that sanctions were lifted, but in general Italo-German contacts were now intensified at several levels. The clearest sign of a change in Mussolini's foreign policy was furnished by his decisions after the successful conclusion of the Abyssinian invasion in May 1936, when the country was annexed to Italy. In July the League of Nations resolved to lift sanctions. Italy was out of her troubles, and Mussolini now got rid of the pro-Westerners Suvich and Aloisi. In June his son-in-law, Count Ciano, became foreign minister. An agreement over Austria was already foreshadowed on 7 January 1936, when Mussolini told the German ambassador that he had no objection to Austria's becoming a satellite of Germany provided she remained formally independent.[24] He now took more definite steps by informing Schuschnigg that the Austrian problem must be solved as it was an obstacle to close links between Italy and Germany.[25] In April he cut off his financial subsidy to the Heimwehr.[26] The long-sought *modus vivendi* was achieved with the German–Austrian agreement of July 1936. Germany recognized Austria's independence and the principle of non-intervention in her internal affairs. The two countries were to pursue a·common foreign policy based on the fact that Austria was a German state. A customs union and military talks were envisaged. Austria did not join the Axis, however, and showed reserve in other matters also. A secret supplementary agreement, also of July 1936, provided that the nationalist opposition would be incorporated in the Vaterländische Front—a move designed in course of time to bring the National Socialists into a convenient position for a take-over. Despite lively distrust on both sides, Hitler now achieved without difficulty what had hitherto eluded his grasp. What a difference in the situation since Stresa! Yet Germany's attitude to the Abyssinian conflict had been far from one of merely friendly neutrality: she had supplied Haile Selassie with arms so as to prolong the campaign, intensifying Italy's involvement and exacerbating her quarrel with the Western powers. The diversionary effect of Abyssinia was exploited for the sake of Central Europe. Now, half-way through 1936, would the two revisionist powers, the winners of the poker game, finally make common cause and create fresh problems for Europe?

2. Involvement in Spain

To this day it cannot be said for certain what caused Hitler to intervene in Spain. Several motives were probably at work. Neither the interest of the German arms industry[27] nor anti-Western strategic aims can have been decisive in themselves. Other motives were, no doubt, the desire to help build up an anti-democratic regime and exclude Communist influence,[28] and to stir up Franco-Italian antagonism.

[23] Bülow's memorandum of 21 Mar. 1936, *DGFP*, c. v, No. 174; Petersen, *Hitler–Mussolini*, 478.
[24] Telegram from Hassell to foreign ministry, 7 Jan. 1936; *DGFP*, c. iv, No. 485, pp. 974 ff.
[25] Gehl, *Austria*, 126.   [26] Petersen, *Hitler–Mussolini*, 483.
[27] Schieder, 'Spanischer Bürgerkrieg'; Volkmann, II.vi.1 above.
[28] Abendroth, *Hitler*.

At all events Hitler swiftly seized the opportunity to intervene in a new European crisis. There was no co-ordination with the foreign ministry, whose views were simply overridden. A considerable share was taken in the decision by Gauleiter Bohle, head of the Party's Auslandsorganisation (organization for Germans abroad).[29] The generals in Spanish Morocco rose against the Popular Front government in Madrid on 17 July 1936. A week later Hitler, speaking at Bayreuth, promised to aid Franco, perhaps expecting a quick victory.[30] The latest reports from the German embassy, which Hitler most probably saw,[31] painted an alarming picture of the threat of a Communist regime which would link Spain firmly to the Franco-Soviet bloc.[32] Franco argued similarly in a letter to Hitler, who took these warnings more seriously than did the foreign ministry.

Deliveries of military equipment soon followed.[33] The foreign ministry and the navy were by no means in favour of intervention.[34] Here, for the first time, there appeared a clear breach between Hitler's wider aims and old-fashioned revisionism, however broadly conceived. Soon there was close co-operation between Hitler, Göring—who had hesitated at first—and Blomberg. But Germany's aid to the insurgents remained far behind Italy's, even with the active intervention of the Condor Legion, which was anxious to improve its experience of strategic bombing.

The German–Italian involvement in Spain, which included overt use of military formations from October–November 1936 onwards,[35] had an important effect on the development of German ascendancy in Europe. On the one hand the outcome of the conflict prevented the formation of a Franco-Spanish Popular Front bloc and improved the economic and strategic positions of the two Fascist powers, whose relations became closer. Secondly, the contrary interests of the Western democracies and the Fascist states were defined more sharply, though the British government, for complex reasons, hesitated to adopt an unambiguous position. The British did not wish to be involved in war alongside the French Popular Front, perhaps in indirect alliance with the Soviet Union, whose aim was to 'force Bolshevism on a shattered Europe'. Sir Maurice Hankey, secretary to the cabinet and the committee of imperial defence and an important adviser to the government on matters of military policy, had no desire to prop up the Spanish republic; nor had the chiefs of staff and others,[36] who wished to mend relations with Mussolini. Even Vansittart, who was uncertain whether Hitler regarded Britain or the USSR as his chief enemy, wanted to gain time for rearmament, by either 'economic appeasement or colonial concessions',[37] and was therefore opposed to intervention in foreign quarrels. He also believed that a war between Germany, France, and Britain would destroy the

---

[29] Merkes, *Deutsche Politik*, 19–20; Jacobsen, *Außenpolitik*, 422–3.
[30] Merkes, *Deutsche Politik*, 363.   [31] Abendroth, 'Deutschlands Rolle', 474.
[32] *DGFP*, D. iii, No. 4.   [33] Maier, *Guernica*, 27 ff., using new sources.
[34] *DGFP*, D. iii, No. 50.
[35] Maier, *Guernica*, is a convenient account of the development and intensification of the Axis commitment; see also Coverdale, *Italian Intervention*. For a survey of international interests see *Der spanische Bürgerkrieg*.
[36] Cowling, *Impact*, 162.
[37] Memorandum of 31 Dec. 1936, 'The World Situation and British Rearmament', cited in Cowling, *Impact*, 158.

social order 'as we know it'. Hitler, by stepping up his anti-Soviet propaganda, knew that he was likely to provoke a sympathetic reaction in Britain and elsewhere; but by this time his credibility was much impaired.

During the Spanish civil war German anti-Soviet propaganda attained its highest peak of intensity, both at home and abroad. Hitler put so much faith in this weapon that he enjoined Goebbels to carry on the campaign so as to create 'right away' an 'adequate foundation' for future German moves in foreign and military policy.[38] This was a specific portent of the future direction of German ambitions.

The key to eastward expansion was to be sought in Britain. Italy, for the present, was only a card in a game played for higher stakes. Hitler's successes led him to think that Britain would not, in the last resort, oppose his East European aims. The Empire meant more to Britain than Europe. In Hitler's own programme, the qualitative leap from continental to global policy would come later, when Germany embarked on overseas enterprises that would bring her into rivalry with the United States. On this basis, though not without frequent doubts, he defined the probable British attitude towards developments in continental Europe.[39] Was he not proved right by British reactions to the Rhineland occupation, the Italian conquest of Abyssinia,[40] and now the events in Spain? At all events, in March 1936 he believed that British 'realism' might enable him to pursue his course, if not with approval from Britain, at least without opposition. In this sense Abyssinia and the Rhineland have rightly been called 'test cases' for Hitler.[41] At the same time these events also demonstrated Britain's aversion to any kind of alliance. As for the principle of equality and non-intervention in each other's affairs, this, in Hitler's view, had been violated in March 1935 when the British White Paper on rearmament had referred to internal events in Germany[42] and, despite its careful formulations, had made it clear that German rearmament was regarded as a threat. Those in Britain who were pressing the urgency of rearmament—Hankey, Vansittart, Fisher, and the chiefs of staff—were at least successful in moving the cabinet towards their ideas,[43] though not in persuading the British public to alter its view of rearmament.

Hitler resented the constant criticism of German affairs in the British press.[44] He could not fail to be aware that strong forces in Britain were opposed to abandoning the Continent to Germany. Viewpoints were driven still further apart by the attitude of the powers to the Spanish war. The ideological fronts became more distinct, and in Britain the conviction gained ground that Hitler was aiming to

[38] Jacobsen, *Außenpolitik*, 457, 821: strictly confidential instruction by the propaganda ministry to the German press, dated 21 Aug. 1936, to step up the campaign against the Soviet Union and the Red Army. On anti-Bolshevik propaganda cf. also Wette, I.II.3 above.

[39] Hillgruber has attempted to trace the 'phases' in Anglo-German relations in 'England in Hitlers außenpolitischer Konzeption', drawing largely on Henke, *England.*

[40] Cf. François-Poncet's impression in *DDF*[2] i, No. 359, 10 Mar. 1936; Henke, *England,* 47.

[41] See esp. Henke, *England,* 48.

[42] *Deutschland und England,* 51 ff.; Henke, *England,* 51; text of the White Paper (Cmd. 4827, 1 March 1935), in *Documents on International Affairs, 1935,* i. 38–47.

[43] See also Meyers, *Sicherheitspolitik,* 253 ff.

[44] Historians differ as to whether the press exercised a favourable or unfavourable influence on Hitler's view of Britain and especially her political strength of purpose: see Aigner, *Ringen,* 98; Kieser, *Appeasementpolitik,* 3.

obtain strategic bases for a coming war against the West.[45] As Hitler's arguments lost credibility, his anti-Bolshevik propaganda was shown up as an exercise in power politics.

The remilitarization of the Rhineland and German intervention in the Spanish civil war have been described as an 'ingenious recipe' for dividing Hitler's opponents and 'introducing turmoil into European conditions'.[46] More precisely, however, it was in both cases a matter of taking advantage of the diversionary effect of the foreign policies of the two Fascist states. Hitler, with far-off aims in view, acted in a decidedly experimental manner and, it must not be overlooked, from a position of relative weakness. He knew, and had been repeatedly assured by Mussolini, that the 'spirit of Stresa' was dead; but it remained to be seen if he had gone too far with the dramatic steps of 1936.

In his Spanish commitment and his attitude to the Italo-Abyssinian war, Hitler had not made a firm choice between Italy and Britain. To this extent too, his initiatives were still experimental. The all-overshadowing anti-Bolshevik campaign was partially aimed at arousing London to great enterprises that were basically the affair of both countries. A major role was assigned to this line of propaganda, if only because Hitler overrated the strains placed on Anglo-French relations by the formation of the Popular Front government.

3. CLARIFICATION OF STANDPOINTS

In the course of 1936 Hitler achieved the maximum extent of treaty revision that could be attained without a military confrontation. Up to that point the leading conservative groups in Germany could also be induced to co-operate without much argument. They might be alarmed at Hitler's methods or precipitate steps, but scarcely realized at any stage that his policy was leading rapidly towards war. Hitler's successes made mock of pessimistic analyses.

Only in the economic sector did the figures not present the desired picture. The stepping up of arms production had not cured all economic difficulties. On the contrary, rearmament showed up the inadequacy of the Reich's supply of raw materials and foreign currency. In 1936 the time had come when, under a long-term policy, the brakes should have been applied if all resources were not to be used up. But Hitler opposed the economic imperialism of Schacht and his followers, whose objective of economic hegemony in Europe called for the application of liberal principles, with cut-backs in consumption and in the arms programme. Instead, Hitler's memorandum of August 1936 on the Four-year Plan[47] called for a total subordination of the economy to the needs of rapid rearmament. As argued in *Mein Kampf*, the function of the economy was to create conditions 'for Germany's self-assertion and the extension of her *Lebensraum*'. The 'military exploitation of our

---

[45] Aigner, *Ringen*, 302.

[46] Fest, *Hitler* (trans.), 484, 500.

[47] Treue, 'Hitlers Denkschrift'; Petzina, *Autarkiepolitik*, 48 ff.; cf. Volkmann, II.v.1, and Deist, III.II.2 (*d*) above.

forces' was to be pursued on the broadest scale and with the utmost speed. Germany must have the 'first army' in the world as regards training, equipment, and organization, and her people must be educated accordingly, or she would be done for. The requirements of speed and quality were basically contradictory and were not studied in the light of an answer to the question 'What kind of war was the object of all the strategic and material preparation?' Unlike the situation before 1914, there was no clear view of which powers would be the adversaries and in what chronological sequence. The military and Hitler took different views as to future eventualities.

During the phase of all-out preparation for war the economy was intended to ensure the satisfaction of the nation's vital needs, but food imports must not take place at the expense of rearmament: the needs of the war economy were paramount. Autarky was to be pursued regardless of economic efficiency. All economic difficulties would be taken care of by the war for *Lebensraum*, which in Hitler's fixed opinion could alone safeguard the nation's future growth and development. The economy was now clearly not geared simply to rearmament for the sake of Germany's equal rights and security, but was overtly programmed for war. The only alternative from this point onwards would have been a complete reversal of course and the abandonment of the policy of expansion by military means.

With the economy thus geared to a future war, Hitler's programme was unalterable in its main lines. Details were not prescribed as yet, but expansion was the goal and war was clearly envisaged. The requirements were that the German army must be operational within four years and that the economy must be on a war footing within the same period. To achieve this, all resources must go into arms production. Piling up stocks, in Hitler's view, was a positive crime. Any management that accumulated stocks instead of making shells 'deserved to be hanged'.[48] Any temporary easing of conditions for the general public must be subordinate to the arms programme. Hitler issued his memorandum as a response to the bottlenecks and shortages that resulted from accelerated rearmament. Accordingly, it is to be regarded not only as a blueprint, but as a document reflecting a situation in which German economic capacity was overstrained by the extent and speed of rearmament, combined with an effort not to allow living standards to sink unacceptably. The Four-year Plan could only be justified on the assumption of an early war. If that war was against the Western powers, the adequacy of the plan was dubious from the start. The policy was bound to create problems of its own, not least owing to shortness of time.

The stages leading to war could not be foreseen in 1936. As long as Hitler still hoped for an arrangement with Britain, a programme of separate 'lightning campaigns' for the conquest of territory hardly seemed logical,[49] since from 1935 onwards France had clearly become dependent on British policy, so that each country had to take greater account of the other. An arrangement could thus in principle have made possible a direct attack on the Soviet Union. But already by

[48] Treue, 'Hitlers Dentschrift', 207.
[49] Hillgruber, 'Weltpolitische Lage', 277.

1936 Hitler did not simply envisage German and British policy working in parallel. He still hoped to achieve his end by pressure on Britain, but as yet he had found no sign of readiness for conversations about the arrangements that interested him. For some time past he had denounced the Soviet Union as the great danger to Europe, especially when he wanted to conceal other designs from the Western powers. He used the same recipe in home affairs. In his memorandum on the Four-year Plan the need for an all-out effort was attributed to the Bolshevik danger, and in the same month (August 1936) secret instructions were given accordingly to the German press. But, considering his low estimation of Soviet fighting power in subsequent years, this is hardly a strong enough basis for the plans, which he may have been fostering as early as 1936, for the first stages of military expansion. On the other hand France, from the point of view of a German policy of *Lebensraum* in the east, had declined to a negative quantity, no longer an object in itself. Was France to be deprived of even that degree of importance, by pressure exerted through Britain? Could the timing and sequence of the expansion now envisaged be altered in that way? Or is the war against France to be regarded as a direct continuation or execution of Hitler's political ideas of the 1920s—which would mean that developments in the 1930s did not modify his aims after all? Certainly many of his statements, e.g. before the occupation of the Rhineland, were essentially tactical in intent. This is true of all his remarks and gestures concerning a final reconciliation between France and Germany, as long as he was still afraid of French intervention against the treaty violations of 1935–6. His statements to Bertrand de Jouvenel can be regarded as an example of such devices, intended to lull the adversary's suspicions and weaken his will to resist. Hitler's present actions, he maintained, were in themselves a refutation of what he had said in former days about France as Germany's hereditary enemy. This seemed to be confirmed by much that he had said and indicated since 30 January 1933, including repeated statements that he had no revengeful feelings and did not hanker after Alsace-Lorraine.

But perhaps the statement to de Jouvenel that France could, if she only wished, 'put an end to the supposed German danger'[50] did actually point to a new conception of policy towards France, which took as its basis her dependence on Britain and was designed to enable Germany to start directly on her eastward drive. The remilitarization of the Rhineland, and the previous return of the Saar to Germany, had in any case narrowed the basis of France's policy towards Germany and made her less capable of applying sanctions.[51]

It is scarcely possible, however, to adduce firm evidence for a policy of this kind, based on new assumptions regarding France, precisely because her policy depended on Britain's, and Hitler had no idea what that might be. Hope and wishes on his part increasingly took the place of those convictions that he had cherished in the 1920s and that had made him feel so much wiser than the statesmen of imperial Germany. So it is only with great caution that one can suggest the possibility of a change of emphasis in Hitler's policy for the phase of expansion beyond the scope of

[50] Interview with B. de Jouvenel, 21 Feb. 1936; Domarus, i. 579 = Baynes, ii. 1266–71.
[51] Knipping, 'Frankreich', 621.

conventional revisionism. All we have is circumstantial evidence,[52] with its known weaknesses; but the possibility of such a change in Hitler's thinking cannot be ruled out.

At all events, after the occupation of the Rhineland Hitler continued to extend olive-branches, though no longer with specifically deceptive intent. He was now acting from a position of relative strength. His assurances that Alsace-Lorraine and other such claims must not stand in the way of good neighbourly relations between France and Germany were no doubt also intended for Britain.[53] The Rhineland occupation was followed by a campaign aimed at securing the confidence of the West: it was for the future to ensure that Germany and France no longer need feel threatened by each other.[54] At an election meeting at Frankfurt am Main on 16 March he declared that he was ready at any time to conclude an agreement with the French government. 'The question which he would put before the German people was: "Do you wish that now at last the hatchet should be buried between us and France and that peace and understanding take the place of war?" (Loud shouts of "Yes!")'[55] The response showed the effect of this propaganda on the German public. The fact that it struck a genuine chord in Germany helped to make it credible abroad.

But these assurances committed Hitler to nothing. Britain wanted a gesture on his part, such as an undertaking not to fortify the Rhineland for the time being. Ribbentrop's experience in London afforded no evidence that British ruling circles were prepared to believe words without deeds.[56] Hitler's formula of a 'permanent' order of peoples enjoying equal rights[57] came up against the British desire to solve Europe's problems within the framework of the League of Nations.

France's view of Germany was still more sceptical. Any intention on Hitler's part of inducing the West to stand aside while he took action in the east must have seemed, even to him, fraught with considerable doubt at this time. The Franco-Soviet treaty could only have increased such doubts, and even the conciliatory government of Laval was unable to dispel them.[58] None the less, he continued with the policy of verbal assurances and gestures. Even with his intimates he maintained that it was not worth fighting France for Alsace-Lorraine, a view perfectly in line with his earlier ideas concerning the purpose of a war.[59] Evidently at this stage he did not want such a profitless war as a preliminary to the war for *Lebensraum*, although it was uncertain whether he could have his wish in the matter. But, if he was after a *modus vivendi*[60] that would enable him to postpone a show-down with

---

[52] As suggested by Knipping, 'Frankreich'.

[53] Thus already in an interview with Ward Price, 9 Mar. 1936: Domarus, i. 600 = Baynes, ii. 1303–4. Phipps to Eden, 11 Mar. 1936, does not mention the point: *DBFP*² xvi, No. 68.

[54] Domarus, i. 600 = Baynes, ii. 1303–4.   [55] Domarus, i. 607 = Baynes, ii. 1310.

[56] Henke, *England*, 48.

[57] Speech in Hamburg, 20 Mar. 1936: Domarus, i. 608 = Baynes, ii. 1311–13.

[58] Cf. Neurath's record of conversation between Hitler and François-Poncet, 21 Nov. 1935, in *DGFP*, c. iv, No. 425, p. 847. For France's policy towards Germany see Duroselle, 'Milieux gouvernementaux'; id., *Décadence*; Renouvin, *Crises du XXᵉ siècle*, pt. 2. *De 1929 à 1945*; Adamthwaite, *France*.

[59] Speer, *Inside*, 120–1.

[60] Knipping, 'Frankreich', 622.

France until after he had achieved his aim in the east, he had little to offer in return. To assure France that he had no designs on her *status possidendi* was hardly a sufficient price to induce her to eschew all concern in Eastern Europe.

Hitler's policy towards France has been described as intended to lull and weaken her will to resist, and as part of a 'sheep's clothing' strategy.[61] At times the primary motive was to forestall retaliation against German treaty violations. After the remilitarization of the Rhineland all these intentions and intermediary aims flowed together into a general policy intended to ensure that options remained open while Hitler pursued his basic objectives.[62] As in 1934,[63] if France was prepared to comply with his ideas it could only suit Hitler's book. Alliances for a limited period, non-aggression pacts or stand-still agreements were, to his mind, perfectly compatible with long-term policies in a contrary sense.[64] In *Mein Kampf* he had already spoken of possible alliances with 'enemies of Germany'. Such moves were part of a political strategy aimed at finally satisfying Germany's vital demands. In Hitler's eyes there was no objection to this, either legal or moral.

Without stating how a Franco-German *rapprochement* fitted into his programme, at the end of November 1935 Hitler had given the French to understand that he considered such a *rapprochement* incompatible with the continuation of the Franco-Soviet pact, and that altogether the Soviet Union ought not to be brought into European affairs. In saying this he probably indicated the limit beyond which he was not prepared to go for the sake of an understanding with France. In his view it was for France to choose, and on her choice would depend his treatment of her at the time of embarking on his anti-Soviet course.

His estimate of Britain's role was also a function of the war he envisaged. However many stages can be traced from 'with Britain' to 'without Britain' to 'against Britain',[65] essentially it is a story of how Hitler's wishful thinking gradually gave place to awareness of the facts. For years he pursued a strategy towards Britain that was basically fruitless. A phase of wooing with an 'offer' of a division of interests, a guarantee of the Empire, and renunciation of a naval or global policy, was followed in and after 1936 by a period of pressure, with revisionist colonial demands and arms competition. As early as 1935 Hitler indicated to journalists his determination not to abandon the claim to colonies,[66] and he did so again in January 1936.[67] He first advanced the claim formally on 7 March 1936. The fact that he did so in the context of his 'peace speech' on the occasion of the Rhineland occupation indicates a tactical intention of causing problems for Britain, no doubt in the expectation that it would make her reconsider her position.[68] From this time on the

---

[61] Jacobsen, *Außenpolitik*, 328, 311 ff.

[62] For a concise recent account of the state of research see Hildebrand, 'Frankreichpolitik'.

[63] Wollstein, *Revisionismus*, 299.   [64] Ibid. 12; Hildebrand, 'Frankreichpolitik', 591 ff.

[65] Kuhn, *Programm*. Henke, *England*, is especially sound; Hillgruber, 'England', gives a recent, carefully argued view.

[66] Interview with Baillie of United Press, Domarus, i. 559 = Baynes, ii. 1255–6.

[67] Interview with Mme Titayna of *Paris-soir*, Domarus, i. 566–7 = Baynes, ii. 1259–63; cf. Kuhn, *Programm*, 180.

[68] Hillgruber, *Strategie*, 242, already sees at this stage preparations for the final objectives of the 'graduated plan'.

colonial demand became a permanent component of Hitler's strategy, at least on the occasion of continental crises.[69] There were, to be sure, elements in Britain who regarded the Empire as the most important issue, and were made uneasy by German colonial claims. But on the whole Hitler was mistaken as to the nature of Britain's primary interests. How would he have reacted if he had known of the calculation of the chiefs of staff that colonies would be 'likely to disperse German naval power'?[70] Whatever concessions the British political and military leaders thought of making, it remained their guiding aim to construct a new, stable European order or at least gain time to rearm. This was Hankey's view and also Chamberlain's in July 1937, when he sought to bring Mussolini back on to Britain's side.

Hitler mistook the British reaction to Mussolini's Ethiopian conquest in a manner characteristic of his preconceived ideas. He saw it as a proof of weakness that Britain, an imperial power, showed hesitancy, sent no troops to protect her sphere of influence, and sought a solution through the League of Nations. Failing to draw the more obvious inference that Africa might be less important in British eyes than Europe, he chose this time to put forward colonial claims as a means of pressure. The more self-confidence Mussolini showed, the less value Hitler placed on Britain as an ally.[71] This effect on British policy was understood in London, and was acutely pointed out by Phipps in his retrospect of April 1937.[72] Mussolini, who had no desire to see an Anglo-German *rapprochement*, encouraged Hitler to think on these lines during his visit to Germany in September 1937. The feebleness of the British reaction to the Italian challenge was to Hitler a matter of astonishment bordering on disappointment, and her invoking of the League appeared to confirm that the Jews had a stranglehold over British policy; but it was not only these considerations that misled Hitler and caused him to modify his programmatic ideas concerning a German–British association. He was at least equally affected by the discovery that Britain was impervious to his approaches. From 1936 or 1937 onwards his timetable involved expansion at an early date, and his own deadlines precluded a long-term process of trying out possibilities of co-operation. He admitted to Speer that the situation had forced him into alliance with Italy: 'I really don't know what I should do.'[73]

The question remains whether Hitler was more concerned in 1936-7 by the 'depreciation'[74] of Britain as a potential partner or by the fact that his approaches had no prospect of success. The question may also be put thus: did he realize that,

[69] Hildebrand, *Foreign Policy*.

[70] Cowling, *Impact*, 162. On the British estimate of Hitler see also Carlton, *Anthony Eden*. For the effect of imperial commitments on British policy see *Retreat from Power*, i; Haggie, *Britannia at Bay;* Holland, *Britain*; Darwin, 'Imperialism'; Peden, 'Burden of Imperial Defence', 405-23. Peden questions Michael Howard's view that the European commitment was much influenced by imperial obligations; he argues that financial stringency and home-defence needs were more important: 'British strategists never forgot that the UK was the heart of the Empire and must be protected at all costs' (p. 415).

[71] Details in Henke, *England*, 40 ff.

[72] Quotation ibid. 41.

[73] Speer, *Inside*, 71.

[74] Henke's term (*England*, 49).

contrary to his misjudgement in the 1920s, Britain would act in accordance with her own traditions and not as he himself liked to imagine? There are various signs that the answer is probably 'yes'. Britain was not willing to adapt: an arrangement with her could only be had on British terms. Any discussion or negotiation prior to such an understanding was, from the British point of view, nothing else than appeasement, a means of gaining time in case it proved impossible, as was suspected, to construct a peaceful order of which National Socialist Germany would be a part. The British aim was to achieve a multilateral guarantee of the European status quo, though the latter was not regarded as sacrosanct. The failure of German attempts to secure an alliance with Britain, which reached their peak in May–June 1936, is basically to be interpreted from this point of view.[75] From January 1936 onwards Hitler sought to achieve new contacts through German–British society. The duke of Saxe-Coburg-Gotha engaged in conversations with key personalities such as Chamberlain, Eden, Duff Cooper (the war minister), and even Edward VIII.[76] Ribbentrop, shortly afterwards, endeavoured to follow these up and to arrange a meeting between Baldwin and Hitler: the matters at issue, he pointed out to Baldwin's adviser Thomas Jones, would 'decide the fate of generations'.[77] The plan failed, however, as it was opposed with determination by Eden.[78]

By these approaches, which were not even interfered with by the occupation of the Rhineland, Hitler evidently hoped to secure British consent to the Anschluss, leading to a still further concerting of interests.[79]

If his wooing of Britain had succeeded Hitler would have achieved ideal conditions, in terms of foreign policy, for the execution of his programme of rearmament and expansion. All Germany's resources could have been concentrated on the intended war in the east. Britain's refusal to co-operate was due to the consistency, much as Hitler might doubt it, of British policy. More lay behind it than a mere difference of opinion as to the opportuneness of a meeting between Hitler and Baldwin. Hitler thus had to realize that he needed contingency plans and more elaborate preparations *vis-à-vis* the Western powers. Time was not on his side. Now that Germany had achieved important revisionist aims, the contrast between warlike and peaceful policies expressed itself in the opposition between Germany's bilateral designs and Britian's endeavour to preserve European peace by means of regional and collective pacts. From the British point of view there was some scope for negotiation over colonies and perhaps south-east Europe. For Hitler, it was a question whether Britain would impose a blockade or connive at Germany's eastward expansion. When, after the Rhineland occupation, the British and French broached the idea of a 'Western pact'[80] to replace the Locarno treaty, Berlin adopted delaying tactics and took care that Eastern Europe was not included in the

[75] Kuhn, *Programm*, 187 ff.

[76] *DGFP*, c. iv, No. 531, pp. 1061–72.

[77] Jones, *Diary*, 194–214.

[78] Eden, *Dictators*, 374.

[79] Neurath to Bullitt, the US ambassador, on 18 May 1936: *IMT* xxxvii. 150-L, p. 589.

[80] Documents on the Western pact negotiations in *DGFP*, c. v, Nos. 489, 515, also Nos. 546–8, 558 etc.; full collection in PA Bonn, Westpakt 1–2; cf. Henke, *England*, 53.

package.[81] The French and British saw the purpose of these tactics, which was not difficult.[82]

During this exploratory period Hitler also looked around for other possible combinations. Britain was still his ideal partner, though she was not to be had for his designs and basically he knew it. Sending Ribbentrop to London as ambassador[83] was a further attempt to bring about the alliance;[84] but pressure of time made it necessary to try out other connections, if possible such as might influence the British attitude. In Hitler's estimation it would soon be 'necessary' for Germany to expand; he needed international cover of some kind, and this explains his ambivalent attitude towards Britain. How exactly did he perceive Germany's situation in 1937? The key documents as regards planning for an early war are, it is generally considered, his memorandum of August 1936 on the Four-year Plan and the Hossbach memorandum of November 1937.[85]

In 1936 Hitler thought he could achieve an alliance on the world scale against the Soviet Union. In proportion as he judged Britain to be weak, his interest centred on Japan. Until 1935 he had fought shy of contacts with Japan lest they endanger his hoped-for alliance with Britain,[86] but from 1936 onwards the German picture of the world balance of forces underwent a change. In Berlin Ribbentrop pressed for an understanding with Japan, and in Tokyo the idea was favoured especially in army circles.[87] The belief that Japan might soon come into conflict with the Soviet Union helped to prepare the ground for an association between the two powers, both striving to enlarge their 'living-space'. Thus, the German–Japanese Anti-Comintern pact was signed in Tokyo on 25 November 1936. Statements by Hitler to British visitors in February 1936[88] indicate that he was speculating on an easing of Anglo-Japanese tension,[89] which would help to bring about a combination of the three powers against the Soviet Union. All Britain need do was to cover the others' rear in Europe and the Far East respectively. Hitler was even prepared to offer military aid to defend the British Empire against any threat from Russia or Japan. Ribbentrop followed up this idea in the summer of 1936;[90] there was even talk of

---

[81] Henke, *England*, 53 ff., referring to numerous important diplomatic moves.

[82] e.g. François-Poncet on 2 July 1936: *DDF*² ii, No. 379.

[83] On Ribbentrop's mission see esp. Hildebrand, *Reich*, 491 ff., where it is seen as an 'attempt at final clarification'; also Henke, *England*.

[84] Ribbentrop, *Memoirs*, 62. For Ribbentrop's role see also *Nationalsozialistische Außenpolitik*, and Michalka, *Ribbentrop*.

[85] For the memorandum see Treue, 'Hitlers Denkschrift'. For the Hossbach record see *DGFP*, D. i, No. 19, Bussmann, 'Hoßbach-Niederschrift'. For a general view of German foreign policy from 1937 onwards see Weinberg, *Foreign Policy*, ii; id., 'Deutschlands Wille zum Krieg', 407–26.

[86] This was in particular Rosenberg's opinion, which Hitler shared until 1935: cf. Rosenberg, *Tagebuch*, 28, 163.

[87] Sommer, *Deutschland und Japan*, 18. For the switch of German Far Eastern policy from China to Japan see Martin, 'Das deutsche Militär', 191–207. The history of German Far Eastern policy is summarized in Fox, *Germany and the Far Eastern Crisis*. Hitler took a stronger interest in Far Eastern policy and in relations with Japan after the conclusion of the anti-Comintern pact: see Bloss, 'Zweigleisigkeit', 55–92.

[88] Lord Londonderry and A. J. Toynbee: cf. Londonderry, *Ourselves*, 50; Toynbee, *Acquaintances*, 279–80; also Frank, *Im Angesicht des Galgens*, 209–10.

[89] Kuhn, *Programm*, 189–90.   [90] Ribbentrop, *Memoirs*, 50.

Germany supplying twelve divisions to help protect the Empire! But the idea of such a three-cornered alliance remained an illusion. Ribbentrop later asserted that in 1936 he had sought to obtain, in return for his offer, a 'free hand' in Eastern Europe and particularly for the solution of the 'Austrian and Czechoslovak question'.[91]

The German approaches were unsuccessful. Reports from the embassy in London referred more and more often to the impossibility of an arrangement allowing Germany a free hand to the east.[92] Britain, as Eden stated publicly in December 1936, could not 'abandon interest in this or that part of the world'.[93] During 1937 Hitler perceived more and more clearly the divergence of German and British policy, confirmed by reports of various kinds and from various quarters. Ribbentrop, whose views had most effect on Hitler, did no more than repeat with emphasis what had always been inherent in the British policy of maintaining an equilibrium of forces. Hitler himself ascribed the abdication of Edward VIII to 'anti-German forces'.[94] Ribbentrop's advice confirmed him in assessments of this kind. In a report on the coronation, dated 21 May 1937, the ambassador stated that further intensive work would be necessary 'to persuade Britain clearly to refrain from interesting herself in East Europe';[95] he also hinted that the attempt might fail, in which case 'the necessary conclusions should be drawn uncompromisingly'.

By the middle of 1937 London and Berlin had more or less come to a conclusion about each other. As a basis of future defence and rearmament measures, the joint planning committee made a study of the situation in the Mediterranean on three assumptions: (1) war with Italy; (2) war in alliance with France and Belgium against Germany and Italy; (3) war in alliance with France and Belgium against Germany, Italy, and Japan, the USSR being neutral or co-operating with the Western powers. And on 5 July 1937 the committee of imperial defence, with Chamberlain present, decided to recommend to the cabinet that priority should be given to building up a deterrent potential against a German attack in Europe.[96]

Anglo-German conversations in mid-July touched on the Anschluss, Danzig, Memel, Eastern Europe in general, and British participation in a 'crusade' against Communism. Eden made it unmistakably clear that Britain could not accept any change in the international status of Austria against the wishes of its people. If the state of opinion there should change it would constitute a new situation affecting the European balance. As to the Sudeten question, Britain could not tolerate interference by force in Czechoslovakia's internal affairs. As to Danzig, Britain would not stand in the way of moderate constitutional evolution. Of especial importance to

---

[91] *DGFP*, D. vi, No. 618, p. 852; also Burckhardt, *Danziger Mission*, 285, 295.

[92] Details in Henke, *England*, 62 ff.

[93] Ibid. 63, quoting DNB report of 14 Dec. 1936.

[94] Speer, *Inside*, 72; Wiedemann, *Feldherr*, 152.

[95] Ribbentrop's report on the coronation: PA, Pol II, England–Deutschland, 4; cf. Henke, *England*, 65. The text is published in A. Ribbentrop, *Kriegsschuld*.

[96] Extract from draft minutes, CID, 296th Meeting, 5th July 1937, PRO Cab 24/270. The cabinet nevertheless decided in Dec. 1937 to give imperial defence priority over European operations. However, this decision had no important effects on rearmament: cf. Peden, 'Burden of Imperial Defence', 405–23, esp. 411 ff.

Germany was what Sir Nevile Henderson, the ambassador in Berlin, called 'expansion to the east', where, in the German view, no British interests were involved. In his instructions to Henderson Eden emphasized that Britain could not join any anti-Soviet combination merely because the Soviet regime was a Communist one. However, the effect of German anti-Bolshevik propaganda was visible in so far as Eden took it for granted that in German eyes the problem of the east and that of Communism were one and the same.[97] It was left to Göring, on 20 July, to disabuse Henderson of this error. Germany needed space and food for her population; she had renounced any idea of westward expansion, so she must now look east. The Slavs were Germany's natural enemies. Göring went on to indicate the next steps. What did peaceful evolution mean? In the Rhineland Germany had only achieved her aim by action, not through the League of Nations. Czechoslovakia would not give up her three and a half million Germans without a struggle, and Germany could not for ever listen to their complaints without coming to the rescue.[98]

As such contacts show, it was no use Britain hoping that the Germans would show patience and willingness to await events in a spirit of compromise; nor could it be expected that Britain would agree to Germany using force to achieve hegemony in Europe. In July 1937 it would have been easier to judge the reasonableness of the doubts Cadogan had expressed after Lord Lothian's visit to Berlin, as to the 'respectability' of Germany's aims.[99]

Abundant evidence in the course of 1937 demonstrated to Hitler that Britain was not to be had as an ally for his eastern policy. The alliance was still a desideratum, but even the doctrinaire Hitler no longer thought it a reasonable expectation. Occasional pieces of good news and gleams of hope could not alter this.[100] Hitler's last resort, basically a fruitless one, was to use pressure and threats. Colonial claims and maritime sanctions were not a valid means of exerting pressure on Britain.[101] Trying to make Britain act against her interests by means of press campaigns was misconceived, chiefly by Nazi agitators, as a demonstration of strength. Colonial claims aroused interest in the international press, but were of far less concern to the British leaders. There was speculation as to whether Germany was shifting the emphasis of her foreign policy, but no greater willingness to talk about Hitler's real aims in the east. Western statesmen, particularly those of Britain, were not prepared 'to sacrifice Europe for Africa'.[102]

4. THE AXIS

Association with Italy had never been more than a second-best solution in Hitler's eyes. In conversations with Count Ciano, the new Italian foreign minister, at the

---

[97] Eden to Henderson, 15 July 1937, PRO Cab 24/271, fo. 46.
[98] Henderson to Eden, 20 July 1937, ibid., fo. 49.   [99] *Cadogan Diaries*, 14.
[100] e.g. report by (later Field Marshal) Milch on the visit of a Luftwaffe delegation to Britain (*IMT* ix. 61); cf. Irving, *Rise and Fall*, 58–9.
[101] Hildebrand, *Reich*, 516, emphasizes this function of colonial policy, taking the view that in Oct. 1937 Hitler still thought he could achieve an alliance with Britain.   [102] Ibid. 515.

end of October 1936, he developed the possibilities of joint action: the Axis thus began to take shape. Mussolini entered into the association with a mixture of national imperialist and vitalistic-biological ideas in mind.[103] Like Hitler, after the success of his Ethiopian venture he fell into the mistake of underrating Britain. To his optimistic mood the Mediterranean seemed destined to be the centre of an Italian empire. Many believed that Italy had freed herself from strategic dependence on Britain.[104] The joint action of Germany and Italy in Spain encouraged the development of a broader partnership, though Hitler still subordinated it to his policy towards Britain. He now sought an offensive alliance with Italy so as to put pressure on Britain to accept Germany's aims. What he offered the Italian foreign minister was the Mediterranean basin as the territory of Fascist imperialism, while Germany claimed the Baltic and Eastern Europe as her own sphere of influence. The 'offensive alliance' proposed by Germany appeared to involve opposition to the Western powers. Hitler saw this very clearly, and therefore advised a camouflage: for propaganda purposes, the alliance was to be represented as a defence against the Bolshevik menace. In this way, he thought, it would present an appeal to third states which would hardly be in favour of German or Italian expansionism as such.

The Italian consent did not go quite so far. The confidential protocol of 23 October 1936, following the Ciano–Neurath conversations, left open many points, such as the two powers' interests in the Danubian area and the question of Austria, with Mussolini still insisting on its independence as a buffer state. Germany sought to obtain commercial advantages in Abyssinia.[105] Thus, the divergence of interests persisted after the conclusion of the agreement, which Mussolini shortly afterwards described as an 'axis around which the other states of Europe might group themselves'.[106] Italy wished to break out of her isolation and was also fearful of an Anglo-German compromise, while Hitler needed his 'Axis partner' as a means of pressure. Ribbentrop's mission to Britain had just begun, and German eyes were fixed on London rather than Rome. Thus, the German press was fairly restrained in its comment on the Axis.[107] The two powers were at one in opposing Communism, as their involvement in Spain made clear; but Hitler's anti-Bolshevism was of a quite different stamp from Mussolini's. Both Berlin and Rome were well aware that National Socialism and Fascism were not on a converging course. Despite the racialist campaign set on foot by Mussolini in the summer of 1938, there could be no question of ideological motives playing the same part in Italy's foreign policy as in that of Germany.

The Axis made no basic changes in the position of Germany or Italy relative to

---

[103] This set of ideas also included the pseudo-political opposition of 'young' and 'old' nations and contempt for the Western democracies. Cf. Nolte, *Fascism*, 226, where this is regarded as the chief reason for Mussolini's turning towards Germany. Important Italian studies of the Axis are De Felice, *Mussolini il Duce*, ii, and Quartararo, *Roma*.

[104] See Petersen, *Hitler–Mussolini*, 486 ff. On the Duce's imperial aspirations cf. Smith, *Roman Empire*, 120 ff.

[105] Text of protocol in *DGFP*, c. v, No. 624, pp. 1136–8; cf. Funke, 'Deutsch-italienische Beziehungen', 834–5.

[106] *Völkischer Beobachter*, 2 Nov. 1936.

[107] Funke, 'Deutsch-italienische Beziehungen', 836.

other European powers. It restricted Mussolini's range of action and made Italy more dependent on German policy. As Italy moved away from the Western powers, Mussolini's influence on the Anschluss question was increasingly nullified.[108] The idea that Italy, Austria, and Hungary might constitute a force of any consequence in Europe on the basis of the Rome protocols was a large overestimation of Italy's possibilities in 1937, especially as Hungary had for some time been gravitating towards Berlin. Germany could afford to avoid closer ties such as were foreseen in Mussolini's proposal for a four-power pact between Germany, Italy, Austria, and Hungary. Neither Hitler nor Neurath approved this idea, which Mussolini put forward as a convincing prelude to his visit to Berlin on 25–9 September 1937. By thus 'supplementing' the Axis[109] in an east–west direction he sought to strengthen Italy and at the same time arrive at a clearer estimation of Germany's influence in south-east Europe. But Berlin rejected the plan, not only because it implied a guarantee of Austrian independence. Neurath for his part wanted no links with weak states, which when it came to the point would only be 'a millstone round our necks'.[110] Berlin wanted in any case to prevent the formation of a bloc against Britain and France.[111] Even during Mussolini's visit, which was made the occasion for a massive display of German military strength, care was taken not to arouse British anxiety. The more pressure Mussolini applied and the more anti-British his arguments,[112] the more Hitler was at pains to keep open the British option. In this the foreign ministry fully agreed with him.[113] A *rapprochement* with Britain was still the theme. An early ending of the Spanish war, which Hitler and Mussolini declared to be desirable, could only be favourable to that purpose. However, Hitler also had a variant policy in mind: to cause Italy to be tied down in Spain as long as possible, so that Germany might take advantage of consequent friction between Italy on the one hand and France or Britain on the other, enabling her to embark on her own expansionist aims.[114]

Germany's lack of enthusiasm for the proposed four-power pact caused much ill-feeling in Rome. Her intention to effect the Anschluss sooner or later could not have been made clearer. The Austrian question disturbed the ostensible harmony between the dictators. An uneasy compromise was reached whereby Italy respected German 'special interests' in Austria, while Germany refrained from broaching any matters that might cause concern in that country. In this way the problem was kept open for a solution according to German wishes. Mussolini's visit secured nothing for Italy except assurances as to German intentions. The much-advertised common

---

[108] Funke, 'Deutsch-italienische Beziehungen', 837; Ciano, *Diary 1937–8*, 79. On Hitler's attitude towards Britain see also Irving, *War Path*, 56.

[109] Funke, 'Deutsch-italienische Beziehungen', 838.

[110] Ibid.

[111] Neurath's circular telegram of 30 July 1937 to German missions in Europe: *DGFP*, D. i, No. 1; Funke, 'Deutsch-italienische Beziehungen', 838.

[112] This attitude of Mussolini's is visible from the report by von Bülow–Schwante of 2 Oct. 1937, on conversations with the Duce during the latter's visit to Germany: *DGFP*, D. i, No. 2.

[113] See also Neurath's telegram of 30 July 1937 (n. 111 above).

[114] Text of the 'Hossbach memorandum' recording Hitler's statements on 5 Nov. 1937 in *DGFP*, D. i, No. 19, and *IMT* xxv. 402–13, PS-386.

interest against disturbers of the peace, and the promises of mutual defence against the Third International, did not amount to much. It cost Hitler nothing to grant Mussolini a free hand in the Mediterranean, and it brought the Italian dictator up against British interests; the result was a short period of attempts by Rome to gain freedom of action *vis-à-vis* Britain. Mussolini realized that his own political weight must be decisively reduced when, after the Anschluss, 'Greater Germany looms on our frontier with the growing strength of its seventy millions.'[115] Italy's accession to the anti-Comintern pact at the beginning of November 1937 did nothing to dispel this mistrust, nor did her withdrawal from the League of Nations. Italy became more dependent on Britain for the security of her Mediterranean interests. How much the verbal demonstrations of the Axis partners meant in practice was uncertain.

From 1936 onwards the German estimate of the European situation was that growing German strength and the application of pressure would succeed in inducing the Western powers to allow Germany a free hand in the east. But the means of pressure were insufficient. Neither armaments nor colonial claims were effective, nor the Axis, nor the illusory power-façade of Berlin, Rome, and Tokyo. Looked at closely, the political result consisted in no more than a hope that the Western powers would refrain from action in a given situation. This meagre achievement was reflected in conjectures and predictions of all kinds, which amounted to an admission of uncertainty as to where Germany really stood. Thus Mackensen, the state secretary for foreign affairs in December 1937, claimed to perceive signs in Britain and France that 'the path towards the realization of every political aim of ours in central and eastern Europe can no longer simply be blocked', a development which he attributed to Germany's recovered freedom of action;[116] while Ribbentrop in London gave a completely different prognosis in a confidential note for Hitler barely two weeks later. In his view an understanding with Britain was unattainable: 'England does not desire in close proximity a paramount (*übermächtig*) Germany which would be a constant menace to the British Isles. On this she will fight.'[117]

Ribbentrop described British policy as a strategy of gaining time for rearmament. Hitler, at the beginning of November 1937, expressed even more clearly than his ambassador the fact that Germany had no further room to manœuvre, given her abandonment of collective security and adoption of a policy of rearmament and autarky. He needed a war soon for economic reasons and because his advantage in arms was otherwise likewise to disappear. Thus, a clear view was reached concerning the attitude of the major powers. However, Hitler did not accept Ribbentrop's assessment without reservation. He was incapable of forming a dispassionate view of Britain. His 'programmatic' idea of her role seems to have shown enduring consistency despite much experience in a contrary sense.

[115] Ciano to the Italian ambassador in London, 16 Feb. 1938, quoted by Felice, 'Beobachtungen', 325; see also Funke, 'Deutsch-italienische Beziehungen', 839.

[116] To the Paris embassy, 21 Dec. 1937: *DGFP*, D. i, No. 88.

[117] Ibid., No. 93, note dated 2 Jan. 1938.

5. DECISION FOR WAR?

The question whether Hitler's 'decision' to embark on expansion by force dates from 1936–7, i.e. the period of the memorandum on the Four-year Plan and the Hossbach memorandum, raises a further problem: what kind of war did he have in mind, and what did he expect would be the attitude of the major powers? In his statement to the four commanders-in-chief and the foreign minister on 5 November 1937 he certainly laid down as a principle that the 'German space question' must be solved by 1943–5 at the latest; but the developments which he went on to discuss in detail were concerned only with an attack on Czechoslovakia or on both Austria and Czechoslovakia. Incidental mention only was made of a conflict with France and the part Czechoslovakia might play in such a case. Hitler's ideas were contradictory.[118] They reflected a mixture of preconceptions about the war for *Lebensraum* and his experiences in foreign policy since 1935, together with an attempt to convince the military leaders of the need to engage the armed forces at an early date.

Hitler argued that a weakening of France by internal social tensions might make it impossible for the French army to invade Germany, or that France might be involved in a military conflict with Italy. In such circumstances it might be possible to round off Germany's position in central Europe in the near future, perhaps even in 1938. In any case 'almost certainly Britain, and probably France as well, had already tacitly written off the Czechs'.

More interesting than his erroneous speculations on a French civil war or a war by Britain and France against Italy were Hitler's statements on 'planned' German action if the preconditions for a speedy solution did not present themselves. War must be waged at the latest in 1943–5 so as to make use of Germany's lead in the arms race, to prevent a fall in the standard of living, and to avoid the risk inherent in the 'ageing of the movement and of its leaders'. According to all that has long been known of Hitler's basic convictions, the war he had in mind could only have been one for *Lebensraum* in the east. Yet in speaking of 'planned action' in 1943–5 the document still refers only to Austria and Czechoslovakia. The conquest of these countries would provide foodstuffs for 5 or 6 million people, assuming that the compulsory emigration of 3 million 'was practicable'; strategically it would improve Germany's frontier, and twelve divisions could be added to her forces.

There was no mention here of a war against Russia. On the contrary, Soviet intervention, it was said, would be countered by the swiftness of the operation. Hitler was at pains to convince the diplomatic and military chiefs that all experience indicated that the Western powers would not intervene. France would not dare, if Britain stood aside, to open an offensive in the west, which would in all probability be halted by the German fortifications. There was a brief mention that Germany 'had to reckon with two hate-inspired antagonists, Britain and France, to whom a German colossus in the centre of Europe was a thorn in the flesh'.

Hitler's varying judgement of British intentions has been described as an

---

[118] On the interpretation cf. Bussmann, 'Hoßbach-Niederschrift', and Henrikson, 'Nürnberger Dokument'. On the lack of co-ordination in political and strategic matters within the German leadership see Messerschmidt *et al.*, 'Tableau de la situation stratégique', 105–26.

'ambivalent intermediate course' on his part,[119] but it is rather to be seen as an adaptation of Hitler's ideas to the British attitude. On his own estimate of future possibilities he had no course left but to continue as he had begun: for economic, financial, and technological reasons he was committed to taking the offensive, with or without Britain and if necessary against her. When the idea of an alliance fell through, he hoped at least not to have to fight Britain in his bid to achieve continental hegemony by force. 'Without Britain' was a short-lived hope that recurred by fits and starts, because an anti-British policy entailed incalculable risks. But from 1937 onwards this variant was objectively impossible, though Hitler did not yet fully perceive it as such. 'Without Britain' was in fact as empty a speculation as the original hope of an alliance[120]—at any rate if German expansion was to go beyond Austria and Czechoslovakia.

The exertion of pressure by means of colonial claims, in the hope of bringing about an alliance, was now devoid of purpose. Accordingly this propaganda was damped down. Hitler realized that such claims were less and less effectual as a foreign-policy weapon. Henceforth they were merely routine imperialist desiderata, which can be disregarded here as they had no effect on Hitler's actions and the course of events that led to war.[121]

It is a decisive feature of Hitler's statements on 5 November 1937 that he was now determined to resort to force as soon as opportunity offered. This can scarcely be called a 'decision' to make war, in the sense of a tangible deviation from former policy, but it expressed that policy in new and concrete terms.

On 21 December 1937 the deployment orders for 'Operation Green' (the attack on Czechoslovakia) were redrafted by the army leaders in accordance with Hitler's offensive thinking. The plan of June 1937, like the general 'Directive for the uniform preparation for war by the Wehrmacht', dated 24 June 1937,[122] had not been geared to specific offensive aims. The partial redrafting of these orders[123] took place without Hitler's participation. Blomberg's doubts, expressed on 5 November, were soon overcome. Blomberg, Keitel, and Jodl used the occasion to emphasize the strategic authority of the Wehrmacht commanders over the separate branches of the armed forces.[124] The link with Hitler's address of 5 November is seen by most historians in the final sentence: 'When Germany has achieved complete preparation for war in all fields, then the military conditions will have been created for carrying out an offensive war against Czechoslovakia, so that the solution of the German

---

[119] Hillgruber, 'England', 75.

[120] On the military-political interpretation of the Hossbach memorandum see also Kielmannsegg, 'Hoßbach-Besprechung', and Dülffer, 'Weisungen'; and cf. Deist, III.III.4 above.

[121] We may agree with Henke (*England*, 107) when he refers to the speculations about Hitler's ultimate aims and argues from the Hossbach memorandum that Hitler's ideas at the end of 1937 were firmly concentrated on the 'continental phase' of his 'programme'. For details on the change of emphasis regarding colonies see Hildebrand, *Reich*, 157 ff., 523.

[122] *IMT* xxxiv. 732 ff., doc. 175-C; cf. Dülffer, 'Weisungen', on the directive and its supplement.

[123] Supplementary directive, repr. in *IMT* xxxiv. 745 ff., doc. 175-C. The revised version of sect. II, pt. 2, of the directive of 24 June 1937 was issued as annex I on 21 Dec. 1937. This deployment order for Operation Green is printed in *DGFP*, D. vii, appendix III, pp. 635 ff.; cf, Müller, *Heer*, 247 ff.

[124] Müller, *Heer*, 246.

problem of living-space can be carried to a victorious end even if one or other of the great powers intervenes against us.'[125] It may be wondered whether Hitler at this time really thought that 'in normal conditions' Germany's space problem could be solved, for two generations to come, by a war against her two south-eastern neighbours. This seems doubtful in the light of his programmatic writings. Possibly he left the point intentionally unclear when approving the revision of the 'Green' deployment plan.

Starting from this basis, the 'graduated plan' so much discussed by historians recedes into an obscure future. If the two neighbour states were to be overrun by lightning campaigns in 1943–5, this still left Russia completely out of account. A confrontation with the United States and, if necessary, with Britain in the later 1940s[126] can hardly have figured in Hitler's calculations towards the end of 1937. It is, however, indicative of the thinking of the defence ministry that it was regarded as possible to make war against Czechoslovakia even if the Wehrmacht was not completely ready and if the Soviet Union should come to that country's aid. Half a sentence is devoted to this question. It would be hard to imagine a more eloquent illustration of the underrating of Moscow and the style in which false diagnoses were expressed in matters of military policy.

On 5 November 1937 scarcely any of Hitler's conditions were met, either in home or in foreign affairs. The equipment of the Wehrmacht and the formation of the officer corps were far from being 'nearly completed', as Hitler's military advisers pointed out. But on one point he was right: the Wehrmacht's lead in terms of modernity and mobility was bound to diminish; German reserves were melting away. Anyone planning short, swift blows could, as Hitler argued, not wait for opportunities indefinitely.

From this point onwards Hitler was not pursuing a policy at the risk of war, but a war policy, which he had thought out in advance and had been preparing since 1933. In this sense he had a 'purpose' and is not to be assigned to the category of a diplomat and strategist lacking a specific aim, such as is postulated by a certain theory of war and foreign policy.[127] But Hitler's analyses were at all times conditioned by historical, political, and psychological prejudices. Wishful thinking, pride in his 'superior' judgement, and the exhilaration of partial successes prevented him from taking a sober view of the chances of achieving his expansionist aims in the least favourable circumstances. Often shrewd, incisive, and successful in particular matters, in his policy as a whole he lacked caution, patience, and clear-sightedness. The military leaders who carried out his ideas did so against their professional judgement. For them too, war had been the intended goal of German

---

[125] Here again the attack on Czechoslovakia is represented as an operation designed to solve Germany's 'space problem'. This misunderstanding of Hitler's thought follows logically from the Hossbach record, which Jodl probably had before him when revising the directive. Cf. Kielmansegg, 'Hoßbach-Besprechung', 268, and Gackenholz, 'Reichskanzlei', 476. Hossbach, *Wehrmacht*, 165, repeats the idea that Hitler intended to solve the 'space problem' by attacking Czechoslovakia and Austria by 1943–5 at the latest. On 'Case Green' see also Deist, III.III.4 above.

[126] Hildebrand, *Foreign Policy*, 54: 'most certainly . . . opposition from the USA.'

[127] e.g. Aron, *Paix et guerre*, 27, 33 ff.

efforts since 1933, but they did not want it so soon. Blomberg and Fritsch, both of whom resigned in the spring of 1938, did not believe the Wehrmacht could win a European war in the near future. After 1937 they had no doubt that such a war was planned; but they did not press for a basic politico-strategic plan which might have made Hitler unfold his future intentions at an earlier date.

6. A Second-best Alliance: The Anti-Comintern Pact

The powers with which Germany, Italy, and Japan had especially to reckon, positively or negatively, in their course towards war were Britain and, more remotely, the United States: both on account of their lack of sympathy for Fascist ideas, and because their political weight enabled them to resist the pull of events in Europe and East Asia respectively.

The anti-Comintern pact of 25 November 1936[128] is of more interest for its prehistory—the German foreign ministry was virtually excluded from its preparation—than for its content. It reflected a move away from China, contrary to the preferences of the military and business leaders, and also the uncertainty of Germany's plan as between Japan and Britain. The 'pact' was no more than an agreement to exchange information on the activities of the Third International, and the 'secret supplementary protocol' was merely a pledge of neutrality and consultation, not a military alliance.[129]

Thus, the anti-Comintern pact, like the Axis, was only a patching together of divergent political interests. As Hitler had hoped to induce Britain, as well as or instead of Italy, to concert her policy with his, so too he initially had ideas of associating Britain with the anti-Comintern pact.[130] This idea also lay behind Ribbentrop's mission to London. The attempt failed, as did a Japanese initiative. The negotiations for the supplementary protocol and the formulation of the preamble were affected by concern for the British attitude. The Japanese government were much more cautious than the army, which pressed for speedy action. The Japanese navy was especially reluctant, on account of British and American reactions. The outbreak of the Spanish civil war spurred Hitler to hasten the conclusion of the pact, while Tokyo was influenced by the fact that the Soviet Union signed a treaty of mutual assistance with Outer Mongolia in April 1936. Shortly before this, Berlin was still hesitant about the supplementary protocol. Even Ribbentrop was concerned 'not to disturb the British line of German policy'.[131]

---

[128] *RGBl.* (1937), ii. 28 ff.; *Documents on International Affairs, 1936,* 297 ff.

[129] Sommer, *Deutschland und Japan,* 45; Martin, 'Deutsch-japanische Beziehungen', 462; id., 'Das deutsche Militär', 191–207.

[130] Sommer, *Deutschland und Japan,* 32; Jones, *Japan's New Order,* 24–5. Earlier British attempts at a *rapprochement* with Japan, emanating from Chamberlain and the Treasury, had failed owing to Japanese lack of interest, foreign office scepticism, and US disapproval. However, the state of Anglo-Japanese relations offered little encouragement to Hitler's global plans: see recently *Anglo-Japanese Alienation,* and Haggie, *Britannia at Bay.*

[131] Sommer, *Deutschland und Japan,* 33 (quoting unpublished notes by H. von Raumer).

In view of the differences of opinion among the Japanese leaders, the pact cannot be regarded as signifying an about-turn in Tokyo's foreign policy. The outbreak of the 'China incident' in July 1937 had in any case narrowed Japan's freedom of action and introduced a fresh source of tension with the West. Altogether the anti-Comintern pact was ineffectual as an instrument against the Soviet Union. Moreover, the attack on China indicated that Japanese policy was shifting in a direction contrary to the intention of the pact. Thus, Chiang Kai-shek was forced to co-operate with the Communists against the Japanese. It became increasingly clear that Berlin would have to choose between Tokyo and Nanking. The Wilhelmstrasse and the war ministry had more and more difficulty in maintaining their old friendly contacts with Chiang and the military and financial aid that went with them.[132] After the conclusion of the anti-Comintern pact Neurath had once more succeeded in convincing Chiang of Germany's good intentions, but, when the Japanese–Chinese war broke out, Hitler and Ribbentrop finally took over the conduct of Far Eastern policy. In this area Ribbentrop was constantly the driving force, while Hitler hesitated for some time.[133] Although the Japanese were unable to convince Berlin that they were pursuing an anti-Comintern policy in China, their pressure was such that the foreign ministry had to give ground. Its assessment of the situation was correct, however: viz. that Japan's successes in China could not be favourable to her strategic position *vis-à-vis* the Soviet Union, because she would have to reckon with the determined hostility of the Chinese and thus risk a war on two fronts.[134]

The only immediate possibility for Berlin was to put more substance into the Axis—an equally nebulous concept—in answer to the cooling of Anglo-German relations since 1937.[135] Thus, Italy's accession to the anti-Comintern pact was logically an expression of the growing solidarity of the Axis powers against Britain rather than against the Soviet Union. None the less, Hitler continued to give Britain first priority in his own designs, whereas Ribbentrop, in the course of 1937, came to the conclusion that his mission was a failure and that German policy should be framed accordingly—a conception which led logically in the direction of the German–Soviet pact.[136]

Ribbentrop's variant of German expansionist policy was aimed above all at countering the illusion that an arrangement could be reached with Britain allowing Germany a free hand in the east. In his despatch on the coronation of George VI (21 May 1937)[137] he already expressed doubts and pointed to German friendship with Italy and Japan, which 'should in every way be taken into account'. Other sceptical

[132] Sommer, *Deutschland und Japan*, 56 ff.; literature cited in Martin, 'Japans Weg'.

[133] Bloss, 'Chinapolitik'.

[134] Weizsäcker to embassy in Tokyo, 28 July 1937; *DGFP*, D. i, No. 472; Sommer, *Deutschland und Japan*, 64.

[135] Henke, *England*, 95 ff.

[136] Hildebrand, *Foreign Policy*, 59.

[137] See Henke's interpretations in *England*, 64–5. Text now published in the apologia by Ribbentrop's widow, A. Ribbentrop, *Kriegsschuld*; this also contains Ribbentrop's report of 28 Dec. 1937 on the conclusion of his mission to Britain, which formed the basis of his report of 2 Jan. 1938 to Hitler (see n. 138): cf Michalka, 'Widerstand'. On Ribbentrop's conception in general see Michalka, *Ribbentrop*.

reports had previously reached Berlin from London. Ribbentrop developed this appraisal into a new prescription for foreign policy. In his end-of-mission report of 28 December 1937 he maintained that Britain would adhere to her traditional balance-of-power policy—a view that Hitler did not necessarily share. Britain, according to Ribbentrop, would always support France's policy in Eastern Europe; she would never accept German ascendancy in Europe, and therefore would join France in fighting Germany if a German–Soviet war broke out. On 2 January 1938 Ribbentrop submitted his recommendations to Hitler: (1) to continue ostensibly to seek an understanding with Britain, while respecting the interests of Germany's own friends; (2) to bring about a system of alliances against Britain, in all secrecy but with great determination—i.e. consolidating the German friendship with Italy and Japan, and extending it to all states whose interests were directly or indirectly in line with Germany's. 'Only thus can we confront Britain, whether it be for a settlement (*Ausgleich*) some day or for a conflict.'

The combination of Ribbentrop's programme with Hitler's, and the changing emphases that resulted, led to a mixture of aggressive expansionism, transparent attempts at deception, and blindness to reality, which was characteristic of the spring of 1938 and ensuing months.

The 'triangle of world powers'—Germany, Italy, and Japan—which Ribbentrop imagined as a concentration of forces that could in some circumstances compel Britain to inaction,[138] remained a dream. To this extent Ribbentrop's warning—'It would be dangerous to renounce secure friendships and not to choose others, because of an uncertain British friendship'—rested on an insecure basis. The ambassador, soon to be foreign minister, urged that 'Germany, Italy, and Japan must hold fast together'; but were these friendships too not 'uncertain'?

It is only relatively the case that Italy's accession to the anti-Comintern pact in November 1937 gave it an anti-British thrust. In its German–Japanese form the pact reflected such divergent interests that one can hardly speak of a 'thrust' of any kind. Japan, after the invasion of China, had not the necessary strength, and Italy could not fill the gap. Formally speaking, Mussolini did not commit himself against the Soviet Union—the supplementary agreement did not apply to Italy—but this did not make the pact any more of a threat to Britain. In design, though not in practice, it seemed to represent a combination that might face Britain with a war on three fronts if she opposed Germany's continental policy. The weakness was, however, that the pact was not a military alliance and that it greatly overrated the extent to which Germany's co-signatories were prepared to act in her interest. There was not the least sign that Japan would let herself be involved in a war with Britain for the sake of German designs in Europe.

Although Japan as a member of this pact could do little to help Germany in her difficulties—her independent activities were much more effective against the West—Hitler allowed himself to be drawn in the direction advocated by Ribbentrop, contrary to his own basic ideas. The withdrawal of German military

---

[138] Memorandum of 2 Jan. 1938 for Hitler: *DGFP*, D. i, No. 93, pp. 162 ff.

advisers from China, the cessation of deliveries to Chiang, and the open support for Japanese policy in October 1937 add up to a course of action that, if not anti-British,[139] was at all events calculated to put a strain on Anglo-German relations.

For Hitler's aims in Europe, Italy came more to the fore as a second-best partner—no longer in an anti-Soviet combination, such as he had hoped ideally to form in concert with Italy and Britain as well, but only as a possible ally against Britain,[140] though in such a case he still hoped that an armed clash could be avoided.

Hitler's attitude to Britain varied to a striking extent as the time of action drew near, that is to say the transition to Germany's expansionist phase. This did not make him more 'uncertain' in his estimate of Britain than Ribbentrop. Their positions were based on quite different long-term perspectives. Hitler was still a long way from the central European imperialism of the Kaiser's Germany, aiming at overseas expansion and eventually world power. His objective was the racial and ideological one of acquiring *Lebensraum* in the East. This aim, he thought, need not necessarily provoke British opposition, provided Britain was governed by statesmen of his calibre and way of thinking. What caused him vexation and doubt was his experiences with 'inadequate' British leaders. But his doubts always left room for hope. This state of uncertainty is perhaps one of the chief reasons why, up to the very start of the expansionist phase, he had achieved no more than an alliance system that did not deserve the name and itself represented a state of political vacillation. His ambivalence *vis-à-vis* Britain was expressed in the often quoted conversations with Carl Jacob Burckhardt in September 1937,[141] which reveal a peculiar love–hate attitude on his part. It angered him that Britain interfered in matters that concerned 'the German sphere'. He was obliged to recognize that his calculations might be frustrated by elements of resistance that appeared to him senseless. Yet he did not make Britain his chief enemy for all that. When he nevertheless said 'England is our No. 1 enemy',[142] he had in mind the desired partner which refused to join in his plans out of political egotism, which thwarted his programme and put him in danger for lack of time. It must be recognized that this love–hate was deeply rooted. What vexed Hitler was not only British interference in 'German' matters but, still more, the realization that Britain would oppose German ascendancy on the Continent, which to him represented the key to still wider ambitions.[143]

For this reason Hitler was all the more amenable to arguments that Britain need not, after all, be reckoned with as an enemy.[144] He was probably also misled by the fact that leading British statesmen generally spoke in cautious, allusive terms that

---

[139] Hillgruber, 'Weltpolitische Lage', 281.

[140] Henke, *England*, 99.

[141] Burckhardt, *Danziger Mission*, 97 ff.

[142] Address to Kreisleiter (circuit leaders), 23 Nov. 1937, on the inauguration of the Ordensburg (party training school) at Sonthofen; Speer, *Inside*, 533; Henke, *England*, 119; Hildebrand, *Reich*, 536.

[143] Cf. his later statement on the connection between hegemony in Europe and the 'way to world domination': *Goebbels Diaries 1942–3*, entry for 8 May 1943.

[144] Details in Henke, *England*, 101 ff.

left room for differences of interpretation. The upshot was that in the spring of 1938 Hitler was less committed to an anti-British view than his newly appointed foreign minister. The 'second-best alliance system' corresponded closely to his picture of the world and to the political possibilities. Given the course he had chosen to pursue, nothing more was to be hoped for in the way of friends or partners. Germany's quest for allies can in a sense be seen as a reflection of British policy as it was perceived in Berlin; but Berlin had no single, doubt-free conception of the problem. Some advocated a change of policy towards Britain, others were for keeping the door open.

7. OVERT EXPANSIONISM AND APPEASEMENT

In London too it proved difficult to co-ordinate varying points of view. Foreign policy was not regarded as the shortest way to mobilize a front against Germany, which was recognized to be the chief potential enemy. London evaded France's constant pressure for more binding military agreements. When, in December 1937, Eden finally recommended closer military contact with the French and Belgians in case Britain had to fulfil her obligation to either country under the Locarno treaty,[145] the chiefs of staff were not in favour. They wanted to leave open the possibility of a *détente* with Germany, and feared France would use any closer co-operation for her own ends, to the detriment of Anglo-German relations. This, however, was not the opinion of the cabinet, which discussed Eden's recommendation and the comments of the chiefs of staff in mid-February, a few days before Eden's resignation. The cabinet confirmed that a British army commitment on the continent was lowest on its list of priorities.[146] The proposal was to send only three divisions at first, to be reinforced later by two more—a force that did not make it worth while holding staff talks.[147] Eden could only secure a decision that the RAF would hold staff talks with the French. In the event of an Anglo-Italian war in the Mediterranean, the chiefs of staff feared that if France were involved Germany would also intervene with the risk of a world war, the outcome of which could be less confidently predicted than that of an Anglo-Italian conflict.[148]

Eden had by now reached the conclusion that it was wiser to make clear British readiness to accept the dictators' challenge. He no longer believed in a *détente*. All experience indicated, in his view, that it could only improve the situation if Britain showed determination to fulfil her treaty commitments. Shortly afterwards, at the beginning of April 1938, the cabinet decided that it was no longer possible to take a merely theoretical view of the country's Locarno obligations. Chamberlain gave

---

[145] Gibbs, *Strategy*, i. 624.
[146] Ibid. 628; PRO Cab. Cons. 5 (38) 12, 51–4. Bond, *British Military Policy*, points out that the capabilities of the British army were deliberately underrated. The government was dominated by wishful thinking and above all by concern for public opinion. On this important aspect see Adamthwaite. 'Le gouvernement britannique', 349–61.
[147] Gibbs, *Strategy*, 628.
[148] Ibid. 627.

approval in principle for staff talks with France. His opinion was much influenced by the suddenness of the German coup in Austria. It was in the interest of Britain and France for each to know what part the other could play in emergency.[149]

Unlike the military, Halifax and Chamberlain believed that a war with Italy could be ruled out. They also thought Japan was too deeply involved in China to be a threat to the Empire. The British position as outlined by Chamberlain on 11 April 1938 may be described as a consensus that staff talks should be based on the assumption of Britain, France, and Belgium going to war with Germany as a result of their Locarno obligations, but that Britain would on no account again send an expeditionary force to the Continent—a view that Duff Cooper in the cabinet criticized as unrealistic.

The weakness of the politico-strategic argument concerning a continental commitment lay in its one-sided preoccupation with West European possibilities. The committee of imperial defence thought that in the event of war Germany would attempt to deliver a knock-out blow in the West—not primarily against France, because of the strength of the Maginot line, but against Britain's industrial and economic potential. Inadequate as this presumption was, all the memoranda and discussions were dominated by one thought: the aggressor whom Britain would have to fight could only be Germany.

As regards possible German coups in Eastern Europe, British policy was not yet fixed. From this point of view Hitler's idea of being able to act 'without Britain' seems to have had some justification. The British, who were only now looking for ways of fulfilling their Locarno commitment if they had to do so, were to need a good deal more experience of Hitler's political practices before they would embark on a policy of curbing German ambitions in the east at the risk of war. For the present Chamberlain sought ways of coming to an understanding with Hitler on East European matters; it appeared that concessions might be made in the south-east, though this policy should be pursued with extreme caution.

Chamberlain's conception of appeasement was intended as a long-term strategy against Hitler. The hopes and disappointments of the period until the outbreak of war arose from the tension between contrary purposes and, especially, each side's failure to comprehend the other's motives. This phase began with a conversation at Berchtesgaden in November 1937 between Hitler and Halifax, who was Eden's deputy in the foreign office and soon to be his successor.[150] Chamberlain's overall design was to involve Hitler in a European peace system, developing an Anglo-German accord into a general one. To secure Germany's participation Britain was prepared to make concessions in Europe and over colonies. If Hitler had not been bent on war there could have been a general clearance of revisionist topics. Halifax

---

[149] Gibbs, *Strategy*, 630. On the general relationship between the Western powers and Nazi Germany see *Die Westmächte und das Dritte Reich*. On the literature of appeasement see important references by Niedhart in *Neue Politische Literatur*, e.g. 'Weltherrschaft versus World Appeasement'. See also Kennedy, *Realities behind Diplomacy*; Kennedy and Spence, 'On Appeasement'; Rock, *British Appeasement*; *The Fascist Challenge*.

[150] Schmidt's record, for Hitler, of the Hitler–Halifax conversation of 19 Nov. 1937, *DGFP*, D. i. No. 31, pp. 55 ff.

indicated that the British government was not wedded to the status quo; there must be 'recognition of changed circumstances, when such need arose', but by means of 'reasonable agreements'. Hitler's attitude to a collective-security system and to disarmament was of interest to Britain. All other matters, Halifax observed, belonged to a category of changes in the European order that would probably come about sooner or later: here Chamberlain's emissary mentioned Danzig, Austria, and Czechoslovakia. Hitler's reaction was one of marked reserve. He spoke with relative coolness about the colonial question, while representing it as the only real issue between Germany and Britain. If it were settled that would be welcome; if not, he could only note the fact with regret. On disarmament and security he spoke evasively and at length. In general his attitude was such as to leave Halifax with no specific indications of how the new British policy might be applied. Hitler's statements, which were often enlightening in themselves, imperfectly concealed his determination not to let his ambitions be thwarted by any international agreements. Only on one point did he abandon his reserve: Germany would 'definitely not return to a League which regarded it as its task to oppose the natural development of political relations'.[151] As for the affairs of Eastern and south-eastern Europe, in his view they were not a matter for talks between Britain and Germany: he was mistrustful of unauthorized intervention.

The dialogue shows clearly to a present-day observer that Hitler was not amenable to the policy of appeasement. Already determined to attack Czechoslovakia when the moment was ripe, he spoke of relations with Prague as a problem that could be solved if the Czechs were 'reasonable'; all they had to do was to treat the Sudeten Germans properly. As regards Austria, it was to be hoped that the treaty of 11 July 1936[152] would 'lead to the removal of all difficulties'. Halifax had tried to make the proposed Anglo-German understanding acceptable by saying that it was not meant to be detrimental either to the Axis or to close Anglo-French relations. Clearly Britain was prepared to make large concessions, but not to guarantee Hitler's rear absolutely, should he embark on warlike action.

The British offer of a 'settlement' was highly inconvenient to Hitler's timetable as it had been planned in 1936, and again fourteen days before the conversation with Halifax. It was, however, a step forward that the British had declared themselves indifferent to changes in south-east Europe. Did this amount to a free hand for Germany in an eastward direction, which Weizsäcker had defined as one of the objects of Germany's policy towards Britain?[153] In Weizsäcker's opinion Britain wanted 'military quiescence, particularly in the West'; it was a question of finding out how much she was prepared to pay for such tranquillity. In matters of rearmament, he added, time was on Britain's side and Germany 'did not have an unlimited period for negotiations'.

Thus, the foreign ministry was also concerned with the 'natural development of political relations'. It assumed, more clearly than Hitler, that a course of action

[151] Ibid. 63.
[152] The so-called 'gentlemen's agreement', *DGFP*, D. i, No. 152, pp. 278 ff.
[153] Note of 10 Nov. 1937 for Bülow, ibid., No. 21, p. 40.

'against Britain' was to be avoided, because a war with Britain could not be contemplated for a long time; but it also pointed out that only limited time was available for a policy of expansion by force, such as Hitler had so clearly announced to his chief subordinates on 5 November. Weizsäcker's recommendations—mutual disclosure of armament programmes, an Anglo-German committee to examine Germany's colonial claims, and consultations among the Locarno powers if and when critical situations arose—might be described as a 'moderate conservative variant of German great power policy',[154] as they were quite different from Hitler's ideas as to the next stages of the German attack; but they were equally based on the consideration that time was short. Shortness of time could only be a problem with calculations that involved the use of force. Weizsäcker exposed himself, at least, to the misunderstanding that such was the logic of his plan. His ideas differed in this respect from those he had developed in June 1937 in preparation for Neurath's visit to London.[155] The premiss that 'We do not want a war' was no longer unambiguously formulated in November, but rather modified to 'We cannot contemplate a war just yet.'

But no opposition was strong enough to obstruct Hitler's chosen course, whether it led to war or not. His purpose was no longer to sound out the extent of British concessions, but to choose a favourable moment for action. Halifax had not gone so far as to offer a settlement of the Danzig, Austrian, and Czechoslovak questions 'in accordance with German wishes',[156] to the extent that Hitler's intentions had figured in the discussion; Hitler had indeed kept those intentions to himself as far as possible. Halifax had in mind a neutralization of Czechoslovakia, a kind of Swiss solution.[157] He considered the Danzig and Corridor situation 'an absurdity' and thought he should mediate between Germany and Poland, but did not desire to see Germany dominant. Yet he hoped to achieve useful results with Chamberlain's strategy, by showing Hitler that he could obtain much of what he wanted if he would abandon the threat of war.[158]

Halifax's visit brought to light the incompatibility of the appeasement policy with Hitler's intentions, either in the middle or the long term. Halifax had the impression that two sets of completely different values had been in contact.[159] Hitler saw more clearly than the British how far the practical aims were irreconcilable. Chamberlain and Halifax for their part saw no reason not to continue as they had begun. They were even 'well satisfied',[160] though recognizing that Hitler did not want a general agreement.[161] Not long after the visit, however, it became clear to the 'appeasers' that Hitler was little impressed by their proposals. The process of expansion by stages was set in motion.

[154] Hildebrand, *Foreign Policy*, 57.
[155] Cf. *Weizsäcker-Papiere*, 115 ff.
[156] Hillgruber, 'Weltpolitische Lage', 282.
[157] Cowling, *Impact*, 276.
[158] Ibid.
[159] Halifax, *Fulness of Days*, 189; Henke, *England*, 117–18.
[160] Letter from Halifax to Henderson, 24 Nov. 1937, quoted in Henke, *England*, 121.
[161] Halifax's report to foreign office; cf. Henke, *England*, 117.

The alterations of the map in 1938 seemed to be an automatic consequence of Germany's growing political and military strength. German pressure on south-east Europe increased. In economic matters it had been systematically exercised since 1933, with a view to political dominance. To this extent, at least, the economic imperialism of the foreign ministry held its ground alongside Hitler's aims, though it did not play more than an auxiliary role. Germany sought to loosen the cohesion of the Little Entente by creating bilateral economic links that were more or less indissoluble, as far as the agricultural countries of south-east Europe were concerned, because of their dependence on the German import market. This was an economic preparation for war and was also intended to secure German influence in the Danube basin against other powers, especially France but also Italy. Important early stages were the commerical treaties of 1 May 1934 with Yugoslavia and agreements with Hungary in February 1934.[162] The preferences granted by Berlin were calculated so as to be a means of political pressure if necessary. This policy took on fresh emphasis as Germany expanded south-eastwards in 1938. Romania was now also drawn more firmly into the German sphere.[163] This successful advance was only possible because of the great mistrust aroused by Soviet policy in the Balkan area.

On the world horizon there were as yet no developments to cause Germany alarm. The Soviet Union seemed for the present to be out of action on account of Stalin's purges. In the United States Roosevelt's government was showing a heightened interest in European events, but the power and influence of the isolationists still seemed unbroken, as was shown by the history of the neutrality acts of 1935-7. The isolationists wished to stay out of a European conflict even it it meant commercial losses, and therefore proposed an arms embargo to be applied against all parties to such a conflict.[164] The president's freedom of action in foreign affairs was restricted by the neutrality laws, as was shown over the Abyssinian conflict and *vis-à-vis* Franco's Spain.[165] Hence, Roosevelt's pressure for closer involvement in security and anti-war measures lacked a solid foundation at this time. Many Americans were not interested in the old continent; Hitler's revisionism did not confront the United States with acute political and strategic problems, at least until 1938. The occupation of the Rhineland, for instance, aroused no anxiety in America;[166]

[162] On trends of trading policy with south-east Europe cf. Volkmann, II.iv.i, II.vi.6 above; also Schröder, 'Hegemonialstellung', citing important literature.

[163] Hillgruber, *Deutsch-rumänische Beziehungen*; Broszat, 'Deutschland'; Marguerat, *Le IIIe Reich*. Kaiser in *Economic Diplomacy* argues that Hitler's foreign economic policy was part of an expansionist foreign policy aiming at war. This view is criticized by Adamthwaite ('War Origins', 110-11) with reference to the well-known controversies concerning National Socialist foreign policy. See also Overy, 'Hitler's War', 272-91. The Western powers pursued a compliant policy in south-east Europe until Munich, after which they sought to regain influence there. Marguerat sees this change as a *point d'appui* for an energetic policy, and there were those in the foreign office too who wished to stop Germany's 'Drang nach Osten'. Schneider, 'Machtpolitik', 211-22, points out that already in Weimar days German governments endeavoured to use economic means to paralyse the French security system. From 1937 onwards the aspect of power politics became increasingly important.

[164] Niedhart, *Großbritannien*, 276 ff.; Schwabe, 'Die entfernteren Staaten'; on US isolationism in general see Schwabe, *Amerikanischer Isolationismus*.

[165] Divine, *Reluctant Belligerent*, 2 ff.   [166] Offner, *Appeasement*.

Roosevelt had viewed Hitler's policy with a critical eye since 1933, but even he saw no threat to his own country. His 'quarantine' speech at Chicago on 5 October 1937 was directed against Japan rather than against Germany, and was more a general warning than an indication of an already formed policy.[167] A trade embargo as a means of curbing aggression was not necessarily a threat to Hitler's plans, and it was not yet systematically applied in any case. The commercial disputes that arose were more the result of German dilatoriness over payment. Roosevelt's idea of a moral front against the totalitarian states[168] also remained a paper scheme only. Yet it was probably already the case, as the German ambassador in Washington, Dieckhoff, reported at the beginning of December 1937, that the United States would throw their weight into the balance in the event of a conflict 'in which the existence of Great Britain is at stake'.[169] The ambassador showed a balanced judgement between the isolationist groups and those that were prepared to assume international responsibilities. But from all this Hitler only drew the conclusion that a policy that was not directly aimed against Britain could be pursued without serious risk. His next steps no longer called for the special preconditions that he had laid down on 5 November 1937.

(a) The Anschluss

From the time of the agreement of 11 July 1936 Hitler's policy towards Austria was one of ideological penetration until the situation became ripe for the Anschluss. Goebbels saw the treaty as 'the necessary condition for [an Austrian version of] 30 January 1933'.[170] The Goebbels-controlled press painted the picture of an Austria that 'belonged' to Greater Germany on grounds of race, politics, history, and ideology. In so doing it touched chords in Germany that did not need to be artificially stimulated. Hitler's foreign policy sought to isolate Austria and avoid

---

[167] Similarly Moltmann, 'Weltpolitische Lage', 153. Moltmann does not regard the guarantee speech as a 'historic turning-point' in pre-war US policy. On US and British appeasement see also Schröder. 'Economic Appeasement', 82–97.

[168] Offner, *Appeasement*, 218 ff.; Helbich, *Roosevelt*, 195 ff.; Schwabe, 'Die entfernteren Staaten', 279.

[169] *DGFP*, D. i, No. 423, pp. 653 ff. (quotation, p. 656). On US policy towards Europe see also Reynolds, *Creation of the Anglo-American Alliance*. Macdonald, in *US, Britain and Appeasement* emphasizes UK–US strategic rivalries. Reynolds criticizes Roosevelt's indecision in the matter of neutrality; but, as Macdonald points out, the difficulty that he had in encouraging Britain to adopt a tougher line was to a great extent due to the lack of general support for an anti-Axis policy. Chamberlain found the 'quarantine' speech unhelpful. See also *Roosevelt and Foreign Affairs*, 2nd Series. Lowenthal, 'Roosevelt', 413–40, speaks of the president's indecision. The naval talks approved by him in Jan. 1938 were directed against Japan; the motto 'Pacific first' held good until the spring of that year. In Sept. Roosevelt sought a peaceful solution to the Czechoslovak crisis; but already in Nov. 1938 he called for an 'air force in being' of 10,000 aircraft and a production capacity of 10,000 planes per annum to safeguard the Western hemisphere. The joint defence board identified Germany as enemy No. 1 from Apr. 1939 onwards: Rainbow Plan I, *Hemispheric Defence*, June 1939 (official document JB, No. 325 (Serial 642-1), RG 225, NA).

[170] Koerner, *Österreich-Anschluß*, 63; Eichstädt, *Dollfuß*, 108 ff.; Jacobsen, *Außenpolitik*, 435 ff. Leopold, the Austrian Nazi leader, took the view that Hitler, by means of the treaty, had pointed the way to the penetration of Austria and its party-political alignment with Germany: letter of 22 Aug. 1937, BA NS 10/281, Adjutantur des Führers. Cf. Schausberger, 'Österreich', 739.

anything that might provoke the Stresa powers to intervene more actively. But tension between the two neighbour states was increasing. The Austrian Nazis under their leader Leopold adopted a challenging attitude. The chancellor, Schuschnigg, refused to take the 'nationalist opposition' into his government. Thus, there were enough internal problems to give Hitler a handle for interference. Did he in fact need an external success[171] to compensate for the events at the beginning of February, the changes at top level of the army and the Wehrmacht,[172] with their adverse effects in and outside the armed forces? Against this is the fact that in March Göring was evidently pressing more strongly than Hitler for an energetic solution of the Austrian problem.[173] But Hitler used the deployment plan to distract the military chiefs from the 'scandal of the generals', and postpone a session of the Reich court martial that was to investigate the latter.[174] The indirect method he adopted, the browbeating of Schuschnigg at Berchtesgaden on 12 February, and the subsequent bogus appeal for help by Seyss-Inquart gave the Western powers no chance to implement their guarantee. The idea of an Austrian 'invitation' evidently came from Weizsäcker; Hitler cast it in the form of a spurious telegram. This was one of his lightning actions. Schuschnigg believed that at Berchtesgaden he had still managed to preserve his country's sovereignty. What had he had to concede? His foreign policy now had to be co-ordinated with Germany's, the ban on the Austrian NSDAP was to be lifted, economic relations were to be stepped up, and general staff talks were to be held regularly.[175] Hitler was certain that with the Berchtesgaden agreement 'the Austrian problem would be automatically solved'.[176] He did not want a solution by force at this time, because Germany's external situation was becoming more and more favourable and her military power greater year by year.

Hitler could be certain that Mussolini would acquiesce: Göring had brought back that assurance from his visit to Rome in January 1937. Italy would not again 'mount guard on the Brenner' against Germany,[177] although Mussolini's reactions to the Rome conversations in general were very reserved. After Mussolini had given a further indication of support on 11 March it was easy to counter Schuschnigg's attempt to hold a plebiscite for a free and independent Austria. The Hungarian and Italian aid that he had hoped for was not forthcoming. His soundings in Rome, Paris, and London were of no avail. After Schuschnigg's resignation, on 11 March, Hitler gave the order for German troops to march in. Austria 'fell back into the Reich'. Directive No. 1 for 'Operation Otto' (it had been feared for a time in Berlin that Archduke Otto was planning an early restoration of the monarchy, and therefore an invasion plan had been drafted in the time of Fritsch and Blomberg)

---

[171] Thus Jacobsen, *Außenpolitik*, 438. An early survey of Anschluss literature is in Hillgruber, 'Anschluß'.

[172] Details in Müller, *Heer*, 255 ff.; cf. also Jodl diary.

[173] Gehl, *Austria*, 188 ff.; *Weizsäcker-Papiere*. [174] Müller, *Heer*, 269.

[175] Text of protocol in *DGFP*, D. i, No. 294, p. 513. On German tactics see also Irving, *War Path*, 80 ff. [176] *DGFP*, D. i, No. 328, p. 548.

[177] Record by Hassell, dated 30 Jan. 1937, of conversation with Göring on 17 Jan.: *DGFP*, D. i, No. 207, pp. 384 ff.

provided for the use of two army corps and the avoidance of force as far as possible. The operation should wear the appearance of a 'friendly entry of German troops welcomed by the population', though its immediate purpose was to forestall the plebiscite. The connection between this piece of expansionist policy and the reshuffle of the supreme command of the Wehrmacht is certainly not to be interpreted as meaning that it was now possible to use more compliant senior officers—in particular the 'unpolitical' and compromised Brauchitsch[178]—to carry out a risky operation. The risk was not in fact very great.

Two weeks later Britain officially recognized the Anschluss, which even Vansittart had considered unavoidable sooner or later.[179] Chamberlain would have preferred other 'methods'; but his policy was one of making concessions on the Continent, and reactions in Germany and Austria showed that Hitler was riding a wave of popular enthusiasm. The German embassy in Paris reported 'a feeling of impotence in face of the closer union of the two German states which is being initiated diplomatically and legally'; opposition found no more than 'Platonic' expression.[180] Even earlier, influential circles in Paris had inclined to a more flexible attitude over Austria. Thus, Georges Bonnet indicated to Papen, the German ambassador in Vienna, who was in Paris at the beginning of November 1937, that the Radical Socialists were 'evolving to the right' and 'turning against Bolshevik tendencies'; according to Papen's account, Bonnet added that he was not opposed to 'progress' in the Austrian question.[181]

The Anschluss marked the attainment of one of the chief aims of old-style revisionism, and also the first move in the expansionist phase. Skilful propaganda laid such stress on the national and historical aspect as to give the impression that the achievement of a long-desired unity would finally contribute to peaceful relations in Europe. The note of national jubilation completely obscured a very important motive for expansion, namely the economic bottlenecks caused by the accelerated rearmament programme.[182] In 1937 there were already shortages of raw materials for the armed forces.[183] It cannot, however, be argued that internal economic crises would have arisen but for the Anschluss. Austria was already to a large extent part of the German economic system, and had been since the agreements of 1936.[184] The technocrats of the Four-year Plan wanted the Anschluss. Austria was of value not only for its raw materials but for its unused industrial capacity, foreign currency, and manpower. In Hitler's eyes, moreover, it was a factor of some importance in his overall plan of economic and strategic expansion. True, at the beginning of May 1938 the war economic staff in the Wehrmacht high command took a highly pessimistic view of the results of the Anschluss. Even as

---

[178] Müller, *Heer*, 268; Messerschmidt, *Wehrmacht*, 210 ff.

[179] Woermann to foreign ministry, 9 Nov. 1937, in *DGFP*, D. ii, No. 14, p. 31: references to statements by Vansittart to Henlein.

[180] Telegram of 16 Feb. 1938 to foreign ministry: *DGFP*, D. i, No. 302, p. 523.

[181] *DGFP*, D. i, No. 22, pp. 41–5, letter of 11 Nov. 1937 from Papen to Neurath; cf. Bariéty, 'Frankreich und die Anschlußfrage'.

[182] Cf. Schausberger, 'Österreich', and id., 'Wirtschaftliche Aspekte'; also Volkmann, II.vi.2 above.

[183] Thomas, *Wehr- und Rüstungswirtschaft*, 94; cf. Volkmann and Deist in Parts II and III above.

[184] Schausberger, 'Österreich', 745–6.

regards production capacity they expected only a transitory benefit. The most valuable increase of war-economic potential, in their opinion, would come from opening up south-east Europe for German war supplies and from the 'improved possibility of throttling Czechoslovakia economically should the need arise'.[185] Thus, analysis purely from the economic and armaments point of view does not yield a satisfactory explanation of German motives. There was in fact an inextricable mixture of economic, politico-tactical, and strategic considerations. As to the method of carrying out the operation, this was not decided until preparations were far advanced.[186]

The French leaders criticized the Anschluss a good deal more severely than the British.[187] This was not especially consistent, as French policy on the matter had long been dependent on that of London; and, as recently as 25 February, Britain had returned a decisive 'no' to a French enquiry concerning a commitment with all its consequences.[188] Thus, the appeals of the French ambassador in Vienna went unheeded. When it was too late, the French asked whether London thought it right to surrender central Europe and the Danube area to the Germans. Did the British think the 'Germanic impetus' could be held up at the Straits if every barrier in the Danubian basin was abandoned? Looking towards Czechoslovakia, Paris already sought to assure herself of British help. The Deuxième Bureau submitted an analysis of German intentions towards that country.[189] General Gamelin considered Germany's politico-strategic position so far improved that he took into account the possibility of German domination over the Balkans and its effects on Turkey. Next to Czechoslovakia he saw Poland within Hitler's immediate grasp, and predicted accurately that she would be overrun in a summer's campaign.[190] Eventually, Gamelin and also Daladier were convinced, Hitler would possess the resources for a long war. The dictator's next objective, as the Western powers clearly saw, would be Czechoslovakia. At that time Hitler was not in fact planning a further push south-eastward, as Gamelin no doubt thought, but intended first to turn against the West. However, Gamelin was not mistaken in his estimate of the importance of the Balkans to Hitler's long-term aims.

(b) *The Sudeten Crisis and the Blitzkrieg Model (Operation Green)*

The Western powers' reaction to the Anschluss could only confirm Hitler in his underestimation of Britain.[191] The appeasers were more upset by Hitler's methods

---

[185] Extract from memorandum of 3 May 1938; Schausberger, 'Wirtschaftliche Aspekte', 165.

[186] An early review of opinions in Hillgruber, 'Anschluß'; an important recent work is Botz, *Eingliederung Österreichs*. On the whole question see also Schausberger, *Griff nach Österreich*.

[187] Telegram from Paul-Boncour to French ambassador in London, 21 Mar. 1938: *DDF²* ix, No. 3. Daladier, the new premier, was surrounded by appeasers such as Chautemps and Bonnet, and was dependent on British support. In public as well as private, in 1938 and well into 1939, the advocates of reconciliation with Germany set the tone: see Poidevin and Bariéty, *Relations franco-allemandes*, 304-5. However, at the top-level Anglo-French talks in London at the end of Apr. 1938 Daladier already urged that political and military forces should be organized to defend Czechoslovakia: cf. *DDF²* ix. 563; 579; also Girault, *Décideurs français*, 23-43.

[188] British memorandum of 25 Feb. 1938: *DBFP²* xix, No. 592.

[189] Report of 28 Mar. 1938: ibid., No. 66.

[190] Note du Vice-Président du Conseil Supérieur de la Guerre, 29 Mar. 1938, ibid., No. 73.

[191] Henke, *England*, 140-1.

than by what they believed to be his aims, and this lessened their credibility, not least among the victims of German expansionism.[192] Hitler's remarks on the Austrian question had evidently made a strong impression on Halifax, who believed that the course of events could only have been altered by a threat of force;[193] but for this no one in Europe was yet ready. Göring, moreover, had let it be understood that the German troops would be withdrawn and free elections held.[194]

Germany's protective tactics, which were a tissue of lies and flimsy deception, did not distract the British government from its course. The 'gravest reactions', foreshadowed in the British protest of 11 March,[195] did not ensue, however. The British ambassador realized that the policy of combining colonial concessions with an attempt to preserve the status quo in central Europe did not work. But the object of appeasement remained basically unaltered, viz. to work on Hitler by way of negotiation and peaceful change in the hope of bringing about a state of security in Europe. It was not a question of blindness, but of the search for peace. Halifax saw very clearly what consequences the annexation might have, and described them in no uncertain terms to Ribbentrop, who was in London at the time.[196] The appeasement policy[197] was henceforth adapted to the realization that the League of Nations was incapable of handling the crises provoked by Hitler.[198] In the attempt to include him in a security system nevertheless, Britain worked for bilateral agreements on the basis that they should not impair the close relations between Britain and France on the one hand and the Axis powers on the other. Soviet participation was not part of the design. It is questionable, however, whether the objective can on that account be termed a 'defensive alliance' against the Soviet Union.[199]

---

[192] Hitler skilfully used Halifax's statements to put pressure on Schuschnigg at Berchtesgaden: Schuschnigg, *Requiem*, 24.

[193] Telegram from Halifax to Henderson, 12 Mar. 1938: *DBFP*[3] i, No. 59.

[194] Telegram from Henderson to Halifax, 12 Mar. 1938; ibid., No. 46.

[195] British embassy in Berlin to Neurath: *DBFP*[3] i, No. 47, p. 24.

[196] Halifax to Henderson, ii. Mar. 1938: ibid., No. 44: 'What we were witnessing was an exhibition of naked force, and the public opinion of Europe would inevitably ask, when the facts were known, what there was to prevent the German government from seeking to apply in similar fashion naked force to the solution of their problems in Czechoslovakia or to any other in which they thought it might be useful. The conclusion must be that German leaders were people who had no use for negotiation but relied solely on the strong hand.'

[197] Herzfeld, 'Appeasement-Politik'; Lundgreen, *Appeasement-Politik*; Wendt, *Economic Appeasement*.

[198] A telegram of 12 Mar. 1938 from Halifax to Phipps, the British ambassador in Paris, said apropos of an appeal to the League of Nations: 'In the view of His Majesty's government such procedure would be of no practical advantage in redressing present situation, and we fear that only result would be to expose League to open humiliation. Moreover to place League in this position now must inevitably prejudice its eventual reconstruction. Please inform French Government that this is the feeling of H.M. Government' (*DBFP*[3] i, No. 57). Delbos agreed: Phipps to Halifax, 13 Mar. 1938, ibid. No. 72.

[199] Though such is the view of Kuhn, *Programm*, 221, and Hillgruber, *Deutschlands Rolle*, 81. There is no foundation for the Soviet and East German assertion (*Deutschland im zweiten Weltkrieg*, i. 116) that the handling of the Sudeten question by Hitler and the Western powers amounted to a plot with the object of directing German expansion against the Soviet Union. Manne, 'Foreign Office', does not support such an interpretation either. The foreign office was indeed fearful of Hitler's reaction to any improvement of relations between the Western Powers and the Soviet Union, and it was susceptible to anti-Comintern propaganda; but there was nothing in the politico-strategic situation to support the idea of a 'defensive

None the less, the attempt to achieve a peaceful settlement of Europe without the Soviet Union made it necessary to rely heavily on British and French preparedness for war. This consideration was in fact one of the chief bases of the appeasement policy. A Soviet offer of collective action against any future aggressor[200] was turned down by Britain.[201] An understanding with Russia, in Chamberlain's opinion, was the one thing Britain could not contemplate.[202] This considerably reduced Britain's freedom of action, on which France depended in her turn; and Britain did not see her way to intervening militarily on the Continent. Hore-Belisha, the war minister, placed an expeditionary force at the bottom of his list of priorities, while Inskip, the minister for the co-ordination of defence, considered the army's main function to be the protection of the Empire. In February 1938 there were only three divisions available for the Continent. Eden, commenting that spring on the reluctance of the military to hold staff talks with France, remarked that they apparently wanted 'to reorientate our whole foreign policy and to clamber on the bandwagon with the dictators'.[203] In March 1938, asked for their views about a possible German attack on Czechoslovakia, the chiefs of staff replied that the integrity of that country could only be restored after a long war with Germany. Such a war could probably not be confined to Europe; it would be a world war, for which Britain did not at present have the resources.[204] Consequently, the British proposal for talks on the Sudeten question was made in the hope of preventing Hitler from taking military action.

On 16 April 1938 Britain concluded an agreement with Italy which removed the principal sources of conflict in the Mediterranean and Africa. The British sought above all to limit possible dangers in the Mediterranean and to strengthen Italy *vis-à-vis* Hitler—an objective clearly perceived by the German foreign ministry.[205]

The attempt to hold talks with Germany was inaugurated with great seriousness. In April Butler, the parliamentary under-secretary of state, informed the German chargé d'affaires that Chamberlain and Halifax were still anxious for a real

alliance' against the Soviet Union. It is questionable, moreover, whether one can agree with Manne (p.751) that Hitler had 'already subdued the civilized policy-makers of the Foreign Office to his famous will'.

[200] Statement to the press by Litvinov, commissar for foreign affairs, on 17 Mar. 1938. The Soviet ambassador in London communicated the text to Halifax, informing him that it represented the Soviet government's view of current international problems: *DBFP*[3] i, No. 90.

[201] Halifax replied to the ambassador on 24 Mar. that in the British view the Soviet proposal 'would not necessarily have a favourable effect upon the prospects of European peace'. On the previous day Halifax had briefly discussed the proposal with the French ambassador, who thought it might contain 'an element of manœuvre': ibid., No. 109.

[202] To General Ironside on 10 July: *Ironside Diaries* 78, quoted in Howard, *Commitment*, 132.

[203] Howard, *Commitment*, 118.

[204] Ibid. 119. However, Britain's growing determination to organize its strength should not be overlooked. Hitler's *faits accomplis* were not simply 'swallowed', but conclusions were drawn from them. To this context belongs the approval of the 'L' scheme by the cabinet on 27 Apr. 1938, authorizing an Air Ministry programme to turn out 12,000 aircraft in the next two years. The bottlenecks of British rearmament were not so much financial as in respect of material and personal capacity, esp. skilled workers. For political and social reasons it was much more difficult in Britain than in Germany to switch from civilian to military production. This important aspect of appeasement is emphasized by Parker, 'British Rearmament', 306–43; see also Höbelt, *Britische Appeasement-Politik*.

[205] Memorandum of 27 Apr. 1938, *DGFP*, D. i, No. 755. The text of the Anglo-Italian agreement is in *Documents on International Affairs, 1938*, ii. 141–56.

understanding with Germany. The events in Austria had done nothing to alter this. As regards Czechoslovakia, Butler reportedly said that 'England was aware that Germany would attain "her next goal" '[206]—meaning by this a solution of the Sudeten problem. Hitler, of course, had already laid down in November 1937 that the incorporation of all Czechoslovakia was to be an early stage in his conquest of *Lebensraum*. In 1938 Germany's attention was focused on Czechoslovakia for strategic and war-economic reasons. The Sudeten problem was a side-issue, though it might afford a convenient pretext at the proper time.

Any form of intervention or participation by the Western powers was contrary to Hitler's wishes. The difference over methods concealed a difference of politico-strategic aims. The willingness now shown by the British to negotiate bilaterally with the dictators was seen by Hitler as interference. Now that he was about to mould Europe to his own intentions, gaining a starting-off point for the eastward march or securing his rear in the west, Czechoslovakia was for him an objective of the first importance. On 28 May 1938 he spoke to defence, government, and party chiefs of the need to eliminate Czechoslovakia without delay. A favourable moment must be chosen, and rearmament was to be stepped up meanwhile.[207] The elimination of Czechoslovakia would 'clear the rear for advancing against the West, England and France'.[208] This was evidently a reaction to the stiffening of the British attitude during the weekend crisis of May 1938, to be mentioned below: the West, it was now decided, must be checkmated before the invasion of the Soviet Union.

In Hitler's opinion Britain and France both needed years before they could 'come on the scene'. Britain, he thought, would be ready for war from about 1941–2. France was to be knocked out once and for all. For the rest, the object of a general war was to 'enlarge our coastal base (Belgium, Holland)'. Thus, Britain's military power was to be expelled from the Continent, not totally destroyed; on Hitler's premises, this had to be achieved before 1941. And so, by a system of alternately covering his rear in each direction, Hitler would first eliminate Czechoslovakia so as to be free to attack the West, finally turning against the Soviet Union.

Hitler's visit to Italy in May 1938 was in part devoted to preparing the way for the solution of the Czechoslovak problem.[209] He wished not only to sound out Mussolini's attitude to a German move towards the south-east, but also to find out whether he could risk a general war with Italian consent. Hitler still took account of the Duce's views in planning his long-term policy. It would even seem that the timetable of German expansion was made dependent on the degree of saturation of Italian imperialism. Hitler expected to return from Italy empty-handed if Mussolini regarded his own 'work' as completed: 'if so, Czechia distant future.' In that case Germany must meanwhile shut off her western frontier and wait. If, however, Mussolini wanted to go forward, the African *impero* was not possible without

---

[206] Woermann to foreign ministry, 22 Apr. 1938; *DGFP*, D. i, No. 750, p. 1092.

[207] Müller, *Heer*, 307–8, from summary notes by Beck: Beck papers, BA-MA N 28/20, fos. 23–6; also Krausnick, 'Vorgeschichte', 311, and Volkmann and Deist, in Parts II and III above.

[208] Memorandum by Wiedemann, *DGFP*, D. vii, app. III, H (v), p. 632; see also Wiedemann, *Feldherr*, 129.

[209] Cf. Schreiber, *Revisionismus*, 131 ff.

German help, which would be conditional on 'Czechia': hence 'return with Czechia in the bag'. Hitler's calculation, which probably dates from April 1938, was that the 'Czech question' could only be settled, against France and British opposition, in close association with Italy, which would deter the Western powers from intervening.[210] Such was the thinking behind the proposed German–Italian pact, which, given Italian agreement, would have been more than a mere 'preliminary' to the 'pact of steel'.[211]

At the beginning of April von Mackensen, the new ambassador to Italy, was given the following guidance. 'Germany's frontiers with Italy, Yugoslavia, and Hungary are fixed. The drive towards the Mediterranean is at an end: we are heading northwards. The Baltic is our objective, after the Sudeten Germans. The Corridor and possibly the border states must be our concern.'[212] Hitler cancelled the permission given to the army to hold staff talks with Italy. Only the Wehrmacht high command was so authorized: 'Secrecy important for tactical purposes.' Hitler did not want any direct military support from Italy, which would have required him to disclose his political plans. Neither the army nor the navy at this time was in fact interested in close co-operation with Italy. Beck and Raeder had a low opinion of her value as an ally, and feared that German policy would be tied to Italian escapades.[213] The internal state of the Axis in 1936–8 was governed by the mutual dependence of politico-strategic aims that each partner kept partially concealed from the other. This lack of frankness prevented the conclusion of specific military agreements, which in 1938 were of more concern to the Italians than to the Germans; the German navy, particularly, judged the value of the Italian alliance very largely from the point of view of relations with Britain. Thus, in a report called for by the OKW on 'co-operation with the Italian armed forces in peacetime and in the case of a war in which Italy is at least benevolently neutral',[214] the navy high command advised against closer contacts.

Hitler's politico-strategic aims against Czechoslovakia, which were not to be disclosed to his Axis partner, were outlined by him to Keitel, chief of the Wehrmacht high command, on 21 April.[215] He referred to the desirability of 'lightning action based on an incident', or 'action after a period of diplomatic discussions which gradually lead to a crisis and to war'; this had the disadvantage that the Czechs could take precautionary measures. A 'strategic attack out of the blue' was too risky because of 'hostile world opinion'. Such a step was, however, 'justified for elimination of the last enemy on the Continent', and was in fact ruthlessly taken against the Soviet Union in 1941.

Hitler hastened the revision of the deployment plan for 'Operation Green'. The draft of mid-May still referred to political events in Europe that might provide an

---

[210] Note by Hitler's adjutant Major Schmundt, 'Observations of the Führer', *DGFP*, D. ii, No. 132.
[211] See also Watt, 'Earlier Model'; Toscano, *Origins*.
[212] *Weizsäcker-Papiere*, 125.
[213] Schreiber, *Revisionismus*, 127 ff.; *Weizsäcker-Papiere*, 123–4.
[214] *Weizsäcker-Papiere*, 123–4.
[215] Note by Major Schmundt: Summary of Hitler–Keitel conversation of 21 Apr. 1938, *DGFP*, D. ii, No. 133.

'especially favourable opportunity that might never recur' for action against Czechoslovakia.[216] After the weekend crisis of 20–1 May 1938, when the Czechs mobilized some units on account of reports and rumours of German troop movements, preparations were again stepped up, with a restatement of political conditions for the attack. The directive of 30 May read: 'It is my unalterable decision to smash Czechoslovakia by military action in the near future. It is the business of the political leadership to await or bring about the suitable moment from a political and military point of view.' The Wehrmacht was instructed to make preparations 'immediately'.[217] The OKW chiefs were aware that the starting-signal would soon be given.[218] Hitler plied the OKW with questions so as to accelerate the work, and ordered rapid progress with the construction of the Westwall.

The deployment plan can be regarded as the model of a lightning war. In the Hitler–Keitel conversation of 21 April it was laid down that the first four days of military action must be politically decisive; tangible successes must be achieved by then, or else 'a European crisis is certain to arise'.[219] The plan therefore provided that 'the whole weight of all forces must be employed against Czechoslovakia'. All Germany's other frontiers must be held defensively or merely watched. Only by using the element of surprise could the sequence of action be carried out. But could Hitler be certain of bringing off the coup, when all the neighbouring states feared that he would strike against the Czechs, or expected it?

Britain made it clear that she felt obliged towards Czechoslovakia only on account of her membership of the League,[220] while France announced that she would honour her specific treaty commitments. Delbos, the foriegn minister, had made clear in London in November 1937 that the Franco-Czechoslovak treaty of 1925 would come into operation if Germany attacked Czechoslovakia by force of arms. The French attitude was confirmed to Halifax in March 1938. The British now felt it necessary to make their position clear. The indication of the maximum extent of British commitment conformed exactly to the possibilities outlined by the military leaders. In this way the statement of Britain's obligations under the covenant was still more circumscribed[221] than indicated by Eden, who already had rejected the idea of any automatic obligation to come to the aid of Czechoslovakia.[222]

While making it clear to the French that Britain felt in no way committed by the Franco-Czechoslovak treaty, Halifax added that she considered herself bound to assist France within the limits of the Locarno treaty, i.e. against an unprovoked

---

[216] *IMT* xxv. 422–3.

[217] *DGFP*, D. ii. 357 ff.; *IMT* xxv, doc. 388-PS, pp. 433 ff.

[218] Jodl diary, *1937–9*, entry for 30 May 1938, p. 373; cf. Müller, *Heer*, 308.

[219] See n. 215.

[220] Thus Chamberlain in the Commons on 16 Mar. 1938. Halifax sent a memorandum with a full statement of the British position to the ambassador in Paris for communication to the French government: *DBFP*[3] i, No. 106.

[221] From the Halifax memorandum (n. 220) cited in the previous note: 'His Majesty's government maintain, and intend to maintain, their membership of the League, and will do their best to fulfil their obligation as a member of the League, within the measure of their capacity and to the extent to which common action can be secured.'

[222] Henke, *England*, 145.

attack. The British offered no more than staff talks between the two air forces. Nothing could more clearly illustrate the British caution and aversion to a continental commitment. As at the end of November 1937, it was again made clear that the British intended to reserve their freedom of decision. It was therefore risky for the French to build any hopes on Halifax's further observation that in case of war the force of events and the threat to vital interests might be stronger than legal obligations.

As the British saw, Hitler was in a position to create *faits accomplis* that could only be reversed by a long war. At the beginning of such a war, British aid must be basically confined to economic pressure. Hence, the British government placed more hopes in an Anglo-French policy of urging Prague to be more conciliatory to its German minority. In other words, London basically thought an initial German success could not be avoided. At the beginning of May Daladier indicated to Bullitt, the American ambassador, what conclusion the French drew from this: they would not be able to fight a war in defence of Czechoslovakia. Their attitude was also affected by fear of German air superiority.[223]

The British policy could, however, be a serious hindrance to Hitler, since he intended to use the minority question as a means of triggering off 'unavoidable events' in Czechoslovakia. Henlein, the Sudeten German leader, was instructed at the end of March to make demands 'which are unacceptable to the Czech government'.[224] British offers of mediation were irreconcilable with Hitler's policy of using ruthlessly for his own purposes the good intentions of the British government and large sections of the British people, who desired to give a helping hand to the principle of self-determination. Halifax's offer of a *démarche* in Prague,[225] or the further suggestion that London would put pressure on the Czechs to accept Germany's terms,[226] still amounted to no more than aid for the vociferous German demands on behalf of the Sudeten minority;[227] and the effect of this was to deprive Hitler of his pretext for an occupation of Czechoslovakia. Hence, Dirksen, the new German ambassador in London, on his initial visit on 3 May informed Halifax that Germany did not regard the Sudeten question as one for mediation: 'We did not desire to take part in these negotiations, and we must refuse any guarantee of their outcome.'[228]

Prague was increasingly resigned to the attitude of the Western powers. Masaryk, the Czechoslovak minister in London, understood Hitler's intentions—those of the British government less well—when he reported: 'The British hate our guts. We are only a nuisance to them, and they curse the day we were founded. . . . I have expressed our position to them as follows: "If it is compatible with British interests

---

[223] Bullitt to the US secretary of state, 9 May 1938: *FRUS* (1938), i. 493–4.

[224] *DGFP*, D. ii, No. 107. On Henlein's role see also Jacobsen, *Außenpolitik*, 442–3, and Rönnefarth, *Sudetenkrise*.

[225] Halifax to the German ambassador on 3 May: *DGFP*, D. ii, No. 145; repeated by Henderson in Berlin on 7 May, ibid., No. 149.   [226] *DGFP*, D. ii, No. 151.

[227] There is no evidence for the statement in the GDR work *Deutschland im zweiten Weltkrieg*, i. 16, that the Western powers intended to abandon Czechoslovakia to Nazi Germany.

[228] *DGFP*, D. ii, No. 145.

to let Hitler have the whole of Europe as far as the Black Sea, tell us so and we shall come to terms with Berlin." ''[229]

Hitler reckoned with the possibility of Western intervention, and the May crisis seems to have confirmed him in this fear. From the military point of view this might be countered by rapidity of action, though with uncertain result, but politically it was necessary to wait for a favourable moment. The plan for 'Operation Green' envisaged October 1938. The OKW settled on 28 September for the attack (X-day);[230] all military preparations were to be completed by that date. The Western powers also figured in the operational plan. The Luftwaffe prepared a study on 25 August 1938 on the assumption of a war with Britain and France,[231] and in the spring of 1939 the navy for the first time conducted manœuvres on the basis of British opposition.[232]

The part played by senior defence chiefs in Germany and Britain respectively during this preliminary phase of the Czechoslovak crisis throws a vivid light on the relationship between the political and military leadership in the two countries. In Britain the chiefs of staff functioned as advisers to the cabinet; they were formally associated with the principal ministers in the committee of imperial defence, and could exercise early influence on debates and decisions. Under Hitler the OKW had declined into a mere instrument, an organ for the execution of decisions that were frequently arbitrary and erratic. Fruitful co-operation was never established between Hitler's military entourage and the army general staff. The two institutions, and their chief personalities, were separated by the unsolved problem of organization at the top level. Beck would have liked, in accordance with tradition, to be Hitler's sole adviser on strategic and politico-strategic questions. As things were, he was unable to find a chink between Hitler and the latter's newly created instrument under Keitel. It is certain that Beck shared Hitler's view that Czechoslovakia was 'intolerable' to Germany, a danger-spot that must be removed by war if necessary.[233] Beck also agreed with Hitler about the need for *Lebensraum* in Europe and the colonies. What made him uneasy was the idea of liquidating Czechoslovakia so soon. Here he was highly critical of the planners or executors of the OKW programme. His views were not far from those of the British military leaders: Germany could win a war against Czechoslovakia, but would lose the resulting European war. Beck assumed, wrongly, that Czechoslovakia could count on military aid from France and Britain; Hitler hoped to avert this danger by skilful manipulation.[234]

---

[229] *Abkommen von München*, 15, quoted in *Deutschland im zweiten Weltkrieg*, i. 117.

[230] *IMT* xxv. 451 ff. At the beginning of May Hitler was informed of a telegram from the US ambassador in London to the effect that Britain would not allow him a free hand in central Europe: see Irving, *War Path*, 98.

[231] 'Extended Case Green', study by Division 5 of the Luftwaffe general staff, *IMT* xxv, 375-PS; see also Deputy Chief of Air Force Operations Jeschonnek, BA-MA PG/33272.

[232] Salewski, *Seekriegsleitung*, i. 40 ff.; Dülffer, *Weimar*.

[233] Memorandum of 29 May, Beck papers, BA-MA N 28/3, submitted by Beck to Brauchitsch on 30 May. This reaction to Hitler's statement of 28 May is described by Müller as 'one of the most important sources for Beck's thinking at that time' (*Heer*, 309).

[234] On the interpretation of the memorandum see, in detail, Müller, *Heer*, 306 ff. Doubts by the navy (Heye and Guse): see Gemzell, *Raeder*, 169 ff.; Dülffer, *Weimar*, 475; Deist, III.ii.3 (*c*) above.

Beck's criticism of the intended policy was addressed to Brauchitsch for Hitler's eyes; his arguments, basically against the OKW and only to a limited extent against Hitler, were not such as to impress the latter, who commented furiously: 'What sort of generals are these, whom I, the head of state, have to force into making war? . . . I don't ask my generals to understand my orders, but to obey them.'[235] Brauchitsch cast himself as a mere 'instrument' when, in mid-June, he informed senior commanders that Hitler had decided that the Czech problem could only be resolved by force.[236] Beck himself thought for a time that the preparations should for the present go ahead as ordered. Other officers shared the view that 'Czechia' must disappear from the map.[237] Manstein, then a divisional commander, declared to Beck that it was entirely a matter for Hitler's decision and responsibility if his judgement of the political situation led him to conclude that it was better to intervene in Czechoslovakia sooner rather than later, because it was more likely then that the Western powers would stand aside.[238] Beck's memorandum of 15–16 July 1938[239] was aimed against the OKW and invited Brauchitsch to represent his views to the Führer; he also suggested a poll of opinions among the generals. On 16 June he tried to put further pressure on Brauchitsch: the military commanders, he suggested, should resign if their warnings were not heeded.[240] This was, as far as ideas went, the acme of the criticism caused by the preparations against Czechoslovakia, directed not against Hitler's objectives but against a strategy and timetable which the chief of the general staff judged to be inadequate. Halder, who was then quartermaster-general and Beck's deputy, rightly pointed out that Hitler was not a man to be influenced by memoranda. But further discussions and approaches led to no better result. Beck and others still thought a distinction must be drawn between Hitler and the party 'bonzocracy', especially the SS. The idea of a 'positive' National Socialism prevented their powers of resistance from developing fully. They were paralysed by the partial identity of aims that had become so unmistakably visible once again in the Czechoslovak question. In the circumstances, substantial opposition to Hitler was hardly thinkable. Brauchitsch set his face against it and rejected Beck's further appeals. At a meeting of generals and army group commanders on 4 August there was basic agreement that war at the present time was to be avoided, since a third world war would mean the end of German civilization, but the question what to do *vis-à-vis* Hitler was left open: no remedy was found. Brauchitsch submitted Beck's memorandum of 16 July to Hitler through the latter's adjutants.[241] Thus, Hitler's plan for a blitzkrieg was not generally accepted by the military chiefs. Senior commanders doubted its feasibility as a combination of political and military surprise; their lack of confidence was due to the inadequacy, in their view, of the armaments situation.

Although many of Beck's arguments were faulty, his views caused Hitler anxiety.

[235] Foerster, *Beck*, 116.
[236] Krausnick, 'Vorgeschichte', 303; Irving, *War Path*, 116.
[237] Letter to Beck, 21 July 1938, in Müller, *Heer*, appendix 42, p. 664.
[238] Ibid. 600.
[239] Beck papers, BA-MA N 28/4; full discussion in Müller, *Heer*, 317 ff.
[240] Note for submission on 16 July: Beck papers, BA-MA N 28/4.
[241] Müller, *Heer*, 337; Foerster, *Beck*, 141.

On 10 August the Führer therefore made a bid to convince the younger generals.[242] Shortly afterwards he explained his views once again to their seniors and tried above all to dispel their fears of Western intervention. But he was unable completely to cure their anxiety concerning the incalculable risk. On 21 August Beck resigned; however, the effect of his gesture was lessened because, at Hitler's wish, he did not at first announce it. Among the German generals, perception was one thing and action another. Beck's successor Halder was still more critical of Hitler's plan. But after Hitler had assumed supreme command, and after Beck's resignation, his scope for action was limited; basically it became a matter for conspiratorial opposition, which Halder soon afterwards tried to set on foot but did not sustain.[243]

The position of the general staff in those decisive months, when Hitler was definitely planning aggression, can only be fully understood in connection with the structural features of the German ruling group. Theoretically the Wehrmacht had the power in some circumstances to push through decisions against Hitler; but in practice it did not exist as a counterweight. There was no military-political co-operation between the army, navy, and air force. The army stood alone. Its leaders had no convincing ideas for an alternative strategy. The commander in chief and the chief of the general staff differed on important questions. There was no unified 'conservative opposition', and no co-ordination with the foreign ministry, which at this time, under Ribbentrop, was steering a course towards conflict with the West. This state of affairs has often been wrongly interpreted as one of 'polycracy' in the National Socialist state. In theory this existed, but in practice particular interest-groups always proved ineffectual when they tried to evolve schemes contrary to Hitler's warlike designs.

Let us briefly look at the tactical moves by which the foreign ministry sought to evade British attempts to achieve a settlement with Prague. Ribbentrop declared to the British ambassador that a 'hollow compromise' between the Sudeten Germans and the Czech government could not conduce to a peaceful solution. If Prague would not 'listen to reason', Hitler would not be deterred by others' threats and 'would not even shrink from a European war'.[244] He informed the ambassador that 'the Sudeten German question was advancing irresistibly towards a solution'. If Britain or France intervened because Germany 'would not look on quietly at the oppression and gradual extermination of those of her own race by the Czechs', their action would be a 'war of aggression'—a distortion of language that was part of the general plan to keep Germany in control of the scenario.

During the May crisis[245] it seemed that Berlin's fears of action by the Western powers were being realized. Hitler was conscious of grave doubts among his own chief officers, and could at first do little to convince them. On 22 May the embassy

---

[242] Jodl diary, *1937–9*, entry of 10 Aug. 1938. Foertsch, *Schuld*, 175–6; Manstein, *Soldatenleben*, 336; Müller, *Heer*, 338; Irving, *War path*, 122 ff.

[243] As regards Beck see the summing-up by Müller, *Heer*, 342; on Halder cf. Ueberschär, 'Halder', with further references.

[244] Memorandum by Ribbentrop, 11 May 1938, *DGFP*, D. ii, No. 154.

[245] On the May crisis see also Braddick, *Germany*, and Irving, *War Path*, 100 ff.

in London reported statements of unmistakable import by the foreign secretary:[246] if German forces entered Czechoslovakia on any account whatever, France would march against Germany, and it was impossible to foresee whether or not Britain would be drawn in. Only those forces which were anxious for the overthrow of European civilization would stand to gain. In the face of these clear warnings, it seems incredible that Hitler should at this very time have taken, or rather reformulated, his 'unalterable decision' to destroy Czechoslovakia. The cementing of his relations with Italy no doubt played a part: his visit to Italy was directly connected with the Czechoslovak question.[247]

The precise effect of the May crisis on Hitler is hard to estimate; a full analysis would have to take account of the Anglo-French attitude, the reactions of the German generals, and numerous reports from London that varied on important points. The German ambassador reported his firm conviction that Britain would not tolerate an invasion of Czechoslovakia.[248] Since the spring of 1938 the reactions of the Chamberlain government to Hitler's abrupt methods had become a theme of British internal politics.[249] But the ambassador was mistaken about Hitler's intentions, though he sought to appeal to the Führer's way of thinking by referring to 'three forces—Jewry, the Communist International, and nationalistic groups in the various countries' which 'wish[ed] to incite a world-wide coalition to war against Germany'.[250] He also mistook his chief Ribbentrop if he thought it useful to suggest an Anglo-German compromise on the basis or condition of a peaceful settlement of the Sudeten question. Ribbentrop had already declared to the French ambassador in June that the great powers should agree about their spheres of interest 'and respect those areas', thus clearly rejecting Western intervention,[251] and he rubuffed British approaches still more firmly. Sir N. Henderson reported to London in August that even French intervention would not deter Hitler if there was a prospect that Britain would stand aside,[252] i.e. if Locarno did not come into operation. Weizsäcker, like Beck, considered a European war over the Sudeten issue, or over wider German aims, to be unthinkable. He preferred the idea of a 'chemical process', the internal dissolution of Czechoslovakia[253] and the application of economic pressure, in short,

---

[246] *DGFP*, D. ii, No. 191. Henderson wrote in almost identical terms to Ribbentrop on 22 May, with a message from Halifax: ibid., No. 189.

[247] Schreiber, *Revisionismus*, 129 ff., emphasizing the change of atmosphere in Rome after the weekend crisis. Hitler's visit to Italy, although apparently not a success, laid foundations which, in the German view, might after all lead to a pact. On the Italian side it was a precondition that Germany should respect Italy's claim to Albania.

[248] See, in detail, Henke, *England*, 162 ff.; very firm statements by Dirksen, *DGFP*, D. i, No. 793. The OKW warned Hitler in May of the army's lack of preparedness.

[249] Aigner, *Ringen*, 322 ff. For these reactions and different attitudes in the cabinet, foreign office, and CID after the departure of Eden, Hankey, and Vansittart see Middlemas, *Diplomacy*, 286 ff. Hore-Belisha, the war minister, was not so strong an advocate for the fighting services as Duff Cooper and Swinton had been.

[250] Report of 18 July 1938, *DGFP*, D. i, No. 793.

[251] Record of conversation on 23 June 1938, *DGFP*, D. ii, No. 264.

[252] *DBFP*[3] ii, No. 613.

[253] Thus already after the May crisis: cf. *Weizsäcker-Papiere*, 129, entry of 31 May.

a combination of old-style imperialism and new forms of indirect rule. These ideas of Weizsäcker's made not the slightest impression on Ribbentrop.

Hitler hesitated. He was not clear as to the strength of British determination. He used the visit to London by his adjutant Wiedemann (which was not his own initiative) to make clear to Halifax that he did not regard the Czech problem as any concern of the British.[254] His instructions to Wiedemann reflected his anger at British behaviour during the May crisis. They can be read as suggesting that he would be glad to reach an arrangement with Britain after the problem of central Europe was solved—i.e. after the elimination of Czechoslovakia. But it is a question whether he had really given up the intention he expressed on 28 May to the chief executants of his military and foreign policy, viz. that once Czechoslovakia was settled he would be free to turn against the Western powers.[255] Do the instructions to Wiedemann imply that these words were merely an outburst of rage over the May crisis?[256] This would be contrary to their tactical purpose, which was fully in accord with Hitler's efforts to isolate Czechoslovakia. Underlining these tactics, Hitler indicated that a subsequent arrangement with Britain must not affect the German–Italian or the Anglo-French relationship. British diplomacy had already suggested the same proviso. But after May 1938 Hitler could not possibly have imagined that an Anglo-French combination would allow him to do as he pleased in Eastern Europe. The chief purpose of the Wiedemann mission was not a long-term bid for German–British understanding; it was an attempt to allay British anxiety over the Czech question. However, it had become only too clear that, once Hitler's designs on Prague were achieved, an arrangement with the Chamberlain government would hardly be possible—and much less with any government that might succeed it.

It was certainly also important to Hitler to show the doubters in his own camp, especially the generals whom Beck's views had infected, that he was right in his assessment of the Western powers. Altogether it is probable that Hitler was so much put out by Chamberlain and by the nervousness in his own camp that he began to consider seriously the idea of expelling Britain from the Continent before he invaded the Soviet Union. It is impossible to say precisely which objectives were dominant in his mind at different stages; but it seems certain that his strategic ideas around this time were confined to the continental dimension. The fact that the German air force and navy began in 1938 to include Britain in their operational planning proves nothing beyond an intention to achieve continental hegemony. Certainly high naval officers hankered after world power and a world role for the navy.[257] But the strategic studies and naval construction programme that were set

---

[254] Directives of 15 July 1938 to Wiedemann, who was probably sent to London at Göring's instance: *DGFP*, D. vii, appendix. III, H (i), pp. 627 ff.

[255] Henke (*England*, 166) takes the view that the directives for Wiedemann 'summed up [Hitler's] current attitude towards England'.   [256] Henke, *England*, 167.

[257] According to the navy chief, Admiral Carls, the naval programme was not only designed for a conflict with Britain but also to achieve 'world-power status'. Cf. Salewski, *Seekriegsleitung*, i. 55. This 'limitation' was also due to structural problems; cf. Messerschmidt, 'Strategisches Lagebild des OKW', 145–58; Schreiber, 'Strategisches Lagebild von Luftwaffe und Kriegsmarine', 175–89; Michalka, 'Machtpolitik', 59–74.

on foot by Hitler's directive of 24 May 1938 and eventually took the form of the 'Z plan' were not, for the time being, designed to serve extra-European ambitions.

The 'Heye memorandum' of 25 October,[258] which was based on Hitler's directives, constitutes the decisive document for the reorientation of naval strategy and construction away from the idea of a war on two fronts against France and Poland or the Soviet Union, and towards that of a deep-sea war against Britain. Heye thought it desirable for Italy to be directly involved against Britain: her overseas bases, which Germany lacked, would be of assistance in the war of supplies. This ran contrary to Hitler's directive that attempts at contact by the Italian armed forces should be treated in delaying fashion.[259] In connection with Hitler's statements of 28 May the reorientation of the naval programme, ordered four days earlier, appears as a component part of a strategy combining rear cover with deterrence. The planned tonnages and types, especially of heavy units and submarines, substantially exceeded the limits of the Anglo-German naval treaty. The stress laid on the U-boat programme pointed to the idea of defence against Britain. The significance of this deterrent becomes fully clear when the question of its purpose is considered: not to preserve peace or the status quo, or as a defence against political pressure, but as part of the biggest power build up ever known on the Continent, and a means of providing Germany with a politico-strategic potential that was bound to endanger Britain's very existence. But was the naval programme, especially as regards large ships, necessarily a sign that Hitler already had in mind the 'later, world-power phase of his programme'[260] in May 1938, during the crisis in the initial phase of his expansionist policy? It cannot be inferred with certainty from the building programme that Hitler would in the mid-1940s have had a navy capable of achieving his more distant aims in the second half of that decade.[261] Such an idea underrates the rearmament capacity of Britain and the United States and overrates German resources, which, according to Hitler's 'programme', had first of all to be applied to the needs of a show-down with the Soviet Union. The effect of such a view is to dissociate the 'programme' from real political needs and to give it an abstract quality, independent of current difficulties and uncertainties.

The further development of the Sudeten question was far from conforming to Hitler's plan. The generals doubted the strength of the Western fortifications. If the French marched, Germany's rear cover would not hold, and the deployment plan could hardly be carried out.[262] Perhaps the belief in a speedy operation was unrealistic. Hitler could not be sure of fighting an isolated war against Czechoslovakia. At the beginning of September he was beset by alternate moods of

[258] The final version, a basic document of naval strategy, is reproduced in Salewski, *Seekriegsleitung*, iii, No. 1, pp. 28–63; cf. Deist, III.III.3 (c) above; Dülffer, *Weimar*, 476 ff. The draft was already in existence in Aug.

[259] Details in Schreiber, *Revisionismus*, 145–6.

[260] Dülffer, *Weimar*, 470.

[261] Hildebrand, *Foreign Policy*, 69–70: 'the attainment of Hitler's long-term aims for the second half of the 1940s moved into the realm of the possible'.

[262] On the Western fortifications see also Bor, *Gespräche*, 119. The Western powers did not overrate their strength as much as Hitler would have liked: cf. report of 17 Aug. 1938 by the French military attaché, Gen. Renondeau, to Daladier, annex II to François-Poncet's dispatch of 18 Aug., in *DDF*² x, No. 411; also Irving, *War Path*, 102, 117 ff.

uncertainty and cold resolution. To Mussolini he professed to be determined that if the Czechs 'provoked' him once again—he had not yet got over the May mobilization—he would let fly at them even if it brought France and Britain into the war. British stubbornness crystallized in his mind into the picture of an adversary 'bent on getting rid of one or other of the two authoritarian nations as soon as she has completed her rearmament'.[263]

One purpose of these communications to Mussolini was do doubt to prepare the Duce for sudden developments. Hitler laid blame on the Czech government in advance. He could not name a date for the action. The 'X-day' envisaged in 'Operation Green' had become extremely problematical owing to the British attitude. At a conference at the Berghof on 3 September which discussed the timing of the 'move-up of the troops to "exercise areas" for "Green"', Brauchitsch proposed that this should be fixed for 28 September. Hitler, however, now demurred to this and wished the troops to assemble 'two days' march away'.[264]

A few days earlier, on 31 August, the British ambassador had once again warned Ribbentrop of the gravity of the situation. France's honour was at stake. If France was drawn in, it would be a serious situation for Britain. Warnings of this kind, which Hitler regarded as threats, had an ambivalent effect on him. He became instinctively more cautious, but also nervous with a tendency to over-compensate, rhetorically at all events. In any case, according to Jodl on 8 September, he no longer believed that the Western powers would stay out of the conflict, but insisted that he would launch his attack nevertheless.[265]

The British representations were not without effect, however. On 11 September Chamberlain described the position to the press in emphatic terms.[266] The Runciman mission in Prague had made considerable progress. 'Any attempt to use force after so great an advance . . . would incur universal condemnation throughout the world.'[267] Germany 'should not . . . count upon it that a brief and successful campaign against Czechoslovakia could be safely embarked on without the danger of the subsequent intervention first of France and later of this country.'[268]

The timing of a serious warning was discussed in the foreign office, and consideration was given to mobilizing the North Sea fleet as a sign of determination.[269] The principal plan, suggested by Churchill, was for a note to be addressed to Germany by four powers, including the Soviet Union. Halifax was

[263] Memorandum for the special mission of Prince Philip of Hesse to Italy: *DGFP*, D. ii, No. 415. This outline of Hitler's political ideas was handed by Prince Philip to the Duce at the beginning of Sept. 1938.
[264] Note of 4 Sept. 1938 by Major Schmundt, *DGFP*, D. ii, No. 424.
[265] Jodl diary, *1937–9*, p. 376.
[266] *DBFP*3 ii, appendix III, pp. 680 ff.
[267] Weizsäcker's belief that Britain and France did not threaten plainly—'at any rate not clearly enough for us to hear the threat or warning' (*Weizsäcker-Papiere*, p. 145, 9 Oct. 1938)—must have been due to a partial lapse of memory.
[268] 'Undoubtedly it is of the first importance that the German government should be under no illusions in this matter and that they should not, as it has been suggested they might, count upon it that a brief and successful campaign against Czechoslovakia could be safely embarked upon without the danger of the subsequent intervention first of France and then of this country': *DBFP*3 ii, appendix III, p. 681.
[269] Middlemas, *Diplomacy*, 298.

inclined to adopt this suggestion, but Chamberlain, relying on his adviser Sir Horace Wilson, obliged the foreign secretary to take a softer line and not to approach the Soviet Union. The cabinet decisions were taken on 30 August. According to Henderson there was still time. The policy was to 'keep Germany guessing'[270]—an expression of Britain's difficulty in attempting to check Hitler despite the inadequacy of her own armament; but this policy was less and less effective in view of the time factor and Hitler's presumed determination (the British government were aware of his statements of 5 November 1937). Berlin correctly assessed the British attitude in this respect. But on both sides determination was inhibited by a final remnant of uncertainty. Chamberlain summed up the situation in this sense.[271] Approaches from German opposition circles or opponents of a war policy, with information about Hitler's and Ribbentrop's intentions,[272] were not quite without effect in London. Halifax, although in increasing disagreement with the premier, was not prepared to make an official *démarche* to Germany as Vansittart advised, without Chamberlain's approval. Such initiatives were ruled out by the premier's decision of 8 September to visit Hitler, a plan which Halifax viewed with much scepticism and which reminded Vansittart of 'going to Canossa'. The German opposition had little chance of persuading Britain to alter her policy, since appeasement presupposed a degree of accommodation, whereas in the view of the opposition, as represented by Halder, Witzleben, and Weizsäcker, the chief precondition of a move against Hitler was that he should suffer a foreign-policy reverse. In any case London did not want to involve the German opposition politically, because it believed the latter to be dominated by 'Prussian Junkers' who were out to restore conservative ideas and policy.[273]

During these September days the determination of the French government crumbled away: it had in fact already been undermined by Bonnet and his political friends.[274] Britain gave no promise of automatic aid,[275] and the Soviet Union reacted evasively.[276] Paris was also perhaps affected by the fear of overwhelming German air superiority:[277] Colonel Lindbergh, the pioneer of transatlantic flight,

[270] Ibid. 300, 317; the line was once more laid down on 30 Aug.

[271] Chamberlain's letter of 3 Sept., quoted ibid. 317: 'While our Foreign Office keep repeating that we must "keep Hitler guessing", that is exactly what he does to us and we have no definite knowledge of his intentions.'

[272] Cf. *DBFP*[3] ii. 683 ff., e.g. minute of conversation between Vansittart and Kleist, submitted to Halifax on 28 Aug. 1938; also Weizsäcker's attempt to make it plain to Henderson that Britain must adopt clear language in the hope of preventing a war: Henderson's telegram of 2 Sept. to Halifax, ibid., No. 748. To this context also belong Kordt's conversations, arranged by Vansittart, with Halifax and Sir H. Wilson, when Kordt advised a broadcast to the German people. Cf. also Middlemas, *Diplomacy*, 276 ff., 321 ff.; Kordt, *Wilhelmstraße*, 245 ff.

[273] Müller, *Heer*, 366 ff.; and esp. Wendt, *München*.

[274] Cf. Girault, 'Französische Außenpolitik', based on new sources.

[275] Middlemas, *Diplomacy*, 330–1; Halifax to Phipps, 12 Sept. 1938, *DBFP*[3] ii. No. 843.

[276] Litvinov had already told the French foreign minister that it was for France to obtain the Poles' and Romanians' consent to the passage of Russian troops: telegram of 31 Aug. 1938 from Bonnet to the French chargé d'affaires in Moscow, *DDF*[2] x, No. 511.

[277] Phipps to Halifax, 13 Sept. 1938, *DBFP*[3] ii, No. 855, p. 310. For the impression made on the French air force chief by a conducted visit to the Luftwaffe see Irving, *War Path*, 125. After the Anschluss the French estimate of the balance of military strength was as follows. AIR FORCE: Germany

had returned from a tour with the gloomy information that 'Germany has 8,000 military aeroplanes and can turn out 1,500 a month.' Phipps in Paris reported the French foreign minister as saying that 'peace must be preserved at any price'; independently of the British appeasement policy, Bonnet hoped, contrary to Daladier's view, that this could be achieved by a direct compromise with Hitler.

According to Albert Speer, Hitler was conducting a large-scale campaign of intimidation: 'War was averted again more because of the compliance of the Western powers than because of any reasonableness on Hitler's part.'[278] But the 'enraged leader of his nation' had little reason to preach to his military chiefs about readiness for war when, on the other hand, he kept on insisting that the Western powers would not intervene. He did not want a repetition of the May crisis. A much more probable diagnosis of Hitler's reactions in August–September is that he was uncertain as to the result of the course which he had set himself and could not abandon without loss of face. It is scarcely possible to distinguish clearly between what Hitler pretended and what he himself believed. The mixture of resolve, rhetoric, self-deception, and blindness evidently spread to his immediate circle. Ribbentrop was in a similar case;[279] Göring took seriously the misgivings of the military leaders, especially as he was well aware of the deficiencies of the air force. On 22 September he was informed in a memorandum by General Felmy that a devastating air war against Britain was at present out of the question.[280] It was doubtless not least because of the shortcomings in his own branch of the armed forces that Göring thought it desirable at this time to advise Hitler against taking the supreme risk. But in March and May 1939 the general staff of the Luftwaffe was to take a much more hopeful view of German preparations.

It is hard to say what effect was produced on Hitler by Chamberlain's offer to travel to Berchtesgaden for discussions.[281] At any rate it might free him from the dilemma of having to choose at once whether to give way or fight a European war. Chamberlain's journey made it clear to the world that Britain wished to intervene or mediate. In his conversation with Hitler on 15 September Chamberlain recognized the Sudeten Germans' right to self-determination; France fell in with this line, so

---

and Italy 5,000 aircraft, France fewer than 500. This gave ground for extreme pessimism. On 15 Jan. 1938 General Vuillemin wrote to the minister, Guy La Chambre: 'Si un conflit éclatait cette année, l'aviation française serait écrasée en quelques jours' (repeated to the Comité permanent de la défense nationale: *DDF*[2] viii, No. 446). ARMY: According to Gamelin's estimate, Germany 126 divisions, including 5 armoured divisions and 92 available for rapid action against France: Italy 66, whereof 42 armoured divisions against France; France 80 divisions. Only in respect of the NAVY was the picture favourable: see Delmas, 'La perception', 127–40 (esp. 129–30). The British general staffs, consulted in Mar. 1938 as to the implications of a German attack on Czechoslovakia, replied that the German divisions were not capable of breaking through the Maginot line. In case of war Germany would probably turn her air force against Britain; Anglo-French bomber capacity was 575 tons, that of Germany 1,825 tons. In other words, Britain could not prevent the 'dog getting the bone' except by a lengthy process of attrition and blockade; see Parker, 'Perceptions de la puissance', 45–54. The cabinet drew the conclusion: no guarantee to Czechoslovakia (22 Mar. 1938).

[278] Speer, *Inside*, 110–11; cf. *Weizsäcker-Papiere*, 144, entry for 9 Oct.
[279] *Weizsäcker-Papiere*, 133, entry for 21 July 1938.
[280] BA-MA RL 3/63, fo. 7440. For more detail see Maier in vol. ii, pt. 2, of the present work, and Deist, III.II.4 (*b*) above.
[281] Details and further references in Henke, *England*, 174–5.

that Prague was virtually faced with an ultimatum. Hitler let it be understood that he was determined to accept a major war for the Sudeten Germans' sake. He evaded the question whether he was aiming at more than a solution of the Sudeten question; however, he did not maintain his position of 28 May, but allowed himself to be pinned down to the 'lesser solution' for the time being.[282] Chamberlain did not receive a clear statement of his intentions, however. Hitler spoke of the 'Czechoslovak question' as the last major problem to be solved. He maintained that National Socialist policy could not be imperialistic, since it was based on racial purity; but his statement that 'in any case Czechoslovakia would cease to exist before long', as the Slovaks were doing their best to break away from it, was an indication that he wanted to release himself from the 'concessions' he had made. Chamberlain evidently misunderstood the intention of this. He assumed that after the Hungarian, Polish, and Slovak territories or spheres of interest had been sliced off, rump Czechoslovakia would continue to exist but would no longer be regarded by Hitler as 'a spear-head in his side'.[283] In general terms Hitler reiterated his desire for good Anglo-German relations, which, he said, he had hoped for for decades on racial grounds.[284]

There was still a possibility that the Czechs would refuse to accept the result of this first Anglo-German conversation and surrender the Sudeten area. Hitler may have speculated on their doing so. Prague yielded, however, and therefore he had to try a new approach. Before the second conversation with Chamberlain he had spoken privately of the 'danger of the Czechs submitting to every demand'.[285] Chamberlain came to Godesberg armed with this information.[286] On 22 September Hitler tried once again to evade the consequence of what he had said at Berchtesgaden by referring to the claims of the Hungarians, Poles, and Slovaks, which he used as a stalking-horse. He also insisted on the immediate entry of German forces into Czechoslovakia and a plebiscite in an area as yet undefined. He succeeded 'only', however, in persuading Chamberlain to take his counter-proposal (the 'Godesberg memorandum') back to London. In it Hitler demanded that the Czechs first withdraw behind a line 'coinciding with the language frontier',[287] and that after the German-language area had been occupied by German troops a plebiscite should be held there on the Saar model. The date he demanded for the preliminary evacuation was 1 October.

[282] Record of conversation, *DGFP*, D. ii, No. 487; Chamberlain's notes, *DBFP*³ ii, No. 895. For Hitler's information as to the state of Western preparedness for war see also Irving, *War Path*, 136–7.

[283] Chamberlain spoke on these lines at the top-level Anglo-French meeting in London on 18 Sept., *DBFP*³ ii, No. 928, pp. 373–400.

[284] Hitler indicated that if Britain persisted in a policy of threats she took the risk of Germany denouncing the naval treaty, and of a return to naval rivalry.

[285] To the Hungarian prime minister on 20 Sept.: *DGFP*, D. ii, No. 554, p. 863, quoted in Henke, *England*, 176.

[286] On the negotiations between London and Prague see e.g. Lundgreen, *Appeasement-Politik*, and Celovsky, *Münchener Abkommen*. The text of the memorandum handed by Hitler to Chamberlain is in *DGFP*, D. ii, No. 584. The discussion in the 'inner group' in London showed that Chamberlain's attitude at Berchtesgaden did not escape criticism: Middlemas, *Diplomacy*, 363; hence, attempts were made to limit his freedom of negotiation.

[287] *DGFP*, D. ii, No. 562; some of the demands emanated from the OKW.

Chamberlain was strongly influenced by the consideration that a settlement of the Sudeten problem might lead to the agreed delimitation of further interests, especially economic ones in the Balkans and elsewhere, as well as a *détente* in the arms question. On this account his handling of the negotiations was viewed benevolently by the City and business circles. Many other observers thought he was pushing his efforts too far. There was criticism in the foreign office,[288] and after Munich this form of appeasement was discredited to an important extent. It can be seen that influential British quarters, including Chamberlain's 'inner circle', saw the crisis in a wider context and did not regard the troubles of Czechoslovakia as a key problem in themselves. But the broad picture could only be stabilized in a world at peace, whereas Hitler was bent on war. In his philosophy, the function of economic policy was to provide the necessary conditions for aggression. The foreign office was thus right in supposing that the German economic offensive in south-east Europe was a spearhead of political and strategic interests.

Hitler endeavoured from the outset to isolate the Czechoslovak problem. It might well seem to him that his tactics were skilfully adapted to that end. By sticking to the principle of self-determination, and at the same time invoking the interests of other claimants, he had gone a long way to outmanœuvre the Czechs. The object was to exhaust their patience. Chamberlain returned to London in deep disappointment. The mood in Britain underwent a sharp change.[289] However, Chamberlain did not confront the nation and the hard-liners empty-handed. He brought the assurance that rump Czechoslovakia was 'of no interest' to Germany. This had led to discussion of an international guarantee of the truncated state; Hitler had to reply that Britain was of course free to give such a guarantee. Clearly his range of action was becoming narrower, and his attempts to evade an international solution more transparent. He was close to the situation he had constantly endeavoured to avoid since 1933: an international system standing in the way of armed German expansion.

However, opposition to Chamberlain's handling of the Sudeten German question was increasingly manifest in the British press and parliament, and in the cabinet itself. After short hesitation—Chamberlain seemed for a time to have recovered the loyalty of his colleagues—an influential group of ministers, including Halifax, took the view that no further pressure should be put on Czechoslovakia. The Russians were suggesting that they, the French, and the British should agree on steps to be taken against Germany if Poland and Romania refused to permit the passage of Soviet troops; London was suspicious of this policy, but the French evidently believed that the Russians might act.[290] Nothing could be expected from the United States in 1938.[291] The Anglo-French talks of 25–6 September[292] revealed strong

---

[288] For a detailed study of the question see Wendt, *Economic Appeasement*, 482 ff.

[289] Henderson, in *Failure*, took the view that Godesberg began a new phase of Anglo-German relations; the leaders of British policy could no longer have any illusions.

[290] Daladier to the US ambassador on 8 Sept.: *FRUS* (1938), i. 581–2. For Daladier's favourable view of Soviet capabilities see also his remarks on 26 Sept. *DGFP*[3] ii, Nos. 1093, 1096.

[291] The American ambassador in London told Halifax on 9 Sept 'We want to keep out of the war': *FRUS* (1938), i. 586.   [292] *DBFP*[3] ii, Nos. 1093, 1096.

differences of opinion. Daladier was for rejecting the German demands. Chamberlain wanted an unambiguous answer as to what France would do if Hitler attacked Czechoslovakia after the rejection of his terms. Would she invade Germany, or entrench herself behind the Maginot line? Would the French air force raid Germany? Could France defend herself? Chamberlain wished to hear General Gamelin, the French chief of staff, on the subject. This was an unusual demand; the talks were almost becoming a cross-examination. Meanwhile the cabinet accepted Chamberlain's proposal to send Sir Horace Wilson to Hitler to make a last appeal for a peaceful settlement; he was to use the argument that the concessions already agreed to by Prague could be reasonably put into effect without applying pressure in the sense of Hitler's memorandum.

The Czechs refused to accept the Godesberg memorandum, and stood pat on their earlier concessions. Prague had ordered general mobilization while the Godesberg talks were still going on.[293] Sir Horace Wilson informed Hitler in Berlin of the Czech government's decision, and a serious discussion followed. Britain, he indicated, was determined to come to France's aid if she were involved in hostilities with Germany in the execution of her treaty obligations to Czechoslovakia.[294] The Czech rejection of the German memorandum, it was now clear, would not cause the British government to desist from its efforts; so that speculation of Hitler's was in vain. Chamberlain had assumed moral responsibility for the execution of the Czech undertaking.[295] This was a blow to Hitler's plan. The Western powers were barring the way in a matter which he regarded as outside their proper sphere. France ostentatiously moved fourteen mobilized divisions to her eastern frontier. The next move might decide between peace and war. Preparations for the German deployment had begun. At noon on 26 September Hitler gave orders for the troops to be moved up to action stations:[296] this was after he had taken cognizance of the letter delivered by Wilson on Chamberlain's behalf. Next day, on 27 September,

[293] Hitler was informed of this during his meeting with Chamberlain on 23 Sept.: *DGFP*, D. ii, No. 583. The possibility of the Czechs mobilizing had previously been mooted in London. Contrary to Halifax's views, Chamberlain had refused his approval; but the 'inner circle' led by Halifax, in agreement with the French, authorized a message to Prague cancelling the advice not to mobilize. Contacts between London and Godesberg were in this respect unsatisfactory. It is also possible that Chamberlain was outwitted by his colleagues on this point: cf. Middlemas, *Diplomacy*, 373.

[294] Record of Sir H. Wilson's meeting with Hitler on 27 Sept. 1938, *DGFP*, D. ii, No. 634.

[295] Ibid., referring to Chamberlain's statement on 26 Sept.: 'Speaking for the British government we regard ourselves as morally responsible for seeing that the promises are carried out fairly and fully, and we are prepared to undertake that they shall be so carried out with all reasonable promptitude, provided that the German government will agree to the settlement of terms and conditions of transfer by discussion and not by force' (*DGFP*, D. ii, No. 618). Prague and the Western powers rejected Hitler's memorandum on 25 Sept. For the Anglo-French negotiations concerning a guarantee of Czechoslovakia against future violent change see Middlemas, *Diplomacy*, 351 ff. On 30 Aug. Chamberlain gave the cabinet a pessimistic assessment of the situation, supported by Inskip, minister for the co-ordination of defence. The change came with the cabinet meeting after Godesberg: the majority now accepted the risk of war and trusted to gaining the upper hand in a long war: cf. Parker, 'Perceptions de la puissance', 50. On conflicting views in the foreign office and the roles of Cadogan and Vansittart, see Steiner, 'Évaluation', 55–71.

[296] *IMT* xxv. 483–4; *DGFP*, D. ii, No. 654. The troops to be moved up amounted to 7 divisions in all. On the military preparations and the extent of Hitler's involvement see also Görlitz, *Keitel*, 188 ff.

Wilson saw Hitler and re-emphasized Britain's determination to stand by France in the case envisaged. The British naval mobilization was a clear signal.[297] The German embassy in Paris reported that the French had already gone far to anticipate total mobilization; deployment of the first sixty-five divisions on the German frontier was expected by the sixth day.[298]

Hitler was now forced to make a move. He had adopted the pose *vis-à-vis* the Western powers, including the British prime minister's envoy whom he had just seen, of a man resolved to the uttermost. To the hesitant officials and generals in his own camp he had repeatedly insisted that the West would not intervene. He believed himself to be infinitely cleverer than the Kaiser's statesmen. Now the world's eyes were upon him. Roosevelt had sent an appeal,[299] so had the king of Sweden. Hitler's whole programme was ready for execution if he forced the issue now. If he drew back he would have to wait for an opportunity that might never present itself. He began to waver.

The first signs of this appeared in a letter of 27 September to Chamberlain. Drafted by Weizsäcker, it actually invited the Western powers to guarantee to Prague that the terms of the German proposals would be strictly carried out. This in itself was an impossibility, but the very mention by Hitler of any further degree of internationalization shows how far he had been disoriented at this point. Further, he offered a guarantee for rump Czechoslovakia.[300] The resigned attitude of the Berlin crowds when battle-ready troops paraded through the streets on Hitler's orders showed, in any case, that there was no popular enthusiasm for war.[301]

Hitler accepted Mussolini's proposal, made at the suggestion of the British government,[302] that a four-power conference be convened to deal with the crisis. He consented to postpone German mobilization by twenty-four hours. On the same day, 28 September, invitations were issued for the next day's meeting. The Munich agreement embodied the main points of Hitler's demands at Berchtesgaden. In an annex to the agreement, signed by all four powers, the British and French reiterated their offer of an international guarantee of the new Czechoslovak frontiers against unprovoked aggression; Germany and Italy undertook to give such a guarantee once the question of the Polish and Hungarian minorities was settled. On 30 September Hitler and Chamberlain signed a joint declaration on Anglo-German relations. The Munich agreement and the Anglo-German naval treaty were described as symbolic

---

[297] The news did not reach Berlin till 28 Sept.: Müller, *Heer*, 374.

[298] Telegram of 27 Sept., *DGFP*, D. ii, No. 647.

[299] Telegram of 26 Sept. 1938, *FRUS* (1938), i. 657: 'The supreme desire of the American people is to live in peace. But in the event of a general war they face the fact that no nation can escape some measure of the consequences of such a world catastrophe . . . I most earnestly appeal to you not to break off negotiations.'

[300] *DGFP*, D. ii, No. 635. Weizsäcker attempted to tie Hitler down to statements in his Sportpalast speech of 26 Sept.: Domarus, i. 924 ff.; Baynes, ii. 1508 ff.; cf. also Kordt, *Wilhelmstraße*, 265.

[301] For the atmosphere in the Reichskanzlei on the morning of 28 Sept. see e.g. Schmidt, *Interpreter*, 105 ff.; Kordt, *Wilhelmstraße*, 272; Weizsäcker, *Memoirs*, 153–4; Wiedemann, *Feldherr*, 170 ff.

[302] *DBFP*³ ii, Nos. 1158–9, 1161, 1165–7, 1174. Chamberlain had at first suggested a five-power conference.

of the desire of the two peoples never to go to war with each other again, and to treat all future problems between them by the method of consultation.[303]

With the Munich agreement Hitler had achieved all those of his aims which lay within the bounds of revisionist thinking and which had been openly acknowledged, most recently in his Sportpalast speech of 26 September. At the same time he had deprived the German opposition of its principal ground for action against him. This might, on the surface, be regarded as yet another success. Strategically, Czechoslovakia was to a great extent eliminated. Its fortifications no longer threatened Germany's flank. Nevertheless, in relation to his own aims Hitler had suffered a repulse, as he himself was well aware.[304] In Britain too the Munich agreement soon met with criticism, of which careful note was taken in Berlin. Hitler gained the impression that he had been duped by Chamberlain, who only wanted time for rearmament. This was no more than a half-truth. The British leaders indeed chafed at the fact that they had to treat Hitler with restraint, carefully anticipating his reactions and calculating their political counter-moves accordingly. But the purpose of the appeasement policy was to organize a stable peace system, not merely to gain time so as to be in a better position to fight Germany.

To Hitler the main thing was that Munich must be the last international conference concerned with German political aims.[305] Never again would he let himself be fobbed off with partial solutions. From now on, however, he could no longer use the pretext of helping a German minority to secure its rights. He intended henceforth to act with lightning swiftness, leaving the other side no time for diplomatic reactions. Given the Anglo-French guarantee of what was left of Czechoslovakia, such a strategy on his part might very quickly bring about an acute crisis.

Hitler was evidently not disturbed by this prospect, perhaps because after Munich he was strongly inclined to the view that the West had been bluffing. Czechoslovakia was now as good as defenceless against a lightning attack. The way to German political and economic domination in south-east Europe lay open; indirect rule could be exercised without the need of force. Poland had shared in the spoils of Czechoslovakia by annexing the Teschen area: this bound her closer to Hitler and affected her moral status in Europe. Nothing seemed to obstruct the preponderance of the Reich. Its authority in eastern Europe was underlined by the 'Vienna award' in the frontier dispute between Czechoslovakia and Hungary: Britain and France were no longer consulted.

For a statesman who declared that he had no more problems to solve and that his country had achieved all its desires, nothing would have been more welcome than a quiet period of consolidation. There was no unsatisfied national ambition that could force his hand. The German nation rejoiced at the Munich settlement. War was the last thing it wanted. But Hitler had other ends in view. Many statements and

[303] For the meetings see *DGFP*, D. ii, Nos. 670, 674. Text of agreement and declarations, Nos. 675, 676.

[304] Details in Henke, *England*, 187 ff.

[305] Kirkpatrick, *Inner Circle*, 135.

speeches bear witness to his feeling of frustration at this time. The national mood was too pacifist for his liking. The desire for peace did not suit his book. He was displeased by the effect on the population, in town and country, of his assurances that Germany had no more claims now that the Sudeten Germans had returned to the Reich. The complicated mechanism of international politics and diplomacy that had saved Europe from catastrophe in September 1938 seemed to him, in retrospect, to have been a mere waste of time. Shortly after Munich he had given Mussolini and Ciano an indication of one of his next aims, by speaking of 'the time . . . when we shall have to fight side by side against France and England'.[306] This was his basic attitude at the moment of signing the declaration of 30 September to the effect that Germany and Britain would never again make war on each other.

Munich was not a signal, however. Only an extreme effort by the major European powers could deter Hitler from embarking on war single-handed. Even Mussolini, who had striven for years to divert Germany's energies eastward, tried to bind Hitler down to a peaceful solution of the Czechoslovak crisis and already made clear what was confirmed in 1939, that he himself was not prepared to be drawn into war. Hitler was not even concerned with justifying his aims, but merely with the immediate political effect of slogans: self-determination, guarantee of Czechoslovakia, renunciation of imperialism, and so forth. The compulsion to act against Europe resulted from the 'necessities' that he had expounded in the memorandum on the Four-year Plan and on 5 November 1937, and the operational plans he had set on foot. Munich had upset Hitler's estimate of the likely reactions of the Western powers, and strengthened his determination never again to allow a conference of that kind to rob him of the fruits of his strategy. The war was merely postponed; peace had won the day at Munich, but it was a Pyrrhic victory.

(c) From Munich to Prague

The Munich agreement, which none of the four powers regarded as ideal, had hardly been concluded when it was subjected to an impatient German strategy designed to undermine it and deprive it of meaning. Hitler no longer took the trouble to adopt a conciliatory pose. The regard he had previously shown for Britain was already missing from his speech at Saarbrücken on 9 October, which was filled with angry outbursts against the British opposition in particular.[307] Chamberlain, Hitler conceded, must be believed when he said he wanted peace; but he might be out of office at any time, and if Eden, Duff Cooper, or Churchill came to power they would do their best to bring about a world war.

This attack was launched partly in the hope of influencing British politics[308] and partly with an eye to German morale. Hitler let it be known that he was stepping up work on the western fortifications. The world, he declared, was still dominated by the spirit of Versailles. Clearly it was his purpose, at home and abroad, to represent

---

[306] Ciano, *Diaries 1937–8*, 166.

[307] Domarus, i. 954 ff.; Baynes ii. 1532 ff. The speech is also to be read in connection with British reactions to Munich. Cf. Irving, *War Path*, 155–6, with references to wire-tapping by the 'Forschungsamt'.

[308] Kuhn, *Programm*, 231 ff.

the material and psychological rearmament of his country as a defensive reaction to challenges from outside. His propaganda directives tell a different story. One of the key documents illustrating his policy after Munich is his address to the German press on 10 November 1938.[309] This was on the morrow of the Reichskristallnacht (night of broken glass), which marked a new ferocity in home affairs and was a clear portent to the outside world. Although Hitler did not say a word about the pogrom to the press representatives, there was an implied psychological connection. The task assigned to them for the coming year was to 'prepare' the German people, i.e. gradually condition it to readiness for war. For decades he had been compelled by circumstances to talk of 'scarcely anything but peace'; only by so doing had he been able to make a start with rearmament, 'which was a necessary precondition for one step after another'. But peace propaganda had its detrimental side: it could take root in people's minds and suggest that the regime was intent on peace in all circumstances. 'That would not only give a false notion of our aims, but above all it would mean that the German nation, instead of being armed to confront events, would be imbued with a defeatist spirit that must in the end destroy the regime's achievements.'

However, the strategy was not to be one of simply extolling the use of force. It was rather a matter of treating foreign affairs in such a way that the German masses came by degrees to feel that things could not go on as they were, that there was nothing for it but to hit out. The four hundred invited journalists were commended for their propaganda work up to the present, and were told that the 'pacifist record' was now played out.

In the orchestration of home and foreign policy and propaganda, the Kristallnacht organized by Goebbels, striking a savage blow at Jews throughout the Reich, was a kind of counterpoint designed to offset the euphoria with which the population at large had greeted the Munich agreement. Minds were also diverted by denunciation of the allegedly pernicious influence of Jews in world affairs.

This was a long way from the atmosphere of reasoned consultation among the major powers. In the period immediately after Munich the Western governments asked themselves what Hitler now wanted and what could be done to keep relations on the Munich basis. Paris, London, and Washington were perplexed.[310] Hugh R. Wilson, the American ambassador in Berlin, reported at the beginning of October his view that, given Hitler's character—'he is a man apart'—it was impossible to make any preconditions about the future until some new indications came into view.

At about the same time, preparations began for a further assault on Czechoslovakia. On 12 October Hitler decided to pursue the aim of holding bilateral negotiations with the Czechs as soon as possible. The international commission supervising the transfer of territory was to be 'done away with' at the earliest

---

[309] Treue, 'Rede Hitlers'; Kotze and Krausnick, *Hitler-Reden*; extracts in Domarus, i. 974 ff.; cf. Wette, I.11.5 above.

[310] Cf. the US ambassador's report of conversations with the British and French ambassadors on 5 Oct. 1938, *FRUS* (1938), i. 713 ff.

possible date.[311] The OKW informed the foreign ministry that a common frontier between Poland and Hungary was undesirable on military grounds. With regard to the 'Czech and Slovak' remainder state, the OKW recommended a policy envisaging future operations. That state would turn to Germany for support, since it felt betrayed by France and Britain. There were elements in favour of breaking up the Czech–USSR relationship, and for this reason the OKW thought it militarily desirable that Slovakia should not be detached from the Czechoslovak state but remain part of it 'under strong German influence'.[312] In the foreign ministry a more dynamic programme was envisaged,[313] viz. an independent Slovakia or, as second best, Slovak autonomy within the existing state. The foreign ministry did not favour attaching Slovakia to Hungary or Poland, but much preferred it to be independent: it would be a weak entity 'and therefore best further the German need for penetration and settlement in the east. Point of least resistance in the east.' If the Czechoslovak solution was adopted temporarily, the preferred one would still be available in the future.

Ribbentrop's primary concern, however, was to deinternationalize the Czechoslovak question. A note prepared for his first conversation with the new Czechoslovak foreign minister suggested ways of circumventing the Western guarantee.[314] It would be best, of course, if Prague were to renounce the French and British guarantees of its own accord. But the matter should be touched on with caution, since public opinion in the West regarded the guarantees as an essential part of the Munich aggreement. Any German guarantee should be so framed as to appear of greater importance than the Western ones.

German policy over-estimated the firmness of the Western powers concerning the guarantee. Chamberlain felt committed to it on moral grounds,[315] but he did not envisage the commitment leading to a confrontation with Germany. The French view was much the same. Bonnet and his political friends wanted an accord with Germany. Halifax considered that they must avoid getting into a position in which Britain and France might be called on to act against Germany and Italy. This was at the beginning of December 1938.[316] The Anglo-French talks on 24 November had shown that guarantees were being discussed that could not in any case become effective. The British, in particular, would rather have had Germany as a co-guarantor than the Soviet Union.[317] Thus, it was in a way consistent that on 15 March 1939, after Hitler's final coup, Chamberlain took the line in cabinet that the *fait accompli* in Prague meant that the state whose frontiers had been guaranteed against unprovoked aggression no longer existed. No guarantee had been given to Czechoslovakia against moral pressure.[318] The British ambassador was not recalled

[311] Memorandum of 12 Oct., *DGFP*, D. iv, No. 53.
[312] Chief of staff, OKW, to foreign ministry, 6 Oct. 1938, ibid., No. 39.
[313] Note for the Führer, 7 Oct. 1938, ibid., No. 45.
[314] Note by Woermann, head of the political department, 12 Oct., ibid., No. 54.
[315] See Aster, *1939*, 24.
[316] Ibid.
[317] Anglo-French conversations, *DBFP*3 iii, No. 325, pp. 300 ff.
[318] Aster, *1939*, 29.

from Berlin. Chamberlain declared, though with misgivings, that Hitler had dealt a blow to confidence but that he himself would continue to prefer discussion to violence. Discussion, however, was just what Hitler sought to avoid, as the events preceding the occupation of the Czech lands had shown.

The main concern of the Wehrmacht high command was that Czechoslovakia should not be able to construct a new system of fortifications: it must 'no longer come into consideration as an opponent in the event of a conflict between Germany and the Western powers'. Here again the idea of alternate rear cover came into play. Leading circles in the Reich sought ways and means of bringing movement into the political situation; if the impulse came from elsewhere, it was on no account to be stopped. On 12 October Hitler laid down that if Hungary mobilized it was 'not our intention to hamper the Hungarians'.[319]

From the outset Hitler had no intention of contenting himself with the Sudeten area. In the talks leading to the Franco-German declaration of 6 December 1938[320] Ribbentrop spoke of the guarantees to Czechoslovakia and the Franco-Soviet alliance, which he described as a hangover from Versailles. The French guarantee to Prague was 'a kind of interference in our sphere of interest' and was not conducive to the policy of understanding on which the two countries had embarked. Shortly afterwards Weizsäcker informed Coulondre, the new French ambassador in Berlin, that the fate of Czechoslovakia was in Germany's hands, and 'nothing other than a German guarantee had any significance for Prague'.[321] Thus, the Franco-German *'rapprochement'* was from the beginning subject to the condition that France respected Germany's East European sphere of interest: this was regarded as an exclusive one, conferring the right to alter frontiers and to unmake states. On this interpretation the 'chemical' solution so far advocated by Weizsäcker came disturbingly close to Hitler's more drastic ideas, or at any rate to a demand that outsiders should keep quiet about future German operations.

In the general context of German foreign policy the Franco-German *'rapprochement'* was of real importance, but only for a limited time.[322] Strategically it was a feature of the system of alternate rear cover. The purely military deterrent effect of the Westwall could be enhanced by a political superstructure. Moreover, the arrangement had a good effect on French public opinion and was a psychological preparation for fresh movement in the south-east. It was, however, only a temporary manœuvre, since the German intention was still to turn westward before attacking the Soviet Union. From the French point of view the *'rapprochement'* was important, not least, as a means if gaining time for rearmament.

---

[319] Cf. n. 311 above. On 14 Oct. Hitler rebuked Darányi, the former Hungarian prime minister, for his country's hesitation: Irving, *War Path*, 153.

[320] *DGFP*, D. iv, Nos. 369, 370.

[321] Weizsäcker's memorandum of 21 Dec. 1938, *DGFP*, D. iv, No. 373.

[322] This is clear from the 'Points for Wehrmacht discussions with Italy' of 26 Nov. 1938, *DGFP*, D. iv, No. 411, envisaging a war by the Axis against France and Britain with the immediate objective of knocking out France and so depriving Britain of her continental base—a strategy Hitler had already devised in May; see also Bloch, 'France', 29. On the Franco-German declaration see now Knipping, 'Deutsch-französische Erklärung'.

The French military at this time viewed the situation with great pessimism.[323] Was the German object in the Paris talks to obtain a free hand in the east, over and above a settlement of the Czechoslovak question[324]—in other words, were Germany's eyes already fixed on the 'major solution'? This must be doubted. The theme of anti-Bolshevism was touched on, but only in relation to Spain. The German side aimed at no more than a loosening of the military alliance between Paris and Moscow, a further undermining of the already uneasy relations between Germany's two strongest neighbours. But there is no trace of Ribbentrop having sought to obtain from France a free hand against the Soviet Union. This would indeed have been quite contrary to the policy he had followed in the May and September crises, based on testing out the determination of the Western powers.

On the other hand, driving a wedge between France and the Soviet Union was an objective that might well have struck an answering chord in Bonnet's mind. To the latter, the break-up of the Popular Front went hand in hand with a policy of increasing coolness between France and Russia. After Munich the outlook for such a policy seemed good. France's system of alliances was in ruins. Her obligations towards Czechoslovakia, the discharge of which depended partly on good relations with Moscow, no longer existed. To the French right wing and the Radical Socialists it appeared a mistake to enter into any more ties in east central Europe. France should execute an 'imperial retreat', turning her attention to the Mediterranean and to her colonies. For this purpose Mussolini's demands for Corsica and Tunis must be damped down. Perhaps Hitler could be approached on the basis of a free hand for Germany in Eastern and south-eastern Europe. As early as October 1938 the French ambassador in Warsaw recommended a loosening of France's ties with Poland. Bonnet saw things in much the same way. The German side had surmised that the French might be thinking on these lines, and for that reason valued the diversionary effect of the Italian demands, which also included Jibuti. As late as 15 March 1939 Weizsäcker sought to interest the French ambassador in this possible division of spheres, thus reverting to the ideas of December 1938.

But the appropriate conditions no longer existed. In December France had sought an arrangement which would recognize Germany's interests in Eastern and south-east Europe—that is to say her political interests, while Paris and London hoped to pursue their economic interests in the area alongside Germany. The Franco-German discussions in Paris on 6–7 December 1938 marked the zenith of these attempts.[325] After Munich the French general staff saw little possibility of halting Germany's eastward expansion, because Poland and the Soviet Union, it was believed, could no longer be relied on. The military recommended a *rapprochement* with Italy. Britain and the Maginot line appeared as France's true defenders. Such was Gamelin's view of the situation.[326] Bonnet's mistake was to suppose that policy

---

[323] Cf. Gamelin's estimate of the situation on 3 Dec. 1938: *DDF*² xiii, No. 23.

[324] Hillgruber, 'Weltpolitische Lage', 285–6; also Bussmann, *Verständigungsversuch*.

[325] Girault, 'Französische Außenpolitik' (also on the attitude of French embassies in the major capitals).   [326] Cf. D'Hoop. 'Politique militaire de la France', 83.

could be concerted with Hitler on the basis of a division of spheres of interests. From Munich onwards, Hitler was bent on further ruthless action against Prague. To that extent the Franco-German talks were an element in his war preparations, though it also seemed at first that they might help to revive economic relations between France and Germany. These had deteriorated since the agreement of 10 July 1937 and had reached their lowest point in 1938. Some improvement was envisaged, but it soon appeared that to Hitler economic matters were of secondary importance—even though both the French government and German industrialists and economists saw them as a means of improving overall relations.[327] France made a serious attempt to follow up the declaration of 6 December 1938 in the economic sphere, particularly by means of the inter-ministerial committee under Daladier, but this was frustrated by Hitler's demand for exclusive control of Eastern Europe. In the same spirit, Weizsäcker told Coulondre on 15 March 1939 that France should 'turn her eyes westward to her empire and not talk of matters where, as experience had shown, her participation had not served the cause of peace'.[328]

All this was in line with Hitler's directives of 21 October[329] and 17 December 1938[330] for the 'liquidation of the remainder of the Czech state'. Three weeks after Munich Hitler had given orders that the Wehrmacht must be prepared at any moment to smash what was left of 'Czechia' and take over the Memel territory. As regards the march on Prague, this must be possible without planned mobilization and so prepared that the Czechs had no opportunity for organized resistance. The whole operation must be based on a surprise attack. A simultaneous deployment of the remaining forces must be prepared against the West. On 17 December Hitler supplemented this with the directive that 'outwardly it must be quite clear that it is only a peaceful action and not a warlike undertaking'. The connection between this scenario and the undermining of Western guarantees is clear.[331] The directive also fits in well with Hitler's general idea of the technique of aggression:[332] 'When I wage war . . . in the midst of peace, troops will suddenly appear in the middle, say, of Paris. . . . The confusion will be beyond belief.'[333]

Hitler also ordered in December that the army should refrain from deployment planning and devote itself wholly to organizational matters.[334] The blitzkrieg concept called for changing priorities in planning and camouflage. Even the top leaders were confused from time to time. The Wehrmacht chief of staff himself was

---

[327] See Poidevin, 'Relations économiques'.
[328] *DGFP*, D. iv, No. 233; cf. Hillgruber, 'Frankreich als Faktor'.
[329] *DGFP*, D. iv, No. 81.
[330] Ibid., No. 152; cf. Deist, III.III.4 above.
[331] Ritter's opinion (*Goerdeler*, 482–3) that in Dec. 1938 there was still no indication of impending action against Czechoslovakia is true enough subjectively, i.e. from the viewpoint of many members of the opposition to Hitler. But it was precisely the element of surprise and the exploiting of a favourable opportunity that was to be decisive. For that very reason no exact dates were mentioned. On the whole question see also Müller, *Heer*, 387.
[332] The term is used by Booms, '*Ursprung*', 332; see also Thies, *Architekt*, 40–1.
[333] Rauschning, *Hitler Speaks*, 17.
[334] *IMT* xxxiv. 477 ff., Doc. C-136; see also Görlitz, *Keitel*, 196.

reduced to conjectures. The anti-Nazi opposition was paralysed by the effects of the September crisis and was incapable of action. There was a striking contrast between this policy of secrecy and Hitler's 'addresses to officers'.[335] During the period of uncertainty, the most instructive of these was probably that delivered to troop commanders on 10 February 1939. Hitler called for confidence in his decisions, which were always carefully thought out and hence unalterable. Many, including even 'some Wehrmacht circles', had failed to understand his decisions of 1938, which had led to the brilliant successes of that year. But 1938 was only a step on a long way 'that is marked out for us'.[336] Hitler was certainly looking into the distant future here—perhaps the next hundred years—but his eye was also on the immediate future. He called for confidence and resistance to future appeals by conservative doubters. The address was a kind of manifesto of his foreign policy, calculated to appeal to an audience composed of officers of the most varied services.

Then suddenly the desired situation came about. Differences between Prague and the Slovak government, excited and exacerbated by Hitler, provided a pretext for the invasion of what was left of the Czech state.[337] On 13 March 1939 the Slovak premier Tiso, dismissed by President Hácha, was received by Hitler in the Reich chancery with the intimation that Slovakia would be left to her fate unless she broke with Prague.[338] Tiso assured Hitler of compliance, and the Slovak parliament declared its own independence on the 14th. Next day Hácha was confronted in Berlin with the news that the order had already been given for German troops to invade Bohemia and Moravia and for their incorporation in the Reich. If the Czech army offered no resistance it would be easy, upon the reconstruction of Czech national life, to accord Czechoslovakia a generous way of life on her own.[339] By a 'declaration' of the two governments on 15 March the Czech president 'placed the fate of the Czech people and their country confidently in the hands of the Führer of the German Reich'. Thus, with lightning rapidity, the act of politico-military blackmail was completed. When Hácha returned to Prague he was saluted by a German guard of honour: Hitler was already installed in the Hradčin. Neurath was appointed to govern the 'Reich Protectorate' of Bohemia and Moravia, which Hitler created against Ribbentrop's advice.

Hitler's triumph provoked further illusions, confirming his preconceived ideas about the Western democracies. But the chagrin of the British and French at their own 'unreadiness' led to a reaction of energy and determination. Ever since Munich, London had contemplated the future with a more realistic eye. The fact, which had been obscured for decades, that France was essential to Britain's military

---

[335] Pointed out in this context by Thies, *Architekt*, 105 ff. The politico-psychological effects of Munich on the German opposition are well reflected in a letter of Goerdeler's of 11 Oct. 1938: cf. Ritter, *Resistance*, 113 ff.

[336] Thies, *Architekt*, 114; see also Groscurth, *Tagebücher*, 166–7; Domarus, ii. 1075.

[337] For the military preparations cf. Umbreit, *Militärverwaltungen*, 50 ff.; for German subversion in Slovakia see Hoensch, *Slowakei*.

[338] *DGFP*, D. iv, No. 202. For Tiso's visit see also Irving, *War Path*, 187.

[339] *DGFP*, D. iv, No. 228, record of Hitler–Hácha meeting of 15 Mar. 1939.

policy and strategy in Europe and the Mediterranean basin was once more clearly recognized. During the evolution that now took place towards new positions it came to be seen that Hitler had much less room for manœuvre than was presupposed by Berlin's visionary plans and aims. The campaign against truth and loyalty was a failure.

VI. 1939: The Initial Position

1. Drawing the Lines

Soon after Munich it became clear that Hitler's foreign policy was doomed to failure, as Britain would not play the role that his plan assigned to her. During Chamberlain's negotiations at Godesberg the committee of imperial defence (CID) had come to the conclusion that it was too early to take up the German challenge. In a year's time, however—in the opinion of General Ismay, who succeeded Hankey as secretary of the committee—Britain's air defences would be strong enough to defeat German hopes of a quick victory.[1] Gradually, too, the chiefs of staff gained acceptance for their view that the army must be substantially enlarged in order to send a force to the Continent in the event of war. They feared that if France were left to herself on the Continent she might give up the 'unequal struggle', and 'it is difficult to say how the security of the UK could be maintained if France were forced to capitulate'.[2] The defence of France and Holland was again seen by the military as part of the defence of the United Kingdom.[3] The cabinet took time to adopt this view. In October–November 1938 the defence of Britain against air attack was still regarded as the army's main function. Chamberlain and Halifax, at talks in Paris in November 1938, were very reserved in their response to French pressure for closer military co-operation. But at a meeting of the CID in mid-December Halifax put the Anglo-French relationship in a new light: 'A time might come when the French would cease to be enthusiastic about their relations with Great Britain if they were left with the impression that it was they who must bear the brunt of the fighting and slaughter on land.'[4]

The Paris talks, which took place shortly before the Franco-German pact of 6

---

[1] Howard, *Commitment*, 123. The Luftwaffe general staff took a similar view of the prospects for the period after the summer of 1939. Cf. report of 23 Apr. 1938 by Oberstleutnant Schmid, head of the 5th division, BA-MA RL 2/534, and Maier in vol. ii of the present work. Schmid's report evidently came to Hitler's knowledge. British rearmament was now pushed forward not only with the object of strengthening peacetime forces but as a direct preparation for war, and with clear priority for the RAF. Between 1934 and 1938 the air force estimates had already risen from £18m. to £133m., while those for the army had only risen from £40m. to £121m.: cf. Peden, 'Burden of Imperial Defence', 144. Peden rightly points out that as regards armoured vehicles the switch to producing medium and heavy tanks had been delayed by politico-strategic considerations, and Germany too did not start on Panzer models III and IV until 1937. According to Kennedy, *Rise and Fall*, 286, 'The RAF rose from being the third service to being the first in the 1930s.' Estimates (£m.) are: (1938) *army*—122.3, *navy*—127.2, *RAF*—133.8. (1939, before outbreak of war) *army*—88.2, *navy*—97.9, *RAF*—105.7. Even so, the comparison with Germany was unfavourable. As against Germany's estimated 5,600 first-line aircraft, Britain had about 2,000 and France about 2,200 (British estimate). The Luftwaffe actually had only 3,300 aircraft: cf. Murray, *Change*, 247; War Office Review, PRO Cab 3/8, p. 2, 301-A, 14 Nov. 1938; CID, appendix III. On British rearmament in the air see also Hyde, *British Air Policy*.

[2] Howard, *Commitment*, 129.

[3] Details in Gibbs, *Strategy*, i. 498 ff. The chiefs of staff argued that the defence of France was vital to the security of the UK, which was the 'corner-stone of our imperial defence policy' (p. 506).

[4] Ibid. i. 494.

December, had clearly made an impression on the foreign secretary, who pointed out that if Britain persisted in refusing to commit herself on the Continent, France might accept German offers for a far-reaching agreement and might even stand aside if Hitler were to attack Britain. After Munich there was in fact no such danger, as is shown by a memorandum of 16 November entitled 'Politique extérieure de la France', used by the French leaders as a brief for their conversations with the British.[5] The memorandum does, however, reflect a new independent line of French foreign policy. After the break-up of the Little Entente, Paris and London both regarded France's strategic position as precarious *vis-à-vis* her over-mighty German neighbour. The British ambassador and the military attaché in Paris repeatedly drew attention to this fact, and intelligence reports painted an alarming picture of Hitler's intentions. A degree of nervousness began to prevail. Halifax for a time even thought Germany might launch an attack on Britain. In any case it was regarded as fairly certain that Hitler would first turn against the Western powers.[6] The British government wondered how long France could withstand a German attack. Consulted on this in January 1939, the chiefs of staff took the view that the Maginot line would hold, but that France would have less hope of resisting an attack through Belgium, which itself might hold out for fourteen days.[7] In another report they recommended on strategic grounds that Britain should intervene if Germany attacked Holland. The cabinet agreed. London now began to press the French to clarify their attitude. The foreign secretary was authorized to state that Britain would come to France's aid if Germany should attack Switzerland and if France took up arms in consequence. The cabinet also agreed to staff talks being held with France to concert action in a war against Germany and Italy.[8]

In February 1939 Chamberlain agreed to a substantial increase in British land forces, and in March it was decided to raise the territorial army from thirteen to twenty-six divisions. At this time Lord Chatfield, the new minister for coordination of defence, recommended universal conscription, which was introduced in the summer. Contacts with the United States and Canada to strengthen the RAF had already taken place in the spring of 1938. Britain began rapidly to organize her defence forces in the hope of stabilizing the situation in Western Europe. This was entirely in accord with French ideas.

Thus, Hitler's plan to bring Western Europe under his own control, to eliminate France, and to keep British military forces off the Continent was opposed by at least the beginnings of a defensive system—although British strategy did not exactly envisage this variant of Hitler's plans, which involved an attack on the West but also a special role for Britain. If Britain were expelled from the Continent but maintained a resolute attitude, this would mean a military stalemate for a limited period but would not gain time for Hitler politically. Thus, in the West the situation foreshadowed that of September 1939 and the defeat of France in 1940.

---

[5] *DDF²* xii, No. 314.
[6] Cf. Niedhart, *Großbritannien*, 391.
[7] Gibbs, *Strategy*, i. 498.
[8] Aster, *1939*, 47.

This was the more so as the relatively independent policy pursued by Bonnet after Munich had collapsed with the Prague coup in March 1939, and French foreign policy was now in the hands of Daladier, who had been sceptical from the outset.

The attempt to bring about closer relations between Berlin and Rome can be seen, from Hitler's point of view, as a reaction to the tightening of Anglo-French relations. The British announcement of intensified rearmament measures shortly after Munich produced corresponding reactions on the German side. The army, navy, and air force were to be considerably strengthened. The navy continued with its building programme, and at the end of January 1939 Hitler agreed to an extended 'Z plan'.[9] The cooling of relations with Britain was also reflected in pressure towards the end of 1938 for submarine parity with Britain.[10] In mid-October 1938 orders were given for a substantial strengthening of the Luftwaffe, directed against Britain and more especially the British navy and supply routes. It was realized in London, however, that Germany did not possess a strategic air force of any consequence.[11]

While London's politico-strategic calculations were based on the possibility of Britain and France fighting a war against Germany, Italy, and perhaps Japan, Hitler and Ribbentrop were seeking to bring about a 'defensive' alliance between Berlin, Rome, and Tokyo. Since the anti-Comintern pact offered no guarantees against a hostile coalition, Ribbentrop wanted a military pact which would counterbalance the combined strength of Britain, France, and the Soviet Union.[12] It was to be 'based on the Führer's view that an armed conflict with the Western democracies must be regarded as being within the bounds of possibility in four to five years' time'. This was the basis of the 'Notes for Wehrmacht discussions with Italy' which the chief of staff communicated to the Reich foreign minister at the end of November 1938.[13] The 'basic military-political object' of a war against France and Britain was first to knock out France, which would prevent Britain continuing the war from the mainland. Belgium, Holland, and Switzerland were to be kept neutral. Spain and Hungary, it was assumed, would be benevolently neutral, the Soviet Union 'hostile'; Poland and the Balkan countries were 'doubtful'. It did not seem necessary for the time being to consider non-European powers. On this basis Hitler and the OKW laid down the following 'outline allocation of tasks'. Germany would concentrate all her forces on the Western front. The object of the land war would be to break through the Maginot line, after which the overthrow of France was expected to present no further military problems. The naval war would be directed against British and French communications in the North Sea and the Atlantic,

---

[9] Salewski, *Seekriegsleitung*, i. 53 ff.; cf. Deist, III.II.3 (*c*) above.

[10] Salewski, *Seekriegsleitung*, i. 65; *DBFP*[3] iii, appendix VII, pp. 662 ff.

[11] Völker, *Luftwaffe*, 75; *IMT* xxvii, doc. 1301-PS. For the Luftwaffe switching to Britain as its contemplated adversary see also Gemzell, *Raeder*, 182. For the British assessment of German air potential cf. interview with Sir Kingsley Wood, secretary of state for air, on 9 Feb. 1939: Hyde, *British Air Policy*, 476.

[12] Ribbentrop–Ciano meeting in Rome, 28 Oct. 1938, *DGFP*, D. iv, No. 400.

[13] Ibid., No. 411, annex. For Hitler's expectation of a war with the West in four or five years see also Irving, *War Path*, 156-7.

while the air offensive would be aimed at Britain, with the air force and navy combining to cut off British sea routes. Italy was to carry out diversionary operations against Britain and France and ward off threats to Germany's southern and eastern flank (Poland).

These plans could not be carried out. Italy refused the division of labour, which would have amounted to preparing for war in German interests alone. The 'pact of steel' signed on 22 May 1939 did not achieve the results for Hitler that the 'Notes' were intended to bring about. Mussolini would not commit himself to any joint activities before 1942. The summer of 1939 also saw the failure of German attempts to persuade Japan to conclude a military alliance against Britain.

The question has often been put as to what Hitler really intended to achieve with his undoubtedly anti-British policy after Munich.[14] The 'Notes' for the German–Italian staff talks indicate that the war against Britain was still contemplated in European terms. Hitler still had some unsolved problems in view, first of all Poland. In view of Munich and Prague, and since he had failed to win over Britain for his plans, a future show-down could affect the interests of both London and Warsaw, so that he might have to reckon with a combination of the two. Hence the uncertainty observed by Weizsäcker in mid-December 1938; Hitler and Ribbentrop were bent on war, but 'it had not yet been decided whether to strike out right away against England, while keeping Poland neutral, or to move first against the East, in order to liquidate the German–Poland and the Ukranian question'.[15]

2. POLISH INTERLUDE: OCTOBER 1938–MARCH 1939

The Polish question appeared for the time being secondary to Hitler's attempts to conclude a military pact with his anti-Comintern partners. Curiously, although the conquest of *Lebensraum* in the east was central to his European policy, he was less preoccupied by Poland than were the 'revisionists' in the foreign ministry and the Wehrmacht. These circles, it is true, were against tackling the Polish problem in 1938, but only because it might cause a conflict with the Western powers. 'Not yet' had been a basic principle of the conservative opposition since 1937.

For quite other reasons, Hitler made an attempt to reach agreement with Poland on his own terms even before the liquidation of Czechoslovakia. The result of this attempt was an important factor in the situation in the spring of 1939, which led directly to the line-up in the following September.

What part could Poland have played in Hitler's plan towards the end of 1938? A week before war broke out, on 22 August 1939, he expounded the reasons for his decision to senior commanders at Berchtesgaden, in an elaborately staged address meant to 'strengthen their confidence'. He was at pains on that occasion to show that he had been consistent throughout. This in itself may tend to cast doubt on the account he gave the generals of his judgement of the situation as it had been at the

[14] Recently Henke, *England*, 204 ff., with numerous references to Hitler's anti-British attitude; also Aigner, *Ringen*, on the 'wave of anti-British feeling' in Germany.
[15] Hassell, *Diaries*, 26.

end of 1938. But his description of the attempt to come to terms with Poland accords well enough with what actually happened between October 1938 and March 1939, so that it seems legitimate to take his remarks of 22 August as a truthful account of what was in his mind. He told the generals that the plan which had 'appealed' to him (*der mir sympathische Plan*) was to 'establish a tolerable relationship with Poland in order to fight first against the West'.[16] This 'first' was of decisive importance in Hitler's eyes. Apparently he had in mind a period of 'some years'. This corresponded to the estimate on which the German–Italian military talks for the proposed alliance had been based, viz. four or five years, and also more or less to the period he had envisaged as the most likely case in November 1937. If the great powers behaved 'normally' as expected, the attack on the West would have taken place in the early 1940s. Thus, an acceleration of the programme in consequence of the Anschluss and the annexation of the Sudeten area was not yet envisaged; the pressure of time due to Western rearmament was evidently not yet co-ordinated with the prerequisites for a short, successful war against the West. Hitler did not have it in mind to turn first against the Soviet Union with Polish help.[17] A striking modification in Hitler's outline of the future stages in his bid for hegemony came in an address of 8 March 1939, shortly before the march on Prague,[18] at the time when he was reaching the decision to crush Poland by force of arms. Announcing this plan to an audience of senior officers, businessmen, and Party functionaries, he justified it on economic grounds. After the fall of Poland pressure could be exercised on Hungary and Romania, which in his view belonged to Germany's *Lebensraum*, so as to dominate them economically; Germany would then have the benefit of their rich agricultural resources and oil. Yugoslavia too would fall into Germany's economic orbit. These problems would be solved by about 1940.

Poland's attitude during the negotiations with Germany, which went on for a month from October 1938, evidently made a considerable difference to Hitler's timing but not to his basic strategy. It was still his intention first to bring Poland under control and then to turn against France as the first major stage in his plan. This, he seemed to assume, would mean a kind of automatic German dominance over Britain, that aged country 'enfeebled by democracy', and by the same token Germany would gain control over Britain's world-wide resources.

This argument seems primarily to have been intended for the businessmen concerned. It is noteworthy how close it came to the actual sequence of events in and after September 1939. True, Germany did not lay hands on Britain's overseas possessions or even those of France. Britain herself was proof against a fatal blow, because German preparations did not basically exceed those required by a

[16] Unsigned record of Hitler's address to Wehrmacht commanders-in-chief on 22 Aug. 1939: *DGFP*, D. vii, No. 192. To the same effect Weinberg, *Foreign Policy*, ii; a critical view in Adamthwaite, 'War Origins', 113.

[17] Thus e.g. Roos, *Polen*; also Booms, 'Ursprung', 329–53, and statement by Coulondre, the French ambassador in Berlin, that Poland was intended by the Axis to spearhead an anti-Soviet offensive: French Government, *Yellow Book*, No. 124.

[18] A record of the address, drawn up in Vienna on 12 Mar. by State Secretary Keppler and Generaldirektor Vogl, came into the possession of W. Bullitt, the US ambassador in Paris, in Sept.: *FRUS* (1939), i. 672 ff. In view of its origin it must be treated with caution as a source.

continental power. Her resources and timetable were in flat contradiction to the feasibility of such a policy.

But the address of 8 March is also noteworthy in another respect. Hitler let it be understood that once he had gained control of British and French overseas possessions, he would settle accounts with the 'dollar Jews'. It was his aim to wipe out the 'Jewish democracy' of the United States. These racist passages strike a similar note to the Reichstag speech of 10 January 1939,[19] with the prophecy that a world war would mean 'the annihilation of the Jewish race in Europe'. But, apart from this essentially negative aim with its *idée fixe* of destroying the 'parasitic Jewish domination' of Europe and the world, the address envisaged a sequence of politico-military decisions that was in no way compatible with the programme of eliminating the Soviet Union and establishing hegemony over the whole of Europe before turning overseas. Again, this notion of Hitler's contrasted curiously with the idea he entertained for a short time after the victory of 1940, of seeking an accommodation with Britain and building up a colonial empire in central Africa, which would constitute an economic zone of world-wide importance when combined with German domination of all Europe west of the Soviet Union.[20] If the latter idea has been judged 'premature' from the point of view of Hitler's 'programme',[21] that must be still more the case with the intentions he adumbrated in March 1939.

In general the discussion of Hitler's programme suffers from the fact that the unrealistic plans and memoranda relating to an extra-European policy take too little account of the actual resources of the Western powers. If Europe is kept in mind as the real field of Hitler's actions and possibilities, the address of 8 March 1939 can be classified more precisely. It is then seen as evidence that Poland was refusing to conform to Hitler's timetable. To all appearances he would not have four years, after eliminating Poland, in which to rearm undisturbed. On the contrary, Britain's attitude in the autumn and winter of 1938 indicated that the Western democracies were alarmed and were hastening to repair their defences. Poland, which Hitler had intended to manipulate for his ends in both the west and the east, refused to become his satellite. She thus upset his strategy of dealing lightning blows with his rear covered, and manœuvred herself into the role of a risk factor of the first order, which Hitler felt he could only eliminate by armed force. At the end of March he was much exercised by this thought, as can be seen from his directive to the military chiefs (discussed below). Poland had not conformed to the strategic model he had in mind for the West, and by the same token he ruled out the idea of using Polish help against the Soviet Union.

The attempts to bring Poland on to the desired course began on 24 October 1938 with a conversation at Berchtesgaden between Ribbentrop and Lipski, the Polish ambassador.[22] After Munich, Poland had sought German approval of a plan to

---

[19] Domarus, ii. 1047 ff. (here 1058) = Baynes, ii. 1567 ff., also (for the present passage) i. 741.

[20] Hillgruber, *Strategie*, 242 ff.

[21] Ibid. 243.

[22] Record by Hewel, *DGFP*, D. v, No. 81.

detach the Carpatho-Ukraine (Sub-Carpathian Ruthenia) from Czechoslovakia and give it to Hungary, which would thus gain a common frontier with Poland. The German foreign ministry, on the other hand, was for applying the right of self-determination. Poland, by sharing in the spoils of Czechoslovakia, had incurred the reputation of collaborating with Hitler, although her aims were basically self-regarding. Was there a chance of encouraging her appetite and turning it in directions convenient to German foreign policy? Apart from the general policy of playing off Poland, Hungary, and Romania against one another and making them dependent on Germany, Ribbentrop hoped to make Poland more directly subservient to German political ambitions. As with Italy and the south Tyrol, a clearing-up of the frontier issue might lead to a general understanding: Danzig would go to Germany, Poland would keep the Corridor, which would be traversed by an autobahn and extraterritorial German railways. In addition, as had been suggested before, Poland would join the anti-Comintern pact.

But it was already clear that the Poles were not amenable to German demands over Danzig, nor were they willing to adopt a directly anti-Soviet stand. Such, however, was the purpose behind Ribbentrop's proposal to Lipski on 19 November, that German–Polish relations should be placed on a 'cast-iron basis' (*eherne Dauerbasis*).[23] Poland was the object of diplomatic offensives by both Berlin and Moscow. On 26 November, a few days after Ribbentrop's second major approach, the Russians reaffirmed their non-aggression pact with Poland. The German ambassador in Moscow reported that this was to guard against Poland joining the anti-Comintern pact. The Russians, who had had fears of a joint German–Polish action against the Soviet Union,[24] now believed that the starting-point for a German eastward offensive had been shifted back from the Soviet–Polish to the Polish–German frontier.

In mid-December Ribbentrop adopted plainer language. He

hoped the Poles would follow a policy based on the tradition of Pilsudski and his breadth of vision. This meant that Poland would take German interests into account and would not resist certain natural phenomena and inevitable developments. Then there would be no further obstacles in the way of a final and stable settlement with Germany and a broad common policy. . . . Germany was anti-Russian and if only for that reason welcomed a strong Poland who would defend her interests against Russia.[25]

On 5 January 1939 Hitler in turn emphasized to Beck, the Polish foreign minister, the importance of the desired territorial settlement for the two countries' future policy. The Soviet Union was the centre of attention; from a purely military point of view the existence of a strong Polish army was a considerable relief to Germany. The Polish divisions standing on the Soviet frontier 'saved Germany just so much additional military expenditure'.[26]

This episode fits in well with Hitler's anti-British strategy of these months.

---

[23] Memorandum by Ribbentrop, *DGFP*, D. v, No. 101.
[24] Schulenburg, Geman ambassador in Moscow, to the foreign ministry, 3 Dec. 1938, ibid., No. 108.
[25] Record of Ribbentrop–Lipski meeting, 15 Dec. 1938, ibid., No. 112.
[26] Record of Hitler–Beck meeting at Berchtesgaden, ibid., No. 119.

According to his plan, Poland would at least to some extent take over the function of covering Germany's rear against the Soviet Union. Her accession to the anti-Comintern pact, which Ribbentrop again broached on the following day, would not necessarily mean an active military role against the Soviet Union. Ribbentrop offered co-operation over the Ukrainian question, which Germany was prepared to regard as a peculiar concern of Poland's. This of course would imply her adopting 'a more and more pronounced anti-Russian attitude', and therefore raised the question whether Poland might not one day join the anti-Comintern pact.[27]

Hitler and Ribbentrop refrained from disclosing that their approach might, in certain circumstances, involve Poland in a policy directed primarily against the West. On the basic questions of Danzig and a more anti-Russian stance, the Poles showed no disposition to agree. Beck informed Ribbentrop that he felt pessimistic for the first time, particularly as regards Danzig. He saw no prospect of agreement on the basis suggested by Hitler.[28] A treaty with Germany against the Soviet Union would be dangerous to Poland, as Beck repeated to Ribbentrop in Warsaw at the end of January.[29] In the ensuing weeks German–Polish relations were marked by increasing tension in Danzig and elsewhere and by further German attempts to persuade the Poles to a general settlement; these, however, were completely fruitless. Lipski repeatedly pointed out that Beck's foreign policy had to take account of difficulties on the home front. Moltke, the German ambassador in Warsaw, had reported in September 1938 that the Polish minister of war, like Marshal Śmigly-Rydz and General Sosnkowski, inspector-general of the army, was not in accord with Beck's policy.[30] As Hitler probably anticipated, the Poles finally refused to give up Danzig or grant the Reich extraterritorial communications with East Prussia, and it was thus clear that the attempt at a 'settlement' had no chance of success.[31]

Hitler thereupon ordered the army commander-in-chief to study the 'question of Poland'.[32] He gave only the general direction that a 'solution in the near future' would require especially favourable political conditions, but that Poland must be so crushed that in the coming decades it need no longer be considered as a political factor. As yet he did not think of incorporating the whole of Poland into Germany or breaking up the Polish state. He thought in terms of a frontier running from the eastern border of East Prussia to the eastern tip of Silesia. He added that a solution of the Polish question in the foreseeable future seemed to him inevitable.[33] What he meant by 'foreseeable' was soon apparent: he ordered the high command of the Wehrmacht to plan 'Operation White' so that 'the operation can be carried out at

[27] Ribbentrop's memorandum, dated 9 Jan., of conversation with Beck on 6 Jan, ibid., No. 120 (quotation, p. 160).
[28] Polish Government, *Official Documents*, No. 49.
[29] Ribbentrop's memorandum, dated 1 Feb., of conversation on 26 Jan., *DGFP*, D. v, No. 126.
[30] Report of 2 Sept. 1938 on anti-German feeling in Poland, ibid., No. 53.
[31] Ribbentrop's memorandum of conversation with Lipski on 26 Mar. 1939, *DGFP*, D. vi, No. 101.
[32] Directive of 25 Mar. 1939, *IMT* xxxviii. 274-6; *DGFP*, D. vi, No. 99. On 'Case White' cf. Deist, III.III.4 above.
[33] See also Krausnick, 'Vorgeschichte', 374, and Müller, *Heer*, 390 ff.

any time as from 1 September 1939'.[34] With the army leaders in particular, he broached his plan much more diplomatically than he had in the case of Czechoslovakia in 1938. Perhaps he hoped to anticipate objection in this way. At all events the army commander and the generals could feel that they were better briefed and would have to cope 'only' with an isolated war if a settlement could not be reached with Poland. This tactic of Hitler's no doubt influenced the attitude of the military chiefs up to the outbreak of war.[35]

The directive for 'Operation White' was issued on 3 April 1939 as a 'Directive of the supreme commander of the Wehrmacht'.[36] It stands in a curious relationship to Hitler's general order of the same date, issued by the Wehrmacht high command and specifying 1 September as the date by which preparations must be complete for the war against Poland. The indefinite formulations in the former directive testify to the intention of waging war against Poland in such a way as to isolate the latter as much as possible. It envisaged that a 'final settlement might become necessary' if Poland were to 'adopt a threatening attitude towards Germany'. The isolation of Poland might be possible—here Hitler reverted to old habits of thought—if a state of crisis were to develop in France, which would have its effect on Britain also. But a blitzkrieg might also achieve the desired effect: 'The isolation of Poland will be all the more easily maintained, even after the outbreak of hostilities, if we succeed in starting the war with sudden, heavy blows and in gaining rapid successes.' Therefore, preparation should be made for a surprise attack. Hitler indicated that a concealed or open mobilization would be ordered at the latest possible moment, on the day before the attack.

The directive followed close on Poland's refusal to conform to the aims of German policy.[37] The connection with Hitler's Western policy was played down in the directive itself, but was recognizable as an overall strategy. The basic object of building up the Wehrmacht—i.e. political and politico-military planning in general—was, according to Hitler, still dictated by the 'antagonism of the Western democracies'. The plan for 'Operation White' was to be seen only as a complement to preparations in general and not as the 'prerequisite for a military conflict with the Western opponents'. Subjectively, this was a kind of wishful programme. After the shock of the march on Prague, Hitler hoped that his first warlike undertaking might likewise be achieved as an isolated action. But, in contrast to September 1938, he himself now planned this move in the framework of a war policy designed to eliminate the West as an obstacle to his advance towards hegemony.

On 23 May 1939 Hitler explained to the commanders-in-chief, the army chief of

---

[34] Directive by chief of high command of the Wehrmacht, *DGFP*, D. vi, No. 149.

[35] This view is taken by Krausnick, 'Vorgeschichte', 374, and Müller, *Heer*, 391. Müller also ascribes importance to Warlimont's role in this connection.

[36] *DGFP*, D. vi, No. 185, annex II; *IMT* xxxiv. 481 ff., doc. C-137; *Hitlers Weisungen*, 17 ff. (=trans., 3). The chief of the high command issued the directive for 'Case White' to the army, navy, and air force commanders-in-chief on 3 Apr.: BA-MA PG 33276, OKW-WFA, copy No. 5. This gave the date fixed by Hitler as 1 Sept.

[37] Görlitz, *Keitel*, 205, makes this connection clear. Hitler is reported as having said more than once in Apr. 'The Polish problem demands . . . to be resolved. The sensible old Marshal Pilsudski died too soon.'

staff, and other officers from different services his views on Germany's situation and the conclusions to be drawn from it.[38] The Polish problem now appeared in a fresh light: it could no longer be 'dissociated from the show-down with the West'. The war might be a long one. If Poland could first be knocked out in an isolated struggle, it would be possible to 'expand our living-space in the east' and 'make food supplies secure'—aims primarily of importance from the point of view of waging war. This was short of the basic solution of the *Lebensraum* problem as Hitler saw it. In any case 'it is not Danzig that is at stake'. In giving vent to his mistrust of Poland, Hitler discredited his efforts of the past months to achieve a comprehensive settlement: Poland would always be on the side of Germany's adversaries and would exploit every opportunity against her. Moreover, Poland was a doubtful barrier against Russian pressure. Clearly there could be 'no question of sparing Poland'; she was to be attacked 'at the first suitable opportunity'. Success in isolating Poland would be decisive.

Consistently with Hitler's focusing on the show-down with the Western powers, the war against Poland was now considered a necessary preliminary on two accounts: to eliminate an uncertain factor in Germany's rear, and to improve her prospects in what would probably be a long war. A 'repetition of Czechia' was not to be counted on, but Hitler aimed to prevent the Western powers intervening in a German–Polish war. If they did so nevertheless, the fight would be primarily against them. It would be better to attack them first and 'finish off Poland at the same time'.

Hitler's exposition of 23 May 1939 shows to what an extent his programme was constrained by his own war and armaments policy. He realized that it could hardly be carried out without a war against the Western powers. 'England sees in our development the establishment of a hegemony which would weaken her. Therefore England is our enemy and the show-down with England is a matter of life and death.' A short war was the object, but Germany must be prepared for a long one—a realization that had to enter into his calculations from now on.

France, in Hitler's mind, was less and less important by comparison with Britain, which he had always seen as the leading Western power. He saw the danger of 'sliding into a war with England on account of Poland'. This would make impossible the idea of dealing Britain at the outset 'a smashing blow or *the* smashing blow' (a fantasy in any case, given the state of German armament). But Hitler's dilemma was that he could not exclude that variant. Poland was to be defeated in a short campaign so as to free Germany's rear and acquire Polish resources, as well as preparing the way for a solution of the 'Baltic problem'. The armament programme for a major war, on the other hand, was geared by Hitler's orders to 1943–4. Long-term armament and short-term foreign-policy objectives were difficult to harmonize. Moreover, Hitler's estimate of the date for a show-down with Britain varied between 1940–1 and 1943–4. In all these calculations the Soviet Union was disregarded. It is thus to be supposed that the accelerated planning for colonies and

---

[38] Schmundt's report in Jacobsen, *1939–1945*, doc. 6, pp. 109 ff.; *IMT* xxxvii. 546 ff., doc L-79: *DGFP*, D. vi, No. 433.

a colonial adminstration[39] which took place during this phase was not a sign that Hitler expected soon to embark on global ambitions after achieving his *Lebensraum* objectives in the east.

3. EASTERN AND SOUTH-EAST EUROPE IN GERMAN AND WESTERN STRATEGY, AND THE BRITISH GUARANTEE TO POLAND

After the Prague coup the entire Eastern European zone between the area of German power and the Soviet Union became an object of politico-strategic interest to the major powers. The West expected Hitler to strike next in this part of Europe, which became of greater economic and strategic importance to him, since it was necessary to his policy of continental hegemony and he was beginning to envisage the possibility of a long-drawn-out war. The *Lebensraum* of which Hitler spoke in May 1939 consisted, besides Poland, of economic opportunities in the Baltic area and above all in south-east Europe. The German–Romanian commercial treaty of 23 March 1939 was an important step towards involving the Balkan countries in an economic system of central and south-east Europe under German control. The Western economic counter-offensive, and the Anglo-French guarantee to Romania of 13 April 1939, prevented Hitler from developing this intention until after the war with Poland, but it remained valid as a programme[40] with wider political implications. The use of the term '*Lebensraum*' in the immediate context is not to be taken as implying the renunciation of longer-term plans. Meanwhile Hitler added another piece to his edifice in a north-easterly direction, also on 23 March, by seizing the Memel district from Lithuania. These moves towards continental hegemony were part of the approach to a degree of autarky in foodstuffs and armaments which would avert the danger of Germany being economically starved out in a long war. In Hitler's view, the navy and air force were the instruments with which to fight such a war against Britain, while it was for the army to secure the necessary strategic positions on the coast facing England. But first the army must be ready to deal a swift blow against France, Belgium, and Holland: 'We must attack Holland with lightning speed.' In general, it must be possible to overrun Germany's neighbour states 'starting from barracks'.

These aims could only be achieved by the rapid and large-scale development of

[39] Reference is generally made in this connection to a letter of 9 Mar. 1939 from Lammers, head of the Reichskanzlei, to von Epp, Reichsleiter of the office for colonial policy. This letter, which was afterwards treated as a directive from the Führer, called for the streamlining of preparations for a future colonial administration. See Hildebrand, *Reich*, 603 ff.; Hillgruber, 'Weltpolitische Lage', 287.

[40] Cf. report by Ministerialdirektor Wohlthat on the conclusion of the state treaty with Romania (23 Mar. 1939), submitted to Göring on 23 Mar.: *DGFP*, D. vi. No. 131, annex, which, however, paints a somewhat exaggerated picture of the persuasive effect of his negotiations. The British government had received a warning of German intentions from Virgil Tilea, the Romanian minister in London, on 17 Mar. According to this, the alleged German attempt to secure a monopoly of Romania's exports in return for a guarantee of her frontiers was viewed in Bucharest as a kind of ultimatum: cf. Halifax's telegram of 17 Mar. to the British missions in Warsaw, Ankara, Athens, and Belgrade, *DBFP*[3] iv, No. 390. The warning, however, was not a true reflection of the situation in Bucharest, where different political views were in conflict. See also Aster, *1939*, 61 ff. The 'programmatic' character of the treaty is emphasized by J. Förster, 'Rumäniens Weg'; see also Volkmann, II.vi.6 above.

armoured and motorized units, artillery, the air force, and the navy; while at the same time Hitler demanded early completion of the western and eastern fortifications. The German economy was insufficient by itself to sustain these purposes, especially as it was desired to cut back the standard of living as little as possible. Hence, more intensive measures were now taken to bind to the German war economy sources of raw materials in Eastern and south-east Europe.

It must be noted that the navy and air force were to be armed with a view primarily to the war against Britain. 'The moment England is cut off from her supplies she is forced to capitulate.' Here Hitler also saw his chance to deal rapid devastating blows at the beginning of a war. Germany must strike at the British navy. Once the army had captured the chief positions on the coast opposite England, 'industrial production will cease to flow into the bottomless Danaid cask of the army's battles and will be available for the benefit of the Luftwaffe and the fleet'.

The fantasy of 'rapid annihilating blows'—overlooking completely that the means for them did not exist—was no doubt rooted in Hitler's mental habits. It must also be related, however, to the optimism of the Luftwaffe commanders, who in the spring of 1939 believed they were well ahead of the British and French air forces in terms of equipment and leadership—a contrast to their pessimism in the previous years. In May–June and again in August 1939, however, in a study prepared by the chief of staff of the formations earmarked for use against Britain,[41] air force advisers warned that for the present only partial success could be counted on and that the Luftwaffe would not become really dangerous to Britain until the second year of war, by which they meant 1941. On 3 July, however, an air force in first-class condition was conjured up for Hitler at the testing station near Rechlin.[42]

According to the Luftwaffe staff at the beginning of May 1939, Germany was the only country that had 'advanced to a total conception of the preparation and conduct of offensive and defensive air warfare as regards equipment, organization, tactics, and leadership'.[43] By May 1940 the staff estimated that Germany would have a decisive lead over the Western powers, but they gave warning of the time factor: soon things would be different. Hitler had not much time left to take advantage of the up-to-dateness of his forces and make political use of Germany's supposed ability to deal annihilating blows. The air staff rated the deterrent effect of the Luftwaffe very highly, and Hitler made much play with it in his efforts to convince the army leaders that the Western powers would not go to war. But his whole political scheme was predicated on Germany's lead in armaments, and he thus brought on himself the risk and compulsion of an all-or-nothing strategy.

The occupation of remnant Czechoslovakia and the creation of the 'Protectorate of Bohemia and Moravia' and the completely dependent vassal state of Slovakia seemed to portend further rapid change in Eastern Europe, while Spain's accession to the anti-Comintern pact on 27 March was a sign of the effects of German policy

[41] BA-MA RL 7/159; cf. Maier, vol. ii of the present work, II.1.
[42] Irving, *Rise and Fall*, 73–4, and Maier, vol. ii of the present work, II.1; Deist, III.11.4 (*b*) above. Cf. also Boog, *Luftwaffenführung*.
[43] Annex to R.d.L. u. Ob.d.L Chef des Genstab., No. 700/39, g.Kdos. (5. Abt. 1), 2 May 1939, 'Die Luftlage in Europe, Stand: Frühjahr 1939', BA-MA RL 2/535.

in the West. Germany's increasing political involvement in south-east Europe was
noted in Britain with mixed feelings. Chamberlain had stated in the Commons on
1 November 1938 his view that it was natural for Germany to enjoy economic
preponderance in that area,[44] and in September 1938 he had used that variant of
appeasement to counter arguments that Germany was again being economically
'encircled'. The foreign office, however, looked beyond Balkan economic problems
to Britain's strategic position in the Mediterranean and the Near East, and was not
inclined to give Germany a free hand in the Balkans. Some feared that Britain, by
her hesitation, would abandon south-east Europe to Germany politically as well as
economically. Thus, the plan to import large quantities of wheat from Romania
appeared to the foreign office very much in the light of a counterweight to
Germany, bringing Romania back in the direction of the world market. Similar
efforts were used in the case of Turkey.[45] The German clearing system did not suit
the ideas of British economic experts and statesmen, not to mention exporters. As
long as Chamberlain's policy was seen as a way of restoring free trade in Europe,
British industry stood behind him, not least because his methods were believed to
have averted war. From this angle the British desire for peace was largely sustained
by economic interests.[46] It was thought that an economic accommodation with
Germany might lead to a political one. Naturally, the interests of exporters
conflicted with those of the arms industry. The two eventually found common
ground in the realization that the hoped-for settlement with Germany was
unattainable. It was not long after Munich before the government came under
pressure on this point. Eden expressed the general mood concisely in the Commons
in November 1938: 'The truth is that democracy as we understand it has to meet a
new challenge in every field. It has to be met in commerce and in other conditions
of life no less than in foreign policy and in armaments.'[47] Anti-German feeling
grew visibly, fed by Goebbels's anti-British propaganda and the effect of the
Reichskristallnacht (the pogrom of 9–10 November 1938).[48] In France this process
did not begin in earnest until after the occupation of Prague, when Bonnet's
conciliatory policy was seen to have failed and more sceptical attitudes were again
dominant.

Plainer language was also being used on the diplomatic front. Halifax declared to
the German ambassador on 15 March 1939 that the Germans, it must be believed,
had little desire for good relations with Britain and were 'seeking to establish a
position in which they could by force dominate Europe and, if possible, the
world'.[49] Chamberlain, in his speech at Birmingham on 17 March 1939, endorsed
this view publicly, not least in order to protect his own conduct against criticism.
He made clear his determination to meet any such challenge from Germany, but did
not on that account give up the policy of appeasement. From now on it was clearer

[44] Henke, *England*, 200.

[45] Wendt, *Economic Appeasement*, 486 ff.

[46] Ibid. 495 ff.

[47] *HC Deb.*[5] 341: 375 ff. (10 Nov. 1938).

[48] Aigner, *Ringen*, 340.

[49] Dispatch of 15 Mar. to Henderson, *DBFP*[3] iv, No. 279.

than before that freedom of action required strength. Given that, Hitler's next move could be met differently.[50] But the attempt to reach a settlement was not to be given up just yet.

Hitler did not assimilate the British premier's warning into his political strategy. His statements to the political and military chiefs show that he thought it no more than a possibility that Britain would be against him, so that there was still a chance of isolating Poland in the intended conflict.

This was realized in London, where Halifax suggested to the American ambassador that it would be well to declare publicly that the German government's new technique of organizing disruption in foreign countries was clearly understood. Halifax also urged that Roosevelt should take urgent steps in regard to American neutrality legislation.[51]

But, despite the enlightenment of the post-Munich period, there were wide differences of view in London as to Hitler's future policy. Some warned against the danger of leaving Germany a free hand in Eastern and south-east Europe. The military attaché in Berlin advised against any economic concessions, which would only be used to accelerate Germany's rearmament programme. He pointed out the risk that such concessions would diminish American confidence in Britain.[52] He thought there was little danger that Hitler would resort to war merely to get out of his economic difficulties. Others, such as Cadogan, advised a 'defensive attitude' to the affairs of central and south-east Europe.[53] Ashton-Gwatkin, the head of the economic relations section of the foreign office, who visited Berlin in the second half of February 1939,[54] reported that Germany was interested in economic co-operation in many fields. While sceptical as to whether Hitler really wanted peace, he saw advantage in such co-operation, as did de la Baume, head of the economic department of the French foreign ministry. Facts could be stronger than men, and Germany might be compelled by circumstances to steer a more moderate course. Ashton-Gwatkin therefore advised aiming at a political settlement by way of economic co-operation. A prominent part was played in the discussions by Hitler's statement in his speech of 30 January 1939 that Germany must increase her exports in order to buy raw materials and foodstuffs. Henderson, the ambassador in Berlin, even recommended giving Hitler a free hand in the east, at least as far as economic domination went, as far as the Ukraine. He thought it 'inevitable' that Germany would want to detach the Ukraine from the Soviet Union. In her own interest, Germany would prefer to have the Ukraine as a buffer state between herself and Russia. A German–Russian war for *Lebensraum* sooner or later was very likely;

[50] This cautious assessment of Chamberlain's reaction to the occupation of Czechoslavakia is probably more accurate than the view taken by Bullock, *Hitler*, Shirer, *Rise and Fall*, and others, that the Birmingham speech marked a turning-point in British policy towards Hitler. On this issue see Hildebrand, *Reich*, 607. Text of Chamberlain's speech in *The Times*, 18 Mar. 1939.

[51] Halifax to Washington embassy, 17 Mar. 1939, *DBFP*[3] iv, No. 394.

[52] Memorandum of 27 Feb. 1939 by Col. Mason-Macfarlane 'respecting the military point of view as regards concessions to Germany in the economic field', *DBFP*[3] iv, No. 172, annex, p. 174.

[53] Aster, *1939*, 41.

[54] *DBFP*[3] iv, appendix II, pp. 597 ff.; *DGFP*, D. iv, Nos. 265, 273, 281; details in Wendt, *Economic Appeasement*, 548 ff.

Germany could contemplate it with relative equanimity if she had a benevolent Britain on her flank, but she greatly feared the contrary. The best way to have good relations with Germany was not to be constantly interfering in matters that did not affect vital British interests. There should be a 'prospect of British neutrality in the event of Germany being engaged in the East', though of course 'we cannot blindly give Germany *carte blanche*'.[55] Any early confrontation in the east was doubtful, as far as could be judged from the conflicting signs that were available in London. Hitler himself seemed capable of anything,[56] but he had to listen to popular opinion, or so Göring told Henderson. The German people clearly wanted peace. The German economy and finances were 'unsound'. In all the circumstances it seemed desirable for Britain to take some action to help Germany on to her feet; Hitler might even be grateful. Such was the advice of Henderson, who evidently wished to tone down the conclusions of his military attaché.

The ambassador's analysis was to a certain extent in line with Hitler's wishes. If the British government had taken Henderson's advice it might even have saved Hitler the need of turning against the West, for the time being at any rate. But the cabinet would not go so far. On 17 March Halifax instructed the ambassador in Moscow to enquire whether the Soviet Union would give Romania active support against a German attack.[57] Was this not a sign of readiness to concert a European policy with the Soviet Union?

London was still under the misapprehension—on which leading members of the German opposition also based their calculations for a long time—that, while Hitler himself might be reasoned with, he could also be driven into dangerous courses by radicals in his entourage, such as Ribbentrop and Himmler. In February 1939 Halifax feared that Germany might be planning to attack the Western powers in the next few months.[58] There was thus ample reason for an approach to the Soviet Union. Britain speeded up her own preparations with a view to a continental commitment.

As a counter to German advances in Romania, after the supposed Berlin ultimatum and the Prague coup, the chiefs of staff on 18 March advised the government to 'get an alliance between Great Britain, Russia, Poland, and France now and issue an ultimatum' to 'deter Germany from her intention to absorb Romania'.[59] They feared that Germany would otherwise gain control of the whole of south-east Europe and threaten the eastern Mediterranean.

The comprehensive review by the chiefs of staff emphasized Hitler's global strategy. They were of the opinion that even if Britain were allied with France and the Soviet Union she could not safely embark on a war against Germany, Italy, and Japan. Chamberlain explained to the cabinet what he had meant to convey by his speech at Birmingham. If, after his warning, Germany continued to use force in

[55] Henderson to Halifax, 9 Mar. 1939, *DBFP*[3] iv, No. 195.

[56] On the diversity of information cf. Aster, *1939*, 38 ff.

[57] Telegram of 17 Mar. 1939 to Sir W. Seeds, *DBFP*[3] iv, No. 389. The exaggerated reports of the threat to Romania had evidently made an impression on Halifax. There was in fact no German 'ultimatum'. See also Förster, 'Rumäniens Weg', and Aster, *1939*, 61 ff., on the 'Tilea affair'.

[58] Aster, *1939*, 47.   [59] Ibid. 76.

pursuit of her policy of dominating Europe, Britain would take up the challenge. The cabinet decided on 18 March to enquire of Russia, Poland, Yugoslavia, Greece, Romania, and Turkey whether they were prepared to join with Britain in resisting any act of German aggression in south-east Europe.[60] Next day this idea was replaced by that of a declaration by Britain, Poland, Russia, and France that they would enter into consultations in case of a fresh threat to any European state. But this was criticized in the Cabinet, and even the next prospective victims, Romania and Poland,[61] did not want any agreement with the Soviet Union. France was prepared to go along with the idea, but thought it very weakly formulated. Then on 31 March Chamberlain declared in the Commons that Britain would come to Poland's aid if the latter's independence were threatened.[62] This was further than he had been prepared to go a few days before; he was apparently alarmed by reports of imminent German action.[63]

Apart from the immediate deterrent effect, Britain's long-term object was to create a more or less stable front in Eastern Europe, from the Baltic to Greece, so as to threaten Hitler with a war on two fronts. It was important to gain time. The chiefs of staff attached importance to the Polish alliance. Unlike the French general staff, they reckoned that Poland could hold out for a relatively long period, three to four months. Poland was the keystone of the hoped-for defensive system in the east. The creation of two fronts would give Britain time to build up her own defences. Chamberlain took the view that a country which fell victim to a German attack could in any case not be liberated quickly; if Britain intervened, it was 'not to save a particular victim, but in order to pull down the bully'.[64] In fact Britain's guarantee to Poland presented not only that country, but also the Soviet Union, with political opportunities, as a result of which London eventually lost control of developments in Eastern Europe; moreover, the guarantee failed to deter Hitler.

Attempts to prise Italy away from the Axis were viewed sceptically by the cabinet. Ministers, and the foreign office, believed that British association with the Soviet Union might strengthen the Axis. The Soviet Union had mixed feelings towards the Chamberlain government. Poland took advantage of the uncertainty on both sides, and stepped into the gap. On 24 March Warsaw, expecting fresh moves by Ribbentrop, asked whether Britain would enter into bilateral consultations. This did not entirely fit in with Britain's East European strategy, but Britain took increasing notice of Poland; she was not informed, however, concerning the secret German–Polish negotiations that had taken place.

[60] Cowling, *Impact*, 296.

[61] Record of an Anglo-French conversation, 22 Mar. 1939, *DBFP*³ iv, No. 484.

[62] Text in *DBFP*³ iv, No. 582. For the background cf. Ritter, *Goerdeler*, 128 ff., criticizing Wheeler-Bennett's view in *Nemesis*, 437.

[63] Cf. e.g. *Cadogan Diaries*, 164–5, entries for 29 and 30 Mar. Kettenacker, 'Diplomatie der Ohnmacht', 223–79 (here 250), refers to the 'reckless backing of Poland'. The failure to involve the Soviet Union on the Western side certainly proved a great disadvantage: but there was scarcely any better course open to the British government in view of the international problems and esp. that of Soviet–Polish relations.

[64] Chamberlain's statement in cabinet, 20 Mar., quoted in Aster, *1939*, 83; see also Howard, *Commitment*, 133.

Chamberlain hoped, in addition to an agreement with Poland, to come to a secret understanding with the Soviet Union that the latter would assist Poland or Romania if they were attacked by Germany. In the cabinet it was Sir Samuel Hoare, the home secretary, who pressed most strongly for an open agreement with the Soviet Union. Halifax thought, however, that if Britain had to choose between Poland and Russia, Poland 'would give the greater value'.[65] Thus, the effect of the guarantee to Poland was to exclude the Soviet Union from the defensive system.

Hitler was confronted by Britain, France, and Poland; but Chamberlain's decision did not have the desired effect on him, as is shown by his statements to the military leaders on 23 May. Now that Britain was, for the first time since 1914, committed to fighting for an East European country, Hitler still hoped to be able to deal with one enemy after the other. British warnings had a curious delayed-action effect. In the autumn of 1938, when the cabinet's policy was to 'keep Hitler guessing', he had felt pretty sure that London would do nothing. After the guarantee to Poland, which Chamberlain had intended to make Britain's position beyond doubt, Hitler began to resort to guessing and conjecture.

4. THE LONDON–BERLIN–MOSCOW TRIANGLE AND THE OUTBREAK OF WAR

The broad line-up of powers in the Second World War was now taking shape. The British government, impelled by vital interests, was gradually overcoming its antipathy towards the Soviet Union. The process was delayed, however, by anti-Communism, the overrating of Poland, and the underrating of the military power of the Soviet Union, which was thought to be of value for defence only. From April 1939 onwards European politics were dominated by the respective positions of London, Berlin, and Moscow. Poland was the politico-strategic 'point of application' of those powers' policies. Beck, the Polish foreign minister, tried during his visit to London to alter the balance by urging that Moscow be excluded from the Anglo-Polish alliance[66] (which he himself proposed instead of a unilateral guarantee); but from the British point of view the alliance continued to involve the question of the Soviet attitude. One thing was clear to both parties: the British guarantee must be honoured this time, or—in view of what had happened in Prague—Britain's credit would be forfeited once and for all.[67]

Britain also considered the strategic position from the point of view of possible effects in the Mediterranean. Besides the guarantee to Poland, she continued her approaches to Romania, Greece, Yugoslavia, and Turkey. Thus, Italy remained an important factor in British eyes. But the Mediterranean also played a part in anti-German strategy, and in that area the Soviet Union was of no direct use to Britain.[68] Hence, London sought to keep the Italians in play. Italy's occupation of Albania

---

[65] Aster, *1939*, 94.

[66] *DBFP*[3] v, No. 1; full discussion in Aster, *1939*, 123 ff.

[67] On this consequence of the betrayal of Czechoslovakia see Taylor, *Origins*, 214.

[68] Howard, *Commitment*, 135–6, referring to the Feb. analysis by the chiefs of staff.

was noted; the time seemed inappropriate for direct action, but London's attention was drawn even more strongly to the Mediterranean, and the approaches to Turkey and Greece were intensified. Halifax informed the Italian chargé d'affaires that if Italy took action against Corfu she would find herself at war with Britain.[69]

But how did London envisage the Soviet role in Europe? The USSR, like Britain, had a treaty relationship with Poland. The Poles and British expected that Russia would at least give economic aid to Poland in the event of war; the British embassy in Moscow did not think this aid would amount to much, however. The embassy gave a pithy estimate of Stalin's long-term strategy: the outcome least welcome to Moscow would be a rapid German victory over the Western powers, 'leaving the victors free to turn eastwards'.[70] As long as London assumed that Hitler would turn eastward in the first place, Anglo-Soviet relations remained cool. A slow change developed in the spring of 1939, as various rumours suggested that Germany was getting ready to attack in the West. Halifax was inclined for closer relations, but Chamberlain at first refused.[71] Britain got word of the forthcoming German–Soviet economic talks.[72] The change of climate in German–Soviet relations lent weight to the foreign office's desire for conversations with Moscow.

But the repeated exclusion of the Soviet Union from the settlement of political problems in Europe made Stalin extremely cautious where Britain was concerned. The guarantee to Poland made Moscow uneasy. Litvinov told the British ambassador that the Soviet Union would take on no further commitments. In Britain, however, it was increasingly realized that no reliable position against Hitler could be built up without the Soviet Union. Churchill, Lloyd George, Eden, and others called in Parliament for a Soviet alliance. The ambassador in Moscow though it desirable to invite the Soviet Union to co-operate in view of the negotiations with Poland and Romania.[73] The chiefs of staffs in their memorandum in March had also called for an alliance with the Soviet Union.

But when, on 18 April, the Soviet Union itself took the initiative by proposing an alliance with Britain and France,[74] the foreign office was thrown into perplexity. France had clearly pronounced for association with the Soviet Union. Moscow now wished to test whether the Western powers were willing to alter their policy. The Russians proposed, among other points, a pact of mutual assistance against any aggressor and a promise of aid to the Soviet Union's East European neighbours between the Baltic and the Black Sea. In this way Stalin offered to replace Poland as the principal East European power in a system of mutual aid against Germany. The British government had envisaged no more than Soviet economic help to Poland in the event of war. It was now in a dilemma—could Stalin be trusted? As Cadogan put

---

[69] *DBFP*[3] v, Nos. 95 ff.

[70] Embassy letter of 20 Feb. 1939, *DBFP*[3] iv, appendix III, pp. 611 ff. 'Fortunately the limited export surplus of the Soviet Union would mean that, in the event of a war, Soviet trade policy would scarcely be a matter of vital importance.' The embassy left open the possibility that the Soviet Union might side with Germany against the West on politico-strategic grounds.

[71] Aster, *1939*, 152 ff.; id., 'Ivan Maisky'.

[72] *DGFP*, D. iv, Nos. 481 ff.; Aster, *1939*, 155.

[73] Telegram from Seeds to Halifax, 6 Apr. 1939, *DBFP*[3], v, No. 13.

[74] Telegram from Seeds to Halifax, 18 Apr. 1939, ibid., No. 201.

it, 'We have to balance the advantage of a paper commitment by Russia to join in a war on our side against the disadvantage of associating ourselves openly with Russia.'[75] What would the Poles say if Russian troops sought permission to cross Poland? Halifax agreed with Cadogan in thinking the Russian proposals 'mischievous'.[76] The government prepared to reject them, as offering no political or military advantage.[77] Chamberlain feared to provoke Hitler unnecessarily; the chiefs of staff underestimated Russian strength, though they had also warned of the risk of a Russo-German understanding. Meanwhile Berlin received information concerning the Soviet–British contacts.

The British government's hesitation was based on deep-seated mistrust of the leading Communist power. An alliance with Soviet Russia did not accord with Chamberlain's philosophy. His political, economic, and social principles seemed to rule out any agreement with the power that stood for their opposite in all respects. His political thinking made it much easier and more natural for him to work for an arrangement with Hitler. A settlement with Berlin offered a better chance of avoiding a war and preventing unpredictable shocks to the social structure of Britain.

The Soviet Union, unpopular with the West and vilified by Hitler, stepped into a role of the first importance by reason of its actual strength, often doubted though it was, and the weight of its strategic position. Even approaches with the limited purpose of not having Moscow as an enemy were more than unusual compared with the past. Hitler's course towards war had accelerated this rise in Soviet prestige and thus brought about a completely new pattern of forces.

In this situation the Soviet Union pursued its old policy of exploiting differences among the powers. Russia's interest in security against Germany had been clearly shown in the autumn of 1938, both before and after Munich. In October the Germans and Russians came to an agreement that neither side would instigate press or radio attacks on the other's head of state. Talks on the prolongation of the trade agreement proceeded without friction. The two sides were not merely pursuing a policy of *détente*. Even in the early phase of these contacts, Stalin's old strategic interest was more in evidence than far-reaching German political designs. Then, at the end of 1938 and beginning of 1939, Hitler suddenly decided to switch his attention to Poland and keep Russia waiting. Stalin, none the less, remained willing to come to terms with Germany.

Before long he was again in a favourable position, owing to the Anglo-French guarantee of Poland and Hitler's decision to make war on the latter. Time was on Stalin's side. Besides his defensive aim he was motivated by the political and strategic importance of extending the Soviet frontier westward. He had in view the Baltic States, Finland, Bessarabia, and, if possible, parts of Poland—as is shown by

---

[75] *Cadogen Diaries*, 175, entry for 18 Apr.

[76] Ibid. The British attitude has been criticized as 'half-hearted': e.g. Kettenacker, 'Diplomatie der Ohnmacht', 255. The estimate of Soviet military strength was a relevant factor. For the French view cf. Vaïsse, 'Perception de la puissance', 18–25.

[77] Aster, *1939*, 164. On France's eastern policy at this stage see H. Bartel, *Frankreich und die Sowjetunion*.

his enquiry, on 18 April 1939, whether Britain's obligation to assist Poland was confined to the case of an attack by Germany.

Manœuvring to gain time was no longer an adequate policy for Britain; but the cabinet persisted in a more than hazardous attempt to keep Russia good-tempered and in play while refusing her offer of an alliance. Too many susceptibilities had to be managed at once: French, Polish, Romanian, and even German. Ministers were anxious not to give a handle to anti-Comintern propaganda. Complicated and artificial reasons were put forward to induce Stalin to declare that he would grant military aid 'if desired' in the event of Britain and France having to implement their guarantees; but they had scarcely been put on paper[78] when a change took place in Moscow. Litvinov, the commissar for foreign affairs, was replaced by Molotov, who, unlike him, was no advocate of collective security. Molotov put his finger on the weak point of the Anglo-French proposal: it contained no provision for reciprocal aid. A German attack on the Soviet Union was not taken into account, nor was there any guarantee of the Baltic States and Finland.[79] Naturally, in view of Stalin's overall policy, this latter point implied a guarantee against Germany only; if Stalin were to go along with Hitler, the states in question would be at Moscow's disposal. This ambiguity in the Soviet position was insufficiently noticed by the West.

The foreign office recognized the importance of the Soviet demands as the precondition of an agreement with the West. The construction of the East European security system would be compromised if these demands were not met. A change of opinion set in. The chiefs of staff produced new strategic recommendations, having for the first time weighed the consequences of securing or failing to secure an alliance with the Soviet Union.[80] They concluded that a full-blown agreement with the Russians would present a solid and formidable front against aggression, while if Russia remained neutral she would be in a dominating position at the end of hostilities.

To Halifax, after conversations with the Soviet ambassador Maisky, it appeared more and more clearly that the choice was between a mutual defensive alliance and no agreement at all.[81] France was willing to conclude a reciprocal agreement, while in London the pros and cons of accepting the Russian terms were still the subject of cautious consideration. A foreign office memorandum of 22 May[82] spoke of the danger that such a pact might be regarded as creating an ideological bloc against the Axis powers, and might even provoke Hitler to aggression. Chamberlain, who was himself of that opinion, was the main obstacle to the proposed treaty, which had been under discussion for weeks; but he finally gave in, though unconvinced. On 27 May Britain accepted the idea of a pact of mutual assistance. Chamberlain attempted to have it couched in the form of declarations of intent, and linked to the

[78] Halifax to Phipps, 28 Apr. 1939, *DBFP*³ v, No. 305.
[79] Seeds to Halifax, 15 May 1939, ibid., No. 520.
[80] Aster, *1939*, 176–7.
[81] Telegram to Cadogan from the UK delegation in Geneva, 22 May 1939, *DBFP*³ v, Nos. 581–2.
[82] Ibid., Nos. 589 and 624.

League of Nations;[83] but the Russians would have none of this. They regarded the latest Western approach as a mere pretext for spinning out discussion,[84] and objected to the reservation as regards Polish and Romanian consent: Britain's offer of assistance was subject to the 'rights and position of other powers'. The Russians' counter-proposal of 2 June went back to their previous demands and also pressed for the early conclusion of a military agreement.[85] London had to yield once more. On 7 June Chamberlain informed the Commons that agreement had been reached on the most important points.[86] The appeasement policy was slowly being jettisoned; Britain was preparing to steer a new course.

The more the danger increased, the less possible it was to ignore the Soviet factor. This in itself gave a new character to British policy, despite the fact that appeasement opportunities were still believed to exist;[87] these related to quite important spheres, and did not even exclude territorial concessions. Chamberlain was determined not to yield to force once more, but he remained prepared at all times to negotiate for the sake of peace. To a man like Hitler this might seem a half-hearted attitude, throwing doubt on British readiness to resist aggression. It also adversely affected Chamberlain's disposition to come to a clear agreement with Moscow, as did his ideological reservations and rooted distrust of the Russians. But he had eventually to bow to the force of circumstances and strategic necessity.

Attempts to reach alliance with the Soviet Union only became possible with the realization that the appeasement policy had been pursued too optimistically.[88] A system which was, at least theoretically, designed to maintain peace and ensure co-operation was replaced by a policy of alliances, which Chamberlain thought more likely to bring about a war. For a long time he would not accept the necessity. Hence, the British ambassador in Moscow was originally instructed to attempt to place Anglo-Soviet relations on a new footing, but not to commit himself in any way as regards Germany's possible eastward expansion.[89] This duality made British policy suspect to the Russians, and lessened the deterrent effect of the Anglo-Soviet negotiations on Hitler. Britain's offer of aid did not satisfy Stalin, because conditions were attached to the British response to a German attack on Finland or the Baltic States: if the Soviet Union intervened in such a case, Britain would not automatically come to its aid. At the crucial point of the Moscow talks, this twofold character of British policy was reflected in several speeches by Halifax. The question in Moscow was: under what conditions would the three powers

---

[83] Halifax to Seeds, 25 May 1939, ibid., No. 609.

[84] Seeds to Halifax, 27 May 1939, ibid., No. 648; 28 May, No. 657; 30 May, Nos. 665 and 670; 1 June, Nos. 681, 689.

[85] Ibid., No. 697.   [86] Halifax to Seeds, 7 June 1939, ibid., No. 735.

[87] Especially noteworthy are the Anglo-German negotiations for an economic settlement in July 1939, which throw a distinctive light on the triangular situation between Britain, Germany, and the Soviet Union. For this reason Wendt, *Economic Appeasement*, 586 ff., speaks of the 'legend' of a radical change in British policy after the occupation of Prague.

[88] On the exclusion of the Soviet Union from the concept of appeasement until 1938 see Niedhart, *Großbritannien*, 335 and *passim*. But serious doubts were still entertained: see Murray, *Change*, 304–5, and e.g. the cabinet meeting of 19 July 1939: PRO Cab 23/100, CAB 38 (39), p. 186.

[89] Niedhart, *Großbritannien*, 392.

respectively come to the aid of Belgium, Greece, Romania, Poland, Turkey, Latvia, Estonia, or Finland? The Russians wanted the obligation to apply whether these states asked to be guaranteed or not, while Britain did not want them mentioned by name. To this the Soviet Union demurred.[90] At this decisive stage—when Chamberlain was already wondering whether to break off negotiations on account of the Russian demands—Halifax spoke publicly of the 'twin foundations of purpose' in British policy: determination to resist force, and the desire to get on with constructive work for peace.[91] In the last stage of the negotiations, at the end of June, Britain sought to extend the guarantee to Switzerland, Holland, and Luxemburg; Chamberlain at this time made the extremely important concession that a state attacked by Germany need not request Soviet aid before such aid could be given under the terms of the alliance. At this point Molotov began to lay great emphasis on a quite new problem, that of indirect aggression. The British government was under strong pressure at home, but it would not yield on this point. Seeds, the ambassador, had already reported from Moscow that Stalin evidently only wanted the cover of the alliance to pursue his own policy towards the small states of Eastern Europe. Apart from this, the British were unwilling to hold military talks at once: they only agreed to do so, under pressure from the French, at the end of July.[92] The negotiations now ran up against what had been a major difficulty from the beginning—the question whether Poland, on whose territory the Soviet guarantee would in all probability have to be executed, would consent to the passage of Soviet troops. The British military delegation were unable to surmount this obstacle. Their instructions afforded little help.[93] Poland was unwilling to have Russian troops on her territory because it was highly uncertain how they could be got out again, not to mention the danger of a Communist infiltration among the populace.

In mid-August the foreign office still had hopes of a favourable outcome, but by now it was negotiating from the point of view of preventing a German–Soviet agreement.[94] Halifax pressed for progress in the military negotiations,[95] as did the French.[96] An occasional gleam of optimism appeared on the Western side, but was groundless in view of the Polish attitude.[97] Warsaw refused to entertain a French proposal that Poland might tacitly allow Russian troops to pass through 'corridors'

[90] *DBFP*[3] vi, No. 35.
[91] Halifax, *Speeches on Foreign Policy*, 283.
[92] *DBFP*[3] vi, Nos. 414, 435, 444.
[93] Ibid., appendix v, pp. 762 ff. (here p. 772).
[94] Meeting of committee on foreign policy, 4 July 1939, PRO Cab 27/625. Halifax had spoken to Kennedy, the US Ambassador in London, on these lines on 5 July. Kennedy reported on that date: 'They would like to tie up Russia so that there is no possibility of the Russians considering a deal with Germany' (*FRUS* (1939), i. 282); accordingly he thought the idea of the negotiations was for 'a negative agreement rather than a positive one'.
[95] Telegram to Seeds, 15 Aug. 1939, *DGFP*[3] vii, No. 6.
[96] Seeds to Halifax, 16 Aug. 1939, ibid., No. 20. Azéma, 'Französische Politik', 280–313, concludes that Paris was becoming more confident and 'somewhat freed from British dominance'. The French wished to make the Soviet Union an important component of the eastern cordon sanitaire against Hitler, thus in a sense continuing Barthou's policy.
[97] Cf. e.g. *DBFP*[3] vii, Nos. 27, 30.

in northern and southern Poland. The Polish general staff disbelieved in Soviet good intentions, as did Beck when appealed to on 19 August.[98] A Russian proposal for 'corridors' in Galicia and in the neighbourhood of Wilno had no chance of acceptance. Despite the important concessions made by the Western powers, the negotiations made no progress. The British and French finally accepted the principle of assistance in case of 'indirect aggression', but this too was of no avail. However, while a definition of indirect aggression was still being debated, Hitler for his part became uneasy. He was now compelled to seek conversations with Stalin—a position into which he had been doggedly manœuvred by the Soviet dictator.

Even after the conclusion of the Hitler–Stalin pact of 23 August the West tried to continue the Moscow negotiations, hopeless though they had now become. On the 25th Voroshilov informed the British and French representatives that in the new political situation there was no purpose in pursuing the discussions.[99]

Hitler, in steering a course between Britain and the Soviet Union, had been untrammelled by ideological scruples. The Anglo-French attempt to secure Romania against a feared German attack in March was described by the foreign ministry as 'action by the British government towards the formation of a united front against Germany'.[100] Hitler spoke in the Reichstag, after Chamberlain's guarantee to Poland, of Britain's 'encirclement policy'. He replied to it by denouncing the naval treaty and the German–Polish agreement of 1934, thus securing a base for propaganda and for further expansionism.

Berlin was, from start to finish, informed of the Anglo-Soviet contacts that began with the initiative over Romania. The possibility of their leading to an agreement had to be taken into account. As the positions of the major powers developed down to September 1939, the strategic situation of the USSR to the rear of Poland became of decisive importance. But the failure of the Anglo-Soviet negotiations was not due to the Russo-Polish deadlock, but to Stalin's calculation that an arrangement with Hitler would afford him greater security. Moreover, the pact with Hitler gave him a free hand *vis-à-vis* Poland and the Baltic States, and left open the possibility of a war between Germany and the Western powers, in which Russia could be a *tertius gaudens*. All this was fully in line with Stalin's long-term strategy.

What account did Hitler take of the guarantee to Poland and the Anglo-Soviet negotiations, and what freedom of action did he have as the coalition of the First World War appeared to be re-forming against him? His address of 23 May shows that in theory there was no alternative policy that offered any promise of success. If Poland could not be isolated, then on his own admission the outcome was doubtful. However, if more closely examined, this formula only meant that Poland must be isolated militarily, i.e. the West must not intervene by force of arms. Hitler certainly also speculated on the deterrent effect of the Westwall.[101] If this

[98] Kennard to Halifax, 18 Aug. 1939, ibid., Nos. 60, 70.

[99] Seeds to Halifax, 25 Aug. 1939, ibid., No. 277.

[100] Circular telegram from the state secretary, 24 Mar. 1939, *DGFP*, D. vi, No. 83.

[101] In his Reichstag speech of 28 Apr. he boasted of these 'strongest fortifications of all time' (Domarus, ii. 1154 = Baynes, ii. 1634). On the actual shortcomings in many sectors see Groscurth, *Tagebücher*, 179.

interpretation is correct, Hitler's calculation was that even if the guarantee came into operation the West would not necessarily intervene and create a second front: it might be possible to eliminate Poland first and fight the West afterwards. Here he was in accord with the basic idea of British strategy, which assumed that Poland could only benefit effectively from the guarantee after victory in a general war. Only Soviet intervention could have held Germany down long enough in the East for a second front to be established.

Although Hitler knew of the Anglo-Soviet talks, he did not include this possibility in his review of 23 May. He touched only lightly on the idea that an alliance between France, Britain, and the Soviet Union must be countered by Germany, Italy, and Japan, i.e. by the semblance of an alliance. In such a case, as Hitler well knew, he would in effect have to rely on his own strength. The more reasonable idea of avoiding a conflict altogether was almost inconceivable to him, given that the resources of the Reich had for years been geared to the prospect of an early war. His conclusion, instead, was that if a three-power alliance were concluded against him, it would force him to attack Britain and France 'with a few annihilating blows'. This was a desperate strategy in view of Germany's economic situation and the state of her armament at sea and in the air. Nor was Hitler himself free from doubt as to whether it would work—as is shown by his statement (mentioned below) that if it came to the worst he would climb down and make a great parade of the 'Party rally of peace'.

If the Soviet Union had allied itself with the West and if Hitler had carried out the intention of which he spoke on 23 May, it would have involved an act of desperation surpassing all the errors of German imperial diplomacy, of which he was so contemptuous. We can hardly suppose he would have acted as he said. As the danger now grew almost tangible, he became hesitant. As Weizsäcker noted on 30 July 1939: 'This summer's decision between peace and war will, it is considered here, depend on whether the doubtful negotiations in Moscow bring Russia into the orbit of the Western powers. If they do not, the depression in that quarter will be such that we can do what we like with Poland.'[102]

On 23 May Hitler used expressions which gave a meaning and context to the German–Soviet trade talks. Economic relations, he said, would only be possible if and when political relations improved. Perhaps, he added, 'Russia might give up interest in the destruction of Poland.' These remarks, in the context of the European situation in the early summer of 1939, leave little doubt that the British guarantee to Poland was causing Hitler concern. He had not yet placed the three-power Moscow negotiations in an overall plan of his own, but he now began to consider making offers to Stalin. Dangerous as the situation potentially was, he was still thinking in terms of rapid solutions: this is shown by the fact that he did not allow for American action in his calculation of developments, although he must have realized what part the United States was bound to play in a show-down between Britain and Germany.

In September 1938 the German chargé d'affaires in Washington had reported on

---

[102] *Weizsäcker-Papiere*, 157.

likely American reactions in the event of war, with no less emphasis than Dieckhoff, the ambassador, before him. He pointed to the naval agreements between the United States and Britain, and the arrangement whereby the British navy looked after the Atlantic and enabled the American navy to concentrate on Japan. His conclusion was that the United States would do everything in its power to prevent a British defeat.[103] Roosevelt repeatedly made clear his interest in stable conditions. His peace appeal of 14 April 1939[104] was sarcastically turned down by Hitler,[105] who did not believe the situation was such as to bring the American potential into play. But American reactions to the Kristallnacht showed that Hitler had lost much ground on the propaganda front. In a kind of over-compensation, the Nazi press intensified its attacks on America.[106]

In 1939 Hitler believed he had sufficient arms superiority to strike short, decisive blows even against the Western powers.[107] In fact he was already placing undue reliance on the feasibility of the blitzkrieg, which involved turning against adversaries one by one.[108] Hitler's belief in the effectiveness of 'rapid blows' was one reason why he never bothered to form an overall politico-military estimate of the intentions and potential of the major powers. It may also explain his surprising diplomatic inaction in the highly dramatic situation of the summer of 1939. He had not the least assurance that the Soviet Union would not come to terms with Britain and France, but as yet he took no firm initiative to nip any such arrangement in the bud. After the British guarantee to Poland he could in any case not think of turning against the Soviet Union until he had first settled accounts with the Western powers, and British diplomacy would have done its best to turn that struggle into a war on two fronts for Germany. Although Hitler for the present had nothing decisive with which to counter the Anglo-French diplomatic offensive, which he denounced as encirclement, his thoughts remained fixed on a show-down with the West,[109] though perhaps he saw this as taking place only after the elimination of Poland, at a time to be chosen by himself.

The 'pact of steel' with Italy, concluded on 22 May, was formulated as a military alliance and carried little additional political weight.[110] Japan's failure to join the alliance[111] placed Hitler's overall strategy on a very insecure footing, as is shown by his very brief reference to Japan on 23 May. Mussolini had no wish to be involved in Hitler's accelerated programme, which had to mean an early attack on Poland. Before 1943, he informed the Führer, Italy was not be be counted on, for reasons of economics and armament.[112] There was not even agreement between the two allies

[103] Hillgruber, 'Faktor Amerika', 8; Hildebrand, Foreign Policy, 85; DGFP, D. i, No. 462.
[104] Moltmann, 'Friedensappell'.
[105] Also in the Reichstag speech, 28 Apr. 1939.
[106] Schröder, 'Drittes Reich', 257.
[107] Frank, Im Angesicht des Galgens, 344; but esp. Hitler's statements of 23 May.
[108] On the concept of a blitzkrieg see also Dülffer, 'Einfluß des Auslandes', 300.
[109] Henke, England, 248-9, with reference to the meeting between Göring and Mussolini in mid-Apr.: record of 15 Apr. 1939 in DGFP, D. vi, No. 205.
[110] Text of treaty ibid., No. 426; Wiskemann, Rome-Berlin Axis.
[111] Sommer, Deutschland und Japan.
[112] Memorandum of 30 May 1939 by Mussolini for Hitler, DGFP, D. vi, No. 459, annex.

on basic strategic assessments. Thus, Mussolini thought the Western powers must be regarded as 'entrenched' (*eingemauert*) and virtually invulnerable to land attacks, so that defensive positions would be required on the Rhine, in the Alps, and in Libya. 'The war can only assume a dynamic character towards the east and south-east.' Thus, Mussolini sought to direct German energies towards Poland in the first instance. That country, and the other guaranteed states in the south-east, could, he observed, be paralysed before any real help could reach them, even from Russia.

Thus, for the present Hitler could not reckon with his Italian ally. Ciano, at the Obersalzberg on 12–13 August, confirmed this state of affairs in more detail.[113] Hitler and Ciano differed from each other on further points of strategic assessment. Ciano assumed that a war against Poland would turn into a European war, while Hitler was 'absolutely convinced that the Western democracies would, in the last resort, recoil from unleashing a general war'. A communiqué drafted by Ciano, which Mussolini had wanted as an expression of the Axis powers' desire for peace, did not meet with Hitler's approval. There was no doubt which member of the Axis would determine the speed and direction of coming events. Hitler explained that his decision whether or not to march against Poland must be taken by the end of August. Use must be made of the late summer period. Danzig was allegedly in great danger. The liquidation of Poland would be as much a gain in strength to the Axis as would the liquidation of Yugoslavia by Italy. Ribbentrop added that once these problems were solved, the Axis powers would have their rear free for a battle with the West. Ciano for his part noted with relief that the Duce probably need take no decision, as Hitler thought he could localize the conflict with Poland; but he now realized that there would soon be a war. Italy had not till then had any idea that matters were so serious.

Hitler's argument combined long-term aims with very precise calculations. The Axis powers needed space; things could not go on as they were. A confrontation with the Western powers was inevitable. The Mediterranean belonged to Italy; Germany must once more follow the 'old Germanic trail' to the east. But the present was an excellent time for the war against Poland. Britain was highly vulnerable from the air, as her anti-aircraft defences were still backward. Germany could hardly be attacked with any hope of success. The Scandinavian countries would certainly remain neutral. The only possible way for the West to attack would be through Holland, and this was very improbable. Hitler's politico-strategic picture was dominated by the priority he assigned to the Western initiative. The 'old Germanic trail' led first to Poland, then towards the Baltic countries; but the great march eastward must be prepared for by an intermediate victory against the Western powers. The Soviet Union was scarcely mentioned in these conversations. Ribbentrop merely stated that the Russians were aware of Germany's intentions towards Poland and had agreed that a German political negotiator should go to Moscow. This much information was given the Italians as to the formation of a new relationship with the Soviet Union.

The approach to Moscow by Hitler and Ribbentrop was based on a strategic

---

[113] Record of meetings of 12 and 13 Aug., *DGFP*, D. vii, Nos. 43, 47.

review of Germany's situation in the summer of 1939. Hitler's statements on 23 May were not the last word concerning the Soviet Union. In June Hitler indicated the significance he attached to what was now an omnipresent factor in European politics. As yet, however, despite repeated Russian hints of readiness to come to an agreement, German feelers had failed to produce any tangible response.[114] Mutual mistrust was to blame. In the foreign ministry opinions differed as to the consequences of a Russo-British alliance. The anti-Nazi opposition clearly saw that Hitler and Stalin in partnership would be a highly dangerous combination. But it was this that came into prospect when the Russians, at the middle of June, intimated that they were 'at the crossroads'. The Soviet chargé d'affaires in Berlin, who used this phrase to the Bulgarian minister, meant that Moscow had to decide whether to come to terms with the Western powers, to drag out the negotiations, or to seek a *rapprochement* with Germany. Stalin had given a hint in his speech of 10 March 1939 to the Eighteenth Congress of the CPSU, by stating that the Ukraine did not feel threatened. Berlin understood his meaning,[115] especially as he added that ideological disputes were no reason for rivalry in international affairs—a maxim that the German foreign ministry had itself made use of for some time after 30 January 1933. These suggestions by Stalin were in accord with his old strategy *vis-à-vis* capitalist and Fascist states, as formulated, for instance, to the Central Committee of the CPSU on 19 January 1925: 'If war breaks out we should not be able to sit with folded arms. We shall have to take action, but we shall be the last to do so. And we shall do so in order to throw the decisive weight in the scales, the weight that can turn the scales.'[116]

Hitler seized his chance. He seems to have contemplated backing down if the Western powers' negotiations in Moscow were successful. In that case he would apparently have called off the operation against Poland[177] and held a much-trumpeted 'Party rally of peace'.[118] If, however, preparations against Poland went ahead as planned, the rally would make it easier to carry out unobtrusive movements of military transport, so that it would be just as convenient in the case of an offensive policy. British attempts at fresh contacts with Berlin also resumed in mid-June;[119] on both the German and the British side these were overshadowed by possibilities in Moscow.[120] Their influence on Hitler was minimal; so was that of the conversations in July between Sir Horace Wilson and Helmuth Wohltat of Göring's office for the Four-year Plan.[121] Offers of colonies, peaceful revision

[114] Kordt, *Wilhelmstraße*, 309.

[115] Hildebrand, *Foreign Policy*, 92–3; Hillgruber, 'Der Zweite Weltkrieg'; J. V. Stalin, Report of 10 Mar. 1939 to the 18th Party Congress on the work of the Central Committee of the CPSU, repr. in *Leninism*, 619 ff. (here 626–7). For the change in May after Litvinov's dismissal see also Irving, *War Path*, 196–7.

[116] Stalin, *Works*, vii. 14.

[117] Kordt, *Wilhelmstraße*, 310.

[118] Weizsäcker, *Memoirs*, 199–200.

[119] Metzmacher, 'Ausgleichsbemühungen'.

[120] Henderson himself put the matter to Weizsäcker in this light: cf. the latter's memorandum of 13 June 1939, *DGFP*, D. vi, No. 521.

[121] Ibid., No. 716.

of Germany's eastern frontiers (the British guarantee applied to Poland's independence but not to her territory), an Anglo-German declaration to refrain from
the use of force, a declaration of non-intervention, economic talks, disarmament
declarations—all this was of no interest to Hitler. It involved far too many
obligations on his part, which an association with Russia would not. The outline of
an Anglo-German settlement was in accord with Weizsäcker's ideas and those of
other foreign ministry officials; Göring could have been persuaded to agree to it, but
not Hitler.[122] There is indeed some indication that after 'smashing Poland' he
would have been ready to talk to the British,[123] but the whole body of evidence only
makes it clearer that he was determined to deal with Poland in his own way even if it
meant war with the West. Before settling accounts with the Poles he did not lend
himself to any soundings of this kind. Set before the choice of war or peace, he
chose war. On 27 July he made it unmistakably clear to Lord Kemsley that he was
not interested in 'appeasement' proposals. He was prepared to give up the Japanese
connection for the sake of a settlement on the basis of his own ideas;[124] this meant
little, however, considering the problems that a German–Soviet understanding
must involve for German–Japanese relations.

The Russians evidently desired to turn the economic conversations, which Berlin
was seeking to accelerate, into a different channel. This seems to be the only
possible interpretation of Mikoyan's provocative remark to an economic expert
from the German embassy, that he was still not sure that the Germans were not
playing 'a political game in which they had an interest just at the present
moment'.[125]

Had it not been for Stalin's strategic disposition to come to terms with Hitler, an
Anglo-Russian combination could not have been prevented. Hitler could expect
little aid from Britain for his political plans, whereas Russia could offer him a free
hand against Poland. This was the deciding factor. Weizsäcker tried to make
London aware of the danger, and stressed the importance of an Anglo-German
agreement.[126] For the German opposition too London's attitude was becoming
crucial.

On 2 August 1939 Ribbentrop, in conversation with the Soviet chargé d'affaires,
directly opened up the possibility of 'remoulding' German–Soviet relations. Given
good will, 'there was no problem from the Baltic to the Black Sea that could not be
solved between the two of us'.[127] He left no doubt as to Germany's plans for Poland:
'in case of Polish provocation we would settle accounts with Poland in the space of a
week.' Ribbentrop went on to give 'a gentle hint at our coming to an understanding
with Russia on the fate of Poland'. Thus, Stalin might be assured from the outset of
the negotiations that an arrangement wih Hitler would be rewarded by a share of
the Polish spoils. On 4 August Molotov was told by the German ambassador that

[122] See Henke, *England*, 268.
[123] Ibid. 272 ff., with references; also Halder, *Diaries* i. 9.
[124] Lenz and Kettenacker, 'Lord Kemsleys Gespräch'.
[125] Record by Hilger of conversation with Mikoyan, 17 June 1939, *DGFP*, D. vi, No. 543.
[126] Weizsäcker, *Memoirs*, 189–90.
[127] Ribbentrop to Schulenburg, 3 Aug. 1939, *DGFP*, D. vi, No. 760.

talks could also cover the Baltic States: 'vital Soviet interests in the Baltic Sea' would be safeguarded, while German 'upheld her well-known demands on Poland'. On 14 August Ribbentrop offered to come to Moscow himself.[128] His argument for a German–Soviet understanding, apart from its stale clichés, reflected the compulsion under which Hitler's policy was labouring. He had no room to manœuvre, and needed the Soviet Union to help him out. 'The crisis which has been produced in German–Polish relations by English policy, as well as English agitation for war and the attempts at an alliance which are bound up with that policy, make a speedy clarification of German–Russian relations necessary.' Ribbentrop spoke of the restoration of 'German–Russian friendship' and the settlement of territorial problems in Eastern Europe.

Molotov, the German ambassador reported, was 'satisfied to a certain extent' by what Ribbentrop had said about the Baltic States, but would not believe that a solution of the Polish question could be forced on Germany. He demanded that Germany cease to support 'Japanese aggression'. Berlin was now pressing for action. The British military delegation was already in Moscow. On 16 August Molotov indicated that the Russians were interested in Ribbentrop's visit. By way of preparation he put various questions, the most important being: 'What would be the German government's attitude to the idea of a non-aggression pact and a joint guarantee of the Baltic States?' The exchange of views which followed[129] brought the positions of Hitler and Stalin closer together, while also making it clear that an alliance with Japan would not be feasible.[130] Hitler urged Moscow to make up its mind quickly:[131] disturbing information was being received from London as to the progress of the Anglo-Soviet negotiations.

Meanwhile, Berlin intensified the pressure on Poland, in such a way as to thrust responsibility on the latter.[132] The worsening of German–Polish relations was part of the tactical approach to Moscow, an argument for haste. Dirksen, the German ambassador in London, reported that Britain would honour her obligation to the Poles and be drawn automatically into a German–Polish conflict. The Soviet draft agreement reached Berlin on 20 August,[133] and on the 23rd Ribbentrop, in Moscow, signed the non-aggression pact and the secret protocol.[134]

The parties promised that if either of them were involved in hostilities with any power, the other would not support that power. The agreement, concluded for ten years, provided for consultation and further guarantees. Each party undertook not to join any group of powers directed in any way against the other. The secret protocol provided for the division of Poland and the Baltic area into Soviet and

---

[128] Ribbentrop to Schulenburg, 14 Aug. 1939, ibid. vii, No. 56.

[129] Ibid., Nos. 88, 105.

[130] Ambassador in Tokyo to foreign ministry, 18 Aug. 1939, ibid., No. 110.

[131] Ribbentrop to Schulenburg, 18 Aug. 1939, ibid., No. 113.

[132] Weizsäcker to the foreign minister's office, 19 Aug. 1939, ibid., Nos. 119, 139. On the press campaign see Irving, *War Path*, 233.

[133] Text in *DGFP*, D. vii, No. 133.

[134] Texts ibid., Nos. 228, 229. On the German–Soviet treaty see Braubach, *Hitlers Weg*; Fabry, *Hitler-Stalin-Pakt*; McSherry, *Stalin, Hitler and Europe*, i; also Sipols, *Vorgeschichte*; Weber, *Entstehungsgeschichte*.

German spheres of interest. Germany declared her complete lack of interest in Bessarabia.

The non-aggression pact meant, first and foremost, war with Poland. Stalin was finally aware of this, and the case was foreseen in the supplementary protocol. The official Soviet work on the history of the Second World War says nothing about the protocol, and gives the treaty a completely different interpretation: viz. that it frustrated the plan to resolve the internal contradictions of the capitalist system at Soviet expense.[135] The essential point, however, was that the Soviet Union could bide its time while the Western powers and the Axis fought each other. This was the conflict between capitalist and Fascist states which had long figured in Moscow's long-term strategy.

In the last days before invading Poland Hitler still tried to persuade the Western powers that the country bore the whole responsibility for the conflict. This attempt to induce Britain to dissociate herself from Poland was of a purely tactical and psychological character, and was ill-suited to manœuvring Britain out of the position she had adopted with the Polish guarantee. Hitler directed no further efforts at the French during the last days of peace, as he now regarded French policy as firmly subordinate to that of London.

The question has been raised whether Hitler's 'alliance' offer to Britain on 25 August 1939[136] marked a return to his original conception of Britain's role. Could it be the case that the war with Poland, which was by no means dropped from Hitler's immediate programme, was after all envisaged as a preliminary to an assault on the Soviet Union, and not as a means of securing Germany's rear so that she could eliminate France and drive Britain off the continent?[137] If such a change of intention took place, it must have happened very quickly. As late as 23 August, in his first, oral comment to the British ambassador on Chamberlain's letter of the 22nd,[138] Hitler declared that Britain had egged the Poles on to pursue an anti-German policy and must now pay the penalty. Any further Polish provocations 'would immediately entail action by the Reich', and if the West mobilized Germany would at once do likewise. According to Henderson, this was said in a tone of violent exaggeration, emphasizing Hitler's readiness to risk a war with the Western powers as well. 'England had made an enemy of the man who had wished to become her greatest friend'; now she would become acquainted with a different Germany. Hitler may have thought that the treaty with Russia, combined with forceful language on his part, might have a deterrent effect. In his reply of 23 August to Chamberlain he took an equally uncompromising tone.[139] Chamberlain had left it in no doubt that

---

[135] Russian *Geschichte des zweiten Weltkrieges*, ii. 346. Beyer, 'Hitler-Stalin-Pakt', 60–108, qualifies Stalin's policy in the summer of 1939 as one of 'yielding, retreat, and conciliation'. On the British view cf. Manne, 'Some British Light'.

[136] Hitler's statement of 25 Aug. 1939 to Henderson, *DGFP*, D. vii, No. 265.

[137] Henke, *England*, 289 ff., followed by Wendt, 'Danzig', 793–4; with reservations Hillgruber, 'England', 77. For more on the role of Danzig in German foreign policy see Denne, *Danzig-Problem*; Levine, *Hitler's Free City*; Kimmich, *Danzig*.

[138] Record, dated 24 Aug., of Halifax–Henderson meeting of 23 Aug., *DGFP*. D. vii, No. 200, with English text of Chamberlain's letter annexed. Henderson's report in *DBFP*3 vii, Nos. 200, 248.

[139] Text in *DGFP*, D. vii, No. 201. For Hitler's knowledge based on wire-taps see Irving, *War Path*, 243–4.

Britain would not tolerate the use of violent methods with Poland, and would not be moved from her purpose by the German–Soviet treaty. Hitler described Danzig and the Corridor as matters of compelling national and psychological importance; a peaceful settlement could not be ensured by Germany, but was the responsibility of those who had constantly opposed peaceful revision. Only a 'change of attitude (*Gesinnung*) on the part of the responsible powers' could bring about any alteration in German–British relations. If there must be war, Hitler declared to Henderson, it had better be at once and not when he was 55 or 60.

Hitler's account of the crisis reflected his wishful thinking and disappointment at the firmness of the British attitude. After the altercation British policy had only the choice between giving in or going to war. Hitler had summed it up: between Britain and Germany there could only be mutual understanding or war.[140] British 'understanding' meant, to him, abandoning Poland and accepting the German way of solving problems. Henderson, usually so sympathetic to German interests, aptly summed up German tactics in a conversation with Weizsäcker on 16 August: 'Germany could never see but one side to any question and always wanted everything modified in her favour.'[141]

As far as relations with Poland were concerned, old animosities in the foreign ministry were so strong that the senior officials saw virtually eye to eye with Hitler. Weizsäcker, who co-operated in the deliberate provocation of Poland over Danzig,[142] was no exception, as is shown e.g. by his proposal to 'take the initiative . . . to stigmatize Polish policy' in foreign capitals.[143] This attitude can still be felt in his *Memoirs*.[144] However, throughout the crisis foreign ministry officials and military chiefs feared, as Hitler did not, that a German–Polish conflict would escalate into a European war.

Hitler's 'cast-iron' conviction that the Western powers would back down did not begin visibly to crumble until he received Chamberlain's letter. When, on the afternoon of 23 August, he told the British ambassador that 'the questions of Danzig and the Corridor will be settled one way or another. Please take note of this', was he really still unaffected by the unmistakable British warning? On the previous day he had painted an ambiguous picture for the supreme commanders.[145] He was evidently not quite so certain as on 14 August,[146] when he told his audience that 'the Munich fellows' (*die Köpfe von München*) would not take the risk. Now, on 22 August, he was concerned to bolster the confidence of his commanders. After the audience he seems to have felt reassured, but ordered the adjutant-in-chief of the Wehrmacht to sound out the generals' reactions to his words.[147] It can be seen from

---

[140] To Henderson on 23 Aug. 1939.

[141] Telegram from Henderson to Halifax, 16 Aug. 1939, *DBFP*³ vii, No. 32.

[142] Not only in exploiting cases of over-reaction by the Poles, such as their note of 10 Aug. on the customs inspectors dispute: *DGFP*, D. vii, No. 10.

[143] Ibid., No. 37; also Nos. 46, 119.

[144] Weizsäcker, *Memoirs*, 197: the Polish note of 10 Aug. 'showed where we had got to'.

[145] Unsigned record of Hitler's address to commanders-in-chief on 22 Aug., *DGFP*, D. vii, Nos. 192, 193. For source-criticism see Hillgruber, 'Quellen', 119 ff.; Baumgart, 'Ansprache Hitlers'; Boehm, 'Ansprache Hitlers'; also Groscurth, *Tagebücher*, 179 ff.

[146] Halder, *Diaries*, i. 6 ff.; Irving, *War Path*, 236.   [147] *Heeresadjutant bei Hitler*, 58.

his words that he was uncertain of the possibility of isolating Poland. It was still very likely that the West would stand aside, but it might be otherwise: 'It is impossible to prophesy with any certainty.'

This was a long way from the 'cast-iron conviction' he had recently shown to Ciano. The stress was on his readiness to take the risk. So that it should not appear too great, he endeavoured to belittle the Western powers' preparedness for war. 'Personal factors' played an important part in his eyes, and most of all 'my existence, because of my political talents'. This was a 'factor of great value . . . But I can be eliminated at any time by a criminal or a lunatic. . . . Our enemies are poor creatures. I saw them at Munich.' Hitler's priorities were still in the order Warsaw–Paris–London. A beginning had been made towards destroying British predominance. Germany need not fear a blockade. The eastern territories would supply the principal raw materials. He had got Poland where he wanted her. 'Iron resolution on our part.' It was now for the soldiers to go ahead. 'I am only afraid that at the last moment some swine or other will submit a plan for mediation.' He was not going to have a second Munich. He himself would give the propaganda signal for the war, credible or otherwise: 'The victor will not be asked afterwards whether he told the truth or not.' And the war must be waged ruthlessly: 'Close your hearts to pity'.[148]

On 23 August the 26th was decided on as the first day of the attack.[149] After everything Hitler had said to the Italians, the British, the Russians, and now to his own commanders, it seemed clear that he accepted the risk of war against the Western powers also; but he did not expect to be faced at once with an effective war on two fronts, because the West could not come quickly to Poland's aid. This was the only correct part of his calculation.

Time was running out. Arrangements were already made for the *casus belli*. A hundred and fifty concentration-camp prisoners, dressed in Polish uniforms, were to carry out a bogus attack and then be liquidated. Agents would stage a raid on Gleiwitz radio station. Himmler had SS men in Polish uniforms, ready for action.[150]

Amid this unscrupulous preparation, Hitler on 25 August burst forth with his 'alliance' offer to Britain. He told the ambassador that once the German–Polish problems were solved he would approach Britain with a 'large comprehensive offer'.[151] In other words, the offer was dependent on being given a free hand against Poland. Hitler left it in no doubt that he was determined to put an end to the 'Macedonian conditions' on Germany's eastern frontier. The 'large offer' was described as a guarantee of the British Empire and a promise of aid to the imperial power 'if necessary'. There were also to be arms limitation and moderate colonial claims.

This initiative had no effect on the British government, since it presupposed a

---

[148] On the reactions of senior army officers see Müller, *Heer*, 411.

[149] Groscurth, *Tagebücher*, 180.

[150] On the procuring of Polish uniforms for Himmler and Heydrich see also Halder, *Diaries*, i. 16, 23; for counter-action by Canaris, *IMT* xxvi. 337. Cf. also Runzheimer, 'Überfall', and Irving, *War Path*, 233.

[151] Unsigned record of statement by Hitler to Henderson, *DGFP*, D. vii, No. 265.

warlike solution of the dispute with Poland. The British answer made this perfectly clear: 'A just settlement of these questions between Germany and Poland may open the way to world peace. Failure to reach it would ruin the hopes of better understanding between Germany and Great Britain.'[152] But Hitler's approach indicated a change of mind on his part as regards the risk to be taken. The British government's firm attitude had its effect. Weizsäcker and Jodl noticed Hitler's uncertainty on 24 August:[153] it was the more striking as the German–Soviet treaty had just been signed in Moscow. In his 'offer' Hitler reverted to a negotiating tactic that the British had used in reverse during the Sudeten crisis, by indicating that once the Sudeten problem was cleared up the way would be open for further negotiations that would also cover arms limitation and colonies. Thus, Hitler now believed he could purchase British inaction by reviving former British 'offers'.

Uncertainty as to Italy's attitude played a part in Hitler's calculations, and no doubt also the imminent need for a decision. It is impossible to be perfectly sure whether he thought of a major change in foreign policy or of turning against the Soviet Union directly after settling with Poland. He was by no means assured that Britain would protect his rear for that purpose. Any such idea would have been even more unrealistic than the attempt to manœuvre Poland into isolation, but it does not follow that it was unthinkable. It would have been in accord with plans cherished by Hitler in the past. His conversation with Carl J. Burckhardt on 11 August also points in that direction. In a 'most extraordinary statement' on that occasion he declared: 'Everything I do is against Russia. If the West is too blind and stupid to see that, I shall have to come to an understanding with the Russians, then defeat the West, and then throw all my forces against the Soviet Union. I need the Ukraine so that we cannot be starved out as we were in the last war.'[154]

Now, however, he had his 'understanding with the Russians'. In Soviet eyes it depended on Hitler's antagonism towards the West. If Hitler had achieved a far-reaching, long-term settlement with Britain, Stalin would have seen the Soviet–German treaty in a new light. But Hitler's intentions towards Britain were of secondary importance at this stage, so long as he was not prepared to desist from his anti-Polish plans. The pact with Stalin did not make it easier for him to do so. Then there was the time-compulsion of which Hitler had spoken to his generals on 22 August: the German economy could only hold out for a few years longer. This was true if the accelerated arms programme was to continue, and was indeed an optimistic assessment. The alternative, of course, was a basically peaceful policy, but Hitler believed this to be the wrong way of securing an adequate power-base.

On 25 August, before receiving the British reply to his 'large offer', Hitler fixed zero hour for 4.30 a.m. on the following day.[155] The military preparations on the 25th were marked by extreme nervousness on the part of the top leaders and especially Hitler himself. Unusual agitation was caused by the conclusion of the

[152] *DBFP*3 vii, No. 426.
[153] Weizsäcker, *Memoirs*, 204; Jodl diary, *1937–9*, 390; Henke, *England*, 288–9.
[154] Burckhardt, *Danziger Mission*, 348.
[155] Halder, *Diaries*, i. 28.

Anglo-Polish treaty of alliance and by the Italian reaction to Hitler's war policy, especially his letter of the same day to Mussolini.[156] The order for the attack, issued in the early afternoon of the 25th, was countermanded that evening. There was just time to cancel the deployment orders. The army high command was in a state of uncertainty; critical voices were raised. The quartermaster-general spoke of 'total irresolution and chaos in the system of command'.[157]

From the time when the Anglo-Polish alliance became known,[158] Hitler could no longer suppose that his initiative would have any effect in Britain—assuming it had ever had any other purpose than to isolate Poland. Hitler learnt of the impending conclusion of the treaty on the afternoon of 25 August.[159] The news had a devastating effect, contradicting all Hitler's recent eloquence and psychological judgement. Mussolini's refusal to join in the war was communicated by Attolico, the ambassador, at about 6 p.m. on the 25th. It contained nothing new: Ciano had already made the position perfectly clear.

Basically only a man like Hitler could really have been surprised by these events, used as he was to thinking and operating on the basis of 'cast-iron convictions'. It is idle to speculate as to the relative effect of the Anglo-Polish alliance and Mussolini's attitude.[160] Hitler was doubly frustrated: his plan to isolate Poland had failed, and the 'pact of steel' was of no use in the imminent contest with the Western powers. Mussolini explained that he thought it inopportune to take any military initiative, for which Italy was not equipped.[161] On the evening of the 25th Hitler, with relief, agreed to Brauchitsch's proposal to postpone the attack.[162] The mobilization went on; the build-up continued.[163] Clearly Hitler was not giving up; the political and military leaders realized it was only a breathing-space. It is hardly conceivable that Hitler still expected a positive answer from London to his 'large offer'. Göring later stated that when he asked Hitler whether the countermanding of the invasion was final, Hitler replied: 'No, I have to see if we can keep the British out.'[164] Even he can at best not have hoped for more than that Britain would draw back once again. To count on this much was an admission of the collapse of his policy. Despite the diplomatic triumph in Moscow, Hitler had no freedom of choice. On 26 August he was not yet certain as to the new date to be fixed for the offensive.[165] Keeping

---

[156] *DGFP*, D. vii, No. 266.   [157] Wagner, *General-Quartiermeister*, 96.

[158] Text of treaty in British Blue Book (*Documents Concerning German–Polish Relations*); with secret protocol, in *Documents on International Affairs, 1939*, i. 469.

[159] It was signed the same afternoon: see Halifax to Kennard, 25 Aug. 1939, *DBFP*[3] vii, No. 309. The information 'that a treaty was now in being', and that consequently Britain could no longer negotiate without Poland, was given by Dahlerus to Bodenschatz and Göring after 10.30 that evening: ibid., No. 299. But the Reichskanzlei had already informed the commander-in-chief, at 7.30, that the treaty had been ratified at about 5 p.m.

[160] See Ribbentrop's evidence at Nuremberg, *IMT* x. 271, and Göring, *IMT* ix. 597; also Jasper, 'Ursachen', 330–1, and Speer, *Inside*, 164.

[161] Mussolini to Hitler, 25 Aug. 1939, *DGFP*. D. vii, No. 271; Italian text in *DDI*[8] xiii, No. 250. See also Vigezzi, 'Mussolini', 89–101; Quartararo, *Roma*; Borejsza, 'Italiens Haltung', 148–94.

[162] Vormann, *Feldzug*, 44.

[163] Halder, *Diaries*, i. 27.

[164] *IMT* xxxix, 090-TC, p. 107.

[165] Halder, *Diaries*, i. 28: 'No decision taken as yet on main problem.'

Britain out became a kind of obsession. Moreover, he needed an alibi with the German people. The British reply of 28 August[166] put an end to any idea there could still have been of separating Britain from her Polish ally. Clearly only a 'just' settlement of the German–Polish question could release Britain from her obligation. In his reply of 29 August Hitler appeared to agree to the proposal for direct German–Polish negotiations,[167] but set a very short time-limit.[168] Henderson observed that the British government could not advise Poland to comply with this procedure: it would be better for the German proposals to be communicated to Warsaw in the normal diplomatic fashion so that the Poles could consider them properly. On 30 August, when Henderson asked to be informed of the German proposals, Ribbentrop replied that they were out of date, as the time-limit had expired.[169] He read out the sixteen points that had been telegraphed on that day to the embassy in London with instructions not to communicate them to the British.[170] The object was to make a show of good will by apparent promises but to make sure that they could not be taken up. In the same way, the sixteen points were broadcast in Germany on the evening of 31 August with a statement that they could no longer be regarded as an offer. As Hitler said later, 'I needed an alibi, especially with the German people.'[171] A Polish rejection of the points was to serve as proof that despite German moderation the Poles were bent on conflict. This was no doubt the main reason why Hitler approved the attempt at mediation by Göring's friend Birger Dahlerus, through whom similar proposals were transmitted to London.[172] This tactic was so timed as not to interfere with the plan for 'Operation White'.

The last days and hours before the outbreak of war show Hitler vacillating between the attempt to keep Britain out and the determination, expressed no doubt in an exaggerated manner, to fight on two fronts if he had to.[173] A clear line of reasoning is hard to find. Mussolini offered mediation, but Hitler would not have it. Attolico, the ambassador, asked on the evening of 31 August 'whether everything was now at an end', to which Hitler replied in the affirmative.[174] He also declined the Italian suggestion for a conference, made on 2 September.[175] The dominant factor in German–Italian relations was Mussolini's refusal to follow Hitler into war.

---

[166] *DGFP*, D. vii, No. 384, annex.

[167] Ibid., No. 421.

[168] Henke, *England*, 293. *DGFP*, D. vii, Nos. 421–2: time-limit 30 Aug.

[169] Record of Henderson–Ribbentrop meeting, 30 Aug. 1939, *DGFP*, D. vii, No. 461.

[170] Schmidt to the chargé d'affaires in London, 30 Aug. 1939, ibid., No. 458.

[171] Schmidt, *Interpreter*, 153.

[172] Dahlerus, *Attempt*; Henke, *England*, 295, with further references. As he suggests, Hitler was willing to negotiate with Britain, but wanted his war with Poland. On Dahlerus's mediation see *DBFP*[3] vii, Nos. 458–9, 467, 477–8, 509, 519, 529. Toland, *Hitler*, 555 ff., gives a vivid picture of the atmosphere in Hitler's entourage.

[173] Statements to Mussolini, Henderson, and others; Halder's note of 29 Aug., *Diaries*, i. 35. Cf. Henke, *England*, 195–6.

[174] Record of Hitler–Attolico meeting, 31 Aug. 1939, *DGFP*, D. vii, No. 478.

[175] *DDI*[8] xiii, No. 571; *DGFP*, D. vii, No. 535. British had demanded on 1 Sept. the cessation of hostilities and withdrawal of German troops (*DGFP*, D. vii, No. 513) and could not accept Mussolini's proposal for an armistice with troops remaining in their positions. The French note was in the same terms (ibid., No. 515).

On 29 August the Duce told Hitler that in his opinion the earlier British proposals afforded a basis for a proper solution.[176] But Hitler was past taking good advice. The 'pact of steel' failed to function. Communications were delayed. On 1 September, the day of the invasion, Hitler sent a message to Mussolini informing him that he did not need military help from Italy.[177] Hitler and Ribbentrop sought to evade Mussolini's proposed conference on the ground that it was irreconcilable with the British and French notes of 1 September, as they 'had the character of an ultimatum'.[178] The actual British and French ultimatums were delivered on 3 September:[179] Britain regarded herself as at war with Germany from 11 a.m. on that day, France from 5 p.m.

Throughout the last days of August the German deployment had been going on, and the blitzkrieg was ready to begin on schedule. Directive No. 1 for the beginning of operations was issued on 31 August.[180] Hitler launched the war with these words: 'Now that every political possibility has been exhausted for ending by peaceful means the intolerable situation on Germany's eastern frontier I have determined on a solution by force.'

Scarcely anyone outside the top leadership knew that Hitler had long determined to use force and had therefore not exhausted the political possibilities of a solution.[181] As he was often to do in later crises, Hitler compared his situation with that of Frederick the Great. To his army adjutant on 29 August he declared that he only wanted his 'first Silesian war',[182] i.e. the war with Poland. He had no wish to fight other powers. If they were stupid and interfered, it was their fault and they must be destroyed. There was also the reflection that the Wehrmacht had to be given its baptism of fire. The standards he had presented to the troops must be embellished with battle honours, or the glorious army would have lost its *raison d'être*.

Hostilities began at dawn on 1 September. German diplomatic missions were informed for guidance that this action was 'in defence against Polish attacks' and was 'for the present not to be described as war'.[183]

The German soldier was sent into battle with a propaganda proclamation by his supreme commander: 'The Polish state has refused the peaceful settlement of relations which I desired and has appealed to arms. . . . A series of violations of the frontier, intolerable to a great power, proved that Poland is no longer willing to respect the frontier of the Reich. In order to put an end to this lunacy I have no other choice than to meet force with force from now on.'[184]

Hitler's decision played into the hands of that power—the Soviet Union—whose

---

[176] Letter of 29 Aug., *DGFP*, D. vii, No. 417.
[177] Ibid., No. 500.
[178] Record of Ribbentrop–Attolico meeting, 2 Sept. 1939, ibid., No. 539.
[179] Ibid., No. 560; *DBFP*³ vii, Nos. 756, 757; *DGFP*, D. vii, No. 563.
[180] *DGFP*, D. vii, No. 493.
[181] For the sequence of events see also Hofer, *War Premeditated*.
[182] *Heeresadjutant bei Hitler*, 60.
[183] Circular telegram from Weizsäcker, 1 Sept. 1939, *DGFP*, D. vii, No. 512.
[184] Proclamation of 1 Sept. 1939, Domarus, ii. 1307; *The Times*, 2 Sept. 1939.

long-term strategy provided for just the war he had unleashed. He thus placed himself in a situation of dependence which was to have a decisive influence on the strategy and final outcome of the war. The effect of his policy was to unite Britain, whom he had wished to have as an ally, with the opponent at whose expense he had hoped to acquire *Lebensraum*. The premisses of his war policy were wrong from the outset. Hitler led Germany into a war that was contrary to his own programme. The causes of this are not to be sought only in his foreign policy. Did the character of the National Socialist state itself precipitate the war, or was the state a mere function of Hitler's own warlike policy? Too many initiatives on all sorts of levels, in economic planning and execution, in armaments, in social and foreign policy, were pursued simultaneously, heightening the pressure and eating up resources. The experts obeyed Hitler's demand for speed, each hoping to fulfil his norm in exemplary fashion or to get the most he could for his own department. Thus, a high degree of friction was immanent in the system, and short-term priorities were set which often did no good to the effort as a whole. But these contradictions were largely dictated by Hitler's own directives. One cannot speak of a 'polycracy' involving Hitler in an unmanageable chaos of conflicting authorities.

The general and unquestioned agreement that the nation's energies were to be mobilized for war enabled Hitler to permit the economy, the Wehrmacht, the Party, and the rest of the state apparatus to enjoy scope for initiatives and rivalries of their own. It is significant that even the advocates of old-fashioned revisionism, a more realistic goal in the light of German possibilities, could not muster the strength to carry through a policy differing from Hitler's and looking further ahead. No one but Hitler commanded mass support after 1934. After one or two failed attempts, no one disputed that it was for Hitler to decide whether there should be war or not. As far as foreign policy was concerned, he forced energies that were often disparate to work in common. Certainly there were 'fields of operations' that Hitler himself could not control absolutely once they had been entrusted to someone's charge: for instance, the pattern and scale of rearmament, with its effects on foreign and social policy. Moreover, he was no doubt bound to some extent by his own 'programme', which he lacked the mental freedom to revise. And another factor was the superior economic strength of the powers which stood in the way of his programme built on false premisses.

Hitler failed, no less completely than the Kaiser's statesmen, to realize that Germany after 1871 must respect the vital interests of her continental neighbours if she did not wish to quarrel with Britain. Her bid for hegemony, which was in the last resort anachronistic, should have been based on preparations for a long war, as regards both the economy and the state of the nation's armament. This was not the case in 1914 and could not be achieved in 1939 either. The whole pattern of the German economy and armament was geared to short continental wars; so was foreign policy, apart from illusory partnerships. Hitler's ruthless campaign against the victors of 1918, who regarded collective security as the only proper way to solve Europe's post-war problems and those of their own national communities, led him to make a fresh bid for hegemony which brought about the Second World War and the second German catastrophe.

The degree of latitude that was open to German foreign policy was in fact roughly that represented by the European aims of the Weimar revisionists. Hitler soon became aware of this. From then on he was confronted by problems whose difficulties he refused to recognize. He succeeded in breaking up the collective-security system, but his further bilateral policy brought only partial success and not the rear cover he needed for the major solution in the east. He entered on the confrontation with Poland without foreign-policy safeguards, relying merely on hopes and suppositions. At the last moment he had to resort to Soviet co-operation, which Stalin had precisely calculated and driven a hard bargain for.

Hitler did not reach this position as a result of balanced politico-strategic calculation. The diplomats and top army leaders were sceptical. Yet the decision to make war was not 'senseless' in every respect, given Hitler's premisses. Germany's lead in armaments was indeed melting away, and the standard of living was bound to decline appreciably before long. Too much had been invested in a war, in concert with the army, the Party, and the business world. And so Hitler chose war even through the cards were not dealt as he would have wished. The course towards war, based on false premisses but represented by propaganda as inevitable, did not permit the German people to raise any serious objection. Many still regarded war as a proper way of vindicating national interests—and perhaps success proved that the Führer was right.

Conclusions

THE academic debate on the causes of the Second World War has never produced such diverse points of view as has research into the causes of the wars of 1864–6, 1870, and 1914–18. Even the provocative theses of a few revisionist historians, which have led to a re-examination of prevailing opinions, have not been able to shake the generally accepted conclusion that it was German policy in the years before 1939 that was the basic cause of the Second World War. Moreover, extensive research into German history of the last 150 years has shown that the founding of the German national state and the attempt to maintain and enlarge it, as well as the renewed efforts to achieve great-power or even world-power status after the catastrophe of 1918, involved a war-oriented policy which fundamentally changed Europe and its political weight in the world. Wars marked the beginning and the end of the seventy-five-year history of the united German state.

This perspective is an important result of the continuing discussion about the decisive structural elements of that state. These developed primarily as a result of specific political conditions in the years after 1871, of the accelerating industrialization, and of combinations of both factors. The question of the continuing importance of these elements has been dealt with in numerous historical studies of imperial Germany. The preliminary conclusion of most of these studies is that in the dominant military, political, and social groups a continuity of foreign- and domestic-policy aims and supporting ideologies can be seen, and that this exerted a powerful influence long after 1918.

To understand the history of the years before the Second World War it is necessary to place these insights in a clear historical framework. The detachment thus achieved permits a more differentiated judgement of the developments, trends, and events of the 1930s which must be considered an integral part of the short history of the united German state. It enables one to see both the continuity and discontinuity of this historical development, in which stability and also changes in the structural elements mentioned above are reflected.

The effects of the military defeat of 1918, the revolution of that year, and the treaty of Versailles must be taken as starting-points for an analysis of the causes of those policies which led to war in September 1939. The collapse of the political and military system, the assumption of power by Social Democrats—former 'enemies of the Reich'—the limiting of the German armed forces to a professional army of 100,000 men and a navy whose only mission seemed to be coastal defence clearly shook traditional German values and ideas of order. Economic and social conditions seemed at first less affected, although even during the war large segments of the middle class had experienced difficulties which threatened their livelihood and were aggravated considerably by the inflation of 1923. Irrespective of whether the changes in political, economic, and social conditions were actually far-reaching, they were felt to be so by those members of the bourgeoisie who shaped public opinion and especially by the nationalist middle class.

The demand for a revision of the treaty of Versailles played a fundamental role in further developments and in the vindication of National Socialist policies after 1933. The issue was raised by all political groups and supported by the mass of the population under the influence of the harsh conditions of the treaty. As a political platform, 'revisionism' had a socially unifying effect, which was, however, short-lived. Very soon it became associated with the most varied foreign- and domestic-policy aims, an ambiguous symbol and propaganda catchword. In nationalist circles it acquired a distinctly domestic emphasis. In a dangerous defiance of reality, the nationalists refused to admit that Germany had been defeated by her enemies in the war; it was 'revolutionary wire-pullers' who had 'stabbed' the undefeated army 'in the back' and brought about the military and political collapse. The condemnation of the 'Versailles dictat' thus came to be allied with traditional anti-parliamentarism and anti-republicanism.

All revisionists were primarily interested in such aims as doing away with reparations, re-establishing German military sovereignty, and regaining the territories lost at Versailles. Here too the number and scope of demands differed from party to party. The important differences were usually to be found in the long-term political goals and the methods with which they were to be attained. Here it became clear that, in spite of the completely changed conditions, the thoughts and actions of many parties in the Weimar Republic, including the Social Democrats, were still determined by plans for achieving great-power status which had been propagated and tried out with varying degrees of success before 1918. Moreover, compared to the situation at the beginning of the century, and despite Germany's immediate weakness, the long-range prospects for a great-power role had improved appreciably. The ideological conflict between Britain and the Soviet Union appeared so deep as to be unbridgeable, the United States had very soon dissociated itself from the Versailles system, the states of east-central Europe were amenable to German economic and political influence, and, finally, the Anglo-French relationship had lost much of the closeness of the war years, especially after the French occupation of the Ruhr in 1923.

To German public opinion and in the minds of almost all Republican politicians, these factors were obscured by the impression that Germany had scarcely any freedom to manœuvre in foreign policy. Even after the Rapallo treaty with the Soviet Union (1922) and Germany's admission to the League of Nations (1926), this assessment of the situation hardly changed. Even Stresemann's promising attempts to exploit economic factors and the collective-security system to create a new basis for a German great-power policy were dismissed by the right-wing parties and similar groups outside parliament as merely a 'policy of fulfilment', i.e. compliance with Versailles. Liberals and Social Democrats, as well as some moderate conservatives, who pursued with different aims a policy of understanding and compromise within the international system represented by the League, failed during the latter years of Weimar to maintain majority support for this policy. The continued vehement rejection of Versailles and the League (the latter seen as an 'organization of the victors'), and demands for a reduction of reparations and for equality in armaments matters, all strengthened the groups favouring traditional power politics.

While the German revolution of 1918–19 and the treaty of Versailles have been suggested as starting-points for a discussion of the causes of German policy after 1933, the world depression of 1929 onwards, with its political, economic, social, and psychological consequences, must be regarded as the decisive factor in the consolidation of the forces which prevailed in German politics until 1939. The clearly strengthening tendencies towards a breaking away from the multilateral system of the League were a consequence of changes in the domestic situation brought about by the economic crisis. These tendencies were accompanied by changes in the military policies of the Reichswehr.

The earlier attempts by General Hans von Seeckt, chief of the army high command, to break out of the Versailles system with the help of the Soviet Union and create a basis for German great-power policy had not, in spite of Rapallo, produced the desired results. After Seeckt's dismissal in 1926 the Reichswehr took the real political and military situation more into account in its plans and actions. Its leaders attempted to draw the proper conclusions from the experience of the First World War by systematic armaments planning, but actual measures remained on a very limited scale. The government's approval of the first armaments programme in 1928 was a reflection of the efforts of the defence minister, Groener, to make the Reichswehr conform to Stresemann's general revisionist policy, whose goals Groener wished to adopt as a framework for operational planning. This relatively consistent policy was gradually abandoned as the foundation of Reichswehr planning after the autumn of 1931. By January 1933 the general political crisis had led to the balance of power in the defence ministry shifting in favour of those who believed that the only way to achieve ambitious military aims and provide a solid base for Germany's claims to be a great power was to abandon the system of collective security. Such ideas—which Groener himself did not basically reject—represented a continuation of Seeckt's foreign policy, itself based on Prusso-German traditions involving a notion of sovereignty and the role of the military that had been obsolete since the First World War. Thus, Groener's original programme was defeated by what were, in this context, reactionary forces.

At the same time the influence of the Reichswehr in home affairs increased notably. In the autumn and winter of 1923 its leaders under Seeckt had failed to use the state of emergency to regain the traditional supremacy of the armed forces within the general power structure, which had been lost at the end of the war. After an interval during the relatively stable years of the republic, General von Schleicher's appointment as defence minister and then chancellor marked the culmination of attempts to restore the supremacy of the military on a much broader organizational base; with the decline of parliamentary government due to the economic crisis these attempts had greater chances of success. Under Schleicher, who enjoyed the confidence of President von Hindenburg, Germany moved towards becoming a military state once more. After the interruption of 1918–19 this traditional factor in German politics seemed, like others, to be regaining its former influence.

The crisis of the parliamentary system was reflected in presidential governments. The first German republic collapsed under the political, economic, and, above all, social problems resulting from the economic crisis. These problems were accompanied by a wave of nationalist and anti-democratic ideas which generally accrued to the benefit of the Nazi Party (NSDAP). A decisive role in the propagation of these ideas was played by the so-called Nationalist Opposition. This included the NSDAP; the Stahlhelm, a league of former front-line soldiers; the German National People's Party (DNVP); the influential literary group headed by Ernst Jünger, known as Soldierly Nationalism; a large part of the student body; and a number of paramilitary organizations and groups. In domestic policy the Nationalist Opposition sought to introduce a 'front-line soldiers' state' organized along military lines, an authoritarian state based on military power. The foreign policy of the Nationalist Opposition was based on a less clearly formulated but nevertheless loudly proclaimed military imperialism, supported by rather vague arguments which stressed national defence and military readiness above all else. The two main churches, the Protestant still more than the Catholic, also belonged far more to the nationalist camp than to the ranks of democratic republicans. The churches' traditional doctrine of a 'just war' prevented the Christian principle of non-violence from carrying any political weight. In spite of the horrors of the First World War, the German official churches tended to accept war uncritically, as if ordained by a natural or divine law. The Catholic Centre Party, the right-liberal German People's Party (DVP), the left-liberal German Democratic Party (DDP), and organizations close to them became increasingly nationalistic during the crisis years of the republic, and dissociated themselves from a foreign policy of peaceful compromise. Only the Social Democrats, who were by now kept out of power, the Reichsbanner Black–Red–Gold, and the trade unions continued to support that policy. Pacifist organizations, especially those which were clearly anti-military, were completely isolated. The German Communists warned constantly of the dangers of an 'imperialist' war, but since their argument was that new (capitalist) wars were inevitable anyway, this only contributed, as did the churches' attitude, to a certain fatalism.

The flood of nationalist books and war films which began in 1929 and increased steadily until the end of 1933 also changed the political climate; the decline in the number of artistic and literary works with pacifist themes at this time reflected a general trend. In spite of the Kellogg–Briand Pact of 1928 outlawing war, the view that military force was a legitimate means of policy was accepted as self-evident. The publications of those years clearly reveal a strong trend towards the militarization of society, which was in accord with and promoted the intentions of the Reichswehr leaders under Schleicher. In this respect 1933 did not represent a break; rather, the National Socialist regime was able to exploit the favourable climate of opinion in its practical policies.

This survey of the situation at the end of 1932 supports the view that, in almost all areas of domestic and foreign policy, groups and individuals who followed traditional ways of thinking as they had developed since 1867–71 had gained influence and were increasingly in control of events, even though conditions at home and abroad had changed completely since 1918. This trend could be observed also in the ideologies of most of these groups and individuals, as well as in economic developments. The crisis of the liberal world trade system resulted in a revival of ideas and plans for more or less self-contained economic areas. In Germany such ideas were a continuation of similar plans of the Wilhelmine era. The idea of a large, autarkic European economy as an alternative to the disintegrating world system gained new significance when the Nazis adopted it as a foundation of their programme, thanks to which they obtained the support of important business circles even before Hitler's appointment as chancellor.

It may seem fair to conclude that after January 1933 the policies of the Nazi regime were essentially a continuation of traditional tendencies and lines of development and were new only in their extreme radicalism; but such an interpretation would be superficial and would carry the continuity thesis too far. It would disregard the programme and political acts of the man who within a few years led the NSDAP to victory over powerful rivals and who was the dominant figure in German politics until 1945: Adolf Hitler. Although individual elements of his world-view may seem heterogeneous and even contradictory, both his racial ideology and his social-Darwinist conviction that 'struggle in all its forms' determined the life of the individuals and nations must be seen as the unchanging basis of his political decisions. Hitler's foreign-policy aims, of which the most important was the conquest of *Lebensraum* in the east, were also determined by this ideological perspective. Peace was desirable only as an opportunity to prepare for war; alliances were valued only in so far as they might be useful in future wars. The ideological determinant in Hitler's political views and his decisions after 1933 constituted a break with previously accepted aims and ideas of order in German policy. In the years after 1933, however, Hitler was careful to conceal from the public the real extent of this change. He was able to avoid conflicts by concentrating on broad areas of agreement with strong revisionist groups in short-term domestic, foreign, economic, and military goals. In the years after 1933 no one talked more about peace than Hitler himself, as his comprehensive programme of 'remilitarization' made it necessary to do so. Only in this way could he hope to achieve an agreement with Britain, an essential element of his programme since the 1920s and a precondition, in his view, for German expansion in the east. But the pace of German rearmament made the attaining of this goal uncertain and thus endangered the political and strategic assumptions of Hitler's policy of aggression.

The contributions to the present volume show that the scale and momentum of the rearmament programme shaped the development of German domestic and foreign policy between 1933 and 1939 to a much greater extent than has previously been assumed. All important measures of the regime supported rearmament directly or indirectly; this was especially true of economic policy and to a lesser degree of foreign policy.

In his conference with Reichswehr commanders on 3 February 1933 Hitler mentioned an additional precondition for successful rearmament: the 'rebuilding of Germany's defence capability', the strengthening by all means of the military spirit (*Wehrwille*). In Hitler's view this could be achieved only through a 'complete reversal' of domestic conditions, by a strict, authoritarian leadership. In this respect the interests of the party and the Reichswehr were identical. The domestic policies of the National Socialist regime clearly served the aim of reorganizing German society for war. Political measures—the elimination of parliamentarism and political parties, the forcing of all interest-groups into line, and the establishment of an authoritarian Führer state—were not ends in themselves but only methods of preparing for war. One consequence of this policy was the corruption and finally the dissolution of the rule of law. Despite all similarities with imperial Germany, the National Socialist break with German traditions is most evident in this sphere.

Even the regime's social policies were affected by the general preparation for war. In this area the NSDAP was strongly influenced by the First World War, during which the working class had protested with increasing force against the continuation of the war and the economic sacrifices required, and had ignited the revolution after the military defeat. Fear of revolution was the main motive of Hitler's policy of maintaining the production of consumer goods in spite of intensive rearmament. But the workers could not be kept in line by propaganda alone; economic concessions were required. When the strategy of social 'bribery' did not work, obedience was enforced by brutal terror.

Hitler left the planning and specific aims of rearmament largely to the military. The new defence minister, von Blomberg, who had determinedly opposed Groener's military policy since 1929, successfully advocated unilateral rearmament. He rejected multilateral or even bilateral agreements which might lead to restrictions on German armament plans. The senior officers of the army and navy quickly took as their point of reference the level of armaments achieved before the First World War. In view of the existing levels of military force in Europe, and the threat of political isolation, it was the first steps towards this goal which were the most dangerous. Hitler himself pointed out the danger of a French preventive strike to the Reichswehr commanders at the beginning of February 1933. The military leaders, particularly von Fritsch and Beck, were of the opinion that this danger could be met only by accelerating the tempo of rearmament; Hitler's intentions in this respect agreed with those of the military leaders. The rejection of all international restrictions on German armaments, the consequent sense of danger, and the military conclusions drawn from this assessment of the situation, gave the rearmament programme a dynamism of its own whose political and economic effects in 1933–9 can hardly be overestimated.

The rearmament of the Wehrmacht up to 1939 was marked by a pronounced lack of co-ordination among the service branches, which considerably reduced its effectiveness. No attempt was made to co-ordinate the programmes of the army, navy, and air force through clear politico-strategic directives. The army programmes of December 1933 and August 1936 were based on the assumption of a European war on several fronts. After the completion of its armaments programme,

Germany would, it was considered, be able to fight such a war with 'some prospect of success'. The offensive aims of the armaments plan of 1936 were obvious. As early as the end of 1935 Beck had spoken of a 'strategic defence' to be carried out aggressively in a war on several fronts. In August 1936 the chief of the general army office considered the armaments plan to be justifiable from the military and economic point of view only if the armed forces were actually to be used after its completion.

At that time the navy had not developed such a comprehensive programme, even allowing for the fact that its expansion would of necessity be a slower process. Since the pre-planning for the Anglo-German naval agreement of June 1935, as well as after its signing, the navy leaders had been involved in the difficult task of developing new strategic assumptions. As with the army, the navy planners considered France and Poland the probable enemies, until the conclusion of the German–Polish non-aggression pact. The strategic implications of the navy's demand for armaments parity with France from 1934 onwards show that it no longer entirely ruled out Britain as a possible long-term enemy. The 'Tirpitz fleet' ideology, to which the leading German naval officers felt bound by tradition, acquired a new relevance. But the change from an orientation towards Britain, which had not been previously questioned, to a policy directed against the superior sea power was a lengthy one. A taboo had to be broken. Only in the summer of 1937 did the naval leaders officially begin to concern themselves with the strategic consequences of a confrontation with Britain. The result of this lack of clarity regarding strategic requirements was a curiously vacillating armaments policy determined more by the impulses of the moment than by the navy's basic long-term aims.

There is no evidence of even a basic co-ordination of armaments efforts between the army and the navy. In contrast, there seemed to be at least the beginning of co-operation between the army and the air force. This was due primarily to the fact that almost all the senior air force officers had come from the army. The two services also shared common strategic ideas; both expected a war on two or more fronts in Europe, with France and Czechoslovakia as the most important states on the other side. The air force considered its main task to be the support of the ground forces rather than an independent air war. In spite of common views there was no co-ordination, as the air force regarded its own armaments programme and related industrial activities as its exclusive domain. The large-scale, well-planned development of the aircraft industry made possible the creation, between 1933 and 1936, of an air force which completely fulfilled its function of deterring other states from taking preventive measures against German rearmament. However, this neither solved the military problems of the new service branch nor helped to master the difficulties resulting from the necessary modernization of aircraft and the systematic application of technical advances to industrial production. After a rapid initial increase, aircraft production stagnated in 1937–8, at which time the British Royal Air Force became the potential enemy. For this war, however, the Luftwaffe was largely deficient in the appropriate armaments.

The rearmament of the German armed forces can be described as an almost uninterrupted build-up and expansion of the service branches which was unprecedented in its speed and dimensions. In 1936–7 economic difficulties necessitated bureaucratic management of the armaments programme in the form of allocations of raw materials. However, such difficulties led neither Hitler nor his military leaders to base their armaments aims on political goals and resulting strategic perspectives. The generally accepted principle was to produce as much as possible as rapidly as possible. Hitler attempted, with some success, to overcome the resulting crises in armaments production by ideological appeals to the armed forces, descriptions of future political perspectives, and excessive production demands. Such efforts, however, also intensified inter-service rivalries. Undoubtedly the armed forces had achieved a very high level of rearmament by the outbreak of the war, when Germany was the strongest military power on the Continent, with the most modern equipment. But the level of armaments did not completely meet the wishes of the military; it was, rather, the result of an unrestrained rearmament of individual service branches. Available resources were thus wasted, although they would certainly have been adequate for a thorough rearmament based on a realistic estimation of the country's economic potential. The causes and preconditions of the German war policy can be explained to a considerable degree by this complex situation and its implications for foreign, economic, and social affairs. In comparison, the ideological differences between the armed forces and the NSDAP, the petty conflicts of authority within the armed forces themselves, and the innumerable organizational problems were of only peripheral importance.

Rearmament was in keeping with Hitler's basic doctrine of struggle, war, and *Lebensraum*. At the beginning of 1933, however, Germany was still afflicted by a depressed economy with several million unemployed, in spite of the nationalist enthusiasm which constituted the psychological basis for the fulfilment of the National Socialist programme. Solving this economic problem was a prerequisite for the consolidation of the regime's domestic power and for an opportunity to realize its military and foreign-policy aims. As Papen and Schleicher had done before him, Hitler adopted a policy of using government funds to stimulate the economy and create new jobs. Typically, however, he saw to it that the corresponding programmes served rearmament directly or indirectly. The close connection between economic recovery and rearmament meant that certain risks had to be taken. The president of the Reichsbank, Schacht, who became the central figure in the first phase of National Socialist economic policy, sought to limit the risks from the beginning. The funds obtained for rearmament by the well-known Mefo bills were limited to a predetermined sum. Although financing for rearmament could be guaranteed in this way for a few years, serious difficulties were soon encountered in obtaining foreign exchange for imports of essential raw materials and even foodstuffs. Schacht attempted to solve this problem through a reorientation of trade policy. Germany largely restricted its exports to countries that could pay for them with the desired raw materials and foodstuffs. The constantly shrinking foreign-exchange reserves could thus be concentrated on rearmament needs. This new element in German policy complemented almost perfectly the efforts to achieve autarky, as relations with the less industrialized states of eastern and south-eastern Europe could now be used to make them more dependent on the German market.

The state regulation of foreign trade which accompanied the 'New Plan' of 1934 had some features of a planned economy, but Schacht and those members of the National Socialist regime concerned with economic questions continued to emphasize the basic responsibility of the employers. In accordance with their view of a 'defence economy' (*Wehrwirtschaft*) they did claim the right to intervene for the purpose of guiding the economic process; they wanted to establish centralized control of all economic organizations. The consideration with which the regime treated both companies and individual capitalists was in sharp contrast to the workers' complete loss of political and economic power. Only in the course of time did the German Labour Front, which had replaced the trade unions, develop social-policy initiatives going beyond its original supervisory function.

The successes of Schacht's economic policy were overtaken by the speed and extent of rearmament as early as the second half of 1935. The National Socialist leaders, above all Hitler and Göring, reacted to the new raw-materials crisis caused by the exhaustion of foreign-exchange reserves by proclaiming an economic mobilization, the Four-year Plan, in September 1936. More than ever, economic policy was subordinated by preparations for war. The programme of exploiting all sources of raw materials within Germany without regard to the profit principle, the build-up and expansion of synthetic-materials industries at almost any cost, and, finally, the goals of achieving a high degree of self-sufficiency in those raw materials of especial importance for armaments and of preparing the whole economy for war within four years must be seen in connection with the army armaments programme of August 1936. As a whole this programme shows clearly the basic social-Darwinist nature of Hitler's ideas and actions: his only solution for economic problems was the conquest of new *Lebensraum*.

Hitler's appeals and his new programme made little difference to the total economic situation. Improvements in some sectors could be expected from individual projects, but the short-term effects achieved by Hitler's dramatic announcement and Göring's energetic efforts soon came to nothing. The raw-materials allocation measures introduced in 1937 completely failed to satisfy the armed forces; it became clear that Hitler himself would have to determine the distribution of available raw materials. Instead, on 5 November 1937 he lectured the commanders of the armed forces on his political ideas for the future. His decisions regarding pressing economic and armaments questions were improvised and provisional. Until the outbreak of war there was no comprehensive armaments programme for all the armed forces. Hitler had already indicated that he did not have much faith in systematic preparations for a total war, as advocated earlier by Ludendorff. In the latter's view based on the experience of the First World War, such a programme involved preparing the entire economy for a long war. Hitler considered it more important to have at his disposal well-equipped, formidable armed forces ready for war at any time; supply depots and logistics capacity were in his eyes matters of only secondary importance.

In the winter of 1937–8 it became increasingly clear that available resources were not sufficient to maintain the volume and speed of rearmament and at the same time overcome the economic crisis, which was now aggravated by a labour shortage. Consequently German economic planners developed a growing interest in neighbouring states, especially Austria and Czechoslovakia. They saw the only possibility of maintaining the desired pace of rearmament in territorial expansion and a resulting enlargement of Germany's economic base. Undoubtedly these arguments influenced the motives and even the timing of Hitler's political decisions to annex Austria and 'smash' Czechoslovakia. The improvement of the general economic situation could not, however, conceal the fact that the crisis persisted and restricted Hitler's freedom of action in making further political decisions. The Führer, of course, considered the economy a mere instrument to be used in the support of his expansionist policies.

A policy directed towards war was also a means of avoiding those social consequences of the constant strain on the economy which Hitler feared. In 1938 and 1939 signs of unrest among workers and of a general dissatisfaction among farmers increased. Refusals to work overtime, high rates of absenteeism due to illness, a decline in productivity, and complaints about the catastrophic migration from rural areas to the cities and the disadvantages of price control were all symptoms of a development which could endanger the political stability of the regime. Although it is not accurate to speak of a dangerous worsening of these conditions in 1939, the possibility of domestic motives in the policies which led to war cannot be completely excluded. The effects described above also show the basic reversal of the traditional values and aims of economic policy that took place under National Socialism.

Preparations for war were the common denominator of the basic decisions of the regime in the areas of domestic, military, and economic policy. It was therefore logical that foreign policy should also be determined by this factor. In accordance with his ideological premises, Hitler never accepted an international order which had as its goal a permanent peaceful coexistence of the various states. In the remilitarization phase, foreign policy assumed the function of providing diplomatic cover for the programme of the new regime. Hitler and the foreign ministry, which was happy to accept this task under the banner of revisionism, managed to avoid international isolation through numerous bilateral initiatives and even achieved significant successes, such as the conclusion of the concordat and the Polish–German non-aggression pact.

This policy was accompanied by the extremely effective use of propaganda under the direction of Joseph Goebbels, whose task was to conceal the personnel and material rearmament measures both from other countries and from the German population, or, if that was not possible, to play them down as purely defensive. For this purpose Goebbels used catch-phrases that had been popular in all German right-wing groups since the 1920s—'revision of Versailles', 'the struggle against Bolshevism', 'equal rights' (for Germany) and 'rebuilding Germany's defence capability' (*Wiederwehrhaftmachung*). Hitler stressed his peaceful intentions at every opportunity, and his propaganda minister saw to it that he received vocal mass support. This deception proved effective both at home and abroad.

Public opinion in foreign countries generally believed that Nazi foreign policy differed from that of the Weimar governments only in its greater determination to realize the same well-known demands. The united front of the Versailles victors had begun to crumble during the 1920s. Even at that time the reaction to German wishes for revision had been varied, and at times sympathetic. In this situation, and in view of the generally weakened condition of most countries as a result of the slump, energetic joint action against German treaty violations was hardly to be expected. The other powers vacillated between attempts to isolate Germany completely, partial co-operation, and efforts to preserve peace by drawing Germany into the international system in spite of her treaty violations.

Hitler and the foreign ministry recognized and thoroughly exploited the opportunities thus offered them for an active foreign policy. The occupation of the demilitarized Rhineland in March 1936 was the high point and also the successful conclusion of the first phase of National Socialist foreign policy. Thereafter its defensive function was largely replaced by attempts to create diplomatic preconditions for the planned conquest of *Lebensraum* in the east. German trade policy towards south-eastern Europe was, in terms of its effects, as much a part of these attempts as the generally less successful courting, at this time, of Italy and Japan.

The relationship with Britain became a decisive factor in Hitler's aims, as he was convinced of the unchanging hostility of France and considered it essential to eliminate or neutralize her before the start of his war of expansion in the east. Hitler clearly found it difficult to assess Britain's attitude to German designs for hegemony in Europe. After 1933 he seems to have continued to assume that Britain would accept German predominance on the Continent if her overseas interests were not affected. The influence of earlier ideas about a possible adjustment of interests between the land and the sea power, with co-operation on a world scale, is obvious. But the uncertainty remained. Hitler and the German naval commanders considered the Anglo-German agreement of 1935 as a relatively short-term, interim measure, and Britain kept her distance in the following years. This threatened to disrupt Hitler's calculations: the absence of a threat in the west was, in his view, the decisive prerequisite for the success of his plan to conquer *Lebensraum* in the Soviet Union, whose military strength he completely underestimated.

Hitler rejected all British offers to help towards a mutually satisfactory peaceful change of the status quo in eastern and south-eastern Europe. Such a policy would have enabled him to achieve Germany's main revisionist goals in Poland, Czechoslovakia, and Austria peacefully—a very far-reaching offer on the appeasers' part. Hitler's refusal to accept such a solution showed his determination to achieve his larger goals by force. His talks with Lord Halifax (soon to be British foreign minister), fourteen days after he had revealed his belligerent intentions to German military leaders in November 1937, show that even at that point he was not prepared to accept what he regarded as no more than a temporary solution. A peace and a war policy here confronted each other with a clarity unusual by diplomatic standards.

Hitler was now carried along by the dynamism of the policy he had initiated. The course of events was accelerated not only by the reactions of Germany's threatened neighbours but by a combination of psychological causes with a variety of factors in military policy and the armaments industry. The events of February–March 1938 and of May and September that year quickly made the timetable of November 1937 obsolete. The British guarantee to Poland in March 1939 reduced Hitler's room for manœuvre even more, as he continued to rule out the alternative of a peaceful compromise.

The question of a connecting link between Hitler's designs and the rapid rearmament programme postulates an overall politico-strategic plan and a timetable agreed upon by Hitler and the military leaders. But Hitler was clearly unable to proceed in such a manner. To do so he would have had to have the compliance of other parties as envisaged in his programme. Even Italy was not prepared to go as far as he wanted; Britain deliberately left him guessing, but made it clear in 1937 that she had no intention of agreeing to military solutions of continental problems. Whatever may be said against appeasement, the British refusal did force Hitler to improvise alternatives. In the autumn of 1938 and the spring of 1939 these even included the attempt to come to an arrangement with Poland. The idea of a political triangle consisting of Berlin, Rome, and Tokyo, which remained an illusion, can also be explained only as a reaction to British policy, an attempt to exert pressure on Britain.

Britain's policy forced Hitler to conclude a pact with Stalin, dependence on which was completely incompatible with his long-term aims. The deterrence component of the 'blitzkrieg strategy' was a political failure on the first occasion of its use: the Western powers declared war, making it impossible for Hitler to prepare his next move according to plan. He could only attempt to improve his military starting position for the realization of his programme. But the qualitative and quantitative German superiority in armaments was sufficient for only the first stages of the war. It permitted solutions on the Continent which only fed a short-lived optimism. Germany was incapable of waging a world war, which is what the conflict soon became.

In exploring the causes of German policy in September 1939 we must note that, unlike August 1914, the German people felt no significant enthusiasm for the war at that time. Contemporary reports in fact suggest the opposite. As early as the Sudeten crisis in the autumn of 1938, Nazi propagandists noted the widespread fear of war among the population. For this reason Hitler ordered in November 1938 that the 'pacifist gramophone record' be turned off and the nation psychologically prepared for military solutions. Consequently the propagandists resorted to fresh themes in 1939. As in 1914, the country was warned of alleged encirclement by hostile powers; it was claimed that Germany was a nation without space, and, to conceal the aggressive intentions of their own government, the propagandists sought to place the blame for 'what was to come' on other countries. None the less, and whatever the reasons for the negative attitude of the German population, it can be said that, in contrast to the situation in 1914, the war policy of the regime did not command widespread support.

This again raises the question of who really supported the German policy of aggression. In seeking an answer we cannot ignore the bourgeois-nationalist groups and their representatives in the foreign ministry, the armed forces, industry, and the universities. In their thoughts and deeds the traditions of the German empire lived on. They had experienced Germany's rise to world-power status before 1914 and their attitudes had been shaped by it; they were familiar with all the variations of German great-power policy and its economic and military principles. They had welcomed and supported rearmament, the 'rebuilding of Germany's defence capability', and the concentration of the economy on preparing for war. They aspired to see an expansion of Germany's position as a great power, over and above a mere revision of the limitations imposed by the treaty of Versailles. They hoped that Germany would establish an *imperium* in the east as the basis of an autarkic defence economy. In these calculations the use of military force was taken for granted. Differences that developed between Hitler and the German diplomatic, economic, and military leaders after 1936–7 involved only the question of the speed at which one should attempt to achieve these goals. As for Hitler's *Lebensraum* programme—the axiomatic basis of his policy, with its social-Darwinist and racist justification—this was outside the framework of traditional German great-power policy and was ignored, played down, or simply not understood by the old leadership groups.

Thus, Hitler's programme was an objective which could be approached in different ways according to such tactics as he chose to dictate. The precondition for a policy of hegemony, viz. the rebuilding of the nation's military capability, affected all areas of life and society and was carried out as a constantly accelerating process with the participation of a growing number of institutions and organizations. The forces involved in this process penetrated the traditional state bureaucracy, competed with and checked each other, but always regarded the Führer and chancellor as the real centre from which they derived their power. The studies in this volume leave no doubt that even Hitler's own decisions were affected by the dynamism of the power-structure that developed in this way.

The step-by-step realization of Hitler's continental programme—historically speaking, a new attempt to establish Germany as a great power and a world power—entered a new phase with the German attack on Poland on 1 September 1939. The expectation that the subjugation of Poland would provoke only formal protests from the Western powers was shattered by their declaration of war on Germany on 3 September. Twenty-five years after the outbreak of the First World War, the lights in Europe were again extinguished. A military machine was set in motion whose destructive power exceeded anything previously known and affected almost every corner of the European continent. This catastrophe was the result of policies pursued by Germany since 1933, which were aimed at expansion and war. These policies were not only based on Hitler's *Lebensraum* ideology, but were also an expression of the claims to power and influence that groups of major importance in Germany had been advancing without interruption since the turn of the century.

WILHELM DEIST
MANFRED MESSERSCHMIDT
HANS-ERICH VOLKMANN
WOLFRAM WETTE

Bibliography

FOR the English edition the Bibliography has been supplemented by works published between 1979 and 1986, as far as they were available to the authors. Edited works which have no single author are listed under titles.

ABEL, KARL-DIETRICH. *Presselenkung im NS-Staat: Eine Studie zur Geschichte der Publizistik in der nationalsozialistischen Zeit*, with preface by Hans Herzfeld (Einzelveröffentlichungen der Historischen Kommission zu Berlin, 2; Berlin, 1968).

ABENDROTH, HANS-HENNING, *Hitler in der spanischen Arena: Die deutsch-spanischen Beziehungen im Spannungsfeld der europaischen Interessenpolitik vom Ausbruch des Bürgerkrieges bis zum Ausbruch des Weltkrieges 1936–1939* (Paderborn, 1973).

—— 'Deutschlands Rolle im spanischen Bürgerkrieg', in *Hitler, Deutschland und die Mächte* (q.v.), 471–88.

ABENDROTH, WOLFGANG, 'Der Widerstand der Arbeiterbewegung', in *Deutscher Widerstand 1933–1945* (q.v.), 76–96.

—— *Sozialgeschichte der europäischen Arbeiterbewegung*[6] (Frankfurt am Main, 1969).

Abkommen von München 1938, Das: Tschechoslowakische diplomatische Dokumente 1937–39, ed. with intro. by Václav Král (Prague, 1968).

ABSOLON, RUDOLF, *Die Wehrmacht im Dritten Reich: Aufbau, Gliederung, Recht, Verwaltung*, 3 vols. (Schriften des Bundesarchivs, 16. 1-3; Boppard, 1963, 1971, 1975).

ACKER, DETLEV, *Walther Schücking (1875–1935)* (Münster, 1970).

ADAMTHWAITE, ANTHONY, *France and the Coming of the Second World War 1936–1939* (London, 1977).

—— 'Le gouvernement britannique et l'opinion publique', in *La Puissance en Europe* (q.v.), 349–61.

—— 'War Origins Again', *JMH* 56 (1984), 100–15.

ADLER, S., 'The War-guilt Question and American Disillusionment, 1918–1928', *JMH* 23 (1951), 1–28.

Adolf Hitler in Franken: Reden aus der Kampfzeit, ed. Heinz Preiss (s.l., n.d. [preface, Nuremberg, 1939]).

AIGNER, DIETRICH, *Das Ringen um England: Das deutsch-britische Verhältnis. Die öffentliche Meinung 1933–1939. Tragödie zweier Völker* (Munich, 1969).

Akten zur deutschen auswärtigen Politik 1918–1945, Series B (*1925–33*) (Göttingen, 1966–78); Series C (*1933–7*), *Das Dritte Reich* (Göttingen, 1971–5); Series D (*1937–45*) (Göttingen, Baden-Baden, and Frankfurt am Main, 1950–70). [For translation of Series C and D see *Documents on German Foreign Policy*.]

ALBERT, RUDOLF, *Nationalwirtschaft: Grundzüge der Gestaltung im Dritten Reich* (Leipzig, 1932).

ALBERT, URSULA, *Die deutsche Wiederaufrüstung der Dreißiger Jahre als Teil der staatlichen Arbeitsbeschaffung und ihre Finanzierung durch das System der Mefawechsel* (diss. Nuremberg, 1956).

ALBERTIN, LOTHAR, *Liberalismus und Demokratie am Anfang der Weimarer Republik: Eine vergleichende Analyse der Deutschen Demokratischen Partei und der Deutschen Volkspartei* (Düsseldorf, 1972).

ALFF, WILHELM, *Der Begriff Faschismus und andere Aufsätze zur Zeitgeschichte* (ed. suhrkamp, 456; Frankfurt am Main, 1971).

ALLARD, SVEN, *Stalin und Hitler: Die sowjetrussische Außenpolitik 1930–1941* (Berne and Munich, 1974).

Allianz Hitler-Horthy-Mussolini: Dokumente zur ungarischen Außenpolitik (1933–1944), ed. M. Adám, G. Juhász, and L. Kerekes (Budapest, 1966).

ALOISI, Baron POMPEO, *Journal (25 juillet 1932–14 juin 1936)*, with intro. and notes by Mario Toscano (Paris, 1957).

ALTHAUS, PAUL, *Staatsgedanke und Reich Gottes* (Langensalza, 1928).

Anatomie des Krieges: Neue Dokumente über die Rolle des deutschen Monopolkapitals bei der Vorbereitung und Durchführung des zweiten Weltkrieges, ed. with intro. by Dietrich Eichholtz and Wolfgang Schumann (East Berlin, 1969).

Anatomie des SS-Staates, ed. Hans Buchheim, 2 vols. (Olten and Freiburg, 1965). [Trans. R. Barry, M. Jackson, and D. Long, *Anatomy of the SS State* (London, 1968).]

ANDERNACH, ANDREAS, *Hitler ohne Maske* (Munich, 1932).

ANDEXEL, RUTH, *Imperialismus: Staatsfinanzen, Rüstung, Krieg. Probleme der Rüstungsfinanzierung des deutschen Imperialismus* (East Berlin, 1968).

ANGERMANN, ERICH, 'Die weltpolitische Lage 1933–1935: Die Vereinigten Staaten von Amerika', in *Weltpolitik 1933–1939* (q.v.), 110–45.

Anglo-Japanese Alienation, 1919–1952: Papers of the Anglo-Japanese Conference on the History of the Second World War, ed. Ian Nish (Cambridge, 1982).

Anleitung für den Pressedienst: Geheim. Erlassen vom Reichsminister der Luftfahrt und Oberbefehlshaber der Luftwaffe, Zentralabteilung Presse, No. 2894/38 dated 2 Dec. 1938 (Berlin, 1938).

ARENDT, HANNAH, *The Origins of Totalitarianism* (New York, 1958).

ARON, RAYMOND, *Paix et guerre entre les nations* (Paris, 1962–3).

ASMUSSEN, HANS, *Politik und Christentum* (Hamburg, 1933).

Aspekte deutscher Außenpolitik im 20. Jahrhundert: Aufsätze Hans Rothfels zum Gedächtnis, ed. Wolfgang Benz and Hermann Graml (Schriftenreihe der VfZG, special No.; Stuttgart, 1976).

ASTER, SIDNEY, 'Ivan Maisky and Parliamentary Anti-appeasement, 1938–39', in A. J. P. Taylor (ed.), *Lloyd George: Twelve Essays* (London, 1971), 317–57.

—— *1939: The Making of the Second World War* (London, 1973).

Auf dem Weg ins Dritte Reich: Kräfte, Tendenzen, Strömungen, ed. Oswald Hirschfeld (Schriftenreihe der Bundeszentrale für politische Bildung, 175; Bonn, 1981).

Ausbürgerung deutscher Staatsangehöriger 1933–45 nach den im Reichsanzeiger veröffentlichten Listen, Die, ed. Michael Hepp, 2 vols. (Munich etc., 1985). [Expatriation lists as published in the Reichsanzeiger 1933–45.]

AZÉMA, JEAN-PIERRE, 'Die französische Politik am Vorabend des Krieges', in *Sommer 1939* (q.v.), 280–313.

BACON, EUGENE HAYWARD, *American Press Opinion of Hitler 1932–1937* (Washington, 1948). 1948).

BAER, G. W., *The Coming of the Italian-Ethiopian War* (Cambridge, Mass., and Oxford, 1967).

BAHNE, SIEGFRIED, '"Sozialfaschismus" in Deutschland: Zur Geschichte eines politischen Begriffs', *International Review of Social History*, 10 (1965), 211–45.

—— 'Einige Bemerkungen zum Gewaltproblem in der Kommunistischen Internationale', in *Frieden, Gewalt, Sozialismus* (q.v.) 680–97.

BALZER, F.-M., *Klassengegensätze in der Kirche* (Cologne, 1973).

BARIÉTY, JACQUES, 'Frankreich und die Anschlußfrage (März 1936–März 1938)', MS for symposium of German and French historians in Bonn, 26–9 Sept. 1978.

—— and BLOCH, CHARLES, 'Une tentative de réconciliation franco-allemande et son échec (1932–1933)', *Revue d'histoire moderne et contemporaine*, 15 (1968), 433–65.

BARKAI, AVRAHAM, *Das Wirtschaftssystem des Nationalsozialismus: Der historische und ideologische Hintergrund 1933–1936* (Bibliothek Wissenschaft und Politik, 18; Cologne, 1977).

BARTEL, HEINRICH, *Frankreich und die Sowjetunion 1938–1940: Ein Beitrag zur französischen Ostpolitik zwischen dem Münchener Abkommen und dem Ende der Dritten Republik* (Stuttgart, 1986).

BARTHEL, HEINZ, *Zur Politik der rüstungswirtschaftlichen Führungsorgane des deutschen Finanz- und Rüstungskapitals beim Aufbau der faschistischen Wehr- und Kriegswirtschaft in den Jahren 1933 bis 1939* (diss. Leipzig, 1962).

BARTHEL, ROLF, *Theorie und Praxis der Heeresmotorisierung im faschistischen Deutschland bis 1939* (diss. Leipzig, 1967).

—— 'Rüstungswirtschaftliche Forderungen der Reichswehrführung im Juni 1934', *ZMG* 9 (1970), 83–92.

BAUM, WALTER, 'Die Reichswehr und das wehrpolitische Amt der Nationalsozialistischen Deutschen Arbeiterpartei', *Allgemeine Schweizerische Militärzeitschrift* (1965), 345–51.

BAUMGART, WINFRIED, 'Zur Ansprache Hitlers vor den Führern der Wehrmacht am 22. August 1939', *VfZG* 16 (1968), 120–49.

Bayern in der NS-Zeit, ed. Martin Broszat, Elke Fröhlich, and Falk Wiesemann, 6 vols. (Munich and Vienna, 1977–83).

BAYNES, NORMAN H., *The Speeches of Adolf Hitler, April 1922–August 1939*, trans. with commentary, 2 vols. (London, 1942).

BECK, LUDWIG, *Studien*, ed. with intro. by Hans Speidel (Stuttgart, 1955).

BECKER, JOSEF, 'Das Ende der Zentrumspartei und die Problematik des politischen Katholizismus in Deutschland', in *Von Weimar zu Hitler* (q.v.), 344–76.

BECKER, WOLFGANG, *Film und Herrschaft: Organisationsprinzipien und Organisationsstrukturen der nationalsozialistischen Filmpropaganda* (Zur politischen Ökonomie des NS-Films, 1; Berlin, 1973).

BÉDARIDA, FRANÇOIS, 'France, Britain and the Nordic Countries', *Scandinavian Journal of History*, 2 (1977), 7–27.

'Begriffe der Wehr-, Friedens- und Kriegswirtschaft, Die', *Militärwissenschaftliche Rundschau*, 1 (1936), 246–60.

BEIN, ALEXANDER, '"Der jüdische Parasit": Bemerkungen zur Semantik der Judenfrage', *VfZG* 13 (1965), 121–49.

BENJAMIN, WALTER, 'Theorien des deutschen Faschismus: Zu der Sammelschrift "Krieg und Krieger", herausgegeben von Ernst Jünger', *Die Gesellschaft* 7/2 (1930), 32–41.

BENNECKE, HEINRICH, *Hitler und die SA* (Munich, 1962).

BENNETT, EDWARD W., *Germany and the Diplomacy of the Financial Crisis of 1931* (Cambridge, 1962).

—— *German Rearmament and the West, 1932–1933* (Princeton, 1979).

BENOIST-MÉCHIN, JACQUES, *Histoire de l'armée allemande*, iii. *L'Essor, 1925–1937* (Paris, 1964).

BENSEL, ROLF, *Die deutsche Flottenpolitik von 1933 bis 1939: Eine Studie über die Rolle des Flottenbaus in Hitlers Außenpolitik* (Beihefte der *Marine-Rundschau*, 3; Berlin and Frankfurt am Main, 1958).

BEREND, IVÁN T., and RÁNKI, GYÖRGY, *Economic Development in East-Central Europe in the 19th and 20th Centuries* (New York and London, 1974).

BERGHAHN, VOLKER R., 'Das Ende des "Stahlhelm"', *VfZG* 13 (1965), 446–51.

—— *Der Stahlhelm: Bund der Frontsoldaten 1918–1935* (Beiträge zur Geschichte des Parlamentarismus und der politischen Parteien, 33; Düsseldorf, 1966).

—— *Der Tirpitz-Plan: Genesis und Verfall einer innenpolitischen Krisenstrategie unter Wilhelm II.* (Geschichtliche Studien zu Politik und Gesellschaft, 1; Düsseldorf, 1971).

—— *Rüstung und Machtpolitik: Zur Anatomie des 'Kalten Krieges' vor 1914* (Mannheimer Schriften zur Politik und Zeitgeschichte, 5; Düsseldorf, 1973).

—— (ed.), *Militarismus* (Neue Wissenschaftliche Bibliothek, 83, Geschichte; Cologne, 1975).

—— *Militarism: The History of an International Debate, 1861–1979* (Leamington Spa, 1982).

BERNDT, ALFRED-INGEMAR, *Gebt mir vier Jahre Zeit! Dokumente zum ersten Vierjahresplan des Führers*[2] (Munich, 1937).

BERNECKER, WALTHER L., 'Kapitalismus und Nationalsozialismus: Zum Problem der Unterstützung Hitlers durch die Wirtschaft', in *1933: Fünfzig Jahre danach. Die nationalsozialistische Machtergreifung in historischer Perspektive*, ed. Josef Becker (Schriften der Philosophischen Fakultäten der Universität Augsburg, 27; Munich, 1983), 49–87.

BERNHARDI, FRIEDRICH VON, *Vom Kriege der Zukunft: Nach den Erfahrungen des Weltkrieges* (Berlin, 1920). [Trans. F.A. Holt, *The War of the Future in the Light of the Lessons of the World War* (London, 1920).]

BERNSTEIN, EDUARD, *Die Wahrheit über die Einkreisung Deutschlands* (Berlin, 1919).

BERTHOLD, LOTHAR, 'Das System des faschistischen Terrors in Deutschland und die Haltung der einzelnen Klassen und Volksschichten', *ZfG* 12/1 (1964), 5–27.

BEST, RICHARD A., 'The Anglo-German Naval Agreement of 1935: An aspect of Appeasement', *Naval War College Review*, 34/2 (1981), 68–85.

Betrogene Generation, Die: Jugend in Deutschland unter dem Faschismus. Quellen und Dokumente, ed. Matthias von Hellfeld and Arno Klönne (Cologne, 1985).

BEYER, GERHARD, 'Der Hitler-Stalin-Pakt vom 23. August 1939 und die sowjetische Außenpolitik', in S. Axel, Gerhard Beyer, and Erwin Steinhauser, *Der 'Hitler-Stalin-Pakt' von 1939* (Oktober-Taschenbuch, 4; Cologne, 1979), 60–108.

BINZ, GERHARD LUDWIG, *Die Erforschung der Wehrgrundlagen: Ein Beitrag zur wehrwissenschaftlichen Begriffsbildung und Aufgabenstellung* (Munich, 1935).

BIRKENFELD, WOLFGANG, *Der synthetische Treibstoff 1933–1945: Ein Beitrag der nationalsozialistischen Wirtschafts- und Rüstungspolitik* (Studien und Dokumente zur Geschichte des Zweiten Weltkrieges, 8; Göttingen, Berlin, and Frankfurt am Main, 1964).

BLAU, ALBRECHT, *Propaganda als Waffe* (NfD: 'for official use only'; Berlin, 1935).

—— *Geistige Kriegführung* (Potsdam, 1937).

BLEUEL, HANS PETER, and KLINNERT, ERNST, *Deutsche Studenten auf dem Weg ins Dritte Reich: Ideologien—Programme—Aktionen 1918–1935* (Gütersloh, 1967).

BLOCH, CHARLES, *Hitler und die europäischen Mächte 1933–34: Kontinuität oder Bruch?* (Hamburger Studien zur neueren Geschichte, 4; Frankfurt am Main, 1966).

—— *Die SA und die Krise des NS-Regimes 1934* (ed. suhrkamp, 434; Frankfurt am Main, 1970).

—— 'La place de la France dans les différents stades de la politique extérieure du troisième Reich (1933–1940)', in *Les Relations franco-allemandes 1933–1939: Strasbourg 7–10 octobre*

1975 (Colloques internationaux du Centre National de la Recherche Scientifique, 563; Paris, 1976), 15–31.

BLOSS, HARTMUT, 'Deutsche Chinapolitik im Dritten Reich', in *Hitler, Deutschland und die Mächte* (q.v.), 407–29.

—— 'Die Zweigleisigkeit der deutschen Fernostpolitik und Hitlers Option für Japan 1938', *MGM* 27 (1980), 55–92.

BOBERACH, HEINZ, *Jugend unter Hitler* (Düsseldorf, 1982).

BÖCKENFÖRDE, ERNST-WOLFGANG, 'Der deutsche Katholizismus 1933: Eine kritische Betrachtung', in *Von Weimar zu Hitler* (q.v.), 317–43.

BOEHM, HERMANN, 'Zur Ansprache Hitlers vor den Führern der Wehrmacht am 22. August 1939', *VfZG* 19 (1971), 294–300.

BOELCKE, WILLI A., 'Probleme der Finanzierung von Militärausgaben', in *Wirtschaft und Rüstung* (q.v.), 14–38.

—— *Die deutsche Wirtschaft 1930–1945: Interna des Reichswirtschaftsministeriums* (Düsseldorf, 1983).

—— *Die Kosten von Hitlers Krieg: Kriegsfinanzierung und finanzielles Kriegserbe in Deutschland 1933–1948* (Sammlung Schöningh zur Geschichte und Gegenwart; Paderborn, 1985).

BÖHM, CHRISTINE, *Zur Entwicklung der sozialen Lage der Arbeiterklasse im faschistischen Deutschland in den Jahren 1933 bis 1935*, (diss. East Berlin, 1973).

BOLLMUS, REINHARD, *Das Amt Rosenberg und seine Gegner: Studien zum Machtkampf im nationalsozialistischen Herrschaftssystem* (Studien zur Zeitgeschichte; Stuttgart, 1970).

BOND, BRIAN, *British Military Policy between the Two World Wars* (Oxford, 1980).

BOOG, HORST, 'Das Offizierkorps der Luftwaffe 1935–1945', in *Das deutsche Offizierkorps 1860–1960: Büdinger Vorträge 1977*, ed. in association with the MGFA by Hanns Hubert Hofmann (Deutsche Führungsgeschichten der Neuzeit, II; Boppard am Rhein, 1980), 269–325.

—— *Die deutsche Luftwaffenführung 1935–1945: Führungsprobleme, Spitzengliederung, Generalstabsausbildung* (Beiträge zur Militär- und Kriegsgeschichte, 21; Stuttgart, 1982).

BOOMS, HANS, 'Die Deutsche Volkspartei', in *Das Ende der Parteien* (q.v.), 523–39.

—— 'Der Ursprung des 2. Weltkrieges: Revision oder Expansion?', *Geschichte in Wissenschaft und Unterricht*, 16 (1965), 329–53.

BOR, PETER, *Gespräche mit Halder* (Wiesbaden, 1950).

BOREJSZA, JERZY W., 'Italiens Haltung zum Deutsch-Polnischen Krieg', in *Sommer 1939* (q.v.), 148–94.

BORK, SIEGFRIED, *Mißbrauch der Sprache: Tendenzen nationalsozialistischer Sprachregelung* (Berne and Munich, 1970).

BORKIN, JOSEPH, *Die unheilige Allianz der I.G. Farben: Eine Interessengemeinschaft im 3. Reich* (Frankfurt am Main and New York, 1979).

BOTZ, GERHARD, *Die Eingliederung Österreichs in das Deutsche Reich: Planung und Verwirklichung des politisch-administrativen Anschlusses (1938–1940)* (Schriftenreihe des Ludwig-Boltzmann-Instituts für Geschichte der Arbeiterbewegung, I; Vienna, Zurich, and Munich, 1972). [This edn. used for Part I of the present vol.; 2nd, enlarged edn. (Vienna, 1976) for Part IV.]

BOUSQUET, GEORGES HENRI, *Autarkie und weltwirtschaftliche Expansion als treibende Kräfte der französischen Wirtschaftspolitik der Gegenwart* (Kieler Vorträge, 31; Jena, 1930).

BOYENS, ARMIN, 'Die Stellung der Ökumene und der bekennenden Kirche zum Problem von

Krieg und Frieden während der Zeit des Dritten Reiches', in *Kirche zwischen Krieg und Frieden* (q.v.), 423–59.

BRACHER, KARL DIETRICH, 'Das Anfangsstadium der Hitlerschen Außenpolitik', *VfZG* 5 (1957), 63–76.

—— 'Stufen der Machtergreifung', in Bracher, Sauer, and Schulz, *Die nationalsozialistische Machtergreifung* (q.v.), 31–368.

—— *Die deutsche Diktatur: Entstehung, Struktur, Folgen des Nationalsozialismus* (Cologne and Berlin, 1969). [Trans. Jean Steinberg, *The German Dictatorship: The Origins, Structure and Effects of National Socialism* (Harmondsworth, 1973).]

—— *Die Auflösung der Weimarer Republik: Eine Studie zum Problem des Machtverfalls in der Demokratie*[5] (Villingen, 1971).

—— 'Der Faschismus', in *Meyers Enzyklopädisches Lexikon*, viii (1973).

—— afterword to Wolfgang Sauer, *Die Mobilmachung der Gewalt* (Frankfurt am Main, Berlin, and Vienna, 1974).

—— *Die Krise Europas 1917–1975* (Propyläen-Geschichte Europas, 6, Frankfurt am Main, Berlin, and Vienna, 1976).

—— *Zeitgeschichtliche Kontroversen: Um Faschismus, Totalitarismus, Demokratie* (Serie Piper, 142; Munich, 1976).

—— *Schlüsselwörter in der Geschichte: Mit einer Betrachtung zum Totalitarismusproblem* (Düsseldorf, 1978).

——SAUER, WOLFGANG, and SCHULZ, GERHARD, *Die nationalsozialistische Machtergreifung: Studien zur Errichtung des totalitären Herrschaftssystems in Deutschland 1933–34* (Schriften des Instituts für politische Wissenschaft, 14; Cologne and Opladen, 1960). [This edn. used for Part IV of the present vol.; later edn. (Ullstein 2992–4; Frankfurt am Main, Berlin, and Vienna, 1974) for Parts I and III.]

BRADDICK, HENDERSON B., *Germany, Czechoslovakia and the 'Grand Alliance' in the May Crisis, 1938* (Monograph Series on World Affairs, 6; Denver, 1969).

BRAMSTED, ERNEST K., *Goebbels and National Socialist Propaganda* (London, 1965).

BRANDENBURG, HANS-CHRISTIAN, *Die Geschichte der HJ: Wege und Irrwege einer Generation* (Cologne, 1968).

BRANDES, DETLEF, *Die Tschechen unter deutschem Protektorat*, i. *Besatzungspolitik, Kollaboration und Widerstand im Protektorat Böhmen und Mähren bis Heydrichs Tod (1938–1942)* (Munich and Vienna, 1969).

BRAUBACH, MAX, *Der Einmarsch deutscher Truppen in die entmilitarisierte Zone am Rhein im März 1936: Ein Beitrag zur Vorgeschichte des zweiten Weltkrieges* (Arbeitsgemeinschaft für Forschung des Landes Nordrhein-Westfalen, Geisteswissenschaften, 54; Cologne and Opladen, 1956).

—— *Hitlers Weg zur Verständigung mit Rußland im Jahre 1939: Rede* (Bonner Akademische Reden, 22; Bonn-Hanstein, 1960).

BRAUN, OTTO, *Von Weimar zu Hitler* (Hamburg, 1949).

BRAUNTHAL, JULIUS, *Geschichte der Internationale*[3], ii (Berlin and Bonn, 1978).

BREIT, GOTTHARD, *Das Staats- und Gesellschaftsbild deutscher Generale beider Weltkriege im Spiegel ihrer Memoiren* (Militärgeschichtliche Studien, 17; Boppard, 1973).

BRINKMANN, RUDOLF, 'Außenhandel und Handelspolitik', *Der Vierjahresplan* (1938), 386–8.

—— *Wirtschaftspolitik aus nationalsozialistischem Kraftquell: Eine Sammlung ausgewählter Vorträge, Reden und Ansprachen* (Jena, 1939).

BROCKDORFF, Count ALEXANDER, 'Weltwirtschaft und Weltrüstung', *Wehrtechnische Monatshefte*, 39 (1935), 492–6.

BROSZAT, MARTIN, *Zweihundert Jahre deutsche Polenpolitik* (Munich, 1963).

—— 'Deutschland — Ungarn — Rumänien', *HZ* 206 (1968), 45–96.

—— *Der Staat Hitlers: Grundlegung und Entwicklung seiner inneren Verfassung* (dtv-Weltgeschichte des 20. Jahrhunderts, 9; Munich, 1969; 1973³). [Trans. John W. Hiden, *The Hitler State* (New York, 1981).]

—— 'Soziale Motivation und Führer-Bindung im Nationalsozialismus', *VfZG* 18 (1970), 392–409.

BRÜNING, HEINRICH, *Memoiren 1918–1934* (Stuttgart, 1970).

—— *Briefe 1946–1960*, ed. Claire Nix in collaboration with Reginald Phelps and George Pettee (Stuttgart, 1974).

—— *Briefe und Gespräche, 1934–1945: Ein historisches Dokument und 'Selbstbildnis' des umstrittenen Reichskanzlers*, ed. Claire Nix in collaboration with Reginald Phelps (Stuttgart, 1974).

BRY, GERHARD, *Wages in Germany 1871–1945* (Princeton, 1960).

BÜCHEL, REGINE, *Der Deutsche Widerstand im Spiegel von Fachliteratur und Publizistik seit 1945* (Schriften der Bibliothek für Zeitgeschichte, 15; Munich, 1975).

BUCHER, PETER, *Der Reichswehrprozeß: Der Hochverrat der Ulmer Reichswehroffiziere 1929–30* (Militärgeschichtliche Studien, 4; Boppard, 1967).

BUCHHEIM, HANS, 'Die SS: Das Herrschaftsinstrument', in *Anatomie des SS-Staates* (q.v.), 13–253. [Trans. R. Barry, 'The SS: Instrument of Domination', 125–301 in English version.]

BUCHHOLZ, W., *Die nationalsozialistische Gemeinschaft 'Kraft durch Freude': Freizeitgestaltung und Arbeiterschaft im Dritten Reich* (diss. Munich, 1979).

BULLOCK, ALAN, *Hitler: A Study in Tyranny* (London, 1952; rev. edn. 1962).

BURCHHARD, ERICH, *Landwirtschaft in Zahlen* (Berlin, 1938).

BURCKHARDT, BERND, *Eine Stadt wird braun: Die nationalsozialistische Machtergreifung in der schwäbischen Provinz* (Hamburg, 1980).

BURCKHARDT, CARL J., *Meine Danziger Mission 1937–1939* (Munich, 1960).

BURDEN, HAMILTON T., *Die programmierte Nation: Die Nürnberger Reichsparteitage* (Gütersloh, 1967). [Trans. *The Nuremberg Party Rallies, 1923 to 1939* (London, 1967).]

Bürgerlichen Parteien in Deutschland, Die: Handbuch der Geschichte der bürgerlichen Parteien und anderer bürgerlicher Interessenorganisationen vom Vormärz bis zum Jahre 1945, ed. Dieter Fricke *et al.*, 2 vols. (East Berlin, 1968, 1970).

BURKE, KENNETH, 'The Rhetoric of Hitler's "Battle"', *The Southern Review*, 5/1 (1939), 1–21.

—— *The Philosophy of Literary Form: Studies in Symbolic Action* (Baton Rouge, 1941; New York, 1957).

BUSSMANN, WALTER, *Ein deutsch-französischer Verständigungsversuch, 6.12.1938* (Nachrichten der Akademie der Wissenschaften in Göttingen, phil.-hist. Klasse, 2; 1953).

—— 'Zur Entstehung und Überlieferung der "Hoßbach-Niederschrift"', *VfZG* 16 (1968), 373–84.

BUTLER, JAMES R., *Lord Lothian (Phillip Kerr) 1882–1940* (London, 1960).

BUTSCHEK, FELIX, *Die österreichische Wirtschaft 1938 bis 1945* (Stuttgart, 1978).

CADOGAN, ALEXANDER, *The Diaries of Sir Alexander Cadogan, O.M., 1938–1945*, ed. David Dilks (London, 1971).

CALIC, ÉDOUARD (ed.), *Ohne Maske: Hitler-Breiting Geheimgespräche 1931* (Frankfurt am Main, 1968).

CAPELLE, HENDRIK VAN, *Economie en buitenlandse handel in Nationaal-socialistisch Duitsland* (Assen, 1978).

CARLTON, DAVID, *Anthony Eden: A Biography* (London, 1981).

CARR, WILLIAM, *Arms, Autarky and Aggression: A Study in German Foreign Policy, 1933-1939* (London, 1972).

—— 'Rüstung, Wirtschaft und Politik am Vorabend des Zweiten Weltkrieges', in *Nationalsozialistische Außenpolitik* (q.v.) 437–54.

CARROLL, BERENICE A., *Design for Total War: Arms and Economics in the Third Reich* (Studies in European History, 17; The Hague and Paris, 1968).

CARSTEN, FRANCIS L., *Reichswehr und Politik 1918–1933* (Cologne and Berlin, 1964). [Trans. *The Reichswehr and Politics 1918–1933* (Oxford, 1966).]

CASPARY, ADOLF, *Wirtschafts-Strategie und Kriegsführung: Wirtschaftliche Vorbereitung, Führung und Auswirkung des Krieges im geschichtlichen Aufriß* (Berlin, 1932).

CELOVSKY, BORIS, *Das Münchener Abkommen 1938* (Quellen und Darstellungen zur Zeitgeschichte, 3; Stuttgart, 1958).

CHECIŃSKI, MICHAEL, 'Die Umstellung der Landwirtschaft und der Ernährungswirtschaft im faschistischen Deutschland auf die Bedürfnisse des Krieges', *ZMG* 6 (1967), 323–34.

'Chemische Industrie und Rohstoffwirtschaft', *Deutsche Wehr*, 39 (1935), 482–3.

CHESI, VALENTIN, *Struktur und Funktionen der Handwerksorganisation in Deutschland seit 1933: Ein Beitrag zur Verbandstheorie* (Untersuchungen über Gruppen und Verbände, 4; Berlin, 1966).

CHRIST, HERBERT, *Der politische Protestantismus in der Weimarer Republik: Eine Studie über die politische Meinungsbildung durch die evangelische Kirche im Spiegel der Literatur und der Presse* (diss. Bonn, 1967).

Christentum und Militarismus, ed. Wolfgang Huber and Gerhard Liedke (Studien zur Friedensforschung, 13; Stuttgart and Munich, 1974).

Chronik der Agrarpolitik und Agrarwirtschaft des Deutschen Reiches von 1933–1945, ed. Werner Tornow (Berichte über Landwirtschaft, NS, special No. 188; Hamburg and Berlin, 1972).

CIANO, GALEAZZO, *Diario 1937–1938* (Bologna, 1948). [Trans. Andreas Mayor, *Ciano's Diary 1937–1938* (London, 1952).]

CLEMENZ, MANFRED, *Gesellschaftliche Ursprünge des Faschismus* (ed. suhrkamp, 550; Frankfurt am Main, 1972).

COMPTON, JAMES V., *Swastika and Eagle: Hitler, the United States and the Origins of the Second World War* (London, 1968).

CONZE, WERNER, 'Die Regierung Brüning', in *Staat, Wirtschaft und Politik in der Weimarer Republik, Festschrift für Heinrich Brüning*, ed. F. A. Hermens and Theodor Schieder (Berlin, 1967), 233–48.

COOPER, MATTHEW, *The German Army 1933–1945: Its Political and Military Failure* (London, 1978).

COSTIGLIOLA, FRANK CHARLES, *The Politics of Financial Stabilization: American Reconstruction Policy in Europe 1924–30* (diss. Cornell University; Ithaca, NY, 1973).

COVERDALE, JOHN F., *Italian Intervention in the Spanish Civil War* (Princeton, 1975).

COWLING, MAURICE, *The Impact of Hitler: British Politics and British Policy 1933–1940* (Cambridge, 1975).

CZICHON, EBERHARD, *Wer verhalf Hitler zur Macht? Zum Anteil der deutschen Industrie an der Zerstörung der Weimarer Republik*[2] (Stimmen zur Zeit, 5; Cologne, 1971).

DAHLE, WENDULA, *Der Einsatz einer Wissenschaft: Eine sprachinhaltliche Analyse militärischer Terminologie in der Germanistik 1933–1945* (Abhandlungen zur Kunst-, Musik- und Literaturwissenschaft, 71; Bonn, 1969).

DAHLERUS, JOHAN B. E., *Sista försöket: London–Berlin sommaren 1939* (Stockholm, 1948). [Trans. Alexandra Dick, *The Last Attempt* (London, 1948).]

DAHM, KARL-WILHELM, *Pfarrer und Politik: Soziale Position und politische Mentalität des deutschen evangelischen Pfarrerstandes zwischen 1918 und 1933* (Dortmunder Schriften zur Sozialforschung, 29; Cologne and Opladen, 1965).

DAHRENDORF, ROLF, *Gesellschaft und Demokratie in Deutschland* (Munich, 1965). [Trans. *Society and Democracy in Germany* (London, 1967).]

DAITZ, WERNER, *Die nationalsozialistische Ostraumpolitik und der Hansa-Kanal: Ein Beitrag zum nationalsozialistischen Arbeitsbeschaffungsprogramm* (Berlin, n.d.).

DARRÉ, RICHARD WALTHER, *Das Bauerntum als Lebensquell der nordischen Rasse* (Munich, 1929).

—— *Erkenntnisse und Werden: Aufsätze aus der Zeit vor der Machtergreifung*, ed. Marie Adelheid Prinzessin Reuß-zur-Lippe (Goslar, 1940).

—— *Um Blut und Boden: Reden und Aufsätze*, ed. Hanns Deetjen and Wolfgang Clauss (Munich, 1940).

DARWIN, JOHN, 'Imperialism in Decline? Tendencies in British Imperial Policy between the Wars', *HJ* 23 (1980), 657–79.

DEDERKE, KARLHEINZ, *Reich und Republik: Deutschland 1917–1933* (Stuttgart, 1969).

DE FELICE, RENZO, 'Beobachtungen zu Mussolinis Außenpolitik', *Saeculum* (1973), 4; 314–27.

—— *Mussolini il Duce*, ii. *Lo stato totalitario, 1936–1940* (Turin, 1981).

DEHIO, LUDWIG, *Deutschland und die Weltpolitik im 20. Jahrhundert* (Munich, 1955). [Trans. Dieter Pevsner, *Germany and World Politics in the Twentieth Century* (London, 1959).]

DEIST, WILHELM, 'Brüning, Herriot und die Abrüstungsgespräche von Bessinge 1932', *VfZG* 5 (1957), 265–72.

—— 'Schleicher und die deutsche Abrüstungspolitik im Juni/Juli 1932', *VfZG* (1959), 163–76.

—— 'Die Politik der Seekriegsleitung und die Rebellion der Flotte Ende Oktober 1918', *VfZG* 14 (1966), 341–68.

—— 'Internationale und nationale Aspekte der Abrüstungsfrage 1924–1932', in *Locarno und die Weltpolitik 1924–1932*, ed. Hans Rössler (Göttingen, 1969), 64–93.

—— *Flottenpolitik und Flottenpropaganda: Das Nachrichtenbureau des Reichsmarineamtes 1897–1914* (Beiträge zur Militär- und Kriegsgeschichte, 17; Stuttgart, 1976).

—— 'De Gaulle et Guderian: L'influence des expériences militaires de la première guerre mondiale en France et en Allemagne', *Études gaulliennes*, 5/17 (1977), 47 ff.

—— 'Die deutsche Aufrüstung in amerikanischer Sicht: Berichte des US-Militärattachés in Berlin aus den Jahren 1933–1939', in *Rußland—Deutschland—Amerika* (Frankfurter Historische Abhandlungen, 17; Wiesbaden, 1978), 279–95.

—— 'Strategic Perspectives and German Military Planning before the Two World Wars', *German History* (Norwich, spring 1987), 4: 69–76.

DELARUE, JACQUES, *Histoire de la Gestapo* (Paris, 1963).

DELMAS, JEAN, 'La perception de la puissance militaire française', in *La Puissance en Europe* (q.v.), 127–40.

DENECKE, HORST, *Die agrarpolitischen Konzeptionen des deutschen Imperialismus beim Übergang vom bürgerlich-parlamentarischen System zur faschistischen Diktatur (Frühjahr 1930 bis Herbst 1934)* (diss. East Berlin, 1972).

DENGG, SÖREN, *Deutschlands Austritt aus dem Völkerbund und Schachts 'Neuer Plan': Zum Verhältnis von Außen- und Außenwirtschaftspolitik in der Übergangsphase von der Weimarer*

Republik zum Dritten Reich (1929–1934) (Europäische Hochschulschriften, 309; Frankfurt am Main, Berne, and New York, 1986).

DENNE, LUDWIG, *Das Danzig-Problem in der deutschen Außenpolitik 1934–39* (Bonn, 1959),

DENNIS, PETER, *Decision by Default: Peacetime Conscription and British Defence 1919–1939* (London, 1972).

DESCHNER, KARLHEINZ (ed.), *Kirche und Krieg: Der christliche Weg zum ewigen Leben* (Stuttgart, 1970).

DEUTSCH, HAROLD C., *The Conspiracy against Hitler in the Twilight War* (Minneapolis and London, 1968). [Trans. Burkhardt Kriegeland, *Das Komplott oder die Entmachtung der Generale: Blomberg- und Fritzsch-Krise. Hitlers Weg zum Krieg* (Zurich, 1974).]

DEUTSCH, JULIUS, *Antifaschismus! Proletarische Wehrhaftigkeit im Kampfe gegen den Faschismus* (Vienna, 1926).

DEUTSCH, KARL W., *Der Stand der Kriegsursachenforschung* (DGFK-Hefte, 2; Bonn-Bad Godesberg, 1973).

Deutsche Kommunismus, Der: Dokumente[3], ed. Hermann Weber (Cologne and Berlin, 1973).

Deutsche Mineralölwirtschaft, Die: Jahrbuch der deutschen Mineralölwirtschaft 1930–1940[2], ed. Karl-Heinz von Thümen (Hamburg, 1956).

Deutsche Parteiprogramme, ed. Wilhelm Mommsen (Munich, 1960).

Deutsche Protestantismus in Revolutionsjahr 1918–19, Der, ed. Martin Greschat (Witten, 1974).

Deutsche Reichsgeschichte in Dokumenten, Urkunden und Aktenstücke zur inneren und äußeren Politik des Deutschen Reiches, ed. Johannes Hohlfeld, iv. *Die nationalsozialistische Revolution, 1931–1934[2]* (Berlin, 1934).

Deutsche Volk klagt an, Das: Hitlers Krieg gegen die Friedenskämpfer in Deutschland. Ein Tatsachenbuch (anon.; Paris, 1936).

Deutsche Widerstand gegen Hitler, Der, ed. W. Schmitthenner and H. Buchheim (Cologne and Berlin, 1966). [Trans. Peter and Betty Ross, *The German Resistance to Hitler* (London, 1970).]

Deutsche Widerstandskämpfer 1933–1945: Biographien und Briefe, 2 vols., ed. Institut für Marxismus-Leninismus beim Zentralkomitee der SED (East Berlin, 1970).

Deutscher Widerstand 1933–1945: Aspekte der Forschung und der Darstellung im Schulbuch. Eine Berichterstattung, ed. Edgar Weick for the Studienkreis zur Erforschung und Vermittlung der Geschichte des deutschen Widerstandes 1933–1945 (Heidelberg, 1967).

Deutschland-Berichte der Sozialdemokratischen Partei Deutschlands (Sopade) 1934–1940, 7 vols. (Salzhausen and Frankfurt am Main, 1980).

Deutschland im zweiten Weltkrieg, i. *Vorbereitung, Entfesselung und Verlauf des Krieges bis zum 22. Juni 1941*, by a group of authors under the direction of Gerhart Hass (Cologne, 1974).

Deutschland in der Weltpolitik des 19. und 20. Jahrhunderts, ed. Immanuel Geiss and Bernd Jürgen Wendt (Düsseldorf, 1973).

Deutschland und England 1933–1939: Die Dokumente des deutschen Friedenswillens[4], ed. Friedrich Berber (Veröffentlichungen des Deutschen Instituts für außenpolitische Forschung, 7; Essen, 1943).

D'HOOP, L. M., 'La politique militaire de la France dans les Balkans de l'accord de Munich au début de la seconde guerre mondiale', *Studia Balkanica*, 7 (Sofia, 1973).

DIBELIUS, OTTO, *Friede auf Erden? Frage, Erwägungen, Antwort* (Berlin, 1930).

DICKERT, DIETRICH, *Die Preisüberwachung 1931–1936* (Untersuchungen des Instituts für angewandte Wirtschaftswissenschaften; Berlin, 1937).

DICKMANN, FRITZ, 'Machtwille und Ideologie in Hitlers außenpolitischen Zielsetzungen vor 1933', in *Spiegel der Geschichte: Festschrift für Max Braubach* (Münster, 1964), 915–41.

DIEHL-THIELE, PETER, *Partei und Staat im Dritten Reich: Untersuchungen zum Verhältnis von NSDAP und allgemeiner innerer Staatsverwaltung 1933-1945* (Münchener Studien zur Politik, 9, Munich, 1969).

DIGNATH-DÜREN, WALTER, *Kirche, Krieg, Kriegsdienst: Die Wissenschaft zu dem aktuellen Problem in der ganzen Welt* (Theologische Forschung, 10; Hamburg, 1955).

DIVINE, ROBERT, *The Reluctant Belligerent: American Entry into World War II* (New York, 1965). [=*America in Crisis.*]

DIX, ARTHUR, 'Neue Wege der Handelspolitik', *Der Deutsche Oekonomist*, 50 (1933), 1129-31.

Documenti diplomatici italiani: Ministero degli affari esteri, Commissione per la pubblicazione dei documenti diplomatici, Series 7 *(1922-1935)* (Rome, 1953-); Series 8 *(1935-1939)* (Rome, 1952-).

Documents Concerning German-Polish Relations and the Outbreak of Hostilities between Great Britain and Germany on September 3, 1939 (Cmd. 6106; HM Stationery Office: London, 1939).

Documents diplomatiques français: Ministère des affaires étrangères, Commission de publication des documents relatifs aux origines de la guerre 1939-1945, *Documents diplomatiques français 1932-1939*, Series 1 (Paris, 1964-); Series 2 (Paris, 1963-).

Documents on British Foreign Policy 1919-1939, ed. Ernest L. Woodward and Rohan Butler (London, 1946-).

Documents on German Foreign Policy, Series C and D (London, 1957-83; 1949-64).

Documents on German Foreign Policy 1918-1945: The Third Reich, Pt. 1, vols. i-v *(1933-1936)* (London and Washington, 1957-66).

Documents on International Affairs, 1928-: ed. Royal Institute of International Affairs (London, 1929-).

Documents on International Affairs 1939-1946, ed. Royal Institute of International Affairs, i (London, 1951).

Documents on Nazism, 1919-1945, ed. Jeremy Noakes and Geoffrey Pridham (London, 1974).

DÖHN, LOTHAR, *Politik und Interesse: Die Interessenstruktur der Deutschen Volkspartei* (Marburger Abhandlungen zur politischen Wissenschaft, 16; Meisenheim am Glan, 1970).

Dokumente der deutschen Politik und Geschichte von 1848 bis zur Gegenwart, ed Johannes Hohfeld, iv. *Die Zeit der nationalsozialistischen Diktatur 1933-1938* (Berlin and Munich, 1954).

Dokumente zur deutschen Geschichte 1929-1933, ed. Wolfgang Ruge and Wolfgang Schumann, rev. by Kurt Gossweiler with the assistance of Margarete Piesche (Frankfurt am Main, 1977. [© Deutscher Verlag der Wissenschaften, East Berlin.]

Dokumente zur Vorgeschichte des Krieges, ed. Ministry of Foreign Affairs (Weißbuch des Auswärtigen Amtes, 2; Berlin, 1939).

DOMARUS, MAX, *Hitler: Reden und Proklamationen 1932-1945: Kommentiert von einem deutschen Zeitgenossen*, i. *Triumph (1932-38)* (Würzburg 1962); ii. *Untergang (1939-45)* (Würzburg, 1963 [for Parts I and IV]; Wiesbaden, 1973 [for Part III]).

DÖNITZ, KARL, *Zehn Jahre und zwanzig Tage*² (Frankfurt am Main, 1963). [Trans. R. H. Stevens and David Woodward, *Memoirs: Ten Years and Twenty Days* (London, 1959).]

DOOR, ROCHUS, *Die Politik des faschistischen Deutschlands gegenüber Ungarn 1943-44* (diss. Leipzig, 1967).

DORPALEN, ANDREAS, *Hindenburg in der Geschichte der Weimarer Republik* (Berlin and Frankfurt am Main, 1966).

DÖRR, MANFRED, *Die Deutschnationale Volkspartei 1925-1928* (diss. Marburg, 1964).

DOUHET, GIULIO, *Il dominio dell'aria* (Verona, 1932). [Trans. Dino Ferrari, *The Command of the Air* (London, 1942).]

DRECHSLER, HANNO, *Die Sozialistische Arbeiterpartei Deutschlands (SAPD): Ein Beitrag zur Geschichte der deutschen Arbeiterbewegung am Ende der Weimarer Republik* (Marburger Abhandlungen zur politischen Wissenschaft, 2; Meisenheim am Glan, 1965).

DRESS, HANS, *Slowakei und faschistische Neuordnung Europas 1939–1941* (East Berlin, 1972).

Dritte Reich, Das: Herrschaftsstruktur und Geschichte, ed. Martin Broszat and Horst Möller (Beck'sche schwarze Reihe, 280; Munich, 1983).

DRÖGE, FRANZ, *Der zerredete Widerstand: Zur Soziologie und Publizistik des Gerüchts im 2. Weltkrieg* (Düsseldorf, 1970).

DUESTERBERG, THEODOR, *Der Stahlhelm und Hitler* (Wolfenbüttel and Hanover, 1949).

DUHNKE, HORST, *Die KPD von 1933 bis 1945* (Cologne, 1972).

DÜLFFER, JOST, 'Weisungen an die Wehrmacht als Ausdruck ihrer Gleichschaltung 1938–39', *WWR* 18 (1968), 651–5, 705–13.

—— 'Überlegungen von Kriegsmarine und Heer zur Wehrmachtspitzengliederung und zur Führung der Wehrmacht im Kriege im Februar-März 1938', *MGM* 9 (1971), 145–55.

—— *Weimar, Hitler und die Marine: Reichspolitik und Flottenbau 1920–1930*, with an appendix by Jürgen Rohwer (Düsseldorf, 1973).

—— 'Der Einfluß des Auslandes auf die nationalsozialistische Politik', in *Innen- und Außenpolitik* (q.v.), 295–313.

—— 'Der Beginn des Krieges 1939: Hitler, die innere Krise und das Mächtesystem', *Geschichte und Gesellschaft*, 2 (1976), No. 4. *Das nationalsozialistische Herrschaftssystem*, 443–70.

—— 'Zum "decision-making process" in der deutschen Außenpolitik 1933–1939', in *Hitler, Deutschland und die Mächte* (q.v.), 186–204.

—— 'Determinants of German Naval Policy, 1920–1939', in *The German Military in the Age of Total War* (q.v.), 152–70.

DURACH, MORIZ, '*Zum Begriff Lebensraum*', *Biographischer Anzeiger*, 40/1 (1939), 288–90.

DUROSELLE, JEAN-BAPTISTE, *La Décadence, 1932–1939: Politique étrangère de la France* (Paris, 1979).

—— 'Les milieux gouvernementaux en face du problème allemand en 1936', in *La France et l'Allemagne* (q.v.), 373–96.

DZIEWANOWSKI, MARIAN KAMIL, *Joseph Pilsudski: A European Federalist, 1918–1922* (Stanford, 1969).

EDEN, R. ANTHONY, *Memoirs: Facing the Dictators* (London, 1962).

EDINGER, LEWIS J., *German Exile Politics: The Social Democratic Executive Committee in the Nazi Era* (Berkeley and Los Angeles, 1956).

EICHHOLTZ, DIETRICH, *Geschichte der deutschen Kriegswirtschaft 1939–1945*, i. *1939–1941* (East Berlin, 1969).

EICHSTÄDT, ULRICH, *Von Dollfuß zu Hitler: Geschichte des Anschlusses Österreichs 1933–1938* (Veröffentlichungen des Instituts für Europäische Geschichte, Mainz, 10; Wiesbaden, 1955).

EILERS, ROLF, *Die nationalsozialistsche Schulpolitik: Eine Studie zur Tradition der Erziehung im totalitären Staat* (Staat und Politik, 4; Cologne and Opladen, 1963).

EMMERSON, JAMES THOMAS, *The Rhineland Crisis: 7 March 1936. A Study in Multilateral Diplomacy* (London, 1977).

Ende der Parteien, Das, ed. Erich Matthias and Rudolf Morsey (Veröffentlichungen der Kommission für die Geschichte des Parlamentarismus und der politischen Parteien; Düsseldorf, 1960).

EPSTEIN, JULIUS, *Das Schicksal der Akkumulation in Deutschland oder der Irrsinn der Autarkie* (Leipzig, 1932).

ERBE, RENÉ, *Die nationalsozialistische Wirtschaftspolitik 1933–1939 im Lichte der modernen Theorie* (Zurich, 1958).

ERBSLAND, KURT, *Die Umgestaltung der deutschen Handelspolitik durch den 'Neuen Plan' und die Möglichkeiten ihrer künftigen Ausgestaltung* (diss. Heidelberg and Speyer, 1937).

ERDMANN, KARL DIETRICH, *Die Zeit der Weltkriege* (=Gebhardt, *Handbuch der deutschen Geschichte*, 9th rev. edn., ed. Herbert Grundmann, iv, in two parts; Stuttgart, 1973, 1976).

Erziehung und Schulung im Dritten Reich, ed. Manfred Heinemann, 2 vols. (Veröffentlichungen der historischen Kommission der Deutschen Gesellschaft für Erziehungswissenschaft, 4; Stuttgart, 1980).

Erziehung zum Wehrwillen: Pädagogisch methodisches Handbuch für Erzieher, ed. Jakob Szliska with aid from the Deutsche Gesellschaft für Wehrpolitik und Wehrwissenschaften (Stuttgart, 1937).

ESENWEIN-ROTHE, INGEBORG, *Die Wirtschaftsverbände von 1933 bis 1945* (Wirtschaftsverbände und Wirtschaftspolitik, Schriften des Vereins für Sozialpolitik, Gesellschaft für Wirtschafts- und Sozialwissenschaften, NS 37; Berlin, 1965).

ESTERS, HELMUT, and PELGER, HANS, *Gewerkschafter im Widerstand* (Schriftenreihe des Forschungsinstituts der Friedrich-Ebert-Stiftung; Hanover, 1967).

FABRY, PHILIPP WALTER, *Der Hitler-Stalin-Pakt 1939–1941: Ein Beitrag zur Methode sowjetischer Außenpolitik* (Darmstadt, 1962).

FARQUHARSON, J. E., *The Plough and the Swastika: the NSDAP and Agriculture in Germany 1928–45* (Sage Studies in 20th Century History, 5; London and Beverly Hills, 1976).

FARRAR, LANCELOT L., Jun., 'The Short-war Illusion: The Syndrome of German Strategy, August–December 1914', *MGM* 12 (1972), 39–52.

Faschismus: Bericht vom Internationalen Antifaschisten-Kongreß, Berlin, 9. bis 10. März 1929, ed. Internationales Antifaschisten-Komitee (Berlin, 1930).

Faschismus als soziale Bewegung: Deutschland und Italien im Vergleich, ed. Wolfgang Schieder (Historische Perspektiven, 3; Hamburg, 1976).

Faschismus in Deutschland, Der: Analysen der KPD-Opposition aus den Jahren 1928–1933, ed. by 13th Plenum of the Executive Committee of the Comintern, Dec. 1933 (Moscow and Leningrad, 1934; repr. Milan, 1967).

Fascist Challenge and the Policy of Appeasement, The, ed. Wolfgang J. Mommsen and Lothar Kettenacker (London, 1933).

FAULHABER, MICHAEL VON (ed.), *Das Schwert des Geistes: Feldpredigten im Weltkrieg* (Freiburg i.Br., 1917).

—— *Waffen des Lichtes: Gesammelte Kriegsreden*[5] (Freiburg, i.Br., 1918).

—— *Rufende Stimmen in der Wüste der Gegenwart: Gesammelte Reden, Predigten, Hirtenbriefe* (Freiburg i.Br., 1931).

FAUST, ANSELM, *Der Nationalsozialistische Deutsche Studentenbund: Studenten und Nationalsozialismus in der Weimarer Republik*, 2 vols. (Düsseldorf, 1973).

FEDER, GOTTFRIED, *Der Deutsche Staat auf nationaler und sozialer Grundlage: Neue Wege in Staat, Finanz und Wirtschaft*[8] (Nationalsozialistische Bibliothek, 35; Munich, 1932).

—— *Das Programm der NSDAP und seine weltanschaulichen Grundgedanken* (Nationalsozialistische Bibliothek, 1; Munich, 1932) [printing of 71st–79th thousand].

FELDMAN, GERALD D., KOLB, EBERHARD, and RÜRUP, REINHARD, 'Die Massenbewegungen der Arbeiterschaft in Deutschland am Ende des Ersten Weltkrieges (1917–1920)', *PVS* 13/1 (1972), 84–105.

FENSCH, DOROTHEA, and GROEHLER, OLAF, 'Imperialistische Ökonomie und militärische Strategie: Eine Denkschrift Wilhelm Groeners', *ZfG* 19 (1971), 1167–77.

FEST, JOACHIM, *Hitler: Eine Biographie*[7] (Frankfurt am Main, 1974). [Trans. Richard and Clara Winston, *Hitler* (New York, 1974).]

Festigung der Handwerkswirtschaft durch Auflösung leistungsunfähiger Betriebe', *Deutsches Handwerk*, 8 (1939), 129–31.

FINKE, HEINRICH, *Unseren Gefallenen zum Gedächtnis: Rede, gehalten am 29. März 1919* (Freiburg i.Br., 1919).

FISCHER, FRITZ, *Bündnis der Eliten: Zur Kontinuität der Machtstrukturen in Deutschland 1871–1945* (Düsseldorf, 1979).

FISCHER, GUIDO, *Wehrwirtschaft: Ihre Grundlagen und Theorien* (Leipzig, 1936).

FISCHER, WOLFRAM, *Deutsche Wirtschaftspolitik 1918–1945*[3] (Opladen, 1968).

FLAIG, HERBERT, *Untersuchung über den Einfluß des 'Neuen Planes' auf den deutschen Außenhandel und die deutsche Außenhandelspolitik* (diss. Freiburg i.Br., 1941).

FLECHTHEIM, OSSIP K., *Die KPD in der Weimarer Republik*, with intro. by Hermann Weber (Offenbach, 1948; repr. Frankfurt am Main, 1969).

FLEMMING, JENS, Artikel zum 40. Todestag Ossietzkys', *Deutsches Allgemeines Sonntagsblatt*, 18 (30 Apr. 1978).

FOERSTER, WOLFGANG, *Generaloberst Ludwig Beck: Sein Kampf gegen den Krieg. Aus nachgelassenen Papieren des Generalstabschefs*[2] (Munich, 1953).

FOERTSCH, HERMANN, *Schuld und Verhängnis (Die Fritsch-Krise 1938)* (Stuttgart, 1951).

Foreign Relations of the United States 1935–1940 (Washington, 1952–).

Forschungen zu Staat und Verfassung: Festgabe für Fritz Hartung, ed. Richard Dietrich and Gerhard Destreich (Berlin, 1958).

FÖRSTER, JÜRGEN, *Stalingrad: Risse im Bündnis 1942–43* (Einzelschriften zur militärischen Geschichte des Zweiten Weltkrieges, 16; Freiburg i.Br., 1975).

—— 'Rumäniens Weg in die deutsche Abhängigkeit: Zur Rolle der Deutschen Militärmission 1940–41', *MGM* 25 (1979), 47–77.

FÖRSTER, OTTO WILHELM, *Das Befestigungwesen: Rückblick und Ausschau* (Wehrmacht im Kampf, 25; Neckargemünd, 1960).

FOX, JOHN PATRICK, *Germany and the Far Eastern Crisis, 1931–1938* (Oxford and London, 1982).

FRAENKEL, EBERHARD, *The Dual State: A Contribution to the Theory of Dictatorship* (New York, London, and Toronto, 1941).

France et l'Allemagne 1932–1936, La: Communications présentées au colloque franco-allemand tenu à Paris du 10 au 12 mars 1977 (Paris, 1980).

FRANK, HANS, *Im Angesicht des Galgens*[2] (Munich-Gräfelfing, 1955). [Trans. (excerpts) S. Piotrowski, *Hans Frank's Diary* (Warsaw, 1961).]

FRANK, WALTER, *Kämpfende Wissenschaft* (Hamburg, 1934).

—— *Deutsche Wissenschaft und Judenfragen: Rede zur Eröffnung der Forschungsabteilung Judenfrage des Reichsinstituts für Geschichte des neueren Deutschland* (Schriften des Reichsinstituts für Geschichte des neueren Deutschland; Hamburg, 1937).

FRASER, LINDLEY, *Germany between Two Wars: A study of Propaganda and War-guilt* (London, 1944).

FRENCH GOVERNMENT, *Livre jaune français: Documents diplomatiques 1938–1939* (Paris, 1939). [Trans. *The French Yellow Book* (London, 1940).]

FRIED, FERDINAND, *Das Ende des Kapitalismus* (Jena, 1931).

—— *Autarkie* (Tatschriften; Jena, 1932).

Frieden, Gewalt, Sozialismus: Studien zur Geschichte der sozialistischen Arbeiterbewegung, ed. Wolfgang Huber and Johannes Schwerdtfeger (Forschungen und Berichte der evangelischen Studiengemeinschaft, 32; Stuttgart, 1976).

FRIEDENSBURG, FERDINAND, 'Das wehrwirtschaftliche Rohstoffpotential des Protektorats Böhmen-Mähren und der Slowakei', *Wehrtechnische Monatshefte* (1939), 146–55.

—— 'Die sowjetischen Kriegslieferungen an das Hitlerreich', *Vierteljahrshefte zur Wirtschaftsforschung* (1962), 331–8.

FRIEDLAENDER-PRECHTL, ROBERT, *Wirtschaftswende: Die Ursachen der Arbeitslosen-Krise und deren Bekämpfung* (Leipzig, 1931).

—— 'Dynamik und Bilanz der Arbeitsbeschaffung', *Wirtschafts-Wende*, spec. No. (Feb. 1933), 5–25.

FRIEDLÄNDER, SAUL, *Pie XII et le IIIᵉ Reich* (Paris, 1964). [Trans. Charles Fullman, *Pius XII and the Third Reich* (London, 1966).]

FROMMELT, REINHARD, *Paneuropa oder Mitteleuropa: Einigungsbestrebungen im Kalkül deutscher Wirtschaft und Politik 1925–1933* (Schriftenreihe der *Vierteljahrshefte für Zeitgeschichte*, 34; Stuttgart, 1977).

FRYE, ALTON, *Nazi Germany and the American Hemisphere, 1933–1941* (New Haven, 1967).

Führers Kampf um den Weltfrieden, Des (Munich, 1936).

'Führerstaat', Der: Mythos und Realität. Studien zur Struktur und Politik des Dritten Reiches — The 'Führer-State': Myth and Reality. Studies on the Structure of Politics of the Third Reich, ed. Gerhard Hirsch and Lothar Kettenacker (Veröffentlichungen des Deutschen Historischen Instituts London, 8; Stuttgart, 1981).

FÜLBERTH, GEORG, and HARRER, JÜRGEN, *Die deutsche Sozialdemokratie 1890–1933* (*Arbeiterbewegung und SPD,* i; Darmstadt and Neuwied, 1974).

FUNKE, MANFRED, *Sanktionen und Kanonen: Hitler, Mussolini und der internationale Abessinienkonflikt 1934–1936²* (Bonner Schriften zur Politik und Zeitgeschichte, 2; Düsseldorf, 1971).

—— 'Die deutsch-italienischen Beziehungen: Antibolschewismus und außenpolitische Interessenkonkurrenz als Strukturprinzip der "Achse"', in *Hitler, Deutschland und die Mächte* (q.v.), 823–46.

—— '7. März 1936: Fallstudie zum außenpolitischen Führungsstil Hitlers', in *Nationalsozialistische Außenpolitik* (q.v.), 227–325.

GABRIEL, S. L., 'Eingliederung der österreichischen Wirtschaft', *Die Bank* (1938), 422–4.

—— Österreich in der großdeutschen Wirtschaft', *Jahrbücher für Nationalökonomie und Statistik,* 147 (1938), 641–94.

GACKENHOLZ, HERMANN, 'Reichskanzlei, 5. November 1937: Bemerkungen über "Politik und Kriegführung" im Dritten Reich', in *Forschungen zu Staat und Verfassung* (q.v.), 459–84.

GAEDE, REINHARD, *Kirche — Christen — Krieg und Frieden: Die Diskussion im deutschen Protestantismus während der Weimarer Zeit* (Hamburg, 1975).

—— 'Die Stellung des deutschen Protestantismus zum Problem von Krieg und Frieden während der Zeit der Weimarer Republik', in *Kirche zwischen Krieg und Frieden* (q.v.), 373–422.

GAEDICKE, HERBERT, and EYNERN, GERT VON, *Die produktionswirtschaftliche Integration Europas: Eine Untersuchung über die Außenhandelsverflechtung der europäischen Länder,* 2 vols. (Zum wirtschaftlichen Schicksal Europas, 1, 3; Berlin, 1933).

GALTUNG, JOHANN, 'Gewalt, Frieden und Friedensforschung', in *Deutsche Friedensforschung,* ed. Dieter Senghaas (Frankfurt am Main, 1971), 55–104.

GAMM, HANS-JOCHEN, *Der braune Kult: Das Dritte Reich und seine Ersatzreligion* (Hamburg, 1962).

—— *Der Flüsterwitz im Dritten Reich* (Munich, 1963).

GANTZEL, KLAUS JÜRGEN, *System und Akteur: Beiträge zur vergleichenden Kriegsur-sachenforschung* (Krieg und Frieden; Düsseldorf, 1972).

GASIOROWSKI, Z. J., 'The German–Polish Non-aggression Pact of 1934', *Journal of Central European Affairs*, 16 (1955), 3–29.

GATZKE, HANS-WILHELM, *Stresemann and the Rearmament of Germany* (Baltimore, 1954).

Gefüge und Ordnung der deutschen Landwirtschaft: Gemeinschaftsarbeit des Forschungsdienstes, ed. and rev. by Konrad Meyer (Berlin, 1939).

GEHL, JÜRGEN, *Austria, Germany and the Anschluss 1931–1938* (London and New York, 1963).

GEHRISCH, WOLFGANG, *Die Entwicklung der Luftfahrtindustrie im imperialistischen Deutschland bis 1945* (diss. East Berlin, 1974).

GEISSLER, ROLF, *Dekadenz und Heroismus: Zeitroman und völkisch-nationalistische Literaturkritik* (Schriften der *Vierteljahrshefte für Zeitgeschichte*, 9; Stuttgart, 1964).

GEMZELL, CARL-AXEL, *Raeder, Hitler und Skandinavien: Der Kampf für einen maritimen Operationsplan* (Bibliotheca Historica Lundensis, 16; Lund, 1965).

—— *Organization, Conflict and Innovation: A Study of German Naval Strategic Planning, 1888–1940* (Lund Studies in International History, 4; Lund, 1973).

GEREKE, GÜNTHER, *Ich war königlich-preußischer Landrat* (Berlin, 1970).

GERLOFF, WILHELM, 'Autarkie als wirtschaftliches Problem', in *Autarkie, 5 Vorträge von Karl Brandt (u.a.). Auf der 1. Kundgebung des 'Deutschen Bundes für freie Wirschaftspolitik' gehalten*, intro. by Carl Petersen (Berlin, 1932), 13–35.

German Military in the Age of Total War, The, ed. Wilhelm Deist (Leamington Spa, 1985).

German Resistance to Hitler: see *Der Deutsche Widerstand gegen Hitler*.

GERSTENBERGER, HEIDE, *Der revolutionäre Konservatismus: Ein Beitrag zur Analyse des Liberalismus* (Sozialwissenschaftliche Abhandlungen, 14; Berlin, 1969).

Geschichte der deutschen Arbeiterbewegung, ed. Institut für Marxismus-Leninismus beim Zentralkomitee der SED, v. *Von Januar 1933 bis Mai 1945* (East Berlin, 1966).

Geschichte des Zweiten Weltkrieges in Dokumenten, i. *Der Weg zum Kriege 1938–1939* (1953); ii. *An der Schwelle des Krieges 1938* (1955); iii. *Der Ausbruch des Krieges 1939* (1956) (Weltgeschichte der Gegenwart in Dokumenten, ed. Michael Freund; Freiburg i.Br. and Munich).

Geschichte des Zweiten Weltkrieges 1939–1945, ed. Institute of Military History, Ministry of Defence, USSR, i. *Die Entfesselung des Krieges: Der Kampf der fortschrittlichen Kräfte für die Erhaltung des Friedens* (Moscow, 1973); ii. *Am Vorabend des Krieges* (Moscow, 1975).

Geschichtliche Grundbegriffe: Historisches Lexikon zur politisch-sozialen Sprache in Deutschland, ed. Otto Brunner, Werner Conze, and Reinhart Koselleck, i. *A–D* (Stuttgart, 1972).

Gesetzblatt der Deutschen Evangelischen Kirche, 19 (1939).

Gesetze des NS-Staates, compiled by Uwe Brodersen with intro. by Dr Ingo von Münch (Gehlen-Texte, 2; Bad Homburg vor der Höhe, Berlin, and Zurich, 1968).

GESSNER, DIETER, *Agrarverbände in der Weimarer Republik: Wirtschaftliche und soziale Voraussetzungen agrarkonservativer Politik vor 1933* (Düsseldorf, 1976).

Gewerkschaften, Friedensvertrag, Reparation (Berlin, 1932).

GEYER, MICHAEL, *Die Landesverteidigung: Wehrstruktur am Ende der Weimarer Republik* (Staatsexamensarbeit; Freiburg i.Br., 1972).

—— 'Die Wehrmacht der Deutschen Republik ist die Reichswehr', *MGM* 14 (1973), 152–99.

—— 'Das Zweite Rüstungsprogramm (1930–1934): Eine Dokumentation', *MGM* 17 (1975), 125–72.

—— 'Militär, Rüstung und Außenpolitik: Aspekte militärischer Revisionspolitik in der Zwischenkriegszeit', in *Hitler, Deutschland und die Mächte* (q.v.), 239–68.

—— *Aufrüstung oder Sicherheit: Die Reichswehr in der Krise der Machtpolitik 1924–1936* (Veröffentlichungen des Instituts für Europäische Geschichte Mainz, Abt. Universalgeschichte, 91; Wiesbaden, 1980).

—— 'Rüstungsbeschleunigung und Inflation: Zur Inflationsdenkschrift des Oberkommandos der Wehrmacht vom November 1938', *MGM* 30 (1981), 121–86.

—— 'Professionals and Junkers: German Rearmament and Politics in the Weimar Republic', in *Social Change and Political Development in Weimar Germany*, ed. Richard Bessel and Edgar J. Feuchtwanger (London, 1981), 77–133.

—— 'The Dynamics of Military Revisionism in the Interwar Years: Military Politics between Rearmament and Diplomacy', in *The German Military in the Age of Total War* (q.v.), 100–51.

GIBBS, NORMAN HENRY, *Grand Strategy*, i. *Rearmament Policy* (London, 1976).

GIES, HORST, *Richard Walther Darré und die nationalsozialistische Bauernpolitik in den Jahren 1930 bis 1933* (diss. Frankfurt am Main, 1966).

—— 'NSDAP und landwirtschaftliche Organisationen in der Endphase der Weimarer Republik', *VfZG* 15 (1967), 341–76.

GIESE, FRITZ E., *Die Deutsche Marine 1920–1945: Aufbau und Untergang* (Frankfurt am Main, 1965).

GILBERT, MARTIN, *The Roots of Appeasement* (London, 1966).

—— *Sir Horace Rumbold: Portrait of a Diplomat 1869–1941* (London, 1973).

—— and GOTT, RICHARD, *The Appeasers: A History of British Policy towards Nazi Germany* (London, 1963).

GIRAULT, RENÉ, 'Die französische Außenpolitik nach München' (MS for symposium of German and French historians in Bonn, 26–9 Sept. 1978).

—— 'Les décideurs français et la puissance française en 1938–1939', in *La Puissance en Europe* (q.v.), 23–43.

GITTIG, H. (ed.), *Illegale antifaschistische Tarnschriften (Zentralblatt für Bibliothekswesen*, suppl. 87; Leipzig, 1972).

GOEBBELS, JOSEPH, *Revolution der Deutschen: 14 Jahre Nationalsozialismus* (Oldenburg, 1933).

—— *'Goebbels spricht': Reden aus Kampf und Sieg* (Oldenburg, 1933).

—— *Nationalsozialistischer Rundfunk* (Munich, 1935).

—— *Signale der neuen Zeit*[4] (Munich, 1938).

—— 'Der Faschismus und seine praktischen Ergebnisse: Vortrag in der Hochschule für Politik am 29. Juni 1933 in Berlin', in id., *Signale der neuen Zeit*[4] (Munich, 1938), 150–76.

—— *Die Zeit ohne Beispiel: Reden und Aufsätze aus den Jahren 1939/40/41* (Munich, 1941).

—— *Tagebücher aus den Jahren 1942–1943* (Zurich, 1948). [Trans. Louis P. Lochner, *The Goebbels Diaries* (London, 1948).]

Goebbels-Reden, ed. Helmut Heiber, i. *1932–1939* (Düsseldorf, 1971).

GOEBEL, OTTO, 'Wege der Durchführung einer Wehrwirtschaft', *Jahrbuch für Wehrpolitik und Wehrwissenschaften 1937/38*, 155–66.

GOETZE, FRITZ, 'Festigung und Mobilisierung des Handwerks als Leistungstand: Zur Verordnung über die Durchführung des Vierjahresplans auf dem Gebiet der Handwerkswirtschaft', *Deutsches Handwerk*, 8 (1939), 123–5.

GÖRING, HERMANN, 'Zur Jahreswende', *Der Vierjahresplan*, 1 (1937), 706-7.

—— 'Wiederaufbau der Ostmark', *Der Vierjahresplan*, 2 (1938), 194-5.

—— *Reden und Aufsätze*[8], ed. E. Gritzbach (Munich, 1943).

GÖRLITZ, WALTER (ed.), *Generalfeldmarschall Keitel: Verbrecher oder Offizier? Erinnerungen, Briefe, Dokumente des Chefs OKW* (Göttingen, Berlin, and Frankfurt am Main, 1961).

GOSSWEILER, KURT, 'Der Übergang von der Weltwirschaftskrise zur Rüstungskonjunktur in Deutschland 1933 bis 1934: Ein historischer Beitrag zur Problematik staatsmonopolistischer "Krisenüberwindung" ', *Jahrbuch für Wirtschaftsgeschichte* (1966), 2: 55-116.

GRAML, HERMANN, 'Resistance Thinking on Foreign Policy', in *The German Resistance to Hitler* (q.v.), 1-54.

GRANZOW, BRIGITTE, *A Mirror of Nazism: British Opinion and the Emergence of Hitler 1929-1933* (London, 1964).

GRÄVELL, WALTER, 'Störungen im Außenhandel?', *Die deutsche Volkswirtschaft*, 8 (1939), 43-50.

GREBING, HELGA, *Geschichte der deutschen Arbeiterbewegung: Ein Überblick* (Munich, 1970).

—— GREIFFENHAGEN, MARTIN, KROCKOW, Count CHRISTIAN VON, and MILLER, JOHANN BAPTIST, *Konservatismus: Eine deutsche Bilanz* (Munich, 1971).

GREIFFENHAGEN, MARTIN, *Das Dilemma des Konservatismus in Deutschland* (Munich, 1971).

—— KÜHNL, REICHHARD, and MÜLLER, JOHANN BAPTIST, *Totalitarismus: Zur Problematik eines politischen Begriffs* (Munich, 1972).

GRIESWELLE, DETLEV, *Propaganda der Friedlosigkeit: Eine Studie zu Hitlers Rhetorik 1920-1933* (Stuttgart, 1972).

Griff nach Südosteuropa: Neue Dokumente über die Politik des deutschen Imperialismus und Militarismus gegenüber Südosteuropa im zweiten Weltkrieg (East Berlin, 1973).

GRIMM, HANS, *Volk ohne Raum*, 2 vols. (Munich, 1926).

GROENER-GEYER, DOROTHEA, *General Groener: Soldat und Staatsmann* (Frankfurt am Main, 1955).

GRONOW, JUKKA, and HILPPÖ, JORMA, 'Violence, Ethics and Politics', *Journal of Peace Research* (1970), 4: 311-20.

GROSCURTH, HELMUTH, *Tagebücher eines Abwehroffiziers 1938-1940*, ed. H. Krausnick and H. C. Deutsch, assisted by H. von Kotze (Quellen und Darstellungen zur Zeitgeschichte, 19; Stuttgart, 1970).

'Großdeutschland in der Energiewirtschaft', *Der Deutsche Volkswirt*, 12 (1938), 1224-7.

GROSSMANN, KURT, R., *Emigration: Geschichte der Hitler-Flüchtlinge 1933-1945* (Frankfurt am Main, 1969).

Großraumwirtschaft: Der Weg zur europäischen Einheit, ed. Wilhelm Gürge and Wilhelm Grotkopp (Berlin, 1931).

GROTKOPP, WILHELM, *Die große Krise: Lehren aus der Überwindung der Wirtschaftskrise 1929/32* (published in co-operation with the Studiengesellschaft für Geld- und Kreditwirtschaft; Düsseldorf, 1954).

GRÜNDEL, GÜNTHER, 'Die Krise des Vernichtungsgedankens in der neuzeitlichen Kriegführung', *Militär-Wochenblatt*, 117/7 (1932-3), 209-12.

GRUNDMANN, FRIEDRICH, *Agrarpolitik im 'Dritten Reich': Anspruch und Wirklichkeit des Reichserbhofgesetzes* (Historische Perspektiven, 14; Hamburg, 1979).

GSCHAIDER, PETER, *Das österreichische Bundesheer 1938 und seine Überführung in die Deutsche Wehrmacht* (diss. Vienna, 1967).

GUDERIAN, HEINZ, *Erinnerungen eines Soldaten*[4] (Heidelberg, 1951). [Trans. Constantine Fitzgibbon, *Panzer Leader* (London, 1970).]

GUNDELACH, KARL, 'Gedanken über die Führung eines Luftkrieges gegen England bei der

Luftflotte 2 in den Jahren 1938/39 (Ein Beitrag zur Vorgeschichte der Luftschlacht um England)', *WWR* 10/1 (1960), 33–46.

GÜNTHER, ALBRECHT ERICH, 'Die Intelligenz und der Krieg', in *Krieg und Krieger*, ed. Ernst Jünger (Berlin, 1930), 69–110.

GUTH, KARL, 'Wirtschaft und Staat: Ein Rück- und Ausblick', *Der Deutsche Volkswirt*, 9 (1934–5), 877–80.

GÜTH, ROLF, *Die Marine des Deutschen Reiches 1919–1939* (Frankfurt am Main, 1972).

—— 'Die Organisation der deutschen Marine in Krieg und Frieden 1913–1933', in Jost Düffler, Rolf Güth, and Wolfgang Petter, *Deutsche Marinegeschichte der Neuzeit* (Handbuch zur deutschen Militärgeschichte 1648–1939, 7; Munich, 1977), 263–336.

—— 'Die Organisation der Kriegsmarine bis 1939', in *Handbuch zur deutschen Militärgeschichte 1648–1939*, ed. Militärgeschichtliches Forschungsamt, iv/7 (Munich, 1979), 401–99.

HADAMOWSKY, EUGEN, *Propaganda und nationale Macht: Die Organisation der öffentlichen Meinung für die nationale Politik* (Oldenburg, 1933).

—— *Der Rundfunk im Dienste der Volksführung* (Gestalten und Erscheinungen der politischen Publizistik, 1; Leipzig, 1934).

—— *Dein Rundfunk: Das Rundfunkbuch für alle Volksgenossen* (Munich, 1934).

—— *Hitler kämpft um den Frieden Europas: Ein Tagebuch von Adolf Hitlers Kampf für Frieden und Gleichberechtigung* (Munich, 1936).

HAFFNER, SEBASTIAN, *Anmerkungen zu Hitler*[5] (Munich, 1978). [Trans. Ewald Osers, *The Meaning of Hitler* (London, 1979).]

HAGEMANN, WALTER, *Publizistik im Dritten Reich: Ein Beitrag zur Methodik der Massenführung* (Hamburg, 1948).

HAGGIE, PAUL, *Britannia at Bay: The Defence of the British Empire against Japan 1931–1941* (Oxford, 1981).

HALDER, FRANZ, *Generaloberst Halder: Kriegstagebuch. Tägliche Aufzeichnungen des Chefs des Generalstabes des Heeres 1939–1942*, ed. Hans-Adolf Jacobsen and A. Philippi, i. *Vom Polenfeldzug bis zum Ende der Westoffensive (14.8.1939–30.6.1940)* (Arbeitskreis für Wehrforschung, Stuttgart; Stuttgart, 1962). [Trans. and ed. Trevor N. Dupuy, *The Halder Diaries* (Boulder, Colo., 1976).]

HALE, ORON JAMES, *The Captive Press in the Third Reich* (Princeton, 1964).

HALIFAX, Earl of, *Speeches on Foreign Policy* [1934–9], ed. H. H. E. Craster (Oxford and Toronto, 1940).

—— *Fulness of Days* (London, 1957).

HALLGARTEN, GEORGE W. F., *Hitler, Reichswehr und Industrie: Zur Geschichte der Jahre 1918–1933*[2] (Frankfurt am Main, 1955).

—— and RADKAU, JOACHIM, *Deutsche Industrie und Politik von Bismarck bis heute* (Frankfurt am Main, 1974).

HALSMAYR, JOSEF, *Die politischen Grundlagen der deutsch-südosteuropäischen Wirtschafts-beziehungen* (diss. Berlin, 1939).

HAMMER, HERMANN, 'Die deutschen Ausgaben von Hitlers "Mein Kampf"', *VfZG* 4 (1956), 161–78.

HAMMER, KARL, *Deutsche Kriegstheologie (1870–1918)* (Munich, 1971).

—— *Christen, Krieg und Frieden: Eine historische Analyse* (Olten and Freiburg i.Br., 1972).

Handwerk, Helfer der Wehrmacht (s.l., [beginning of 1939]).

HANSEN, ERNST WILLI, *Reichswehr und Industrie: Rüstungswirtschaftliche Zusammenarbeit und wirtschaftliche Mobilmachungsvorbereitungen 1923–1932* (Wehrwissenschaftliche Forschungen, Abt. Militärgeschichtliche Studien, 24; Boppard, 1978).

HARPER, GLENN T., *German Economic Policy in Spain During the Spanish Civil War, 1936–1939* (The Hague and Paris, 1967).

HARTTUNG, ARNOLD (ed.), *Der Friedens-Nobelpreis, Stiftung und Verleihung: Die Reden der vier deutschen Preisträger Gustav Stresemann, Ludwid Quidde, Carl von Ossietzky und Willy Brandt* (Berlin, 1972).

HASSELL, ULRICH VON, *Vom anderen Deutschland: Aus den nachgelassenen Tagebüchern 1938–1944* (Zurich and Freiburg i.Br., 1946). [Trans. High Gibson, *The von Hassell Diaries, 1938–1944* (London, 1948).]

HAUSER, KARL, 'Wehrwirtschaft und Ernährungspolitik', *Der Deutsche Volkswirt*, 10 (1936), 2089–91.

HAUSER, OSWALD, *England und das Dritte Reich: Eine dokumentierte Geschichte der englisch-deutschen Beziehungen von 1933 bis 1939 auf Grund unveröffentlichter Akten aus dem britischen Staatsarchiv*, i. *1933 bis 1936* (Stuttgart, 1972).

HECKER, HANS, *'Die Tat' und ihr Osteuropa-Bild 1909–1939* (Cologne, 1974).

HEER, HANNES, *Burgfrieden oder Klassenkampf: Zur Politik der sozialdemokratischen Gewerkschaften 1930–1933* (Sammlung Luchterhand, 22; Neuwied and Berlin, 1971).

Heeresadjutant bei Hitler 1938–1943: Aufzeichnungen des Majors Engel, ed. Hildegard v. Kotze (Schriftenreihe der *Vierteljahrshefte für Zeitgeschichte*, 29; Stuttgart, 1974).

HEGELHEIMER, ARMIN, *Wirtschaftslenkung und Preisintervention: Ziele und Probleme der staatlichen Preispolitik in einer gelenkten Wirtschaft, dargestellt am Beispiel der deutschen Wirtschaftslenkung und der französischen Planification* (Berlin, 1969).

HEIBER, HELMUT, *Joseph Goebbels* (Berlin, 1962). [Trans. John E. Dickinson, *Joseph Goebbels* (London, 1973).]

HEIMANN, BERNHARD, and SCHUNKE, JOACHIM, 'Eine geheime Denkschrift zur Luftkriegskonzeption Hitler-Deutschlands vom Mai 1933', *ZMG* 3 (1964), 72–86.

HEINKEL, ERNST, *Stürmisches Leben*[4], ed. Jürgen Thorwald (Stuttgart, 1953).

HEINRICHSBAUER, AUGUST, *Schwerindustrie und Politik* (Essen, 1948).

HELBICH, WOLFGANG J., *Franklin D. Roosevelt* (Berlin, 1971).

HELLMER, HEINRICH, 'Kohlehydrierung aus wehrwirtschaftlichen Gründen', *Der Deutsche Volkswirt*, 10 (1935–6), 1479–81.

HENDERSON, NEVILE, *Failure of a Mission: Berlin, 1937–1939* (London, 1940).

HENKE, JOSEF, *England in Hitlers politischem Kalkül 1935–1939* (Schriften des Bundesarchivs, 20; Boppard, 1973).

—— 'Hitlers England-Konzeption: Formulierung und Realisierungsversuch', in *Hitler, Deutschland und die Mächte* (q.v.), 584–603.

HENNIG, EIKE, 'Industrie, Aufrüstung und Kriegsvorbereitung im deutschen Faschismus (1933–1939): Anmerkungen zum Stand "der" neueren Faschismusdiskussion', in *Gesellschaftliche Beiträge zur Marxschen Theorie*, 5 (Frankfurt am Main, 1975), 68–148.

HENNING, F.-W., *Landwirtschaft und ländliche Gesellschaft in Deutschland*, ii. *1750–1976* (Paderborn, 1978).

HENNING, HANSJOACHIM, 'Kraftfahrzeugindustrie und Autobahnbau in der Wirtschaftspolitik des Nationalsozialismus 1933–1936', *Vierteljahrschrift für Sozial- und Wirtschaftsgeschichte*, 2 (1978), 217–42.

HENRIKSON, GÖRAN, 'Das Nürnberger Dokument 386-PS (Das "Hoßbach-Protokoll")', *Probleme deutscher Zeitgeschichte* (Lund Studies in International History, 2; Stockholm, 1971), 151–94.

HENTSCHEL, VOLKER, *Weimars letzte Monate: Hitler und der Untergang der Republik* (Düsseldorf, 1978).

Herbell, Hajo, *Staatsbürger in Uniform 1789 bis 1961: Ein Beitrag zur Geschichte des Kampfes zwischen Demokratie und Militarismus in Deutschland* (East Berlin, 1969).

HERFERTH, WILHELM, *Der Reichsnährstand: Ein Instrument des Faschismus zur Vorbereitung des zweiten Weltkrieges (unter besonderer Rücksicht des Aufbaues des Reichsnährstandes in den Jahren 1933 bis 1935)* (diss. East Berlin, 1961).

—— 'Der faschistische "Reichsnährstand" und die Stellung seiner Funktionäre im Bonner Staat', *ZfG* 10 (1962), 1046–76.

HERZFELD, HANS, 'Politik, Heer and Rüstung in der Zwischenkriegszeit', in id., *Ausgewählte Aufsätze: Dargebracht als Festgabe zum siebzigsten Geburtstage von seinen Freunden und Schülern* (Berlin, 1962), 255–77.

—— 'Zur Problematik der Appeasement-Politik', in *Geschichte und Gegenwartsbewußtsein: Festschrift für Hans Rothfels* (Göttingen, 1963), 161–97.

HESS, ERNST, 'Die Zonen der Wehrwirtschaft', *Der Deutsche Volkswirt*, 10 (1935–6), 1479–81.

HESSE, KURT, *Der Feldherr Psychologos: Ein Suchen nach dem Führer der deutschen Zukunft* (Berlin, 1922).

—— *Persönlichkeit und Masse im Zukunftskrieg: Eine Diskussion jüngerer Offiziere über den Krieg und seine psychologischen Probleme* (Berlin, 1933).

—— 'Die Entwicklung der wirtschaftlichen Kriegsvorbereitungen', in *Rüstung und Abrüstung: Eine Umschau über das Heer- und Kriegswesen aller Länder* (Berlin, 1934), 292–303.

HEUSS, THEODOR, *Hitlers Weg* (Stuttgart, Berlin, and Leipzig, 1933; repr. 1968).

HEYDORN, HEINZ-JOACHIM, 'Begrüßung der Teilnehmer' (p. 11), 'Vorbemerkung zur Schulbuchkonferenz' (pp. 19–23), 'Schlußbemerkung' (pp. 137–9), in *Deutscher Widerstand 1933–1945* (q.v.).

HIELSCHER, FRIEDRICH, 'Die große Verwandlung', in *Krieg und Krieger*, ed. Ernst Jünger (Berlin, 1930), 125–34.

HIERL, CONSTANTIN, *Grundlagen einer deutschen Wehrpolitik*[3] (Nationalsozialistische Bibliothek, 12; Munich, 1931).

—— *Im Dienst für Deutschland 1918–1945* (Heidelberg, 1954).

HIGHAM, ROBERT, *Armed Forces in Peacetime Britain 1918–1939* (London, 1962).

HILDEBRAND, KLAUS, *Vom Reich zum Weltreich: Hitler, NSDAP und koloniale Frage 1919–1945* (Veröffentlichungen des Historischen Instituts der Universität Hamburg, 1; Munich, 1969).

—— *Deutsche Außenpolitik 1933–1945: Kalkül oder Dogma?* (Stuttgart, 1971). [Trans. Anthony Fothergill, *The Foreign Policy of the Third Reich* (London, 1973).]

—— *Das Deutsche Reich und die Sowjetunion im internationalen System 1918–1932: Legitimität oder Revolution?* (Frankfurter historische Vorträge, 4; Wiesbaden, 1977).

—— 'Die Frankreichpolitik Hitlers bis 1936', *Francia*, 5 (1977), 591–625.

HILFERDING, RUDOLF, 'Krieg, Abrüstung und Milizsystem', *Die Gesellschaft*, 3 (1926), i. 385–98.

HILGER, GUSTAV, *The Incompatible Allies: A Memoir-History of German-Soviet Relations, 1918–1941* (New York, 1953).

HILLER VON GAERTRINGEN, Baron FRIEDRICH, 'Groener', in *Neue Deutsche Biographie*, vii (Berlin, 1966), 111–14.

—— 'Das Ende der Deutschnationalen Volkspartei im Frühjahr 1933', in *Von Weimar zu Hitler* (q.v.), 246–78.

—— 'Zur Beurteilung des "Monarchismus" in der Weimarer Republik', in *Tradition und Reform in der deutschen Politik: Gedenkschrift für Waldemar Besson*, ed. Gotthard Jasper (Frankfurt am Main, Berlin, and Vienna, 1976), 138–86.

HILLGRUBER, ANDREAS, 'Der "Anschluß" Österreichs 1938', *Neue Politische Literatur*, 9 (1964), 984–8.

—— 'Quellen und Quellenkritik zur Vorgeschichte des Zweiten Weltkrieges', *WWR* 14 (1964), 110–26.

—— *Hitler, König Carol und Marschall Antonescu: Die deutsch-rumänischen Beziehungen 1938–1944*[2] (Veröffentlichungen des Instituts für Europäische Geschichte Mainz, 5; Wiesbaden, 1965).

—— *Hitlers Strategie, Politik und Kriegführung 1940–41* (Frankfurt am Main, 1965).

—— 'Der Faktor Amerika in Hitlers Strategie 1938–1941', in *Aus Politik und Zeitgeschichte* (suppl. to weekly *Das Parlament*), B 19 (1966), 3–21.

—— *Deutschlands Rolle in der Vorgeschichte der beiden Weltkriege* (Die deutsche Frage in der Welt, 7; Göttingen, 1967). [Trans. William C. Kirby, *Germany and the Two World Wars* (Cambridge, Mass., 1981).]

—— 'Der Zweite Weltkrieg, 1939–1945', in *Osteuropa-Handbuch, Sowjetunion: Außenpolitik 1917–1955* (q.v.), 270–342.

—— 'Die weltpolitische Lage 1936–1939: Deutschland', in *Weltpolitik 1933–1939* (q.v.), 270–92.

—— 'England in Hitlers außenpolitischer Konzeption', *HZ* 218 (1974), 65–84.

—— *Großmachtpolitik und Militarismus im 20. Jahrhundert: 3 Beiträge zum Kontinuitätsproblem* (Düsseldorf, 1974).

—— 'Kontinuität und Diskontinuität in der deutschen Außenpolitik von Bismarck zu Hitler', in id., *Großmachtpolitik*, 11–36.

—— 'Militarismus am Ende der Weimarer Republik und im "Dritten Reich"', in id., *Großmachtpolitik*, 37–51.

—— 'Frankreich als Faktor der deutschen Außenpolitik im Jahre 1939' (MS for symposium of German and French historians in Bonn, 26–9 Sept. 1978).

HILLMAN, H. C., 'Comparative Strength of the Great Powers', in *Survey of International Affairs 1939–1946: The World in March 1939* (London, New York, and Toronto, 1952), 366–507.

HIMMLER, HEINRICH, *Geheimreden 1933 bis 1945 und andere Ansprachen*, ed. Bradley F. Smith and Agnes F. Peterson, with introduction by Joachim C. Fest (Frankfurt am Main, Berlin, and Vienna, 1974).

HITLER, ADOLF, *Der Weg zum Wiederaufstieg* (1927); repr. in Turner, *Faschismus* (1972) (q.v.), 41–59.

—— *Mein Kampf* (Munich, 1930; [394th thousand by 1939; *Jubiläumsausgabe* 1939]). [Trans. James Murphy, *Mein Kampf* (London, 1939).]

—— *Frieden und Sicherheit: Rede, gehalten am 17. Mai 1933 im Deutschen Reichstag* (Die Erhebung; Berlin, 1933).

—— *Deutschland will Frieden und Gleichberechtigung: Die Friedensreden unseres Volkskanzlers*, ed. Erich Unger (Langensalza, 1934).

—— *Reden für Gleichberechtigung und Frieden* (Munich, 1934).

Hitler, Deutschland und die Mächte: Materialien zur Außenpolitik des Dritten Reiches, ed. Manfred Funke (Bonner Schriften zur Politik und Zeitgeschichte, 12; Düsseldorf, 1976).

Hitler Rearms, ed. Dorothy Woodman (Paris, 1934). [English equivalent of *Hitler treibt zum Krieg*, q.v.]

Hitlers Luftflotte startbereit: Enthüllungen über den tatsächlichen Stand der Hitlerschen Luftrüstungen (Paris, 1935).

Hitlers Machtergreifung 1933: Vom Machtantritt Hitlers, 30. Januar 1933 bis zur Besiegelung des Einparteienstaates 14. Juli 1933, ed. Josef and Ruth Becker (Munich, 1983).

Hitler's Secret Book: see *Hitlers zweites Buch*.

Hitlers Städte: Baupolitik im Dritten Reich. Eine Dokumentation, ed. Jost Dülffer, Jochen Thies, and Josef Henke (Cologne and Vienna, 1978).

Hitler's Table Talk, trans. Norman Cameron and R. H. Stevens, intro. by H. R. Trevor-Roper (London, 1953).

Hitlers Weisungen für die Kriegführung 1939–1945: Dokumente des Oberkommandos der Wehrmacht, ed. Walther Hubatsch (Frankfurt am Main, 1962). [Trans. H. R. Trevor-Roper, *Hitler's War Directives* (London, 1964).]

Hitlers zweites Buch: Ein Dokument aus dem Jahre 1928, with intro. by Gerhard L. Weinberg (Quellen und Darstellungen zur Zeitgeschichte, 7; Stuttgart, 1961). [Trans. Salvator Attanasio, *Hitler's Secret Book*, with introduction by Telford Taylor (New York, 1962).]

Hitler treibt zum Krieg: Dokumentarische Enthüllungen über Hitlers Geheimrüstungen, ed. Dorothy Woodman (Paris, 1934). [German equivalent of *Hitler Rearms*, q.v.]

HÖBELT, LOTHAR, *Die britische Appeasementpolitik: Entspannung und Nachrüstung 1937–1939* (Vienna, 1983).

HOEFT, KLAUS-DIETER, 'Die Agrarpolitik des deutschen Faschismus als Mittel zur Vorbereitung des zweiten Weltkrieges', *ZfG* 7 (1959), 1205–30.

—— *Zur Agrarpolitik des deutschen Imperialismus von 1933 bis zur Gegenwart* (Dresden, 1960).

HOENSCH, JÖRG K., *Die Slowakei und Hitlers Ostpolitik: Hlinkas Slowakische Volkspartei zwischen Autonomie und Separation. 1938/1939* (Beiträge zur Geschichte Osteuropas, 4; Cologne and Vienna, 1965).

HOFER, WALTHER, *Die Entfesselung des Zweiten Weltkrieges: Eine Studie über die internationalen Beziehungen im Sommer 1939*, 3rd enlarged edn. (Frankfurt am Main, 1964). [Trans. Stanley Goodman, *War Premeditated, 1939* (London, 1955).]

HOFFMANN, FRIEDRICH, 'Der Ruf nach Autarkie in der deutschen politischen Gegenwartsideologie', *Weltwirtschaftliches Archiv*, 36/2 (1932), 496–511.

HÖHNE, HEINZ, *Der Orden unter dem Totenkopf: Die Geschichte der SS* (Gütersloh, 1967, and Frankfurt am Main, 1969). [Trans. R. Barry, *The Order of the Death's Head* (London, 1969).]

—— *Mordsache Röhm: Hitlers Durchbruch zur Alleinherrschaft 1933–34* (Spiegel-Buch, 52; Reinbek, 1984).

HOLLAND, R. F., *Britain and the Commonwealth Alliance 1918–1939* (London, 1981).

HOLLDACK, HEINZ, *Was wirklich geschah: Die diplomatischen Hintergründe der deutschen Kriegspolitik. Darstellung und Dokumente* (Munich, 1949).

HOMZE, EDWARD L., *Arming the Luftwaffe: The Reich Air Ministry and the German Aircraft Industry, 1919–39* (Lincoln, Nebr., 1976).

HONIGBERGER, ROLF, *Die wirtschaftspolitische Zielsetzung des Nationalsozialismus und deren Einfluß auf die deutsche Wirtschaftsordnung: Dargestellt und kritisch untersucht am Beispiel des deutschen Arbeitsmarktes von 1933 bis 1939* (diss. Freiburg i.Br., 1949).

HORN, WOLFGANG, *Führerideologie und Parteiorganisation in der NSDAP* (Geschichtliche Studien zu Politik und Gesellschaft, 3; Düsseldorf, 1972).

—— *Der Marsch zur Machtergreifung: Die NSDAP bis 1933* (Athenäum-Droste-Taschenbücher, 7234; Königstein and Düsseldorf, 1980).

HOSSBACH, FRIEDRICH, *Zwischen Wehrmacht und Hitler*[2] (Wolfenbüttel, 1965).

HOWARD, MICHAEL, *The Continental Commitment: The Dilemma of British Defence Policy in the Era of Two World Wars. The Ford Lectures in the University of Oxford 1971* (London, 1972).

HÜBENER, ERHARD, *Die Finanzierung der Arbeitsbeschaffung, der Aufrüstung und des Krieges in der deutschen Finanzpolitik 1933-1945* (diss. Halle, 1948).

HUBER, WOLFGANG, 'Evangelische Theologie und Kirche beim Ausbruch des Ersten Weltkrieges', in *Historische Beiträge zur Friedensforschung*, ed. Wolfgang Huber (Stuttgart and Munich, 1970), 134-215.

—— 'Kirche und Militarismus', in *Christentum und Militarismus* (q.v.), 158-84.

—— and SCHWERDTFEGER, JOHANNES, 'Möglichkeiten und Grenzen des Friedenshandelns von Kirchen und christlichen Gruppen', in *Kirche zwischen Krieg und Frieden* (q.v.), 543-86.

Hugenbergs innenpolitisches Programm[3] (Deutschnationale Flugschrift, 353; Berlin, 1931).

Hugenbergs weltwirtschaftliches Programm: Mahnung an das Ausland[3] (Deutschnationale Flugschrift, 352; Berlin, 1931).

HUMMELBERGER, WALTER, 'Die Rüstungsindustrie der Tschechoslowakei 1933 bis 1939', in *Wirtschaft und Rüstung* (q.v.), 308-30.

HUNKE, 'Die Lage', *Die Deutsche Volkswirtschaft*, 3 (1934), 481-2.

HÜRTEN, HEINZ, *Reichswehr und Ausnahmezustand: Ein Beitrag zur Verfassungsproblematik der Weimarer Republik in ihrem ersten Jahrfünft* (Vorträge, Rheinisch-Westfälische Akademie der Wissenschaften: Geisteswissenschaften, G 222; Opladen, 1977).

HÜTTENBERGER, PETER, *Die Gauleiter: Studie zum Wandel des Machtgefüges in der NSDAP* (Schriftenreihe der *Vierteljahrshefte für Zeitgeschichte*, 19; Stuttgart, 1969).

—— 'Nationalsozialistische Polykratie', *Geschichte und Gesellschaft*, 2 (1976), No. 4. *Das nationalsozialistische Herrschaftssystem*, 417-42.

HYDE, H. MONTGOMERY, *British Air Policy between the Wars 1918-1939* (London, 1976).

ILGNER, MAX, *Exportsteigerung durch Einschaltung in die Industrialisierung der Welt* (Kieler Vorträge, 53; Jena, 1938).

ILLERT, HELMUT, *Die deutsche Rechte der Weimarer Republik im Urteil der englischen Presse 1928-1932* (diss. Cologne, 1966).

IMT (International Military Tribunal): see *Trial*.

'Industrie, Die', in *Motor und Sport*, A/32 (1933), 27.

Innen- und Außenpolitik unter nationalsozialistischer Bedrohung: Determinanten internationaler Beziehungen in historischen Fallstudien, ed. Erhard Forndran, Frank Golczewski, and Dieter Riesenberger (Düsseldorf, 1976).

Ironside Diaries 1937-1940, The, ed. Roderick Macleod and Denis Kelly (London, 1962).

IRVING, DAVID, *The Rise and Fall of the Luftwaffe: The Life of Luftwaffe Marshal Erhard Milch* (London, 1973).

—— *The War Path: Hitler's Germany, 1933-9* (London, 1978).

JÄCKEL, EBERHARD, *Hitlers Weltanschauung: Entwurf einer Herrschaft* (Tübingen, 1969).

—— *Hitlers Herrschaft: Vollzug einer Weltanschauung* (Stuttgart, 1986).

JACOBSEN, HANS-ADOLF, *1939-1945: Der Zweite Weltkrieg in Chronik und Dokumenten* (Darmstadt, 1959; 1961[5]).

—— *Der Zweite Weltkrieg: Grundzüge der Politik und Strategie in Dokumenten* (Fischer Bücherei, Bücher des Wissens, 645-6; Frankfurt am Main, 1965).

—— *Die nationalsozialistische Außenpolitik 1933-1938* (Frankfurt am Main and Berlin, 1968).

—— 'Die Rolle Deutschlands in der Weltpolitik 1933-1935', in *Weltpolitik 1933-1939* (q.v.), 255-69.

—— Krieg in Weltanschauung und Praxis des Nationalsozialismus', in *Beiträge zur Zeitgeschichte: Festschrift für Ludwig Jedlicka*, ed. Rudolf Neck and Adam Wandruszka (St. Pölten, 1976, 237–46.

Jahrbuch der deutschen Sozialdemokratie [SPD] für das Jahr 1930.

Jahrbuch 1930 des Allgemeinen Deutschen Gewerkschaftsbundes (Berlin, 1931).

Jahrbuch 1931 des Allgemeinen Deutschen Gewerkschaftsbundes (Berlin, 1932).

Jahrbuch 1939, vol. i, ed. by Arbeitswissenschaftliches Institut der Deutschen Arbeitsfront (Berlin, n.d.).

JAMIN, MATHILDE, *Zwischen den Klassen: Zur Sozialstruktur der SA-Führerschaft* (Wuppertal, 1984).

JÄNICKE, MARTIN, *Totalitäre Herrschaft: Anatomie eines politischen Begriffs* (Soziologische Abhandlungen, 13; Berlin, 1971).

JARAUSCH, KONRAD J., *The Four Power Pact* (New York, 1965).

JASPER, GOTTHARD, 'Über die Ursachen des Zweiten Weltkrieges: Zu den Büchern von A. J. Taylor und David L. Hoggan', *VfZG* 10 (1962), 311–40.

[JODL, ALFRED], Diary: 'Von Jodl verfaßtes dienstliches Tagebuch (Chef L) vom 4. Jan. 1937 bis 25. August 1939 (Exhibit VS-72), Doc. 1780-PS, *IMT* xxviii. 345–90 [see *Trial*].

JOHE, WERNER, *Die gleichgeschaltete Justiz: Organisation des Rechtswesens und Politisierung der Rechtssprechung 1933–1945 dargestellt am Beispiel des Oberlandesgerichtsbezirks Hamburg* (Veröffentlichungen der Forschungsstelle für die Geschichte des Nationalsozialismus in Hamburg, 5; Frankfurt am Main, 1967).

JOHNSON, FRANKLIN ARTHUR, *Defence by Committee: The British Committee of Imperial Defence 1885–1959* (London, 1960).

JONES, FRANCIS CLIFFORD, *Japan's New Order in East Asia: Its Rise and Fall, 1937–45* (London, 1954).

JONES, THOMAS, *A Diary with Letters 1941–1950* (London, New York, and Toronto, 1954; repr. London, 1969).

JOOS, JOSEF, *Die politische Ideenwelt des Zentrums* (Wissen und Wirken: Einzelschriften zu den Grundfragen des Erkennens und Schaffens, 54; Karlsruhe, 1928).

Junge Deutschland will Arbeit und Frieden, Das: Reden des Reichskanzlers Adolf Hitler, des neuen Deutschlands Führer, with preface by Dr Josef Goebbels (Berlin, [1933]).

JÜNGER, ERNST, *Feuer und Blut: Ein kleiner Ausschnitt aus einer großen Schlacht*[4] (Berlin, 1929).

—— *Das Wäldchen 125: Eine Chronik aus den Grabenkämpfen 1918*[4] (Berlin, 1929).

—— 'Deutsche Mobilmachung', in *Krieg und Krieger*, ed. E. Jünger (Berlin, 1930), 9–30.

JÜNGER, FRIEDRICH GEORG, *Aufmarsch des Nationalismus* (Berlin, [1928]).

—— 'Krieg und Krieger', in *Krieg und Krieger*, ed. Ernst Jünger (Berlin, 1930), 51–67.

JUNKER, DETLEF, *Die deutsche Zentrumspartei und Hitler 1932–33: Ein Beitrag zur Problematik des politischen Katholizismus in Deutschland* (Stuttgarter Beiträge zur Geschichte und Politik, 4; Stuttgart, 1969).

JUSTROW, KARL, *Feldherr und Kriegstechnik: Studien über den Operationsplan des Grafen Schlieffen und Lehren für unseren Wehraufbau und unsere Landesverteidigung* (Oldenburg, 1933).

KAAS, LUDWIG, 'Außenpolitik des Reiches', in *Politisches Jahrbuch 1927–28*, ed. Gerhard Schreiber (München-Gladbach, 1928), 11–62.

—— 'Der Völkerbund als deutsche Aufgabe', in *Nationale Arbeit* (q.v.), 119–40.

KADRITZKE, NIELS, *Faschismus und Krise: Zum Verhältnis von Politik und Ökonomie im Nationalsozialismus* (Campus Studium, 528; Frankfurt am Main and New York, 1976).

KAISER, DAVID E., *Economic Diplomacy and the Origins of the Second World War: Germany, Britain, France, and Eastern Europe, 1930–1939* (New York, 1981).

KAISER, GERHARD, '"Geistige Kriegsführung" und die Amtsgruppe Wehrmacht-propaganda des OKW im Zweiten Weltkrieg', in *Der deutsche Imperialismus und der Zweite Weltkrieg*, iii (East Berlin, 1962), 171–9.

KANTOROWICZ, HERMANN, *Der Geist der englischen Politik und das Gespenst der Einkreisung Deutschlands* (Berlin, 1929).

KASPER, HANNS-HEINZ, *Die Erdölgewinnung Deutschlands in der Zeit von 1933–1945* (diss. Dresden, 1974).

KATER, MICHAEL H., *Studentenschaft und Rechtsradikalismus in Deutschland 1918–1933: Eine sozialgeschichtliche Studie zur Bildungskrise in der Weimarer Republik* (Hamburg, 1975).

—— 'Ansätze zu einer Soziologie der SA bis zur Röhm-Krise', in *Soziale Bewegung und politische Verfassung: Beiträge zur Geschichte der modernen Welt*, ed. Ulrich Engelhardt, Volker Sellin, and Horst Stuke (Stuttgart, 1976), 798–831.

Katholische Kirche im Dritten Reich: Eine Aufsatzsammlung zum Verhältnis von Papsttum, Episkopat und deutschen Katholiken zum Nationalsozialismus 1933–1945, ed. Dieter Albrecht (Mainz, 1976).

Keesings Archiv der Gegenwart (1938).

Keesing's Contemporary Archives (1938).

KEHRIG, MANFRED, *Die Wiedereinrichtung des deutschen militärischen Attaché-Dienstes nach dem Ersten Weltkrieg (1919–1933)* (Wehrwissenschaftliche Forschungen, Abt. Militär-geschichtliche Studien, 2; Boppard, 1966).

KEHRL, HANS, *Krisenmanager im Dritten Reich: 6 Jahre Frieden, 6 Jahre Krieg. Erinnerungen* (Düsseldorf, 1973).

KELLER, THEO, 'Sinn und Unsinn der Autarkie', *Schweizerische Rundschau*, 32 (1932–3), 769–83.

KENNEDY, PAUL M., '"Splendid Isolation" gegen "Continental Commitment": Das Dilemma der britischen Deutschlandstrategie in der Zwischenkriegszeit (1931–1939)', in *Tradition und Neubeginn: Internationale Forschungen zur deutschen Geschichte im 20. Jahrhundert*, ed. Joachim Hütter, Reinhard Meyers, and Dietrich Papenfuss (Cologne, Berlin, Bonn, and Munich, 1975), 151–72.

—— *The Realities behind Diplomacy: Background Influences on British External Policy, 1865–1980* (London, 1981).

—— *The Rise and Fall of British Naval Mastery* (London, 1983).

—— and SPENCE, J. E., 'On Appeasement', *British Journal of International Studies*, 6 (1980), No. 3.

KENS, KARLHEINZ, and NOWARRA, HEINZ JOACHIM, *Die deutschen Flugzeuge 1933–1945*[2] (Munich, 1964).

KERN, WOLFGANG, *Die innere Funktion der Wehrmacht, 1933–1939* (Militärhistorische Studien, NS 20; East Berlin, 1979).

KERNIG, CLAUS D., 'Das Verhältnis von Kriegslehre und Gesellschaftstheorie bei Engels', in *Friedrich Engels 1820–1970: Referate, Diskussionen, Dokumente* (Schriftenreihe des Forschungsinstituts der Friedrich-Ebert-Stiftung, 85; Hanover, 1971), 77–92.

KERSHAW, IAN, *Der Hitler-Mythos: Volksmeinung und Propaganda im Dritten Reich* (Schriften der *VfZG*, 41; Stuttgart, 1980). [Trans. *Popular Opinion and Political Dissent in the Third Reich: Bavaria 1933–1945* (Oxford, 1983).]

KETTENACKER, LOTHAR, *Nationalsozialistische Volkstumspolitik im Elsaß* (Studien zur Zeitgeschichte, 4; Stuttgart, 1973).

—— 'Die Diplomatie der Ohnmacht', in *Sommer 1939* (q.v.), 223–79.

KIELMANSEGG, Count PETER, 'Die militär-politische Tragweite der "Hoßbach-Besprechung"', *VfZG* 8 (1960), 268–75.

KIESER, ROLF, *Englands Appeasementpolitik und der Aufstieg des Dritten Reiches im Spiegel der britischen Presse (1933–1939): Ein Beitrag zur Vorgeschichte des Zweiten Weltkrieges* (diss. Zurich, 1964).

KIMMEL, ADOLF, *Der Aufstieg des Nationalsozialismus im Spiegel der französischen Presse 1930–1933* (Abhandlungen zur Kunst-, Musik- und Literaturwissenschaft, 70; Bonn, 1969).

KIMMICH, CHRISTOPH M., *The Free City: Danzig and German Foreign Policy 1919–1934* (New Haven, 1968).

KINDLEBERGER, CHARLES POOR, *The World in Depression, 1929–1939* (New York, 1973).

KIRCHBERG, PETER, 'Typisierung in der Kraftfahrzeugindustrie und der Generalbevollmächtigte für das Kraftfahrwesen', *Jahrbuch für Wirtschaftsgeschichte* (1969), ii. 117–42.

Kirche im Krieg: Der deutsche Protestantismus am Beginn des 2. Weltkrieges, ed. Günter Brakelmann (Studienbücher zur kirchlichen Zeitgeschichte, 1/2; Munich, 1979).

Kirche und das Dritte Reich, Die: Fragen und Forderungen deutscher Theologen, ed. Leopold Klotz, 2 vols. (Gotha, 1932).

Kirche zwischen Krieg und Frieden: Studien zur Geschichte des deutschen Protestantismus, ed. Wolfgang Huber and Johannes Schwerdtfeger (Stuttgart, 1976).

KIRKPATRICK, IVONE, *The Inner Circle* (London, 1959).

KLEIN, BURTON H., *Germany's Economic Preparations for War* (Cambridge, 1959).

KLEINAU, WILHELM, *Stahlhelm und Staat: Eine Erläuterung der Stahlhelm-Botschaften* (Berlin, 1929).

—— *Soldaten der Nation: Die geschichtliche Sendung des Stahlhelms* (Berlin, 1933).

KLEMPERER, KLEMENS VON, *Germany's New Conservatism: Its History and Dilemma in the Twentieth Century* (Princeton, 1957).

KLIETMANN, KURT-GERHARD, *Die Waffen-SS: Eine Dokumentation* (Osnabrück, 1965).

KLÖNNE, ARNO, *Hitlerjugend: Die Jugend und ihre Organisation im 3. Reich* (Schriftenreihe des Instituts für wissenschaftliche Politik in Marburg an der Lahn, 1; Hanover and Frankfurt am Main, 1957).

—— *Jugend im Dritten Reich: Die Hitler-Jugend und ihre Gegner* (Düsseldorf and Cologne, 1982).

KLOSE, WERNER, *Generation im Gleichschritt: Ein Dokumentarbericht* (Oldenburg and Hamburg, 1964).

KLOTZBACH, KURT, *Gegen den Nationalsozialismus: Widerstand und Verfolgung in Dortmund 1930–1945. Eine historisch-politische Studie* (Schriftenreihe des Forschungsinstituts der Friedrich-Ebert-Stiftung; Hanover, 1969).

KLOTZBÜCHER, ALOIS, *Der politische Weg des Stahlhelm, Bund der Frontsoldaten, in der Weimarer Republik: Ein Beitrag zur Geschichte der 'Nationalen Opposition' 1918–1933*, (diss. Erlangen-Nuremberg, 1965).

KNICKERBOCKER, HUBERT RENFRO, *The German Crisis* (New York and London, 1932) [British title *Germany: Fascist or Soviet?*].

KNIPPING, FRANZ, 'Frankreich in Hitlers Außenpolitik 1933–1939', in *Hitler, Deutschland und die Mächte* (q.v.), 612–27.

—— 'Die deutsch-französische Erklärung vom 6. Dezember 1938' (MS for Symposium of German and French historians in Bonn, 26–9 Sept. 1978).

KOCH, HANS-JOACHIM W., *Geschichte der Hitlerjugend* (Percha am Starnberger See, 1975).

KOCH-WESER, ERICH, *Deutschlands Außenpolitik in der Nachkriegszeit 1919–1929* (Berlin-Grunewald, 1929).

KOCKA, JÜRGEN, *Klassengesellschaft im Krieg: Deutsche Sozialgeschichte 1914–1918* (Kritische Studien zur Geschichtswissenschaft, 8; Göttingen, 1973).

KOELBLE, JOSEF, *Grundzüge der neuen deutschen Wirtschaftsordnung* (Leipzig, 1939).

KOERNER, RALF RICHARD, *So haben sie es damals gemacht . . . Die Propagandavorbereitungen zum Österreich-Anschluß durch das Hitlerregime 1933–1938* (Vienna, 1958).

KOGON, EUGEN, *Der SS-Staat: Das System der deutschen Konzentrationslager* (Munich, 1946). [Trans. Heinz Norden, *The Theory and Practice of Hell: The German Concentration Camps and the System behind them* (London, 1950).]

KÖHLER, BERNHARD, *Des Führers Wirtschaftspolitik: Rede*[3] (Hier spricht das neue Deutschland, 8–9; Munich, 1935).

KÖHLER, KARL, 'Operativer Luftkrieg: Eine Wortbildung zur Bezeichnung unterschiedlicher Vorstellungen', *Wehrkunde*, 16 (1967), 265–9.

—— and HUMMEL, KARL-HEINZ, 'Die Organisation der Luftwaffe 1933–1939', in *Wehrmacht und Nationalsozialismus 1933–1939* (Handbuch zur deutschen Militärgeschichte 1648–1939, Munich, 1978), 7: 501–79.

KÖLLNER, LUTZ, *Rüstungsfinanzierung: Dämonie und Wirklichkeit* (Frankfurt am Main, 1969).

KOLSHORN, Major (retd.), 'Die Erfassung deutscher Bodenschätze', *Deutsche Wehr*, 39 (1935), 263.

Komintern und Faschismus 1920–1940: Dokumente zur Geschichte und Theorie des Faschismus, ed. Theo Pirker (Schriftenreihe der *Vierteljahrshefte für Zeitgeschichte*, 10; Stuttgart, 1965).

Konjunkturstatistisches Handbuch 1936 (Hamburg, 1935).

KORBEL, JOSEF, *Poland between East and West: Soviet and German Diplomacy toward Poland, 1919–1939* (Princeton, 1963).

KORDT, ERICH, *Wahn und Wirklichkeit*[2] (Stuttgart, 1948).

—— *Nicht aus den Akten . . . Die Wilhelmstraße in Frieden und Krieg: Erlebnisse, Begegnungen und Eindrücke 1928–1945* (Stuttgart, 1950).

KORFES, OTTO, *Grundsätze der Wehrwirtschaftslehre: Allgemeine Grundlagen der Wehrwirtschaft und Kriegswirtschaft* (Schriften zur kriegswirtschaftlichen Forschung und Schulung, 10; Hamburg, 1936).

KOSZYK, KURT, *Zwischen Kaiserreich und Diktatur: Die sozialdemokratische Presse von 1914 bis 1933* (Heidelberg, 1958).

—— *Deutsche Presse 1914–1945: Geschichte der deutschen Presse*, Pt. 3 (Abhandlungen und Materialien zur Publizistik, 7; Berlin, 1972).

KOTZE, HILDEGARD VON, and KRAUSNICK, HELMUT (eds.), *Es spricht der Führer: Sieben exemplarische Hitler-Reden mit Erläuterungen* (Gütersloh, 1966).

KRACAUER, SIEGFRIED, *Von Caligari bis Hitler: Ein Beitrag zur Geschichte des deutschen Films* (Rowohlts Deutsche Enzyklopädie; Reinbek, 1958).

KRANIG, ANDREAS, *Lockung und Zwang: Zur Arbeitsverfassung im Dritten Reich* (Schriftenreihe der *VfZG*, 47; Stuttgart, 1983).

KRAUSE, WERNER, *Wirtschaftstheorie unter dem Hakenkreuz: Die bürgerliche politische Ökonomie in Deutschland während der faschistischen Herrschaft* (East Berlin, 1969).

KRAUSNICK, HELMUT, 'Vorgeschichte und Beginn des militärischen Widerstandes gegen Hitler', in *Vollmacht des Gewissens*, ed. Europäische Publikation (Frankfurt am Main and Berlin, 1960), i. 177–384.

—— 'Judenverfolgung', in *Anatomie des SS-Staates* (q.v.). [Trans. D. Long, 'The Persecution of the Jews', 1–124.]

—— and GRAML, HERMANN, 'Der deutsche Widerstand und die Alliierten', in *Aus Politik und Zeitgeschichte* (suppl. to weekly *Das Parlament*) B 29 (1961), 413–40.

KRIECK, ERNST, *Nationalpolitische Erziehung* (Leipzig, 1933).

Kriegspropaganda 1939–1941: Geheime Ministerkonferenzen im Reichspropagandaministerium, ed. with intro. by Willi A. Boelcke (Stuttgart, 1966).

Kriegswirtschaft und Rüstung 1939–1945, ed. Friedrich Forstmeier and Hans-Erich Volkmann (Düsseldorf, 1977).

Krieg und Krieger, ed. Ernst Jünger (Berlin, 1930).

KROCKOW, Count CHRISTIAN VON, *Scheiterhaufen: Größe und Elend des deutschen Geistes* (Berlin, 1983).

KROLL, GERHARD, *Von der Weltwirtschaftskrise zur Staatskonjunktur* (Berlin, 1958).

KRUEDENER, JÜRGEN, 'Zielkonflikt in der nationalsozialistischen Agrarpolitik: Ein Beitrag zur Diskussion des Leistungsproblems in zentralgelenkten Wirtschaftssystemen', *Zeitschrift für Wirtschafts- und Sozialwissenschaften* (1974), 335–61.

KRÜGER, ANNELIESE, *Der berufsständische Gedanke in der Wirtschaftsorganisation des Nationalsozialismus* (diss. Münster and Quakenbrück, 1936).

KRÜGER, ARND, *Die Olympischen Spiele 1936 und die Weltmeinung: Ihre außenpolitische Bedeutung unter besonderer Berücksichtigung der USA* (Sportwissenschaftliche Arbeiten, 7; Berlin, Munich, and Frankfurt am Main, 1972).

KRÜGER, PETER, *Deutschland und die Reparationen 1918/19: Die Genesis des Reparationsproblems in Deutschland zwischen Waffenstillstand und Versailler Friedensschluß* (Schriftenreihe der *Vierteljahrshefte für Zeitgeschichte*, 25; Stuttgart, 1973).

—— 'Friedenssicherung und deutsche Revisionspolitik: Die deutsche Außenpolitik und die Verhandlungen über den Kellogg-Pakt', *VfZG* 22 (1974), 227–57.

—— *Die Außenpolitik der Republik von Weimar* (Darmstadt, 1985).

—— and Hahn, Erich J., 'Der Loyalitätskonflikt des Staatssekretärs Wilhelm von Bülow im Frühjahr 1933', *VfZG* 20 (1972), 376–410.

KUBE, ALFRED, *Pour le mérite und Hakenkreuz: Hermann Göring im Dritten Reich* (Quellen und Darstellungen zur Zeitgeschichte, 24; Munich, 1986).

KUCZYNSKI, JÜRGEN, *Studien zur Geschichte des staatsmonopolistischen Kapitalismus in Deutschland 1918 bis 1945* (=id., *Die Geschichte der Lage der Arbeiter unter dem Kapitalismus*, xvi; East Berlin, 1963).

—— *Darstellung der Lage der Arbeiter unter dem Kapitalismus*, vi/1. *Darstellung der Lage der Arbeiter in Deutschland von 1933 bis 1945* (East Berlin, 1964).

KUCZYNSKI, THOMAS, *Das Ende der Weltwirtschaftskrise in Deutschland 1932/33* (diss. East Berlin, 1972).

—— 'Die unterschiedlichen wirtschaftspolitischen Konzeptionen des deutschen Imperialismus zur Überwindung der Wirtschaftskrise in Deutschland 1932/33 und deren Effektivität', in *Wirtschaft und Staat im Imperialismus* (q.v.), 215–51.

KÜGELGEN, CARLO VON, 'Deutschland-Rußland: Die Entwicklungsmöglichkeiten des deutsch-russischen Handels mit der Sowjetunion', *Deutsche Wirtschaftszeitung*, 37 (1940), 44–6.

KUHN, AXEL, *Hitlers außenpolitisches Programm: Entstehung und Entwicklung 1919–1933* (Stuttgarter Beiträge zur Geschichte und Politik, 5; Stuttgart, 1970).

—— 'Das nationalsozialistische Deutschland und die Sowjetunion', in *Hitler, Deutschland und die Mächte* (q.v.), 639–53.

KÜHN, HELMUT, *Die Verlagerungen in der deutschen Lebensmittel- und Rohstoffeinfuhr 1933 bis 1938 (Ein Problem nationalsozialistischer Außenhandelspolitik)* (diss. Berlin, Würzburg, and Aumühl, 1939).

KÜHNL, REINHARD, *Die nationalsozialistische Linke 1925-1930* (Marburger Abhandlungen zur politischen Wissenschaft, 6, Meisenheim am Glan, 1966).

—— Zur Programmatik der nationalsozialistischen Linken: Das Strasser-Programm von 1925/26', *VfZG* 16 (1966), 317-33.

—— *Der deutsche Faschismus in Quellen und Dokumenten* (Kleine Bibliothek: Politik, Wissenschaft, Zukunft, 62; Cologne, 1975).

KUPISCH, KARL, 'Strömungen der Evangelischen Kirche in der Weimarer Republik', *Archiv für Sozialgeschichte*, ed. by the Friedrich-Ebert-Stiftung, 11 (1971), 373-415.

LADEMACHER, HORST, 'Gewalt der Legalität oder Legalität der Gewalt: Zur Theorie und Politik der SPD von Kiel (1927) bis Prag (1934)', in *Frieden, Gewalt, Sozialismus* (q.v.), 404-60.

Lageberichte der Geheimen Staatspolizei über die Provinz Hessen-Nassau 1933-1936, Die, ed. Thomas Klein (Veröffentlichungen aus den Archiven Preußischer Kulturbesitz, 22/1, 2; Cologne and Vienna, 1986).

Lagevorträge des Oberbefehlshabers der Kriegsmarine vor Hitler 1939-1945, ed. Gerhard Wagner (Munich, 1972).

LAMPE, ADOLF, *Allgemeine Wehrwirtschaftslehre* (Jena, 1938).

LANGE, KARL, 'Der Terminus "Lebensraum" in Hitlers "Mein Kampf"', *VfZG* 13 (1965), 426-37.

—— *Hitlers unbeachtete Maximen: 'Mein Kampf' und die Öffentlichkeit* (Geschichte und Gegenwart; Stuttgart, Berlin, Cologne, and Mainz, 1968).

LÄRMER, KARL, *Autobahnbau in Deutschland 1933-1945: Zu den Hintergründen* (East Berlin, 1975).

LAURENS, FRANKLIN D., *France and the Italo-Ethiopian Crisis 1935-1936* (The Hague, 1967).

Lautlose Aufstand, Der: Bericht über die Widerstandsbewegung des deutschen Volkes 1933-1945, ed. Günther Weisenborn, enlarged and rev. edn. (Hamburg, 1954).

LEAGUE OF NATIONS, *Conference for the Reduction and Limitation of Armaments*, Series B. *Minutes of the General Commission*, ii (Geneva, 1933).

—— *Conference for the Reduction and Limitation of Armaments, Draft Convention Submitted by the United Kingdom Delegation* (Geneva, 1933).

Lebensgeschichte und Sozialkultur im Ruhrgebiet 1930-1969, ed. Lutz Niethammer, i. *'Die Jahre weiß man nicht, wo man die heute hinsetzen soll': Faschismuserfahrungen im Ruhrgebiet* (Berlin and Bonn, 1983).

LE BON, GUSTAV, *La Psychologie des foules* (Paris, 1895). [Trans, *The Crowd: A Study of the Popular Mind* (London, 1896).]

LEEB, Generalfeldmarschall WILHELM RITTER VON, *Tagebuchaufzeichnungen und Lagebeurteilungen aus zwei Weltkriegen*, ed. from his papers and with a biographical note by Georg Meyer (Beiträge zur Militär- und Kriegsgeschichte, 16; Stuttgart, 1976).

LEMHÖFER, LUTZ, 'Gegen den gottlosen Bolschewismus: Zur Stellung der Kirchen zum Krieg gegen die Sowjetunion', in *'Unternehmen Barbarossa': Der deutsche Überfall auf die Sowjetunion 1941*, ed. Gerd. R. Ueberschär and Wolfram Wette (Paderborn, 1984), 131-9.

LENEL, HANS OTTO, *Ursachen der Konzentration: Unter besonderer Berücksichtigung der deutschen Verhältnisse*[2] (Wirtschaftswissenschaftliche und wirtschaftsrechtliche Untersuchungen, 2; Tübingen, 1968).

LENIN, VLADIMIR ILYICH, *Works*, 45 vols. (London, 1960-70).

LENK, KURT, *'Volk und Staat': Strukturwandel politischer Ideologien im 19. und 20. Jahrhundert* (Stuttgart etc., 1971).

LENZ, WILHELM, and KETTENACKER, LOTHAR, 'Lord Kemsleys Gespräch mit Hitler Ende Juli 1939', *VfZG* 19 (1971), 305–21.

LEUCHTENBURG, WILLIAM E., *Franklin D. Roosevelt and the New Deal: 1932–1939* (New York, 1963).

LEVINE, HERBERT S., *Hitler's Free City: A History of the Nazi Party in Danzig, 1925–39* (Chicago, 1973).

LEWY, GUENTHER, *The Catholic Church and Nazi Germany* (London and New York, 1964).

LEY, ROBERT, *Soldaten der Arbeit* (Munich, 1938).

L'HUILLIER, FERNAND, *Dialogues franco-allemands 1925–1933* (Publications de la Faculté des Lettres de l'Université de Strasbourg, Le petit format, 5; Paris, 1971).

LINK, WERNER, *Die amerikanische Stabilisierungspolitik in Deutschland 1921–1932* (Düsseldorf, 1970).

LINK, WILHELM, 'Deutsche Außenhandelspolitik', in *Nationalsozialistisches Denken und Wirtschaft*, ed. Rudolf Heinel *et al.* (Kulturpolitische Schriftenreihe, 3; Stuttgart, 1932), 71–88.

LINNEBACH, KARL, *Die Wehrwissenschaften, ihr Begriff und ihr System: Im Auftrag der deutschen Gesellschaft für Wehrpolitik und Wehrwissenschaften* (Berlin, 1939).

LIPGENS, WALTER, 'Europäische Einigungsidee 1923–1930 und Briands Europaplan im Urteil deutscher Akten', *HZ* 203 (1966), 46–89, 316–63.

LIPSKI, JÓZEF, *Diplomat in Berlin 1933–1939: Papers and Memoirs of Józef Lipski, Ambassador of Poland*, ed. Waclaw Jędrzejewicz (New York, 1968).

Locarno und die Weltpolitik 1924–1932, ed. H. Rössler (Göttingen, 1969).

LONDONDERRY, Marquess of, *Ourselves and Germany* (London, 1938).

LOOCK, HANS-DIETRICH, 'Nordeuropa zwischen Außenpolitik und "großgermanischer" Innenpolitik', in *Hitler, Deutschland und die Mächte* (q.v.), 684–706.

LOWENTHAL, MARK M., 'Roosevelt and the Coming of the War: The Search for United States Policy 1937–42', *JCH* 16/3 (1981), 413–40.

LÜDECKE, HELLMUT, *Die Sicherung der wirtschaftlichen Unabhängigkeit Großdeutschlands (Ein Beitrag zur Klärung des Autarkieproblems)* (diss. Vienna and Würzburg, 1939).

LUDENDORFF, F. W. ERICH, *Meine Kriegserinnerungen 1914–1918* (Berlin, 1919). [Trans. *My War Memories 1914–1918* (London, 1919).]

—— *Der totale Krieg* (Munich, 1935). [Trans. A. S. Rappoport, *The Nation at War* (London, 1936).]

LUDWIG, KARL-HEINZ, *Technik und Ingenieure im Dritten Reich* (Düsseldorf, 1974).

—— 'Strukturmerkmale nationalsozialistischer Aufrüstung bis 1935', in *Wirtschaft und Rüstung* (q.v.), 39–64.

LUKÁCS, GYÖRGY, *Die Zerstörung der Vernunft: Der Weg des Irrationalismus von Schelling zu Hitler* (Berlin, 1955). [Trans. of *Az ész trónfosztása: As irracionalista filozófia kritikája* (Budapest, 1954).]

LUNDGREEN, PETER, *Die englische Appeasement-Politik bis zum Münchener Abkommen: Voraussetzungen, Konzeption, Durchführung* (Studien zur europäischen Geschichte, 7; Berlin, 1969).

LÜTTGENS, CARL-MAX, *Autarkie und Arbeitsbeschaffung* (Berlin, 1932).

LUTZ, GÜNTHER, *Das Gemeinschaftserlebnis in der Kriegsliteratur* (diss. Greifswald, 1936).

LUTZ, HENRICH, *Demokratie im Zwielicht: Der Weg der deutschen Katholiken aus dem Kaiserreich in die Republik 1914 bis 1925* (Munich, 1963).

MAAS, LIESELOTTE, *Handbuch der deutschen Exilpresse: 1933–1945*, i. *Bibliographie A–K* (Munich, 1975).

MACDONALD, C. A., *The United States, Britain and Appeasement, 1936–1939* (New York, 1981).

Machtbewußtsein in Deutschland am Vorabend des Zweiten Weltkrieges, ed. Franz Knipping and Klaus-Jürgen Müller (Sammlung Schöningh zur Geschichte und Gegenwart; Paderborn, 1984).

MACKSEY, KENNETH J., *Guderian, Panzer General* (London, 1975).

McSHERRY, JAMES E., *Stalin, Hitler and Europe*, i. *The Origins of World War II: 1933–1939* (Cleveland and New York, 1968).

MÄGERLEIN, HEINZ, *Der Wehrsport: Nach den Richtlinien des Reichskuratoriums für Jugendertüchtigung* (Lehrmeister-Bücherei, 975; Leipzig, 1933).

MAIER, KLAUS A., *Guernica, 26.4.1937: Die deutsche Intervention und der 'Fall Guernica'* (Einzelschriften zur militärischen Geschichte des Zweiten Weltkrieges, 17; Freiburg i.Br., 1975).

—— 'Der Aufbau der Luftwaffe und ihre strategisch-operative Konzeption, insbesondere gegenüber Frankreich' (MS for symposium of German and French historians in Bonn, 26–9 Sept. 1978).

—— 'Total War and German Air Doctrine before the Second World War', in *The German Military in the Age of Total War* (q.v.), 210–19.

MANGELS, 'Facharbeitermangel und Bekämpfung der Arbeitslosigkeit', *Der Vierjahresplan*, 1 (1937), 349–51.

MANN, THOMAS, *Schriften zur Politik*, selected by Walter Boehlich (Bibliothek Suhrkamp, 243; Frankfurt am Main, 1973).

MANNE, ROBERT, 'The Foreign Office and the Failure of Anglo-Soviet Rapprochement', *JCH* 16/4 (1981), 725–55.

—— 'Some British Light on the Nazi–Soviet Pact', *European Studies Review*, 11 (1981), 83–102.

MANSFELD, WERNER, 'Grundsätze einer realen Lohnpolitik', *Der Vierjahresplan*, 6 (1942), 29–31.

MANSILLA, H. C. F., *Faschismus und eindimensionale Gesellschaft* (Sammlung Luchterhand, 18; Neuwied and Berlin, 1971).

MANSTEIN, ERICH VON, *Aus einem Soldatenleben: 1887–1939* (Bonn, 1958).

MARCON, HELMUT, *Arbeitsbeschaffungspolitik der Regierungen Papen und Schleicher: Grundsteinlegungen für die Beschäftigungspolitik im Dritten Reich* (Moderne Geschichte, 3; Berne and Frankfurt am Main, 1974).

MARGUERAT, PHILIPPE, *Le IIIᵉ Reich et le pétrole roumain 1938–1940: Contribution à l'étude de la pénétration économique allemande dans les Balkans à la veille et au début de la Seconde Guerre mondiale* (Geneva and Leiden, 1977).

MARTENS, ERIKA, *Zum Beispiel 'Das Reich': Zur Phänomenologie der Presse im totalitären Regime* (Cologne, 1972).

MARTENS, STEFAN, *Hermann Göring: 'Erster Paladin des Führers' und 'Zweiter Mann im Reich'* (Sammlung Schöningh zur Geschichte und Gegenwart; Paderborn, 1985).

MARTIN, BERND, 'Die deutsch-japanischen Beziehungen während des Dritten Reiches', in *Hitler, Deutschland und die Mächte* (q.v.), 454–70.

—— 'Japans Weg in den Krieg: Bemerkungen über Forschungsstand und Literatur zur japanischen Zeitgeschichte', *MGM* 23 (1978), 183–209.

—— 'Das deutsche Militär und die Wendung der deutschen Fernostpolitik von China auf Japan', in *Machtbewußtsein in Deutschland* (q.v.), 191–207.

MASER, WERNER, *Adolf Hitler: Legende—Mythos—Wirklichkeit* (Munich, 1971). [Trans. Peter and Betty Ross, *Hitler* (London, 1973).]

MASON, TIMOTHY W., *Arbeiterklasse und Volksgemeinschaft: Dokumente und Materialien zur deutschen Arbeiterpolitik 1936–1939* (Schriften des Zentralinstituts für sozialwissenschaftliche Forschung der Freien Universität Berlin, 22; Opladen, 1975).

MASSAKAS, ALEXANDER, *Präferenzzölle als Mittel der Annäherungspolitik der bedeutendsten Wirtschaftsgebiete Europas* (diss. Königsberg, 1933).

MASTNY, VOJTECH, *The Czechs under Nazi Rule: The Failure of National Resistance* (New York and London, 1971).

MATTHIAS, ERICH, *Sozialdemokratie und Nation: Ein Beitrag zur Ideengeschichte der sozialdemokratischen Emigration in der Prager Zeit des Parteivorstandes 1933–1938* (Stuttgart, 1952).

—— 'Die Sozialdemokratische Partei Deutschlands', in *Das Ende der Parteien* (q.v.), 101–278.

—— 'Der Untergang der alten Sozialdemokratie 1933', in *Von Weimar zu Hitler* (q.v.), 281–316.

MATZ, ULRICH, *Politik und Gewalt: Zur Theorie des demokratischen Verfassungsstaates und der Revolution* (Freiburg i.Br. and Munich, 1975).

MAURER, EMIL, *Grundlagen und Zukunft der deutschen Nationalwirtschaft* (Leipzig, 1932).

MAXELON, MICHAEL-OLAF, *Stresemann und Frankreich: 1914–1929. Deutsche Politik der Ost-West-Balance* (Geschichtliche Studien zu Politik und Gesellschaft, 5; Düsseldorf, 1972).

MEIER, MANFRED, *Deutsche Außenhandelsregulierung von 1933 bis 1939* (diss. Basle and Bergen-Enkheim, 1956).

MEIER-DÖRNBERG, WILHELM, *Die Ölversorgung der Kriegsmarine 1935–1945* (Einzelschriften zur militärischen Geschichte des Zweiten Weltkrieges, 11; Freiburg i.Br., 1973).

MEIER-WELCKER, HANS, 'Aus dem Briefwechsel zweier junger Offiziere des Reichsheeres 1930–1938', *MGM* 14 (1973), 57–100.

MEINCK, GERHARD, 'Der Reichsverteidigungsrat', *WWR* 6 (1956), 411–22.

—— *Hitler und die deutsche Aufrüstung 1933–1937* (Veröffentlichungen des Instituts für Europäische Geschichte Mainz, 19; Wiesbaden, 1956).

MEINECKE, FRIEDRICH, *Die deutsche Katastrophe* (Wiesbaden, 1946). [Trans. Sidney B. Fay, *The German Catastrophe: Reflections and Recollections* (Cambridge, Mass., 1959).]

MEINHOLD, WILLY, *Grundlagen der landwirtschaftlichen Marktordnung* (Berichte über Landwirtschaft, NS, spec. No. 134; Berlin, 1937).

—— 'Volkswirtschaftliche Grundsätze der Preisbildungspolitik im Vierjahresplan', *Jahrbücher für Nationalökonomie und Statistik*, 150 (1939), 569–91.

—— *Die landwirtschaftlichen Erzeugungsbedingungen im Kriege* (Jena, 1941).

Meldungen aus dem Reich 1938–1945: Die geheimen Lageberichte des Sicherheitsdienstes der SS, ed. Heinz Boberach, 17 vols. (Herrsching, 1984–5).

MELZER, ROLF, *Studien zur Agrarpolitik der faschistischen deutschen Imperialisten in Deutschland im System der Kriegsplanung und Kriegführung 1933 bis 1941* (diss. Rostock, 1966).

MENDELSSOHN, PETER DE, *Die Nürnberger Dokumente: Studien zur deutschen Kriegspolitik 1937–45* (Hamburg, 1947).

MERKEL, HANS, *Agrarpolitik* (Leipzig, 1942).

—— and WÖHRMANN, OTTO, *Deutsches Bauernrecht*[3] (Neugestaltung von Recht und Wirtschaft, 32. 2; Leipzig, 1940).

MERKES, MANFRED, *Die deutsche Politik gegenüber dem spanischen Bürgerkrieg 1936–1939*, 2nd rev. and enlarged edn. (Bonner historische Forschungen, 18; Bonn, 1969).

MESSERSCHMIDT, MANFRED, 'Organisation und Entwicklung der "Öffenlichkeitsarbeit" in

Reichswehr und Wehrmacht: Pressearbeit, Wehrpropaganda, Zensur 1919–1945', typed memorandum (Freiburg i.Br., 1969).

MISSERSCHMIDT, MANFRED, 'Zur Militärseelsorgepolitik im Zweiten Weltkrieg', *MGM* 5 (1969), 37–85.

—— *Die Wehrmacht im NS-Staat: Zeit der Indoktrination* (Hamburg, 1969).

—— 'Revision, Neue Ordnung, Krieg: Akzente der Völkerrechtswissenschaft in Deutschland 1933–1945', *MGM* 9 (1971), 61–95.

—— *Militär und Politik in der Bismarckzeit und im Wilhelminischen Deutschland* (Erträge der Forschung, 43; Darmstadt, 1975).

—— 'Das strategische Lagebild des OKW (Hitler) im Jahre 1938', in *Machtbewußtsein in Deutschland* (q.v.), 145–58.

—— *et al.*, '*Tableau de la situation stratégique chez les dirigeants allemands en 1938*', in *La Puissance en Europe* (q.v.), 105–26.

METZMACHER, HELMUT, 'Deutsch-englische Ausgleichsbemühungen im Sommer 1939', *VfZG* 14 (1966), 369–412.

MEYERS, REINHARD, *Britische Sicherheitspolitik 1934–1938: Studien zum außen- und sicherheitspolitischen Entscheidungsprozeß* (Bonner Schriften zur Politik und Zeitgeschichte, 11; Düsseldorf, 1976).

MICHALKA, WOLFGANG, 'Die nationalsozialistische Außenpolitik im Zeichen eines "Konzeptionen-Pluralismus": Fragestellungen und Forschungsaufgaben', in *Hitler, Deutschland und die Mächte* (q.v.), 46–62.

—— 'Widerstand oder Landesverrat? Literaturbericht', *MGM* 21 (1977), 207–14.

—— *Ribbentrop und die deutsche Weltpolitik 1933–1940: Außenpolitische Konzeptionen und Entscheidungsprozesse im Dritten Reich* (Veröffentlichungen des Historischen Instituts der Universität Mannheim, 5; Munich, 1980).

—— 'Machtpolitik und Machtbewußtsein politischer Entscheidungsträger in Deutschland 1938', in *Machtbewußtsein in Deutschland* (q.v.), 59–74.

MICHALON, C., and VERNET, C., 'L'armée française et la crise du 7 mars 1936' (MS for Franco-German symposium in Paris, 1978).

MIDDLEMAS, KEITH, *Diplomacy of Illusion: The British Government and Germany, 1937–39* (London, 1972).

MILATZ, ALFRED, *Wähler und Wahlen in der Weimarer Republik*² (Bonn, 1968).

'Miles' (i.e. HERBERT ROSINSKI), *Deutschlands Kriegsbereitschaft und Kriegsaussichten?* (Zurich and New York, 1939).

Militär und Militarismus in der Weimarer Republik, ed. Klaus-Jürgen Müller and Eckhardt Opitz (Düsseldorf, 1978).

MILWARD, ALAN S., *The German Economy at War* (London, 1965).

MISCH, CARL, *Gesamtverzeichnis der Ausbürgerungslisten 1933–1938: Nach dem amtlichen Abdruck des Reichsanzeigers* (Paris, 1939).

MISSALLA, HEINRICH, '*Gott mit uns*': *Die deutsche katholische Kriegspredigt 1914–1918* (Munich, 1968).

Mit dem Gesicht nach Deutschland: Eine Dokumentation über die sozialdemokratische Emigration. Aus dem Nachlaß Friedrich Stampfers ergänzt durch andere Überlieferungen, ed. Erich Matthias, rev. Werner Link (Düsseldorf, 1968).

MITROVIĆ, ANDREJ, 'Ergänzungswirtschaft: The Theory of an Integrated Economic Area of the Third Reich and Southeast Europe (1933–1941)', in *The Third Reich and Yugoslavia 1933–1945* (Belgrade, 1977), 7–45.

MODEL, HANSGEORG, *Der deutsche Generalstabsoffizier: Seine Auswahl und Ausbildung in Reichswehr, Wehrmacht und Bundeswehr* (Frankfurt am Main, 1968).

MOHLER, ARMIN, *Die Konservative Revolution in Deutschland 1918–1932: Ein Handbuch*, 2nd rev. and enlarged ed. (Darmstadt, 1972).

MÖLLER, HORST, *Exodus der Kultur: Schriftsteller, Wissenschaftler und Künstler in der Emigration nach 1933* (Beck'sche schwarze Reihe, 293; Munich, 1984).

MOLTKE, Count HELMUTH VON, *Gesammelte Schriften und Denkwürdigkeiten des Generalfeldmarschalls Grafen Helmuth v. Moltke*, iii (Berlin, 1892–3).

MOLTMANN, GÜNTER, 'Weltherrschaftsideen Hitlers', in *Europa und Übersee: Festschrift für Egmont Zechlin*, ed. Otto Brunner and Dietrich Gerhard (Hamburg, 1961), 197–240.

—— 'Franklin D. Roosevelts Friedensappell vom 14. April 1939: Ein fehlgeschlagener Versuch zur Friedenssicherung', *Jahrbuch für Amerikastudien* (1964), 91–109.

—— 'Die weltpolitische Lage 1936–1939: Die USA', in *Weltpolitik 1933–1939* (q.v.), 146–66.

MOMMSEN, HANS, 'Der Reichstagsbrand und seine politischen Folgen', *VfZG* 12 (1964), 351–413.

—— *Beamtentum im Dritten Reich: Mit ausgewählten Quellen zur nationalsozialistischen Beamtenpolitik* (Schriftenreihe der *Vierteljahrshefte für Zeitgeschichte*, 13; Stuttgart, 1966). 1966).

—— review of Hans-Adolf Jacobsen, *Nationalsozialistische Außenpolitik 1933 bis 1938*, in *MGM* 7 (1970), 180–5.

—— 'Nationalsozialismus', in *Sowjetsystem und demokratische Gesellschaft: Eine vergleichende Enzyklopädie*, ed. C. D. Kernig, iv. *Lenin bis Periodisierung* (Freiburg i.Br., Basle, and Vienna, 1971), 695–713.

MORITZ, A., 'Wertvolle Ergänzungen der Erzeugungsschlacht', *Der Vierjahresplan*, 3 (1939), 117–19.

MORSEY, RUDOLF, 'Die Deutsche Zentrumspartei', in *Das Ende der Parteien 1933* (q.v.), 281–453.

—— *Der Untergang des politischen Katholizismus: Die Zentrumspartei zwischen christlichem Selbstverständnis und 'Nationaler Erhebung' 1932/33* (Stuttgart and Zurich, 1977).

MOYER, L. V., *The Kraft durch Freude Movement in Nazi Germany, 1933–1939* (Ann Arbor, 1984).

MUELLER-HILLEBRAND, BURKHART, *Das Heer 1933–1945: Entwicklung des organisatorischen Aufbaues*, i. *Das Heer bis zum Kriegsbeginn* (Darmstadt, 1954).

MÜLLER, GEORG WILHELM, *Das Reichsministerium für Volksaufklärung und Propaganda* (Berlin, 1940).

MÜLLER, HELMUT, *Die Zentralbank: Eine Nebenregierung. Reichsbankpräsident Hjalmar Schacht als Politiker der Weimarer Republik* (Schriften zur politischen Wirtschafts- und Gesellschaftslehre, 5; Opladen, 1973).

MÜLLER, KLAUS-JÜRGEN, 'Reichswehr und "Röhm-Affäre": Aus den Akten des Wehrkreiskommandos (Bayer.) VII', *MGM* 3 (1968), 107–44.

—— *Das Heer und Hitler: Armee und nationalsozialistisches Regime 1933–1940* (Beiträge zur Militär- und Kriegsgeschichte, 10; Stuttgart, 1969).

—— 'Staat und Politik im Denken Ludwig Becks', *HZ* 215 (1972), 607–31.

—— *Armee, Politik und Gesellschaft in Deutschland 1933–1945: Studien zum Verhältnis von Armee und NS-System* (Sammlung Schöningh zur Geschichte und Gegenwart; Paderborn, 1979).

—— 'Militärpolitik in der Krise: Zur militärpolitischen Konzeption des deutschen Heeres-Generalstabes 1938', in *Deutscher Konservatismus im 19. und 20. Jahrhundert: Festschrift für Fritz Fischer*, ed. Dirk Stegmann *et al.* (Bonn, 1983), 333–45.

MÜLLER, KLAUS-JÜRGEN, 'Militärpolitische Konzeptionen des deutschen Generalstabes 1938', in *Machtbewußtsein in Deutschland* (q.v.), 159–74.

—— 'Die Reichswehr und die "Machtergreifung" ', in *Nationalsozialistische Machtergreifung* (q.v.), 137–51.

—— *General Ludwig Beck: Studien und Dokumente zur politisch-militärischen Vorstellungswelt und Tätigkeit des Generalstabschefs des deutschen Heeres 1933-1938* (Schriften des Bundesarchivs, 30; Boppard, 1980).

MÜLLER, ROLF-DIETER, *Das Tor zur Weltmacht: Die Bedeutung der Sowjetunion für die deutsche Wirtschafts- und Rüstungspolitik zwischen den Weltkriegen* (Wehrwissenschaftliche Forschungen, Abt. Militärgeschichtliche Studien, 32; Boppard, 1984).

MURAWSKI, ERICH, *Die Presse als Hilfsmittel zur Wehrerziehung* (Stuttgart, 1937).

MURRAY, WILLIAMSON, 'German Air Power and the Munich Crisis', *War and Society*, 2 (1977), 107–18.

—— 'The German Response to Victory in Poland: A Case Study in Professionalism', *Armed Forces and Society*, 7/2 (1981), 285–98.

—— *The Change in the European Balance of Power, 1938-1939: The Path to Ruin* (Princeton, 1984).

NADOLNY, RUDOLF, *Mein Beitrag* (Wiesbaden, 1955).

NAMIER, LEWIS B., *Diplomatic Prelude 1938-1939* (London, 1948).

Nationale Arbeit: Das Zentrum und sein Wirken in der deutschen Republik, ed. Karl Anton Schulte (Berlin and Leipzig, 1929).

Nationale Außenpolitik: Rede, gehalten auf der Reichsführertagung der DNVP zu Berlin am 25. Juni 1932 von Dr. Freiherrn von Freytagh-Loringhoven (Deutschnationale Flugschrift, 369; Berlin, 1932).

'Nationale Handelspolitik statt Weltwirtschaftspolitik: Programmatische Forderungen der NSDAP', *Neue Wirtschaft*, 6/15 (1932), 6–8.

Nationalsozialistische Außenpolitik, ed. Wolfgang Michalka (Wege der Forschung, 297; Darmstadt, 1978).

Nationalsozialistische Diktatur 1933-1945: Eine Bilanz, ed. Karl Dietrich Bracher, Manfred Funke, and Hans-Adolf Jacobsen (Schriftenreihe der Bundeszentrale für politische Bildung, 192; Bonn, 1983).

Nationalsozialistische Machtergreifung, Die, ed. Wolfgang Michalka (Paderborn etc., 1984).

NEEBE, REINHARDT, *Großindustrie, Staat und NSDAP 1930-1933: Paul Silverberg und der Reichsverband der Deutschen Industrie in der Krise der Weimarer Republik* (Kritische Studien zur Geschichtswissenschaft, 45; Göttingen, 1981).

NEHRING, WALTHER K., *Die Geschichte der deutschen Panzerwaffe 1916 bis 1945* (Berlin, 1969).

NELL-BREUNING, OSWALD VON, 'Autarkie', *Stimmen der Zeit*, 63/124 (1932), 28–39.

1933: Wie die Republik der Diktatur erlag, ed. Volker Rittberger (Stuttgart etc., 1983).

NICLAUSS, KARLHEINZ, *Die Sowjetunion und Hitlers Machtergreifung: Eine Studie über die deutsch-russischen Beziehungen der Jahre 1929 bis 1935* (Bonner Historische Forschungen, 29; Bonn, 1966).

NIEDHART, GOTTFRIED, *Großbritannien und die Sowjetunion 1934-1939* (Munich, 1972).

—— (ed.), *Kriegsbeginn 1939: Entfesselung oder Ausbruch des Zweiten Weltkrieges?* (Wege der Forschung, 374; Darmstadt, 1976).

—— 'Weltherrschaft versus World Appeasement', *Neue Politische Literatur*, 23 (1978), 281–91.

NITSCHKE, NUGENT, *Der Feind: Erlebnis, Theorie und Begegnung. Formen politischen Handelns im 20. Jahrhundert* (Stuttgart, 1964).

NOLTE, ERNST, *Der Faschismus in seiner Epoche: Die Action française. Der italienische Faschismus. Der Nationalsozialismus* (Munich, 1963). [Trans. Leila Vennewitz, *Three Faces of Fascism* (London, 1965).]

Nürnberger Prozeß, Der: Aus den Protokollen, Dokumenten und Materialen des Prozesses gegen die Hauptkriegsverbrecher vor dem Internationalen Militärgerichtshof³, selected with intro. by P. A. Steininger, 2 vols. (East Berlin, 1958).

NUSS, KARL, and SPERLING, HEINZ, 'Eine Rüstungskonzeption des deutschen Generalstabes aus dem Jahre 1934', *Militärgeschichte*, 17 (1978), 203-13.

OBST, ERICH, *Die Großraumidee in der Vergangenheit und als tragender politischer Gedanke unserer Zeit* (Vorträge der Friedrich-Wilhelms-Universität zu Breslau im Kriegswinter 1940-1; Breslau, 1941).

OEHME, WALTER, and CARO, KURT, *Kommt das Dritte Reich?* (Berlin, 1930).

OESTERHELD, ALFRED, *Wirtschaftsraum Europa* (Oldenburg and Berlin, 1942).

OESTREICH, PAUL, *Walther Funk: Ein Leben für die Wirtschaft* (Munich, 1940).

Offiziere im Bild von Dokumenten aus drei Jahrhunderten (Beiträge zur Militär- und Kriegsgeschichte, 6; Stuttgart, 1964).

OFFNER, ARNOLD A., *American Appeasement: United States Foreign Policy and Germany, 1933-1938* (Cambridge, Mass., 1969).

O'NEILL, ROBERT J., *The German Army and the Nazi Party 1933-1939* (London, 1966).

OSSIETZKY, CARL VON, 'Abschied von Stresemann' (1929), in *Gustav Stresemann, Schriften*, with preface by Willy Brandt, ed. Arnold Harttung (Schriften großer Berliner; Berlin, 1976), 409-11.

—— 'Die Pazifisten', in id., *Rechenschaft: Publizistik aus den Jahren 1912-1933*, ed. Bruno Frei (Frankfurt am Main, 1972), 38-42.

Osteuropa-Handbuch: Sowjetunion. Außenpolitik 1917-1955, ed. Dietrich Geyer (Cologne and Vienna, 1972).

OVERY, RICHARD JAMES, 'The German Pre-war Aircraft Production Plans: November 1936-April 1939', *English Historical Review*, 90 (1975), 778-97.

—— 'Hitler's War and the German Economy: A Reinterpretation', *Economic History Review*, 35/2 (1982), 272-91.

—— *Göring: 'The Iron Man'* (London, 1984).

PARKER, R. A. C., 'British Rearmament 1936-39: Treasury, Trade Unions and Skilled Labour', *English Historical Review*, 96 (1981), 306-43.

—— 'Perceptions de la puissance par les décideurs britanniques 1938-1939: Le Cabinet', in *La Puissance en Europe* (q.v.), 45-54.

Parteitag der Arbeit vom 6. bis 13. Sept. 1937, Der: Offizieller Bericht über den Verlauf des [9.] Reichsparteitages mit sämtlichen Kongreßreden (Munich, 1938).

Parteitag der Ehre vom 8.-14. September 1936, Der: Offizieller Bericht über den Verlauf des Reichsparteitages mit sämtlichen Kongreßreden² (Munich, 1936).

Parteitag der Freiheit vom 10. bis 16. September 1935, Der⁴ (Munich, 1936).

Pazifismus: Stellung der D.D.P. zum Pazifismus, ed. by the national headquarters of the German Democratic Party (Schriftenreihe für politische Werbung, Deutsche Demokratische Partei, 12; Berlin, 1928).

Pazifismus in der Weimarer Republik: Beiträge zur historischen Friedensforschung, ed. Karl Holl and Wolfram Wette (Sammlung Schöningh zur Geschichte und Gegenwart; Paderborn, 1981).

PEDEN, G. C., *British Rearmament and the Treasury, 1932-1939* (Edinburgh, 1979).

PEDEN, G. C., 'The Burden of Imperial Defence and the Commitment Reconsidered', *Historical Journal*, 27/2 (1984), 405–23.

PENTZLIN, HEINZ, *Hjalmar Schacht: Leben und Wirken einer umstrittenen Persönlichkeit* (Berlin, Frankfurt am Main, and Vienna, 1980).

PESE, WALTER WERNER, 'Hitler und Italien 1920–1926', *VfZG* 3 (1955), 113–26.

PETERSEN, JENS, *Hitler–Mussolini: Die Entstehung der Achse Berlin–Rom 1933–1936* (Bibliothek des Deutschen Historischen Instituts in Rom, 43; Tübingen, 1973).

PETZINA, DIETMAR, 'Hauptprobleme der deutschen Wirtschaftspolitik 1932/33', *VfZG* 15 (1967), 18–55.

—— *Autarkiepolitik im Dritten Reich: Der nationalsozialistische Vierjahresplan (1936–1942)* (Schriftenreihe der *Vierteljahrshefte für Zeitgeschichte*, 16; Stuttgart, 1968).

—— 'Die Mobilisierung deutscher Arbeitskräfte vor und während des Zweiten Weltkrieges', *VfZG* 18/4 (1970), 443–55.

—— *Die deutsche Wirtschaft in der Zwischenkriegszeit* (Wiesbaden, 1977).

—— ABELSHAUSER, WERNER, and FAUST, ANSELM, *Sozialgeschichtliches Arbeitsbuch*, iii. *Materialen zur Statistik des Deutschen Reiches 1914–1945* (Statistische Arbeitsbücher zur neueren deutschen Geschichte; Munich, 1978).

PFAFF, ALFRED, *Der Wirtschafts-Aufbau im Dritten Reich* (Munich, 1932).

PHELPS, REGINALD H., 'Hitler als Parteiredner im Jahre 1920', *VfZG* 11 (1963), 274–330.

Ploetz: Das Dritte Reich. Ursprünge, Ereignisse, Wirkungen, ed. Martin Broszat and Norbert Frei (Freiburg i.Br. and Würzburg, 1983).

PLUM, GÜNTER, *Gesellschaftsstruktur und politisches Bewußtsein in einer katholischen Region 1928–1933: Untersuchung am Beispiel des Regierungsbezirks Aachen* (Studien zur Zeitgeschichte, ed. by Institut für Zeitgeschichte; Stuttgart, 1972).

POHLE, HEINZ, *Der Rundfunk als Instrument der Politik: Zur Geschichte des deutschen Rundfunks von 1923 bis 1938* (Wissenschaftliche Schriftenreihe für Rundfunk und Fernsehen, 1; Hamburg, 1955).

POIDEVIN, RAYMOND, 'Vers une relance des relations économiques franco-allemandes 1938–1939', in *Deutschland und Frankreich 1936–1939: 15. Deutsch-französisches Historikerkolloquium des Deutschen Historischen Instituts Paris (Bonn, 26.–29. September 1979)*, ed. Klaus Hildebrand and Karl Ferdinand Werner (Beihefte der Francia, 10; Munich, 1981), 351–63.

—— and BARIÉTY, JACQUES, *Relations franco-allemandes 1815–1975* (Paris, 1977).

POLISH GOVERNMENT, *Official Documents Concerning Polish–German and Polish–Soviet Relations 1933–1939* (London, 1940).

POSSE, HANS-ERNST, 'Möglichkeiten der Großraumwirtschaft', *Die nationale Wirtschaft*, 1–2 (1933–4), 282–3.

POST, GAINES, Jun., *The Civil-Military Fabric of Weimar Foreign Policy* (Princeton, 1973).

PREDÖHL, ANDREAS, 'Die Epochenbedeutung der Weltwirtschaftskrise 1929 bis 1931', *VfZG* 1 (1953), 97–118.

PRESSEL, WILHELM, *Die Kriegspredigt 1914–1918 in der evangelischen Kirche Deutschlands* (Arbeiten zur Pastoraltheologie, ed. Martin Fischer and Robert Frick, 5; Göttingen, 1967).

Probleme der Geschichte des zweiten Weltkrieges: Referate und Diskussionen zum Thema: Die wichtigsten Richtungen der reaktionären Geschichtsschreibung über den 2. Weltkrieg, ed. Leo Stern (Kommission der Historiker der DDR und der UdSSR, *Protokoll der wissenschaftlichen Tagung in Leipzig vom 25.–30. November 1957*, ii; East Berlin, 1958).

Programme der deutschen Sozialdemokratie (1863–1863), ed. Bundessekretariat der Jungsozialisten (Hanover, 1963).

Pross, Helge, *Die deutsche akademische Emigration nach den Vereinigten Staaten 1933–1941* (Berlin, 1955).

Protektorat Böhmen und Mähren im deutschen Wirtschaftsraum, Das, ed. Volkswirtschaftliche Abteilung der Deutschen Bank (printed as manuscript early Apr. 1939).

Protokoll der Verhandlungen des XII. Parteitages der KPD (Berlin, 1929).

Protokoll des 6. Weltkongresses der kommunistischen Internationale, Moskau 1928, i. *Die internationale Lage und die Aufgaben der Komintern: Der Kampf gegen die imperialistische Kriegsgefahr* (Hamburg and Berlin, 1928).

Protokolle der Reichstagsfraktion und des Fraktionsvorstandes der deutschen Zentrumspartei 1926–1933, Die, ed. Rudolf Morsey (Veröffentlichungen der Kommission für Zeitgeschichte bei der Katholischen Akademie in Bayern, Series A, Quellen, 9; Mainz, 1969).

Prümm, Karl, *Die Literatur des Soldatischen Nationalismus der 20er Jahre (1918–1933): Gruppenideologie und Epochenproblematik*, 2 vols. (Theorie—Kritik—Geschichte, 3/1, 2; Kronberg (Taunus), 1974).

Puchert, Berthold, 'Die Entwicklung der deutsch-sowjetischen Handelsbeziehungen von 1918 bis 1939', *Jahrbuch für Wirtschaftsgeschichte* (1937), 4; 11–36.

Puissance en Europe 1938–1940, La, ed. René Girault and Robert Frank (Publications de la Sorbonne, international series, 23; Paris, 1984).

Quaroni, Pietro, *Valigia diplomatica: Ricordi di un ambasciatore* (Milan, 1956). [Trans. Anthony Rhodes, *Diplomatic Bags: An Ambassador's Memoirs* (London, 1956); German trans. *Diplomatengepäck* (Frankfurt am Main, 1956).]

Quartararo, Rosaria, *Roma tra Londra e Berlino: La politica estera fascista dal 1930 al 1940* (I fatti della storia. Saggi, 6; Rome, 1980).

Rahn, Werner, *Reichsmarine und Landesverteidigung 1919–1928: Konzeption und Führung der Marine in der Weimarer Republik* (Munich, 1976).

Rammstedt, Otthein (ed.), *Gewaltverhältnisse und die Ohnmacht der Kritik* (Frankfurt am Main, 1974).

Ránki, György, 'Das ungarische Wirtschaftsleben im Dienste der deutschen Kriegswirtschaft zur Zeit des zweiten Weltkrieges', in *Probleme der Geschichte des zweiten Weltkrieges* (East Berlin, 1958), 238–59.

Rasch, Manfred, 'Zur Mineralölpolitik der Kriegsmarine: Dokumente aus dem Jahre 1935', *MGM* 37 (1985), 71–101

Raupach, Hans, 'Strukturelle und institutionelle Auswirkungen der Weltwirtschaftskrise in Ost-Mitteleuropa', *VfZG* 24 (1976), 38–52.

Rauschning, Hermann, *Hitler Speaks* (London, 1939; repr. Vienna, 1973).

Rautenberg, Hans-Jürgen, *Deutsche Rüstungspolitik vom Beginn der Genfer Abrüstungskonferenz bis zur Wiedereinführung der allgemeinen Wehrpflicht 1932–1935* (diss. Bonn, 1973).

—— 'Drei Dokumente zur Planung eines 300.000 Mann-Friedensheeres aus dem Dezember 1933', *MGM* 22 (1977), 103–39.

—— and Wiggerhaus, N., 'Die "Himmeroder Denkschrift" vom Oktober 1950', *MGM* 21 (1977), 135–206.

Reden Hitlers als Kanzler, Die: Das junge Deutschland will Arbeit und Frieden (Munich, 1934).

Regierung Hitler, Die, ed. Karl-Heinz Minuth, pt. 1. *1933/34*, 2 vols. (Akten der Reichskanzlei: Regierung Hitler 1933–38; Boppard, 1983).

Reichhardt, Hans-Joachim, *Die Deutsche Arbeitsfront: Ein Beitrag zur Geschichte des nationalsozialistischen Deutschlands und zur Struktur des totalitären Herrschaftssystems* (diss. Berlin, 1956).

REICHHARDT, HANS-JOACHIM, 'Möglichkeiten und Grenzen des Widerstandes der Arbeiterbewegung', in *Der deutsche Widerstand* (q.v.), 169–213.

'Reichsparteitag und Wirtschaft', *Die nationale Wirtschaft*, 3 (1935), 291–9.

Reichstags-Handbuch, IV. Wahlperiode 1928 (Berlin, 1928).

REIMANN, VIKTOR, *Dr Joseph Goebbels* (Vienna, Munich, and Zurich, 1971).

REINHARDT, FRITZ, *Die Arbeitsschlacht der Reichsregierung* (Berlin, 1933).

REISCHLE, HERMANN, *Kann man Deutschland aushungern?* (Schriftenreihe der NSDAP, Series 2, 2; Berlin, 1940).

—— *Nationalsozialistische Agrarpolitik* (Großdeutsche Reihe; Munich, 1941).

Relations franco-allemandes 1933–1939, Les: Strasbourg, 7–10 octobre 1975 (Colloques internationaux du Centre National de la Recherche Scientifique, 563; Paris, 1976).

RENOUVIN, PIERRE, *Les Crises du XXe siècle*, pt. 2. *De 1929 à 1945* (Histoire des relations internationales, 8; Paris, 1958).

Retreat from Power: Studies in Britain's Foreign Policy, ed. David Dilks, i. *1906–1939* (London, 1981).

REUPKE, HANS, *Der Nationalsozialismus und die Wirtschaft* (Berlin, 1931).

REYNOLDS, DAVID, *The Creation of the Anglo-American Alliance, 1937–1941* (London, 1981).

REYNOLDS, NICHOLAS, *Treason was no Crime: General Ludwig Beck, Chief of the German General Staff* (London, 1976).

RIBBENTROP, ANNELIES VON, *Die Kriegsschuld des Widerstandes: Aus britischen Geheim-dokumenten 1938/39²*, ed. Rudolf von Ribbentrop (Leoni am Starnberger See, 1975).

RIBBENTROP, JOACHIM VON, *Zwischen London und Moskau: Erinnerungen und letzte Aufzeichnungen*, ed. Annelies von Ribbentrop (Leoni am Starnberger See, 1953). [Trans. Oliver Watson, *The Ribbentrop Memoirs* (London, 1954).]

RICKHOFF, HARALD VON, *German–Polish Relations, 1919–1933* (Baltimore and London, 1971).

RIEDEL, MATTHIAS, 'Die Rohstofflage des Deutschen Reiches im Frühjahr 1936', *Tradition*, 14 (1969), 310–34.

—— *Eisen und Kohle für das Dritte Reich: Paul Pleigers Stellung in der NS-Wirtschaft* (Göttingen, Frankfurt am Main, and Zurich, 1973).

RIESENBERGER, DIETER, *Die katholische Friedensbewegung in der Weimarer Republik*, with a preface by Walter Dirks (Düsseldorf, 1976).

RINGER, ALFRED, *Handel und Außenhandel: Neubau des Außenhandels im nationalsozialistischen Deutschland* (Berlin, 1933).

RITTER, GERHARD, *Carl Goerdeler und die deutsche Widerstandsbewegung* (Stuttgart, 1956). [Trans. (abr.) R. T. Clark, *The German Resistance: Carl Goerdeler's Struggle against Tyranny* (London, 1958).]

ROBERTSON, ESMONDE M., 'Zur Wiederbesetzung des Rheinlandes 1936', *VfZG* 10 (1962), 178–205.

—— *Hitler's Pre-war Policy and Military Plans 1933–1939* (London, 1963).

ROCK, WILLIAM R., *British Appeasement in the 1930s* (London, 1977).

ROHDE, HORST, *Das deutsche Wehrmachttransportwesen im Zweiten Weltkrieg: Entstehung—Organisation—Aufgaben* (Beiträge zur Militär- und Kriegsgeschichte, 12; Stuttgart, 1971).

—— 'Das Eisenbahnverkehrswesen in der deutschen Kriegswirtschaft 1939–1945', in *Kriegswirtschaft und Rüstung 1939–1945*, ed. Friedrich Forstmeier and Hans-Erich Volkmann (Düsseldorf, 1977), 134–63.

ROHE, KARL, *Das Reichsbanner Schwarz Rot Gold: Ein Beitrag zur Geschichte und Struktur der politischen Kampfverbände zur Zeit der Weimarer Republik* (Beiträge zur Geschichte des Parlamentarismus und der politischen Parteien, 34; Düsseldorf, 1966).

ROLFES, MAX, 'Landwirtschaft 1914-1970', in *Handbuch der deutschen Wirtschafts- und Sozialgeschichte*, ii. *Das 19. und 20. Jahrhundert* (Stuttgart, 1976), 741-95.

RÖNNEFARTH, HELMUTH K. G., *Die Sudetenkrise in der internationalen Politik: Entstehung—Verlauf—Auswirkung*, 2 vols. (Veröffentlichungen des Instituts für Europäische Geschichte Mainz, 21; Wiesbaden, 1961).

ROOS, DIETER, *Hitler und Dollfuß: Die deutsche Österreich-Politik 1933-1934* (Hamburger Beiträge zur Zeitgeschichte, 3; Hamburg, 1966).

ROOS, HANS, *Polen und Europa: Studien zur polnischen Außenpolitik 1931-1939* (Tübingen, 1957).

Roosevelt and Foreign Affairs, Franklin D., 2nd Series. *1937/39*, ed. Donald B. Schewe, iv-xvii (New York and Toronto, 1979).

ROSAR, WOLFGANG, *Deutsche Gemeinschaft: Seyss-Inquart und der Anschluß* (Vienna, Frankfurt am Main, and Zurich, 1971).

ROSENBERG, ALFRED, *Der Zukunftsweg einer deutschen Außenpolitik* (Munich, 1927).

—— *Der Mythus des 20. Jahrhunderts: Eine Wertung der seelisch-geistigen Gestaltenkämpfe unserer Zeit* (Munich, 1934) [printing of 17th-20th thousand].

—— *Das politische Tagebuch Alfred Rosenbergs 1934/5 und 1939/40*, ed. Hans-Günther Seraphim (dtv-dokumente, 219; Munich, 1964).

ROSENBERG, ARTHUR, *Geschichte der Weimarer Republik*[13], ed. Kurt Kersten (Frankfurt am Main, 1972). [Trans. Ian F. D. Morrow and L. Marie Sieveking, *A History of the German Republic* (London, 1936); first German publication 1961.]

ROSINSKI, HERBERT: *see* 'Miles'.

ROSKILL, STEPHEN, *Hankey: Man of Secrets*, i. *1877-1919* (London, 1970); ii. *1919-1931* (London, 1972); iii. *1931-1963* (London, 1974).

RUBBERT, HANS-HEINRICH, 'Die "gelenkte Marktwirtschaft" des Nationalsozialismus', *Hamburger Jahrbuch für Wirtschafts- und Gesellschaftspolitik* (1963), 215-34.

RUGE, WOLFGANG, *Deutschland von 1917-1933: Von der Großen Sozialistischen Oktoberrevolution bis zum Ende der Weimarer Republik* (Lehrbuch der deutschen Geschichte (Beiträge), 10; East Berlin, 1967).

RUNGE, WOLFGANG, *Politik und Beamtentum im Parteienstaat* (Stuttgart, 1965).

RUNZHEIMER, JÜRGEN, 'Der Überfall auf den Sender Gleiwitz im Jahre 1939', *VfZG* 10 (1962), 408-26.

RUPRECHT, PAUL, 'Staatliche oder private Rüstungsindustrie?', *Militär-Wochenblatt*, 120 (1935-6), 242-5.

RUSSELL, ELBERT W., *Christianity and Militarism* (Oakville, Ont., 1971).

—— 'Christentum und Militarismus' (1974), in *Christentum und Militarismus* (q.v.), 21-109.

SAAGE, RICHARD, 'Antisozialismus, Mittelstand und NSDAP in der Weimarer Republik', in *Internationale wissenschaftliche Korrespondenz zur Geschichte der deutschen Arbeiterbewegung*, 11 (1975), 146-77.

—— *Faschismustheorien: Eine Einführung* (Munich, 1976).

Sachwörterbuch der Geschichte Deutschlands und der deutschen Arbeiterbewegung, i. *(A-K)* (East Berlin, 1969).

SALDERN, ADELHEID VON, *Mittelstand im 'Dritten Reich': Handwerk, Einzelhändler, Bauern* (Frankfurt am Main and New York, 1979).

SALEWSKI, MICHAEL, *Entwaffnung und Militärkontrolle in Deutschland 1919-1927* (Schriften des Forschungsinstituts der deutschen Gesellschaft für Auswärtige Politik, 24; Munich, 1966).

SALEWSKI, MICHAEL, 'Selbstverständnis und historisches Bewußtsein der deutschen Kriegsmarine', *MR* 67 (1970), 65–88.

—— *Die deutsche Seekriegsleitung 1935–1945*, i. *1935–1941* (Frankfurt am Main, 1970).

—— 'Marineleitung und politische Führung 1931–1935', *MGM* 10 (1971), 113–58.

—— 'Das Ende der deutschen Schlachtschiffe im Zweiten Weltkrieg', *MGM* 12 (1972), 53–73.

—— *Die deutsche Seekriegsleitung 1935–1945*, iii. *Denkschriften und Lagebetrachtungen 1938–1944* (Frankfurt am Main, 1973).

—— 'Zur deutschen Sicherheitspolitik in der Spätzeit der Weimarer Republik', *VfZG* 22 (1974), 121–47.

—— 'England, Hitler und die Marine', in *Vom Sinn der Geschichte*, ed. Otmar Franz (Stuttgart, 1976), 163–84.

—— 'Die bewaffnete Macht im Dritten Reich 1933–1939', in *Wehrmacht und Nationalsozialismus 1933–1939* (Handbuch zur deutschen Militärgeschichte 1648–1939, 7; Munich, 1978), 13–287.

SANDHOFER, GERT, 'Das Panzerschiff "A" und die Vorentwürfe von 1920 bis 1928', *MGM* 3 (1968), 35–62.

SÄNGER, FRITZ, *Politik der Täuschungen: Mißbrauch der Presse im Dritten Reich. Weisungen, Informationen, Notizen 1933–1939* (Vienna, 1975).

SARHOLZ, THOMAS, *Die Auswirkungen der Kontingentierung von Eisen und Stahl auf die Aufrüstung der Wehrmacht von 1936 bis 1939* (diss. Darmstadt, 1983).

SAUER, WOLFGANG, 'Die Mobilmachung der Gewalt', in Bracher, Sauer, and Schulz, *Die nationalsozialistische Machtergreifung* (q.v.), 685–972.

SAWKA, GEORGE, 'The Franco-Polish Alliance and the Remilitarization of the Rhineland', *Historical Journal*, 16 (1973), 125–46.

SCHACHT, HJALMAR, *Grundsätze deutscher Wirtschaftspolitik* (Stalling-Bücherei 'Schriften an die Nation', 1; Oldenburg, 1932).

—— *Deutschland in der Weltwirtschaftskrise* (Berlin, 1935).

—— *'Finanzwunder' und 'Neuer Plan'* (Berlin, 1938).

—— *76 Jahre meines Lebens* (Bad Wörishofen, 1953). [Trans. Diana Pyke, *My First 76 Years* (London, 1955.]

SCHAUMBURG-LIPPE, FRIEDRICH CHRISTIAN Prince ZU, *Dr G: Ein Porträt des Propagandaministers* (Wiesbaden, 1963; 1972³).

SCHAUSBERGER, NORBERT, 'Wirtschaftliche Aspekte des Anschlusses Österreichs an das Deutsche Reich (Dokumentation)', *MGM* 8 (1970), 133–64.

—— 'Der wirtschaftliche Anschluß Österreichs 1938', *Österreich in Geschichte und Literatur*, 15 (1971), 249–73.

—— 'Die Bedeutung Österreichs für die deutsche Rüstung während des Zweiten Weltkrieges', *MGM* 11 (1972), 57–84.

—— 'Österreich und die nationalsozialistische Anschlußpolitik', in *Hitler, Deutschland und die Mächte* (q.v.), 728–56.

—— *Der Griff nach Österreich: Der Anschluß* (Vienna and Munich, 1978).

SCHAUWECKER, FRANZ, 'Das Erlebnis des Krieges', in Franz Seldte (ed.), *Der Stahlhelm: Erinnerungen und Bilder* (Berlin, 1932; new edn. in 2 vols., 1934), 176–80.

SCHEEL, KLAUS, 'Der Aufbau der faschistischen PK-Einheiten vor dem Zweiten Weltkrieg', *ZMG* (1965), 444–55.

—— *Krieg über Ätherwellen: NS-Rundfunk und Monopole 1933–1945* (East Berlin, 1970).

SCHEER, FRIEDRICH-KARL, *Die Deutsche Friedensgesellschaft (1892–1933): Organisation—*

Ideologie—politische Ziele. Ein Beitrag zur Entwicklung des Pazifismus in Deutschland (diss. Bochum, 1974).

SCHELER, EBERHARD, *Die politischen Beziehungen zwischen Deutschland und Frankreich zur Zeit der aktiven Außenpolitik Hitlers Ende 1937 bis zum Kriegsausbruch* (diss. Frankfurt am Main, 1962).

SCHELER, MAX, *Der Genius des Krieges und der Deutsche Krieg* (Leipzig, 1915).

—— *Die Idee des Friedens und der Pazifismus* (Berlin, 1931).

SCHELL, ADOLF VON, 'Krieg und Motorisierung', *Die Straße*, 23–4 (1940), 506.

SCHERKE, FELIX, and VITZTHUM, Countess URSULA, *Bibliographie der geistigen Kriegsführung*, with intro. by Air Force General von Cochenhausen (Berlin, 1938).

SCHIAN, MARTIN, *Die Arbeit der evangelischen Kirche in der Heimat* (Die deutsche evangelische Kirche im Weltkriege, 2; Berlin, 1925).

SCHIEDER, WOLFGANG, 'Spanischer Bürgerkrieg und Vierjahresplan: Zur Struktur national-sozialistischer Außenpolitik', in *Der Spanische Bürgerkrieg in der internationalen Politik (1936-1939)*, ed. Wolfgang Schieder and Christof Dipper (Munich, 1976), 162–90.

SCHIFRIN, ALEXANDER, 'Gedankenschatz des Hakenkreuzes', *Die Gesellschaft*, 8 (1931), i. 97–116.

—— 'Die Krise der deutschen Gegenrevolution', *Die Gesellschaft*, 9 (1932), ii. 387–405.

SCHILDT, AXEL, *Militärdiktatur mit Massenbasis? Die Querfrontkonzeption der Reichs-wehrführung um General von Schleicher am Ende der Weimarer Republik* (Campus Forschung, 225; Frankfurt am Main and New York, 1981).

SCHILDT, GERHARD, *Die Arbeitsgemeinschaft Nord-West: Untersuchungen zur Geschichte der NSDAP 1925/26* (diss. Freiburg i.Br., 1964).

SCHILLER, KARL, *Arbeitsbeschaffung und Finanzordnung in Deutschland* (Zum wirt-schaftlichen Schicksal Europas, 2. 4; Berlin, 1939).

SCHIRACH, BALDUR VON, *Die Hitler-Jugend: Idee und Gestalt* (Berlin, 1934).

—— *Revolution der Erziehung: Reden aus den Jahren des Aufbaus* (Munich, 1938).

SCHLANGEN, WALTER, 'Der Begriff totalitäre Herrschaft und seine politisch-theoretischen Bezüge: Anmerkungen zur Methodik der Analyse eines sozialwissenschaftlichen Begriffs', *PVS* (1972), 429–48.

SCHMIDT, GUSTAV, 'Strategie und Außenpolitik des "Troubled Giant" ', *MGM* 14 (1973), 200–20.

SCHMIDT, PAUL, *Statist auf diplomatischer Bühne 1923-1945: Erlebnisse des Chefdolmetschers im Auswärtigen Amt mit den Staatsmännern Europas* (Bonn, 1954). [Trans. (abr.) R. H. C. Steed, *Hitler's Interpreter* (London, 1951).]

SCHMIDT-PAULI, EDGAR VON, *Die Männer um Hitler* (Berlin, 1932).

SCHMÖLDERS, GÜNTER, 'Probleme und Kräfte des erweiterten Wirtschaftsraumes', *Jahrbuch der Akademie für Deutsches Recht*, 5 (1938), 106–202.

SCHNEIDER, HANS-JÜRGEN, 'Machtpolitik und Ökonomie: Zur nationalsozialistischen Außenpolitik im Jahre 1938', in *Machtbewußtsein in Deutschland* (q.v.), 211–22.

SCHNEIDER, MICHAEL, *Unternehmer und Demokratie: Die freien Gewerkschaften in der unternehmerischen Ideologie der Jahre 1918-1933* (Schriftenreihe des Forschungsinstituts der Friedrich-Ebert-Stiftung, 116; Bonn-Bad Godesberg, 1975).

SCHOENBAUM, DAVID, *Hitler's Social Revolution: Class and Status in Nazi Germany, 1933-1939* (London, 1967).

SCHOLDER, KLAUS, 'Die Kirchen im Dritten Reich', in *Aus Politik und Zeitgeschichte* (suppl. to weekly *Das Parlament*) B 15 (1971), 3–31.

—— *Die Kirchen und das Dritte Reich*, i. *Vorgeschichte und Zeit der Illusionen 1918-1934* (Frankfurt am Main, Berlin, and Vienna, 1977).

SCHOLDER, KLAUS, 'Otto Dibelius (1880–1980)', *Zeitschrift für Theologie und Kirche*, 78 (1981), 90–104.

SCHOLTZ, HARALD, *Erziehung und Unterricht unterm Hakenkreuz* (Kleine Vandenhoeck-Reihe, 1512; Göttingen, 1985).

SCHÖNFELD, ROLAND, 'Deutsche Rohstoffsicherungspolitik in Jugoslawien 1934–1944', *VfZG* 24 (1976), 215–58.

SCHOTTELIUS, HERBERT, and CASPAR, GUSTAV-ADOLF, 'Die Organisation des Heeres 1933–1939', in *Wehrmacht und Nationalsozialismus 1933–1939* (Handbuch zur deutschen Militärgeschichte 1648–1939, vii; Munich, 1978); 289–399.

SCHRAMM; WILHELM VON, 'Schöpferische Kritik des Krieges: Ein Versuch', in *Krieg und Krieger*, ed. Ernst Jünger (Berlin, 1930), 31–49.

SCHREIBER, GERHARD, 'Die Rolle Frankreichs im strategischen und operativen Denken der deutschen Marine' (MS for symposium of German and French historians in Bonn, 26–9 Sept. 1978).

—— 'Reichsmarine, Revisionismus und Weltmachtstreben', in *Militär und Militarismus in der Weimarer Republik: Beiträge eines internationalen Symposiums an der Hochschule der Bundeswehr Hamburg am 5. und 6. Mai 1977* (Düsseldorf, 1978), 149–76.

—— 'Die Rolle Frankreichs im strategischen und operativen Denken der deutschen Marine' (MS for symposium of German and French historians in Bonn, 26–9 Sept. 1978).

—— *Revisionismus und Weltmachtstreben: Marineführung und deutsch-italienische Beziehungen 1919–1944* (Beiträge zur Militär- und Kriegsgeschichte, 20; Stuttgart, 1978).

—— 'Zur Kontinuität des Groß- und Weltmachtstrebens der deutschen Marineführung', *MGM* 26 (1979), 101–71.

—— *Hitler-Interpretationen 1923–1983: Ergebnisse, Methoden und Probleme der Forschung* (Darmstadt, 1984).

—— 'Das strategische Lagebild von Luftwaffe und Kriegsmarine im Jahre 1938', in *Machtbewußtsein in Deutschland* (q.v.), 175–89.

SCHRÖDER, HANS-JÜRGEN, *Deutschland und die Vereinigten Staaten 1933–1939: Wirtschaft und Politik in der Entwicklung des deutsch-amerikanischen Gegensatzes* (Veröffentlichungen des Instituts für Europäische Geschichte Mainz, 59; Wiesbaden, 1970).

—— 'Das Dritte Reich, die USA und Lateinamerika 1933–1941', in *Hitler, Deutschland und die Mächte* (q.v.), 339–64.

—— 'Der Aufbau der deutschen Hegemonialstellung in Südosteuropa 1933–1936', in *Hitler, Deutschland und die Mächte* (q.v.), 757–73.

—— 'Economic Appeasement: Zur britischen und amerikanischen Deutschlandpolitik vor dem Zweiten Weltkrieg', *VfZG* 30 (1982), 82–97.

SCHUBERT, GÜNTER, *Anfänge nationalsozialistischer Außenpolitik* (Cologne, 1963).

SCHULMEISTER, OTTO, *Werdende Großraumwirtschaft: Die Phasen ihrer Entwicklung in Südosteuropa* (Berlin, 1943).

SCHULTE, KARL ANTON, 'Das Zentrum und die neue Zeit: Grundsätze und politischer Ideegehalt der Partei', in *Nationale Arbeit* (q.v.), 31–53.

Schulthess' Europäischer Geschichtskalender, NS, vols. for 1929, 1930, 1931, 1932.

SCHULZ, GERHARD, *Faschismus-Nationalsozialismus: Versionen und theoretische Kontroversen 1922–1972* (Frankfurt am Main, Berlin, and Vienna, 1974).

—— *Aufstieg des Nationalsozialismus: Krise und Revolution in Deutschland* (Frankfurt am Main, Berlin, and Vienna, 1975).

—— 'Die Anfänge des totalitären Maßnahmenstaates', in Bracher, Sauer, and Schulz, *Die nationalsozialistische Machtergreifung* (q.v.), 31–368.

SCHULZE, HAGEN, *Anpassung oder Widerstand? Aus den Akten des Parteivorstandes der deutschen Sozialdemokratie 1932/33* (Archiv für Sozialgeschichte, suppl. 4; Bonn-Bad Godesberg, 1975).

SCHUMANN, HANS-GERD, *Nationalsozialismus und Gewerkschaftsbewegung* (Hanover and Frankfurt am Main, 1958).

SCHUMANN, WOLFGANG, 'Aspekte und Hintergründe der Handels- und Wirtschaftspolitik Hitlerdeutschlands gegenüber Jugoslawien 1933 bis 1945', *Bulletin des Arbeitskreises 'Zweiter Weltkrieg'* (1973), 3: 5–38.

SCHÜRMANN, A. W., 'Der Weg zur Autarkie: Übergangsstadium oder Dauersystem?', *Neue Wirtschaft*, 6/8 (1932), 1–3.

SCHUSCHNIGG, KURT VON, *Ein Requiem in Rot-Weiß-Rot* (Zurich, 1946). [Trans. Franz von Hildebrand, *Austrian Requiem* (London, 1947).]

SCHUSTER, KURT G. P., *Der Rote Frontkämpferbund 1924–1929: Beiträge zur Geschichte und Organisationsstruktur eines politischen Kampfbundes* (Beiträge zur Geschichte des Parlamentarismus und der politischen Parteien, 55; Düsseldorf, 1975).

SCHUSTEREIT, HARTMUT, 'Unpolitisch—Überparteilich—Staatstreu: Wehrfragen aus der Sicht der Deutschen Demokratischen Partei 1919–1930', *MGM* 16 (1974), 131–72.

—— *Linksliberalismus und Sozialdemokratie in der Weimarer Republik: Eine vergleichende Betrachtung der Politik von DDP und SPD 1919–1930* (Geschichte und Gesellschaft: Bochumer Historische Studien; Düsseldorf, 1975).

SCHÜTZLE, KURT, *Reichswehr wider die Nation: Zur Rolle der Reichswehr bei der Vorbereitung und Errichtung der faschistischen Diktatur in Deutschland (1929–1933)* (East Berlin, 1963).

SCHWABE, GERDA, *Der deutsch-rumänische Wirtschaftsvertrag vom 23. März 1939* (diss. East Berlin, 1968).

SCHWABE, KLAUS, *Der amerikanische Isolationismus im 20. Jahrhundert: Legende und Wirklichkeit* (Frankfurter historische Vorträge, 1; Wiesbaden, 1975).

—— 'Die entfernteren Staaten am Beispiel der Vereinigten Staaten von Amerika: Weltpolitische Verantwortung gegen nationale Isolation', in *Innen- und Außenpolitik* (q.v.), 277–94.

SCHWARTE, MAX, *Der Krieg der Zukunft* (Leipzig, 1931).

SCHWARZ, HANS-PETER, *Der konservative Anarchist: Politik und Zeitkritik Ernst Jüngers* (Freiburger Studien zu Politik und Soziologie; Freiburg i.Br., 1962).

SCHWARZ, SALOMON, *Handbuch der deutschen Gewerkschaftskongresse (Kongresse des Allgemeinen Deutschen Gewerkschaftsbundes)* (Berlin, 1930).

SCHWEITZER, ARTHUR, 'Der ursprüngliche Vierjahresplan', *Jahrbücher für Nationalökonomie und Statistik*, 160 (1956), 348–96.

—— 'Die wirtschaftliche Wiederaufrüstung Deutschlands von 1934–1936', *Zeitschrift für die gesamte Staatswissenschaft*, 114 (1958), 594–637.

—— 'Organisierter Kapitalismus und Parteidiktatur 1933 bis 1936', *Schmollers Jahrbuch für Gesetzgebung, Verwaltung und Volkswirtschaft*, 79 (1959), i. 37–79.

—— 'Der organisierte Kapitalismus: Die Wirtschaftsordnung in der ersten Periode der nationalsozialistischen Herrschaft', *Hamburger Jahrbuch für Wirtschafts- und Gesellschaftspolitik*, 7 (1962), 32–47.

—— *Big Business in the Third Reich* (Bloomington, Ind., 1964).

SCHWEND, KARL, 'Die Bayerische Volkspartei', in *Das Ende der Parteien* (q.v.), 457–519.

SCHWENDEMANN, KARL, *Abrüstung und Sicherheit: Handbuch der Sicherheitsfrage und der Abrüstungskonferenz. Mit einer Sammlung der wichtigsten Dokumente*[2], 2 vols. (Berlin, 1933).

SCHWICHOW, VON, 'Die Ernährungswirtschaft als Wehrproblem', *Deutsche Wehr*, 39 (1935), 257–60.

SCHWICHTENBERG, HELMUT, *Die wirtschaftlichen Voraussetzungen und Methoden der Erzeugungsschlacht* (diss. Cologne and Würzburg, 1937).

SCOTT, WILLIAM EVANS, *Alliance against Hitler: The Origins of the Franco-Soviet Pact* (Durham, NC, 1962).

SEABURY, PAUL, *The Wilhelmstrasse: A Study of German Diplomats under the Nazi Regime* (Berkeley and Los Angeles, 1954).

Secret Book: see *Hitlers zweites Buch*.

SEIDEL, RICHARD, *Die Gewerkschaftsbewegung in Deutschland* (Internationale Gewerkschaftsbibliothek, 7–8; Amsterdam, 1929).

SELDTE, FRANZ (ed.), *Der Stahlhelm: Erinnerungen und Bilder* (Berlin, 1932; new edn. in 2 vols., 1934).

—— (ed.), *Sozialpolitik im Dritten Reich 1933–1938* (Munich and Berlin, 1939).

SENFF, HUBERTUS, *Die Entwicklung der Panzerwaffe im deutschen Heer zwischen den beiden Weltkriegen: Eine Untersuchung der Auffassungen über ihren Einsatz an Hand von Vorschriften, literarischer Diskussion und tatsächlichem Heeresaufbau* (Frankfurt am Main, 1969).

SENGER UND ETTERLIN, FERDINAND M. VON, *Die Kampfpanzer von 1916–1966* (Munich, 1966).

SENGHAAS, DIETER, *Abschreckung und Frieden: Studien zur Kritik organisierter Friedlosigkeit* (Kritische Studien zur Politikwissenschaft; Frankfurt am Main, 1969).

SHELDON, WILLIAM F., 'Das Hitler-Bild in der "Time" 1923–1933', in Joachim Hütter, Reinhard Meyers, and Dietrich Papenfuß (eds.), *Tradition und Neubeginn: Internationale Forschungen zur deutschen Geschichte im 20. Jahrhundert* (Cologne, Berlin, Bonn, and Munich, 1975), 67–81.

SHIRER, WILLIAM L., *The Rise and Fall of the Third Reich* (London and New York, 1960).

SIEBURG, ḤEINZ-OTTO, 'Das Gespräch zu Thoiry 1926', in *Gedenkschrift M. Göhring: Studien zur europäischen Geschichte*, with intro. by Jacques Droz, ed. Ernst Schulin (Veröffentlichungen des Instituts für Europäische Geschichte Mainz, 50; Wiesbaden, 1968), 317–37.

SIPOLS, VILNIS JANOVIĆ, *Die Vorgeschichte des deutsch-sowjetischen Nichtangriffsvertrages* (Cologne, 1981).

SMITH, DENIS MACK, *Mussolini's Roman Empire* (London and New York, 1976).

SNELL, JOHN L., *Illusion and Necessity: The Diplomacy of Total War, 1939–1945* (Boston, 1963).

SOHL, KLAUS, 'Die Kriegsvorbereitungen des deutschen Imperialismus in Bulgarien am Vorabend des zweiten Weltkrieges', *Jahrbuch für Geschichte der UdSSR und der volksdemokratischen Länder Europas*, 3 (1959), 91–119.

SOHN-RETHEL, ALFRED, *Ökonomie und Klassenstruktur des deutschen Faschismus: Aufzeichnungen und Analysen*, ed. Johannes Agnoli *et al.* (ed. suhrkamp, 630; Frankfurt am Main, 1973).

SOLDAN, GEORGE, *Der Mensch und die Schlacht der Zukunft* (Oldenburg, 1925).

SOMMER, THEO, *Deutschland und Japan zwischen den Mächten 1935–1940: Vom Antikominternpakt zum Dreimächtepakt* (Tübinger Studien zur Geschichte und Politik, 15; Tübingen, 1962).

Sommer 1939: Die Großmächte und der europäische Krieg, ed. Wolfgang Benz and Hermann Graml (Schriftenreihe der *VfZG*, spec. No.; Stuttgart, 1979).

SONTHEIMER, KURT, *Antidemokratisches Denken in der Weimarer Republik: Die politischen Ideen des deutschen Nationalismus zwischen 1918 und 1933* (Munich, 1962).

Sowjetsystem und demokratische Gesellschaft: Eine vergleichende Enzyklopädie, ed. C. D. Kernig, 6 vols. (Freiburg i. Br., 1966–72), iii. Ideologie bis Leistung (1969).

Sozialdemokratischer Parteitag in Leipzig 1931. Vom 31. Mai bis 5. Juni im Volkshaus. Protokoll. (Leipzig, 1931; repr. Glashütte im Taunus, Berlin, Bonn, and Bad Godesberg, 1974).

Sozialdemokratischer Parteitag in Magdeburg 1929 vom 26. bis 31. Mai in der Stadthalle. Protokoll (Berlin, 1929).

Spanische Bürgerkrieg in der internationalen Politik (1936–1939), Der, ed. Wolfgang Schieder and Christof Dipper (Nymphenburger Texte zur Wissenschaft, 23; Munich, 1976).

SPEER, ALBERT, *Erinnerungen* (Frankfurt am Main, 1969). [Trans. Richard and Clara Winston, *Inside the Third Reich* (London, 1970).]

SPENGLER, OSWALD, *Der Untergang des Abendlandes: Umrisse einer Morphologie der Weltgeschichte*, 2 vols. (Munich, 1919–22). [Trans. Charles F. Atkinson, *The Decline of the West* (London, 1926–9).]

Staat und NSDAP 1930–1932: Quellen zur Ära Brüning, with intro. by G. Schulz, rev. by Ilse Maurer and Udo Wengst (Quellen zur Geschichte des Parlamentarismus und der politischen Parteien, 3rd series, 3, Die Weimarer Republik, Düsseldorf, 1977).

Staats- und Wirtschaftskrise des Deutschen Reiches 1929/33, Die (Stuttgart, 1967).

STADTLER, EDUARD, *Seldte, Hitler, Hugenberg: Die Front der Freiheitsbewegung* (Berlin, 1930).

STALIN, J. V. [Iosif Vissarionovich], *Report on the Work of the Central Committee of the Communist Party of the Soviet Union at the Seventeenth and Eighteenth Congresses of the CPSU* (London, 1939).

—— *Leninism* (London, 1940).

—— *Works*, 13 vols. (London, 1946–55).

Stand und Problematik der Erforschung des Widerstandes gegen den Nationalsozialismus (Studien und Berichte aus dem Forschungsinstitut der Friedrich-Ebert-Stiftung; Bad Godesberg, 1965).

STARCKE, GERHARD, *NSBO und Deutsche Arbeitsfront* (Berlin, 1934).

STARK, GEORG, *Moderne politische Propaganda* (Schriftenreihe der Reichspropaganda-Abteilung der NSDAP, 1; Munich, 1930).

Statistisches Handbuch von Deutschland 1928–1944 (Munich, 1944).

STEGMANN, DIRK, 'Zum Verhältnis von Großindustrie und Nationalsozialismus 1930–1933: Ein Beitrag zur Geschichte der sog. Machtergreifung', *Archiv für Sozialgeschichte*, 13 (1973), 339–482.

STEINBERG, F., *Die deutsche Kriegsstärke: Wie lange kann Hitler Krieg führen?* (Paris, 1939).

STEINBERG, HANS-JOSEPH, *Widerstand und Verfolgung in Essen 1933–1945* (Schriftenreihe des Forschungsinstituts der Friedrich-Ebert-Stiftung, Series B, Historisch-politische Schriften; Hanover, 1969).

STEINBERGER, HANS, 'Wirtschaft, Raum und Wehrmacht', *Deutsche Wehr*, 6 (1933), 484–5.

STEINER, ZARA, 'Evaluation des rapports de force en Europe occidentale en 1938: Le point de vue du Foreign Office', in *La Puissance en Europe* (q.v.), 55–72.

STEINERT, MARLIS G., *Hitlers Krieg und die Deutschen: Stimmung und Haltung der deutschen Bevölkerung im Zweiten Weltkrieg* (publication of the Institut Universitaire de Hautes Études Internationales, Geneva, Düsseldorf and Vienna, 1970).

STELLRECHT, HELMUT, *Soldatentum und Jugendertüchtigung* (Schriften der deutschen Hochschule für Politik, 1. 16; Berlin, 1935).

—— 'Die Wehrerziehung der deutschen Jugend', in *Nationalpolitischer Lehrgang der Wehrmacht vom 15. bis 23. Januar 1937* (Berlin, [c. 1937]).

Stellung der Sozialpolitik in der europäischen Neuordnung, Die, ed. Arbeitswissenschaftliches Institut der DAF (Berlin, 1944).

Stellung des evangelischen Christen zum Pazifismus, Die: Vortrag, gehalten auf der Tagung des Evangelischen Reichsausschusses der Deutschnationalen Volkspartei in Stettin am 19. September 1931 von Pfarrer Wilm (Deutschnationale Flugschrift, 358; Potsdam and Berlin, 1931).

STELZNER, JÜRGEN, *Arbeitsbeschaffung und Wiederaufrüstung 1933–1936: Nationalsozialistische Beschäftigungspolitik und Aufbau der Wehr- und Rüstungswirtschaft* (diss. Tübingen and Bamberg, 1976).

STEPHAN, WERNER, *Aufstieg und Verfall des Linksliberalismus 1918–1933: Geschichte der Deutschen Demokratischen Partei* (Göttingen, 1973).

STRESEMANN, GUSTAV, *Vermächtnis: Der Nachlaß,* 2 vols., ed. Henry Bernhard (Berlin, 1932).

—— *Diaries, Letters and Papers,* ed. and trans. Eric Sutton, 3 vols. (London, 1935, 1937, 1940).

—— *Schriften,* with preface by Willy Brandt, ed. Arnold Harttung (Schriften großer Berliner; Berlin, 1976).

STUEBEL, HEINRICH, 'Die Finanzierung der Aufrüstung im Dritten Reich', *Europa-Archiv,* 6 (1951), 4128–36.

STUMPF, REINHARD, 'Die Luftwaffe als drittes Heer: Die Luftwaffen-Erdkampfverbände und das Problem der Sonderheere 1933 bis 1945', in *Industrielle Welt,* spec. vol., *Soziale Bewegung und politische Verfassung,* ed. Ulrich Engelhardt, Volker Sellin, and Horst Stuke (Stuttgart, 1976), 857–94.

SUNDHAUSSEN, HOLM, 'Südosteuropa in der nationalsozialistischen Kriegswirtschaft am Beispiel des "Unabhängigen Staates Kroatien"', *Südost-Forschungen,* 32 (1973), 233–66.

SURÁNYI-UNGER, THEO, 'Ungarische Wehrwirtschaft', *Weltwirtschaftliches Archiv,* 53/1 (1941), 75–III.

Survey of International Affairs, 1920–, ed. Royal Institute of International Affairs (London, 1925–).

SWATEK, DIETER, *Unternehmenskonzentration als Ergebnis und Mittel nationalsozialistischer Wirtschaftspolitik* (Volkswirtschaftliche Schriften, 181; Berlin, 1972).

SYRUP, FRIEDRICH, 'Maßnahmen zur Versorgung der Landwirtschaft mit Arbeitskräften', *Der Vierjahresplan,* 1 (1937), 208–10.

—— 'Neue Maßnahmen zur Regelung des Arbeitseinsatzes', *Der Vierjahresplan,* 2 (1938), 143–6.

SYWOTTEK, JUTTA, *Mobilmachung für den totalen Krieg: Die propagandistische Vorbereitung der deutschen Bevölkerung auf den Zweiten Weltkrieg* (Studien zur modernen Geschichte, 18; Opladen, 1976).

TARNOW, F., *Die Stellungnahme der freien Gewerkschaften zur Frage der Wirtschaftsdemokratie* (Jena, 1929).

Taschenkalender für den Bergbau auf Braunkohle, Erz, Salz, Erdöl 1956 (Düsseldorf, n.d.).

TAYLOR, A. J. P., *The Origins of the Second World War* (London, 1961).

TEICHERT, ECKART, *Autarkie und Großraumwirtschaft in Deutschland 1930–1939: Außenwirtschaftspolitische Konzeptionen zwischen Wirtschaftskrise und Zweitem Weltkrieg* (Studien zur modernen Geschichte, 30; Munich, 1984).

TESSIN, GEORG, *Deutsche Verbände und Truppen 1918–1939: Altes Heer, Freiwilligenverbände, Reichswehr, Heer, Luftwaffe, Landespolizei,* ed. with assistance from the Bundesarchiv and the Arbeitskreis für Wehrforschung (Osnabrück, 1974).

Texte zur Faschismusdiskussion, i, *Positionen und Kontroversen,* ed. Reinhard Kühnl (rororo aktuell, 1824; Reinbek, 1974).

THALMAN, RITA, *Protestantisme et nationalisme en Allemagne 1900–1945* (Paris, 1976).

THÄLMANN, ERNST, *Der revolutionäre Ausweg und die KPD* (Berlin, 1932).

THAMER, HANS-ULRICH, *Verführung und Gewalt: Deutschland 1933–1945* (Die Deutschen und ihre Nation, 5; Berlin, 1986).

Theorien über den Faschismus, ed. Ernst Nolte (Neue Wissenschaftliche Bibliothek, 21, Geschichte; Cologne and Berlin, 1970).

THÉVOZ, ROBERT, BRANIG, HANS, and LOWENTHAL-HENSEL, CÉCILE, *Pommern 1934/35 im Spiegel von Gestapo-Lageberichten und Sachakten*, i. *Darstellung*; ii. *Quellen* (Veröffentlichungen aus den Archiven Preußischer Kulturbesitz, 11, 12; Cologne and Berlin, 1974).

THIELE, WALTER, *Großraumwirtschaft in Geschichte und Politik* (Dresden, 1938).

THIES, JOCHEN, *Architekt der Weltherrschaft: Die 'Endziele' Hitlers* (Düsseldorf, 1976).

—— 'Adolf Hitler in Offenburg (8. November, 1930): Zur Diskussion über Hitlers politische Endziele. Eine Dokumentation', in *Die Ortenau* (Veröffentlichungen des historischen Vereins für Mittelbaden, 57; Offenburg, 1977), 296–312.

THIMME, ANNELIESE, *Gustav Stresemann: Eine politische Biographie zur Geschichte der Weimarer Republik* (Hanover and Frankfurt am Main, 1957).

THOMAS, GEORG, *Geschichte der deutschen Wehr- und Rüstungswirtschaft (1918–1943/45)*, ed. Wolfgang Birkenfeld (Schriften des Bundesarchivs, 14; Boppard, 1966).

THÖNE, KARIN, *Entwicklungsstadien und Zweiter Weltkrieg: Ein wirtschaftswissenschaftlicher Beitrag zur Frage der Kriegsursachen* (Schriften zur Wirtschafts- und Sozialgeschichte, 22; Berlin, 1974).

TIRPITZ, ALFRED VON, *Erinnerungen* (Deutsche Denkwürdigkeiten; Leipzig, 1919). [Trans. *My Memoirs* (London, 1919).]

TOLAND, JOHN, *Adolf Hitler* (New York, 1976).

TOSCANO, MARIO, *The Origins of the Pact of Steel* (Baltimore, 1967).

TOYNBEE, ARNOLD JOSEPH, *Acquaintances* (London, 1967).

TRAUB, GOTTFRIED, 'Der Geisteskampf der Gegenwart', *Eiserne Blätter*, 40–1 (1930).

TREUE, WILHELM, *Gummi in Deutschland: Die deutsche Kautschukversorgung und Gummi-Industrie im Rahmen weltwirtschaftlicher Entwicklungen*, ed. for Continental Gummi-Werke AG Hanover (Munich, 1955).

—— 'Hitlers Denkschrift zum Vierjahresplan 1936', *VfZG* 3 (1955), 184–210.

—— 'Rede Hitlers vor der deutschen Presse (10. November 1938)', *VfZG* 6 (1958), 175–91.

—— *Wirtschaftsgeschichte der Neuzeit*³, ii (Stuttgart, 1973).

TREVOR-ROPER, HUGH R., 'Hitlers Kriegsziele', *VfZG* 8 (1960), 121–33.

Trial of Major War Criminals by the International Military Tribunal sitting at Nuremberg, Germany, 42 vols. (London, 1947–9).

TROMPKE, EBERHARD, *Der Arbeitseinsatz als Element deutscher Wehr- und Kriegswirtschaft* (diss. Seestadt-Rostock, 1941).

TRUMPP, THOMAS, *Franz von Papen, der preußisch-deutsche Dualismus und die NSDAP in Preußen: Ein Beitrag zur Vorgeschichte des 20. Juli 1932* (Tübingen, 1964).

TURNER, HENRY ASHBY, *Stresemann and the Politics of the Weimar Republic* (Princeton, 1963).

—— *Faschismus und Kapitalismus in Deutschland: Studien zum Verhältnis zwischen Nationalsozialismus und Wirtschaft* (Göttingen, 1972).

—— 'Verhalfen die deutschen "Monopolkapitalisten" Hitler zur Macht?', in id., *Faschismus*, 9–32.

—— *German Big Business and the Rise of Hitler* (Oxford, 1985).

TUTAS, HERBERT E., *Nationalsozialismus und Exil: Die Politik des Dritten Reiches gegenüber der deutschen politischen Emigration 1933-1939* (Munich, 1975).

UEBERHORST, HORST, *Von Athen bis München: Die modernen Olympischen Spiele—Der olympische Gedanke—Der deutsche Beitrag*[2] (Berlin, Munich, and Frankfurt am Main, 1971).

—— *Elite für die Diktatur: Die Nationalpolitischen Erziehungsanstalten 1933-1945. Ein Dokumentarbericht* (Düsseldorf, 1974).

UEBERSCHÄR, GERD, 'Generaloberst Halder im militärischen Widerstand 1938-1940', *Wehrforschung* (1973), 20-31.

UMBREIT, HANS, *Deutsche Militärverwaltungen 1938/39: Die militärische Besetzung der Tschechoslowakei und Polens* (Beiträge zur Militär- und Kriegsgeschichte, 18; Stuttgart, 1977).

United States Strategic Bombing Survey, ii (New York and London, 1976).

Urkunden zur letzten Phase der deutsch-polnischen Krise, ed. Ministry of Foreign Affairs (Weißbuch des Auswärtigen Amts, 1; Berlin, 1939).

Ursachen und Folgen: Vom deutschen Zusammenbruch 1918 und 1945 bis zur staatlichen Neuordnung Deutschlands in der Gegenwart. Eine Urkunden- und Dokumentensammlung zur Zeitgeschichte, ed. and rev. by Herbert Michaelis and Ernst Schraepler with the assistance of Günter Scheel, ix (Berlin, 1964).

VAÏSSE, MAURICE, *Sécurité d'abord: La politique française en matière de désarmement, 9 décembre 1930-17 avril 1934* (Paris, 1981).

—— 'La perception de la puissance soviétique par les militaires français en 1938', *Revue historique des armées*, 3 (1983), 18-25.

Verhandlungen des Reichstages: Stenographische Berichte, V. Wahlperiode 1930, vol. 446 *(von der 53. Sitzung am 13. Okt 1931 bis zur 64. Sitzung am 12. Mai 1932)* (Berlin, 1932).

VIGEZZI, B., 'Mussolini, Ciano, la diplomatie italienne et la perception de la politique de puissance au début de la Deuxième Guerre mondiale', in *La Puissance en Europe* (q.v.), 89-101.

VOGELSANG, THILO, 'Neue Dokumente zur Geschichte der Reichswehr 1930-1933', *VfZG* 2 (1954), 397-436.

—— 'Hitlers Brief an Reichenau vom 4. Dezember 1932', *VfZG* 7 (1959), 429-37.

—— *Reichswehr, Staat und NSDAP: Beiträge zur deutschen Geschichte 1930-32* (Quellen und Darstellungen zur Zeitgeschichte, 11; Stuttgart, 1962).

—— *Kurt von Schleicher, ein General als Politiker* (Persönlichkeit und Geschichte, 39; Göttingen, 1965).

VOGT, MARTIN, *Das Kabinett Müller II (1928-1930)*, 2 vols. (Akten der Reichskanzlei, Weimarer Republik, ed. for the Historische Kommission bei der bayerischen Akademie der Wissenschaften by K.-D. Erdmann and for the Bundesarchiv by Hans Booms; Boppard, 1970).

VÖLKER, KARL-HEINZ, 'Die Entwicklung der militärischen Luftfahrt in Deutschland 1920-1933: Planung und Maßnahmen zur Schaffung einer Fliegertruppe in der Reichswehr', in *Beiträge zur Militär- und Kriegsgeschichte*, 3 (Stuttgart, 1962), 121-292.

—— *Die deutsche Luftwaffe 1933-1939: Aufbau, Führung und Rüstung der Luftwaffe sowie die Entwicklung der deutschen Luftkriegstheorie* (Beiträge zur Militär- und Kriegsgeschichte, 8; Stuttgart, 1967).

—— *Dokumente und Dokumentarfotos zur Geschichte der deutschen Luftwaffe: Aus den Geheimakten des Reichswehrministeriums 1919-1933 und des Reichsluftfahrtministeriums 1933-1939* (Beiträge zur Militär- und Kriegsgeschichte, 9; Stuttgart, 1968).

VOLKMANN, HANS-ERICH, 'Außenhandel und Aufrüstung 1933 bis 1939', in *Wirtschaft und Rüstung* (q.v.), 81–131.

—— 'Politik und ökonomisches Interesse in den Beziehungen der Weimarer Republik zum Königreich Spanien', in *Aspekte deutscher Außenpolitik im 20. Jahrhundert: Aufsätze Hans Rothfels zum Gedächtnis*, ed. Wolfgang Benz and Hermann Graml (Schriftenreihe der Vierteljahrshefte für Zeitgeschichte, spec. No.; Stuttgart, 1976), 41–67.

—— 'Politik, Wirtschaft und Aufrüstung unter dem Nationalsozialismus', in *Hitler, Deutschland und die Mächte* (q.v.), 269–91.

—— 'Ökonomie und Machtpolitik: Lettland und Estland im politisch-ökonomischen Kalkül des Dritten Reiches (1933–1940)', *Geschichte und Gesellschaft*, 2 (1976), 471–500.

—— 'Das außenwirtschaftliche Programm der NSDAP 1930–1933', *Archiv für Sozialgeschichte*, 17 (1977), 251–74.

—— *Wirtschaft im Dritten Reich: Eine Bibliographie*, pt. 1. *1933–1939* (Schriften der Bibliothek für Zeitgeschichte, 20; Munich, 1980).

—— 'Zur rüstungsökonomischen und großraumwirtschaftlichen Motivation der Eingliederung der Sudetengebiete und Böhmen-Mährens in das Deutsche Reich', *Studia Historiae Oeconomicae*, 14 (1979); Poznań, 1980), 161–86.

—— 'Zum Verhältnis von Großwirtschaft und NS-Regime im Zweiten Weltkrieg', in *Nationalsozialistische Diktatur 1933–1945: Eine Bilanz*, ed. Karl Dietrich Bracher, Manfred Funke, and Hans-Adolf Jacobsen (Düsseldorf, 1983), 480–508.

Volksgemeinschaft — Wehrgemeinschaft: 'Was sind wir? Pimpfe! Was wollen wir werden? Soldaten!' ed. Werner Knackmuss (Eine Veröffentlichung zum Schülerwettbewerb des Nationalsozialistischen Lehrerbunds; Berlin, 1936).

Vollmacht des Gewissens, ed. Europäische Publikation, i (Frankfurt am Main and Berlin, 1960).

VOLLMER, BERNHARD, *Volksopposition im Polizeistaat: Gestapo- und Regierungsberichte 1934–1936* (Quellen und Darstellungen zur Zeitgeschichte, 2; Stuttgart, 1957).

VÖLTZER, FRIEDRICH, 'Vom Werden des deutschen Sozialismus', *Zeitschrift für die gesamte Staatswissenschaft*, 96 (1936), 1–48.

VONDUNG, KLAUS, *Magie und Manipulation: Ideologischer Kult und politische Religion des Nationalsozialismus* (Göttingen, 1971).

Von Weimar zu Hitler 1930–1933, ed. Gotthard Jasper (Neue Wissenschaftliche Bibliothek, 25, Geschichte; Cologne and Berlin, 1968).

VORMANN, NIKOLAUS VON, *Der Feldzug 1939 in Polen* (Weissenburg, 1958).

Vortrag Adolf Hitlers vor westdeutschen Wirtschaftlern im Industrie-Club zu Düsseldorf am 27. Januar 1932 (Munich, 1932), 11

VORWERCK, Major, 'Berufsständische Ordnung und Landesverteidigung', *Wissen und Wehr*, 17 (1936), 323–8.

WACKER, WOLFGANG, *Der Bau des Panzerschiffs 'A' und der Reichstag* (Tübinger Studien zur Geschichte und Politik, 11; Tübingen, 1959).

WAGEMANN, ERNST, *Zwischenbilanz der Krisenpolitik: Eine international vergleichende konjunkturpolitische Studie* (Berlin, 1935).

WAGENFÜHR, ROLF, *Die deutsche Industrie im Kriege 1939–1945²* (Berlin, 1963).

[WAGNER, EDUARD], *Der Generalquartiermeister: Briefe und Tagebuchaufzeichnungen des Generalquartiermeisters des Heeres General der Artillerie Eduard Wagner*, ed. Elisabeth Wagner (Munich and Vienna, 1963).

WAGNER, RAIMUND, 'Die Wehrmachtführung und die Vierjahresplanpolitik im faschistischen Deutschland vor der Entfesselung des Zweiten Weltkrieges', *Militärgeschichte*, 12 (1973), 180–8.

WAHL, KARL, '...*es ist das deutsche Herz*': *Erlebnisse und Erkenntnisse eines ehemaligen Gauleiters* (Augsburg, 1954).

WALDE, KARL J., *Guderian* (Frankfurt am Main, 1976).

WALLACH, JEHUDA L., *Das Dogma der Vernichtungsschlacht: Die Lehren von Clausewitz und Schlieffen und ihre Wirkungen in zwei Weltkriegen* (Frankfurt am Main, 1967).

WALSDORFF, MARTIN, *Westorientierung und Ostpolitik: Stresemanns Rußlandpolitik in der Locarno-Ära* (Bremen, 1971).

Warum bekämpfen wir Deutschnationalen den Pazifismus? (Deutschnationale Flugschrift, 199; Berlin, 1924).

WATT, DONALD CAMERON, 'The Anglo-German Naval Agreement of 1935: An Interim Judgement', *JMH* (June 1956), 155–75.

—— 'An Earlier Model for the Pact of Steel: The Draft Treaties Exchanged between Germany and Italy during Hitler's Visit to Rome in May 1938', *International Affairs*, 33/2 (1957), 185–97.

—— 'German Plans for the Reoccupation of the Rhineland: A Note', *JCH* 1 (1966), 193–9.

WATZDORF, BERNHARD, 'Dokumente über die militärischen Hintergründe des Autobahn-baues im faschistischen Deutschland', *ZMG* 8 (1969), 66–9.

WEBER, ECKHARD, *Stadien der Außenhandelsverflechtung Ostmittel- und Südosteuropas* (Ökonomische Studien, 19; Stuttgart, 1971).

WEBER, HERMANN, *Hauptfeind Sozialdemokratie: Strategie und Taktik der KPD 1929–1933* (Düsseldorf, 1982).

WEBER, MAX, *Gesammelte politische Schriften*, with intro. by Theodor Heuss, repr. by Johs. (F.) Winckelmann, 2nd enlarged edn. (Tübingen, 1958).

—— 'Parlament und Regierung im neugeordneten Deutschland: Zur politischen Kritik des Beamtentums und Parteiwesens', in id., *Gesammelte politische Schriften*, 294–431.

WEBER, REINHOLD W., *Die Entstehungsgeschichte des Hitler-Stalin-Paktes 1939* (Europäische Hochschulschriften, series 3, 141; Frankfurt am Main and Berne, 1980).

WEDEL, HASSO VON, *Die Propagandatruppen der Deutschen Wehrmacht* (Die Wehrmacht im Kampf, 34; Neckargemünd, 1962).

WEGNER, BERND, 'Die Garde des "Führers" und die "Feuerwehr" der Ostfront: Zur neueren Literatur über die Waffen-SS', *MGM* 23 (1978), 210–36.

—— *Hitlers politische Soldaten: Die Waffen-SS 1933–1945. Studien zu Leitbild, Struktur und Funktion einer nationalsozialistischen Elite* (Sammlung Schöningh zur Geschichte und Gegenwart; Paderborn, 1982).

—— '"My Honour is Loyalty": The SS as a Military Factor in Hitler's Germany', in *The German Military in the Age of Total War* (q.v.), 220–39.

WEHBERG, HANS, *Die Ächtung des Krieges* (Schriften der deutschen Liga für Völkerbund; Berlin, 1930).

WEHLER, HANS-ULRICH, '"Absoluter" und "totaler" Krieg: Von Clausewitz zu Ludendorff', *PVS* (1969) 2–3: 220–48.

WEHNER, HEINZ, 'Die Rolle des faschistischen Verkehrswesens in der ersten Periode des zweiten Weltkrieges', *Bulletin des Arbeitskreises Zweiter Weltkrieg* (1966), 2: 37–61.

WEIDEMANN, HANS, *Die Gestaltung der deutschen Außenwirtschaft unter dem Neuen Plan* (diss. Frankfurt am Main and Emsdetten, 1938).

WEIDENFELD, WERNER, *Die Englandpolitik Gustav Stresemanns* (Mainz, 1972).

WEIGMANN, HANS, 'Zur gegenwärtigen Problemlage der Wirtschaftsplanung', *Archiv für Wirtschaftsplanung*, 1 (1941), 9–45.

WEIL, FELIX, 'Neuere Literatur zur deutschen Wehrwirtschaft', *Zeitschrift für Sozialforschung*, 7 (1938), 200–18.

Weimars Ende: Prognosen und Diagnosen in der deutschen Literatur und politischen Publizistik 1930–1933, ed. Thomas Koebner (Frankfurt am Main, 1982).

WEINBERG, GERHARD L., *The Foreign Policy of Hitler's Germany: Diplomatic Revolution in Europe 1933–1936* (Chicago and London, 1970).

—— *The Foreign Policy of Hitler's Germany: Starting World War II, 1937–1939* (Chicago and London, 1980).

—— 'Deutschlands Wille zum Krieg', in *Nationalsozialistische Diktatur* (q.v.), 407–26.

—— 'Friedenspropaganda und Kriegsvorbereitung', in *Deutschland 1933: Machtzerfall der Demokratie und nationalsozialistische 'Machtergreifung'*, ed. Wolfgang Treue and Jürgen Schmädeke (Einzelveröffentlichungen der historischen Kommission zu Berlin, 42; Berlin, 1984), 119–35.

WEJNGARTNER, THOMAS, *Stalin und der Aufstieg Hitlers: Die Deutschlandpolitik der Sowjetunion und der Kommunistischen Internationale 1929–1934* (Beiträge zur auswärtigen und internationalen Politik, 4; Berlin, 1970).

WEIZSÄCKER, ERNST VON, *Erinnerungen: Mein Leben*, ed. R. von Weizsäcker (Munich, Leipzig, and Freiburg i.Br., 1950). [Trans. John Andrews, *Memoirs of Ernst von Weizsäcker* (London, 1951).]

Weizsäcker-Papiere 1933–1950, Die, ed. Leonidas E. Hill (Frankfurt am Main, Berlin, and Vienna, 1974).

Weltherrschaft im Visier: Dokumente zu den Europa- und Weltherrschaftplänen des deutschen Imperialismus von der Jahrhundertwende bis Mai 1945, ed. with intro. by Wolfgang Schumann and Ludwig Nestler, with the assistance of Willibald Gutsche and Wolfgang Ruge (East Berlin, 1975).

Weltpolitik 1933–1939: 13 Vorträge, ed. Oswald Hauser for the Ranke-Gesellschaft-Vereinigung für Geschichte im öffentlichen Leben (Göttingen, Frankfurt am Main, and Zurich, 1973).

WENDT, BERND-JÜRGEN, *München 1938: England zwischen Hitler und Preußen* (Hamburger Studien zur neueren Geschichte, 3; Frankfurt am Main, 1965).

—— *Economic Appeasement: Handel und Finanz in der britischen Deutschland-Politik 1933–1939* (Studien zur modernen Geschichte, 3; Düsseldorf, 1971).

—— 'England und der deutsche "Drang nach Südosten": Kapitalbeziehungen und Warenverkehr in Südosteuropa zwischen den Weltkriegen', in *Deutschland in der Weltpolitik des 19. und 20. Jahrhunderts*, ed. Immanuel Geiss and Bernd-Jürgen Wendt (Düsseldorf, 1973), 483–512.

—— 'Danzig: Ein Bauer auf dem Schachbrett nationalsozialistischer Außenpolitik', in *Hitler, Deutschland und die Mächte* (q.v.), 774–94.

Westmächte und das Dritte Reich 1933–1939, Die: Klassische Großmachttrivialität oder Kampf zwischen Demokratie und Diktatur?, ed. Karl Rohe (Sammlung Schöningh zur Geschichte und Gegenwart; Paderborn, 1983).

WETTE, WOLFRAM, *Kriegstheorien deutscher Sozialisten: Marx, Engels, Lassalle, Bernstein, Kautsky, Luxemburg. Ein Beitrag zur Friedensforschung* (Stuttgart, Berlin, Cologne, and Mainz, 1971).

—— 'Mit dem Stimmzettel gegen den Faschismus? Das Dilemma des sozialdemokratischen Antifaschismus in der Endphase der Weimarer Republik', in *Frieden, Gewalt, Sozialismus* (q.v.), 358–403.

WETTE, WOLFRAM, 'Probleme des Pazifismus in der Zwischenkriegszeit', in *Pazifismus in der Weimarer Republik* (q.v.), 9–25.

—— 'From Kellogg to Hitler (1928–1933): German Public Opinion Concerning the Rejection or Glorification of War', in *The German Military in the Age of Total War* (q.v.), 71–99.

—— 'Sozialdemokratie und Pazifismus in der Weimarer Republik', *Archiv für Sozialgeschichte*, 26 (1986), 281–300.

—— 'Difficult Persuasion: The Psychological Mobilization of the German Population for World War II (1933–1939)', in *UNESCO Yearbook on Peace and Conflict Studies 1986* (Paris, 1987).

WHALEY, BARTON, 'Covert Rearmament in Germany 1919–1939: Deception and Misperception', *Journal of Strategic Studies*, 5/1 (1982), 3–29.

WHEELER-BENNETT, JOHN W., *The Nemesis of Power: The German Army in Politics, 1918–1945* (London, 1953).

Widerstand gegen den Nationalsozialismus, Der: Die deutsche Gesellschaft und der Widerstand gegen Hitler, ed. Jürgen Schmädeke and Peter Steinbach (Munich and Zurich, 1985).

Widerstand und Verfolgung in Wien 1934–1945: Eine Dokumentation, ed. by Dokumentationsarchiv des österreichischen Widerstandes, 3 vols. (Vienna, 1975).

WIEDEMANN, FRITZ, *Der Mann, der Feldherr werden wollte: Erlebnisse und Erfahrungen des Vorgesetzten Hitlers im 1. Weltkrieg und seines späteren persönlichen Adjutanten* (Velbert-Kettwig, 1964).

WIGGERSHAUS, NORBERT, review of E. Calic, *Ohne Maske: Hitler-Breiting Geheimgespräche 1931*, in *MGM* 8 (1970), 217.

—— *Der deutsch-englische Flottenvertrag vom 18. Juni 1935: England und die geheime deutsche Aufrüstung 1933–1935* (diss. Bonn, 1972).

—— 'Enttarnung der Luftwaffe und Wiedereinführung der allgemeinen Wehrpflicht in Deutschland', *Information für die Truppe*, 10 (1976), 69–75, 80–3.

WILLIAMS, WILLIAM A., 'The Legend of Isolationism in the 1920s', *Science and Society* (1954), 1–20.

WILLIKENS, WERNER, *Nationalsozialistische Agrarpolitik* (Munich, 1931).

WILM: see *Stellung des evangelischen Christen zum Pazifismus*.

WINCKLER, LUTZ, *Studie zur gesellschaftlichen Funktion faschistischer Sprache* (ed. suhrkamp, 417, Frankfurt am Main, 1970; 1971²).

WINKLER, HEINRICH AUGUST, 'Unternehmerverbände zwischen Ständeideologie und Nationalismus', *VfZG* 17 (1969), 341–71.

—— *Mittelstand, Demokratie und Nationalsozialismus: Die politische Entwicklung von Handwerk und Kleinhandel in der Weimarer Republik* (Cologne, 1972).

—— 'Vom Protest zur Panik: Der gewerbliche Mittelstand in der Weimarer Republik', in *Industrielles System und politische Entwicklung in der Weimarer Republik: Verhandlungen des Internationalen Symposiums in Bochum vom 12.–17. Juni 1973*, ed. Hans Mommsen, Dietmar Petzina, and Bernd Weisbrod (Düsseldorf, 1974), 779–91.

—— *Revolution, Staat, Faschismus: Zur Revision des Historischen Materialismus* (Göttingen, 1978).

WINSCHUH, JOSEF, *Gerüstete Wirtschaft* (Berlin, 1939).

WIPPERMANN, WOLFGANG, *Faschismustheorien: Zum Stand der gegenwärtigen Diskussion²* (Erträge der Forschung, 17; Darmstadt, 1975).

WIRSING, GISELHER, 'Zwangsautarkie', *Die Tat*, 23 (1931), 428–38.

—— *Zwischeneuropa und die deutsche Zukunft* (Tat-Schriften; Jena, 1932).

WIRTH, JOSEF, *Reden während der Kanzlerschaft*, with intro. by Heinrich Hemmer (Berlin, 1925).

Wirtschaftliches Sofortprogramm der N.S.D.A.P., ausgearb. von der Hauptabt. 4 der Reichs-organisationsleitung der N.S.D.A.P. (Kampfschrift, 16; Munich, 1932).

Wirtschaftsdemokratien: Ihr Wesen, Weg und Ziel, ed. for the Allgemeiner Deutscher Gewerkschaftsbund (ADGB) by Fritz Naphtali (Berlin, 1928).

Wirtschaft und Rüstung am Vorabend des Zweiten Weltkrieges, ed. Friedrich Forstmeier and Hans-Erich Volkmann (Düsseldorf, 1975).

Wirtschaft und Staat im Imperialismus: Beiträge zur Entwicklungsgeschichte des staatsmonopolistischen Kapitalismus in Deutschland, ed. Lotte Zumpe (Forschungen zur Wirtschaftsgeschichte, 91; East Berlin, 1976).

WISKEMANN, ELIZABETH, *The Rome-Berlin Axis: A History of the Relations between Hitler and Mussolini,* rev. edn. (London, 1966).

WITT, PETER-CHRISTIAN, *Die Finanzpolitik des Deutschen Reiches von 1903 bis 1913: Eine Studie zur Innenpolitik des Wilhelminischen Deutschland* (Historische Studien, 415; Lübeck, 1970).

WITTMANN, KLAUS, *Schweden in der Außenwirtschaftspolitik des Dritten Reiches 1933-1945* (diss. Hamburg, 1976).

WOERMANN, EMIL, 'Zehn Jahre Erzeugungsschlacht und Ernährungswirtschaft', *Deutsche Agrarpolitik,* 2 (1943-4), 115-20.

WOHLFEIL, RAINER, 'Wehr-, Kriegs- oder Militärgeschichte?', *MGM* 1 (1967), 21-9.

—— 'Heer und Republik', in Edgar Graf von Matuschka and Rainer Wohlfeil, *Reichswehr und Republik (1918-1933)* (Handbuch zur deutschen Militärgeschichte 1648-1939, 6; Frankfurt am Main, 1970), 11-303.

WOLFFSOHN, MICHAEL, 'Arbeitsbeschaffung und Rüstung im nationalsozialistischen Deutschland 1933', *MGM* 22 (1977), 9-21.

—— 'Großunternehmer und Politik in Deutschland: Der Nutzen der Arbeitsbeschaffung der Jahre 1932/33 für die Schwer- und Chemieindustrie', *Zeitschrift für Unternehmensgeschichte,* 22 (1977), 109-33.

—— *Industrie und Handwerk im Konflikt mit staatlicher Wirtschaftspolitik? Studien zur Politik der Arbeitsbeschaffung in Deutschland 1930-1934* (Berlin, 1977).

WOLLSTEIN, GÜNTER, 'Eine Denkschrift des Staatssekretärs Bernhard von Bülow vom März 1933: Wilhelminische Konzeption der Außenpolitik zu Beginn der nationalsozialistischen Herrschaft', *MGM* 13 (1973), 77-94.

—— *Vom Weimarer Revisionismus zu Hitler: Das Deutsche Reich und die Großmächte in der Anfangsphase der nationalsozialistischen Herrschaft in Deutschland* (Reihe Argo, 2; Bonn-Bad Godesberg, 1973).

—— 'Die Politik des nationalsozialistischen Deutschland gegenüber Polen 1933-1939/45', in *Hitler, Deutschland und die Mächte* (q.v.), 795-810.

WORTMANN, MICHAEL, *Baldur von Schirach: Hitlers Jugendführer* (Cologne, 1982).

WRIGHT, J. R. C., *'Above Parties': The Political Attitude of the German Protestant Church Leadership 1918-1933* (London, 1974).

WUESCHT, JOHANN, *Jugoslawien und das Dritte Reich: Eine dokumentierte Geschichte der deutsch-jugoslawischen Beziehungen von 1933 bis 1945* (Stuttgart, 1969).

WULF, JOSEPH, *Presse und Funk im Dritten Reich: Eine Dokumentation* (Kunst und Kultur im Dritten Reich, 5; Gütersloh, 1964).

YANO, HISASHI, *Hüttenarbeiter im Dritten Reich: Die Betriebsverhältnisse und soziale Lage bei der Gutehoffnungshütte Aktienverein und der Fried.-Krupp-AG 1936 bis 1939* (Zeitschrift für Unternehmungsgeschichte, suppl. 34; Stuttgart, 1986).

YOUNG, ROBERT J., *In Command of France: French Foreign Policy and Military Planning, 1933-1940* (Cambridge, Mass., and London, 1978).

ZAHN, GORDON C., *German Catholics and Hitler's Wars* (London, 1963).

10. Mai 1933: Bücherverbrennung in Deutschland und die Folgen, ed. Ulrich Walberer (Frankfurt am Main, 1983).

ZENTNER, KURT, *Illustrierte Geschichte des Dritten Reiches* (Munich, 1965).

ZINNEMANN, C., 'Wechselwirkungen zwischen Kriegswirtschaft und Wirtschaftskrieg', *Deutsche Technik*, 7 (1939), 491–2.

ZIPFEL, FRIEDRICH, 'Gestapo und SD in Berlin', in *Jahrbuch für die Geschichte Mittel- und Ostdeutschlands*, ix–x (Tübingen, 1961), 263–92.

—— 'Hitlers Konzept einer "Neuordnung" Europas: Ein Beitrag zum politischen Denken des deutschen Diktators', in *Aus Theorie und Praxis der Geschichtswissenschaft: Festschrift für Hans Herzfeld zum 80. Geburtstag*, ed. Dietrich Kurze (Berlin, 1972), 154–74.

ZMARZLIK, HANS-GÜNTER, 'Der Sozialdarwinismus in Deutschland als geschichtliches Problem', *VfZG* 11 (1963), 246–73.

ZORACH, JONATHAN, 'Czechoslovakia's Fortifications: Their Development and Role in the 1938 Munich Crisis', *MGM* 20 (1976), 81–94.

ZUMPE, LOTTE, *Wirtschaft und Staat in Deutschland 1933 bis 1945* (Wirtschaft und Staat in Deutschland, 3; East Berlin, 1980).

Index of Names

MAP 2. German Political and Economic Influence at the Outbreak
of the Second World War

The gradation from more to less intensive
influence is shown as follows :

NORTH SEA

N.
IRELAND

IRISH
FREE
STATE

GT. BRITAIN   NETHERLANDS

The
Hague

London

Brussels

BELGIUM

Luxemburg

Paris

Seine

Loire

F R A N C E   Ber

SWITZE
LAN

Rhine

AND.

Lisbon   Madrid

S P A I N   Corsica
(Fr.)

Balearic Is.

Sardinia

Tangier   Gibraltar (Br.)
(internat.)
SP. MOROCCO   M E D I T E

Rabat   Algiers

MOROCCO   A L G E R I A   TUN
(Fr.)   (Fr.)   (Fr.
Pro

0   200   400   600   800 km